1 MONTH OF
FREE
READING

at

www.ForgottenBooks.com

ISBN 978-0-331-33751-8
PIBN 11090280

MONTHLY BULLETIN

OF THE

INTERNATIONAL BUREAU OF THE AMERICAN REPUBLICS

INTERNATIONAL UNION OF AMERICAN REPUBLICS

Vol. XXIV.

JANUARY–JUNE

1907

WASHINGTON
GOVERNMENT PRINTING OFFICE
1907

Bull No. 6—07——18

91839

INDEX

TO THE

MONTHLY BULLETIN

OF THE

INTERNATIONAL BUREAU OF THE AMERICAN REPUBLICS.

Vol. XXIV.   **Nos. 160-165, inclusive.**

Whole No. 160.   Vol. XXIV.   No. 1.

Monthly Bulletin

OF THE

International Bureau

OF THE

American Republics.

INTERNATIONAL UNION OF AMERICAN REPUBLICS.

———

While the utmost care is taken to insure accuracy in the publications of the International Bureau of the American Republics, no responsibility is assumed on account of errors or inaccuracies which may occur therein.

———

JANUARY, 1907.

———

WASHINGTON, D. C., U S. A.:
GOVERNMENT PRINTING OFFICE.
1907.

GENERAL INDEX.

["

INDEX.

INDICE.

TABLE DES MATIÈRES.

HONORARY CORRESPONDING MEMBERS OF THE INTERNATIONAL UNION OF AMERICAN REPUBLICS.

Countries.	Names.	Residence.
Argentine Republic..	Señor Dr. Don Estanislao S. Zeballos.......	Buenos Ayres.
Bolivia..............	Señor Don Manuel V. Ballivián<i>a</i>..........	La Paz.
Brazil..............	Dezembargador Antonio Bezerra...........	Pará.
	Firmino da Silva	Florianopolis.
Chile...............	Señor Don Moisés Vargas	Santiago.
Colombia...........	Señor Don Rufino Gutiérrez...............	Bogotá.
Costa Rica..........	Señor Don Manuel Aragón	San José.
Cuba...............	Señor Don Antonio S. de Bustamante	Havana.
	Señor Don Lincoln de Zayas..............	Havana.
Dominican Republic.	Señor Don José Gabriel García<i>b</i>...........	Santo Domingo.
Ecuador............	Señor Don Francisco Andrade Marín.......	Quito.
	Señor Don Luis Alberto Carbo	Guayaquil.
Guatemala..........	Señor Don Antonio Batres Jáuregui........	Guatemala City.
	Señor Don Rafael Montúfar	Guatemala City.
Haiti...............	Monsieur Georges Sylvain	Port au Prince.
Honduras	Señor Don E. Constantino Fiallos	Tegucigalpa.
Mexico.............	Señor Don Francisco L. de la Barra........	City of Mexico.
	Señor Don Antonio García Cubas	City of Mexico.
	Señor Don Fernando Ferrari Pérez	City of Mexico.
Nicaragua	Señor Don José D. Gámez.................	Managua.
Paraguay...........	Señor Don José S. Decoud	Asunción.
Panama	Señor Don Samuel Lewis..................	Panama.
	Señor Don Ramón M. Valdés..............	Panama.
Peru	Señor Don Alejandro Garland.	Lima.
Salvador............	Señor Dr. Don Salvador Gallegos	San Salvador.
Uruguay............	Señor Don José I. Schiffiano	Montevideo.
Venezuela	Señor General Don Manuel Landaeta Rosales.	Caracas.
	Señor Don Francisco de Paula Alamo.......	Caracas.

a Honorary corresponding member of the Royal Geographical Society of Great Britain.
b Corresponding member of the Academia Nacional de la Historia de Venezuela

LATIN-AMERICAN REPRESENTATIVES IN THE UNITED STATES.

AMBASSADORS EXTRAORDINARY AND PLENIPOTENTIARY.

Brazil..............................Mr. JOAQUIM NABUCO,
    Office of Embassy, 1710 H street, Washington, D. C.
Mexico.............................Señor Don ENRIQUE C. CREEL,
    Office of Embassy, 1415 I street, Washington, D. C.

ENVOYS EXTRAORDINARY AND MINISTERS PLENIPOTENTIARY.

Argentine Republic ....Señor Don EPIFANIO PORTELA,
    Absent. Office of Legation, 2109 Sixteenth street, Washington, D. C.
Bolivia ....Señor Don IGNACIO CALDERÓN,
    1833 Sixteenth street, Washington, D. C.
Chile...............................Señor Don JOAQUÍN WALKER-MARTÍNEZ,
    Absent.
Colombia.......................Señor Don ENRIQUE CORTES,
    1312 Twenty-first street NW., Washington D. C.
Costa Rica.........................Señor Don JOAQUÍN BERNARDO CALVO,
    1329 Eighteenth street NW., Washington, D. C.
Cuba...............................Señor Don GONZALO DE QUESADA,
    Office of Legation, "The Wyoming," Washington, D. C.
Ecuador...........................Señor Don LUIS FELIPE CARBO,
    Office of Legation, 1222 Connecticut avenue, Washington, D. C.
Haiti ....Mr. J. N. LÉGER,
    1429 Rhode Island avenue, Washington, D. C.
Honduras ....Señor Dr. Don JOSÉ ROSA PACAS,
    Absent.
Nicaragua ....Señor Don LUIS F. COREA,
    Office of Legation, 2003 O street, Washington, D. C.
Panama ....Señor Don J. DOMINGO DE OBALDÍA,
    Office of Legation, "The Highlands," Washington, D. C.
Peru ....Señor Don FELIPE PARDO,
    Office of Legation, 2171 Florida avenue, Washington, D. C.
Salvador...........................Señor Dr. Don JOSÉ ROSA PACAS,
    Absent.
Uruguay ....Señor Dr. Don LUÍS MELIAN LAFINUR,
    Office of Legation, 1752 M street, Washington, D. C.

MINISTER RESIDENT.

Dominican Republic ....Señor Don EMILIO C. JOUBERT,
    "The Shoreham," Washington, D. C.

CHARGÉS D'AFFAIRES.

Chile...............................Señor Don ALBERTO YOACHAM,
    Office of Legation, "The Rochambeau," Washington, D. C.
Guatemala..........................Dr. RAMÓN BENGOECHEA,
    Office of Legation, in care Consulate-General, 2 and 4 Stone street, New York City.
Venezuela ....Señor Dr. RAFAEL GARBIRAS GUZMAN,
    "The Rochambeau," Washington, D. C.

DIRECTOR OF THE INTERNATIONAL BUREAU OF THE AMERICAN REPUBLICS.
JOHN BARRETT.

UNITED STATES REPRESENTATIVES IN THE LATIN-AMERICAN REPUBLICS.

AMBASSADORS EXTRAORDINARY AND PLENIPOTENTIARY.

Brazil ....Irving B. Dudley, Rio de Janeiro.

Mexico ....David E. Thompson, Mexico.

ENVOYS EXTRAORDINARY AND MINISTERS PLENIPOTENTIARY.

Argentine Republic ....A. M. Beaupré, Buenos Ayres.

Bolivia ....William B. Sorsby, La Paz.

Chile ....John Hicks, Santiago.

Colombia ....Thomas C. Dawson, Bogotá.

Costa Rica ....William L. Merry, San José.

Cuba ....Edwin V. Morgan, Havana.

Ecuador ....Williams C. Fox, Quito.

Guatemala ....Joseph W. J. Lee, Guatemala City.

Haiti ....Henry W. Furniss, Port au Prince.

Honduras...............................(See Guatemala.)

Nicaragua..............................(See Costa Rica.)

Panama ....Herbert G. Squiers, Panama.

Paraguay ....(See Uruguay.)

Peru ....Leslie Combs, Lima.

Salvador...............................(See Costa Rica.)

Uruguay................................Edward C. O'Brien, Montevideo.

Venezuela ....W. W. Russell, Caracas.

MINISTER RESIDENT AND CONSUL-GENERAL.

Dominican Republic.....................Fenton R. McCreery, Santo Domingo.

RATES OF POSTAGE FROM THE UNITED STATES TO LATIN-AMERICAN COUNTRIES.

The rates of postage from the United States to all foreign countries and colonies (except Canada, Mexico, and Cuba) are as follows:

		Cents.
Letters, per 15 grams (½ ounce)		5
Single postal cards, each		2
Double postal cards, each		4
Newspapers and other printed matter, per 2 ounces		1
Commercial papers	Packets not in excess of 10 ounces	5
	Packets in excess of 10 ounces, for each 2 ounces or fraction thereof	1
Samples of merchandise	Packets not in excess of 4 ounces	2
	Packets in excess of 4 ounces, for each 2 ounces or fraction thereof	1
Registration fee on letters and other articles		10

Ordinary letters for any foreign country (except Canada, Mexico, and Cuba) must be forwarded, whether any postage is prepaid on them or not. All other mailable matter must be prepaid, at least partially.

Matter mailed in the United States addressed to Mexico is subject to the same postage rates and conditions as it would be if it were addressed for delivery in the United States, except that articles of miscellaneous merchandise (fourth-class matter) not sent as bona fide trade samples should be sent by "Parcels Post;" and that the following articles are absolutely excluded from the mails without regard to the amount of postage prepaid or the manner in which they are wrapped:

All sealed packages, other than letters in their usual and ordinary form; all packages (including packages of second-class matter) which weigh more than 4 pounds 6 ounces, except such as are sent by "Parcels Post;" publications which violate any copyright law of Mexico.

Single volumes of printed books in unsealed packages are transmissible to Mexico in the regular mails without limit as to weight.

Unsealed packages of mailable merchandise may be sent by "Parcels Post" to Bolivia, British Guiana, British Honduras, Chile, Colombia, Costa Rica, Guatemala, Honduras, Mexico, Nicaragua, Salvador, and Venezuela, at the rates named on page XV.

PROHIBITED ARTICLES TO ALL FOREIGN COUNTRIES.

Poisons, explosives, and inflammable articles, live or dead animals, insects (especially the Colorado beetle), reptiles, fruit or vegetable matter liable to decomposition, and substances exhaling a bad odor, excluded from transmission in domestic mails as being in themselves, either from their form or nature, liable to destroy, deface, or otherwise injure the contents of the mail bags, or the persons of those engaged in the postal service; also obscene, lewd, or lascivious books, pamphlets, etc., and letters and circulars concerning lotteries, so-called gift concerts, etc. (also excluded from domestic mails); postal cards or letters addressed to go around the world; letters or packages (except those to Mexico) containing gold or silver substances, jewelry or precious articles; any packet whatever containing articles liable to customs duties in the countries addressed (except Cuba and Mexico); articles other than letters which are not prepaid at least partly; articles other than letters or postal cards containing writing in the nature of personal correspondence, unless fully prepaid at the rate of letter postage; articles of a nature likely to soil or injure the correspondence; packets of commercial papers and prints of all kinds, the weight of which exceeds 2 kilograms (4 pounds 6 ounces), or the size 18 inches in any direction, except rolls of prints, which may measure 30 inches in length by 4 inches in diameter; postal cards not of United States origin, and United States postal cards of the largest ("C") size (except as letters), and except also the reply halves of double postal cards received from foreign countries.

There is, moreover, reserved to the Government of every country of the Postal Union the right to refuse to convey over its territory, or to deliver, as well, articles liable to the reduced rate in regard to which the laws, ordinances, or decrees which regulate the conditions of their publication or of their circulation in that country have not been complied with.

☞ Full and complete information relative to all regulations can be obtained from the United States Postal Guide.

FOREIGN MAILS.

TABLE SHOWING THE RATES OF POSTAGE CHARGED IN LATIN-AMERICAN COUNTRIES ON ARTICLES SENT BY MAIL TO THE UNITED STATES.

Countries.	Letters, per 15 grams, equal to one-half ounce.		Single postal cards, each.a		Other articles, per 50 grams, equal to 2 ounces.		Charge for registration.	Charge for return receipt.
	Currency of country.	Centimes.	Currency of country.	Centimes.	Currency of country.	Centimes.		
Arg...ine Republic	16 centavos	35	6 centavos	15	3 tamos	10	24 centavos	12 t sas.
Bolivia via Panama	22 centavos	55	6 centavos	20	6 tamos	15	20 centavos	10 centavos.
...via ...ther routes	20 centavos	50	6 centavos	15	sma	10	sma	200 reis.
Brazil	300 reis	35	100 reis	10	50 reis	5	400 reis	200 reis.
Kile	10 centavos	50	3 centavos	15	2 tamos	10	10 en tamo	5 centavos.
Gabia	20 centavos	50	4 centavos	10	2 tamos	5	10 centavos	5 centavos.
Sta Rica	10 centimos	25	3 centimos	7½	2 centimos	5	10 centimos	5 t ms.
Cuba b								
Ecuador	10 centavos	25	3 tamos	10	2 cen imos	5	10 ...	5 t cms.
...dian Republic (Santo Domingo)	10 tamos	25	2 centavos	10				
Falkland Inds.	4 pace	40	1 pay	15	1 pay	10	2 pence.	2½ ...
Guatemala	10 centavos	50	3 centavos	15	3 tamos		10 centavos	5 t cms.
Haiti	10 ...cimes de gorde.	50	3 ...imes de gate.	15	3 cen imos de rge.	10	2 cen imes de gourde.	5 nétimes de gourde.
Honduras	15 centavos	50	3 centavos	15	2 tamos	10	10 e... ms.	5 centavos.
Honduras, British	5 centavos	25	2 cts.	10	2 cts.	10	10 cts.	6 cms.
Mex...	15 centavos	50	5 centavos	15	1 centavo	10	10 cen avo	5 centavor.
N...egia	60 centavos		3 centavos	15	2 centavo	10	20 cuavor	10 t cms.
Paraguay	20 centavos	50	8 centavos	15	8 cen imos	10	40 e ados	20 t ms.
Peru via San Francisco	22 centavos	55	8 tamos	20	6 centavos	15	... smos	5 cen tas.
Peru via ...ma								
Porto ...b								
Sal ador via Panama	11 centavos	55	3 centavos	15	3 tamos	10	10 centavos	5 tamos.
Salvador via other l...ties	10 centavos	50	3 centavos	15	2 tamos	10	10 centavos	5 t cms.
Uruguay	10 centimos	50	3 centimos	15	cmos	10	i cms.	25 cel cm.
British ...sia	50 centimos	50	15 centimos	15	10 centimos	10		
Dutch Guiana	5 cents	25	2 cents	10	1 cent	5	10 cents itch	10 cnts Dmb.
...sia	25 cents Dutch	50	7½ cents Dutch	15	5 cents Dutch	10	10 cents itch	10 cents Dmb.
	25 centimes		10 centimes		5 centimes		25 centimes	10 centime.

a The rate for a reply-paid (double) card is double the rate named in this col um.

b United States domestic rates and conditions.

PARCELS-POST REGULATIONS.

TABLE SHOWING THE LATIN-AMERICAN COUNTRIES TO WHICH PARCELS MAY BE SENT FROM THE UNITED STATES; THE DIMENSIONS, WEIGHT, AND RATES OF POSTAGE APPLICABLE TO PARCELS, AND THE EXCHANGE POST-OFFICES WHICH MAY DISPATCH AND RECEIVE PARCELS-POST MAILS.

COUNTRIES.	ALLOWABLE DIMENSIONS AND WEIGHTS OF PARCELS.				POSTAGE.		EXCHANGE POST-OFFICES.	
	Greatest length.	Greatest length and girth combined.	Greatest girth.	Greatest weight.	For a parcel not exceeding ½ pound.	For every additional pound or fraction of a pound.	UNITED STATES.	LATIN AMERICA.
	Ft. in.	Ft.	Ft.	Lbs.	Cents.	Cents.		
Bolivia	3 6	6	......	11	20	20	New York and San Francisco.	La Paz.
Chile	3 6	6	......	11	20	20	New York and San Francisco.	Valparaiso.
Colombia	2 0	......	4	11	12	12	All offices authorized to exchange mails between the two countries.	
Costa Rica	2 0	......	4	11	12	12		
Guatemala	3 6	6	......	11	12	12	New York, New Orleans, and San Francisco.	Guatemala City, Retalhulen, and Puerto Barrios.
Guiana, British	3 6	6	......	11	12	12	All offices authorized to exchange mails.	
Honduras	3 6	6	......	11	12	12	New York, New Orleans, and San Francisco.	Tegucigalpa, Puerto Cortez, Amapala, and Trujillo.
Honduras, British	3 6	6	......	11	12	12	New Orleans	Belize.
Mexico	2 0	......	4	11	12	12	All offices authorized to exchange mails.	
Nicaragua	3 6	6	......	11	12	12	New York, New Orleans, and San Francisco.	Bluefields, San Juan del Norte, and Corinto.
Salvador	3 6	6	......	11	12	12	New York and San Francisco.	San Salvador.
Venezuela	3 6	6	......	11	12	12	All offices authorized to exchange mails.	

UNITED STATES CONSULATES IN LATIN AMERICA.

Frequent application is made to the Bureau for the address of United States Consuls in the South and Central American Republics. Those desiring to correspond with any Consul can do so by addressing "The United States Consulate" at the point named. Letters thus addressed must be delivered to the proper person. It must be understood, however, that it is not the duty of Consuls to devote their time to private business, and that all such letters may properly be treated as personal, and any labor involved may be subject to charge therefor.

The following is a list of United States Consulates in the different Republics (consular agencies are given in italics):

ARGENTINE REPUBLIC—
Bahia Blanca.
Buenos Ayres.
Cordoba.
Rosario.

BRAZIL—
Aracaju.
Bahia.
Ceara.
Maceio.
Manaos.
Maranhão.
Natal.
Para.
Pernambuco.
Rio de Janeiro.
Rio Grande do Sul.
Santos.
Victoria.

CHILE—
Antofagasta.
Arica.
Caldera.
Coquimbo.
Coronel.
Iquique.
Punta Arenas.
Talcahuano.
Valdivia.
Valparaiso.

COLOMBIA—
Barranquilla.
Bogotá.
Bucaramanga.
Cali.
Cartagena.
Cucuta.
Honda.
Santa Marta.
Quibdo.

COSTA RICA—
Puerto Limon.
Punta Arenas.
San José.

CUBA—
Banes.
Baracoa.
Caibarien.
Cardenas.
Cienfuegos.
Habana.
Manzanillo.
Matanzas.
Nuevitas.
Sagua la Grande.
Santa Clara.
Santiago.

DOMINICAN REPUBLIC—
Azua.
Macoris.
Monte Christi.
Puerto Plata.

DOMINICAN REPUBLIC—Cont'd.
Samana.
Sanchez.
Santo Domingo.

ECUADOR—
Bahia de Caraquez.
Esmeraldas.
Guayaquil.
Manta.

GUATEMALA—
Champerico.
Guatemala.
Livingston.
Ocos.
San José de Guatemala.

HAITI—
Aux Cayes.
Cape Haitien.
Gonaives.
Jacmel.
Jeremie.
Miragoane.
Petit Godve.
Port au Prince.
Port de Paix.
St. Marc.

HONDURAS—
Amapala.
Bonacca.
Ceiba.
Puerto Cortes.
San Juancito.
San Pedro Sula.
Tegucigalpa.
Trla.
Trujillo.
Ruatan.
Utilla.

MEXICO—
Acapulco.
Aguascalientes.
Alamos.
Campeche.
Cananea.
Chihuahua.
Ciudad Juarez.
Ciudad Porfirio Diaz.
Coatzacoalcos.
Durango.
Ensenada.
Frontera.
Guadalajara.
Guanajuato.
Guaymas.
Hermosillo.
Jalapa.
Laguna de Terminos.
La Paz.
Manzanillo.
Matamoras.
Mazatlan.
Mexico.

MEXICO—Continued.
Monterey.
Nogales.
Nuevo Laredo.
Oaxaca.
Parral.
Progreso.
Puebla.
Saltillo.
San Luis Potosi.
Sierra Mojada.
Tampico.
Tlacotalpan.
Topolobampo.
Torreon.
Tuxpan, Vera Cruz.
Veracruz.
Victoria.
Zacatecas.

NICARAGUA—
Bluefields.
Cape Gracias á Dios.
Corinto.
Managua.
Matagalpa.
San Juan del Norte.
San Juan del Sur.

PANAMA—
Bocas del Toro.
Colon.
David.
Panama.
Santiago.

PARAGUAY—
Asunción.

PERU—
Callao.
Chimbote.
Eten.
Iquitos.
Mollendo.
Paita.
Salaverry.

SALVADOR—
Acajutla.
La Libertad.
La Unión.
San Salvador.

URUGUAY—
Montevideo.

VENEZUELA—
Barcelona.
Caracas.
Carupano.
Ciudad Bolivar.
Coro.
La Guayra.
Maracaibo.
Puerto Cabello.
Tovar.
Valera.

CONSULATES OF THE LATIN-AMERICAN REPUBLICS IN THE UNITED STATES.

ARGENTINE REPUBLIC.

Alabama	Mobile.
California	San Francisco.
District of Columbia	Washington.
Florida	Fernandina.
	Pensacola.
Georgia	Savannah.
Illinois	Chicago.
Louisiana	New Orleans.
Maine	Portland.
Maryland	Baltimore.
Massachusetts	Boston.
Mississippi	Gulf Port and Ship Island.
	Pascagoula.
Missouri	St. Louis.
New York	New York City.
Pennsylvania	Philadelphia.
Philippine Islands	Manila.
Virginia	Norfolk.

BOLIVIA.

California	San Diego.
	San Francisco.
Illinoi	Chicago.
Maryland	Baltimore.
Missouri	Kansas City.
New York	New York City.
Pennsylvania	Philadelphia.

BRAZIL.

Alabama	Mobile.
California	San Francisco.
Florida	Fernandina.
	Pensacola.
Georgia	Brunswick.
	Savannah.
Louisiana	New Orleans.
Maine	Calais.
Maryland	Baltimore.
Massachusetts	Boston.
Mississippi	Gulfport.
	Pascagoula.
Missouri	St. Louis.
New York	New York City.
Pennsylvania	Philadelphia.
Porto Rico	San Juan.
Virginia	Norfolk.
	Richmond.

CHILE.

California	San Francisco.
Canal Zone	Panama.
Georgia	Savannah.
Hawaii	Honolulu.
Illinois	Chicago.
Maryland	Baltimore.
Massachusetts	Boston.
New York	New York City.
Oregon	Portland.
Pennsylvania	Philadelphia.
Philippine Islands	Manila.
Porto Rico	San Juan.
Washington	Port Townsend.
	Tacoma.

COLOMBIA.

Alabama	Mobile.
California	San Francisco.
Connecticut	New Haven.
Florida	Tampa.
Illinois	Chicago.
Louisiana	New Orleans.
Maryland	Baltimore.
Massachusetts	Boston.
Michigan	Detroit.
Missouri	St. Louis.
New York	New York City.
Pennsylvania	Philadelphia.
Porto Rico	San Juan.
Virginia	Norfolk.

COSTA RICA.

Alabama	Mobile.
California	San Francisco.
Canal Zone	Colon.
	Panama.
Colorado	Denver.
Illinois	Chicago.
Louisiana	New Orleans.
Maryland	Baltimore.
Massachusetts	Boston.
Missouri	St. Louis.
New York	New York City.
Oregon	Portland.
Pennsylvania	Philadelphia.
Porto Rico	San Juan.
Texas	Galveston.
Virginia	Norfolk.

CUBA.

Alabama	Mobile.
California	Los Angeles.
Florida	Fernandina.
	Jacksonville.
	Key West.
	Pensacola.
	Tampa.
Georgia	Brunswick.
	Savannah.
Illinois	Chicago.
Kentucky	Louisville.
Louisiana	New Orleans.
Maine	Portland.
Maryland	Baltimore.
Massachusetts	Boston.
Michigan	Detroit.
Mississippi	Gulfport.
Missouri	St. Louis.
New York	New York City.
Ohio	Cincinnati.
Pennsylvania	Philadelphia.
Porto Rico	Arecibo.
	Mayagüez.
	Ponce.
	San Juan.
Texas	Galveston.
Virginia	Newport News.
	Norfolk.

DOMINICAN REPUBLIC.

Illinois	Chicago.
Maryland	Baltimore.
Massachusetts	Boston.
New York	New York City.
North Carolina	Wilmington.
Pennsylvania	Philadelphia.
Porto Rico	Aguadilla.
	Arecibo.
	Humacao.
	Mayaguez.
	Ponce.
	San Juan.
	Vieques.

ECUADOR.

California	Los Angeles.
	San Francisco.
Illinois	Chicago.
Louisiana	New Orleans.
Massachusetts	Boston.
New York	New York City.
Ohio	Cincinnati.
Pennsylvania	Philadelphia.
Philippine Islands	Manila.
South Carolina	Charleston.
Virginia	Norfolk.

GUATEMALA.

Alabama	Mobile.
California	San Diego.
	San Francisco.
Florida	Pensacola.
Illinois	Chicago.

CONSULATES OF THE LATIN-AMERICAN REPUBLICS—Continued.

GUATEMALA—Continued.

Kansas	Kansas City.
Kentucky	Louisville.
Louisiana	New Orleans.
Maryland	Baltimore.
Massachusetts	Boston.
Missouri	St. Louis.
New York	New York City.
Pennsylvania	Philadelphia.
Porto Rico	San Juan.
Texas	Galveston.
Washington	Seattle.

HAITI.

Alabama	Mobile.
Georgia	Savannah.
Illinois	Chicago.
Maine	Bangor.
Massachusetts	Boston.
New York	New York City.
North Carolina	Wilmington.
Porto Rico	Mayagüez.
	San Juan.

HONDURAS.

Alabama	Mobile.
California	Los Angeles.
	San Diego.
	San Francisco.
Illinois	Chicago.
Kansas	Kansas City.
Kentucky	Louisville.
Louisiana	New Orleans.
Maryland	Baltimore.
Michigan	Detroit.
Missouri	St. Louis.
New York	New York City.
Ohio	Cincinnati.
Pennsylvania	Philadelphia.
Texas	Galveston.
Washington	Seattle.

MEXICO.

Alabama	Mobile.
Arizona	Bisbee.
	Clifton.
	Douglas.
	Naco.
	Nogales.
	Phoenix.
	Solomonsville.
	Tucson.
	Yuma.
California	Calexico.
	Los Angeles.
	San Diego.
	San Francisco.
Canal Zone	Ancon.
Colorado	Denver.
Florida	Pensacola.
Hawaii	Honolulu.
Illinois	Chicago.
Kentucky	Louisville.
Louisiana	New Orleans.
Maryland	Baltimore.
Massachusetts	Boston.
Mississippi	Pascagoula.
Missouri	Kansas City.
	St. Louis.
New York	New York City.
Ohio	Cincinnati.
Oregon	Portland.
Pennsylvania	Philadelphia.
Philippine Islands	Manila.
Porto Rico	Mayagüez.
	Ponce.
	San Juan.
Texas	Brownsville.
	Eagle Pass.
	El Paso.
	Galveston.
	Laredo.
	Port Arthur.
	Rio Grande City.
	Sabine Pass.
	San Antonio.
	Solomonsville.

MEXICO—Continued.

Virginia	Norfolk.
Washington	Tocoma.

NICARAGUA.

Alabama	Mobile.
California	Los Angeles.
	San Diego.
	San Francisco.
Illinois	Chicago.
Kansas	Kansas City.
Kentucky	Louisville.
Louisiana	New Orleans.
Maryland	Baltimore.
Massachusetts	Boston.
Michigan	Detroit.
Missouri	St. Louis.
New York	New York City.
Pennsylvania	Philadelphia.
Philippine Islands	Manila.
Porto Rico	Ponce.
	San Juan.
Texas	Galveston.
Virginia	Norfolk.
	Newport News.
Washington	Seattle.

PANAMA.

Alabama	Mobile.
California	San Francisco.
Georgia	Atlanta.
Hawaii	Hilo.
Illinois	Chicago.
Louisiana	New Orleans.
Maryland	Baltimore.
Massachusetts	Boston.
Missouri	St. Louis.
New York	New York City.
Pennsylvania	Philadelphia.
Porto Rico	San Juan.
Tennessee	Chattanooga.
Texas	Galveston.
	Port Arthur.
Washington	Puget Sound.

PARAGUAY.

Alabama	Mobile.
Delaware	Wilmington.
District of Columbia	Washington.
Georgia	Savannah.
Illinois	Chicago.
Indiana	Indianapolis.
Maryland	Baltimore.
Michigan	Detroit.
Missouri	Kansas City.
	St. Louis.
New Jersey	Newark.
	Trenton.
New York	Buffalo.
	New York City.
	Rochester.
Ohio	Cincinnati.
Pennsylvania	Philadelphia.
Porto Rico	San Juan.
Virginia	Norfolk.
	Richmond.

PERU.

California	Los Angeles.
	San Diego.
	San Francisco.
Canal Zone	Panama.
Georgia	Savannah.
Hawaii	Honolulu.
Illinois	Chicago.
Louisiana	New Orleans.
Maryland	Baltimore.
Massachusetts	Boston.
New York	New York City.
Oregon	Portland.
Pennsylvania	Philadelphia.
Porto Rico	San Juan.
South Carolina	Charleston.
Washington	Port Townsend.

CONSULATES OF THE LATIN-AMERICAN REPUBLICS—Continued.

SALVADOR.

California	San Diego.
	San Francisco.
Louisiana	New Orleans.
Massachusetts	Boston.
Missouri	St. Louis.
New York	New York City.

URUGUAY.

Alabama	Mobile.
California	San Francisco.
Florida	Apalachicola.
	Fernandina.
	Jacksonville.
	Pensacola.
	St. Augustine.
Georgia	Brunswick.
	Savannah.
Illinois	Chicago.
Louisiana	New Orleans.
Maine	Bangor.
	Calais.
	Portland.
Maryland	Baltimore.
Massachusetts	Boston.

URUGUAY—Continued.

Mississippi	Pascagoula.
Missouri	St. Louis.
New York	New York City.
Ohio	Cincinnati.
Pennsylvania	Philadelphia.
Philippine Islands	Manila.
South Carolina	Charleston.
Texas	Galveston.
	Port Arthur and
	Sabine Pass.
Virginia	Norfolk.
	Richmond.

VENEZUELA.

California	San Francisco.
Illinois	Chicago.
Louisiana	New Orleans.
New York	New York City.
Pennsylvania	Philadelphia.
Philippine Islands	Cebu.
Porto Rico	Arecibo.
	Mayagüez.
	Ponce.
	San Juan.

WEIGHTS AND MEASURES.

The following table gives the chief weights and measures in commercial use in Mexico and the Republics of Central and South America, and their equivalents in the United States:

Denomination.	Where used.	United States equivalents.
Are	Metric	0.02471 acre.
Arobe	Paraguay	25 pounds.
Arroba (dry)	Argentine Republic	25.3171 pounds.
Do	Brazil	32.38 pounds.
Do	Cuba	25.3664 pounds.
Do	Venezuela	25.4024 pounds.
Arroba (liquid)	Cuba and Venezuela	4.263 gallons.
Barril	Argentine Republic and Mexico	20.0787 gallons.
Carga	Mexico and Salvador	300 pounds.
Centaro	Central America	4.2631 gallons.
Cuadra	Argentine Republic	4.2 acres.
Do	Paraguay	78.9 yards.
Do	Paraguay (square)	8.077 square feet.
Do	Uruguay	2 acres (nearly).
Cubic meter	Metric	35.3 cubic feet.
Fanega (dry)	Central America	1.5745 bushels.
Do	Chile	2.575 bushels.
Do	Cuba	1.599 bushels.
Do	Mexico	1.54728 bushels.
Do	Uruguay (double)	7.776 bushels.
Do	Uruguay (single)	3.888 bushels.
Do	Venezuela	1.599 bushels.
Frasco	Argentine Republic	2.5096 quarts.
Do	Mexico	2.5 quarts.
Gram	Metric	15.432 grains.
Hectare	do	2.471 acres.
Hectoliter (dry)	do	2.838 bushels.
Hectoliter (liquid)	do	26.417 gallons.
Kilogram (kilo)	do	2.2046 pounds.
Kilometer	do	0.621376 mile.
League (land)	Paraguay	4.633 acres.
Libra	Argentine Republic	1.0127 pounds.
Do	Central America	1.043 pounds.
Do	Chile	1.014 pounds.
Do	Cuba	1.0161 pounds.
Do	Mexico	1.01465 pounds.
Do	Peru	1.0143 pounds.
Do	Uruguay	1.0143 pounds.
Do	Venezuela	1.0161 pounds.
Liter	Metric	1.0567 quarts.
Livre	Guiana	1.0791 pounds.
Manzana	Costa Rica	1.73 acres.
Marc	Bolivia	0.507 pound.
Meter	Metric	39.37 inches.
Pie	Argentine Republic	0.9478 foot.
Quintal	do	101.42 pounds.
Do	Brazil	130.06 pounds.
Do	Chile, Mexico, and Peru	101.61 pounds.
Do	Paraguay	100 pounds.
Quintal (metric)	Metric	220.46 pounds.
Suerte	Uruguay	2,700 cuadras. (*See* Cuadra.)
Vara	Argentine Republic	34.1208 inches.
Do	Central America	33.874 inches.
Do	Chile and Peru	33.367 inches.
Do	Cuba	33.384 inches.
Do	Mexico	33 inches.
Do	Paraguay	34 inches.
Do	Venezuela	33.384 inches.

METRIC WEIGHTS AND MEASURES.

METRIC WEIGHTS.

Milligram (1/1000 gram) equals 0.0154 grain.
Centigram (1/100 gram) equals 0.1543 grain.
Decigram (1/10 gram) equals 1.5432 grains.
Gram equals 15.432 grains.
Decagram (10 grams) equals 0.3527 ounce.
Hectogram (100 grams) equals 3.5274 ounces.
Kilogram (1,000 grams) equals 2.2046 pounds.
Myriagram (10,000 grams) equals 22.046 pounds.
Quintal (100,000 grams) equals 220.46 pounds.
Millier or tonneau—ton (1,000,000 grams) equals 2,204.6 pounds.

METRIC DRY MEASURE.

Milliliter (1/1000 liter) equals 0.061 cubic inch.
Centiliter (1/100 liter) equals 0.6102 cubic inch.
Deciliter (1/10 liter) equals 6.1022 cubic inches.
Liter equals 0.908 quart.
Decaliter (10 liters) equals 9.08 quarts.
Hectoliter (100 liters) equals 2.838 bushels.
Kiloliter (1,000 liters) equals 1.308 cubic yards.

METRIC LIQUID MEASURE.

Milliliter (1/1000 liter) equals 0.27 fluid dram.
Centiliter (1/100 liter) equals 0.338 fluid ounce.
Deciliter (1/10 liter) equals 0.845 gill.
Liter equals 1.0567 quarts.
Decaliter (10 liters) equals 2.6417 gallons.
Hectoliter (100 liters) equals 26.417 gallons.
Kiloliter (1,000 liters) equals 264.17 gallons.

METRIC MEASURES OF LENGTH.

Millimeter (1/1000 meter) equals 0.0394 inch.
Centimeter (1/100 meter) equals 0.3937 inch.
Decimeter (1/10 meter) equals 3.937 inches.
Meter equals 39.37 inches.
Decameter (10 meters) equals 393.7 inches.
Hectometer (100 meters) equals 328 feet 1 inch.
Kilometer (1,000 meters) equals 0.62137 mile (3,280 feet 10 inches).
Myriameter (10,000 meters) equals 6.2137 miles.

METRIC SURFACE MEASURE.

Centare (1 square meter) equals 1,550 square inches.
Are (100 square meters) equals 119.6 square yards.
Hectare (10,000 square meters) equals 2.471 acres.

PRICE LIST OF PUBLICATIONS.

PRICE.

Bulletin of the Bureau, published monthly since October, 1893, in English,
Spanish, Portuguese, and French. Average 225 pages, 2 volumes a year.
  Yearly subscription (in countries of the International Union of American
    Republics and in Canada)... $2.00
  Yearly subscription (other countries).................................. 2.50
  Single copies... .25
  Orders for the Bulletin should be addressed to the Chief Clerk of the
  Bureau.
American Constitutions. A compilation of the political constitutions of the
  independent States of America, in the original text, with English and Span-
  ish translations. Washington, 1906. 3 vols., 8°.
    Paper ....each.. 1.00
    Bound in cloth...do.... 1.50
    Bound in sheep ....do.... 2.00
      Vol. I, now ready, contains the constitutions of the Federal Republics of the United
      States of America, of Mexico, of the Argentine Republic, of Brazil, and of Venezuela, and
      of the Republics of Central America, Guatemala, Honduras, El Salvador, Nicaragua, Costa
      Rica, and Panama. Vols. II and III will be ready shortly.
      Vol. II will contain the constitutions of the Dominican Republic, Haiti, Cuba, Uruguay,
      Chile, Peru, Ecuador, Colombia, Paraguay, and Bolivia.
      Vol. III will contain Articles of Confederation of the United States, First Constitution
      of Venezuela 1811, Fundamental Law of Republic of Colombia 1819, Ditto of 1821, Consti-
      tution of Colombia of 1821, Constitution of Central American Confederation of 1824, Con-
      stitution of the Grenadian Confederation of 1858, Constitution of the United States of
      Colombia of 1863, Pro Constitution of Guatemala of 1876, Convention between United
      States and Republic of Panama for construction of ship canal to connect the waters of the
      Atlantic and the Pacific Oceans.
Code of Commercial Nomenclature, 1897. (Spanish, English, and Portuguese.)
  645 pages, 4°, cloth.. 2.50
Code of Commercial Nomenclature, 1897. (Portuguese, Spanish, and English.)
  640 pages, 4°, cloth.. 2.50
      NOTE.—Designates in alphabetical order, in equivalent terms in the three languages,
      the commodities of American nations on which import duties are levied. The English,
      Spanish, and Portuguese edition is entirely exhausted.
Leyes y reglamentos sobre privilegios de invención y marcas de fábrica en los
  países hispano-americanos, el Brasil y la República de Haití. Revisado hasta
  agosto de 1904. Washington, 1904. 415 pages, 8°.......................... 1.00
Patent and trade-mark laws of the Spanish American Republics, Brazil, and
  the Republic of Haiti. Revised to Aug., 1904, Washington, 1904.......... 1.00
  The above two works bound together in sheep 3.00

SPECIAL BULLETINS.

Money, Weights, and Measures of the American Republics, 1891. 12 pages, 8°. .05
Report on Coffee, with special reference to the Costa Rican product, etc.
  Washington, 1901. 15 pages, 8°... .10
El café. Su historia, cultivo, beneficio, variedades, producción, exportación,
  importación, consumo, etc. Datos extensos presentados al Congreso relativo
  al café que se reunirá en Nueva York el 1° de octubre de 1902. 167 páginas,
  8°... .50

Coffee. Extensive information and statistics. (English edition of the above.)
108 pages, 8°.. $0.50
Intercontinental Railway Reports. Report of the Intercontinental Railway
Commission. Washington, 1898. 7 vols. 4°, three of maps.............. 25.00

HANDBOOKS (GENERAL DESCRIPTION AND STATISTICS).

Argentine Republic. A geographical sketch, with special reference to economic
conditions, actual development, and prospects of future growth. Washington, 1903. 28 illustrations, 3 maps, 366 pages, 8°...................... 1.00
Bolivia. Geographical sketch, natural resources, laws, economic conditions,
actual devolopment, prospects of future growth. Washington, 1904. Illustrated, 214 pages, 8°.. 1.00
Brazil. Geographical sketch, with special reference to economic conditions
and prospects of future development. 1901. 233 pages, 8°.............. .75
Cuba. A short sketch of physical and economic conditions, government, laws,
industries, finances, customs tariff, etc., prepared by Señor Gonzalo de
Quesada, minister from Cuba, with bibliography and cartography of 198
pages. Washington, November, 1905. Map and 42 illustrations, 541 pages, 8°. 1.00
Guatemala. 1897. (2d edition revised.) Illustrated, 119 pages, 8°......... .25
Honduras. Geographical sketch, natural resources, laws, economic condi-
tions, actual development, prospects of future growth. Washington, 1904.
Illustrated, economic and telegraphic maps, 252 pages, 8°................. 1.00
Mexico. Geographical sketch, natural resources, laws, economic conditions,
actual development, prospects of future growth. Washington, 1904. Illus-
trated, 454 pages, 8°.. 1.00
Paraguay. Second edition, revised and enlarged, with a chapter on the native
races. 1902. Illustrated, map, 187 pages, 8°. Bibliography, page 141.... .75
Venezuela. Geographical sketch, natural resources, laws, economic conditions, actual development, prospects of future growth. Washington, 1904.
Illustrated, railway map, 608 pages, 8°................................. 1.00

BIBLIOGRAPHICAL BULLETINS.

Chile. A list of books, magazine articles, and maps relating to Chile. Washington, 1903. 110 pages, 8°... 1.00
Paraguay. A list of books, magazine articles and maps relating to Paraguay.
53 pages, 8°. Washington, 1904... 1.00

MAPS.

Guatemala. From official and other sources. 1902. Scale of 12.5 miles to
1 inch (1:792,000). In 2 sheets, each sheet 71 x 76 cm. No. 1. General
features. No. 2. Agricultural.. 1.00
Mexico. From official Mexican and other sources. 1900. Scale of 50 miles
to 1 inch. In 2 sheets, each sheet 108 x 80 cm. No. 1. General map.
No. 2. Agricultural areas.. 1.00
Nicaragua. From official and other sources. 1904. Scale of 12.5 miles to
1 inch (1:192,000). In 2 sheets, each sheet 80 x 80 cm. No. 1. General
map. No. 2. Agricultural.. 1.00
Bolivia. Mapa de la república de Bolivia, mandado organizar y publicar por
el Presidente Constitucional General José Manuel Pando. Scale 1:2,000,000.
La Paz, 1901. (Reprint International Bureau of the American Republics,
1904)... 1.00

PRICE.
Costa Rica. From official and other sources. 1903. Scale of 12.5 miles to 1 inch (792,000) $0. 50
Brazil. From official and other sources. 1905. Scale of 75 miles to 1 inch (1:4,752,000). In one sheet 96 x 93 cm 1. 00

LIST OF BOOKS AND MAPS IN COURSE OF PREPARATION.

LAW MANUALS.

Leyes Comerciales de América Latina: Código de Comercio de España comparado con los Códigos y Leyes Comerciales de Pan América.
Land and Immigration Laws of American Republics. (To replace edition of 1893.)

HANDBOOKS.

Chile.
Dominican Republic.

MAPS.

Maps are in course of preparation of the Republics of Honduras and Salvador.
Payment is required to be made in cash, money orders, or by bank drafts on banks in New York City or Washington, D. C., payable to the order of the INTERNATIONAL BUREAU OF THE AMERICAN REPUBLICS. Individual checks on banks outside of New York or Washington, or postage stamps, can not be accepted.

FOR FREE DISTRIBUTION.

The Bureau has for distribution a limited supply of the following, which will be sent, free, upon written application:
The case of the United States of Venezuela before the Tribunal of Arbitration to convene at Paris under the provisions of the Treaty between the United States of Venezuela and Her Britannic Majesty, signed at Washington, February 2, 1897, in 10 vols., of which 2 are maps.
Message from the President of the United States, transmitting a communication from the Secretary of State submitting the report, with accompanying papers, of the delegates of the United States to the Second International Conference of American States, held at the City of Mexico from October 22, 1901, to January 22, 1902. Washington, 1902. 243 pages. 8°. (57th Congress, 1st session, Senate Doc. No. 330.)
Message from the President of the United States, transmitting a report from the Secretary of State, with accompanying papers, relative to the proceedings of the International Congress for the study of the production and consumption of coffee, etc. Washington, 1903. 312 pages. 8° (paper). (57th Congress, 2d session, Senate Doc. No. 35.)
Message from the President of the United States, transmitting a report by the Secretary of State, with accompanying papers, relative to the proceedings of the First Customs Congress of the American Republics, held at New York in January, 1903. Washington, 1903. 195 pages. 8° (paper). (57th Congress, 2d session, Senate Doc. No. 180.)

NOTE.—Senate documents, listed above, containing reports of the various International American Congresses, may also be obtained through members of the United States Senate and House of Representatives.

Brazil at St. Louis Exposition. St. Louis, 1904. 160 pages. 8° (paper).

Chile—A short description of the Republic according to official data. Leipzig, 1901. 106 pages.   Map and 37 illustrations. 8° (cloth).

Chile—Breve descripción de la República escrita según datos oficiales. Leipzig, 1901. 106 páginas. Mapa y 36 grabados. 8° (en tela).

Chile at Pan-American Exposition. Buffalo, 1901. 252 pages (paper).

Guatemala—The Country of the future. By Charles M. Pepper. Washington, 1906. 80 pages. 8° (paper).

VALUE OF LATIN-AMERICAN COINS.

The following table shows the value, in United States gold, of coins representing the monetary units of the Central and South American Republics and Mexico, estimated quarterly by the Director of the United States Mint, in pursuance of act of Congress:

ESTIMATE JANUARY 1, 1907.

Countries.	Standard.	Unit.	Value in U. S. gold or silver.	Coins.
ARGENTINE REPUBLIC.	Gold	Peso	$0.965	Gold—Argentine ($4.824) and ½ Argentine. Silver—Peso and divisions.
BOLIVIA *	Silver ...	Boliviano	.510	Silver—Boliviano and divisions.
BRAZIL	Gold	Milreis ..	.546	Gold—5, 10, and 20 milreis. Silver—½, 1, and 2 milreis.
CENTRAL AMERICAN STATES— Costa Rica......	Gold	Colon ...	.465	Gold—2, 5, 10, and 20 colons ($9.307). Silver—5, 10, 25, and 50 centimos.
Guatemala...... Honduras ...... Nicaragua ...... Salvador	Silver ...	Peso	.510	Silver—Peso and divisions.
CHILE	Gold	Peso	.365	Gold—Escudo ($1.825), doubloon ($3.650), and condor ($7.300). Silver—Peso and divisions.
COLOMBIA..........	Gold	Dollar...	1.000	Gold—Condor ($9.647) and double condor. Silver—Peso.
ECUADOR	Gold	Sucre....	.487	Gold—10 sucres ($4.8665). Silver—Sucre and divisions.
HAITI	Gold	Gourde..	.965	Gold—1, 2, 5, and 10 gourdes. Silver—Gourde and divisions.
MEXICO..............	Gold	Peso a ...	.498	Gold—5 and 10 pesos. Silver—Dollar b (or peso) and divisions.
PANAMA	Gold	Balboa ..	1.000	Gold—1, 2½, 5, 10, and 20 balboas. Silver—Peso and divisions.
PERU	Gold	Libra ...	4.866½	Gold—½ and 1 libra. Silver—Sol and divisions.
URUGUAY	Gold	Peso	1.034	Gold—Peso. Silver—Peso and divisions.
VENEZUELA	Gold	Bolivar..	.193	Gold—5, 10, 20, 50, and 100 bolivars. Silver—5 bolivars.

a 75 centigrams fine gold.   b Value in Mexico, 0.498.

*[By the new Bolivian law enacted September 14, 1906, the gold peso of one-fifth of a pound sterling (1.5976 grams, 916⅔ fine) is made the unit of value.—EDITOR.]

ERNATIONAL BUREAU
IPUBLICS.

ard of the International Union of
or 19, 1906, Mr. JOHN BARRETT.
was unanimously elected Director
rcan Republics, in place of Mr.
1 to accept the position of United
.RRETT entered upon the discharge

, continuously in the foreign serv-
aving held the following positions:
34-1898; Special Commissioner of
in China, Japan, and the Philip-
ad States to the Second Pan-Amer-
; Commissioner General to Asia
rld's Fair, 1902-3; United States
iited States Minister to Panama,
olombia, 1905-6.
n, State of Vermont, in 1866, but
tland, Oregon, where he entered
from Dartmouth College in 1889.
legrees, respectively, of Bachelor
(M. A.) from Dartmouth College.
of the Republic of Colombia con-
tor of Laws and Political Science,
iote better relations between Latin

RECEPTION OF THE MINISTER OF URUGUAY IN THE UNITED STATES.

Dr. LUIS MELIAN LAFINUR, Envoy Extraordinary and Minister Plenipotentiary of Uruguay near the Government of the United States, was received in his capacity as such by President ROOSEVELT on January 5, 1907.

Upon presenting his credentials Doctor LAFINUR spoke as follows:

"MOST EXCELLENT MR. PRESIDENT: I have the honor to place in your hands the credentials which invest me with the quality of Envoy Extraordinary and Minister Plenipotentiary of the first class of the Republic of Uruguay near Your Excellency's Government. I also hand you the autograph letter by which the mission of my predecessor, Don EDUARDO ACEVEDO DIAZ, is terminated.

"Uruguay, Most Excellent Sir, ever maintains the purpose of tightening the bonds of brotherhood which happily join her to the powerful nation over whose destinies you preside. She prides herself on the friendship of your noble country, from which she has always received evidence of good will and consideration alike, and endeavors to follow in the path of its colossal progress, desiring, to that end, that the industry and trade of both peoples may combine in the solidarity of reciprocal advantages.

"Relying on your benevolence, I have come to aid in accomplishing this aim of my Government, in whose name I make wishes for the prosperity of your people and the personal happiness of Your Excellency."

The President's reply was as follows:

"MR. MINISTER : I am glad to welcome you to Washington and to receive from your hands the letter accrediting you in the quality of Envoy Extraordinary and Minister Plenipotentiary of Uruguay near the Government of the United States.

"The sentiments to which you have given utterance of the friendly and fraternal good will of Uruguay toward the United States coincide with the impressions which Mr. ROOT received during his visit to your country and find response in the reciprocal feelings which this Government and people entertain for the Government and people of Uruguay. In all that will tend to maintain and strengthen these good relations and to add to the development of mutually advantageous trade and industrial intercourse between the two countries it will be this Government's pleasure to give you its hearty cooperation.

"I thank you for the good wishes which you make in the name of your Government, and in turn beg that you will convey to your worthy President the expression of my own wish for his personal

eased that you and your colleagues of
have done me the honor to suggest that
me in Washington for the Bureau of

ication by the governing board of the
dent ROOSEVELT'S hearty expression of
·.

my membership of the First Pan-
ocacy of the Pan-American Railway,
slowly filled. The importance of this
and more upon me, and I hope to see

ating that it will be one of the pleasures
on of all the Republics of this Hemi-
50,000), from time to time as may be
an international home in Washington.
Republic is seen in the appropriation
urchase of the site, and in the agree-
or the maintenance of the Bureau we
cooperation, so that the forthcoming
be the joint work of all the Republics.
em drawing closer together.
it all these are for the first time to be
Hague Conference. Henceforth they
ee aim is the settlement of international
nations' or other similar tribunal.
d all of them my heartfelt thanks for
New Year gift as this. I have never
New Year morning how much more
sive, and I consider myself highly hon-

ored by being considered worthy to provide the forthcoming union home, where the accredited representatives of all the Republics are to meet and, I trust, to bind together their respective nations in the bonds of unbroken peace.

"Very truly, yours,

"ANDREW CARNEGIE."

Hon. ELIHU ROOT,

Secretary of State and ex-Officio Chairman of the Governing Board of the Bureau of South American Republics, Washington, D. C.

"THE WHITE HOUSE,
"*Washington, January 2, 1907.*

"MY DEAR MR. CARNEGIE: I am so much pleased at learning from Secretary ROOT what you are going to do for the Bureau of American Republics. You have already done substantially the same thing for the cause of peace at The Hague. This new gift of yours has an almost, or quite, equal significance as far as the cause of peace in the Western Hemisphere is concerned, for the Bureau of American Republics is striving to accomplish for this Hemisphere what The Hague Peace Tribunal is striving to accomplish for both Hemispheres. I thank you heartily.

"Wishing you many happy new years, believe me, sincerely yours,

"THEODORE ROOSEVELT."

About three years ago the Governing Board of the Bureau of American Republics resolved upon the purchase of a site to erect a new building for the use of the Bureau which is now occupying a rented building in the city of Washington. The amount fixed upon to be expended was $125,000. This amount was allotted to the different Republics in proportion to their population, being the same proportion in which they paid the expenses of the Bureau. Fifteen Republics other than the United States announced their readiness to pay their proportion and some of them sent the money, so that there has been for several years some $20,000 or $30,000 in the Treasury of the United States to be expended for the building.

Mr. HAY, at that time Secretary of State of the United States, wrote to the President stating these facts, and the President sent a message to Congress asking for an appropriation for the share of the United States, which would have been about $71,000. The appropriation passed the Senate, but did not pass the House. The matter then rested until the last session. When Secretary ROOT was preparing for the Rio conference he found this state of affairs—this message of the President to Congress which had not been acted upon—and he asked the committees of Congress to go on and make the appropriation. As it seemed to him that the basis of $125,000 was inadequate to the work which he hoped the Bureau would do, and as he hoped to secure additional money from outside sources, he secured from Congress an appropriation of $200,000. It is put in the form for the purchase of land and is the entire contribution of the United States toward the new building for the Bureau of the American Republics, payable to the order of the Secretary of State.

So that there is at the present time available for the purchase of a site and erection of the new building—First, the contributions of the Latin-American Republics on the basis of the original allotment; second, the appropriation by Congress of $200,000, and, third, Mr. Carnegie's gift of $750,000. The idea is to have the building a notable example of Latin-American architecture, and to have in it offices which may be the headquarters of each Latin-American nation or group of nations as they may arrange it. There are to be in it also reading rooms, in which the leading Latin-American newspapers and magazines will be found, and quarters for the library, which has already reached something over 12,000 volumes, so that the library can be readily consulted, and to have it serve as a meeting place for all the Latin Americans who come to the United States.

BOUNDARY TREATIES BETWEEN COSTA RICA AND PANAMA.

The following treaties executed in the city of Panama on March 6. 1905, between the representatives of Costa Rica and Panama, were ratified by the Congress of Panama on January 25, 1907:

"The Governments of Costa Rica and Panama, for the purpose of friendly and definitely settling any questions that might arise in the future concerning their respective territorial rights, and prompted by the desire of putting an end forever to the differences that during many years have constituted a source of uneasiness between the two nations herein represented—differences, by the way, which should henceforth be forever extinguished because the brotherly and reciprocal interests of both countries so demand it; for the aforesaid purpose His Excellency the President of the Republic of Costa Rica has granted full powers to his Excellency LEONIDAS PACIIECO, Envoy Extraordinary and Minister Plenipotentiary before the Government of Panama, and His Excellency the President of the Republic of Panama has likewise given full powers to His Excellency General SANTIAGO DE LA GUARDIA, Secretary of Foreign Relations, who, after having fulfilled the requisite formalities, make the following declaration in the name of their respective Governments:

"I. The signatory Republics do hereby solemnly declare that in accordance with the purport of the provisions of the respective laws

and treaties, as well as with the official declarations made by the high
contracting parties, the question of boundaries maintained during
many years by the Republic of Colombia, which was the former owner
of the territory in litigation—at present belonging to the Republic of
Panama and that of Costa Rica—was settled by the award of His
Excellency the President of the French Republic at Rambouillet on
the 11th day of September, 1900, and by virtue of which, the boundary line having been fixed by the arbiter by means of general indications only, the practical fixing of the same remained to be done by a
mutual agreement which would be reached in view of the spirit of conciliation and good understanding which has heretofore inspired the
two interested nations.

"In witness whereof we have hereunto set our hands and seals, in
duplicate, at the city of Panama on the 6th day of March, 1905.

"LEONIDAS PACHECO.

"SANTIAGO DE LA GUARDIA."

"The Governments of the Republics of Costa Rica and Panama, in
view of the purport of the declaration made by them on this day with
reference to the award made by the President of the French Republic
on the 11th day of September, 1900, and being desirous of drawing
still closer and of strengthening the brotherly relations which happily
exist between both Republics, and taking into consideration that one
of the most expeditious and efficient means to obtain the desired end
is to fix in a final and solemn manner the boundary line of their respective territories, taking into account, in so doing, both the reciprocal
friendly feelings and the interests of the two countries; and that
whereas, by virtue of the separation of the Isthmus, effected of the
3d of November, 1903, the circumstances which obtained at the time
the award herein referred to was made were widely different from
those prevailing at the present time; that said circumstances render it
necessary for both Republics to establish a boundary line better suited
to their present and future interests; that the cordial feelings by
which the signatory Powers are prompted, and the reciprocal desire
that their development, prosperity, and progress may continue without hindrance and with the mutual support and cooperation of each
other suggest the advisability of consulting, in the new survey the
wishes, expectations, and wants of both countries; that on being
inspired in a spirit of conciliation and good understanding, to establish
the basis upon which the survey of the boundary line should rest the
Republics of Costa Rica and Panama show due regard for the wise
counsel of the high arbiter who made the aforesaid award. Now,
therefore, in view of the foregoing, said high contracting parties have
agreed to conclude the following treaty, and for the carrying out of
which His Excellency the President of Costa Rica has commissioned

ɛco and DE LA GUARDIA, after the exchange
in good and due form, have this day agreed
ine of the territories of the nations repre-
form stated in the following article:
en the Republics of Costa Rica and Panama
which, starting from Punta Mona, on the
inue in a southwesterly direction until it
down along Cuabre. From this point the
along the left bank of said Sixaola River to
with the Yurquin or Zhorquin River. At
ne shall cut through the thalweg of the
n the left bank of the Yurquin, and shall
ction into the divide of the watersheds, first
Yurquin to the east and of the Uren to the
se of the latter and those of the Tararia or
e summit of the great Cordillera which
Atlantic Ocean from those of the Pacific
ie line shall follow in an east-southeasterly
l summit, to a point called 'Cerro Pando,'
of the division of the waters between the
ai Viejo rivers. Thence the boundary line
mit of the Santa Clara Mountains, follow-
rs between the coto of Terraba and Esqui-
l the Chiriqui mejo and coto of the Gulf
saches the headwaters of the Golfito River,
line shall continue to its mouth in Golfo
mouth called Golfito. Between this latter
straight imaginary line shall divide the
lce Gulf), the western portion of the latter
sive control of Costa Rica and the eastern
mmon control of both signatory Republics,
it in their respective coasts is called the lit-
sidered an integral part of the contiguous

ention to the present treaty shall establish
in order to make the demarcation of the
foregoing article.
treaty shall have been ratified by the respec-
re months following the date of the last of
proceed to effect their proper exchange,

which shall take place at the city of San Jose, Costa Rica, or at the city of Panama.

"In witness whereof we sign and seal the present document, in duplicate, at the city of Panama, on the 6th day of March, 1905.

" LEONIDAS PACHECO.

"SANTIAGO DE LA GUARDIA."

"The Republics of Costa Rica and Panama, for the purpose of adopting the most expeditious manner of surveying and fixing the boundary line set forth in the treaty of boundaries, signed by the same contracting parties on this day, have decided to enter into the present agreement, for which purpose His Excellency the President of Costa Rica has appointed His Excellency LEONIDAS PACHECO, Envoy Extraordinary and Minister Plenipotentiary near the Government of Panama, and His Excellency the President of Panama has likewise appointed His Excellency Gen. SANTIAGO DE LA GUARDIA, Secretary of State for Foreign Relations.

"The said Messrs. DE LA GUARDIA and PACHECO, after the exchange of their full powers, found in good and due form, have made the following agreement:

"I. For the purpose of properly surveying and demarcating the boundary line-established by Article I of the treaty of boundaries, entered into between the signatory Republics on this day, the contracting Governments respectively bind themselves to appoint a commission, composed of the necessary personnel, which shall execute its mission within the terms and in the manner set forth in the following articles:

"II. The commissions created in accordance with the foregoing article shall be completed by an engineer, whose appointment shall be made in the manner hereinafter indicated, and whose duties shall be limited as follows: Should the Costa Rican and Panamanian commissions disagree as to the practicability of the operations, the point or points discussed shall be submitted to the opinion of said engineer. who shall have full power to decide any difference that should arise. The operations in question shall be carried out in accordance with the decision of said engineer.

"III. Within three months after the exchange of the present convention, which shall have been duly ratified by the respective Congresses, the representatives in Washington of both contracting Governments shall jointly proceed to request the President of the United States of North America to consent to appoint the engineer herein referred to, and to make said appointment. Should one of the two Governments have no representative at Washington, or if for any other reason they should fail to make the joint request within the aforesaid term, after the expiration of the latter either of the representatives of Costa Rica or Panama may separately make said request,

d setting of the boundary line shall be made
g from the date of the appointment of the
operation shall be completed within twelve
which the work was begun.   The commis-
ng parties shall hold meetings at Colon
nat purpose, and shall begin their work at
lary line which, in accordance with Article
es herein referred to, starts from Punta

.

ties agree that if for any reason either of
ica or Panamá should fail to appear at the
he work is to be begun, said work shall be
tion of the other Republic which may be
of the engineer herein referred to, and
n and. there shall be valid and final, the
commissioners having no right to bring
same procedure shall be followed in case
mers of the contracting Republics should
tarting of the work, or in case they should
same in the form set forth in the present
the decision of the appointed engineer.
irties agree that the term fixed for the
f the landmarks is not peremptory, and
ifter the expiration of said term, shall be
irm may not have been sufficient for the
erations, or because the commissions of
have agreed between themselves, and in
of the appointed engineer, to temporarily
ie the remainder of the term fixed may
nish said work.
of setting the landmarks be temporarily
en done up to that date shall be considered
a boundaries in the respective parts shall
fixed, even though, owing to unforeseen
inces, said suspension should continue

s of the operations carried out, which shall
by the commissioners, shall, without the
lity on the part of the signatory Republics,
e of their boundary.
d to in the foregoing article shall be drawn
Every day, at the completion of the work,
y noted down, stating the starting point of

the day's operations, the kind of landmarks constructed or adopted, the distance at which one landmark is set from another, the bearing or direction of the line which determines the common boundary, etc.   In case any discussion should arise between the Costa Rican and Panamanian commissions concerning any point, said question or questions, as well as the decision of the engineer herein referred to, shall be stated in the respective minutes.   Said minutes shall be kept in triplicate, the Costa Rican commission keeping one of the copies, another to be kept by the Panamanian commission, and the third one by the engineer, to be deposited, after the completion of the operations, with the Government of the United States of America.

"X. Each of the signatory Republics shall pay one-half of such expenses as may be incurred on account of the assignment and stay of the engineer herein referred to, as well as such salary as may be due him during all the time he may spend in the fulfillment of his duties.

"XI. The failure to execute the work within the terms herein referred to shall not cause the nullification of the present convention, and the omission shall be filled within the shortest possible time by the Republic called upon to do so.

"XII. After the present convention shall have been ratified by the respective congresses and within three months from the date of the last of the ratifications, the contracting parties shall proceed to make their corresponding exchange, which shall take place at San Jose, Costa Rica, or at the city of Panama.

"In witness whereof, we sign and seal, in duplicate, the present convention, at Panama, on the 6th day of March of 1905.

"LEONIDAS PACHECO.
"SANTIAGO DE LA GUARDIA."

TRADE CONDITIONS IN CENTRAL AMERICA.

The following is an extract from the report of Mr. LINCOLN HUTCHINSON, Special Agent of the United States Department of Commerce and Labor:

CENTRAL AMERICA.

GENERAL CONDITIONS.

The geography of the six Central American States is so well known as to call for little comment in this place.   In order, however, to understand certain features of the commercial development of these countries, it is necessary to emphasize one or two points which are sometimes overlooked.   The six States of Guatemala, Honduras, British Honduras, Salvador, Nicaragua, and Costa Rica together form

be entire length runs a backbone of moun-
ruptly from the coast, reaching in places
) feet, inclosing many plateau regions, and
te of much of the interior.

nt effect, commercially, of the presence of
ie difficulty which it presents to transpor-
ts or from either coast into the interior.
 to coast is in Nicaragua, with an eleva-
 feet. In the other countries far greater
ie; in Costa Rica, for example, over 4,000
y 5,000. These altitudes have prevented
 from coast to coast, and have maintained
ion between the west and the east slopes of
slope belongs still to the commercial sphere
rn to that of the Atlantic. There is at
 the whole of the very short distance from
ide. In some cases such roads have been
d a greater or less distance from one side
 one or two cases, as in Costa Rica and in
cts of an early completion. In the main,
ssage of goods from the one coast to the
sibility; and even in districts near either
oods is a costly and uncertain affair. Ox
e burden bearers, and many of the roads,
in the dry season, become virtually impas-
is. This commercial separation of the two
cal consequences, which will be discussed

TION AND COMMERCE.

States is, in general, very sparse, the total
estimated at about 4,100,000. This popu-
evenly distributed. The smallest of the
an area of but 7,225 square miles, has a
per square mile, while the largest, Nica-
0 square miles, shows a density of only 8.5

per mile.   In both area and population British Honduras is insignificant (7,562 square miles and about 37,000 inhabitants), but her nearest neighbors, Honduras, Guatemala, and Salvador, constituting the northern half of Central America, form the most important group among the six States.   The combined area of these three is about one-half of the total area of the six, but their population is 80 per cent of the total.

DEVELOPMENT WILL INCREASE TRAFFIC.

The commercial activity of the people as a whole is not great.   The total imports of the six countries probably reach a value of about $16,000,000 per annum, or a little less than $4 per capita.   The exports are estimated at $26,000,000, or a little more than $6 per capita.   But in this respect, again, we find great differences.   Costa Rica is the most active in proportion to population, her export and import trade together reaching nearly $30 per capita.   The others are far behind, except British Honduras, whose commercial statistics are, however, swelled by a large transit trade, and are therefore misleading.   The exports and imports of Nicaragua reach a value of about $10 per capita; of Guatemala, $9; Salvador, $7, and Honduras, $6.30.

Three of the countries in question have been going through a period of commercial depression in the past two or three years, due, in part at least, to poor crops of coffee, combined with low prices in the world market.   Those most affected have been Guatemala and Honduras.   Nicaragua has suffered in less degree, at least so far as the effect on foreign trade movement has been concerned.   Costa Rica has felt the coffee depression less than any of the others, because of the development there of another great industry—banana raising.   Thus we find that in some sections foreign trade has declined in recent years, while in others it has grown rapidly.   It is probable that the growing sections represent the more normal condition of the whole, for where decline has taken place it can be traced to causes which are mostly of temporary character.   The countries all have great resources.   New investments of foreign capital are taking place, and new enterprises are being developed.   It is safe to assume that the next few years will see a fairly rapid growth of trade in all the countries.

UNITED STATES LEADS IN IMPORTS.

The imports of Central America are such as are always characteristic of countries whose industries are chiefly extractive: Textiles, implements, tools, machinery, and foodstuffs.   In this respect Central America does not differ materially from most of the countries of South America.   It does differ from them, however, in that the United States holds the lion's share of the trade.   Taking the six countries as a whole, it is probable that the United States supplies at least 50 per

represent average annual values for the
~~table~~ gold.

..ed States, the United Kingdom, and Germany to
..States, for specified periods.

...tes.	United Kingdom.		Germany.	
1900-1904.	1894-1898.	1899-1903.	1897-1899.	1900-1904.
$....,000	$...,000	$644,000	$350,000	$247,000
...,000	1,549,000	468,000	466,000	452,000
...,000	376,000	313,000	......	......
1,...,000	313,000	286,000	......	......
1,...,000	862,000	674,000	445,000	619,000
...784,000	1,421,000	1,071,000		

.. United States stands first in all of the
England takes second place except in Sal-
Germany stands third. In Costa Rica,
and Nicaragua we have made great gains,
..Guatemala and Salvador, the decline is
.line in the trade of those countries.

.TIVE INDUSTRIES.

..ed that the industries of these Central
.tractive. The products are mainly trop-
the uplands some few commodities com-
re also exploited. Manufactures in any
wholly lacking, but in some of the towns
brewing, ice making, the manufacture of
re to be found. The demand for foreign
.y, etc., is therefore connected almost
t not of these embryo manufactures but
.l industries and the exploitation of the
.und in some districts.
.industries as well as the lines in future
.ountries is perhaps best illustrated by
.and industry in one of them, which, as
. the greatest commercial activity—Costa
.ctory to do this, as the statistical depart-
.veloped a high degree of efficiency, which
.ery complete data.

COSTA RICA.

BANANAS AND COFFEE CHIEF EXPORTS.

The chief exports of Costa Rica are coffee and bananas, these two items together making up over 90 per cent in value of all shipments abroad. Hard woods, hides, and small quantities of precious metals supply the major part of the remaining 10 per cent. In the other five countries the exports comprise nearly the same list, but in different proportions. In most of them coffee occupies the leading place, while in Costa Rica bananas have risen to a point of equality with coffee and bid fair soon to surpass it. The value of coffee exports has remained nearly stationary during the past ten years; in 1896 it was $4,310,000 and in 1905 only $3,774,000. Banana exports, on the other hand, have grown with astonishing rapidity from $565,000 in 1896 to $3,648,000 in 1905. The market for Central American bananas is extending rapidly, the last few years having seen large sales in England, and it is certain that the success of the industry in Costa Rica will stimulate the development of the banana lands of the other five countries.

IMPORTS BY COUNTRIES.

The decline in the value of coffee exports from Costa Rica has been more than offset by the increase in banana exports, and the total value of shipments of all commodities to foreign countries has therefore increased from $5,333,000 in 1896 to $8,148,000 in 1905. And this growth in exports has naturally been accompanied by a development of the import trade through general increase of purchasing power, as well as through the increased demand for the paraphernalia needed by the expanding industries. In this growing import trade the United States has played a more and more important part, as is well illustrated by the following table showing the percentage of imports from the principal countries:

Share of leading countries in the import trade of Costa Rica, 1894-1905.

Year.	Eng-land.	United States.	Ger-many.	France.	Year.	Eng-land.	United States.	Ger-many.	France.
	Per cent.	Per cent.	Per cent.	Per cent.		Per cent.	Per cent.	Per cent.	Per cent.
1894......	32.03	34.59	19.21	7.79	1901	21.93	46.77	13.50	5.43
1897......	26.92	33.64	21.01	10.00	1902	23.94	54.08	12.47	5.25
1898......	19.61	44.80	15.50	10.80	1903	21.57	50.20	11.07	6.47
1899......	19.60	54.00	14.35	5.90	1904	19.27	52.20	12.50	4.60
1900......	37.30	46.50	13.50	5.94	1905	19.73	46.88	12.90	5.24

The share of the United States has increased from a bare superiority over that of England to an excess of some 9 per cent over England, Germany, and France combined.

....	$1,171,150	$942,674	20.8
in, wilson, etc...............	1,073,363	670,382	62.7
....	777,388	520,576	67.5
....	157,630	92,577	58.7
....	147,306	66,461	45.1
....	111,389	31,814	28.6
....	100,000	66,694	66.5
....	73,393	71,699	97.9
....	76,874	55,126	71.7
....	66,187	65,728	99.4
....	501,601	501,601	100.0
....	985,625	314,599	31.9
....	5,289,477	2,705,063	45.9

ficiently clear idea of the chief classes of
osta Rica from the United States, but a
ains—the growth or decline of our trade
lowing table throws light on this point.
s, in United States gold, of the principal
es for the five-year periods stated.

*d articles into Costa Rica from the United States,
1895-1904.*

10-1904.	Article.	1895–1899.	1900–1904.
100,400	Leather, and manufactures of	$22,400	$34,400
101,600	Scientific instruments and apparatus..................	19,400	39,000
349,329	Oils..........................	19,200	30,800
45,630	Carts, carriages, other vehicles, and parts............	18,000	51,200
215,600	Paper, and manufactures of.	17,400	24,000
47,800	Paints, pigments, and colors.	2,600	4,600

nstitute the bulk of American trade with
marked increase. There are, however,
them included in one or another of the

above groups) in which our trade has declined.   The more important of them are:

Articles.	1895–1899.	1900–1904.	Articles.	1895–1899.	1900–1904.
Live animals....................	$9,200	$8,600	Wines, spirits, and liquors.....	$44,600	$29,200
Books, maps, engravings,			Paraffin and paraffin wax.....	26,200	23,000
etchings, etc..................	7,400	4,800	Perfumery and cosmetics.....	4,600	3,400
Fish...........................	21,600	16,000	Vegetables.....................	15,600	15,000

INCREASES AND DECREASES.

The decline in our exports of live animals seems to be merely a part of a general decline in purchases of such animals.   Larger numbers are being raised within the country itself and in the neighboring Republics, and it is not probable that any considerable supplies will be brought from the United States.   The demand must be confined to a few animals for breeding purposes.

Books, maps, engravings, etchings, etc. (of which the largest item is books), do not present a very promising field for American exporters. American illustrated papers, chromos, lithographs, etc., have a certain sale, but books imported are, of course, printed chiefly in Spanish or French, and American publishers, with a rather limited market for works in those languages, can hardly compete with Spanish, French, and German houses.

In fish the United States continues to hold the larger part of the market in spite of the decline.   The falling off is difficult to explain. It seems likely to be only temporary, though Spain, France, Germany, and Italy are sending considerable quantities, especially of sardines and canned shellfish.

In perfumery and cosmetics the share of the United States is small at best.   France is the chief source of supply and seems likely to remain so.

The falling off in our sales of vegetables is so slight as to be of little significance.   The same can not be said, however, in regard to the decline in our sales of wines, liquors, etc.   A few years ago there were indications that we were building up a fair trade in these goods, especially in wines.   The foothold then obtained seems now to have been lost in favor of Portugal, Spain, and France.

HONDURAS.

SHARE OF THE UNITED STATES IN EXPORTS AND IMPORTS.

The statistical office of the Government of Honduras has recently prepared a statement of the foreign trade of the country for the fiscal year ended July 31, 1905.   The figures are of considerable interest as nce of the United States in the commerce

country for the year were valued at
nt the United States furnished $1,689,900,
xports were more than twice as large as
United States taking $4,622,700, or more
e of other countries is shown by the fol-

s, year ended July 31, 1905, by countries.

Exports from Honduras.	Country.	Imports into Honduras.	Exports from Honduras.
,602,700	Japan	$1,800	
600	Guatemala	1,600	$120,000
27,400	Cuba	900	391,100
74,600	Panama	200	1,300
5,600	Costa Rica		2,800
15,600	All others	15,000	
35,600	Total	2,362,800	5,564,000

xport are the various natural vegetable
e reaching a value of $2,593,700. Mineral
)98,700, and animal exports at $909,000.
ts exported, bananas are by far the most
shipments being $2,078,400. Cocoanuts
hen hard woods, with $128,100; rubber,
2,700, and sarsaparilla, $30,000.
t is copper, $1,154,000; gold and silver
e, $813,700. The only important animal
, $595,600, and hides and skins, $298,000.

ITION OF THE UNITED STATES.

ie above figures are compiled illustrates
nited States in the markets of Honduras,
ally important fact that the commanding
s has been attained only in recent years.
the United States to Honduras were not
te amount, but they constituted a far less
al purchases of that country. And the
ot merely in one or two classes of goods,
ant item of our trade. The following
ment of exports from the United States,
ited States gold. The figures represent
-year periods.

Average annual imports of specified classes of articles into Honduras from the United States, 1895–1904.

Class.	1895–1899.	1900–1904.	Class.	1895–1899.	1900–1904.
All foodstuffs, including breadstuffs, provisions, wines, liquors, etc..........	$131,600	$220,300	Explosives.......	$21,700	$42,900
Cotton goods	181,400	278,900	Quicksilver	43,300	47,900
Iron and steel, and manufactures of.......................	92,600	151,100	Wood, and manufactures of..	20,000	38,900
Chemicals, drugs, medicines, etc	35,400	51,300	Leather, and manufactures of	14,700	33,200
			Sugar and molasses..........	14,400	20,400
			Oils	10,500	19,100
			All goods	657,200	1,057,200

The only goods showing a decline between the two periods are a few unimportant ones: Scientific instruments and apparatus, $5,700 to $4,500; notions, $2,300 to $1,900; soap, $8,100 to $6,600; and bottled wines, $2,100 to $1,400.

Besides the foregoing more important classes of goods there are many others which show a similar increase—paper, candles, cars, carriages and other vehicles, coal, earthen and china ware, glassware, rubber manufactures, lamps and chandeliers, matches, oilcloths, paints, etc., perfumery and cosmetics, manufactures of straw and palm leaf, tinware, etc. The rapid rise of the United States to the controlling position in the commerce of Honduras is but one of many illustrations of what our exporters may do in time in many parts of Spanish America.

GUATEMALA.

REVIVAL OF COMMERCIAL LIFE.

In 1897 the United States sent to Guatemala goods to the value of $2,992,000; in 1898 this figure dropped to $1,163,000, and in 1900 to $765,000. England in 1896 sent $2,000,000; in 1899, $640,000. Germany in 1897, $800,000; in 1898, $440,000; and in 1899, $250,000. The lowest ebb of the import trade was reached in 1899 and 1900. Since then there has been a gradual recovery.

The official figures of imports for the year 1904 showed considerable increase over previous years. Those for 1905, which have just been published by the Guatemalan Government, exhibit still further advance. Beginning with the years immediately following the crisis the figures are shown in the annexed table, which represent annual average values for the three-year periods stated and for 1904 and 1905 separately:

Foreign trade of Guatemala, 1899–1905.

Year.	Imports.	Exports.	Year.	Imports.	Exports.
1899–1901...................	a$3,714,500	a$7,761,100	1904	$5,041,100	$7,551,900
1902–1904..................	a 4,009,900	a 7,767,400	1905	6,841,400	8,237,800

a Average annual value.

	1905.		1894–1904.		1905.	
ent.		cent.	Value.	Per cent.	Value.	Per cent.
36.6	$3,067,000	44.5	$2,166,600	26.9	$2,675,300	34.9
22.6	1,570,100	22.9	1,287,400	15.4	1,050,500	12.8
20.0	1,405,500	20.5	4,508,000	58.8	4,078,600	48.5
9.2	269,500	3.9	201,300	2.4	25,300	.3

nala has sunk almost into insignificance;
emained nearly stationary, with a slight
imports and some decline in their share
the United States has increased in both
import trade in 1905 was nearly as large
y, and France combined.

OWTH OF IMPORTS.

that American exports to Guatemala con-
I I have repeatedly been told by persons
ie facts that the reason for the recent
the shortage of Guatemalan maize crops,
the purchase of foreign supplies. An
roves this to be but partial truth. It is
e the largest single item in our exports to
ue that a very considerable part of the
rts in 1905 consisted of these same goods,
of the tale, for there are other extremely
de with Guatemala which show similar
n 1905, when Guatemala's purchases of
tates were abnormally large, they formed
total purchases from us; at least an equal
undry manufactured goods, of which the
textiles. On the other hand, the growth
n many lines of goods which offer us a
ie Guatemalan maize crop affected mainly
s, the increase for the year being $558,000

(from $450,000 in 1904 to $1,008,000 in 1905), but other increases are scarcely less significant, as will be seen from the following:

Principal articles of import into Guatemala showing increases in 1905.

Article.	1904.	1905.	Article.	1904.	1905.
Other foodstuffs	$168,000	$409,000	Glassware and porcelain.	$17,000	$48,000
Iron and steel	176,000	422,000	Coal	49,000	69,000
Textiles	1,249,000	1,467,000	Tallow	39,000	73,000

There were also many other smaller items. In most of these classes of goods in which Guatemalan purchases have made marked gains the United States has contributed largely increased amounts, and in all of them except textiles and glassware the United States already holds the bulk of the trade. We furnish 89 per cent of the breadstuffs, 50 per cent of the other foodstuffs, 42 per cent of the iron and steel, 92 per cent of the coal, 98 per cent of the tallow, 22 per cent of the glassware, and 21 per cent of the textiles.

KINDS OF GOODS NEEDED.

A clear idea of the kinds of goods in demand in Guatemala and the position of the United States in the trade may be obtained from the following table, which includes all principal items of Guatemalan import (values in United States gold):

Principal imports into Guatemala and share of the United States therein for specified years.

Article.	1905.			Average per annum from United States.		
	All countries.	United States.		1899–1901.	1902–1904.	Increase (+) or decrease (−).
		Value.	Per cent.			
Foodstuffs:						Per cent.
Breadstuffs	$1,054,800	$937,500	88.8			
Beverages	210,100	45,400	21.6			
Provisions	128,000	116,200	90.8			
Fruits and vegetables	38,400	29,500	76.8			
Sundry preserved goods	89,600	48,400	54.0			
All others	25,700	4,800	18.8			
Total	1,546,600	1,181,800	76.4	$439,500	$445,100	+ 1.3
Textiles:						
Cottons	1,447,600	317,300	21.9	171,600	239,900	+ 39.8
Woolens	143,600	800	.5			
Silks	163,600	68,800	41.9			
Linens	12,400	1,000	7.9			
Sacks	135,000	18,600	13.8			
All other	11,300	1,000	8.9			
Total	1,913,500	407,500	21.3			
Iron and steel:						
Machinery	152,200	78,600	51.6			
Agricultural and laborers' tools	107,600	21,700	20.2			
Mechanics' tools	24,300	9,400	38.7			
Railway materials	93,800	68,200	72.7			
Household utensils	76,400	16,800	22.0			
Galvanized roofing	60,550	6,800	11.2			
Pipes and fittings	19,300	11,200	58.0			

Principal imports into Guatemala and share of the United States therein for specified years—Continued.

Article.	1905	United States.		Average per annum from United States.		
	All countries.	Value.	Per cent.	1899–1901.	1902–1904.	Increase (+) or decrease (−).
Iron and steel—Continued.						*Per cent.*
Fence wire.............................	$30,000	$22,400	74.9	....	....	....
Hardware.............................	13,300	6,500	48.7	....	....	....
Iron and steel for industrial uses..	32,400	23,000	70.9	....	....	....
All other.............................	92,400	33,600	36.4	....	....	....
Total.............................	702,100	298,000	42.4	$139,200	$180,000	+ 29.6
Paper................................	104,500	18,600	17.8	16,500	20,800	+ 26.1
Glass and glassware.................	38,700	8,700	22.4	6,300	9,400	+ 49.2
Cars, carriages, etc.................	5,700	3,100	54.8	14,100	11,300	− 19.9
Wood:						
Unmanufactured	42,700	42,300	99.1	....	....	....
Manufactures......................	27,300	9,200	33.8	....	....	....
Total.......	70,000	51,500	73.7	40,200	84,200	+109.4
Leather:						
Unmanufactured...................	51,500	33,000	64.1	....	....	....
Boots and shoes...................	6,500	4,900	76.9	....	....	....
Other manufactures...............	14,400	1,900	12.9	....	....	....
Total.............................	72,400	39,800	55.0	18,700	30,900	+125.5
Coal................................	69,300	63,900	92.2	7,700	32,000	+315.6
Oils................................	72,000	54,300	75.4	31,300	40,900	+ 30.7
Paints, pigments, colors, etc........	25,400	15,800	62.3	12,500	13,500	+ 8.0
Chemicals, drugs, medicines, etc.....	128,200	59,100	46.1	35,300	33,400	− 5.4
Explosives..........................	22,000	21,700	98.6	19,000	22,200	+ 16.8
Copper manufactures................	16,400	4,100	25.0	1,300	2,600	+100.0

HINTS FOR AMERICAN EXPORTERS.

The bulk of American trade with Guatemala is seen to be in food-stuffs and in iron and steel goods, and in both of these classes of commodities as a whole we supply a larger share than any other country. There are many separate items included in these headings in which we are, however, far behind some of our competitors. A more detailed examination of these latter may offer hints to our exporters as to lines in which their trade might be increased. The annexed table shows specified imports into Guatemala, share of the United States therein, and principal sources of competition in 1905:

Articles.	All countries.	United States.	Chief competitors.
Breadstuffs:			
Rice	$37,100	$26,500	Germany.
Malt...	32,300	21,700	Chile.
Crackers, etc	5,600	3,900	England, Germany.
Paste preparations	4,100	1,800	Italy.
Provisions:			
Butter..	4,600	2,800	Germany.
Cheese	8,300	3,500	Italy, Germany.
Hams, bacon, sausages..................................	4,700	500	Spain.
Sundry preserved goods:			
Wooden coverings......................................	9,800	8,200	Germany, Spain
Other coverings.......................................	79,800	40,200	Germany.
Sweets and comfits	11,000	4,200	England, Germany.

Articles.	All coun-tries.	United States.	Chief competitors.
Beverages:			
Mineral waters	$6,500	$1,600	England, France.
Beer	44,800	6,400	Germany.
Spirits	54,600	18,200	France.
Ginger ale	2,600	600	England.
Liquors	7,800	400	France.
Cider	1,600	400	Spain.
Wine, red	41,700	14,500	France, Spain.
Wine, white	35,700	2,600	Spain, France, Germany.
Wine, sparkling	12,500	65	France.
Table oil	9,900	3,200	France, Spain.
Iron and steel:			
Electrical material and apparatus	20,700	5,900	Germany.
Firearms—revolvers	6,600	6,000	Spain.
Others	6,100	670	Germany. Belgium, England.
Household utensils	76,400	16,800	Germany.
Pumps	2,400	1,100	Germany, England.
Pipes and fittings	19,300	11,200	England, Belgium.
Hardware	18,300	6,500	Germany.
Tools and implements	131,900	31,100	Germany, England.
Galvanized roofing	60,500	6,800	Germany.
Machinery driven by animal, water, or steam power	113,300	45,200	England, Germany.
Typewriters	3,075	2,774	Germany.

COMPETITION IN TEXTILES.

In textiles the United States holds but 21 per cent of the total trade, yet there are certain lines of these goods in which we are making progress, which is prophetic of considerable changes in the near future. In woolen, linen, and jute manufactures we hardly compete at all, but in silks we already hold the largest share, and in several classes of cottons we have made marked progress. The table on page 78 shows imports of silk and cotton goods into Guatemala, share of the United States therein, and principal sources of competition in 1905.

Articles.	All coun-tries.	United States.	Chief competitors.
Silk goods:			
Ready-made goods	$63,300	$38,900	China, Japan.
Shawls and mufflers	32,100	20,200	Japan.
Ribbons	19,500	85	Germany, England.
Umbrellas and parasols	4,500	750	Germany, Italy.
Silk floss	16,500	7,100	England, Japan.
Piece goods	18,300	1,300	Japan, France, Germany.
Cotton Goods:			
Ready-made goods	45,900	3,600	England, Germany.
Ribbons	4,700	130	Germany.
Corsets	4,500	600	Germany, England.
Drills	135,200	58,500	England, Germany.
Blankets	24,300	4,000	Do.
Thread and yarn	190,200	1,800	England.
Umbrellas and parasols	4,700	1,800	Germany.
Underclothing	56,600	4,200	Do.
Piece goods—			
Unbleached	372,200	134,700	England.
Bleached	114,800	8,200	Do.
Dyed	92,700	38,500	England, Germany.
Prints	124,600	43,900	England.
Twills	33,500	300	Do.
All other	120,300	10,400	England, Germany.
Towels	10,100	250	England.

In cottons the United States makes the best showing in drills, unbleached and dyed goods, and in prints.   There is a steadily increasing demand for American goods of this sort not only in Guatemala but in all Central America.   The difficulties which stand in the way of increased business are chiefly those which affect the sale of our cotton goods in all Spanish America.   They have been repeatedly alluded to.

NICARAGUA, SALVADOR, AND BRITISH HONDURAS.

Little need be added as to the trade of Nicaragua, Salvador, and British Honduras.   The conditions existing there are similar to those already described as pertaining to the neighboring States, Nicaragua and British Honduras belonging to the group whose commerce has advanced in recent years, and Salvador to the group where commercial depression has made itself felt.

A considerable portion of the trade of British Honduras is probably transit trade to Guatemala.   The United States has made definite advances in nearly all important commodities, our total exports rising from an average of $511,000 for the five years 1895–1899 to $813,000 for the years 1900–1904, the increase affecting all chief classes of commodities with the single exception of malt liquors, which have decreased from an average of $11,800 per annum to $9,300.

In Nicaragua there has been a total increase from $1,005,000 per annum to $1,405,000, but it has not been quite so general for all classes of commodities.   In addition to malt liquors, which have dropped from $20,900 per annum to $17,200, must be mentioned wines, which have fallen from $19,300 to $11,600; and cars, carriages, etc., which show a decrease from $10,300 to $7,800 per annum.

Salvador presents directly opposite conditions.   Our total exports have decreased from $1,163,000 per annum to $794,000, and the decline affects all commodities except cotton goods, explosives, and leather manufactures.   Even iron and steel, in which lies our greatest strength in Spanish America, have fallen from $252,000 to $152,000 per annum. The decline is part of a general movement, however, and can not be regarded as permanent or affecting the United States alone, and its significance is more than offset by the growth from $179,000 to $233,000 per annum which has taken place of our sales of cotton goods.   It is said that in prints, especially, in spite of the depression in Salvador, American goods are rapidly ousting the European.

ARGENTINE REPUBLIC.

IMPORTS AND EXPORTS FIRST NINE MONTHS 1906.

The trade report of the Argentine Republic for the first nine months of the year 1906, as compared with the same period of 1905, is as follows:

[Values in gold.]

	1905.	1906.	Increase (+) or decrease (−).
Imports	$155,651,460	$197,315,514	+$41,664,054
Exports	247,110,183	224,631,261	− 22,478,872
Total	402,761,593	421,946,775	+ 19,185,182

EXPORTS FIRST TEN MONTHS 1906.

The export figures of Argentine Republic for the first ten months of 1906 are as follows, corresponding returns for the same period of the previous year being also furnished for purposes of comparison:

Articles.	Ten months—	
	1906.	1905.
Oxhides:		
Dry ....number..	2,144,319	1,524,521
Salt..do....	1,275,075	1,496,451
Horsehides:		
Dry..do....	141,114	84,896
Salt..do....	14,736	112,301
Sheepskins..bales..	43,733	46,647
Hair...do....	8,749	5,025
Tallow..pipes..	17,972	26,219
Do..casks..	58,542	85,770
Do..hogsheads..	8,601	15,748
Goatskins..bales..	8,226	11,393
Wool ....do....	272,521	336,190
Wheat ....tons..	2,135,860	2,576,285
Maize...do....	2,073,068	1,938,848
Linseed..do....	449,746	559,536
Flour..do....	100,883	103,537
Bran..do....	145,276	122,885
Pollards...bags..	45,972	85,856
Oilseed..do....	170,651	169,062
Hay...bales..	1,320,668	759,884
Quebracho...tons..	241,889	221,967
Quebracho extract ....do....	46,614	24,577
Butter ....cases..	110,001	159,440
Mutton, carcasses..................................number..	2,492,763	2,942,866
Beef..quarters..	1,673,700	1,564,376

MOVEMENT OF THE PORT OF BUENOS AYRES, OCTOBER, 1906.

During October, 1906, there arrived at Buenos Ayres, 137 ocean-going steamers, of 323,718 tons net register, carrying 37,899 passengers, 169,804 tons coal, and 232,457 tons general merchandise.

6, it is provided that after January 1,
imported into the Argentine Republic
spected in order to guarantee that the
cts are derived did not suffer from con-
products are in sound condition and fit
ucts must be accompanied by a certifi-
ntine consul from the country of origin,
is from a factory subject to sanitary
orced in Argentina.

of factories in the Argentine Republic
all animal food products intended for
1, which shall affix thereto a stamp show-
ertificate also must be produced showing
oduct is prepared has undergone sani-
nust bear a stamp showing the place of

OLIVIA.

DIETARY LAW.

ember 14, 1906, approved the following

rees:

lished as the monetary unit of account
ound sterling—that is, of 1.5976 grams,
grams, 1.000 fine.
ivided into 100 centavos.
gold to be struck shall be the piece of
7.988 grams, 0.916⅔ fine; and the piece

of 2 pesos, 50 centavos, with a weight of 3.994 grams of a like fineness. The diameter of both shall be exactly equal to the English sovereign and half sovereign.

"ART. 4. The tolerance allowed both in the weight and in the fineness of national gold coin to be emitted shall be the same as fixed by English law for the sovereign and half sovereign—that is, 0.002 for fineness and 2 milligrams for weight.

"ART. 5. English sovereigns and half sovereigns and Peruvian libras and half libras shall have legal circulation in Bolivia and shall have an unlimited legal tender value of 5 and of 2½ pesos gold, respectively.

"ART. 6. The expenses of coining gold coin are to the account of the State, so that the national mint shall pay in coined gold, reduced to the fineness of 1.000, an amount equal to that received in ingots at the same fineness.

"ART. 7. Coinage of gold is unlimited. The mint shall receive, to be converted into coin, all which may be presented.

"ART. 8. Loss in weight by abrasion of gold coin shall be borne by the holder thereof. There shall be retired from circulation 5-peso pieces which have lost in weight as much as 50 milligrams and 2½-peso pieces which have lost 30 milligrams, and for these the national mint shall pay the value thereof proportioned to the weight remaining.

" For the purposes of this article foreign coins mentioned in article 5 of this law are considered as national money.

"ART. 9. Silver money is of three kinds:

"1. The piece of 50 centavos of the gold peso, with a weight of 15 grams and diameter of 32 millimeters.

"2. The piece of 20 centavos, with a weight of 6 grams and diameter of 25 millimeters.

"3. The piece of 10 centavos, with a weight of 3 grams and diameter of 20 millimeters.

"ART. 10. The standard of fineness of silver coin is 0.900. The tolerance in fineness above or below shall not exceed 0.003. The tolerance in weight may not be more or less than 3 milligrams in 50-centavo pieces, and 4 milligrams in 20 and 10 centavo pieces.

"ART. 11. Nickel coins are of three kinds:

"1. The piece of 4 centavos, with weight of 5 grams and diameter of 25 millimeters.

"2. The piece of 2 centavos, with weight of 2.50 grams and diameter of 15 millimeters.

"3. The piece of 1 centavo, with weight of 1.75 grams and diameter of 15 millimeters.

"ART. 12. The alloy of nickel coin shall be the same as that of the pieces at present in circulation.

"ART. 13. The Executive, keeping in view conditions of art and of

shall receive and exchange for gold all
o them.

worn by use shall be exchanged at par by
s drilled therein or intentionally mutilated
culation and shall be retired, paying there-
lue as metal.

s which by use have lost 5 per cent in
for new coins.

s is authorized to issue silver money up to
loney up to 1,700,000 pesos in the following

	Pesos.
....	1,000,000
....	3,000,000
....	3,000,000
....	800,000
....	800,000
....	100,000

liary coin under authority of the preceding
Executive, taking care not to exceed the
in the circulation thereof.

of silver money shall be made from the
be withdrawn. Any excess in the latter
educed to bars and sold abroad on account

present conversion value of bolivianos at
le value of the present boliviano is fixed at
peso ($0.40), the rate at which conversion
the country shall be made.

of December, 1908, the State will exchange
liary coinage all the present silver and cop-
e all that is then remaining in circulation
erchandise and will be reduced to bars on
of.

as the Executive may deem expedient the
be continued in circulation with a fixed
or the pieces of 10 centavos of a boliviano
r the pieces of 5 centavos of a boliviano.
binage enters into free circulation, the pres-
recoined with the new die.

"TRANSITORY PROVISIONS.

"ART. 24. From the date of the promulgation of this law coinage of the present silver money shall be suspended.

"The national mint shall pay within the maximum period of ninety days the amounts unpaid due for imports of bullion already received.

"ART. 25. After January 1, 1907, banks of discount and of issue (Bancos Hipotecarios y de Emisión) shall keep their accounts, designating values in gold pesos.

"ART. 26. Banks of issue may emit bills of 1, 5, 10, 20, 50, and 100 pesos gold.

"ART. 27. Every bank within the limit of its legal authority to issue shall have the power to supply the public, in proportion as necessities may demand, with bills of the denominations enumerated in the preceding article.

"ART. 28. Up to January 1, 1908, the existing issue of banks shall be entirely changed for the new issue in pesos gold, exception being made of bills of 1 boliviano, which may continue circulating until December 31 of the present year with the fixed value of $0.40, provided the Executive may deem it desirable, and in his judgment this may be necessary in order to avoid disturbances which may arise on account of the new monetary unit.

"ART. 29. Bills subject to be retired and not so retired prior to the date set out in the preceding article, shall be taxed as against the holders thereof 2 centavos gold per boliviano.

"ART. 30. After January 1, 1908, banks shall pay all obligations and convert their bills into gold; until this date they may continue making use of the present money.

"ART. 31. After January 1, 1908, the metallic reserve of banks shall be made up of gold coin or ingots of the same metal, and subsidiary money (silver and nickel) shall form no part thereof, except in the proportion of 1 per cent on the subscribed capital.

"ART. 32. Amounts which the banks may have on January 1, 1908, of the present coinage of silver, copper, and nickel shall be exchanged by the State for gold.

"ART. 33. The provisions contained in articles 26, 27, 30, and 31 of this law shall be incorporated in the law concerning banks of issue.

"ART. 34. After January 1, 1907, all imports shall be reduced to the new monetary unit, and in relation thereto the State shall effectuate all its collections and payments, for which all fiscal offices shall carry from the indicated date their accounts in pesos gold.

"ART. 35. From the same date the peso gold shall begin to be in force for all transactions and shall have the conversion value for all obligations at the exchange fixed in article 21 of this law.

shall adopt rules for putting in force this
d to take all steps which may be necessary
mplishing without embarrassment the con-
████ ███.

may be in conflict with this law are hereby

BRAZIL.

MOREIRA PENNA was born in the town of
inas Geraes, on November 30, 1847. He
o do Garaça, and in 1866 entered the Law
ating from there in 1870. While pursuing
is friend and fellow-pupil, Dr. RODRIGUES
rvsa Academico," a political and literary

urned to Minas to take up the practice of
Santa Barbara, afterwards settling at Bar-
ried MARIA GUILHERMINA DE OLIVEIRA
er began the year previous to his marriage,
y to the Provincial Assembly for the term
reelected, serving from 1876 to 1877, and
as affiliated with the Liberal party which
Sinimbú Ministry on January 5, 1878. He
ably as Deputy from the Third District of
erving consecutively from that year up to
as proclaimed.
AMPOS Ministry he occupied the War port-
YETTE Ministry, the portfolio of Agricul-
During the second SARAIVA cabinet, Doctor
over the Department of Justice, and it was
Department that the law of September 28,
freedom to all slaves over 60 years of age.

In 1888, he was invited to become a member of the committee appointed to draw up the Civil Code.

After the proclamation of the Republic, Doctor Penna retired to private life for a short time, but soon again entered the political arena. He was elected Deputy to the Legislature of the State of Minas and was chairman of the committee appointed to draft the State constitution.

In 1892 he was elected, by a unanimous vote, governor of the State of Minas. While holding this office be founded the city of Bello Horizonte and removed the capital from Ouro Preto to that city. He also founded the first law school in the State of Minas.

In 1895 he accepted the presidency of the Bank of the Republic, which office he held until 1898. In 1902 he was appointed to substitute Silviano Brandão as Vice-President of the Republic.

INAUGURAL MESSAGE OF PRESIDENT AFFONSO PENNA.

President Affonso Penna, in his inaugural message of November 15, 1906, expresses his grateful acknowledgments to his countrymen for the high honor they have bestowed upon him, and he says he will endeavor to deserve this honor, and will employ all his energies to promote the welfare and prosperity of the Brazilian people. He is not unmindful of the great responsibility he has assumed, and prays that he may be able to perform his arduous duties and merit the confidence reposed in him.

The President next refers to the visit he made to several of the States during the past summer, and expresses his gratitude to the governments and people for the affectionate demonstrations with which he was received everywhere. Everything that he saw, read, and heard strengthened his conviction that the country is progressing firmly toward its great destiny.

The economic awakening which the people are witnessing at home and abroad is a sure sign that they are entering upon a new era, which promises rich results for the general happiness. It is necessary to obey this movement, which already holds the modern world in vassalage, and no nation can keep itself aloof without seriously compromising its future. In his programme he has already indicated in a general way the course he would pursue in order to stimulate this movement, and his personal observation of the agricultural, commercial, and industrial conditions in the States has strengthened his purpose of vigorously forwarding the political policy which he has there outlined.

The constant complaints made by farmers that the price of their products does not compensate the labor employed have deeply engaged the public attention during the last few years. This is indeed a matter calling for profound study, and is closely connected with the welfare and progress of the nation. These complaints are well founded.

According to the statistics of the export trade for 1905, the value in gold of the Brazilian exports of coffee, rubber, cotton, sugar, tobacco, herva-maté, etc., was £44,658,000, or 685,456,000 *milreis* national currency, while in 1904 the export value in gold was £39,489,000, or 776,548,000 *milreis* national currency. That is, while the exports in 1905 were greater than in 1904, the producers received 91,087,000 *milreis* less than in 1904, whereas if the rate of exchange had been the same as in 1904, they would have received 208,000 *milreis* more. So marked a difference in the short space of one year can not fail to cause great disturbances in the national economy, placing the producers in a critical situation. Public officials can not remain indifferent to these facts. The cause of the evil is, in the opinion of the President, in the poor quality of the national currency, which is subject to constant oscillations in value. What the country needs is a stable currency, and this is to be obtained by substituting a gold currency for a paper currency. He points out that while there has been an increase of 25 per cent in the value of Brazilian currency, the price of imported articles has not decreased in the same proportion, so that the rise in exchange has not benefited consumers, but middlemen. He does not wish to be understood by this as favoring a low rate of exchange for the purpose of increasing the price of national products, but he thinks that the rise in the value of the national currency should be effected slowly and gradually. It must be remembered that sudden changes in the rate of exchange, whether upward or downward, are always ruinous in their consequences. In order to avoid this, the law of 1899 authorized the Government to withdraw the paper currency from circulation in order to increase its value. This policy, the President thinks, should be continued, but it should be supplemented by measures which will prevent the disturbances occasioned by a rapid valorization, such as occurred last year.

Referring to the manufacturing industry of Brazil, the President states that although it is in its infancy it seems to be progressing toward prosperity. During his visit to the States he observed that factories were springing up everywhere and were perfectly equipped for the production of high-class goods. These factories employ many thousands of operatives and represent an investment of hundreds of thousands of *contos*. He recommends that the manufacturing industries be protected by a moderately high tariff.

During his administration special attention will be given to the development of the railway system and to the improvement of the ports.

He refers to the heavy export taxes maintained in some of the States which prevent the circulation of national products, and cites Mexico as an example to be followed, whose economic progress is attributed to the abolition of such duties. The agricultural and manufacturing industries are counseled to adopt labor-saving machinery which will enable them to increase their production, and the formation of cooperative credit associations and the establishment of commercial schools and institutions for technical and professional training are urgently recommended. He says: "The youth of the nation should be afforded the means of equipping itself in order to exercise with intelligence and profit the noble profession which is exercising such a powerful influence in the modern world."

The conflict between capital and labor, which is of such a grave and serious character in other countries, happily does not exist in Brazil owing to the scarcity of labor. It is easy for all to find employment. However, he thinks they should not rest apathetically in the security of the present, but should see that the laws of Brazil, with respect to mutual-aid associations and trades unions, are on a par with the progress in these lines made in other countries.

Touching on the subject of immigration, he calls attention to the urgent need of foreign immigrants in Brazil and says that any sacrifices the country may make to this end will be abundantly compensated for. As proof of this statement he cites the flourishing condition of many colonies which are agricultural and industrial centers of the first order. Immigrants should be encouraged to remain permanently in the country by aiding them to acquire property.

The President declares it his intention to give special consideration to the subject of education and that he will endeavor to put an end to the confusion and uncertainty which now reigns as the result of obscure and contradictory rules and regulations.

The President emphasizes the importance to Brazil of the works undertaken by the preceding administration for the sanitation and embellishment of the capital of the Republic and thinks they should be supplemented by an abundant water supply.

Referring to the Pan-American Conference of Rio de Janeiro, he says:

"The meeting of the International American Conference at Rio de Janeiro and the visit with which the eminent statesman and Secretary of State of the United States, Mr. ELIHU ROOT, honored our country and other countries of South America are events of extraordinary political importance, marking a new era in the relations of the peoples of the New World.

"To base these relations on a broad policy of mutual confidence, to promote the development of trade by the exchange of products peculiar to each region, to abandon misconceptions and prejudices which are wholly unjustifiable, is the rigorous duty of all the American Governments and the rule of conduct of Brazil in its international relations.

"In the period of formation of our political existence the statesmen of Brazil realized the great importance of establishing closer relations

with the young and lively flourishing Republic of the United States
of America, which was the first among the colonies of the New World
to proclaim its independence. This traditional policy has received a
great impetus in recent years, and I am convinced will continue to merit
the solicitous attention of both nations.

"Between the Republic of Brazil and its sister Republics there exist
no differences which can not be decided amicably and without fear of
serious conflict.

"In this blessed American Continent—one may affirm it boldly—
there can be emulation only in the field of economic prosperity, of
moral and material progress, and in conquests of civilization, each
nation seeking to draw the greatest advantage from its splendid natural
gifts, so as to grow in greatness and offer the largest sum of benefits
to humanity.

"Happily there are wanting here the factors which explain the
system of armed peace, that scourge which leads to ruin the nations
which are compelled to adopt it. We, on our part, have maintained
a traditional policy of peace and harmony, and in the calm deliberations
of Cabinets or in arbitration tribunals have succeeded in settling controversies which have come down to us from colonial times. The fact
that our naval and land forces have been maintained at the same size
for many years, notwithstanding the great increase in the area under
cultivation and the great development in our national and foreign
trade, eloquently attests our pacific purposes. This does not mean,
however, that we should neglect to put our military force, with its
splendid traditions of bravery and patriotism, in a condition to fulfill its
high and noble mission as defenders of the national honor and vigilant
guardians of the Constitution and laws. The loss of valuable war vessels
which our navy suffered some years ago abundantly justifies the action
of the Government in seeking to replace them with vessels constructed
in accordance with the needs of modern naval warfare. In the same
way, to improve the military organization and renew the war material
within the limits prescribed by the state of our finances, it is the duty
of our Government, as it is that of every government conscious of its
responsibilities, and it ought to be able to perform this duty without
having attributed to it purposes of aggression, for it has been and
always will be our aim to promote closer relations with all nations."

The President concludes his message with the following:

"To govern within the Constitution and the laws, to respect the
rights and legitimate interests of all, to practice justice, these are rules
I have endeavored to observe whenever it has been given to me to
exercise any portion of the public power, and I shall continue to follow
them in the high position in which the confidence of my compatriots
has placed me."

SPEECH OF BARON DO RIO BRANCO.

The following is an extract from the speech of Baron Do Rio Branco, Minister of Foreign Affairs, to the officers of the Brazilian army, delivered at Rio de Janeiro on November 10, 1906, the translation being furnished by the Brazilian Embassy at Washington.

"The movement of friendliness that acquired greater strength of late between the United States of America and Brazil is due, undoubtedly, to the rare accomplishments of our Ambassador in Washington, to the skill with which he knows how to express the sentiments of the Government of this country.   But above all, it is due to the growing opinion acquired by Brazil in the esteem of the world in a few years of international peace, in which she gained the opportunity of throwing herself resolutely forward in every kind of moral and material improvement.   Without this, which is really the work of the whole nation and of its best advisers and political leaders, the spontaneous and almost unanimous vote of the Republics of our continent would not have been given to the city of Rio de Janeiro as the meeting place of the Third International American Conference.   Nor could we have had the privilege of the visit of the eminent statesman, ELIHU ROOT, eloquent champion of the policy of friendship among nations, which the great President ROOSEVELT represents—a policy that the United States of Brazil, as well as the United States of America, wish warmly to see accepted and consolidated in this section of the world.

"The demonstration that you have made recently to the President of the Republic and the one with which you honor me to-day are not of the kind that could give cause of suspicion or inquietude abroad. As Brazilians, you military men, praising the remarkable words addressed by Secretary ROOT to the Conference, give a proof of your sentiments of American solidarity, of loving affection for peace and concord, of friendliness toward all the nations of our Continent, all which Brazil would like to see more and more prosperous and strong, enjoying all the blessings that we wish for our own country.

"You are the soldiers of a nation that from the very beginning of its life has shown invariably not to have any ideas of hegemony or territorial conquests.

"Our first foreign war was made for the defense of a land whose people, tired of anarchy and of military caudillos, had vountarily joined themselves to Brazil, while we were not yet a sovereign nation.   Peace was arrived at and Brazil and her adversary, renouncing the contention which they defended by the sword, agreed to make of that land an independent State.   Since then gallant Uruguay never had a more true and disinterested friend nor a more ardent partisan of its independence than the Brazilian nation.

"Ever since, in 1851 and 1852, as well as between 1864 and 1870, we only fought to avenge our national honor or to promote the reestablishment of democratic institutions in the countries of the River Plate and the Paraguay. Owing to these the illustrious General MITRE, who knew intimately the convenience for his country of the Brazilian alliance, as we appreciate the good to the general interests of this part of the world of the Argentine friendship, could say in 1880 that Brazil was in the past a destroyer of tyrannies and a liberator of peoples.

"If, while we were the first military power in South America, never the superiority of our strength constituted a danger for our neighbors, and we never entered upon any wars of conquest, less could we think of them now that our Constitution expressly forbids them. We always settled our boundary disputes through friendly agencies, and never went in our pretensions as far as our mother country did. In our late understanding with Bolivia, owing to which we reacquired a part of the large territories that we had transferred to her in 1867, we offered her considerable compensations which, I feel certain, will secure her commercial prosperity in the immediate future. We have ample room within the frontiers that close the territories in which our language is spoken and which were discovered and peopled by our own people.

"Our love of peace is not, however, a reason for us to remain in the condition of military inefficiency to which we have been brought by our civil struggles and in a period of political agitation consequent to the change of our form of government. a period, we believe, happily closed forever. It is not in the power of one nation alone to avoid international conflicts. Even neutralized States, like Switzerland and Belgium, care seriously and patriotically for their military defenses in case of possible attack. The large extent of our littoral and that of our interior, the example given us by our neighbors, who armed themselves while our attention was engaged in internal politics, impose on us the duty of creating the elements necessary for our defense. We are bound to organize our national safety, to preserve our dignity, and to look for the guaranty of our rights, which sometimes force only can give. We require an efficient army and considerable military reserves; we must replace our navy in its former standing."

EXPORTS, FIRST NINE MONTHS, 1906.

The "*Serviço do Estatistica Commercial*" publishes the following statistics of the exports of Brazil for the first nine months of 1906 compared with those for the same period of 1905.

Article.	Quantity.		Value in milreis.	
	1905.	1906.	1905.	1906.
Raw cotton ....kilos..	11,770,007	23,378,642	7,896,822	13,142,943
Monazitic sands ....do....	3,264,790	3,347,940	1,112,357	1,126,674
Sugar........................do....	24,079,346	53,715,272	4,956,863	5,220,220
Castor oil beans ....do....	2,092,426	1,660,347	311,104	279,347
Rubber:				
Mangabeira ....do....	455,013	459,588	1,571,058	1,628,734
Maniçoba ....do....	1,740,902	1,730,571	8,319,808	8,080,341
Seringa.................do....	23,428,933	23,666,670	156,317,234	142,465,795
Cacáo........................do....	12,659,526	17,430,121	9,264,432	12,212,802
Coffee ....bags..	6,649,807	7,820,900	204,284,406	219,724,780
Cotton seed ....kilos..	32,550,990	26,246,733	1,477,221	1,523,261
Chestnuts ....hectoliters..	197,887	95,700	3,510,796	2,015,862
Carnaúba wax ....kilos..	1,485,218	2,096,478	2,530,707	3,055,117
Horns ....do....	931,866	932,075	487,824	591,640
Salted hides.................do....	16,051,980	19,549,122	10,227,811	12,050,595
Dry hides....................do....	5,581,791	6,884,808	6,669,097	8,561,671
Hair.........................do....	296,320	357,231	348,178	355,483
Beef extract.................do....	85,642	83,078	148,589	176,867
Bran ....do....	19,284,482	19,086,721	1,894,434	1,585,330
Mandioca flour...............do....	4,255,749	5,131,545	928,599	995,007
Medicinal plants ....do....	135,105	108,881	79,190	96,621
Fruits..........................			757,574	980,554
Tobacco ....kilos..	18,709,218	22,445,305	12,145,009	13,287,678
Herva maté ....do....	27,507,393	40,004,886	11,935,776	19,177,489
Ipecacuanha ....do....	15,132	21,567	167,392	297,805
Wool ....do....	197,285	425,333	194,252	484,135
Woods			464,111	408,413
Manganese ....tons..	191,203	103,689	4,354,652	2,275,217
Old metal ....kilos..	3,507,560	4,848,780	270,258	442,739
Gold bars....................grams..	3,039,680	3,649,440	5,142,160	5,771,896
Precious stones			752,482	1,961,121
Skins ....kilos..	1,671,468	1,189,306	5,818,730	5,998,772
Piassava.....................do....	996,152	1,167,162	472,972	493,656
Miscellaneous....................			2,941,136	2,705,266
Total......................			467,703,001	498,691,472
Value of coins exported			49,386	196,297
General total			467,752,387	498,887,769

COFFEE MOVEMENT, OCTOBER, 1906.

["*Boletim da Associação Commercial*," of November 13, 1906.]

The coffee movement at the ports of Rio de Janeiro and Santos for the month of October, 1906, compared with that of the same month of the previous year, was as follows:

	Rio de Janeiro.		Santos.	
	1906.	1905.	1906.	1905.
Entries...............................	536,596	470,760	1,963,423	1,178,604
Shipments.............................	486,293	472,988	1,698,314	1,059,018
Sales.................................	157,000	144,000	1,209,335	350,415
Daily average of entries..............	17,309	13,250	63,981	38,019
Daily average of shipments............	14,800	19,493	54,784	34,151
Entries from July 1	1,720,410	1,536,577	6,275,204	4,172,612
Shipments from July 1.................	1,276,054	1,476,844	4,463,215	3,308,899
Stock on hand October 31..............	589,866	362,996	2,117,600	1,507,007

orts for the same period of 1905 were
1,173,092 *milreis*, paper, or $46,471,671
rage value of the paper *milreis* in gold
higher than in 1905.

IDE IMPORTS.

al G. E. ANDERSON, of Rio de Janeiro,
ment of the United States, says:
lerable leather, but it also imports exten-
sing 1,451,056 pounds, valued at about
urnished a little over one-half, Germany
ted States about one-twelfth. Of the
ame to Rio de Janeiro and about one-
Santos. There was also imported sole
pounds, valued at $7,292.
mostly for shoemaking, and there is a
s in the shoemaking industry of Brazil.
n shoemaking machinery has been in

SCHOOL AT CAMPOS.

been started at Campos, Brazil, by the
NILO PEÇANHA. The school will give
aking, gardening, etc., and will be thor-

CHILE.

TIONS AND STATISTICS.

ict from the report of Mr. LINCOLN
of the United States Department of

PURCHASING POWER OF CHILE.

The recent growth of the general import trade of Chile has been extensively commented on by our consular representatives to the Department of State, and it is unnecessary, therefore, in this place to make more than passing reference to the broader features of the development. It is well known that the foreign purchases of the country have increased most markedly in the past few years, the total in 1904, according to Chilean official figures, rising to $57,360,000 United States gold, and exceeding that of 1903 by about 10 per cent. The full returns for 1905 are not yet in, but every indication points toward an equal or even greater increase for that year. The total population of the country is estimated at something over 3,000,000, and the per capita importation is therefore low ($19) compared with that of the other temperate climate countries of South America. In Uruguay the per capita imports amount to about $25, and in Argentina to over $40. There is every reason to suppose that the present wave of prosperity in Chile will raise her purchases at least to the point reached by her eastern neighbors, bringing the grand total within the next few years up to $75,000,000 or $80,000,000.

NATURAL CONDITIONS AND THE IMPORT TRADE.

To understand fully, however, the character and prospects of Chilean import trade it is not sufficient to consider totals only. The country, geographically and economically, is divided into several distinct sections whose climatic and industrial characteristics create demands for quite different classes of foreign commodities. Confined as it is to a narrow strip of territory between the mountains and the sea, and stretching north and south over 2,000 miles, it includes within its borders every variety of climatic condition, and its products and industries differ in the various districts as much as do those of Scotland and the plateau of Mexico. A clear idea of these differences as reflected in commercial possibilities can best be obtained by analyzing the character of the imports into the various sections. These sections are in rough outline: (1) The arid and semiarid mineral section of the north, from Coquimbo northward; (2) the commercial and industrial section of the center, including the two largest cities of the country, Santiago and Valparaiso; (3) the agricultural and pastoral section of the south central region, between Santiago and Temuco; (4) the forest section, from Temuco southward nearly to the Straits of Magellan; (5) the cold zone of the far south, Tierra del Fuego and Chilean Patagonia, whose chief industries are pastoral and mining.

IMPORTS CLASSIFIED.

In the Chilean official statistics imports are divided into eleven primary classes, and the relative importance of each of these is indicated in the following table, compiled from the latest available data (1904):

Per cent·

    I. Animal products (live animals, food products, raw material, and manu-
       factures) 7.5
   II. Vegetable products (plants, etc., food products, raw materials, manu-
       factures, wood, and tobacco).................................... 11.9
  III. Mineral products (precious metals, etc., iron and steel, other metals,
       stone, earths, etc.)... 17.1
   IV. Textiles, and manufactures of (straw, hemp, jute, etc., cotton, linen,
       wool, and silk)... 28.4
    V. Industrial oils, polishes, combustibles, paints, etc................... 14.2
   VI. Paper and cardboard, and manufactures thereof..................... 3.1
  VII. Beverages and liquors.. 1.0
 VIII. Perfumery, drugs, and chemicals................................... 2.0
   IX. Machinery, instruments, tools, and apparatus (for arts and sciences,
       mining, agriculture, industries, and locomotion).................. 13.3
    X. Arms, ammunition and explosives................................. .9
   XI. Sundries... .6

         Total ($57,360,000) 100.0

It is clear from the above figures that, as in other South American countries, textiles head the list, with 28.4 per cent of the total foreign purchases. Iron and steel, if we include machinery and arms, come second, with 24.6 per cent. The third place is taken by oils, varnishes, paints, etc., with 14.2 per cent, and the fourth by foodstuffs (portions of Classes I and II), with 7.4 per cent. These four together make up 75 per cent of the total importations.

WHERE IMPORTS GO.

The table below indicates the distribution of the demand for these imports in the five sections of the country described, stated in percentages of the total imports of all commodities into each section.

Distribution of imports into Chile in 1904, by ports and classes.

Class.	Coquimbo northward (section 1).	Valparaiso (section 2).	Talcahuano and Coronel (section 3).	Valdivia, Port Montt, and Ancud (section 4).	Punta Arenas (section 5).
	Per cent.	Per cent.	Per cent.	Per cent.	Per cent.
I. Animal products...................	2.7	4 5	4.5	2.7	7.1
II. Vegetable products	9.9	12.9	15.4	13.2	16.9
III. Mineral products	15.7	17.4	19.2	28.6	12.0
IV. Textiles	11.9	36.0	36.1	26.2	14.1
V. Oils, etc	36.0	7.6	6.6	6.1	4.4
VI. Paper	1.1	4.2	2.4	2.8	.7
VII. Beverages and liquors	1.9	.9	.6	.8	8.1
VIII. Perfumery, drugs, chemicals, etc..	.8	2.8	1.3	1.1	5.8
IX. Machinery, etc....................	18.0	12.2	13.2	16.7	4.1
X. Arms, etc	1.7	.7	.4	.8	....
XI. Sundries	.3	.8	.3	1.0	a 26.8
Total	100.0	100.0	100.0	100.0	100.0

a Punta Arenas being a free port, the imports of "Sundries" appear abnormally large.

RELATIVE IMPORTANCE OF SECTIONS.

The great differences between the imports of the various sections of the country will be noticed at once. In the northern section the order of importance is oils, etc., machinery, mineral products (mostly iron and steel), textiles, and vegetable products (mostly foodstuffs). In the commercial, pastoral, and agricultural sections (2 and 3) textiles head the list, while machinery, metal products, and vegetable products follow. In the far south foodstuffs and textiles occupy leading places, though machinery, except in section 5, is also important. The relative commercial importance of the various sections also differs greatly. Valparaiso entries constitute no less than 57.4 per cent of the total imports of the entire country. The northern mining region (section 1) comes second, with 25.2 per cent of the total. Section 8 takes 12 per cent; section 4, 1.8 per cent, and section 5, 3.6 per cent. The exports from the various sections of course show like differences. Exports are classified in the statistics simply as animal, vegetable, and mineral products, with two minor classes of no importance. The northern section of the country (section 1) exports 95.7 per cent of the mineral products; the second, third, and fourth sections 83.5 per cent of the animal products, and the second and third sections 89 per cent of the vegetable products. The exports of Patagonia and Tierra del Fuego are as yet small, and consist almost wholly of animal products.

The following tables are compiled from the official export statistics of the United States, England, Germany, France, Belgium, and Italy. They show the average annual exports of domestic merchandise to Chile for the periods stated. The values are given in United States dollars.

Average annual exports to Chile from specified countries, 1894–1904.

Country.	1894–1898.	1899–1903.	Increase (+) or decrease (−).	1904.
			Per cent.	
United States	$2,680,000	$3,680,000	+ 37.3	$4,825,000
England	11,934,000	14,579,000	+ 22.3	a16,200,000
Germany	7,444,000	8,883,000	+ 19.3	a11,620,000
France	3,016,000	2,860,000	− 4.9	a3,500,000
Belgium	1,356,000	1,304,000	− 3.8	a2,250,000
Italy	452,000	1,056,000	+133.6	a1,152,000
All six	26,882,000	32,362,000	+ 20.4	39,547,000

a Partly estimated.

SHARE OF THE UNITED STATES.

The share of the United States in the total trade is therefore comparatively small, but it is increasing far more rapidly than that of any other country, with the single exception of Italy. From fourth place it has risen in the past ten years to third place, having passed France by a considerable margin. All local information obtainable in Chile at present indicates that since 1904 our trade has grown even more rapidly, and we may expect the figures for 1905 and 1906[a] to place us more nearly on an equality with Germany. Italy's large increase has been due mainly to cheap cotton goods and wines, her share in other trade being relatively small.

Analyzing further the trade of the United States we find that our exports to Chile consisted of the articles mentioned in the following table, which includes all items except those so small as to be negligible. The increase or decrease of our trade is shown by a comparison of the two five-year periods, 1894–1898 and 1899–1903, with the year 1904. The figures stated are United States gold.

Average annual exports of specified articles from the United States to Chile, 1894–1904.

Article.	1894–1898.	1899–1903.	1904.
Mowers and reapers	$39,000	$12,000	$22,000
Plows and cultivators	19,000	46,000	76,000
All other agricultural implements, etc	49,000	53,000	150,000
Total	107,000	111,000	248,000
Wheat	96,000	121,000	
Wheat flour	2,000	119,000	2,000
Oat meal (1 year)	400	1,200	2,300
Wheat flour preparations (1 year)	600	800	1,700
Cars for steam and other railways	3,000	65,000	19,000
Other carriages and cycles	27,000	12,000	93,000
Total	30,000	77,000	112,000
Patent or proprietary medicines	66,000	71,000	97,000
All other chemicals, drugs, and medicines	31,000	29,000	48,000
Clocks and watches:			
Clocks	7,000	9,000	16,000
Watches	35,000	37,000	28,000
Total	42,000	46,000	44,000
Bituminous coal	4,000	77,000	78,000
Cotton cloths:			
Colored	29,000	116,000	293,000
Uncolored	553,000	411,000	381,000
Total	582,000	527,000	674,000
Cordage	11,000	23,000	19,000
Salmon, canned	17,000	47,000	72,000
Glass and glassware	10,000	19,000	22,000
Soap grease and grease scraps, and all soap stock	17,000	38,000	42,000
Scientific instruments and apparatus, including electric	33,000	41,000	69,000
Leather: Buff, grain, splits, and all other upper	1,200	12,800	33,000
Boots and shoes	1,200	3,000	11,000
Iron and steel, and manufactures of:			
Pig	1,000	600	
All other manufactured		5,000	
Bar iron	600	24,000	
All other bar and rod	200	20,000	2,000
Hoop, band, and scroll		1,400	5,000
Steel rails	16,000	69,000	

[a] Since Mr. HUTCHINSON's report was written, later figures are available which bear out his anticipation of expansion of American trade with Chile. The declared exports of domestic and foreign merchandise from the United States to Chile, which for the fiscal year 1904, ending June 30, amounted to $4,824,857, aggregated in 1905 $5,391,357. The fiscal year 1906, which ended June 30, almost doubled the 1904 trade, the total amount of exports to Chile being $8,667,227.

Average annual exports of specified articles from the United States to Chile, 1894–1904—Continued.

Article.	1894–1898.	1899–1903.	1904.
Iron and steel, and manufactures of—Continued.			
Sheets and plates—			
Iron	$1,600	$2,000	....
Steel	....	8,400	....
Structural iron and steel	....	1,600	$2,000
Wire	11,000	77,000	96,000
Locks, hinges, and other builders' hardware	63,000	45,000	88,000
Saws and tools	38,000	60,000	78,000
Total	101,000	105,000	166,000
Car wheels	2,400	4,400	1,000
Castings, not elsewhere specified	1,600	600	2,000
Cutlery (very little "table")	4,000	13,000	35,000
Firearms	18,000	18,000	36,000
Printing presses	2,600	5,600	16,000
Sewing machines	20,000	29,000	69,000
Locomotives	105,000	101,000	37,000
Stationary engines	5,000	7,000	21,000
Boilers and parts of engines	9,000	19,000	8,000
Cash registers	....	a 2,600	5,000
Electric machinery (1 year)	16,000	3,200	20,000
Laundry machinery	....	a 400	4,000
Metal-working machinery (1 year)	9,000	3,000	1,000
Pumps and parts (1 year)	3,000	5,600	11,000
Shoe machinry (1 year)	2,000	2,400	1,000
Typewriters (2 years)	6,000	19,200	32,000
Wood-working machinery	....	....	11,000
All other machinery	158,000	147,000	222,000
Total	361,600	377,000	532,000
Cut nails and spikes	58,000	78,000	104,000
Wrought nails and spikes, including tacks	7,000	19,000	36,000
Scales and balances	17,000	20,000	35,000
Stoves, ranges, etc	12,000	13,000	23,000
Pipes and fittings (1 year)	22,000	26,000	33,000
Safes	....	200	....
All other iron and steel	35,000	45,000	55,000
Total iron and steel, and agricultural implements and machinery	706,000	986,000	1,363,000
Rosin	16,000	17,000	29,000
Spirits of turpentine	25,000	38,000	71,000
Lard:			
Edible	29,000	55,000	58,000
Other	27,000	3,400	2,000
Oil, mineral:			
Naphthas	800	2,000	7,000
Illuminating	278,000	423,000	654,000
Lubricating	87,000	133,000	182,000
Total	365,800	558,000	843,000
Oil, cotton-seed	2,000	15,000	10,000
Paints, pigments, and colors, all other	3,000	7,000	11,000
Writing paper and envelopes	4,000	11,000	17,000
All other paper	26,000	76,000	119,000
Total	30,000	87,000	136,000
Plated ware	16,000	14,000	26,000
Tallow	2,000	31,000	14,000
Toilet or fancy soap	4,000	7,000	21,000
All other soap	3,000	6,000	9,000
Refined sugar	3,000	....	....
Sawed wood	5,000	10,000	18,000
Boards, deals, and planks	171,000	188,000	429,000
Staves and heading	14,000	18,000	29,000
All other wood	15,000	8,000	26,000
Furniture, not elsewhere specified	31,000	14,000	22,000
Total	236,000	288,000	524,000
Grand total of above items	2,408,000	3,313,000	4,420,000
Grand total of all items	2,689,000	3,680,000	4,796,000

a Three years.

COTTON AND OTHER TEXTILES.

In 1904 Chile imported cottons to the value of $8,756,000; woolens, $3,993,000; silks, $995,000, and linens, $287,000. The United States supplied so insignificant a quantity of the woolens, silks, and linens that we can not be said to compete at all in these goods. In general, conditions in Chile are similar to those in Argentina, and the usual comment among business men is that the United States has not done a larger trade in cottons because we have not yet adopted the thorough-going methods of our competitors in catering to the peculiar needs of the market. A comparison of American sales of cotton goods to Chile with those of our principal competitors shows the following (values in United States dollars):

Average annual exports of cotton goods from specified countries to Chile, 1894–1903.

Country.	1894–1898.	1899–1903.	Increase (+) or decrease (−).
			Per cent.
United States	$562,000	$627,000	9.4
England	4,056,000	4,460,000	+ 9.9
Germany	1,509,000	1,758,000	+ 17.2
France	716,000	524,000	− 26.8
Italy	100,000	364,000	+261.0
Total	6,957,000	7,683,000	+ 9.7

As in other South American countries the United States showed in the above period a decline in sales of cotton goods as a whole. England, Germany, and Italy are gaining a stronger foothold, the most marked development being that of the last-mentioned country. However, an upward trend has since been in evidence in the American cotton-goods trade with Chile. The declared exports from the United States for the three last fiscal years were: In 1904, a total of $673,593; in 1905, a total of $742,771, and in 1906, a total of $871,272. One class of goods in which the United States is meeting with considerable success is colored cotton cloths. Our share in the total trade in this article is still small, but it is growing with a rapidity which demonstrates our ability to compete with Europe. A considerable part of these colored goods seems to be prints.

IRON AND STEEL MANUFACTURES.

In 1904 Chile imported iron and steel goods to the value of $14,110,000. The share of the United States in this trade, though smaller than that of either England or Germany, is growing rapidly and gives good promise for the future. The best outlook is in machinery, both agricultural and sundry industrial machines. Of machinery other than agricultural the chief imports are printing presses ($130,000), mining machinery ($1,185,000), sundry machinery for industries, light, and power ($2,674,000), sundry parts and repairs for machines ($344,000). The United States figure prominently in a number of the items which make up these general classes as well as in many smaller items, as follows: Scales and balances, 57 per cent of a total of $48,000; typewriters, cash registers, etc., 80 per cent of a total of $34,000; printing presses, etc., 50 per cent of a total of $130,000; bicycles, etc., 43 per cent of a total of $6,000.

Of mining machinery the United States supplies but 2 per cent, the reason undoubtedly being that the mining industries of the country are mainly in the hands of Europeans. In fact, it may be stated as a general rule that one of the greatest handicaps to the expansion of American trade in iron and steel goods in Chile is the lack of American capital investment in the predominating industries of the country. Purchases are made from Europe, except in those cases in which the United States is so preeminent as to make it imperative to draw supplies from that source. Our partial success in the face of this obstacle gives good promise for the future.

MISCELLANEOUS PRODUCTS OF IRON AND STEEL.

The principal items of iron and steel in which the United States is already taking a share of the trade have already been mentioned, and it only remains to add a few comments as to some of them. "Unmanufactured" iron and steel, such as pig, bar, hoop, band, scroll, and sheet iron, etc., are imported in considerable quantities for the use of the protected local factories. The total purchases in 1904 amounted to $1,984,000. The United States supplied but an insignificant quantity—one-half of 1 per cent.

In wire we made a much better showing, furnishing 18 per cent of the total of $693,000. Germany sent 44 per cent and England 26 per cent. The sales of the United States are increasing rapidly, however, the reason being, as alleged by prominent importers, that our manufacturers are beginning to give close heed to instructions and suggestions as to details of packing, weight, etc.

In general hardware, nails, nuts, screws, bolts, etc., our trade is growing, in spite of alleged higher prices in many lines. Of general hardware we furnished, in 1904, 13 per cent of a total of $97,000; of nails, nuts, screws, bolts, etc., 28 per cent of a total of $527,000. There is particular complaint as to the packing of such goods, and loss through the breaking of cases. Sales of American cutlery are also increasing, reaching, in 1904, 13 per cent of a total of $64,000. Hollow ware is almost wholly English and German, American goods not being able to compete in price.

Firearms are mainly American. In 1904 the United States supplied 44 per cent of the total of $57,000; England's share being less than 2 per cent, and Germany's 31 per cent. The more legitimate trade is

l margin, but her supremacy is being
riod her sales were nearly three times as
econd period considerably less than twice
s and Germany both show a phenomenal
has grown the more rapidly of the two,
period were two-thirds as large as Ger-
third as large as England's. American
s to Chile for the fiscal year 1905 were
ark in that trade.

D OF THE FUTURE.

a of Chilean trade several important con-

lation and the development of industries
nd increasing purchases of iron and steel
er than of other classes of goods. The
apidly, as in Argentina, for instance, and
t to see any very great increase in the
oods with which the people are fed and
ary foodstuffs can be, and to a large extent
d the purchases of clothing materials can
d the present amount until there are more
ing, of course, the more costly classes of
d through the increasing wealth of the
he demand of the future will be for goods
levelopment of the national industries.
country are such as to require increasing
l goods, especially machinery. Chile is
: nearly 88 per cent of her exports to-day

are of mineral products; nearly every important mineral of commerce is to be found somewhere within her borders, and there are signs of increasing activity in the extraction of every one of them. Mining operations until recently have in the main been of the simplest kind, requiring relatively little modern machinery and appliances, but a very noticeable change is going on. The richer and more accessible deposits have been partly worked out, and owners are learning the necessity of effecting economies by introducing new processes. These new processes must demand foreign purchases of machinery or the material from which machinery is made.

The other chief industries of the country—agricultural, horticultural, pastoral, and lumbering—though of small importance compared with mining, and not likely to develop for many years, at least beyond the point of supplying home demands, have this in common with the mining industry, that in order to grow they require the introduction of modern methods and machinery. Probably the greatest obstacle to progress in the country is the extreme scarcity of efficient labor, and only the adoption of labor-saving methods will permit of competition with imported goods. These industries, therefore, just as truly as the mining industry, will continue to increase the demand for iron and steel products, especially machinery.

(3) Though the present condition of Chile is such as to make it certain that iron and steel and manufactures thereof are to become more and more prominent among the imports, and thus improve the trade prospects of the United States, there are numerous other lines along which American trade is prospering and may be expected to continue to improve. Cars and carriages, medicines and drugs, colored cotton goods, canned salmon, glassware (cheaper grades), scientific instruments and apparatus, naval stores, mineral oils, paper, lumber, and various other articles, all show encouraging increase. In some of these we hold a virtual monopoly of the trade; in the others we have made sufficient advance to indicate that we are beginning to be able to meet European competition.

AGRICULTURAL IMPLEMENTS AND MACHINERY.

In general, American goods are preferred, and our total trade in these articles shows most satisfactory increase, but in mowers and reapers our trade declined from $39,000 per annum for the five years 1894–1898 to $12,000 for the years 1899–1903, with a rise again in 1904 to $22,000.

There seem to be several causes for this decline. The older farms got themselves well stocked with these machines a few years ago and are not therefore in need of new supplies, and the newer places, consisting mainly of small patches of clearing in the forest region of the south, have not yet reached a stage where the employing of such machines is profitable. The purchases, as a whole have therefore declined, and this accounts in part for the decline of American sales. There is, however, another cause—the substitution of a Canadian machine for the American. There is much complaint that the American machines are too light and not sufficiently able to stand the rough handling given them by the unskilled Chilean laborer. The harvesting season is rainless in Chile, and there is no such need of haste in getting the crop in as there is in Argentina, and the heavier, more durable machines are therefore preferred.

FARM AND DAIRY PRODUCTS.

As stated above, it is only in years of bad harvest that Chile is now obliged to import any considerable quantity of cereals. She produces her own supply. The same is true of most foodstuffs, but there are certain lines of finer grade goods in which American trade is growing and may be expected to increase. Various breakfast foods and cereal preparations are among these, and a larger trade could be done, in spite of the 25 per cent import duty, if greater care were exercised in packing for the long journey through the moist Tropics.

Lard is imported to the value of about $180,000 per annum. It comes mainly from Uruguay, which supplies over 60 per cent of the total, while the United States supplies only about 22 per cent. We are handicapped by the necessity of transportation through the Tropics. Only by the most careful refining and packing can we assure arrival in good condition. Our trade has been much injured by carelessness in this respect. The import duty is 35 per cent on a valuation of 5.9 cents per pound.

CANNED FISH AND FRUIT.

Canned salmon is rapidly becoming an article of large consumption, the total imports in 1904 being valued at $129,000. The United States has been most successful in this trade, supplying about 94 per cent of the total, or $122,000 worth. It is probable that this amount could be doubled, even with the present population of Chile, if our canners could see their way to putting up the goods in a greater variety of small tins, especially to meet the needs of the poorer portions of the population, and by the organization of a systematic propaganda.

Some business is also done in canned fruits and vegetables from California, but the trade is seriously handicapped by the ability of Chile to produce these goods herself and her determination to protect the industry. The Chilean goods are inferior to the American, but not sufficiently inferior to enable us to overcome the duty of 60 per cent on a valuation of 9 cents per pound on vegetables and 11.4 cents per pound on fruits. We have a certain amount of trade, but it is confined to the demands of the richer classes only.

MATERIALS FOR RAILWAYS.

There are several factors operating against the sale of American railway material. In the first place, about one-half the total railway mileage of Chile is owned and controlled by European mining enterprises, especially English, and there is a strong tendency to favor European material for these lines. Then, for the remaining half of the railways owned by the Chilean Government, there are two powerful influences working against us, the strong hold which the German manufacturers have obtained in the past year or two, and the interests of a large Chilean concern which has been quite successful in the manufacture of freight cars and a few locomotives, and the construction of bridges, etc. Freight cars are protected by a duty of 25 per cent, and this seems to have enabled the local builders to gain a fairly strong hold, though large numbers, chiefly of European cars, are still imported. There is a strong feeling in nearly all quarters that bids for all such materials—rails, cars, locomotives, etc.—are not considered wholly on their merits, and that American interests are suffering considerably in consequence. Whether this be true or not, it is certain that American manufacturers are not getting as large a share of the business as the excellence of the American products would warrant, and that if steps are not taken soon to gain a stronger hold on the market, the United States is certain to be left behind in the expansion of railway construction in Chile, which has already begun and is certain to continue for a good many years to come.

RAILWAY CONSTRUCTION PROGRESSIVE.

Proposals for new railways have been reported on by our diplomatic and consular officers, and scarcely a day passes which does not bring forth some new scheme of construction. While some of these many plans may prove abortive, there can be no doubt that a good many of them will eventually be carried out, for one of the crying needs of the country is for better transportation facilities, and there is a growing recognition of the fact. Recent experience seems to indicate that there are serious obstacles standing in the way of American construction of new government lines, so that the gaining of a foothold thus directly may be out of the question, but there are many openings for the building of private or semiprivate lines for which government concessions could probably be obtained. The demonstration of superior excellence of construction and operation on these lines would be a valuable object lesson, and would greatly increase American chances in government construction as well. This is particularly true of electric roads.

Most of Chile from Santiago southward abounds in water power as yet undeveloped, which, by electric transmission over distances, in

many cases at least not excessive, could be turned to good use for
locomotion and other purposes. An American firm is about to begin
the construction of an electric road from Talcahuano to Concepcion,
and an English-Chilean corporation has just obtained a concession for
a similar road from Valparaiso to Santiago. The latter claims to have
a minimum of over 20,000 horsepower available at a point within 30
miles of Santiago.   .

CARRIAGES AND CYCLES.

American sales are increasing satisfactorily, but the business is not
likely to become a very large one, for the country roads in general
are poor and the city pavements extremely bad. Such carriages as
are imported are chiefly French and American (about $8,500 of the
former and $6,500 of the latter in 1904), while wagons are mainly
American ($3,100 in 1904). There is a large local manufacture, the
protective duty varying from 15 to 60 per cent ad valorem, the value
being appraised at the custom-house. Cycles are imported to only a
very limited amount ($5,000 in 1904), chiefly from the United States,
though Germany also furnishes a considerable number.

CHEMICALS, DRUGS, AND MEDICINES.

The United States plays but a very small part in the trade in chemicals, drugs, and medicines, except in the last named, and even in these
our sales are confined mainly to a few lines. American medicinal oils
(chiefly cod-liver oil), patent and proprietary medicines, medicinal
soaps, and medicinal plasters make up the bulk of our sales. In
chemicals we do but little, for the reason that most of our products are
required for home use.

CLOCKS AND WATCHES.

Clocks are imported to the extent of about $30,000 per annum, Ger-
many furnishing about three-fifths and the United States one-third.
Cheap American alarm clocks seem to be in particular demand, and
there is evidence that our sales of other grades are increasing as well.
The imports of watches are about three times as large as of clocks.
Gold and silver watches are credited chiefly to France, but it is
probable that many of them are of Swiss origin. Switzerland stands
second, selling about half as many as France, while the share of the
United States is small—10 per cent of the total. In watches of "other
metals," however, the United States leads with 42 per cent of the
total of $32,000 worth in 1904. France and Switzerland together
send about the same amount as the United States. The strength of
the United States, therefore, seems to lie in the sales of more inexpen-
sive grades of both clocks and watches, good movements in cheap

cases, and a larger trade could probably be done by catering to this demand. The duty on clocks varies from 25 to 35 per cent; on watches, 15 per cent on a valuation which for gold watches varies from $12.60 to $18 each, for silver watches from $3.25 to $7.20, and for those of "other metals" from $1.08 to $4.32.

AMERICAN COAL.

There seems to be but little opportunity for the introduction of American coal. Our sales are growing, it is true, but their amount is insignificant compared with the consumption of the country. The total consumption is estimated at about 1,600,000 tons per annum, of which one-half is imported and one-half produced in the country. Of the imported coal, 75 per cent comes from England and 22 per cent from Australia. The United States in 1904 furnished only 15,000 tons out of a total of 822,000 tons. The same complaints are heard in Chile as have been mentioned in the reports on other countries, that the American coal (Pocahontas), though good, requires more careful firing, and is liable to heating and deterioration during the voyage from the United States. The local coal is of an inferior, quick-burning quality, but its cheapness is gaining for it rapidly increasing sales. There is no import duty on coal.

CORDAGE AND TWINE.

England supplies nearly 70 per cent of the total cordage and twine imports of about $190,000 per annum; the United States 11 per cent, consisting largely of binders' twine. The importation of all but the best grades of cordage and twines is being reduced considerably by the growth of a successful local industry using native-grown flax as its raw material. This industry is protected by a duty which ranges from 25 to 35 per cent on valuations which vary from 8.2 to 16.4 cents per pound.

GLASS AND GLASSWARE.

The United States is just beginning to meet with some success in table and ornamental glassware of the cheaper sorts. The prices are said to be satisfactory, and the principal drawbacks are the prejudice in favor of European shapes, etc., the greater variety of European patterns, and the carelessness of our exporters in the matter of packing. Other glass and glassware comes chiefly from Europe, the United States furnishing only insignificant quantities of any sort. The difficulty is mainly a question of price. Our manufacturers could probably do a better business by pushing energetically their sales of table and ornamental glassware alone. The duties on most of these articles vary from 25 to 35 per cent on a valuation of a little over 4 cents per pound.

cent on a valuation of $1.63 per pound;
) 25 per cent on a valuation of 82 cents per
r, unspecified, 25 per cent on a valuation
)st classes of boots and shoes the duty is 60
ch varies from $5.40 per dozen pairs on
ld use to $51.85 per dozen pairs for fancy

)nsiderable industry has already been built
t the best grades of boots and shoes are
es to supply the home market, and at least
:mplating entering neighboring markets.
: hope for American trade must lie in the
:s of goods demanded by the better classes
; leather and machinery for the native
:d leather is not yet satisfactory, and the
, though made with American machinery
: durability. There is therefore still an
American goods could be more energet-
, could be reduced somewhat. American
: at from $3.50 to $5 a pair, are sold in the
)ps at from $7.50 to $8.50. The duty and
r so great a difference. There is also a
American manufacturers do not send their
: materials, to these markets. It is certain
ight in Chile do not last as long as those
 made in Chilean factories with American
leather retail at $4 a pair, but they are at
le than those which can be purchased at
d if the prices on imported goods could
could be done toward meeting the local

WOOD AND WOODENWARE.

In 1904, Chile imported building lumber to the value of $655,000 and wooden furniture to the value of $134,000. These were the two chief items of wood import, all other articles together reaching a value of only $200,000. Virtually all the building lumber is Oregon pine, and the United States of course supplies this, the amount of our trade being limited only by the variations of Chilean demand. The only question, therefore, which arises as to the future is connected with the possibility of development of Chilean home supplies. Southern Chile, from about Temuco southward, abounds in dense forests, which have only in recent years begun to be exploited to any considerable extent, and the entire central section of the country raises great quantities of alamo (poplar), which, it is said, was introduced by the early Spaniards. The alamo and several of the native woods of the south are fairly well adapted for some building purposes, and are already being used to the injury of the import trade in those sections. Nearly 75 per cent of the lumber imports in 1904 went to ports from Coquimbo northward. For the south, therefore, the home supplies have already made a long advance toward meeting the home demand, and we can not expect to see much development of our business there. But the question at once arises whether American lumber is to be driven out of the northern markets as well. There are many reasons for believing that this is not likely to happen, at least for many years to come. The alamo need hardly be considered. It is a poor timber for construction, and its use must always be limited to comparatively few purposes. Some of the southern timbers, however, are more formidable rivals to the American product, but even here there are almost insurmountable obstacles to its extensive use, except in regions within fairly easy reach of the forests.

MEAGER TRANSPORTATION FACILITIES.

The first difficulty is lack of cheap transportation. Much of the lumber is at present carried to the building centers by rail, and the freights are high. It is possible that some time in the future companies will be organized to transport the lumber from the mills to ports on the coast by means of the numerous rivers of the south, and thence northward on auxiliary steam schooners similar to those in use on our own northwest coast. But even if this be done there will remain the other great obstacle to the extensive use of this lumber—the impossibility of properly cutting and seasoning it. The best woods are heavy and full of sap. The rainfall is so excessive that it has thus far been found impossible to get laborers to work in the forests, except during the spring and early summer months. The timber is cut wet and sawn wet, and the process of seasoning is extremely slow. A furniture

:ates furnishes comparatively little. The
Germany, though most of it is probably
stitutes 44 per cent of the total, while
cent, England's 14.6 per cent, and the
There is evidence, however, that Ameri-
ef items being office furniture and ordi-
goods. The shipments of manufactures
tes to Chile showed a steady rise in value
ar 1:01, to $86,043 in 1905. The largest
twood furniture, and this comes mainly
trade is hampered by a high import duty
local factories. It is 60 per cent on a
4.9 cents per pound on chairs, benches,
s and backs, to 32.7 cents per pound on

L AND OTHER OILS.

heavy, the British Statesmen's Yearbook
oreign purchases of industrial oils, etc.,
215 gold). The declared exports of oils
hile for the fiscal years 1903 to 1905 were

the United States to Chile, 1903–1905.

b	1903.	1904.	1905.
....	$2,001	$1,668	$5,044
....	485,817	653,995	649,272
....	140,062	188,165	199,870
....	12,821	9,709	44,952
....	640,701	853,537	899,138

dmitted free of duty, and comes almost
contract has recently been made for sup-
pply by large shipments from California.

There should be a good opening for this oil for fuel purposes in the mining districts of both Chile and Bolivia, for native fuel in these regions is almost unknown.

MOSS AS A FUEL.

Some of the nitrate and borax establishments of the interior of northern Chile are at present using a very inferior native fuel—a thick moss which grows on the rocks only at elevations of over 13,000 feet. It is poor material, but is found more economical than coal brought from the coast. The supplies are rather limited and are being rapidly reduced without possibility of renewal for many decades. In some of the Bolivian mines anthracite gas is used in gas engines for power, the anthracite being brought from Wales, landed at Antofagasta, freighted by rail to between 12,000 and 13,000 feet elevation at Oruro or some near-by point, and then carried to the mines on carts or on mule back. Power thus obtained is very costly, and it seems probable that a systematic effort to introduce the more extensive use of fuel oil, if done on a large scale so that economical methods of transportation could be used, would prove successful.

Refined oil for illuminating purposes comes, of course, almost wholly from the United States. Its use is likely to grow with the population throughout all northern Chile, for, there being no water power and no cheap supplies of gas coal, lighting must continue to be done by kerosene. The duty is 25 per cent on a valuation of 1.64 cents per pound gross weight.

Lubricating oils imported are almost wholly petroleum oils. The United States supplied in 1904 77 per cent, most of the remainder being furnished by England (14 per cent), and Germany (8 per cent). The duty is 25 per cent on a valuation of 6.55 cents per pound gross weight.

PAPER AND ITS MANUFACTURES.

The total imports of paper, cardboard, and their manufactures amounted to $1,695,000 in 1904. Germany furnished nearly 56 per cent, England 13 per cent, and the United States 18 per cent. The largest items of import are newspaper, $505,000; blotting and wrapping paper, $166,000; printed books, etc., $195,000, and writing and book paper, $154,000. The United States has been making particularly good progress in newspaper, supplying 36 per cent of the total, compared with Germany's 57 per cent. In blotting and wrapping paper Germany has almost a monopoly, selling 80 per cent of the total. Printed books, etc., come mainly from England, Germany, and France, while Germany and England together furnish 82 per cent of the writing and book paper. Thus, among the larger items of paper imported into Chile, the United States takes a prominent part in the supply of only one—newspaper.

ɔt so much a matter of price as of cus-
made to familiarize the people with
trade would result.

f duty; printed books, etc., are also,
most writing and book paper bears a
tion of 11.45 cents per pound; wrap-
25 to 50 per cent; cardboard, 25 per
30 per cent, on valuations which are

ENTS, AND COLORS.

tins, etc., are imported to the extent of
'hey come mostly from England and
rnishing less than 4 per cent in 1904.
uels, in small tins, tubes, etc., the United
, though the total imports are small.
the United States furnishing 28 per
Germany 36 per cent.
Ʒerman, the nearest competitor being
are only about one-fourth as large as
ᴤ furnishes only an insignificant quan-
class of goods in 1904 were valued at

for American varnishes, though our
ill. The total imports in 1904 were
States supplied 17 per cent, England
per cent.

American shoe blacking and polishes are also in growing demand. Of the total imports in 1904 of $33,000, the United States furnished 20 per cent, England and Germany each 34 per cent, and France 12 per cent.

The import duties are: On mixed paints, 25 per cent on valuations varying from 3.93 cents per pound on common paints mixed with oil to 32.7 cents per pound on fine black leather paints; on dry paints, 25 per cent on valuations from 3.27 cents per pound on white and red lead to 98.2 cents per pound on indigo; on varnishes, 25 per cent on valuations from 4.9 cents per pound on common varnishes to 21.3 cents on copal. On shoe polish, 35 per cent on valuations from 3.93 cents to 32.7 cents per pound.

ADMONITION TO MANUFACTURERS.

In closing it remains to repeat what has so often been emphasized before, that one of the greatest obstacles to American success is the attitude of American manufacturers who, being assured of a home market, are indifferent to the peculiarities of the foreign market. If our exporters will learn to give the closest attention to the suggestions and instructions which are constantly being given them by their customers and agents as to the minutiæ of packing, shipping, marking, making out of invoices, etc., there can not be the slightest doubt that their trade will advance by leaps and bounds. The persistent disregard of such instructions and the failure to recognize responsibility when losses result is doing as much to hamper American trade as any other single cause.

RAILROAD CONSTRUCTION.

The Joint Committee on Appropriations of both houses of the Chilean Congress, in one of its sessions of November, 1906, approved the expenditure of 12,000,000 *pesos* for the construction of the following railroad lines:

From Animas to Los Pozos; from Inca to Copiapo; from Vallenar to Viscachitas; from Serena to Rivadavia; from Ovalle to Trapiche; from Palomas to San Marcos; from Choapa to Salamanca; from Rayado to Los Vilos; from Rayado to Papudo; from Cabildo to Pedehua; from Santiago to Cerriles; Santiago belt railroad; from San Bernardo to the volcano; from Melipilla to San Antonio; from Alcones to Pichilemu; from San Vicente to Peralillo; from Curico to Hualañe; from San Clemente to Panimavida, with a branch road to Colorado; from Cauquenes to Curanipe, or other point on the coast; from Cauquenes to Coelemu; from Angeles to Antuco; from Cohiue to Nacimiento; from Pua to Curacautin; from Nueva Imperial to Carahue; and from Gorbea to Antilhue.

CUSTOMS REVENUES, FIRST TEN MONTHS OF 1906.

According to statistics published in the "*Diario Oficial*" of Chile the various custom-houses of the Republic collected during the month of October, 1906, a total revenue of 11,960,011.67 *pesos*, of which sum 3,982,083.42 *pesos* were for import duties, 7,765,050.80 *pesos* for export duties, and 212,877.45 for miscellaneous receipts.

During the same month of 1905 the amount collected for import duties was 2,913,322.10 *pesos;* for export duties, 7,256,474.99 *pesos*, and for miscellaneous receipts, 256,401.41 *pesos*, making a total of 10,426,198.50.

A comparison of the receipts of October, 1906, with those of the same month of 1905 shows an increase in import duties of 1,068,761.32 *pesos* and in export duties of 508,575.81 *pesos*, and a decrease in miscellaneous receipts of 43,523.96 *pesos*. The total increase was 1,533,813.17 *pesos*.

The following table shows the amount collected by each custom-house during the month under review, the figures for the same month of 1905 being also given by way of comparison:

Custom-houses.	October—	
	1905.	1906.
I. Export duties:	*Pesos.*	*Pesos.*
Pisagua	1,026,362.73	1,287,615.57
Iquique	3,999,465.63	3,791,300.81
Tocopilla	922,117.25	1,292,331.10
Antofagasta	385,106.38	523,729.04
Taltal	923,423.00	960,074.28
Total	7,256,474.99	7,765,050.80
II. Import duties:		
Arica	32,370.68	76,427.28
Pisagua	22,700.20	36,707.32
Iquique	347,750.14	377,081.64
Tocopilla	10,631.91	27,129.20
Antofagasta	187,409.76	351,709.70
Taltal	25,967.98	75,116.71
Caldera	5,767.07	21,660.00
Carrizal Bajo	1,021.88	11,037.15
Coquimbo	56,856.60	137,507.64
Valparaiso	1,645,491.76	2,112,598.87
Talcahuano	436,701.13	536,237.17
Coronel	15,166.48	51,332.62
Valdivia	75,408.11	127,731.86
Puerto Montt	4,640.68	5,974.89
Frontier custom-houses	45,437.72	80,501.38
Total	2,913,322.10	3,982,083.42
III. Miscellaneous receipts	256,401.41	212,877.45
Total general	10,426,198.50	11,960,011.67

During the first ten months of 1906 the custom-houses of the Republic collected a total revenue of 80,643,145.09 *pesos*. During the same period of 1905 the revenue collected amounted to 73,105,158.31 *pesos;* a comparison of these figures shows an increase in 1906 of 7,537,986.78 *pesos*.

LIVE-STOCK CENSUS OF 1906.

The Bureau of Statistics and Agricultural Information, Department Industry and Public Works, of the Republic of Chile, has published recently the live-stock census taken during the last months of 1906. The following figures show the numerical values of each class: Horses, 698,880; cattle, 2,477,064 heads; sheep, 2,405,584; goats, 461,908; hogs, 287,612.

The figures for the Provinces of Tacna, Tarapaca, Antofagasta, Coquimbo, Valparaiso, and Chiloe, and Territory of Magallanes were not included in this census.

The annual consumption of meat in the Republic is estimated as follows: 400,000 heads of cattle, 545,517 sheep, and 145,741 hogs.

THE PROMOTION OF IMMIGRATION.

On November 15, 1906, the Chilean Senate approved a proposed law authorizing the expenditure of 500,000 *pesos* for the promotion of immigration, and of 50,000 *pesos* for the construction, in Valparaiso, of lodgings for immigrants, and empowering the Executive to invest said amounts in the objects for which they were appropriated.

TRADE WITH GREAT BRITAIN, 1901-1905.

The following figures relating to the commerce between Chile and Great Britain from 1901 to 1905 have been taken from a report submitted on August 7, 1906, by the Chilean Consul-General at Glasgow to the Minister of Foreign Relations:

Year.	Value.	Year.	Value.
1901	£7,739,595	1904	£8,955,218
1902	7,587,142	1905	10,850,418
1903	7,929,948		

An examination of these figures shows the considerable increase of the commercial relations between Chile and the United Kingdom, being more pronounced in 1905, an increase of nearly £3,000,000 over 1903 and of £2,000,000 over 1904.

The value of the exports from Chile to Great Britain during the years under comparison was as follows:

Year.	Value.	Year.	Value.
1901	£4,318,095	1904	£5,422,941
1902	4,521,376	1905	6,008,031
1903	4,597,812		

f $1,000,000. The object of the com-
ght in Chile to be the control of the

_____

OMBIA.

CLIMATE OF THE REPUBLIC.

y United States Minister to Colombia,
:906, Director of the Bureau of the
e published in the "Southern Lum-

nly 950 miles from the southernmost
somprehend its strategic position, its
esources. It is the only South Amer-
the Atlantic and Pacific; it has an area
:, France, and Belgium combined, or,
ge as the State of Texas; and there is
n America that has such unexploited
, copper, gold, silver, platinum, and
. At the same time its agricultural
account of the richness of the soil,
the variety of the climate. Although
the Tropical Zone and a large portion
it has many different sections —com-
at as Tennessee and Alabama—which,
a climate as cool all the year round as
n the latter part of October."
:uated at an altitude of 8,500 feet on a
he State of Massachusetts, is as cool

through the whole year as Boston in September. The average man thinks of Colombia as being like Panama or like the hot low coasts of the country, when he visits its principal ports, not understanding that when he gets into the interior he goes upon those high plateaus with their cool temperature."

FOREIGN COMMERCE OF BARRANQUILLA, FIRST NINE MONTHS OF 1906.

The following statistics, relating to the foreign commerce of Barranquilla, from January to September, 1906, have been taken from the latest official data received.

The exports from said port during the period in reference amounted to 22,860,936.155 kilos, valued at 4,878,268 gold *pesos*.

The principal products exported were: Hides and skins, 1,730,565; coffee, 17,313,435 sacks; divi-divi, 1,190,476 packages; cotton, 109,212 sacks; silver ores, 139,974 packages; plants, 127,113, and 132,796 alligator skins. Besides these exports, there are the exports of cattle, which were itemized separately, amounting to 187,820 gold *pesos*, value of 9,391 head of cattle exported to Cuba, at the rate of 20 gold *pesos* each.

The imports during the period under review amounted to 21,269,-458.035 kilos, valued at 4,408,271 gold *pesos*, the countries of origin being Great Britan, United States, France, Spain, and others.

A comparison of exports and imports shows a balance of trade in favor of Barranquilla of 379,987 gold *pesos*.

EXPORTS OF HIDES FROM PUERTO VILLAMIZAR, FIRST NINE MONTHS OF 1906.

During the months of January to September, 1906, there were exported from Puerto Vallamizar, Department of Santander, Colombia, 8,791 hides, as follows: January, nothing; February, nothing; March, 2,000; April, 748; May, 1,962; June, 620; July, 400; August, 1,790; September, 1,271.

COSTA RICA.

CUSTOMS REVENUES, APRIL-NOVEMBER, 1906.

According to statistics published in the "*Gaceta Oficial*" of Costa Rica, December 19, 1906, the various custom-houses of the Republic collected a revenue of 2,837,453.79 *colones* during the eight months from April to November, 1906, which, compared with 2,520,447.84 *colones* collected during the same period of 1905, show an increase of 317,005.95 *colones*. The customs revenues for the period under review were estimated in the Budget at 2,800,000 *colones;* therefore, the actual amount collected yielded a surplus of 37,453.79 *colones*.

Governor MAGOON as follows:

NOR: The honorable Diplomatic Corps
the Cuban Republic, although it can not
rmal situation created in the country by
duty not to break the practice of inter-
vith the greatest pleasure to salute your
ovisionally the chief magistracy of the
faculties by delegation of the President
ica the powers and government of this

nce and no personal merits of any kind
the honor to-day of addressing your
ver, that the few words I am about to
ression of the thought and good will of
f the high corps here assembled.
an Republic, accept the sincere felicita-
r august sovereigns and of the heads of
hich we respectively represent, we offer
' the year 1907; and at the same time
es for the early and complete reestab-
condition in the island of Cuba, a basis
the rehabilitation of its independence,
rity.
lency's self the most cordial felicitations
h especially on this occasion wishes you
story success in the arduous and noble
our high abilities and integrity has been

e following reply in English:
the Dean of the Diplomatic Corps, and
rs of that Corps accredited to the Repub-
ccept my sincere thanks and profound
pressions of friendship and good will,
ndation voiced by the dean of this hon-

orable Corps, and for the spirit of friendship and kindly consideration which prompts their utterance. The exceptional circumstances which bring us together at this time and place impel the belief that your congratulations and good wishes are prompted by something greater and better than mere formal courtesy; that, in fact, they are prompted by a sympathetic friendship for the people and Republic of Cuba in their endeavor to maintain a place in the family of nations, and good will toward the United States in its efforts to assist them.

"As Provisional Governor of Cuba, exercising by designation of the President of the United States the powers delegated to the United States by the Constitution of Cuba, it is my duty, as well as privilege and pleasure, to thank you for and on behalf of the people and Republic of Cuba for your recognition of the fact that the Republic continues in existence, moves along the lines of national endeavor, preserves its international relations, and, with but slight changes in personnel, discharges the duties for which governments are instituted.

"I join with you in the wish for the early and complete reestablishment of the political tranquillity of the island of Cuba, and rejoice that on every hand throughout the island evidences appear that political passion and prejudice are passing away and that reason and judgment are taking their places; that peace and prosperity have returned, and the people have again assumed their ordinary vocations and are reaping the abundant harvests which God in His goodness has given them.

> " 'There's a divinity that shapes our ends,
> Rough hew them how we will,'

and it seems that Providence has intervened at this critical juncture in the affairs of Cuba to give an unmistakable example of the benefits to be derived from pursuing the arts of peace. Providence directing, the sympathy of the world supporting, and the great Republic of the United States directly assisting, there should be no doubt that the remaining difficulties will be removed and the way opened by which the high purposes and ultimate destinies of Cuba are to be attained.

"Again I thank you, officially and personally, and especially the Dean of your high Corps."

THE HENEQUEN INDUSTRY.

United States Consul MAX J. BAEHR, of Cienfuegos, reports as follows:

"Although there is in the island of Cuba considerable land planted in henequen (hemp) and three or four industrial plants with the necessary machinery to prepare the fiber for market, the output is yet limited and insufficient to furnish raw material for existing manufactories, these being compelled to used imported fiber, principally from Yucatan. The number of henequen plantations in Cuba, has been

ll be sufficient for the consumption of
d day the factory makes 35,000 pounds
and, with the exception of the tarred
taly, the factories at Regla and Havana
he rope consumed in Cuba, and they
ba, which in 1904 amounted to 550,000

ing the sea, thus facilitating the unload-
erial and its transportation by means of
The establishment contains all kinds of
factured from the finest to the heaviest
d other purposes. It is provided with
amos, has a repair shop, boiler rooms,
capacity for 5,000 bales of henequen.
in five or six years the production of
ent for the national consumption and
orted.
s known in Cuba, *Agave americana* and
elding a hard, tough filament, applied
ope and cordage. Both grow sponta-
lands, unfit for any other kind of cul-
ineral composition of the soil abounds
cultivation, including the price of the
at about $836 per *caballeria* (33 acres),
ing, and packing, $2,248, or a total of

arge plantation of 25 *caballerias* shows
,000 plants. These, after three years,

the time when they attain their most perfect development, yield on an average three leaves monthly, and as it is calculated that each leaf contains one and a half ounces of fiber, 1,000,000 leaves gathered from a caballeria during one year will yield 420 bales of 4 quintals (400 pounds each).

"Surrounding the plantation referred to and where the leaves are gathered, cleaned, and the bales prepared there are many smaller plantations where the leaves are sold on the plant at the rate of 50 cents silver per thousand, the purchaser paying for cutting, gathering, and cartage. The leaves, collected in bunches of ten each, are paid for at the rate of $1 currency per thousand. The life of a plant is calculated at fifteen years, but as each plant disappears it leaves an offshoot or young plant, which at the end of three years will again commence to give the same yield for another fifteen years."

TRADE OF CIENFUEGOS, 1905-6.

United States Consul MAX J. BAEHR furnishes a detailed statement showing imports and exports at the port of Cienfuegos during the fiscal year 1905-6. The total trade amounted to $20,262,849, imports $7,432,827, exports $12,830,022. The imports from the principal countries were as follows:

United States	$2,928,635	Colombia	$687,278
England	1,093,852	Uruguay	426,959
Spain	688,806	Germany	418,832

The principal articles imported from the United States were: Machinery, breadstuffs, provisions, coal, lumber, oils, shoes, barbed wire, and cement. The most remarkable increase over last year's importation is that of American shoes, from $51,363 in 1905 to $128,178 in 1906, or 125 per cent.

The most notable decrease is in American rice. Its price compared with that for the Indian article is so high as to eliminate it from this market altogether, especially since the native prefers the Indian to the American rice. In 1905 Cienfuegos imported $168,804 worth of American rice, and during the last fiscal year not one pound entered this harbor from the United States.

Of the $12,830,022 exports $12,738,892 went to the United States, $57,249 to England, and $33,881 to Germany. It will thus be seen that while the United States took practically all the exports of this market, it received less than 40 per cent of its trade; while England, Spain, and Germany, without taking anything from them, so to speak, were favored with 14, 9, and 6 per cent, respectively.

The imports from Colombia were cattle solely, and those from Uruguay "jerked beef" only.

FIRST HALF OF 1906.

oreign trade of the Dominican Repub-
ine 30, 1906, with comparative tables

the foreign trade carried on by the
e first six months of 1906, compared
s a falling off of $764,917, the returns
agricultural activities of the country
d that the reduction in values is due
es received for the products exported,
nerally increased.

of sugar was increased by 8,749,230
$1,033,594 less for the entire quantity
uantity shipped during the first half
3,204,000 pounds of cacao shipped, by
ing to heavy rains during the season
9,397 less than the 17,388,000 pounds
period. Nor do the decreased exporta-
g off in production, which was to the
op being unusually late the apparent
year must appear as an excess during

howing of this particular period, which
y misleading circumstances, is sound,
of industrial progress than has been
iod in recent years.

Local products were sold abroad to the value of $4,007,158, against importations, not counting currency, valued at $1,887,268, leaving the proportionately large balance of trade for the half year in favor of the Republic of $2,119,890.

The total transfers of gold and silver currency consisted of an importation of $176,800 in money of the United States, and although $738,724.27 was sent abroad in the form of exchange for deposit as a trust fund with reference to the public debt, no currency was required to be exported on that account.

In the aggregate foreign trade of the Republic during the first six months of 1906, amounting to $5,890,426. the United States participated to the extent of $3,833,678, or 65 per cent of the whole, receiving products to the value of $2,839,525, and supplying merchandise invoiced at $994,153, which is about the same proportion of trade enjoyed by that country during the corresponding period of 1905.

The trade with Germany was of the next greatest importance, aggregating $1,285,328, of which $436,105 represents merchandise sold to, and $849,223, products purchased from the Republic.   The total trade with Germany shows an increase of $371,075 over the comparative period, which advances the percentage of trade with that country from 13 to 21 per cent of the whole.   This was facilitated by the employment of a suitable local steamer by the Hamburg-American Line to connect the commerce of the Republic with its through steamers touching at St. Thomas.

France received $332,063 of the trade, representing exports to the Republic invoiced at $101,630 and imports from it valued at $230,433, having dropped in the percentage of the whole trade received from 11 to 5 per cent.

The trade with Great Britain was increased from $260,844 to $282,692, and that with Italy and Spain, while still small, shows a considerable increase, as may be seen from the accompanying comparative tables.

While a decrease of $1,253,018 in the value of exports is shown by the statistical returns, the aggregate trade values were supported by a striking increase in the value of imports of approximately 50 per cent; the imports for the first half of 1906, omitting currency, having been invoiced at $1,887,268 as against $1,252,866 for the first half of 1905. This large increase recorded in imports indicates, no doubt, a much wider demand for foreign merchandise, but the conditions of local trade induce the belief that the showing results to some extent as well from the fact that the large importations formerly made by way of the land frontier without record have been checked, and that such traffic has, through the activity of the frontier customs patrol, been forced into regular channels.

gest amount of rice, the ship-
icreased in value from $56,258
om the United States ($26,933)
Britain ($10,956) decreased in
om France, Spain, and "Other

he only class of imports espe-
in value during the half year,
ig valued at but $96,908 and
, as against values from those
iod of $118,974 and $43,476,
iany ($36,878) show a slight
also participated in supplying

which aggregated in invoice
lucts valued at $12,518, were
, that country furnishing all of
dstuffs to the value of $11,166.
nd dairy products imported is
United States and Germany—
tively—as well as from France,

d, illuminating and lubricating
d in the United States, Euro-
ty of olive and other oils.

The invoice values of manufacturers of vegetable fibers were nearly double those of the first half of 1905, the increase being principally in consignments from the United States, valued at $34,672, and Germany $29,411; those from Great Britain showing a decrease from $19,141 to $17,735.

Preserved fish, one of the principal articles of diet, is still largely supplied from the United States, that commodity from America being invoiced at $64,533, while an increase in demand for German products of this nature is apparent. Spain and France also furnished small quantities, although the values from the latter country and from Italy decreased.

There was an increase in the value of manufactures of wood imported, to the extent of $7,655, most of which, invoiced at $50,981, came from the United States, while Germany furnished these manufactures to the value of $4,762. The importations from other countries were inconsiderable.

Leather goods to the value of $52,133, an increase over that of the previous period, were received, $42,129 coming from the United States, $3,729 from Germany, $2,251 from France, $1,943 from Spain, and $1,847 from the United Kingdom.

Chemicals, drugs, and dyes invoiced at $30,219 were imported, those from the United States being of the largest quantity and valued at $20,443. French products were received to the value of $4,295, British $3,365, and German $1,889, the remainder coming from "Other countries."

The only marked change in the value of agricultural implements received from the principal sources—Great Britain and Germany—is seen in the increase in value of those imported from Germany from $9,163 to $17,878, making the total value, including those from all other countries, $28,124.

German beer found a greater demand than that of any other make, the receipts showing an increase in value from $11,889 to $20,333, while the United States supplied but $5,599, the total value received having been $27,027, of which the United Kingdom and Spain furnished the remainder.

Imports of German paper manufactures increased in value to $8,358, exceeding those from the United States, invoiced at $5,882, and with those from Spain, invoiced at $1,321, from France, Italy, the United Kingdom, and "other countries" in smaller quantities, aggregated in value $16,675, as against $13,000 for the first half of 1905.

Hats and caps from Italy, invoiced at $9,621, as formerly, exceeded in value the receipts of that class of merchandise from other countries. Those from France were valued at $3,897, the United States $1,379, Germany, Spain, Porto Rico, and Great Britain furnishing the remainder.

ung consignments to France decreased
f $65,188, to 2,475,983 pounds, val-

ncreased from 356,481 pounds during
5 1,203,444 pounds during the first
at $25,164 and $76,945, while those
pounds, valued at $34,031, show no
r value. The amount sent to France
ounds, valued at $39,792, to 316,527
[pounds were shipped to Cuba, and
xported was distributed among "all

orts of tobacco, owing to the lateness
ed during the first half of 1906. The
st noticeable in the quantity shipped
3,362,684 pounds sent to that country
[44,180 exported thereto during the
the United States, however, exceeded
o the latter country during the com-
ls, or 1,000 per cent, the exportations
half of 1905 having been less than
of the tobacco exportations went prin-
ipments aggregating 349,174 pounds.
United States were increased from
,500 bunches during the first half of

ent abroad show an increase in value
! which went to Germany.
out of a total value of $3,610, and
ported to Germany. Goatskins and
,176 and $15,099, respectively, were

consigned to the United States, while Germany purchased the latter to the value of $26,964.

Wax to the extent of 221,335 pounds, valued at $51,375 was shipped to Germany, the United States, and France.

For the various kinds of hard woods, mahogany, lignum-vitæ, etc., the United States, United Kingdom, Germany, and France afforded markets for the exportation to the aggregate value of $39,679.

NATIONALITIES OF IMPORTING VESSELS.

Of the total imports, values to the extent of $1,135,950, or 55 per cent, were brought in American vessels; $652,078, or 32 per cent, were imported in German, $146,882, or 7 per cent, in French, $42,342 in Norwegian, $33,131 in British, and the remainder in vessels of nationalities as shown by the corresponding table, annexed.

American vessels brought substantially all of the cargoes imported from the United States, as well as transit cargoes valued at $50,470.

NATIONALITIES OF EXPORTING VESSELS.

Of the export values amounting to $4,007,158, American vessels carried $1,416,652, or 35 per cent, and Norwegian vessels were second with cargoes valued at $1,218,198, or 30 per cent, all bound for the United States. Following the Norwegian vessels, in the order named, were German with $855,451, French with $240,860, British with $236,179, etc.

TONNAGE.

The aggregate foreign tonnage of the several ports of the Republic for the half year was 726,511 tons, representing 822 entrances and clearances of vessels engaged in the foreign trade. The total coastwise tonnage of the various entry ports was 60,133 tons, representing 3,335 coastwise entrances and clearances.

Imports into the Dominican Republic during the first six months of the calendar year 1906, showing the values and principal countries of origin, in comparison with those of the corresponding period of 1905.

Article and country.	January 1 to June 30, 1905.		January 1 to June 30, 1906.	
	Quantity.	Value.	Quantity.	Value.
Agricultural implements:				
United States	....	$7,570	....	$7,390
United Kingdom	....	2,045	....	2,164
Germany	....	9,183	....	17,875
France	....	15	....	68
Cuba	....	....	....	3
Porto Rico	....	....	....	302
Other countries	....	1,272	....	327
Total	....	20,065	....	28,129

Imports into the Dominican Republic during the first six months of the calendar year 1906, etc.—Continued.

Article and country.	January 1 to June 30, 1905.		January 1 to June 30, 1906.	
	Quantity.	Value.	Quantity.	Value.
Animals:				
Horses and mules—	*Number.*		*Number.*	
United States	40	$5,900	1	$500
Porto Rico	27	994	2	290
Total	67	6,894	3	790
Cattle—				
Porto Rico	91	2,755		
All other—				
United States		2		
Books, maps, and other printed matter:				
United States		1,046		1,551
United Kingdom		5		61
Germany		1,097		1,329
France		495		3,315
Italy				182
Spain		208		264
Cuba		48		469
Porto Rico				9
Other countries				3,500
Total		2,899		10,680
Breadstuffs:				
Wheat flour—	*Barrels.*		*Barrels.*	
United States	18,633	102,406	30,288	132,222
Porto Rico	10	50		
Other countries	43	257	20	90
Total	18,686	102,713	30,708	132,312
All other—				
United States		10,966		11,196
United Kingdom		40		31
Germany		20		155
France		166		701
Italy		187		449
Spain		3		
Porto Rico		4		6
Other countries				8
Total		11,386		12,519
Chemicals, drugs, and dyes:				
United States		15,573		20,443
United Kingdom		2,195		3,365
Germany		1,358		1,889
France		5,417		4,295
Italy		3		5
Spain		72		182
Cuba		45		
Porto Rico		65		
Other countries		241		40
Total		24,969		30,219
Coal:	*Tons.*		*Tons.*	
United States	1,753	5,899	3,401	12,674
United Kingdom	1,986	6,164		
Other countries	425	2,485		
Total	4,164	11,847	3,401	12,674
Cotton, manufactures of:				
United States		110,559		195,275
United Kingdom		94,540		173,503
Germany		31,056		66,150
France		19,557		28,249
Spain				18,813
Italy		3,144		10,569
Belgium		90		
Cuba				21
Porto Rico		30		3,296
Other countries		1,665		4,272
Total		260,641		500,158

Imports into the Dominican Republic during the first six months of the calendar year 1906, etc.—Continued.

Article and country.	January 1 to June 30, 1905.		January 1 to June 30, 1906.	
	Quantity.	Value.	Quantity.	Value.
Earthen, stone, and china ware:				
United States		$184		$287
United Kingdom		489		1,664
Germany		7,940		10,771
France		617		236
Italy				32
Spain		14		22
Porto Rico				7
Other countries				12
Total		9,241		13,131
Fibers, vegetable, manufacturers of:				
United States		17,829		34,672
United Kingdom		19,141		17,734
Germany		4,043		29,413
France		3,553		270
Italy				438
Spain		277		425
Other countries		2,816		61
Total		47,256		83,013
Fish, preserved, and fish products:				
United States		54,701		64,533
United Kingdom		10		
Germany		347		1,040
France		991		203
Italy		196		6
Spain		265		868
Porto Rico		140		92
Other countries		136		147
Total		56,886		66,889
Fruits and nuts:				
United States		833		2,854
United Kingdom		15		23
Germany		26		124
France		218		1,125
Italy		18		474
Spain		183		2,935
Cuba		30		240
Porto Rico				6
Total		1,323		7,772
Glass and glassware:				
United States		1,154		8,182
United Kingdom		100		100
Germany		910		5,879
France		236		711
Italy				8
Spain		3		288
Belgium		7		
Porto Rico				4
Total		2,429		15,72
Gold and silver currency:				
United States		298,300		176,500
Grease and grease scraps for soap stock:				
United States		16,726		7,574
Germany		496		
France		8		
Porto Rico		2,077		918
Total		19,307		8,492
Gums and resins:				
United States		5,202		6,663
United Kingdom		60		316
Germany		7		936
Total		5,269		7,915

Imports into the Dominican Republic during the first six months of the calendar year 1906, etc.—Continued.

Article and country.	January 1 to June 30, 1905.		January 1 to June 30, 1906.	
	Quantity.	Value.	Quantity.	Value.
Hats and caps:				
United States		$3,829		$1,379
United Kingdom		348		102
Germany		1,554		911
France		2,186		3,897
Italy		4,022		9,621
Spain				209
Porto Rico		356		189
Other countries		12		
Total		12,307		16,308
Iron and steel, manufactures of:				
United States		118,974		96,908
United Kingdom		43,476		23,241
Germany		21,322		36,878
France		6,830		4,068
Spain		252		89
Belgium		1,129		1,831
Cuba		18		45
Porto Rico		551		8
Other countries		76		70
Total		192,628		163,133
Jewelry, including watches and clocks:				
United States		29		348
United Kingdom		91		16
Germany		645		495
France		1,252		2,410
Italy		300		4,963
Spain				10
Porto Rico		81		
Total		2,398		8,242
Leather, and manufactures of.				
United States		28,663		42,129
United Kingdom		2,148		1,847
Germany		1,463		3,729
France		1,952		2,251
Italy				165
Spain		281		1,943
Porto Rico		10		69
Other countries		61		
Total		34,579		52,133
	Dozen bottles.		Dozen bottles.	
Malt liquors, beer in bottles:				
United States	1,667	2,007	4,885	5,599
United Kingdom	90	190	572	910
Germany	8,398	11,889	13,827	20,333
France	500	2,028	111	178
Spain	12	15		
Other countries	15	18	6	7
Total	10,682	16,147	19,431	27,027
Metals and manufactures of (not elsewhere specified):				
United States		3,065		5,207
United Kingdom		513		924
Germany		516		2,338
France				583
Italy				3
Spain				25
Cuba		15		
Porto Rico		75		
Other countries		81		3
Total		4,265		9,033
Oils.				
United States		74,102		95,016
United Kingdom		325		663
Germany		773		372
France		219		831
Italy		123		422

Imports into the Dominican Republic during the first six months of the calendar year 1906, etc.—Continued.

Article and country.	January 1 to June 30, 1905.		January 1 to June 30, 1906.	
	Quantity.	Value.	Quantity.	Value.
Oils—Continued.				
Spain		$370		$4,997
Porto Rico		19		130
Other countries		167		313
Total		76,128		102,774
Paints, pigments, and colors:				
United States		3,682		4,412
United Kingdom		1,510		1,680
Germany		747		2,455
France		26		120
Spain		80		
Total		6,045		8,667
Paper and manufactures of.				
United States		5,583		5,982
United Kingdom		176		31
Germany		3,363		8,358
France		1,563		664
Italy		106		412
Spain		2,078		1,321
Porto Rico				9
Cuba		182		
Other countries				98
Total		13,000		16,675
Perfumery and cosmetics:				
United States		652		458
Germany		136		420
France		4,018		4,700
Italy		74		49
Spain		100		26
Porto Rico				185
Other countries		19		
Total		4,944		5,838
Provisions, comprising meats and dairy products				
United States		30,570		53,044
United Kingdom		290		294
Germany		24,511		44,716
France		1,305		2,565
Italy		156		577
Spain		39		64
Cuba				969
Porto Rico		648		1,789
Other countries		10		81
Total		57,529		104,103
Rice:	*Pounds.*		*Pounds.*	
United States	621,199	12,551	1,268,580	26,933
United Kingdom	1,471,929	23,286	655,742	10,956
Germany	2,562,319	56,258	6,972,922	135,982
France	30,620	486	246,431	4,461
Italy	100	7		
Spain	2,173	50	4,315	151
Other countries	11,000	212	133,172	3,281
Total	4,699,340	92,820	9,281,112	181,764
Rubber, manufactures of:				
United States		1,165		1,614
United Kingdom		319		181
Germany		608		644
France		354		239
Total		2,446		2,721
Soap:				
United States		11,431		14,512
United Kingdom		27		2
Germany				9
France		68		118
Italy				10

Imports into the Dominican Republic during the first six months of the calendar year 1906, etc.—Continued.

Article and country.	January 1 to June 30, 1905.		January 1 to June 30, 1906.	
	Quantity.	Value.	Quantity.	Value.
Soap—Continued.				
Porto Rico		$8		$13
Other countries		103		336
Total		11,688		15,000
Sugar and confectionery:				
United States		5,544		21,628
United Kingdom		362		299
Germany		280		1,638
France				2,065
Italy				197
Spain				557
Total		6,186		28,804
Tobacco, manufactured:				
United States		246		14
Cuba		1,238		1,101
Total		1,484		1,115
Umbrellas and canes:				
United States		3		91
United Kingdom		415		606
Germany		646		1,586
France		729		1,807
Italy		616		1,274
Spain				23
Other countries		38		42
Total		2,447		5,429
Vegetables:				
United States		6,561		12,019
United Kingdom		110		719
Germany		119		148
France		744		1,170
Italy		21		78
Spain		793		5,352
Cuba		2,352		3,009
Porto Rico		840		1,294
Total		11,540		23,816
Vehicles:				
United States		912		2,291
Germany				169
France				10
Other countries		400		
Total		1,312		2,470
Wines, liquors and distilled spirits:				
United States		1,151		690
United Kingdom		304		
Germany		1,191		2,241
France		3,824		10,935
Italy		648		1,728
Spain		2,362		7,761
Cuba				114
Other countries				336
Total		9,780		23,808
Wood and manufactures of:				
United States		43,430		50,981
United Kingdom		3,062		381
Germany		2,215		4,762
France		411		543
Italy				33
Spain				20
Cuba		118		195
Porto Rico				4
Other countries		45		15
Total		49,281		56,934

Imports into the Dominican Republic during the first six months of the calendar year 1906, etc.—Continued.

Article and country.	January 1 to June 30, 1905.		January 1 to June 30, 1906.	
	Quantity.	Value.	Quantity.	Value.
Wool and manufactures of:				
United States		$306	....	$402
United Kingdom..........		2,400	....	6,405
Germany..........		1,196	....	8,818
France..........		1,929	....	4,345
Spain..........			....	34
Other countries		4	....	
Total..........		5,775	....	20,004
All other articles not elsewhere specified:				
United States..........		24,513	....	33,470
United Kingdom..........		1,714	....	2,415
Germany..........		11,941	....	24,105
France..........		7,223	....	14,670
Italy..........		256	....	1,086
Spain..........		186	....	1,907
Belgium..........			....	400
Cuba			....	1
Porto Rico		937	....	95
Other countries..........		2,564	....	3,511
Total..........		49,334	....	81,610

RECAPITULATION.

Country.	Value first six months—	
	1905.	1906.
United States	$1,033,421	$1,160,963
United Kingdom..........	206,139	250,626
Germany..........	186,345	436,105
France..........	80,575	101,630
Italy..........	9,876	32,760
Spain	7,217	48,283
Belgium..........	1,226	2,231
Cuba	4,046	6,197
Porto Rico	9,640	8,713
Other countries..........	12,681	16,580
Total..........	1,551,166	2,064,068

NOTE.—The total value of imports from the United States includes gold and silver currency amounting to $298,300 for the first six months of 1905, and $176,900 for the corresponding period of 1906.

Exports from the Republic of Santo Domingo, during the first six months of the calendar year 1906, showing the values and principal countries of destination, in comparison with those of the corresponding period of 1905.

Article and country.	January 1 to June 30, 1905.		January 1 to June 30, 1906.	
	Quantity.	Value.	Quantity.	Value.
Animals, live stock:				
Cuba..........	....	$23,510	....	$5,309
Other countries..........	....		....	155
Total..........	....	23,510	....	5,464
Bananas:	*Bunches.*		*Bunches.*	
United States..........	357,000	178,500	434,500	217,500
Other countries..........			100	5
Total..........	357,000	178,500	434,600	217,505

Exports from the Republic of Santo Domingo during the first six months of the calendar year 1906, etc.—Continued.

Article and country.	January 1 to June 30, 1905.		January 1 to June 30, 1906.	
	Quantity.	Value.	Quantity.	Value.
Cacao:	*Pounds.*		*Pounds.*	
United States	4,323,119	$350,681	6,125,341	$395,362
United Kingdom	58,002	4,871		
Germany	6,483,986	503,453	9,602,621	638,100
France	6,528,169	563,138	2,475,983	179,302
Total	17,388,276	1,422,143	18,203,945	1,212,764
Chemicals, drugs and dyes, raw materials for:				
United States		632		4,377
United Kingdom				420
Germany		13,394		36,576
France		177		
Other countries		5,013		1,651
Total		19,216		43,024
Cocoanuts:	*Pounds.*		*Pounds.*	
United States	11,184	108	5,648	52
Germany	247,208	2,138	280,169	3,558
Total	258,392	2,246	285,817	3,610
Coffee:	*Pounds.*		*Pounds.*	
United States	395,716	33,476	392,070	34,031
Germany	356,481	25,164	1,203,444	76,945
France	529,051	39,792	316,527	18,344
Cuba			56,607	4,507
Other countries	121,261	6,430	112,222	12,011
Total	1,402,609	104,862	2,080,870	145,838
Copra:	*Pounds.*		*Pounds.*	
Germany	72,042	1,088	32,499	444
Gums and resins:	*Pounds.*		*Pounds.*	
United States	5,517	1,019	3,405	291
United Kingdom	2,565	50		
Other countries	1,150	89	10,541	969
Total	9,232	1,158	13,946	1,260
Hides and skins:				
Goatskins—	*Pounds.*		*Pounds.*	
United States	66,547	18,698	86,328	22,176
Germany			18,650	1,243
Other countries	1,685	392	5,468	1,260
Total	68,232	19,090	110,446	24,579
Hides of cattle—	*Pounds.*		*Pounds.*	
United States	43,623	5,692	156,893	15,099
Germany	89,245	9,169	281,658	26,964
France	65,412	6,379	32,740	4,544
Other countries	2,924	296	4,772	502
Total	201,234	21,536	476,063	47,109
Honey:	*Gallons.*		*Gallons.*	
United States	94,920	6,176	17,670	4,572
Germany	530	113	6,060	1,755
France	120	36		
Other countries	5,930	1,079		
Total	101,500	7,404	23,730	6,327
Sisal and other vegetable fibers:	*Pounds.*		*Pounds.*	
United States	72,705	9,106	56,899	4,943
Germany				274
Cuba		10,559		11,924
France		425		
Other countries		450		250
Total		20,540		17,391

Exports from the Republic of Santo Domingo during the first six months of the calendar year 1906, etc.—Continued.

Article and country.	January 1 to June 30, 1905.		January 1 to June 30, 1906.	
	Quantity.	Value.	Quantity.	Value.
Sugar (raw):	*Pounds.*		*Pounds.*	
United States	98,840,685	$3,105,855	107,126,108	$2,086,560
United Kingdom	1,086,900	41,870	1,250,250	24,408
Germany	71,979	2,715	28,301	643
Other countries	500	14	348,640	5,249
Total	99,999,064	3,150,454	108,746,294	2,116,860
Tobacco (leaf):	*Pounds.*		*Pounds.*	
United States	56,608	2,557	659,374	26,328
Germany	3,362,684	132,396	744,180	22,850
France	360,014	21,248	349,174	11,021
Total	3,779,306	156,201	1,752,728	60,199
Wax:	*Pounds.*		*Pounds.*	
United States	45,713	10,559	43,467	11,545
United Kingdom				
Germany	80,942	19,813	146,197	33,154
France	65,657	11,972	26,637	5,320
Other countries	2,564	613	6,034	1,376
Total	194,876	42,957	221,335	51,375
Wood:				
Mahogany—	*Feet.*		*Feet.*	
United States	82,584	1,668	3,153	135
United Kingdom	113,180	4,900	58,834	2,936
Germany			12,229	622
France	46,708	3,585	7,544	325
Other countries	3,358	119	26,152	498
Total	196,524	10,272	107,981	4,516
Lignum vitæ—	*Tons.*		*Tons.*	
United States	477	21,298	352	5,476
United Kingdom	222	2,326	204	2,240
Germany	16	235	125	1,494
France	3	20	460	5,268
Other countries	295	6,280	168	1,708
Total	1,013	30,119	1,319	16,386
All other woods:				
United States		9,311		5,354
United Kingdom		648		1,862
Germany		521		4,071
France		3,180		5,430
Cuba		100		
Other countries		2,378		2,060
Total		16,178		18,777
All other exports:				
United States		11,995		5,724
Germany		17		550
France		186		879
Cuba		103		1,772
Other countries		3,204		4,705
Total		15,505		13,630

RECAPITULATION.

Countries.	January 1 to June 30, 1905.	January 1 to June 30, 1906.
United States	$3,767,331	$2,839,525
United Kingdom	54,705	32,006
Germany	710,206	849,223
France	650,198	230,433
Cuba	34,272	23,512
Other countries	26,357	32,399
Total	5,243,009	4,007,158

Origin and values of imports, and nationality of vessels carrying same, during the six months January 1 to June 30, 1906.

Countries.	Dominican.	American.	British.	Dutch.	French.
United States		$1,085,480	$33,131		
United Kingdom		3,513			$64,969
Germany		414			3,928
France		1,199			71,728
Italy		32,737			13
Belgium					
Spain	$2,799	12,587			
Cuba	30				
Porto Rico	2,014				
Other countries	2,907	20		$9,686	3,267
Total	7,740	1,136,950	33,131	9,586	146,892

Countries.	German.	Norwegian.	Cuban.	All other.	Total.
United States		$42,342			$1,160,953
United Kingdom	$182,154				250,626
Germany	431,763				436,105
France	25,703				101,630
Italy					32,750
Belgium	2,231				2,231
Spain	6,246			$25,535	48,283
Cuba			$1,126		6,197
Porto Rico			6,167		8,713
Other countries	3,968		3,432	99	16,580
Total	652,078	42,342	10,725	25,634	2,064,068

Destination and value of exports, and nationality of vessels carrying same, during the six months, January 1 to June 30, 1906.

Countries.	Dominican.	American.	British.	Dutch.	French.
United States	$500	$1,385,810	$235,517		
United Kingdom		6,818			4,049
Germany		19,029			225,134
France		4,995			
Cuba	4,432		662		
Porto Rico	360				3,651
Other countries	3,111			12,898	7,720
Total	8,403	1,116,652	235,179	12,898	240,860

Countries.	German.	Norwegian.	Cuban.	All other.	Total.
United States		$1,218,198			$2,839,525
United Kingdom	$24,748				32,066
Germany	826,145				819,223
France					230,433
Cuba			$18,418		23,512
Porto Rico					4,013
Other countries	4,558			$99	28,386
Total	856,451	1,218,198	18,418	99	4,007,158

Number and tonnage of vessels engaged in the foreign trade, by ports, during the six months, January to June, 1906.

Ports.	Entrances.				Clearances.			
	Sailing.		Steam.		Sailing.		Steam.	
	Number.	Tonnage.	Number.	Tonnage.	Number.	Tonnage.	Number.	Tonnage.
Azua	7	2,071	23	27,290	5	1,214	22	26,660
Barahona	4	492			5	585		
Macoris	57	4,058	53	60,669	56	3,259	56	63.697
Monte Cristi	5	832	21	35,161	10	391	19	31,499
Puerto Plata	17	2,128	75	102,690	12	1,739	76	106,539
Samana	3	425	25	44,757	3	405	25	44,757
Sanchez			37	68,458	1	40	37	68,458
Santo Domingo	28	4,901	62	60,891	22	4,059	56	58,385
Total	121	14,908	296	399,916	114	11,692	291	399,995

Number and tonnage of vessels engaged in the coastwise trade, by ports, during the six months, January to June, 1906.

Ports.	Entrances.				Clearances.			
	Sailing.		Steam.		Sailing.		Steam.	
	Number.	Tonnage.	Number.	Tonnage.	Number.	Tonnage.	Number.	Tonnage.
Azua	99	2,653	18	768	93	1,666	18	768
Barahona	61	777	4	492	61	777	4	492
Macoris	277	5,789	72	1,941	319	5,922	76	2,079
Monte Cristi	33	407	4	172	42	564	4	172
Puerto Plata	208	1,954	8	307	233	1,979	9	350
Samana	136	1,622	7	301	157	1,612	9	215
Sanchez	189	2,240	8	344	189	2,299	9	387
Santo Domingo	401	7,901	80	2,395	417	8,255	83	2,543
Total	1,404	23,343	201	6,720	1,511	23,064	219	7,006

HAITI.

AMENDMENTS TO CUSTOMS TARIFF.

The customs tariff act of September 4, 1905, published in the MONTHLY BULLETIN of October, 1906, has been amended as follows:

Law of September 3, 1906.

ARTICLE 1. The following third paragraph is added to Article 27 of the customs law dated September 4, 1905:

"Any differences found in excess shall be immediately noted in a supplementary statement and the Government shall require application of the legal penalties provided for in the case of smuggling. The State shall not take provisional security by way of attachment, bond, or otherwise, on chattels or goods the property of the exporter, except under a judgment enforceable notwithstanding opposition or appeal.

"Agents of lines established in Haiti are required, under forfeiture of their license and without prejudice to all other penalties, to duly and regularly report within three months the weight furnished to them on which freight of any article shipped in Haiti has been paid in the port of destination."

ART. 2. The present law repeals all laws or provisions of law inconsistent therewith. It shall be enforced at the instance of the Secretary of State for Finance and Commerce.

Law of September 6, 1906, establishing a minimum and maximum tariff.

ARTICLE 1. The minimum tariff is declared to be the tariff of import duties annexed to the law dated September 4, 1905, regulating the customs of the Republic, together with the wharfage dues, weighing dues, consular fees, tonnage dues, watch dues, pilotage dues inward, sanitary inspection dues, the surtaxes of 50 per cent, 33⅓ in national currency and 25 per cent in gold, on such aggregate charges and surtaxes, or said tariff as modified by subsequent laws.

ART. 2. A maximum tariff is hereby established, and is to consist of the tariff now existing or which may be modified by subsequent laws, increased by 50 per cent leviable on the aggregate of such charges and surtaxes.

ART. 3. The minimum tariff shall not apply to the statistical due applicable to coined money.

ART. 4. The Government are authorized to issue a decree with the object of applying the maximum tariff to such countries as charge excessive rates upon our goods and products and to rescind any decrees issued by them so soon as the causes which prompted the resolutions have ceased.

ART. 5. The present law repeals all laws or provisions of law inconsistent therewith. It shall be enforced at the instance of the Secretary of State for Finance and Commerce.

Decree of September 21, 1906, reestablishing the former import duties on soap.

ARTICLE 1. The duties leviable on soap prior to the law of August 21, 1906, are reestablished from November 1 next.

ART. 2. The proceeds of these duties shall be exclusively applied to the current service. They shall be entered in a special return.

ART. 3. The present decree shall be enforced at the instance of the Secretary of State for Finance and Commerce.

MEXICO.

FOREIGN COMMERCE, SEPTEMBER, 1906.

According to figures issued by the Statistical Division of the Treasury Department of the Republic of Mexico, the foreign commerce of the Republic for September, 1906, and for the first three months of the current fiscal year, 1906-7, was represented by the following valuations, the figures for the corresponding periods of the preceding year being also given for purposes of comparison:

The total value of importations during the three months under review was $50,920,045.77 in Mexican currency, as declared in the customhouses, an increase of $12,019,610.45 as compared with the preceding year.

The exports for the three months were valued at $53,767,800.74, showing a decrease of $5,980,877.17 as compared with the same period of 1905-6.

IMPORTS.

[Silver valuation.]

Articles.	September—		First three months—	
	1906.	1905.	1906-7.	1905-6.
Animal substances	$2,045,371.30	$1,370,206.77	$4,739,176.92	$4,064,068.08
Vegetable substances	1,824,181.68	2,217,579.69	6,582,754.75	6,012,009.47
Mineral substances...................	6,888,719.51	3,857,766.26	16,411,071.84	10,172,410.34
Dry goods............................	3,151,614.92	2,078,149.42	7,027,720.66	5,617,448.40
Chemical and pharmaceutical substances	731,771.32	570,501.00	2,048,079.60	1,755,708.76
Beverages............................	522,334.96	660,722.00	1,652,364.12	1,851,009.05
Paper and its applications	401,285.86	485,439.32	1,268,999.98	1,331,771.11
Machinery and apparatus	1,720,643.65	1,450,607.63	6,248,335.84	4,472,769.07
Vehicles.............................	668,056.04	226,983.38	1,709,946.06	743,707.24
Arms and explosives.................	364,121.55	228,005.43	943,147.84	1,039,399.77
Miscellaneous........................	871,382.47	663,648.95	2,289,448.66	1,820,134.08
Total	19,189,483.26	13,339,609.85	50,920,045.77	38,900,435.82

EXPORTS.

[Silver valuation.]

Articles.	September—		First three months—	
	1906.	1905.	1906-7.	1905-6.
Precious metals	$7,712,201.37	$9,515,509.76	$27,284,234.39	$30,823,585.23
Other articles	8,631,413.15	9,000,247.53	26,483,566.35	28,925,092.68
Total	16,343,614.52	18,515,757.29	53,767,800.74	59,748,677.91

The details of the export trade for the periods under comparison show the following classification and figures:

	September—		First three months—	
	1906.	1905.	1906-7.	1905-6.
Mexican gold coin	$28,623.00		$29,990.00	
Foreign gold coin	4,354.00		5,908.00	$3,400.83
Gold in bars	1,290,663.44	$2,523,272.25	4,427,536.94	7,856,227.20
Gold in other forms	411,112.30	78,867.08	1,257,882.18	485,357.62
Total gold	1,734,752.74	2,602,139.28	5,721,317.12	8,344,985.65
Mexican silver coin	1,256,250.90	1,203,500.00	4,720,798.00	2,213,065.00
Foreign silver coin	4,760.08	5,825.00	27,434.00	30,159.17
Silver in bars	3,807,421.28	5,048,246.15	14,047,372.5b	17,921,535.15
Silver in other forms	909,017.37	655,799.33	2,767,312.72	2,310,840.26
Total silver	5,977,448.63	6,913,370.48	21,562,917.27	22,478,599.58
Total gold and silver	7,712,201.37	9,515,509.76	27,284,234.39	30,823,585.23
Antimony	73,899.00	29,208.00	293,864.00	240,380.96
Copper	2,801,547.00	3,304,685.90	6,846,168.00	8,055,203.55
Marble	10.00	25,000.00	5,530.00	60,496.00
Plumbago	3,600.00		8,400.00	1,000.00
Lead	224,695.00	287,840.25	800,143.56	1,538,329.05
Zinc	118,115.00	11,643.00	365,937.12	44,767.99
Other metals	1,785.00	22,703.00	1,022,706.38	121,267.11
Total	10,935,892.37	13,196,589.91	36,626,943.45	40,845,031.89
Vegetable products:				
Coffee	115,478.90	230,269.00	891,974.00	1,671,685.50
Cascalote and tanning barks	3,500.00		3,800.00	20,147.00
Rubber	380,445.00	66,312.38	890,917.00	227,864.18
Chicle	71,156.00	56,161.20	143,186.40	156,349.65
Beans	30,480.00	90,012.82	125,627.00	205,122.82
Fruits	10,998.30	23,467.10	27,783.28	40,403.40
Chick peas	351,526.00	307,100.00	1,827,409.00	1,240,746.00
Guayule	500.00	5,055.00	626.00	10,987.00
Horse beans	2,000.00	25,030.00	2,300.00	104,074.00
Henequen	2,097,375.91	2,264,602.00	6,429,097.91	7,253,871.00
Ixtle	312,900.00	341,737.00	881,677.00	954,315.88
Woods	332,340.00	166,272.10	563,757.10	355,218.40
Maize	357.20	581.00	2,530.20	10,561.00
Mahogany	3,619.00	4,846.00	14,713.00	12,261.00
Dyewoods	23,575.00	21,690.20	106,640.00	109,965.93
Xacaton	227,174.00	136,442.00	463,137.00	542,159.00
Leaf tobacco	191,611.00	61,161.00	481,048.00	290,297.00
Vanilla	70,776.00	374,968.99	569,570.00	1,852,213.99
Other vegetables	100,839.40	67,724.23	325,998.65	143,864.16
Total	4,326,645.81	4,263,456.02	13,751,811.49	15,201,478.91
Animal products:				
Cattle	88,852.00	248,841.00	517,343.00	1,042,200.00
Skins and hides	668,766.29	545,214.42	1,945,671.53	1,666,437.10
Other animal products	36,987.25	43,767.00	108,290.25	110,060.04
Total	794,605.54	837,822.42	2,571,304.78	2,818,097.14
Manufactured articles:				
Sugar	25,180.00	3,126.00	155,049.00	259,681.00
Flour and pastes	15,606.00		117,790.00	52,600.00
Rope	125.00		457.00	
Dressed skins	2,164.00	14,168.00	25,952.00	49,816.00
Straw hats	83,477.00	36,678.54	145,599.00	113,187.54
Manufactured tobacco	38,135.00	27,713.00	119,582.00	89,107.76
Other manufactures	34,651.80	57,810.10	69,937.02	107,851.48
Total	199,338.80	139,525.64	634,366.02	672,513.77
Miscellaneous articles	87,172.00	78,363.50	183,335.00	170,926.20

Following is a résumé of the valuations of Mexican imports during the periods under comparison, with reference to their countries of origin:

Country.	September—		First three months—	
	1906.	1905.	1906-7.	1905-6.
Europe	$7,644,822.03	$5,930,941.15	$19,326,927.67	$17,342,480.44
Asia	80,771.18	119,575.86	318,214.91	348,394.6
Africa	16,879.00	1,545.00	50,785.30	10,459.00
North America	11,393,952.97	7,186,562.00	31,108,697.30	20,977,474.11
Central America	671.51	1,084.75	8,420.94	2,765.24
South America	10,817.88	38,151.15	44,977.41	101,577.00
West Indies	28,321.69	25,290.77	46,181.24	71,785.13
Oceania	13,347.00	34,458.77	15,841.00	44,588.77
Total	19,189,483.26	13,339,009.85	50,920,045.77	38,900,435.22

Following is a résumé of the valuations of Mexican exports during the periods under comparison, with reference to their countries of destination:

Country.	September—		First three months—	
	1906.	1905.	1906-7.	1905-6.
Europe	$5,269,689.81	$5,116,715.31	$16,899,725.00	$16,316,289.22
North America	10,838,912.46	12,945,540.75	35,938,320.54	41,758,707.61
Central America	75,882.25	97,976.23	260,492.60	354,146.02
South America	3,582.00	6,521.00	28,775.00	27,734.09
West Indies	95,548.00	349,004.00	650,487.00	1,296,806.09
Total	16,843,614.52	18,515,757.29	53,767,800.74	59,748,677.91

RESERVE FUND OF THE TREASURY.

Señor LIMANTOUR, Secretary of Finance and Public Credit of the Mexican Republic, in presenting a proposal for expenditure of $24,000,000 Mexican currency, from the reserve fund of the Treasury, $1,500,000 in school buildings in the Federal District, $2,500,000 in water systems, and $20,000,000 in port works, gave the following account of the Mexican national finances before the Chamber of Deputies in its session of December 10, 1906:

"Now that the discussion of the projected law wherein the expenditure of $24,000,000 is proposed, I think it might be of interest to the members of the House to know the present condition of the Federal finances.

"As the honorable Deputies know, the accounts of the previous fiscal year will be closed at this time, and the Executive is preparing the projected budget for the coming year. Therefore, I may state that the data collected by the Treasury refer to the latest period—that is to say, the period from July 1, 1905, to June 30, 1906.

"The results of the last fiscal year are excellent; the receipts, as the President of the Republic stated in his message of September 16, 1906, exceeded 100,000,000 *pesos*. The receipts in cash have actually amounted to ____ 100,000,000 pesos. The increase of expenditures was not perceptible, being almost equal to those of the previous fiscal year—that is to say, 20,000,000 pesos, in round numbers. The superavit was therefore 22,000,000 pesos. This amount is not the final balance, as there are some explanations that I will include in the report which, together with the projected budget, I will have the honor to submit to the Chamber on the 14th of this month; but, anyhow, said superavit may be estimated at 20,000,000 pesos.

"Under these circumstances the Executive has deemed it his duty to submit to Congress these two propositions: First, a reduction in the taxes for the next fiscal year, and, second, an increase in the salaries of certain officers and employees of the Government.

"In regard to the first proposition—i. e., the reduction of taxes—it will be suggested that the Federal tax paid by the taxpayers of the different States be reduced from 25 per cent to 20 per cent, in which case its name will be the 'Federal fifth' instead of the 'Federal fourth.'

"But as this tax is not collected in the Federal District and the Territories, the action of the Executive in finding out which of the municipal taxes in the District and Territories ought to be reduced, was just, believing that the taxes on food products should be preferred for this purpose; therefore he will have the honor to propose to the Chamber the abolition of the tax on bread, a tax that has yielded over 200,000 pesos every year, and the reduction of the tax on meat, if the efficient way by which the object of said reduction could be secured is found—that is to say, that the consumer, and not the seller, should be benefited.

"Finally, there are certain municipal taxes the collection of which is troublesome, innumerable difficulties arising therefrom; but, as there are many details in these taxes, it is absolutely necessary that the Executive be authorized to revise them. if such a course is deemed convenient by the Chamber.

"This is in regard to the reduction of taxes, and in this respect I will take the liberty to remind the Chamber that during the current year, at the time of the passage of the stamp law, certain quotas have been considerably reduced and the amount of this reduction in one single year will exceed 1,000,000 pesos.

"It has been, therefore, very satisfactory for the Government to see that in the period of a few months the amount of reductions made and initiated exceeds 3,000,000 pesos.

*　　·*　　*　　*　　*　　*　　*

"The contracts that are being executed in the ports of Salina Cruz and Coatzacoalcos were signed five years ago, and the cost of the works amounts to 64,000,000 pesos. Upon their completion the Republic will have two magnificent ports on both extremes of the Isthmus of Tehuantepec. On the Pacific, Salina Cruz will be the first port of the whole American Continent, and on the Atlantic, Coatzacoalcos will also be able to admit steamers with a draft of 30 feet, as all first-class ports. These sacrifices have been made in order to increase our interoceanic trade to its largest possible extent. To this end contracts have been signed for a period of nine years, which will bring about a movement of at least 300,000 tons annually. The Hawaiian sugar, which to this date has been transported through Cape Horn, will, from the first months of 1907, be transported through the Isthmus of Tehuantepec.

"Mention might be made of other contracts, but what has been stated is sufficient to give the honorable Deputies an idea of the importance of this matter, and to acquaint them with the necessity of making a considerable effort to place our interoceanic route in a condition adequate to realize the hopes of all nations.

"Of said 65,000,000 *pesos*, the total cost of the existing contracts, works have already been executed amounting to nearly 40,000,000 *pesos*, the authorizations requested from this Chamber at different periods having been for the purpose of applying in the construction of these ports all the money available, in order to obtain the desired result as soon as possible.

"Therefore, there is yet to be spent on said works 25,000,000 *pesos*, perhaps one or two millions more, and of these 25,000,000 we request you to appropriate 20,000,000 from the reserve fund of the Treasury. This reserve fund was, on June 30, 1906, 62,000,000 *pesos* in cash money, available at any moment.

"I do not refer to the other funds which, although belonging to the Government, have a definite application, such as the fund for the amortization of the debt; I refer only to the funds which are absolutely at the disposal of the Government.

"Of these 62,000,000, 12,000,000, more or less, constitute the currency-standard fund, which was created by the monetary laws enacted by Congress, and the purpose of which is to maintain the parity of the currency. Six or eight million *pesos* are necessary for the operation of all bureaus of the Government, such as post-offices, telegraph service, disbursing offices, etc. These 8,000,000 *pesos*, added to the other 12,000,000, leave us 20,000,000 *pesos*. From the balance the Congress has already, from time to time, made appropriations outside of the budget for the work of construction of the Legislative Palace and the water system of the Federal District.

"As I have already stated, we request authority to take 20,000,000 *pesos* more from the Treasury reserve fund. After withdrawing this amount there will be left in the reserve fund 10,000,000 or 15,000,000 *pesos*, a sum which, the Government thinks, must not be touched in order to meet any future emergency.

the Chamber may well understand, the reduction of taxes and
e of salaries proposed are questions in which the Government
t with wisdom, as it is one thousand times preferable to have
le cash on hand than to rely upon an increase of revenues dur.
next fiscal year without bearing in mind that perhaps it will
ssary to make certain extraordinary expenditures.
r this reason the President thinks that, with the measures that
just stated, and which will be initiated upon the presentation of
ar's budget, we can be proud of having taken a step which very
tions can take—the reduction of taxes and at the same time the
e of salaries."

CUSTOM-HOUSE RECEIPTS, NOVEMBER, 1906.

ican custom-house receipts for the month of November, 1906,
$4,555,162.42, of which $113,093.55 were export duties,
,492.42 import duties, and $78,577.45 port dues.

orts of entry the import duties were as follows:

uz	$1,520,778.77	Manzanillo	$6,726.91
)	852,209.43	San Blas	5,384.67
	445,869.47	Matamoras	5,183.83
o	306,252.19	Salina Cruz	4,176.03
	303,421.62	Altata	3,911.69
	255,852.51	La Paz	2,407.54
Diaz	204,274.07	Isla del Carmen	2,092.94
n	90,150.97	Chetumal	1,336.66
	76,799.88	Topolobampo	1,007.46
ita	75,511.46	Tijuana	951.15
s	58,133.97	Guerrero	732.29
a	30,406.21	Las Vacas	650.32
rieta	21,045.61	Tuxpam	600.42
o	17,233.76	Tonala	445.91
he	16,301.26	Camago	252.70
oalcos	16,091.06	Mier	233.55
aco	10,014.55	La Ascension	191.28
li	9,752.51	Zapaluta	167.19
da	8,971.13		
osalia	7,969.95	Total	4,363,492.42

RECEIPTS FROM THE STAMP TAX, 1897-1906.

following table taken from official statistics recently pub-
, shows the receipts yielded by the stamp tax in the Mexican
lic during the fiscal years 1897-98 to 1905-6:

Fiscal year.	Total.	Fiscal year.	Total.
	Pesos.		*Pesos.*
	21,698,895.81	1902-3	29,798,951.78
	23,245,840.97	1903-4	30,983,107.74
	24,869,270.61	1904-5	31,799,207.75
	25,187,106.98	1905-6	33,001,423.23
	26,991,558.55		

FINE CATTLE IMPORTS.

The "Mexican Investor" states that since the removal of the duty on cattle from the United States there have been very large shipments by carloads of both dairy and beef cattle received in the Republic.

Most of the cattle imported from Texas and points farther north are fine bred. Of late many fine milch cows have been shipped in from Illinois, Kentucky, and other States noted for fine cattle. These are going to Mexico City and vicinity for the dairies which are springing up in that part of the Republic. Most of the fine breed of cattle are coming from the Northern States of the United States, and cattle for the ranches are being shipped mostly from Texas, Arizona, and other Southwestern States. At the present rate it will not take long to supply Mexico with fine cattle, both for the range and the dairies.

SILVER BASIS OF THE STAMP AND CUSTOMS TAXES FOR JANUARY, 1907.

The usual monthly circular issued by the Treasury Department of the Mexican Government announces that the legal price per kilogram of pure silver during the month of January, 1907, is $45.10, according to calculations provided in the decree of March 23, 1905. This price will be the basis for the payment of the stamp tax and customs duties when silver is used throughout the Republic.

CONSULAR TRADE REPORTS.

The Consul-General of Mexico at New York reports that during the month of November, 1906, 10 vessels proceeding from Mexican ports entered the harbor of New York City, bringing 99,036 packages of merchandise. During the same month the vessels clearing from the port of New York numbered 13, carrying 220,666 packages of merchandise consigned to Mexican ports. The imports in detail from Mexico to New York in November, 1906, were as follows:

Articles.	Quantity.	Articles.	Quantity.
Henequen ....bales..	13,391	Lead bullion ....bars..	50,185
Coffee ....sacks..	537	Metals.....................boxes..	316
Hides.....................bales..	7,399	Sarsaparilla ....packages..	180
Hides.....................loose..	953	Vanilla....................boxes..	32
Ixtle.....................bales..	4,815	Alligator skins ....do....	25
Goatskins ....do....	1,209	Bones....................packages..	300
Deerskins ....do....	209	Honey ....barrels..	42
Rubber....................do....	1,161	Cedar ....logs..	1
Leaf tobacco ....do....	411	Mahogany ....do....	185
Cigars....................boxes..	31	Jalap ....sacks..	7
Broom root ....bales..	390	Copper ....bars..	8,580
Chicle ....do....	2,361	Oranges..................boxes..	5,561
Hair......................do....	10	Chili....................sacks..	592

The Mexican Consul at Philadelphia advises that the shipments of merchandise from that port to the Mexican ports of Tampico and Veracruz during the month of November, 1906, amounted to $67,297.80, and consisted entirely of shipments of coal.

The following table shows the importations of foreign merchandise through the custom-house of Nogales, State of Sonora, Mexico, in the month of November, 1906:

Animal substances	$31,647.35
Vegetable substances	61,944.93
Mineral substances	36,779.26
Textiles and manufactures thereof	17,011.16
Chemical products	11,920.56
Spirituous beverages	1,663.15
Paper and paper products	3,257.64
Machinery and apparatus	27,968.65
Vehicles	7,768.70
Firearms and explosives	19,952.27
Miscellaneous articles	17,314.67
Total	237,228.34

Countries of origin:

United States of America	$231,411.40
Germany	562.80
England	5,075.25
France	178.89
Total	237,228.34

Custom-house duties collected during said month, $77,041.50.

The following table shows the exports of merchandise from the State of Sonora, Mexico, through the American custom-house at Nogales, Arizona, during November, 1906:

Sugar	$36	Corn	$151
Paper manufactures	3	Oranges	180
Mescal	159	Feathers	6
Mineral waters	5	Fresh fish	15
Fowls	13	Pastes	31
Portland cement	200	Lead ores	121
Rawhides	10,652	Potatoes	56
Fresh meat	29	Cheese	10
Iron and steel waste	878	Ready-made cotton clothing	8
Spices, not specially mentioned	16	Common salt	15
Beans	8,420	Straw hats	9
Preserved fruits	25	Leaf tobacco	785
Cattle	28	Total	21,935
Lemons	50		
Pickles	34		

Imports of foreign merchandise through the port of Nogales, Mexico, to the State of Sonora, Mexico, in October, 1906:

Animal substances	$40,790.86
Vegetable substances	42,356.61
Mineral substances	347,606.96
Cloth, and manufactures thereof	49,535.03
Chemical products	16,972.84
Spirituous beverages	2,775.52
Paper and paper products	5,221.09
Machinery and apparatuses	39,809.06
Vehicles	9,131.43
Arms and explosives	9,704.28
Miscellaneous	22,494.42
Total	586,398.12

Countries from which the merchandise referred to was shipped:

United States	$539,637.46
Germany	15,183.54
France	13,177.56
England	15,788.55
Austria	1,105.50
Japan	1,123.59
Switzerland	381.90
Total	586,398.12

The duties collected at the port referred to, in October, 1906, amounted to $129,488.11.

Exports through the port of Nogales, Mexico, from the State of Sonora, into the United States, through the port of Nogales, Ariz., in in October, 1906:

Fowls	$198	Milk	$10
Mezcal	45	Corn	20
Sugar	66	Oranges	402
Leather belting	3	Forage	356
Fresh meats	45	Fresh fish	77
Portland cement	56	Potatoes	256
Rawhides	5,949	Cheese	1
Candies	52	Coal	240
Scrap iron and steel	380	Ready-made cotton clothing	10
Spices	30	Salt	15
Fruits	11	Raw tobacco	378
Beans	18	Gold dust and gold bullion	184,214
Preserved fruits	67	Silver bullion	128,772
Cattle	1,054		
Pottery	10	Total	323,035
Lemons	120		

NICARAGUA.

COMMERCIAL TREATY WITH ITALY.

The ratifications of the treaty of friendship, commerce, and navigation between Nicaragua and Italy, signed at Managua on January 25, 1906, were exchanged on the 28th of September of the same year. The treaty provides for reciprocal most-favored-nation treatment in all matters of commerce, navigation, and import and export duties, with the exception of coastwise trade and fishing. As regards import, export, and transit dues, the most-favored-nation clause is not applicable to the privileges which Nicaragua has accorded, or may in the future accord, to other Central American Republics. The treaty shall remain in force for the period of ten years, or until one year after denunciation.

IMPORTS AND EXPORTS.

United States Vice-Consul A. O. WALLACE, of Managua, reports that the total exports from the several ports of Nicaragua during the last six months of 1905 amounted to $1,074,939, of which the United States took articles valued at $769,723; France, $101,236; England, $86,457; Germany, $51,212; Italy, $15,976; the Netherlands, $15,768, and other countries the remainder. The imports into Nicaragua for the same period amounted to $1,687,913, distributed among the leading countries as follows: United States, $952,211; England, $336,394; Germany, $214,360, and France, $121,503.

The exports, exclusive of coffee, from Corinto and San Juan del Sur during the last six months of 1905 amounted to $243,504; for the previous six months, $343,375. The imports into the same ports for the same period were valued at $1,179,935, and for the preceding six months the amount was $1,259,750. The exports of coffee from these two ports for the last six months of 1905 amounted to $228,589, of which the United States took $20,711 worth; France, $98,312; Germany, $49,491; England, $15,618; Italy, $15,178; the Netherlands, $15,769, and Chile and Austria the remainder.

The imports into Corinto and San Juan del Sur from the United States during the last six months of 1905 amounted to $521,403, of which the ten principal articles are shown in the following statement:

Articles.	Value.	Articles.	Value.
Cotton goods, etc.	$99,197	Oil, all kinds	$21,498
Drugs, etc.	15,278	Paper	3,681
Flour	181,611	Provisions	21,167
Iron and steel manufactures	90,823	Rice	46,452
Leather and leather goods	15,189	Silk goods	11,080

The exports from the same ports to the United States for the six months amounted to $139,665. The principal articles were: Hides, valued at $44,013; rubber, $57,649; and deerskins, $25,641.

MINING INDUSTRIES.

United States Vice-Consul ARTHUR O. WALLACE, of Managua, reports to the Secretary of State regarding the mining industry of Nicaragua as follows:

"There has been a remarkable revival of activity in the mining industries, shown by the fact of the large importations of mining machinery, by the reworking of abandoned mines, and by the discovery and opening up of new properties.

"It may be safely said that the returns from this industry will be in a very few years one of the principal resources of wealth for the country at large and to the Government in revenues, perhaps even more than agriculture and stock raising, which have been somewhat abated of late."

PANAMA.

RECEPTION OF PRESIDENT ROOSEVELT.

The United States battle ship *Louisiana* arrived at Colon on Wednesday, November 14, 1906, with President ROOSEVELT on board. He was visited on board by the President of the Republic, Doctor AMADOR, accompanied by Mrs. AMADOR and Secretary of State ARIAS. On the next day, the 15th, President ROOSEVELT visited the city of Panama and received a magnificent reception. He was received by President AMADOR and the citizens of Panama at the Plaza in front of the cathedral.

President AMADOR said:

"Mr. PRESIDENT: The visit with which you honor the people of Panama would make the most powerful and haughty nation of the world feel proud, and is an evident proof of the cordial interest they inspire in you.

"Understanding and appreciating this to its full value, we thank you from the bottom of our hearts, as it is additional cause for us to admire, love, and respect you, as you are admired, loved, and respected by your fellow-citizens, and even more, if it is possible, because a sentiment of deep gratitude binds us.

"In olden times the nations achieved their independent life amidst the thunder of battles, bathing their soil with the blood of their martyrs, their heroes, and the victims of their wrath.

"The Republic of Panama, daughter of a modern civilization, was not born under these conditions. She has come to life by virtue of this self-same civilization, and as the result of the struggle between advancement and retrogression, and in pursuance of her manifest destiny has allied her forces to those of the great nation whose path you guide in the most stupendous undertaking of latter-day progress—the construction of the interoceanic canal, wide highway for universal navigation—and the great marvel of the century.

"A rare alliance is this, Mr. President, that of the great Colossus of the north, with its immense riches, unlimited credit, its vast store of knowledge, and numerous elements that contribute to make it the only entity capable of successfully carrying on such a great enterprise, with the small and the youngest republic of America, owner of the land, which she gladly lends for the work; and nestling it, as we do, in our country's bosom, we feel that its safe keeping in a large measure devolves upon us.

"To harmonize the various elements that had to be united, to overcome the opposition and obstacles that arose, to reorganize the great work, to grasp, in a word, its immense magnitude, a superior man was necessary, and you were this man. Firm in your endeavors, you now come as commander in chief of our allied forces to review them and infuse in them the enthusiasm which you possess, so that the victory of toil and science may soon crown our sacrifices and efforts for the common glory of your country and mine, in proportion to the contingent of each.

"In passing through the Canal Zone this morning you have, no doubt, rapidly reviewed your legions, and in your countenance I read the satisfaction of this first examination.

"You have heard frequent and thundering detonations, but they were not those of the murderous cannon, but instead the explosive energy with which science knocks at the door of the Andes, demanding of them free passage for the commerce of the world.

"You have noticed the movement of trains in different directions, similar to those that in time of war carry the destructive elements where they better serve their accursed end, but here this does not happen. On the contrary, their mission is for the benefit of man; it is the tribute that the mountains themselves pay at the demand of engineering science to change the topography of the country, to convert the ravines into valleys and the valleys in turn into lakes, the sweet kisses of which will counteract the brine of the two oceans and will serve as a silvery link between the betrothed of the future—the Atlantic and the Pacific.

"God be blessed, sir, for permitting his own work to be thus altered by the hand of man for the benefit of mankind.

"You have been able to see that the staff under the indefatigable Stevens attends assiduously to the directions of the work, and assigns to each his post and duty; that the numerous body of engineers, mechanics, and clerks obey and cheerfully fulfill the orders they receive, and that everyone, even the humble laborers, seem inspired by one sole purpose, all protected by the tireless corps under Colonel GORGAS, the guardian of the health and life of the soldiers of toil and all the inhabitants of this tropical land.

"I should now have the honor to offer to you the forces of our own contingent, but I shall not enumerate them because they are well known to you. But I do believe this is the occasion for me to say, supported by the testimony of all your representatives, that the Panamanian people and government not only strictly fulfill the obligations contracted toward you, but that we are filled with enthusiasm and willingness to facilitate all the means at our disposal, whether it be our written duty or not, to make your immense task lighter and even pleasant.

" I ermit, sir, the people of Ianama to acclaim you as commander in chief of the allied American-Ianamanian forces, in this great struggle of progress and civilization.

"We are a grateful people, and the remembrance that in you we have had a generous defender remains indelibly impressed upon our hearts.

"The qualities that have chiefly strengthened your character are two—courage and justice—and you have displayed both in our favor, when it has been necessary, against your own people and foreigners.

" Ianama is aware, through your utterances, that as long as we continue along the path of honor and duty we shall not lack your powerful support.

"Therefore we ask you to receive this expression of our sincere gratitude.

" Be welcome and consider yourself in the midst of your best friends and admirers."

To this address of welcome I resident ROOSEVELT responded:

" MR. PRESIDENT, Señora AMADOR, and you citizens of Ianama: For the first time in the history of the United States it has become advisable for a I resident of the United States to step on territory not beneath the flag of the United States, and it is in the territory of Ianama that this has occurred, a symbol and proof of the closeness of the ties that unite the two countries, because of their peculiar relations to the gigantic enterprise of digging the Ianama Canal.

" In the admirable address of I resident AMADOR to which we have just listened the I resident rightly said that the United States and Ianama are partners in the great work which is now being done here on this Isthmus. We are joint trustees for all the world doing that work, and, President Amador, I hereby pledge on behalf of my country to you and your people the assurance of the heartiest support and of assistance on a basis of a full and complete and generous equality between the two Republics. Nowhere else in the world at this moment is a work of such importance taking place as here on the Isthmus of Panama, for here is being performed the giant engineering feat of the ages, and it is a matter for deep gratitude that I am able, I am happy to say, that it is being well and worthily performed.

"It is but a few weeks since the Secretary of State of the American Republic, Secretary Root, was your guest here in this city, he having at that time finished a tour of South America, which in its interest and in its far-reaching importance dwarfed anything of the kind that had ever hitherto been done by a Secretary of State of the American Republic, save only on the one or two occasions of absolute national importance in the great crises of the past. Mr. ROOT, President AMADOR, at that time spoke to you and your people, giving his assurance of the hearty friendliness of spirit of the Republic of the North in its relations toward you and your people; and I wish here with all the emphasis possible to make Mr. ROOT's words mine and to reiterate what he has said to you already, that the sole desire of the United States as regards the Republic of Panama is to see it increase in wealth, in numbers, in importance, until it becomes, as we earnestly hope it will become, one of the Republics whose history reflects honor upon the entire western world. Such progress and prosperity, Mr. President, can come only through the preservation of both order and liberty; through the observance by those in power of all their rights, obligations, and duties to their fellow-citizens, and through the realization of those out of power that the insurrectionary habit, the habit of civil war, ultimately means destruction to the Republic.

"I now wish to thank you, President AMADOR, and all your people for the reception that has been accorded us. Not only have I been immensely impressed with the tremendous work being done so successfully on this Isthmus, but I have also been immensely impressed with the beauty and fertility of your country; and I prophesy for it a great future, a future which, when the canal is completed, will be of such a kind, and will attain such dimensions, as to make it indeed a proud boast to claim citizenship in Panama.

"And now, Mr. President, in closing, I have but to say that not only do our people heartily wish well to Panama, but that we shall never interfere with her save to give her our aid in the attainment of her future."

MINTING OF NICKEL COINS.

On November 27, 1906, the National Assembly of Panama enacted a law providing for the minting of subsidiary nickel coins to the amount of 25,000 balboas (1 balboa is equal to $1). The coins to be minted will be of two denominations, to-wit, one of the nominal value of 2½ cents, and another of the nominal value of half a cent. The coins of the first denomination will be minted to the amount of 20,000 balboas, or a total of 800,000 pieces. Of the latter denomination 5,000 balboas will be coined, giving 1,000,000 coins of that value. The metal from which these are to be made is an alloy composed of 75 per cent nickel and 25 per cent copper.

EXPORTATION OF SILVER COINS PROHIBITED.

Under date of October 25, 1906, the Secretary of Finance of Panama issued the following order forbidding the exportation of silver coins:

"[Department of Finance—Resolution No. 1031.]

" Whereas it is known that the subsidiary silver coins recently minted, among them being the peso or half balboa, are being shipped abroad, and, furthermore, considering that the scarcity of these coins makes commercial transactions difficult, and is prejudicial to the inhabitants in general, and, furthermore, that section 13 of the Colombian law, No. 70 of 1894, which is in force in this Republic, prohibits the exportation of subsidiary silver coins; be it

"*Resolved*, That notification is hereby made to the public in general, and especially to the business enterprises and agents of navigation companies, that the exportation of silver coins of the Republic of any denomination whatsoever is absolutely prohibited, and consequently all those who should even attempt to violate such prohibition will be dealt with in accordance with the existing laws concerning this matter.

"To be registered, published, and communicated to whom it may concern for its legal effect.

" F. V. DE LA ESPRIELLA,
" *Secretary of Finance.*"

PARAGUAY.

PRESIDENT FERREIRA'S CABINET.

President FERREIRA, of Paraguay, in a decree dated November 25, 1906, organized his cabinet as follows:

Minister of the Interior, Doctor MANUEL BENITEZ,

Minister of Foreign Relations, Doctor CECILIO BÁEZ.

Minister of Finance, Señor Don ADOLFO R. SOLER.

Minister of Justice, Worship, and Public Instruction, Doctor CARLOS LUIS ISASI.

Minister of War and Marine, Señor Don GUILLERMO DE LOS RÍOS.

CENTRAL RAILWAY REPORT.

The report of the Iaraguay Central Railway for the year ending May 1, 1906, shows receipts of $275,000, gold, an increase of $66,000 over the preceding year. Operating expenses were $162,000, an increase of $29,000, leaving net receipts $113,000, gold.

PERU.

THE PROMOTION OF IMMIGRATION.

The President of the Peruvian Republic issued on August 10, 1906, the following decree, the principal object of which is to promote immigration to the Republic:

"The President of the Republic, considering that it is necessary to regulate the investment of the amount appropriated in the general budget in force for the promotion of immigration, and in the most efficient way to accomplish the purpose to which said amount is destined, decrees:

"First. The Government shall furnish third-class transportation to natives of Europe and America, the introduction of whom is sought by industrial corporations or individuals, and who must have the following qualifications:

"(a) They must be from 10 to 50 years old, if men, and from 10 to 40 years old, if women, besides having the conditions of morality and health prescribed by the provisions in force.

"(b) They shall engage in agriculture, mining, or any other industry, for themselves or for colonization, immigration, or irrigation companies.

"Second. The payment for transportation shall be made by the respective consul of the Republic in the port of embarkation, upon receipt of the cable order from the Minister of Improvements (Fomento), to whom the interested parties shall apply in writing, requesting said payment, and stating the number of immigrants to whom transportation is furnished, the agricultural or industrial establishment to which they will be assigned, and agreeing to furnish said immigrants with lodging, food, and medical attendance from the port of landing to their points of destination.

"Third. The Consuls of the Republic, upon receipt of the order from the Minister of Improvements, shall make the payments directly to the steamship company, and after assuring themselves, personally, that each immigrant has all the qualifications required in section 1 of this decree; for the purposes of this section they shall issue to each immigrant a certificate to be delivered to the maritime authority of the port of landing for transmittal to the Minister of Improvements.

"Fourth. There shall be kept in the Division of Agriculture and Colonization of the Department of Improvements a general registry of immigrants, in accordance with the forms and instructions which the Minister may prescribe.

"Fifth. The expenditures caused by the enforcement of this decree shall be charged to paragraph 13 of the extraordinary appropriation for the Department of Improvements, in the general budget in force.

"Given in the Executive Mansion at Lima, on the tenth day of the month of August, nineteen hundred and six.

"JOSÉ IARDO.

"DELFÍN VIDALÓN,
   "*Minister of Improvements.*"

CONCESSION FOR THE EXPLOITATION OF GUANO.

In October, 1906, the Minister of Finance of Peru granted a concession to Messrs. LARCO HERRERA BROTHERS for the extraction of guano, to the amount of 2,000 tons, from the Guañape Islands.

SALVADOR.

ADHERENCE TO THE SANITARY CONVENTION OF 1905.

Under date of November 5, 1906, President ESCALÓN, of Salvador, issued a decree announcing the adherence of the Republic to the Sanitary Convention concluded in Washington on October 14, 1905, by the representatives of Chile, Costa Rica, Cuba, Dominican Republic, Ecuador, United States, Guatemala, Mexico, Nicaragua, Peru, and Venezuela. Notification of this adherence will be made to the Legislative Assembly for its approval.

COMMERCIAL TREATY WITH ITALY.

The "*Diario Oficial,*" of Salvador, in its issue of November 9, 1906, publishes the text of the treaty of friendship, commerce, and navigation between the Governments of Salvador and Italy, signed in the city of Guatemala by the respective plenipotentiaries on the 14th of April, 1906. The President of the Republic approved this treaty on the 26th of the same month, submitting it, at the same time, to the ratification of the National Assembly.

RATIFICATION OF THE AGRICULTURAL CONVENTION OF ROME.

On November 5, 1906, the President of the Republic of Salvador approved and submitted to the ratification of the Legislative Assembly the convention for the establishment of an international institute of agriculture, concluded in Rome on June 7, 1905, by the representatives of the various countries taking part therein, Salvador being one of them.

UNITED STATES.

TRADE WITH LATIN AMERICA.

STATEMENT OF IMPORTS AND EXPORTS.

Following is the latest statement, from figures compiled by the Bureau of Statistics, United States Department of Commerce and Labor, showing the value of the trade between the United States and the Latin-American countries. The report is for the month of November, 1906, with a comparative statement for the corresponding month of the previous year; also for the eleven months ending November, 1906, as compared with the same period of the preceding year. It should be explained that the figures from the various custom-houses, showing imports and exports for any month, are not received by the Treasury Department until about the 20th of the following month, and some time is necessarily consumed in compilation and printing, so that the returns for November, for example, are not published until some time in January.

IMPORTS OF MERCHANDISE.

	November—		Eleven months ending November—	
	1905.	1906.	1905.	1906.
Cocoa (*Cacao; Coco ou cacao crû; Cacao*):	*Dollars.*	*Dollars.*	*Dollars.*	*Dollars.*
Central America	497	2,353	22,615	22,226
Brazil	226,217	380,178	847,944	1,917,991
Other South America	44,428	189,082	1,630,928	1,974,056
Coffee (*Café; Café; Café*):				
Central America	30,711	43,091	5,825,422	5,888,987
Mexico	122,973	14,707	2,636,827	2,064,580
Brazil	7,896,329	8,720,654	70,275,545	42,527,697
Other South America	718,195	504,004	7,197,189	8,831,394
Copper (*Cobre; Cobre; Cuivre*):				
Cuba	9,562	22,149	53,134	68,383
Mexico	1,173,851	1,055,095	15,478,627	16,685,767
South America	51,648	49,199	826,672	1,630,637
Fibers:				
Cotton, unmanufactured (*Algodón en rama; Algodáo em rama; Coton, non manufacturé*):				
South America	18,975	81,816	311,821	401,172
Sisal grass (*Henequén; Henequen; Henuequen*):				
Mexico	1,701,771	1,485,725	14,305,614	12,683,182
Fruits:				
Bananas (*Plátanos; Bananas; Bananes*):				
Central America	359,336	417,906	3,866,710	5,143,576
Cuba	25,936	1,682	1,230,454	1,322,979
South America	27,305		189,834	309,429
Oranges (*Naranjas; Laranjas; Oranges*):				
Mexico	8,778	14,650	45,591	31,436
Cuba	2,306	1,431	4,359	8,749
Fur skins (*Pieles finas; Pelles; Fourrures*):				
South America	51,578	15,433	143,552	280,815
Hides and skins (*Cueros y pieles; Couros e pelles; Cuirs et peaux*):				
Central America	54,673	45,878	504,382	517,823
Mexico	238,013	278,865	3,412,214	4,079,055
South America	1,251,855	1,159,871	12,637,509	12,950,794

IMPORTS OF MERCHANDISE—Continued.

	November—		Eleven months ending November—	
	1905.	1906.	1905.	1906.
India rubber, crude (*Goma elástica; Borracha cruda; Caoutchouc*):	Dollars.	Dollars.	Dollars.	Dollars.
Central America	69, 208	52, 837	785, 787	712, 152
Mexico	28, 080	154, 175	276, 197	1, 378, 520
Brazil	2, 509, 572	2, 711, 451	25, 107, 831	24, 447, 264
Other South America	74, 924	129, 772	1, 082, 491	1, 168, 079
Lead, in pigs, bars, etc. (*Plomo en galápagos, barras, etc.; Chumbo em linguados, barras, etc.: Plomb en saumons, en barres, etc.*):				
Mexico	248, 839	122, 872	3, 098, 295	2, 050, 078
South America	683		20, 583	7, 001
Sugar, not above No. 16 Dutch standard (*Azúcar, inferior al No. 16 del modelo holandes; Assucar, não superior ao No. 16 de padrão hollandez; Sucre, pas au-dessus du type hollandais No. 16*):				
Mexico	434	316	610, 660	78, 882
Cuba	1, 843, 931	668, 289	69, 573, 899	56, 344, 473
Brazil	3, 276	178, 966	1, 335, 769	507, 602
Other South America	469, 120	746, 928	1, 981, 935	1, 737, 019
Tobacco, leaf (*Tabaco en rama; Tabaco não manufacturado; Tabac non manufacturé*):				
Mexico	593	11, 945	10, 947	46, 859
Cuba	1, 269, 195	1, 239, 302	10, 699, 854	14, 098, 105
Wood, mahogany (*Cuoba; Mogno; Acajou*):				
Central America	58, 482	77, 291	481, 418	448, 520
Mexico	35, 960	38, 234	321, 429	454, 888
Cuba	438	28, 619	71, 397	167, 475
Wool (*Lana; Lã; Laine*): South America—				
Class 1 (clothing)	11, 786	1, 429	8, 469, 593	6, 529, 807
Class 2 (combing)	41, 144	31, 847	615, 007	295, 838
Class 3 (carpet)	120, 883	277	995, 765	759, 188

EXPORTS OF MERCHANDISE.

	November—		Eleven months ending November—	
	1905.	1906.	1905.	1906.
Agricultural implements (*Instrumentos agrícolas; Instrumentos de agricultura; Machines agricoles*):				
Mexico	34, 479	41, 201	390, 713	499, 970
Cuba	16, 239	3, 570	235, 520	110, 363
Argentine Republic	759, 274	268, 385	5, 153, 427	4, 201, 637
Brazil	8, 030	9, 159	168, 161	93, 607
Chile	3, 888	25, 061	255, 696	404, 814
Other South America	33, 567	13, 149	237, 610	268, 683
Animals: Cattle (*Ganado vacuno; Gado; Bétail*).				
Mexico	49, 019	84, 659	427, 704	775, 219
Cuba	70, 279	19, 825	1, 941, 452	991, 082
South America	9, 074	6, 140	71, 523	69, 984
Hogs (*Cerdos; Porcos; Pores*):				
Mexico	16, 143	35, 737	86, 232	204, 219
Horses (*Caballos; Cavallos; Chevaux*):				
Mexico	9, 554	59, 375	226, 124	321, 361
Sheep (*Ovejas; Ovelhas; Brebis*):				
Mexico	360	1, 630	37, 055	100, 845
Breadstuffs: Corn (*Maíz; Milho; Maïs*):				
Central America	4, 326	1, 073	467, 508	52, 418
Mexico	94, 008	89, 889	669, 461	1, 107, 326
Cuba	105, 129	153, 941	1, 004, 115	1, 190, 830
South America	258	499	148, 281	11, 897
Oats (*Avena; Aveia; Avoine*):				
Central America	4, 552	1, 381	17, 587	24, 215
Mexico	783	1, 396	19, 843	50, 737
Cuba	15, 562	26, 765	183, 835	267, 722
South America	697	234	23, 958	19, 138
Wheat (*Trigo; Trigo; Blé*):				
Central America	7, 643		23, 210	25, 325
Mexico	176, 629	60, 178	616, 089	1, 473, 714
South America	117, 771	10, 507	208, 394	324, 573

EXPORTS OF MERCHANDISE—Continued.

	November—		Eleven months ending November—	
	1905.	1906.	1905.	1906.
Wheat flour (*Harina de trigo; Farinha de trigo; Farine de blé*):	*Dollars.*	*Dollars.*	*Dollars.*	*Dollars.*
Central America	140,282	93,177	1,880,148	1,494,286
Mexico	19,576	9,187	253,494	111,717
Cuba	330,635	272,982	3,185,872	2,613,034
Brazil	73,526	164,847	984,184	1,164,714
Colombia	102,794	12,997	613,884	118,694
Other South America	216,453	165,550	2,358,511	2,299,449
Carriages, etc.:				
Automobiles (*Automóviles; Automoviles; Automobiles*):				
Mexico	12,738	64,827	162,780	678,280
South America	6,974	19,929	54,912	142,311
Carriages, cars, etc., and parts thereof (*Carruajes, carros y sus accesorios; Carruagems,carros e partes de carros; Voitures, wagons et leurs parties*):				
Central America	37,820	174,685	395,322	2,059,493
Mexico	110,533	332,117	1,083,181	2,267,102
Cuba	67,157	72,159	598,185	1,122,869
Argentine Republic	113,792	277,869	1,184,399	1,864,091
Brazil	32,796	11,092	108,166	255,940
Chile	109,437	37,857	111,318	190,129
Colombia	10,177	1,557	39,001	33,130
Venezuela	487	645	7,255	9,965
Other South America	12,277	11,480	114,663	250,659
Clocks and watches (*Relojes de pared ë bolsillo; Relogios de bolso e parede; Horloges et montres*):				
Central America	1,114	1,856	11,343	15,999
Mexico	7,076	2,003	57,000	66,982
Argentine Republic	2,728	4,976	54,432	71,224
Brazil	5,657	9,826	58,003	73,081
Chile	4,819	6,149	43,351	43,117
Other South America	2,830	2,777	54,688	38,220
Coal (*Carbón; Carvão; Charbon*).				
Mexico	257,523	209,675	2,569,034	2,928,496
Cuba	181,378	137,439	1,177,763	1,758,657
Copper (*Cobre; Cobre, Cuivre*):				
Mexico	99,346	53,319	1,100,103	960,041
Cotton:				
Cotton, unmanufactured (*Algodon en rama; Algodão em rama, Coton non manufacturé*).				
Mexico	208,359	314	2,516,114	522,372
Cotton cloths (*Tejidos de algodón; Fazendas de algodão; Coton manufacturé*):				
Central America	127,328	165,902	1,422,053	1,333,724
Mexico	24,470	22,211	283,562	218,731
Cuba	64,787	82,224	1,110,001	892,560
Argentine Republic	47,459	34,544	416,913	238,841
Brazil	32,378	48,466	679,134	442,708
Chile	38,866	92,299	763,921	779,924
Other South America	43,888	75,305	453,835	736,400
Wearing apparel (*Ropa de algodón; Fazendas de algodão; Vêtements en coton*):				
Central America	53,840	77,236	600,380	669,097
Mexico	44,156	42,791	583,010	513,692
Cuba	33,208	76,203	383,911	484,130
Argentine Republic	28,025	9,301	307,569	212,397
Brazil	2,079	5,473	58,000	49,712
Chile	1,033	5,335	19,362	31,336
Colombia	5,327	2,719	43,684	30,241
Venezuela	2,657	1,579	22,120	25,228
Other South America	3,303	7,789	48,466	65,495
Electric and scientific apparatus (*Aparatos eléctricos y científicos; Apparelhos electricos e scientificos; Appareils électriques et scientifiques*):				
Central America	13,976	20,452	149,745	222,183
Mexico	86,644	118,068	773,523	1,269,068
Argentine Republic	44,701	39,274	214,651	145,006
Brazil	26,641	86,108	410,833	768,535
Chile	16,810	23,353	121,792	184,469
Venezuela	5,412	11,697	90,375	97,208
Other South America	28,129	28,764	234,741	280,062

EXPORTS OF MERCHANDISE—Continued.

	November—		Eleven months ending November—	
	1905.	1906.	1905.	1906.
Electrical machinery (*Maquinaria eléctrica; Machines électricas; Machines électriques*):	*Dollars.*	*Dollars.*	*Dollars.*	*Dollars.*
Central America	1,021	4,909	12,035	38,892
Mexico	69,269	60,371	947,227	953,103
Cuba	13,180	6,238	78,602	436,681
Argentine Republic	22,556	12,106	150,528	162,402
Brazil	10,452	44,175	190,474	497,212
Other South America	9,161	11,498	93,079	128,920
Iron and steel, manufactures of:				
Steel rails (*Carriles de acero; Trilhos de aço; Rails d'acier*):				
Central America	824	2,000	272,336	493,998
Mexico	159,483	114,689	1,361,212	721,855
South America	244,231	130,903	2,625,484	2,572,779
Builders' hardware, saws and tools (*Materiales de metal para construcción, sierras y herramientas; Ferragens, serras e ferramentas; Matériaux de construction en fer et acier, scies et outils*):				
Central America	23,136	34,966	278,311	214,701
Mexico	117,427	87,060	974,473	997,179
Cuba	40,171	46,389	567,074	580,998
Argentine Republic	79,017	68,713	583,016	762,613
Brazil	24,208	57,631	336,387	431,314
Chile	6,490	32,634	142,673	261,391
Colombia	8,829	5,733	53,210	68,689
Venezuela	4,444	3,451	30,621	54,464
Other South America	26,035	28,279	223,766	275,750
Sewing machines, and parts of (*Máquinas de coser y sus accesorios; Machinas de coser e accessorios; Machines à coudre et leurs parties*):				
Central America	9,161	11,498	91,079	128,920
Mexico	32,497	77,455	536,206	756,167
Cuba	10,259	26,479	334,565	310,187
Argentine Republic	53,063	59,572	578,748	535,308
Brazil	23,109	70,849	159,461	283,465
Other South America	23,322	30,590	321,085	386,955
Steam engines, and parts of (*Locomotoras y accesorios; Locomotivas e accessorios; Locomotifs et leurs parties*):				
Central America		101,763	152,068	1,197,209
Mexico	20,500	321,839	242,808	963,174
Cuba	31,500	143,498	439,109	468,509
Argentine Republic	8,840	8,126	216,288	216,481
Brazil		36,517	147,292	596,016
Other South America		15,285	124,461	512,375
Typewriting machines, and parts of (*Mecanógrafos y accesorios; Machinas de escribir e accessorios; Machines à écrire et leurs parties*).				
Central America	2,808	3,153	19,588	43,252
Mexico	25,560	21,073	308,807	339,865
Cuba	3,492	2,344	62,027	67,572
Argentine Republic		12,245	84,757	102,644
Brazil	399	7,458	40,245	57,583
Colombia	1,152	2,857	10,522	10,850
Other South America	8,042	17,916	112,661	153,419
Leather, other than sole (*Cuero distinto del de suelas; Ouro, não para sola; Cuirs, autres que pour semelles*):				
Central America	12,306	17,712	140,439	193,411
Mexico	19,981	8,345	87,767	65,988
Cuba	17,246	24,689	288,514	248,345
Argentine Republic	31,962	15,719	261,212	263,382
Brazil	11,799	22,977	123,411	154,301
Chile		5,687	50,114	85,979
Colombia	7,059	4,919	84,629	59,872
Venezuela	4,207	9,824	41,287	70,332
Other South America	6,123	8,395	73,949	159,455
Boots and shoes (*Calzado; Calçado; Chaussures*):				
Central America	39,814	48,809	271,563	447,223
Mexico	86,263	132,658	1,350,319	1,358,907
Colombia	4,925	4,379	52,858	54,345
Other South America	55,294	41,990	239,779	317,160
Naval stores:				
Rosin, tar, etc. (*Resina, alquitrán, etc.; Resina e alcatrão; Résine et goudron*):				
Central America	1,960	2,140	19,724	23,322
Mexico	3,128	1,116	15,800	16,901
Cuba	5,722	10,129	62,583	71,889

EXPORTS OF MERCHANDISE—Continued.

	November—		Eleven months ending November—	
	1905.	1906.	1905.	1906
Naval stores—Continued.	*Dollars.*	*Dollars.*	*Dollars.*	*Dollars.*
Rosin, tar, etc.—Continued.				
Argentine Republic................	156,176	88,233	229,125	443,293
Brazil...........................	14,085	57,061	425,788	601,251
Chile............................	7,921	4,414	33,542	58,409
Colombia	2,570	1,774	19,886	26,622
Venezuela	2,021	6,257	30,390	39,457
Other South America	8,055	32,174	147,380	129,839
Turpentine (*Aguarrás; Aguaraz; Térébenthine*):				
Central America.................	8,463	1,840	33,764	43,854
Cuba............................	5,443	11,896	59,042	75,791
Argentine Republic..............	19,169	1,358	124,415	270,551
Brazil...........................	6,146	13,920	102,392	118,150
Chile............................	5,124	8,510	61,068	81,188
Other South America	3,013	7,984	45,553	74,931
Oils, mineral, crude (*Aceites minerales, crudos; Oleos mineraes, crús; Huiles minérales, brutes*):				
Mexico..........................	61	847	679,754	933,642
Cuba............................	21,658	60,153	388,348	545,518
Oils, mineral, refined or manufactured (*Aceites minerales, refinados ó manufacturados; Oleos mineraes, refinados ou manufacturados; Huiles minérales, raffinées ou manufacturées*):				
Central America.................	31,667	31,483	295,429	375,312
Mexico..........................	31,862	65,488	250,670	179,923
Cuba............................	31,335	43,941	298,136	271,898
Argentine Republic..............	387,305	149,632	2,072,931	2,401,277
Brazil...........................	222,284	291,687	2,352,116	2,653,195
Chile............................	26,164	61,780	854,782	858,041
Colombia	10,310	10,036	102,475	118,588
Venezuela	9,435	14,093	126,676	130,555
Other South America	54,232	106,161	787,062	863,040
Paper (*Papel; Papel; Papier*):				
Central America.................	11,430	13,927	171,487	158,815
Mexico..........................	86,308	52,920	521,590	601,695
Cuba............................	30,630	43,431	363,899	443,519
Argentine Republic..............	45,451	20,143	257,778	351,369
Brazil...........................	4,021	5,967	66,540	77,810
Chile............................	11,360	31,247	211,367	225,477
Colombia	1,186	2,259	31,399	22,921
Venezuela	2,697	7,856	39,152	44,369
Other South America	9,598	9,019	101,790	112,758
Books (*Libros; Livros; Livres*):				
Central America.................	12,918	11,274	55,817	100,917
Mexico..........................	40,021	34,314	272,215	240,107
Cuba............................	42,964	22,533	251,832	263,129
Argentine Republic..............	12,918	11,271	55,817	100,917
Brazil...........................	14,028	10,304	44,466	102,939
Chile............................	2,712	12,815	165,988	173,448
Other South America	4,669	6,959	55,847	70,710
Provisions, comprising meat and dairy products:				
Beef, canned (*Carne de vaca en lata; Carne de vacca em latas; Boeuf conservé*):				
Central America.................	2,100	5,502	25,835	62,558
Mexico..........................	1,333	6,114	34,724	26,498
Cuba............................	2,218	754	16,195	19,751
South America	4,770	4,478	33,258	12,640
Beef, salted or pickled (*Carne de vaca, salada ó adobada; Carne de vacca, salgada; Boeuf salé*):				
Central America.................	9,006	10,255	76,325	107,555
South America	6,526	26,318	198,245	237,872
Tallow (*Sebo; Sebo; Suif*):				
Central America.................	6,899	1,255	117,191	125,426
Mexico..........................	2,715	497	82,118	20,467
Cuba............................	1,861	978	7,215	10,780
Chile............................	1,088	3,653	32,911	92,190
Other South America	2,646	7,155	55,910	49,381
Bacon (*Tocino; Toucinho; Lard fumé*):				
Central America.................	1,574	5,526	11,909	29,585
Mexico..........................	3,332	3,969	36,738	43,516
Cuba............................	14,132	63,621	368,879	178,937
Brazil...........................	10,446	11,673	101,814	162,264
Other South America	1,005	480	12,708	10,128
Hams (*Jamones, Presuntos; Jambons*):				
Central America.................	6,306	11,168	71,071	103,956
Mexico..........................	10,961	7,336	120,468	90,229
Cuba............................	30,314	58,389	419,867	503,315
Venezuela	7,556	7,216	34,867	41,526
Other South America	2,198	7,073	48,429	64,064

EXPORTS OF MERCHANDISE—Continued.

	November—		Eleven months ending November—	
	1905.	1906.	1905.	1906.
Provisions, etc.—Continued.	*Dollars.*	*Dollars.*	*Dollars.*	*Dollars.*
Pork (*Carne de puerco; Carne de porco; Porc*):				
Central America	11,885	17,740	141,032	210,387
Cuba	58,015	70,800	420,275	634,028
Brazil	220		28,496	218
Colombia			7,240	688
Other South America	9,497	21,752	192,901	229,964
Lard (*Manteca; Banha; Saindoux*):				
Central America	17,589	58,763	414,751	461,976
Mexico	74,419	44,503	386,923	479,236
Cuba	179,582	293,304	2,068,819	2,562,484
Brazil	5,718	99,478	101,262	602,481
Chile	2,847	11,304	69,784	157,713
Colombia	79,074	2,653	355,171	65,653
Venezuela	32,905	26,529	342,627	282,625
Other South America	46,921	38,641	381,181	557,565
Butter (*Mantequilla; Manteiga; Beurre*):				
Central America	7,163	12,768	88,624	137,439
Mexico	10,857	11,240	119,988	124,817
Cuba	4,149	6,232	29,282	54,628
Brazil	8,951	7,096	122,106	109,164
Venezuela	15,633	2,968	76,005	90,136
Other South America	1,049	5,131	32,236	42,068
Cheese (*Queso; Queijo; Fromage*):				
Central America	5,398	6,488	55,447	69,293
Mexico	3,668	2,207	36,794	38,602
Cuba	687	2,202	14,990	14,205
Paraffin (*Parafina; Parafina; Paraffine*):				
Central America	5,221	11,450	45,636	60,879
Mexico	19,732	11,293	342,090	477,865
South America	1,321	3,396	26,426	36,434
Tobacco, unmanufactured (*Tabaco en rama; Tabaco não manufacturado; Tabac non manufacturé*):				
Central America	8,891	3,552	60,127	64,353
Mexico	6,628	7,729	104,166	92,147
Argentine Republic	16,800	1,288	49,556	30,804
Colombia	1,014		8,691	15,128
Other South America	2,311	9,216	70,895	77,717
Tobacco, manufactures of (*Tabaco elaborado; Tabaco manufacturado; Tabac manufacturé*):				
Central America	1,225	28,872	108,307	139,103
Mexico	1,598	998	21,133	28,426
Cuba	6,111	12,531	95,770	102,736
Argentine Republic	214	72	12,269	4,463
Colombia	91	865	6,651	4,250
Other South America	2,193	6,590	43,158	54,117
Wood, and manufactures of:				
Wood, unmanufactured (*Madera sin labrar; Madeira não manufacturada; Bois brut*):				
Central America	16,551	106,780	343,546	616,601
Mexico	80,329	72,311	761,306	1,188,451
Cuba	16,488	836	74,699	165,817
Argentine Republic	2,242	15,200	95,960	163,927
Other South America	11,077	88,662	151,001	195,363
Lumber (*Maderas; Madeiras; Bois de construction*):				
Central America	57,032	139,148	107,697	1,031,879
Mexico	115,915	106,148	1,170,177	1,971,083
Cuba	197,062	132,957	1,700,867	2,175,156
Argentine Republic	421,588	641,482	2,237,020	4,611,986
Brazil	51,992	84,830	414,347	772,315
Chile	42,960	10,545	421,947	649,255
Other South America	63,669	103,431	685,544	1,073,936
Furniture (*Muebles; Mobilia; Meubles*):				
Central America	21,710	23,080	232,098	271,978
Mexico	58,895	99,004	642,346	828,180
Cuba	63,590	45,070	617,342	530,632
Argentine Republic	36,267	30,968	286,345	316,018
Brazil	4,918	7,180	35,460	59,270
Chile	968	3,488	57,512	-69,245
Colombia	2,083	1,913	33,830	17,176
Venezuela	9,516	2,626	35,638	18,292
Other South America	5,622	14,378	85,468	97,264

November—		Eleven months ending November—	
1905.	1906.	1905.	1906.
Dollars.	Dollars.	Dollars.	Dollars.
13, ███, 716	13, 579, 936	107, 663, 897	101, 819, 7
145, 003	160, 335	2, 815, 943	3, 102, 6
29, 794, 573	30, 367, 724	271, 839, 119	296, 321, 2
7, ███, 370	10, 218, 441	74, 302, 954	98, 537, 0
3, 434, 495	2, 364, 715	22, 846, 542	25, 749, 2
565, 041	340, 331	4, 041, 317	5, 487, 4
46, 647, 695	57, 011, 477	482, 758, 292	536, 017, 4
3, 031, 091	3, 353, 663	17, 943, 898	19, 512, 3
19, 716, 513	12, 360, 945	142, 128, 743	121, 542, 0
6, 964, 945	8, 064, 596	97, 958, 945	105, 932, 1
9, 346, 100	12, 344, 085	105, 405, 156	129, 576, 1
21, 399, 494	26, 291, 953	228, 990, 742	277, 435, 9
645, 507	377, 898	2, 818, 925	3, 143, 4
51, 636, 619	61, 802, 046	596, 246, 459	666, 142, 3
16, 010, 809	16, 733, 521	124, 972, 705	121, 332, 3
10, 809, 061	12, 520, 270	144, 944, 706	127, 644, 7
29, 769, 488	38, 452, 310	369, 798, 111	402, 253, 4
16, 839, 479	22, 542, 529	179, 608, 110	228, 118, 1
25, 820, 919	28, 696, 668	251, 837, 254	303, 185, 2
931, 558	918, 219	8, 840, 742	8, 630, 8
99, 281, 514	119, 818, 517	1, 079, 031, 751	1, 186, 159, 8

The imports and exports of gold and silver during November and eleven months of 1906 were as follows, compared with those of the same month and period of the year 1905:

Gold and silver.	November—		Eleven months ending November—	
	1905.	1906.	1905.	1906.
Gold:				
Imports..............................	$5,202,790	$8,850,223	$46,264,524	$147,907,092
Exports..............................	1,137,318	1,963,757	44,125,935	44,831,203
Silver:				
Imports..............................	4,306,838	3,263,519	31,246,389	40,140,110
Exports..............................	5,361,819	4,561,830	49,316,953	53,550,248

EXPORTS OF DOMESTIC PRODUCTS, 1903–1906.

The Bureau of Statistics furnishes the following statistics of exports of domestic products during the years 1903–1906, inclusive:

Month.	Breadstuffs.	Meat and dairy products.	Cattle, hogs, and sheep.
1903—January................................	$19,116,959	$16,503,837	$2,890,797
February................................	17,093,473	13,385,597	2,667,277
March................................	18,340,281	14,353,561	2,381,151
April................................	18,289,718	11,542,958	2,984,891
May................................	16,859,779	11,870,950	3,374,801
June................................	13,798,862	13,371,397	3,770,962
July................................	11,366,699	12,388,863	3,783,279
August................................	13,025,713	12,688,503	2,763,798
September................................	15,599,622	13,676,064	2,898,832
October................................	18,895,439	13,866,878	3,432,331
November................................	15,205,867	13,192,250	2,971,284
December................................	16,328,204	14,941,505	3,767,791
Total, 12 months................................	193,920,616	161,782,372	37,690,193
1904—January................................	13,481,129	14,353,431	4,055,793
February................................	11,024,975	12,624,752	3,500,337
March................................	11,557,451	14,461,672	4,052,630
April................................	6,974,723	11,846,302	3,970,162
May................................	4,734,801	10,860,152	3,806,858
June................................	4,515,859	12,759,968	3,509,325
July................................	4,326,115	9,258,949	2,988,255
August................................	5,341,836	11,219,518	2,937,732
September................................	6,419,915	11,984,822	3,115,670
October................................	7,458,126	12,799,591	3,526,660
November................................	6,771,649	11,961,403	3,000,084
December................................	9,705,229	14,088,942	3,594,131
Total, 12 months................................	92,311,812	148,219,515	42,057,657
1905—January................................	12,440,131	13,170,049	3,905,168
February................................	10,594,405	12,585,561	3,850,397
March................................	12,631,494	14,985,316	3,872,472
April................................	10,821,564	14,130,090	3,489,071
May................................	8,347,110	12,793,605	3,162,222
June................................	6,249,.	13,533,014	3,562,832
July................................	5,126,508	14,314,568	2,992,491
August................................	7,814,769	14,212,278	2,834,519
September................................	12,980,243	12,799,893	3,110,117
October................................	15,255,671	14,118,210	2,881,877
November................................	17,374,026	15,313,240	3,109,495
December................................	26,472,121	20,267,621	4,067,339
Total, 12 months................................	146,107,883	172,243,385	40,838,000
1906—January................................	26,253,558	20,542,799	3,480,390
February................................	19,460,320	17,094,589	3,605,967
March................................	15,531,743	15,661,905	3,805,055
April................................	13,079,594	16,366,772	3,831,903
May................................	10,605,000	14,999,492	3,765,842
June................................	7,102,461	15,377,807	3,818,581
July................................	7,910,925	14,975,996	2,644,870
August................................	12,933,698	16,768,067	2,634,245
September................................	17,430,420	16,011,831	2,471,544
October................................	18,988,719	14,741,273	1,916,006
November................................	15,191,121	11,809,455	2,655,234
December................................	15,369,873	13,588,089	2,922,039
Total, 12 months................................	180,462,232	187,880,650	37,551,626

PORTS OF COTTON.

covering exports of cotton from the United
e Bureau of Statistics, Department of Com-

		Other cotton.			
les.	**Price per pound.**	**Bales.**	**Pounds.**	**Values.**	**Price per pound.**
lars.	*Cents.*			*Dollars.*	*Cents.*
2,132	22.5	4,441,180	2,142,816,819	202,963,616	9.5
5,295	20.9	4,685,995	2,252,574,992	211,397,296	9.3
7,000	21.7	4,813,374	2,358,796,100	234,581,134	9.9
8,937	24.7	4,978,412	2,456,176,284	246,382,297	10.1
5,797	21.0	5,817,980	2,910,343,407	288,362,322	9.9
8,989	17.6	5,998,692	2,980,221,771	255,998,351	8.7
9,732	22.0	4,472,206	2,234,592,318	180,016,511	8.5
5,897	20.4	5,898,466	2,929,818,430	295,250,022	7.9
4,610	18.2	6,850,227	3,465,456,536	197,972,696	5.7
4,682	18.9	4,702,784	2,361,504,208	195,144,948	8.1
4,819	19.0	5,085,712	3,040,261,516	225,776,966	7.4
5,781	17.7	7,645,690	3,898,258,638	235,951,899	6.9
5,294	14.7	7,420,229	3,799,968,084	209,591,357	5.5
5,490	36.4	6,909,757	8,065,686,612	342,678,838	7.9
5,499	19.5	6,617,464	3,390,905,778	315,879,294	9.3
5,299	28.8	6,706,276	3,423,084,348	283,089,261	8.3
3,152	26.5	6,716,322	3,435,197,778	306,398,039	8.9
5,897	22.7	5,086,682	2,104,980,611	3772,501,491	12.0
5,271	20.3	8,732,661	4,512,792,189	399,896,721	8.9
8,680	20.5	6,732,449	8,471,984,650	381,918,642	11.0

**GOLD AND SILVER ARTICLES FALSELY
MARKED PROHIBITED.**

ation, exportation, or carriage in interstate commerce
ed articles of merchandise made of gold or silver or
poss.

enate and House of Representatives of the
n Congress assembled, That it shall be unlaw-
corporation, or association, being a manu-
r retail dealer in gold or silver jewelry or
r silverware, or for any officer, manager,
firm, corporation, or association to import
imported into or exported from the United
lling or disposing of the same, or to deposit
a the United States mails for transmission
use to be delivered to any common carrier
ne State, Territory, or possession of the
ict of Columbia, to any other State, Terri-
United States, or to said District, in inter-
sport or cause to be transported from one
sion of the United States, or from the Dis-
ther State, Territory, or possession of the
istrict, in interstate commerce, any article
red after the date when this Act takes effect
irt of gold or silver, or any alloy of either

of said metals, and having stamped, branded, engraved, or printed thereon, or upon any tag, card, or label attached thereto, or upon any box, package, cover, or wrapper in which said article is incased or inclosed, any mark or word indicating or designed or intended to indicate that the gold or silver or alloy of either of said metals in such article is of a greater degree of fineness than the actual fineness or quality of such gold, silver, or alloy, according to the standards and subject to the qualifications set forth in sections two and three of this Act.

SEC. 2. That in the case of articles only of merchandise made in whole or in part of gold or of any of its alloys so imported into or exported from the United States, or so deposited in the United States mails for transmission, or so delivered for transportation to any common carrier, or so transported or caused to be transported as specified in the first section of this Act, the actual fineness of such gold or alloy shall not be less by more than one-half of one carat than the fineness indicated by the mark stamped, branded, engraved, or printed upon any part of such article, or upon any tag, card, or label attached thereto, or upon any box, package, cover, or wrapper in which such article is incased or inclosed; except that in the case of watch cases and flat ware, so made of gold or of any of its alloys, the actual fineness of such gold or alloy shall not be less by more than three one-thousandth parts than the fineness indicated by the mark stamped, branded, engraved, or printed upon such article, or upon any tag, card, or label attached thereto, or upon any box, package, cover, or wrapper in which such article is incased or inclosed: *Provided*, That in any test for the ascertainment of the fineness of any article mentioned in this section, according to the foregoing standards, the part of the article taken for the test, analysis, or assay shall be such part or portion as does not contain or have attached thereto any solder or alloy of inferior fineness used for brazing or uniting the parts of said article: *Provided further*, That in the case of any article mentioned in this section, in addition to the foregoing tests and standards, the actual fineness of the entire quantity of gold or of its alloys contained in such article, including all solder and alloy of inferior fineness used for brazing or uniting the parts of such article (all such gold, alloys, and solder being assayed as one piece), shall not be less by more than one carat than the fineness indicated by the mark stamped, branded, engraved, or imprinted upon such article, or upon any tag, card, or label attached thereto, or upon any box, package, cover, or wrapper in which such article is incased or inclosed, it being intended that the standards of fineness and the tests or methods for ascertaining the same provided in this section for articles mentioned therein shall be concurrent and not alternative.

SEC. 3. That in the case of articles of merchandise made in whole or in part of silver or any of its alloys so imported into or exported from

VENEZUELA.

IMPORTS FROM NEW YORK, MARCH, 1906.

The Consul-General of Venezuela at New York reports that in March, 1906, 4,729,487 kilograms of merchandise, valued at 1,729,909 *bolivares*, were shipped from the port of New York to Venezuelan ports, in comparison with 3,557,675 kilograms, valued at 1,489,858 *bolivares*, shipped from the port of New York in March, 1905, consigned to Venezuelan ports.

FOREIGN TRADE OF VARIOUS COUNTRIES.

The following table has been prepared by the British Board of Trade and published in the Board of Trade Journal for December 20, 1906:

Foregin trade of various countries for nine months ending September, 1906, compared with the same period for the years 1904 and 1905.

[Values in pounds sterling.]

	Imports.			Exports.		
	1904.	1905.	1906.	1904.	1905.	1906.
Germany	230,560,000	243,579,000	288,999,000	189,161,000	201,297,000	221,309,000
Belgium	79,753,000	85,376,000	91,945,000	59,886,000	61,692,000	71,715,000
France	131,397,000	140,251,000	152,963,000	127,668,000	139,587,000	147,400,000
Switzerland	34,495,000	37,018,000	39,456,000	25,495,000	27,635,000	30,669,000
Italy	55,070,000	59,610,000	70,053,000	44,856,000	48,556,000	53,774,000
Egypt	13,926,000	15,100,000	16,888,000	14,081,000	13,213,000	13,998,000
United States	156,541,000	181,724,000	197,568,000	201,128,000	225,332,000	253,964,000
Japan	27,094,000	40,069,000	33,002,000	22,285,000	22,691,000	25,807,000
British India	45,851,000	48,220,000	52,620,000	77,906,000	76,701,000	81,025,000
United Kingdom	345,856,000	352,633,000	380,107,000	221,189,000	242,396,000	278,054,000

NOTE.—In the case of Belgium the value of principal articles only is given, and in the case of Germany, Belgium, France, Switzerland, Egypt, Japan, and the United Kingdom the import figures given in the above summary represent imports for home consumption only, i. e., excluding reexports. In all cases the exports figures are intended to represent exports of domestic products. In most cases, however, they include a certain amount of nationalized goods, i. e., goods originally imported for consumption, and which, if dutiable, have been charged with duty, but which are subsequently reexported.

COFFEE MOVEMENT.

The following statistics of the coffee trade are taken from "The Tea and Coffee Trade Journal," and were compiled from figures received by the Coffee Exchange of New York.

The world's visible supply on December 1, 1906, was as follows:

	Bags.
Europe (all kinds)	5,000,451
Rio	492,000
Santos	1,762,000
Bahia	68,000
United States (all kinds)	3,422,385
Total	10,744,836

brazed or otherwise affixed thereto a plating, covering, or sheet composed of gold or silver, or of an alloy of either of said metals, and known in the market as rolled gold plate, gold plate, gold filled, silver plate, or gold or silver electroplate, or by any similar designation, so imported into or exported from the United States, or so deposited in the United States mails for transmission, or so delivered to any common carrier, or so transported or caused to be transported as specified in the first section of this act, no such article, nor any tag, card, or label attached thereto, nor any box, package, cover, or wrapper in which such article is incased or inclosed, shall be stamped, branded, engraved, or imprinted with any word or mark usually employed to indicate the fineness of gold, unless such word or mark be accompanied by other words plainly indicating that such article or part thereof is made of rolled gold plate, gold plate, or gold electroplate, or is gold filled, as the case may be, and no such article, nor any tag, card, or label attached thereto, nor any box, package, cover, or wrapper in which such article is incased or inclosed, shall be stamped, branded, engraved, or imprinted with the word "sterling" or the word "coin" either alone or in conjunction with other words or marks.

* * * * * * *

SEC. 8. That this act shall take effect one year after the date of its passage.

Approved, June 13, 1906.

———

URUGUAY.

DECREES REGULATING THE IMPORTATION OF CATTLE.

The provisions regulating the importation of cattle into Uruguay have been modified by a decree reducing from ten years to one year the period for sanitary observation of suspected countries. Formerly the certificates from these countries had to show that the bovine diseases do not and have not existed for ten years past. Considering this period to be excessive the Institute of Hygiene has been making efforts to have it reduced to conform with the legislation adopted in other importing countries, and a Presidential decree to that effect has been issued.

Two other decrees appearing almost simultaneously, one the 26th of October and the other the 13th of October, relate to the inspection of animals on their landing and to the creation of a register of pedigrees.

VENEZUELA.

IMPORTS FROM NEW YORK, MARCH, 1906.

The Consul-General of Venezuela at New York reports that in March, 1906, 4,729,487 kilograms of merchandise, valued at 1,729,909 *bolivares*, were shipped from the port of New York to Venezuelan ports, in comparison with 3,557,675 kilograms, valued at 1,489,858 *bolivares*, shipped from the port of New York in March, 1905, consigned to Venezuelan ports.

FOREIGN.TRADE OF VARIOUS COUNTRIES.

The following table has been prepared by the British Board of Trade and published in the Board of Trade Journal for December 20, 1906:

Foregin trade of various countries for nine months ending September, 1906, compared with the same period for the years 1904 and 1905.

[Values in pounds sterling.]

	Imports.			Exports.		
	1904.	1905.	1906.	1904.	1905.	1906.
Germany	230,590,000	243,579,000	288,999,000	189,161,000	201,297,000	221,309,000
Belgium	79,753,000	85,376,000	91,945,000	59,886,000	61,692,000	71,715,000
France	131,397,000	140,251,000	152,963,000	127,668,000	139,587,000	147,400,000
Switzerland	34,496,000	37,018,000	39,486,000	25,495,000	27,635,000	30,669,000
Italy	55,070,000	59,610,000	70,053,000	44,856,000	48,556,000	53,774,000
Egypt	13,926,000	15,100,000	16,688,000	14,081,000	13,213,000	13,998,000
United States	156,511,000	181,724,000	197,568,000	201,128,000	225,332,000	253,964,000
Japan	27,094,000	40,069,000	33,002,000	22,265,000	22,691,000	28,807,000
British India	45,851,000	48,220,000	52,620,000	77,906,000	76,701,000	81,025,000
United Kingdom	345,858,000	352,633,000	380,107,000	221,189,000	242,896,000	278,054,000

NOTE.—In the case of Belgium the value of principal articles only is given, and in the case of Germany, Belgium, France, Switzerland, Egypt, Japan, and the United Kingdom the import figures given in the above summary represent imports for home consumption only, i. e., excluding reexports. In all cases the exports figures are intended to represent exports of domestic products. In most cases, however, they include a certain amount of nationalized goods, i. e., goods originally imported for consumption, and which, if dutiable, have been charged with duty, but which are subsequently reexported.

COFFEE MOVEMENT.

The following statistics of the coffee trade are taken from "The Tea and Coffee Trade Journal," and were compiled from figures received by the Coffee Exchange of New York.

The world's visible supply on December 1, 1906, was as follows:

	Bags.
Europe (all kinds)	5,000,451
Rio	492,000
Santos	1,762,000
Bahia	68,000
United States (all kinds)	3,422,385
Total	10,744,836

Afloat for—

United States from Brazil	891,000
United States from Java and East	3,000
Europe from Java and East	55,000
Europe from Brazil	1,800,000
Europe from United States	4,000

Shipments:

Rio	59,000
Santos	252,000
Total	13,808,836
Against November 1	13,165,786
Against December 1, 1905	13,090,849

Stocks of coffee in the principal ports, Europe.

Months.	Bags in—		
	1906-7.	1905-6.	1904-5.
July	4,840,577	5,740,122	7,550,722
August	4,585,459	5,496,584	7,286,863
September	4,946,052	5,525,045	7,067,798
October	4,430,772	5,311,493	6,857,106
November	4,556,769	5,189,101	6,478,773
December	5,000,451	5,140,725	6,476,073
January		5,821,080	6,446,069
February		5,380,152	6,277,041
March		5,217,813	6,188,106
April		5,108,472	6,104,501
May		5,091,026	6,092,763
June		5,059,033	5,857,761

Visible supply of the world on the first of each month.

Month.	1906-7.	1905-6.	1904-5.
July	9,364,562	11,465,641	12,361,496
August	9,948,058	11,265,540	12,561,149
September	10,756,653	12,102,496	13,492,192
October	12,153,621	12,624,093	14,256,096
November	13,165,786	13,006,841	14,350,000
December	13,808,836	13,090,849	14,086,729
January		12,647,595	13,916,390
February		11,931,631	13,612,723
March		11,324,561	13,271,745
April		10,747,916	12,967,170
May		10,356,157	12,297,490
June		10,171,979	11,632,586

BOOK NOTES.

Books and pamphlets sent to the Bureau of the American Republics, and containing subject-matter bearing upon the countries of the International Union of American Republics, will be treated under this caption in the Monthly Bulletin.

"Through Five Republics of South America: A Critical Description of Argentina, Brazil, Chile, Uruguay, and Venezuela in 1905." By PERCY F. MARTIN, F. R. G. S., with 128 illustrations and 8 maps. London, 1906.

Mr. MARTIN is a journalist by profession and this, as he says in his preface, is his first book. It is one of the most unfair and prejudiced attacks on South America and South Americans which has appeared in a decade. The writer seems to possess no balance, as will be evident from a few of the coarser extracts from his book. He says that "incompetency, dishonesty, and corruption are not yet abandoned by some of the official class. These I have attempted to identify, and have not hesitated to condemn when detected or suspected. I do not anticipate a pleasurable reception of my candor among these particular sections of my readers, but I accept full responsibility for such opinions."

Let us see what are some of Mr. MARTIN's opinions as to South America and South Americans. As to the latter, he says in general: "The Argentine can show a far more attractive race of people, both physically and mentally, while Chile and Uruguay are also more fortunate in the character and appearance of their people. The fine old Spanish blood can still be traced in the inhabitants of these States, as well as those of Venezuela, and something—I may say, perhaps a good deal—of the Hidalgo's native courtesy and dignity of manner are still met with in the Spanish-American Republics. In Brazil, however, the habits of the Indian, combined with the contaminating influence of much bastard blood, are too pronounced to render the inhabitants in any way agreeable or attractive."

What he says here of the Spanish-speaking people is among the more favorable of his comments. In his more candid moments what he says is: "The amenities of war are but little understood or, if understood, are but little practiced between the various contestants in South American Republics. Under ordinary circumstances such amenities, if even desirable, are purely artificial, and while we may lament the lack of chivalry among these otherwise picturesque ruffians of the Sunny South, it is not difficult to understand its absence."

It is scarcely to be expected that the administration of affairs in the five Republics would be pleasing to Mr. MARTIN. The "picturesque ruffians" in time of peace could be expected to be only a degree less ruffianly than in war. So we have his opinion of the port officials of Buenos Ayres in these words:

"The Prefecture of Marine have it practically in their own hands, and they manage to 'do' some of the shipowners and captains pretty thoroughly. The minor officials demand just whatever they want for their own private requirements—coal for their launches, paint for their boats, and provisions for their own consumption. To refuse their exactions would mean persecution and obstruction, including an entirely unnecessary overhauling of a ship's stores and equipments on the pretext of seeing if anything has been omitted from the store list.

If an accusation can be brought home—and by false swearing and manufactured evidence it generally can—fines are imposed on the ship-owners and bills of health and other papers are aggravatingly delayed. On the whole, it pays better to satisfy the rascally blackmailers and thus get rid of them. The abuses, I am credibly informed, are daily augmenting in both number and seriousness."

The judiciary fares somewhat better at the hands of Mr. MARTIN. As for it and for the police, at least, he sees hope in the future.

"Several accusations of bribery and blackmail have been proved against lesser fry of the Argentine judges, while any foreign resident in 'the camp'—that is, the open country, where the estancias are situated—can tell stories of highway robbery by the police, assisted and even directed by the local commissary. Argentina is, no doubt, emerging by degrees from her dark days in regard to legal abuses, but she has not quite come out into the daylight yet."

The judicial situation seems to Mr. MARTIN less hopeful in Chile.

" Many and various are the stories current throughout Chile as to the deplorable condition of justice, or what passes as such, in the Republic. Even allowing for the usual exaggeration and prejudice which must inevitably be imported into ex parte statements, there can be no doubt that the administration of the law in Chile is, for the most part, in the hands of a very pliable and corrupt body of men, to whom bribes are as their daily bread, and, indeed, form the prin-cipal method of their earning it."

Mr. MARTIN devotes a chapter of his book to the city of Rosario in Argentina. He finds but little to praise, and, as usual, much to con-demn, most of all the city government.

"I know of no municipality of any town in the Argentine Republic which has earned for itself a more unenviable reputation for dishon-esty, except it be that of Córdoba, than Rosario. Certainly no town that I have visited shows anything approaching · the neglect of the public welfare."

Against Brazil, Mr. MARTIN seems to have an especial grudge. The "picturesque ruffians" of the South become, in Brazil, "red-handed assassins."

But in truth he makes but little difference between the five Repub-lics. He says:

"In point of character and disposition, I should say that there exists but little difference between one Latin-American nation and another. Some of the inhabitants of the South are, perhaps, more refined and more gentle than the inhabitants of the North, but beyond that, the characteristics, tastes, and manners of the whole of the South American nations are much alike, and offer but little occasion for choice."

But of Brazil: "It may be said that the present Government of Brazil, like so many others before it, is supported by a political system which leans entirely upon brute force—undiscipline and wholly unreliable. Every prominent office holder knows that his term rests wholly and solely upon the amount of physical force available behind him and his colleagues, and consequently the highest as well as the lowest is in league with the very dregs of the military and the police. Merce-naries by the thousand are to be hired in Brazil, as in some other of the South American States, and your cook or butler of to-day may, for a small consideration, become a red-handed assassin or a successful leader of a *coup d'état* to-morrow."

What can one say of such a book as this, except to regret its publication?

Englishmen on occasions marvel that they are disliked outside of their own country. When such books as this are published, read, and applauded in England how can they marvel?

English writers often complain that Americans, both of the North and of the South, are thin skinned. Perhaps this is true, but there seems, after reading books of this type, to be something to be said on the other side. It may be asked of Mr. MARTIN whether it comports with British fair play unhesitatingly to condemn men as dishonest and corrupt upon mere suspicion, and whether such suspicions so easily entertained, and so freely expressed as facts, are entertained by any other person than Mr. MARTIN himself.

"Spanish Honduras. Report of the chief engineer of the American-Honduras Company." Illustrated. New York, 1906.

This very interesting and valuable report of Mr. J. FRANCIS LE BARON, which is in reality a handbook of the Republic of Honduras, is here published in book form. One interested in the natural resources of Honduras can not afford to overlook this little volume of 183 pages.

"*Saint-Domingue à la veille de la Révolution et la question de la Représentation Coloniale aux États-Généraux,*" par P. BOISSONNADE, *professeur à l'Université de Poitiers.* Paris and New York, 1906.

The period covered by the study of Professor BOISSONNADE is from January, 1788, to July, 1789. The opening chapter on the planters of the French section of the island, now known as Haiti, and of the political causes leading to their agitation for representation in the States-General is well and briefly told.

Guadeloupe and Martinique, under the royal government, had colonial assemblies wherein the interests of the planter class had direct representation. Haiti practically had no such assembly. Two or three chambers of agriculture and of commerce, established about thirty years before, covered all there was of representative institutions in Haiti. These acted, so far as they acted at all, on behalf of the twenty-five or thirty thousand whites, planters, factors, and merchants, for the most part. An equal or greater number of mulattoes, and a half million of negro slaves, of course, had no representation. The government was, for all practical purposes, absolutely in the hands of the governor-general and the intendant. It was on account of this state of affairs and the evils necessarily attending absolutism that the majority of the white planters took sides with the revolutionary party of France. That this action would in the end bring about their own destruction they failed to see. The period covered by the study of Professor BOISSONNADE closes with the triumphant admission of the delegates, very irregularly chosen, to the National Assembly.

ADDITIONS TO THE COLUMBUS MEMORIAL LIBRARY DURING DECEMBER, 1906.

ARGENTINE REPUBLIC.

AMBROSETTI, JUAN B.: Por el valle Calchaquí. Conferencia con proyecciones luminosas leída el 28 de julio de 1897 con motivo del xxv. aniversario de la Sociedad científica Argentina . . . Buenos Aires, Imprenta de Pablo E. Coni é hijos, 1897. 19 p. plates. 8°.
(Artículo publicado en los "Anales de la Sociedad científica Argentina," t. 44, p. 289.)

—— Un viaje á Misiones. Conferencia dada en el Teatro Nacional en el xxii. aniversario de la Sociedad científica Argentina con el concurso de la Sociedad Argentina de Enseñanza por medio de las proyecciones luminosas. Buenos Aires, Imprenta de Pablo E. Coni é hijos, 1894. 24 p. illus. 8°.

AMEGHINO, FLORENTINO: Presencia de mamíferos diprotodontes en los depósitos terciarios del Paraná. Por Florentino Ameghino . . . Buenos Aires, Imprenta de Coni Hermanos, 1900. 8 p. 8°.
(Artículo publicado en los "Anales de la Sociedad científica Argentina," t. 49, p. 235.)

ARGENTINE REPUBLIC. DIVISIÓN ELECTORAL de la República Argentina y división administrativa, parroquial y escolar del municipio de Buenos Aires. (Decretos vigentes.) Buenos Aires, Imprenta de Juan A. Alsina, 1903. 64 p. maps. 8°.

—— MINISTERIO DE AGRICULTURA: Escuela nacional de agricultura y ganadería de Villa Casilda. Su contribución á la segunda esposición del Rosario de Santa Fe, organizada por la Sociedad rural Santafecina. Buenos Aires, Establecimiento tip. "Roma," 1903. 45 p. illus. 12°.

—— WEATHER BUREAU: Weather reports. Feb.-Dec., 1902. Buenos Aires. 3 v. f°. (Daily charts, bound.)

BERNÁRDEZ, M.: The Argentine estancia. A review of the live-stock and agricultural industries and of the rural prospects of the Argentine Rupublic. By M. Bernardez. Buenos Aires, Printed by Ortega and Radaelli, 1903. viii, 123 p. maps. illus. plates. 8°.

CANDIOTI, MARCIAL R.: Revista del archivo de la Sociedad científica Argentina por Marcial R. Candioti. Primera parte, 1872-1878. Buenos Aires, Imprenta de Pablo E. Coni é hijos, 1894. (2) 287 p. 8°.

█████ █ provincia de Mendoza. El Patamillo
██████ ████ . . . Memoria presentada á la
███ ███ de Aires, Imprenta de Pablo E. Coni
███ ████. Argen. 8°.

█ ████ y ganado. Buenos Aires, Compañía
██ de Banco, 1892. 14-635 p. front. (port.). 8°.
██ ████ de la provincia por Abraham
█████ por el mismo. gobierno de la provincia
████ de París en 1889. Mendoza, Tip. de "Los
███ ██. map. 8°.
████ fossiles de la République Argentine par
█████ Ayres, Imprimerie de P. Coni et fils, 1897.
███ . . . .

"Anales de la Sociedad científica Argentina," t. 43.)
siles de carnassiers primitifs de Monte Hermoso
Buenos Aires, Imprenta de Pablo E. Coni é hijos,

"Anales de la sociedad científica Argentina," t. 47, p. 56.)
public. Written in German by Richard Napp,
██████ for the Central Argentine commission on
█ at Philadelphia. Buenos Ayres, Printed by the
. 463, xcvii p. maps. 8°.
█ la conferencia del teniente coronel Don Luis
███, imp. del Departamento nacional de agricul-

letin del Departamento nacional de agricultura, t. 10, no. 12,

e de fósiles en la pampa Argentina por el Dr. Juan
Aires, Imprenta de Pablo E. Coni é hijos, 1897.

"Anales de la Sociedad científica Argentina," t. 44.)
al y el interior." Observaciones sobre ganadería
i E. Villanueva. Obra editada bajo los auspicios
grícola de "La Plata." Buenos Aires, Tip. lit. y
de artes y oficios, 1887. xvii, 872 p. 12°.
ws and live stock. By Robert Wallace . . .
oyd, 1904. 154 p. front. (port.). illus. plates.

BOLIVIA.

Patrón de oro. Mensaje del ejecutivo é informe de
La Paz, Tip. lit. "Iris," 1906. 42 p. 8°.
INDUSTRIA: Informe de las comisiones de hacienda
rato ferroviario con el City Bank y los Srs. Speyer
ngo Heitmann. 55 pp. 8°.
ational City Bank, Speyer & Ca. Artículos pub-
" Texto del contrato. La Paz, Imp. de "El

Bolivia.   Ministerio de colonización y agricultura: Memoria que presenta el
Ministro de colonización y agricultura al Congreso ordinario de 1906.   La
Paz, Imprenta de " El Comercio de Bolivia," 1906. 45, lxxi p. 8°.

Carvajal, Walter: . . . Noche de duda. La Paz, Imp. Velarde, 1906. 39 p. 16°.

Daza, Lizandro Alvarez: Cultivo de la coca. Por Lizandro Alvarez Daza. (Artículos publicados en el "Comercio de Bolivia.") La Paz, Tall. Gráficos
" La Prensa" (1899). cover-title. 19 p. 8°.

Godchaud, G.: . . . Progrès et développement de la Bolivie. Par G. Godchaud
. . . J. de Lemoine . . . Extrait du bulletin de la Société Belge
d'études coloniales. Brussels, l'Imprimerie Nouvelle, 1906. 21 p. Map.
8°.

Marchant Y., Victor E.: . . . Estudio sobre la climatología de La Paz. Por
Victor E. Marchant Y. . . . La Paz, Tip. " La Patria," 1906. 48 p.
tables. 8°.
(At head of title: "Ministerio de Colonización y Agricultura.")

Nordenskiold, Erland: Sobre los mamíferos fósiles del valle de Tarija por Erland
Nordenskiold. . . . Buenos Aires, Imprenta de Coni hermanos, 1903.
10 p. illus. 8°.
(Artículo publicado en los "Anales de la Sociedad científica Argentina," t. 55, p. 255.)

Pinilla, Claudio: Contrato ferrocarrilero. Discusión del contrato Speyer en el H.
Senado nacional. Discurso pronunciado por el Ministerio de Relaciones
Exteriores, Don Claudio Pinilla. La Paz, Imp. y lit. Boliviana, 1906.
53 p. 8°.

Canal Zone.

United States Isthmian Canal Commission: Annual report of the Isthmian canal
commission for the year ending December 1, 1906. Washington, Government Printing Office, 1906. 153 p. 8°.

—— Special Message of the President of the United States concerning the
Panama canal. Communicated to the two Houses of Congress on December 17, 1906. (2d sess. of the 59th Congress.) Washington, Government
Printing Office, 1906. 33 p. map. illus. obl. 8°.

Chile.

Chile.   Dirección fiscal de alcantarillado: Breve exposición del trabajo realizado por la sección técnica. Presentada al delegado fiscal por . . .
Gerardo Van M. Brockman, noviembre 1905. Santiago de Chile, Sociedad "Imprenta y lit. Universo," 1906. 58 p. diagrs. maps. 4°.

—— Oficina central de estadística: Sinópsis estadística i jeográfica de la República de Chile en 1904. Santiago de Chile, Imprenta Cervantes, 1906.
576 p. 8°.

Comisión mixta Italo-Chilena: Alegato del ajente Chileno ante la excma. Comisión
mixta Italo-Chilena en la reclamación No. 351 de Don Felipe Diego
Schiattino contra el gobierno de Chile. Santiago de Chile, Imprenta
Nacional, 1887. 92 p. 8°.

Gautier, Ferdinand: Chili et Bolivie. Étude économique et minière. Paris, E.
Guilmoto, 1906. vi, 228 (1) p. map. 8°.

Orrego, José Manuel: Memoria sobre la civilización de los Araucanos leída el once
del corriente ante el consejo de la Sociedad evanjélica por el . . . Dr. B.
José Manuel Orrego . . . Santiago, Imprenta de la Sociedad, 1854. 39
(1) p. 12°.

Strain, Isaac G.: Sketches of a journey in Chili, and the Argentine provinces, in
1849. By Isaac G. Strain . . . New York, Horace H. Moore, 1853. xi,
295 p. 8°.

Costa Rica.

Gabb, William M.: Informe sobre la exploración de Talamanca. Verificada durante los años de 1873–74. Por William M. Gabb. San José, Tip. Nacional, 1894. 89 (4) p. 8°.

Pittier, H.: . . . Nombres geográficos de Costa Rica. I. Talamanca. (Primera contribución.) Por H. Pittier. San José, Tip. Nacional, 1895. 46 p. 8°.

—— Die sprache der Bribri-Indianer in Costa Rica von H. Pittier de Fabrega. Herausgegeben und mit einer vorrede versehen von Dr. Friedrich Müller . . . Wien, Carl Gerold's Sohn, 1898. 149 p. Map. 8°.

—— . . . Primitiæ floræ costaricensis. Par H. Pittier. Tome 2. San José, Tip. Nacional, 1898–1900. 405 p. 8°.

—— —— Same. Tome 3, no. 1 . . . San José, Tip. Nacional, 1901. cover-title. 62 (4) p. 8°.

Thiel, Bernardo A.: . . . Viajes á varias partes de la República de Costa Rica por el Dr. Bernardo A. Thiel, Obispado de Costa Rica, 1881–1896. San José, Tip. Nacional, 1896. 93 p. 8°.

(At head of title: "Instituto físico-geográfico nacional.")

Cuba.

Cuba. Ministerio de hacienda: Estadística general. Comercio exterior, primer semestre del año 1905 y año fiscal de 1904–1905. Habana, "La Universal," 1906. xiii, 188 p. diagr. 4°.

—— —— Regulations for the method procedure in the payment of interest coupons of bonds. Habana, November 22nd, 1906. [3] p. caption-title. 8°. (Text in Spanish and English.)

Dominican Republic.

[Customs service of Santo Domingo]: Customs receivership. Republic of Santo Domingo. Regulations and decisions. Administrative circulars nos. 1 to 39. Circular letters nos. 1 to 47. Volume 1. April 1, 1905, to June 30, 1906. Washington, Press of W. F. Roberts Company, 1906. 250 p. 8°. (Text in Spanish and English.)

Ecuador.

Guayaquil. Cámara de comercio: Memoria que presenta el presidente de la Cámara de comercio á la junta general de 17 de mayo de 1906. Guayaquil, Imprenta Mercantil, 1906. 79 p. 8°.

Haiti.

Ménos Solon [and others]: Œuvre des écrivains Haïtiens. Auteurs Haïtiens. Morceaux choisis précédés de notices biographiques par MM. Solon Ménos, Dantès Bellegarde, A. Duval, Georges Sylvain. Poésie. Port-au-Prince, Imprimerie de Mme. F. Smith, 1904. vi. 7–162 p. 8°.

Honduras.

American Honduras Company: Spanish Honduras, its rivers, lagoons, savannahs mountains, minerals, forests, fish, game, agricultural products, fruits, transportation and natives. New York, W. R. Gillespie, 1906. 183 p. illus. 8°.

Mexico.

Conkling, Howard: Mexico and the Mexicans; or notes of travel in the winter and spring of 1883. By Howard Conkling. New York, Taintor Brothers, Merrill & co., 1883. x, 298 p. front. plates. 8°.

FÖRSTEMANN, ERNST: ... Commentary on the Maya manuscript in the Royal public library of Dresden by Dr. Ernst Förstemann. Translated by Miss Selma Wesselhoeft and Miss A. M. Parker. Translation revised by the author. Cambridge, Mass., Published by the [Peabody] Museum, October, 1906. 266 (2) p. 8°.

(At head of title: "Papers of the Peabody Museum'. . . Harvard University. v. 4, no. 2.)

[GARCÍA, GENARO, ed.]: El Clero de México y la guerra de independencia. Documentos del Arzobispado de México. México, Ch. Bouret, 1906. 272 p. 12°.

(At head of title: "Documentos inéditos ó muy raros para la historia de México," t. 9.)

GRAY, ALBERT ZABRISKIE: Mexico as it is: being notes of a recent tour in that country; with some practical information for travellers in that direction, as also some study on the church question, by Albert Zabriskie Gray ... New York, E. P. Dutton & co., 1878. 148 p. front. illus. 8°.

GREAT BRITAIN. FOREIGN OFFICE: Report for the year 1905 on the trade and commerce of the consular district of Mexico. London, Harrison & Sons, 1906. 40 p. 8°.

———— Report for the year 1905–06 on the trade of Mexico. London, Harrison & Sons, 1906. 8 p. 8°. (Dip. & cons. repts. ann. ser. no. 3733.)

MÉXICO. DIRECCIÓN GENERAL DE ESTADÍSTICA: ... Anuario estadístico de la República Méxicana. 1904. Formado por la Dirección general de estadística ... México, Imprenta y fototipía do la Secretaría de fomento, 1906. 567 p. 4°.

———— Censo y división territorial del territorio de la Baja California verificados en 1900. México, Imprenta y fototipía de la Secretaría de fomento, 1905. 72, 21 p. 4°.

———— Same. Estado de Jalisco. . . . México, Imp. y fototipía de la Secretaría de fomento, 1905. 332, 159 p. 4°.

———— Same. Territorio de Tepic. México, Imprenta y fototipía de la Secretaría de fomento, 1905. 78, 29 p. 4°.

[POINSETT, JOEL ROBERTS]: Notes on Mexico, made in the autumn of 1822. Accompanied by an historical sketch of the revolution, and translations of official reports on the present state of that country . . . By a citizen of the United States. Philadelphia, H. C. Carey and I. Lea, 1824. vi, 359 p. map. 8°.

NICARAGUA.

MOSQUITO RESERVATION: Municipal constitution and annual laws of the Mosquito reservation for the seven years 1883 to 1891, inclusive. Savannah, Ga., The Morning News Print, 1892. vi, 119 p. 8°.

STOUT, PETER F.: Nicaragua: past, present, and future; a description of its inhabitants, customs, mines, minerals, early history, modern filibusterism, proposed inter-oceanic canal and manifest destiny. By Peter F. Stout. . . . Philadelphia, J. E. Potter, 1859. 372 p. map. 8°.

PARAGUAY.

PARAGUAY. DIRECCIÓN GENERAL DE CORREOS Y TELÉGRAFOS: Memoria de correos y telégrafos de la República del Paraguay presentada al P. E. de la nación por el Director general del ramo correspondiente al año de 1904. Asunción, Tip. "La Unión," 1906. 241 (1), ii p. maps. 4°.

———— PRESUPUESTO GENERAL DE GASTOS de la nación para el año 1907. Asunción, Tip. "La Unión," 1906. 68 p. 4°. (Anexo al No. 1791 del "Diario Oficial.")

PERU.

ADAMS, GEO. I.: . . . Caudal, procedencia y distribución de aguas de los Departamentos de la Libertad y Ancachs. Por Geo. I. Adams, Lima, Imprenta de "El Lucero," 1906. 58 p. maps. 8°.

(Boletín del Cuerpo de Ingenieros de Minas del Perú, No. 40.)

COMISIONES MIXTAS PERUANO-BRASILERAS: . . . Informes de las Comisiones mixtas Peruano-Brasileras. Encargadas del reconocimiento de los ríos Alto Purús i Alto Yurúa, de conformidad con el acuerdo provisional de Río Janeiro del 12 de julio de 1904. Lima, Oficina tip. de "La Opinión Nacional," 1906. xiii, 373 p. plates. maps. 8°.

PERÚ. MINISTERIO DE HACIENDA Y COMERCIO: Memoria que el Ministro de hacienda y comercio . . . presenta al congreso ordinario de 1906. Lima, Imprenta del Estado, 1906. cxxvii, 458 p. 8°.

STILES, ALBERTO I.: . . . Examen técnico de la laguna de Huarochiri del Departamento de Lima por Alberto I. Stiles. Lima, Imprenta La Industria, 1906. 128 p. maps. 8°.

(Boletín del Cuerpo de Ingenieros de Minas del Perú, No. 42.)

SUTTON, C. W.: . . . Informes sobre aguas del Departamento de Piura. Por C. W. Sutton y Alberto I. Stiles. Lima, Imprenta Carlos Prince, 1906. 26 p. maps. 8°.

(Boletín del Cuerpo de Ingenieros de Minas del Perú, No. 43.)

PHILIPPINE ISLANDS.

BLAIR AND ROBERTSON: The Philippine Islands. 1700-1736. Vols. 44 and 55. Cleveland, Arthur H. Clark Company, 1906. 2 v. 8°.

SOUTH AMERICA.

EISENSTEIN, RICHARD: Reise nach Panama, Peru, Chile mit Feuerland, Argentinien, Paraguay, Uruguay, und Brasilien. Tagebuch mit erörterungen, um zu überseeischen reisen und unternehmungen anzuregen. Von Richard, freiherr von und zu Eisenstein . . . Mit 310 abbildungen, 7 landkarten, 3 plänen und 2 verzeichnissen im text, 10 tabellen mit meteorologischen beobachtungen und einer reisekarte. Wien, K. Geroldssohn, 1906. (2) 380 p. illus. map. 8°.

MARTIN, PERCY F.: Through five republics of (South America) a critical description of Argentina, Brazil, Chile, Uruguay, and Venezuela in 1905. By Percy F. Martin . . . London, W. Heinemann, 1906. xxiv, 487 p. 92 pl. (incl. front.). 4 port. 3 fold. maps. 8°.

UNITED STATES.

ALEXANDER, LUCIEN HUGH: James Wilson, patriot, and the Wilson doctrine. By Lucien Hugh Alexander . . . Reprinted from the North American Review, mid-November issue, 1906. Vol. 183, no. 8. cover-title. 19 p. 8°.

BIRKINBINE, JOHN: . . . The production of iron ores in 1905. By John Birkinbine. Advance chapter from mineral resources of the U. S. 1905 . . . Washington, Government Printing Office, 1906. 38 p. 8°.

(At head of title: Dept. of the Interior, U. S. Geological survey.)

FOSTER, JOHN W.: The practice of diplomacy as illustrated in the foreign relations of the United States. By John W. Foster . . . Boston and New York, Houghton, Mifflin and company, 1906. 401 p. 8°.

LAKE MOHONK CONFERENCE OF FRIENDS OF THE INDIAN and other dependent peoples: Proceedings of the 24th annual meeting of the . . . conference . . . 1906. Published by the conference, 1906. 155 p. 8°.

NEW YORK PRODUCE EXCHANGE: Report of the New York Produce Exchange. With the charter, by-laws, and the several trade rules adopted by the exchange, and a list of its members. From July 1, 1905, to July 1, 1906. No imprint. 384 p. 8°.

PARKER, EDWARD W.: . . . The production of coal in 1905. By Edward W. Parker. Advance chapter from Mineral resources of the U. S., 1905 . . . Washington, Government Printing Office, 1906. 266 p. 8°.

(At head of title: Dept. of the Interior, U. S. Geological Survey.)

UNITED STATES. BUREAU OF THE CENSUS: Census of Manufactures: 1905. Ohio. Washington, Government Printing Office, 1906. 61 p. 4°. (Bull. 53.)

—— —— Child labor in the District of Columbia. Based on unpublished information derived from the schedules of the Twelfth Census: 1900. Washington, Government Printing Office, 1906. 21 p. 4°. (Bull. 68.)

—— BUREAU OF CORPORATIONS: Annual report of the Commissioner of Corporations to the Secretary of Commerce and Labor for the fiscal year ended June 30, 1906. Washington, Government Printing Office, 1906. 17 p. 8°.

—— BUREAU OF INSULAR AFFAIRS: Report of the Chief of the Bureau of Insular Affairs to the Secretary of War. 1906. Washington, Government Printing Office, 1906. 32 p. 8°.

—— BUREAU OF NAVIGATION: Annual report of the Commissioner of Navigation to the Secretary of Commerce and Labor. November 20, 1906. Washington, Government Printing Office, 1906. cover-title. 313 p. 8°.

—— CIVIL SERVICE COMMISSION: Civil service act, rules, and executive orders. Revision of the rules of April 15, 1903, with notes on the rules by the Commission, and legal decisions. Edition of November, 1906 . . . Washington, Government Printing Office, 1906. 89 p. 8°.

—— COMMISSION OF NATURALIZATION: Report to the president of the commission on naturalization. Submitted November 8, 1905 . . . Washington, Government Printing Office, 1906. 115 p. 8°. (U. S. 59th Cong., 1st sess., House doc. 46.)

—— CONGRESS: Official Congressional directory for use of the U. S. Congress. Compiled under the direction of the Joint Committee on Printing by A. J. Halford. 59th congress, 2d session. 1st ed. Corrections made to November 30, 1906. Washington, Government Printing Office, 1906. xix, 426 p. front. map. 8°.

—— DEPARTMENT OF THE INTERIOR: Report of the Secretary of the Interior for the fiscal year ended June 30, 1906. Washington, Government Printing Office, 1906. x, 336 p. 8°.

—— DEPARTMENT OF JUSTICE: Annual report of the Attorney-General of the U. S. for the year 1906. Washington, Government Printing Office, 1906. 47 p. 8°.

—— LIBRARY OF CONGRESS: Report of the Librarian of Congress and report of the Superintendent of the library building and grounds for the fiscal year June 30, 1906. Washington, Government Printing Office, 1906. 175 p. 8°.

—— MESSAGE OF THE PRESIDENT of the United States communicated to the two Houses of Congress at the beginning of the second session of the 59th Congress. Washington, Government Printing Office, 1906. 60 p. 8°.

—— TREASURY DEPARTMENT: Annual report of the Secretary of the Treasury on the state of the finances for the fiscal year ended June 30, 1906. Washington, Government Printing Office, 1906. 110 p. 8°.

UNIVERSITY OF PENNSYLVANIA: Transactions of the Department of Archaeology, Free Museum of Science and Art. Vol. 2, pt. 1. Philadelphia, Published by the Department of Archaeology, 1906. 105 p. plates. 4°.

URUGUAY.

ARAÚJO ORESTES: Historia de la escuela Uruguaya por Orestes Araújo . . . Tomo 2. Montevideo, Imp. Dornaleche y Reyes, 1906. 230, cviii p. 12°.

ASOCIACIÓN RURAL DEL URUGUAY: Catálogo de la gran exposición nacional anual de ganadería á celebrarse en Montevideo en los días 11, 12, 13 y 14 de noviembre de 1906 . . . Montevideo, Imprenta "Rural," 1906. 111 p. 8°.

GREAT BRITAIN. FOREIGN OFFICE. Report for the year 1905 on the trade and finance of the Republic of Uruguay . . . London, Harrison and Sons, 1906. 16 p. 8°. (Dip. & cons. repts. ann. ser. no. 3735.)

MONTEVIDEO. DIRECCIÓN DE CENSO Y ESTADÍSTICA DE MONTEVIDEO: Resumen anual de estadística municipal. Año 3 1905. Montevideo, "La Prensa," 1906. 289 (1) p. 4°.

URUGUAY. MINISTERIO DE RELACIONES EXTERIORES: Memoria presentada á la honorable asamblea general en el primer período de la xxii legislatura por el Ministro de relaciones exteriores. 1903–1904. Tomos 1 & 2. Montevideo, Tip. de la Escuela Nacional de Artes y Oficios, 1905. 2 v. 8°.

VENEZUELA.

LA FIESTA DEL ÁRBOL EN EL ESTADO ZULIA. 23 de mayo de 1905. No imprint. half-title. front. (port.). 158 p. 8°.

GIL FORTOUL, José: Historia constitucional de Venezuela. Por José Gil Fortoul. Tomo primero. La Colonia, la Independencia, la gran Colombia. Berlín, Carl Heymann, 1907. xi, 570 p. 8°

VENEZUELA. MENSAJE DEL PRESIDENTE al Congreso. 1894. 1895. 1896. 1902. Caracas. 4 pamphlets. 8°.

WEST INDIES.

STARK, JAMES H.: Stark's illustrated Bermuda guide; containing a description of everything on or about these places of which the visitor or resident may desire information, including their history, inhabitants, climate, agriculture, geology, government and resources . . . By James H. Stark. Boston, James H. Stark [1897]. viii, 153 (6) p. maps. plates. front. 8°.

GENERAL WORKS, REFERENCE BOOKS, AND BIBLIOGRAPHIES.

ALMANACH DE GOTHA. Annuaire généalogique, diplomatique et statistique. 1907. Gotha, Justus Perthes [1906]. xxiv, 1200 p. 16°.

ALMANACH POPULAR BRAZILERO para o anno de 1907. . . . Pelotas, Echenique Irmãos & cia., 1906. 284, xxxxi p. 12°.

BAKER AND TAYLOR COMPANY: Standard library catalogue of 2,500 approved books selected from the lists of all publishers, forming a complete and well balanced library of books recommended by the highest library authorities, and affording through its classification of subjects a basis of selection for libraries of a smaller number of books or for additions to established libraries. (2d revision.) New York, The Baker and Taylor Company, [1906]. 130 p. 12°.

BARTNETT, Walter J.: The federation of the World. By Walter J. Bartnett . . . San Francisco, The Murdock press, 1906. 16 p. 8°.

CUBA. DEPARTAMENTO DE ESTADO: Actas de la Tercera Conferencia International Americana y reseña de la sesión de clausura. Reunida en julio de 1906. Habana, Imprenta de Rambla y Bouza, 1906. 112 (1) p. 8°.

204 INTERNATIONAL BUREAU OF THE AMERICAN REPUBLICS.

Evans, A. E.: . . . A catalogue of the Aburi gardens, being a complete list of all the plants grown in the government botanical gardens at Aburi, Gold Coast, West Africa, together with their popular or local names, uses, habits and habitats: prepared for the Institute of commercial research in the Tropics by A. E. Evans, Curator of the Gardens. London, Williams & Norgate, 1906. 40 p. 8°.

Danvila y Collado, Manuel: Estudios críticos acerca de los orígenes y vicisitudes de la legislación escrita del antiguo reino de Valencia por el Dr. Don Manuel Danvila y Collado. Madrid, Jaime Ratés, 1905. 376 p. 4°.

Hutchinson, Lincoln: Report on trade conditions in Central America and on the west coast of South America. By Lincoln Hutchinson, special agent of the Department of Commerce and Labor. Washington, Government Printing Office, 1906. 113 p. 8°.

International Bureau of the American Republics: Annual report of the Director. 1906. Washington [Government Printing Office], 1906. 17 p. 8°.

———— ———— Same. In Spanish. 8p.

———— Monthly Bulletin. November, 1906. Vol. 23, no. 5. pp. 1027-1338. port. 8°.

CONTENTS.

Death of Señor Don José Muñoz.
Annual report of the Director.
The Central American Peace Conference.
Reception of the new Minister from Colombia in the United States.
Argentine Republic. Exports, first eight months, 1906; movement of the port of Rosario, first half, 1906, sugar output of Tucumán, unloading of inflammable material at Buenos Ayres; projected free zone.
Bolivia. Imports from New York and San Francisco; revenues of Tarija, first half of 1906, proposed public health law, tin from the Malay Peninsula.
Brazil. New President of the Republic, cabinet; customs revenues, January-June, 1906; commerce of Santos, January-August, 1906; the coffee market in September, 1906; coffee movement, August, 1906; report on Perini fiber, the jerked beef industry; port improvement works of Rio Grande do Sul; United States consular reports on rubber growing.
Chile. The production of nitrate in 1906, bank statement, July 31, 1906; comparative trade values, 1905, port movement of Valparaiso 1905, trade with Uruguay during 1905, postal movement during 1905, trade with Ecuador in 1905.
Colombia. Fiscal revenues, February-July, 1906 patents granted to American inventors; registration of United States trade-marks, mission of a foreign agricultural agent.
Costa Rica. Budget for 1906-7, agricultural and pastoral statistics; appraisement of sheet iron for chimneys.
Cuba. Revenues from consular fees, 1903-4 to 1905-6, analysis of foreign trade, report of the Cuban railway.
Ecuador. Suspension of the new tariff, telegraph rates railroad from Huigra to Cuenca.
Guatemala. Coffee shipments from Champerico.
Haiti. Payment of import duties in gold.
Mexico. Foreign commerce, July 1906 details of the trade with the United States during 1905-6; silver basis of the stamp and customs taxes for November, 1906 customs revenues, first quarter of 1906-7, consolidation of narrow-gauge lines, operations of the Mexican railway, first half of 1906 ; trade of Porfirio Diaz, gold and silver production, 1900-1906; school statistics, utilization of guayule refuse; customs surtax at specified ports, concession for the exploitation of guano, consular reports.
Nicaragua. Mining code, exports in 1906, gold mining in the Republic.
Panama. Public revenues from September, 1904, to June, 1906.
Paraguay Foreign trade, 1 03-1905, and first half of 1906.
Peru. Trade with New York, first half of 1906, exports and imports of Iquitos, first half of 1906 rubber exports from Iquitos, first half of 1906, United States consular reports on quinine cultivation.
Salvador. Budget for 1906-7, revenues during the first quarter of 1906; commerce in 1905.

CONTENTS—continued.

LEONARD, JOHN W.: Who's who in America. A biographical dictionary of notable
living men and women of the United States. 1906–1907. . . . Edited
by John W. Leonard. Chicago, A. N. Marquis & company, [1906].
xxxii, 2080 p. 8°.

POOR'S MANUAL OF THE RAILROADS OF THE UNITED STATES. 1906. Street railway
and traction companies, industrial and other corporations and statements
of the debts of the United States, the several states, municipalities, etc.
New York, Poor's Railroad Manual Co., 1906. 124, xvi, 1808, 13 p.
maps. 8°.

PURCHAS, SAMUEL: Hakluytus posthumus or Purchas, his pilgrimes . . . By Samuel
Purchas. Glasgow, James MacLehose and sons, 1906. Vols. 17, 18, and
19. 3 v. 8°.

ROOT, ELIHU: Speeches incident to the visit of Secretary Root to South America.
July 4 to September 30, 1906. Washington, Government Printing Office,
1906. xv, 300 p. 8°.

ROTHWELL, RICHARD P.: Mineral industry; its statistics, technology, and trade.
Founded by Richard P. Rothwell . . . 1905. New York and London,
The Engineering and Mining Journal, 1906. xix, 739 p. 8°.

SUBERCASEAUX, B. VICUÑA: Los congresos Pan-Americanos. Artículos publicados en
"El Mercurio" por B. Vicuña Subercaseaux, Secretario de la delegación
de Chile á la Tercera Conferencia International Americana. Santiago de
Chile, Sociedad "Imprenta y lit. Universo," 1906. 113 p. 18°.

PERMANENT LIBRARY FILES.

Those publications marked with an asterisk have no recent numbers on file.

Persons interested in the commercial and general news of foreign countries will find the following among the official and periodical publications on the permanent files in the Columbus Memorial Library, International Bureau of the American Republics:

ARGENTINE REPUBLIC.

Boletín de la Cámara Mercantil. Barracas al Sud. Weekly.
Boletín Consular. (Ministerio de relaciones exteriores.) Buenos Ayres. Irregular.
Boletín de la Unión Industrial Argentina. Buenos Ayres. Monthly.
* Boletín del Instituto Geográfico Argentino. Buenos Ayres.
* Boletín Demográfico Argentino. Buenos Ayres. Monthly.
* Boletín Oficial de la República Argentina. Buenos Ayres. Daily.
Boletín de Precios Corrientes. [Buenos Aires.] Weekly.
Bollettino Mensile della Camera Italiana di Commercio ed Arti in Buenos Aires. Buenos Ayres. Monthly.
Buenos Aires Handels-Zeitung. Buenos Ayres. Weekly.
Buenos Aires Herald. Buenos Ayres. Daily and weekly.
* El Comercio Exterior Argentino. Buenos Ayres.
La Ilustración Sud-Americana. Buenos Ayres. Semimonthly.
Monthly Bulletin of Municipal Statistics of the City of Buenos Ayres. Buenos Ayres. Monthly.
La Nación. Buenos Ayres. Daily.
Patentes y Marcas, Revista Sud-Americana de la Propiedad Intelectual é Industrial. Buenos Ayres. Monthly.
La Prensa. Buenos Ayres. Daily
Review of the River Plate. Buenos Ayres. Weekly.
Revista Mensual de la Cámara Mercantil. Barracas al Sud. Monthly.
Revista Nacional. Buenos Ayres. Monthly.
The Standard. Buenos Ayres. Mail supplement.

BELGIUM.

Recueil consulaire. Bruxelles. Quarterly.

BOLIVIA.

Boletín de la Oficina Nacional de Inmigracion, Estadística y Propaganda Geográfica. La Paz. Quarterly.
Boletín de la Sociedad Geográfica de la Paz. La Paz. Irregular.
* El Comercio. La Paz. Daily.
El Estado. (Diario Oficial.) La Paz. Daily.
* Revista Comercial é Industrial de la República de Bolivia. La Paz. Monthly.
Revista del Ministerio de Colonización y Agricultura. La Paz. Quarterly.

BRAZIL.

Boletim da Agricultura. Secretario da Agricultura, Commercio e Obras Publicas do Estado de São Paulo. Sao Paulo. Monthly.

Boletim do Museo Goeldi. Pará. Monthly.

Boletim da Secretaria de Agricultura, Viação, Industria e Obras Publicas do Estado da Bahia. Bahia. Monthly.

* Boletim de Serviço da Estatistica Commercial da Republica dos Estados Unidos do Brazil. Rio de Janeiro. Irregular.

* Brazilian Mining Review. Ouro Preto. Irregular.

Brazilian Review. Rio de Janeiro. Weekly.

Diario da Bahia. Bahia. Daily.

Diario do Congresso Nacional. Rio de Janeiro. Daily.

Diario Oficial. Rio de Janeiro. Daily.

* Gazeta Commercial e Financeira. Rio de Janeiro. Weekly.

* Jornal do Commercio. Rio de Janeiro. Daily.

Jornal do Recife. Pernambuco. Daily.

Jornal dos Agricultores. Rio de Janeiro. Semimonthly.

O Paiz. Rio de Janeiro. Daily.

Provincia (A) do Pará. Belem. Daily.

Revista Agricola. Sao Paulo. Monthly.

* Revista Brazileira. Rio de Janeiro. Monthly.

* Revista Industrial e Mercantil. Pernambuco. Monthly.

Revista Maritima Brazileira. Rio de Janeiro. Monthly.

CHILE.

Anales de La Universidad. Santiago. Monthly.

Boletín del Ministerio de Relaciones Esteriores. Santiago. Monthly.

Boletín de la Sociedad Agrícola del Sur. Concepción. Semimonthly.

Boletín de la Sociedad de Fomento Fabril. Santiago. Monthly.

Boletín de la Sociedad Nacional de Agricultura. Santiago. Weekly.

Boletín de la Sociedad Nacional de Minería. Santiago. Monthly.

Chilian Times. Valparaiso. Semiweekly.

Diario Oficial de la República de Chile. Santiago. Daily.

El Mercurio. Valparaiso. Daily.

El Noticiero Comercial. Santiago de Chile. Monthly.

El Pensamiento. Santiago. Monthly.

* Revista Comercial é Industrial de Minas. Santiago. Monthly.

COLOMBIA.

Diario Oficial. Bogota. Daily.

Revista de la Instrucción Pública de Colombia. Bogota. Monthly.

COSTA RICA.

Boletín Judicial. San Jose. Daily.

La Gaceta. (Diario Oficial.) San Jose. Daily.

Limon Weekly News. Port Limon. Weekly. (Suspended until further notice.)

CUBA.

Boletín Oficial de la Cámara de Comercio, Industria y Navegación de la Isla de Cuba. Habana Monthly.

Boletín Oficial del Departamento del Estado. Habana. Monthly.

Diario de la Marina. Habana. Daily.

Derecho y Sociología. Habana. Monthly.

El Estudio. Boletín de Derecho, Legislación, Jurisprudencia y Administración.
   Habana. Trimonthly.
La Gaceta Económica. Habana. Semimonthly.
Gaceta Oficial de la República de Cuba. Habana. Daily.
Informe Mensual Sanitario y Demográfico de la República de Cuba. Habana.
   Monthly.
Informe Mensual Sanitario y Demográfico de Cienfuegos. Cienfuegos. Monthly.
Informe Mensual Sanitario y Demográfico de Matanzas. Matanzas. Monthly.
Revista Municipal y de Intereses Económicos. Habana. Semimonthly.

DOMINICAN REPUBLIC.

Gaceta Oficial. Santo Domingo. Weekly.
Revista de Agricultura. Santo Domingo. Monthly.

ECUADOR.

Anales de la Universidad Central del Ecuador. Quito. Monthly.
Gaceta Municipal. Guayaquil. Weekly.
Registro Oficial de la República del Ecuador. Quito. Daily.

FRANCE.

Les Annales Diplomatiques et Consulaires. Paris. Monthly.
Bulletin American Chamber of Commerce. Paris. Monthly.
Bulletin de la Chambre de Commerce de Paris. Paris. Weekly.
Bulletin de la Société de Géographie Commerciale de Paris. Paris. Irregular.
La Géographie. Bulletin de la Société de Géographie. Paris. Semimonthly.
Journal d'Agriculture Tropicale. Paris. Monthly.
Moniteur Officiel du Commerce. Paris. Weekly.
Le Nouveau Monde. Paris. Weekly.
Rapports commerciaux des agents diplomatiques et consulaires de France. Paris.
   Irregular. [Sup. to "Moniteur officiel du commerce."]
La Revue. Paris. Semimonthly.
* Revue du Commerce Extérieur. Paris. Semimonthly.

GERMANY.

Berichte über handel und industrie. Berlin. Irregular.
* Deutsche Kolonialzeitung. Berlin. Weekly.
Petermann's Mitteilungen. Gotha. Monthly.
Südamerikanische Rundschau. Berlin. Monthly.
Der Tropenpflanzer. Berlin. Monthly.
Zeitschrift der Gesellschaft für Erdkunde zu Berlin. Berlin. Monthly.

GREAT BRITAIN.

Board of Trade Journal. London. Weekly.
British Trade Journal. London. Monthly.
Commercial Intelligence. London. Weekly.
Diplomatic and Consular Reports. London.
Geographical Journal. London. Monthly.
Mining (The) Journal, Railway and Commercial Gazette. London. Weekly.
The Scottish Geographical Magazine. Edinburgh. Monthly.
South American Journal. London. Weekly.
Times (The). London. Daily. (Filed for one year.)
Tropical Life. London. Monthly.

GUATEMALA.

Boletín de Agricultura. Guatemala. Irregular.
El Guatemalteco. Guatemala. Daily. (Diario Oficial.)
La Locomotora. Guatemala. Monthly.
*La República. Guatemala. Daily.

HAITI.

*Bulletin Officiel de l'Agriculture et de l'Industrie. Port au Prince. Monthly.
*Le Moment. (Journal politique.) Port au Prince, Haiti. Weekly.
Le Moniteur. (Journal officiel de la République d'Haïti.) Port au Prince, Haiti.
   Biweekly.
Revue de la Société de Législation. Port au Prince, Haiti. Monthly.

HONDURAS.

Boletín Legislativo. Tegucigalpa. Daily.
El Estado. Tegucigalpa. (3 nos. per week.)
La Gaceta. Tegucigalpa. Daily. (Official paper.)
*Gaceta Judicial. Tegucigalpa. Semiweekly.
*El Pabellón de Honduras. Tegucigalpa. Weekly.
*El Republicano. (Semi-official.) Tegucigalpa. Three times a week.
Revista del Archivo y Biblioteca Nacional de Honduras. Tegucigalpa, Honduras.
   Monthly.

ITALY.

Bollettino del Ministro degli Affari Esteri. Roma. Irregular.

MEXICO.

El Agricultor Mexicano. Ciudad Juarez. Monthly.
Anales del Museo Nacional de México. Mexico. Monthly.
Boletín de Estadística. Merida. Semimonthly.
Boletín del Instituto Científico y Literario. Toluca. Monthly.
Boletín Oficial del Distrito sur de la Baja California. La Paz. Weekly.
Boletín de la Secretaría de Fomento colonización é industria. Mexico. Monthly.
Boletín Oficial de la Secretaría de Relaciones Exteriores. Mexico. Monthly.
Diario Oficial. Mexico. Daily.
El Economista Mexicano. Mexico. Weekly.
*El Estado de Colima. Colima. Weekly.
El Hacendado Mexicano. Mexico. Monthly.
Mexican Herald. Mexico. Daily. (Filed for one year.)
Mexican Investor. Mexico. Weekly.
Mexican Journal of Commerce. Mexico City. Monthly.
Periódico Oficial del Gobierno del Estado de Guerrero. Chilpancingo, Mexico.
   Weekly.
Periódico Oficial del Gobierno del Estado de Michoacán de Ocampo. Morelia.
   Mexico. Semiweekly.
*Periódico Oficial del Gobierno del Estado de Oaxaca. Oaxaca de Juarez, Mexico.
   Semiweekly.
Periódico Oficial del Gobierno del Estado de Tabasco. San Juan Bautista, Mexico.
   Semiweekly.
El Republicano. Aguascalientes. Weekly.
Semana Mercantil. Mexico. Weekly.

NICARAGUA.

The American. Bluefields. Weekly.
El Comercio. Managua. Daily.
Diario Oficial. Managua. Daily.

PANAMA.

Gaceta Oficial. Panama. Daily.
Star and Herald. Panama. Weekly.
La República. Panama. Weekly.
Registro Judicial, Organo del Poder Judicial de la República. Panama. Irregula

PARAGUAY.

* Boletín Quincenal de la Cámara de Comercio de la Asunción.* Asuncion. Sem
monthly.
Diario Oficial. Asuncion. Daily.
Paraguay Rundschau. Asuncion. Weekly.
* Revista del Instituto Paraguayo. Asuncion. Monthly.
Revue Commerciale. Assumption. Semimonthly.

PERÚ.

Auxiliar del Comercio. Callao. Biweekly.
Boletín de Minas, Industrias y Construcciones. Lima. Monthly.
Boletín del Ministerio de Fomento. Dirección de Fomento. Lima. Monthly.
―――― Dirección de Obras Públicas. Lima. Monthly.
Boletín de la Sociedad Geográfica de Lima. Lima. Quarterly.
Boletín de la Sociedad Nacional de Agricultura. Lima. Monthly.
Boletín de la Sociedad Nacional de Minería. Lima. Monthly.
* El Economista. Lima. Weekly.
* El Peruano. (Diario Oficial.) Lima. Daily.
Padrón General de Minas. Lima. Semiannual.
Revista de Ciencias. Lima. Monthly.
Revista Pan-Americana. Lima. Monthly.

PHILIPPINE ISLANDS.

Boletín de la Cámara de Comercio Filipina. Manila. Monthly.
El Mercantil. Manila. Daily.
Official Gazette. Manila. Weekly. (Also issued in Spanish.)

PORTO RICO.

La Correspondencia de Puerto Rico. San Juan. Daily.

EL SALVADOR.

Anales del Museo Nacional. San Salvador. Monthly.
Boletín de Agricultura. San Salvador. Semimonthly.
Boletín de la Dirección General de Estadística. San Salvador. Irregular.
Diario del Salvador. San Salvador. Daily.
Diario Oficial. San Salvador. Daily.
* Revista de Derecho y Jurisprudencia. San Salvador. Monthly.

SWITZERLAND.

La Propriété Industrielle. Berne. Monthly.

UNITED STATES.

American Druggist. New York. Semimonthly.
American Exporter. New York. Semimonthly. (Alternate Spanish and English editions.)
American Historical Review. New York. Quarterly.
American Made Goods. New York. Quarterly.
American Review of Reviews. New York. Monthly.
Anna's of the American Academy of Political and Social Science. Philadelphia. Bimonthly.
El Boletín Comercial. St. Louis. Monthly.
Bookman (The). New York. Monthly.
Bulletin of the American Geographical Society. New York.
Bulletin of Books added to the Public Library of the City of Boston. Boston. Monthly.
Bulletin of the Geographical Society of Philadelphia. Philadelphia. Monthly.
Bulletin of the New York Public Library. Monthly.
Century Magazine. New York. Monthly.
El Comercio. New York. Monthly.
Current Literature. New York. Monthly.
Dun's Review. New York. Weekly.
Dun's Review. International edition. New York. Monthly.
Engineering Magazine. New York. Monthly.
Engineering and Mining Journal. New York. Weekly.
Engineering News. New York. Weekly.
Export Implement Age. Philadelphia. Monthly.
Exporters and Importers Journal. New York. Monthly.
Field Columbian Museum Publications. Chicago.
Forum (The). New York. Quarterly.
Independent (The). New York. Weekly.
India Rubber World. New York. Monthly.
International Buyer. New York. Semimonthly. (Alternate Spanish and English editions.)
Journal of Geography. New York. Monthly.
Library Journal. New York. Monthly.
Literary Digest. New York. Weekly.
* Mexican Industrial Review. Chicago. Monthly.
Mines and Minerals. Scranton, Pa. Monthly.
Mining Magazine. New York. Monthly.
Mining World. Chicago. Weekly.
Modern Mexico. St. Louis. Monthly.
Monthly Consular and Trade Reports. (Department of Commerce and Labor.) Washington. Monthly.
National Geographic Magazine. New York. Monthly.
North American Review. New York. Monthly.
Las Novedades. New York. Weekly.
Outlook (The). New York. Weekly.
Pan-American Review. New York. Monthly.
Patent and Trade Mark Review. New York. Monthly.
Records of the Past. Washington, D. C. Monthly.
Scientific American. New York. Weekly.
Scientific American. Export Edition. New York. Monthly.
Sister Republics. Denver, Colo. Monthly.
Tea and Coffee Trade Journal. New York. Monthly.

Technical World (The). Chicago. Monthly.
United States Tobacco Journal. New York. Weekly.
World To-day (The). Chicago. Monthly.
World's Work. New York. Monthly.

URUGUAY.

Anales del Departamento de Ganadería y Agricultura. Montevideo. Monthly.
* Montevideo Times. Montevideo. Daily.
Revista de la Asociación Rural del Uruguay. Montevideo. Monthly.
Revista de la Unión Industrial Uruguaya. Montevideo. Semimonthly.

VENEZUELA.

Boletín de Estadística. Caracas. Monthly.
El Fonógrafo. Maracaibo. Daily.
El Heraldo Industrial. Caracas. Semimonthly.
Gaceta Oficial. Caracas. Daily.
* Venezuelan Herald. Caracas.

BALDWIN, SIMEON E.: The comparative results in the advancement of private international law of the Montevideo congress of 1888–9 and The Hague conference of 1893, 1894, 1900, and 1904. By Simeon E. Baldwin . . . Baltimore, 1906. Cover-title. 15 p. 8°.
(Reprinted from the Proceedings of the American Political Science Association.)

BARTNETT, WALTER J.. The federation of the World. By Walter J. Bartnett . . . San Francisco, The Murdock press, 1906. 16 p. 8°.

BENAVIDES, RAFAEL: La Prusia Militar . . . por el General Mejicano Rafael Benavides. New York, Imprenta de Hallett & Breen, 1873. xv, 704, vi (1) p. 8°.

BLUE BOOK OF AMERICAN SHIPPING: Marine [and] naval directory of the United States. 1906. 11th annual edition . . . Cleveland, The Penton publishing company, [1906]. 509 p. front. 4°.

BOLLAERT, WILLIAM: Antiquarian, ethnological, and other researches in New Granada, Ecuador, Peru, and Chile, with observations on the pre-Incarial, Incarial, and other monuments of Peruvian nations. By William Bollaert . . . London, Trübner & co., 1860. 279 p. pls. map. 8°.

CANADIAN YEARBOOK FOR 1906. Toronto, Printed at the office of the Canadian Yearbook, [1906]. Cover-title. 406 p. 8°.

CONGRESSO SCIENTIFICO LATINO-AMERICANO (terceira reunião) celebrado na cidade do Rio de Janeiro em 6 a 16 de agosto de 1905. Relatio geral . . . 1° tomo. Trabalhos preliminares e inauguração do Congresso. Rio de Janeiro, Imprensa Nacional, 1906. 207 p. 8°.

CUBA. DEPARTAMENTO DE ESTADO: Actas de la tercera Conferencia internacional Americana y reseña de la sesión de clausura. Reunida en Rio de Janeiro en julio de 1906. Habana, Imprenta de Rambla y Bouza, 1906. 112, (1) p. 8°.

DANVILA Y COLLADO, MANUEL: Estudios críticos acerca de los orígenes y vicisitudes de la legislación escrita del antiguo reino de Valencia por el Dr. Don Manuel Danvila y Collado. Madrid, Jaime Ratés, 1905· 376 p. 4°.

DRAGO, LUIS M.: . . . Cobro coercitivo de deudas públicas. Buenos Aires, Coni Hermanos, 1906. 169, (1) p. 8°.

EISENSTEIN, RICHARD: Reise nach Panama, Peru, Chile mit Feuerland, Argentinien, Paraguay, Uruguay und Brasilien. Tagebuch, mit erörterungen, um zu überseeischen reisen und unternehmungen anzuregen. Von Richard, freiherr von und zu Eisenstein . . . Mit 310 abbildungen, 7 landkarten, 3 planen und 2 verzeichnissen im text, 10 tabellen mit meteorologischen beobachtungen und einer reisekarte. Wien, K. Gerolds sohn, 1906. (2), 380 p. illus. map. 8°.

EVANS, A. E.: . . . A catalogue of the Aburi gardens, being a complete list of all the plants grown in the government botanical gardens at Aburi, Gold Coast, West Africa, together with their popular or local names, uses, habits, and habitats; prepared for the Institute of Commercial Research in the Tropics by A. E. Evans, Curator of the Gardens. London, Williams & Norgate, 1906. 40 p. 8°.

EXPORTERS' ENCYCLOPÆDIA COMPANY: Exporters' encyclopædia. New York. Published by the Exporters' encyclopædia company, 1907. xvi, 633 p. 8°.

GARCIA, ANDRES J. R. V.: Dictionary of engineering terms in English and Spanish, indexes in both languages. Containing 3,000 technical terms. By Andres J. R. V. Garcia. New York, Spon & Chamberlain, 1906. xxxvi, 150 p. 12°.

GEOLOGICAL SURVEY OF CANADA: Annual report. New series. vols. 14 and 15. 1901–1903. Ottawa, Printed by S. E. Dawson, 1905–1906. 2 v. 8°.

—— Maps to accompany annual report, vol. 15. 21 maps in case.

HART, J. HINCHLEY: Cacao. A treatise on the cultivation and curing of "cacao By J. Hinchley Hart . . . Second edition. Trinidad, Printed at t "Mirror" office, Port of Spain, 1900. vi, 117 p. 8°.

HELPER, HINTON ROWAN: . . . Projected intercontinental railway through t three Americas. . . . Letter from Mr. Hinton Rowan Helper . . Washington, Government Printing Office, 1906. 21 p. 8°.
(U. S. Senate, 59th cong., 1st sess., doc. no. 504.)

HEYNE, PAUL: Practical dictionary of electrical engineering and chemistry in G man, English, and Spanish. Treating especially of modern machi industry, the foundry, and metallurgy. By Paul Heyne . . . In volumes. Dresden, Published by Gerhard Kühtmann, 1899. 3 v. 8°.

HUTCHINSON, LINCOLN: Report on trade conditions in Argentina, Paraguay, and U1 guay, by Lincoln Hutchinson. Washington, Government Printing Offi 1906. 101 p. 8°.

—— Report on the trade conditions in Central America and on the west coast South America. By Lincoln Hutchinson, special agent of the Departme of Commerce and Labor. Washington, Government Printing Office, 190 113 p. 8°.

HISTORY OF SIMON BOLIVAR, Liberator of South America. London, Printed by Cls ton & Co., 1876. 56 p. front. (port.). 12°.

INTERNATIONAL AMERICAN CONFERENCE: La adhesión de la Segunda Conferencia Int nacional Americana á las convenciones de La Haya. Incidente prom vido por la Delegación de Chile en México con motivo de la publicaci del protocolo de adhesión á las Convenciones de La Haya en el volum titulado: "Recomendaciones, Resoluciones y Tratados" de la Conferen México, Tipografía de la Oficina Impresora de Estampillas, Palacio Nacion 1902. 69 p. 4°.

—— . . . Crónica social, 1901. México, [F. Laso y comp., Impresores, 1902 379 p. plates. photos. 4°.

—— Resolutions of the Third International American Conference relating to t International Bureau of American Republics. [Reprinted from "Ac geral Terceira Conferencia Internacional Americana" Rio de Janeir Imprenta Nacional, 1906.] caption title. 8 p. 8°.

—— —— Same. Spanish translation.

INTERNATIONAL BUREAU OF THE AMERICAN REPUBLICS: Annual report of the Directc 1906. Washington, Government Printing Office, 1906. 17 p. 8°.

—— —— Same. In Spanish. 8 p.

—— Monthly Bulletin. July, 1906. Vol. 23, no. 1. Washington, Governme Printing Office, 1906. 338 p. 8°. (Appendix: "Additions to the Colu bus Memorial Library, January–June, 1906." xlvii p.)

CONTENTS.

Tuberculosis Congress.

Argentine Republic. Foreign commerce, first quarter of 1906; exports first fc months of 1906; pastoral and agricultural census of the national territories; li stock census of Entre Rios; internal revenue, first quarter, 1906; State licenses commercial travelers; Rosario port works.

Bolivia. Trade with the United States, first half of 1906; merchandise exported fr New York and San Francisco to Bolivia in the months of April, May, and June, 19

Brazil. Boundary treaty with Dutch Guiana; commerce of Santos, first four mont of 1906, exports of hides from Rio Grande do Sul; port movements of Para a Manaos; the mineral industry.

Chile. Message of President Riesco; purchase of railway material.

Colomb's. New Cabinet.

Costa Rica. Inaugural message of President Gonzales Viquez; sketch of Preside Viquez; message of President Esquivel; the mining industry in 1905.

Ecuador. Construction of a sewage system: new honorary corresponding member

Guatemala. Land laws.

Honduras. New consular charges.

of land in 1905; wool clip of 1905-6; condi-
...

...bushing enterprise; merchandise shipped

...import duties on United States products;
...in 1905; status of the flour trade; immi-
...of Mangabeira rubber; exports of hides from
...first five months, 1906; rubber entries at
...; status of the wine market; extension of

...; United States market for nitrate of soda;

...les and telegraphs; exploitation of subma-

...; new cabinet.
...bonus statistics; tariff changes; encourage-
...he clearance of crude petroleum.
...nditures during 1905.
...dustries; abolition of certain Government
...d Bahia de Caraquez; bids for railroad from
...mote immigration.
...Transcontinental Railway.

...s in 1906; suspension of free entry for certain
...d.
...06; foreign commerce, first nine months,
...nths, 1905-6; shipment of zinc ore in bond;
...months, 1905-6; basis of the stamp tax for
..., July-December, 1906; postal service, May,
...s; customs receipts, June, 1906; extension
...ntana Roo; ratification of the Sanitary Con-
...and Industry; communication facilities of
...turalization of foreigners; new smelter at
...ents at Veracruz; railroad construction in

...th New York.

...f public revenues during the years 1896 to
...tamp duty on imports; La Libertad-Nueva
...ons; tariff changes.
...ca; foreign commerce, fiscal year, 1906; dis-
...regulations for the supply of construction
...of Philippine commerce.

INTERNATIONAL BUREAU OF THE AMERICAN REPUBLICS: Monthly Bulletin. September, 1906. Vol. 23, no. 3. Washington, Government Printing Office, 1906. pp. 583–773. 8°.

CONTENTS.

——— Monthly Bulletin. October, 1906. vol. 23, No. 4. pp. 775–1026. 8°.

CONTENTS.

er, 1906; bank statement; exports to Spain in

rica; foreign commerce, August, 1906; report
mparative exports of British and American
our York custom-house, 1906; increased imports

it; distribution of seed wheat; free entry of
promises in Montevideo, improved shipping ·

used Puerto Cabello, second half, 1906; bounty
on earthenware.

mmmmmm Monthly Bulletin. Novem-
gton, Government Printing Office, 1906.

s.
lombia in the United States.
ight months, 1906; movement of the port of
of Tucumán; unloading of inflammable mate-
nas.
San Francisco; revenues of Tarija, first half of
from the Malay Peninsula.
de; Cabinet; customs revenues, January-June,
August, 1906; the coffee market in September
report on Parini fiber; the jerked beef industry;
inde do Sul; United States consular reports on

06; bank statement, July 31, 1906; comparative
f Valparaiso, 1906; trade with Uruguay during
rade with Ecuador in 1906.
July, 1906; patents granted to American invent-
rade-marks; mission of a foreign agricultural

INTERNATIONAL BUREAU OF THE AMERICAN REPUBLICS: Monthly Bulletin. December, 1906. vol. 23, No. 6. Washington, Government Printing Office, 1906. pp. 1339-1608. 8°.

CONTENTS.

ied goods, 1905–6; exports of farm products and oils, October,
first nine months, 1906; postals-post convention with Peru;
for the extension of foreign commerce; conditions of the
cts; the wealth of the country.
the production of sugar; internal development and fluvial

shipping appointment of certain agricultural implements;
k, February, 1906.

rtion, 1905: Transactions of the Second International
f the American Republics. Held at the New Willard
). C., October 9, 10, 12, 13, and 14, 1905, under the
ing Board of the International Union of the Ameri-
gton, Government Printing Office, 1906. 460 p. 8°.
INTERNATIONAL ARBITRATION: Report of the twelfth
) . . . Conference. 1906. . . . Published by the
ence . . . 1906. 177 p. 8°.
in America. A biographical dictionary of notable
en of the United States. 1906–7. Edited by John
o, A. N. Marquis & Co., [1906]. xxxii, 2080 p. 8°.
or naturalización. Tokio, 1903. 416 (2) p. 12°.
republics of (South America); a critical description
Chile, Uruguay, and Venezuela in 1905. By Perry
don, W. Heinemann, 1906. xxiv, 487 p. 92 pl.
. 3 fold maps. 8°.
covery in America. By Charles Morris . . . Phila-
. B. Lippincott Co., 1906. 344 p. front. pls. 12°.
Americanismo. Rio de Janeiro, Typ. do "Jornal
. 220 p. 8°.
ADS OF THE UNITED STATES, 1906: Street railway and
ndustrial and other corporations, and statements of
l States, the several States, municipalities, etc. New
Manual Co., 1906. 124. xvi, 1808, 13 p. maps. 8°.
soit international public européen et américain . . .
. . . Tome 8. Paris, A. Pedone, 1906. 965 p. 8°
sthumus; or, Purchas his Pilgrimes. Contayning a
in sea voyages and lande travells, by Englishmen
uel Purchas. Vols. 13–19. Glasgow, James Mac-
7 v. 8°.
s irregulares da lingua portugueza . . . Compilado
lo R. . . . Rio de Janeiro, Typ. Nacional, 1880.

seasons Company (publishers): Railway appliances
. For the promotion of export trade. . . . Pub-
lailway Equipment and Publication Company. New
8°.
cretary of State of the United States of America as
nt of the Third Conference of American Republics
ly 31, 1906. Half-title. No imprint. 11 p. 8°.
visit of Secretary Root to South America. July 4
3. Washington, Government Printing Office, 1906.

ROTHWELL, RICHARD P.: Mineral industry, its statistics, technology, and trade. Founded by Richard P. Rothwell . . . New York and London, The Engineering and Mining Journal, 1906.   xix, 739 p.   8°.

[SEABRA, ALBERTO]: Ensaios de pan-americanismo.   S. Paulo, Typ. Anesio Azambuja & Ca., 1906.   84 (1) p.   8°.

SIMMONDS, P. L.: Tropical agriculture.   A treatise on the culture, preparation, commerce, and consumption of the principal products of the vegetable kingdom.   By P. L. Simmonds . . . London, E. & F. N. Spon, 1889.   539 p. 8°.

SIVERS, JEGÓR VON: Ueber Madeira und die Antillen nach Mittelamerika.   Reisedenkwürdigkeiten und Forschungen von Jegór von Sivers.   Leipzig, C. F. Fleischer, 1861.   xii, 389 p.   8°.

SUBERCASEAUX, B. VICUÑA: Los congresos pan-americanos.   Artículos publicados en "El Mercurio" por B. Vicuña Subercaseaux, secretario de la delegación de Chile á la Tercera Conferencia Internacional Americana.   Santiago de Chile, Sociedad "Imprenta y Lit. Universo," 1906.   113 p.   12°.

UNITED STATES.   ARMY WAR COLLEGE: Author and title list of accessions to the Army War College library, including maps and index of periodicals, for the fiscal year 1906.   [Washington, Government Printing Office, 1906.]   52 p.   8°.

—— BUREAU OF MANUFACTURES: Reports by American consular officers relative to trade conditions in Latin America.   Published in Daily Consular and Trade Reports, July 1, 1905, to April 20, 1906.   With index prepared in Bureau of Trade Relations, Department of State, May, 1906.   405 numbered p. 8°.

—— —— Same.   April 21 to June 20, 1906.   194 numbered pages.   vii p.   8°.

—— BUREAU OF STATISTICS (Department of Agriculture): Report on the agriculture of South America, with maps and latest statistics of trade.   Prepared under the direction of the statistician by Almont Barnes . . . Washington, Government Printing Office, 1892.   189 p.   8°.

—— BUREAU OF STATISTICS (Department of Commerce and Labor): . . . Commercial America in 1905, showing commerce, production, transportation, finances, area, and population of each of the countries of North, South, and Central America and the West Indies . . . Washington, Government Printing Office, 1906.   117 p.   4°.

—— DEPARTMENT OF AGRICULTURE: Index to the yearbooks of the Department . . . 1894–1900.   Prepared by Charles H. Greathouse . . . Washington, Government Printing Office, 1902.   196 p.   8°.

—— —— Same.   List by titles of publications of the . . . Department of Agriculture from 1840 to June, 1901, inclusive.   Compiled and compared with the originals by R. B. Handy and Minna A. Cannon . . . Washington, Government Printing Office, 1902.   216 p.   8°.

—— LIBRARY OF CONGRESS: List of books (with references to periodicals) relating to child labor.   Compiled under the direction of Appleton Prentiss Clark Griffin, Chief Bibliographer.   Washington, Government Printing Office, 1906.   66 p.   4°.

—— —— List of discussions of the fourteenth and fifteenth amendments with special reference to negro suffrage.   Compiled under the direction of Appleton Prentiss Clark Griffin, Chief Bibliographer.   Washington, Government Printing Office, 1906.   18 p.   4°.

—— —— List of works relating to the American occupation of the Philippine Islands. 1898–1903.   By Appleton Prentiss Clark Griffin, Chief Bibliographer.   Reprinted from the list of books (with references to periodicals) on the Philippine Islands, 1903.   With some additions to 1905.   Washington, Government Printing Office, 1905.   100 p.   8°.

aa. **Surgeon**: Alphabetical list of abbre-
ilation employed in the index-catalogue
eral's Office, U. S. A.   From vols. 1 to
nment Printing Office, 1895.   282 p.   4°.
r.   Washington, Government Printing

r.   **Washington**, Government Printing

' pronouncing dictionary of the Spanish
d by **Mariano** Velásquez de la Cadena
Edward Gray . . . and Juan L. Iribas
Co., 1906.   2 v.   4°.

aphique, historique & philologique de
aint-Martin.   Paris, H. Welter, [1906].
ana.]
the new world of his discovery.   A nar-
note on the navigation of Columbus's
ven, K. P.   Philadelphia, J. B. Lippin-
maps.   8°.

–

república Argentina, Chile y Bolivia, en la
tados de límites y protocolos existentes
la diferencia entre la línea de las altas
m.   Tomado del mapa general que se
nal de la República.   Por Manuel Cruz.
nteniendo los tratados y protocolos y
aa con arreglo al censo de 1895.   Buenos
1:5,750,000.   6 x 30 inches.
Norte.   Organizada pela Commissão de
o Rio Grande do Norte . . . 1903.   Scale

Valparaiso, Oficina Hidrográfica, julio
16½ inches.
survey in 1902.   Washington, U. S.
23 x 37½ inches.

CHILE. Port Barrow, Cockburn Channel. From Chilian surveys in 1901 and 190 Washington, U. S. Hydrographic Office, June, 1906. 8 x 9½ inches.

—— Port Soffia, Cockburn Channel. From Chilian surveys in 1901 and 190 Washington, U. S. Hydrographic Office, June, 1906. 8 x 9½ inches.

—— Puertos de las islas Guaitecas . . . 1904. Escala 1:20,000. Valparais Oficina Hydrográfica, marzo 1906. (4 small maps on 1 sheet.) 27½ x 2 inches. (Puerto Low, Puerto Rhone, Puerto Barrientos, Melinca.)

—— Sholl Bay. From Chilian surveys in 1901 and 1903. Washington, U. l Hydrographic Office, June, 1906. 11 x 15½ inches.

—— Port Taltal. From a Chilean survey in 1903. Washington, U. S. Hydr graphic Office, August, 1906. 18½ by 14½ inches.

CUBA. Habana to Port Mariel. Compiled from the latest information. Washin ton, U. S. Hydrographic Office, February, 1906. 26 x 37 inches.

—— Port Mariel to Gobernadora Point. Compiled from the latest informatio Washington, Hydrographic Office, February, 1906. 26 x 37 inches.

DOMINICAN REPUBLIC: Cape Engaño to Cape Samaná. From a survey in 1905 . . Washington, U. S. Hydrographic Office, February, 1906. 25½ x 38 inche

—— Cape Samaná to Cape Viejo Frances. From a survey in 1905 . . . Was ington, U. S. Hydrographic Office, February, 1906. 23 x 36 inches.

—— Manzanillo Bay and approaches. From surveys in 1905 . . . Washingto U. S. Hydrographic Office, February, 1906. 28½ x 42½ inches.

—— Mapa de la isla de Santo Domingo y Haití por el General Casimiro ¦ de Moya. Oficialmente adoptado por resolución del Congreso Nacion Dominicano fecha 18 mayo de 1905. Chicago, Rand, McNally & C(1906. Scale 1:400,000′. 65 x 37½ inches. (Contains small maps of tl cities of Santo Domingo and Port-au-Prince.)

HAITI. Jeremie Bay. From an examination in 1904 by the officers of the U. S. *Newark* and U. S. S. *Denver.* Washington, U. S. Hydrographic Offi(August, 1906. 18½ by 13½ inches.

MEXICO. Carta general de la República Mexicana, formada en la Secretaría ¦ Fomento, con mejoramiento de datos, por disposición del Secretario d Ramo. Ingeniero Manuel Fernández Leal, 1899. Scale 1:2,000,000. sheets, each 22½ x 33½ inches.

—— — Carta topográfica general de los alrededores de Puebla. Formada por comisión geográfico-exploradora. Edición de 1884. 3ᵃ serie, letra A- Scale 1:50,000. Size 19½ x 25½ inches.

—— Port Morelos (Yucatan). From a Mexican Government survey published 1905. Washington, U. S. Hydrographic Office, Aug., 1906. 13½ by 1 inches.

NICARAGUA. Mapa de la República de Nicaragua revisado, levantado por orden de Exa. el Presidente de la República . . . Por Maximiliano v. Sonnenste . . . 1895. In 4 sheets, each 29 x 29 inches.

PANAMA. Map of the Republic of Panama, prepared in the War Department, Offi of Chief of Staff, Second (Military Information) Division, General Sta U. S. A., January, 1904. Size 22½ x 44 inches.

PARAGUAY. Mapa de la República del Paraguay levantado por Félix Daum Ladouce. 1906. Escala 1:1,200,000. Buenos Aires, Compañía Sud-Am ricana de Billetes de Banco. 29 by 41½ inches.

—— Plano de Asunción. 8½ by 5½ inches. (On verso, "Ley de inmigración.")

Modern Mexico.   Vols. 17–18.   April, 1904–March, 1905.
Monthly Consular Reports.   Washington.   Nos. 304–307.   January–March, 1906.
——— Nos. 307–309.   April–June, 1906.
——— [All Series].   Vol. 65.   January–April, 1901.
Review of the River Plate.   Buenos Aires.   Vol. 23.   July–December, 1905.
Revista Agricola.   São Paulo.   Vol. 10.   January–December, 1905.
Scientific American.   New York.   Vol. 91.   July–December, 1904.
——— Vol. 92.   January–June, 1905.
——— Vol. 93.   July–December, 1905.
——— Vol. 94.   January–June, 1906.
South American Journal.   London.   Vol. 57.   July–December, 1904.
——— Vol. 58.   January–June, 1905.
——— Vol. 59.   July–December, 1905.
The World To-day.   Chicago.   Vol. 10.   January to June, 1906.
World's Work.   New York.   Vol. 11.   November, 1905, to April, 1906.

O

International Union of American Republics

Monthly Bulletin

OF THE

International Bureau

OF THE

American Republics

VOL. 24, NO. 2

FEBRUARY, 1907

WHOLE NO. 161

WASHINGTON, D C., U. S. A.

GOVERNMENT PRINTING OFFICE

1907

GENERAL TABLE OF CONTENTS.

TABLE OF CONTENTS.

. ÍNDICE.

ÍNDICE.

INDICE.

TABLES DES MATIÈRES.

La sección castellana comienza en la página 408.
A secção portugueza encontra-se á pagina 501.
On trouvera la section française à la page 525.

HIS EXCELLENCY ENRIQUE C. CREEL, AMBASSADOR OF MEXICO TO THE UNITED STATES.

Mexican Ambassador to the United
to President Roosevelt on February
y Secretary Root and was attended
taché of the Embassy. Felicitous
1 the President and the Ambassador,

nor of handing to Your Excellency
lits me as Ambassador Extraordinary
'ernment of the Mexican Republic,
tter of recall of my predecessor, the
o, by reason of his ill health, was

ve granted me any other commission
me as that of its representative near
3tates of America, instructing me at
ngthen the already close ties existing
sides being neighbors, possess iden-
, common interests, and numerous
ication.
of Chihuahua, where I have lived since
been in charge of its government, I
us qualifications of the people of the

261

United States of America, with whom, for reasons clearly to be explained, my own people have been in touch and have friendly feelings which are growing all the time with more vitality.

"I have known for a long time your wonderful development, your great resources as a nation, your honorable political policy, your noble and fruitful initiative, and all the gifts which give your people such a worthy and high standing. My country, under the protection of peace and under the influence of credit, has moved during the last thirty years over a path of radical and increasing development, and wishes very sincerely the friendship of her important neighboring country; a friendship which she knows will bring her great benefits.

"To attain such a success I will use every effort within my power, as by so doing I will satisfy the impulse of my old love for the great people under your wise government, and I will also, I am sure, convey the feelings of my country and especially those of my president, as both wish with keen interest to give more life and strength to the cordial relations cultivated with your country and her representatives.

"In behalf of my Government, in the name of the Mexican people and in my own, I present to Your Excellency our best wishes for your personal happiness and for the growing prosperity of the people of the United States of America."

President Roosevelt made the following reply:

"Mr. Ambassador, it affords me sincere gratification to welcome you as the honored representative of a country to which we are bound by many and strong ties of friendship and neighborhood, and to receive from your hands the letter of credence you present as Ambassador Extraordinary and Plenipotentiary of the Government of the Mexican Republic.

"In choosing you as its intimate agent in this capital I feel that your Government has borne in mind no less earnestly than we ourselves constantly consider the singularly close interests which should naturally exist between countries in actual touch with each other across the broad expanse of the continent from sea to sea, and which have developed and grown stronger year by year, through similarity of institutions, identity of aims, and mutually beneficial interchanges. Your long experience of these conditions and the administrative part you have played in contributing to their enlargement has not only enabled you to know our people, but has led them to know you and to appreciate the apt qualities you bring to the fulfillment of the congenial work of still further strengthening the bonds of good-fellowship in the high office to which you are now called. In all that may tend to the realization of that most desirable end you may rest assured of the hearty cooperation of this Government, even as the Mexican people may confidently count upon the friendliness and esteem of the American people, who cordially wish for the constant advance of

Mexico in the paths of peace, material prosperity, and enduring welfare.

"Accepting the letter you present recalling your predecessor, Señor CASASUS, I take occasion to express high personal regard for him as a man and esteem for his eminent qualities of statesmanship. While regretting his retirement and sympathizing with him because of the ill health which has constrained him to this step, I bespeak for you, Mr. Ambassador, an equally cordial place in our regards and equal success in sharing the confidence and gaining the good will of all with whom your mission brings you into association.

"In conclusion, Mr. Ambassador, I beg you to convey to the President of the Mexican Republic the wishes I am glad to express, for myself as well as on behalf of this Government and people, for his personal well-being and for the happiness and good fortune of his country and his countrymen."

NEW BUILDING FOR THE BUREAU OF THE AMERICAN REPUBLICS.

The Governing Board of the Bureau of the American Republics at a special meeting held on January 30, 1907, in reply to the letter dated January 1, 1907, from Mr. ANDREW CARNEGIE, announcing a donation of $750,000 for the erection of a new building for the use of the Bureau, unanimously passed the following resolutions by acclamation:

"*Resolved*, That the letter of Mr. ANDREW CARNEGIE to the Chairman of the Board, dated January 1, 1907, be received and filed and spread upon the minutes of the Board.

"*Resolved*, That the Governing Board of the Bureau of the American Republics express to Mr. ANDREW CARNEGIE its acceptance and grateful appreciation of his generous and public-spirited engagement to supply the funds for the proposed new building for the Union of American Republics. The Board shares with Mr. CARNEGIE the hope that the institution whose work will thus be promoted may further the cause of peace and justice among nations and the sincere and helpful friendship of all the American Republics for each other.

"*Resolved*, That the Chairman of the Board communicate a copy of the foregoing resolutions to Mr. CARNEGIE;" and

"I. That the letter of the Honorable the Secretary of State, Mr. ELIHU ROOT, addressed to Mr. ANDREW CARNEGIE; the answer of this distinguished philanthropist, and the resolution of the Governing Board accepting his splendid gift be kept on file with the important documents of the Bureau; and

"II. That the text of these letters and the resolutions thereon be artistically engrossed, under the title of 'CARNEGIE'S Gift to the

International Bureau of the American Republics,' and properly framed, to form a part of the exhibits of the Bureau at the Jamestown Ter-Centennial Exposition."

The first resolution was introduced by the Hon. ELIHU ROOT, Secretary of State and Chairman of the Board, and the second by Señor DON LUIS FELIPE CARBO, Minister of Ecuador.

THE DEVELOPMENT OF INTELLECTUAL AND EDUCATIONAL RELATIONS BETWEEN THE COUNTRIES OF AMERICA.

At a special meeting of the Governing Board of the International Bureau of the American Republics, held on January 30, 1907, Mr. JOHN BARRETT, Director of the Bureau, announced that, in accordance with the new and enlarged programme of the Bureau to develop closer relations with Latin America on the intellectual and educational, as well as the commercial and material side, and by the authority of Dr. NICHOLAS MURRAY BUTLER, of Columbia University, New York City, Dr. WILLIAM R. SHEPHERD, Professor of History in Columbia University, whose special interests and studies lie in Spanish and Spanish-American history, will make a trip as a representative of Columbia University to the leading South American commercial and political capitals during the summer of 1907. The object of Doctor SHEPHERD'S trip will be to cultivate personal relations with the leading statesmen, men of letters, and men of affairs in South America, and to carry to them knowledge of the educational resources and opportunities of American colleges and universities, with a view of bringing about closer relationship between the Latin-American Republics and the United States. While absent, Doctor SHEPHERD will also collect material for the course of lectures on South America, which he is to deliver in Cooper Union, New York City, during the spring of 1908 as the Hewitt Lecturer of Columbia University.

The Director of the Bureau is in correspondence with Latin-American officials and universities to perfect the arrangements for Doctor SHEPHERD'S visit. It is hoped that Doctor SHEPHERD'S visit will reciprocally result in the sending of South American men of letters to the United States.

Dr. SHEPHERD was born in Charleston, South Carolina, June 12, 1871, and was graduated from Columbia University in 1893. He held a university fellowship in American history at Columbia from graduation until 1895. He has given instruction in history at the university since 1896, in which year he received the degree of doctor of philosophy. At the present time he conducts courses on the history of Latin

America and of those portions of the United States which were formerly under Spanish rule. He has also given a number of public lectures on the history and institutions of Spanish America. Doctor Shepherd spent one year in 1902 and 1903 in Spain searching the archives for documents relating to Spanish America and the United States. He published in 1904, in the Annual Report of the American Historical Association, an article entitled "The Spanish archives and their importance for the history of the United States." In the following summer he was sent by the Carnegie Institution, of Washington, to gather data for a guide to the materials in the Spanish archives which concern the United States.

Doctor Shepherd has published numerous articles dealing with the history of Spain in America and has edited an historical atlas, soon to be published, which will give to English-speaking students a more adequate conception of the historical geography of Latin America than has ever before appeared in a work of this kind.

He is a member of the Hispanic Society of America and is American correspondent for the historical section of *Cultura Española*. He has served since their foundation as judge for the JOHN BARRETT prizes on the relations of Latin America and the United States.

DR. JOSÉ IGNACIO RODRIGUEZ.

In the death of Dr. José IGNACIO RODRIGUEZ, Librarian and Chief Translator of the International Bureau of the American Republics, this institution has sustained a great loss, and Latin America mourns one of its most accomplished men of letters whose modesty was equal to his exceptional qualifications. Doctor RODRIGUEZ was born in Havana in 1831, and resided there until 1869, when, on account of his convictions and untiring work in favor of the freedom of the Cuban slaves, he was compelled to leave for the United States, where he afterwards permanently lived. In Cuba, Doctor RODRIGUEZ was the recipient of many honors and degrees from colleges and universities, and filled important offices in a judicial capacity. Upon his arrival in the United States he studied law under Caleb Cushing, being admitted to the bar of the District of Columbia and the United States Supreme Court. As an international lawyer his work was always highly appreciated by the Latin-American diplomatic corps.

Doctor RODRIGUEZ was Secretary to the First International American Conference, which created the Bureau, from February, 1890, to the end of the Conference; Chief Translator and head of Spanish Department of the Bureau until 1897; Secretary of the International

American Monetary Commission, 1891; went to Paris with the American Peace Commission as private confidential adviser in matters of Spanish law, September to December, 1898, and was Chief Translator and Librarian of the Columbus Memorial Library of the International Bureau of the American Republics until his death.   He was the author of several important works on Cuba and also contributor to numerous American-Cuban papers.   Doctor RODRIGUEZ died on February 1, 1907, and upon his death the following resolutions were adopted by the Governing Board of the International Bureau of the American Republics:

"*Resolutions regarding the death of Dr. José Ignacio Rodriguez, Librarian and Chief Translator of the International Bureau of the American Republics.*

" Whereas the International Bureau of the American Republics has been deprived by death of the services of Dr. José IGNACIO RODRIGUEZ, Librarian and Chief Translator, and
" Whereas Doctor RODRIGUEZ performed distinguished work in the Bureau, covering the whole period since its establishment; be it
" *Resolved*, That the Governing Board of the Bureau hears with profound regret the news of Doctor RODRIGUEZ's demise, and extends its sincere sympathy to his widow and family in the irreparable loss they have sustained, and directs that copies of these resolutions be respectively spread on the minutes of the Governing Board and forwarded to the family of the deceased."

TER-CENTENARY OF ENGLISH SETTLEMENT IN THE UNITED STATES.

The following extract from the address of Señor NICOLAS VELOZ-GOITICOA, Special Commissioner of the Jamestown Exposition to Latin America, delivered in Washington January 15, 1907, before the National Convention for the Extension of the Foreign Commerce of the United States, on the effect of the Jamestown Exposition, is given:
" For the purpose of celebrating the ter-centenary of the establishment of the first permanent English colony in the northern half of the Western Hemisphere, there will be held the Jamestown International Exposition from April 26 to November 30 of the present year.
"All the Governments of the world have been invited by President ROOSEVELT, through the Department of State, to commemorate this great historical event by sending officers and vessels of their navies

and representations of their armies to participate in the greatest peaceful gathering of this kind that has ever been recorded in the history of the universe.

"This invitation has been accepted by practically all the nations of both hemispheres, and in conjunction and accord with this friendly meeting there will be held a great international, historical, commercial, and industrial exhibition.

"A special invitation was extended by the Exposition Management to the Governments and peoples of Latin America to exhibit their great natural wealth and manufactured products.

" Of the twenty Latin-American Republics fifteen will be represented either by delegations from their armies and navies or by creditable displays of their natural resources, suitably housed either in special buildings they will erect for this purpose in a certain portion of the exposition grounds or in separate booths in a convenient section that has been set apart to this effect in one of the exposition buildings.

" In the same manner as former expositions have stimulated the trade relations of the United States with foreign countries, the Jamestown Exposition—where all the agricultural, commercial, and industrial products of the United States will be conveniently displayed by practically all the States of the Federal Union—will serve as an object lesson not only to the foreign delegates of the better cultured classes who will attend the naval and military celebration, but to all other alien visitors, all of whom will surely describe to their fellow-countrymen on their return to their respective homes the wonderful progress they have seen exhibited at Jamestown of the agricultural and other American commercial commodities and the trade possibilities resulting therefrom.

" The Jamestown Exposition has the additional advantage over all former American world's fairs in the fact that within a given radius it can be more conveniently reached by a much larger number of millions of people, both from the United States and from abroad.

" All these attendant conditions will undoubtedly be conducive to considerable expansion of the domestic and foreign commerce of the United States, and will produce the most profitable effect on the latter commerce.

"On the other hand, Latin America will be represented at Jamestown by a much larger number of countries than has ever taken part in any previous American world's fair, and the fact of the ready response of said countries to the efforts of the Jamestown Exposition to secure their attendance has been most gratifying to the management, as it was only commenced three months ago and the participation of practically all is already an accomplished fact."

The Director of the Bureau of the American Republics has appointed Mr. F. J. YANES, Secretary of the Bureau, as the representative of the Bureau on the United States Government Board of the Jamestown Tercentennial Exposition. This appointment was approved by the Governing Board of the Bureau at a special meeting of the Board held on January 30, 1907. Mr. YANES, in connection with Mr. CARLTON Fox, will prepare the exhibit of the Bureau at the Exposition.

ARGENTINE REPUBLIC.

FOREIGN TRADE, FIRST NINE MONTHS, 1906.

The figures covering the foreign trade of the Argentine Republic for the nine months—January to September, 1906—show a balance of trade in favor of the Republic to the amount of $27,315,747 gold. An excess of gold and silver imports over exports is reported to the extent of $17,901,475.

Total imports for the period in reference figured for $197,315,514 gold; $136,585,756 being for dutiable merchandise and $58,729,758, free of duty. Imports of precious metals were valued at $17,985,128. While imports in general for the first nine months of 1906 show an increase of $41,664,054, as compared with the corresponding period of 1905, imports of gold and silver show a decrease of $8,419,625.

Exports in general show a total valuation of $224,631,261 gold in the nine months of 1906, as compared with $247,039,158 during the same period of the preceding year, a decline of $22,478,872 being thus noted. Of the merchandise shipped abroad, $224,550,286 were free of duty and $80,975 dutiable. Exports of gold and silver were valued at $83,653, being $662,261 less than last year. The countries of origin for the imports were, with their respective quotas:

Great Britain, $69,160,935; Germany, $28,513,581; United States, $27,196,249; France, $20,664,625; Italy, $18,586,772; Belgium, $9,209,785; Spain, $5,549,405; Brazil, 4,875,872; Holland, $1,189,677; Uruguay, $1,353,770; Paraguay, $898,825; Cuba, $520,129; Chile, $446,365, and Bolivia, $94,595.

Comparing these figures with those of 1905, an increase is shown in the following countries: Great Britain, $17,241,263; Germany, $6,359,459; United States, $5,401,664; France, $368,370; Italy, $2,222,210; Belgium, $2,217,496; Spain, $1,170,426; Uruguay, $656,225; Brazil, $643,262; Holland, $435,780; Cuba, $111,689, and a decrease in the following: Chile, $19,368; Bolivia, $7,615; Africa, $6,589, and Paraguay, $6,882.

The destination of exports was as follows: Great Britain, $31,260,840; Germany, $29,183,935; France, $24,639,892; Belgium, $19,610,516; United States, $10,329,253; Brazil, $8,790,003; Italy, $4,810,475;

Uruguay, $3,816,882; Africa, $3,283,821; Holland, $2,037,114; Spain, $1,861,187; Chile, $1,115,693; Bolivia, $297,777; Cuba, $199,310, and Paraguay, $134,848.

The increase over the exports of the first nine months of 1905 was as follows: Belgium, $3,337,469; Germany, $2,608,081; Italy, $455,670; Spain, $185,202, and Chile, $71,764, while the following countries show a decrease: Great Britain, $2,696,207; Uruguay, $2,088,691; France, $1,156,812; Africa, $969,605; Holland, $689,550; Brazil, $414,778; Bolivia, $184,651; Cuba, $125,235; United States, $114,254; Paraguay, $114,211.

TRADE WITH BRAZIL.

Statistics showing the intertrade relations between the Argentine Republic and Brazil indicate an enormous preponderance in favor of Argentine exports. For the first nine months of 1906, Brazil received Argentine products valued at $8,790,003 gold, as against $4,875,872 gold, the value of Brazilian shipments to that Republic.

For the preceding five years, although the reciprocal trade between the two countries follows an ascending scale, the difference is always in favor of the Argentine Republic, as is demonstrated by the following figures:

	1901.	1902.	1903.	1904.	1905.
Argentine exports to Brazil	$6,185,507	$9,702,488	$8,368,742	$4,545,127	$10,427,012
Brazilian exports to the Argentine Republic	3,741,877	4,386,047	4,583,645	5,350,976	6,032,973

National statistics do not show what proportion of coffee is imported by the Republic from Brazil, but the total imports for the first nine months of the year 1906 aggregated 6,683,240 kilograms, presumably in the greater part from that country. The other principal articles of import from Brazil are tobacco and herba mate. Statistics show that from January to September, 1906, tobacco was imported by the Argentine Republic to the extent of 2,998,000 kilograms, of which 471,322 were from Habana, 562,614 from Paraguay, and 1,964,123 kilograms from "other countries," the bulk being undoubtedly of Brazilian origin. As regards herba mate, the quantity imported from Brazil in the months in reference amounted to 29,424,786 kilograms, an increase as compared with the corresponding months of 1905 of 6,158,272 kilograms. The quantities from Paraguay were: 2,388,272 kilograms of "canchada," a diminution of 329,886 kilograms, and 292,470 kilograms of the elaborated article, an increase of 202,130 kilograms.

Argentine shipments to Brazil consist chiefly of wheat, flour, and jerked beef.

COLLECTION OF CROP STATISTICS.

The Argentine Government, with the purpose of collecting data concerning the crop returns for the year 1906–7, has issued a circular to the assessment offices of each province, directing that all licensed owners of thrashing and reaping machines be furnished with blank forms on which the agricultural statistics of the respective properties shall be entered and forwarded to the central office. Unlicensed owners of agricultural machines are required to forward to the assessor's office certified statements as to the number and make of their machines. All the information thus collected is to be sent to the Statistical Division of the Department of Agriculture of the Republic.

NATIONAL RAILWAY REVENUES.

The Minister of Public Works of the Argentine Republic has prepared a report on the revenue of the national railways for 1905 and 1906 (approximate), the results being as follows: Andine, 1905, $1,848,062; 1906, $2,460,000; increase, 33.1 per cent; *Argentino del Norte*, 1905, $684,801; 1906, $970,000; increase, 49.6 per cent; Central Northern, 1905, $4,388,419; 1906, $6,070,000; increase, 38.3 per cent. The totals for 1905 are thus shown to have aggregated $6,844,820 national currency, as compared with $9,500,000 in 1906, an increase in the latter period of 38 per cent. The calculated revenue for 1907 is based on a 15 per cent increase over the returns for 1906.

CUSTOMS RECEIPTS AT BUENOS AYRES, NOVEMBER AND FIRST ELEVEN MONTHS OF 1906.

According to latest statistics published in the "*Boletin Oficial*" of the Argentine Republic, the customs receipts at the port of Buenos Ayres for the month of November, 1906, amounted to 8,575,544.55 *pesos* national currency and 242,979 *pesos* gold. The receipts for the same month of 1905 amounted to 7,626,514 *pesos*, national currency and 279,017.50 *pesos* gold.

During the first eleven months of 1906, the total collection was 103,367,423.38 *pesos* national currency and 3,073,526 *pesos* gold, as compared with 87,119,873.23 *pesos* national currency and 3,836,290.78 *pesos* gold in the same period of 1905.

IMMIGRATION DURING NOVEMBER AND FIRST ELEVEN MONTHS OF 1906.

The Immigration Division of the Department of Agriculture of the Argentine Republic has recently published the following figures relating to immigration during the month of November and first eleven months of 1906:

Passengers from foreign countries 2,092
Passengers from Montevideo 3,613
Immigrants from foreign countries 42,784
Immigrants from Montevideo 4,272

Total 52,761

From January 1, 1906, to November 30, 1906, 209,767 immigrants entered the port of Buenos Ayres. It is expected that the total for 1906 will amount to nearly 250,000 immigrants.

RAILWAY MILEAGE AND GAUGE.

The following table shows the gauge and the miles of roadbed in operation of the various railways of the Argentine Republic:

Railway.	Gauge.	Miles in operation.	
		1905.	1906.
	Ft. in.		
Argentine Great Western	5 6.	464	464
Argentine Northeastern	4 8½	411	411
Argentino del Norte	3 3.37	663	673
Buenos Aires Great Southern	5 6.	2,481	2,543
Buenos Aires and Pacific	5 6.	1,065	1,166
Buenos Aires Western	5 6.	966	1,060
Buenos Aires Rosario	5 6.	2,347	2,361
Central Córdoba (eastern section)	3 3.37	128	128
Central Córdoba (northern section)	3 3.37	549	549
Central Northern	3 3.37	773	882
Central Northern (Chaco Branch)	3 3.37	200	209
Córdoba Northwestern	3 3.37	95	95
Córdoba and Rosario	3 3.37	180	180
East Argentine	4 8½	99	99
Entre Rios Railways	4 8½	472	501
National Andine	5 6.	300	300
Northwest Argentine	3 3.37	94	94
Province of Santa Fé	3 3.37	891	891
Total		12,078	12,577

RAILWAY CONSOLIDATION.

The Argentine Congress has authorized the Executive of the Republic to approve the consolidation of the East Argentine and the Argentine Northeastern railroads, the new company thus constituted to be known under the name of "Argentine Northeastern Railroad" (*Ferrocarril Nord-este Argentino*).

At present both railroads, including their branch lines, run from the city of Concordia to Santo Tomé and Corrientes, with the point of bifurcation about 9 kilometers northwest of the city of Monte Caseros, in the Province of Corrientes.

The present capital of the consolidated companies is based upon the value per kilometer as fixed in the respective contracts, in the following manner: East Argentine, 160,318 kilometers and 50 centimeters, at the rate of $31,317.69 gold per kilometer, equal to $5,020,305.08 gold; Argentine Northeastern, 662,731 kilometers and 85 centimeters, at the rate of $30,500 gold per kilometer, equal to $20,213,321.42 gold.

BUDGET OF BUENOS AYRES FOR 1907.

The budget of the city of Buenos Ayres, Argentine Republic, for 1907 was submitted to the municipal commission in the early part of December, 1906. The total amount of expenditure is fixed at 18,341,926.67 *pesos*, distributed as follows: Personnel, 6,807,080 *pesos*; general expenditures, 6,805,000 *pesos*; subventions, 1,345,800 *pesos*; amortization of the loan, 2,932,807.10 *pesos*; extraordinary appropriation, 451,649.57 *pesos*.

The revenues are estimated at 19,662,600 *pesos*, the surplus over expenditures being, therefore, 1,320,673.33 *pesos*, which will be applied to the appropriation for the municipal commission and other expenditures which it may provide for by special ordinances.

CENSUS OF ROSARIO.

A census of the city of Rosario, taken on October 19, 1906, showed the population to be 150,686. The census of 1895 showed 91,669, an increase of 59,017, or 64 per cent in eleven years being thus noted.

CENSUS OF BAHÍA BLANCA.

The municipal census for 1906 taken by the city of Bahía Blanca shows a population of 37,755. The national census, taken in 1901, gave only 14,238 inhabitants.

BOLIVIA.

COMMERCIAL MOVEMENT OF VARIOUS CUSTOM-HOUSES, 1906.

The following figures, taken from official statistics recently received from Bolivia, refer to the commercial movement of various custom-houses of the Republic in the periods of 1906 as stated in the following paragraphs:

Oruro custom-house: From January, 1906, to September, 1906, there were imported through this custom-house merchandise of a total weight of 5,573,917 kilograms, from the following countries: Germany, 1,722,294 kilograms; United States, 1,113,960 kilograms; England, 1,087,873 kilograms; Peru, 871,462 kilograms; Chile, 211,360 kilograms; Belgium, 160,836 kilograms; Italy, 114,769 kilograms; Panama, 189,687 kilograms; Spain, 35,598 kilograms; France, 43,552 kilograms; Ecuador, 20,076 kilograms; Portugal, 2,450 kilograms.

Uyuni custom-house: The imports through this custom-house during the first half of 1906 amounted to 17,745,983.500 kilograms, valued at 2,546,606.41 *bolivianos*. The total weight of exports during the same period was 1,073,002.003 kilograms, and the value 843,095.90 *bolivianos*.

During the first quarter of 1906
kilograms of merchandise,
00.74 *boliviano*.

exported during the first quar-
worth of silver ores.

during the first half of 1906 exported
2,493.76 marcs of silver ores.

exported during the third quarter of

BRAZIL.

FIRST NINE MONTHS, 1906.

rade for the first nine months of 1906
,934,983 *milreis* ($184,512,500.718), as
175,319,804.478) in the corresponding
ations during the same periods were
44.512) and 467,703,001 *milreis* ($255,-
he estimated value of the Brazilian
$0.546 United States currency.

FIRST NINE MONTHS OF 1906.

from the latest official statistics re-
lected by the various custom-houses of
sths of 1906:

		1906.	1905.
		Milreis.	*Milreis.*
	Rio de Janeiro...........	61,198,226	58,742,171
	Santos....................	30,132,772	26,066,824
	Paranagua	1,759,729	1,066,180
	Florianopolis.............	953,664	831,908
	Rio Grande..............	6,407,798	6,847,018
	Porto Alegre..............	6,422,564	5,723,900
	Uruguayana..............	880,416	937,902
	Santa Anna do Livra-	180,114	266,685
	mento.		
	Corumba	999,652	1,088,580
	Total	175,425,014	109,491,102

s shows an increase for the first nine
lreis.

BUDGET LAW AND CUSTOMS PROVISIONS FOR 1907.

The "*Diario Official*" for January 1, 1907, contains the Budget Law of the United States of Brazil for the fiscal year 1907, as approved by the Brazilian Congress. The following is a translation of the principal provisions of this law:

"ARTICLE 1. The general revenue of the Republic of the United States of Brazil is estimated at 69,575,280 *milreis* gold and 228,355,086 *milreis* paper, and the revenue applied to the special funds is estimated at 13,921,000 *milreis* gold, and 18,991,913 *milreis* paper, to be realized from the amounts collected within the same fiscal year from the following sources:

	Gold.	National paper.
	Milreis.	*Milreis.*
Importations, ordinary	66,900,000	111,950,000
Light-house dues	290,000	
Wharf dues	110,000	10,000
Additional tax of 10 per cent on the clearance of goods free from duty		200,000
Five per cent of the export duties of Acre Territory		1,825,086
Internal revenues	1,560,666	70,883,000
Excise taxes		35,680,000
Extraordinary revenues	714,614	7,825,000
Paper-money redemption fund		4,200,000
Paper-money guarantee fund	9,311,000	6,573,913
Sinking fund for redemption of railway bonds	160,000	1,638,000
Amortization of internal debts		3,030,000
Port-improvement fund		3,530,000

"ART. 2. With regard to the manner of collecting the import duties for consumption, the provision contained in No. 111, article 2, of the law No. 1452, of December 30, 1905, shall be observed with the following changes: (1) The law No. 1499, of September 1, 1906, shall be observed in collecting duties on the articles enumerated in No. 124 of the tariff; (2) the duties shall be payable 50 per cent in gold whenever the rate of exchange remains above 14 pence per *milreis* for thirty consecutive days, and in the same way will cease to be payable only after the exchange shall have been maintained below 14d. for the same period. The average exchange rate for the thirty days shall be taken for the effects of this provision. If the exchange falls to 14 pence or below, the duties shall be payable 35 per cent in gold.

"ART. 3. The president of the Republic is authorized—

"I. To issue in anticipation of the revenue in the fiscal year treasury notes to the amount of 25,000,000 *milreis*, to be redeemed before the close of the fiscal year.

"II. To receive and to restore, in conformity with article 41 of the law No. 628, of September 17, 1851, the money on deposit for orphans, property of the dead and absent, lottery premiums, the deposits of savings banks and of mutual-benefit associations, and the deposits from other sources. Any surplus resulting from same shall be applied to the amortization of the internal loans, and any deficit shall be charged to expenditure of the fiscal year.

"III. To collect for the fund destined for harbor improvements to be made by the Union—

"(1) A tax of 2 per cent gold on the official value of imports at the port of Rio de Janeiro and at the custom-houses of Rio Grande do Sul, except on the articles mentioned in article 1, No. 2. This tax may be collected at the other ports and frontier custom-houses as soon as it has been decided to undertake systematically the improvement works in the ports and navigable rivers.

"(2) A tax of 1 to 5 *reis* per kilogram of merchandise loaded or unloaded, according to its value, destination, or origin from other ports.

"*Sole paragraph.* To hasten the progress of said works, the President of the Republic will be permitted to accept gifts or aid offered by States, municipalities, or associations interested in the improvements, providing the charges resulting from such aid shall not exceed the amount of the respective dues.

"IV. To modify the present taxes collected for the water service of the Federal capital to the limit provided for by the law No. 2639 of September 22, 1875. The number of service pipes may be increased, but the daily supply of 1,200 liters for each pipe must be maintained.

"V. To modify the tax for the sewerage service of the capital, so as to establish as nearly as possible an equilibrium between the amount of the taxes collected and the amount paid to the City Improvements Company for this service.

"VI. To revise the regulations contained in decree No. 5874 of January 27, 1906, making the transportation tax of 20 per cent applicable to all tickets of whatever price except those of suburban trains of the Federal capital and of the capitals of the States, those which serve for urban tramways of animals, steam or electric traction, and those referred to under letters c, d, e, f, and g of article 4 of the above decree. The provisions contained in article 2 respecting the maximum tax to be collected and the percentage of reductions established on season tickets shall, however, remain in force.

"VII. To modify the service of inspection of consumption duties, revising the respective regulations and issuing new regulations, without increase of expenditure.

"VIII. To revise the regulations No. 5072 of December 12, 1903, on the following basis:

"(a) To consolidate in a single regulation the provisions of decree No. 4270 of December 10, 1901, as modified by decree No. 5072 of December 12, 1903, in conformity with law No. 953 of December 29, 1902, article 2, No. 12, which authorized its revision and that of article 25, sections 1 and 2, of law No. 1144 of December 30, 1903 and article

20, No. 14, of law No. 1316 of December 31, 1904. In this revision the following provisions shall be observed:

"1. The expenses of the Department for the Supervision of Insurance shall be defrayed by means of a tax, which shall be collected from all insurance companies, national or foreign, which are now doing business or which may hereafter do business in Brazil. This tax shall be the same for all companies, and is independent of the tax paid by foreign companies by virtue of article 54 of the regulations No. 5072, of December 12, 1903.

"2. Companies which desire to renew operations, reopen agencies that have already been authorized, or establish new agencies, can only do so after having complied with the laws in force.

"3. Insurance companies doing business under the provisions of articles 8 and 9 of regulations No. 5072, of December 12, 1903, which renew or extend the terms of terrestrial and maritime insurance contracts issued up to the date of the consolidation, or which make new insurance contracts subsequent to this date, shall be required to have a reserve fund in Brazil formed of 20 per cent of the net annual profits as provided for in article 2, No. 2, of the regulations No. 5072, of 1903, under penalty of having their authority to do business revoked.

"4. An insurance contract is null and void when, being a part of a larger amount insured, it does not contain a specific declaration of the amounts insured, the terms, and the names of the insuring companies.

"5. In case of violation of the above section, each of the contracting parties, as shown from the contract or from any other document which may be produced, shall be punished by a fine equal to 10 per cent of the amount of the contract.

"6. All insurance companies are required to keep a register of all policies issued or renewed, which shall be sealed and marked in accordance with the terms of the Commercial Code, and be subject to examination at any time by the Inspector of Insurance.

"(b) Articles intended for export may be cleared from the customhouses of the Union only on the exhibition of a document of insurance made by any national or foreign insurance company authorized to do business in the country.

"(c) The exhibition of the insurance document mentioned in letter b may be dispensed with, provided the owner of the article makes a declaration to the effect that the exportation is made at the risk of the Treasury.

"IX. For the purpose of safeguarding the interests of national production—

"1. To revise the rates of the Federal railways which are under its immediate administration.

"2. To enter into an agreement with the concessionaires of the

res railways or river navigation for the
sg consumption from customs duties (except
i port improvements and clearance) may
orted by such companies for use in the
their lines.
iconvent—
ants of the Republics of Uraguay and
iquidation by these Governments of their

as of those States producing monazitic
ulating the exploitation and the trade of

f import duties, even granting free entry
i deemed necessary, to articles of foreign
ate with similar articles produced in the

sailing privilege—
cations of an agricultural, industrial, and
hed by the governments of the States, or
'ree distribution, and on publications and
onal Agricultural Association and other

l matter of any kind sent to the Federal,
libraries; to the *A Revista do Instituto
?io Grande do Norte;* to the *Boletim do*
publications for free distribution of the
ociation and of the Anti-Tuberculosis
al, Bahai, and Pernambuco.
customs duties—
nts and machinery destined to the manu-
icultural products, also apparatus for the
cts imported direct by agriculturists or
d machinery and apparatus for the equip-
e manufacture of *xarque* (dried meat) and
om the pulp of the sugar cane, subject to
at.
ts imported for the use of associations or
berculosis.
f fodder plants employed for the improve-
, sheep, and hogs.

"5. Material imported by the Leopoldina Railway Company for the extension, operation, and improvement of its lines, except when similar articles are produced in the country. The same privilege shall be enjoyed by all the railways which have made or shall make reductions on the freight rates on articles of national production equivalent to those made by that company, subject, however, to the clearance tax of 10 per cent and the special taxes for the port-improvement fund. This provision shall remain in force until the Government carries out the provision of No. IX, section 3.

"6. Rowing and sailing boats destined exclusively for nautical sports, with movable seats and their accessories, such as oars, sails, oarlocks, boat hooks, braces, masts, hammocks, tillers, life belts, halyards, sheets, etc., imported directly by regatta clubs.

"7. Material imported for the construction of central sugar mills, also for the construction and extension of railways and port works executed by private concession, being subject to 10 per cent of the clearance tax when the duty on the articles is not less than this amount.

"8. Stamped tin plates and their accessories for the manufacture of tins for butter, lard, bacon, sweets, or meats, when imported directly by the producers of these articles, subject to a clearance tax of 10 per cent.

"9. Material imported by companies or individuals who propose to undertake the economic cultivation of coffee, cocoa, tobacco, cotton, and animal and vegetable fibers for textiles, and establish central factories, suitably equipped, for their treatment. The President of the Republic shall also use his influence with the Federal railway companies and the navigation companies subsidized or in any way aided by the State, for the purpose of obtaining a reasonable reduction in the transportation rates on the products of such establishments.

"(a) If such establishments are founded by agricultural syndicates, organized under the law of January 6, 1903, the materials shall be subject to an *ad valorem* duty of 5 per cent as established by the custom-house laws, independently of any order of the Minister of the Treasury.

"(b) The central factories and their products shall enjoy the privileges established by the present article only when the local governments of the States or of the Federal district in which they are established, also grant them favors.

"10. All machinery and apparatus imported by the States, municipalities, and private parties for silk factories, provided that in the spinning and weaving only cocoons of national production are used.

"11. Objects imported for the Goeldi Museum in the State of Pará, and those imported by the State governments for the national colonies and the civilization of the Indians.

...governments of States, municipalities,
...exemption from import duties shall be
ported by them to be used in the construction
vement works, whether executed direct by the
to private persons, subject to the clearance
...for waterworks; metallic material for
rial for paving streets, including stone-break-
respective motors and macadamizing rollers;
ar improvements; for the construction of fur-
on of garbage, bridges, lighting service, railways, including the material destined to the
ower for the same; material imported for the
...and prisons; animals and material destined
d fire brigade; material destined for labora-
and material; material for the pilot service
f which the governments of the States, of the
he Federal District may have immediate need

y the Federal Union for works under its juris-
itted free of duty.
r ceramic material required for sewers in the
, Maranhão, Pernambuco, Santa Catharina,
lo Sul, and Parana, and in the city of Nitheroy,
, in accordance with the terms of the decree
dy cited.
l kinds for raising water, including the respec-
pumps, pumps, pipes, and other accessories
on works in the municipal districts of Geara
ich suffer from drought. The same privilege
persons who may import such articles, on his
use, in the above-mentioned States.
...est for exemption from duties, including the
nade to the Minister of the Treasury by the

...tors, stoves, chafing dishes, lamps, and any
alcohol as fuel, either in its pure form or car-
...ing subject to a clearance duty of 10 per cent.
l for the zoological gardens and those imported
...life expositions.
e animals mentioned in this number after death
...ums situated in the vicinity of the garden or
n.
other objects required in the games of foot-
directly imported by sporting clubs, while the
...orce.

"18. Material intended for the market to be built in *praia* D. Manoel, in the Federal capital.

"19. Apparatus destined for the lighting and power service by means of alcohol.

"XIV. If deemed expedient to decree that the customs duties on the articles enumerated in Nos. 124, 130, 131, and 136 of the tariff be collected exclusively in gold.

"ART. 4. Article 3 of the law No. 1452 of December 30, 1905, shall continue in force, with the following modifications:

"In addition to the articles specified in article 2, paragraphs 33 and 36 of the preliminary provisions of the tariff, smooth wire, whether galvanized or not, No. 7 for fences and No. 14 to wrap cotton, fodder, and other agricultural products, wire to support grape vines, the following articles shall pay only 5 per cent *ad valorem* import duties.

"(1) Agricultural engines; (2) rubber valves for air pumps, or other apparatus of any form or description; (3) copper or brass wire cloth, pasteboard, or leather cones for turbines and component parts of diffusion batteries; (4) iron or brass wire brushes, or scrapers for cleaning pipes; (5) manometers for determining steam pressure or vacuum, temperature indicators; (6) tubes of copper, iron, or brass for boilers, concentrators, and evaporators; (7) mills for breaking and crushing sugar; (8) screens and stands as well as crossbars for furnaces; (9) pans, mills, and gearings, with their accessories; (10) power and transmission apparatus, including pulleys, shafts, cranks, axle journals, coupling clutches, pins, rings, and suspension collars; (11) rails with all their accessories, such as clamps, fish plates, screws, switches, counter rails, junction rails, switch points, and apparatus for operating same; (12) locomotives and cars with their accessories; (13) stills and distilling columns with their accessories; (14) molds, filters, crystallizers for purifying and refining sugar and special lime for the maufacture of sugar; (15) pumps of iron or other metal for liquids or pulps of all kinds or for hot or cold water supply; (16) glasses and tubes of glass for evaporating and condensing apparatus, to indicate the height of water or other liquid in boilers or other apparatus; (17) barbed wire and oval wire measuring 18 by 16 and 19 by 17, including the sheaves of iron or steel and their respective winders; (18) alcohol and denaturing and carburetting substances; (19) hogsheads of tinned iron for transporting alcohol, and also apparatus used for the industrial application of alcohol; (20) tools, hoes, and scythes for agricultural use. The above-mentioned machinery, apparatus, and articles are exempted from duties when imported by agricultural syndicates or directly by agriculturists, managers of agricultural companies, owners of stock farms, and also when imported by state and municipal governments.

regulations are issued in substitution of
the decree No. 5890 of February 10, 1906,
mentioned in article 108 of these regula-
7 per cent, the provision of this article in
; in force.
n .duty may be collected on articles of
milar articles of foreign manufacture are
; injurious to the public health, inasmuch
vhether national or foreign, is prohibited,
:les shall incur the penalties prescribed in
3.
uganda written in a foreign tongue and
il shall be included under article 2, para-
; provisions of the tariff.
emptions from import duties in cases per-
the provisions of the decree No. 917A of
le to railway and tramway cars, shall be

use clearances on gold coin and gold bars
ect to the stamp tax of 2 per cent on the
the rate of exchange is below 15d. per
educed to 1½ per cent whenever exchange

n bars or in powder exported directly by
cted from their mines is exempted from
vision, the President being authorized to
llection of the tax created by the present

"ART. 12. Roasted and ground artificial coffee can not be exposed for sale unless this condition is expressly stated on the wrapper, and such coffee is subject to a tax of 500 reis per kilogram or fraction of a kilogram, which shall be collected by means of stamps placed on the wrapper.

"Manufacturers and merchants violating this provision shall be punished by a fine of 3,000 milreis whenever the nature of artificial coffee is not declared or when such coffee is exposed for sale without being duly stamped, the fiscal agent denouncing such violation to receive half the fine.

"Coffee shall be considered artificial which has not been manufactured exclusively from the coffee bean.

"ART. 13. The period referred to in article 20 of law No. 1144, of December 30, 1903, is hereby extended to cover the present fiscal year.

"ART. 14. A consumption duty is hereby created on the following articles: 1½ milreis per kilogram of butter of domestic manufacture which is not made of pure milk; 610 reis per kilogram of artificial lard of domestic production.

"1. This tax shall be collected in accordance with the regulations in force and the instructions which the Government may issue.

"2. The butter and lard referred to in the present article may be exposed for consumption only when the words 'artificial butter' and 'artificial lard' are clearly written on the respective tins or other coverings.

"3. Articles injurious to the public health can not be delivered for consumption.

"4. Products which do not contain the declaration referred to in paragraph 2 shall be seized and destroyed after having been analyzed.

"5. Persons violating this provision shall be punished by fines of 1,000 to 5,000 milreis, and in case of repetition of the offense double this amount, without prejudice to the criminal penalties in which they may incur, such fines to be collected in accordance with the regulations in force.

"ART. 15. The railways of the Union shall give free transportation to insane persons destined to the asylums which are maintained or subsidized by the Federal or State governments.

"SEC. 1. A request for free transportation shall be made by the chiefs of police of the States or of the Federal district to the director of the railway on which transport is desired.

"SEC. 2. Free transportation will only be granted to patients who, on account of their poverty, have to be treated in the asylums free of charge.

"ART. 16. Article 15 of law No. 953 of December 29, 1902, shall continue in force, being extended to cover the West of Minas Railway.

"ART. 17. The provisions of Nos. VII, VIII, X, XI, XV, XVI, article 2, of law No. 1452 of December 30, 1905, and articles 17 and 18 of said law, and also all provisions of previous budget laws will remain in force, except those referring particularly to the fixing of receipts and expenditures, the stipulation or increase of salaries, reform of departments, or fiscal legislation that have not been expressly revoked.

"ART. 18. All contrary provisions are hereby revoked.

"GENERAL EXPENDITURES.

"ARTICLE 1. The general expenditures of the Republic of the United States of Brazil for the fiscal year 1907 is fixed at 315,478,637 *milreis* paper and 52,224,247 *milreis* gold, which will be divided among the different departments as specified in the following clauses:

	Gold.	National paper.
	Milreis.	*Milreis.*
Department of Justice and the Interior	10,700	31,379,813
Department of Foreign Relations	1,951,661	1,485,800
Navy Department	1,300,004	35,024,561
War Department	100,000	58,893,497
Department of Industry, Ways and Public Works	6,413,633	82,214,406
Treasury Department	42,442,349	106,480,558

RUBBER EXPORTS, 1905-6.

United States Consul G. E. ANDERSON, of Rio Janeiro, commenting on the annual message of the Governor of the State of Para, Dr. AUGUSTO MONTENEGRO, says:

" Embodied in the message of the governor is a table showing the amount of rubber produced and shipped abroad in the great Amazon rubber country, including not only the Brazilian ports of Para and Manãos, but the Peruvian port of Iquitos as well. This table shows the total exports July, 1905, to June, 1906, inclusive, to be as follows in pounds:

	Fine.	Medium.	Sernamby.	Caucho.	Total.
To Europe via—	*Pounds.*	*Pounds.*	*Pounds.*	*Pounds.*	*Pounds.*
Iquitos	1,457,911	302,552	1,500,969	1,855,372	5,116,806
Manãos	10,201,998	2,070,821	2,400,492	4,175,610	19,119,053
Para	11,969,643	1,367,561	8,879,471	2,546,571	19,763,253
Total	23,629,553	3,741,038	7,780,933	8,887,587	41,029,112
To the United States via—					
Iquitos	33,066	660	126,772	2,565	163,064
Manãos	6,757,115	1,647,374	2,158,591	2,311,848	12,872,999
Para	6,836,403	1,432,849	9,135,634	882,343	18,287,229
Total	13,626,584	3,080,913	11,415,998	3,197,757	31,323,293
Total to Europe and the United States	37,256,137	6,821,882	19,196,931	12,077,314	75,352,396

"It will be noted that of the 75,852,895 pounds sent by the three ports the United States received about 40 per cent. The proportion of the Brazilian rubber crop for 1904 taken by the United States was nearly 60 per cent, American manufacturers taking nearly 6,000,000 pounds more during that year than they did during the fiscal year ending June 30, 1906. Present figures indicate a very material change in the course of Brazil's rubber trade with the United States. The United States not only continues to take a larger quantity of rubber than any other nation, but it continues to take almost as much as all other markets, shipments from other ports being considered.

"The gold value of the rubber produced in the State of Para alone in the year ending June 30, 1906, was, according to the governor of the State, $18,117,200. The highest prices were realized in the New York market in September, at $1.28 for fine island rubber, and the lowest in June last, at $1.17 for the same grade. The total exports from the State of Para for the year ending June, 1906, were of a total value of 54,166,505$270, or something like $13,500,000."

COFFEE MOVEMENT, NOVEMBER, 1906.

["*Boletim da Associação Commercial*" of December 11, 1906.]

The coffee movement at the ports of Rio de Janeiro and Santos, for the month of November, 1906, compared with that of the same month of the previous year, was as follows:

	Rio de Janeiro.		Santos.	
	1906.	1905.	1906.	1905.
	Bags.	Bags.	Bags.	Bags.
Entries	462,644	356,826	1,676,955	872,644
Shipments	544,840	315,955	2,175,540	1,016,325
Sales	133,000	121,000	740,227	667,000
Daily average of entries	15,421	11,894	55,898	29,088
Daily average of shipments	20,728	12,209	72,518	33,874
Entries from July 1	2,183,054	1,898,403	7,952,156	5,045,256
Shipments from July 1	1,897,980	1,845,140	6,838,755	4,395,134
Stock on hand Nov. 30	502,670	593,677	1,676,660	1,458,863

CREATION OF CONVERSION OFFICE.

The following decree, No. 6267, of December 13, 1906, sets forth the regulations for the execution of law No. 1575 of December 6, 1906, creating the conversion office:

"PART I.—*The conversion office.*

"ARTICLE 1. The conversion office created by law No. 1575, of December 6, 1906, is specially intended to receive gold coin in accordance with article 5 of said law, and to deliver against same notes payable to bearer of exact value of the coins received at the rate of 15d. per *milreis* or equivalent in the moneys referred to in article 5 of the said law.

r. 2. The notes issued by the conversion office shall be legal in every part of the territory of the Republic, and shall be in for fulfilment of all contracts and payments, except those d to in article 2 of the above-mentioned law, and shall be d and paid at sight to bearer to be exchanged in gold coin at l office.

r. 3. The gold which the conversion office shall receive in ge for notes issued will be kept in deposit, and shall not be l upon any account nor upon any order for any other purpose ng conversion at the specified rate of exchange of the notes under the personal responsibility of the officials of the conver- ice and on the guaranty of the National Treasury.

r. 4. For diversion of the deposits referred to in the previous the officials of the conversion office shall be liable under article the Penal Code, in addition to the personal liability established article.

r. 5. The gold deposited in the conversion office will be pre- in suitable cases or parcels, with the amount of each marked l, and be duly numbered, dated, sealed, and deposited.

r. 6. Marks, francs, lire, dollars, as well as sovereigns, shall) make up the deposit referred to in the preceding article, and for the purposes of issue and conversion at the rate of 15d. lreis per pounds sterling and at corresponding rates for the oins.

r. 7. The amounts to credit of the 'redemption' and 'guar- f paper-money' funds, created under law 581 of June 20, 1899, ; transferred to the conversion office.

The redemption fund shall continue to be applied according to l of the above law.

The guarantee fund shall also be utilized for the redemption of money, which shall be replaced by notes issued by the conver- fice to the value of said fund, in conformity with paragraph 2 :le 9 of the law No. 1575 of December 6.

The administration and movement of the two funds, to which :icle refers, shall continue under the charge of the minister of isary.

"PART II.—*Issue of notes.*

r. 8. The value of the notes issued by the conversion office shall ond exactly to the amount of the deposits in gold existing in ice.

r. 9. In no case may notes be issued against deposits of silver of notes convertible in gold, or against bills of exchange.

r. 10. The notes issued shall be of the value of 10 *milreis* up to payable to bearer at sight.

"Paragraph 1. Such notes shall bear, besides the value they represent, the following declaration: 'The conversion office will pay to bearer, at sight, in Rio de Janeiro, the value of this note in gold coin at the rate of 15d. per *milreis* against value received in accordance with decree No. 1575 of December 6, 1906.

"Paragraph 2. If found convenient, the notes of 10 *milreis* and 20 *milreis* may be withdrawn from circulation and the issue be confined to notes of other denominations, ranging from 50 *milreis* up to 1 *conto*

"Art. 11. Fractional values without corresponding equivalent in gold coin shall be paid in national silver, nickel, or copper coin. The administration of the conversion office shall post in a prominent position within the building of the office tables showing the equivalents of foreign gold coins and of the fractions of same payable in national silver, nickel, or copper coin, in accordance with the table attached to this regulation relating to English coin.

"Art. 12. No notes shall be issued a second time.   When presented for exchange they shall be immediately inutilized by perforation or other convenient means, be noted in the corresponding books, and be burned, in accordance with the formalities to be established by the administration of the office.

"Art. 13. A sufficient supply of notes shall always be maintained in the safes, signed and ready to meet all demands.

"Paragraph 1. Signature of the notes shall be effected by employees of the conversion office or of the treasury, should the Minister of the Treasury so determine, and shall fill the greater part of the space allowed on same.

"Paragraph 2. The notes received by the office shall be duly examined, made up into labeled bundles, and be signed and stamped by the officials who examined them.

"Art. 14. All issues shall be entered in special books, wherein shall be specified the values of the notes, numbers, series, signatures, etc.

"Art. 15. For the exchange, substitution, remittance, or burning of notes, the instructions contained in decree No. 9370 of February 14, 1885, shall be observed so far as, in the judgment of the Minister of the Treasury, is advisable.

"Art. 16. The redemption of notes presented for payment shall be effected in such manner as to guarantee the authenticity of the notes and the regularity of the payment.

"Art. 17. The issue of notes by the conversion office shall cease when the total value of same shall amount to 320,000,000 *milreis* (equivalent to 20,000,000), when, in accordance with the law approved by Congress, the rate of 15d. per *milreis*, determined by Article 1 of law No. 1575 of 1906, may be altered.

"Art. 18. When the limit referred to in the preceding articles has been attained and the rate been altered, all the notes issued shall be

~~when maturing while not less~~ than one year from the date ~~the Minister of Finance.~~

~~If the time limit has expired,~~ notes shall continue to be ~~redeeming five years,~~ counting from initial date for same at a ~~on the inscribed value.~~

~~discount shall be 5 per cent for the first half year, 10 per cent~~ he second, 15 per cent during the third, and 20 per cent dur~~ing.~~ After five years the notes shall be proscribed and ant revert in favor of the fund mentioned in article 9 of law ~~b of 1906.~~

19. The conversion office shall keep a special account of all ued and the gold received, of which a balance sheet shall be the close of every week.

paragraph. After the closing of the Department the presi the conversion office shall forward to the Minister of the ɣ a daily report of the movement and the balance of deposits forward.

20. Until special notes for issue by the conversion office be unused notes of the Treasury shall be utilized, duly signed, d, and bearing the following declaration: 'At the conversion ll be paid to bearer the sum of —— value received in gold, lance with law No. 1575 of December 6, 1906.'

"PART III.—*Administration of the office.*

21. All employees in the conversion office are appointed nmission, and their services will be retained as long as found

22. The conversion office, which will be under the direct ion of the Minister of the Treasury, shall be administered by ent, vice-president, secretary, treasurer, and three assistants, nt, assistant accountant, six clerks, balance clerk, porter, two ers, and two porter's assistants. If necessary the services of t shall be engaged for verification of coins.

23. It shall be the duty of the president—

To direct and supervise all the work of the Department.

To put the present regulations into execution and all other ns of laws relating to the Department, as well as all instruc ed by the Minister of the Treasury.

To give balance accounts of cash in safes.

To communicate by letter with the public departments when ~~he requires it.~~

To make an annual report of the operations of the office and of atters of interest connected therewith.

To sign balance sheets and estimates and to open, close, and

" (7) To sign accounts, notes, or orders and modify same as deemed necessary.

" (8) To decide without appeal, with the assistance of the treasurer and the expert he may appoint, if necessary, upon the genuineness or spuriousness of coins presented at the office.

" (9) To propose to the Minister of the Treasury the nomination of employees for vacancies and the substitution of those he may consider incapable.

" (10) To advise, reprehend, or dismiss any employee of the department, and impose fines in accordance with these regulations.

" (11) To extend the office hours of the department.

" (12) To appoint experts in accordance with article 22.

" (13) To order the detention of any person who shall be discovered on the premises '*in flagrante delicto*' or shall commit acts prejudicial to the order of the department or to the preservation of its material, notify the respective authorities, and deliver over to them the delinquent.

"ART. 24. It shall be the duty of the vice-president to assist the president and to substitute him when necessary.

"ART. 25. It shall be the duty of the secretary to conduct all the official correspondence, register and file the same, and carry out the instructions of the president.

" ART. 26. It shall be the duty of the treasurer—

" (1) To propose the appointment of his assistants, to serve under his guarantee and responsibility, and he may require from them such guarantees as he may deem proper.

" (2) To receive, deposit, and keep all coins, notes, or other values received by the department.

" (3) To effect payments due at the department, as also of receipts or payment values of exchange of notes, and see that all such transactions are properly made.

" (4) To name the assistant to act as his substitute.

" (5) To prepare a daily report of the movement in the treasury.

" ART. 27. The treasurer shall be responsible for all values received and for all false notes or coins received in exchange by the conversion office.

"ART. 28. It shall be the duty of the assistants—

" (1) To substitute the treasurer when absent and assist him in all the duties appertaining to the department.

" (2) Perform the duties delegated to them by the treasurer in matters regarding receipts, payments, and safe-keeping of values.

"ART. 29. By designation of the treasurer one of his assistants may act as receiving and another as paying cashier.

" ART. 30. The duties of the accountant shall be as follows—

" (1) To direct and inspect all accounts.

ı the treasurer all balance sheets and
he books, as also those to be entered

ties of the clerks.
ties of the porter.
ties of the messengers.
vice-president, and treasurer shall be
resident of the Republic, and the other
ıd by the Secretary of the Treasury.
the treasurer shall be 100 *contos*, and
 way as that of the Treasurer of the

—*General provisions.*

 the Treasury, whenever he shall deem
erations of the conversion office to be
ıals whom he may select, and give the
) regulating of the work of the depart-
ı instructions.
 of the conversion office shall be from
ing day.
safes shall be held by the president and
s necessary in order to open the same.
ıf the conversion office shall be subject
in Section XI of decree No. 5390, of

t shall have the power to establish in
version office, according to the terms of
) law No. 1575, of December 6, 1906.
e conversion office shall have the power
 in London.
reasury shall issue instructions respect-
ncy and select the form of notes to be

ıcy has been formed, the salaries of
ıll be submitted to the approval of the

'reasury an exchange department will be
ı No. 3 of article 10 of law No. 1,575

"*Sole paragraph.* In order to institute this department the Government will have the right to utilize up to £3,000,000 of the gold reserves against paper, in case it resolves not to apply immediately the balance of the said fund to the amortisation of the paper money, according to the terms of paragraph 2 of article 9 of law No. 1,575 of December 6, 1906.

"ART. 43. The operations of the exchange department shall consist of the following:

"(1) Purchase and sale of bills at sight, at 90 days and at 120 days, on all European and American centers.

"(2) Purchase and sale of gold in coin or bar.

"ART. 44. The management of the exchange department will be confided to a director appointed by decree of the President of the Republic.

"ART. 45. The staff to be appointed for the exchange department shall consist of assistant director, bills payable clerk, five assistants to the above, bills receivable clerk, one assistant to the same, correspondence clerk, accountant, assistant accountant, treasurer, two receiving cashiers, one cash paying clerk, two messengers.

"ART. 46. All correspondence will be signed by the director, and all drafts will bear his signature and that of the accountant or assistant director, in case the director be not present.

"ART. 47. The directors of the exchange department will present weekly to the Minister of the Treasury a balance sheet of the operations of the department, and, daily, a report upon the movement of the cash.

"ART. 48. Until further deliberation by the Government the exchange department will continue to transact business as hitherto at the Banco do Brazil.

"ART. 49. To commence the work of the conversion office the Minister of the Treasury may appoint for the services of that department any employees of departments subordinate to the ministry, giving them instructions as he may consider necessary, and stipulating their gratification, which shall not exceed the half of the amount of their salaries.

"Rio de Janeiro, December 13, 1906.

"DAVID CAMPISTA."

PREMIUMS OFFERED TO GROWERS OF CACAO.

For the purpose of encouraging the cultivation of cacao in São Paulo, the legislature of this State has recently passed a law authorizing the government to pay premiums during the next three years to those engaged in cacao cultivation in the southern part of this State. Those competing for the premiums must have at least 25 hectares of land suitable for cacao raising and not less than 1,000 trees.

'is each. At the close of the second year
year of age will receive 200 *reis* each, and
age will receive 100 *reis* each. The pre-
re as follows: 15,000 trees of one year, 200
years, 100 *reis*; 50,000 trees of 3 years,

ION OF FOREIGNERS.

ition of the decree of January 7, 1907, rela-
signers from Brazil:
r who for any reason shall compromise the
c tranquility, may be expelled from a part
l territory.
are considered causes sufficient for expul-

or prosecution by foreign courts for ordi-

i, at least, by the Brazilian courts for ordi-

idicancy, and seduction, when adequately

who shall reside in the territory of the
ive years or for less time may be expelled
married to a Brazilian woman, or is a wid-
rilian woman.
Power may prevent the entrance into the
f any foreigner whose antecedents author-
ong those referred to in articles 1 and 2.
ance may not be denied a foreigner under
article 3, if he has withdrawn from the

il be individual and in the form of an act
ustice and the Interior.
Power shall make an annual statement to
int of this law, giving the names of those
and stating also the cases in which he has
s of the State authorities and the reasons

Power shall notify officially the foreigner
xpel from the country, giving his reasons

therefor, and granting him from three to thirty days in which to withdraw, and he may, as a measure of public safety, order his detention up to the moment of departure.

"ART. 8. Within the term granted, the foreigner may have recourse to the authority ordering the expulsion when the causes of the expulsion are those specified in article 1, or to the judicial power, when the expulsion is ordered in accordance with the provision of article 2. Only in the latter case shall the appeal have suspensive effect.

" *Sole paragraph*. The appeal to the judicial power shall consist in proving the falsity of the reasons alleged before the sectional judge.

"ART. 9. The foreigner who shall return to the territory from which he has been expelled shall be prosecuted by the sectional judge and sentenced to imprisonment of from one to three years, and after filling the sentence, he shall again be expelled.

"ART. 10. The Executive power may revoke the order of expulsion when the causes determining it have ceased to exist."

THE BRAZILIAN LLOYD.

The Brazilian Lloyd which inaugurated its monthly steamship service between Rio de Janeiro and New York last August has already made three trips. The first trip was made with the steamer *Goyaz*, which carried 13,768 packages of freight, for which it received in freight charges $12,233. The *Sergipe*, which made the second trip, had a cargo of 24,072 packages, the freight rates amounting to $13,100. On the third trip the steamer started from Rio de Janeiro with a cargo of 14,703 packages.

RUBBER FORESTS IN STATE OF PIAUHY.

There have been discovered recently in the forests along the banks of the Parnahyba River, in the State of Piauhy, great areas covered with rubber trees of the maniçoba variety, which it is expected, when developed, will be a source of great revenue to that State.

NEW DEPARTMENT CREATED.

The President of Brazil issued a decree on December 29, 1906, authorizing the creation of a new department to be known as the Department of Agriculture, Industry, and Commerce. The Department of Industry, Ways, and Public Works will hereafter be known as the Department of Ways and Public Works.

PRIZES OFFERED FOR AGRICULTURAL MACHINERY.

The government of the State of São Paulo has been authorized by its legislature to offer prizes of different amounts to manufacturers of agricultural machinery, who shall, during the next five years, manull leaves, sticks, and stones.

FFEE CROP FOR 1907-8.

respectively by the Coffee Association
Commercial Association of Santos. to
azil for the year 1907-8, recently sub-
The crop to be exported from Santos,
e Janeiro, 3,500,000 bags.

F BELLO HORIZONTE.

Minas Geraes recently issued a decree
o industrial enterprises for the estab-
Horizonte, the capital of that State.
l industrial companies which establish
'ill be furnished, free of charge, with
f ten years and will be given the land
s. They will also be exempt from the
of five years. As the result of these
and a collar and cuff factory are now
sed to build shortly a shoe factory and
fruits, etc.
naugurate a period of great industrial
but 10 years old:

FAMBUCO, NOVEMBER, 1906.

e Commercial Association of Pernam-
atistics of the export movement at that
er, 1906:

13	Skins .... bales..	127
156	Castor-oil seed .... bags..	784
14	Cacao ....do....	3
46	Coffee ....do....	3,238
475	Soap ....boxes..	8,900
385	Oile ....do....	790
407	Do ....barrels..	356

IMMIGRATION.

According to figures published in the *"Diario Official,"* of December 27, 1906, the number of immigrants entering Brazil and the Argentine Republic during the years from 1880 to 1904 was as follows:

	Brazil.	Argentine Republic.		Brazil.	Argentine Republic.
1880	29,729	41,651	1894	63,294	80,67
1881	11,054	47,484	1895	161,371	80,98
1882	27,197	51,503	1896	158,179	135,20
1883	28,670	63,243	1897	44,355	105,12
1884	20,087	77,805	1898	27,650	95,19
1885	30,135	108,722	1899	29,920	111,08
1886	25,741	93,116	1900	13,801	105,92
1887	54,900	120,842	1901	15,724	125,95
1888	131,745	155,632	1902	14,558	96,08
1889	65,187	260,909	1903	14,950	112,67
1890	107,100	110,594	1904	19,914	161,78
1891	216,659	52,097			
1892	86,213	73,294	Total	1,512,399	2,555,24
1893	123,926	84,420			

TARIFF MODIFICATION, 1906.

I.—*Decree No. 1499, of September 1, 1906, relating to the mode of payment of the taxes on foreign beer.*

["*Diario Official,*" No. 205, of September 4, 1906.]

ARTICLE 1. Under the present decree, beer mentioned in tariff No. 124 is subject to the provisions of article 1, No. 1, and of article 2, letter *a*, III, of the decree No. 1452, dated December 30, 1905. Guiness' stout is, however, excepted, and shall pay the duty stated in the tariff, at the rate of 50 per cent in gold, according to the stipulations contained in letter *a*, No. 3, of article 2 of the decree aforesaid.

ART. 2. All contrary provisions are hereby repealed.

COMMERCIAL AGREEMENT WITH ITALY.

In pursuance of an exchange of notes between the Italian Legation and the Ministry for Foreign Affairs of Brazil, the provisional commercial agreement resulting from the notes exchanged on July 5, 1900, is maintained in force until December 31, 1908. Consequently, Italian products entering Brazil shall continue to enjoy the rates of the minimum tariff so long as the import duties applicable in Italy to coffee originating from Brazil shall not exceed 130 *francs* per 100 kilograms.

IMPROVEMENT WORKS AT PARA.

By the decree of December 20, 1906, the Brazilian Government authorizes the *Port of Para Company* to operate in Brazil. This company was organized in September, 1906, at Portland, Maine, for the purpose of building or leasing and operating port works in Brazil and

ital of $27,500,000, of which $7,500,000 are
00 common stock. The par value of both
$100. The preferred stock is guaranteed a

FOR PRINTING NEW NOTES.

reasury has entered into a contract with the
olland, and WATERLOW & SONS, of England,
tes to be used by the conversion department
otes of the denominations of 1,000 *milreis*
ade by the Holland firm, and those of other
glish firm.

NEW STATE LOANS.

lo recently negotiated a loan of £3,000,000
ER & Co., of London, and the National City
e loan is made at 95, at 5 per cent interest,
years.
announced, according to advices from Brazil,
ent will guarantee the loan of £5,000,000 in
o de Janeiro and Minas Geraes, the proceeds
nnection with the coffee valorization scheme.
have been in progress during the past sixty
ment of the Federal guarantee has been
pletion of the arrangements for this money
will be immediate united action on the part
he three States of São Paulo, Rio, and Minas
rization.
le do Sul is preparing to negotiate two loans,
of 1,850,000 *milreis* paper, and the second,
aring 7 per cent interest. This last is to be
ilways of the State and leasing the same.

SURTAX ON MERCHANDISE.

l issued a decree on January 12, 1907, estab-
gold on all imports made through the custom-
io Grande do Sul. The product of this tax
rt works which are soon to be begun at the
l. This tax will be collected beginning with

ADHERENCE TO THE HAGUE CONVENTION.

Brazil has made public its adherence to the conventions signed at The Hague July 29, 1899, the one relating to the laws and usages of war on land, the other extending the principles of the Geneva Convention of August 22, 1864, to maritime wars.

CHILE.

CUSTOMS REVENUES, NOVEMBER AND FIRST ELEVEN MONTHS OF 1906.

According to official statistics the various custom-houses of Chile collected during the month of November, 1906, a total revenue of 10,764,975.30 *pesos*, of which sum 3,554,842.52 *pesos* were for import duties, 7,009,610.84 *pesos* for export duties, and 200,521.94 *pesos* for miscellaneous receipts.

During the same month of 1905 the amount collected for import duties was 2,983,176.52 *pesos;* for export duties, 6,013,508.19 *pesos*, and for miscellaneous receipts, 196,746.79 *pesos*, making a total of 9,193,431.50 *pesos*.

A comparison of the receipts of November, 1906, with those of the same month of 1905 shows an increase in import duties of 561,666 *pesos*, in export duties of 996,102.65 *pesos*, and in miscellaneous receipts of 3,775.15 *pesos*, a total increase of 1,561,543.80 *pesos*.

The following table shows the amount collected by each custom-house during the month under review, the figures for the same month of 1905 being also given for purposes of comparison:

Custom-houses.	November—	
	1905.	1906.
I. Export duties:	*Pesos.*	*Pesos.*
Pisagua	1,008,308.46	936,242.94
Iquique	2,479,775.82	2,992,172.65
Tocopilla	776,235.76	849,786.63
Antofagasta	943,872.69	1,504,302.83
Taltal	805,315.96	727,096.51
Total	6,013,508.19	7,009,610.84
II. Import duties:		
Arica	33,648.71	97,976.96
Pisagua	19,631.71	25,492.19
Iquique	240,107.92	330,270.33
Tocopilla	16,726.93	20,467.94
Antofagasta	219,282.77	214,383.76
Taltal	30,147.90	79,676.34
Caldera	9,859.25	11,585.04
Coquimbo	63,691.99	128,597.77
Valparaiso	1,736,002.17	1,908,428.31
Talcahuano	469,578.61	499,800.17
Coronel	13,419.43	68,155.16
Valdivia	78,823.21	84,907.42
Puerto Montte	2,100.89	2,622.00
Ancud		122.55
Frontier custom-houses	45,180.03	39,404.68
Total	2,983,176.52	3,554,842.52
III. Miscellaneous receipts	196,746.79	200,521.94
Grand total	9,193,431.50	10,764,975.30

uonths of 1906 the revenue collected by the
o a total of 91,407,120.39 pesos, as against
ed during the same period of the previous
530.58 pesos.

... OF GRAPHITE OR PLUMBAGO.

n its issue for December 5, 1906, announces
... deposits of graphite or plumbago on
...; situated in the Department of Castro
f Chiloe Island, at a latitude of 42° 28'.
it pure plumbago, of steely and metallic
:ional quantity. They do not differ from
irrowdale mines at Cumberland, already
:onsidered the best in the world.
various industries, for the manufacture of
:ducing metals, as well as for lubricating
.et and cast iron to prevent it from rusting,
i to be electrotyped. In view of the indus-
;ubstance in its various applications this
source of wealth for the country.

...DING OF VALPARAISO.

ie Minister of the Interior promulgated a
nstruction of the city of Valparaiso, Chile,
quake occurred in the summer of that year.
ed, and conduits for gas, water, and sewer-
iance with modern sanitary methods. The
in lines approved by the Executive and the
  expropriation of such properties as are
:ing decreed as provided by the law of June

:public is authorized to contract a loan of
) be spent on public improvements through-
ied that £300,000 shall be employed for the
)ublic edifices. Private individuals are to
: leveling and paving their properties, and
rintended by a commission composed of the
;, the municipal governor, and five persons
it of the Republic.
·e been granted to Chilean citizens and to
r the construction of new electric car lines
utility.

APPROVAL OF IMMIGRATION CONTRACT.

The Minister of Colonization, on December 31, 1906, approved the contract celebrated between the Government of Chile and Señor Cme FANTINI for the introduction into the country through the ports of Valparaiso and Talcahuano of 30,000 workmen, with or without their families. The nationalities specified are Italian, French, and Spanish.

The contractor must indicate the trade or occupation of each intending immigrant, and must certify as to his good physical condition and his immunity from any criminal legal process.

The Chilean Government guarantees the payment of £9 to each adult, £10 for each son 12 years of age, and £4 for each child under 1 years old.

Liberal land grants have been made to corporations with the understanding that a certain number of immigrants shall be located thereon within a certain time. This scheme is meeting with fair success.

UNIFORMITY OF CONSULAR REPORTS.

The Minister of Foreign Relations of the Chilean Government, under date of October 11, 1906, issued a departmental circular to the various consuls of Chile in foreign countries, setting forth the rules to be followed in the preparation of statistical data covering the foreign trade of the Republic. The uniform preparation of this data is especially insisted upon in order to facilitate comparison in successive years.

Eight general headings for the classification of information are given, as follows: Imports—covering year, quantity, and value; exports—year, quantity, and value; imports by countries—year, country of origin, and value; exports—year, country of destination, and value; nature of imports; nature of exports; maritime movement—entries, departures.

Comparative figures for five years are to be furnished and a uniform nomenclature for articles of trade is required.

FACTORY CENSUS OF SANTIAGO, 1906.

The following figures were taken from the factory census of Santiago of 1906: Number of factories, 945; capital invested in machinery, 7,506,846 *pesos;* total capital invested, 31,741,310 *pesos;* raw material consumed in one year, 23,451,209 *pesos;* number of motors, 206; horsepower of motors, 3,296; average production, 37,857,517 *pesos.*

The number of factories does not include all those operating within the city of Santiago; small factories employing less than five laborers were omitted.

COLOMBIA.

TARIFF MODIFICATIONS.

I.—*Ordinance No. 993, of July 10, 1906, classifying for duty camel's-hair belting.*

["*Diario Oficial,*" No. 12705, of July 27, 1906.]

Camel's-hair belting shall be dutiable as "Tissues of horsehair or other material not specially mentioned" under Class X of the tariff.

II.—*Decree No. 912, dated July 31, 1906, granting free importation to certain machines and apparatus.*

["*Diario Oficial,*" No. 12722, of August 18, 1906.]

SOLE ARTICLE. Machines and apparatus not made in the country, imported for the manufacture of sugar, shall be exempted from import duty.

Paragraph. The present decree shall enter into operation on the day of its publication in the "*Diario Oficial,*" but any machines of the kind referred to imported on or after June 20, 1906, will also be entitled to the privileged treatment.

III.—*Decree No. 950, of August 14, 1906, as to the exportation of male neat cattle.*

["*Diario Oficial,*" No. 12725, of August 22, 1906.]

ARTICLE 1. Male neat cattle exported through the ports of the Republic on the Atlantic coast shall pay 3 *pesos* each.

ART. 2. This shall be applicable ten days after the publication of the present decree in the "*Diario Oficial.*"

ART. 3. Article 1 of decree No. 285, dated March 5, 1906, is modified accordingly.

IV.—*Ordinance No. 1006, dated July 26, 1906, classifying for duty paraffin candles.*

["*Diario Oficial*" No. 12737, of September 5, 1906.]

In accordance with the decree No. 603, dated May 25, 1906, candles of paraffin or spermaceti are to be dutiable under Class IX of the tariff.

V.—*Decree No. 1026, of October 28, 1906, reducing the import duty on certain articles.*

["*Diario Oficial*" No. 12742, of September 12, 1906.]

SOLE ARTICLE. For tariff purposes, the following goods are to be deemed to belong to the under-noted classes:

Class II: Galvanized iron wire gauze, perforated for the treatment of coffee; manures with azote, phosphate of lime, and ammonia basis;

pita ("fique") bags; niter, arsenious acid, regulus of antimony, black oxide, cobalt, oxide of manganese, boracic acid, enamel paints, nitrate of potassium, bichromate of potassium, metallic arsenic, antimony, and uranium; plows.

Class III: Steel, in bars or rods, when intended to be further manufactured.

Class IV: Carbonic acid gas; oil of mirbane.

Paragraph. The present decree shall enter into operation on the day of its publication in the "*Diario Oficial.*"

PROHIBITED EXPORTATION OF SILVER AND GOLD COINS.

In view of the increase which has been noticed lately in the exportation of silver and gold coins from Colombia, and of the fact that such exportation is detrimental to the national interests, the President of the Republic, in a decree dated December 8, 1906, has prohibited the same. Persons violating this decree shall be punished as defrauders of the national treasury.

IMPROVEMENT OF THE CAUCA AND NECHÍ RIVERS.

The President of the Republic, on November 5, 1906, approved the contract entered into by the Ministers of Public Works and of Finance on October 27, 1906, with the "*Compañía Colombiana de Transportes,*" located at Barranquilla, for the improvement of the Cauca and Nechí rivers.

The principal provisions of the contract as published in the "*Diario Oficial,*" of December 28, 1906, are as follows:

The company shall clean out and make navigable the river Cauca from Valdivia down to its junction with the Magdalena and the river Nechí from Zaragoza to its junction with the Cauca, and shall establish regular steam transport on the said rivers sufficient for the needs of the traffic.

The work of dredging the rivers shall begin within two years and be terminated within two years thereafter.

The company is obliged to construct the necessary buildings, dwelling houses for its employees, offices and warehouses wherever it may be necessary. Public lands may be taken without cost for this purpose.

The company shall keep open the channel of the rivers for the term of the contract, and at the termination thereof the Government shall receive the rivers in a navigable condition."

Navigation of the parts of the rivers covered in the contract is the exclusive monopoly of the company.

The employees of the company are, in time of peace, exempt from military and police duty.

The Government grants importation, free of duties, of steamboats, dredges, tools, utensils, machines and parts thereof, diving suits, and other things intended exclusively for the indicated work.

The Government grants $6,000 gold a year in aid of the enterprise for the term of fifteen years, counting from the date of the first voyage made by steamboat.

The company is required to give bond for $3,000 gold.

The contract may be assigned, with the permission of the Government, to anyone except to a foreign nation or Government.

The maximum prices for transport by the company shall not exceed $6 gold for each first-class passenger, and $16 per metric ton or for 2 cubic meters in bulk of freight, as the company may elect.

The prices given are for the whole distance on the Canca. Transit from intermediate points shall pay in proportion. Mail matter shall be carried free, as also Government employees on official business.

Government property, officials, and soldiers shall be carried for one-half the regular rate.

The contract shall continue for fifty years.

COSTA RICA.

TARIFF MODIFICATIONS, 1906.

I.—*Decree of February 2, 1906, in reference to prohibited imports.*

["La Gaceta" No. 29, of February 4, 1906.]

ARTICLE 1. The provisions of article 9 of the Fiscal Code are to read as follows:

"ART. 9. No arms, ammunition or equipments of war, dynamite or nitroglycerine, foodstuffs discovered to be in a state of corruption or of a quality injurious to public health may be imported nor articles which form or may in future form a monopoly. The mere fact that such goods are landed in the country, even though it may only be a question of a mere transit, or are introduced or transshipped on vessels of small tonnage in territorial waters, shall be properly looked upon as a case of actual importation as regards the responsibilities and the penalties provided by law."

ART 2. Vessels of large tonnage are those of more than 600 tons burden and vessels of small tonnage those of less than 600 tons. Before any person can be allowed to transship nonprohibited goods from a vessel of large tonnage to a vessel of small tonnage or from one to another vessel of small tonnage, he will be required to pay the import duties and quay dues designated in the tariff in connection with the merchandise to be transshipped. This provision likewise applies to persons desiring to reship goods on vessels of small tonnage, or in case the latter are to enter territorial waters with foreign products or merchandise. Transshipment between vessels of large tonnage or reshipment on one of them shall not be subject to other duties than those leviable under article 93 of the Fiscal Code.

ART. 3. The present decree shall enter into force on the day of its publication, save as to article 2 which shall only take effect on March 1, next.

II.—*Circular dated February 13, 1906, relating to the importation of maize-grinding mills.*

["*La Gaceta*" No. 37, of February 14, 1906.]

According to this circular, mills for grinding crude or cooked maize, called by certain importers under the name of "*molinillos para tortillas*," are to be dutiable at the rate of 3 *centimes* of a *colon* per kilogram under No. 14 of the tariff.

III.—*Decree of February 20, 1906, respecting the importation of "iztepeque" tobacco.*

["*La Gaceta*" No. 43, of February 21, 1906.]

SOLE ARTICLE. From and after April 1, 1907, tobacco called "*iztepeque*" may be imported by private persons on payment at the custom-house of the duty fixed by decree No. 3 of August 12, 1896, namely, 1 *colon* and 75 *centimes* per kilogram, in addition to the quay and theater dues leviable thereon.

IV.—*Decree of March 21, 1906, assessing duty on school bags and office clips and portfolios.*

["*La Gaceta*" No. 68, of March 22, 1906.]

ARTICLE 1.—The underdescribed articles are dutiable as follows:

(*a*) Scholars' satchels or bags for carrying their books and requisites, at the rate of 11 *centimes* per kilogram.

(*b*) Clips for holding papers, at the rate of 16 *centimes* per kilogram.

(*c*) Office portfolios, at the rate of 43 *centimes* per kilogram.

ART. 2. The above-named duties shall not be subject to the surtax of 50 per cent, and any goods of this description lying at the custom-house, or as to which a dispute may have arisen, shall be cleared in accordance with the provisions of the present decree.

V.—*Decree of June 5, 1906, relating to the importation of dynamite and other explosives for industrial purposes.*

["*La Gaceta*" No. 129, of June 7, 1906.]

SOLE ARTICLE. This decree sanctions decree No. 17 issued on April 19, 1906, by the permanent commission sanctioning the agreement entered into between the Executive and the Standard Explosives Company (Limited), by which dynamite and other explosives are admitted to importation and warehousing in the country, when destined for industrial purposes.

VI.—*Decree of June 7, 1906, determining the classification of liquefied carbonic acid.*

["*La Gaceta*" No. 130, of June 8, 1906.]

SOLE ARTICLE. From and after July 1, 1906, liquefied carbonic acid shall be dutiable at the rate of 5 *centimes* per kilogram, without being subject to the surtax of 50 per cent.

Decree No. 10, of January 26, last, is amended accordingly.

VII.—*Decree of July 6, 1906, exempting certain machines from import duty.*

["*La Gaceta*" No. 11, of July 13, 1906.]

SOLE ARTICLE. Machines of all kinds used for the treatment of coffee, cocoa, sugar, starch, rice, and "*panelas*," as also for the manufacture of brooms, alimentary pastes, and beer shall be admitted free of duty for a period of five years.

VIII.—*Decree of August 4, 1906, as to the importation of oiled cotton clothing.*

["*La Gaceta*" No 31, of August 5, 1906.]

SOLE ARTICLE. From September 1, 1906, cotton clothing, oiled for the purpose of protecting from rain, shall be dutiable at the rate of 30 *centimes* per kilogram, without being subject to the surtax of 50 per cent.

IX.—*Decree of August 16, 1906, classifying the specific called "santyl (knoll.)"*

["*La Gaceta*" No. 41, of August 17, 1906.]

SOLE ARTICLE. The specific called "*santyl (knoll)*" shall pay 3 *colons* 50 *centimes* per kilogram, without being subject to the surtax of 50 per cent.

X.—*Decree of September 21, 1906, establishing the classification
iron sheets for chimney stacks.*

["*La Gaceta*" No. 69, of September 22, 1906.]

SOLE ARTICLE. Iron sheets for chimney stacks shall be dutiable
the latter, from October 15, 1906.

Sheets of the kind, imported perforated, between the date of t
present decree and October 15, shall be dutiable according to t
established practice.

EXPORT TRADE OF PUNTARENAS, APRIL TO NOVEMBER, 1906

According· to statistics published in "*La Gaceta*" of Costa Rica,
its number for December 22, 1906, the export trade of the port
Puntarenas, from April 1, 1906, to November 30, 1906, amounted
250,295 kilograms, valued at 186,179.69 *colones.* The principal artic
exported were the following: Gold in bars, 57,377.50 *colones;* co
43,246.80 *colones;* rubber, 31,883.40 *colones;* cocoa, 14,964.80 *colone*
skins, 18,606.55 *colones;* leather, 10,491.80 *colones.* The rest is d
tributed among other products of lesser importance.

CUBA.

THE PUBLIC TREASURY ON DECEMBER 31, 1906.

Following is a statement recently published by the Department
Finance of Cuba, and it shows the situation of the Treasury of t
Republic on December 31, 1906:

DEBIT.

Orders of advance funds in transit	$1, 121, 467.
External-debt bonds	1, 000, 600.
Special laws	7, 875, 862.
Postal money-order fund	231, 336.
Pending obligations	4, 262.
Fund for honorary consuls	465.
Loan tax fund	1, 806, 867.
Loan deposit fund, first 50 per cent	67, 421.
Balance fund of army salaries, second 50 per cent	1, 121, 494.
Revenue fund	864, 898.
Total	14, 117, 611.

CREDIT.

In cash	13, 009, 368.
In external-debt bonds	1, 000, 600.
Remittances in transit	107, 642.
Total	14, 117, 611.

SUGAR CROP OF 1905-6.

According to figures published by the "Official Bulletin" of the Department of Agriculture, Industry, and Commerce of Cuba, a general statement of the sugar output of the Republic during 1905-6, as compared with the preceding year, was as follows:

	Exports.		Stock on hand.	
	1904-5.	1905-6.	1904-5.	1905-6.
	Sacks.	*Sacks.*	*Sacks.*	*Sacks.*
Havana	997,031	1,182,751	146,955	3,615
Matanzas	1,269,007	1,353,125	96,137	772
Cardenas	1,150,784	1,108,015	120,908	
Cienfuegos	1,219,459	1,604,713	100,527	835
Sagua	622,155	666,947	18,198	
Caibarien	576,174	620,587	18,936	
Guantanamo	325,628	309,207		1,200
Cuba	113,335	82,618	312	
Manzanillo	313,060	327,177		
Santa Cruz del Sur	71,019	76,005		
Nuevitas	85,159	143,980		
Gibara y Puerto Padre	497,201	488,717		
Zaza		18,200	13,700	
Trinidad	70,996	71,191		
	7,311,008	8,053,263	515,673	6,322

SUMMARY.

	1904-5.	1905-6.
	Tons.	*Tons.*
Exports	1,044,430	1,150,466
Stock on hand	73,668	903
Total	1,118,098	1,151,369
Domestic consumption in 12 months	45,160	46,830
	1,163,258	1,198,199
Old stock on hand January 1		19,450
Total production	1,163,258	1,178,749

Increase in 1905-6, 15,491 tons, or 1.314 per cent.

EXPORTS OF TOBACCO DURING 1906.

The exports of tobacco from the Republic of Cuba during the calendar year 1906, compared with those of 1905, were as follows, according to official statistics:

	Leaf tobacco.		Manufactured tobacco.		Cut tobacco.
			Cigars.	Cigarettes.	
Jan. 1 to Dec. 31—	*Bales.*	*Kilos.*	*Number.*	*Packages.*	*Kilos.*
1906	277,426	12,636,836	256,738,029	15,643,275	169,260
1905	317,087	14,776,139	227,028,521	11,829,076	119,337
Increase or decrease	39,661	2,139,303	29,709,508	3,814,199	49,923

Following is a statement showing the exports of leaf tobacco and cigars from Cuba during the eight years from 1899 to 1906:

Year.	Leaf tobacco.	Cigars.	Year.	Leaf tobacco.	Cigars.
	Bales.	Number.		Bales.	Number.
1899	144, 264	193, 166, 736	1903	303, 106	208, 607, 410
1900	223, 516	204, 971, 383	1904	250, 638	217, 645, 082
1901	238, 479	213, 425, 089	1905	317, 087	227, 028, 321
1902	260, 982	208, 508, 550	1906	277, 426	256, 738, 029

FISCAL REVENUES DURING 1906.

According to statistics published by the Department of Finance of the Cuban Republic, the collection of public revenues during the calendar year 1906 was as follows, by months:

January	$2, 524, 762. 40	August	$2, 392, 288. 36
February	2, 453, 036. 99	September	1, 674, 170. 73
March	2, 686, 501. 62	October	1, 951, 893. 36
April	2, 109, 281. 55	November	2, 211, 869. 22
May	2, 577, 942. 08	December	2, 303, 529. 50
June	2, 177, 059. 71		
July	2, 356, 099. 62	Total	27, 418, 435. 14

The special tax for the amortization of the loan yielded, during the year, under review, a total revenue of $3,683,742.84, distributed as follows:

January	$323, 307. 96	August	$338, 850. 18
February	278, 756. 35	September	186, 462. 78
March	312, 700. 22	October	292, 712. 39
April	271, 455. 50	November	380, 503. 21
May	297, 710. 64	December	347, 506. 37
June	309, 350. 17		
July	365, 427. 07	Total	3, 683, 742. 84

CONCESSION FOR A SUBMARINE CABLE.

The "*Gaceta Oficial*" of Cuba for December 26, 1906, publishes a decree granting a concession to the Commercial Cable Company of Cuba, an organization of United States origin, to lay submarine cables between the continental coast of the United States and Cuba, and to work and maintain a cable service between those countries from January 10, 1907.

EXTRADITION TREATY WITH THE DOMINICAN REPUBLIC.

The "*Gaceta Oficial*" of Cuba, in its issue of January 15, 1907, publishes the text of the treaty for the extradition of criminals between the Cuban and Dominican Republics, concluded and signed by the respective plenipotentiaries in the city of Havana on the 29th of June, 1905, and approved by the Cuban Senate on January 10, 1906. The ratifications of this treaty were exchanged in Havana on January 11, 1907, and it shall take effect thirty days thereafter, continuing in force for one year from the date of the denunciation thereof by either of the contracting parties.

AMERICAN AND ENGLISH CAPITAL IN THE REPUBLIC.

According to latest statistics, the American capital invested in Cuba amounts to $141,000,000, distributed as follows: Railroads, $34,000,000; sugar and tobacco industries, $68,000,000; real estate, $18,000,000; small agricultural industries, $4,000,000; mining, $3,500,000; commerce and manufactures, $4,000,000; banking, $5,000,000; navigation companies, $1,500,000; mortgages, $3,500,000.

The English capital invested in the Republic amounts to $100,-000,000, of which $90,000,000 are in railroads, $5,000,000 in steamers, and $5,000,000 in real estate.

ECUADOR.

INAUGURATION OF PRESIDENT ELOY ALFARO.

The inauguration of Gen. ELOY ALFARO, Acting President of Ecuador, as Constitutional President of the Republic occurred on January 1, 1907.

GUATEMALA.

CONCESSION FOR THE EXPLOITATION OF NATIONAL FORESTS.

"*El Guatemalteco*," an official publication of the Republic of Guatemala, in its issue of November 2, 1906, publishes the text of contract entered into between the Government and Mr. JOSÉ WER, authorizing the latter to fell timber and extract rubber, chicle, and other rosins from the national forests located in the Department of Peten. The term of the contract is five years, and the concessionaire shall pay 500 *pesos* annually besides the export duties specified in the concession.

This contract was approved by the Executive on October 20, 1906.

HAITI.

RAILROAD CONTRACT.

"*Le Moniteur*," official journal of Haiti, publishes the text of a contract granting a concession by the Government for the construction of a railroad line from Port au Prince to Cayes, passing through Leogane, Grand Goave, Petit Goave, Miragoane, Anse-a-Veau, Asile, and Cavaillon. This line will be about 240 kilometers in length and measure 42 inches between rails.

REESTABLISHMENT OF THE FORMER DUTIES ON SOAP.

According to the terms of a governmental decree, the import duties on soap are modified as follows:

According to the terms of the present tariff, a duty of $2.15 per 50 kilograms is levied on soap.

Since the 1st of November the duty is only 50 cents per 50 kilograms.

The greater part of the soaps used for laundry purposes are imported from the United States, while the better grades of toilet soaps are imported from France.

MEXICO.

FOREIGN COMMERCE, OCTOBER, 1906.

According to figures issued by the Statistical Division of the Treasury Department of the Republic of Mexico, the foreign commerce of the country for October, 1906, and for the first four months of the fiscal year, 1906-7, was represented by the following valuations, the figures for the corresponding periods of the preceding year being also given for purposes of comparison:

The total value of imports for the four months under review amounted to $69,195,817.76 as compared with $53,014,426.92 in the corresponding period of 1905-6, an increase being thus shown of $16,181,390.84.

Total exports for the period amounted to $72,768,991.91 as against $79,126,225.20 in the first four months of 1905-6, a decline of $6,357,233.29.

Details of the trade from July to October, 1906, inclusive, show the following results:

IMPORTS.

[Silver valuation.]

Articles.	October—		First four months—	
	1906–7.	1905–6.	1906–7.	1905–6.
Animal substances	$1,641,341.65	$1,097,179.32	$6,380,518.57	$5,181,247.35
Vegetable substances	1,995,321.55	2,257,764.19	8,549,079.30	8,269,773.66
Mineral substances	7,681,073.91	4,352,790.70	23,442,145.75	14,525,201.04
Dry goods	2,317,608.47	1,988,333.14	9,375,329.13	7,605,781.54
Chemical and pharmaceutical substances	653,064.51	639,437.58	2,701,144.11	2,395,146.34
Beverages	420,810.81	507,205.10	2,083,174.93	2,858,214.15
Paper and its applications	489,604.65	458,755.68	1,758,694.63	1,790,526.79
Machinery and apparatus	1,910,715.34	1,599,718.95	8,158,651.18	6,072,488.02
Vehicles	760,417.75	315,255.67	2,470,393.81	1,058,942.91
Arms and explosives	366,996.99	283,695.63	1,250,144.33	1,323,095.40
Miscellaneous	737,688.36	613,875.64	3,027,142.02	2,434,009.72
Total	18,275,771.99	14,113,991.60	69,195,817.76	53,014,426.92

EXPORTS.

[Silver valuation.]

Articles.	October—		First four months—	
	1906-7.	1905-6.	1906-7.	1905-6.
Precious metals	$10,345,546.17	$10,222,497.79	$37,629,780.56	$41,046,083.02
Other articles	8,655,645.00	9,155,049.50	35,139,211.35	38,080,142.18
Total	19,001,191.17	19,377,547.29	72,768,991.91	79,126,225.20

PRICE OF PUBLIC LANDS, 1907-8.

According to the schedule issued by the Department of Fomento of Mexico on January 21, 1907, the price of public lands throughout the Republic for the year 1907-8 shall range as follows:

Department.	Price per hectare,a Mexican currency.	Department.	Price per hectare,a Mexican currency.
Aguascalientes	$7.00	Puebla	$11.00
Campeche	4.00	Queretaro	9.00
Chiapas	4.00	San Luis Potosi	4.00
Chihuahua	3.00	Sinaloa	4.00
Coahuila	3.00	Sonora	4.00
Colima	6.00	Tabasco	7.00
Durango	4.00	Tamaulipas	3.00
Guanajuato	12.00	Tlaxcala	17.00
Guerrero	5.00	Veracruz	12.00
Hidalgo	5.00	Yucatan	4.00
Jalisco	9.00	Zacatecas	3.00
Mexico	21.00	Federal District	100.00
Michoacan	14.00	Territory of Tepic	4.00
Morelos	27.00	Territory of Lower California	2.00
Nuevo Leon	3.00	Territory of Quintana Roo	2.00
Oaxaca	5.00		

a 2.471 acres.

SILVER EQUIVALENTS OF THE MEXICAN PESO.

The President of the Mexican Republic has established, for the six months commencing January 1, 1907, and for use in statistical calculations only, the following table of equivalents between the Mexican *peso* and the coins of the countries where the silver standard obtains:

Country.	Coin.	Value in Mexican currency.	Country.	Coin.	Value in Mexican currency.
Bolivia	Boliviano	0.98	Nicaragua	Peso	0.98
Guatemala	Peso	.98	Persia	Kran	.18
Salvador	do	.98	China	Tael	1.705
Honduras	do	.98			

OPENING OF THE TEHUANTEPEC RAILROAD.

The inauguration of the Mexican trans-Isthmian railway across the Isthmus of Tehuantepec in the last week of January, 1907, was made the occasion of national ceremonial. On January 23 the President of the Republic, accompanied by the members of his cabinet, representatives of the diplomatic corps, and other representative men, opened the line at its Pacific terminus, Salina Cruz, and then journeyed across the Isthmus to Coatzacoalcos, the Atlantic port, to be present at the arrival of the first cargo carried on the new road, on January 25. On both occasions suitable and congratulatory addresses were made, and the firm of Sir Weetman Pearson & Son, Limited, was warmly commended for its triumph over the difficulties which had attended the inception of the enterprise.

The actual distance in a straight line between Coatzacoalcos (hereafter to be known as Puerto de Mexico) and Salina Cruz, the two termini of the road, is only 125 miles, but owing to the configuration of the land a lengthening of the course to about 190 miles was necessitated. The bridges are numerous and of steel construction, the sleepers being either of creosoted pine, native hardwood or California redwood. The gauge is of standard type, and the rolling stock--most of which has been built in the United States—is of special type adapted to the cargoes of sugar which will form the leading item of transport. The locomotives are of the new oil-burning variety, and as extensive oil wells have been discovered in the vicinity of the road it is anticipated that the use of imported oil will soon be unnecessary.

The American-Hawaiian Steamship Line, operated in connection with the Tehuantepec road was also inaugurated on the 25th of January, the steamship company having signed a freight contract for the annual shipment of 500,000 tons of sugar from Honolulu to New York, Philadelphia, and New Orleans via Tehuantepec.

TEHAUNTEPEC RAILROAD TRAFFIC.

On December 18, 1906, the President of the Mexican Republic issued the following decree, regulating the transit of merchandise through the Tehuantepec Railroad:

"Section 1. From January 1, 1907, the transit of foreign, national, and nationalized merchandise which the Tehuantepec Railroad may receive, either at Coatzacoalcos for transportation and reshipment at Salina Cruz, or at Salina Cruz for transportation and reshipment at Coatzacoalcos, is authorized.

"Sec. 2. The interoceanic transit of merchandise transported by the Tehuantepec Railroad shall be subject to the conditions which may be prescribed by the respective regulations, and the only duties to be paid by ships and merchandise shall be those specified in sections 88 and 89 of the contract of May 16, 1902, as amended by the contract of May 20, 1904, in accordance with the law of May 31, 1904.

"Sec. 3. The transshipment of foreign merchandise which, being destined to other national port or ports, and which requires to be transported through the Isthmus of Tehauntepec, may be made at the ports of Acapulco, Progreso, Tampico, and Veracruz."

Section 88 of the contract of May 16, 1902, as amended by the contract of May 20, 1904, is as follows:

SEC. 88. The vessels, passengers, and merchandise hereinafter mentioned shall be subject to the following taxes:

"I. Vessels entering the ports of Coatzacoalcos or Salina Cruz, laden with foreign merchandise subject to the taxes referred to in Paragraph V and in article 89, provided such vessels are not included in the exemptions specified in the second paragraph of article 61 and in the fourth paragraph of article 70, shall pay as a sole tax the sanitary dues, which dues shall be reduced to one-half of the lowest quota in force at either of the ports of Tampico or Veracruz; and vessels shall pay pilot dues when a pilot is requested, but vessels not requesting a pilot are exempt from said dues.

"II. All vessels entering at the ports of Coatzacoalcos or Salina Cruz, laden with merchandise to which the taxes referred to in Paragraph V do not apply, and which vessels are not excepted from all taxes in accordance with the second paragraph of article 61 and Paragraph IV of article 70, shall be subject to all taxes and port dues, according to the lowest tariff in force at either of the ports of Tampico or Veracruz, and at the two principal ports of the Pacific.

"III. Should vessels arriving at the ports of Coatzacoalcos or Salina Cruz bring merchandise subject to the taxes mentioned in Paragraph V, together with other merchandise not subject to said taxes, they shall only be entitled to the exemption referred to in the first paragraph of this article, with respect to the part of the cargo corresponding to the merchandise subject to said taxes, and shall observe, in regard to the part which corresponds to the merchandise which is not subject to taxes, the provisions contained in the foregoing paragraph.

"IV. Passengers arriving at Coatzacoalcos or Salina Cruz, with through transit tickets across the Isthmus for the purpose of reembarking at the other end of the road, shall pay a transit tax of 40 cents a person.

"V. Foreign merchandise arriving at either Coatzacoalcos or Salina Cruz, to be transported across the Isthmus by rail and to be reembarked at the other end of the road consigned abroad, shall be exempt from all taxes or dues, except the two following:

"A. A transit tax of 40 cents per ton of 1,000 kilograms of merchandise.

"B. A tax for loading and unloading, in each port, of 25 cents per ton of 1,000 kilograms of merchandise, loaded or unloaded in the said ports, except merchandise transferred from one ship to another in the same port, which merchandise shall not be subject to any tax"

Section 89 of the contract of May 16, 1902, was not changed by the contract of May 20, 1904, and is as follows:

"SEC. 89. The Government shall have the right to increase the transit and the loading and unloading taxes in accordance with the following prescriptions and proportion:

"I. Both taxes may be increased 25 per cent when the railroad company shall have received each year, during three consecutive years, distributable net prcfits amounting to a sum equivalent at least to 5 per centum of the social capital or of the part thereof that has been subscribed. If the entire capital has not been subscribed, the Government shall have power to increase both taxes 25 per cent more.

"II. The transit and loading and unloading taxes may be increased 50 per cent more if the amount of distributable net profits received by the company each year during three consecutive years is equivalent to 7½ per cent.

"III. The above-mentioned taxes may be increased 75 per cent if the company shall have received each year during three consecutive years 10 per cent.

"IV. If the amount of distributable net profits received by the company each year, for a period of three consecutive years, is equivalent to 12½ per cent, both taxes may be increased 100 per cent.

"V. If by increasing both taxes 25 per cent, in accordance with Paragraph I, the company should receive for distributable net profits an amount equivalent to less than 5 per cent of the subscribed capital, then the amount necessary to complete the 5 per cent shall be taken from the revenue produced in one year by said increase.

"VI. If by increasing both taxes 50, 75, or 100 per cent, in accordance with Paragraphs II, III, and IV, the company should receive, in one year, for distributable net profits an amount equivalent to less than 6 per cent of the subscribed capital, then the amount necessary to complete the 6 per cent shall be taken from the revenue produced during said year by the increase.

"VII. In no case shall the transit tax be increased to more than 80 cents per ton of merchandise, or 80 cents per passenger, nor the tax for loading and unloading to more than 50 cents per ton in each port."

REGULATIONS FOR THE TRANSIT OF MERCHANDISE ACROSS THE ISTHMUS OF TEHUANTEPEC.

[Promulgated December 18, 1906.]

CHAPTER I.—*Concerning transit.*

SECTION 1.

ARTICLE 1. Transit of merchandise through the Isthmus of Tehuantepec is subject to the provisions of the present regulations, and is divided, for the effects thereof, into the following classes:

I. Transit of merchandise shipped from a foreign port and consigned to a foreign port.

II. Foreign merchandise shipped from a foreign port and consigned to a national [a] port.

III. Transit of foreign merchandise transferred, or unloaded and again reembarked, at a national port, consigned to another national port.

IV. Transit of domestic, or nationalized [b] merchandise, shipped from a national port and consigned to another national port.

V. Transit of national, or nationalized merchandise, shipped from a national port and consigned to a foreign country.

SECTION 2.

ART. 2. For the transit of merchandise shipped from a foreign port and consigned to a foreign country the following rules shall be observed:

I. The captain of the vessel shall have prepared, for delivery to the chief of the customs' guard at the time of the anchorage inspection visit, the following documents:

A. An entrance manifest, in quadruplicate, of the merchandise on board the vessel for the said traffic, which manifest, arranged in accordance with Form No. 1, shall specify the number of each bill of lading, the number of packages, the class of packages, the generic specification of the goods that they contain, the gross weight of the merchandise covered by each bill of lading, and three blank columns with the following headings: "Date of reshipment," "Vessel in which reshipment was made," and "Number of the clearance manifest."

B. Two numbered copies of each of the bills of lading shown in the manifest.

C. A list, in triplicate, of the passengers in transit, giving the number of packages of which their baggage consists and whose transpor-

---

[a] A Mexican port.

[b] Merchandise imported in accordance with the customs laws, and forming a part of the general stock of the merchandise of the country.

tation is for account of the company (Form No. 2), since only a simple statement of hand baggage shall be made.

II. The administrator of the custom-house, on receiving from the chief of the customs' guard the documents referred to, shall send them to the auditing department in order that they may be checked and numbered, and shall immediately issue a written order permitting the unloading, which unloading shall take place within the terms specified in section 1 of Chapter II of these regulations.

III. When the unloading is completed the result thereof shall be entered on the four copies of the manifest, and the National Railway Company of Tehuantepec, through its agent and under his signature, shall certify on the aforesaid copies that he receives the cargo in accordance therewith, which cargo, while it remains in the country, shall be under the exclusive responsibility of said company.

IV. The administrator of the custom-house shall forward by registered mail to the administrator of the custom-house through which the merchandise is to be cleared one of the copies of the manifest, together with a copy of each of the bills of lading shown in said manifest. Should the company wish to ship at once the part of the cargo that has been loaded on the railway cars, the custom-house shall forward, by the conductor of the train, to the custom-house through which the merchandise is to be cleared, a copy of the manifest with its respective bills of lading, even though, owing to the fact that unloading has not been finished, the corresponding entries have not been made. The importing custom-house shall give notice of said entries or annotations to the exporting custom-house, in a statement which the latter shall attach to the manifest, and which statement shall certify to the agreement or conformity of the company, and the company, in the meanwhile, shall issue provisional receipts covering the packages that it may have shipped.

V. The shipment of merchandise by rail, and the unloading thereof in the export custom-house, shall be under the supervision of the fiscal (customs) employees in accordance with the provisions of Section II, Chapter II, of these regulations.

VI. When merchandise is to be reshipped in the vessel that is to transport it to its final destination, the Tehuantepec Railway Company shall deliver, in triplicate, to the custom-house, a clearance manifest containing the same date comprised in the entry manifest, and, in addition thereto and immediately preceding each entry of packages, the number of the entrance manifest and the name of the vessel corresponding to this document.

VII. The administrator of the custom-house, on receiving the said manifest, shall send it to the auditing department to be compared and numbered, and shall immediately issue a written order permitting the shipment under the inspection of the customs guards.

VIII. When the loading is finished, the captain of the ship, or, in his name, the agent or representative of the respective maritime company, shall certify, under his signature, on all the copies of the clearance manifest, that he has received, in accordance therewith, the packages enumerated in said document.

IX. The custom-house, in accordance with the data certified to on the clearance manifest, shall fill in in the copy of the entrance manifest which it possesses, in the blank columns remaining on said copy, noting in each entry under their respective headings, the date of the reshipment of the packages, the name of the vessel in which the reshipment was made, and the number of the clearance manifest. Said custom-house shall retain copies of the last-named document, and shall remit a duplicate to the importing custom-house in order that the said custom-house may make the same annotations on the other three copies of the entrance manifest.

X. It is not essential that all the packages reshipped in the same vessel be declared in the entrance manifest, but it is indispensable that the total of these packages be reshipped within a period of two months, counting from the date of unloading at the entrance or importing custom-house. If, after this time has elapsed, the company should not prove that the package or packages are not still in the warehouses, due to the lack of means in reshipping them or to any other justifiable cause, it shall pay the corresponding duties in accordance with the provisions of article 18 of these regulations.

XI. When the merchandise referred to in this section does not come direct from a foreign port, but has been transferred to the vessel at a national port, the custom-house of said port shall issue to the captain a certified copy of the request of transshipment, and the captain shall attach it to the entrance manifest.

SECTION 3.

ART. 3. For the transit of merchandise coming from a foreign port and consigned to a national port, the rules hereinafter set forth shall be observed :

I. The merchandise must come protected by the manifest referred to in article 23 of the general customs' ordinance, and said manifest shall state that the goods are being transported to the port of final destination via the Tehuantepec Isthmus route. The captain of the vessel shall deliver this manifest to the chief of the customs guard at the time of making the anchorage inspection visit.

II. In addition to the manifest referred to, the captain of the vessel shall deliver the entrance manifest to the commander of the customs guard, especially for the transit, made out in accordance with the provisions of paragraph A, division I, of article 2 of these regulations, together with two numbered copies of each of the bills of lading shown in said manifest.

III. The administrator of the custom-house, on receiving the documents referred to in the foregoing paragraphs I and II (pars. I and II of art. 3, sec. 3), shall deliver them to the auditing department to be numbered and compared with the copies of the entrance manifest, so as to be sure that the information contained in the latter agrees with the consular manifest. Should differences occur, the administrator shall require that the entrance manifest be replaced with a new manifest which does not contain the differences, and if no differences occur the administrator shall accept the two documents and make the following annotations upon them: On the consular manifest, "Corresponds to the transit of —— to —— on entrance manifest No. —— ;" and on the entrance manifest: "Corresponds to manifest No. —— from (point of shipment abroad), presented on (date), on the arrival of (name of vessel bringing the goods), in charge of captain (insert name of captain)."

IV. The administrator, after delivering the documents to the auditing department, shall issue a written order to proceed with the unloading, which latter shall be done in accordance with the provisions of section 1, Chapter II, of these regulations.

V. When the loading is finished, the result shall be noted on the entrance as well as the consular manifest, and on all the copies of the former the Tehuantepec Railway Company, through its agent and under his signature, shall certify on the aforesaid copies that he receives the cargo in accordance therewith, which cargo, while it remains in the country, shall be under the exclusive responsibility of said company.

VI. The administrator of the custom-house shall immediately forward, by registered mail, to the administrator of the custom-house through which the merchandise is to be cleared, one of the copies of the entrance manifest, together with one each of the bills of lading of the shipment and of the consular manifest.

VII. The operations concerning the shipment of the merchandise by rail, its transit, unloading at the port through which it is to be exported, and, finally, its reloading on the vessel that is to convey it to its final destination, shall be subject to the provisions of Divisions V, VI, VII, and VIII of article 2 of these regulations, with the sole difference that the company shall deliver one more copy of the export manifest, on which the captain of the vessel, or, in his name, the agent or representative of the respective maritime company, shall also certify, under signature, his conformity in having received the packages.

VIII. The administrator of the export custom-house shall deliver the consular manifest to the captain of the ship, and shall deliver to him in a closed and sealed envelope a copy of the clearance manifest, so that these documents may be delivered to the custom-house where the merchandise is to be despatched. The administrator referred to shall see that the provisions of Division IX of said article 2 of these rules and regulations are complied with.

If between the cargo and consular manifest, differences, such as a greater or less number of packages, incorrect marking, alteration in the weights of the packages, etc., should occur at the custom-house, the provisions relating to the general customs ordinance shall apply, since neither the corrections and additions to the said manifest, the annotations placed thereon for transit purposes solely by the custom-house authorizing or approving the manifest, nor the declaration of the Tehuantepec Railway Company in the clearance manifest, shall be considered. As a sole exception to this rule, there shall be deducted from the consular manifest the packages which, taking as a basis those of the entrance manifest, have not been reshipped at the export custom-house on account of having been lost, or for any other cause, while in transit, and the duties on which, for said reason, must be paid by the railway company. The deduction in this case shall be proved by a certificate which the remitting custom-house shall attach to the copy of the clearance manifest, and said certificate shall specify the marks, numbers, and classes of the packages that may be missing, and shall also state that the payment of the corresponding duties are for account of the said company.

XI. The consular invoices corresponding to the goods shipped in transit across the Isthmus of Tehuantepec, to be dispatched at some national port, shall be consigned by the shippers to the consignees in said port; but if the consular invoices should be presented to the custom-house whose duty it is to authorize the transit, the latter shall receive them and shall attach them to the consular manifest in order that they may be forwarded, through the export custom-house, to the custom-house of final destination.

ART. 4. The transit of foreign merchandise transshipped or unloaded and again reloaded, at any of the national ports designated for this purpose, shall be subject to the formalities established in the foregoing article, provided that in the custom-house where the transshipment or reloading is effected the requisites for such operations, according to the general customs ordinance, have been observed.

ART. 5. When the merchandise under consideration comes either from Coatzacoalcos with destination Salina Cruz, or from Salina Cruz with destination Coatzacoalcos, its transit is subject to the provisions of Divisions I, II, III, IV, V, VI, X, and XI of article 3, as well as, in so far as may apply thereto, to the provisions of Divisions VII, VIII, and IX of said article. The forwarding of merchandise at the custom-house of destination shall be effected in accordance with the provisions of the general ordinance of the respective Department, and the entrance manifest shall specify the number and date of the request of clearance, instead of the date required by Division IX of article 2, concerning merchandise which should be reshipped.

SECTION 4.

ART. 6. The transit of national or nationalized merchandise coming from a national port and consigned to another national port, as well as national or nationalized merchandise coming from a national port and consigned to a foreign country, shall be subject to the stipulations of section 3 of these regulations, with the following variations:

I. If the transit consists of merchandise included in the first of the specified classes, in place of the consular manifest to which division I of article 3 refers, the captain of the vessel shall deliver to the chief of the customs' guard the documents required for coastwise traffic by article 303 of the general customs' ordinance.

II. If the transit consists of national or nationalized merchandise consigned to a foreign country, the captain of the vessel shall deliver to the chief of the customs' guard a copy of the clearance request that the shipper presented or filed in the custom-house of origin, in conformity with the provisions of article 325 of the general customs' ordinance, which copy shall be certified to by said office.

SECTION 5.

ART. 7. Passengers' baggage that is to be reembarked at the export custom-house shall be carried under the following conditions:

I. The administrator of the entrance custom-house shall deliver to the chief of the customs guard the three copies of the list presented by the captain of the vessel in compliance with the provisions of paragraph C, division I, article 2 of these regulations, so that on finishing the unloading of the packages the number unloaded may be compared with the total shown in the manifest list. If there should be no differences, or in case there are differences and after the same have been explained, the chief of the customs guard and the agent of the railway company shall manifest, under their signatures at the bottom of the three copies of the list, their conformity with the result of the unloading.

II. The chief of the customs guard shall return the three copies of the list to the administrator of the custom-house, who shall deliver them to the auditing department to be numbered, certifying on the same, at the request of the representative of the company, that the packages have been received and are under the exclusive care of the company until reembarked for the point of final destination.

III. The packages shall be shipped in the railway cars free of charge by the company, but must be wired and sealed by the watchmen appointed for that purpose.

IV. The conductor of the train shall receive from the custom-house, in a sealed envelope, a duplicate copy of the list, and on arriving at his destination he shall deliver it to the chief of the customs guard, who, in turn, shall hand it to the administrator who shall order the packages counted, and permit, under the inspection of the watchmen, the moving of the same either to the vessel which is to reembark them or to the proper warehouse. Should the number of packages not be complete, or some of them come with wires or seals broken, the custom-house shall impose a fine on the company not to exceed $500 Mexican silver.

V. The reembarkation of the baggage shall be checked from the lists sent by the entrance custom-house, noting before each item and in the proper column the name of the vessel which is to transport the baggage. Whenever the total number of packages declared on a list has been reembarked, the exporting custom-house shall send it to the entrance custom-house, in order that it may be attached to the original copy and the additional data copied in triplicate.

VI. When the company requests that the baggage be checked in the entrance custom-house, the application of the preceding rules will not be necessary, unless one or more of the packages contain merchandise subject to the payment of duties, in which case the custom-house shall indicate on the list the baggage which is in that condition, in order that the requirements provided for in Divisions II, III, IV, and V of this article may be observed.

CHAPTER II. — *Concerning the unloading and embarking of merchandise.*

SECTION 1.

ART. 8. When the chief of the customs' guard receives from the administrator of the custom-house the respective order, he shall direct that the transit merchandise be unloaded, in the unloading of which the following formalities shall be observed:

1. The watchmen appointed for that purpose, on the one hand, and the employees of the National Tehuantepec Railway Company, on the other hand, shall note, in indexed memorandum books prepared beforehand and which the captain of the vessel or the company shall furnish, the packages that are being unloaded.

II. Packages as they are unloaded shall be placed either in the box cars of the railway or in the respective warehouses, according to the classification of the merchandise and the kind of transit for which it is intended, bearing in mind the provisions of Chapter III of these regulations.

III. When the unloading is finished, the memorandum books kept by the watchmen shall be compared with those kept by the employees of the company, and any differences that may occur shall be explained, so that when they agree in all their records they may be signed by the watchmen, the employees of the company, and the captain of the vessel or his representative.

IV. The memorandum books kept by the watchmen shall be attached by the chief of the customs' guard to the general report of unloading that the administrator shall make.

V. The railway company, through its representative authorized for that purpose, shall examine the report of unloading made by the chief of the customs' guard, and, if he finds it agrees with that which, in turn, was rendered him by his employees, he shall certify his conformity on both documents. In the contrary case he shall investigate the discrepancies with the custom-house until the differences disappear or are found.

VI. When the reports are entirely in accord and have been signed by the employees and the representative of the company, the indexed memorandum books and the general report of unloading shall be sent to the auditing department, so that the latter may make the proper annotations thereon.

VII. As a general rule the operations of unloading and loading merchandise shall take place on working days between 6 a. m. and 6 p. m.; but they may be continued during the night and even on holidays, except national holidays, provided the railway company give proper notice to the custom-house, so that the latter may promptly arrange for the service of the customs' guard. Employees of the customs' guard shall receive payment for special work in accordance with the provisions of the general customs' ordinance.

VIII. Should the administrator deem proper to deny permission for special work, he shall report thereon immediately by telegraph to the custom-house bureau (dirección de aduanas), giving the reasons for his refusal.

IX. During the unloading, preference shall be given the baggage and other goods belonging to the passengers.

ART. 9. Should any vessel, in addition to the merchandise in transit, bring other merchandise that must be transshipped, the provisions of Section II, Chapter VII, of the general customs ordinance shall apply, but should it be necessary to convey the last-named merchandise ashore, either to wait for the vessel which is to transport it to its final destination or for any other cause, said merchandise shall be subject to the formalities prescribed in the foregoing article, but if the transshipment is made from ship to ship direct or by means of lighters, it shall be sufficient that the operation be witnessed by the proper customs employees.

ART. 10. The loading of transit merchandise in the vessel which is to carry it to its final destination, after the chief of the customs guard has received the proper order from the administrator, shall be effected by the company free of charge, but the operation shall be witnessed by watchmen appointed for that purpose.

SECTION 2.

ART. 11. The shipment of merchandise in transit shall be made in the cars of the railway company free of charge, but the operation shall be witnessed by watchmen that the custom-house appoints for that purpose, who, when the loading of each car is finished, shall close it with padlocks of the Treasury Department and shall note the number of each one of these.

ART. 12. When the merchandise, due to its class or size or for any other reason, can not be loaded for transportation in box cars, and if for this reason it should be necessary to transport it on platform or open cars, the watchmen shall keep a record of the number of the car as well as of the class of the merchandise.

ART. 13. The custom-house shall make a report, covering each train, showing the number of the treasury padlocks placed on the closed or box cars, the numbers of the platform or open cars, and the class of merchandise which the last-named cars convey. The entrance custom-house shall forward, by the conductor of the train and in a closed and sealed envelope, the aforesaid report to the export custom-house, to be used in connection with the unloading of the merchandise.

ART. 14. The railway company shall furnish and attach to each car a railway label 10 centimeters in length by 8 centimeters in width, which shall bear, in black letters, the following inscription:

> Merchandise in transit:
> From......(place of shipment).
> To ....(place of destination).
> Date ......(date of shipment).

This car shall not be opened without the intervention of the fiscal or customs' employees, except in case of superior force duly proved.

Whoever violates this provision shall be brought before the proper authority for punishment.

ART. 15. On the arrival at the custom-house of destination of any train transporting merchandise in transit, the administrator shall deliver to the chief of the customs' guard the report he received from the entrance custom-house, so that the watchmen can see whether the numbers of the fiscal padlocks and those of the platform or open cars, as well as the merchandise transported, agree with the information given in the report. If there should be no differences, the padlocks shall be opened and the railway company shall be permitted, in the presence of the watchmen, to unload the packages. If, on the

contrary, the padlocks should not be in good condition, or any other
abnormal circumstances should be observed, a certificate shall be drawn
up, signed by the chief of the customs' guard, the agent of the railway company, and two witnesses, stating in detail the differences
encountered. This certificate shall be delivered to the administrator
of the custom-house who shall make the corresponding investigation,
citing the conductor of the train and such employees of the company
as may be necessary. If from the investigation it should result that
the damage suffered by the padlocks or that the abnormal circumstances noted were caused by fraud, he shall report the same to the
district judge.

ART. 16. Only in case of superior force shall cars sealed with the
custom-house seals or locked with the fiscal padlocks be opened en
route. If the superior force should be of such a nature as to neces-
sitate the transshipment of the merchandise, the station agent of the
nearest station shall take part in the operation. In all cases a report
shall be prepared relating the circumstances, which report shall be
delivered by the conductor to the administrator of the custom-house.

If for any reason it should be necessary to break the seals or to
unlock the fiscal padlocks placed on the doors of the cars, and provided
the train continue its journey under the inspection of the fiscal
employees, the latter shall break the seals and open the padlocks,
immediately notifying the administrator of the custom-house of the
port where the train is destined, giving in detail the cause of the
accident, the losses or damages suffered, and the place where the freight
was stored, in case it was necessary to take it from the cars in which
it came, and said employees shall sign the report referred to in the
first paragraph of this article.

ART. 17. When foreign merchandise in transit is contained in a car
that shows signs of having been broken open, or whose seal or official
padlock has been broken, destroyed, or unduly opened, as well as
when uncrated merchandise transported in open cars does not correspond to the class indicated in the report, the railway company shall
pay, in accordance with the provisions of article 18 of these regulations, the amount of the duties corresponding to the missing packages
or which show signs of having been substituted or broken open.

ART. 18. In cases in which, for any of the reasons indicated in
these regulations, the National Tehuantepec Railway Company shall
have to pay the import duties corresponding to the merchandise in
transit the proper liquidation sheet shall be made up from data from
consular invoices or private invoices; if there should be no consular invoices, from the waybills covering the shipment; or from
data from documents which the company may file or which it may be
necessary to request of the company. The liquidation and payment

he indebtedness is discovered, ~~but shall not be~~
~~~~ ~~customs has appeared~~ or ~~verified~~
~~~~ ~~in all cases shall~~ be sent said
~~~~ ~~the custom-house~~ for examination.
~~~~ ~~in this article, the missing mer-~~
~~~~ ~~and this is duly proved to the~~
~~~~ ~~ing to the merchandise which~~
~~must be paid.~~
~~custom-house shall~~ verify the collection of the
~~~~le 16, ~~without preventing~~ thereby the imme-
~~~~ ~~respective manifest~~ that the corresponding
~~~~ ~~subject~~ to the payment of duties, and said
~~~~e the entrance custom-house so that the latter
annotation on the ~~other~~ copies of the manifest.

~~~~ning the extent of the custom-house grounds.

~~of Coatzacoalcos~~ and Salina Cruz the National
~~~~ball inclose, by means of fences solidly con-
~~~~ for custom-house operations.
~~:~~ entrances of any kind which give access to
~~~~ all the warehouses located in the same, shall
~~~~rent from each other, the keys to which shall
~~~~in possession of the employee or employees
~~~~n-house, and, on the other hand, in possession
~~~~ted by the company.
~~~~yees of the custom-house and of the customs'
~~~~ccess from the land side, as well during the
~~~~, to the fenced grounds. From the water side
~~~~ shall be permitted during the day to said
~~~~f their rank; but during the night only the
~~~~ custom-house and their customs' guard, and
~~~~f the railway company, as well as the water
~~~~ necessary in the performance of their duties,

~~~~ervice, within the fenced inclosure, shall be in
~~~~ in so far as concerns the caring for merchan-
~~~~but the employees of the customs' guard shall
~~~~to prevent the carrying away of the said mer-
~~~~ any other act that might injure the interests

~~~~houses shall arrange the watch service in such
~~~~ehouses and places of deposit of merchandise
~~~~hed by the employees of the customs' guard,

taking care, however, that the vigilance that the latter exercise shall
not interfere with the operations of the company in quickly dispatching the merchandise.

ART. 25. The distribution of transit merchandise shall be effected in
the places selected by the company with the approval of the administrator of the custom-house, which administrator shall see that said
merchandise is entirely separated from that which is to be dispatched
in the port, inasmuch as the place designated for the inspection of the
latter merchandise shall be separate from the rest of the fenced
inclosure and shall be accessible to the public at such times and hours
as the custom-house may determine.

ART. 26. The records of the entrance and departure of packages
consigned in transit shall be kept by the railway company, but during
the first ten days of each month the company shall submit a balance
sheet showing the debits and credits and the packages on hand on the
last day of the previous month.

For this purpose the books necessary to be kept shall be a daybook
and a ledger, which may be divided into several volumes consecutively
numbered, which the administrator of the custom-house shall authorize.

ART. 27. The administrator of the custom-house may at any time
satisfy himself of the correctness of the entries made in said books
and may proceed to recount and inspect the marks and numbers of the
stored packages.

CHAPTER IV.—*Concerning duties and taxes and the verification of
their collection.*

SECTION 1.

ART. 28. The vessels, passengers, and merchandise hereinafter
mentioned shall be subject to the following charges:

I. Vessels arriving at the ports of Coatzacoalcos or Salina Cruz,
laden with foreign merchandise subject to the payment of the charges
referred to in division V of this article, and which are not comprised
in the exemptions mentioned in the second division of article 61 and
in the fourth paragraph of article 70 of the contract of May 20, 1904,
concerning the Tehuantepec Railway, shall pay as a sole tax the sanitary dues, which shall be reduced to the lowest charge in force at
either of the ports of Tampico or Veracruz, and shall pay pilot dues
only in case a pilot shall have been requested by them.

II. All vessels arriving at the ports of Coatzacoalcos or Salina Cruz
laden with merchandise to which the charges referred to in Division V
do not apply, and which vessels are not exempt from all charges in
accordance with Division II of article 61 and paragraph 4 of article 70
of said contract, shall be subject to all taxes and port dues according

ither of the ports of Tampico or Vera-
ll ports of the Pacific.

ng at the ports of Coatzacoalcos or Salina
ject to the taxes mentioned in Division V,
adise not subject to said taxes, they shall
ferred to in the first division of this article
) the merchandise subject to said taxes,
art which corresponds to the merchandise
the provisions contained in the foregoing
se the taxes due, according to the number
asures, shall be determined by calculating
etween the number of tons and the gross
handise.

Coatzacoalcos or Salina Cruz with through
hmus, to be reembarked at the other end of
tax of 40 cents per person.

arriving at Coatzacoalcos or Salina Cruz
e Isthmus by rail and to be reembarked
consigned abroad shall be exempt from
xception of the following:

ents per ton of 1,000 kilograms of mer-

or loading or unloading of 25 cents per
erchandise loaded or unloaded in the said
merchandise transferred from one vessel
port, which merchandise shall not be sub-

nt may increase the transit and loading
l'to in Division V of the foregoing article,
n prescribed in article 89 of the contract
Railway.

comprised in Division V, article 28, shall
the payment of taxes and duties to the
following rules:

ming from aboard arriving at Coatzacoal-
nsported by rail for the purpose of being
of the railway, consigned to any Mexican
o the transit tax, nor to any other charge
Salina Cruz. Customs duties, port dues,
ich said merchandise is subject, shall be
of final destination.

coming from abroad, imported through
uz for local consumption or commerce at
ilway, shall pay at the port of entry the

duties and imposts to which the said merchandise is subject accordance with the law.

III. Domestic merchandise coming from a Mexican port and shipped to Coatzacoalcos or Salina Cruz to be transported by rail for the purpose of being reembarked at the other end of the railway, consigned to another Mexican port, is not subject to the transit tax nor to duties and imposts at Coatzacoalcos or Salina Cruz.

IV. Domestic merchandise coming from a Mexican port and shipped to Coatzacoalcos or Salina Cruz to be transported by rail for the purpose of being exported at the other end of the railway, and merchandise coming from a point on the railway, shipped to either of said ports to be exported, is not liable to the transit tax and is not subject to greater duties than those which, other circumstances being equal, apply to similar merchandise in other Mexican ports.

V. Domestic merchandise coming from a Mexican port, shipped to Coatzacoalcos or Salina Cruz for local consumption or commerce at points on the line of the railway, shall pay the duties and imposts to which it is subject in conformity with the law.

ART. 31. All documents required by these regulations for the transit of merchandise across the Isthmus of Tehuantepec are exempt from the stamp tax.

ART. 32. The traffic of foreign merchandise transshipped, or unloaded and again reembarked, at a national port, consigned to another national port, and passing across the Isthmus of Tehuantepec, shall not be considered as a portion of the coastwise trade, and, therefore, may be effected aboard foreign vessels, without, for that reason, being subject to the internal maritime tax on traffic referred to in the decree of July 1, 1898.

ART. 33. The traffic of national or nationalized merchandise, coming from a national port and consigned to another national port, passing across the Isthmus of Tehuantepec, shall be considered, in accordance with article 291 of the general customs ordinance, as a part of the coastwise trade, and, therefore, if said merchandise is reshipped in any foreign vessel, said vessel shall be liable to the interior maritime traffic tax referred to, except when the vessel belongs to the maritime service which the railway company has established at Tehuantepec.

ART. 34. Neither consular invoices, declarations, nor formalities of any kind, before consuls or other Mexican officials in foreign countries, concerning merchandise transported by the railway to be consigned abroad, shall be required.

SECTION 2.

ART. 35. The charges referred to in Divisions IV and V of article 28 shall be collected by the railway company, taking as a basis for the calculation of the charges comprised in the last of said divisions the declared weights of the corresponding bills of lading of the shipment, provided always there be no doubt or suspicion concerning their correctness, since, in the latter case, the company as well as the administrator of the custom-house may order the packages weighed.

ART. 36. On the 15th of each month the railway company shall deliver to the custom-houses in which the goods were unloaded the amount of the collection of the previous month, accompanying same with a statement in duplicate showing the name of the carrying vessel, the number of the entrance manifest, the numbers of the bills of lading, the number of packages, their gross weight, and the amount of the duties or charges of each entry, placing in separate columns that which corresponds to the transit charges collected for loading and unloading. Said statement shall show the total number of passengers and the transit tax they may have paid. The company shall attach as a voucher a copy of each bill of lading referred to in said statement.

ART. 37. The custom-house at Coatzacoalcos and Salina Cruz shall keep a book in which accounts shall be opened for each of the vessels that bring foreign merchandise consigned to a foreign country. On the debit side of said account there shall be entered, in separate columns, the number of each bill of lading, the number of packages it covers, the gross weight of the packages, and the transit and loading and unloading charges to which the merchandise is subject. Following this there shall be entered the number of passengers in transit for foreign countries, as well as the amount of the taxes they should pay. On the credit side of the account there shall be entered, in separate items, the amounts the company may deliver corresponding to the vessel in question, which should agree with the entries on the debit side, and if any differences should occur a proper explanation shall be required of the company.

ART. 38. If within the term of two months, counting from the date of the entrance of the vessel, the company should not have delivered the total amount of the charges corresponding to that vessel, the custom-house in interest shall demand the immediate delivery of said sum, even though the company, for any reason, should not have collected it.

SECTION 3.

ART. 39. The custom-houses shall prove to the Bureau of the Department (dirección del ramo) the correctness of the receipts from transit dues and from loading and unloading by filing a copy of the reports

submitted by the company and attach to said copy copies of the bills
of lading and of the corresponding quadruplicates of the entrance
manifests, with the understanding that if within the reports entries
should appear already shown in prior entrance manifests, these entries
shall form the proper notice with respect thereto.

ART. 40. The custom-house shall have a separate series of numbers
for the entrance and clearance manifests in accordance with the class
of transit specified in article 1 of these regulations, in such a manner
that each class shall have, in the same fiscal year, different consecutive
numbers.

ART. 41. The custom-houses shall forward to the Treasury Bureau
(dirección del ramo) triplicate copies of the entrance and clearance
manifests corresponding to the completed transit shipments, as well
as triplicate copies of the passenger lists.

ART. 42. The National Tehuantepec Railway Company shall file
with the customs bureau a bond for an unlimited amount to guarantee
the duties to be collected and the penalties to which the company may
be subject either on account of its own acts or those of its employees
or workmen.

ART. 43. The National Tehuantepec Railway Company shall be
responsible to the Public Treasury and to the persons in interest for
all freight it receives to be unloaded, transported, or reloaded.

ART. 44. It is the duty of the company to perform such operations
as the merchandise may require at the ports of Coatzacoalcos and
Salina Cruz, such as carting, transporting, unloading, filing of documents, dispatching, and unpacking, from the time the unloading of the
vessel is authorized up to the time of the dispatching or reshipment
of said merchandise in the vessels that are to carry it to its final destination.

ART. 45. It is also the duty of the company to observe the provisions of the general customs ordinance concerning the guarding
necessary to be done to insure the legality of the traffic, without other
restrictions than the notification to the fiscal employees of the operations that are going to be performed, or the securing of permission,
when permission is necessary, from said fiscal employees for the purpose of carrying out the operations referred to.

ART. 46. The fiscal employees, on the one hand, shall confine their
duties solely to watching or guarding, and shall not interfere in any
of the operations connected with the handling of the freight, said
operations belonging exclusively to the company.

ART. 47. The railway company shall, without delay, furnish the
employees, foremen, and laborers that may be necessary for the fulfillment of the requirements prescribed by the law in general, and by
these regulations in particular, as well as for the purpose of carrying

ɴ ᴍᴀɪɴᴛᴇɴᴀɴᴄᴇ ᴛʜᴀᴛ may be required in the
ᴊᴏᴀᴛᴋ.

ᴏꜰ ᴜɴᴀᴠᴏɪᴅᴀʙʟᴇ circumstances or superior
ꜰᴀᴄᴛɪᴏɴꜱ ᴏꜰ ᴡᴏʀᴋᴍᴇɴ, the delays incurred by
ᴏns owing to a lack of sufficient personnel
t the company to the payment of a fine not
a fine shall be imposed by the administrator
he Treasury Department, which shall hear

 of the company shall be well instructed in
al customs' ordinance and of these regula-
rance in this respect shall not be a legal
the company from the liability in which it

ily identify the higher employees of the
any shall give them credentials stating the
oyee. These credentials shall be counter-
company appoints, due notice being given
atzacoalcos and Salina Cruz, for that pur-

ployees of the company, whose duty it is
id to have constant access to the fenced
rm or a badge by which they can be easily

of the company shall report their acts to
yees of the customs' guard to the customs'
chief of said guard. All differences aris-
be explained by the manager of the com-
; he may appoint, and by the administrator
case of a disagreement between them, the
the director-general of customs, who shall
ulting with the Treasury Department.
railway company sees or suspects that any
 pretext of performing his duties, should
amit any abuse or infringement, he shall
lministrator of the custom-house in order
 the necessary steps in the matter. The
stom-house and of the customs' guard shall
espect to the employees of the company.
company shall properly light, at its own
night work is done, and shall also install,

for its own account, two electric searchlights of uniform movement, one at Coatzacoalcos and the other at Salina Cruz.

ART. 55. Whenever the custom-house at Coatzacoalcos or Salina Cruz deem proper that one or more of their employees should watch the transit of merchandise, the railway company shall provide them with the necessary passes, for which reason the conductor of the train shall permit them to ride in the caboose. The duties of employees in such cases are limited to watching the fiscal padlocks and the platform or flat cars.

CHAPTER VI.—General rules.

ART. 56. In all kinds of traffic carried on across the Isthmus each and everyone of the stipulations relating to said traffic contained in the contract made between the Federal Government and Messrs. S. Pearson & Son (Limited) on May 16, 1902, amended May 20, 1904, shall be strictly observed.

ART. 57. The railway company, in order to have a sufficient stock of fuel on hand in barges or scows, shall consult with the administrator of the custom-house at the place where said barges or scows are to anchor. The company shall not permit, for any reason whatever, that there be unloaded from said barges or scows merchandise other than fuel, and the employees of the custom-house shall take care to avoid any undue manipulation or use of said barges or scows, but the loading and unloading of fuel shall be made without hindrance or delay, but a previous notice to that effect in writing shall be given by the company to the chief of the customs' guard, who shall at once transmit it to the customs' administrator.

ART. 58. Whenever, in accordance with treaties or conventions, private agents appointed for the purpose by foreign governments shall have to fulfill any formalities concerning freight which, after having left the respective country, is to be reimported into it or into any of its possessions, the custom-house at Coatzacoalcos and Salina Cruz shall give said agents all the help possible in the performance of their duties.

ART. 59. Infractions of these regulations, for which no special penalty is prescribed in the same, shall be punished administratively with a fine which shall not exceed $50 silver.

ART. 60. The provisions of these rules apply exclusively to traffic operations between Coatzacoalcos and Salina Cruz, since goods imported for dispatch at the ports mentioned, as well as the vessels carrying same, are subject to the rules and procedure prescribed in the general customs' ordinance.

SILVER BASIS OF THE STAMP AND CUSTOMS TAXES FOR FEBRUARY, 1907.

The usual monthly circular issued by the Treasury Department of the Mexican Government announces that the legal price per kilogram of pure silver during the month of February, 1907, is $45.03 Mexican currency, according to calculations provided in the decree of March 25, 1905. This price will be the basis for the payment of the stamp tax and customs duties when silver is used throughout the Republic.

BUDGET ESTIMATE FOR 1907-8.

In presenting the estimates of revenues and expenditures for the year beginning July 1, 1907, and ending June 30, 1908, the Minister of Finance of the Mexican Republic places the normal revenue for the year at $98,835,000, while the appropriations submitted for approval aggregate only $92,966,595.02, thus leaving a surplus of revenue amounting to $5,868,404.98. As, however, governmental approval is sought for a bill authorizing a reduction of taxation in certain branches and of various advances in salaries, for which an allowance of $5,000,000 is made, the probable excess of revenue over expenditure for the year in question is reduced to $868,404.98.

The total receipts from taxes on foreign commerce are placed at $48,375,000, distributed as follows:

Import duties	$45,000,000	Dues for storage, etc	$80,000
Export duties	960,000	Pilotage dues	20,000
Sundry port dues	730,000	Sanitary dues	105,000
Transit dues	80,000	Consular fees	920,000

Stamp revenues are calculated at $31,540,000, including stamp sales, $12,500,000; Federal contributions, $8,250,000; taxes on mining properties, $1,400,000; internal tax on gold and silver, $2,590,000; tax on tobacco, $3,050,000; tax on alcohol, $920,000; tax on cotton yarns and goods, $2,550,000; trade-mark and patent dues and tax on explosives, $280,000.

Assay, melting, separating and refining dues are fixed at $140,000.

Special taxes in the Federal District and territories are estimated at $10,630,000, while the earnings of the various branches of the public service, including postal and telegraph lines are placed at $5,850,000. Real estate and minor sources are calculated to produce $2,050,000.

The total revenues from the public service under the heads noted during the fiscal year 1905-6 amounted to $101,972,623.70, and the budget estimate for 1906-7 was fixed at $90,073,500, though in the report for the year the figures cited are $91,000,229.48.

In apportioning the various governmental expenditures for the year 1907-8, the following distribution is made of the public moneys:

Department.	1907-8.	1906-7.
Legislative...	$1,225,277.26	$1,225,277.26
Executive..	289,394.50	332,521.48
Judiciary..	527,906.75	465,681.31
Ministry of Foreign Relations........................	1,568,857.63	1,827,472.78
Ministry of the interior:		
Ministry in general................................	1,544,001.00	2,244,001.00
Public health......................................	533,298.90	509,698.30
Rural police.......................................	1,471,327.75	1,313,108.50
Charities, Federal District........................	1,290,685.50	1,199,162.25
Administration, Federal District...................	7,630,729.48	7,618,822.25
Administration, Federal Territories................	367,670.75	348,357.55
Ministry of Justice..................................	1,340,940.50	1,307,222.55
Public Instruction and Fine Arts....................	6,288,790.90	5,873,561.72
Ministry of Fomento..................................	2,003,957.75	2,101,005.55
Communications and Public Works.....................	14,201,271.53	12,337,321.98
Ministry of Finance:		
Administrative.....................................	8,562,349.50	8,662,768.50
Public debt..	26,489,873.39	26,785,673.23
Ministry of War and Marine...........................	17,662,762.87	16,924,088.50
Total	92,966,595.02	91,000,223.43

ECONOMIC CONDITIONS DURING 1905-6.

A review of economic conditions prevailing throughout the Republic of Mexico during the fiscal year 1905-6 was made by the Mexican Minister of Finance on the occasion of presenting the budget statement for the fiscal year 1907-8 to Congress on December 14, 1906.

Minister LIMANTOUR states that the foreign commerce of the Republic did not undergo any substantial change during the period in reference as compared with the preceding year, the total imports being valued at $220,651,074.49 as compared with $178,204,962.45, and the exports at $271,138,809.32 as against $208,520,451.43 in the year 1904-5.

The principal item of increase on the import list is "mineral substances," which advanced from $52,758,614.20 in 1904-5 to $90,937,430.56 in 1905-6. The exceptional importation of gold due to the operations of the exchange and currency commission readily explains the difference in question. The returns of customs-houses show that the importations of American gold coins and of Mexican coins struck at Philadelphia represent alone an amount in excess of $38,000,000. Therefore, leaving out of consideration the gold introduced from abroad in 1905-6 in exchange for hard silver pesos, it is seen that the imports exceeded those of the preceding year by about $4,000,000. If the value in silver pesos paid for said coins be deducted from the export figures—that is to say, the 49,000,000 hard silver pesos—it reduces the exports valuations for the year to $232,000,000. A diminution in the imports of foreign explosives is due to the manufacture of dynamite on a large scale within the Republic, while an apparent

machinery and apparatus is occasioned by a
cation from "Machinery and apparatus" to

of gold in 1905–6 was $31,695,777.38 bullion,
0.26, and the balance consisting of ore, gold
Native gold presented to the Exchange and
or coinage amounted to $4,718,666.66, so that
the year was $36,414,444.04.
1 of silver is placed at $125,400,083.77, but
be deducted the $49,671,025 hard pesos paid
$123,453.50, representing foreign silver coin
)05,605.27 as the total silver output of the

ucts other than gold and silver, there was a
1 was not compensated by the increase in the
tals.
le products, there was a marked gain in rubber,
)n amounted to $1,671,000, a figure greater
ling year, but this was largely due to the ex-
known as guayule, which has recently been
itutes a new source of wealth to the country.
:reased, a gain of more than 75 per cent being
is in the foreign sugar market, the shipments
exico suffered a sharp decline, the valuation
00,000 to less than $1,000,000. The domestic
ived sufficiently to make the crop remunerative.
al products make a very satisfactory showing,
anned hides, for which there was a very active

oad traffic, Minister LIMANTOUR states that in
s the number of passengers carried increased
id the number of tons of freight rose from
The gross earnings from passengers and cargo
impanies were $50,500,000 in 1903 and nearly
The data for the first six months of 1906 are

e nation was reduced to the extent of $4,465,-
MANTOUR states that all forms of the national
exception of the interior redeemable debt, are
lished by means of sinking funds, the total on
46,760,455.51.
ilation of the currency gained $1,600,000, and
s abroad increased by more than $4,000,000.
financial status of the country, the Executive

sire: from July 1, 1907, the Federal contribution—a tax
during c   ult years rose as high as a 30 per cent basis—shall
be collected on a basis of 20 per cent only.

Summing up the revenues and disbursements for the year 1905-6
it appears that the Federal exchequer, out of its normal resources,
which totaled $101,972,623.70, and with the extraordinary receipts,
which aggregated $977,190.67, met all the budget appropriations, and
moreover devoted $17,550,449.50 to extraordinary expenditures,
mainly for works of public utility, and nevertheless had a substantial
surplus to meet other important outlays during the year. Minister
LIMANTOUR expresses the opinion that the economic and financial situation of the Republic throughout the coming fiscal year will continue
upon the basis of prosperity inaugurated by the new monetary régime.

REVIEW OF THE MININ   [DUSTRY, 1906.

In its issue for January, 1907, "Mod. n Mexico" publishes a comprehensive review of the mining con   ..s and output of the Mexican
Republic during 1906, additional data being also furnished for purposes of comparison. While maintai   r its position as the greatest
producer of silver, Mexico, during the   ar 1906, advanced to sixth
place in the production of gold, from fifth to fourth in the production
of lead, and is second only to the United States as a producer of
copper. Zinc, to whose exploitation attention has been given only
recently, was exported during the year to the amount of nearly
60,000 tons, more than half of which went to the United States and
the remainder to England, France, and Belgium. Estimates for the
year 1907 indicate that an appreciable increase in this class of exports
will be made.

The following tables show the relative output of the various countries producing gold, silver, and copper in 1905 and 1906:

Country.	Gold.		Change in value.
	1905.	1906.	
Australasia	$85,470,779	$82,851,561	$3,119,218
British India	11,924,308	10,655,674	1,268,634
Canada	14,486,833	12,000,000	2,486,833
Mexico	14,526,855	15,430,000	903,145
Russia	22,197,155	21,500,000	697,155
Rhodesia	7,203,865	10,201,327	2,997,462
Transvaal	101,225,558	119,605,922	18,380,364
United States	88,180,700	97,155,201	8,974,501
All others	34,151,823	35,250,000	1,098,177
Total	379,867,873	404,649,685	$1,782,872

ı shows the following valuation in the
l in American currency:

١7, 123	1903–1904	$60, 193, 958
١0, 752	1904–1905	60, 890, 276
١4, 545	1905–1906 (six months)	48, 178, 898

lver in Mexico for the calendar year 1906
ıe output showed a reduction of 6,156,000
ıtion is due to the rise in the value of
ring 1906 having been 66.791 cents per
١52 cents in the preceding year.
ıt of copper in 1906 was more than com-
ın the price of that metal, which averaged
ımpared with 15.590 cents in 1905.

ENTION WITH CANADA.

been made in the "*Diario Oficial*" of
ınt entered into between the Mexican and
ch becomes effective on March 1, 1907.
ıs:
orders issued either in Mexico or in Can-
money of the country in which they are
frequent fluctuations of exchange, the
shall be converted into the proper equiv-
ıdministration.
r which a money order can be drawn in
ır shall be $100 gold or its equivalent in

countries shall have the right to fix the
ıey orders issued by them. The services
ıstem shall be performed exclusively by
ıange. On the part of México the office
ı the part of Canada, Montreal.
ıs of all money orders issued shall be
cepted) between the two countries.
ın error shall be corrected or that the
ıall be repaid to the remitter, application

must be made to the post-office in which the order was issued. Duplicate orders shall only be issued by the post-office of the country of payment.

Repayments, whether of an original or of a duplicate order, shall not be made to the remitter until it has been ascertained that the order has not been paid.

Orders which shall not have been paid within twelve months from the month of issue shall become void, and the sum received shall accrue to the country of origin.

The Postmaster-General in either country shall be authorized to adopt any additional rules for greater security against fraud or for the better working of the system. All such additional rules shall, however, be communicated to the Postmaster-General of the other country.

Each administration is authorized, in extraordinary circumstances, to suspend temporarily the money-order service in whole or in part, but this must be communicated immediately to the other office, by wire if necessary.

POSTAL RECEIPTS, OCTOBER, 1906.

The revenues produced by the Mexican mail service during the month of October, 1906, are thus reported by the Postmaster-General of the Republic to the secretary of public communications and works, the figures for the same month of 1905 being also stated by way of comparison:

	August.	
	1906.	1905.
	Pesos.	*Pesos.*
Sales of postage stamps	285,440.26	261,363.94
Rent of post-office boxes	28,514.00	21,112.09
Fines, etc	2,778.66	4,568.10
Premiums on money orders:		
International	1,084.12	745.35
Domestic	26,080.88	22,812.65
Editors'	3,291.20	3,011.74
Total	341,089.14	314,153.78

NEW STEAMSHIP CONTRACT.

On December 5, 1906, the Mexican Congress approved a contract between the Government and Mr. THOMAS HERBERT WORNSOP for the establishment of a steamship service between Victoria, British Columbia, and the Mexican ports of Mazatlan, Manzanillo, Acapulco, and Salina Cruz, with privilege of touching at other Mexican ports. The steamers must make one trip, at least, each month, and monthly con-sections in Cabila with steamship lines to Europe, Japan, China, and Australia, in accordance with the itinerary to be approved by the Government.

The operation of this service shall commence eight months from the approval of the contract, and the steamers of the concessionaire may touch at other foreign ports, subject to the approval of the Government.

The Government shall pay the concessionaire, or the company that he may organize, the amount of $8,888.33 for each round trip from Victoria to Mazatlan, Manzanillo, Acapulco, and Salina Cruz on the Pacific Ocean, or a total subsidy of $100,000, Mexican currency, per year, but no payment shall be made for more than twelve round trips per year.

The duration of the contract is two years, and the concessionaire has made a deposit of 2,000 *pesos*, in bonds of the consolidated public debt, to guarantee the fulfillment of the conditions thereof.

CUSTOMS REVENUE, FIRST HALF OF 1906-7.

Official statistics recently published show that the revenues collected by the various custom-houses of the Republic of Mexico during the first half of the fiscal year 1906-7 were as follows; the figures for the same period of 1905-6 being also given for purposes of comparison:

	First half of fiscal year—	
	1906-7.	1905-6.
	Pesos.	*Pesos.*
Import duties	24,757,267.08	20,431,885.58
Export duties	524,240.70	468,015.42
Port dues	519,841.31	428,667.19
Total	24,801,349.09	21,328,508.19
	$12,351,071.83	$10,621,607.00

BANK HOLDINGS AND CIRCULATION.

The reports of the six chartered banks of the City of Mexico show that at the close of business on November 30, 1906, the specie and notes held, were as shown below:

Bank.	Gold.	Silver pesos.	Fractional coin.	Notes.	Total.
National	$14,392,512.00	$6,407,329.00	$1,085,708.00	$969,440.00	$25,044,985.00
London and Mexico	9,065,490.00	3,571,838.00	91,142.13	1,654,825.00	14,986,295.13
Central	1,053,680.00	151,264.00	16,265.33	1,446,141.00	2,697,333.33
Commerce and Industry	95,870.00	16,354.00	51,934.57	71,975.00	236,133.57
International and Mortgage	95,700.00	17,787.00	15,031.62	555,680.00	684,198.62
Lincoln Hypotecario	107,540.00	566.00	535.81	5,630.00	114,071.81
Total	25,668,873.00	12,165,138.00	1,260,612.46	4,703,694.00	43,763,017.46

> following figures show the total paper circulation of the City of
~ICO banks on the date given:

Notes:
National	$34, 031, 664
London and Mexico	17, 049, 622
Bonds:	
Central	2, 383, 400
International and Mortgage	12, 888, 200
Agricola ó Hipotecario	3, 451, 400
Total	69, 804, 292

MEAT CONSUMPTION IN THE FEDERAL DISTRICT IN 1905.

Official statistics recently published give the following figures relat-
ing to the meat consumption of the Fe___ral District of the Mexican
Republic during the year 1905. The number and value of the animals
killed during the year in reference in t [laughterhouse of the city of
Mexico and in the slaughterhouses of the eight municipalities of the
Federal District was as follows:

	Heads.	Value, Mexican currency.
Cattle	130, 018	$6, 500, 900. 00
Sheep	167, 166	794, 043. 25
Goats	10, 599	37, 096. 50
Hogs	76, 852	2, 305, 560. 00
Total	384, 635	9, 637, 599. 75

SANITATION WORKS AT MAZATLAN.

On December 20, 1906, the Mexican Executive approved a contract
entered into between the Government of the Republic, the State of
Sinaloa, and the municipality of Mazatlan, on one side, and Messrs.
Pearson & Son (Limited), on the other, for the construction of the
sanitation works at the city of Mazatlan. The total cost of these has
been fixed in the contract at 600,000 *pesos*, and for the payment of
said sum the State of Sinaloa has been authorized to issue bonds of
indebtedness to the nominal value of 698,000 *pesos*, sufficient to cover
at 86 per cent of its nominal value the price agreed upon for the
works. The construction thereof must be commenced within three
months after the approval of the plans and specifications and completed within two years. The concessionaires have made a deposit of
25,000 *pesos* to guarantee the fulfillment of the conditions stipulated
in the contract.

FRONTIER TRAFFIC WITH THE UNITED STATES, 1905-6.

According to statistics published by the Treasury Department of the
Mexican Republic, the number of freight cars and the amount of
traffic tonnage which entered Mexico across the Rio Grande from the

United States during the fiscal year 1905-6 aggregated 36,850 cars and 601,517 tons of merchandise. The aggregate number of cars and amount of freight tonnage which passed from Mexico to the United States during the same period was 18,368 cars with 238,598 tons of merchandise. Thus a surplus of tonnage amounting to 458,019 in favor of the United States is reported for the period under review.

NEW FIBER PLANT.

A fiber plant of Mexico known popularly as *"cadillo"* has recently been made the subject of investigation with the result that naturalists claim for it the same qualities as the best known jute producers. Its resistant powers are said to be as great as the Brazilian hemp plant and if it can be produced in commercial quantities a good market is assured. The plant grows in great abundance in the tropical regions of Mexico.

ELECTRIC LIGHT AND POWER CONCESSION.

The Congress of the Mexican Republic approved on November 26 a contract entered into between the Bureau of Public Works of the Federal District, the Mexican Light and Power Company (Limited), the Mexican Electric Light Company (Limited), on June 30, 1906, granting said companies the sole right, for a period of twenty years, of supplying electric power and light in the Federal District. The contract provides for the rescission of all contracts previously entered into, the above-mentioned companies having acquired the concessions previously held by the "*Compañia Mexicana de Electricidad*," the *Compañia Explotadora de las Fuerzas Hidro-eléctricas de San Ilde-fonso*," and the "*Compañia de Gas y Luz Eléctrica*."

MOTIVE POWER CONCESSION.

On December 12, 1906, the Mexican Government entered into a contract with the firm of S. Pearson & Son authorizing this company to utilize for motive power 340,000 liters of water per second from the River Antigua, Canton of Jalapa, State of Veracruz.

The plant may be placed on the riverside anywhere between a point 20 kilometers above the Puente National, and another point 10 kilometers below the bridge. The company shall commence within six months from the date of the signing of the contract, and the construction within twenty-four months. All the works must be completed within seven years.

GAS CONCESSION.

In November, 1906, the Mexican Government granted Messrs. Doheny, Canfield & Bridge a concession to erect and operate in any city or town of the Republic gas plants for the manufacture and distribution of crude-oil gas. The concessionaires obligate themselves to commence the actual construction work within six months, to invest $500,000 Mexican currency, and to furnish gas to the districts of Santa Maria, San Rafael, Juarez, and Roma within four years. The establishment of the gas factory in the city of Mexico and the pipe lines connected therewith must be completed within ten years, and upon such completion the company shall invest at least $100,000 in any plant which it may establish in any other town or city in the Republic.

The company organized to operate under this gas concession will be known as the "Mexican National Gas Company."

CONSULAR TRADE REPORTS.

The Consul-General of Mexico at New York reports that during the month of December, 1906, 12 vessels proceeding from Mexican ports entered the harbor of New York City, bringing 76,122 packages of merchandise. During the same month the vessels clearing from the port of New York numbered 12, carrying 207,274 packages of merchandise consigned to Mexican ports. The imports in detail from Mexico to New York in December, 1906, were as follows:

Articles.	Quantity.	Articles.	Quantity.
Henequen ....bales..	9,612	Metals.................boxes..	388
Coffee ....sacks..	2,304	Ores..................sacks..	134
Hides ....bales..	6,561	Sarsaparilla ....packages..	48
Hides ....loose..	5,314	Vanilla................boxes..	4
Ixtle................bales..	6,235	Alligator skins ....do...	34
Goatskins ....do...	2,515	Bones................packages..	52
Deerskins ....do...	544	Honey................barrels..	119
Rubber................do...	5,381	Cedar.................logs..	140
Leaf tobacco ....do...	183	Mahogany.............do...	739
Cigars.................boxes..	38	Jalap.................sacks..	4
Broom root ....bales..	903	Copper................bars..	3,832
Chicle ....do...	3,088	Oranges...............boxes..	1,717
Fustete ....logs..	13,064	Chile.................sacks..	82
Hair..................bales..	20	Mexican dollars ....boxes..	346
Lead bullion ....bars..	10,758	Asphalt ....barrels..	1,336

The Mexican Consul at Nogales, Arizona, reports that the exportation of merchandise from the State of Sonora, Mexico, to the United States, in December, 1906, was as follows:

Fowls	$6	Oranges........................	$920
Stationery	4	Potatoes	65
Mescal........................	100	Lead ores	3,474
Cane sugar.....................	1	Fresh fish......................	67
Rawhides......................	15,613	Cheese.........................	1
Portland cement.................	24	Ready-made cotton clothing....	21
Fresh meat	186	Wheat..........................	68
Beans	42	Leaf tobacco	368
Preserved fruits	11	Gold and silver, and gold dust..	107,713
Lemons........................	70	Silver bullion	159,056
Canned vegetables..............	19		
Corn	206	Total	288,035

The imports of foreign merchandise through the custom-house of Nogales, Mexico, to the State of Sonora in December 1906, were as follows:

Animal products	$46,770.93
Vegetable products	51,553.63
Mineral products	242,266.44
Textiles, and manufactures thereof	46,537.05
Chemical products	12,199.21
Spirituous beverages	2,488.29
Paper and paper products	5,303.39
Machinery and apparatus	49,916.34
Vehicles	9,179.67
Arms and explosives	15,066.96
Miscellaneous	19,186.05
Total	500,467.96

The countries of origin of the foregoing merchandise are as follows:

United States of America	$436,569.83
Germany	12,999.88
France	11,483.16
England	35,269.47
Spain	128.64
Austria	1,062.28
Japan	2,954.70
Total	500,467.96

The customs duties collected during the month amounted to $123,296.45 silver.

NICARAGUA.

CENSUS OF THE DEPARTMENT OF GRANADA, 1906.

According to the last census, taken in November, 1906, the population of the Department of Granada, Republic of Nicaragua, numbers 28,093 inhabitants. The former census fixed the population at 18,938 inhabitants. There has been, therefore, an increase of 9,045 inhabitants, or 48 per cent.

In said department there are 60 Hondurians, 34 Salvadorians, and 27 Costa Ricans.

PANAMA.

REPORT OF THE PANAMA RAILROAD COMPANY.

The report of the workings of the Panama Railroad during the fiscal year ended June 30, 1906, was made public in December of that year, showing the following results:

For the railroad proper the total earnings for the year were $2,570,828, an increase of $311,990 over the previous year. The expenditures for the same period amounted to $1,731,888, exceeding that for the previous year by $552,948. The difference between earnings and expenses for the year is $838,940, showing a decrease of $240,953 from the net earnings of the preceding year.

The steamship line operated in connection with the railroad reports earnings to the amount of $1,347,012, an increase of $31,178 over the previous year. The expenses of the line, however, aggregated $1,384,170, being $225,582 more than the year before and $37,158 in excess of the earnings for the year under review.

Combining the figures for the two branches of the service it is seen that the total earnings amount to $3,917,840 and the total expenses to $3,116,058, showing a balance on the credit side of the company of $801,782, representing the total profit for the year's operations.

During the year progress was made in improving and enlarging the facilities of the railroad, and since the middle of December, 1905, no congestion of freight on the Isthmus has been reported. Old tracks were reconstructed and the line double tracked throughout nearly its whole extent. With the completion of new wharves and docks and the addition of larger equipment and heavier power which is constantly arriving, Isthmian traffic over this route is amply provided for.

PARAGUAY.

CONCESSION FOR NEW RAILWAY.

The Paraguayan Congress has granted a concession for building a new railway from Los Medanos to the western boundary of Paraguay. The railway begins at the port of Los Medanos, on the property of the American Quebracho Company, and is to be 1-meter gauge. The concession is for ninety-nine years, at the end of which time the railway reverts to the State.

MUNICIPAL IMPROVEMENTS IN ASUNCIÓN.

The Paraguayan Government, in a decree dated October 5, 1906, granted the concessions for the construction and exploitation of sanitation works, electric light, power, and tramways in the city of Asunción, to Mr. EDUARDO MOELER, in accordance with the terms prescribed in the law of August 30, 1906. The concessions granted are the following:

First. The right to establish the water and sewer systems in the capital.

Second. The right to construct and exploit a plant for the manufacture, distribution, and sale of electric current and power.

Third. The right to construct and exploit a street-railway system within the capital.

PERU.

CUSTOM REVENUES AT CALLAO, 1906.

The official statistics recently received show that during the calendar year 1906 there were collected at the custom-house of Callao, Republic of Peru, for customs duties, £735,941.483, as compared with £612,744.638 collected during 1905, an increase of £123,196.845. During the month of December, 1906, the customs revenues collected amounted to £69,781.637, as against £54,490.265 collected during the same month of 1905, an increase of £15,291.872.

RAILROAD FROM LIMA TO HUACHO.

President PARDO, of Peru, has promulgated a law for the construction of a new line of railway from Lima to Huacho, with branch lines to the ports of Supe and Chaucay. The concessionaires are guaranteed 6 per cent a year on their investment, and thirty years' exclusive control of the railway.

SALVADOR.

REVENUES AND EXPENDITURES, 1905-6.

The "*Diario Oficial*" of Salvador for November 19, 1906, contains a table showing the fiscal revenues and expenditures of the Republic during the fiscal year from June 1, 1905, to May 31, 1906, as follows:

Revenues.	Pesos.	Expenditures.	Pesos.
Import duties................	5,073,810.64	Legislative power.........................	48,366.49
Export duties................	788,997.14	Chief Executive	57,360.00
Liquor tax...................	1,943,494.56	Department of the Interior...............	1,446,889.56
Stamp tax....................	252,426.21	Department of Improvements.............	777,733.72
Miscellaneous...............	480,515.30	Department of Public Instruction	695,691.06
Posts, telegraphs, etc.........	377,173.97	Department of Beneficence...............	204,745.00
		Department of Foreign Relations	71,879.20
		Department of Justice	653,648.82
		Department of Finance....................	603,845.90
		Department of Public Credit	4,941,016.97
		Department of War.......................	1,877,478.78
Total	8,916,417.82	Total.............................	11,382,155.25

Deficit against revenues, 2,465,737.43 pesos.

SHORTAGE OF CROPS IN THE REPUBLIC.

The "*Diaro Oficial*" of Salvador for December 20, 1906, publishes statistics showing the losses entailed upon the Republic by reason of the great storm of October. The approximate losses are fixed at $6,266,105, and the coffee crop, instead of aggregating 74,295,544 pounds, with a value of $12,295,605 silver, as in 1905, is estimated at 49,530,363 pounds, whose value is $4,098,535.

The maize crop is reduced almost one-half, or from 160,806.8 *medios* to 90,648.8, while rice figures for but 72,872.5 *tareas*, as compared with 117,287.5 in 1905.

UNITED STATES.

TRADE WITH LATIN AMERICA, 1906.

STATEMENT OF IMPORTS AND EXPORTS.

Following is the latest statement, from figures compiled by the Bureau of Statistics, United States Department of Commerce and Labor, showing the value of the trade between the United States and the Latin-American countries. The report is for the month of December, 1906, with a comparative statement for the corresponding month of the previous year; also for the twelve months ending December, 1906, as compared with the same period of the preceding year. It should be explained that the figures from the various custom-houses, showing imports and exports for any one month, are not received at the Treasury Department until about the 20th of the following month, and some time is necessarily consumed in compilation and printing, so that the returns for December, for example, are not published until some time in February.

IMPORTS OF MERCHANDISE

Articles and countries.	December—		Twelve months ending December—	
	1905.	1906.	1905.	1906.
Cocoa (*Cacao; Coco ou cacao cru; Cacao*):	Dollars.	Dollars.	Dollars.	Dollars.
Central America......	919	5,074	23,534	27,300
Brazil..	128,958	251,335	976,902	2,169,328
Other South America	95,360	186,223	1,726,315	2,160,279
Coffee (*Café; Café; Café*):				
Central America..................................	169,563	198,885	6,010,066	6,087,872
Mexico	68,622	69,762	2,695,449	2,134,182
Brazil..	6,292,253	9,041,313	56,567,788	51,569,010
Other South America	613,306	580,832	7,810,792	9,412,228
Copper (*Cobre; Cobre; Cuivre*):				
Cuba...	2,575	4,947	55,689	73,330
Mexico	1,387,962	1,470,675	16,896,589	18,156,442
South America	77,760	41,978	210,144	785,664
Fibers:				
Cotton, unmanufactured (*Algodón en rama; Algodão em rama; Coton, non manufacturé*):				
South America	40,911	77,059	352,732	578,581
Sisal grass (*Henequén; Henequen; Henequen*):				
Mexico	1,373,291	1,803,387	15,678,935	14,486,569

IMPORTS OF MERCHANDISE—Continued.

Articles and countries.	December— 1905.	December— 1906.	Twelve months ending December— 1905.	Twelve months ending December— 1906.
	Dollars.	Dollars.	Dollars.	Dollars.
Fruits:				
Bananas (*Plátanos; Bananas; Bananes*):				
Central America	285,219	342,017	4,152,929	5,485,698
Cuba	71	5,734	1,290,225	1,208,713
South America	30,352	....	520,186	309,429
Oranges (*Naranjas; Laranjas; Oranges*):				
Mexico	2,622	5,712	48,213	87,148
Cuba	1,444	1,062	5,803	9,801
Fur skins (*Pieles finas; Pelles; Fourrures*):				
South America	59,877	9,365	542,427	300,180
Hides and skins (*Cueros y pieles; Couros e pelles; Cuirs et peaux*):				
Central America	56,950	32,146	561,332	549,469
Mexico	361,873	533,267	3,804,087	4,612,822
South America	765,868	999,644	13,408,457	13,950,438
India rubber, crude (*Goma elástica; Borracha cruda; Caoutchouc*):				
Central America	100,994	60,949	836,731	773,101
Mexico	24,677	158,565	800,874	1,827,085
Brazil	2,297,295	3,869,999	27,404,626	28,317,263
Other South America	128,450	171,664	1,210,941	1,839,743
Lead, in pigs, bars, etc. (*Plomo en galápagos, barras, etc.; Chumbo em linguados, barras, etc.; Plomb en saumons, en barres, etc.*):				
Mexico	316,213	377,488	3,414,508	3,223,566
South America	44,881	1,600	64,964	8,601
Sugar, not above No. 16 Dutch standard (*Azúcar, no superior de la escala holandesa; Assucar, não superior ao No. 16 de padrão hollandez; Sucre, pas au-dessus du type hollandais No. 16*):				
Mexico	929	763	611,589	79,345
Cuba	3,075,919	279,261	72,649,818	56,624,164
Brazil	....	458,331	1,335,769	965,933
Other South America	134,606	580,575	2,116,541	2,267,594
Tobacco, leaf (*Tabaco en rama; Tabaco em folha; Tabac en feuilles*):				
Mexico	113	7,745	11,121	54,604
Cuba	1,181,892	1,235,681	11,879,938	15,333,786
Wood, mahogany (*Caoba; Mogno; Acajou*):				
Central America	36,552	20,517	517,970	469,037
Mexico	42,004	54,970	363,433	509,836
Cuba	17,807	2,246	89,204	169,721
Wool (*Lana; Lã; Laine*):				
South America—				
Class 1 (clothing)	379,035	91,481	8,848,628	6,621,298
Class 2 (combing)	16,044	....	631,091	301,195
Class 3 (carpet)	4,121	134	999,886	759,322

EXPORTS OF MERCHANDISE.

Articles and countries.	December— 1905.	December— 1906.	Twelve months ending December— 1905.	Twelve months ending December— 1906.
Agricultural implements (*Instrumentos de agricultura; Instrumentos de agricultura; Machines agricoles*):				
Mexico	40,635	29,602	431,348	529,572
Cuba	18,430	3,750	253,920	114,118
Argentine Republic	580,188	50,985	5,733,615	4,703,622
Brazil	10,202	10,343	178,363	103,950
Chile	26,027	25,906	281,723	430,749
Other South America	25,302	18,746	263,709	287,429
Animals:				
Cattle (*Ganado vacuno; Gado; Bétail*):				
Mexico	79,585	65,146	507,289	840,365
Cuba	41,700	12,810	1,983,152	1,003,842
South America	19,817	8,374	94,340	78,358
Hogs (*Cerdos; Porcos; Porcs*):				
Mexico	30,813	21,844	117,045	226,063
Horses (*Caballos; Cavalhos; Chevaux*):				
Mexico	48,233	42,348	274,357	868,709
Sheep (*Ovejas; Ovelhas; Brebis*):				
Mexico	....	1,120	37,055	101,8..

EXPORTS OF MERCHANDISE—Continued.

Articles and countries.	December—		Twelve months ending December—	
	1905.	1906.	1905.	1906.
	Dollars.	Dollars.	Dollars.	Dollars.
Breadstuffs:				
Corn (Maíz; Milho; Maïs):				
Central America	4,903	2,785	472,411	55,262
Mexico	33,373	41,070	702,884	1,148,296
Cuba	115,726	114,263	1,119,841	1,305,073
South America	2,147	1,430	150,428	13,327
Wheat (Trigo; Trigo; Blé):				
Central America	4,145	7,868	29,355	23,308
Mexico	286,216	62,873	902,305	1,586,587
South America	175,298	36,970	383,692	361,548
Wheat flour (Harina de trigo; Farinha de trigo; Farine de blé):				
Central America	184,808	147,558	2,064,956	1,611,844
Mexico	9,683	6,726	263,177	118,448
Cuba	76	295,912	3,443,048	2,906,948
Brazil	16	127,923	1,141,800	1,292,637
Colombia	92	9,746	661,286	128,440
Other South America	29 78	125,406	2,595,089	2,424,855
Carriages, etc.:				
Carriages, cars, etc., and parts of (Carruajes, carros y sus accesorios; Carruagens, carros e partes de carros; Voitures, wagons et leurs parties):				
Central America	112,654	15,900	508,978	2,075,260
Mexico	135,301	283,585	1,218,482	2,540,620
Cuba	186,057	61,208	774,142	1,184,077
Argentine Republic	95,163	631,630	1,579,552	2,366,741
Brazil	32,487	30,064	140,653	296,904
Chile	42,192	34,980	452,510	225,109
Colombia	7,103	872	45,104	34,002
Venezuela	997	924	8,252	10,889
Other South America	35,573	25,366	180,236	276,025
Automobiles and parts of (Automóviles; Automóviles; Automobiles):				
Mexico	29,672	39,243	192,452	717,923
South America	5,507	24,503	60,419	166,814
Coal (Carbón; Carvão; Charbon):				
Mexico	346,872	209,484	2,915,806	3,137,980
Cuba	131,130	263,335	1,608,892	2,021,972
Copper (Cobre; Cobre; Cuivre):				
Mexico	121,980	85,538	1,322,083	1,045,579
Cotton:				
Cotton, unmanufactured (Algodón non manufacturado; Algodão não manufacturado; Coton non manufacturé):				
Mexico	349,387		2,855,733	522,872
Cotton cloths (Tejidos de algodón; Fazendas de algodão; Coton manufacturé):				
Central America	138,472	129,956	1,560,525	1,663,680
Mexico	20,751	15,835	304,313	254,066
Cuba	72,318	44,103	1,212,319	936,663
Argentine Republic	23,880	32,643	440,823	271,484
Brazil	64,358	36,630	743,492	479,388
Chile	107,812	208,103	871,733	988,027
Colombia	63,095	82,504	516,928	830,604
Venezuela	30,676	35,481	397,891	470,962
Other South America	46,858	67,565	505,703	470,702
Wearing apparel (Ropa de algodón; Roupa de algodão; Vêtements en coton):				
Central America	90,207	81,195	690,587	749,892
Mexico	40,920	49,212	623,980	562,304
Cuba	49,118	56,416	433,032	540,546
Argentine Republic	14,156	14,796	321,745	227,193
Brazil	7,123	6,216	65,323	54,923
Chile	2,009	2,931	21,371	34,257
Colombia	3,361	2,473	47,045	82,717
Venezuela	6,821	1,829	28,941	27,057
Other South America	9,695	9,625	58,161	65,030
Electric and scientific apparatus (Aparatos eléctricos y científicos; Apparelhos electricos e scientíficos; Appareils électriques et scientifiques):				
Central America	18,751	27,096	168,496	249,579
Mexico	75,230	132,719	848,753	1,401,787
Argentine Republic	34,628	33,869	249,179	478,875
Brazil	101,007	67,769	611,854	836,304
Chile	19,450	19,692	141,242	204,152
Venezuela	11,898	13,361	102,273	110,569
Other South America	45,305	47,181	280,049	327,243

EXPORTS OF MERCHANDISE—Continued.

Articles and countries.	December—		Twelve months ending December—	
	1905.	1906.	1905.	1906.
Iron and steel, manufactures of:	Dollars.	Dollars.	Dollars.	Dollars.
Steel rails (*Carriles de acero; Trilhos de aço; Rails d'acier*):				
Central America...............................	34,829	147,240	307,165	611,178
Mexico...	125,049	142,246	1,486,261	864,141
South America.................................	269,178	435,099	2,894,662	3,008,778
Builders' hardware, and saws and tools (*Materiales de metal para construcción, sierras y herramientas; Ferragens, serras e ferramentas; Matériaux de construction en fer et acier, scies et outils*):				
Central America...............................	32,034	29,083	310,345	343,784
Mexico...	81,668	82,216	1,056,141	1,079,395
Cuba...	61,735	86,109	628,809	567,097
Argentine Republic............................	59,669	65,927	642,685	828,540
Brazil...	47,177	49,723	383,564	481,037
Chile..	26,814	86,110	169,457	277,411
Colombia.......................................	4,651	7,385	57,861	76,344
Venezuela......................................	4,209	3,901	34,830	58,368
Other South America...........................	17,822	32,405	241,588	308,155
Electrical machinery (*Máquinas eléctricas; Machinas eléctricas; Machines électriques*):				
Central America...............................	1,361	10,849	13,396	47,741
Mexico...	109,796	95,856	1,057,023	1,048,959
Cuba...	111,735	646	190,337	437,327
Argentine Republic............................	4,141	5,854	154,669	168,256
Brazil...	24,829	33,282	215,303	530,494
Other South America...........................	35,546	13,058	150,827	147,381
Sewing machines, and parts of (*Máquinas de coser y accesorios; Machinas de coser e accesorios; Machines à coudre et leurs parties*):				
Central America...............................	7,507	9,280	98,586	138,200
Mexico...	50,701	39,550	586,907	795,717
Cuba...	35,791	7,876	370,356	318,063
Argentine Republic............................	78,957	68,125	657,705	603,433
Brazil...	15,414	46,974	174,875	330,439
Colombia.......................................	4,861	6,965	69,073	76,929
Other South America...........................	23,137	86,132	347,222	423,027
Steam engines, and parts of (*Locomotoras y accesorios; Locomotivas e accesorios; Locomotifs et leurs parties*):				
Central America...............................	59,180	104,663	211,248	1,301,872
Mexico...	29,891	267,054	272,702	1,230,224
Cuba...	189,722	178,900	628,831	647,498
Argentine Republic............................	8,646	265,835	224,931	482,316
Brazil...	....	....	147,292	596,046
Other South America...........................	3,100	89,705	127,561	602,080
Typewriting machines, and parts of (*Máquinas de escribir y accesorios; Machinas de escribir e accesorios; Machines à écrire et leurs parties*):				
Central America...............................	4,945	3,215	54,533	46,467
Mexico...	20,992	33,707	329,799	373,572
Cuba...	7,854	4,680	69,881	72,261
Argentine Republic............................	9,549	13,581	94,306	116,225
Brazil...	5,942	5,436	46,187	62,969
Colombia.......................................	1,557	954	12,079	11,804
Other South America...........................	8,838	13,945	151,499	167,364
Leather, other than sole (*Cuero distinto del de suelo; Couro, não para solas; Cuirs, autres que pour semelles*):				
Central America...............................	18,016	25,043	156,455	218,454
Mexico...	10,318	7,664	98,085	73,682
Cuba...	29,016	27,787	267,530	276,132
Argentine Republic............................	44,852	17,091	306,061	280,473
Brazil...	10,435	13,031	133,846	166,432
Chile..	1,192	30,077	51,506	116,056
Colombia.......................................	6,277	4,629	40,906	64,501
Venezuela......................................	4,975	4,911	46,263	75,243
Other South America...........................	6,922	6,900	80,871	166,564
Boots and shoes (*Calzado; Calçado; Chaussures*):				
Central America...............................	47,296	67,218	318,859	514,141
Mexico...	84,583	105,791	1,411,902	1,464,698
Colombia.......................................	2,874	4,847	55,732	59,192
Other South America...........................	28,293	54,512	268,072	371,672
Naval stores:				
Rosin, tar, etc. (*Resina, y alquitrán; Resina e alcatrão; Résine et goudron*):				
Central America...............................	3,343	1,789	23,067	25,111
Mexico...	2,969	1,240	18,760	18,141
Cuba...	6,802	8,565	69,335	80,394

Articles and countries.	1905.
	Dollars.
Naval stores—Continued.	
Rosin, tar, etc.—Continued.	
Argentine Republic	21,029
Brazil	
Chile	
Colombia	
Venezuela	
Other South America	
Turpentine (*Aguarrás; Aguaraz; Térébenthine*):	
Central America	3,781
Cuba	7,353
Argentine Republic	51,395
Brazil	
Chile	4,385
Other South America	6,488
Oils, mineral, crude (*Aceites minerales, crudos; Oleos mineraes, crús; Huiles minérales, brutes*):	
Mexico	60,879
Cuba	32,858
Oils, mineral, refined or manufactured (*Aceites minerales, refinados ó manufacturados; Oleos mineraes, refinados ou manufacturados; Huiles minérales, raffinées ou manufacturées*):	
Central America	32,976
Mexico	50,183
Cuba	62,884
Argentine Republic	142,449
Brazil	245,683
Chile	50,627
Colombia	6,885
Venezuela	12,771
Other South America	154,701
Oils, vegetable (*Aceites vegetales; Oleos vegetaes; Huiles végétales*:)	
Central America	3,611
Mexico	102,380
Cuba	11,685
Argentine Republic	359
Brazil	39,167
Chile	1,281
Other South America	7,686
Paper (*Papel; Papel; Papier*):	
Central America	38,605
Mexico	42,579
Cuba	42,561
Argentine Republic	37,788
Brazil	19,804
Chile	18,488
Colombia	2,615
Venezuela	4,470
Other South America	6,368
Provisions, comprising meat and dairy products:	
Beef, canned (*Carne de vaca en latas; Carne de vacca em latas; Bœuf conservé*):	
Central America	4,045
Mexico	1,000
Cuba	4,035
Other South America	5,843
Beef, salted or pickled (*Carne de vaca, salada ó en salmuera; Carne de vacca, salgada ou em salmoura; Bœuf salé ou en saumure*):	
Central America	3,741
South America	30,821
Tallow (*Sebo; Sebo; Suif*):	
Central America	20,291
Mexico	2,858
Cuba	1,075
Chile	10,213
Other South America	4,688
Bacon (*Tocino; Toucinho; Lard fumé*):	
Central America	1,970
Mexico	6,999
Cuba	43,798
Brazil	19,854
Other South America	866
Hams (*Jamones; Presunto; Jambons*):	
Central America	8,626
Mexico	13,178
Cuba	48,975
Venezuela	8,918
Other South America	10,786

TS OF MERCHANDISE—Continued.

	December—		Twelve months ending December—	
	1905.	1906.	1905.	1906.
	Dollars.	Dollars.	Dollars.	Dollars.
		17,894	154,586	226,651
		67,272	45,661	701,728
		78	45,661	236
			7,846	682
	99,135	97,897	228,019	227,661
		62,675	434,050	598,661
		67,840	665,748	347,175
		984,460	2,281,680	2,020,200
	89,077	125,964	121,685	794,442
	7,248	17,691	77,811	176,404
	87,778	2,848	662,944	48,866
	39,504	13,077	275,551	264,728
	70,897	48,861	464,565	602,934
	19,129	14,800	101,744	158,029
	29,298	12,748	128,297	126,570
	8,080	8,138	32,918	42,808
	19,904	18,179	123,040	119,348
	14,478	2,028	84,451	72,300
	2,808	9,380	94,561	51,306
	6,128	6,206	61,615	75,560
	4,849	4,232	40,828	48,454
	1,488	1,446	18,436	15,661
	9,868	4,074	70,115	66,427
	4,814	17,989	108,380	110,086
	5,040	658	58,596	81,464
	1,988		10,617	15,128
	2,688	10,972	79,981	86,688
	12,409	12,896	121,776	177,999
	1,689	2,472	28,062	30,398
	13,008	8,656	108,808	111,282
	1,798	43	14,061	4,506
		21	70	606
	812	60	7,163	4,810
	8,897	6,191	47,055	60,308
	102,694	26,072	446,240	642,678
	96,249	91,810	859,555	1,280,261
	32,498	7,560	97,192	178,377
	34,170		120,130	163,927
	96,263	23,340	187,264	218,708
	67,195	173,970	474,892	1,205,849
	148,582	169,270	1,619,709	2,140,353
	206,155	204,388	1,904,022	2,379,544
	361,664	495,899	2,618,684	5,110,885
	70,116	97,669	484,463	870,014
	52,603	182,203	479,550	831,458
	47,645	115,690	713,188	1,189,626
	24,909	16,614	257,007	288,592
	73,100	89,785	715,446	917,965
	79,237	44,218	696,579	574,860
	90,796	55,029	517,081	851,047
	2,491	4,282	87,951	63,542
	4,728	10,364	62,240	79,609
	2,288	956	36,113	18,132
	11,663	1,563	47,801	19,855
	5,203	11,355	90,671	108,619

FOREIGN COMMERCE IN 1906.

Figures issued by the Bureau of Statistics of the United States fo the foreign commerce of the country during the calendar year 190 show that the volume of trade aggregated $3,118,857,193 as compare with $2,806,135,345 in 1905.

Total imports figured in 1906 for $1,320,609,250 as against $1,179 144,550 in 1905, an increase of $141,464,700 for the year, while expo advanced from $1,626,990,795 in 1905 to $1,798,247,943 in 1906.

Of the total imports of $1,320,609,250 cited for 1906, more than ha or $700,053,785, were from Europe, $240,722,414 from North Americ countries (most largely Canada), $148,050,955 from South Ameri (nearly three-fifths of which was from Brazil), and $219,331,374 fr Asia and Oceania, the small remnant of $12,450,722 being from Afri The relative increase was decidedly larger in the trade with Europe th in that with other countries. Of European imports, $231,458,430 we from Great Britain, $150,894,393 from Germany, and $119,900,329 fr France. The preponderance in the case of exports was still great Of a total of $1,798,247,943 no less than $1,246,590,946 went to Euro compared with $325,871,044 to North America, $78,822,379 to Sou America, $128,593,906 to Asia and Oceania, and $18,369,668 to Afri Of European countries the United Kingdom took by far the larg share, $587,465,219, or nearly one-half, being one-third of all expor Germany took $242,922,487, France $103,623,431, and Netherlan $104,396,865. To Canada, the United States sent $168,699,070, wh imports from there were $71,647,500. The increase in trade wi Europe is out of all proportion to that with other countries; trade wi China and Japan for the year shows a decrease. With China, impo increased from $28,113,811 to $30,775,557, but exports fell off fr $58,574,793 to $29,934,015, and with Japan imports increased fr $50,703,377 to $64,791,485, while exports fell from $55,757,868 $34,405,978.

With the countries of Central America, trade for the twelve mon ending December, 1906, was represented by the following figur comparative statistics for the preceding year being also furnished:

Country.	Imports.		Exports.	
	1905.	1906.	1905.	1906.
Costa Rica	$4,111,476	$4,715,510	$1,973,796	$2,473
Guatemala	3,243,629	2,822,020	2,875,579	2,98
Honduras	1,671,773	2,204,692	1,563,084	1,58
Nicaragua	1,433,815	1,331,172	1,833,595	2,041
Panama	879,145	1,448,686	7,831,564	14,30
Salvador	921,857	1,216,262	1,473,822	1,33
Total Central American States	12,264,695	13,738,342	17,571,440	24,98

Dominican Republic, and Haiti, shows the
two periods under comparison.

	Imports.		Exports.	
	1905.	1906.	1905.	1906.
.....	$90,457,600	$95,655,184	$44,580,711	$48,491,844
.....	4,682,913	3,464,425	1,840,600	2,271,282
.....	1,171,308	1,086,390	2,914,879	3,266,425

South America figured as follows on the
United States during the years 1905 and

	Imports.		Exports.	
	1905.	1906.	1905.	1906.
.....	$17,063,166	$18,291,368	$28,434,360	$33,271,569
.....			144,480	242,616
.....	90,648,908	96,476,959	12,351,236	16,517,375
.....	14,823,584	15,146,282	7,006,977	9,392,458
.....	6,285,939	6,669,461	3,685,417	2,961,671
.....	2,382,775	3,251,684	1,907,699	1,834,766
.....	2,205	1,200	6,719	110,496
.....	2,603,685	1,963,508	4,297,228	5,198,455
.....	3,529,495	2,453,013	2,748,761	3,160,606
.....	7,010,357	7,780,898	3,206,564	3,310,618
.....	144,990,099	148,000,965	66,405,368	78,822,379

and exports, with the respective valua-

	12 months ending December—	
	1905.	1906.
animals...............	$133,561,944	$128,113,168
....	154,718,814	140,520,131
....	404,577,756	447,908,822
turing...............	196,290,557	249,555,019
....	277,187,403	334,810,699
....	7,788,076	9,686,411
....	1,179,144,550	1,310,609,250
animals...............	155,216,866	177,216,254
....	315,664,895	344,096,464
....	490,129,393	521,902,516
turing...............	213,108,894	248,897,752
....	429,781,924	470,093,398
....	5,520,650	7,574,147
....	1,599,422,632	1,772,720,530
....	27,568,173	25,527,413
....	1,621,990,795	1,798,247,945

Countries other than those of Latin America show the following returns of trade values during the periods under comparison:

Country.	Imports.		Exports.	
	1905.	1906.	1905.	1906.
United Kingdom	$191,078,377	$221,468,430	$642,532,317	$697,681
Germany	134,127,448	180,684,388	212,684,529	
France	98,621,668	115,900,339	90,080,346	
Netherlands	33,355,687	61,177,684	78,311,483	
Canada	68,927,323	71,547,590	144,670,682	
Chinese Empire	38,138,611	50,778,457	56,574,789	
Japan	50,708,377	54,792,485	56,767,693	

EFFECTS OF BRAZILIAN PREFERENTIAL TARIFF.

Article 17 of the Brazilian budget law, promulgated on January 1 1907, continues in force the provisions of article 18 of the budget law of December, 1905, and of article 6 of the law of December, 1904 providing for a differential tariff in compensation for concessions made to Brazilian products. Under the provisions in reference, a decree of June 30, 1906, was passed by the Brazilian Government whereby a 20 per cent reduction was made on certain articles of United States origin imported into Brazil. The items affected by this reduction are as follows:

Wheat flour; condensed milk; manufactures of rubber under art. 1033 of the tariff act, including rubber and celluloid; gutta-percha basins, funnels, capsules, and bottles; walking sticks, canes, whips etc.; pouches, dolls, toys of all kinds; buttons, saws, engine packing combs, rulers, penholders, fans, belts, braces, garters, cords, tape dentists' rubber, sticks, tubes, and branches for flowers; rubber sheet ing, tubes, threads, sheets, and mats, all of rubber; inks, under art 173 of the tariff act, except writing inks, but including marking ink designers' inks, drawing inks, and other liquid inks, and printers' in in tubes or cylinders; paints and varnishes; typewriters, ice box pianos, scales, windmills, and watches and clocks.

These preferentials in favor of United States products over all other are continued, and by the terms of the law just passed the item typewriters is defined to include linotypes and cash registers, the bringing these two United States products within the scope of the per cent preferentials.

The only feature of the law unfavorable to United States interest seems to be in the increase in the duty on grape juice, as a result which the duty now charged exceeds considerably 100 per cent valorem. United States grape juice has had and may still be able maintain the chief hold on the Brazilian market in such goods. increase in the duty charged is made for the benefit of the small gr juice preserving factory in São Paulo.

The new law provides that motor cars and motor boats used industrial purposes shall be admitted at 5 per cent ad valorem.

	Unit of measure.	1905.			Changes in quantity.	
		Quantity.	Value.		Increase.	Decrease.
			Total.	Per unit.		
MANUFACTURED.						
Alundum	Pound	4,331,233	$308,186	$0.07	719,251	
Arsenic, white	Ton of 2,000 pounds	831	88,150	100.00	355,566	
Bromine	Pound	1,230,000	168,750	.036		
Coke	Ton of 2,000 pounds	32,568,926	99,960,968	3.05	4,164,914	
Copper sulphate	Pound	48,534,129	3,009,106	.062		1,734.85
Copperas	Ton of 2,000 pounds	18,346	129,822	7.80		4.12
Crushed steel	Pound	837,000	58,590	.07	25,000	
Graphite, artificial	do	4,868,000	312,784	.064	272,500	
Lead, sublimated white	Ton of 2,000 pounds	8,000	3,000,000	188.68	1,683	
Zinc oxide	do	61,142	4,452,332	72.82	3,148	
Zinc-lead, white	do	5,743	468,685	81.69		1.62
METALLIC.						
Aluminum	Pound	14,350,000	5,166,000	.36	3,000,000	
Copper	do	915,000,000	178,699,500	.1950	61,238,780	
Gold	Ounces, fine	4,702,525	97,135,201	20.67	438,489	
Iron, pig	Ton of 2,240 pounds	25,521,911	490,275,910	19.21	2,818,514	
Lead	Ton of 2,000 pounds	364,324	48,962,692	106.34	44,552	
Quicksilver	Flasks	27,276	1,063,764	39.00		4.23
Silver	Ounces, fine	57,858,367	38,201,160	.66791	1,256,667	
Zinc	Ton of 2,000 pounds	225,898	27,899,964	123.95	23,947	

NATIONAL CONVENTION FOR THE EXTENSION OF THE FOREIGN COMMERCE OF THE UNITED STATES.

The National Convention for the Extension of the Foreign Commerce of the United States, met at the new Willard Hotel in Washington on January 14, 1907, and was in session three days, concluding with a banquet on the evening of the 16th, at which President ROOSEVELT delivered the principal address, and speeches were delivered by the Hon. JOSEPH G. CANNON, Speaker of the House of Representatives, Governor WARFIELD, of Maryland, and Governor Swanson, of Virginia.

The call for the convention was issued by the New York Board of Trade and Transportation. Delegates to the number of more than one thousand were appointed by the governors of the States, all the important chambers of commerce, commercial clubs, boards of trade, and national associations.

The convention was called to order by Mr. E. S. A. DE LIMA, chairman of the committee on organization, and Mr. WILLIAM McCARROL was chosen president of the convention.

A number of prominent men were invited to address the convention; among these were Hon. ELIHU ROOT, Secretary of State, Dr. JACOB G. SCHURMAN, president of Cornell University; Hon. OSCAR S. STRAUS, Secretary of Commerce and Labor; and Hon. JOHN BARRETT, Director of the Bureau of the American Republics.

u the United States in 1000 as 00,010,170,

in 1905, and the amount of wool produced
nds, as compared with 126,527,121 pounds

WITH PORTO RICO.

ie trade of the United States with Porto
ing with October, 1906, compared with
preceding years stated:

ports United ieo.	Ten months ending with October—	Imports from Porto Rico.	Exports from United States.
12,831 712,491 87,604 84,129	1904	$12,090,682	99,350,885
	1905	16,576,118	13,384,431
	1906	19,920,137	16,509,946

T OFFICE IN 1905-6.

States Commissioner of Patents for the
6, shows the business transacted through
year. There were received during the
ipplications for mechanical patents, 172
3 caveats, 10,888 applications for trade-
labels, and 438 applications for prints.
ted, including reissues and designs, was
ered during the year 10,408 trade-marks,
'he number of patents which expired was
which had been allowed were forfeited
ayment of the final fee.
ice from all sources amounted to $1,811,-
itures were $1,538,149.40, leaving a sur-
tures of $273,148.44.

RUGUAY.

IONTEVIDEO FOR 1905.

Montevideo, Republic of Uruguay, for
ults:
irtment at the end of 1904 was estimated
: the end of 1905 it amounted to 298,533,
it an increase in 1904 of 6,329. Persons
video numbered 94,220, as against 84,317

departures. Comparatively, the birth rate was low, it being o
25.82 per thousand, the number of births being 7,709. A compari
of the births in Montevideo with the remainder of the Republic sho
that from the year 1900 to 1904 the births in the capital numbe
38,924, and in the other parts of the country 114,459, making a to
for the whole Republic of 153,383. The illegitimate birth rate
slightly reduced, being 17.47 per thousand of the total, as against 18
per thousand in 1904. Of the total number of births, 3,996 w
boys and 3,713 girls. There was shown a great increase in the nu
ber of marriages, which amounted to 1,803, as compared with 1,
in 1904. The death rate confirms the reputation that the capital
the Republic has always had of being a healthy city. The deaths
1905 were 4,402, which, compared with those of 1904, show a red
tion of 236; the rate is 14.74 per thousand. Of this total, 2,582 w
males and 1,820 females. The deaths from infectious diseases n
bered 831, being 383 less than in 1904. Of these 831, 621 died fi
consumption.

The superficial area upon which the capital is built represents
hectares, and that of streets and roads 541 hectares.

Montevideo has 8 theaters, and during 1905 1,070 performan
were given, the number of spectators having been 784,975.

The race track held 33 meetings, and 25,757 persons atten
thereto. The number of spectators at other entertainments
325,898.

There were 774 new buildings erected during 1905, with a front
of 8,695 lineal meters.

The tramway lines of Montevideo in 1904 carried 23,162,879 p
sengers, and in 1905 carried 27,438,719, an increase of 4,275,8
For the month of October, 1906, they carried 2,425,236.

FISH CULTURE IN THE REPUBLIC.

With the purpose of developing the possibilities of fish culture
the waters of the Republic, the President of Uruguay has direc
Señor VIRGILIO SAMPAGNARO, Uruguayan Consul at Cherbou
France, to make a thorough investigation of the various syste
employed for the exploitation of this industry in Northern, Cen
and Southern Europe. An Executive decree bearing date of Dec
ber 15, 1906, has been issued to this effect through the Ministry
Fomento.

The industry is to be studied from its technical and economic sta
point, and a report made as to the maritime fauna and flora of
waters visited and their comparative bearings upon the culture
Uruguay. It is the purpose not only to develop the species nativ
the Republic, but also to introduce other varieties of fish.

VENEZUELA.

FOREIGN TRADE OF CARUPANO, FIRST HALF OF 1906.

he foreign trade of the port of Carupano, Venezuela, during the
. half of the year 1906, amounted to 1,508,084 *bolivares*, of which
3,546 *bolivares* were for imports and 434,538 *bolivares* for exports.
ing the same period of 1905 the imports amounted to 605,461 *boli-
s*, and the exports to 384,972 *bolivares*, a total trade of 990,433
ares. A comparison of the trade of 1905 with that of 1906 shows
ncrease over the former of 517,651 *bolivares.*

REVENUES FROM DUTIES ON PARCELS POST, 1905-6.

uring the fiscal year 1905-6 there were collected in the various
om-houses of the Republic of Venezuela, for duties on the impor·
on of parcels post, 216,896.14 *bolivares*, distributed as follows, by
om-houses: La Guaira, 162,375.21 *bolivares;* Puerto Cabello,
322.47 *bolivares;* Maracaibo, 18,197.03 *bolivares;* Ciudad Bolivar,
389.96 *bolivares;* Carupano, 4,284.47 *bolivares;* total, 216,869.14
ares.

TARIFF MODIFICATIONS.

*·Resolution of September 20, 1906, relating to the importation of
wire gauze.*

["*Gaceta Oficial*" No. 9878, of September 21, 1906.]

his resolution provides that in future, whenever wire gauze is to
mported, the goods or a drawing must be produced to the Federal
cutive, so that the Government may determine whether the goods
to pay duty or not.

*-Resolution dated September 21, 1906, determining the classifica-
tion of empty sacks of duck and similar cloth.*

["*Gaceta Oficial*" No. 9878, of September 21, 1906.]

y virtue of this resolution empty sacks of duck ("*loneta*," "*lien-
*") and similar cloth shall be dutiable under the fifth class of the
f when imported into the Republic.

*—Resolution dated September 26, 1906, determining the customs
treatment of component parts of carts.*

["*Gaceta Oficial*" No. 9883, of September 27, 1906.]

nder this resolution cast-iron wheels with their rubber tires, not
eding 30 centimeters in diameter, axles and irons for carts
nded to be used in plantations of coffee, cocoa, or other agricul-
l purposes are to be included in the second class of the tariff, pro-
d such carts are built in the country.

EXPORT OF PEARLS.

The latest published statistics of the export of pearls from Venez are for the year ending July 1, 1904. The total amount in w was 301,147 grams, valued at the ports of export at $286,409. export by countries and by custom-houses was as follows:

BY COUNTRIES.

	Grams.
Great Britain and colonies	139,182
France	152,625
Italy	5,900
United States	3,440
Total	301,147

BY CUSTOM-HOUSES.

	Grams.
Porlamar	139,182
La Guaira	142,765
Carupano	13,450
Puerto Cabello	5,760
Total	301,147

RULES AND REGULATIONS OF THE MINING LAW.

[From the "Gaceta Oficial" of March 6, 1906.]

Gen. CIPRIANO CASTRO, President of the United States of Vene and Restorer of Venezuela, decrees:

In compliance with article 10 of the mining law decreed by National Congress on August 3, 1905, said law is subject to the fo ing rules and regulations:

"SECTION I.—*Classification.*

"ARTICLE 1. In conformity with article 1 of the mining law mineral beds or deposits are classified as follows:

"Mines of gold, silver, copper, platinum, lead, tin, zinc, mer antimony, chrome, cobalt, nickel, arsenic, iron, manganese, ba strontium, cadmium, molybdenum, sulphur, graphite, uranium, dium, tungsten, asbestos, kaolin, alum, alkaline sulphates, colum potassium salts, phosphates, apatite, phosphorite, nitrates, copr guano and other fertilizers; mines of coal, anthracite, lignite, succ or yellow amber, mineral resin, oxokerite or mineral wax, nap petroleum, bitumin, asphalt, tar, and other fossil fuels, and mi precious stones used in jewelry.

"SECTION 1. In order that such beds or deposits may be consi mines, whether they be veins, lodes, alluvions, pockets, etc., necessary that they be susceptible of being industrially and com cially worked.

the works themselves, and the stability

Concerning mining property.

be exploited, not even by the owner of
concession made therefor by the Federal

e and subsurface in every zone or dis-
at the surface and extending in a verti-
s, and the latter starting at a depth of 3
ndefinite depth.
ry owner of a mining claim terminates
ag claim. Nevertheless, he who, while
whether they be lodes or alluvion placers,
nted or comprised in a mining claim, the
eady been forfeited, has the preferred
ining claim in the adjacent ground.
he course of exploitation, an individual or
mining claim of another, he shall dicon-
tely on becoming aware of it, or as soon
r the owner, and shall divide by halves the
l in good faith; but should he maliciously
nother, he shall have no right whatever
ll pay to the owner of the mining claim
of said ore, and the owner of the claim
faith in an opposing judicial action.
within the limits of vein or lode mining
ces referred to in Sections XIV and XV
i, belong to the owner of the mining claim,
ne without a new concession. In mining
d the owners shall have the preference
denouncement and acquisition of all the
in, in accordance with the provisions of

exists between two or more mining claims
round, they shall be granted to that owner
who first applies for the same; and if the
ncessions renounce them, they shall be
for them.

"ART. 7. The title of each mining claim shall be issued by the President of the Republic, sealed with the seal of the Federal Executive, and countersigned by the Minister of Fomento in the following manner: 'The President of the Republic, inasmuch as it appears that the —— —— citizens (persons or firm) has applied to the Government for the adjudication of a mining claim of —— class, called ——, of —— extent, located at ——, State (Territory or district) of ——, the boundary lines of which, in accordance with the respective plans drawn by the engineer or surveyor —— ——, are as follows: ——; and, inasmuch as all the requisites prescribed by the mining law and its rules and regulations have been complied with, has seen fit to declare in favor of —— ——, his heirs or assigns, the mining claim of —— extent, located in the municipality of —— district, of —— State or Territory or of the federal district, to which reference is made in docket No. ——. In case that both the grantee or grantors of the mining claims are foreigners, as well as some or all the members of the companies that may be organized for the exploitation thereof, they shall always be considered as Venezuelans and shall be subject to the laws of the Republic and to the jurisdiction of its courts in all business relating to the mining claim and its exploitation, and in no case and for no cause whatever shall there be room for diplomatic action or international claim, and such members shall necessarily have their domicile in the Republic, without prejudicing their domicile out of the Republic, and, so far as the exploiting company is especially concerned, they shall always continue in the territory of the nation and in accordance with its laws. The present title shall be recorded at the proper register office corresponding to the place in which the mining claim is located, and entitles the grantee and his successors for —— years to the use and enjoyment of said mining claim as long as they comply with the provisions specified in the mining law and rules and its regulations now in force.'

"ART. 8. The new mining claim granted on public or common lands includes both the surface and mining property, and the owner may freely use in its exploitation the forests, waters, and other materials contained therein in the working of the mines, being bound only to strictly comply with the legal provisions relating to the matter.

"ART. 9. Whenever the owner needs the surface belonging to a private party in the exploitation of his mine, he shall have a friendly understanding with the owner of said surface, but if they can not agree, and the necessity for the use of the land being sufficiently proved, he shall proceed to expropriate said surface, submitting the question to experts, in conformity with the provisions of the laws, in order to appraise such portion of the land as may be necessary to take, as well as the losses and damages caused to the owner.

the surface important crops or precious woods,
shall only be entitled to such portion as he may
installation of the houses, buildings, machinery,
ly and other essential works.

ely mining districts the owners of mines and
guards are bound to take care of the forests
iction to the detriment of the mines.

*ning the necessary requisites for acquiring and
working mining claims.*

alt, naphtha, petroleum, bitumen, oxokerite or
l not be acquired nor worked except as pre-
and XV of these rules and regulations.
ing are prohibited from acquiring or having
mining claims:
mployed in the department of mines, and min-
within the zone in which they render services

ites, governors of territories and of the Federal
of the respective mining zone.
th the administration of justice in mining

do not apply to mines acquired before the
esaid offices, nor to those which, during their
cials may acquire by inheritance or will.
ns desiring to make explorations for discover-
s, shall act in conformity with the provisions
of these rules and regulations, at the risk of
l in addition to such indemnity for losses and
ed thereby.
n competent to acquire mines may freely make
Government, common, and on uncultivated
te parties and which are unfenced.
o explorations shall be made in the yards, gar-
s, fenced lots of houses located in towns or
spective owners or other persons authorized

lorations are to be made on cultivated or fenced
te parties, the interested party shall apply for
e owner or of his representative, who, in case
in writing to the explorer the proper permit,
ndaries of the land wherein the exploration
rner or his representative should refuse to give

said permit, the interested party shall request the same from the president of the state, governor of the territory or federal district, through the first civil authority of the locality, stating in his petition the kind of bond he is willing to give for such losses and damages as may be caused by making such explorations. The applicant shall likewise state his name, nationality, and domicile, as well as the location and conditions of the land for which he requests the permit.

"ART. 16. The president of the state, governor of the territory or of the federal district, shall report to the owner of the land or his representative concerning the application, and either of them shall, within the fifteen days following said notification, set forth the reasons they may have for denying the permit. In view of the statement of the interested parties and after the report of the three experts has been made, if the case should warrant it, the aforesaid authorities shall grant or refuse the exploration permit. The three experts referred to shall be appointed as follows: One by each of the interested parties and the other by the president of the state, governor of the territory or of the federal district. If after the expiration of the aforesaid fifteen days, the owner of the land or his representative should fail to appear before the proper authority, the latter shall grant the explorer the permit applied for for the term of three months, stating therein the limits of the land wherein the exploration is to be made. Said permit shall entitle the holder thereof to the exclusive right to make explorations during the three months referred to, which term may be extended an additional three months at the discretion of the proper authority.

"ART. 17. On mining claims, whether they are being exploited or not, no prospecting for mines can be carried on except with the special permit of the grantee.

"*Sole paragraph.* The inhibition prescribed in this article does not include the right to roads or rights of way that another mine or mining prospect, whether it is being exploited or not, may be entitled to establish or which already exist in the mining claims in order to facilitate the exploitation thereof.

"ART 18. A prospect pit or other mining works shall not be made within a shorter distance than 20 meters from a building, railroad, walled inclosure, wagon road, canal, bridge, watering place or any other public or private easement, nor less than 2,000 meters from fortified places, without the previous permission of the proper authorities or of the owner.

"ART. 19. With reference to towns built near mines in exploitation, the first civil authority of the locality shall issue the necessary permit to execute the works referred to in the foregoing article, provided no damages result therefrom to the town.

RT. 20. Any person who, excluding all others, desires to make ...rations in Government or uncultivated lands, shall apply to the ...ary of Fomento for a permit, who is able to grant it for the term ...xtent of land that he may deem proper. Said permit shall entitle ...rson to whom it is issued, for the term stated therein, the right ...ference to denounce and acquire such mines as may be found on ...nd granted.

RT. 21. After the exploration is completed, if the party in interest ...scovered any deposit that may be considered a mine in accord-...with the mining law, he shall take four samples of the vein, ..., or ore deposit, each of said samples to weigh not less than 500 ...s (1 pound). In the case of alluvion gold in any kind of a placer ...posit, the parties in interest shall furnish from the mine the four ...les referred to of the soil containing nuggets or grains. These ...les shall be delivered, in the presence of two witnesses, to the ...ivil authority of the municipality or parish of the jurisdiction in ...the mine is located, together with a written statement prepared ...e party in interest or his legal representative, drawn on stamped ...'of the kind on which said statement and application should be ..., in accordance with the respective state, territory, or federal ...ct law, and with the proper stamps duly canceled. The state-...referred to shall specify the kind of mine or ore deposit believed ...re been discovered; that the samples were taken from a given ..., comprised in the jurisdiction of the municipality or parish, and ...n said place a mining claim can be surveyed which shall be com-...l, more or less, in a square of so many meters on each side, or a ...gle so many meters long by so many meters in width, or equal ...many hectares, with the following boundaries. He shall also ...on the best known places in said mining claim, as well as the ...of the contiguous mines, should there be any, and the number of ...he desires the ownership of the mine.

...ole paragraph.—Should the persons or companies making said ...ncements be foreigners, they shall state in said application that ...are willing to submit themselves entirely to the provisions of the ...g law and its regulations. Should they fail to comply with this ...site, the denouncement shall be void and of no value, and the ...r civil authority shall so declare in writing at the bottom of the ...ation, retaining said application in order to copy it, together ...the statement of nullity, in a book kept for that purpose, and to ...rd afterwards the original to the Department of Fomento where ...shall be established a special file of mine denouncements which ...been declared null and of no value.

RT. 22. The chief of the municipality or parish shall at once, with-...y excuse or pretext, under the penalty of dismissal from office, the imposition of a fine of from 1,000 to 4,000 *bolívares*, and the payment of any damages caused to the interested party, except in case of superior force or unavoidable circumstances duly justified, and, in the latter case, the chief civil officer of the place (who, should it be necessary, shall appoint a delegate for this purpose), shall cause to be entered in the respective book, in the presence of the interested party and two witnesses, a minute, in accordance with Form No. 1.

"Thereupon notices shall be posted in the most public places of the municipality or parish, by order of the civil chief, reading: (See Form No. 2.)

"ART. 23. The local authority shall record in a book kept for that purpose the minutes referred to in the foregoing article, and shall deliver to the interested party an original copy of the same, signed by the aforesaid authority and his secretary, the witnesses, and the interested party, and shall forward a certified copy of the minutes to the chief authority of the respective district of the municipality or parish, and, through the president or governor of the state, territory, or federal district, to the Department of Fomento, together with a sample taken from those he delivered to the interested party or discoverer. The sending of the sample shall be by mail, in a registered envelope, or by express, if the interested party is willing to pay the expenses incurred thereby. The express company shall return the receipts of delivery to the proper person.

"ART. 24. As soon as the civil chief of the district in the jurisdiction of which the municipality or parish in which the discovery and denouncement of the mine belongs, receives the copy of the respective minutes, he shall post in his office, and in the most conspicuous places of the town for forty days, notices similar to those provided for in article 22, and shall publish said minutes in the official papers of the district, should there be any, or in those of the nearest place, or in the newspaper having the largest circulation in the locality, or of the nearest locality, four times at least within a period of thirty days from the date of the denouncement, and a copy of each publication should be added to the docket.

"The chief of the district shall, without delay, forward in turn, to the Department of Fomento, through the president of the state, governor of the territory, or of the federal district, by registered mail, an exact copy of the whole docket of the denouncement.

"ART. 25. The chief of the district and the Department of Fomento shall cause said minutes to be copied in the book for the registration of mines, and they shall acknowledge receipt, at the place of destination, by registered mail to the authorities who sent the document, and shall advise the interested party accordingly.

"ART. 26. On the expiration of the forty days prescribed in article 24, and within the following sixty days, the denouncer shall address

epartment of Fomento a communication requesting that he be
asession of the mine.

paragraph.—The above application must contain: The Chris-
ne, the surname, residence, and nationality of the applicant;
icity in which he makes his representation; the date of the
ement before the civil chief of the municipality or parish; the
mine he applies for, and the name of the latter; the boundaries
and wherein the mine is located; the number of hectares, or
th of the sides of the square applied for, and all other features
racteristics which may be necessary to clearly define the min-
ns applied for. He shall, likewise, state the number of years
as to possess the mining claim.

. 27. On the receipt of the application referred to in the fore-
ticle, the Secretary of Fomento shall acknowledge receipt of
a to the interested party, and if the former is satisfied that the
uents established by the mining law and its regulations have
uplied with, and that the term of forty days to which article
a has elapsed, and that there has been no justifiable opposition,
. communicate with the respective president of the state, or
r, in order that the latter may direct the civil chief of the dis-
which the mine is located to proceed, within the term of eight
make the survey of the mining claim applied for and to give
on of the same to the interested party.

. 28. The chief of the district, upon the receipt of the order
e president of the state, governor of the territory or federal
shall fix, three days in advance, the day and hour on which
l chief of the municipality or parish and other persons who
e present at the act of the taking possession, shall go to the
ere the mine is located; and, on arriving there, shall commu-
rith the chief of the municipality or parish and, through its
bannel, to the watchman or guard of the mine, if there be any;
iterested party, to two experts appointed by the same chief of
rict, and to the contiguous owners of mines, and shall decree
ame act and at the same time shall direct the delivery of pos-
of said mining concession to the interested party or his legal
itative. (Circular form No. 3.)

adjacent mine owners shall be summoned by tickets express-
eon the number of hectares, the boundaries, the name of the
er, and the date and hour fixed. The neighboring mine own-
l sign at the bottom of the ticket, or, if unable to sign, shall
me one else sign for them, and these tickets shall be added to
ket made. If the adjacent mine owners refuse to sign the
and should fail to attend, or should they be absent and fail to
asented, in spite of the publications made in the official or other
para, as soon as these circumstances are verified by creditable

witnesses, they shall not be able to claim any right with regard
act of taking possession in which they shall be considered prese

"*Sole paragraph.*—The chiefs of the district are authoriz
appoint a temporary mine watchman or guard, in case the E
Executive should not have made said appointments, within the r
tive boundaries.

"ART. 29. It is the duty of the chief of the municipality or
to serve the summons referred to in the foregoing article, so th
parties summoned may meet at the place of the discovery of the
on the day fixed. If, because of carelessness or malice, the ch
the municipality or parish should fail to comply with the prev
of this article, the chief of the civil district shall impose upon
fine of 1,000 *bolivares* and suspend him from office.

"ART. 30. If the chief of the municipality or parish or the
watchman or guard should have any justifiable legal impediment
would prevent them from complying with the order of the ch
the district to give possession of the denounced mine on the da
hour prescribed by the said authority they shall duly advise the
of the district, so that the latter may appoint substitutes to take
places in said act.

"*Sole paragraph.*—Said functionaries are responsible for the
ages that the interested party may sustain on account of the de
the due compliance of the provisions of these Rules and Regul
concerning the acquisition of the right of possession of a mine.

"Art. 31. In case of excuses based on physical disabilitie
other legal causes, the chiefs of the district are authorized to ap
in the capacity of acting substitutes, the persons who must be p
at the act of taking possession of a mine, in cases where the
formalities have been complied with. The chief of the district
also appoint an acting Secretary in case the Secretary can not be p
at said act.

"ART. 32. The chief of the municipality, or parish, respective
secretary, the mine watchman or guard, the party in interest, tl
experts appointed, and the adjoining mine owners, should th
any, assembled and installed in the place in which the mine w
covered, shall go through the ceremony of entering into posses
the following manner: The chief of the municipality or parish,
panied by the experts, shall fix the boundary lines and determi
number of hectares or the length of each side of the square
tangle that the interested party has applied for, in order to se
his mining claim; in each angle a landmark shall be placed, i
formity with the provisions of article 53 of these rules and regul
and the land of the claim in a single body shall be designa
the place preferred by the party in interest. Before this i
the experts and the mine watchman or guard must accompa

nd have samples taken from the vein, deposit or
r orechamber, at the place where the party in
e samples submitted by him, in order that it may
be hereinafter referred to if the examination and
th have made clearly show that there exist in that
ogous or similar to those of the samples which the
bmitted, of which samples the chief civil authority
remaining in his possession; and they shall also
es whether the approximate number of hectares, or
side of the square, or the base and height of the
requested is well calculated, and whether the land-
nts prescribed in the rules and regulations have
being done, the chief of the municipality or parish
ed to complete the act of possession and to comply
s of the mining law and of these rules and regula-
locket from the proceedings made and using the
State of the proper class. (Form for the act of

hief of the municipality or parish, after the act of
nated, shall immediately forward by registered mail
xpense of the interested party if sending by express
ertified copy of the act of entering into possession
district, and, through the President of the State,
erritory or of the Federal District, to the Minister
chief of the district, as well as the Minister of
nediately acknowledge receipt, and each shall have
kept for that purpose the act of entering into
ollowing terms:
o-day ———— I have received from the chief of the
irish of ———— a certified copy of the entry by
vas given to Mr. (or company) ———— of a mine
h is ———— (such and such) ———— ore and is situated
or parish of ————, located in ———— place, having
ndaries: ————; that the denouncer chose -————
ere surveyed in a square of ———— per side (or a
- base by ———— height), and signed by the Minis-
the chief of the district.
ssion gives the right to the denouncer to explore
r deem convenient and to have made a topographic
n accordance with the provisions of these rules and

in ninety days, counting from the date of the act
ossession, the party in interest shall have made a
of the claim and shall send it, certified to by the
r guard and by an engineer or surveyor, to the

Department of Fomento, with a copy of the docket relating to
denouncement, in order to obtain from the President of the Repu
the deed or title to the mining claim, with all the rights and privile
granted him by the mining law and these rules and regulations
shall also send to the said Department the certificate and rep
given him by the National Laboratory regarding the analysis mad
the ore taken from the shaft prescribed in these rules and regulatic
Said deed or title shall be issued within the term of thirty-days, provi
the docket and the plan have been made in conformity with the p
visions of the mining law and of these rules and regulations. If
discrepancies are found they shall be duly noted, and the docket
plan shall be returned to the party in interest, so that they can be
rected within the term of sixty days. If the interested party corr
said discrepancies, the deed or title shall be issued to him within
thirty days following the filing of the new proceedings.

"ART. 36. The map or plan of the mining claim, the perimete
which shall be ascertained in conformity with article 4 of the min
law, shall be made on drawing paper of good quality and on a s
that will show the necessary details of the land. Said plan s
specify the location of the mine, its extent and boundaries, the len
and direction of the sides, the topographic position of the monume
at least with respect to the most salient points of the land; shall s
whether it is on government or private land and give data regard
the shaft, in accordance with the provisions of article 37 of these n
and regulations, and all other data and information that may be ne
sary to fix with all exactness, on the general plan that these rules
regulations prescribe, shall be furnished to the technical inspecto
mines, the place that the mining claim occupies on the land.

"ART. 37. During the ninety days allowed, after entering into
session, in which to request the deed or title to the property,
denouncer shall, if a vein or lode mine, sink a shaft one and one-
meters square at the surface and of the necessary depth to cut the v
This work shall precede the drawing of the plan, in order that
engineer or surveyor who makes the same can show on it all the
concerning the vein. As soon as the shaft is finished, the part
interest shall advise the respective mine watchman or guard, who
examine it, take a sample of it, and send the same to the Ministe
Fomento. Said functionary shall send the sample to the Nati
Laboratory to be duly examined, in order to be sure that it is the s
ore that the interested party had analyzed, at his own expense, at
time of requesting the deed or title to the property.

"ART. 38. The proceeding of entering into possession of m
shall be for account of the interested person, who shall furnish to
chief of the municipality or parish, to his Secretary, to the
watchman or guard, and to two experts, who must participate the

provisions and horses necessary to convey them to the location
he mine.

Each of the four following functionaries, namely, the civil chief,
Secretary, and the two experts, shall also receive, as compensa-
, 20 *bolivares* for part taken by them in the proceedings made for
possession of each claim.

The approximate survey that may be made of each claim is under-
d to be included in the aforesaid proceedings, but if said proceed-
should be annulled for any omission imputable to the functionaries
xperts who take part in them, the proceedings must be repeated
is, and if this should not be possible, they shall return to the party
iterest the compensation received, except in case of superior force
lly proved.

All the proceedings and steps taken in the acquisition of mines shall
iade on sealed paper of the last class, according to the respective
of the State, Territory, or of the Federal District, and the stamps
iired on the same shall be duly canceled.

Sole paragraph.—One person may obtain several claims.

ART. 39. The Federal Executive may lease, in accordance with the
iulations that he may deem proper, the mines that, through for-
ure, abandonment or any other cause, may have reverted to the
iership of the Nation.

"FORM NUMBER 1.

The municipality or parish of ———, of the state or territory
——— (or of the federal district).

I, ——— ———, first civil authority of this place, certify that on
——— day of ———, at ——— hours, appeared before me Mr.
company) ——— ———, a Venezuelan citizen (or of such and such
itionality) ——— ———, of legal age, residing at ———, and
——— profession or occupation, accompanied by ——— ———
iess, and ——— ——— witness, residing in this municipality or
ih, who declare and certify that Mr. (the solicitor or his legal
·esentative) ——— ——— with (or without) permission of explora-
, discovered a mine, in accordance with the mining law and the
s and regulations concerning the subject, from which mine he
ents and deposits in this office, under ——— numbers, the respec·
samples of the vein or deposit (or of washed alluvion gold) that
mine seems to contain; that these samples were taken from (such
such) a place, within the jurisdiction of the municipality or parish;
that the denouncer selects for a term of ——— years, a mining
i of ——— hectares, contained within a square of ——— meters
side (or a rectangle of ——— meters in length or base by ———
rs in width or height) having the following boundaries: ———

In witness whereof, the legal denouncement of the land on which to
t the mine referred to having been made, to which mine the dis-

coverer gives the name of ——— ———, complying thereby with the provisions of the mining law and its rules and regulations, we, the undersigned, sign as follows:

"The local authority: ——— ———.

"The party in interest: ——— ———.

"Witness: ——— ———.

"Witness: ——— ———.

"*Note.*—In case the denouncer is a foreigner, there shall be added to the above form, before the space left for signatures, the following: Mr. (or Messrs. or company) ——— ——— declares that in his capacity as a foreigner he submits to all the provisions contained in articles 6 and 7 of the mining law and to the sole paragraph of article 21 and articles 48, 49, 50, and 51 of these rules and regulations.

"*Note.*—Should the denouncer be unable to sign his name, he shall appoint some one to sign for him.

"FORM NO. 2.

"On this - ——— day of ———— at ——— hours, appeared before me Mr. ——— ————, a Venezuelan citizen (or foreigner), in the presence of the witness ——— ——— and the witness ——— ———, denouncing the discovery of a free mine of ——— ore in ——— place, and bounded as follows: ———.

"In compliance with the law, this notice shall be displayed on the bulletin board for a period of forty days.

"The chief civil authority: ——— ———.

"The secretary: ——— ———.

"MODEL NO. 3.

"Circular.

"I ——— ———, chief of the district, in compliance with a superior order, and all the provisions of the mining law and its rules and regulations, having been complied with concerning the denouncement and delivery of possession of ——— - mine, denounced by Mr. ——— ———— (or whoever legally represents him), order that you, in conjunction with your Secretary, and Mr. ——— - ———, mine watchman, and of Messrs. ——— ———, whom I have appointed experts, proceed to the place where said mine is situated, the respective owners of the adjoining property having been previously summoned, if there are such owners, within the peremptory term of eight days, counting from the date on which this communication is received; and, for the necessary legal effect, I command you to do all that is necessary in order that the persons appointed may attend, so that all the provisions of the mining law, and its rules and regulations, may be complied with relating to this act of entry, making you responsible for failure to comply with all of these provisions.

"(Date)

"The chief civil authority ——— ———.

. "MODEL No. 4.—*Concerning the act of entry.*

"I, ——— ———, chief of the municipality or parish of ———,
accompanied by my Secretary, by ——— ———, mine watchman or
guard, and by Messrs. ——— ———, experts appointed for this act,
and by Mr. ——— ———, who has requested, in accordance with the
formalities prescribed by the mining law and its rules and regulations,
the possession of this mine called ———, and with the concurrence of
the adjoining owners (if they are present, and if they should not be
present it shall be so stated), solemnly declare in the name of the law and
. by order of the Minister of Fomento of the United States of Venezuela,
that, all the legal requisites having been complied with, I put in
possession Mr. (or company) ——— ——— of the mine that he has discovered and which is embraced within the following boundaries: ———;
and that in each angle of the survey of the mining concession a corner-
stone has been placed, in conformity with article 53 of the rules and
regulations of the mining law; that the party in interest has chosen
——— hectares of land that are surveyed in a square of ——— meters
on each side (or in a rectangle having a base of ——— meters by ———
meters in height), more or less; that the samples which the interested
party submitted on making the respective denouncement of the said
mine have been verified, and that said samples are of the same class
and grade as those encountered in said location; and, finally, there
being no legal opposition, Mr. (or company) ——— ——— is hereby
declared to be in peaceful possession of said mine, in accordance with
the requirements of the law.

"We sign three of the same tenor.

"(Date).

"The chief civil authority of the municipality or parish.

——— ———.

"The Secretary.

——— ———.

"The party in interest.

——— ———.

"The mine watchman or guard.

——— ———.

"The experts and the adjoining property owners, should there be
any of the latter.

——— ———.

"SECTION IV.—*Concerning opposition.*

"ART. 40. By first denouncer, and with unquestioned right to obtain
the ownership of a mine, is understood to be the first person who may
have made the denouncement and presented the samples referred to
in these rules and regulations, in accordance with the formalities prescribed therein and in the mining law, unless there has been a legal

decision to the contrary. In the case of discussion or question at t time of the denouncement the samples shall be compared and th identity verified, examining them in comparison with those of i place from which they have been extracted, taken from the same ve lode, outcrop, or deposit of washed gold, respecting their quality i conditions and making the assays or tests of the same.

" *Sole paragraph.*—Whoever denounces a mine in the name of anotl person should show the power authorizing him to do so. Said do ment shall be used by the empowered in case of opposition.

"ART. 41. The opposition may be made orally at the time the i coverer files the denouncement, or in writing at any time before i day fixed for entry into possession.

"In the first instance the authority before whom the denounce is made shall enter the proceedings in a register which shall be k for that purpose, which shall be signed by the public functioni together with the parties thereto.

"ART. 42. After the filing of the document, or the recording of proceedings of opposition, a term of fifteen days shall elapse in wh the parties in interest shall prove to the mine watchman, or guard, to the officer who substitutes him, who has the best right to the mi the decision being rendered on the last day of the term referred to

"The party not satisfied with this decision may appeal, within term of five days, to the technical inspector, who shall decide wit the term of fifteen days after having received the proceedings relat thereto; and should one of the parties still be dissatisfied, he may t the case, as a last resort, to the Minister of Fomento; but in no c shall the proceedings which these rules and regulations establish the acquisition of mines be stopped, and whoever obtains the l favorable decision, in case of an appeal from the first, shall be owner of the mine.

"If the opposition should not treat of priority in the discovery, should be founded on rights of another kind already acquired, person believing himself to be wronged with the decision of i administrative proceedings, may maintain his rights in an ordin suit before the courts.

"ART. 43. The owners of adjoining mines may make opposition the time of entering into possession, when the survey embraces al part of their mines; but in this case the suit concerns the survey shall be tried and decided in accordance with the provisions of civil procedure, the act of entry, or the effects thereof, remainin suspense during the pendency of the suit.

" *Sole article.*—In the case referred to in the foregoing article parties shall be summoned before the judge having jurisdiction, the opposing party shall, within eight days and the term of the tance, formulate the petition of survey.

"Section V.—Concerning the title of the property.

r. 44. The Minister of Fomento, in accordance with the docket, the claim, and the analysis of the ore, provided he finds that visions of the mining law and its rules and regulations have mplied with, shall issue, on national sealed paper of the value bolivars, the title of ownership, and shall cancel stamps to the f 40 bolivars.

is deed or title shall be legalized with the signature of the Presi-
: the Republic, sealed with the seal of the Federal Executive, untersigned by the Minister of Fomento, and a record of it made in the proper register.

paragraph.—The docket referred to in this article shall con-tified copies of all the documents relating to the denouncement juisition of the mine.

r. 45. After the issuance of the title to the property, the r of Fomento shall order that two certified copies be made of le and two of the respective plan of the claim. One of the of the title, as well as one of the copies of the plan, shall be the archives of the Department, and the other shall be sent to nical inspector of mines of the Republic. The title and origi-n shall be delivered to the party in interest. The plan shall ertification of the proper Bureau, stating that it was the one th the application for the title of the property.

r. 46. All the expenses incurred for sealed paper and stamps in ng the title to the property, and for the copies made in accord-ith the provisions of the foregoing article, shall be for account interested party.

r. 47. The title to the property shall be protocolized in the ition office of the jurisdiction in which the mining claim is

"Section VI.—*Duties of the grantee.*

r. 48. Companies formed for the exploitation of mines are civil and are subject to the civil jurisdiction of the Republic.

r. 49. Corporations issuing shares, and limited stock companies nerships formed for the purpose of exploiting a mining claim, organized in conformity with the provisions of the commer-de, without losing for that reason their character as civil l.

r. 50. Natural persons domiciled abroad who desire to exploit the referred to in the mining law and its regulations shall, before ncing their operations, legally appoint an agent or attorney l the powers necessary, who shall represent them and be respon-r the obligations that they may contract in the country. The power of attorney of the agent must always be registered in the office of the Public Registry, in the respective Division of the Tribunal of Commerce, and shall be published in full in the official newspaper, or in another newspaper in the jurisdiction of the Tribunal of Commerce to whom the registry appertains.

"ART. 51. The property, rights, and shares that natural or juridical persons domiciled abroad may have in the Republic, shall be directly liable for the operations and transactions, concerning their respective branches, that their agents in Venezuela may make.

"ART. 52. Whoever furnishes funds for the exploration or discovery of mines, as well as for the workings, machinery, and construction of buildings, has a mortgage on the mining claim. In order that this mortgage be valid it must be registered in the Office of the Registry where the mine is situated, stating therein the amount advanced and the object or purpose for which it was made.

"ART. 53. The denouncers must, at their own expense, fix the boundaries of the mines denounced, previous to the issue of the title to the property.

"The boundaries of the mines must be determined at the angles, with corner stones of masonry or posts of wood from the heart of the tree, these landmarks being at least 65 centimeters in circumference, and each post or corner stone shall be marked with the initials of the denouncer.

"ART. 54. The denouncers, after having erected the corner stones or posts referred to in the foregoing article, shall advise the mine guard or watchman, in order that he may see whether the provisions of said article have been complied with, and to enable him to inform the Minister of Fomento of the result of his inspection.

"ART. 55. The owner of any claim, on becoming aware that any corner stone or post is lacking, shall immediately replace it, and each year shall clear the dividing lines or those that form the perimeter of the claim.

"ART. 56. The denouncers who should fail to comply with the provisions of the foregoing articles shall pay a fine of 500 *bolivares*, which shall be collected in the form indicated in Section IX of these rules and regulations as soon as the mine watchman or guard reports the infraction to the Minister of Fomento.

ART. 57. Within the period of four years, which shall be counted from the day of the issue of the title to the property, the owner shall begin the exploitation of the mine and shall verify this fact before the Minister of Fomento, by means of a certificate that shall be issued by the mine watchman or guard.

"~~Chapter VIII.—Penalties imposed on infringers.~~"

58. Should the four years referred to in article 57 of these
d regulations elapsed without the owner of the mine having
d it he shall pay the National Government as a fine the sum of
livares, which shall give him the right to an extension of four
ore, counted from the date of the expiration of the first four

If this fine is not paid within the sixty days following the
ion of the first four years the Federal Executive shall declare
feiture of the claim, through the organ of the Department of
o, who shall publish in the Official Gazette the resolution taken
espect.

uring the extension of the four years that the party in interest
s by the payment of the fine he should fail to exploit the mine
eral Executive shall declare it forfeited.

order that a mine may be considered in exploitation it is
d that at least ten workmen be daily employed in the workings.

r. 59. The forfeiture of the mining claim having been declared,
rmity with the provisions of the foregoing article, the Min-
Fomento shall have inserted in the book in which the titles to
re inscribed a marginal note to this effect, and for the same
notice shall be given to the register in whose office the title
tocolized. Like notice shall be sent the president of the state,
ernor of the territory, or the federal district in whose jurisdic-
mine belongs.

r. 60. In addition to the cases of forfeiture established in this
, the persons who solicit a mining claim will lose *ipso jure* their
obtain title to the property:

If the sixty days referred to in article 26 should expire without
overer of the mine or his concessionary having requested of the
r of Fomento the possession of the claim;

If the ninety days referred to in article 35 should expire without
rested party having requested of the Minister of Fomento the
the property; and

If the party in interest should not correct, within the term pre-
by article 35, the errors that the Department finds in the docket
n of the claim, and does not obtain in said case the title to the
y within the term indicated in the latter part of the same article.

loss of the rights to which this article refers shall occur with-
necessity of a special resolution of the Department of Fomento.

r. 61. The mining taxes referred to in Section IX of these rules
ulations shall be paid quarterly.

owners of mining claims who do not pay said taxes in the
indicated, shall pay as a fine to the National Government double
unt due therefor from the first quarter that they fail to pay.

"*Sole paragraph.*—Should two years elapse without the owner of the claim paying the taxes the Government shall decree the forfeiture of the mine or request that it be sold at auction with all its machinery, apparatus, and tools for the purpose of paying the amount of the taxes and fines.

"ART. 62. The mining claims that revert to the Government by virtue of these rules and regulations may be leased or acquired by their first owner, provided he pay a fine of 5,000 bolivars and acts in conformity with the provisions of the mining law and of these rules and regulations. The new owners of forfeited mining claims can not sell them to the first owners or to their heirs without said first owners or their heirs paying to the National Government the fine of 5,000 bolivars referred to in this article.

"SECTION VIII.—*Concerning the manner of establishing the registry of mines in public offices.*

"ART. 63. The chief of the municipality or parish shall keep a book in which shall be recorded the denouncements made before him in conformity with the provisions of article 21.

"This book shall be bound and arranged in such manner that it will neither be easy to add to or take from it one or more leaves, and it shall be paged, and each page shall be rubricated by the president of the state, governor of the territory or federal district, who shall place, furthermore, on the first page of each book, a statement or writing signed by them, specifying the number of folios that it contains and stating that each one has been rubricated by them.

"ART. 64. The annotation referred to in the foregoing article shall be made in the following manner:

"First, there shall be written therein the number of the entry, commencing with one and following upward in strict numerical order.

"Immediately following this the date shall be inserted, expressing the hour in writing.

"Following this the corresponding entry shall be made, stating the circumstances referred to in article 21 in accordance with the manifestations made by the denouncer.

"No erasure, correction, nor interlineations shall be made. If any mistake should have occurred, it shall be corrected at the bottom of the page by means of a note in which shall be expressed the word or mistaken phrase and the form in which it should remain.

"Lastly, the statement or writing shall be signed by the chief of the municipality or parish, by the denouncer, the two witnesses, and the secretary. If the denouncer should not know how to sign his name, this shall be noted, stating in the note that the statement or writing was read to him by the person he requested to sign for him.

"Witnesses will not be accepted who do not know how to sign.

al authority of the municipality or
in which he shall enter the denounce-
ine, in accordance with the provisions

l and shall be kept in conformity with
articles.

the making of the denouncement
cretary shall spread upon the record
rticle 64, and shortly after the legal
igs the original copy shall be issued,
erred to in article 23, delivering the
remitting the certified copies to the
h the president of the state, governor
district, to the Minister of Fomento,
these rules and regulations.

spective entry of the book mentioned
f the discovery of the mine, and shall
ollection of the taxes caused by reason
s a legal decision to the contrary.

ecorded in the book referred to in
hentic, unless they appear with cor-
ures that alter the sense of the entry,
d to the party in interest, but in all
igainst such a presumption as well as
iity of the proceedings. This without
e of the procedure, inasmuch as the
r or the impediment which caused it,
for costs, damages, and injuries.

Territorial Wealth, Agriculture, and
f Fomento shall keep the following

ments;
ents;
ession;
erty, showing where these documents

orfeited or auctioned, and

the form ordered in this section, and
ter of Fomento.

"SECTION IX.—*Concerning taxes and franchises.*

"ART. 70. Alluvion gold, in whatever class of deposits or beds that may be found in the beds of rivers and on public lands, is free to be worked when not adjudicated by concessions of the Federal Executive; this is the case as long as the exploitation is made with pans, and this system of exploitation is especially declared to be free from all taxes.

"ART. 71. Each mining claim, of vein or lode, of whatever character it may be, shall pay a tax of 2 bolivars annually per hectare, whether the land belongs to the nation or to private persons, and if in exploitation it shall pay an additional tax of 3 per cent on the gross output of the mine.

"Mining claims of alluvion gold, in whatever class of deposit or bed they may be found, shall pay 10 per cent on the gross product of exploitation, and, in addition, an area tax of 2 bolivars annually per hectare, whether the land belongs to the nation or to private persons.

"ART. 72. All the taxes and fines provided for in these rules and regulations shall be paid at the nearest custom-house to the mining district in which the mine is situated, or in any collection office when so ordered by the Federal Executive. If the mining claim should be situated in the Federal district, the taxes and fines shall be paid into the National Treasury.

"ART. 73. The Federal Executive, through the medium of the Minister of Fomento, shall order the creation of a stamp which shall be called the 'National Stamp of Mines.'

"The issue of said stamps shall be in the form that the Federal Executive may deem proper, and of the following denominations: Five centimes of a bolivar, twenty-five centimes of a bolivar, one bolivar, ten bolivars and one-hundred bolivars.

"ART. 74. All taxes and fines referred to in these rules and regulations shall be paid in said stamps.

"The Minister of Fomento shall send to the respective collection offices some policies sealed and numbered by the Department of Fomento, in order that in every case stamps may be canceled in said offices to the value of the amount of the taxes and fines.

"Each stamp shall be canceled with the date on which the taxes are paid.

"The policy shall be in the following form:

"*Policy of mining taxes.*

"On this date Mr. (or company) —— —— has paid the respective mining taxes (or fine) (from such and such a date) on mining claim of —— mining district, called —— (insert name of mine), consisting of — — — hectares, situated in the municipality of —— district of —— state, territory, or federal district. (At the bottom,

ng into consideration the pro-
enterprises in the develop-
intry, may relieve from the
may deem it proper, the im-
sils that are needed for the
kinds of explosive materials
ubject to the regulations and
of mines being obligated to
meters in depth, the roofs of
ce, and shall establish them
tilometers, according to the
towns or mining centers, for
e shall also free from duties

he contracts which he makes,
g taxes fixed by these rules
given to the nature of the
ession, to their location and
such cases, he shall always

i, buildings, machinery, and
primarily liable for the taxes
ions and for the payment of
except for the importations
, provided the goods of said
itation of the mines, or, when
exploitation, within the term

"SECTION X.—*Barrancos, or placers.*

"ART. 79. In the exploitation of auriferous clays or alluvions in any kind of a deposit or bed, a "barranco," or placer, is understood to be a solid 10 meters long by 10 meters wide and of indefinite depth.

"ART. 80. In investigating mines by the system of 'barrancos' or shafts for the exploitation of alluvion gold, works shall not be undertaken in the direction of an uncovered vein, whether the same is or is not in industrial exploitation, nor within the space of 100 meters on either side of it—that is to say, the owner of the vein has the right to retain and guard within his claim a zone of 200 meters wide, through the center of which the vein runs.

"ART. 81. The exploitation referred to in the foregoing article is preferably restricted to the washing of alluvion gold in pans, and as in these works there are frequently found loose stones, pebbles, or fragments of veins, and other exploitable minerals that may be broken or crushed by means of a mortar or by hand, the owner of the 'barranco' or shaft has the right to the use of all these classes of minerals, with the exception of defined veins or lodes that can only be acquired through the procedure prescribed in these rules and regulations.

"ART. 82. Any person capable of contracting, and who works for the purpose of discovering mines in the subsoil, may employ the 'barranco' or shaft system in said exploration or exploitation without being subject to any other restrictions than those prescribed in these rules and regulations.

"ART. 83. The 'barranco' or shaft system shall not be begun within the confines of towns and public highways, nor within buildings, aqueducts, reservoirs, plantations, and gardens, either public or private, it being understood that this prohibition is limited to a distance of 100 meters from the things herein specified.

"ART. 84. When a deposit of alluvion gold is discovered the mine watchman or guard, accompanied by the first civil authority of the place, shall visit the locality of the discovery, and, after making an ocular inspection in conformity with the provisions of the foregoing article, shall establish the order of the workings for the purpose of preventing the miners from injuring each others' interests; to this end he shall make the corresponding demarkations by means of posts inclosing a surface area of 100 square meters for each 'barranco' or deposit that is to be worked.

"One person may have several 'barrancos' or deposits.

"Crushers or 'alfarjetas' are also applicable to the 'barrancos' or shaft system of exploitation.

"ART. 85. In mining works carried on for the purpose of making explorations of any kind, with the exception of 'barrancos,' in mines having veins situated on government or uncultivated land, and on lands of private persons or mining claims, the exploiters must properly close the excavations that they make before abandoning the mines, and may be compelled to do so by the proper authority of the jurisdiction by means of fines or arrests, according to circumstances.

"SECTION XI. *Concerning water for mines.*

"ART. 86. Whoever makes the denouncement referred to in Section III of these rules and regulations acquires the right to take the water necessary for the working of a mine, provided the discovery is on government or vacant lands, in accordance with the provisions of this section.

"The use of water, without prejudice to the rights of third parties legitimately acquired, is always included in mining claims of alluvion gold.

"ART. 87. The first denouncer of a mine found in any place whatever has the preferred right, over all later discoverers, to take the necessary water for the use of his establishment and for the persons connected therewith, subject to the decision of experts, and he may make good this right at any time, even though he has not worked the mine, provided always, in the latter case, that the mining claim has not been declared forfeited, even though, in order to secure said right, it may be necessary to suspend the working of an establishment erected at a mine discovered subsequently.

"ART. 88. The other discoverers acquire equal rights, subordinated to the rights of the prior discoverers and with preference over those of subsequent discoverers, in the strict order of priority. This right is acquired by the act of making the denouncement.

"ART. 89. Every denouncer of a mine has, furthermore, the right to use the water that he desires, provided it does not prejudice rights granted in the foregoing articles to those who may have denounced mines before the water referred to was used, and provided he needs the water for the exploitation of his mines. In this case those who denounce mines after the use of said water have no right to use it unless there is an excess in the deposits or existing water courses.

"ART. 90. On making use of the rights referred to in the preceding articles, the owners of mines can never deprive the owners of the surface lands, who were there when the denouncement or denouncements were made, of the water necessary for their families, for their stock, for whatever kinds of machinery they may have established or commenced to establish, and for the irrigation of their crops. Those who afterwards become owners of the surface lands shall only be entitled to the surplus water for the uses indicated; neither can the owners of mines prevent the free enjoyment of the easements of aqueducts that are established on the land where the mine is located in favor of a town, settlement, farm, or installation of machinery of a third person.

"ART. 91. If differences should arise between the owners of mines because of the fact that some persons claim that there is excess water in a deposit or current, and others affirm to the contrary, the doubt shall be settled by three experts appointed for that purpose, one by each of the parties in interest and one by the chief civil authority of the district.

"ART. 92. Whenever it is necessary to decide whether there is a surplus in a current or deposit, to the end that an individual may use it, said surplus shall be the water remaining after separating the water which belongs to the owners of the mines first denounced.

"ART. 93. The right to surplus water granted by articles 89 and 90 shall not be denied in any way whatever by miners and persons engaged in the aforesaid industrial pursuits, unless it be for the purpose of enlarging their original establishments within the boundary of their mining claim.

"ART. 94. The differences that occur between miners and owners of land concerning water, or between persons enjoying any easement of aqueduct, shall be adjusted in the manner provided for in these rules and regulations.

"ART. 95. If a mine should be denounced which can not possibly be worked without the water with which another mine formerly denounced is exploited, the new denouncer shall have the right to take said water, provided he comply with the two following requisites:

"1. That he convey, at his own expense, to the aforesaid mine other water sufficient for the exploitation thereof.

"2. That he pay the owner of the aforesaid mine the damages said owner may have sustained because of the change of water, either on account of the larger trench or ditch said owner has to maintain, or because of the quality of the land that said water traverses, or, lastly, for any other cause whatever.

"ART. 96. If the owner of a large establishment should suspend the working of the mines, retaining the ownership of the same, the miners of smaller establishments may use the water that said owner may have conveyed to the aforesaid establishment, previously paying him therefor the value thereof, according to the appraisement of the experts, for said use, and shall, at their own expense, keep the trench or ditch in good order, without acquiring, for this reason, in any case, any right whatever to the ownership of the same.

"In such case the owner of the larger mine also has the right to compensation by the owner of the smaller mine for any damages the former may suffer by the use of the trench or ditch, and that the latter previously guarantee said indemnity or compensation in accordance

f civil authority of the place wherein

passes with the right to the mines,
mines is lost, and becomes, like the
though this fact should not be set
e seller of a mine should need the
g to him and at the time of making
ter right.
f a mine changes the water which he
nt for other water taken from a dif-
'everts by virtue of this fact to its
ownership, and thereafter becomes
s section.
aim be forfeited in conformity with
wner of a mine may take for another
by the forfeited mine, provided he
acquisition of said mine being able to
rmerly obtained, unless said water
said acquisition.
mines farther up the stream upon
already been installed may freely
establishments, provided he return
int above that which the owners of
wn the stream take their water supply,
he water by the first establishments
wer establishments.
ines that are situated farther up the
hip prior to that of the owner of the
stream, and who has taken for the
after having passed by his establish-
using thereby damages to the owner
pelled by the latter to convey said
to a point below that where it can

e possible to comply with the provi-
manager of the upper mines shall
er mines for the damages sustained,
ould it be necessary, by three experts
rties in interest, and the other by the

hese rules and regulations shall be
ment and indemnities occasioned by

"SECTION XII. — *Concerning the working and policing of mines.*

"ART. 104. Each State of those composing the Union, and each territory, as well as the federal district, constitutes a mining zone or circumscription, subdivided into as many mining districts as there are districts in the respective state, territory, or federal district.

"ART. 105. In the mining districts the police, who are under the control of the authorities of the state, territory, or federal district, are obliged to give immediate aid to the technical inspector and to the mine guards, provided they so request it, in the fulfillment and execution of their functions.

"ART. 106. The owners or administrators of mines are obliged to exploit same in conformity with the rules of the art, in such manner that the lives of the workmen shall not be endangered, and for the purpose of complying with the orders which, in each special case, the proper authorities may issue in addition to the following:

"1. To maintain well ventilated the places where the work of exploitation is carried on, so that the miners will neither drown nor suffocate from the accumulation or retention of gases or miasmas, or from the infiltrations or accumulations of water. Consequently, the necessary communication for ventilation, drainage, and extraction of materials shall be established with the surface.

"2. To insure the ceilings and walls or sides of the transit workings and of the workings from which ore is taken by means of timbering, masonry, or timber walls, as the nature of the ground may require. These works shall be inspected from time to time for the purpose of making the repairs that solidity requires them to have. The natural pillars which serve to support the mine shall not be removed except on the condition of replacing them with artificial pillars of equal resistance.

"3. To facilitate the entrance and exit and the general transit of the workmen. For this purpose, if the transit works or openings have a greater incline than 35°, they shall be provided with a railing, and if the incline is as much as 40°, in addition to the railings they shall have a stairway—that is to say, steps in the rock, or formed artificially. The ladders placed in the openings, drafts, or shafts for transit shall have the proper conditions of safety, and every 5 meters shall be provided with a rest or platform, to prevent the passage of a person or object that may roll down them. If the workmen should have to descend into the mines in cars, cages, or buckets, cables of first-class quality shall be employed, and the necessary safety apparatus shall be used to prevent accidents.

"4. The placing of blasts or charges in rock or gangue, crevices or holes that have already been charged or fused shall not be permitted.

tamping rods, the ends of which are of iron,
capable of producing sparks when used, be

in galleries or levels, tunnels, drifts, cross-
all not be permitted to pitch the ore to a lower
viously advised the workmen who may be in

le exploitation of the mine, the twenty-four
to three shifts, namely, from 7 a. m. to 3 p. m.;
and from 11 p. m to 7 a. m., employing in each
fficient number of workmen, overseers, and
all be men, and in no case shall persons under
en, be employed.
having a wire passing through the several
transit workings, shall be placed in the upper
ft. The prescribed signals of the mine shall
le following stroke: 1 stroke of the bell indi-
r car should stop; 2 strokes is the signal to
signal to ascend; 4 strokes means to ascend
ith care, and 5 strokes or a continued ringing
or other grave occurrence has taken place in

descent to the galleries or excavations and
well as admission to the mills and machinery
strictly prohibited to all persons except the
vorks, or miners, except with the permission
technical inspector of mines and the mine
t or circumscription, who may enter at any
are excepted from the foregoing prohibition.
occasioned to a mine by the exploitation of
imbursed by the owner of the latter, accord-
three experts appointed, one by each of the
he other by the civil authority of the locality.
dent occurs in a mine, which causes the death,
ng of a miner unfit to work, damages shall be
erest. Should the parties be unable to agree as
nages, said amount shall be fixed by three ex-
; purpose, one each by the parties in interest
ef civil authority of the place.
e of the mines is in charge of the director of
rity shall not extend beyond the limits of his
ler to take action he must request aid from the
ho will cooperate with him in the furtherance
le mine, and he may appeal to the authorities

of the locality in all cases in which the procedure is not comprised within the sphere of his powers.

"ART. 110. It is the duty of mining companies to keep their books in Spanish and in accordance with the formalities prescribed by the commercial code.

"SECTION XIII.—*Concerning functionaries.*

"ART. 111. In the capital of the Republic there shall be a technical inspector of mines, who shall establish, for account of the Government, an office in due form. This functionary, who must be a graduate engineer, shall have an official archivist who shall act as secretary whenever necessary.

"ART. 112. In every mining district or circumscription, there shall be a mine guard who shall have practical knowledge in mining matters, shall know how to interpret a plan, and shall be of legal age.— These same conditions are required in order to be eligible for appointment as official archivist of the inspection office.

"ART. 113. In the technical inspection office of mines the following books shall be kept: A title register of mining property; an index of mines in which shall be recorded the name of the mine, its class, number of hectares of which it consists, the name of the owner, the date of the adjudication, number of the docket, place in which the mine is situated, transfer and other observations regarding the mine; a register of transfers; a register of executive orders of forfeiture, and a register of the decisions made by the technical inspector of mines in opposition suits.

"ART. 114. The mine guards shall keep a book with an index of the mining claims in the territory of their jurisdiction, recording in same all the data relating to said mines in accordance with the book kept by the technical inspector.

"ART. 115. The plan filed by the party in interest, together with the respective docket of the Department of Fomento, shall be subjected to the examination of the technical inspector of mines, who, on finding said plan in accordance with the law, shall approve it. Should it not be found in conformity with the law, or should there be lacking the information and details required, in order that the position of the mining claim on the land be well defined, the technical inspector of mines shall so report to the Department of Fomento to the end that the proper steps may be taken in the matter.

"ART. 116. When the Federal Executive shall deem it necessary, the technical inspector of mines shall visit the mining districts or circumscriptions of the Republic, shall record in detail the methods employed in the working of the mines and the treatment of the different ores, and shall make a report on each district or circumscription, setting

are endangered, said officer shall take the
‹ the cause of the danger.   Should a claim
gineers, appointed by the first civil authority
e of the parties in interest, shall be heard,
‹or, in conformity with the opinion of the
shall render a decision in the least possible

r, or the representative of one or more mining
lisposal of the technical inspector of mines,
means and methods necessary to inspect the
ng him the plans, the pay roll of the work-
1 other information as may be of use to him
of the exploitation.   The director, or the
›, shall also show the inspector the title to
ier documents which may substantiate the
iing claim, when the inspector desires them
iny circumstances that may affect the rights
arties.
:epresentative of one or more mines, shall
›f the mine guard, or of the employee that
ignates, his books of account for the pur-
rectness of the liquidations and quarterly
ə proved from an examination of the books
ise is defrauding the public treasury, the
nse shall pay a fine ten times greater than
shall, in addition, be subject to the orders
iediction thereof in bringing the proper suit.
ir, or legal representative of the mining
y to the mine guard, and the latter shall see
. report setting forth the quantity of ore ex-
useful substances produced, the number of
heir nationality, and all other expenses in-
ι of the mine.   This report, after having
ı of the company, shall be sent by the mine
of Fomento to be preserved in the archives
copy thereof shall be sent to the office of
mines, and shall serve as a basis for com-
nch of territorial wealth.   This report shall
the verification of the accounts presented

"*Sole article.*—In case there are no mine guards, the duties imposed upon them by virtue of this article shall be for account of the first civil authority of the locality.

. "ART. 120. The technical inspector of mines and the mine guards shall likewise intervene in the demarcation of the mining claims when there is reason to doubt the correctness of the surveys, and in all such acts and claims of the miners that may affect the property of the Nation concerning the mines or their direct interest in the exploitation thereof.

"ART. 121. In cases of disputes with workmen the mine guard shall inquire into the causes of the same, and if he can not settle them amicably he shall proceed to protect the interests of both parties, and when necessary, for the preservation of public order in the mine and its vicinity, shall solicit the aid of the civil authority having immediate jurisdiction, which authority shall lend him its aid.

"ART. 122. The certified copies of the plans of mining claims requested of the Minister of Fomento shall be issued by the office of the technical inspector of mines, and shall afterwards be legalized by the signature of the director of territorial wealth, agriculture, and stock-raising of said office.

"ART. 123. The technical inspector of mines shall be under the immediate orders of the Minister of Fomento.

"ART. 124. The mine guards shall be paid the monthly salary assigned them in the budget of rents and public expenses, and shall have the right to collect the following emoluments:

" For assisting at the act of entering into possession and survey of each mining claim, 100 *bolivars.*

" For investigating and rendering a decision in administrative opposition suits, 150 *bolivars.*

" For verifying on the ground the plan of the mining claim and viséing or indorsing the same, 20 *bolivars.*

"For certifying that a mining claim is in exploitation, 100 *bolivars.*

"*Sole paragraph.*—Furthermore, for each act or investigation in which the mine guard takes part, the party in interest shall supply him with the food and horses necessary.

"ART. 125. If a mine guard should unduly prolong the certification of the exploitation of mines, he shall be deprived of his office, an there shall be imposed upon him a fine of from 200 to 500 *bolivars* according to the gravity of the offense.

SECTION XIV.—*Concerning asphalt mines.*

"ART. 126. Asphalt, naphtha, petroleum, bitumin, oxokerite, on mineral wax mining claims in force on the date of the promulgation of these rules and regulations continue in all their legal strength and effect and subject to all the provisions that these rules and regulation

d in the stamps provided for by these
yment of mining taxes.

and other substances referred to in
d by special contracts made with the
tracts shall stipulate the amounts the
sderal Treasury.

in this article shall be considered as
consequently, in future shall not be
ne National Congress.

Concerning coal mines.

nes of stone, coal, coke, anthracite and
epublic, shall be exploited only by the
no new titles shall be issued covering

ly acquired under titles of ownership
titles are in full force and effect on the
become operative, remain in full legal

lich the Federal Executive shall exploit
aferred to in this section shall be set

—General provisions.

mining claim shall be made without
tee, having previously and separately
ster of Fomento. Should those who
im be foreigners, either private per-
ate in the said notice that they subject
the provisions, concerning the aquisi-
contained in the mining law and its
consequently, transactions relating to
itation, shall in no case nor for any
lomatic intervention nor to any inter-

of the notice referred to. If they should not comply with this requisite, the respective register shall not protocolize said document of transfer, and shall immediately advise the Department of Fomento of the occurrence.

"*Paragraph 1.*—Under no condition shall transfers of mining claims be made to foreign Governments or States, nor shall the latter be admitted as partners.

"*Paragraph 2.* Any infraction of the provisions of this article will make the transfer of the mining claim absolutely and completely null and of no effect.

"*Paragraph 3.* The Minister of Fomento shall order that the notices which the parties in interest and the respective register give to the Department of Fomento, in accordance with the present article, be filed in the proper archive separately from other documents. He shall also have filed with the said documents the certified copies of the deeds of transfer of the mines, which, in accordance with the following article, the registers or recorders shall send him as soon as the deeds referred to are protocolized.

"ART. 133. The registers of the district in which the mining claims are situated, immediately upon recording the definite titles and transfers of the mining claims, shall, in their official capacity, send certified copies of the same to the Minister of Fomento and the technical inspector of mines.

"ART. 134. The Minister of Fomento, the technical inspector of mines, the president of the state, the governor of the territory and of the Federal District, the registers and chiefs of districts, the municipalities, and parishes, shall carefully comply with the obligations imposed upon them by the mining law and its rules and regulations, and shall guard the books of record that must be kept in accordance with the requirements of the law.

"ART. 135. The superintendents or directors of mines shall formulate rules and regulations for the internal government of the mines, specifying therein the working hours of the miners and other employees, the wages or salaries, the pay days, and the prices of articles of first necessity should the owner of the mine furnish such articles personally or through the intervention of a third party.

"Three copies of the rules and regulations referred to in the foregoing paragraph shall be posted in the most public places of the office, and a copy shall be sent to the mine guard of the circumscription or district, another copy to the technical inspector of mines, and another to the Department of Fomento.

"*Sole paragraph.* Every contract that the Federal Executive makes with a private person or company, shall be in conformity with the provisions of articles 6 and 7 of the mining law and with the provisions of article 132 of these rules and regulations.

VII.—*Transitory provisions.*

vein or lode mining claims, and the con-
l Executive for the exploitation of alluvion
:e and effect, made in conformity with the
rce at the time of their issue, are hereby
cted to the provisions of the mining law
d regulations on and after the date of the

as forfeited in conformity with the laws
nted, and which by reason of said forfeit-
y a third party and the ownership granted
on of the former owner, belong to the new
nate owner.
o already have a provisional title, and who,
e in a position to obtain the title to the
e issued to them in conformity with the
w and its rules and regulations.
procedure concerning mines that are now
is hereby declared valid, but the parties in
ckets conform to the procedure prescribed
ns.

XVIII.—*Final provisions.*

nd regulations shall become effective from
n in the Official Gazette.
e with article 11 of the mining law decreed
on August 3, 1905, the mining code of
of March 24 of the same year sanctioning
s relating to the matter are hereby repealed.
of Fomento is charged with the execution

alace in Caracas, February 23, 1906, ninety-
nce and forty-eighth of the Federation.

CIPRIANO CASTRO.

DIEGO BTA. FERRER,
The Minister of Fomento.

UNITED STATES OF VENEZUELA,
DEPARTMENT OF FOMENTO,
BUREAU OF TERRITORIAL WEALTH,
AGRICULTURE, AND STOCK RAISING,
Caracas, March 5, 1906.

(Ninety-fifth year of Independence and forty-eighth of Federation.)

Resolved: ARTICLE 1. That, in conformity with the provisions of article 73 of the regulative decree of the mining law issued on the 23d of the past month, a national mining stamp is hereby created. This stamp shall bear the coat of arms of the Republic within a circle 17 millimeters in diameter. The following inscriptions shall be placed in the annular space formed by this circle and another concentric circle 22 millimeters in diameter: In the u part, "United States of Venezuela," and in the lower part "Nat Mining Stamp;" this space shall be within a rectangle having f 25 millimeters and a height of 28 millimeters, suitably adorned, in le lower part of which there shall be indicated in figures the respective value of the stamp, and in letters on both sides.

ART. 2. The first issue of the national mining stamp shall be to the amount of 1,000,000 *bolivares*, and shall be lithographed in the lithographing establishments of this city, the proper requirements as to size being observed, and shall be of the following colors:

Number of stamps.	Denomination in bolivars.	Color.	Amount in bolivars.
1,750	100	Yellow	175,000
15,000	10	Blue	150,000
400,000	1	Red	400,000
1,000,000	.25	Green	250,000
500,000	.05	Purple	25,000
			1,000,000

Let it be communicated and published.

DIEGO. BTA. FERRER,
For the Federal Executive.

TRADE OF AMERICA AND GREAT BRITAIN, 1906.

The "Accounts Relating to Trade and Navigation of the United Kingdom," published in December, 1906, contain a detailed statement of the commercial intercourse between Great Britain and the various countries of America during the year 1906, as compared with the two preceding years.

The classification of imports is as follows:

Articles and countries.	1904.	1905.	1906.
Animals, living (for food).			
Cattle:			
United States................................	£7,160,062	£7,149,139	£6,937,410
Sheep and lambs:			
United States..............	456,630	226,628	127,401
Articles of food and drink.			
Wheat:			
Argentine Republic.........	7,522,331	8,282,388	6,678,413
Chile...........................	327,303	57,672	285
United States................	2,517,425	2,453,575	8,040,290
Wheat flour:			
United States................	4,095,749	2,896,317	4,744,970
Barley:			
United States................	1,220,287	754,090	826,333
Oats:			
United States................	46,971	689,975	985,551
Maize:			
Argentine Republic...........	5,518,683	5,090,862	5,943,585
United States................	1,956,137	4,686,676	4,603,767
Beef, fresh:			
Argentine Republic...........	2,492,704	3,751,780	4,136,819
United States................	5,130,286	4,814,611	5,235,663
Mutton, fresh:			
Argentine Republic...........	2,491,210	2,458,915	2,440,996
Pork, fresh:			
United States................	262,450	292,390	268,804
Bacon:			
United States................	6,209,009	5,828,392	6,859,061
Beef, salted:			
United States................	178,098	190,839	197,238
Hams:			
United States................	2,606,129	2,409,993	2,808,823
Coffee:			
Brazil.......................	241,693	282,975	251,498
Central America..............	831,405	716,921	851,674
Sugar, unrefined:			
Brazil.......................	32,294	80,634	391,296
Cuba........................	....	....	41,943
Peru........................	508,422	720,608	243,129
Tobacco.			
Tobacco, unmanufactured:			
United States........	2,416,494	1,740,800	2,556,776
Tobacco, manufactured:			
United States................	1,188,342	1,145,123	1,284,313
Metals.			
Copper:			
Chile........................	236,245	356,085	354,158
United States................	2,648	5,659	5,813
Regulus and precipitate:			
Chile........................	144,857	241,525	158,014
Peru........................	155,996	87,135	102,419
United States................	178,123	149,388	223,398
Wrought and unwrought:			
Chile........................	950,459	1,187,200	1,026,476
United States................	2,831,437	1,908,635	2,311,769
Iron, pig:			
United States................	61,516	....	....
Lead, pig and sheet:			
United States................	437,066	325,664	307,782
Raw materials for textile manufactures.			
Cotton, raw:			
Brazil.......................	629,988	805,597	1,488,896
United States................	40,197,242	38,314,379	38,546,295
Wool, sheep or lamb's:			
Argentine Republic...........	410,230	962,328	1,205,836
South America................	567,065	553,349	689,678
Uruguay.....................	152,095	119,497	126,883
Alpaca, vicuña, and llama:			
Chile........................	82,628	112,367	158,664
Peru........................	194,625	119,321	154,378
Raw materials for sundry industries.			
Hides, wet:			
Argentine Republic and Uruguay................	52,268	253,755	374,693
Brazil.......................	49,222	49,361	37,800
Tallow and stearin:			
Argentine Republic...........	472,175	471,527	351,859
United States................	411,516	426,667	631,262

The classification of exports is as follows:

Articles and countries.	1904.	1905.	190.
Articles of food and drink.			
Beer and ale:			
United States...	£221,159	£240,642	£20,664
Salt, rock and white:			
United States...	58,123	57,304	61,827
Spirits:			
United States...	395,790	413,082	426,123
Raw materials.			
Coal, coke, etc.:			
Argentine Republic...	1,019,510	1,194,911	1,630,414
Brazil...	707,564	730,966	834,254
Chile..	261,620	840,662	835,172
United States..	68,326	87,164	85,462
Uruguay...	281,663	236,588	439,773
Wool, sheep and lamb's:			
United States..	1,044,545	1,138,579	875,102
Articles manufactured wholly or in part.			
Cotton manufactures, all classes:			
Argentine Republic...	2,354,040	2,148,345	2,840,611
Brazil...	1,621,987	1,611,140	1,675,596
Central America..	487,917	472,634	438,023
Chile..	864,302	1,048,419	1,238,906
Colombia and Panama.......................................	478,298	813,046	629,755
Haiti and Dominican Republic..............................	208,201	151,096	197,842
Mexico..	306,876	290,140	371,035
Peru..	385,549	461,336	452,325
United States..	1,847,811	2,022,342	2,216,130
Uruguay...	628,064	604,660	586,653
Venezuela...	467,566	287,504	453,035
Jute yarn:			
Brazil...	235,254	833,080	208,888
United States..	84,983	81,824	
Jute manufactures:			
Argentine Republic...	306,614	161,620	
Brazil...	5,185	5,168	
United States..	978,097	1,101,606	
Linen yarn:			
United States..	84,816	86,888	77,807
Linen piece goods:			
Argentine Republic...	102,952	111,425	
Brazil...	82,394	90,477	
Colombia and Panama.......................................	21,170	27,493	
Mexico..	20,088	27,624	
United States..	2,166,672	2,634,864	2,675,779
Woolen tissues:			
Argentine Republic...	430,683	465,628	
Brazil...	124,163	141,464	
Chile..	204,492	216,060	
Mexico..	45,168	64,606	
Peru..	62,428	53,324	
United States..	298,387	362,364	
Uruguay...	77,718	94,068	
Worsted tissues:			
Argentine Republic...	404,604	376,643	
Brazil...	81,026	89,127	
Chile..	107,682	104,498	
Mexico..	51,700	42,921	
Peru..	34,151	24,317	
United States..	965,287	1,045,442	
Uruguay...	46,549	61,194	

Articles and countries.	1904.	1905.	1906.
: manufactured wholly or in part—Continued.			
e Republic...	£38,688	£61,047	£75,920
....	31,245	82,648	64,327
ates...	39,165	53,426	88,441
tals and articles manufactured therefrom.			
e Republic...	31,085	29,460	32,598
	84,130	33,728	41,373
	18,466	15,464	15,748
	27,021	27,135	22,924
ates...	81,208	79,695	91,066
ienumerated:			
e Republic...	71,972	90,842	134,625
	96,402	119,384	121,104
	34,152	37,330	47,338
ates...	30,641	31,840	33,372
ates...	269,496	763,395	1,668,538
rle, bolt, and rod:			
e Republic...	31,552	60,936	85,756
	27,644	29,620	41,941
....	27,471	28,896	40,471
ates...	53,526	66,120	61,957
heets:			
e Republic...	561,796	747,497	1,006,862
merica...	23,113	34,976	35,860
	92,605	167,163	327,326
	71,210	93,354	78,170
....	26,519	72,221	79,698
d sheets:			
ates...	890,406	796,626	797,064
Machinery and millwork.			
ierica...	877,030	824,805	1,547,093
ates...	25	696	1,180
machinery (engines):			
ierica...	93,923	323,742	289,789
ates...	2,112		2,847
arious:			
ierica...	254,917	330,072	511,923
ates...	30,508	19,829	9,429
implements:			
ierica...	252,857	250,597	282,181
ates...	1,245	3,210	1,964
lines:			
ierica...	66,740	72,004	57,570
inery:			
ierica...	38,300	40,592	72,006
ates...	1,493	1,470	870
inery:			
ierica...	233,365	165,019	210,860
ates...	360,094	411,312	596,983
Miscellaneous.			
e Republic...	24,877	28,326	55,150
	12,321	23,157	50,952
ates...	12,210	22,680	166,692
china ware:			
e Republic...	101,258	133,356	184,883
	82,906	104,422	119,638
ates...	555,549	508,053	572,165
....	47,050	18,601	64,529

IE WORLD'S RUBBER OUTPUT, 1906.

rld's supply of rubber in 1906, according to British estimates,
y 65,000 tons, and consumption almost as much. New plants
ncreased and will produce much more in the near future.
nd planting (but some mixed with tea and cocoa and coffee) is
l at: Ceylon, 100,000 acres; Malaya, Malacca, Sumatra, etc.,

90,000 acres; Borneo, 12,000 acres; Java, 20,000 acres. Mexico has some large plantations, also Nicaragua and Honduras, and some in Colombia, Ecuador, Bolivia, and Peru. India has 10,000 to 20,000 acres in planting, Burma and Mergui are beginning; the Philippines, Samoa, Hawaii, and other Pacific isles, and Seychelles and West Coast Africa will add to the supply, also the West Indies. In the Kongo and German West Africa plantations are in progress. The supply from the Amazonas (Brazil) shows no sign of reduction; Brazil exported 38,000 tons. Stimulus is given to the production of other rubbers in Brazil, such as maniçoba, etc., by various companies working with large capital, and supplies in 1906 considerably increased. Large quantities of guayule from Mexico have been disposed of in America and Europe. English manufacturers have as yet scarcely used it, not being attracted by it, but are making further experiments. There has been a sustained demand throughout the year and manufacturers have been busy. Motor vehicles of all descriptions have largely increased tire makers' demands.

As summarized by the chairman of the Brazilian rubber trust, the world's rubber production for 1906 is estimated to amount to 70,000 tons, of which quantity 60 per cent, or 42,000 tons, is the anticipated output of South America. Of these 42,000 tons, Brazil will provide 35,000 tons or more, or 50 per cent of the whole world's production, the value of the Brazilian output being, roughly, £17,000,000 ($82,730,000). Nearly the whole of the 42,000 tons from South America is natural-grown rubber, and nearly the whole of the 35,000 tons is the product of the Amazon and its tributaries. This production is absolutely essential to the manufacturing industry, for, notwithstanding occasional temporarily lower prices, there is no question that the demand is increasing at a ratio in excess of that of the supply. All the plantation rubber will be required, and more than can be grown. At present the output of plantation rubber is about 1,000 tons per annum, or about 1½ per cent of the whole, while Brazil provides 50 per cent of the whole.

A London firm's review of the rubber market of India in 1906 states that the rapid increase of supply has been beyond expectation, amounting probably to 160 tons Ceylon and 350 tons Malay against, in 1905, 70 tons Ceylon and 75 tons Malay.

RUBBER CULTIVATION IN THE MALAY PENINSULA.

A correspondent from Penang, in the "British Trade Journal" of December 1, 1906, says:

"The rubber industry here is in a most flourishing condition. It is, I am pleased to say, encouraged by the present Government, which seems wisely bent upon making agriculture the mainstay of the country. During the past three years extensive tracts of land have been

rubber cultivation, and as capital has flowed,
his purpose, all that human ingenuity can
establish the industry on a firm and lasting
 rubber (parcels of Para sheet, from Perak)
in the London market, and at the Rubber
in Ceylon it was exhibits from the Malay
most coveted of all the prizes—the gold medal
l sample in the show. In addition to this
rs can boast that this land of their adoption
ig country in existence, experts from various
ng come to this conclusion after carefully
lalayan plantations and comparing what they
and experience gained elsewhere—in Ceylon,

BOOK NOTES.

t to the International Bureau of the American
ig subject-matter bearing upon the countries of
l of American Republics, will be treated under
hly Bulletin.

lfacturing in South America is the problem
. M. L. BROWN and FRANKLIN ADAMS in their
lew of Reviews" for February, 1907. While
ally upon the effect of recent developments in
ommercial dealings with South America, the
vakening a possibility of rivalry between the
lections of the Western Hemisphere so far as
are concerned. In support of this contention
er of imports by South American countries is
the marked development of natural resources
ransport facilities. In the Argentine Republic
commodities as flour, sugar, beer, butter, and
ictically ceased, and of the 20,000,000 liters of
country in 1905 the native output is credited
An annual home production of 186,000,000
iturally limits this class of imports, while the
et by the 256,000,000 boxes turned out by the
Cotton and cloth mills have been established;
ireasingly produced, and local furniture fac-
crease the demand for native lumber. The
 in Brazil is the manufacture of cotton goods,
 products, more than 100 mills employing

40,000 of natives being reported. Sugar refineries are second only to cotton mills, while cigarette factories, shoe and leather establishments, iron works, silk mills, breweries, furniture factories, and flour mills are distributed throughout the leading cities. Other articles manufactured in increasing quantities are glass and porcelain ware, stoves, implements, nails, coffee, machinery, chemicals, gloves, perfumery, watches, and war ships. Chile maintains a large free list for manufactures from other countries, as her enormous nitrate industry provides her with ample outlet for energetic effort. Peru, Uruguay, and Venezuela are also encouraging home industries, and Ecuador, in September, 1906, passed a law granting so many privileges to native manufacturers that foreign goods are in danger of practical exclusion. Colombia, in the effort to force a native production of flour has doubled the import duty on the foreign article, and other countries are showing the same determination to meet the requirements of their industrial life. The discovery of new coal areas, the application of petroleum and alcohol as fuel, and their availability as demonstrated by recent discoveries and experiments; the undoubted water power, as yet unapplied, of the great rivers and falls of the southern continent—all these are cited as evidences of the existent possibilities. In reviewing the statistics of exports of manufactured products, it is shown that Uruguay has increased her shipments of meat extracts more than 100 per cent in five years; that the Argentine Republic shows an advance in the same industry of more than 400 per cent in ten years; that in ten years the latter's exports of butter have grown from $119,000 to $2,081,000, and of flour, from $1,816,000 in 1895 to $5,186,000 in 1905; also that quebracho tanning extract exported, rose from 402 metric tons in 1895, valued at $38,000, to 29,408 tons in 1905, valued at $2,343,000. Leaving the established facts, the authors see no reason to doubt that the Argentine and Chilean wine trade may be a factor of the future; that Ecuador and Venezuela, through the medium of their raw cacao and sugar, may compete with the chocolate manufacturers of Europe; that Brazil's bamboo forests may contribute to the growing demand for paper, even as her new fiber plant promises a cheap substitute for linen; that her manganese deposits combined with her iron may form the nucleus of a vast steel industry, and that the dockyards of Rio de Janeiro may vie with those of Europe in the construction of steel ships.

The first quarterly number of "The American Journal of International Law" has just made its appearance from the Waverly Press, of Baltimore. This stately periodical is published by the American Society of International Law, and is edited by a distinguished company of teachers, jurists, and diplomats. Its object is to record and to discuss current topics of moment in the domain of international relationships and thus to diffuse among the general public a more correct comprehension of international rights and duties and to promote a popular habit of thinking about international affairs. In seeking to perform the work thus outlined, the journal does not confine itself to academic essays on abstract topics of international law, but pays most attention to the issues which are at the present time of special interest. Thus the CALVO and DRAGO doctrines are explained and discussed by AMOS S. HERSHEY, professor of international law in the University of Indiana; "International Responsibility to Corporate Bodies for Lives Lost by Outlawry" is considered by JOHN W. FOSTER, formerly Secretary of State; "Insurgency and International Maritime Law" are treated of by GEORGE GRAFTON WILSON, professor of international law in Brown University, and the "Doctrine of Continuous Voyages" is discussed by CHARLES BURKE ELLIOTT, a justice of the supreme court of Minnesota. In the section devoted to editorial comment a biographical sketch of CARLOS CALVO is published, while the peace of the *Marblehead*, Mr. ROOT's South American trip, and the nature of government in Cuba are among the subjects treated. The first issue of the "Quarterly" aims to cover the year 1906 *in toto*, but succeeding numbers will deal wholly or principally with the quarter. In a prefatory note on the need of a popular understanding of international law, Secretary ROOT says: "The more clearly the people of a country understand their own international rights, the less likely they are to take extreme and extravagant views of their rights and the less likely they are to be ready to fight for something to which they are not really entitled. The more clearly and universally the people of a country realize the international obligations and duties of their country, the less likely they will be to resent the just demands of other countries that those obligations and duties be observed. The more familiar the people of a country are with the rules and customs of self-restraint and courtesy between nations which long experience has shown to be indispensable for preserving the peace of the world, the greater will be the tendency to refrain from publicly discussing controversies with other countries in such a way as to hinder peaceful settlement by wounding sensibilities or arousing anger and prejudice on the other side." A supplement, uniform with the journal itself, but separately paged and sewed, contains the full texts of numerous official documents, including treaties, agreements, declarations, instructions, national laws affecting international relations, and the diplomatic list of the United States. The initial document of the supplement reproduces, under the head of the Argentine Republic, "Instructions of the Minister of Foreign Relations to the Minister to the United States," December 29, 1902, being what is known as the DRAGO Doctrine.

"The Engineering Magazine" for February, 1907, publishes an instructive résumé of the Panama Canal work and the workers, being a personal study of actual conditions made by Mr. FULLERTON WALDO in December, 1906. The writer regrets that he can not furnish the reader with a sensation as to the ineffectiveness of the work on the Isthmus. On the other hand, he reports the paving of streets, abundant potable water, a bakery capable of turning out 24,000 loaves of bread daily, a cold-storage plant, and a laundry as among the modern conveniences recently installed in Colon. The city of Panama he reports as having been completely transformed since the United States has interested itself in the work there. Extensive paving contracts have been carried out, a fine modern hotel has been erected and thoroughly equipped, and the comforts of the inhabitants fully provided for. When over 30,000 workmen are to be housed and fed it is evident that suitable preparations must be made in order that the physical conditions of the people should be equal to their tasks. Such preparations, Mr. WALDO claims, have been looked after as one of the most important preliminaries to the building of the canal. In regard to the latter, he states that during the year ending December, 1906, excavations to the extent of 1,500,000 cubic yards were made, or about twice the record of the preceding year. The installation of an adequate storage depot has also been accomplished at Mount Hope and forms the center of distribution of supplies. Tribute is paid to the work of Chief Engineer STEVENS and the chief sanitary officer, Col. WILLIAM C. GORGAS, U. S. Army, and pleasant reference made to a meeting with President AMADOR.

The "Twenty-third Annual Report of the Council of the Corporation of Foreign Bondholders," issued in January, 1907 (London), contains not only exhaustive statements of the external indebtedness of the various countries of Latin America whose bonds are held by the Corporation, but also, in the appendix, covers the economic bases on which the credit of the respective nations rests. The approximate amount of loans in default to the Corporation (exclusive of arrears of interest) is stated to have been £300,000,000 in 1876, in which sum Latin America was represented by £84,000,000. In 1906 the total had been reduced to £16,000,000, of which the share of Latin-American countries was £9,000,000. An interesting statement is made as to the settlement of the Cedula question in regard to the Argentine debt, which is regarded as the principal feature of the Corporation's transactions in 1906. A résumé setting forth the British view of the influence of the MONROE Doctrine as applied to the settlement of financial questions is published as pertinent to the matter. Although the Corporation of Foreign Bondholders extends its influence to every country where national securities have gone into default, it has exercised an especially strong influence in Latin America.

In the *"Revista de Derecho, Historia y Letras"* for January, 1907 (Buenos Ayres), the initial article deals with the words and actions of President ROOSEVELT in relation to the following subjects: The Navy in war; the power of money; and the habit of insurrection. The writer has collected from various publications of the United States the presidential utterances on the topics treated, and reproduces them in Spanish, with appropriate comments thereon. This review of the North American press by an Argentine writer is apt and profitable, as it tends to a better understanding of subjects of mutual interest. The same periodical also publishes an interesting paper concerning the claims of the United States against Venezuela, as well as a translation from the French, of a careful consideration of imperialism in the United States in relation to the Monroe Doctrine.

A large portion of "The Mining World" (Chicago) for January, 1907, is devoted to a consideration of Mexican mines and their development. The Cananea copper workings are described; the mining industry of the State of Chihuahua is reported in detail, and northern Mexico, the States of Jalisco, Sinaloa, Tepic, and Durango are covered from the mineral standpoint. In South America, Peru and Colombia and the respective values of their mining output are treated, in each case the information furnished affording an adequate review of the statistics and data for the year 1906.

The petroleum deposits of Peru are extensively reported in the *"Boletin del Ministerio de Fomento"* for September, 1906, and received by the Columbus Memorial Library on January 21, 1907. Their situation and geological character is said to be similar to those of Pennsylvania and Russia, while their exploitation is conducted in the same manner as those of the United States. Though some of the wells are credited with an output of 100 barrels of 160 liters daily, the average yield is placed at 5 to 7 barrels. Piura and Zorritos are named as the chief producing oil sections, though other portions of the Republic and the respective output are exhaustively described.

The *"Boletin del Ministerio de Relaciones Exteriores"* of the Argentine Republic, covering the year 1905 and received by the Columbus Memorial Library on February 20, 1907, is a public document of more than ordinary interest, dealing with the foreign trade relations of the country as reported by its various consular representatives abroad. From Odessa Señor GARCÍA MANSILLA reports upon the standing of Argentine quebracho and its competitors in the hide-curing industry of that district. The maritime movements between Manchester, England, and the ports of the Republic are covered, while from Bremen not only is the year completely reviewed in its relation to Argentine

Brazilian districts make a valuable résumé of conditions existir the two Republics.

The consul of Guatemala, at Paris, Mr. CHARLES H. STEPHAN prepared a valuable book of trade reference, a copy of which has received by the Columbus Memorial Library. This "*Manuel Co aire*" (Consular Handbook) comprises a list of the consular c resident in Paris, a list of the various merchants and the articl which they deal, a directory of commission merchants of the city, also the various shipping formalities to be observed in the trans of goods. As a practicable guide of the trade it is invaluable.

ʟᴀ. Mɪɴɪsᴛᴇʀɪᴏ ᴅᴇ Fᴏᴍᴇɴᴛᴏ ʏ Oʙʀᴀs Púʙʟɪᴄᴀs: Memoria que el Secretario de fomento y obras públicas presenta á la Asamblea Nacional en sus sesiones ordinarias de 1906. Panama, Tip. Sosa y Paredes, [1906]. vi, 186 p. illus. 4°.

-Mɪɴɪsᴛᴇʀɪᴏ ᴅᴇ Iɴsᴛʀᴜᴄᴄɪóɴ Púʙʟɪᴄᴀ ʏ Jᴜsᴛɪᴄɪᴀ: Anexos de la Memoria presentada . . . á la asemblea nacional en sus sesiones ordinarias de 1906. Panama, Tip. Moderna, [1906]. 107 p. 8°.

PARAGUAY.

McMᴀʜᴏɴ's Oᴘɪɴɪᴏɴs ɪɴ Rᴇɢᴀʀᴅ ᴛᴏ ᴛʜᴇ Pᴀʀᴀɢᴜᴀʏᴀɴ Wᴀʀ. A few remarks in answer to his assertions. [Washington? 1869]. 12 p. 8°. Caption title.

Esᴄᴀʟᴀᴅᴀ, Jᴀɪᴍᴇ: 25 de noviembre de 1906. El General Ferreira. Apuntes biográficos sacados de la obra inédita: Política brasilera en el Paraguay y Río de La Plata por Jaime Sosa Escalada, escrita en Buenos Aires en 1893 y completados con otros datos. Asunciòn, Tip. de Jordon y Villaamil, 1906. 56 p. 8°.

PHILIPPINE ISLANDS.

ᴏ ᴅᴇ Tᴀᴠᴇʀᴀ, T. H.: Una memoria de Anda y Salazar. Por T. H. Pardo de Tavera. Manila, Imprenta "La Democracia," 1899. 102 p. 8°.

PORTO RICO.

ʟᴅ ʏ Lᴀsɪᴇʀʀᴀ, Iɴᴏɢᴏ]: Historia geográfica, civil y política de la isla de S. Juan Bautista de Puerto Rico. Dada á luz Don Antonio Valladares de Sotomayor. Madrid, Impr. de A. Espinosa, 1788. 403 p. 8°.

SALVADOR.

ᴅᴏʀ. Mɪɴɪsᴛᴇʀɪᴏ ᴅᴇ Rᴇʟᴀᴄɪᴏɴᴇs, Jᴜsᴛɪᴄɪᴀ ʏ Bᴇɴᴇғɪᴄᴇɴᴄɪᴀ: Memoria de los actos del ejecutivo en los Departamentos de Relaciones Exteriores, Justicia ᴢ Beneficencia presentada á la honorable Asamblea Nacional . . . el día 21 de febrero de 1905. San Salvador, Imprenta nacional [1907]. 418 p. 8°.

UNITED STATES.

ɪᴄᴀɴ Mᴇᴛʀᴏʟᴏɢɪᴄᴀʟ Sᴏᴄɪᴇᴛʏ: . . . The metric system. Opinions in favor of its adoption, expressed by representatives of the leading industries, interests, trade and manufactures. Caption title. 18 p. 8°.

ʟʟ Uɴɪᴠᴇʀsɪᴛʏ Lɪʙʀᴀʀʏ: Librarian's report. 1905-1906. Half-title. No. imprint. 55 p. 8°.

ɪʀ Mɪʟɪᴛᴀʀʏ Aᴄᴀᴅᴇᴍʏ. Illustrated catalogue. Culver, Indiana, 1906. 100, (1) p. Plates. Illus. Maps. 4°.

ɪʀ Sᴜᴍᴍᴇʀ Nᴀᴠᴀʟ Sᴄʜᴏᴏʟ: Catalogue of the . . . school . . . Culver, 1906. [16] p. Plates. 4°.

ʀʀ, L. A.: . . . History of standard weights and measures of U. S. By L. A. Fischer . . . Washington, (Government Printing Office, 1905. pp. 365-381. 8°. (Reprint No. 17, Bull. No. 3. Bureau of Standards.)

ᴅ, Bᴇɴᴊᴀᴍɪɴ Aᴘᴛʜᴏʀᴘ: Address on the metric system of weights and measures. By Benjamin Apthorp Gould. Delivered before the Commercial Club of Boston, February 18, 1888, at its 184th regular meeting. Half-title. 15 p. 8°.

HONORARY CORRESPONDING MEMBERS OF THE INTERNATIONAL UNION OF AMERICAN REPUBLICS.

Countries.	Names.	Residence.
Argentine Republic..	Señor Dr. Don Estanislao S. Zeballos.......	Buenos Ayres.
Bolivia..............	Señor Don Manuel V. Ballivián*..........	La Paz.
Brazil..............	Dezembargador Antonio Bezerra...........	Pará.
	Firmino da Silva	Florianopolis.
Chile..............	Señor Don Moisés Vargas	Santiago.
Colombia..........	Señor Don Rufino Gutiérrez...............	Bogotá.
Costa Rica..........	Señor Don Manuel Aragón	San José.
Cuba..............	Señor Don Antonio S. de Bustamante	Havana.
	Señor Don Lincoln de Zayas...............	Havana.
Dominican Republic.	Señor Don José Gabriel García *..........	Santo Domingo.
Ecuador............	Señor Don Francisco Andrade Marín.......	Quito.
	Señor Don Luis Alberto Carbo	Guayaquil.
Guatemala..........	Señor Don Antonio Batres Jáuregui........	Guatemala City.
	Señor Don Rafael Montúfar	Guatemala City.
Haiti..............	Monsieur Georges Sylvain	Port au Prince.
Honduras	Señor Don E. Constantino Fiallos	Tegucigalpa.
Mexico............	Señor Don Francisco L. de la Barra........	City of Mexico.
	Señor Don Antonio García Cubas..........	City of Mexico.
	Señor Don Fernando Ferrari Pérez	City of Mexico.
Nicaragua	Señor Don José D. Gámez.................	Managua.
Paraguay...........	Señor Don José S. Decoud	Asunción.
Panama	Señor Don Samuel Lewis..................	Panama.
	Señor Don Ramón M. Valdés..............	Panama.
Peru	Señor Don Alejandro Garland.............	Lima.
Salvador...........	Señor Dr. Don Salvador Gallegos	San Salvador.
Uruguay...........	Señor Don José I. Schiffiano	Montevideo.
Venezuela	Señor General Don Manuel Landaeta Rosales.	Caracas.
	Señor Don Francisco de Paula Alamo.......	Caracas.

*Honorary corresponding member of the Royal Geographical Society of Great Britain.
*Corresponding member of the Academia Nacional de la Historia de Venezuela

URUGUAY. *Laws, statutes, etc.:* PRESUPUESTO GENERAL DE GASTOS para en año económico de 1904–1905. Montevideo, Imprenta "El Siglo," 1904. 278 p. 4°.

—— MINISTERIO DE HACIENDA: . . . Situación del tesoro al clausurar el ejercicio de 1905–1906. Importante superávit destinado a vialidad y obras públicas. Discurso pronunciado por el señor Ministro de hacienda . . . en la sesión del día 25 de septiembre de 1906 . . . de la H. Cámara. Montevideo, Imp. "El Siglo Ilustrado," 1906. 16 p. 8°. (At head of title, "H. Cámara de representantes.")

—— MINISTERIO DE RELACIONES EXTERIORES: Memoria . . . 1905. Montevideo, Tall. tip. de "La Prensa," 1906. xxxvi, 68 p. 4°..

VENEZUELA.

VENEZUELA. MINISTERIO DE HACIENDA Y CRÉDITO PÚBLICO: Estadística mercantil y marítima. Año económico de 1905 á 1906. Caracas, Imprenta Bolivar, 1906. 254 (2) p. 4°.

ZULIA, ESTADO DE: Mensaje que el . . . Presidente constitucional del Zulia presenta á la asamblea legislativa del estado en sus sesiones de 1906. Maracaibo, Imprenta Americana, 1906. 11 (2) p. 4°.

—— SECRETARIO GENERAL DEL ESTADO: Memoria que presenta á la legislatura del estado Zulia, por disposición del ciudadano Presidente constitucional, el Secretario general del estado en 1906. Maracaibo, Imprenta del Estado, 1906. 150 p. 4°.

WEST INDIES.

WARD, C. J.: . . . Jamaica at World's Fair, Chicago. An account descriptive of the colony of Jamaica, with historical and other appendices. Comp. under the direction of Lieut. Col. the Hon. C. J. Ward . . . New York, W. J. Pell, printer, 1893. 95 p. illus. fold. map. 8°.

GENERAL WORKS, REFERENCE BOOKS, AND BIBLIOGRAPHIES.

BOSTON PUBLIC LIBRARY: Annual list of new and important books added to the public library of the city of Boston. Selected from the Monthly Bulletins, 1905–1906. Boston, Published by the Trustees, 1907. vii, 264 p. 8°.

CENTRAL AND SOUTH AMERICAN TELEGRAPH Co.: The Central & South American Telegraph Co. via Galveston. [New York, 1895]. 9, [1] p. 31 plates. Map. Cover title. obl. 8°. [Views of Mexico, Central & South America.]

CURTIS, WILLIAM ELEROY: . . . The relics of Columbus. An illustrated description of the historical collection in the Monastery of La Rabida. By William Eleroy Curtis . . . Washington, Lowdermilk company, 1893. 216 p. Illus. 8°. (At head of title, "Souvenir of La Rabida, World's Columbian exposition.")

HOSTOS, EUGENIO M. DE: Moral social por, Eugenio M. de Hostos . . . Segunda edición. Madrid, Imprenta de Bailly-Balliere é hijos, 1906. 262 p. 12°.

PRESS PUBLISHING COMPANY: The World almanac and encyclopedia, 1907. Issued by the Press Publishing company. New York, 1906. 608 p. 8°.

PUTNAM, FREDERIC WARD: Address by Federico Ward Putnam, the retiring president of the American association for the advancement of science, Columbus meeting, . . . August, 1899 . . . Easton, Pa., The Chemical publishing company, 1899. 17 p. 8°. (Reprinted from the proceedings of the Association, vol. 48, 1899.)

Romero, Carlos V: Tercera conferencia panamericana. Informe dirigido á su gobierno por el delegado de Bolivia, Carlos V. Romero. Buenos Aires, Imprenta de J. Peuser, 1906. 12 p. 8°.

U. S. Library of Congress: Publications. December, 1906. Half-title. No imprint. 28 p. 8°.

Whitaker, Joseph: An almanack for the year . . . 1907 by Joseph Whitaker . . . London, 1907. 1015 p. 12°.

MAPS.

Montevideo. Novísimo Plano de la Cuidad de Montevideo: Reducido de los originales existentes en la Junta E. Administrativa. 1897. Montevideo, A. Barreiro y Ramos. 18 by 17 inches.

RATES OF POSTAGE.

?ATES OF POSTAGE FROM THE UNITED STATES TO LATIN-AMERICAN COUNTRIES.

The rates of postage from the United States to all foreign countries and colonies (except Canada, Mexico, and Cuba) are as follows:

	Cents.
Letters, per 15 grams (½ ounce)	5
Single postal cards, each	2
Double postal cards, each	4
Newspapers and other printed matter, per 2 ounces	1
Commercial papers........ Packets not in excess of 10 ounces	5
Packets in excess of 10 ounces, for each 2 ounces or fraction thereof	1
Samples of merchandise.. Packets not in excess of 4 ounces	2
Packets in excess of 4 ounces, for each 2 ounces or fraction thereof	1
Registration fee on letters and other articles	8

Letters for any foreign country (except Canada, Mexico, and Cuba) must be forwarded, whether postage is prepaid on them or not. All other mailable matter must be prepaid, at least

mailed in the United States addressed to Mexico is subject to the same postage rates and conditions as it would be if it were addressed for delivery in the United States, except that articles of miscellaneous merchandise (fourth-class matter) not sent as bona fide trade samples should be sent by "Parcels Post;" and that the following articles are *absolutely excluded* from the mails without regard to amount of postage prepaid or the manner in which they are wrapped:

All sealed packages, other than letters in their usual and ordinary form; *all* packages (including packages of second-class matter) which weigh more than 4 pounds 6 ounces, except such as are sent by "Parcels Post;" publications which violate any copyright law of Mexico.

Single volumes of printed books *in unsealed packages* are transmissible to Mexico in the regular mails without limit as to weight.

Unsealed packages of mailable merchandise may be sent by "Parcels Post" to Bolivia, British Guiana, British Honduras, Chile, Colombia, Costa Rica, Guatemala, Honduras, Mexico, Nicaragua, Salvador, and Venezuela, at the rates named on page xv.

PROHIBITED ARTICLES TO ALL FOREIGN COUNTRIES.

Poisons, explosives, and inflammable articles, live or dead animals, insects (especially the Colorado beetle), reptiles, fruit or vegetable matter liable to decomposition, and substances exhaling a bad odor, excluded from transmission in domestic mails as being in themselves, either from their form or nature, liable to destroy, deface, or otherwise injure the contents of the mail bags, or the persons of those engaged in the postal service; also obscene, lewd, or lascivious books, pamphlets, etc., and letters and circulars concerning lotteries, so-called gift concerts, etc. (also excluded from domestic mails); postal cards or letters addressed to go around the world; letters or packages (except those to Mexico) containing gold or silver substances, jewelry or precious articles; any packet whatever containing articles liable to customs duties in the countries addressed (except Cuba and Mexico), articles other than letters which are not prepaid at least partly; articles other than letters or postal cards containing writing in the nature of personal correspondence, unless fully prepaid at the rate of letter postage; articles of a nature likely to soil or injure the correspondence; packets of commercial papers and prints of all kinds, the weight of which exceeds 2 kilograms (4 pounds 6 ounces) or the size 18 inches in any direction, except *rolls* of prints, which may measure 30 inches in length by 4 inches in diameter; postal cards not of United States origin, and United States postal cards of the largest ("C") size (except as letters), and except also the reply halves of double postal cards received from foreign countries.

There is, moreover, reserved to the Government of every country of the Postal Union the right to refuse to convey over its territory, or to deliver, as well, articles liable to the reduced rate in regard to which the laws, ordinances, or decrees which regulate the conditions of their publication or of their circulation in that country have not been complied with.

☞ Full and complete information relative to all regulations can be obtained from the United States Postal Guide.

FOREIGN MAILS.

TABLE SHOWING THE RATES OF POSTAGE CHARGED IN LATIN-AMERICAN COUNTRIES ON ARTICLES SENT BY MAIL TO THE UNITED STATES.

Countries.	Letters, per 15 grams, equal to one-half ounce.		Single postal cards, each.a		Other articles, per 50 grams, equal to 2 ounces.		Charge for registration.	Charge for return receipt.
	Currency of country.	Centimes.	Currency of country.	Centimes.	Currency of country.	Centimes.		
Argentine Republic	15 centavos	25	6 centavos	15	3 centavos	10	24 centavos	12 centavos.
Bolivia viâ Panama	22 centavos	55	8 centavos	20	6 centavos	15	20 centavos	10 centavos.
Bolivia viâ other routes	20 centavos	50	6 centavos	15	4 centavos	10		
Brazil	300 reis	35	100 reis	10	50 reis	5	400 reis	200 reis.
Chile	10 centavos	50	3 centavos	15	2 centavos	10	10 centavos	5 centavos.
Colombia	20 centavos	50	4 centavos	10	2 centavos	5	10 centavos	5 centavos.
Costa Rica	10 centimos	25	3 centimos	7½	2 centimos	5	10 centimos	5 centimos.
Cuba b								
Dominican Republic (Santo Domingo)	10 centavos	25	3 centavos	10	2 centavos	5	10 centavos	5 centavos.
Ecuador	10 centavos	50	2 centavos	10	1 penny	10	2 pence	2½ pence.
Falkland Islands	4 pence	40	1 penny	15	1 penny	10	10 centavos	5 centavos.
Guatemala	10 centavos	50	3 centavos	15	2 centavos	10	2 centièmes de gourde	5 centièmes de gourde.
Haiti	10 centimes de gourde	50	3 centièmes de gourde	15	2 centièmes de gourde	10		
Honduras	15 centavos	15	3 centavos	10	2 centavos	10	10 centavos	5 centavos.
Honduras, British	5 cents	25	2 cents	10	1 cent	10	10 cents	6 cents.
Mexico	15 centavos	60	5 centavos	15	1 centavo	10	10 centavos	5 centavos.
Nicaragua	60 centavos		8 centavos	15	8 centavos	10	40 centavos	10 centavos.
Paraguay	20 centavos	50	6 centavos	15	4 centavos	10	10 centavos	20 centavos.
Peru viâ San Francisco	22 centavos	55	8 centavos	20	4 centavos	15	10 centavos	5 centavos.
Peru viâ Panama					6 centavos			
Porto Rico b								
Salvador viâ Panama	11 centavos	55	3 centavos	15	3 centavos	15	10 centavos	5 centavos.
Salvador viâ other routes	10 centavos	50	3 centavos	15	2 centavos	10	10 centavos	5 centavos.
Uruguay	10 centavos	50	3 centavos	15	2 centavos	10	50 centimos	25 centimes.
Venezuela	50 centimos	50	15 centimos	15	10 centimos	10		
British Guiana	5 cents	25	2 cents	15	1 cent	6		
Dutch Guiana	25 cents Dutch	50	7½ cents Dutch	15	5 cents Dutch	10	10 cents Dutch	10 cents Dutch.
French Guiana	25 centimes		10 centimes		5 centimes		25 centimes	10 centimes.

a The rate for a reply-paid (double) card is double the rate named in this column.
b United States domestic rates and conditions.

PARCELS-POST REGULATIONS.

TABLE SHOWING THE LATIN-AMERICAN COUNTRIES TO WHICH PARCELS MAY BE SENT FROM THE UNITED STATES; THE DIMENSIONS, WEIGHT, AND RATES OF POSTAGE APPLICABLE TO PARCELS, AND THE EXCHANGE POST-OFFICES WHICH MAY DISPATCH AND RECEIVE PARCELS-POST MAILS.

COUNTRIES.	ALLOWABLE DIMENSIONS AND WEIGHTS OF PARCELS.			POSTAGE.		EXCHANGE POST-OFFICES.	
	Greatest girth.	Greatest length.	Greatest weight.	For a parcel not exceeding 1 pound.	For every additional pound or fraction of a pound.	UNITED STATES.	LATIN AMERICA.
	Ft. in.		Ft.	Lbs.	Cents.	Cents.		
Bolivia	3 6	6	......	11	20	20	New York and San Francisco.	La Paz.
Chile	3 6	6	......	11	20	20	New York and San Francisco.	Valparaiso.
Colombia..........	2 0	.	4	11	12	12	All offices authorized to exchange mails between the two countries.	
Costa Rica.........	2 0	.	4	11	12	12		
Guatemala	3 6	6	......	11	12	12	New York, New Orleans, and San Francisco.	Guatemala City, Retalhuleu, and Puerto Barrios.
Guiana, British....	3 6	6	......	11	12	12	All offices authorized to exchange mails.	
Honduras	3 6	6	......	11	12	12	New York, New Orleans, and San Francisco.	Tegucigalpa, Puerto Cortez, Amapala, and Trujillo.
Honduras, British .	3 6	6	......	11	12	12	New Orleans	Belize.
Mexico.............	2 0	.	4	11	12	12	All offices authorized to exchange mails.	
Nicaragua.........	3 6	6	......	11	12	12	New York, New Orleans, and San Francisco.	Bluefields, San Juan del Norte, and Corinto.
Salvador	3 6	6	......	11	12	12	New York and San Francisco.	San Salvador.
Venezuela.........	3 6	6	......	11	12	12	All offices authorized to exchange mails.	

UNITED STATES CONSULATES IN LATIN AMERICA.

Frequent application is made to the Bureau for the address of United States Consuls in the South and Central American Republics. Those desiring to correspond with any Consul can do so by addressing "The United States Consulate" at the point named. Letters thus addressed must be delivered to the proper person. It must be understood, however, that it is not the duty of Consuls to devote their time to private business, and that all such letters may properly be treated as personal, and any labor involved may be subject to charge therefor.

The following is a list of United States Consulates in the different Republics (consular agencies are given in italics):

ARGENTINE REPUBLIC—
Bahia Blanca.
Buenos Ayres.
Cordoba.
Rosario.

BRAZIL—
Aracaju.
Bahia.
Ceara.
Maceio.
Manaos.
Maranhão.
Natal.
Para.
Pernambuco.
Rio de Janeiro.
Rio Grande do Sul.
Santos.
Victoria.

CHILE—
Antofagasta.
Arica.
Caldera.
Coquimbo.
Coronel.
Iquique.
Punta Arenas.
Talcahuano.
Valdivia.
Valparaiso.

COLOMBIA—
Barranquilla.
B gota.
Bucaramanga.
Cali.
Cartagena.
Cucuta.
Honda.
Santa Marta.
Quibdo.

COSTA RICA—
Puerto Limon.
Punta Arenas.
San José.

CUBA—
Banes.
Baracoa.
Caibarien.
Cardenas.
Cienfuegos.
Habana.
Manzanillo.
Matanzas.
Nuevitas.
Sagua la Grande.
Santa Clara.
Santiago.

DOMINICAN REPUBLIC—
Azua.
Macoris.
Monte Christi.
Puerto Plata.

DOMINICAN REPUBLIC—Cont'd.
Samana.
Sanchez.
Santo Domingo.

ECUADOR—
Bahia de Caraques.
Esmeraldas.
Guayaquil.
Manta.

GUATEMALA—
Champerico.
Guatemala.
Livingston.
Ocos
San José de Guatemala.

HAITI—
Aux Cayes.
Cape Haitien.
Gonaives.
Jacmel.
Jeremie.
Miragoane.
Petit Godve.
Port au Prince.
Port de Paix.
St Marc.

HONDURAS—
Amapala.
Bonacca.
Ceiba.
Puerto Cortes.
San Juancito.
San Pedro Sula.
Tegucigalpa.
Tela
Truxillo.
Ruatan
Utila.

MEXICO—
Acapulco.
Aguascalientes.
Alamos
Campeche.
Cananea.
Chihuahua.
Ciudad Juarez.
Ciudad Porfirio Diaz.
Coatzacoalcos.
Durango.
Ensenada.
Frontera.
Guadalajara.
Guanajuato.
Guaymas.
Hermosillo.
Jalapa.
Laguna de Terminos.
La Paz.
Manzanillo.
Matamoras.
Mazatlan.
Mexico.

MEXICO—Continued.
Monterey.
Nogales.
Nuevo Laredo.
Oaxaca.
Parral.
Progreso.
Puebla.
Saltillo.
San Luis Potosi.
Sierra Mojada.
Tampico.
Tlacotalpan.
Topolobampo.
Torre m.
Tuxpan, Vera Cruz.
Veracruz.
Victoria.
Zacatecas.

NICARAGUA—
Bluefields.
Cape Gracias á Dios.
Corinto.
Managua.
Matagalpa.
San Juan del Norte.
San Juan del Sur.

PANAMA—
Bocas del Toro.
Colon.
David.
Panama.
Santiago.

PARAGUAY—
Asunción.

PERU—
Callao.
Chimbote.
Eten.
Iquitos.
Mollendo.
Paita.
Salaverry.

SALVADOR—
Acajutla.
La Libertad.
La Unión.
San Salvador.

URUGUAY—
Montevideo.

VENEZUELA—
Barcelona.
Caracas.
Carupano.
Ciudad Bolivar.
Coro.
La Guayra.
Maracaibo.
Puerto Cabello.
Tovar.
Valera.

CONSULATES OF THE LATIN-AMERICAN REPUBLICS IN THE UNITED STATES.

ARGENTINE REPUBLIC.

Alabama	Mobile.
California	San Francisco.
District of Columbia	Washington.
Florida	Fernandina.
	Pensacola.
Georgia	Savannah
Illinois	Chicago.
Louisiana	New Orleans.
Maine	Portland.
Maryland	Baltimore.
Massachusetts	Boston.
Mississippi	Gulf Port and Ship Island.
	Pascagoula.
Missouri	St. Louis.
New York	New York City.
Pennsylvania	Philadelphia.
Philippine Islands	Manila.
Virginia	Norfolk.

BOLIVIA.

California	San Diego.
	San Francisco.
Illinoi	Chicago.
Maryland	Baltimore.
Missouri	Kansas City.
New York	New York City.
Pennsylvania	Philadelphia.

BRAZIL.

Alabama	Mobile.
California	San Francisco.
Florida	Fernandina.
	Pensacola.
Georgia	Brunswick.
	Savannah.
Louisiana	New Orleans.
Maine	Calais.
Maryland	Baltimore.
Massachusetts	Boston.
Mississippi	Gulfport.
	Pascagoula.
Missouri	St. Louis.
New York	New York City.
Pennsylvania	Philadelphia.
Porto Rico	San Juan.
Virginia	Norfolk.
	Richmond.

CHILE.

California	San Francisco.
Canal Zone	Panama.
Georgia	Savannah.
Hawaii	Honolulu.
Illinois	Chicago.
Maryland	Baltimore.
Massachusetts	Boston.
New York	New York City.
Oregon	Portland.
Pennsylvania	Philadelphia.
Philippine Islands	Manila.
Porto Rico	San Juan.
Washington	Port Townsend.
	Tacoma.

COLOMBIA.

Alabama	Mobile.
California	San Francisco.
Connecticut	New Haven.
Florida	Tampa.
Illinois	Chicago.
Louisiana	New Orleans.
Maryland	Baltimore.
Massachusetts	Boston.
Michigan	Detroit.
Missouri	St. Louis.
New York	New York City.
Pennsylvania	Philadelphia.
Porto Rico	San Juan.
Virginia	Norfolk.

COSTA RICA.

Alabama	Mobile.
California	San Francisco.
Canal Zone	Colon.
	Panama.
Colorado	Denver.
Illinois	Chicago.
Louisiana	New Orleans.
Maryland	Baltimore.
Massachusetts	Boston.
Missouri	St. Louis.
New York	New York City.
Oregon	Portland.
Pennsylvania	Philadelphia.
Porto Rico	San Juan.
Texas	Galveston.
Virginia	Norfolk.

CUBA.

Alabama	Mobile.
California	Los Angeles.
Florida	Fernandina.
	Jacksonville.
	Key West.
	Pensacola.
	Tampa.
Georgia	Brunswick.
	Savannah.
Illinois	Chicago.
Kentucky	Louisville.
Louisiana	New Orleans.
Maine	Portland.
Maryland	Baltimore.
Massachusetts	Boston.
Michigan	Detroit.
Mississippi	Gulfport.
Missouri	St. Louis.
New York	New York City.
Ohio	Cincinnati.
Pennsylvania	Philadelphia.
Porto Rico	Arecibo.
	Mayaguez.
	Ponce.
	San Juan.
Texas	Galveston.
Virginia	Newport News.
	Norfolk.

DOMINICAN REPUBLIC.

Illinois	Chicago.
Maryland	Baltimore.
Massachusetts	Boston.
New York	New York City.
North Carolina	Wilmington.
Pennsylvania	Philadelphia.
Porto Rico	Aguadilla.
	Arecibo.
	Humacao.
	Mayaguez.
	Ponce.
	San Juan.
	Vieques.

ECUADOR.

California	Los Angeles.
	San Francisco.
Illinois	Chicago.
Louisiana	New Orleans.
Massachusetts	Boston.
New York	New York City.
Ohio	Cincinnati.
Pennsylvania	Philadelphia.
Philippine Islands	Manila.
South Carolina	Charleston.
Virginia	Norfolk.

GUATEMALA.

Alabama	Mobile.
California	San Diego.
	San Francisco.
Florida	Pensacola.
Illinois	Chicago.

CONSULATES OF THE LATIN-AMERICAN REPUBLICS—Continued.

GUATEMALA—Continued.

Kansas	Kansas City.
Kentucky	Louisville.
Louisiana	New Orleans.
Maryland	Baltimore.
Massachusetts	Boston.
Missouri	St. Louis.
New York	New York City.
Pennsylvania	Philadelphia.
Porto Rico	San Juan.
Texas	Galveston.
Washington	Seattle.

HAITI.

Alabama	Mobile.
Georgia	Savannah.
Illinois	Chicago.
Maine	Bangor.
Massachusetts	Boston.
New York	New York City.
North Carolina	Wilmington.
Porto Rico	Mayagüez.
	San Juan.

HONDURAS.

Alabama	Mobile.
California	Los Angeles.
	San Diego.
	San Francisco.
Illinois	Chicago.
Kansas	Kansas City.
Kentucky	Louisville.
Louisiana	New Orleans.
Maryland	Baltimore.
Michigan	Detroit.
Missouri	St. Louis.
New York	New York City.
Ohio	Cincinnati.
Pennsylvania	Philadelphia.
Texas	Galveston.
Washington	Seattle.

MEXICO.

Alabama	Mobile.
Arizona	Bisbee.
	Clifton.
	Douglas.
	Naco.
	Nogales.
	Phoenix.
	Solomonsville.
	Tucson.
	Yuma.
California	Calexico.
	Los Angeles.
	San Diego.
	San Francisco.
Canal Zone	Ancon.
Colorado	Denver.
Florida	Pensacola.
Hawaii	Honolulu.
Illinois	Chicago.
Kentucky	Louisville.
Louisiana	New Orleans.
Maryland	Baltimore.
Massachusetts	Boston.
Mississippi	Pascagoula.
Missouri	Kansas City.
	St. Louis.
New York	New York City.
Ohio	Cincinnati.
Oregon	Portland.
Pennsylvania	Philadelphia.
Philippine Islands	Manila.
Porto Rico	Mayagüez.
	Ponce.
	San Juan.
Texas	Brownsville.
	Eagle Pass.
	El Paso.
	Galveston.
	Laredo.
	Port Arthur.
	Rio Grande City.
	Sabine Pass.
	San Antonio.
	Solomonsville.

MEXICO—Continued.

Virginia	Norfolk.
Washington	Tocoma.

NICARAGUA.

Alabama	Mobile.
California	Los Angeles.
	San Diego.
	San Francisco.
Illinois	Chicago.
Kansas	Kansas City.
Kentucky	Louisville.
Louisiana	New Orleans.
Maryland	Baltimore.
Massachusetts	Boston.
Michigan	Detroit.
Missouri	St. Louis.
New York	New York City.
Pennsylvania	Philadelphia.
Philippine Islands	Manila.
Porto Rico	Ponce.
	San Juan.
Texas	Galveston.
Virginia	Norfolk.
	Newport News.
Washington	Seattle.

PANAMA.

Alabama	Mobile.
California	San Francisco.
Georgia	Atlanta.
Hawaii	Hilo.
Illinois	Chicago.
Louisiana	New Orleans.
Maryland	Baltimore.
Massachusetts	Boston.
Missouri	St. Louis.
New York	New York City.
Pennsylvania	Philadelphia.
Porto Rico	San Juan.
Tennessee	Chattanooga.
Texas	Galveston.
	Port Arthur.
Washington	Puget Sound.

PARAGUAY.

Alabama	Mobile.
Delaware	Wilmington.
District of Columbia	Washington.
Georgia	Savannah.
Illinois	Chicago.
Indiana	Indianapolis.
Maryland	Baltimore.
Michigan	Detroit.
Missouri	Kansas City.
	St. Louis.
New Jersey	Newark.
	Trenton.
New York	Buffalo.
	New York City.
	Rochester.
Ohio	Cincinnati.
Pennsylvania	Philadelphia.
Porto Rico	San Juan.
Virginia	Norfolk.
	Richmond.

PERU.

California	Los Angeles.
	San Diego.
	San Francisco.
Canal Zone	Panama.
Georgia	Savannah.
Hawaii	Honolulu.
Illinois	Chicago.
Louisiana	New Orleans.
Maryland	Baltimore.
Massachusetts	Boston.
New York	New York City.
Oregon	Portland.
Pennsylvania	Philadelphia.
Porto Rico	San Juan.
South Carolina	Charleston.
Washington	Port Townsend.

CONSULATES OF TH

ARGENTINE REPUBLIC.

Alabama	Mobil
California	San F
District of Columbia	Washi
Florida	Fernat
	Pensac
Georgia	Savant
Illinois	Chicago
Louisiana	New Or
Maine	Portlant
Maryland	Baltimo
Massachusetts	Boston.
Mississippi	Gulf P
	ship Is
	Pascagou
Missouri	St. Louis
New York	New York
Pennsylvania	Philadelph
Philippine Islands	Manila.
Virginia	Norfolk.

BOLIVIA.

California	San Diego.
	San Francisco
Illinoi	Chicago.
Maryland	Baltimore.
Missouri	Kansas City.
New York	New York City
Pennsylvania	Philadelphia

BRAZIL.

Alabama	Mobile.
California	San Francisco.
Florida	Fernandina.
	Pensacola.
Georgia	Brunswick.
	Savannah.
Louisiana	New Orleans.
Maine	Calais
Maryland	Baltimore.
Massachusetts	Boston.
Mississippi	Gulfport.
	Pascagoula.
Missouri	St. Louis.
New York	New York City.
Pennsylvania	Philadelphia.
Porto Rico	San Juan.
Virginia	Norfolk.
	Richmond.

CHILE.

California	San Francisco.
Canal Zone	Panama.
Georgia	Savannah.
Hawaii	Honolulu.
Illinois	Chicago.
Maryland	Baltimore.
Massachusetts	Boston.
New York	New York City.
Oregon	Portland.
Pennsylvania	Philadelphia.
Philippine Islands	Manila.
Porto Rico	San Juan.
Washington	Port Townsend.
	Tacoma.

COLOMBIA.

Alabama	Mobile.
California	San Francisco.
Connecticut	New Haven.
Florida	Tampa.
Illinois	Chicago.
Louisiana	New Orleans.
Maryland	Baltimore.
Massachusetts	Boston.
Michigan	Detroit.
Missouri	St. Louis.
New York	New York City.
Pennsylvania	Philadelphia.
Porto Rico	San Juan.
Virginia	Norfolk

WEIGHTS AND MEASURES.

The following table gives the chief weights and measures in commercial use in Mexico and the Republics of Central and South America, and their equivalents in the United States:

Denomination.	Where used.	United States equivalents.
	Metric	0.02471 acre.
	Paraguay	25 pounds.
(dry)	Argentine Republic	25.3171 pounds.
Do	Brazil	32.38 pounds.
Do	Cuba	25.3664 pounds.
Do	Venezuela	25.4024 pounds.
(liquid)	Cuba and Venezuela	4.263 gallons.
	Argentine Republic and Mexico	20.0787 gallons.
	Mexico and Salvador	300 pounds.
	Central America	4.2631 gallons.
	Argentine Republic	4.2 acres.
	Paraguay	78.9 yards.
	Paraguay (square)	8.077 square feet.
	Uruguay	2 acres (nearly).
meter	Metric	35.3 cubic feet.
(dry)	Central America	1.5745 bushels.
	Chile	2.575 bushels.
	Cuba	1.599 bushels.
	Mexico	1.54728 bushels.
	Uruguay (double)	7.776 bushels.
	Uruguay (single)	3.888 bushels.
	Venezuela	1.599 bushels.
	Argentine Republic	2.5096 quarts.
	Mexico	2.5 quarts.
	Metric	15.432 grains.
	do	2.471 acres.
(dry)	do	2.838 bushels.
(liquid)	do	26.417 gallons.
(kilo)	do	2.2046 pounds.
	do	0.621376 mile.
land)	Paraguay	4.633 acres.
	Argentine Republic	1.0127 pounds.
	Central America	1.043 pounds.
	Chile	1.014 pounds.
	Cuba	1.0161 pounds.
	Mexico	1.01465 pounds.
	Peru	1.0143 pounds.
	Uruguay	1.0143 pounds.
	Venezuela	1.0161 pounds.
	Metric	1.0567 quarts.
	Guiana	1.0791 pounds.
	Costa Rica	1.73 acres.
	Bolivia	0.507 pound.
	Metric	39.37 inches.
	Argentine Republic	0.9478 foot.
	do	101.42 pounds.
	Brazil	130.06 pounds.
	Chile, Mexico, and Peru	101.61 pounds.
	Paraguay	100 pounds.
	Metric	220.46 pounds.
	Uruguay	2,700 cuadras. (*See* Cuadra.)
	Argentine Republic	34.1208 inches.
	Central America	33.874 inches.
	Chile and Peru	33.367 inches.
	Cuba	33.384 inches.
	Mexico	33 inches.
	Paraguay	34 inches.
	Venezuela	33.384 inches.

CONSULATES OF THE LATIN-AMERICAN REPUBLICS—Continued.

SALVADOR.		URUGUAY—Continued.	
California	San Diego.	Mississippi	Pascagoula.
	San Francisco.	Missouri	St. Louis.
Louisiana	New Orleans.	New York	New York City.
Massachusetts	Boston.	Ohio	Cincinnati.
Missouri	St. Louis.	Pennsylvania	Philadelphia.
New York	New York City.	Philippine Islands	Manila.
		South Carolina	Charleston.
URUGUAY.		Texas	Galveston.
			Port Arthur and
Alabama	Mobile.		Sabine Pass.
California	San Francisco.	Virginia	Norfolk.
Florida	Apalachicola.		Richmond.
	Fernandina.		
	Jacksonville.	**VENEZUELA.**	
	Pensacola.		
	St. Augustine.	California	San Francisco.
Georgia	Brunswick.	Illinois	Chicago.
	Savannah.	Louisiana	New Orleans.
Illinois	Chicago.	New York	New York City.
Louisiana	New Orleans.	Pennsylvania	Philadelphia.
Maine	Bangor.	Philippine Islands	Cebu.
	Calais.	Porto Rico	Arecibo.
	Portland.		Mayagüez.
Maryland	Baltimore.		Ponce.
Massachusetts	Boston.		San Juan.

WEIGHTS AND MEASURES.

The following table gives the chief weights and measures in commercial use in Mexico and the Republics of Central and South America, and their equivalents in the United States:

Denomination.	Where used.	United States equivalents.
Are	Metric	0.02471 acre.
Arobe	Paraguay	25 pounds.
Arroba (dry)	Argentine Republic	25.3171 pounds.
Do	Brazil	32.38 pounds.
Do	Cuba	25.3664 pounds.
Do	Venezuela	25.4024 pounds.
Arroba (liquid)	Cuba and Venezuela	4.263 gallons.
Barril	Argentine Republic and Mexico	20.0787 gallons.
Carga	Mexico and Salvador	300 pounds.
Centaro	Central America	4.2631 gallons.
Cuadra	Argentine Republic	4.2 acres.
Do	Paraguay	78.9 yards.
Do	Paraguay (square)	8.077 square feet.
Do	Uruguay	2 acres (nearly).
Cubic meter	Metric	35.3 cubic feet.
Fanega (dry)	Central America	1.5745 bushels.
Do	Chile	2.575 bushels.
Do	Cuba	1.599 bushels.
Do	Mexico	1.54728 bushels.
Do	Uruguay (double)	7.776 bushels.
Do	Uruguay (single)	3.888 bushels.
Do	Venezuela	1.599 bushels.
Frasco	Argentine Republic	2.5096 quarts.
Do	Mexico	2.5 quarts.
Gram	Metric	15.432 grains.
Hectare	do	2.471 acres.
Hectoliter (dry)	do	2.838 bushels.
Hectoliter (liquid)	do	26.417 gallons.
Kilogram (kilo)	do	2.2046 pounds.
Kilometer	do	0.621376 mile.
League (land)	Paraguay	4.633 acres.
Libra	Argentine Republic	1.0127 pounds.
Do	Central America	1.043 pounds.
Do	Chile	1.014 pounds.
Do	Cuba	1.0161 pounds.
Do	Mexico	1.01465 pounds.
Do	Peru	1.0143 pounds.
Do	Uruguay	1.0143 pounds.
Do	Venezuela	1.0161 pounds.
Liter	Metric	1.0567 quarts.
Livre	Guiana	1.0791 pounds.
Manzana	Costa Rica	1.73 acres.
Marc	Bolivia	0.507 pound.
Meter	Metric	39.37 inches.
Pie	Argentine Republic	0.9478 foot.
Quintal	do	101.42 pounds.
Do	Brazil	130.06 pounds.
Do	Chile, Mexico, and Peru	101.61 pounds.
Do	Paraguay	100 pounds.
Quintal (metric)	Metric	220.46 pounds.
Suerte	Uruguay	2,700 cuadras. (See Cuadra.)
Vara	Argentine Republic	34.1208 inches.
Do	Central America	33.874 inches.
Do	Chile and Peru	33.367 inches.
Do	Cuba	33.384 inches.
Do	Mexico	33 inches.
Do	Paraguay	34 inches.
Do	Venezuela	33.384 inches.

METRIC WEIGHTS AND MEASURES.

METRIC WEIGHTS.

m (1/1000 gram) equals 0.0154 grain.
...am (1/100 gram) equals 0.1543 grain.
ram (1/10 gram) equals 1.5432 grains.
... equals 15.432 grains.
Decagram (10 grams) equals 0.3527 ounce.
Hectogram (100 grams) equals 3.5274 ounces.
Kilogram (1,000 grams) equals 2.2046 pounds.
iagram (10,000 grams) equals 22.046 pounds.
ital (,000 grams) equals 220.46 pounds.
... onneau—ton (1,000,000 grams) equals 2,204.6 pounds.

METRIC DRY MEASURE.

liliter (1/1000 liter) equals 0.061 cubic inch.
Centiliter (1/100 liter) equals 0.6102 cubic inch.
Deciliter (1/10 liter) equals 6.1022 cubic inches.
... equals 0.908 quart.
ecaliter (10 liters) equals 9.08 quarts.
ectoliter (100 liters) equals 2.838 bushels.
Kiloliter (1,000 liters) equals 1.308 cubic yards.

METRIC LIQUID MEASURE.

Milliliter (1/1000 liter) equals 0.27 fluid dram.
Centiliter (1/100 liter) equals 0.338 fluid ounce.
Deciliter (1/10 liter) equals 0.845 gill.
Liter equals 1.0567 quarts.
Decaliter (10 liters) equals 2.6417 gallons.
Hectoliter (100 liters) equals 26.417 gallons.
Kiloliter (1,000 liters) equals 264.17 gallons.

METRIC MEASURES OF LENGTH.

Millimeter (1/1000 meter) equals 0.0394 inch.
Centimeter (1/100 meter) equals 0.3937 inch.
Decimeter (1/10 meter) equals 3.937 inches.
Meter equals 39.37 inches.
Decameter (10 meters) equals 393.7 inches.
Hectometer (100 meters) equals 328 feet 1 inch.
Kilometer (1,000 meters) equals 0.62137 mile (3,280 feet 10 inches).
Myriameter (10,000 meters) equals 6.2137 miles.

METRIC SURFACE MEASURE.

Centare (1 square meter) equals 1,550 square inches.
Are (100 square meters) equals 119.6 square yards.
Hectare (10,000 square meters) equals 2.471 acres.

PRICE LIST OF PUBLICATIONS.

Price.

Bulletin of the Bureau, published monthly since October, 1893, in English, Spanish, Portuguese, and French. Average 225 pages, 2 volumes a year.

Yearly subscription (in countries of the International Union of American Republics and in Canada).. $2.00

Yearly subscription (other countries)................................... 2.50

Single copies... .25

Orders for the Bulletin should be addressed to the Chief Clerk of the Bureau.

American Constitutions. A compilation of the political constitutions of the independent States of America, in the original text, with English and Spanish translations. Washington, 1906. 3 vols., 8°.

Paper ....each.. 1.00

Bound in cloth...do.... 1.50

Bound in sheep ....do.... 2.00

    Vol. I, now ready, contains the constitutions of the Federal Republics of the United States of America, of Mexico, of the Argentine Republic, of Brazil, and of Venezuela, and of the Republics of Central America, Guatemala, Honduras, El Salvador, Nicaragua, Costa Rica, and Panama. Vols. II and III will be ready shortly.

    Vol. II will contain the constitutions of the Dominican Republic, Haiti, Cuba, Uruguay, Chile, Peru, Ecuador, Colombia, Paraguay, and Bolivia.

    Vol. III will contain Articles of Confederation of the United States, First Constitution of Venezuela 1811, Fundamental Law of Republic of Colombia 1819, Ditto of 1821, Constitution of Colombia of 1821, Constitution of Central American Confederation of 1824, Constitution of the Grenadian Confederation of 1858, Constitution of the United States of Colombia of 1863, Pro Constitution of Guatemala of 1876, Convention between United States and Republic of Panama for construction of ship canal to connect the waters of the Atlantic and the Pacific Oceans.

Code of Commercial Nomenclature, 1897. (Spanish, English, and Portuguese.) 645 pages, 4°, cloth... 2.50

Code of Commercial Nomenclature, 1897. (Portuguese, Spanish, and English.) 640 pages, 4°, cloth... 2.50

    Note.—Designates in alphabetical order, in equivalent terms in the three languages, the commodities of American nations on which import duties are levied. The English, Spanish, and Portuguese edition is entirely exhausted.

Leyes y reglamentos sobre privilegios de invención y marcas de fábrica en los países hispano-americanos, el Brasil y la República de Haití. Revisado hasta agosto de 1904. Washington, 1904. 415 pages, 8°.......................... 1.00

Patent and trade-mark laws of the Spanish American Republics, Brazil, and the Republic of Haiti. Revised to Aug., 1904, Washington, 1904.......... 1.00

The above two works bound together in sheep 3.00

SPECIAL BULLETINS.

Money, Weights, and Measures of the American Republics, 1891. 12 pages, 8°. .05

Report on Coffee, with special reference to the Costa Rican product, etc. Washington, 1901. 15 pages, 8°... .10

El café. Su historia, cultivo, beneficio, variedades, producción, exportación, importación, consumo, etc. Datos extensos presentados al Congreso relativo al café que se reunirá en Nueva York el 1° de octubre de 1902. 167 páginas, 8°... .50

PRICE.

Costa Rica. From official and other sources. 1903. Scale of 12.5 miles to 1
inch (792,000) $0. 50
Brazil. From official and other sources. 1905. Scale of 75 miles to 1 inch
(1:4,752,000). In one sheet 96 x 93 cm 1. 00

LIST OF BOOKS AND MAPS IN COURSE OF PREPARATION.

LAW MANUALS.

Leyes Comerciales de América Latina: Código de Comercio de España comparado
con los Códigos y Leyes Comerciales de Pan América.
Land and Immigration Laws of American Republics. (To replace edition of 1893.)

HANDBOOKS.
Chile.
Dominican Republic.

MAPS.

Maps are in course of preparation of the Republics of Honduras and Salvador.
Payment is required to be made in cash, money orders, or by bank drafts on banks
in New York City or Washington, D. C., payable to the order of the INTERNATIONAL
BUREAU OF THE AMERICAN REPUBLICS. Individual checks on banks outside of New
York or Washington, or postage stamps, can not be accepted.

FOR FREE DISTRIBUTION.

The Bureau has for distribution a limited supply of the following, which will be
sent, free, upon written application:
The case of the United States of Venezuela before the Tribunal of Arbitration to
convene at Paris under the provisions of the Treaty between the United States of
Venezuela and Her Britannic Majesty, signed at Washington, February 2, 1897, in
10 vols., of which 2 are maps.
Message from the President of the United States, transmitting a communication from
the Secretary of State submitting the report, with accompanying papers, of the
delegates of the United States to the Second International Conference of American
States, held at the City of Mexico from October 22, 1901, to January 22, 1902.
Washington, 1902. 243 pages. 8°. (57th Congress, 1st session, Senate Doc. No.
330.)
Message from the President of the United States, transmitting a report from the Sec-
retary of State, with accompanying papers, relative to the proceedings of the Inter-
national Congress for the study of the production and consumption of coffee, etc.
Washington, 1903. 312 pages. 8° (paper). (57th Congress, 2d session, Senate
Doc. No. 35.)
Message from the President of the United States, transmitting a report by the Secre-
tary of State, with accompanying papers, relative to the proceedings of the First
Customs Congress of the American Republics, held at New York in January, 1903.
Washington, 1903. 195 pages. 8° (paper). (57th Congress, 2d session, Senate
Doc. No. 180.)

NOTE.—Senate documents, listed above, containing reports of the various International American
Congresses, may also be obtained through members of the United States Senate and House of Representatives.

PUBLICATIONS.

xition. St. Louis, 1904. 160 pages. 8° (paper).

jon of the Republic according to official data. Leipzig, 1901.
37 illustrations. 8° (cloth).

ión de la República escrita según datos oficiales. Leipzig,
inas. Mapa y 36 grabados. · 8° (en tela).

le at Pan-American Exposition. Buffalo, 1901. 252 pages (paper).

mala—The Country of the future. By Charles M. Pepper. Washington,
80 pages. 8° (paper). .

VALUE OF LATIN-AMERICAN COINS.

The following table shows the value, in United States gold, of coins representing the monetary units of the Central and South American Republics and Mexico, estimated quarterly by the Director of the United States Mint, in pursuance of act of Congress:

ESTIMATE JANUARY 1, 1907.

Countries.	Standard.	Unit.	Value in U. S. gold or silver.	Coins.
ARGENTINE REPUBLIC.	Gold	Peso	$0.965	Gold—Argentine ($4.824) and ½ Argentine. Silver—Peso and divisions.
BOLIVIA *	Silver ...	Boliviano	.510	Silver—Boliviano and divisions.
BRAZIL	Gold	Milreis ..	.546	Gold—5, 10, and 20 milreis. Silver—½, 1, and 2 milreis.
CENTRAL AMERICAN STATES— Costa Rica......	Gold	Colon ...	.465	Gold—2, 5, 10, and 20 colons ($9.307). Silver—5, 10, 25, and 50 centimos.
Guatemala...... Honduras ...... Nicaragua ...... Salvador	Silver ...	Peso	.510	Silver—Peso and divisions.
CHILE	Gold	Peso	.365	Gold—Escudo ($1.825), doubloon ($3.650), and condor ($7.300). Silver—Peso and divisions.
COLOMBIA...........	Gold	Dollar...	1.000	Gold—Condor ($9.647) and double condor. Silver—Peso.
ECUADOR	Gold	Sucre....	.487	Gold—10 sucres ($4.8665). Silver—Sucre and divisions.
HAITI	Gold	Gourde..	.965	Gold—1, 2, 5, and 10 gourdes. Silver—Gourde and divisions.
MEXICO.............	Gold	Peso a ...	.498	Gold—5 and 10 pesos. Silver—Dollar b (or peso) and divisions.
PANAMA	Gold	Balboa..	1.000	Gold—1, 2½, 5, 10, and 20 balboas. Silver—Peso and divisions.
PERU	Gold	Libra ...	4.866½	Gold—½ and 1 libra. Silver—Sol and divisions.
URUGUAY	Gold	Peso	1.034	Gold—Peso. Silver—Peso and divisions.
VENEZUELA	Gold	Bolivar..	.193	Gold—5, 10, 20, 50, and 100 bolivars. Silver—5 bolivars.

a 75 centigrams fine gold.   b Value in Mexico, 0.498.

*[By the new Bolivian law enacted September 14, 1906, the gold peso of one-fifth of a pound sterling (1.5976 grams, 916⅔ fine) is made the unit of value.—EDITOR.]

O

International Union of American Republics

Monthly Bulletin

OF THE

International Bureau

OF THE

American Republics

VOL. 24, NO. 3

MARCH, 1907

WHOLE NO. 162

WASHINGTON, D. C., U. S. A.

GOVERNMENT PRINTING OFFICE

1907

International Union of American Republics

Monthly Bulletin

OF THE

International Bureau

OF THE

American Republics

VOL. 24, NO. 3

MARCH, 1907

WHOLE NO. 162

WASHINGTON, D. C., U. S. A.

GOVERNMENT PRINTING OFFICE

1907

Secretary.   Chief Clerk.

GENERAL TABLE OF CONTENTS.

INDEX.

INDICE.

INDICE.

TABLE DES MATIÈRES.

VIII

MR. JOAQUIM NABUCO, AMBASSADOR OF BRAZIL TO THE UNITED STATES, PRESIDENT OF
THE THIRD PAN-AMERICAN CONGRESS.

MONTHLY BULLETIN

OF THE

INTERNATIONAL BUREAU OF THE AMERICAN REPUBLICS,

International Union of American Republics.

| VOL. XXIV. | MARCH, 1907. | No. 3. |

The Director of the International Bureau of the American Republics, in the broadening work of the institution, hopes for the cooperation of all persons interested not only in the promotion of trade among the American Republics but in the development of closer diplomatic, intellectual, and social relations. He trusts that the Latin American as well as the North American press and people will aid all they can, through the Bureau, the advancement of the cause of international American commerce, good will, and mutual acquaintance. Any suggestions which may come from editors, professional men, scholars, business men, and other representative persons, either in public or private life, of the American Republics will be gladly welcomed and carefully considered. If such suggestions can not be followed they will be none the less respected, and they may contain the inspiration for some effort, akin or slightly different, which will be productive of much good.

A NEW PROGRAMME ON LIMITED INCOME.

The new programme for the Bureau, outlined by the last Pan-American Conference at Rio Janeiro, is an ambitious one which will require for complete execution more time than might at first be expected. It will be necessary for those watching the growth and progress of the Bureau to be patient and not to expect great results at once. Despite the fact that this programme plans for the enlargement and extension of its work and for the establishment of a department of statistics, with the consequent increasing demands on the present staff, there has been provided as yet no increase in the annual income of the Bureau. It will be impossible, moreover, to provide the institution with more money, in the form of larger appropriations

»publics, until the new budget has been submitted
only by the Governing Board of the Bureau but
᛫ Governments and Congresses. This means that
year must pass before the revenues of the Bureau
meet the rapidly growing wants.

‛ PERMANENT HOME OF THE BUREAU.

᛫d progress is being made toward the construction of the Bureau's
home, or Temple of Peace, as Mr ANDREW CARNEGIE describes
One of the best sit·   the   ᛫   shington for this edifice has
᛫n secured. It is a   ly 5 acres, bounded by Seventeenth, Eighteen , ᛫   ᛫   ᛫nd Virginia avenue, about
three squares below the   ᛫   ᛫ar, ᛫   ᛫avy building, facing, on the
Seventeenth street side, the park belt   ᵉ White House and fronting,
on the B street and Virginia avenue   ᷟ, the new park system along
the Potomac River. Although thi   ᛫   ᵒn of Washington is not yet
fully improved, it will in the course   ᛫᛫᛫w years be one of the beautiful parts of the capital. The corner on which the new building will
be erected is one of the most important in the Burnham plan for making a "City Beautiful." By the time the structure is completed, work
should also be well under way for the Lincoln memorial statue or
monument and the Grant memorial bridge, the approaches to which
will be close at hand. It is expected that the general scheme of the
building to be submitted to the architects as a basis for the competitive design will be ready before this BULLETIN is off the press, but too
late for publication.

PRACTICAL WORK OF THE BUREAU.

As evidence of the new practical work of the Bureau, the Director
has pleasure in stating that within the last sixty days, or since the
beginning of the new administration of the Bureau, over a dozen leading American manufacturers and exporters have, through the advice
and suggestion of the Bureau, decided to send representatives to
Latin America for the purpose of studying carefully the field and
arranging for closer business connections. Several important commercial publications, like "The American Exporter," "The Bankers'
Magazine," and others, are planning, with the assistance of the
Bureau, a series of articles on all of the American Republics and specific discussions of the opportunities for investment and the extension .
of the markets for North American manufactured products. "Mun-

sey's Magazine" will shortly print an article, prepared by this Bureau, on the "New South America," while the "North American Review" has requested the Bureau to discuss the intellectual development of Latin America, which is now so little appreciated in the United States. In this latter connection it can be said that, in addition to Prof. WILLIAM R. SHEPHERD, of Columbia University, whose mission to South America was described in the last number of the BULLETIN, there are now in that part of the world, for the same purpose of study, investigation, and acquaintance, Professor L. S. ROWE, of the University of Pennsylvania, and Professor BERNARD MOSES, of the University of California.

CHANGES IN THE BULLETIN.

Those persons who are especially interested in the MONTHLY BUL-LETIN will note that the Bureau is endeavoring to make this publication more attractive in appearance. A change has been effected in the cover, which is an improvement over the somber appearance of former issues. Photographs of representative men connected with Pan-American activities are being placed in its pages, and in this issue there are a few paragraphs in the nature of editorial comment which are intended to keep the BULLETIN in closer touch with its constituency and to call the attention of its readers to the work that the Bureau is carrying on. The English section has been placed first rather than the Spanish, because the greatest need at the present moment is to educate or inform the people of the United States who speak only English about the resources, possibilities, conditions, and progress of their sister Latin American Republics. The knowledge which the average Latin American has of the United States is far greater than that which the average person in the United States has of the nations to the south.

PROMOTION OF THE MINISTER OF ECUADOR.

The Bureau extends its congratulations to the Minister of Ecuador in Washington, Señor Don LUIS FELIPE CARBO, on his promotion to the position of Minister of Foreign Affairs at Quito, but it regrets that it must lose him from the Supervisory Committee, of which he has been an active member. The Bureau also felicitates Hon. WILLIAMS C. FOX, its late Director, on the assumption of his duties as United States Minister to Ecuador. Minister CARBO and Mr. Fox left Washington together about the middle of March and should now have arrived at their new posts.

omes the arrival in Washington and to the mem-
erning Board the new Ambassador of Mexico,
: C. Creel, and the Ministers, respectively, of Uru-
a, Señor Dr. Don Luis Melian Lafinur and Señor
ᴜ ᴸᵁᴵᴮ EDO Herrarte, and hopes that they will take a
) interest ᴸ᷾ o welfare and development of the Bureau. All
aᴵᵒ men represeₐ tive of the best statesmanship of their respective
countries.

EXHIBIT AT ᵎᵎᵎ ᶠ EXPOSITION.

Good progress is being n ᵉparation of the exhibit of
the Bureau at the Jamestow᷾ ᴵᴵnial Exposition. It is in
the hands of Mr. Francisco J ᴵ ᴵe efficient Secretary of the
Bureau, assisted by Mr. Carlton ᵉcial Agent.

A WORD TO CORRESPᴼ ᴳ MEMBERS.

The Director takes advantage of this opportunity to urge upon
the Corresponding Members of the Bureau in the different Republics
that they will provide it, without delay, with any new and interesting
data concerning their respective countries, which will be of interest
for publication in the Bulletin.

ADDRESS BY THE BRAZILIAN AMBASSADOR, MR. JOAQUIM NABUCO.

At Buffalo on February 20, 1907, the Brazilian Ambassador to
the United States, Mr. Joaquim Nabuco, delivered an interesting
address in English on the subject of "Lessons and Prophecies of the
Third Pan-American Conference." In the course of his remarks he
paid a beautiful tribute to the Secretary of State of the United States,
which is given below:

"As its President all I can tell you is that its surface was as smooth
as possible, but your distinguished fellow-citizen, Mr. Buchanan,
the head of the American delegation, who so ably and silently worked
in the recess of the committees, could tell you, I feel sure, that the
depths were as still as the surface. To that quiet nothing has contributed more than the attitude of the Secretary of State, as the head
of the Washington Pan-American Board, when the plans for the meeting were laid out, and than his personal visit to the seat of the conference and to other South American capitals. Mr. Root was indeed

the ideal representative this country could send on such a mission. His sincerity, his earnestness, his love of equity, his high-mindedness, his considerateness, together with his powerful intellect and with what, in the broader geographical sense of the word, can be called his genuine Americanism, a most generous sympathy with all the nations of our Continent, could not fail to create among them an impression of confidence likely to last long after his passage. He went to us animated with the spirit of a BLAINE, yet speaking the language of a MARSHALL. His words were received everywhere as political oracles, studied as constitutional lessons on the nature and the working of the institutions we all copied from you. With his presence our nations well realize that your Secretaries of State are still cast on the same mold as in the times of the JEFFERSONS, the MONROES, the WEBSTERS, and the CLAYS. That above all has assured the success of the Rio Conference.''

ADDRESS BY THE BOLIVIAN MINISTER, MR. IGNACIO CALDERÓN, BEFORE THE NATIONAL GEOGRAPHIC SOCIETY.

In a recent address before the National Geographic Society, of Washington, the Bolivian Minister, Mr. IGNACIO CALDERON, concluded with words of such interest and significance that the BULLETIN quotes in full that portion of his speech:

"Before concluding this already too long address permit me to call your attention to the fact that what is being done in Bolivia is also in progress in the majority of the South American Republics. The Argentine Republic, for instance, by receiving an increasing current of immigration is rapidly developing her wonderful resources. If some of them have not yet succeeded in getting over the fatal disease of internal turmoil, it will not be long before they will enter the road of order, and Mr. ROOT's prophecy that the twentieth century will be South America's century will be fulfilled.

"Slowly but surely the onward march of progress will bring closer and closer the Southern Republics, guided by the eternal force of liberty and the broadest sentiments of universal fellowship and community of interests. I venture the hope that in no distant future a confederation of Peru, Bolivia, Chile, the Argentine Republic, Uruguay, and Paraguay, as the United States of South America, will be established, and that Ecuador, Venezuela, and Colombia, reunited, and Brazil will form a trinity of nations that with their sisters of the north will be the beacon light of the world, shining with the undimmed brightness of human rights, peace, and happiness.

"Asia is already populated by many hundreds of millions of people whose races, civilization, and traditions will never, perhaps, assimilate

)po. Africa has been carved among the powers of
r World, then, remains, where the political conditions
re broken and the forward march of the democracy
h America will be supreme.

re proclaimed a more vital, lasting, or grander prin-
tne   tree Doctrine, which in its purest interpretation is
isecration f all America to democratic life—that is to say, the
ation of man and the empire of justice and the right to work
it his own destiny without the tutelage of kings or classes or any
other sovereignty than that of citizen and ballot.

"We are thankful and render our tribute of admiration to the history and civilization of Europe; we su   y the books of her thinkers;
enjoy the magnificent works of her artist of her poets, and of all those
who have so highly elevated the i   tual level of mankind. We
desire and solicit the concourse of her no le races; but in the political
order the whole America is destined to be the throne of liberty and
right, where mankind will advance to the highest ideals of his divine
mission in the world. And when the barrier separating this grand
Republic from her sisters of the South is removed by the completion of
the Panama Canal, the two great oceans made one, it is necessary that
the bonds of union and of mutual interest and respect be already established on the firm basis of peace and justice.

"The Panama Canal will open a new horizon to commerce, and it
might be said that it will be the material consecration of the Monroe
Doctrine, that excludes conquest from America, where, under the
inspiration of democracy, freedom, and justice, the Christian brotherhood of mankind will be perpetuated."

ARGENTINE REPUBLIC.

FOREIGN COMMERCE, 1906.

The figures compiled by the Bureau of Statistics of the Argentine
Republic relating to the foreign trade of the country during the calendar year 1906 and published recently, state that aggregate value of
imports and exports during the year amounted to $562,224,450 gold
as compared with $527,998,261 in 1905. Imports are credited with
a value of $269,970,521 gold, an increase over 1905 of $64,816,101
gold, and exports with $292,253,829 gold, a decrease of $30,590,012
gold. Despite this decrease, the balance of trade is in favor of the
Republic, amounting, in 1906, to $22,283,308 gold, as against
$117,689,421 gold, in 1905.

The imports of gold and silver were $14,347,217 gold less than in
1905.

The increase in imports is noted in all items, while exports of the principal national products decreased in the following manner: Cattle, $3,484,833 gold less than in 1905; wool, $5,910,156 gold less; jerked beef, $3,141,801 gold less; animal products, 16,906,547 *pesos* less; flax, 317,990 *pesos* less; wheat, 19,321,960 *pesos* less; wheat flour, 595,735 *pesos* less; all other agricultural products, $12,580,543 gold less.

The imports from the United States were $39,000,000 gold, approximately, and the exports thither nearly $13,000,000 gold. That country holds second rank for imports and seventh for exports. The increase of imports from the United Kingdom amounted to about $26,000,000 gold and from the United States $10,000,000.

CROP ESTIMATES FOR 1906-7.

A preliminary estimate upon the 1906-7 wheat and flaxseed crops of the Argentine Republic was issued on January 21, 1907, by the Argentine Ministry of Agriculture. The estimate is based upon thrashing-machine returns received up to January 10, and indicates for each crop an abundant harvest. From the data at hand it is estimated that the wheat yield will be 155,000,000 bushels, as compared with final estimates of 135,000,000 bushels in 1905-6 and 154,000,000 bushels in 1904-5. The flaxseed crop is put at 26,000,000 bushels. The final figures for 1905-6 and 1904-5 were, respectively, 23,000,000 and 29,000,000 bushels.

THE SUGAR CROP OF 1906.

The total production of sugar in the Argentine Republic during the crop year ended August 31, 1906, was 114,500 tons, while the amount estimated in April, 1906, was 125,000, as minimum.

Of said 114,500 tons, 91,500 more or less were produced by the sugar mills of Tucuman and the rest by those of Salta, Jujuy, Chaco, and Formosa, the sugar districts of the Republic.

This crop has been sufficient to meet the demands of domestic consumption, which is estimated at about 100,000 or 110,000 tons per annum.

According to official statistics recently published, the amount of sugar cane milled from the 1906 crop at the 28 factories of the province of Tucuman until December 31, 1906, shows an increase of 95,791,471 kilograms over that of 1905, while the quantity of sugar manufactured during the same period was 14,917,151 kilograms less than that of the previous year, in spite of the fact that the amount of milled sugar was larger.

The total amount of the cane milled of the crop of 1906 was 1,671,388,411 kilograms. Down to November, 1906, there were manufactured 100,506,206 kilograms of sugar, which, added to 525,375

kilograms manufactured by 9 factories in December, 190
total of 101,031,681 kilograms of manufactured sugar.

The amount of sugar exported to December 31, 1906, was
kilograms.

BUDGET FOR 1907.

The committee on appropriations of the Argentine Con
mitted, on the latter part of December, 1906, its report on
for 1907. The following figures, relating to the revenues an
tures for said year, having been taken therefrom:

EXPENDITURES.

	Gold currency.
Congress	
Interior	
Foreign Relations	
Finance	$60,581.20
Public debt	
Justice and Public Instruction	23,256,392.79
War	
Navy	
Agriculture	17,088.00
Public Works	500,000.00
Pensions	
Total	34,443,088.99
In bonds:	
Justice and Public Instruction	
Public Works	2,412,860.82

Import duties:	
In general	$44,000,000.00
Two per cent surtax	2,700,000.00
Storage and hoisting	2,000,000.00
Light-houses and beacons	325,000.00
Sanitary inspections	50,000.00
Port, wharf, and dock dues	2,000,000.00
Hydraulic hoists	400,000.00
Consular fees	500,000.00
Statistics and stamps	450,000.00
Fines and incidentals	25,000.00
Buenos Ayres Province, repayments on account of debt of	986,873.44
National Bank	348,232.00
Total	53,830,105.44
Tax on alcohol	
Tax on tobacco	
Tax on matches	
Tax on beer	
Tax on insurance	
Tax on cards	
Tax on artificial beverages	
Sanitation works	
Land tax	
License tax	
Stamp tax	
Cartage	
Postal service	
Telegraph service	
Forest concessions	
Public land sales and leases	
Fines and incidentals	
Railroads	
Health tax (Act No. 4039)	
Bond revenue (Act No. 3782, National Bank)	
Matriculation and examination fees, etc	
Fees for registration of real estate, attachments, official and judicial bulletins, etc	
National transports	

REVENUES—Continued.

	Gold currency.	Paper currency.
Military tax..........................	....	$250,000.00
Unexpended appropriations..........................	....	250,000.00
Repayments on account of loan:		
Entre Rios Province..........................	....	100,000.00
Santa Fe Province..........................	....	150,000.00
Mendoza Province..........................	....	50,000.00
Cordoba Province..........................	....	150,000.00
Tucuman Province..........................	....	50,818.75
Total..........................	$55,530,105.44	53,846,368.75
In bonds:		
Various laws..........................	....	11,730,910.00
Act No. 4064..........................	2,412,980.22	....

COLLECTIONS OF INTERNAL REVENUE IN 1906.

The report of the Collector-General of Internal Revenue of the Argentine Republic for the calendar year 1906 shows that the collections amounted to 40,470,574.12 *pesos*, an increase of 10.8 per cent over 1905 and an increase of 21.51 per cent on the budget estimates. Following is a detailed account of the amounts yielded by the various taxes in 1906, as compared with the preceding year:

[Argentine peso=$0.965, United States currency.]

Taxes.	1906.	1905.
	Pesos.	*Pesos.*
Alcohol..........................	15,615,869.84	15,586,123.90
Tobacco..........................	15,700,975.20	14,535,981.21
Beer..........................	3,051,804.20	2,228,126.39
Matches..........................	2,263,325.96	2,495,655.96
Playing cards..........................	159,334.93	157,964.56
Artificial drinks..........................	7,062.85	11,214.77
Wines..........................	69,111.01	66,343.05
Insurance..........................	452,127.56	412,627.08
Patent medicines..........................	677,690.25	537,917.55
Fines..........................	26,380.87	42,309.67
Interests..........................	332,816.65	436,475.53
Official publications sold..........................	2,119.56	1,866.06
Hoisting dues..........................	34.97	316.12
Storage dues..........................	2,816.34	1,335.00
Roads..........................	3,923.45	7,534.87
Denaturalization fees..........................	52,401.19	67,806.00
Incidentals..........................	....	52.00
Total..........................	....	....

THE MATCH INDUSTRY.

In a report made by the Chief of the Industrial Section of the Argentine Department of Agriculture it is stated that the Republic maintains ten match factories, giving employment to more than 3,500 workmen, and whose total capital is about 5,000,000 *pesos*. The average tax paid by those establishments amounts to more than 2,000,000 *pesos* annually.

The bearing of this industry upon other national enterprises is shown by the fact that the manufacture of matches in the Republic

ı 700 tons annually of stearin; that more than
xpended each year in pasteboard boxes and litho-
! that native cotton is employed for the wicks of
las," or wax tapers, with match heads.

—᷈, variᴏᴜᴏ establishments pay customs duties of 5 per cent on
g and of 28 per cent and upward on chemical products such
rate of potash, antitoxic phosphorus, gums, glue, etc.

DEVELOPMENT OF COMMERCE WITH BRAZIL.

_n order to meet the "favored-nation" clause in the new Brazilian
ıtom-house law, the Argentine Republic is preparing to make a
ıᴇᴄiprocal reduction on coffee, yerba maté, and tobacco. The Brazilian law authorizes the Government to grant rebates on duty on
merchandise or produce not indigenous to the country as follows:
ꞁ   ᴀnty per cent to countries which do not impose duties on Brazilian
ucts under similar conditions; 10 per cent to countries which
a 50 per cent rebate on Brazilian products, and when these
ıcts are imported in vessels flying the Brazilian flag, a further
ıᴇ of 5 per cent will be allowed.
, three articles mentioned as the subject of Argentine legislation
not only among the leading articles of Brazilian export, but also
constitute an important factor in the Argentine market. It is calculated that the loss occasioned by placing them on the Argentine
free list will, however, be more than compensated by increased sales
to Brazil of grain, flour, and meat products.

During the five years ending with 1905, Argentine products entering
Brazil have paid duties amounting to $7,863,852, gold, and during
the same period Brazilian products have paid duty in the Argentine
Republic amounting to $6,951,383.

THE FROZEN-MEAT INDUSTRY IN 1906.

The "*Frigorificos*" or frozen-meat establishments of the Argentine
Republic report the following shipments of produce during 1906:
Carcasses of frozen sheep and lambs, 2,951,812; quarters of frozen
beef, 1,576,833, and quarters of chilled beef, 455,459. These figures
are compared with 3,468,043 mutton carcasses; 1,507,995 quarters
of frozen beef, and 426,002 quarters of chilled beef in 1905, showing
a considerable decline in the first-named item and a slight advance
in the other two.

The Argentine freezing industry is reported to be passing through
a crisis, and the purpose of the Buenos Ayres Provincial Government
to levy a tax on every animal slaughtered is regarded with disfavor.

IMMIGRATION IN 1906.

The Director of Immigration of the Argentine Republic has issued statistics showing that the year 1906 established a "record" as to the number of immigrants arriving in the country. Passengers and immigrants debarking at the port of Buenos Ayres numbered 366,309, while departures are entered for 164,145, leaving 202,164 persons as additions to the population. · It is presumable, however, that some of these were en route to other South American countries, as the total figures for the year place the number of immigrants at 252,536.

The nationalities of the new citizens of the Republic were: Italians, 127,578; Spaniards, 79,287; Russians, 17,424; Syrians, 7,177; Austrians, 4,277; French, 3,698; Germans, 2,178; British, 1,690; Montenegrians, 1,081; Greeks, 945; Portugese, 885; Brazilians, 608; Swiss, 503, and other nationalities, in smaller numbers. The department reports that it had no difficulty in placing the immigrants in the various provinces.

MOVEMENT OF POSTS AND TELEGRAPHS, 1906.

Statistics concerning the Argentine Post and Telegraph Department show that at the close of 1906 the Republic had in operation 2,010 offices, 86 having been opened during the year and 4 closed. Letters were delivered numbering 535,906,474, an increase of 35,518,611 over the preceding year. Registered letters, with a value of $4,511,596, paper, were sent and postal drafts for $6,035,733.25 issued. International drafts were drawn for $244,693.44, paper, and $279,848.34 were paid, while postal orders amounted to $770,436, paper. The Parcels Post movement at the central office was 289,171 packages. Employees numbered 8,586.

A total length of telegraph lines is reported at the close of the year of 53,157 kilometers, covering an area of 24,358 kilometers, the number of messages sent being 9,413,014.

The Departmental revenue was $9,130,000 (national currency), of which $7,061,561 was for post-offices and $2,068,439 for telegraph service. In 1905 the revenue for these sources amounted to $8,030,852, so that an increase is noted for 1906 of $1,099,148, although, according to the Budget estimate, a greater advance had been anticipated.

MEASURES AGAINST BOVINE TUBERCULOSIS.

The Argentine Government has recently entered into a contract with the famous bacteriologist, Doctor BEHRING, for the right to apply his method curative of bovine tuberculosis in the city of Buenos Ayres. By virtue of this contract Doctor BEHRING sends to the capital his first assistant, Dr. PAUL ROEMER, who shall be charged with

he applications of the treatment to all animals
riod of one year, at the expiration of which the
:cinded by either party. The Government will
nection a hospital for consumptive animals.

ROM LA PLATA TO BUENOS AYRES.

Department of Public Works of the Argentine Republic states
report,   is, specifications, and estimates for the construc-
canal i.   La Plata to Buenos Ayres have been submitted
e engineer in charge of the surveys. The cost of the work is
ated at $21,00 ,000, gold, the annual maintenance at $1,688,260,
a, and the revenues at $1,800,000 per year, a probable surplus of
,1,740.

BOLIVIA.

ESTIMATE OF REVENUES FOR 1907.

The Legislative Power of the Republic of Bolivia has approved the
estimate of fiscal revenues for 1907, which amounts to 13,303,333
bolivianos.

One *boliviano* is equal to $0.510, United States currency.

THE IMPORTATION OF SILVER BULLION IN 1906.

The National Mint of the Bolivian Republic has published recently
the following figures relating to the importation of silver bullion during the calendar year 1906:

Month.	Quantity.	Value.	Month.	Quantity.	Value.
	Kilos.	*Bolivianos.*		*Kilos.*	*Bolivianos.*
January	763,755	34,487.73	August	521,407	23,545.16
February	710,648	32,091.44	September	315,627	14,259.04
March	751,035	33,900.23	October	613,646	28,154.13
April	385,030	17,376.83	November	407,187	18,755.71
May	830,265	37,491.34	December	334,985	15,438.94
June	427,324	19,304.80			
July	627,065	28,307.81	Total	6,687,974	303,115.16

COINAGE IN 1906.

According to statistics published by the National Mint of Bolivia,
there were coined during the year 1906, 316,003 *bolivianos,* the distribution of which, by months, is as follows:

	Bolivianos.		Bolivianos.
January	35,871	August	1,087
February	32,610	September	35,784
March	860	October	23,914
April	16,305	November	27,175
May	43,480	December	19,566
June	30,436		
July	48,915	Total	316,003

MINERAL EXPORTS OF POTOSI, 1906.

Total shipments of tin reported for the year 1906 by the Potosi custom-house amount to 132,509.43 quintals, on which duties to the value of 356,276.32 *bolivianos* were collected. Duties on silver exported, amounted to 1,606.03 *bolivianos*, making the total receipts from mineral exports 357,882.35 *bolivianos*.

CONSULAR REPORTS ON TRADE WITH THE UNITED STATES.

The merchandise exported from New York and San Francisco, consigned to Bolivia, during the months of November and December, 1906, according to Bolivian consular reports, was as follows:

	November.		December.	
	Packages.	Value.	Packages.	Value.
New York via—				
Mollendo	10,580	$61,483.31	12,105	$76,595.99
Antofagasta	2,853	32,431.14	4,272	37,847.22
Para	709	6,124.82	116	1,206.20
Rosario	134	5,676.77	115	3,510.00
Arica	81	765.13	79	1,004.00
Montevideo			49	635.75
Total	14,357	106,481.17	16,736	120,799.16
San Francisco via—				
Mollendo		78,513.26		16,332.73
Antofagasta		11,459.13		9,235.55
Arica		85.00		
Total		90,057.39		25,568.28

Exports from the United States to Bolivia in 1906.

	New York.		San Francisco.	
	Packages.	Value.	Packages.	Value.
January	2,700	$48,036.50	21,668	$12,038.23
February	2,695	26,610.40	18,312	23,290.29
March	2,339	27,789.42	30,225	18,312.07
April	3,601	48,709.39		30,000.00
May	7,009	63,754.68		8,125.00
June	1,896	27,769.91		9,204.83
July	4,251	56,540.14		17,228.47
August	5,005	57,574.06		11,535.17
September	6,628	87,413.80		67,072.11
October	17,329	116,141.27		36,552.17
November	14,357	106,481.17		90,057.39
December	16,736	120,799.16		25,568.28
Total	84,346	787,619.90	70,205	348,984.01

EW YORK AND SAN FRANCISCO, JANUARY
AND FEBRUARY, 1907.

tatement showing the shipments of merchandise
ew York and San Francisco to Bolivia during the
u. a u y and February, 1907, as reported by the Bolivian
at the ports mentioned:

Month.	Via—	Value.
....	Port of New York: Mollendo....................	$286,194.40
	Antofagasta	29,458.72
	Para....................	7,601.73
	Rosario....................	5,727.96
	Manaos....................	1,887.85
	Montevideo	503.42
	Total	331,364.08
February	Mollendo....................	209,313.16
	Antofagasta	27,411.49
	Rosario....................	4,815.00
	Para....................	4,158.38
	Arica....................	508.86
	Puerto Juarez....................	522.00
	Montevideo	135.36
	Total	246,924.25
....	Port of San Francisco: Mollendo....................	53,268.22
	Antofagasta	243.86
	Total	53,512.08
February	Mollendo....................	24,310.07
	Antofagasta	1,781.75
	Total	26,091.82
	Total, port of New York....................	578,288.33
	Total, port of San Francisco....................	79,603.90
	Grand total....................	657,892.23

SALE OF THE GUAQUE-LA PAZ RAILWAY.

The United States Minister to Bolivia has informed the Department of State that an executive decree has been issued, by authority
of the Bolivian Congress, for the sale of the Guaque-La Paz Railroad.
The proceeds of the sale are to constitute a fund to guarantee interest
on the cost of the railway that the Executive may contract for from
Potosi to Sucre, or from Macha, Bartolo, or other point that the technical studies indicate as the most practical for the starting and route
for the railway to said capital.

RAILROAD LINE TO TARIJA.

On November 28, 1906, the National Congress of the Republic of
Bolivia passed a law authorizing the Executive to order the construction, as soon as possible, of a railroad to the city of Tarija, starting

from the Central Northern Argentine Railway, or from the Oran Line. For this purpose the Executive is further authorized to make the necessary combinations, and to raise loans, subject to the approval of the Legislative Power. The receipts from the national custom-house of Tarija, and other national revenues, if necessary, shall be applied exclusively to the amortization of the loans thus raised.

CUSTOMS REVENUES, SECOND QUARTER OF 1906.

Official statistics published in December, 1906, show that the custom-houses of the Republic of Bolivia collected during the second quarter of 1906 the amount of 1,053,628.39 *bolivianos*. This sum is thus distributed among the various custom-houses:

	Bolivianos.
Antofagasta	582, 114. 22
Arica	14, 705. 65
La Paz and Pelechuco	395, 444. 23
Tarija	15, 653. 05
Uyuni	25, 866. 60
Puerto Suarez	2, 898. 73
Oruro	16, 945. 91
Total	1, 053, 628. 39

BRAZIL.

CUSTOMS REVENUES IN 1906.

The customs revenue of the Republic of Brazil for the calendar year 1906 was 247,413,386 *milreis*, of which 84,960,996$ was gold and 162,452,391$ paper. During the year 1905, the revenue was 239,689,-327$, of which 53,775,501$ was gold and 185,913,826$ paper. The aggregate increase in 1906 was, therefore, 7,724,059$. The revenue from exports from the Acre district, was 9,177,815$, as against 8,177,975$ in 1905, an increase in favor of 1906 of 999,840$.

COFFEE SHIPMENTS IN 1906-7.

For the twelve months, January–December, 1906, total entries of coffee at the Brazilian ports of Rio de Janeiro, Santos, Victoria, Bahia, and other smaller ports, aggregated 15,347,660 bags of 60 kilograms. The shipments from the same ports amounted to 13,965,800 bags, as against 10,820,604 bags recorded for the preceding year. These clearances to foreign ports in 1906 were valued at 418,399,742 *milreis* or £27,615,883, the values for 1905 being 324,678,601 *milreis* or £21,420,330.

izil for the first half of the last five crop years show

alf year.	Total crop.			Half year.	Total crop.
Bags.	*Bags.*			*Bags.*	*Bags.*
), 637,309	16, 276, 465	1904–5		8, 135, 155	10, 507, 089
5, 532, 076	12, 993, 559	1905–6		8, 238, 498	11, 035, 378
5, 615, 500	11, 193, 505	1906–7		12, 550, 837	

average 1   of the half yearly report to the total crop for the
cover(1. 1.8 per cent, and on this basis the total output
year 1906–7 would be 17,480,274 bags.
nenting   he above figures the "Brazilian Review" states
the figures 1   of   le current crop year are so
and so surprising as to disturb   ldgment, it being evident
le yield will surpass all previous re rds. . ,
lary, 1907, shipments from the ports of Santos and Rio de
aggregated 1,740,203 bags; as compared with 421,016 in the
nonth of 1906.

PORTS OF HIDES FROM RIO GRANDE DO SUL, 1906.

and dry hides shipped from Rio Grande do Sul during 1906
L   ered 861,120, the United States taking 28,000 of the last-named
class.   In 1905 the total number shipped was 723,235, of which dry
hides for the United States amounted to 14,513.

RUBBER EXPORTS IN 1906.

Figures covering the shipments of Para rubber from Manaos, and
in transit from Peru and Bolivia through Para, for the year 1906
aggregate 34,767,755 kilograms, of which 16,192,304 went to the
United States and 18,575,451 kilograms were consigned to European
parts.

Manaos shipments figure for 17,150,410 kilograms, consigned in the
following manner: New York, 7,162,444 kilograms; Liverpool,
6,118,460; Havre and Hamburg, 3,869,506.

The export of rubber from the port of Para for the month of
December, 1906, were: To the United States, 3,454,582 kilograms;
to Europe, 1,080,530 kilograms.   The exports to Europe during the
six months July to December, 1906, amounted to 4,616,823 kilograms.   The quantity exported during the year was: To the United
States, 9,430,234 kilograms; to Europe, 8,204,158 kilograms.

CREATION OF A GEOLOGICAL AND MINERALOGICAL BUREAU.

In connection with the Department of Ways and Public Works
recently established by the Brazilian Government, a Bureau of
Geological and Mineralogical Research has been created by an Execu-
tive decree of January 10, 1907.

The principal objects of the new Bureau are as follows:

To make a scientific study of the geology and mineral resources of the Republic, with special attention to surface and subsoil waters. Such information·is to serve as a basis for the organization of communications and other public works, particularly for counteracting the effects of drought. A laboratory and museum are to be maintained in connection with the actual surveys; maps, diagrams, and statistics are to be prepared and issued for the benefit of governmental offices and duly authorized persons, and, in fact, every possible measure is to be taken for the systematic propaganda of the mineral wealth of the country.

EXPLOITATION OF MANGANESE DEPOSITS.

The "Brazilian Review" for February 5, 1907, reports the organization at Ougree, Belgium, of a Belgian-Brazilian company having for its object the extraction of manganese and iron and the treatment of the same, and, in general, the development of all business appertaining to the manganese and iron industries and of their derivatives. A capital of 4,700,000 *francs* has been divided into 4,700 shares of 1,000 *francs* each, of which 3,000 shares and 200,000 *francs* in bullion have been remitted for the purchase of manganese concessions in Brazil.

The company, whose duration is fixed at thirty years, also proposes to exploit such other products of the soils as may be included in their concessions.

IMMIGRATION AT RIO DE JANEIRO, 1906.

The number of immigrants entering the port of Rio de Janeiro during 1906, exclusive of persons brought into the country through the agents of the government of the State of São Paulo, was 27,147. Their nationalities were as follows: Portuguese, 16,795; Italians, 4,318; Spaniards, 4,074; Turks, 1,110; Germans, 225; Russians, 199; Belgians, 15; Argentines, 14; Swiss, 10; other, 80. Of the total, 23,344 were males and 3,803 females.

ERECTION OF A SMOKELESS-POWDER FACTORY.

The Minister of War of the Brazilian Government has approved the contract made with a United States firm for the establishment of a smokeless-powder factory at Piquete.

CUSTOMS REVENUE AT RIO DE JANEIRO, DECEMBER, 1906.

The total customs revenue at the port of Rio de Janeiro for the month of December, 1906, amounted to 8,813,608$812, of which 3,488,240$050 was gold and 5,325,368$762 paper. These figures show a decline of 842,112$845 as compared with December, 1905, when receipts aggregated 9,655,721$157.

DIAMOND MINES OF SALOBRO.

' published by the Department of Agriculture of
t   of July, contains a description and brief history of
nond ı   s of Salobro, in the State of Bahia.
ıse mines were discovered in 1881. A professor from Canna-
s, while engaged in prospecting at a place called Salobro, found
ı gravel of a small tributary of the Pardo River a number of
ımonds of rare color and of the first water.
ı news of the discovery soon spread, and in a short time a mining
ın of several thousand inhabitants sprang into existence.

The mines are situated at a distance of about 70 kilometers from
Cannavieiras and 6 or 7 kilometers from ᴄacaranda, the nearest point
on the Pardo River. This region differs greatly from. the other
diamond-bearing regions of Brazil, because of its close proximity.to
the sea (about 60 kilometers distant), and the absence of hills, which
are generally associated with the occurrence of diamonds. The
region is traversed by both the Pardo and Jequitinhonha rivers. The
geological formation of this region consists of several strata of sand-
stone and clay schists, and having intercalated between them a thick
layer of conglomerate consisting of different kinds of granitic and
gneissic rocks. This series is several hundred meters thick, with a
marked incline to the east. In the bed of the Salobro River and its
tributaries this conglomerate outcrops at different points, and the
mines are in the immediate vicinity of these outcrops.

Thus, according to the author, there seems to be no doubt that the
diamond is directly connected with this conglomerate. It is probable
that this formation extends over a large area of this zone and there
is strong ground for the belief that at many, if not at all, its points
of outcrop, it will be found diamond-bearing, as at Salobro. This last-
mentioned district, however, still offers a large field for mining operations and is undoubtedly destined to a brilliant future.

The production of the mines of Salobro from 1881 to 1890 has been
estimated at about 54,000 *oitavas* (193,644 grams).[a] Since 1886 there
has been a decline in the production, due to several causes, the main
one being the difficulties encountered in working the deposits. The
entire region is covered with a thick forest growth and it is necessary
first to clear the land and then dig down a distance of about 2 meters
before the diamond-bearing gravel is reached.

While the diamonds from the Salobro mines have neither the bril-
liance nor the hardiness of those from the Diamantinas mines they are
nevertheless considered very fine and obtain a good price.

Two or three French and English companies have been working
these mines for a number of years at a good profit.

---

[a] Oitava equivalent to 3.586 grams.

MINING NOTES.

"The São José Diamonds and Carbons Limited" is the title of a company that has been organized for the purpose of working the diamond alluvial deposits in the valley of Rio São Jose, in the municipal district of Lencoes, Bahia. The "cascalho" in which the diamonds are found is from 20 to 40 centimeters thick, and is from 8 to 10 meters below the surface.

By a decree of January 3, 1907, the President of Brazil authorized the Datas Diamond and Gold Company to operate in Brazil. This company was incorporated at Wilmington, Delaware, July, 1906. It has a capital of $100,000.

A commission of mining experts, of which Dr. ORVILLE DERBY is chief engineer, has been appointed to study and report on the manganese and gold deposits situated between Miguel Burnier and Sabara and other points in the vicinity of the Central Railway.

FLOATING EXHIBIT OF JAPANESE PRODUCTS.

The Japanese Steam Navigation Company, "Tokio Kisen Kwaiska," has inaugurated a service for the exhibition of Japanese products in the principal ports of the South American Republics. The exhibits will be made in vessels especially built for this purpose. The company is to receive aid from the Japanese Government for this service.

INDUSTRIAL USE OF PERINI FIBER.

In order to promote the industrial use of the new Perini fiber, the government of the State of Rio de Janeiro offers an annual subsidy of 30,000 milreis, for a period of four years, to anyone who shall establish a paper or rope factory in this State and shall use this fiber in the manufacture of its products.

CHILE.

CUSTOMS RECEIPTS IN 1906.

Customs receipts at the various ports of the Republic of Chile for the calendar year 1906 aggregated $103,507,555.71 (Chilean currency), as compared with $91,321,900.98 in 1905, an increase during the twelve months of $12,185,654.73.

Export duties in 1906 figure for $60,153,596.41, as against $57,127,954 in 1905, while import dues for the two periods are reported at $41,443,545.48 and $32,265,679.22, respectively.

ipts throughout the two years were as follows:

Month.	1905.	1906.
....	$8,004,494.00	$9,191,353.00
....	7,200,859.00	6,136,190.00
....	7,060,441.61	8,618,323.59
....	5,909,326.14	7,018,808.22
....	5,577,290.47	7,668,383.48
....	6,030,051.13	7,022,879.33
....	7,717,045.77	8,928,493.70
....	8,714,596.00	6,758,133.65
....	8,153,669.71	7,077,541.81
....	10,426,198.50	11,960,011.57
....	9,193,431.50	10,764,975.30
....	6,023,311.17	12,099,435.32

al receipts at ᵇaraiso, the principal port of entry, during ᵃber, 19C e ᵇ 008,039.33, as compared with $1,712,997.36 5, while to ᵉᵗᵃ, through which the bulk of shipments ᵃⁿᵈ are m d with $1,004,740.96 in 1906, as against '40.24 in 1ᵗ he month of December.

GET FOR 1907.

aᵣ ᵃˢ approved by the National Congress, proᵃ, during the year 1907, of 134,830,532.36 papeᵣ ᵣᵥᵥ .83, gold, distributed among the various branches of public service, as follows:

	Paper.	Gold.
	Pesos.	Pesos.
Ministry of the Interior........	20,605,528.65	5,820,961.33
Ministry of Foreign Affairs, Worship, and Colonization..............	3,277,367.42	937,397.09
Ministry of Justice........	6,911,202.93	....
Ministry of Instruction........	16,086.55	161,666.46
Ministry of the Treasury........	10,829,096.92	28,349,166.23
Ministry of War........	16,192,780.47	99,733.33
Ministry of the Navy........	10,460,781.41	6,315,731.27
Ministry of Industry and Public Works........	9,532,988.10	117,433.32
Ministry of Communications (railroads)...	40,934,273.91	16,984,671.00

COPPER PRODUCTION IN 1906.

Chilean copper exports during 1906 aggregated 28,000 tons, a diminution of 1,600 tons being noted as compared with the preceding year.

THE WHEAT AND BARLEY CROPS IN 1906.

According to the Bureau of Agricultural Statistics of Chile the wheat and barley crops gathered in 1906 were as follows, compared with those of 1904 and 1905:

[Metric quintals. 1 quintal=220.46 pounds.]

	1904.	1905.	1906.
Wheat........	5,454,361.70	4,002,393.15	4,293,497.99
Barley........	1,134,048.41	1,060,541.64	978,664.32

STATUS OF THE NITRATE INDUSTRY.

The fiscal delegate charged by the Chilean Government with an investigation of the nitrate beds of the Republic reports that the State still possesses some 2,000,000 hectares (hectare, 2.47 acres) of nitrate grounds. "It may be safely estimated," he says, "that 1,000,000 hectares of ground contain 10,000,000,000 Spanish quintals (Castile and Chile quintal, 101.41 pounds) of nitrate. So that if the yearly exportation of nitrate be put at the absurdly high figure of 80,000,000 quintals—it has never yet reached 40,000,000—there is sufficient nitrate in the supposed 1,000,000 hectares for one hundred an seventy-five years. If to these 1,000,000 hectares, belonging to the State," says the delegate, "there be added the grounds belonging to private persons, the number of years of duration would be three or four times greater."

STATUS OF CHILEAN BANKS.

Deposits in Chilean banks on September 30, 1906, aggregated 376,997,423 *pesos*, or $113,992,268 United States gold, on a capital and reserve fund of 170,421,121 *pesos*, or $51,126,336 United States gold.

At that time the cash on hand amounted to 75,300,956 *pesos*, or $22,590,287 United States gold, of which 5,096,138 *pesos*, or $1,528,841 United States gold, was in gold or silver. The loans amounted to 422,266,645 *pesos*, or $126,679,994 United States gold.

Of the 25 banks in Chile 13 are either located in Valparaiso or have important branches there. Several of them pay from 3 to 6 per cent interest on deposits, as follows: At sight, 3 per cent; on current account, 3 per cent; two or three months, 4 per cent; four months, 5 per cent, and six months, or thirty days' notice after three months, 6 per cent. Interest settlements are made the last of June and December.

The bank loan rate is from 9 to 12 per cent and in a few extreme cases it was even found to be higher. The usual rate for individual loans is from 10 to 14 per cent and in some cases 3 per cent per month is paid. There is a good opening here for money, and it will pay investigating.

RAILROAD FROM OSORNO TO PUERTO MONTT.

On December 12, 1906, a law was promulgated authorizing the President of the Republic to advertise for bids for the construction of a railroad line from Osorno to Puerto Montt, the cost of which must exceed 12,000,000 *pesos*, national gold currency of 18 pennies. The bids must be presented within two months from the publication in the "*Diario Oficial*" of the law referred to.

MOVEMENT OF VALPARAISO, 1906

ent of Valparaiso, Chile, during the year 1906 was
s, ... ng to official statistics:
:ries: ...mers, 1,030, with 1,728,381 tons; sailing vessels, 181,
251,482 tons; total, 1,211 vessels, with 1,979,863 tons.

arances: Steamers, 1,048, with 1,706,681 tons; sailing vessels,
vith 259,488 tons; total, 1,220 vessels, with 1,966,169 tons.

CUSTOMS TARIFF.

The "*Feuille officielle suisse*" of commerce publishes the following
notice:

The Chilean customs tariff in effect since 1903 will also be applied
without modification during the year 1907.

SCARCITY OF LABOR.

United States Consul ALFRED A. WINSLOW, of Valparaiso, reports:
"There is a great lack of laborers both in the city and on the farm,
and because of this workmen demand very high wages and are so
independent that in many cases they are of little service. There are
no labor organizations, but workmen are so scarce that anyone who
wishes to work can demand and obtain almost any price. Common
laborers have been paid 8 and 10 pesos per day, which means from
$2.40 to $3 United States gold. The usual wage is from 5 to 6 pesos
($1.50 to $1.80) per day and skilled labor in proportion. Even at
these prices it is impossible to get near enough men.

"One firm in this city with very large interests in this country has
arranged to bring over 2,000 coolies on contract, and a corporation is
considering the matter of bringing in a like number of workmen from
the Argentine Republic. It is conservatively estimated that 10,000
men could be given employment for the next two or three years in
rebuilding the city of Valparaiso. Where these men are to come from
is a mystery. The Government realizes this, and is considering the
question of immigration. It is proposed to grant liberal land concessions to actual settlers. There is still much valuable land not
occupied, and the agricultural products are needed for the country to
supply food for workmen in the cities and in the mines at a reasonable
price. As it is, living is very expensive here."

COLOMBIA.

RAILWAYS IN THE REPUBLIC.

According to figures published in the *"Diario Oficial,"* of Colombia, for August 29, 1906, the railways of the Republic, and their respective length, were as follows:

Kilometers.

Antioquia Railway	58
Bolivar Railway	28
Cartagena Railway	105
Cauca Railway	37
Cúcuta Railway	70
La Dorada Railway	33
Girardot Railway	78
Northern Railway	50
Sabana Railway	40
Santa Marta Railway	67
Southern Railway	29
Tolima Railway	22
Total	**617**

DENATURED ALCOHOL CONCESSIONS.

Under date of August 27 and October 22, 1906, the President of the Republic of Colombia approved two concessions for the exclusive privilege of distilling and selling denatured alcohol in the country, to be used in the production of light, power, heat, or other industrial methods.

The first concession is to CHARLES J. EDER and is limited to the Department of Cauca, and the other to LEO J. KOPP and others for the Department of Cundinamarca and the Federal District.

Both grants are for five years, dating from January 1, 1907, and limit the selling price of the article to 18 *centavos* gold per liter.

CUBA.

CUSTOMS REVENUES, CALENDAR YEAR 1906.

A statement recently published by the Department of Finance of the Cuban Republic shows that the various custom-houses collected, during the calendar year 1906, a total revenue of $25,090,084.05, as compared with $25,258,005.44 in 1905, a decrease of $69,910.19.

ile shows the different amounts collected during
year in reference: ·

,...	$2, 395, 296. 25	August....................	$2, 159, 197. 54
....	2, 240, 081. 70	September................	1, 501, 388. 95
,...	2, 462, 204. 54	October....................	1, 720, 145. 71
....	2, 006, 211. 58	November...............	2, 009, 085. 76
,...	2, 419, 977. 97	December...............	2, 008, 613. 87
... .	1, 951, 724. 31		
....	2, 126, 155. 87	Total...............	25, 090, 084. 05

THE TOBACCO MARKET IN 1906.,

view of the tobacco market of Cuba for the calendar year 1906
٨s ٠t from January 1 to December 31 Cuba exported to the
ٮ ٲte ٳ ٳrmany, Canada,. the Argentine Republic, France,
ٮ, ٲ hile, Holland, and Australia 277,426 bales of
tobacc nose total weight was 12,636,836 kilograms, as against
ٳ ٳle ٳg a total weight of 14,776,139 kilograms in 1905.
ٳٳٳٳ٠٠٠ٳ tor ٳr of 89,661 bales with a weight of 2,139,303
is tl ٳ s٠٠٠./n.

king Cuban tobacco, but failing to import it
., Honduras, Gibraltar, the Canaries, Dutch
-- ٳٳٳ British Antilles, and French Africa. For these
markets 706 bales, weighing 35,385 kilograms, were reported in 1905.
New markets in 1906 were: The Dominican Republic, China, and
Brazil, taking 111 bales with an aggregate weight of 4,875 kilograms.

Cigars were exported to the number of 256,738,029 in 1906 to
England, the United States, Germany, France, Canada, Belgium,
British Africa, Hungary, and Italy, as against 227,028,621 in the preceding year, thus showing an increase of 29,709,508 cigars. The
countries failing to import Cuban cigars during 1906 were the Ber-
mudas, the Azores, French Oceania, Korea, and Portuguese Africa,
whose purchases in 1905 had amounted to 107,871 cigars. New
markets credited with 329,930 cigars of Cuban origin during the year
were: European Turkey, Sweden, Trinidad, British Columbia, various regions of Asia, China, Russia, British India, Asiatic Turkey,
German Africa, Norway, Ecuador, and Spanish Africa.

Shipments of cigarettes aggregated 15,643,275 packs, as compared
with 3,814,199 packs in 1905. Favoring import duties in Colombia—
a great market for cigarettes—had important bearing on the trade.
Exportation to Mexico, Chile, the Dutch Antilles, Canaries, Venezuela, British Antilles, United States, Peru, England, Costa Rica,
Panama, and Gibraltar also increased notably. New markets were
found in Trinidad, Egypt, countries of Asia, Australia, Japan,
British Indies, and Guayaquil, sales aggregating 36,360 packs, while
Auckland, Roumania, British Africa, and Denmark made no pur-
٢٠ ٠٠ though in 1905 they had received 50,822 packs.

Cut tobacco was exported to the United States, Colombia, France, England, Chile, and French Africa to the extent of 169,260 kilograms, as compared with 119,337 kilograms in 1905, a gain of 49,923 kilograms being thus shown. Among new importers were: Bolivia, Panama, various sections of Africa, Mexico, Salvador, and Ecuador, with a total of 3,070 packs.

The production of all the tobacco districts of the Republic was 286,288 bales in 1906, against 473,617 bales in 1905, a decrease of 187,239 bales, of which, 130,315 were for Vuelta Abajo, 13,818 for Semi Vuelta, 32,147 for Villas or Remedios, and 15,016 for Partidos.

The production of the following districts had an increase in 1906: Santiago de Cuba, 2,755 bales; Puerto Príncipe, 961, and Matanzas, 251.

The value of the tobacco exported during 1906 was as follows:

Leaf tobacco, 277,426 bales, at $70 each	$19,419,820.00
Cigars, 256,738,029, at $65 per 1,000	16,688,571.88
Cigarettes, 15,643,275 packages, at $25 per 1,000	391,081.87
Cut tobacco, 169,260 kilograms, at $1.20 each	203,112.00
Total	36,702,585.75

The value of the tobacco exports in the previous year was $29,415,961.16, the increase in 1906 being, therefore, $7,286,624.59.

The value of the manufactured tobacco consumed during the year under review was $12,334,154.72. Adding this sum to the value of exported tobacco, the amount of $49,036,740.47 is obtained, which, compared with the value of tobacco exported and consumed during 1905, amounting to $42,275,113.42, gives an increase in 1906 of $6,761,627.05.

Estimating the value of tobacco, cigars, cigarettes and cut tobacco consumed and given away in factories, or which passengers carry away with them or which producers and members of their families consume in the plantations, and adding it to the amount of $49,036,740.47, the production, industry, and trade of tobacco in the Republic would have a total value of over $51,000,000.

REPORT ON YELLOW FEVER.

A report issued January 17, 1907, by Dr. E. B. BARNET, chief of the local health board of Havana, states that there were 112 cases of yellow fever in Cuba for the year 1906, of which 33 were fatal. In Havana there were 71 cases and 12 deaths, and in the provinces 41 cases and 21 deaths, showing a mortality rate of 17 per cent for Havana and 51 per cent for the remainder of the island. There were in Havana from January 1 to October 1 21 cases of yellow fever, of which 6 died, a rate of 29 per cent, and from October 1 to December 31 there were 50 cases and 6 deaths, a rate of only 12 per cent.

DOMINICAN REPUBLIC.

FINANCIAL STATUS OF THE REPUBLIC, 1906.

President CACERES, in his annual message to the National Congress for the year 1907, says:

"The receipts for the last year to December 31 have amounted to more than $3,800,000.

"The sums deposited in the National City Bank of New York by virtue of the decree of March 31, 1905, amount, with interest up to December 31, 1906, to $2,317,607.40.

"Cash on hand in the office of the Auditor of the Treasury and in other public offices amounts to more than $280,000.

"It is the first time that the annual balance of the public treasury of the country is closed with a sum equal to that estimated in the Report of the Minister of Finance, a sure guaranty of the immutability of the peace and of the credit that we have attained as a base for the future economic redemption of the Republic, finding therein the means to free it from debt, and to undertake all the improvements which must give an impulse to its productive capacity, on which depends the sure advancement of its prosperity and settled policy.

"The exports for the year represent in value $6,543,872 and the imports $4,281.337."

FOREIGN COMMERCE FOR THE YEAR 1906.

According to figures issued by the Controller and Receiver-General of the Customs Service of the Dominican Republic, the year 1906 was one of advancing prosperity to the country as a whole, as attested by the fact that its industrial and commercial activities, during that period, surpassed those of any previous year in the history of the country. Both its production and consumption were increased to a marked degree.

The general application of the revenue laws furnished the Government with the necessary funds to make many needed improvements, especially in the building of roads. Substantial private enterprises, particularly in agriculture, were generally successful and enlarged in scope. Notable progress was made in every branch of commerce toward orderly and natural business conditions. More people were employed or engaged in profitable labor than ever before and the resulting increased demand for supplies stimulated both the internal trade and foreign importations.

The total value of the foreign trade of the Republic during the calendar year 1906, not including imports and exports of gold, silver, and paper currency, was $10,601,815, an increase of approximately one million over 1905, which exhibited a greater volume of business *than any other* year up to that time.

The value of merchandise purchased abroad and imported was $4,065,437, against local products exported to the value of $6,536,378, leaving a balance of trade in favor of the Republic of $2,470,941.

The credits resulting from this accumulating balance enabled the Government to deposit abroad during the year, without the exportation of currency, $1,476,116 to apply on the public debt. In addition to this the volume of American currency circulating in the country was increased by the net importation of $208,406, leaving still an apparent foreign credit in favor of the Republic, as a result of the year's transaction, of $786,424.

All of the principal local products were increased both in quantities and values over those of preceding years except sugar, which, although the output exceeded that of 1905 by 7,781 tons, suffered a considerable decline in value.

Thus while the exportations of 1905, aggregating 47,309 tons, yielded an average net price of $3.10 per hundredweight, or a total of $3,292,470, the 55,090 tons shipped during 1906 netted but $1.93 per hundredweight, or $2,392,406 for the entire exportation, showing a decrease in value for the larger quantity exported during the latter year of $900,064. This served to offset the gains in values of other products shipped and reduced the total value of exports to $6,543,872, as against $6,896,098 exported during 1905, a net decrease of $352,226. And as almost the entire sugar exportation was, as usual, to the United States, the principal decrease in export values, amounting to $734,987, is shown in the products shipped to that country, while it continued to receive by far the greatest quantity of products exported and more than half of the entire values produced.

The production of cacao showed a continued steady increase and a gain for the year of approximately 3,000,000 pounds, the total exportations reaching 14,295 tons. The general prices obtained for this product have also been good, netting an average of slightly more than $7 per hundredweight and advancing until at the close of the year it was in good demand for export at $11 per hundredweight, placing it, for the time, at the head of the list as the country's product of greatest value. And, in view of the peculiar suitability of the climate and soil to the production of the highest grades of this article, which has as yet received comparatively little attention, as well as the growing demand for it as a staple both in Europe and America, it seems destined to take its place permanently as the most valuable and profitable product of the Republic.

The production of tobacco leaf, bananas, coffee, hides and skins, wax and dye woods was also considerably increased and the prices received generally higher than those of 1905, as shown by the annexed comparative tables.

But the most striking feature of the year's trade is the marked increase in imports, which were considerably larger than those of any preceding year, consisting almost exclusively of staple merchandise and food supplies, and indicating a greatly increased purchasing power on the part of the general public.

The total value of imports, exclusive of currency, was $4,281,337, against $2,736,828 during 1905, showing a net increase of $1,328,609, or 49 per cent, over the comparative period, which was the record year of the Republic in general commerce and imports up to that time.

Of this *increase* in trade the United States received $685,938, consisting of larger purchases in that country of general merchandise, but especially of cotton goods, which were more than doubled. Increased purchases were made in Germany to the value of $382,676, considerably more than half of which represented increased rice importation. Great Britain enjoyed an increased trade to the extent of $160,143, consisting almost entirely of larger sales of cotton goods. The importations from France were increased 25 per cent, or $59,196, and those from Spain $50,315, doubling the trade with the latter country. Other changes in trade of less importance took place, as shown by the annexed tables.

The total values of the commercial transactions of the Republic with foreign countries during 1906 were distributed as follows:

	Values.	Percentage of the whole.
United States	$6,252,707	57.8
Germany	2,923,942	27.0
France	771,916	7.2
United Kingdom	572,714	5.2
Spain	93,732	.9
Italy	50,842	.5
Cuba	47,751	.4
Porto Rico	32,986	.3
All other countries	78,669	.7
Total	10,825,209	100.0

Trade in ordinary textiles, miscellaneous hardware, foodstuffs, and other similar merchandise of first necessity made up the greater part of the importations of the year.

The aggregate declared values of cotton goods, manufactures of iron and steel, rice, wheat flour, provisions, including meat and dairy products, oils, manufactures of vegetable fibers, fish and fish products, and articles of wood and leather manufacture, of relative importance in the order enumerated, constitute 74 per cent of the total value of imported merchandise, the remaining 26 per cent being represented by that of miscellaneous articles of every nature.

Imports under the leading class, cotton goods, were invoiced at $1,136,358, as against $552,774 for 1905, the increase having been due principally to larger receipts from the United States and Great Britain.

In manufactures of iron and steel, the United States, while furnishing more than half of the total values imported, showed a decrease in its shipments from those of 1905, although the purchases in Great Britain, Germany, and France were increased in considerable proportions. The total value of imports under this heading was $474,200, of which $238,561 came from the United States, $86,789 from Great Britain, $57,161 from Germany, and $34,736 from France.

Rice was the principle food product imported during 1906, and the amount received during the year—18,874,116 pounds, invoiced at $370,668—shows an increase over importations of the same commodity during the previous twelve months of 8,857,000 pounds. Of this increase, practically all came from Germany, which furnished 15,390,595 pounds of the total importation, while the remainder was divided principally between the United States and Great Britain.

The United States supplied substantially all of the flour imported, consisting of 58,622 barrels, valued at $250,390, as against 41,172 barrels imported during 1905 at a cost of $208,968.

The same country led in furnishing the meat and dairy products, the value of these purchased from that source having been $117,546, or $35,512 in excess of that of the previous year. The values of provisions from Germany, France, and Porto Rico of this class also show an increase, the total value of meat and dairy products having been $226,855, as against $138,195 during the comparative period.

The United States was, as usual, the principal source of the mineral oil supply, which reached a value of $202,378, or 38 per cent over the invoice value of receipts therefrom during 1905. Spain's trade in olive oil increased from $2,013 to $7,738, while the value of the oil trade with the United Kingdom, France, Italy, and "other countries" was a little more than that of the previous year.

Manufactures of vegetable fibers purchased by the Republic from other countries consisted mostly of bagging, in which to export products, and cordage, invoiced at $149,027, against $85,721 for 1905. Formerly the United Kingdom controlled the largest portion of this trade, but during 1906 the value of fiber manufactures received from that country were slightly decreased, as well as that from France, while the values of such importations from the United States, Germany, and Spain were more than doubled for each country.

Among the imported foodstuffs consumed were comparatively large quantities of fish and fish products, the bulk of these being salt and dried fish from the United States, the value of which was $126,299, or $16,844 more than for 1905. The contributions of Germany and

France to this class were also increased, but the importations from those countries are as yet relatively unimportant.

The aggregate value of manufactures of leather received from all sources was $118,579, as against $72,964 during 1905, the increase being due to larger receipts from nearly all countries furnishing these goods, but more especially to those from the United States, the value of which was $101,833, an increase of 68 per cent over that of the previous year.

The United States also furnished most of the wood manufactures, as was the case in 1905, the shipments therefrom being valued at $95,780, out of a total of $110,925. The remainder was supplied principally by Germany. The manufactures included under this heading consist mostly of barrel heads and staves and box shooks, used for export packing.

The remainder of the merchandise imported during 1906 was of a miscellaneous nature and minor importance, distributed throughout some thirty different classes of articles, as may be seen by reference to the accompanying schedules. The largest proportion of this came from the United States, although Germany, as usual, led in the values of malt liquors, woolen goods, and chinaware supplied; Spain in dried fruits and nuts; Italy in hats and caps, and France in wines and liquors.

The principal products sold to other countries were, in the order of their relative value, sugar, cacao, tobacco, bananas, coffee, hides and skins, wax, tropical hard woods, and raw materials for drugs and dyes.

The 123,401,271 pounds of sugar exported, with an invoice value of $2,392,406, was nearly all destined to the United States, the total shipments to that country aggregating 117,491,975 pounds, declared at $2,291,527. Of the remainder, 1,754,175 pounds were sent to the United Kingdom, 801,876 pounds to Germany, 304,605 to France, and smaller quantities, aggregating 348,640 pounds, to various other countries.

Cacao beans, valued at $2,262,912, representing shipments of 32,022,460 pounds, were exported, of which 17,502,961 pounds went to Germany, 9,821,512 to the United States, and the remainder to France.

The total quantity of tobacco exported amounted to 14,965,799 pounds, with a valuation of $837,057, all of which was divided between the three countries named, as follows: Germany, 8,946,053 pounds, declared at $528,897; the United States, 3,746,162 pounds, at $189,279, and France, 2,273,584 pounds, invoiced at $118,881.

Practically all of the 669,100 bunches of bananas shipped and invoiced at $334,005 went to the United States.

There were 2,916,727 pounds of coffee exported, with a declared value of $220,051. Of this, 1,562,193 pounds, invoiced at $98,997, went to Germany; 569,215 pounds, at $50,030, to France; 564,291 pounds, at $49,556, to the United States, and 86,608 pounds, at $7,957, to Cuba; the remainder, in all, 134,442 pounds, valued at $13,511, having been distributed in small lots among all "other countries."

Hides of goats and cattle declared at $150,440 were sold abroad, principally in the United States, Germany, and France, shipments thereto having been declared at $78,335, $60,849, and $7,521, respectively.

The value of the 514,825 pounds of wax shipped was $125,599. Of this product, 281,288 pounds went to Germany, 154,233 pounds to the United States, 65,584 pounds to France, and all "other countries," 13,720 pounds.

Shipments of tropical hard woods were made to the United States aggregating in value $27,773, while smaller consignments were generally distributed among the United Kingdom, France, and "other countries," making a total invoice value of woods exported $72,859.

The remainder of the total declared value of exports represented shipments of cattle, $12,359; materials for the manufacture of drugs and dyes, $56,061; vegetable fibers, $20,630; honey $15,985, and of cocoanuts, $5,814, as well as of many other minor tropical products itemized in the annexed tables.

The maritime movement by means of which the year's foreign commerce was effected were represented by 1,538 entrances and clearances at the eight seacoast entry ports of the Republic of vessels having an aggregate registered tonnage of 1,656,002 tons.

Import cargoes, valued at $2,445,429, or 57 per cent of the total value of imports, were brought in American bottoms; values to the extent of $1,308,338, or 32 per cent, were carried in German; $272,111 in French; $95,680 in British, and $55,421 in Norwegian vessels. Cuban, Dutch, and Dominican ships brought cargoes to the value of $29,628, $13,316, and $11,246, respectively, while the remainder of the receipts were distributed among vessels of various other nationalities.

Export cargoes to the value of $1,102,519, or 32 per cent of the total value of exports, were transported by vessels sailing under the German flag. The export values carried in American vessels amounted to $2,091,480, also approximately 32 per cent of the whole. Norwegian steamers received cargoes aggregating $1,412,623 in value, or 21 per cent, while French ships obtained freight invoiced at $579,723; British, $311,931; Dutch, $23,496, the remainder of the exports having been shipped in Dominican vessels.

In the coastwise trade 6,657 entrances and clearances were recorded at the various entry ports of the Republic, representing a total tonnage movement in local traffic carried on by Dominican vessels thereat of 122,219 tons.

Seventy-five per cent of this trade was carried on by small sailing vessels and the remainder by steamers of less than 60 tons burden.

This branch of commerce has increased in activity to meet the advanced requirements of the country.

Imports into the Republic of Santo Domingo during the calendar year 1906, showing the values and principal countries of origin, in comparison with those of the calendar year 1905.

Articles, by classes.	Jan. 1, 1905, to Dec. 31, 1905.		Jan. 1, 1906, to Dec. 31, 1906.	
	Quantity.	Value.	Quantity.	Value.
Agricultural implements:				
United States		$15,394		$15,450
United Kingdom		2,427		4,068
Germany		19,230		24,519
France		321		60
Cuba				3
Porto Rico		97		344
Other countries		1,362		327
Total		38,831		44,771
Animals:				
Horses and mules—	*Number.*		*Number.*	
United States	52	7,529	3	800
Cuba	20	400		
Porto Rico	27	1,344	12	1,305
Total	99	9,273	15	2,105
Cattle—				
United States	2	365		
Porto Rico	134	4,075		
Total	136	4,440		
All other—				
United States		96		82
Germany		32		
Porto Rico				819
Total		128		901
Books, maps, and other printed matter:				
United States		2,563		5,664
United Kingdom		5		83
Germany		1,542		2,512
France		1,445		4,791
Italy		30		182
Spain		463		697
Cuba		388		1,013
Porto Rico				119
Other countries				3,500
Total		6,436		18,561
Breadstuffs (wheat flour):	*Barrels.*		*Barrels.*	
United States	41,172	208,968	58,622	250,390
Germany				1
Porto Rico	10	50		
Other countries	231	805	20	90
Total	41,413	209,823	58,642	250,481
All other—				
United States		20,508		19,438
United Kingdom		70		103
Germany		74		153
France		433		946
Italy		820		710
Spain		305		157
Porto Rico		4		6
Other countries		12		58
Total		22,226		21,571

Imports into the Republic of Santo Domingo during the calendar year 1906, showing the values and principal countries of origin, in comparison with those of the calendar year 1905—Continued.

Articles, by classes.	Jan. 1, 1905, to Dec. 31, 1905.		Jan. 1, 1906, to Dec. 31, 1906.	
	Quantity.	Value.	Quantity.	Value.
Chemicals, drugs, and dyes:				
United States	....	$39,022	....	$46,331
United Kingdom	....	4,460	....	5,962
Germany	....	2,969	....	3,218
France	....	10,856	....	7,083
Italy	....	375	....	84
Spain	....	85	....	206
Cuba	....	113	....	
Porto Rico	....	74	....	108
Other countries	....	275	....	40
Total	....	58,260	....	65,152
Coal:	*Tons.*		*Tons.*	
United States	4,280	12,803	5,742	21,701
United Kingdom	2,336	8,582	805	3,191
Porto Rico	2	20	....	
Other countries	425	2,485	50	375
Total	7,043	23,890	6,596	25,267
Cotton, manufactures of:				
United States	....	218,100	....	596,347
United Kingdom	....	190,074	....	339,811
Germany	....	69,450	....	97,109
France	....	36,347	....	45,361
Spain	....	20,102	....	31,782
Italy	....	14,591	....	13,482
Belgium	....	90	....	
Cuba	....		....	45
Porto Rico	....	1,038	....	7,052
Other countries	....	2,982	....	4,479
Total	....	552,774	....	1,126,388
Earthen, stone, and china ware:				
United States	....	589	....	802
United Kingdom	....	1,915	....	2,185
Germany	....	13,144	....	19,838
France	....	1,001	....	611
Italy	....		....	82
Spain	....	14	....	26
Belgium	....	73	....	
Porto Rico	....		....	7
Other countries	....		....	12
Total	....	16,736	....	23,533
Fibers, vegetable, manufactures of:				
United States	....	29,770	....	60,310
United Kingdom	....	32,409	....	31,000
Germany	....	12,943	....	54,325
France	....	6,466	....	726
Italy	....	471	....	464
Spain	....	766	....	2,040
Other countries	....	2,896	....	162
Total	....	85,721	....	149,027
Fish, preserved, and fish products:				
United States	....	109,455	....	126,299
United Kingdom	....	10	....	
Germany	....	933	....	2,129
France	....	1,590	....	1,072
Italy	....	522	....	18
Spain	....	1,264	....	1,712
Porto Rico	....	140	....	92
Other countries	....	220	....	155
Total	....	114,134	....	131,477
Fruits and nuts:				
United States	....	3,240	....	5,685
United Kingdom	....	15	....	23
Germany	....	99	....	337
France	....	1,464	....	1,797
Italy	....	108	....	630

Imports into the Republic of Santo Domingo during the calendar year 1906, showing the values and principal countries of origin, etc.—Continued.

Articles by classes.	Jan. 1, 1905, to Dec. 31, 1905.		Jan. 1, 1906, to Dec. 31, 1906.	
	Quantity.	Value.	Quantity.	Value.
Fruits and nuts—Continued.				
Spain		$1,487		$6,582
Cuba		105		240
Porto Rico		49		6
Other countries				
Total		6,567		15,290
Glass and glassware:				
United States		5,605		13,473
United Kingdom		209		105
Germany		3,099		8,399
France		441		1,022
Italy		176		166
Spain		3		515
Belgium		7		
Porto Rico		23		54
Other countries				88
Total		9,563		23,822
Gold and silver currency:				
United States		350,435		215,900
Grease and grease scraps for soap stock:	*Pounds.*		*Pounds.*	
United States	972,205	37,856	503,213	26,875
Germany	22,926	503		
France	357	8		
Spain	1,130	150		
Porto Rico	238,637	5,005	31,883	918
Total	1,235,255	43,522	535,096	27,793
Gums and resins:				
United States		13,583		17,149
United Kingdom		60		415
Germany		7		1,319
France		12		21
Spain				56
Total		13,662		18,960
Hats and caps:				
United States		9,070		2,162
United Kingdom		553		137
Germany		2,292		1,199
France		4,626		7,444
Italy		47,364		15,767
Spain		144		212
Porto Rico		652		311
Other countries		829		
Total		65,530		27,232
Iron and steel, manufactures of:				
United States		287,381		283,561
United Kingdom		63,568		86,789
Germany		37,022		57,161
France		10,438		34,736
Italy		709		7
Spain		262		928
Belgium		3,752		3,834
Cuba		93		45
Porto Rico		581		7,067
Other countries		353		72
Total		404,159		474,200
Jewelry, including watches and clocks:				
United States		1,532		795
United Kingdom		111		15
Germany		846		1,883
France		3,588		5,553
Italy		1,141		7,193
Spain				10
Porto Rico		81		
Total		7,299		15,449

Imports into the Republic of Santo Domingo during the calendar year 1906, showing the values and principal countries of origin, in comparison with those of the calendar year 1905—Continued.

Articles, by classes.	Jan. 1, 1905, to Dec. 31, 1905.		Jan. 1, 1906, to Dec. 31, 1906.	
	Quantity.	Value.	Quantity.	Value.
Leather, and manufactures of:				
United States		$59,455		$101,833
United Kingdom		3,860		4,034
Germany		3,188		6,015
France		4,968		4,243
Italy				175
Spain		1,312		2,210
Porto Rico		89		69
Other countries		72		
Total		72,964		118,579
Malt liquors; beer in bottles:	*Dozen.*		*Dozen.*	
United States	4,175	5,240	9,252	11,006
United Kingdom	450	600	912	1,458
Germany	20,061	30,572	28,987	45,172
France	810	2,601	667	945
Spain	12	15		
Other countries	55	34	281	430
Total	25,563	39,152	40,099	59,011
Metals, and manufactures of (not elsewhere specified):				
United States		7,939		13,745
United Kingdom		1,016		1,204
Germany		2,348		3,904
France		244		727
Italy		40		3
Spain		126		29
Cuba		85		
Porto Rico		97		
Other countries		81		3
Total		11,976		119,615
Oils:				
United States		147,309		202,378
United Kingdom		1,057		1,506
Germany		1,609		1,379
France		1,653		1,854
Italy		465		819
Spain		2,013		7,738
Belgium		22		
Porto Rico		19		1,302
Other countries		1,787		483
Total		155,934		217,459
Paints, pigments, and colors:				
United States		9,117		9,182
United Kingdom		2,577		3,431
Germany		2,507		4,174
France		41		126
Spain		82		
Other countries		41		
Total		14,365		16,913
Paper and manufactures of:				
United States		13,170		13,165
United Kingdom		299		53
Germany		7,945		18,670
France		3,053		1,007
Italy		760		982
Spain		2,837		2,145
Porto Rico				9
Cuba		182		
Other countries		3		176
Total		28,249		36,207
Perfumery and cosmetics:				
United States		3,078		1,560
United Kingdom		200		6
Germany		1,062		671
France		10,822		8,495
Italy		221		105
Spain		130		112

Imports into the Republic of Santo Domingo during the calendar year 1906, showing the values and principal countries of origin, etc.—Continued.

Articles, by classes.	Jan. 1, 1905, to Dec. 31, 1905.		Jan. 1, 1905, to Dec. 31, 1905.	
	Quantity.	Value.	Quantity.	Value.
Perfumery and cosmetics—Continued.				
Porto Rico				$185
Other countries		$19		
Total		15,552		11,134
Provisions, comprising meat and dairy products:				
United States		72,834		137,546
United Kingdom		1,216		539
Germany		56,101		89,245
France		4,870		9,108
Italy		653		931
Spain		526		610
Cuba		1,241		969
Porto Rico		648		7,549
Other countries		106		358
Total		138,195		226,855
Rice:	*Pounds.*		*Pounds.*	
United States	1,552,319	31,613	1,533,985	32,527
United Kingdom	2,203,707	35,554	1,310,836	23,000
Germany	5,913,424	127,704	15,290,595	302,616
France	271,517	4,868	462,801	8,249
Italy	1,100	29		
Spain	4,032	124	10,149	305
Other countries	90,913	1,657	165,750	3,881
Total	10,017,012	201,329	18,874,116	370,668
Rubber, manufactures of:				
United States		4,286		5,130
United Kingdom		822		219
Germany		1,300		764
France		466		251
Spain		12		
Total		6,886		6,364
Soap:				
United States	707,286	22,382	741,757	25,872
United Kingdom	652	27	60	2
Germany	82	16	228	9
France	801	116	1,822	119
Italy			430	17
Cuba	308	64		
Porto Rico	200	8	30	13
Other countries	9,280	309	10,640	336
Total	718,609	22,922	754,967	26,368
Sugar and confectionery:				
United States		22,265		48,614
United Kingdom		411		517
Germany		1,549		2,016
France		1,457		3,378
Italy		246		509
Spain		669		1,924
Total		26,597		56,958
Tobacco, manufactured:				
United States		368		133
Germany		61		
Cuba		2,365		1,489
Other countries				30
Total		2,794		1,652
Umbrellas and canes:				
United States		960		156
United Kingdom		1,396		1,788
Germany		1,319		2,986
France		1,730		3,188
Italy		8,017		3,213
Spain		799		297
Other countries		38		254
Total		14,229		11,882

Imports into the Republic of Santo Domingo during the calendar year 1906, showing the values and principal countries of origin, in comparison with those of the calendar year 1905—Continued.

Articles, by classes.	Jan. 1, 1905, to Dec. 31, 1905.		Jan. 1, 1906, to Dec. 31, 1906.	
	Quantity.	Value.	Quantity.	Value.
Vegetables:				
United States....	....	$16,620	....	$20,963
United Kingdom....	....	271	....	833
Germany....	....	382	....	590
France./....	....	2,149	....	3,981
Italy....	....	302	....	378
Spain....	....	3,654	....	14,004
Cuba....	....	4,937	....	4,284
Porto Rico....	....	889	....	4,505
Other countries....	....	85	....	
Total....	....	29,349	....	49,438
Vehicles:				
United States....	....	14,914	....	9,188
Germany....	....		....	169
France....	....		....	10
Porto Rico....	....	50	....	
Other countries....	....	400	....	120
Total....	....	15,364	....	9,487
Wines, liquors, and distilled spirits:				
United States....	....	2,693	....	1,429
United Kingdom....	....	325	....	29
Germany....	....	2,988	....	6,367
France....	....	10,290	....	17,370
Italy....	....	2,142	....	3,271
Spain....	....	4,384	....	14,972
Cuba....	....		....	115
Porto Rico....	....		....	38
Other countries....	....	68	....	416
Total....	....	22,900	....	44,017
Wood, and manufactures of:				
United States....	....	87,355	....	96,780
United Kingdom....	....	3,072	....	2,601
Germany....	....	4,712	....	10,440
France....	....	598	....	1,413
Italy....	....	130	....	103
Spain....	....		....	147
Cuba....	....	135	....	302
Porto Rico....	....		....	124
Other countries....	....	170	....	15
Total....	....	96,182	....	110,925
Wool, and manufactures of:				
United States....	....	969	....	949
United Kingdom....	....	5,105	....	7,390
Germany....	....	6,461	....	14,643
France....	....	2,667	....	7,452
Italy....	....	549	....	96
Spain....	....	535	....	486
Belgium....	....	50	....	
Other countries....	....	17	....	
Total....	....	16,412	....	31,516
All other articles not elsewhere specified:				
United States....	....	155,568	....	181,143
United Kingdom....	....	4,568	....	3,810
Germany....	....	25,394	....	40,193
France....	....	18,655	....	25,461
Italy....	....	982	....	1,495
Spain....	....	1,144	....	3,710
Belgium....	....	410	....	1,355
Cuba....	....	56	....	1,997
Porto Rico....	....	1,139	....	874
Other countries....	....	4,627	....	8,400
Total....	....	112,513	....	166,438

lic of Santo Domingo during the calendar year 1906, showing the
nd principal countries of origin, etc.—Continued.

	Jan. 1, 1905, to Dec. 31, 1905.		Jan. 1, 1906, to Dec. 31, 1906.	
	Quantity.	Value.	Quantity.	Value.
]LATION.				
	....	$1,061,020	....	
	....	366,684	....	
	....	441,450	....	
	....	150,304	....	
	....	80,873	....	
	....	43,417	....	
n........	....	4,443	....	
	....	10,167	....	
Rico......	....	16,123	....	
.or countries....	....	21,782	....	
Total..................	....	3,096,263	....	4,281,337

nited States includes gold and silver currency amount-
ear 1906.

Domingo, during the calendar year 1906, showing the
lestination, in comparison with those of the calendar

Article.	Jan. 1, 1905, to Dec. 31, 1905.		Jan. 1, 1906, to Dec. 31, 1906.	
	Quantity.	Value.	Quantity.	Value.
...mals, live stock:				
Cuba..........	....	$41,937	....	$12,604
Other countries...............	....	160	....	255
Total........................	....	42,097	....	12,859
Bananas:	Bunches.		Bunches.	
United States............	514,000	257,000	608,000	334,000
Other countries...........	33	17	100	5
Total.....................	514,033	257,017	668,100	334,005
Cacao:	Pounds.		Pounds.	
United States............	7,816,441	587,812	9,821,512	699,462
United Kingdom...........	197,720	19,343	....	
Germany.................	11,840,612	859,653	17,502,961	1,220,353
France...................	8,981,591	745,065	4,696,927	343,033
Other countries............			1,000	64
Total.....................	28,836,364	2,211,873	32,022,460	2,262,912
Chemicals and dyes, raw materials for:				
United States............	....	2,784	....	6,005
United Kingdom...........	....	5,416	....	4,875
Germany.................	....	18,061	....	43,430
France...................	....	222	....	
Cuba....................	....	228	....	15
Other countries...........	....	5,093	....	1,736
Total.....................	....	31,798	....	56,061
Cocoanuts:	Pounds.			
United States............	15,984	133	37,040	266
Germany.................	360,392	3,400	577,598	5,500
Other countries...........			5,219	48
Total.....................	376,376	3,533	619,857	5,814
Coffee:	Pounds.			
United States............	458,591	39,992	564,291	49,556
Germany.................	770,691	47,856	1,562,193	98,997
France...................	681,958	51,151	569,213	50,030
Cuba....................	102,587	10,434	86,608	7,957
Other countries...........	135,361	7,530	134,422	13,511
Total.....................	2,149,188	156,963	2,916,727	220,051

Exports from the Republic of Santo Domingo, during the calendar year 1906, showing the values and principal countries of destination, etc.—Continued.

Article.	Jan. 1, 1905, to Dec. 31, 1905.		Jan. 1, 1906, to Dec. 31, 1906.	
	Quantity.	Value.	Quantity.	Value.
Copra:	*Pounds.*		*Pounds.*	
United States			4,252	$127
Germany	128,595	$2,024	74,693	1,896
Total	128,595	2,024	78,945	2,023
Gums and resins:				
United States	14,967	2,249	6,751	758
United Kingdom	2,555	50		
France			1,289	90
Other countries	15,237	903	11,831	1,058
Total	32,759	3,202	19,871	1,906
Hides and skins:				
Goatskins—				
United States	168,594	46,149	181,655	52,874
Germany			27,546	2,471
France			2,546	351
Other countries	4,852	981	22,837	2,826
Total	173,446	47,130	234,584	58,522
Hides of cattle—				
United States	167,567	17,565	261,347	25,461
Germany	248,056	24,278	555,157	58,378
France	167,247	21,591	63,006	7,170
Other countries	5,111	511	9,104	909
Total	587,981	63,945	888,614	91,918
Honey:	*Gallons.*		*Gallons.*	
United States	111,018	9,786	39,611	10,474
United Kingdom	680	68		
Germany	1,030	213	9,357	2,995
France	945	160	5,000	1,724
Other countries	9,330	1,759	4,100	792
Total	123,003	11,956	58,068	15,985
Sisal and other vegetable fibers:	*Pounds.*		*Pounds.*	
United States	77,515	9,393	69,522	5,857
Germany			2,000	274
Cuba	62,722	11,509	75,125	14,142
France	5,950	425	980	107
Other countries	33,000	450	1,200	250
Total	179,187	21,777	148,797	20,630
Sugar (raw):				
United States	104,612,601	3,243,437	117,491,975	2,291,527
United Kingdom	1,186,700	43,896	1,754,175	31,978
Germany	127,199	4,221	801,876	58,963
France			304,605	4,669
Other countries	45,900	926	348,640	5,249
Total	105,972,400	3,292,470	123,481,271	2,392,406
Tobacco, leaf:				
United States	3,719,458	143,951	3,746,162	189,279
Germany	5,890,665	244,147	8,946,053	526,507
France	1,900,639	92,389	2,273,584	118,881
Total	11,510,762	480,487	14,965,799	837,057
Wax:				
United States	111,462	25,164	154,233	41,714
United Kingdom	14,406	1,055		
Germany	182,783	42,614	281,288	67,601
France	152,550	23,850	65,584	13,403
Other countries	9,721	1,986	13,720	2,791
Total	470,922	94,669	514,825	125,509
Wood:				
Mahogany—	*Feet.*		*Feet.*	
United States	186,519	6,936	22,719	1,070
United Kingdom	202,031	7,085	56,534	2,926
Germany	27,728	1,609	19,893	990
France	58,111	4,653	10,733	453
Other countries	62,739	1,951	45,968	1,398
Total	536,628	22,235	157,947	6,847

Exports from the Republic of Santo Domingo during the calendar year 1906, showing the values of and principal countries of destination, etc.—Continued.

Articles.	Jan. 1, 1905, to Dec. 31, 1905.		Jan. 1, 1906, to Dec. 31, 1906.	
	Quantity.	Value.	Quantity.	Value.
Wood—Continued.				
Lignum-vitæ—	Feet.		Feet.	
United States	1,942	$51,674	811	$16,655
United Kingdom	270	2,564	231	2,980
Germany	89	815	175	1,893
France	115	2,108	70	5,494
Other countries	604	12,821	403	6,051
Total	3,020	69,982	1,690	33,073
All other woods—				
United States		18,522		10,048
United Kingdom		3,279		3,118
Germany		2,897		5,958
France		10,537		8,338
Cuba		100		
Other countries		7,602		5,477
Total		42,937		32,939
All other exports:				
United States		21,754		14,141
United Kingdom		59		
Germany		9,218		1,110
France		934		8,673
Cuba		2,859		2,531
Other countries		5,179		6,800
Total		40,003		33,255
RECAPITULATION.				
United States		4,484,271		3,749,284
United Kingdom		82,800		45,887
Germany		1,261,006		2,099,816
France		953,065		562,416
Cuba		67,067		37,249
Other countries		47,889		49,220
Total		6,896,098		6,543,872

NOTE.—Under the heading "All other exports," during the year 1906 is included $7,493.73 worth of gold and silver currency exported to the United States.

Origin and value of imports and nationality of vessels carrying same during the calendar year 1906.

Country.	Dominican.	American.	British.	Dutch.	French.	German.	Norwegian.	Cuban.	All other.	Total.
United States		$2,377,050	$74,143		$124,337	$371,286	$52,230			$2,503,423
United Kingdom		6,476	21,537			816,331	3,191			526,827
Germany		414			7,381					824,126
France		1,299			127,643	80,558				200,500
Spain	$2,917	15,661			1,096	22,637		$1,350	$50,071	93,732
Italy		44,479			2,140	4,223				50,842
Belgium						5,189				5,189
Cuba	30							10,472		10,502
Porto Rico	4,089			$1,529	9,514			17,804		32,936
All other countries	4,210	50		11,787		8,114			99	24,260
Total	11,246	2,445,429	95,680	13,316	272,111	1,308,338	55,421	29,626	50,170	4,281,337

Destination and value of exports and nationality of vessels carrying same during the calendar year 1906.

Country.	Dominican.	American.	British.	Dutch.	French.	German.	Norwegian.	Cuban.	All other.	Total.
United States......		$2,053,268	$310,501	$2,730			$1,382,735			$3,749,284
United Kingdom...	$500	7,569		600	$8,015	$24,748	4,455			45,887
Germany..........		24,601			4,049	2,071,166				2,099,816
France...........		6,042			554,326	2,047				562,415
Cuba.............	10,387			1,430			25,433			37,250
Porto Rico.......	360				5,613					5,973
All other countries.	10,754			20,116	7,720	4,558			$99	43,247
Total........	22,001	2,091,480	311,931	23,496	579,723	2,102,519	1,412,623	......	99	6,543,872

Number and tonnage of vessels engaged in the foreign trade, by ports, during the calendar year 1906.

Ports.	Entrances.				Clearances.			
	Sailing.		Steam.		Sailing.		Steam.	
	Number.	Tonnage.	Number.	Tonnage.	Number.	Tonnage.	Number.	Tonnage.
Azua...............	10	2,641	42	51,602	10	2,641	42	51,602
Barahona..........	10	1,691	23	27,290	10	1,691	23	27,290
Macoris...........	82	5,388	96	117,975	82	5,388	96	117,975
Monte Cristi......	15	1,021	45	76,381	15	1,021	45	76,381
Puerto Plata......	31	3,953	140	205,185	31	3,953	140	205,185
Samaná...........	5	611	53	95,831	5	611	53	95,831
Sanchez..........	6	660	68	120,083	6	660	68	120,083
Santo Domingo....	35	5,692	108	111,397	35	5,692	108	111,397
Total.........	194	21,657	575	806,344	194	21,657	575	806,344

Number and tonnage of vessels engaged in the coastwise trade, by ports, during the calendar year 1906.

Ports.	Entrances.				Clearances.			
	Sailing.		Steam.		Sailing.		Steam.	
	Number.	Tonnage.	Number.	Tonnage.	Number.	Tonnage.	Number.	Tonnage.
Azua...............	169	4,833	57	2,406	157	3,564	58	2,448
Barahona..........	157	2,111	25	1,374	155	1,845	25	1,374
Macoris...........	551	10,611	181	5,066	591	10,476	180	5,050
Monte Cristi......	93	1,081	4	172	105	1,143	4	172
Puerto Plata......	397	4,228	8	307	478	4,522	9	350
Samaná...........	245	3,391	7	301	294	3,468	6	215
Sanchez..........	364	4,379	8	344	365	4,602	9	387
Santo Domingo....	759	14,411	204	6,226	782	14,858	210	6,504
Total.........	2,735	45,045	494	16,196	2,927	44,478	501	16,500

CUSTOMS RECEIPTS, 1906.

The following report of the administration of customs affairs of Santo Domingo has been received in the Bureau of Insular Affairs of the War Department. This brings the statement up to December 31, 1906. Because of the fact that the present administration of customs affairs of Santo Domingo was begun on April 1, 1905, it is impossible to make a comparison with previous calendar years, but

made with the year ending March 31, 1906, and
months ending December 31, 1905. The compar-
owing results:

s for the calendar year 1906, $3,192,000
g December 31, 1905, $1,650,655.62; for the twelve
rch 31, 1906, $2,502,154.31. Paid to the Domin-
for twelve months ending December 31, 1906,
the Dominican Government for the nine months
31, 1906, $770,641.38; paid to the Dominican Gov-
for the t elve months ending March 31, 1906, $1,056,368.53.

ECUADOR.

RECEIPTS, 1906.

year 1906, the following figures are
s of the Government of Ecuador:

REVENUE.

	Sucres.
es, with surtaxes	6,275,000
es, with surtaxes	2,423,000
est, fines, and extraordinary receipts	75,000
Light-house dues	10,000
Tax on removal of goods	240,000
Tax on freights and passengers	20,000
Tax on life insurance	2,000
Tax on fire insurance	12,000
Tax on issues of banks	6,000
Tax on profits	15,000
Pawnbroking establishments	30,000
Product of consulates	420,000
Salt revenue	450,000
Aguardiente revenue	620,000
Matches	300,000
Powder and dynamite revenue	80,000
Cigarette paper	60,000
General contribution and tax on personal estate	360,000
Stamps and stamped paper	260,000
Postal and telegraphic stamps	110,000
Taxes assigned to the Board of Health	25,000
Octrois	200,000
Various	195,000
Total	12,188,000

EXPENDITURE.

Legislative power	83,490
Executive power	47,872
Council of State	1,800
Foreign affairs	337,560

	Sucres.
Public instruction.............	1, 584, 490
Justice, etc...................	353, 568
Interior.......................	1, 057, 284
Charity........................	407, 480
Finance and public credit......	4, 592, 606
Public works...................	1, 180, 200
War and marine.................	2, 650, 948
Post-office and telegraphs.....	529, 840
Sundries.......................	110, 042
Extraordinary expenditure......	300, 000
Total......................	13, 237, 180

In making the estimate of expenditure for 1907 the sum is fixed at 13,000,000 *sucres*.

FOREIGN COMMERCE, 1903-5.

According to statistics recently received, the total foreign trade of the Republic of Ecuador, during the year 1905, was represented by imports valued at 15,733,891 *sucres* and exports, 18,565,668 *sucres*.

In the preceding year, imports figured for 15,338,170 *sucres*, as compared with 11,069,814 *sucres* in 1903, and exports for 23,284,193 *sucres*, as against 18,626,354 in 1903.

The increased imports in 1904 as compared with 1903 are stated to be mainly due to the importation of large quantities of cotton, woolen, and silk goods, machinery, hardware, shoes, foodstuffs, china and glass, clothing and candles.

PHYSICAL ASPECTS AND COMMERCIAL POSSIBILITIES.

The following paper, containing an interesting account of life and economic conditions in Ecuador, was delivered before the National Geographic Society, at Washington, on November 30, 1906, by Hon. JOSEPH W. J. LEE, then United States Minister to Ecuador. It is reproduced in the BULLETIN, in both Spanish and English, at the request of Señor Don LUIS FELIPE CARBO, Envoy Extraordinary and Minister Plenipotentiary to the United States from Ecuador:

"The Republic of Ecuador lies at the northwestern corner of the South American continent, between Colombia and Peru.

"As its name implies, it is situated upon the Equator.

"Ecuador possesses an area of 429,000 square miles, including the Galapagos Archipelago. It is nearly twice the size of France, and as large as Texas, New York, Pennsylvania, and Nebraska combined. The population is 1,500,000. Although the country is comprised between 1° north and 4° south latitude, almost every variation of climate is obtainable, from the torrid lands of the coast to the chilly plains at an elevation of 12,000 feet at the foot of the snow-clad peaks of the Andes.

"Both the eastern and western ranges of the Andes traverse the Republic. Between these ranges lie extensive high valleys, yielding the products of the Temperate Zone. To the west of the Cordillera stretch the low tropical lands on the Pacific, and to the east the country gradually descends to the low Amazon Valley and the frontiers of Brazil.

"Guayaquil, the principal seaport of the Republic, is situated on the River Guayas, the most important stream in South America emptying into the Pacific, about 60 miles above its mouth. It has a population of 50,000. It is the emporium of Ecuador. All imports and exports pass through Guayaquil. The houses are built of wood owing to the lack of other material. They are constructed in the southern style, with balconies protruding over the sidewalks and resting upon wooden pillars, thus forming piazzas, which afford protection against sun and rain. As fires under the circumstances are particularly dangerous, Guayaquil has perhaps a more extensive fire department than any city of its size, and ample reservoirs of water on a hill behind the town. It is improbable that Guayaquil will ever again be visited by such disastrous conflagrations as in the past.

"The hospitals of Guayaquil are as complete as any in South America. The great new general hospital with its modern appliances compares most favorably with Ancon Hospital at Panama. Although the Cathedral, the churches, the great municipal buildings, and theaters are built of wood, they are imposing and are decorated in perfect taste. The Union Club of Guayaquil is, with the exception of the Hongkong Club, the best I have ever seen in the Tropics. Under the bright light of the moon these buildings appear to be constructed of rare marbles. The public squares are beautifully kept and filled with rare specimens of the rich vegetation of Ecuador.

"The harbor is always busy with shipping. Two steamers each week sail for Panama and two arrive from the Isthmus.. Fleets of tugboats, lighters, canoes, and balsas cover the water. The canoes, laden deep with fruit and country produce, come down river on the swift tide and return on the turn of the tide with scarcely the necessity to move a paddle. The balsas are used to a great extent. They are a maritime contrivance invented by the ancient Peruvians and made of five, seven, and nine trunks of an exceedingly light tree called balsa, in sizes as required. Large balsas go with safety to sea as far as Paita in Peru. The logs are lashed together with vines and are fastened so firmly that they can ride almost any sea. The whole machine adapts itself to the waves and no water rises between the logs. Houses are generally built upon them and form homes for a literally 'floating population.'

"The dry season lasts from June to December. The weather is very pleasant and the nights and mornings are often cold. The mean temperature of Guayaquil is about 78°.

"On clear summer days Chimborazo may be seen, rising 21,000 feet above the long chain of the Cordillera, covered with ice and snow, whose dazzling whiteness is intersected by black lines, formed by the sharp edges of frightful rocks, upon which the snow can not gather.

"Guayquil exports one-third of the world's supply of cocoa. It is raised along the River Guayas and its tributaries and is the principal staple of Guayaquil. Ivory nuts, from which bone buttons of commerce are made, are exported in enormous quantities. Panama hats, so called because they are distributed to the United States and Europe by way of the Isthmus of Panama, are manufactured in the Province of Manabi. The lowlands of the coast also produce cinchona bark, from which we obtain quinine (Countess of Chinchon), rice, coffee, sugar, tobacco, rubber, copal gum, vanilla, sarsaparilla, salt, petroleum, and cotton. It is interesting to note that during our civil war England was supplied with cotton from Ecuador. Of course every variety of tropical fruit is produced and fine timber for house and shipbuilding.

"The daily papers of Guayaquil, the ' Nacion,' ' Telegráfo,' ' Grito del Pueblo,' and ' Tiempo,' are well patronized, well published, and of much influence. A satisfactory daily telegraphic service is maintained with the rest of the world. It is to be regretted that our newspapers do not devote an equivalent amount of space to events in South America.

"Across the river from Guayaquil is Duran, the terminus of the Guayaquil and Quito Railroad, a company incorporated under the laws of the State of New Jersey. This railroad, built by American engineers, is completed for a distance of 140 miles and rises to a height of 12,000 feet under the shadow of Chimborazo. The roadbed is leveled into the city of Quito, 260 miles from the coast, and track is being laid at the present time at the rate of a mile per day.

"Leaving Duran at 7 a. m., the train proceeds over flat and gently rising country to the foothills of the Andes. In the level country are the great sugar estates, stretching for miles on either side of the track and equipped with lines of miniature railway for hauling cane, and with large sugar factories. Leaving the plains, the ascent is gradual through dense tropical forests plentifully watered by streams and cascades which can supply unlimited water power.

"At an elevation of from 4,000 to 5,000 feet there rises a mass of colossal, bald, rounded hills almost shutting out the sunlight, and it appears impossible that the railroad can proceed farther. The mountains seem an unsurmountable wall 9,000 or 10,000 feet high. But American engineers have found a way and have accomplished one of the most difficult feats known in railroad construction. A sugar-loaf peak stands out in front of the towering hills. Cut zigzag in the sheer face of the granite, a switchback of four levels has solved the problem of rising to 9,000 feet. This level attained, the line advances through volcanic country seamed with ravines and surrounded by sulphur-covered hills until a similar cul-de-sac is reached. This, in turn, is surmounted by means of a switchback loop with a grade of 7 per cent and we reach the pass of Palmyra, on the roof of the world at 12,000 feet. Wild wastes of shifting sand surround the track. Stiff grass, like rushes on the seashore, is the only vegetation. Fossil shells are found here, and the general appearance of the country is that of the seacoast.

"From this point there is a gradual descent until the present end of the road is reached at Cajabamba, 11,000 feet above the level of the sea and at the foot of mighty Chimborazo. At this place there are some of the few existing remains of buildings erected by the ancient Incas. They are built of great masses of stone, fastened together with cement. The stone can be broken, but it is impossible to make any impression upon the cement. Strange to relate, I found living here a former Rough Rider whom I had known in Cuba. He is engaged in the purchase of hides for the New York market.

"It is necessary to spend the night in this village and to set out for Quito early next morning by automobile or diligence. I have always found it more satisfactory to travel by diligence. In this way baggage can accompany the traveler, and a long wait at the journey's end is avoided.

"The wagons are drawn by teams of five or six mules. Sixty mules, with changes, are used to reach Quito. Two drivers occupy the box seat, one furnished with a long-handled whip for the leaders, the other with a short whip for the wheelers. The animals are urged on with whistles and shouts without intermission. It is the most thrilling, exciting, and hair-raising locomotion I know. The mules are kept at full gallop down the long slopes of the Andes. It is often as much as they can do to keep ahead of the coach. However, I have never heard of an accident. The drivers are men long trained in the business and do not know what fear is.

"Formerly, before the days of the railroad and carriage road, it took ten days, on mule back, from Guayaquil to Quito. Now by rail and coach the time is three days. I have made the journey with automobile and train in twenty hours.

"The country is on a colossal scale. It seems a land made for giants. High in the air the tops of the rounded hills are one patchwork of cultivated fields. At the foot of the hills lie smiling green valleys. There is abundant water and the dry places are well irrigated. Along the roadside water is carried for long distances by means of tunnels cut in the volcanic soil, with arched openings at certain intervals. The scarlet wool ponchos worn by the Indian laborers make it possible to pick them out, in the marvelous, clear atmosphere, on the hills and in the valleys at surprising distances.

"It is necessary to spend the night at the city of Ambato (8,000 feet). The town lies in a deep cauldron. The climate is delightful. Here apples, plums, and peaches flourish as well as the vegetables and cereals of the Temperate Zone. Ambato has several cotton mills producing the coarse white cotton cloth universally used by the Indians for shirts and wide, baggy trousers. Water power is abundant and the mills pay well. Ambato is also headquarters for the trade from the Oriente, or the lowlands toward the east stretching to the valley of the Amazon. Line for a railroad to tap this district, rich in rubber and gold, has been surveyed and work will begin soon.

"Leaving Ambato in the early morning, we can see one of the most glorious sights in the world—sunrise on Chimborazo. The majestic giant stands out against the dawn, his mantle of snow washed with crimson and gold. The road winds over gigantic hills, around precipices, and down steep descents until we reach the great plain of Latacunga stretching to the foot of dread Cotopaxi. The fields as well as the broad roads crossing the wide valleys are inclosed by adobe walls surmounted by the broad-leaved American aloe. The aloe, sometimes called the century plant, is one of the most useful and important plants in the country. It is an erroneous idea that it flowers only once in a hundred years. The Indians thatch their huts with its leaves. The leaves, when tapped, yield sirup; they can also be used as soap and the spines as pins. The fiber is woven into sacks and from it are made the coarse sandals worn by the common people. The tall flower stalks are used for beams and ladders. The flowers, boiled and soaked in vinegar, make an agreeable pickle. The cochineal is found in abundance upon the leaves of the plentiful cactus. Its name is derived from its supposed resemblance to a little pig (cochinillo). It is used by the Indians for dyeing ponchos and shawls.

"As we approach the city of Latacunga the country becomes more sterile. The plain is covered with volcanic sand and pumice stone, indicating the neighborhood of Cotopaxi. The houses and churches are built of pumice stone thrown out by the mountain, which in the past has caused much destruction to this part of the country. There is a legend that the great earthquake of 1698 was predicted by a priest seven years before it took place. The Carmelite nuns of Latacunga believed in the prophecy and slept in tents in their garden for seven years. The convent fell but the nuns were saved. Latacunga is the starting point of the most romantic gold legend in Ecuador. The lost treasure of the Incas is supposed to be hidden in the neighboring hills. One Valverde, a Spaniard, was informed of the secret by his sweetheart, an Incas maiden, and he became suddenly very rich. He left a description and guide of the hiding place. This document was preserved in the archives of the city until it was stolen. Many expeditions have been made in search of the lost treasure, but without success. From this city we journey over rolling country to the foot of Cotopaxi (18,890 feet). The mountain presents a beautiful appearance, clad in its robe of snow. Its shape is that of a regular truncated cone with a flat summit. The crater is uninterrupted in activity, and volumes of white and gray smoke continually issue from it. Generally, the smoke assumes the form of an enormous tree with trunk and branches, until a current of air tears it away from the mountain and it floats away a cloud, while by night the smoke forms a pillar of fire. Near the snow line is a huge mass of rock called the Inca's head. According to legend, this was the original summit of the mountain, torn off and hurled down by an eruption on the day the Inca Atahuallpa was executed by the Viceroy of Peru.

"After crossing the high pass of Chasqui, above the clouds, the road lies through rich pastures and fertile fields. The green pastures of the beautiful valley of Machachi spread around us, dotted with countless herds of cattle and horses. Beautiful villas set in gardens and groups of trees nestle at the foot of great hills.

"Houses are closer together as we near Quito, the capital. Numberless Indians, men and women, carrying burdens or driving laden mules, form an endless procession. For the entire length of the great Ecuadorian highway human beings are always in sight.

"The Indians carry everything on their backs. The load is supported by a strap passing across the forehead. Their strength lies in the muscles of the neck, not in their arms. Their gait is a dogtrot, which they can keep up all day. They are very polite and submissive.

"Quito is built in a bowl-shaped valley at the foot of Mount Pichincha. The altitude of the city is 9,600 feet above the sea. The mountain rises in the background to a height of 16,000 feet. The view which presents itself from the summit of this mountain is one of the most superb and imposing possible to conceive. Twenty snow-clad peaks rise before you, ranging from 15,000 to 22,000 feet. It is truly a council of the patriarchs of the Andes.

"There are three entrances to the city, two from the south and one from the north. We enter from the south by a picturesque bridge spanning the river Machangara. The direct rays of the equatorial sun are white as limelight, and the first impression of Quito is that of a snow-white city, relieved by roofs of rich red tiles. In the streets and plazas are thousands of people, continually moving. The majority are Indians in scarlet or orange ponchos, wide white cotton trousers, and broad-brimmed white felt hats. There are Indians from a hundred different villages, marked by the cut of the hair, the turn of a hat, or the shape of a poncho. The streets are thronged from morning to evening with mules, horses, oxen, donkeys, and llamas with loads of every description.

"Ladies in smart victorias, drawn by Chilean or native horses, drive to and from the shops filled with merchandise from Paris, New York, London, Vienna, and Berlin. Handsome officers in full regimentals stroll along the streets. Gentlemen in frock coats and top hats are everywhere.

"The city is traversed from east to west by two deep ravines, through which Pichincha sends down its torrents of melted snow. The land upon which the city is built is in shape like the inside of an oval bowl, at the bottom of which is the Plaza Major. The course of the streets is generally regular, running east and west and north and south. The streets are paved with cobbles. The houses, of stone and brick, are mostly built in the Spanish-Moorish style, with courtyards within. The roofs project over the sidewalk and afford protection from rain. Balconies overhang the streets from every window. The ground on the street has no connection with the rest of the house, and is usually occupied by shops. The entrance is always high enough to admit a mounted horseman with ease. Around the courtyards are galleries supported by arches or pillars. The living rooms open upon these galleries. Servants are cheap and faithful. There are several good hotels in Quito—the Royal Palace, Hotel de Paris, Hotel Americano, and the Casa Azul. The people of Quito are charming, courteous, and hospitable. I do not know any city of its size which contains as many intelligent and cultivated people. Their hospitality is proverbial. I have continually received presents of sweetmeats, butter, cakes, venison, and even fish. There are no fish in or near Quito. They must be brought from Guayaquil, frozen in blocks of ice, a journey of six days. I shall always be indebted to my courteous, cultivated friends of Quito for their constant kindness to me.

"The population of Quito is computed to be about 70,000. Being the capital of the Republic, the Government buildings and offices are here and also the Presidential palace. The handsome Government and municipal buildings, the Bishop's palace, and the Cathedral surround the Great Plaza. There are many beautiful churches and convents in Quito. The church of the Jesuits is superb, with its interior a mass of scarlet and real gold. Singers from Europe are attached to the choir. Here in the capital above the clouds is one of the prettiest theaters in South America.

"The 'Comercio' and 'Tiempo,' the leading newspapers, are progressive, well edited, and influential.

The mean temperature of the city is about 60°. The thermometer scarcely ever rises above 70° or sinks below 50°. The mornings and

;he middle of the day warm. The climate is delight-
)ver cold; a perpetual spring. Consumption and
s are practically unknown. Many marvelous cures
lished in cases of consumption where hope had been
are many people who would pay any price to be
.) great white plague. Quito seems to be a cure.
hts are of twelve hours' duration the year round.
ꜱᴇ ᴠᴇᴛween sun and shade is 10°. This difference is felt
ᴀᴅ ᴜy moving from sun to shade, or vice versa. A journey of
ours from the city will place the traveler in the region of eternal
or in the space of half a day he can descend the deep and sultry
ys which separate the mighty chains of the Andes. This varia-
n of temperature depe   ᴀᴊ   tion and occurring between
rrow limits furnishes a Qꜱᴜᴠ   α   rsified supply of vegetable
, from the banana, pine   ιnd plantain to wheat, corn,
toes, cabbages, salads,   ,, grapes, and strawberries.
lay so persistently that medicine ᴛᴀs to be given to them to save
ives. As the climate is cool   houses unheated, daily and
t exercise on foot or on horseback is absolutely necessary. On
the city it is difficult to avoid the sun, as trees are scarce. But
)ke is unknown. Mosquitoes, snakes, scorpions, tarantulas,
, rats are unheard of. There are no bugs or beetles.

"The flora of Quito is beautiful and inexhaustible. Roses bloom
all the year round; wild flowers cover the sides of courtyards and
ruins; tulips, orchids, pinks, and lilies bloom winter and summer, and
geraniums run riot over walls and roofs.

"COMMERCIAL.

"Ecuador is a sound-money country, and has never issued paper
money. As the Ecuadorians have demonstrated in the past their
good sense in this matter the actual currency, which is on a gold
basis, is unlikely to be disturbed in the future.

"Ecuador has no foreign debt. The only foreign debt incurred has
been paid off. This was the money borrowed during the struggle for
independence. The only obligation of the Government at present is
the interest on the bonds issued for the construction of the Guayaquil
and Quito Railroad. Development always follows the railroad.

"Ecuador is the principal producer of cocoa and ivory nuts in the
world. On the coast coffee, rubber, bananas, sugar cane, rice, cotton,
and tobacco grow luxuriantly. Upon the plateaux of the high districts are produced wheat, corn, oats, beans, potatoes, and all the
principal cereals of the temperate Zone. This section also supplies
cattle, horses, sheep, and pigs. There is abundant pasture all the
year. It is an agricultural country.

"The establishment of industries is welcomed. The rivers on the coast and the streams in the mountains furnish ample cheap water power. Some of the industries which would give results are banana planting on the coast, where land and labor are cheap and the crop finding a ready market; lard refining—immense quantities are imported by way of Panama and Cape Horn to supply Ecuador, Peru, and Chile; cotton and woolen mills for the same markets; cement works to supply public construction and railroad building; furniture factories; china and glass works; distilleries, and canning and preserving factories. All these industries would find the necessary elements—raw material of the best quality and cheap labor. For cement the country provides all the materials; also for china and glass ware; for shoes, fine leather and hides; for furniture, a great variety of useful and precious woods. There is enough land on the coast available to supply the banana market of the world. The fisheries around the Galapagos Islands, which belong to Ecuador, are well stocked with turtle and codfish. The climate is mild, the sea is calm, and there is abundant salt. There are extensive coal deposits in the Province of Azuay and gold and silver in the provinces of Loja, El Oro, and Esmeraldas. Ecuador is a rich country awaiting development, where there are opportunities for the capital and spirit of foreigners.

"The Republic has good currency, cheap labor, plenty of water power, abundant raw material of superior quality, many rivers on the coast for transportation, and a railroad into the interior.

"But the doors of trade can not be opened unless the merchants and capitalists of this country heed the invitation and enter the markets in which they are· assured a preferred place, and lay the lines of mutual trade relations that will redound to the advantage of the countries concerned.

"This initiative must be found here, and it is certain that commercial interests of this country and the American investors will put the sickle into the field sowed by our great Secretary of State, the Hon. ELIHU ROOT, and already ripening.

"Germany, Great Britain, and France are in the field, Great Britain having a larger trade balance to her credit than this country enjoys. The success of the European trader is due to his closer study of the needs of the people. They have their particular predilections in trade, and these can only be ascertained by a careful study of their lives and wants.

"America has the world as her market, but it is in the line of self-interest that she should stimulate, encourage, and develop the South American trade."

PARCELS POST CONVENTION WITH THE UNITED STATES.

The provisions of the Parcels Post Convention between Ecuador and the United States, becoming effective on March 1, 1907, relate only to parcels of mail matter to be exchanged as provided in the agreement and do not affect existing arrangements under the Universal Postal Convention, which are to continue as heretofore. The convention provides:

"There shall be admitted to the mails articles of merchandise and mail matter (except letters, post cards, and written matter) of all kinds that are admitted under any conditions to the domestic mails of the country of origin, except that no packet may exceed $50 in value, 11 pounds in weight, nor the following dimensions: Greatest length in any direction, 3 feet 6 inches; greatest length and girth combined, 6 feet, and must be so wrapped or inclosed as to permit contents to be easily examined by postmasters and customs officers. The following articles are prohibited admission to the mails:

"Publications which violate the copyright laws of the country of destination; poisons and explosive or inflammable substances; fatty substances, liquids, and those which easily liquify; confections and pastes; live and dead animals, except dead insects and reptiles thoroughly dried; fruits and vegetables which will easily decompose, and substances which exhale a bad odor; lottery tickets, lottery advertisements, or circulars; all obscene or immoral articles; articles which may destroy or in any way damage the mails, or injure the persons handling them.

"All admissible articles of merchandise mailed or received shall be free from any detention or inspection whatever, except such as is required for collection of customs duties.

"A letter or communication of the nature of personal correspondence must not accompany, be written on, or inclosed with any parcel. If such be found the letter will be placed in the mails, if separable, and if the communication be inseparably attached, the whole package will be rejected. No parcel may contain packages intended for delivery at an address other than the one borne by the parcel itself.

"Rates of postage shall in all cases be fully prepaid with postage stamps of the country of origin. In the United States, for a parcel not exceeding 1 pound, the rate shall be 20 cents; and for each additional 1 pound or fraction thereof, 20 cents.

"In Ecuador, for a parcel not exceeding 460 grams in weight, 50 milesimos of an Ecuadorian cóndor gold, and for each additional 460 grams or fraction thereof, 50 milesimos de Ecuadorian cóndor gold.

"The country of destination may, at its option, levy and collect from the addressee for interior service and delivery a charge the amount of which is to be fixed according to its own regulations, but which shall in no case exceed 5 cents in the United States nor 50 milesimos of an Ecuadorian cóndor gold, in Ecuador for each parcel whatever its weight.

"The sender will, at the time of mailing, receive from the post-office where the parcel is mailed a 'certificate of mailing.'

"The sender may have a parcel registered by paying, in addition to the postage, the registration fee required for registered articles in the country of origin.

"The addressees of a registered parcel shall be advised of the arrival of the parcel by a notice from the post-office of destination.

"The sender of each parcel shall make a customs declaration, pasted upon or attached to the parcel, giving a general description of the parcel, an accurate statement of contents and value, date of mailing, and sender's signature and place of residence.

"Parcels shall be subject to all customs duties and regulations in force for the protection of customs revenues; and the customs duties properly chargeable shall be collected on delivery, in accordance with the customs regulations of the country of destination.

"Articles admitted should be so carefully packed as to be safely transmitted in the ordinary mails of either country. If a parcel can not be delivered as addressed, or is refused, it must be returned without charge, directly to the dispatching office of exchange, at the expiration of thirty days from its receipt at the office of destination. When the contents of a parcel which can not be delivered are liable to deterioration or corruption they may be destroyed at once, if necessary; or, if expedient, sold, without previous notice or judicial formality, for the benefit of the right person. The post-office department will not be responsible for the loss or damage of any parcel."

HAITI.
GENERAL TRADE CONDITIONS.

United States Consul L. W. LIVINGSTON, of Cape Haitien, reports that practically all the imports into Haiti come from the United States, England, France, and Germany, in the order named.

"The great bulk of imports from the United States consists of provisions, kerosene, tobacco, drugs and medicines, cotton goods, leather, carriages, shoes, machinery, etc. England supplies cotton and woolen goods, alpaca, crockery, roofing material, and other articles. The greatest variety of goods come from France.

"Considerable logwood is exported, quite an amount going to the United States. Practically all the coffee and cacao goes to Havre, France, although the ultimate destination of a large proportion is Germany. After the ratification of the reciprocity treaty between France and Haiti, Germany applied the maximum tariff rates to Haitian coffee, which prohibited its importation into that country."

Consular Agent CARL ABEGG, reporting from Port de Paix, says:

"Imports have increased slightly, but consist only of the very cheapest grades of goods, with very few exceptions. England supplies cotton goods, prints, coffee bags, corrugated iron, porter, and stout; Germany, matches, iron pots, hats, vinegar, mineral water, and bottled beer; France, wine, olive oil, perfumery, cigarette paper and tobacco, millinery, etc. The total of these imports amount to one-tenth of those from the United States. Among the articles arriving from the United States was a plow, the first one to be landed here. The exports consist of cedar wood, lignum-vitæ, and sisal.

"The island of Tortuga has been leased by a Belgian company, which will establish plantations thereon. The company has the privilege of cutting the timber on the island."

Consular Agent J. W. WOËL, of Gonaives, reports that one of the most notable concessions ever granted to foreigners by the Haitian Government was that for the building of a railroad from Gonaives to Hirche, with a branch to Gros Morne.

"The total length of the road will be about 100 miles. The company, which is made up chiefly of Americans, also obtained a land grant of 1½ kilometers (0.93 mile) on each side of the line for the purpose of cutting ties and providing lumber. This grant only holds good when the railroad passes through Government property. It also includes the right to build telephone and telegraph lines and a wharf at Gonaives and a steamship service around the island exclusively for the coastwise trade. To encourage the enterprise, the Government guarantees 6 per cent interest on an expenditure of $24,200 per mile for a period of fifty years."

According to United States Consul JOHN B. TERRES, nearly two-thirds of the imports at Port au Prince are received from the United States, the remainder coming mainly from France, Germany, and England. He also states that the amount of export trade of this exceedingly fertile island is very small, though with development it might in a short time be increased twentyfold.

For some years considerable attention has been paid to cotton planting, with a gradual increase in production. There are vast fields suitable for cotton growing, and it is hoped that the crop will make up for the deficiency in coffee. All the gins and presses used come from the United States.

The production of sugar has gradually increased and a fair light-brown grade is produced for home consumption, the price being equal to 8 cents gold per pound. It is sometimes difficult to meet the demand. No refinery for the finer grades of white sugar has as yet been established. All sugar machinery is of United States origin.

Tobacco growing shows little change, although there are large tracts of land capable of producing a very fine grade of tobacco.

Hard woods are exported in quantities which are increasing yearly. Large areas of forest lands filled with valuable trees have not yet been explored, but with the extension of the present railroad enterprises and the completion of those under way these districts will be opened up.

In the dry-goods trade the United States continues to supply the greater part of the demand.

Among the food products imported, codfish, salt pork, beef, flour, herrings, cooking butter, and lard are received from the United States. Table butter is imported, for the most part, from Copenhagen and Germany, as the United States article has not given satisfaction. The importation of cheese is shared by the United States, France, and Germany. Canned goods come in largest quantities from the United States, though France and Germany furnish some, such as sausages, pâté de fois gras, and other expensive kinds.

A large amount of laundry soap is being made in the country; the materials for making it are imported from the United States. However, a large quantity, of a better quality, is imported, and it commands a higher price. France has the largest trade in fancy toilet soaps, yet the United States furnishes much of this article. The United States has almost the entire trade in carriages and harness. The native suppy of lumber is very small, the United States continuing to supply most of the demand for pine.

HONDURAS.

MESSAGE OF PRESIDENT BONILLA.

On January 1, 1907, President BONILLA delivered an address to the Congress of Honduras covering his policy and administration, the following being extracts therefrom:

"The Government has maintained its foreign relations with all other countries in the best spirit of cordiality, has striven to fulfill its international obligations, and has endeavored, as is the duty of sister Republics to whom the future reserves a common destiny, to strengthen more and more the bonds that unite Honduras with the other States of Central America.

*　　*　　*　　*　　*　　*

"I am pleased to inform you that our boundary question with the sister Republic of Nicaragua was settled by the award made, on the 24th of last month (December, 1906), by His Majesty the King of Spain. In that award the Royal arbitrator fixed the boundary line as follows: From Portillo of Teotecacinte to the confluence of the Guineo with the Poteca River, thence down the latter and the Segovia River to their outlet into an arm of the Atlantic near Cape Gracias á Dios. Thus that question is terminated, leaving clear to Nicaragua and to Honduras their boundary line. I now state with pleasure tnat when the Government of Nicaragua received notice of the award of His Majesty the King of Spain, the President, Gen. José Santos Zelaya, hastened to congratulate me, showing in this manner another evidence of his culture and sentiments of Central American confraternity.

"Last May the meeting of the Sixth Universal Postal Congress was held in Rome, where the representative of Honduras, Mr. Juan Giordano, Duke of Oratino, signed the text of the new convention proposed for the countries that compose the Postal Union, which convention will soon be submitted to your consideration.

*   *   *   *   *   *   *

"Likewise at the Geneva Conference, in session from the 11th of June to the 26th of July last, for the revision of the convention of 1864 concerning the attention and care of ill and wounded soldiers of armies in the field, our Delegate, in representation of the Government, signed the new convention that will be put in force, the text of which will be submitted to you at the proper time.

*   *   *   *   *   *   *

"On the 23d of last July the Third International American Conference was solemnly inaugurated in the city of Rio de Janeiro, United States of Brazil. Our representative, Dr. Fausto Dávila, in compliance with his instructions, signed several documents in the form of conventions, resolutions, and recommendations, which he considered of advantage to our country, all of which will be submitted to your consideration. It is to be hoped that the proceedings of said Congress will meet with the approval of the Governments represented therein for the purpose of attaining, even though slowly, a true American solidarity.

"The discourse of His Excellency Elihu Root, Secretary of State of the United States, to the delegates of the Congress, explaining clearly the policy of his Government concerning the other nations of America, is worthy of the highest consideration and respect. The declarations contained in that notable document, as lofty and just as they are significant, will always form one of the most brilliant pages in the history of the Third International American Conference.

*   *   *   *   *   *   *

"Peace and order have been maintained in the Republic, and under their protecting influence the election of the local officers of the Government in accordance with the new law was held. The Honduranean people have dedicated themselves to habits of industry, are contented, and full of confidence in the future. The Government rests confiding in public opinion, and continues in the work of progress it has so vigorously undertaken.

"On the 1st of last March the new political Constitution, decreed by the National Constituent Assembly on September 2, 1904, became operative, and in accordance with decree No. 76 of that same assembly, issued on January 19, 1906, the codes and laws adopted in decree No. 65 of that same august body were promulgated. The provisions of the fundamental as well as of the supplementary laws have encountered no obstacle whatever in their application, having been received, in general, with marked favor, which shows that the principles which they contain are more in harmony with our social conditions and with our political education than were our former laws and perhaps erroneous legislation.

"The general hospital, established under the immediate protection of the Government and now under the able management of Dr. GUSTAVO A. WALTER, the present head of the institution, has been notably improved, not only in the condition of the buildings, but also in the effectiveness of the service. With the object of increasing its personnel by a corps of competent teachers, the Government contracted in Europe with Dr. CARLOS KOPP, a medical professor who has commenced to render expert and valuable services. Various other charitable institutions in the country have been properly protected by granting them subventions for their support and conservation, to the end that they may answer the purposes for which they were intended.

"The Government printing office, which has been considerably improved, has continued to give useful service by editing a great number of national publications and by printing the official documents of the Government. In said office the Constitution and other laws of the Republic, to the number of 17 books, aggregating 67,200 volumes, costing only $9,830—a relatively small amount when compared with the cost of former works of the same kind—have been published.

"The Central Bureau of Statistics ordered the taking of a national census, which operation was effected on December 30, 1905. The result obtained showed the population to be 500,114 souls. This number, compared with the number of inhabitants shown by the former censuses of 1881 and 1897, shows a considerable increase in the population.

"The present administration, with the view of omitting no means that may tend to the development of the country, has appropriated the amount of $155,301.44 to some of the municipalities for the construction of city halls, schools, and other works of public utility that the scant resources of the aforesaid municipalities would not permit them to carry out with their own funds, as well as for the construction and repair of various national buildings.

"During the last fiscal year the sum of $32,429.25 was expended in the disinfection and cleansing of the ports of Cortez, and San Pedro Sula, towns that were, during the past year, scourged by yellow fever, and which disease did not subsequently reappear, due to the efficient hygienic measures and the strict sanitary orders enforced by the Government.

"It is a pleasure to inform you that a large number of public works undertaken by the Government, or under its immediate protection, have been completed, and that other new works of great benefit to the country have been initiated and are about to be terminated.

"The wagon road to the south, which connects the capital with the port of San Lorenzo on the Pacific, has been permanently opened to public use. This highway has been repaired and changed so as to be suitable for the transit of automobiles, a method of transportation which is beginning to be actively developed in Honduras, to which end the Government has granted concessions to the New York-Honduras Rosario Mining Company, Santos Soto & Co., and J. Rössner & Co. On this road, and on that which is being constructed toward the north, there have been expended during the last three years of my administration $930,275.25, of which sum $315,433.39 corresponds to the last fiscal year, not including various other amounts spent on bridle paths and subsidies for the preservation of various country roads.

"The Northern Railway, since it has been taken over by the Government, has maintained and preserved itself out of its own receipts, and daily improvements are being made from its own funds. Last year one locomotive and twenty flat cars, together with other accessories bought out of the profits of the railroad, were purchased, leaving a balance in favor of the company. The locomotives and cars ordered of Mottey, Green & Co., New York, amounted to $41,679.50. At the present time rules and regulations are being prepared for the government of the railway, and the auditing of the accounts during the Government's administration has been ordered.

"In addition to the potable water service already established at Choluteca, Cedros, La Venta, Trujillo, Trinidad de Santa Barbara, and San Pedro Sula, toward the installation of which the Government gave the piping, assisting the last-named town to the amount of $10,000, orders have been given for the installment at an early date of the water service at Comayagua, Nacaome, and San Marcos de Colon, the necessary material for the installation at the first-named town being now at the capital, the actual cost of which amounts to $46,178.27.

"For the purpose of developing the country the Government has granted concessions to A. D. Baird, Desiderio Alvarez, Eduardo Ordoñez Portal, Rio Montagua Development Company, Diego Robles, Mariano Ortez, Carlos C. Bolet, J. J. Fernandez, Luicci & Ferracuti, Vacaro Bross & Co., Virgil C. Reynolds, and Federico

Girbal, which concessions will be submitted to you for consideration by the respective Department.

"In addition to the concessions named, and bearing in mind that Puerto Cortez, owing to its present hygienic conditions, suffers constantly from the effects produced by the epidemics of yellow fever that have several times developed therein, causing many deaths and paralyzing commerce, due to the alarm felt in the United States, one of its principal markets, the Government has granted concessions to Mr. Armando Gavorit and Capt. J. W. Grace for the introduction of potable water and the drainage of the Puerto Cortez swamps, respectively. The completión of the work covered by these two concessions, for which there has arrived and is now arriving the necessary material, will be a positive advantage to the Atlantic coast, and especially will Puerto Cortez be enabled to enjoy that development which its natural conditions warrant.

"On August 21, 1906, a contract was made with the Planters Steamship Company for the construction of a wharf at Tela Bay, and of a railroad from said port or bay, through El Progreso, in the Department of Yoro, to the Comayagua River in the same Department. On the completion of the work covered by the contract referred to, a large tract of uncultivated land will be open for agricultural and commercial uses, and the whole region will be considerably benefited thereby.

"There has been a notable improvement in the telegraphic service. New offices have been opened at Oropoli, Department of El Paraiso; at Victoria, Department of. Yoro; at Orica, Guayape, and Olancho, Department of Tegucigalpa; at San Francisco of Yojoa, Department of Cortes, and at La Labor, Department of Ocotepeque, representing a total length of telegraph line constructed during the last fiscal year of 102 miles. There are now 181 telegraph offices in the Republic, and the length of the system of telegraph wires is 3,363 miles.

"Notwithstanding the damages done to agriculture and commerce on the north coast of the Republic on account of the epidemics of the past few years, the scarcity of cereals and the alarm felt in July last concerning an international conflict, all of which diminish our sources of revenue, it is a fact, nevertheless, that our public revenues, though small in comparison with those of other countries, were, because administered with honesty and economy, sufficient to encourage national progress in a safe and perceptible manner.

"The gross revenues of the last fiscal year were $4,004,497.28. Deducting the cost of collection, $469,414.13, makes the net receipts of the Government during the period referred to $3,535,078.15, an excess over the budget of $491,578.15. The expenditures, including those for account of the public credit, were $3,294,747.40, and notwithstanding there was an excess of $251,147.40 over the actual expenses incurred. and the amount estimated in the budget, nevertheless, taking into account the increase in the revenues of $491-578.15 over the receipts estimated in the budget, there still remains a surplus of $240,430.75. Comparing the receipts of the past year with those of 1904–5, there is a balance of $230,715.89 in favor of the former year, and in the expenses incurred there is a decrease of $46,845.40 in favor of 1905–6.

"The internal debt in July 31, 1905, was $2,287,720.74, which amount, added to that of $643,634.73, authorized by the Legislative Assembly, makes a total of $3,471,355.47; but as during the fiscal year 1905–6 there was paid on account thereof the sum of $345,362.71, the present internal debt amounts to $3,125,992.76.

"The subject of public instruction has received my special attention. In my former message I informed the National Constituent Assembly that I intended to open a normal school for males on the 1st of last May. It is with pride and satisfaction that I now state that the plan referred to has been realized. The administration has spent on the building in which the school is located the sum of $81,134.37 in putting the edifice in proper condition and in supplying the necessary conveniences required by science. The sum of $42,816.81 has been spent for instruction materials, furniture, and apparatus. The school opened at the time stated with 154 scholarships supported by the Government, and with a total number of 201 students in attendance. I hope that not only said establishment but also the normal school for girls, in which instruction is being given to 236 students, will constitute a firm foundation for the intellectual future of the young people of the Republic.

"The Government is supporting abroad a number of students who are preparing for useful and practical careers in the Republic. During the last fiscal year the outlay for this purpose was $24,103.51. Primary instruction in the Republic is being carried out in accordance with the provisions of the new code, and the Government has granted subventions to the municipalities in order to secure the diffusion of knowledge as an efficient measure of future progress."

MEXICO.

FOREIGN COMMERCE IN NOVEMBER, 1906.

According to figures issued by the Statistical Division of the Treasury Department of the Republic of Mexico, the foreign commerce of the Republic for November, 1906, and for the first five months of the current fiscal year, 1906–7, was represented by the following valuations, the figures for the corresponding periods of the preceding year being also given for purposes of comparison:

The total value of imports during the five months under review was

$88,853,411.16 in Mexican currency, as declared in the custom-houses, an increase of $21,013,316.67, as compared with the preceding year.

The exports for the five months were valued at $96,141,669.80, showing a decrease of $3,654,668.15, as compared with the same period of 1905–6.

IMPORTS.
[Silver valuation.]

Articles.	November—		First five months—	
	1906.	1905.	1906–7.	1905–6.
Animal substances..................	$1,876,202.52	$1,373,191.29	$8,256,721.09	$6,554,438.64
Vegetable substances................	2,655,763.68	2,810,478.66	11,204,842.98	11,080,252.32
Mineral substances.................	5,741,502.15	4,530,715.41	29,183,647.90	19,055,916.45
Dry goods.......................	2,035,375.95	1,759,604.47	11,410,705.08	9,365,386.01
Chemical and pharmaceutical substances..........................	791,819.04	505,132.92	3,492,963.15	2,900,279.26
Beverages.......................	669,087.28	529,676.50	2,752,262.21	2,887,590.65
Paper and its applications..........	574,098.72	463,570.54	2,332,793.35	2,254,097.33
Machinery and apparatus...........	3,280,760.44	1,477,331.41	11,438,811.62	7,549,819.43
Vehicles........................	910,321.35	272,384.80	3,380,715.16	1,331,327.71
Arms and explosives...............	380,393.87	397,116.14	1,630,538.20	1,720,211.54
Miscellaneous....................	742,263.40	706,465.43	3,769,410.42	3,140,475.15
Total.....................	19,657,593.40	14,825,667.57	88,853,411.16	67,840,004.49

EXPORTS.
[Silver valuation.]

Articles.	November—		First five months—	
	1906.	1905.	1906–7.	1905–6.
Precious metals....................	$12,380,813.52	$13,151,310.50	$50,010,594.08	$54,197,393.52
Other articles....................	10,991,864.37	7,518,802.25	46,131,075.72	45,598,944.42
Total.....................	23,372,677.89	20,670,112.75	96,141,669.80	99,796,337.95

The details of the export trade for the periods under comparison show the following classification and figures:

	November—		First five months—	
	1906.	1905.	1906–7.	1905–6.
Mexican gold coin.....................			$29,990.00	
Foreign gold coin....................			6,209.00	$4,588.98
Gold in bars......................	$1,620,787.95	$2,807,813.50	8,235,520.76	13,994,593.07
Gold in other forms................	550,126.63	104,976.40	2,194,383.85	709,248.32
Total gold	2,170,914.58	2,912,789.90	10,466,163.61	14,708,430.37
Mexican silver coin..................	3,523,521.00	5,567,906.00	9,129,137.00	7,890,957.00
Foreign silver coin..................	19,833.00	6,636.00	58,187.00	47,508.62
Silver in bars......................	5,609,978.36	4,310,727.44	25,830,416.65	28,504,287.43
Silver in other forms................	1,056,566.58	353,251.16	4,526,689.82	3,046,210.10
Total silver...................	10,209,898.94	10,238,520.60	39,544,430.47	39,488,963.15
Total gold and silver..........	12,380,813.52	13,151,310.50	50,010,594.08	54,197,393.52
Antimony........................	114,593.00	58,546.00	577,124.00	449,254.96
Copper...........................	2,821,164.00	1,750,613.74	11,685,615.00	11,965,902.60
Marble..........................	15,020.00		20,550.00	73,098.00
Plumbago........................	18,220.00	8,204.00	37,420.00	12,204.00
Lead............................	395,234.00	211,190.00	1,615,528.56	2,288,816.67
Zinc............................	45,770.00	16,960.00	509,303.12	93,032.99
Other metals.....................	13,162.00	22,386.00	1,049,999.38	171,362.11
Total.....................	15,803,976.52	15,219,210.24	65,566,134.14	69,251,064.85
Vegetable products:				
Coffee......................	209,080.00	385,554.00	1,153,074.00	2,363,912.50
Cascalote and tanning barks......	1,234.00		7,824.00	20,147.00
Rubber.....................	464,788.00	79,256.84	1,674,229.00	378,160.52
Chicle......................	168,127.60	101,717.06	420,018.00	328,243.58

	November—		First five months—	
	1906.	1905.	1906–7.	1905–6.
Vegetable products—Continued.				
Beans	$92,465.00	$70,353.00	$323,259.00	$331,563.82
Fruits	64,379.20	54,108.50	135,563.43	162,896.60
Chick peas	244,466.00	137,938.00	2,455,050.00	1,695,104.00
Guayule	4,640.00	3,886.00	5,460.00	18,272.00
Horse beans		216.00	2,200.00	104,546.09
Heniquen	4,007,838.86	2,438,774.00	12,840,803.77	12,587,436.00
Ixtle	379,497.00	331,592.00	1,773,232.00	1,630,182.88
Woods	196,765.40	196,116.10	776,142.50	757,660.56
Maize	48.00	3,885.00	2,887.80	14,694.00
Mahogany	5,030.00	4,302.00	31,894.00	21,801.00
Dyewoods	40,868.12	35,930.76	193,210.12	181,987.61
Xacaton	106,045.00	159,484.00	717,170.00	965,402.00
Leaf tobacco	112,887.35	106,396.00	711,926.35	495,055.74
Vanilla	44,210.00	133,900.00	889,695.00	2,221,870.99
Other vegetables	228,747.55	168,944.75	779,257.20	576,357.51
Total	6,373,139.66	4,421,354.01	24,901,996.17	24,703,960.69
Animal products:				
Cattle	109,128.00	322,745.00	705,576.00	1,614,357.50
Skins and hides	700,171.50	439,490.60	3,301,102.03	2,673,954.68
Other animal products	74,067.34	32,553.40	214,699.59	193,959.19
Total	883,366.84	794,789.00	4,221,377.62	4,482,271.37
Manufactured articles:				
Sugar		200.00	155,049.00	259,926.00
Flour and pastes			457.00	
Rope	96,553.00	52,009.00	278,526.00	167,973.00
Dressed skins	571.00	18,675.00	30,569.00	96,385.00
Straw hats	72,497.80	39,095.00	284,145.80	136,602.79
Manufactured tobacco	40,010.60	31,954.00	210,408.60	144,237.75
Other manufactures	44,517.80	29,579.00	181,436.82	207,390.10
Total	256,150.20	171,512.00	1,140,592.22	1,062,514.64
Miscellaneous articles	56,044.65	63,247.50	311,569.65	296,526.20

Following is a résumé of the valuations of Mexican imports during the periods under comparison, with reference to their countries of origin:

Country.	November.		First five months—	
	1906.	1905.	1906–7.	1905–6.
Europe	$6,733,630.24	$5,634,701.32	$32,665,984.58	$28,905,532.57
Asia	214,343.26	104,636.51	627,028.35	581,092.27
Africa	33,080.00	2,290.20	86,696.48	13,335.38
North America	12,641,796.38	9,039,593.14	55,293,191.45	38,048,429.94
Central America	1,798.14	10,951.74	11,080.84	17,550.81
South America	11,281.85	14,273.09	70,774.06	126,004.47
West Indies	21,663.53	19,221.57	79,684.40	103,189.43
Oceania			18,971.00	44,959.62
Total	19,657,593.40	14,825,667.57	88,853,411.16	67,840,094.49

Following is a résumé of the valuations of Mexican exports during the periods under comparison, with reference to their countries of destination:

Country.	November.		First five months—	
	1906.	1905.	1906–7.	1905–6.
Europe	$6,575,790.58	$3,754,423.73	$27,701,118.89	$23,960,668.35
Asia	796.00		796.00	
North America	16,446,197.40	16,405,890.10	66,855,643.40	73,208,341.04
Central America	88,303.91	119,051.92	437,941.51	568,150.56
South America	15,150.00	3,035.00	62,115.00	34,309.00
West Indies	246,440.00	387,712.00	1,084,055.00	2,024,869.00
Total	23,372,677.89	20,670,112.75	96,141,669.80	99,796,337.95

SILVER BASIS OF THE STAMP AND CUSTOMS TAXES FOR MARCH, 1907.

The usual monthly circular issued by the Treasury Department of the Mexican Government announces that the legal price per kilogram of pure silver during the month of March, 1907, is $44.66, according to calculations provided in the decree of March 25, 1905. This price will be the basis for the payment of the stamp tax and customs duties when silver is used throughout the Republic.

INCREASED AND DECREASED EXPORTS OF AGRICULTURAL PRODUCTS, 1905-6.

A comparison of the statistics of Mexican exports of agricultural products during the fiscal years 1904-5 and 1905-6 shows the following increases and decreases:

Agricultural products the exports of which have increased in 1905-6.	Pesos.	Agricultural products the exports of which have decreased in 1905-6.	Pesos.
Coffee	31,841.65	Cascalote and tanning barks	38,179.00
Rubber	1,671,321.00	Horse beans	107,774.00
Chicle	73,056.92	Timber	315,853.75
Beans	91,152.72	Maize	217,986.50
Fruits	72,559.58	Blackberry wood	2,819.13
Spanish peas	707,314.25	Logwood	156,128.71
Guayule	117,026.00	Grass root	139,494.00
Sisal grass	48,190.38	Leaf tobacco	509,097.94
Ixtle	172,175.33	Several animal products	47,465.97
Vanilla	1,871,721.98	Sugar	5,043,210.76
Various	479,221.19	Henequen rope	41,770.00
Cattle	122,517.00	Manufactured tobacco	42,115.75
Untanned hides	1,143,555.09		
Flour and cotton-seed paste	2,892.00		
Palm hats	233,478.29		
Miscellaneous	155,769.91		

The total of exports of agricultural products during 1905-6 was 78,429,623.33 *pesos*, and in 1904-5 78,216,473.34 *pesos*.

REDUCTION OF IMPORT DUTY ON WHEAT.

An Executive decree issued on February 9, 1907, reduces the rate of wheat imported into Mexico to $1.50 (Mexican) per hundred gross kilograms. This rate is to continue in force until June 30, 1907, and became effective on February 15, 1907. The former rate, which has ruled since September, 1904, was $3 (Mexican) per hundred kilograms, gross weight, or one-half the present schedule.

;OAD IN THE STATE OF SONORA.

ɼernment has authorized Mr. A. S. MACKENZIE,
d into on August 9, 1906, to construct and exploit
ιe State of Sonora, starting from the Carbo Sta-
Railroad, and terminating at the mines of Copete,
st be completed within five years. The conces-
.ɵ a deposit of 3,000 *pesos*, in bonds of the consoli-
uɛ   to guarantee the fulfillment of the terms of the
ɪᴛ.

RAILROAD IN GUANAJUATO AND MICHOACAN.

ˉirtue of contract made with the] xican Government, Messrs.
ᵢ & Co. and Mr. Zaldivar y Florez have been authorized
, exploit a railroad line in the State of Guanajuato,
ɀ from Salv   ɛrra and terminating at Yuririapúndaro, which
'   ex   to Morelon, in said ſtate, or to Puruandiro, in
            ᴜ   The line must be completed within five
1 ɪꜰ ɪ   ᴵⁿcessionaires choose to construct the authorized
          ᴵᴿ for their completion shall be fixed by the
      ᴜ   ⟩rks.   The bond furnished by the concession-
ɂ ᴀmounts to 15,000 pesos.

CONSULAR TRADE REPORTS, JANUARY, 1907.

The Mexican consul at Philadelphia advises that the shipments
of merchandise from that port to the Mexican ports of Tampico and
Veracruz during the month of January, 1907, amounted to $141,381.11
and consisted of coal, petroleum, and powder invoiced at $74,706.35,
$61,874.76, and $4,800, respectively.

The consul-general of Mexico at New York reports that during the
month of January, 1907, 11 vessels, proceeding from Mexican ports,
entered the harbor of New York City, bringing 71,656 packages of
merchandise.   During the same month the vessels clearing from the
port of New York numbered 15, carrying 167,089 packages of merchandise, consigned to Mexican ports.   The imports in detail from
Mexico to New York in January, 1907, were as follows:

Articles.	Quantity.	Articles.	Quantity.
Henequen..............bales..	9,692	Fustete....................logs..	9,163
Coffee..................sacks..	1,853	Hair......................bales..	32
Hides..................bales..	8,554	Lead bullion..............bars..	16,737
Hides..................loose..	3,764	Metals...................boxes..	612
Ixtle..................bales..	3,268	Sarsaparilla...........packages..	127
Goatskins..............do....	1,944	Vanilla..................boxes..	50
Deerskins..............do....	130	Alligator skins..........do....	22
Rubber.................do....	2,667	Honey..................barrels..	304
Leaf tobacco............do....	418	Cedar....................logs..	310
Cigars.................boxes..	25	Mahogany.................do....	371
Sugar.................sacks..	5,000	Copper...................bars..	2,620
Broom root............bales..	310	Pepper...................sacks..	420
Chicle................do....	3,130	Mexican dollars..........boxes..	133

The Mexican consul at Nogales, Arizona, reports that the exportation of merchandise from the State of Sonora, Mexico, to the United States in January, 1907, was as follows:

Fowls.	$26	Corn.	$81
Cane sugar.	16	Oranges.	853
Mescal.	80	Soup pastes.	275
Portland cement.	161	Fresh fish.	43
Rawhides.	9, 574	Lead ores.	587
Fresh meat.	86	Ready-made cotton clothing.	10
Scrap iron and steel.	395	Salt.	6
Cotton lace.	2	Wheat.	2
Preserved fruits.	58	Leaf tobacco.	250
Beans.	3	Gold bullion and dust.	82, 613
Cattle.	6, 549	Silver bullion.	85, 222
Earthenware.	9	Total.	186, 906
Lemons.	5		

The imports of foreign merchandise through the custom-house of Nogales, Mexico, to the State of Sonora in January, 1907, were as follows:

Animal products.	$65, 148.64	Paper and paper products.	$6, 929.81
Vegetable products.	63, 531.20	Machinery and apparatus.	89, 971.80
Mineral products.	449, 973.64	Vehicles.	10, 285.17
Textiles, and manufactures		Arms and explosives.	5, 935.53
thereof.	37, 179.46	Miscellaneous.	22, 143.18
Chemical products.	27, 779.93	Total.	775, 049.12
Spirituous beverages.	3, 170.76		

The countries of origin of the foregoing merchandise are as follows:

United States.	$730, 151.07	Spain.	$44.22
Germany.	6, 426.09	Austria.	679.38
France.	9, 296.28	Total.	775, 049.12
England.	27, 876.20		
Italy.	578.88		

The customs duties collected during the month amounted to $130,967.46 silver.

THE HENEQUEN MARKET IN 1906.

The "Secretaria de Comunicaciones," of the Mexican Government, has been requested by the Chamber of Commerce of Merida to urge all members of the Mexican consular force to collect information concerning possible new markets for the fiber known as henequen or sisal hemp. It is proposed not only to enter new fields for the sale of the raw product but also to ship manufactures thereof. The Argentine Republic, England, and Japan have already been exploited as possible purchasing countries, and in the twelve months ending with December, 1906, the United States took $14,486,569 worth of sisal grass.

During the calendar year 1906 exports of henequen from Progreso amounted to 597,966 bales, which, added to the 28,819 reported for

a total from the Yucatan district of 626,785 bales.
the United States took 595,024 bales and Canada
remainder being distributed in a decreasing ratio
ngland, Germany, Belgium, France, Italy, Spain,

<blockquote>
th
a1.
are a'
</blockquote>

ts and manufacturers are not only applying new
»reparation of sisal for the markets of the world,
illy studying the qualities of such other fiber plants
»r similar usage.

CUSTOMS REVENUES, JANUARY, 1907.

The customs reve—..s at ——'ous Mexican ports during the month
January, 1907, aggregated 1 552,524.91, of which $4,446,052.23
.s credited for imports and $106,472.63 to exports.

POSTAL RECEIPTS, N(;MBER, 1906.

Total receipts from the postal service of the Mexican Republic, as
ted by the Postmaster-General to the Department of Communi-
is and Public Works, show a net increase over the corresponding
·d of the preceding year of $28,921.36; November, 1906, figures
$317,008.52, and November, 1905, $288,087.16.

. the five months' period ending with November, 1906, the total
receipts from this branch of the public service are placed at
$1,597,934.86, as compared with $1,461,993.74 in the same period
of 1905, an increase of $135,941.12, or 9.30 per cent.

COPPER MINING IN THE REPUBLIC.

According to statistics published by the Ministry of Improvements, there are 796 copper mines in the Republic, distributed as
follows among the different States and Territories:

Jalisco	302	Tamaulipas	11
Sonora	234	Coahuila	5
Michoacan	95	Oaxaca	5
Lower California	65	Puebla	5
Chihuahua	53	Hidalgo	5
Durango	51	Guanajuato	4
Aguacalientes	49	Mexico	3
Guerrero	44	Nuevo Leon	3
Sinaloa	25	Tepic	2
Zacatecas	14		
San Luis Potosi	14	Total	796
Colima	12		

QUICKSILVER IN THE REPUBLIC.

In the State of Jalisco, Mexico, is situated what is claimed to be
the largest single deposit of quicksilver in the world. In 1905 the
property came into the possession of Messrs. Lawson & Page, and
large furnaces and retorts for the treatment of mercury were installed.

In commenting upon the development of the mines, "*El Economista Mexicano*," of February 2, 1907, finds the cheap exploitation of quicksilver as one of the most important features in the development of the gold and silver properties of the Republic, according to the cyanide process.

Messrs. Lawson & Page have constructed a large reduction mill and cyanide plant on their San Jeronimo *hacienda*, and crushers, with other necessary machinery, are under orders.

RAILROAD CONCESSIONS.

The "*Diario Oficial*" of the Mexican Republic, in its issues for December 7 and 14, 1906, and January 11, 1907, respectively, contains the texts of the following railroad concessions:

Concession granted to the Mexican National Railroad Company for the construction and exploitation of a railroad line in the State of Nuevo Leon, starting from the town of Colombia and terminating at the station of Jarita of the Mexican National. The entire line must be completed within two years, and its length is estimated at 30 kilometers. The company has made a deposit of 5,000 *pesos* to guarantee the fulfillment of the conditions of the concession.

Concession granted to the Nacozari Railroad Company for the construction and exploitation of the following railroad lines: (1) One starting from the port of Guaymas and terminating at San Pedro Batuc on the Moctezuma River, District of Ures; (2) one starting from a convenient point of the line referred to in paragraph (1) and terminating at the city of Hermosillo, or near it, to connect with the Sonora Railroad; (3) one starting also from a convenient point of the first line and terminating at the city of Ures, or near it. The first line must be completed on December 31, 1914, and upon its completion the company shall proceed to construct the other two lines, at the rate of 40 kilometers per year, on either line, or on both at the same time. The total length of these three lines has been estimated at 360 kilometers. The bond furnished by the concessionaire amounts to 42,000 *pesos*.

Concession granted to the Cananea Consolidated Copper Company for the construction and exploitation of a railroad line between the States of Chihuahua and Sonora, starting from a point called "Madera," terminus of the Nallucharic Railroad branch line to the San Pedro stream, in the State of Chihuahua, and terminating at Bacerac, or another point near the Babispe River, in the State of Sonora. This line must be completed within six years; its length is estimated at 180 kilometers.

The term of the three concessions above referred to is the usual one of ninety-nine years, in accordance with the railroad law of April 29, 1899.

RAILROAD IN THE MUNICIPALITY OF MEXICO.

A contract entered into on the 14th of August, 1906, grants the Mexican National Railroad Company a concession for the construction and exploitation of a railroad line in the municipality of Mexico, starting from a point of the Interoceanic Railroad, near the station of San Lazaro, and connecting with the San Rafael and Atlixco Railroad. The company is further authorized to construct two branch lines, one starting from a convenient point of the main line and running in a westerly direction to the east shore of the Viga Canal, with extensions to "*La Union*" and "*La Victoria*" factories, and another, starting from the main line also, and terminating at "*El Salvador*" factory.

The construction of the main line must be completed within one year from the date of the concession.

RAILROAD IN THE STATE OF VERACRUZ.

On August 16, 1906, the Mexican Government entered into a contract with Messrs. S. Pearson & Son, authorizing the latter to construct and exploit a railroad line in the State of Veracruz, starting from the city of Minatitlan and terminating at a point between the twenty-fifth and thirty-fifth kilometers of the Tehuantepec Railroad.

Five kilometers of the line must be completed within the first year, five more within the second, and the whole line within the third year.

The company has made a deposit of 3,000 *pesos*, in bonds of the consolidated public debt, to guarantee the fulfillment of the terms of the concession.

NICARAGUA.

ARBITRAL AWARD OF THE BOUNDARY QUESTION BETWEEN THE REPUBLICS OF HONDURAS AND NICARAGUA.

I, Alfonso XIII, King of Spain, by the grace of God and the Constitution;

Whereas the pending boundary question between the Republics of Honduras and Nicaragua having been submitted to my decision, in conformity with articles 3, 4, and 5 of the Treaty of Tegucigalpa of October 7, 1894, and pursuant to the communications addressed by my Secretary of State, under date of November 11, 1904, to the Secretaries of Foreign Affairs of said Powers;

Actuated by the desire of reciprocating the confidence that both of the said Republics have equally confided in the ancient Mother Country, by submitting to my decision a matter of such importance;

Resulting therefrom, and from the Royal Decree of April 17, 1905, *in the* appointing of a commission to examine into the **aforesaid** boundary question, in order that it may make clear the points in litigation and render a preliminary report of the arbitral award;

Resulting that the high parties in interest submitted in due time their respective allegations and replies, accompanied by the corresponding documents in support of that which is considered the rights of each;

Resulting that the boundary between the Republics of Honduras and Nicaragua, from the coast of the Pacific Ocean to the Portillo of Teotecacinte, is already definitely fixed by the mutual agreement of both parties; .

Resulting that, according to the proceedings of Amapala on September 14, 1902, and August 29, 1904, a common boundary point on the coast of the Atlantic Ocean was to have been chosen by the mixed Honduran-Nicaraguan commission in order to trace from that point the boundary of the frontier to the said Portillo of Teotecacinte, which could not be carried out inasmuch as no agreement was arrived at;

Resulting that the territory in litigation embraces an extensive zone which includes:

To the north, a zone which, starting from Portillo of Teotecacinte, continues across the summit of the cordillera, following the line or intersection that divides the rainfall of each side until it terminates at Portillo, in the spring that forms the source of the Frio River, then following the bed of said spring and of said river to the junction of the latter with the Guayambre River, and thence along the bed of the Guayambre River to the point where the latter unites with the Guayape River, and from there to the point where the Guayape and the Guayambre rivers take the common name of Patuca River, follows the water course of this river to the meridian that passes through Cape Camaron, and continues on this meridian to the coast;

And to the south, from the Portillo of Teotecacinte to the headwaters of the Limon River, downstream, along the bed of this river, and thence along the bed of the Poteca River to its confluence with the Segovia River, following the water course of the latter river to a point situated at a distance of 20 geographic miles in a straight and perpendicular line from the Atlantic coast, turning at this point toward the south upon the astronomic meridian until it intercepts the parallel of geographic latitude that passes through the mouth of the Arena River and the Sandy Bay Lagoon, on which parallel it continues toward the east from the said intersection to the Atlantic Ocean; resulting that the question, which is the object of this arbitration, consists, then, in fixing the dividing line of both Republics, included between a point on the Atlantic coast and the said Portillo of Teotecacinte;

Whereas according to the agreement of both parties set forth in rule 3 of article 2 of the Treaty of Tegucigalpa or Gámez-Bonilla of 1894, by which this arbitration is governed, it should be understood that one of the Republics of Honduras or Nicaragua is owner of the territory belonging to Spain, which at the time of their independence constituted the Provinces of Honduras and Nicaragua, respectively;

Whereas the Spanish Provinces of Honduras and of Nicaragua were formed by historic evolution, until they were constituted in two separate districts (*intendencias*) of the captaincy general of Guatemala, in conformity with the provisions of the royal ordinance of intendants of the Province of New Spain of 1786, which applied to Guatemala, and under whose régime of intendant provinces they were at the time of freeing themselves from Spain in 1821;

Whereas by royal decree of July 24, 1791, on petition of the intendant governor of Comayagua and in conformity with the orders of the superior board of Guatemala, by virtue of the provisions of articles 8 and 9 of the royal ordinance of intendants of New Spain, the incorporation of the larger jurisdiction (*alcaldía mayor*) of Tegucigalpa to the intendancy and government of Comayagua (Honduras), with all the territory of his bishopric, in regard to said larger jurisdiction of the Province annexed to the Province of Honduras and united with the latter ecclesiastically, as well as in the collection of taxes, was approved;

Whereas by virtue of this royal ordinance the Province of Honduras was formed in 1791 out of all the territories of the original Province of Comayagua, the territories annexed to Tegucigalpa, and the rest of the bishopric of Comayagua, comprising in this manner a region that bordered on the south with Nicaragua, on the southwest and west with the Pacific Ocean, San Salvador, and Guatemala, and on the north, northeast, and east with the Atlantic Ocean, except that part of the coast occupied at the time by Indians, Mesquite Indians, Indian and mulatto half-breeds, *Payas*, etc.;

Whereas prior to the provisions of said royal decree of 1791, the demarcation made by two other royal decrees of August 23, 1745, must be considered, one of which appointed Don JUAN DE VERA governor and general commander of the Province of Honduras for the government of this Province and of the other Provinces comprised in the entire bishopric of Comayagua and the district of the larger jurisdiction (alcaldia mayor) of Tegucigalpa, and of all the territories and coasts that are included from the place where the jurisdiction of the Province of Yucatan to the Cape of Gracias a Dios terminates; and in the other decree appointed Don ALONSO FERNANDEZ DE HEREDIA, governor and general commander of the province of Nicaragua, of Costa Rica, of the district of Corregidor of Realejo, of *alcadias mayores* or of the greater jurisdiction of Sutiaba, of Nicoya, and of the other territories included between the Cape of Gracias a Dios and the Chagre River, exclusive; in said documents therefore is shown the Cape of Gracias a Dios as the boundary point of the jurisdictions conferred on the said governors of Honduras and of Nicaragua in the capacity in which they were appointed;

Whereas the communication of the captain general of Guatemala, Don PEDRO DE RIVERA, addressed to the King on November 23, 1742, concerning the Mesquite Indians, in which he affirms that the Cape of Gracias a Dios is on the coast of the Province of Comayagua (Honduras), is also an antecedent worthy of consideration;

Whereas by virtue of the treaty with England in 1786, the English vacated the Mesquite country, at the same time that the port of Trujillo was again opened and laws were adopted for its government, four Spanish towns were ordered created on the Mesquite coast at Rio Tinto, Cape Gracias a Dios, Bluefields, and at the mouth of the San Juan River, and although these places remained directly subject to the military authority of the captaincy general of Guatemala, both parties have agreed that this did not alter in any way the territories of the Provinces of Nicaragua and Honduras, the latter Republic having shown by numerous certified records and accounts that before and after 1791 the intendent government of Comayagua intervened in all matters over which it had jurisdiction at Trujillo, Rio Tinto, and Cape Gracias a Dios;

Whereas the seventh law of title 2 of book 2 of the Digest of Indias, on specifying the manner of making the division of the discovered territories, provided that it should be made in such manner that the division for temporal use should conform with that for spiritual purposes, the archbishoprics corresponding to the districts of the audiencias (courts), the bishoprics to the governments and districts of larger jurisdiction, and parishes and curates to the ordinary districts of the corregidors and alcaldes;

Whereas the bishopric of Comayagua or of Honduras, which, prior to 1791, had exercised acts of jurisdiction on the lands now in dispute, performing such acts in an unquestioned manner from the said date of the demarcation by the Government intendency of the same name, having proved that it governed in matters concerning the collection of tithes, issued matrimonial licenses, furnished curates, and attended to ecclesiastical claims at Trujillo, Rio Tinto, and Cape Gracias a Dios;

Whereas the village or town of Cape Gracias a Dios, situated somewhat to the south of the cape of the same name and on the south bank of the most important mouth of the river now called Coco or Segovia, was, prior to 1791, included in the ecclesiastical jurisdiction of the bishopric of Comayagua, formed a part of said jurisdiction at the time that the ancient Spanish province of Honduras organized itself into an independent state;

Whereas the constitution of the State of Honduras of 1825, adopted at the time it was united to Nicaragua, forming, with other States, the Federal Republic of Central America, provides that "its territory comprises all that corresponds and has always corresponded to the bishopric of Honduras;"

Whereas the demarcation fixed for the province or intendency of Comayagua or of Honduras by the aforesaid royal decree of July 24, 1791, continued without change at the time the provinces of Honduras and Nicaragua obtained their independence; therefore, even though the King approved by royal decree of January 24, 1818, the reestablishment of the greater jurisdiction (alcaldia mayor) of Tegucigalpa, with certain features of autonomy in economic matters, said greater jurisdiction continued to form a division of the province of Comayagua or Honduras, under the jurisdiction of the political chief of the province, and as such division took part in the election held on November 5, 1820, for a deputy to the Spanish Cortes and a substitute deputy for the province of Comayagua, and likewise took part with the other divisions of Gracias, Choluteca, Olancho, Yoro, with Olanchito and Trujillo, Tencoa, and Comayagua, in the election of the provincial deputies of Honduras, said election being held on November 6, 1820;

Whereas on organizing the Government and intendency of Nicaragua, in conformity with the royal ordinance of intendents of 1786, there were formed the five political divisions of Leon, Matagalpa, El Realejo, Subtiaga, and Nicoya, not including in this division nor in that which the intendent governor, Don Juan de Ayassa, proposed in 1788—territories that are now claimed on the north and west of Cape Gracias a Dios by Nicaragua—nor does it appear that the jurisdiction of the bishopric of Nicaragua extended to this cape, and it should be borne in mind that the last intendent governor of Nicaragua, Don MIGUEL GONZALEZ SARAVIA, on describing the province that was under his command in his book entitled "Political and Statistical Sketch of Nicaragua," published in 1824, stated that the boundary line of said province on the south runs from the Gulf of Fonseca in the Pacific to the Perlas River in the sea of the north (Atlantic);

Whereas, even though at any period it may have been thought that the jurisdiction of Honduras extended to the south of Cape Gracias a Dios, the examining commission has found that such extension of dominion was never well determined, and that, at all events, was ephemeral below the town and port of Cape Gracias a Dios, and, therefore, it does not follow that the common boundary on the *Atlantic coast is* Sandy Bay, as is claimed by Honduras;

Whereas, in order to arrive at the place called Cape Camaron, as well as that of Sandy Bay, it would be necessary to resort to artificial boundary lines that in no manner coincide with the well-marked natural boundaries recommended in the Gámez-Bonilla Treaty;

Whereas all the maps (Spanish and foreign) that the commission appointed by royal decree of April 17, 1905, has examined referring to the territories of Honduras and Nicaragua prior to the date of independence show the separation between both territories at Cape Gracias a Dios or to the south of that cape, and that, in a period subsequent to independence, maps such as those of Squier (New York, 1854); Baily (London, 1856); Dussieux (made under the supervision of Stieler, Riepert, Petermann & Begghaus, Paris, 1868); Dunn (New Orleans, 1884); Colton, Ohman & Co. (New York, 1890); Andrews (Leipzig, 1901); Armour's (Chicago, 1901), indicate the boundary at the Cape of Gracias a Dios;

Whereas of the maps examined relating to the question only five show the boundary between Honduras and Nicaragua on the Atlantic side to the north of Cape Gracias a Dios, and these five maps are all subsequent to the date of independence and even of the period in which litigation was commenced between the two States referred to; that of these five maps three are Nicaraguan and the other two (one German and the other North American), although they place the boundary to the north of Cape Gracias a Dios, indicate it at a point very near this cape, or at the extreme northern part of the delta of the Segovia River;

Whereas geographic authorities, such as López de Velasco (1571–1574), Tomás López (1758), González Saravia (governor of Nicaragua, 1823), Squier (1856), Reclus (1870), Sonnenstern (1874), Bancroft (1890), have indicated the outlet of the Segovia River, or the Cape Gracias a Dios, or a point to the south of this cape, as the common boundary between Honduras and Nicaragua on the Atlantic coast;

Whereas the Cape of Gracias a Dios has been acknowledged as the common boundary between Nicaragua and Honduras in various diplomatic documents originating in the latter Republic, such as the circulars addressed to foreign governments by Don FRANCISCO CASTELLON, Minister Plenipotentiary of Nicaragua and Honduras (1844); Don SEBASTIAN SALINAS, Minister of Foreign Relations of Nicaragua (1848), and Don JOSÉ GUERRERO, Supreme Director of the State of Nicaragua (1848), and the instructions conferred by the Government of Nicaragua on its Envoy Extraordinary in Spain, Don JOSÉ DE MARCOLETA, for the recognition of the independence of said Republic (1850);

Whereas, as is deduced from the foregoing exposition, the point that best responds to the reasons of historic right, of equity, and of geographic position, for the purpose of serving as a common boundary between the two litigious States on the coast of the Atlantic, is Cape Gracias a Dios, and that this cape marks that which has practically been the limit of extension or conquest of Nicaragua toward the north and of Honduras toward the south;

Whereas, after the adoption of the Cape of Gracias a Dios as the common boundary on the Atlantic coast between the two litigious States, it is proper to fix the frontier boundary line between this point and Portillo of Teotecacinte, which was the point reached by the mixed Honduran-Nicaraguan commission;

Whereas, contiguous to the Cape of Gracias a Dios on the Atlantic there exists no great cordillera which by its nature and direction could be taken as a frontier between both States starting from said point, and that, on the contrary, there is found at this same place as a perfectly marked boundary the outlet and channel of so large and important a river as that called Coco, Segovia, or Wanks;

Whereas, that afterwards the course of this river, for at least a considerable part thereof, offers, because of its direction and the circumstances of its channel, the most natural and exact boundary that could be desired;

Whereas this same Coco, Segovia, or Wanks River for a large part of its course has figured and figures in many maps, public documents, and geographic descriptions as the frontier between Honduras and Nicaragua;

Whereas, in the volumes of the Blue Book corresponding to the years 1856 and 1860, presented by the Government of His Britannic Majesty to Parliament, and which are included among the documents submitted by Nicaragua, it is stated that according to the communication of the representative of England in the United States, who intervened in the negotiations for the purpose of settling the question of the Mosquito territory (1852), Honduras and Nicaragua had mutually acknowledged the Wanks or Segovia River as the frontier; that in article 2 of the convention between Great Britain and Honduras on August 27, 1859, His Britannic Majesty acknowledged the middle of the Wanks or Segovia River, that empties at the Cape of Gracias a Dios, as the boundary between the Republic of Honduras and the territory of the Mesquite Indians, and that in article 4 of the treaty with Great Britain and the United States of America of October 17, 1856, it was declared that all the territory to the south of the Wanks or Segovia River, not included in the part reserved for the Mesquite Indians, and without prejudging the rights of Honduras, should be considered within the boundaries and under the sovereignty of the Republic of Nicaragua;

Whereas it is necessary to establish a point at which the course of the Coco, Segovia, or Wanks River must be abandoned before said river, turning toward the southwest, enters acknowledged Nicaraguan territory;

Whereas the point having the best conditions required in this case is the place where the said Coco or Segovia River receives on its left bank the waters of its tributary, the Poteca or Bodega River;

Whereas the place of the confluence of the Poteca with the Segovia River has also been adopted by various authorities, and singularly by the Nicaraguan engineer, Don MAXIMILIANO V. SONNENSTERN, in his "Geography of Nicaragua for use in the primary schools of the Republic" (Managua, 1874);

Whereas, on following the channel of the Poteca River upstream to its junction with the Guineo or Namaki River, there is encountered the south site of Teotecacinte, to which the document filed by Nicaragua, dated August 26, 1720, refers, and according to which said site belonged to the jurisdiction of the city of New Segovia (Nicaragua);

Whereas the point where Guineo River enters and forms a part of the Poteca River can be taken as the frontier boundary, which corresponds to the survey of the said site of Teotecacinte up to its juncture with the Portillo of the same name, but in such a manner that the aforesaid site remains within the jurisdiction of Nicaragua;

Whereas the selection of the confluence of the Poteca with the Coco or Segovia River as the point at which the channel of the last-named river should be abandoned, in order to arrive at the Portillo of Teotecacinte in the manner referred to, might be the cause of doubt and controversy, due to the assumption that it would result beneficially to Honduras in the narrow region in the northern part of the basin of the Segovia River, which would thus remain within the boundaries of Honduras; to offset this and as compensation for having adopted the outlet or mouth of the Segovia River in the manner hereinbefore expressed, the bay and town of Gracias a Dios, which, according to prior evidence, would belong by better right to Honduras, remain within the domain of Nicaragua; and

Whereas, lastly, that although rule 4 of article 2 of the treaty of Gámez-Bonilla or Tegucigalpa directs that in order to fix the boundaries between both Republics the dominion or ownership of territory fully proved will be respected without acknowledging the juridical value to possession in fact that either of the parties might allege, rule 6 of the same article provides that, if expedient, compensation may be made and even indemnifications fixed to endeavor to establish, as far as possible, well-defined natural boundaries.

In accordance with the solution proposed by the examining commission and in conformity with the opinion of the full council of state and with that of my council of ministers—

Declare that the dividing line between the Republic of Honduras and Nicaragua from the Atlantic to the Portillo of Teotecacinte, where the mixed boundary commission left it in 1901, because they could not agree as to its continuation in their subsequent meetings, is fixed in the following manner: The extreme common boundary point on the Atlantic coast shall be the outlet into the sea of the Coco, Segovia, or Wanks River, contiguous to the Cape of Gracias a Dios, considering as the mouth of the river the mouth of its principal arm between Hara and the island of San Pio, where the said cape is situated, Honduras retaining the islets or keys existing within said principal arm before arriving at the bar, and conserving for Nicaragua the south shore of the said principal mouth with the aforesaid island of San Pio, together with the bay and population of the Cape of Gracias a Dios and the entire arm called Gracias that flows into the Bay of Gracias a Dios between the mainland and the aforesaid island of San Pio.

Starting from the mouth of the Segovia or Coco River the boundary line will follow the water course or *Talweg* of this river upstream without interruption to its confluence with the Poteca or Bodega River, and from that point the said boundary line will leave the Segovia River, follow the watercourse of the said Poteca or Bodega tributary and continue upstream to its junction with the Guineo or Namashi River.

From this junction the boundary line shall take the direction that corresponds to the demarcation of the site of Teotecacinte, in accordance with the survey made in 1720, in order to arrive at Portillo of Teotecacinte, so that said site remains integrally within the jurisdiction of Nicaragua.

Given, in duplicate, at the Royal Palace of Madrid on December 23, 1906.

ALFONSO.

JUAN PEREZ CABALLERO,
Secretary of State.

CONCESSION OF LAND AND WATER PRIVILEGES.

A valuable concession has been made by the Nicaraguan Government to a New York company's representative for the development of the commercial, agricultural, and mineral resources of Nicaragua.

A summary of the report made on the subject by the United States consul at Managua is as follows:

The company obligates itself to deepen the passage over the bar of the Rio Grande to 14 feet in order that vessels suited to the banana and fruit trade may enter the stream, and is granted the period of four years in which to complete the work, which shall represent an expenditure of not less than $100,000 gold. Within eighteen months the company shall run its first steamer on the river, and thereafter keep up navigation for all the time the concession is in force.

The company agrees to construct a wharf and a custom-house at the mouth of the river, upon the completion of which the Government will declare the place an open port with the name Port Zelaya.

The right to denounce and acquire 50,000 *manzanas* (about 86,500 acres) of land suitable for banana growing along the river and its tributaries is allowed the company, which land may be subdivided into lots of 100 or more manzanas each. Special rights and privileges in this connection are provided for colonists whom the company proposes to induce to settle upon their lands, it being stipulated that such shall be exempt for a period of ten years from the payment of duties on all domestic necessities, machinery, and live stock, and that their property and products be exempt from tax and, with a few exceptions, from export duties.

For the purpose of facilitating the loading and discharging of cargo during the period in which the bar of the river is being opened the company binds itself to construct a wharf and warehouse on Man-of-war Key (an island close by), in deep water, which shall constitute a part of Port Zelaya. After the river improvements have been consummated the structures on said island are to be maintained as a safeguard to commerce and navigation in the event of accident or damage to interior waterway facilities.

The foregoing contract relates to a section of this Republic that is celebrated for the richness of its agricultural lands, its undeveloped mineral resources, and opportunities for extensive water transportation.. At a distance of 80 miles inland from its mouth the Rio Grande is reported to have a good navigable depth. The main river, its branches and tributaries, covered by this concession, penetrate a large territory. Wild rubber abounds along the banks of these streams, as also valuable hard woods, such as mahogany, cedar, rosewood, etc., which latter the company and its colonists are granted the right to cut for domestic purposes. It is estimated that over $50,000 gold per month is produced by miners in the mineral zone extending through the central part of the Republic bisected by the Rio Grande water system.

INCREASED PRICE OF PUBLIC LANDS.

Under date of December 14, 1906, the President of Nicaragua issued a decree whereby the price of public lands in the Republic was advanced 50 per cent over the rate fixed in the previous decree regulating such sales and bearing date of July 28, 1903.

It is officially stated that:

"The President of the Republic, considering that the price fixed by law for vacant lands is very low and consequently not in proportion with the opening and importance which the industrial, agricultural, transportation, and commercial industries of the country

with the expenses caused to the public adminis-
erprises, decrees:

om the 1st of January next the price of vacant
reased 50 per cent over the tariff established by
28, 1903.

. 2. ryment for said lands shall be effected in the fol-
manner, vwo-thirds in current money and the other third
..ments of public credit.

ᴀᴛ. 3.–All lands which up to date have not been paid for in
itional treasury, are comprehended in this decree."

amendment to the existing Agrarian law of the Republic also
.ies that an advance shall be made over previously established
ɴ for property sold for cattle raising, agricultural purposes, or
o which irrigation may be easily effected. It is furthermore de-
that forest lands producing timber capable of being utilized
et or dyewoods, for the production of rubber or resinous
.ances, shall be paid for with an advance of $1 per hectare over
nary cost of the land.

BUDGET FOR THE YEARS 1906 AND 1907.

Nicaraguan budget for the two years' term—1906 and 1907—
was promulgated on February 21, 1906, and contained the following
estimates of revenue and expenditure for the period:

Estimated revenues for 1906 and 1907.

Customs revenue	$12,000,000
Liquor revenue	4,800,000
Tobacco revenue	433,333
Slaughter tax	738,900
Stamped paper	350,000
Monopolies (powder, etc.)	210,000
Sale of waste lands	190,000
National railways and steamers (rent)	760,000
Other national services	376,000
Fines, etc	82,000
Sundry receipts	554,000
Total	20,434,233

Estimated expenditures for 1906 and 1907.

Department of—

Government	1,101,903
Police	2,725,890
Charity	94,840
War and marine	3,721,642
Finance and public credit	4,900,280
Internal development	4,762,954
Justice	1,080,236
Foreign affairs	206,240
Public instruction	2,467,466
Total	20,941,451

PANAMA.

TRADE WITH THE UNITED STATES.

The growth of United States trade with Panama is shown by the fact that imports from that Republic in the calendar year 1904, the first year of its existence, were $812,947; in 1905, $879,145; and in 1906, $1,448,686; and the exports to Panama were, in 1904, $2,683,801; in 1905, $7,831,564; and in 1906, $14,239,471.

Exports from the United States to Panama now average more than $1,000,000 a month, and the total trade with that Republic seems likely to aggregate $16,000,000 in the fiscal year which ends with the month of June.

Bananas are the largest single item of the practically $1,000,000 worth of merchandise imported therefrom in the seven months ending with January, 1907, the value of bananas alone being $741,870, against $338,217 in the corresponding months of the preceding year. India rubber, of which the United States is steadily increasing her importations and consumption, amounted to $91,720, against $55,028 in the corresponding months of the preceding year. Of vegetable ivory the imports from Panama were nearly 2,000,000 pounds in the seven months, against a little over half a million pounds in the same months of last year. Of hides the figures were nearly a half million pounds against less than 300,000 pounds in the corresponding months of the preceding year, and of coffee 178,000 pounds against but 25,000 pounds in the same months of last year.

The fact that meat and dairy products aggregated $750,000, boots and shoes nearly $200,000, lard over $250,000, shows that the exports to Panama are not by any means exclusively for the canal or for the use of the Government in building it, but that a large proportion is for individual and personal consumption by persons residing in Panama.

INSTALLATION OF TELEPHONES AT PANAMA.

The President of the Republic on January 17, 1907, approved a contract with the *Compañia de Teléfonos* to take effect February 1, and to continue for five years, providing for the installation of telephones in the fire and police departments and other public offices of the city of Panama.

Fifty instruments are to be installed, for which the Government will pay five balboas per month for each.

PARAGUAY.

BUDGET ESTIMATES FOR 1907.

Following are the details of the Paraguayan estimates of revenue and expenditure for 1907 as sanctioned by the Government on September 17, 1906:

REVENUE.

	Gold.	Currency.
Import duties	$1,675,000	
Export duties	615,000	
Wharf dues	115,000	
Warehouse dues	30,000	
Transit dues on foreign maté	27,000	
Consular fees	20,300	
Tax on timber	70,000	
Sundries	14,700	
Tax on internal consumption		$1,500,000
Stamps and stamped paper		905,000
Succession duty		70,000
Post-office		131,000
Telegraph service		240,000
"Contribución directa"		2,500,000
Fines re "Contribución directa"		80,000
Sales of national timber		410,000
Sundries		244,000
Total	2,567,000	6,080,000

EXPENDITURE.

	Gold.	Currency.
Legislative Congress	$492	$1,247,040
Presidency of the Republic		314,400
Department of the Interior	7,336	7,986,026
Department of Foreign Affairs	114,148	1,633,920
Department of Finance	600	2,513,160
Department of Justice and Public Worship and Instruction	52,234	6,086,360
Department of War and Marine	24,720	7,347,900
Special laws	180,457	2,880,000
Total	389,037	30,008,806

The item "Special laws" includes in the estimate of $189,457 gold the service of the external debt at the maximum rate of 3 per cent interest which commences with the July, 1907, coupon.

POSTPONEMENT OF AGRICULTURAL EXHIBITION.

Paraguay's Agricultural Exhibition, to be held in Asuncion, is postponed until the end of March, 1907, owing to the depressed aspect of native industries consequent upon the locust invasion and the protracted drought during the year 1906.

Machinery for the exhibit will be received until February 28, 1907, and should, in general character, be sufficiently cheap to be within the use of purchasers on a small scale. Economical machinery for making cheese, butter, preparing coffee for the market, breaking palm nuts, small cotton gins, small flour mills, starch-making machines, fiber machinery and oil apparatus, rice cleaners, and saws used in tree felling are all sure of a favorable opportunity if properly placed on the Paraguayan market.

NEW STAMP LAW.

The new stamp law of the Paraguayan Republic, promulgated December 8, 1906, abrogates that of October 6, 1896, and provides for the following distribution of the new revenues:

Thirty-five per cent for the general expenditures of the Republic, 25 per cent for the construction of a chief law court, and 25 per cent for the construction of schools.

The following are extracts from the law:

"All private documents involving the payment or return of a certain amount of money, by one single party, shall pay one per thousand on the value stated therein, if they are payable on sight or within ninety days, and two per thousand if they are payable within a longer period.

"If the amount to be paid or returned is not stated in such documents, a stamp of 50 *pesos* shall be affixed thereto.

"Permits issued by local authorities for the free transit of timber, tobacco, yerba maté, and hides, and bills of sale, or barter, of cattle and horses shall have affixed thereto one 50-*centavo* stamp.

"A 20-*centavo* stamp shall be affixed to checks drawn on banks.

"Lawyers, accountants, translators, and amanuenses shall affix a 20-*centavo* stamp to every document presented by them in the performance of their duties. Solicitors shall pay 10 *centavos*.

"Contracts of bargain and sale, barter, transfer of stocks and rights, and all other documents transferring or modifying the ownership of real estate, shall pay a tax of three per thousand ad valorem.

"Conditional gifts and transfers of real estate shall pay a tax of two per thousand ad valorem. If such gifts or transfers are made without consideration, the benefited party shall pay one per thousand ad valorem.

"A tax of one per thousand ad valorem shall be paid on the following: Leases of more than one year; contracts of partnership and extensions thereof; contracts for services and contracts for work."

PERU.

FOREIGN COMMERCE, FIRST FOUR MONTHS OF 1906.

Figures covering the commerce of Peru for the first four months of 1906 give import values as £1,717,282, as compared with £1,265,025 in the corresponding period of 1905. The figures for export are £1,739,575 in the first third of 1906, as against £1,702,654 in the same months of the preceding year, a gain in both branches of foreign trade thus being shown.

als, and metals, coal, machinery, and tools, and
,ading items on the import list, while sugar, min-
in and hides lead among the exports.

f origin for the various imports were as follows,
es net   n Peruvian pounds:

	1906.	1905.
,y	£288,118,689	£212,745,145
lla	93,441,682	38,823,042
a	65,798,215	48,955,123
	126,772,537	60,382,223
	12,318,427	28,953,581
	19,453,131	16,502,630
alos	307,530,068	179,443,200
	166,952,622	53,915,232
n	448,728,900	436,490,581
	19,254,625	26,640,504
	61,013,335	47,147,034
	77,992,769	72,853,405

of destination were:

	1906.	1905.
	£148,352,652	£140,271,204
	25,877,684	45,664,658
	21,000	26,229,000
	75,676,771	43,333,802
	453,276	27,680,542
		14,246,568
Chile	434,773,084	228,240,373
United States	158,650,035	152,063,172
France	144,889,001	123,996,382
Great Britain	668,672,804	803,862,923
Others	81,209,072	24,058,410

EXPORTS TO NEW YORK, FIRST TEN MONTHS OF 1906.

The total value of Peruvian products shipped for the port of New
York during the first ten months ending October, 1906, was $1,647,547.
The items of export, with their respective values, were as follows:

Cotton	$397,042	Guano	$24,145
Sugar	127,460	Furniture	105
Coffee	25	Goatskins	238,283
Copper	247,204	Deerskins	8,229
Cocoa leaves	203,052	Straw hats	107,128
Hides	1,096	Leaf tobacco	25
Rubber	60,261	Sundries	9,077
Alpaca wool	224,076		
Sheep wool	1,236	Total	1,647,547
Lumber	103		

EXPORT DUTY ON SILVER COINS.

The Peruvian Government has promulgated a law authorizing the
Executive to impose on exports of silver coins a duty exceeding by 50
per cent, the difference between its legal value, established by the law
of October 13, 1900, and its intrinsic value, which is to be transmitted

weekly to the Minister of Finance by the Chamber of Commerce of the city of Lima.

Travelers and the members of ships' crews are prohibited from carrying with them on leaving national territory more than 10 silver *soles;* any excess will be confiscated.

SALVADOR.

FOREIGN COMMERCE, FIRST QUARTER, 1906.

Latest statistics of the foreign commerce of Salvador cover the first quarter of the calendar year 1906, showing total export valuations for the three months of 7,243,086.11 *colones,* and imports valued at 1,056,163.59 *colones.*

Coffee was by far the largest single item of export, the shipments figuring for 6,565,515.62 *colones,* while cotton textiles, valued at 362,567.30, stand at the head of the import list. Following "sundries," which form the next important classification, come flour, 63,004.20 *colones,* and hardware valued at 62,944.98 *colones.*

The countries of destination for the various exports, with the valuations received, were as follows:

	Colones.		Colones.
Germany	1,546,307.85	Holland	4,520.40
British America	99,636.35	Honduras	23,425.50
Austria-Hungary	339,292.90	Italy	1,043,429.36
Costa Rica	4,630.00	Nicaragua	250.00
Chile	732.00	Norway	40,417.40
Denmark	2,268.75	Panama	34,270.60
Spain	342,603.40	Peru	11,570.00
United States	1,810,521.00	Sweden	9,120.00
France	1,612,471.85		
Great Britain	416,064.35	Total	7,243,086.11
Guatemala	555.00		

Following are the countries of origin for the merchandise imported into the Republic during the quarter in reference:

	Colones.		Colones.
Germany	106,523.91	Guatemala	1,295.00
Austria-Hungary	4.232.68	Holland	6,905.00
Belgium	29,068.50	Honduras	17,009.35
Brazil	27.45	Italy	31,086.22
Costa Rica	7,142.40	Japan	3,551.40
Cuba	846.75	Mexico	15,104.56
Chile	650.00	Nicaragua	11,330.70
China	20,400.09	Portugal	919.25
Denmark	336.87	Russia	102.75
Ecuador	100.00	Sweden	1,139.80
Spain	16,822.84	Switzerland	1,140.00
United States	335,925.47		
France	87,200.67	Total	1,056,163.59
Great Britain	357,345.95		

SUBSIDY FOR GERMAN STEAMSHIPS.

The "*Diario Oficial*" for January 10, 1907, of the Republic of Salvador, publishes the text of a contract made between the Government and the German steamship line *Kosmos*, as approved by the President on January 8, whereby a subsidy of 500 *pesos* per month is granted for specified service.

By the terms of the contract the steamers of the company are obliged to touch at the Salvadorian ports at least twice a month; to grant a rebate of 50 per cent in tariff rates for the transport of army personnel and war material between the ports of the Republic, either in time of peace or war; to transport the President of the Republic and the secretaries of state between the ports of Central America, Mexico, and California free of charge;·and to provide free transport between the ports of the Republic for the chiefs and administrators of customs.

This contract is to continue in force for two years, unless one of the contracting parties gives a preliminary notice of four months indicating a desire·to terminate the same.

PROPAGANDA FOR SALVADOR COFFEE.

The "*Diario Oficial*" for January 12, 1907, publishes the Executive decree of the Government of Salvador, authorizing the Consul-General of the Republic in San Francisco to pay to the Salvador Coffee Company the sum of $200 gold per month for the purpose of placing before the public in a more adequate manner the merits of the coffee grown in Salvador.

QUALIFICATIONS FOR THE PRACTICE OF MEDICINE.

Natives or foreigners resident in Salvador, who have obtained, or who may obtain in future, a diploma conferring upon them the degree of doctor in medicine or its equivalent, the degree of doctor in pharmacy and natural sciences, or the degree of dental surgeon in any foreign school or university, may, under the following conditions, become members of the school of medicine, pharmacy, natural sciences, and dental surgery:

1. File in due form, properly certified, the respective diploma, and establish the identity of the respective person. The applicant shall also prove that he is in the enjoyment of the rights conferred upon him by the diploma.

2. Present proof of good deportment.

3. The diploma shall not have been obtained contrary to Salvadorian laws.

4. He shall pass an examination, unless exempted therefrom by the *provisions of* a treaty or treaties. The examination shall consist of a *thesis which* the applicant must submit in accordance with this law,

and of questions upon any subjects the committee may deem proper to ask him.

Persons on whom the school of medicine, pharmacy, natural sciences, and dental surgery has conferred an honorary degree, shall be considered members of said school.

Only persons of undoubted qualifications and character, who have distinguished themselves in writing scientific works of acknowledged merit in any of the branches included in the curriculum of the school, shall be honorary members.

The degrees mentioned in the foregoing articles shall only be conferred in Salvador by the school of medicine, pharmacy, natural sciences, and dental surgery.

UNITED STATES.

TRADE WITH LATIN AMERICA.

STATEMENT OF IMPORTS AND EXPORTS.

Following is the latest statement, from figures compiled by the Bureau of Statistics, United States Department of Commerce and Labor, showing the value of the trade between the United States and the Latin American countries. The report is for the month of January, 1907, with a comparative statement for the corresponding month of the previous year; also for the seven months ending January, 1907, as compared with the same period of the preceding year. It should be explained that the figures from the various custom-houses, showing imports and exports for any month, are not received by the Treasury Department until about the 20th of the following month, and some time is necessarily consumed in compilation and printing, so that the returns for January, for example, are not published until some time in March.

IMPORTS OF MERCHANDISE.

Articles and countries.	January—		Seven months ending January—	
	1906.	1907.	1906.	1907.
Cocoa (*Cacao; coco ou cacao; cacao*):	Dollars.	Dollars.	Dollars.	Dollars.
Central America	526	8,252	5,546	24,506
Brazil	248,665	65,384	802,147	1,581,827
Other South America	184,193	168,800	1,027,169	1,080,622
Coffee (*Café; Café; Café*):				
Central America	685,881	509,091	1,959,311	1,222,369
Mexico	127,091	93,671	1,044,566	495,434
Brazil	3,784,488	5,037,466	35,384,721	37,082,211
Other South America	930,168	856,357	5,565,305	5,237,881
Copper (*Cobre; Cobre; Cuivre*):				
Cuba	10,491	4,169	45,477	44,659
Mexico	1,694,333	1,545,433	10,208,341	10,405,289
South America	74,176	157,195	278,425	442,584

IMPORTS OF MERCHANDISE—Continued.

Articles and countries.	January—		Seven months ending January—	
	1906.	1907.	1906.	1907.
Fibers:				
Cotton, unmanufactured (*Algodon en rama; Algodao em rama; Coton non manufacture*):	*Dollars.*	*Dollars.*	*Dollars.*	*Dollars.*
South America	71,193	121,062	276,709	207,226
Sisal grass (*Henequén; Henequem; henequen*):				
Mexico	976,060	1,508,899	9,139,998	9,376,069
Fruits:				
Bananas (*Plátanos; Bananas; Bananes*):				
Central America	209,028	327,893	2,293,092	1,993,999
Cuba	33	32	270,028	349,160
South America	24,661	30,894	209,096	67,729
Oranges (*Naranjas; Laranjas; Oranges*):				
Mexico	800	2,365	46,801	34,677
Cuba	661	2,114	5,349	6,215
Hides and skins (*Cueros y pieles; couros e pelles; Cuirs et peaus*):				
Mexico	492,208	531,774	2,165,808	2,631,083
Cuba	14,418	31,941	57,274	196,165
Brazil	150,768	142,967	1,085,408	1,308,828
Other South America	930,526	1,545,185	5,991,975	6,559,127
India rubber, crude (*Goma elástica; Borracha cruda; Caoutchouc*):				
Central America	74,794	97,592	432,302	445,463
Mexico	76,062	146,683	240,060	971,673
Brazil	2,987,310	2,912,074	12,334,937	16,720,378
Other South America	93,753	46,106	709,495	863,046
Lead, in pigs, bars, etc. (*Plomo en galapagos, barras, etc.; Chumbo em linguados; barras, etc.; Plomb en saumons, en barres, etc.*):				
Mexico	352,190	197,502	1,754,259	1,872,698
Sugar, not above No. 16 Dutch standard (*Azucar, inferior al No. 16 del modeloholandes; Assucar, nao superior no No. 16 de padrao hollandez; Sucre, pas au-dessus du type hollandais No. 16*):				
Mexico	618	30,349	26,442	94,107
Cuba	2,337,909	5,045,581	23,032,142	22,156,101
Brazil	167,644	188,366	237,178	828,053
Other South America	170,875	171,151	1,537,380	1,728,006
Tobacco (*Tabaco; Tabaco; Tabac*):				
Cuba	1,772,012	1,657,050	9,549,778	11,821,397
Wood, mahogany (*Caoba; Mogno; Acajou*):				
Central America	30,330	21,349	300,126	247,212
Mexico	67,348	86,216	251,881	346,567
Cuba	10,275	4,958	65,500	109,702
Wool (*Lana; Lã; Laine*):				
South America—				
Class 1 (clothing)	1,408,102	776,422	2,456,820	879,758
Class 2 (combing)	20,858	111,214	160,562	246,322
Class 3 (carpet)	2,783	900	474,155	419,421

EXPORTS OF MERCHANDISE.

Agricultural implements (*Instrumentos agricolas; Instrumentos de agricultura; Machines agricoles*):				
Mexico	33,857	27,839	264,828	247,162
Cuba	10,442	2,985	125,164	38,219
Argentine Republic	539,873	302,507	4,405,195	2,967,737
Brazil	4,322	6,402	59,125	61,184
Chile	26,594	29,478	268,595	308,687
Other South America	35,615	16,492	201,778	147,144
Animals:				
Cattle (*Ganado vacuno; gado; Betail*):				
Mexico	73,057	68,276	382,590	551,202
Cuba	26,335	11,031	1,301,011	372,461
South America	7,626	9,341	77,273	37,289
Hogs (*Cerdos; Porcos; Porcs*):				
Mexico	32,924	24,076	95,937	145,766
Horses (*Caballos; Cavallos; Chevaux*):				
Mexico	11,695	42,800	150,430	245,423
Sheep (*Orejas; Orelhas; Brebis*):				
Mexico	7,403		24,655	56,618

EXPORTS OF MERCHANDISE—Continued.

Articles and countries.	January—		Seven months ending January—	
	1906.	190".	1906.	1907.
	Dollars.	Dollars.	Dollars.	Dollars.
Breadstuffs:				
Corn (Maíz; Milho; Maïs):				
Central America............	4,624	1,768	72,361	16,996
Mexico....................	80,684	112,327	519,376	707,565
Cuba.....................	196,808	145,242	783,016	804,157
South America...........	992	390.	12,791	5,888
Oats (Avena; Aveia; Avoine):				
Central America..........	682	6,272	19,234	14,660
Mexico...................	2,704	8,509	16,149	32,803
Cuba....................	15,240	35,216	132,577	224,679
South America...........	2,842	788	16,585	5,602
Wheat (Trigo; Trigo; Blé):				
Central America..........	6,570	1,608	32,006	19,463
Mexico...................	125,917	124,565	1,020,502	426,690
South America...........	30	15,753	383,644	296,929
Wheat flour (Harina de trigo; Farinha de trigo; Farine de blé):				
Central America..........	108,474	149,324	1,094,522	951,351
Mexico...................	13,602	10,786	122,313	72,467
Cuba....................	224,169	230,256	1,896,004	1,713,428
Brazil...................	144,369	102,609	737,500	776,496
Colombia................	5,522	19,216	470,670	93,878
Other South America.....	150,571	107,064	1,512,262	1,260,601
Carriages, etc.:				
Automobiles (Automóviles; Automoviles; Automobiles):				
Mexico...................	30,935	55,932	145,179	445,073
South America...........	3,588	23,839	40,490	131,381
Carriages, cars, etc., and parts thereof (Carruaje, carros y sus accesorios; Carruagens, carros e partes de carros; Voitures, wagons, et leurs parties):				
Central America..........	246,503	198,945	521,284	660,397
Mexico...................	212,116	184,938	602,226	1,353,228
Cuba....................	173,127	70,452	603,973	467,855
Argentine Republic......	73,843	297,918	263,457	1,296,088
Chile...................	5,114	5,801	365,635	78,944
Other South America.....	17,102	38,060	203,995	261,306
Clocks and watches (Relojes de pared y bosillo; Relogios de bolso e parede; Horloges et montres):				
Central America..........	1,113	1,682	9,856	9,817
Mexico...................	5,449	5,788	33,945	29,095
Argentine Republic......	5,790	2,230	45,986	30,776
Brasil..................	6,883	7,664	40,873	56,171
Chile...................	4,746	2,234	41,904	26,292
Other South America.....	5,496	3,352	32,434	34,546
Coal (Carbón; Carvão; Charbon):				
Mexico...................	293,473	259,080	1,688,088	1,777,333
Cuba....................	211,465	187,091	1,092,082	1,144,401
Copper (Cobre; Cobre; Cuivre):				
Mexico...................	111,728	90,695	780,052	540,369
Cotton:				
Cotton unmanufactured (Algodón en rama; Algodão em rama; Coton non manufacturé):				
Mexico...................	214,051	2,740	1,343,085	33,683
Cotton cloths (Tejidos de algodón; Fazendas de algodão; Coton manufacturé):				
Central America..........	167,235	166,624	909,518	1,000,796
Mexico...................	23,266	24,182	178,728	149,646
Cuba....................	58,329	86,636	745,369	660,933
Argentine Republic......	26,327	11,695	214,095	179,280
Brazil..................	24,945	33,774	362,237	360,397
Chile...................	186,756	87,493	670,717	688,209
Colombia................	69,194	86,683	313,406	515,566
Venezuela...............	26,073	41,407	206,742	294,492
Other South America.....	42,814	47,384	283,186	317,196
Wearing apparel (Ropa de algodón; Fazendas de algodão; Vêtements de coton):				
Central America..........	19,853	30,179	140,458	199,918
Mexico...................	14,056	20,257	182,058	143,366
Cuba....................	20,832	22,492	140,633	196,748
Other South America.....	10,957	10,113	55,136	69,886
Twine (Bramante; Barbante; Ficelle):				
Argentine Republic......	1,629	13,120	2,141,271	1,095,819
Other South America.....	14,757	14,285	180,026	181,990

EXPORTS OF MERCHANDISE—Continued.

Articles and countries.	January—		Seven months ending January—	
	1906.	1907.	1906.	1907.
Electric and scientific apparatus (*Aparatos eléctricos y cientificos; Apparatos electricos e scientificos; Appareils électriques et scientifiques*):	*Dollars.*	*Dollars.*	*Dollars.*	*Dollars.*
Central America	8,163	21,345	68,665	121,752
Mexico	55,657	89,243	285,001	566,022
Cuba	33,218	33,693	283,856	341,249
Argentine Republic	8,390	18,761	108,020	200,981
Brazil	46,615	110,205	285,206	414,669
Other South America	43,203	65,957	276,893	355,503
Electrical machinery (*Maquinaria eléctrica; Machinas electricas; Machines électriques*):				
Central America	—3,009	226	10,934	31,136
Mexico	87,758	143,452	531,151	661,556
Cuba	81,175	1,505	244,533	73,625
Argentine Republic	4,516	5,947	74,564	97,827
Brazil	9,507	45,743	106,012	275,172
Other South America	29,241	1,793	105,378	80,092
Iron and steel, manufactures of:				
Steel rails (*Carriles de acero; Trilhos de aço; Rails d'acier*):				
Central America	105,286		237,128	167,487
Mexico	141,928	165,468	1,032,198	639,197
Cuba	260,366	265,377	2,111,582	1,562,695
Builders' hardware; saws and tools (*Materiales de metal para construcción, sierras, y herramientas; Ferragens, serras e ferramentas; Materiaux de construction en fer et en acier, scies et outils*):				
Central America	35,348	30,617	210,677	216,972
Mexico	91,181	93,940	665,937	605,096
Cuba	42,486	62,656	397,086	332,983
Argentine Republic	61,764	73,029	401,210	507,282
Brazil	36,863	38,151	228,347	292,902
Chile	38,295	26,110	137,194	186,010
Colombia	9,400	7,462	35,901	43,459
Venezuela	4,304	5,100	24,188	39,603
Other South America	22,203	27,158	141,666	180,256
Sewing machines and parts of (*Maquinas de coser y sus accesorios; Machinas de coser e accesorios; Machines à coudre et leurs parties*):				
Central America	11,536	9,749	65,747	73,018
Mexico	49,845	65,314	358,516	473,159
Cuba	29,723	38,119	186,235	189,795
Argentine Republic	40,034	20,964	435,187	304,846
Brazil	16,504	32,829	122,554	274,623
Colombia	9,941	3,836	38,167	43,140
Other South America	30,432	28,333	201,526	243,977
Steam engines and parts of (*Locomotoras y accesorios; Locomotivas e accesorios; Locomotifs et leurs parties*):				
Central America	89,190		281,338	362,090
Mexico	10,000	19,000	175,284	947,976
Cuba	52,242	101,911	628,190	623,720
Argentine Republic	30,000	86,025	47,486	396,776
Brazil	53,816	24,600	102,208	122,680
Other South America	19,876	75,706	82,974	222,930
Typewriting machines and parts of (*Mecanógrafos y accesorios; Machinas de escribir e accesorios; Machines à écrire et leurs parties*):				
Central America	4,284	4,586	34,170	26,177
Mexico	18,147	29,620	183,893	230,866
Cuba	6,226	12,573	41,418	47,058
Argentine Republic	7,004	7,510	55,167	72,775
Brazil	3,181	8,495	29,485	37,321
Colombia	450	1,674	7,020	9,161
Other South America	21,940	22,190	83,338	116,976
Leather, other than sole (*Cuero distinto del de suelas; Couro, não para solas; Cuirs, autres que pour semelles*):				
Central America	23,282	28,148	96,561	124,535
Cuba	22,230	14,419	142,730	76,914
Argentine Republic	27,578	14,725	203,326	142,308
Brazil	6,075	8,677	79,354	77,544
Other South America	23,603	9,772	130,409	109,583
Boots and shoes (*Calzado. Calçado; Chaussures*):				
Central America	47,558	54,231	237,726	340,505
Mexico	101,844	149,801	909,509	1,369,006
Colombia	4,649	1,142	27,912	28,237
Other South America	19,496	24,224	176,945	245,385

EXPORTS OF MERCHANDISE—Continued.

Articles and countries.	January—		Seven months ending January—	
	1906.	1907.	1906.	1906.
Naval stores:	Dollars.	Dollars.	Dollars.	Dollars.
Rosin, tar, etc. (Resina, alquitrón, etc.; Resina e alcatrão; Résine et goudron):				
Cuba	6,700	7,600	42,641	51,622
Argentine Republic	96,187		282,803	306,518
Brazil	124,276	40,733	352,346	318,177
Other South America	47,486	12,689	186,500	180,344
Turpentine (Aguarras; Aguaraz; Terebenthine):				
Central America	6,791	1,666	31,826	24,945
Cuba	6,038	8,579	30,185	51,929
Argentine Republic	31,069	13,709	121,985	115,294
Brazil	9,453	12,206	59,838	94,589
Chile	4,969	10,627	50,241	60,674
Other South America	10,311	2,984	32,449	44,896
Oils, mineral, crude (Aceites minerales, crudos; Oleos mineraes crûs; Huiles minéral brutes):				
Mexico	70,193	134,233	379,305	644,194
Cuba	47,955		196,962	287,932
Oils, mineral, refined or manufactured (Aceites minerales, refinados ó manufacturados; Oleos mineraes, refinados ou manufacturados; Huiles minérales, raffinées ou manufacturées):				
Central America	21,880	37,701	137,763	154,574
Mexico	12,644	15,380	91,209	162,864
Cuba	19,656	90,794	203,345	266,022
Argentine Republic	46,307	70,474	1,264,693	1,380,334
Brazil	182,453	227,860	1,897,260	1,764,073
Chile	104,969	82,108	501,391	404,321
Other South America	65,795	59,184	681,206	675,436
Oils, vegetable (Aceites vegetales; Oleos vegetaes; Huiles végétales):				
Central America	2,433	5,202	18,186	26,985
Mexico	72,080	87,030	555,673	536,390
Cuba	15,051	28,515	84,683	107,101
Argentine Republic	374	5,025	12,260	45,548
Brazil	5,696	134,016	91,612	240,175
Chile	3,389	1,317	12,110	30,051
Other South America	8,096	16,440	84,169	76,285
Paper (Papel; Papel; Papier):				
Mexico	2,401	6,579	25,807	33,492
Cuba	13,225	21,380	75,890	117,031
Argentine Republic	23,558	16,029	121,692	183,644
Brazil	2,227	414	16,065	9,382
Chile	26,847	11,775	93,892	91,806
Other South America	13,948	16,002	57,539	57,625
Books (Libros; Livros; Livres):				
Central America	5,230	3,624	34,392	31,603
Mexico	26,473	26,966	231,987	163,268
Cuba	35,684	46,201	209,076	193,005
Argentine Republic	6,824	5,258	38,960	60,561
Brazil	13,136	4,092	67,029	56,534
Chile	1,709	47,368	112,074	193,209
Other South America	11,101	23,230	55,853	57,947
Provisions, comprising meat and dairy products:				
Beef, canned (Carne de vaca en lata; Carne de vacca em latas; Boeuf conservé):				
Central America	2,424	7,042	20,156	41,782
Mexico	2,163	2,030	17,573	17,931
Cuba	3,642	1,063	16,697	11,238
South America	4,897	2,927	25,822	26,552
Beef, salted or pickled (Carne de vaca, salada ó adobada; Carne de vacca, salgada; beuf salé):				
Central America	8,138	15,159	56,536	71,373
South America	19,717	10,184	161,774	155,391
Tallow (Sebo; Sebo; Suif):				
Central America	16,136	12,191	103,056	77,269
Mexico	3,196	2,813	74,322	14,042
Cuba	51	487	5,522	4,285
Chile	2,260	2,317	41,066	52,060
Other South America	4,504	4,040	33,069	33,345
Bacon (Tocino; Toucinho; Lard fumé):				
Central America	1,494	2,674	11,029	19,129
Mexico	3,617	7,918	27,098	33,369
Cuba	43,419	69,407	256,949	352,639
Brazil	21,987	16,456	102,895	116,171
Other South America	949	448	6,963	3,444

EXPORTS OF MERCHANDISE—Continued.

Articles and countries.	January—		Seven months ending January—	
	1906.	1907.	1906.	1907.
Provisions, etc.—Continued.	*Dollars.*	*Dollars.*	*Dollars.*	*Dollars.*
Hams (*Jamones; Presuntos; Jambons*):				
Central America	4,247	18,691	48,079	82,559
Mexico	9,146	15,023	79,654	67,234
Cuba	44,919	49,538	290,553	348,044
Venezuela	3,580	3,303	33,194	29,186
Other South America	4,754	3,214	43,884	35,854
Lard (*Manteca; Banha; Saindoux*):				
Central America	26,424	72,843	268,469	395,964
Mexico	71,890	86,797	348,781	382,116
Cuba	236,542	352,166	1,449,683	1,699,233
Brazil	11,999	49,605	70,401	584,308
Chile	6,422	6,864	46,143	111,785
Colombia	4,853	4,333	273,376	28,499
Venezuela	28,775	9,726	244,200	153,363
Other South America	45,295	28,125	335,848	341,223
Butter (*Mantequilla; Manteiga; Beurre*):				
Central America	8,133	13,434	66,227	100,163
Mexico	12,443	15,201	71,755	81,625
Cuba	5,998	11,165	23,970	41,653
Brazil	10,737	1,920	82,059	52,319
Venezuela	9,323	1,326	66,660	37,956
Other South America	3,404	2,109	20,968	33,880
Cheese (*Queso; Queijo; Fromage*):				
Central America	5,242	7,959	38,072	40,293
Mexico	3,967	3,639	23,019	24,125
Cuba	925	2,610	6,657	10,052
Paraffin (*Parafina; Paraffina; Paraffine*):				
Central America	9,442	6,972	35,524	37,361
Mexico	33,895	110,032	206,527	359,781
South America	1,268	4,613	16,025	32,499
Tobacco, unmanufactured (*Tabaco en rama; Tabaco não manufacturado; Tabac non manufacturé*):				
Central America	8,125	6,258	47,523	36,607
Mexico	3,229	18,636	55,076	81,655
Argentine Republic	2,600	3,359	42,298	27,713
Colombia	1,192	1,060	6,272	10,362
Other South America	4,731	3,793	47,599	50,850
Tobacco, manufactures of (*Tabaco elaborado; Tabaco manufacturado; Tabac manufacturé*):				
Central America	4,687	10,096	32,949	48,883
Wood and manufactures of:				
Wood, unmanufactured (*Madera sin labrar; Madeira não manufacturada; Bois brut*):				
Central America	39,874	36,996	289,190	387,916
Mexico	94,842	141,709	519,726	709,138
Cuba	34,263	3,156	109,979	77,686
Argentine Republic	322	15,000	96,456	108,334
Other South America	17,016	15,492	105,608	193,576
Lumber (*Maderas; Madeiras; Bois de construction*):				
Central America	48,967	87,629	325,600	740,014
Mexico	126,622	167,530	926,116	1,178,086
Cuba	241,587	268,972	1,280,331	1,206,283
Argentine Republic	305,880	598,198	1,911,179	3,762,531
Brazil	27,121	145,120	242,411	729,755
Chile	38,574	48,117	329,838	530,947
Other South America	152,834	130,795	426,109	775,318
Furniture (*Muebles; Mobilia; Meubles*):				
Central America	16,130	28,460	182,196	167,576
Mexico	74,947	97,794	435,059	527,592
Cuba	75,420	65,488	457,207	301,787
Argentine Republic	20,877	42,012	199,637	289,968
Brazil	2,816	6,855	29,096	42,334
Chile	7,932	6,581	46,165	48,087
Colombia	1,195	789	13,276	9,442
Venezuela	1,604	6,299	26,867	14,457
Other South America	8,182	4,370	43,206	65,817

FOREIGN COMMERCE, JANUARY, 1907.

Figures issued by the United States Bureau of Statistics for the
month of January, 1907, and for the seven months of the fiscal year
1907 show increased imports and exports of manufactured goods and

of crude materials for use in manufactures, as compared with the same periods of the preceding year. Total imports for the seven months of 1907 aggregated $809,740,176 as against $695,724,641 in 1906, while total exports for the two periods amounted in value to $1,129,709,062 and $1,056,624,825, respectively. For the month of January, 1907, imports figure for $126,586,934 and exports for $189,306,356, as compared with $106,521,526 and $170,603,053 recorded for the two branches of commerce in the same month of 1906.

The distribution of trade for the periods in reference was as follows:

Countries.	January.			
	Imports.		Exports.	
	1906.	1907.	1906.	1907.
Europe	$57,989,151	$63,853,831	$125,954,168	$141,863,997
North America	16,607,973	20,182,314	25,923,978	28,616,226
South America	13,508,185	15,113,946	5,984,711	6,549,597
Asia	14,474,517	19,687,025	7,642,806	7,585,725
Oceania	1,687,796	2,966,346	3,307,106	2,856,520
Africa	2,163,903	4,783,472	1,790,282	1,533,589
Central American States:				
Costa Rica	651,999	322,115	218,281	207,942
Guatemala	115,732	268,745	268,501	256,197
Honduras	94,487	111,173	164,660	175,896
Nicaragua	83,908	84,283	153,364	169,637
Panama	73,331	136,200	1,059,574	1,115,632
Salvador	83,446	106,312	129,578	140,314
Mexico	4,437,717	4,997,158	5,356,440	5,764,217
West Indies:				
Cuba	4,544,172	7,228,734	4,267,975	4,957,931
Haiti	92,120	142,384	324,519	204,220
Santo Domingo	300,741	277,447	126,809	394,290
South America:				
Argentine Republic	2,331,391	1,821,624	2,325,194	2,610,751
Bolivia			13,702	22,363
Brazil	7,591,655	8,517,465	1,105,751	1,511,748
Chile	1,751,944	1,857,743	886,879	831,597
Colombia	467,541	618,866	238,800	278,115
Ecuador	230,062	252,565	165,871	139,666
Paraguay	750	724	1,648	19,651
Peru	181,145	512,631	507,415	462,776
Uruguay	145,215	705,319	253,851	287,568
Venezuela	726,264	651,673	233,192	254,723

Countries.	Seven months ending January.			
	Imports.		Exports.	
	1906.	1907.	1906.	1907.
Europe	$364,957,024	$437,585,717	$739,620,561	$801,937,521
North America	120,323,072	139,275,622	174,156,346	194,352,629
South America	83,010,164	92,044,830	44,282,366	48,509,950
Asia	107,095,350	128,561,809	67,192,180	50,780,837
Oceania	13,163,172	12,634,267	20,138,125	24,002,333
Africa	7,175,859	9,618,341	11,235,267	10,085,792
Central American States:				
Costa Rica	1,796,396	1,549,506	1,293,846	1,418,600
Guatemala	1,261,091	849,807	1,509,444	1,660,487
Honduras	812,777	-1,309,300	541,867	1,117,056
Nicaragua	740,429	593,568	1,046,060	1,232,732
Panama	535,406	961,077	5,853,336	7,701,576
Salvador	170,845	278,230	860,355	791,570
Mexico	29,103,433	30,696,964	32,353,628	36,853,048
West Indies:				
Cuba	35,648,715	38,406,640	26,744,431	28,160,343
Haiti	732,769	633,886	2,070,806	1,909,094
Santo Domingo	926,068	1,280,881	1,151,631	1,572,153

| | Seven months ending January. | | | |
| | Imports. | | Exports. | |
	1906.	1907.	1906.	1907.
....	$8,370,778	$7,782,316	$19,929,014	$20,812,881
....			86,564	192,063
....	51,034,995	58,021,240	7,665,334	10,088,235
....	9,780,146	10,977,827	5,179,260	5,949,204
....	3,953,035	3,689,334	2,302,189	1,808,955
....	1,340,828	2,012,819	1,179,782	978,474
....	750	1,174	6,781	83,363
....	1,493,635	2,303,686	2,906,834	3,242,333
y............................	1,237,416	1,538,963	1,674,219	1,962,969
sla..........................	4,527,717	4,208,318	1,812,205	1,886,121

RATIO OF TRADE INCREASE WITH LATIN AMERICA.

total foreign commerce of the Latin American Republics,
ting both exports and imports, is now valued at nearly $2,000,-
-. The annual totals of the sales made by the merchants of
ted States to Latin America stand as follows, the figures being
.iendar years:

....	$116,475,877
....	146,849,361
....	218,077,809

sales to South America alone have increased from $42,500,000
in 1901 to $78,800,000 in 1906. Sales to Mexico have increased from
$36,800,000 in 1901 to $62,300,000 in 1906. Sales to the five Central
American States have increased from $6,500,000 in 1901 to $10,-
700,000 in 1906. The exports to Brazil have taken on a new life.
The largest sales of earlier years were made in 1895, about $15,000,000.
For the next ten years they show a steady decline to $10,700,000 in
1904. Last year lifted them to $16,547,000, a record mark. Argen-
tine purchases from the United States of about $6,000,000 in 1896
are increased to $33,271,000 in 1906. Within a decade Chile's pur-
chases have increased from a little more than $3,000,000 to $9,390,000,
while the trade of Peru during the same time has jumped from
$1,000,000 to a little more than $5,000,000.

An important feature of this commerce appears in the fact that a
large percentage of it consists of manufactured products. Of such
wares Latin America bought from the United States last year about
the same quantity that the United Kingdom did, and about three-
quarters as much as did all the countries of continental Europe.
About 86 per cent of the sales of the United States to South America
were manufactured wares. The Argentine account shows 98.6 per
cent of manufactures. The Mexican account shows 70 per cent, the
Brazilian account 83 per cent, and the Chilean account 85.5 per cent.
The average for the total American commerce with all nations was
40 per cent. London financial papers have estimated that $1,000,-
000,000 of foreign capital will be invested in South America during

the next five years. Already $150,000,000 of European capital is earning good interest in Argentina.

INTERNAL REVENUE, FEBRUARY, 1907.

The comparative statement of the Government receipts and expenditures of the United States shows that for the month of February, 1907, the receipts were $53,925,496 and the disbursements $45,720,315, leaving a surplus for the month of $8,205,000, against a surplus of $4,475,000 for the corresponding month last year.

The receipts from customs last month amounted to $27,553,801, a gain over February, 1906, of nearly $4,000,000.

Internal revenue, $20,505,201, a gain of $2,200,000; miscellaneous, $5,866,493, a loss of $267,000. The expenditures were almost exactly $2,000,000 in excess of those for February, 1906, the increases being in the public works, civil and miscellaneous and pension items. For the eight months of the present fiscal year a surplus is shown of $40,666,348, as against a surplus one year ago of a little over $1,000,000.

THE LEATHER INDUSTRY IN 1906.

The leather industry contributed $150,000,000 to the foreign commerce of the United States in the year 1906, against less than $55,000,000 a decade earlier. In imports of hides and skins and exports of leather and manufactures from that article the growth of the decade has been extremely rapid. Hides and skins form the largest single item in the record of imports, and leather and manufactures thereof stand third in the list of manufactures exported.

The value of hides and skins imported in the calendar year 1906 was practically $84,000,000, and in 1896, a decade earlier, was but $21,000,000, having thus quadrupled in ten years.

Of leather and its manufactures exported the figures for 1906 were over $45,000,000 and in 1896 were less than $19,000,000. Add to this $84,000,000 of hides and skins imported and $45,000,000 of leather and manufactures thereof exported the $18,000,000 worth of leather and manufactures thereof imported and the nearly $2,000,000 worth of hides and skins exported, the grand total which leather and the materials for its manufacture form in the foreign trade of the United States aggregates in the calendar year 1906 about $150,000,000.

ARMY SUPERVISION OF PANAMA CANAL CONSTRUCTION.

On February 26, 1907, it was announced officially that all the bids offered for the construction of the Panama Canal had been rejected and that the work would be intrusted to the supervision of army engineers.

Maj. GEORGE WASHINGTON GOETHALS, Corps of Engineers, U. S. Army, was appointed Chief Engineer, assisted by Maj. DAVID DuBos

aj. WILLIAM LUTHER SIBERT, both of the Corps of
Admiral H. H. ROSSEAU, civil engineer, U. S. N.;
JORGAS, Army Medical Corps; ex-Senator BLACK-
ana ON SMITH, who is at present head of the Depart-
r s d Quarters on the Isthmus, are the other members
mission.
r   JTT   ss, in addition to his duties as Chief Engineer, will
u of t e Canal Commission.

PHILIPPINE COMMERCE IN 1906.

he commerce of the Philippine Islands for the fiscal year 1906 was
716,400, of which $25,799,266 was imports and $31,917,134 was
rorts. Analyzing the export trade for the calendar year 1905, it
years that out of a total export of $33,454,744 all except about 3½
ent was represented by four articles: Hemp, 65 per cent; sugar, 15
nt; copra, nearly 10 per cent, and tobacco, about 6½ per cent.
, valued at $21,757,344, represented nearly two-thirds of the
.. This product is virtually a monopoly of the islands, and its
vation might be largely increased. The special need of the
ustry is a practical mechanical device for extracting the fiber
i plant. This is now done by hand, in crude and wasteful
..y, by which about one-third of the fiber is spoiled and an additional and large percentage is reduced to inferior grades.
The islands produced a 350,000 ton sugar crop for the year, and
could undoubtedly, all conditions being favorable, produce a good deal
more than that. The success of the tobacco industry, so far as the
American market is concerned, depends chiefly upon the possible cultivation of a wrapper leaf that would take the place of the Sumatra.
The $4,000,000 trade in copra might be doubled, and probably will
be. This is the dried or desiccated "meat" of the common cocoanut.
When treated it yields cocoanut oil, extensively used in soap making,
and it is now used in Europe as the base of dietetic compounds, particularly an imitation butter, for which a large market has already
been created. As a "butter" it is regarded as much superior to margarine or margarine compounds, and it does not melt in the tropics as
do dairy butter and the margarine products.
Tea, coffee, cocoa, rubber, raw silk, and spices present their respective but limited possibilities. So do wool, hides, and goatskins.

EXPORTS OF MANUFACTURES, 1906.

The total value of the exports of United States manufactures for
the calendar year 1906 was $719,000,000, as compared with $571,-
410,497 for 1905, according to figures issued by the Bureau of Statistics. The total of all exports for the fiscal year ending with June
was $2,403,976,551, of which $1,717,953,382 was domestic products

and $686,023,169 manufactures. In the distribution by countries and grand divisions the percentage which manufactures form of the exports varies greatly, their proportion being smallest in the exports to European countries.

The table which follows shows the exports of domestic products to each of the principal countries and the share which manufactures formed thereof in the last fiscal year.

Country.	Exports of domestic products.	Exports of manufactures.	Per cent of manufactures.
			Per cent.
United Kingdom	$578,023,505	$133,459,935	23.09
Germany	232,403,778	55,632,220	23.93
Canada	146,175,015	90,485,933	61.90
France	96,453,755	30,002,357	31.11
Netherlands	95,197,392	43,431,231	45.62
Mexico	57,418,646	40,406,657	70.38
Belgium	49,208,063	15,132,479	30.76
Italy	47,362,491	12,723,262	26.87
Cuba	46,377,277	25,624,220	55.25
Chinese Empire	43,660,764	41,812,222	95.98
Japan	37,956,290	21,318,797	56.17
Argentine Republic	32,575,950	32,120,383	98.60
British Australasia	28,936,236	25,674,635	88.74
Denmark	22,902,135	3,372,633	14.72
Spain	19,091,070	2,294,236	12.02
Russia	18,756,096	9,188,474	48.00
Austria-Hungary	14,764,131	6,356,741	43.06
Brazil	14,422,089	11,990,315	83.15
Panama	12,410,108	10,069,715	81.14
British South Africa	11,609,508	8,421,805	71.96
British West Indies	9,616,665	3,404,307	35.40
Chile	8,657,723	7,905,391	85.53
Sweden	7,435,051	3,201,778	43.06
Hongkong	7,032,833	2,080,184	29.70
Norway	6,012,026	1,324,480	22.03
Philippine Islands	5,458,867	3,759,688	68.87
GRAND DIVISIONS.			
Europe	1,189,254,885	318,503,047	26.78
North America	294,546,176	182,121,776	61.83
Asia	104,804,873	78,530,251	74.93
South America	74,745,589	64,328,906	86.06
Oceania	35,060,348	29,711,707	84.74
Africa	19,541,511	12,827,488	65.64
Grand total	1,717,953,382	686,023,169	39.93

The exports of manufactures for the calendar year 1906 amounted to 41 per cent of the total exports, as compared with 35.73 per cent in 1905.

CONVENTION FOR THE EQUITABLE DISTRIBUTION OF WATERS OF THE RIO GRANDE.

The President of the United States, on January 16, 1907, promulgated the following convention between the United States and Mexico, providing for the equitable distribution of the waters of the Rio Grande for irrigation purposes. The convention was signed at Washington, May 21, 1906, ratification advised by the Senate June 26, 1906, ratified by President Roosevelt December 26, 1906. It was approved by the Mexican Senate December 3, 1906, and ratified by President Diaz on January 5, 1907. Ratifications were exchanged in Washington, January 16, 1907, and the convention promulgated by President Diaz on January 26, 1907.

"The United States of America and the United States of Mex
being desirous to provide for the equitable distribution of the wat
of the Rio Grande for irrigation purposes, and to remove all causes
controversy between them in respect thereto, and being moved
considerations of international comity, have resolved to conclud
Convention for these purposes and have named as their Plenipote
tiaries:

"The President of the United States of America, ELIHU Ro
Secretary of State of the United States; and

"The President of the United States of Mexico, His Excellen
Señor Don JOAQUÍN D. CASASÚS, Ambassador Extraordinary a
Plenipotentiary of the United States of Mexico at Washington;

"Who, after having exhibited their respective full powers, which w
found to be in good and due form, have agreed upon the followi
articles:

"ARTICLE I.

"After the completion of the proposed storage dam near Eng
New Mexico, and the distributing system auxiliary thereto, a
as soon as water shall be available in said system for the purpo
the United States shall deliver to Mexico a total of 60,000 acre-fi
of water annually, in the bed of the Rio Grande at the point wh
the head works of the Acequia Madre, known as the Old Maxic
Canal, now exists above the city of Juarez, Mexico.

"ARTICLE II.

"The delivery of the said amount of water shall be assured by t
United States and shall be distributed through the year in the sai
proportions as the water supply proposed to be furnished from t
said irrigation system to lands in the United States in the vicini
of El Paso, Texas, according to the following schedule, as nearly
may be possible:

January	
February	
March	
April	
May	
June	
July	
August	
September	
October	
November	
December	
Total for the year	2,613.80 cubic

"In case, however, of extraordinary drought or serious accident to the irrigation system in the United States, the amount delivered to the Mexican Canal shall be diminished in the same proportion as the water delivered to lands under said irrigation system in the United States.

"ARTICLE III.

"The said delivery shall be made without cost to Mexico, and the United States agrees to pay the whole cost of storing the said quantity of water to be delivered to Mexico, of conveying the same to the international line, of measuring the said water, and of delivering it in the river bed above the head of the Mexican Canal.   It is understood that the United States assumes no obligation beyond the delivering of the water in the bed of the river above the head of the Mexican Canal.

"ARTICLE IV.

"The delivery of water as herein provided is not to be construed as a recognition by the United States of any claim on the part of Mexico to the said waters; and it is agreed that in consideration of such delivery of water, Mexico waives any and all claims to the waters of the Rio Grande for any purpose whatever between the head of the present Mexican Canal and Fort Quitman, Texas, and also declares fully settled and disposed of, and hereby waives, all claims heretofore asserted or existing, or that may hereafter arise, or be asserted, against the United States on account of any damages alleged to have been sustained by the owners of land in Mexico, by reason of the diversion by citizens of the United States of waters of the Rio Grande.

"ARTICLE V.

"The United States, in entering into this treaty, does not thereby concede, expressly or by implication, any legal basis for any claims heretofore asserted or which may be hereafter asserted by reason of any losses incurred by the owners of land in Mexico due or alleged to be due to the diversion of the waters of the Rio Grande within the United States; nor does the United States in any way concede the establishment of any general principle or precedent by the concluding of this treaty.   The understanding of both parties is that the arrangement contemplated by this treaty extends only to the portion of the Rio Grande which forms the international boundary, from the head of the Mexican Canal down to Fort Quitman, Texas, and in no other case.

"ARTICLE VI.

"The present Convention shall be ratified by both contracting parties in accordance with their constitutional procedure, and the ratifications shall be exchanged at Washington as soon as possible.

ereof, the respective Plenipotentiaries have signed
oth in the English and Spanish languages and have
their seals.

icate at the City of Washington, this 21st day of
ᵾ ᴅᴏᴜ   ᴅᴅ nine hundred and six.

ned: ELIHU ROOT   [SEAL.]
gned: JOAQUIN D CASASUS   [SEAL.]

URUGUAY.

THE NEW PRESIDENT OF THE REPUBLIC.

On March 1, 1907, Dr. CLAUDIO WILLIMAN was elected President
the Oriental Republic of Uruguay, his inauguration taking place
he same day.

e new President is about 45 years old, and has rendered his
y valuable and meritorious services as a statesman and as a
. as well.

octor WILLIMAN, after receiving the degree of LL. D., was appointed, through a competitive examination, to the professorship of
physics in the University of Montevideo, which he held for twenty-five
years. During the administration of President CUESTAS he was
offered a position in the Cabinet, which he refused to accept, and for
two years before his election to the Presidency he performed the functions of Minister of the Interior.

CUSTOMS REVENUES, 1906.

The customs revenues of Uruguay for the calendar year 1906
amounted in value to $12,897,261 gold, as compared with $11,496,742
in the preceding year, an increase of $1,400,519.

Previous to 1905 the highest recorded receipts had been for 1895,
when $10,660,515 represented the total revenues from customs.

PROMOTION OF IMMIGRATION.

A bill has recently been presented to the Uruguayan Congress providing for the establishment of an immigrants' hotel and offering free
landing, lodging, and board for a fortnight to prospective immigrants
into the Republic. Furthermore, facilities for obtaining work and
free transport to interior destinations are among the inducements
held out to incoming travelers, while consular officers abroad are
charged with propaganda in the emigrating centers of Europe.

SEALING REGULATIONS.

A law recently passed by the Uruguayan Congress prohibits unlicensed sealing in territorial waters and is a part of a general purpose to develop the piscatorial resources of the Republic.

ADDITIONAL DUTY ON IMPORTS.

The *"Bulletin Bi-mensuel"* of the Chamber of Commerce of Montevideo publishes a copy of a Uruguayan law, whereby the fee for the certification of invoices as established by the law of May 12, 1906, is suppressed. As a substitute therefor the law creates an additional duty of one-half per cent on the value of articles imported into the Republic, with the exception of live animals, articles destined for consumption on war vessels, goods intended for reshipment, and goods in transit; also articles which are free of duty by virtue of special laws.

The full text of the consular tariff was published in the MONTHLY BULLETIN for November, 1906.

THE CEREAL AND FLAX CROP OF 1905-6.

The Department of Stock Raising and Agriculture of the Uruguayan Republic has published recently the statistics relating to the cereal and flax crop of the agricultural year 1905-6. According to said data the cultivated area was distributed as follows: Wheat, 288,468 hectares; maize, 166,361 hectares; other cereals, 5,353 hectares, and flax, 18,485 hectares.

The area dedicated to wheat increased in more than 27,000 hectares over that of 1904-5, but the space of land cultivated with maize shows a decrease of more than 10,000 hectares as compared with the preceding year, and the area devoted to flax shows also a decrease of 1,600 hectares.

The cereals which, besides wheat and maize, were cultivated—such as barley, oats, canary seed, and rye—cover a small extension of land, but it increased to such an extent that it reached in 1905-6 an importance which it never had. The increase since 1904-5 was 1,600 hectares, most of which is devoted to canary seed.

The total cultivated area in the year under review was 478,667 hectares, 18,000 more than the previous year.

The average production per hectare was as follows: Wheat, 434 kilograms; maize, 492 kilograms; flax, 583 kilograms; oats, 648 kilograms; barley, 675 kilograms; canary seed, 569 kilograms.

VENEZUELA.

COMMERCIAL MOVEMENT OF THE REPUBLIC DURING 1905-6.

The Department of Finance and Public Credit of Venezuela published in the latter part of 1906 the "Mercantile and Maritime Statistics" for the fiscal year 1905-6, the following résumé having been made therefrom:

The total value of the foreign trade of the Republic during 1905-6 amounted to 125,934,987.54 *bolivares*, of which 44,952,867.66 *bolivares* were for imports and 80,982,119.88 *bolivares* for exports, a difference in favor of the latter being thus shown of 36,029,252.22 *bolivares*. The imports consisted of all kinds of merchandise, such as machinery, apparatus, instruments, tools, piece goods, clothing, furniture, beverages, food products, chemical products, drugs, medicines, etc. The greatest portion of exports was of the following national products: Coffee, cacao, cattle, horses, mules, asphalt, timber, india rubber, cinchona bark, mangrove, horns, hides, sugar, fish, mother-of-pearl, tortoise shell, dividivi, sernambi, cotton, tar, balatá, quartz, cocoanut, bananas, maize, heron plumes, pearls, gold, medicines, sarsaparilla, etc. The principal articles of export were: Coffee, 37,104,451.75 *bolivares;* cocoa, 14,655,986.45 *bolivares;* cattle, 8,992,021 *bolivares;* hides and skins, 7,558,648.03 *bolivares;* balata, 3,640,594.25 *bolivares;* gold, 2,987,313.95 *bolivares.*

The various costom-houses of the Republic collected during the year under review a total revenue of 19,480,312.63 *bolivares.*

During the fiscal year in reference 675 steamers, with 1,593,515 tons, and 291 sailing vessels, with 26,503 tons, entered the various ports of the Republic, and 714 steamers, with 1,206,626 tons, and 421 sailing vessels, with 30,935 tons, were cleared therefrom.

The coastwise trade between the different Venezuelan ports during the year amounted to 116,312,961.68 *bolivares.*

The following table shows the countries of origin of the imports during 1905-6, with the respective values:

Countries of origin.	Value.
	Bolivares.
United States	13,585,469.04
Great Britain	13,385,982.76
German Empire	8,852,398.37
Netherlands	3,094,862.48
France	2,738,806.93
Spain	2,152,088.98
Italy	965,872.50
Belgium	112,875.00
Austria-Hungary	36,922.20
Cuba	20,814.40
Ecuador	5,400.00
Panama	1,375.00
Total	44,952,867.06

Following were the countries of destination of exports:

Countries of destination.	Value.
	Bolívares.
United States	25,191,270.22
France	20,558,671.10
Netherlands and colonies	11,827,211.60
Great Britain and colonies	6,551,466.81
Cuba	8,971,650.00
German Empire	4,310,862.85
Spain	2,882,509.60
Italy	302,076.90
Brazil	145,300.00
Austria-Hungary	113,556.00
Belgium	79,278.00
Panama	41,838.80
Morocco	2,259.00
Costa Rica	1,789.00
Dominican Republic	1,700.00
Colombia	680.00
Total	80,982,119.88

CACAO PRODUCTION AND CONSUMPTION.

The raw material forming the principal ingredient of the chocolate and cocoa of commerce is the nut of the cacao tree, indigenous to the tropical climates of Ecuador, Brazil, Venezuela, and other South American countries. The variety of cacao most valued in the preparation of chocolate comes from Caracas; that from Guayaquil, from Trinidad and Ocana most nearly approach the first-named, and are followed by the product of Manaos and Para. Cuba and Ceylon also produce fine grades of cacao, and the rise in the price of chocolate manufactures has stimulated the growing of the plant in other sections of the world.

Figures of production and consumption of cacao during the year 1905 and estimates for 1906, based upon six months' returns, show the following results:

Production of cacao.

Country.	1905.	1906.
	Kilos.	*Kilos.*
San Thomé (P. W. Africa)	25,379,320	23,500,000
Ecuador	21,127,833	24,900,000
Brazil	21,090,088	27,400,000
Trinidad	20,018,560	15,900,000
Santo Domingo	12,784,660	13,700,000
Venezuela	11,700,555	11,000,000
Gold Coast	5,665,820	6,100,000
Grenada	5,455,600	4,700,000
Ceylon	3,542,613	3,800,000
Cuba and Porto Rico	3,000,000	3,000,000
Haiti	2,343,200	2,500,000
Surinam	1,611,851	2,000,000
Dutch East Indies	1,491,795	1,700,000
Jamaica	1,484,509	2,200,000
French Antilles	1,200,000	1,400,000
Kamerun and Samoa	1,185,400	1,600,000
Santa Lucia	700,000	800,000
Dominica	596,700	600,000
Kongo	194,638	200,000
Other countries	800,000	1,000,000
Total	141,373,142	148,000,000

consumption for the foregoing crops are as follows:

Country.	1905.	1906.
	Kilos.	*Kilos.*
	34,958,420	35,600,000
	29,663,100	34,200,000
	21,747,600	22,250,000
	21,100,000	21,500,000
	19,294,550	21,200,000
	6,101,712	6,200,000
	5,218,400	6,400,000
	3,018,097	3,200,000
	2,668,500	3,000,000
	2,230,400	2,500,000
	1,125,000	1,200,000
	971,500	1,100,000
	900,000	1,000,000
	700,000	750,000
	600,000	650,000
	493,813	550,000
	138,000	150,000
	60,000	65,000

al exports of Venezuelan cacao amount to 40,000 , markets being France and Spain. From Trinided each year to America, France, and ayaquil exports from 100,000 to 200,000 is a aulv to Spain and Germany. New York, Hamburg, three great cacao importing markets. credited with manufacturing more chocolate than all other countries combined and the average annual exports are valued at $6,000,000. Of this quantity, the yearly exports to the United States are about $1,000,000 and to England, more than $2,000,000. Consumption of chocolate within the Swiss Republic is estimated as worth $2,500,000 annually, a larger per capita ratio being also reported than for any other consuming country.

The nutritive qualities of chocolate as a beverage and as a food product have been widely exploited as have the usage of such by-products of the cacao plant as cocoa butter and other semimedicinal substances.

When the Spaniards achieved the conquest of Mexico, the natives reported that from time immemorial the beverage known locally as "chocolate" had been made from the cacao bean in that country and its alimentary merits were quickly recognized, first by Spain, then by Italy and France.

WORLD'S COPPER OUTPUT.

A statement published in the London "Financial Times" gives the estimated production of copper of the world in 1906 at 730,000 tons, as against 708,000 tons in 1905 (presumably long tons of 2,240 pounds each).

The output of the United States increased from 391,400 to 413,000 tons, and there was exported 211,100 tons, as against 247,100 tons in 1905. American official figures, however, show that the exports of copper in 190£ were 238,798 long tons and in 1906 203,014 long tons, a decrease in exports of 35,784 tons. The total imports into Europe increased 20,500 tons, of which no less than 12,700 tons came from Japan. Australia sent 8,100 tons and Mexico 1,000 tons more than the previous year. On the other hand, consignments from Chile decreased 2,300 tons, from Peru 2,100 tons, and from Cape Colony 1,000 tons.

The principal countries consuming copper were: United States, 300,300 tons, as against 273,792 tons in 1905; United Kingdom, 80,451 tons, as against 60,491 tons; Germany, 165,107 tons, as against 136,875 tons; and France, 56,328, as against 48,619 tons.

The requirements of England were so heavy during 1906 that there was a material falling off in transshipment business, exports having declined 7,800 tons. Germany increased her exports over 4,000 tons. Throughout the year the average of stocks in England and France was 6,600 tons, as against 10,500 tons in 1905, and the average total visible supply was 11,800 tons, as compared with 16,400 tons. The record of average deliveries was 7,900 tons, as against 7,300 tons. The average price of standard was $425.42 per ton, as compared with $338.67 in 1905, and the average price of ingots was $449.12.

THE WORLD'S WHEAT CROP.

In September, 1906, the Beerbohm "London List" indicated 437,600,000 quarters, or 3,500,800,000 bushels as the total for the world's wheat crop of 1906. The revised exhibit, now presented, recognizing the later evidence as to harvests in Argentina, Australia, etc., while changing some of the details, does not essentially change the aggregate, which is made to appear as 437,480,000 quarters, or 3,499,840,000 bushels. This compares with 3,362,560,000 bushels shown for the preceding year, and an annual average of 3,198,000,000 bushels for five years prior to 1906.

npilation, based on Beerbohm statements from
tes the progress of wheat production for the past
resenting bushels:

....	. 1,800,000,000	1891	2,376,000,000
....	. 1,808,000,000	1892	2,411,000,000
....	. 1,960,000,000	1893	2,474,000,000
....	. 2,000,000,000	1894	2,562,000,000
....	1,856,000,000	1895	2,496,000,000
....	1,960,000,000	1896	2,437,000,000
....	1,960,000,000	1897	2,281,000,000
....	2,200,000,000	1898	2,918,000,000
....	2,040,000,000	1899	2,788,000,000
....	2,240,000,000	1900	2,610,000,000
....	2,080,000,000	1901	2,940,000,000
....	2,160,000,000	1902	3,195,000,000
....	2,280,000,000	1903	3,292,000,000
....	2,224,000,000	1904	3,202,000,000
....	2,144,000,000	1905	3,362,000,000
....	2,264,000,000	1906	3,500,000,000

BOOK NOTES.

**Books and pamphlets sent to the Bureau of the American Republics, and
containing subject-matter bearing upon the countries of the International Union of American Republics, will be treated under this caption
in the Monthly Bulletin.**

The "Boletín de la Sociedad de Fomento Fabril" (Santiago) publishes in its issue for January, 1907, an interesting and instructive
paper prepared by EUGENIO AUTRAN concerning the highly valued
Eriomys laniger, the Chilean rodent which furnishes the chinchilla
of commerce. The latter name was presumably applied to the
animal by the Spaniards during their early conquests in America, in
honor of one of the invading conquerors who was so called. Ranging in length from 28 to 40 centimeters and furnishing a fur of varying values, it has been supposed that there were several varieties of
the chinchilla; but there is really but one species, the size and quality
of the pelt differing according to season and development. In the
Argentine Republic, hunters classify the skins as Chilean, royal, and
Bolivian chinchilla. Chilean skins are similarly classed as royal,
Bolivian, and coast. In the latter Republic the animal is found
from the Department of Illapel to the northern limit of the country
and from the coast to the upper ranges of the Cordilleras. The royal
chinchilla inhabits an altitude of 300 to 2,000 meters, the Bolivian

an elevation of 5,000 meters, and the coast variety between 80 and 1,000 meters. The Argentine finds are made on the upper Andean table-lands in the Provinces of Catamarca, Salta, and Jujuy as far north as the Bolivian frontier. The first skins were sent to Spain in the early years of the nineteenth century, and in 1857 these pelts were valued at from $5 to $6 a dozen. At present their value ranges, according to quality, from $10 to $50. From the Chilean Department of Combarbalá annual exports of chinchilla skins reach 3,506 dozens, while Vallenar and Elqui furnish a sufficient quantity to bring the yearly shipments up to more than half a million skins. Coquimbo, the principal Chilean port of shipment for these furs, is credited in 1905 with exports of 12,000 dozens, the prices being almost double those of the previous year.

In "*El Florecimiento de México*" (The Prosperity of Mexico), the Columbus Memorial Library has received a valuable compendium of general information regarding the Mexican Republic. Edited by Francisco Trentini and published by the authority of the Government, the work is a reference book of unquestioned importance. Parallel columns reproduce the subject-matter in both English and Spanish, and innumerable illustrations, maps, and statistical tables add to the beauty and utility of the volume. The fine letterpress, binding, and photo-engravings are specimens of the best class of Mexican workmanship, even the paper being of native manufacture. Dating the present prosperous condition of his country from the inauguration of President Díaz's Government, the author makes adequate reference to the public service of the Executive, and finds, in the details of the economic status of the Republic, proof of his exceptional qualifications as a man and a citizen. These details cover the entire field of government and political organization and of geographical information, embraced in Volume I, while Volume II treats of the various States and Federal Territories separately, with reference to their natural resources, their industrial development and capabilities, and the constitutional regulations governing the same.

The "North American Review" for March 1, 1907, publishes a consideration of "Our Trade Relations with South America" by Dr. L. S. Rowe. The writer is professor of political science at the University of Pennsylvania and served as a delegate on the part of the United States to the Third Pan-American Conference at Rio de Janeiro. He finds that in spite of careless trade methods on the part of the United States that country has advanced its relative position in the markets of South America from year to year. It is his opinion, however, that a large increase in trade can not be anticipated unless it is accompanied by a corresponding investment in the great quasi-public works of Latin America, such as railroad building, street railroads, and electric light plants One of the reasons for the great shipments of machinery, etc., from European centers to South America lies in the fact that such countries as England and Germany have large capital invested, and naturally the equipment is purchased in the countries controlling the investment. A commercial background is one of the necessary elements to continental solidarity, and Doctor Rowe states that much of the actual achievement of the conference presupposes that the years to come will develop a unity of sentiment based upon closer commercial and industrial relations.

In a paper on "The Cause of Earthquakes" published in the "North American Review" for March 1, 1907, the writer, Prof. RALPH S. TARR, quotes the word of Count DE MONTESSUS DE BALLORE to the effect that outside of two great belts the world is practically immune from earthquakes. One of these two belts, in which have occurred 53 per cent of all recorded shocks, includes the Mediterranean region, Asia Minor, the Caucasus, the Himalayas, the East Indies, Central America, and the West Indies. The other almost encircles the Pacific Ocean. Passing along the Andes, it crosses the other belt in the Central American region; thence extends up the western coast of North America, passes across to Asia along the Aleutian chain; thence down through Kamchatka, the Japanese Islands, and the Philippines, and, crossing the other belt in the East Indies, extends on to New Zealand. Forty-one per cent of all recorded shocks occur in this latter belt.

As its name indicates, Mr. WILLIS FLETCHER JOHNSON's book, "Four Centuries of the Panama Canal," is designed to cover the history of that projected waterway from the time of BALBOA's discovery of the Pacific from "a peak in Darien" to the present day. At the same time, the history, both technical and otherwise, is adapted to the needs of the ordinary seeker after information. The voyages of COLUMBUS, the early Spanish conquests, the speedily advanced views of explorers as to the value of a trans-Isthmian route, the various surveys and reports thereon, the diplomatic and political influences affecting the different enterprises suggested, the international treaties and claims, and the final development of the present status of affairs on the Isthmus—all are narrated with a grasp of the situation and a clarity of expression that makes the volume a distinct boon to the lay reader of canal literature. The author has collected his data both at first hand and through authoritative sources in Washington, Panama, New York, Paris, and Bogotá, and official documents and personages are quoted with freedom and discretion.

Señor RICARDO FERNANDEZ GUARDIA has prepared an attractive little volume concerning the discovery and conquest of Costa Rica (*Historia de Costa Rica—El Descubrimiento y la Conquista*), his aim being, as frankly stated in the preface, to increase the general knowledge of the primitive history of his country. Prior to 1883, when the works of Señores Don LEÓN FERNÁNDEZ and Don MANUEL M. DE PERALTA appeared, no historical record of the early conditions of the country was in existence, with the exception of certain pages devoted to Costa Rica in Oviedo's History of the Indies. ·Since that date, research has been carried on, notably by Bishop THIEL and Señor Don CLETO GONZALEZ VÍQUEZ, the present President of the Republic. From the various sources at his command the author has compiled and rearranged into a small handbook all facts reaching from the discovery of the Atlantic shore by Columbus, through the story of conquest and colonial government, until the final abandonment of the province, in 1573, to the native owners, who had fought valiantly against the yoke of invasion.

An interesting book, entitled "*Reise nach Panama, Peru, Chile, Argentinien, Paraguay, Uruguay, und Brasilien,*" by RICHARD FREIHERR VON UND ZU EISENSTEIN, has been received by the Columbus Memorial Library. This is a diary with explanations written for the purpose of encouraging foreign travel and enterprises. Besides the abovementioned countries, which are treated more extensively, the author also gives a general review of Ecuador and Bolivia. The description of each country comprises a historical sketch, geographical description, area and population, climate, agriculture, minerals, commerce, and miscellaneous information, such as price of transportation, etc. The book contains 310 excellent views, 7 maps, 10 tables of meteorological observations, and one map of the entire voyage.

The bulk of the December, 1906, "*Boletín de la Secretaría de Fomento*" (Mexico), IV, is devoted to a review of the Tehuantepec Railway enterprise from the time HERNANDO CORTÉS reported to his King, CHARLES V, of Spain, the necessity of an interoceanic highway to the successful inception of the line under President DIAZ. The governmental decrees in furtherance of the work under Messrs. S. PEARSON & SON, the conditions of construction, and the saving in sea travel brought about through the completion of the road are covered, while numerous cuts and plans aid in a thorough comprehension of the subject-matter.

The "*Boletín de Historia y Antiguedades*" (Colombia) for November, 1906, contains a list of the treaties, conventions, and protocols celebrated between the Republic of Colombia and other nations. The compiler, Señor EDUARDO PASADO, states that three previous

ECUADOR.

Anales de la Universidad Central del Ecuador. Quito. Monthly.
Gaceta Municipal. Guayaquil. Weekly.
Registro Oficial de la República del Ecuador. Quito. Daily.

GREAT BRITAIN.

Board of Trade Journal. London. Weekly.
Commercial Intelligence. London. Weekly.
Diplomatic and Consular Reports. London.
Geographical Journal. London. Monthly.
Mining (The) Journal, Railway and Commercial Gazette. London. Weekly.
The Scottish Geographical Magazine. Edinburgh. Monthly.
South American Journal. London. Weekly.
Times (The). London. Daily. (Filed for one year.)
Tropical Life. London. Monthly.

FRANCE.

Les Annales Diplomatiques et Consulaires. Paris. Monthly.
Bulletin American Chamber of Commerce. Paris. Monthly.
Bulletin de la Chambre de Commerce de Paris. Paris. Weekly.
Bulletin de la Société de Géographie Commerciale de Paris. Paris. Irregular.
La Géographie. Bulletin de la Société de Géographie. Paris. Semimonthly.
Journal d'Agriculture Tropicale. Paris. Monthly.
Moniteur Officiel du Commerce. Paris. Weekly.
Le Nouveau Monde. Paris. Weekly.
Rapports commerciaux des agents diplomatiques et consulaires de France. Paris.
    Irregular. [Sup. to "Moniteur Officiel du Commerce."]
La Revue. Paris. Semimonthly.
*Revue du Commerce Extérieur. Paris. Semimonthly.

GERMANY.

Berichte über Handel und Industrie. Berlin. Irregular.
*Deutsche Kolonialzeitung. Berlin. Weekly.
Petermann's Mitteilungen. Gotha. Monthly.
Sudamerikanische Rundschau. Berlin. Monthly.
Der Tropenpflanzer. Berlin. Monthly.
Zeitschrift der Gesellschaft für Erdkunde zu Berlin. Berlin. Monthly.

GUATEMALA.

Boletín de Agricultura. Guatemala. Irregular.
El Guatemalteco. Guatemala. Daily. (Diario Oficial.)
La Locomotora. Guatemala. Monthly.
*La República. Guatemala. Daily.

HAITI.

*Bulletin Officiel de l'Agriculture et de l'Industrie. Port au Prince. Monthly.
*Le Moment. (Journal politique.) Port au Prince, Haiti. Weekly.
Le Moniteur. (Journal officiel de la République d'Haiti.) Port au Prince, Haiti.
    Biweekly.
Revue de la Société de Législation. Port au Prince, Haiti. Monthly.

HONDURAS.

Boletín Legislativo. Tegucigalpa. Daily.
El Estado. Tegucigalpa. (3 nos. per week.)
La Gaceta. Tegucigalpa. Daily. (Official paper.)

icigalpa. Semiweekly.
ras. Tegucigalpa. Weekly.
ni-official.) Tegucigalpa. Three times a week.
Biblioteca Nacional de Honduras. Tegucigalpa, Honduras.

ITALY.

del 1   legli Affari Esteri. Roma. Irregular.

MEXICO.

iltor Mexicano. Ciudad Juarez. Monthly.
co 1   nal de México. Mexico. Monthly.
d   Merida. Semimonthly.
iei ins   entífico y Literario. Toluca. Monthly.
ii Oficial uei i   to sur de la Baja California. La Paz. Weekly.
n de la Secretaria ue Fom   iustria. Mexico. Monthly.
i Oficial de la Secretaría ue Relac   E: ires. Mexico. Monthly.
Oficial. Mexico. Daily.
nomista Mexicano. Mexico. Wee .
ado de Colima. Colima. Weekly.
endado Mexicano. Mexico. Monthly.
Herald. Mexico. Daily. (Filed for one year.)
Investor. Mexico. Weekly.
Journal of Commerce. Mexico City. Monthly.
o Oficial del Gobierno del Estado de Guerrero. Chilpancingo. Mexico.
y.
ico Oficial del Gobierno del Estado de Michoacán de Ocampo. Morelia. Mexico. Semiweekly.
*Periódico Oficial del Gobierno del Estado de Oaxaca. Oaxaca de Juarez, Mexico. Semiweekly.
Periódico Oficial del Gobierno del Estado de Tabasco. San Juan Bautista, Mexico. Semiweekly.
El Republicano. Aguascalientes. Weekly.
Semana Mercantil. Mexico. Weekly.

NICARAGUA.

The American. Bluefields. Weekly.
El Comercio. Managua. Daily.
Diario Oficial. Managua. Daily.

PANAMA.

Gaceta Oficial. Panama. Daily.
Star and Herald. Panama. Weekly.
*La República. Panama. Weekly.
Registro Judicial, Órgano del Poder Judicial de la República. Panama. Irregular.

PARAGUAY.

*Boletín Quincenal de la Cámara de Comercio de la Asunción. Asuncion. Semimonthly.
Diario Oficial. Asuncion. Daily.
Paraguay Rundschau. Asuncion. Weekly.
*Revista del Instituto Paraguayo. Asuncion. Monthly.
Revue Commerciale. Assumption. Semimonthly.

PERU.

Auxiliar del Comercio. Callao. Biweekly.
Boletín de Minas, Industrias y Construcciones. Lima. Monthly.

Boletín del Ministerio de Fomento. Dirección de Fomento. Lima. Monthly.
—— Dirección de Obras Públicas. Lima. Monthly.
Boletín de la Sociedad Geográfica de Lima. Lima. Quarterly.
Boletín de la Sociedad Nacional de Agricultura. Lima. Monthly.
Boletín de la Sociedad Nacional de Minería. Lima. Monthly.
*El Economista. Lima. Weekly.
*El Peruano. (Diario Oficial.) Lima. Daily.
Padrón General de Minas. Lima. Semiannual.
Revista de Ciencias. Lima. Monthly.
Revista Pan-Americana. Lima. Monthly.

PHILIPPINE ISLANDS.

Boletín de la Cámara de Comercio Filipina. Manila. Monthly.
El Mercantil. Manila. Daily.
Official Gazette. Manila. Weekly. (Also issued in Spanish.)

PORTO RICO.

La Correspondencia de Puerto Rico. San Juan. Daily.

EL SALVADOR.

Anales del Museo Nacional. San Salvador. Monthly.
Boletín de Agricultura. San Salvador. Semimonthly.
Boletín de la Dirección General de Estadística. San Salvador. Irregular.
Diario del Salvador. San Salvador. Daily.
Diario Oficial. San Salvador. Daily.
*Revista de Derecho y Jurisprudencia. San Salvador. Monthly.

UNITED STATES.

American Druggist. New York. Semimonthly.
American Exporter. New York. Semimonthly. (Alternate Spanish and English editions.)
American Historical Review. New York. Quarterly.
American Made Goods. New York. Quarterly.
American Review of Reviews. New York. Monthly.
Annals of the American Academy of Political and Social Science. Philadelphia. Bimonthly.
El Boletín Comercial. St. Louis. Monthly.
Bookman (The). New York. Monthly.
Bulletin of the American Geographical Society. New York.
Bulletin of Books added to the Public Library of the City of Boston. Boston. Monthly.
Bulletin of the Geographical Society of Philadelphia. Philadelphia. Monthly.
Bulletin of the New York Public Library. Monthly.
Century Magazine. New York. Monthly.
El Comercio. New York. Monthly.
Current Literature. New York. Monthly.
Dun's Review. New York. Weekly.
Dun's Review. International edition. New York. Monthly.
Engineering Magazine. New York. Monthly.
Engineering and Mining Journal. New York. Weekly.
Engineering News. New York. Weekly.
Export Implement Age. Philadelphia. Monthly.
Exporters and Importers Journal. New York. Monthly.

Field Columbian Museum Publications.   Chicago.
Forum (The).   New York.   Quarterly.
Independent (The).   New York.   Weekly.
India Rubber World.   New York.   Monthly.
International Buyer.   New York.   Semimonthly.   (Alternate Spanish and English
   editions.)
Journal of Geography.   New York.   Monthly.
Library Journal.   New York.   Monthly.
Literary Digest.   New York.   Weekly.
*Mexican Industrial Review.   Chicago.   Monthly.
Mines and Minerals.   Scranton, Pa.   Monthly.
Mining Magazine.   New York.   Monthly.
Mining World.   Chicago.   Weekly.
Modern Mexico.   St. Louis.   Monthly.
Monthly Consular and Trade Reports.   (Department of Commerce and Labor.)
   Washington.   Monthly.
National.Geographic Magazine.   New York.   Monthly.
North American Review.   New York.   Monthly.
Las Novedades.   New York.   Weekly.
Outlook (The).   New York.   Weekly.
Pan-American Review.   New York.   Monthly.
Patent and Trade Mark Review.   New York.   Monthly.
Records of the Past.   Washington, D. C.   Monthly.
Scientific American.   New York.   Weekly.
Scientific American.   Export Edition.   New York.   Monthly.
Sister Republics.   Denver, Colo.   Monthly.
Tea and Coffee Trade Journal.   New York.   Monthly.
Technical World (The).   Chicago.   Monthly.
United States Tobacco Journal.   New York.   Weekly.
World To-day (The).   Chicago.   Monthly.
World's Work.   New York.   Monthly.

URUGUAY.

Anales del Departamento de Ganadería y Agricultura.   Montevideo.   Monthly.
*Montevideo Times.   Montevideo.   Daily.
Revista de la Asociación Rural del Uruguay.   Montevideo.   Monthly.
Revista de la Unión Industrial Uruguaya.   Montevideo.   Semimonthly.

VENEZUELA.

Boletín de Estadística.   Caracas.   Monthly.
El Fonógrafo.   Maracaibo.   Daily.
El Heraldo Industrial.   Caracas.   Semimonthly.
Gaceta Oficial.   Caracas.   Daily.
*Venezuelan Herald.   Caracas.

HONORARY CORRESPONDING MEMBERS OF THE INTERNATIONAL UNION OF AMERICAN REPUBLICS.

Countries.	Names.	Residence.
Argentine Republic..	Señor Dr. Don Estanislao S. Zeballos.......	Buenos Ayres.
Bolivia	Señor Don Manuel V. Ballivián*a*..........	La Paz.
Brasil	Dezembargador Antonio Bezerra...........	Pará.
	Firmino da Silva	Florianopolis.
Chile...............	Señor Don Moisés Vargas	Santiago.
Colombia...........	Señor Don Rufino Gutiérrez..............	Bogotá.
Costa Rica	Señor Don Manuel Aragón	San José.
Cuba	Señor Don Antonio S. de Bustamante	Havana.
	Señor Don Lincoln de Zayas..............	Havana.
Dominican Republic.	Señor Don José Gabriel García *b*..........	Santo Domingo.
Ecuador............	Señor Don Francisco Andrade Marín.......	Quito.
	Señor Don Luis Alberto Carbo	Guayaquil.
Guatemala..........	Señor Don Antonio Batres Jáuregui........	Guatemala City.
	Señor Don Rafael Montúfar	Guatemala City.
Haiti...............	Monsieur Georges Sylvain	Port au Prince.
Honduras	Señor Don E. Constantino Fiallos	Tegucigalpa.
Mexico.............	Señor Don Francisco L. de la Barra........	City of Mexico.
	Señor Don Antonio García Cubas..........	City of Mexico.
	Señor Don Fernando Ferrari Pérez	City of Mexico.
Nicaragua	Señor Don José D. Gámez.................	Managua.
Paraguay...........	Señor Don José S. Decoud	Asunción.
Panama	Señor Don Samuel Lewis..................	Panama.
	Señor Don Ramón M. Valdés..............	Panama.
Peru	Señor Don Alejandro Garland.	Lima.
Salvador...........	Señor Dr. Don Salvador Gallegos	San Salvador.
Uruguay............	Señor Don José I. Schiffiano	Montevideo.
Venezuela	Señor General Don Manuel Landaeta Rosales.	Caracas.
	Señor Don Francisco de Paula Alamo.......	Caracas.

a Honorary corresponding member of the Royal Geographical Society of Great Britain.
b Corresponding member of the Academia Nacional de la Historia de Venezuela

LATIN-AMERICAN REPRESENTATIVES IN THE UNITED STATES.

AMBASSADORS EXTRAORDINARY AND PLENIPOTENTIARY.

Brazil ....Mr. Joaquim Nabuco,
Office of Embassy, 1710 H street, Washington, D. C.

Mexico................................Señor Don Enrique C. Creel,
Office of Embassy, 1415 I street, Washington, D. C.

ENVOYS EXTRAORDINARY AND MINISTERS PLENIPOTENTIARY.

Argentine Republic ....Señor Don Epifanio Portela,
Office of Legation, 2108 Sixteenth street, Washington, D. C.

Bolivia ....Señor Don Ignacio Calderón,
Office of Legation, 1683 Sixteenth street, Washington, D. C.

Chile.................................Señor Don Joaquín Walker-Martínez,
Absent.

Colombia.............................Señor Don Enrique Cortes,
Office of Legation, 1312 Twenty-first street NW., Washington D. C.

Costa Rica...........................Señor Don Joaquín Bernardo Calvo,
Office of Legation, 1329 Eighteenth street NW., Washington, D. C.

Cuba.................................Señor Don Gonzalo de Quesada,
Office of Legation, "The Wyoming," Washington, D. C.

Ecuador..............................Señor Don Luis Felipe Carbo,
Absent.   Office of Legation, 1222 Connecticut avenue, Washington, D. C.

Guatemala............................Señor Dr. Don Luis Toledo Herrarte,
Office of Legation, The Arlington, Washington, D. C.

Haiti ....Mr. J. N. Léger,
Office of Legation, 1429 Rhode Island avenue, Washington, D. C.

Honduras ....Señor Dr. Don José Rosa Pacas,
Absent.

Nicaragua ....Señor Don Luis F. Corea,
Office of Legation, 2003 O street, Washington, D. C.

Panama ....Señor Don J. Domingo de Obaldía,
Office of Legation, "The Highlands," Washington, D. C.

Peru ....Señor Don Felipe Pardo,
Office of Legation, 2171 Florida avenue, Washington, D. C.

Salvador.............................Señor Dr. Don José Rosa Pacas,
Absent.

Uruguay ....Señor Dr. Don Luís Melian Lafinur,
Office of Legation, 1416 Twenty-first street, Washington, D. C.

MINISTER RESIDENT.

Dominican Republic ....Señor Don Emilio C. Joubert,
"The Shoreham," Washington, D. C.

CHARGÉS D'AFFAIRES.

Chile................................Señor Don Alberto Yoacham,
Office of Legation, "The Rochambeau," Washington, D. C.

Honduras.............................Señor Dr. Salvador Córdova,
Office of Legation, care of Consulate-General of Honduras, New York City.

Venezuela ....Señor Dr. Rafael Garbiras Guzman,
"The Rochambeau," Washington, D. C.

UNITED STATES REPRESENTATIVES IN THE LATIN-AMERICAN REPUBLICS.

AMBASSADORS EXTRAORDINARY AND PLENIPOTENTIARY.

Brasil ....IRVING B. DUDLEY, Rio de Janeiro.

Mexico ....DAVID E. THOMPSON, Mexico.

ENVOYS EXTRAORDINARY AND MINISTERS PLENIPOTENTIARY.

Argentine Republic ....A. M. BEAUPRÉ, Buenos Ayres.

Bolivia ....WILLIAM B. SORSBY, La Paz.

Chile ....JOHN HICKS, Santiago.

Colombia.................................THOMAS C. DAWSON, Bogotá.

Costa Rica ....WILLIAM L. MERRY, San José.

Cuba ....EDWIN V. MORGAN, Havana.

Ecuador ....WILLIAMS C. FOX, Quito.

Guatemala................................JOSEPH W. J. LEE, Guatemala City.

Haiti ....HENRY W. FURNISS, Port au Prince.

Honduras.................................(See Guatemala.)

Nicaragua................................(See Costa Rica.)

Panama ....HERBERT G. SQUIERS, Panama.

Paraguay ....(See Uruguay.)

Peru ....LESLIE COMBS, Lima.

Salvador.................................(See Costa Rica.)

Uruguay.................................EDWARD C. O'BRIEN, Montevideo.

Venezuela ....W. W. RUSSELL, Caracas.

MINISTER RESIDENT AND CONSUL-GENERAL.

Dominican Republic.......................FENTON R. McCREERY, Santo Domingo.

RATES OF POSTAGE FROM THE UNITED STATES TO LATIN-AMERICAN COUNTRIES.

The rates of postage from the United States to all foreign countries and colonies (except Canada, Mexico, and Cuba) are as follows:

	Cents.
Letters, per 15 grams (½ ounce)	5
Single postal cards, each	2
Double postal cards, each	4
Newspapers and other printed matter, per 2 ounces	1
Commercial papers { Packets not in excess of 10 ounces	5
Packets in excess of 10 ounces, for each 2 ounces or fraction thereof	1
Samples of merchandise { Packets not in excess of 4 ounces	2
Packets in excess of 4 ounces, for each 2 ounces or fraction thereof	1
Registration fee on letters and other articles	8

Ordinary letters for any foreign country (except Canada, Mexico, and Cuba) must be forwarded, whether any postage is prepaid on them or not. All other mailable matter must be prepaid, at least partially.

Matter mailed in the United States addressed to Mexico is subject to the same postage rates and conditions as it would be if it were addressed for delivery in the United States, except that articles of miscellaneous merchandise (fourth-class matter) not sent as *bona fide* trade samples should be sent by "Parcels Post;" and that the following articles are *absolutely excluded* from the mails without regard to the amount of postage prepaid or the manner in which they are wrapped: *all* sealed packages, other than letters in their usual and ordinary form; *all* packages (including packages of second-class matter) which weigh more than 4 pounds 6 ounces, except such as are sent by "Parcels Post;" publications which violate any copyright law of Mexico.

Single volumes of printed books *in unsealed packages* are transmissible to Mexico in the regular mails without limit as to weight.

Unsealed packages of mailable merchandise may be sent by "Parcels Post" to Bolivia, British Guiana, British Honduras, Chile, Colombia, Costa Rica, Guatemala, Honduras, Mexico, Nicaragua, Salvador, and Venezuela, at the rates named on page xv.

PROHIBITED ARTICLES TO ALL FOREIGN COUNTRIES.

Poisons, explosives, and inflammable articles, live or dead animals, insects (especially the Colorado beetle), reptiles, fruits or vegetable matter, liable to decomposition, and substances exhaling a bad odor, excluded from transmission in domestic mails as being in themselves, either from their form or nature, liable to destroy, deface, or otherwise injure the contents of the mail bags, or the persons of those engaged in the postal service; also obscene, lewd, or lascivious books, pamphlets, etc., and letters and circulars concerning lotteries, so-called gift concerts, etc. (also excluded from domestic mails); postal cards or letters addressed to go around the world; letters or packages (except those to Mexico) containing gold or silver substances, jewelry or precious articles; any packet whatever containing articles liable to customs duties in the countries addressed (except Cuba and Mexico); articles other than letters which are not prepaid at least partly; articles other than letters or postal cards containing writing in the nature of personal correspondence, unless fully prepaid at the rate of letter postage; articles of a nature likely to soil or injure the correspondence; packets of commercial papers and prints of all kinds, the weight of which exceeds 2 kilograms (4 pounds 6 ounces), or the size 18 inches in any direction, *except rolls* of prints, which may measure 30 inches in length by 4 inches in diameter; postal cards not of United States origin, and United States postal cards of the largest ("C") size (except as letters), and except also the reply halves of double postal cards received from foreign countries.

There is, moreover, reserved to the Government of every country of the Postal Union the right to refuse to convey over its territory, or to deliver, as well, articles liable to the reduced rate in regard to which the laws, ordinances, or decrees which regulate the conditions of their publication or of their circulation in that country have not been complied with.

☞ Full and complete information relative to all regulations can be obtained from the United States Postal Guide.

FOREIGN MAILS.

TABLE SHOWING THE RATES OF POSTAGE CHARGED IN LATIN-AMERICAN COUNTRIES ON ARTICLES SENT BY MAIL TO THE UNITED STATES.

Countries.	Letters, per 15 grams, equal to one-half ounce.		Single postal cards, each.a		Other articles, per 50 grams, equal to 2 ounces.		Charge for registration.	Charge for return receipt.
	Currency of country.	Centimes.	Currency of country.	Centimes.	Currency of country.	Centimes.		
Argentine Republic	15 centavos	35	6 centavos	15	3 centavos	10	24 centavos	12 t ms.
Bolivia via Panama	22 centavos	35	8 centavos	20	6 tmos.	15	20 centavos	10 das.
Bolivia via other routes	20 cms.	50	cms.	16	4 cms.	10		200 reis.
Brazil	300 reis	35	100 reis	10	50 reis	5	400 reis	5 cm.
Chile	10 centavos	50	3 cms.	15	2 centavos	10	10 centavos	5 t cm.
Bolivia	20 centavos	50	4 cms.	15	2 centavos	10	10 centavos	5 t fm.
Costa Rica	10 cms.	25	3 centimos.	7½	2 centimos.	5	10 cms.	5 centavos.
Ecuador	10 cms.	25	3 centavos	10	2 cms.	5	10 cms.	5 centavos.
Dominican Republic (Santo Domingo)	10 cms.	25	2 centavos	10	2 cms.		10 cms.	2½ cpe.
Falkland Islands	4 pence	40	1 penny	15	1 penny	10	2 pence	5 centavos.
Haiti	10 centavos	50	3 centavos	15	2 cms.	10	10 cms.	5 times de
...	10 centavos de gourde.	50	3 centavos de gourde.	15	1 ryds. de gourde.		2 cms. de gourde.	gourde.
Honduras	15 centavos	50	3 centavos	15	2 cents.	10	10 centavos	5 das.
..., British	5 cents.	25	5 cm.	10	1 centavo	10	10 cm.	6 t cm.
Mexico	5 centavos	50	5 centavos	15	5 centavos	10	10 centavos	5 t mi.
Paraguay	60 cms.		8 centavos	15	cms.	10	40 cms.	10 t mi.
Peru via San Francisco	20 centavos	60	6 cen tavos	15	5 tavos	10		20 t mi.
Peru via Panama	22 centavos	55	8 cms.	20	6 centavos	15	10 centavos	5 centavos.
Porto Rico b								
Salvador via Panama	11 cms.	55	3 centavos	15	3 centavos	15	10 centavos	5 t cm.
Salvador via other routes	10 centavos	50	3 centavos	15	2 centavos	10	10 centavos	5 centavos.
Uruguay	50 centimes	50	cms.	15	10 centimes.	10	50 centimos.	25 das.
British Guiana	5 cents.	25	2 cents.	10	1 cent	5	10 cents Dutch	10 cents Dah.
Dutch, ulna	25 cents Dutch	50	7½ cents Dutch	15	5 cents Dutch	10	25 centimes.	10 centimes.
Dutch, Rina	25 centimes.		10 centimes.		times.			

a The rate for a reply-paid (double) card is double the rate named in this column.

b See domestic rates and conditions.

Bolivia............	New York and San Francisco.	La Paz.
Chile..............	New York and San Francisco.	Valparaiso.
Colombia..........	All offices authorized to exchange mails between the two countries.	
Costa Rica.........		
Guatemala........	New York, New Orleans, and San Francisco.	Guatemala City, Retalhuleu, and Puerto Barrios.
Guiana, British....	All offices authorized to exchange mails.	
Honduras........	New York, New Orleans, and San Francisco.	Tegucigalpa, Puerto Cortes, Amapala, and Trujillo.
Honduras, British .	New Orleans.........	Belize.
Mexico............	All offices authorized to exchange mails.	
Nicaragua.........	New York, New Orleans, and San Francisco.	Bluefields, San Juan del Norte, and Corinto.
Salvador..........	New York and San Francisco.	San Salvador.
Venezuela.........	All offices authorized to exchange mails.	

UNITED STATES CONSULATES IN LATIN AMERICA.

Frequent application is made to the Bureau for the address of United States Consuls in the South and Central American Republics. Those desiring to correspond with any Consul can do so by addressing "The United States Consulate" at the point named. Letters thus addressed must be delivered to the proper person. It must be understood, however, that it is not the duty of Consuls to devote their time to private business, and that all such letters may properly be treated as personal, and any labor involved may be subject to charge therefor.

The following is a list of United States Consulates in the different Republics (consular agencies are given in italics):

ARGENTINE REPUBLIC—
Bahia Blanca.
Buenos Ayres.
Cordoba.
Rosario.
BRAZIL—
Aracaju.
Bahia.
Ceara.
Madeia.
Manaos.
Maranhao.
Natal.
Para.
Pernambuco.
Rio de Janeiro.
Rio Grande do Sul.
Santos.
Victoria.
CHILE—
Antofagasta.
Arica.
Caldera.
Coquimbo.
Coronel.
Iquique.
Punta Arenas.
Talcahuano.
Valdivia.
Valparaiso.
COLOMBIA—
Barranquilla.
Bogota.
Bucaramanga.
Cali.
Cartagena.
Corozal.
Honda.
Santa Marta.
Quibdo.
COSTA RICA—
Puerto Limon.
Punta Arenas.
San José.
CUBA—
Banes.
Baracoa.
Caibarien.
Cardenas.
Cienfuegos.
Habana.
Manzanillo.
Matanzas.
Nuevitas.
Sagua la Grande.
Santa Clara.
Santiago.
DOMINICAN REPUBLIC—
Azua.
Macoris.
Monte Christi.
Puerto Plata.

DOMINICAN REPUBLIC—Cont'd.
Samana.
Sanchez.
Santo Domingo.
ECUADOR—
Bahia de Caraquez.
Esmeraldas.
Guayaquil.
Manta.
GUATEMALA—
Champerico.
Guatemala.
Livingston.
Ocos.
San José de Guatemala.
HAITI—
Aux Cayes.
Cape Haitien.
Gonaives.
Jacmel.
Jeremie.
Miragoane.
Petit Godre.
Port au Prince.
Port de Paix.
St. Marc.
HONDURAS—
Amapala.
Bonacca.
Ceiba.
Puerto Cortes.
San Juancito.
San Pedro Sula.
Tegucigalpa.
Tela.
Truxillo.
Ruatan.
Utilla.
MEXICO—
Acapulco.
Aguascalientes.
Alamos.
Campeche.
Cananea.
Chihuahua.
Ciudad Juarez.
Ciudad Porfirio Diaz.
Coatzacoalcos.
Durango.
Ensenada.
Frontera.
Guadalajara.
Guanajuato.
Guaymas.
Hermosillo.
Jalapa.
Laguna de Terminos.
La Paz.
Manzanillo.
Matamoros.
Mazatlan.
Mexico.

MEXICO—Continued.
Monterey.
Nogales.
Nuevo Laredo.
Oaxaca.
Parral.
Progreso.
Puebla.
Saltillo.
San Luis Potosi.
Sierra Mojada.
Tampico.
Tlacotalpam.
Topolobampo.
Torreon.
Tuxpan, Vera Cruz.
Veracruz.
Victoria.
Zacatecas.
NICARAGUA—
Bluefields.
Cape Gracias á Dios.
Corinto.
Managua.
Matagalpa.
San Juan del Norte.
San Juan del Sur.
PANAMA—
Bocas del Toro.
Colon.
David.
Panama.
Santiago.
PARAGUAY—
Asuncion.
PERU—
Callao.
Chimbote.
Eten.
Iquitos.
Mollendo.
Paita.
Salaverry.
SALVADOR—
Acajutla.
La Libertad.
La Union.
San Salvador.
URUGUAY—
Montevideo.
VENEZUELA—
Barcelona.
Caracas.
Carupano.
Ciudad Bolivar.
Coro.
La Guayra.
Maracaibo.
Puerto Cabello.
Tovar.
Valera.

CONSULATES OF THE LATIN-AMERICAN REPUBLICS IN THE UNITED STATES.

ARGENTINE REPUBLIC.

Alabama	Mobile.
California	San Francisco.
District of Columbia	Washington.
Florida	Fernandina.
	Pensacola.
Georgia	Savannah.
Illinois	Chicago.
Louisiana	New Orleans.
Maine	Portland.
Maryland	Baltimore.
Massachusetts	Boston.
Mississippi	Gulf Port and Ship Island.
	Pascagoula.
Missouri	St. Louis.
New York	New York City.
Pennsylvania	Philadelphia.
Philippine Islands	Manila.
Virginia	Norfolk.

BOLIVIA.

California	San Diego.
	San Francisco.
Illinoi	Chicago.
Maryland	Baltimore.
Missouri	Kansas City.
New York	New York City.
Pennsylvania	Philadelphia.

BRAZIL.

Alabama	Mobile.
California	San Francisco.
Florida	Fernandina.
	Pensacola.
Georgia	Brunswick.
	Savannah.
Louisiana	New Orleans.
Maine	Calais.
Maryland	Baltimore.
Massachusetts	Boston.
Mississippi	Gulfport.
	Pascagoula.
Missouri	St. Louis.
New York	New York City.
Pennsylvania	Philadelphia.
Porto Rico	San Juan.
Virginia	Norfolk.
	Richmond.

CHILE.

California	San Francisco.
Canal Zone	Panama.
Georgia	Savannah.
Hawaii	Honolulu.
Illinois	Chicago.
Maryland	Baltimore.
Massachusetts	Boston.
New York	New York City.
Oregon	Portland.
Pennsylvania	Philadelphia.
Philippine Islands	Manila.
Porto Rico	San Juan.
Washington	Port Townsend.
	Tacoma.

COLOMBIA.

Alabama	Mobile.
California	San Francisco.
Connecticut	New Haven.
Florida	Tampa.
Illinois	Chicago.
Louisiana	New Orleans.
Maryland	Baltimore.
Massachusetts	Boston.
Michigan	Detroit.
Missouri	St. Louis.
New York	New York City.
Pennsylvania	Philadelphia.
Porto Rico	San Juan.
Virginia	Norfolk.

COSTA RICA.

Alabama	Mobile.
California	San Francisco.
Canal Zone	Colon.
	Panama.
Colorado	Denver.
Illinois	Chicago.
Louisiana	New Orleans.
Maryland	Baltimore.
Massachusetts	Boston.
Missouri	St. Louis.
New York	New York City.
Oregon	Portland.
Pennsylvania	Philadelphia.
Porto Rico	San Juan.
Texas	Galveston.
Virginia	Norfolk.

CUBA.

Alabama	Mobile.
California	Los Angeles.
Florida	Fernandina.
	Jacksonville.
	Key West.
	Pensacola.
	Tampa.
Georgia	Brunswick.
	Savannah.
Illinois	Chicago.
Kentucky	Louisville.
Louisiana	New Orleans.
Maine	Portland.
Maryland	Baltimore.
Massachusetts	Boston.
Michigan	Detroit.
Mississippi	Gulfport.
Missouri	St. Louis.
New York	New York City.
Ohio	Cincinnati.
Pennsylvania	Philadelphia.
Porto Rico	Arecibo.
	Mayagüez.
	Ponce.
	San Juan.
Texas	Galveston.
Virginia	Newport News.
	Norfolk.

DOMINICAN REPUBLIC.

Illinois	Chicago.
Maryland	Baltimore.
Massachusetts	Boston.
New York	New York City.
North Carolina	Wilmington.
Pennsylvania	Philadelphia.
Porto Rico	Aguadilla.
	Arecibo.
	Humacao.
	Mayagüez.
	Ponce.
	San Juan.
	Vieques.

ECUADOR.

California	Los Angeles.
	San Francisco.
Illinois	Chicago.
Louisiana	New Orleans.
Massachusetts	Boston.
New York	New York City.
Ohio	Cincinnati.
Pennsylvania	Philadelphia.
Philippine Islands	Manila.
South Carolina	Charleston.
Virginia	Norfolk.

GUATEMALA.

Alabama	Mobile.
California	San Diego.
	San Francisco.
Florida	Pensacola.
Illinois	Chicago.

CONSULATES OF THE LATIN-AMERICAN REPUBLICS—Continued.

GUATEMALA—Continued.

Kansas	Kansas City.
Kentucky	Louisville.
Louisiana	New Orleans.
Maryland	Baltimore.
Massachusetts	Boston.
Missouri	St. Louis.
New York	New York City.
Pennsylvania	Philadelphia.
Porto Rico	San Juan.
Texas	Galveston.
Washington	Seattle.

HAITI.

Alabama	Mobile.
Georgia	Savannah.
Illinois	Chicago.
Maine	Bangor.
Massachusetts	Boston.
New York	New York City.
North Carolina	Wilmington.
Porto Rico	Mayaguez.
	San Juan.

HONDURAS.

Alabama	Mobile.
California	Los Angeles.
	San Diego.
	San Francisco.
Illinois	Chicago.
Kansas	Kansas City.
Kentucky	Louisville.
Louisiana	New Orleans.
Maryland	Baltimore.
Michigan	Detroit.
Missouri	St. Louis.
New York	New York City.
Ohio	Cincinnati.
Pennsylvania	Philadelphia.
Texas	Galveston.
Washington	Seattle.

MEXICO.

Alabama	Mobile.
Arizona	Bisbee.
	Clifton.
	Douglas.
	Naco.
	Nogales.
	Phoenix.
	Solomonsville.
	Tucson.
	Yuma.
California	Calexico.
	Los Angeles.
	San Diego.
	San Francisco.
Canal Zone	Ancon.
Colorado	Denver.
Florida	Pensacola.
Hawaii	Honolulu.
Illinois	Chicago.
Kentucky	Louisville.
Louisiana	New Orleans.
Maryland	Baltimore.
Massachusetts	Boston.
Mississippi	Pascagoula.
Missouri	Kansas City.
	St. Louis.
New York	New York City.
Ohio	Cincinnati.
Oregon	Portland.
Pennsylvania	Philadelphia.
Philippine Islands	Manila.
Porto Rico	Mayaguez.
	Ponce.
	San Juan.
Texas	Brownsville.
	Eagle Pass.
	El Paso.
	Galveston.
	Laredo.
	Port Arthur.
	Rio Grande City.
	Sabine Pass.
	San Antonio.
	Solomonsville.

MEXICO—Continued.

Virginia	Norfolk.
Washington	Tacoma.

NICARAGUA.

Alabama	Mobile.
California	Los Angeles.
	San Diego.
	San Francisco.
Illinois	Chicago.
Kansas	Kansas City.
Kentucky	Louisville.
Louisiana	New Orleans.
Maryland	Baltimore.
Massachusetts	Boston.
Michigan	Detroit.
Missouri	St. Louis.
New York	New York City.
Pennsylvania	Philadelphia.
Philippine Islands	Manila.
Porto Rico	Ponce.
	San Juan.
Texas	Galveston.
Virginia	Norfolk.
	Newport News.
Washington	Seattle.

PANAMA.

Alabama	Mobile.
California	San Francisco.
Georgia	Atlanta.
Hawaii	Hilo.
Illinois	Chicago.
Louisiana	New Orleans.
Maryland	Baltimore.
Massachusetts	Boston.
Missouri	St. Louis.
New York	New York City.
Pennsylvania	Philadelphia.
Porto Rico	San Juan.
Tennessee	Chattanooga.
Texas	Galveston.
	Port Arthur.
Washington	Puget Sound.

PARAGUAY.

Alabama	Mobile.
Delaware	Wilmington.
District of Columbia	Washington.
Georgia	Savannah.
Illinois	Chicago.
Indiana	Indianapolis.
Maryland	Baltimore.
Michigan	Detroit.
Missouri	Kansas City.
	St. Louis.
New Jersey	Newark.
	Trenton.
New York	Buffalo.
	New York City.
	Rochester.
Ohio	Cincinnati.
Pennsylvania	Philadelphia.
Porto Rico	San Juan.
Virginia	Norfolk.
	Richmond.

PERU.

California	Los Angeles.
	San Diego.
	San Francisco.
Canal Zone	Panama.
Georgia	Savannah.
Hawaii	Honolulu.
Illinois	Chicago.
Louisiana	New Orleans.
Maryland	Baltimore.
Massachusetts	Boston.
New York	New York City.
Oregon	Portland.
Pennsylvania	Philadelphia.
Porto Rico	San Juan.
South Carolina	Charleston.
Washington	Port Townsend.

CONSULATES OF THE LATIN-AMERICAN REPUBLICS—Continued.

SALVADOR.		URUGUAY—Continued.	
California	San Diego.	Mississippi	Pascagoula.
	San Francisco.	Missouri	St. Louis.
Louisiana	New Orleans.	New York	New York City.
Massachusetts	Boston.	Ohio	Cincinnati.
Missouri	St. Louis.	Pennsylvania	Philadelphia.
New York	New York City.	Philippine Islands	Manila.
		South Carolina	Charleston.
URUGUAY.		Texas	Galveston.
			Port Arthur and
Alabama	Mobile.		Sabine Pass.
California	San Francisco.	Virginia	Norfolk.
Florida	Apalachicola.		Richmond.
	Fernandina.		
	Jacksonville.	**VENEZUELA.**	
	Pensacola.		
	St. Augustine.	California	San Francisco.
Georgia	Brunswick.	Illinois	Chicago.
	Savannah.	Louisiana	New Orleans.
Illinois	Chicago.	New York	New York City.
Louisiana	New Orleans.	Pennsylvania	Philadelphia.
Maine	Bangor.	Philippine Islands	Cebu.
	Calais.	Porto Rico	Arecibo.
	Portland.		Mayaguez.
Maryland	Baltimore.		Ponce.
Massachusetts	Boston.		San Juan.

WEIGHTS AND MEASURES.

The following table gives the chief weights and measures in commercial use in Mexico and the Republics of Central and South America, and their equivalents in the United States:

Denomination.	Where used.	United States equivalents.
Are	Metric	0.02471 acre.
Arobe	Paraguay	25 pounds.
Arroba (dry)	Argentine Republic	25.3171 pounds.
Do	Brazil	32.38 pounds.
Do	Cuba	25.3664 pounds.
Do	Venezuela	25.4024 pounds.
Arroba (liquid)	Cuba and Venezuela	4.263 gallons.
Barril	Argentine Republic and Mexico	20.0787 gallons.
Carga	Mexico and Salvador	300 pounds.
Centaro	Central America	4.2631 gallons.
Cuadra	Argentine Republic	4.2 acres.
Do	Paraguay	78.9 yards.
Do	Paraguay (square)	8.077 square feet.
Do	Uruguay	2 acres (nearly).
Cubic meter	Metric	35.3 cubic feet.
Fanega (dry)	Central America	1.5745 bushels.
Do	Chile	2.575 bushels.
Do	Cuba	1.599 bushels.
Do	Mexico	1.54728 bushels.
Do	Uruguay (double)	7.776 bushels.
Do	Uruguay (single)	3.888 bushels.
Do	Venezuela	1.599 bushels.
Frasco	Argentine Republic	2.5096 quarts.
Do	Mexico	2.5 quarts.
Gram	Metric	15.432 grains.
Hectare	do	2.471 acres.
Hectoliter (dry)	do	2.838 bushels.
Hectoliter (liquid)	do	26.417 gallons.
Kilogram (kilo)	do	2.2046 pounds.
Kilometer	do	0.621376 mile.
League (land)	Paraguay	4.633 acres.
Libra	Argentine Republic	1.0127 pounds.
Do	Central America	1.043 pounds.
Do	Chile	1.014 pounds.
Do	Cuba	1.0161 pounds.
Do	Mexico	1.01465 pounds.
Do	Peru	1.0143 pounds.
Do	Uruguay	1.0143 pounds.
Do	Venezuela	1.0161 pounds.
Liter	Metric	1.0567 quarts.
Livre	Guiana	1.0791 pounds.
Manzana	Costa Rica	1.73 acres.
Marc	Bolivia	0.507 pound.
Meter	Metric	39.37 inches.
Pie	Argentine Republic	0.9478 foot.
Quintal	do	101.42 pounds.
Do	Brazil	130.06 pounds.
Do	Chile, Mexico, and Peru	101.61 pounds.
Do	Paraguay	100 pounds.
Quintal (metric)	Metric	220.46 pounds.
Suerte	Uruguay	2,700 cuadras. (See Cuadra.)
Vara	Argentine Republic	34.1208 inches.
Do	Central America	33.874 inches.
Do	Chile and Peru	33.367 inches.
Do	Cuba	33.384 inches.
Do	Mexico	33 inches.
Do	Paraguay	34 inches.
Do	Venezuela	33.384 inches.

METRIC WEIGHTS AND MEASURES.

METRIC WEIGHTS.

Milligram (1/1000 gram) equals 0.0154 grain.
Centigram (1/100 gram) equals 0.1543 grain.
Decigram (1/10 gram) equals 1.5432 grains.
Gram equals 15.432 grains.
Decagram (10 grams) equals 0.3527 ounce.
Hectogram (100 grams) equals 3.5274 ounces.
Kilogram (1,000 grams) equals 2.2046 pounds.
Myriagram (10,000 grams) equals 22.046 pounds.
Quintal (100,000 grams) equals 220.46 pounds.
Millier or tonneau—ton (1,000,000 grams) equals 2,204.6 pounds.

METRIC DRY MEASURE.

Milliliter (1/1000 liter) equals 0.061 cubic inch.
Centiliter (1/100 liter) equals 0.6102 cubic inch.
Deciliter (1/10 liter) equals 6.1022 cubic inches.
Liter equals 0.908 quart.
Decaliter (10 liters) equals 9.08 quarts.
Hectoliter (100 liters) equals 2.838 bushels.
Kiloliter (1,000 liters) equals 1.308 cubic yards.

METRIC LIQUID MEASURE.

Milliliter (1/1000 liter) equals 0.27 fluid dram.
Centiliter (1/100 liter) equals 0.338 fluid ounce.
Deciliter (1/10 liter) equals 0.845 gill.
Liter equals 1.0567 quarts.
Decaliter (10 liters) equals 2.6417 gallons.
Hectoliter (100 liters) equals 26.417 gallons.
Kiloliter (1,000 liters) equals 264.17 gallons.

METRIC MEASURES OF LENGTH.

Millimeter (1/1000 meter) equals 0.0394 inch.
Centimeter (1/100 meter) equals 0.3937 inch.
Decimeter (1/10 meter) equals 3.937 inches.
Meter equals 39.37 inches.
Decameter (10 meters) equals 393.7 inches.
Hectometer (100 meters) equals 328 feet 1 inch.
Kilometer (1,000 meters) equals 0.62137 mile (3,280 feet 10 inches).
Myriameter (10,000 meters) equals 6.2137 miles.

METRIC SURFACE MEASURE.

Centare (1 square meter) equals 1,550 square inches.
Are (100 square meters) equals 119.6 square yards.
Hectare (10,000 square meters) equals 2.471 acres.

PRICE LIST OF PUBLICATIONS.

Price.

Bulletin of the Bureau, published monthly since October, 1893, in English, Spanish, Portuguese, and French. Average 225 pages, 2 volumes a year.

    Yearly subscription (in countries of the International Union of American Republics and in Canada)... $2.00

    Yearly subscription (other countries).................................. 2.50

    Single copies.. .25

    Orders for the Bulletin should be addressed to the Chief Clerk of the Bureau.

American Constitutions. A compilation of the political constitutions of the independent States of America, in the original text, with English and Spanish translations. Washington, 1906. 3 vols., 8°.

    Paper..each.. 1.00

    Bound in cloth..do.... 1.50

    Bound in sheep...do.... 2.00

      Vol. I, now ready, contains the constitutions of the Federal Republics of the United States of America, of Mexico, of the Argentine Republic, of Brazil, and of Venezuela, and of the Republics of Central America, Guatemala, Honduras, El Salvador, Nicaragua, Costa Rica, and Panama. Vols. II and III will be ready shortly.

      Vol. II will contain the constitutions of the Dominican Republic, Haiti, Cuba, Uruguay, Chile, Peru, Ecuador, Colombia, Paraguay, and Bolivia.

      Vol. III will contain Articles of Confederation of the United States, First Constitution of Venezuela 1811, Fundamental Law of Republic of Colombia 1819, Ditto of 1821, Constitution of Colombia of 1821, Constitution of Central American Confederation of 1824, Constitution of the Grenadian Confederation of 1858, Constitution of the United States of Colombia of 1863, Pro Constitution of Guatemala of 1876, Convention between United States and Republic of Panama for construction of ship canal to connect the waters of the Atlantic and the Pacific Oceans.

Code of Commercial Nomenclature, 1897. (Spanish, English, and Portuguese.) 645 pages, 4°, cloth.. 2.50

Code of Commercial Nomenclature, 1897. (Portuguese, Spanish, and English.) 640 pages, 4°, cloth.. 2.50

      NOTE.—Designates in alphabetical order, in equivalent terms in the three languages, the commodities of American nations on which import duties are levied. The English, Spanish, and Portuguese edition is entirely exhausted.

Leyes y reglamentos sobre privilegios de invención y marcas de fábrica en los países hispano-americanos, el Brasil y la República de Haití. Revisado hasta agosto de 1904. Washington, 1904. 415 pages, 8°.......................... 1.00

Patent and trade-mark laws of the Spanish American Republics, Brazil, and the Republic of Haiti. Revised to Aug., 1904, Washington, 1904.......... 1.00

    The above two works bound together in sheep.......................... 3.00

SPECIAL BULLETINS.

Money, Weights, and Measures of the American Republics, 1891. 12 pages, 8°. .05

Report on Coffee, with special reference to the Costa Rican product, etc. Washington, 1901. 15 pages, 8°... .10

El café. Su historia, cultivo, beneficio, variedades, producción, exportación, importación, consumo, etc. Datos extensos presentados al Congreso relativo al café que se reunirá en Nueva York el 1° de octubre de 1902. 167 páginas, 8°.. .50

PRICE.

Coffee. Extensive information and statistics. (English edition of the above.)
108 pages, 8°.. $0.50
Intercontinental Railway Reports. Report of the Intercontinental Railway
Commission. Washington, 1898. 7 vols. 4°, three of maps................ 25.00

HANDBOOKS (GENERAL DESCRIPTION AND STATISTICS).

Argentine Republic. A geographical sketch, with special reference to economic
conditions, actual development, and prospects of future growth. Washington, 1903. 28 illustrations, 3 maps, 366 pages, 8°....................... 1.00
Bolivia. Geographical sketch, natural resources, laws, economic conditions,
actual devolopment, prospects of future growth. Washington, 1904. Illustrated, 214 pages, 8°.. 1.00
Brazil. Geographical sketch, with special reference to economic conditions
and prospects of future development. 1901. 233 pages, 8°............... .75
Cuba. A short sketch of physical and economic conditions, government, laws,
industries, finances, customs tariff, etc., prepared by Señor Gonzalo de
Quesada, minister from Cuba, with bibliography and cartography of 198
pages. Washington, November, 1905. Map and 42 illustrations, 541 pages, 8°. 1.00
Guatemala. 1897. (2d edition revised.) Illustrated, 119 pages, 8°......... .25
Honduras. Geographical sketch, natural resources, laws, economic condi-
tions, actual development, prospects of future growth. Washington, 1904.
Illustrated, economic and telegraphic maps, 252 pages, 8°.............. 1.00
Mexico. Geographical sketch, natural resources, laws, economic conditions,
actual development, prospects of future growth. Washington, 1904. Illus-
trated, 454 pages, 8°... 1.00
Paraguay. Second edition, revised and enlarged, with a chapter on the native
races. 1902. Illustrated, map, 187 pages, 8°. Bibliography, page 141 .... .75
Venezuela. Geographical sketch, natural resources, laws, economic conditions, actual development, prospects of future growth. Washington, 1904.
Illustrated, railway map, 608 pages, 8° 1.00

BIBLIOGRAPHICAL BULLETINS.

Chile. A list of books, magazine articles, and maps relating to Chile. Washington, 1903. 110 pages, 8°... 1.00
Paraguay. A list of books, magazine articles and maps relating to Paraguay.
53 pages, 8°. Washington, 1904.. 1.00

MAPS.

Guatemala. From official and other sources. 1902. Scale of 12.5 miles to
1 inch (1:792,000). In 2 sheets, each sheet 71 x 76 cm. No. 1. General
features. No. 2. Agricultural......:................................... 1.00
Mexico. From official Mexican and other sources. 1900. Scale of 50 miles
to 1 inch. In 2 sheets, each sheet 108 x 80 cm. No. 1. General map.
No. 2. Agricultural areas 1.00
Nicaragua. From official and other sources. 1904. Scale of 12.5 miles to
1 inch (1:192,000). In 2 sheets, each sheet 80 x 80 cm. No. 1. General
map. No. 2. Agricultural.. .... 1.00
Bolivia. Mapa de la república de Bolivia, mandado organizar y publicar por
el Presidente Constitucional General José Manuel Pando. Scale 1:2,000,000.
La Paz, 1901. (Reprint International Bureau of the American Republics,
1904)... 1.00

LIST OF BOOKS AND MAPS IN COURSE OF PREPARATION.

LAW MANUALS.

Leyes Comerciales de América Latina: Código de Comercio de España comparado con los Códigos y Leyes Comerciales de Pan América.
Land and Immigration Laws of American Republics. (To replace edition of 1893.)

HANDBOOKS.

Chile.
Dominican Republic.

MAPS.

Maps are in course of preparation of the Republics of Honduras and Salvador.

Payment is required to be made in cash, money orders, or by bank drafts on banks in New York City or Washington, D. C., payable to the order of the INTERNATIONAL BUREAU OF THE AMERICAN REPUBLICS. Individual checks on banks outside of New York or Washington, or postage stamps, can not be accepted.

FOR FREE DISTRIBUTION.

The Bureau has for distribution a limited supply of the following, which will be sent, free, upon written application:

The case of the United States of Venezuela before the Tribunal of Arbitration to convene at Paris under the provisions of the Treaty between the United States of Venezuela and Her Britannic Majesty, signed at Washington, February 2, 1897, in 10 vols., of which 2 are maps.

Message from the President of the United States, transmitting a communication from the Secretary of State submitting the report, with accompanying papers, of the delegates of the United States to the Second International Conference of American States, held at the City of Mexico from October 22, 1901, to January 22, 1902. Washington, 1902. 243 pages. 8°. (57th Congress, 1st session, Senate Doc. No. 330.)

Message from the President of the United States, transmitting a report from the Secretary of State, with accompanying papers, relative to the proceedings of the International Congress for the study of the production and consumption of coffee, etc. Washington, 1903. 312 pages. 8° (paper). (57th Congress, 2d session, Senate Doc. No. 35.)

Message from the President of the United States, transmitting a report by the Secretary of State, with accompanying papers, relative to the proceedings of the First Customs Congress of the American Republics, held at New York in January, 1903. Washington, 1903. 195 pages. 8° (paper). (57th Congress, 2d session, Senate Doc. No. 180.)

NOTE.—Senate documents, listed above, containing reports of the various International American Congresses, may also be obtained through members of the United States Senate and House of Representatives.

VALUE OF LATIN-AMERICAN COINS.

The following table shows the value, in United States gold, of coins representing the monetary units of the Central and South American Republics and Mexico, estimated quarterly by the Director of the United States Mint, in pursuance of act of Congress:

ESTIMATE JANUARY 1, 1907.

Countries.	Standard.	Unit.	Value in U. S. gold or silver.	Coins.
ARGENTINE REPUBLIC.	Gold	Peso	$0. 965	Gold—Argentine ($4.824) and ¼ Argentine. Silver—Peso and divisions.
BOLIVIA *	Silver ...	Boliviano	.510	Silver—Boliviano and divisions.
BRAZIL	Gold	Milreis ..	.546	Gold—5, 10, and 20 milreis. Silver—½, 1, and 2 milreis.
CENTRAL AMERICAN STATES— Costa Rica......	Gold	Colon ...	.465	Gold—2, 5, 10, and 20 colons ($9.307). Silver—5, 10, 25, and 50 centimos.
Guatemala...... Honduras ...... Nicaragua ...... Salvador	Silver ...	Peso	.510	Silver—Peso and divisions.
CHILE	Gold	Peso	.365	Gold—Escudo ($1.825), doubloon ($3.650), and condor ($7.300). Silver—Peso and divisions.
COLOMBIA..........	Gold	Dollar...	1.000	Gold—Condor ($9.647) and double condor. Silver—Peso.
ECUADOR	Gold	Sucre....	.487	Gold—10 sucres ($4.8665). Silver—Sucre and divisions.
HAITI	Gold	Gourde..	.965	Gold—1, 2, 5, and 10 gourdes. Silver—Gourde and divisions.
MEXICO..........	Gold	Peso a ...	.498	Gold—5 and 10 pesos. Silver—Dollar b (or peso) and divisions.
PANAMA	Gold	Balboa ..	1.000	Gold—1, 2½, 5, 10, and 20 balboas. Silver—Peso and divisions.
PERU	Gold	Libra ...	4.866½	Gold—½ and 1 libra. Silver—Sol and divisions.
URUGUAY	Gold	Peso	1.034	Gold—Peso. Silver—Peso and divisions.
VENEZUELA	Gold	Bolivar..	.193	Gold—5, 10, 20, 50, and 100 bolivars. Silver—5 bolivars.

a 75 centigrams fine gold.   b Value in Mexico, 0.498.

*[By the new Bolivian law enacted September 14, 1906, the gold peso of one-fifth of a pound sterling (1.5976 grams, 916⅔ fine) is made the unit of value.—EDITOR.]

International Union of American Republics

Monthly Bulletin

OF THE

International Bureau

OF THE

American Republics

VOL. 24, NO. 4

APRIL, 1907

WHOLE NO. 163

WASHINGTON, D. C., U. S. A.

GOVERNMENT PRINTING OFFICE

1907

FRANCISCO J. YÁNES,
                Secretary.

WILLIAM C. WELLS,
                Chief Clerk.

GENERAL TABLE OF CONTENTS.

INDEX.

ÍNDICE.

INDICE.

TABLE DES MATIÈRES.

SEÑOR DR. DON CLAUDIO WILLIMAN, THE NEW PRESIDENT OF URUGUAY.

MONTHLY BULLETIN

OF THE

INTERNATIONAL BUREAU OF THE AMERICAN REPUBLICS,

International Union of American Republics.

| VOL. XXIV. | APRIL, 1907. | No. 4. |

The appreciative comment on the improved appearance and character of the MONTHLY BULLETIN, which the Director of the International Bureau has received since the publication of the March issue, has been most gratifying. From North, Central, and South America have come congratulations on the efforts to make it more interesting, attractive, and practical. In the United States especially, where the chief work must be done to inform the people in regard to the other American nations, there has been a pleasing response to the plan of the Bureau to put the BULLETIN into closer touch not only with manufacturers, exporters, and merchants, but with educators, scholars, and writers. The reproduction of photographs of the Latin-American ambassadors and ministers in Washington is giving the people of the United States a better opportunity to become acquainted in person, as it were, with these men who represent the best statesmanship and intellectuality of the sister nations. We hope in due time to follow these portraits with those of presidents, leading statesmen, and public men in Latin America. In his connection, the Director expresses the hope that readers of the BULLETIN will send to the Bureau, from time to time, photographs of leading men in their respective countries which can be used as occasion may arise.

PHOTOGRAPHS OF PROGRESS AND DEVELOPMENT.

There is no better way of proving practically the actual progress and development of any section of America than that of publishing photographs of scenes, buildings, and localities which are evidence of material, industrial, and intellectual movement. The Bureau has therefore decided to make a collection of recent photographs taken in all parts of Latin America. The constituency of the BULLETIN will confer a favor upon it and upon the Bureau itself if it will send any pictures, private or official, which are in line with this idea. It is desirable that all persons who come to the Bureau for tangible information about different cities and sections of Latin America may find there a complete set of representative photographs. If anybody sending pictures should wish to make sure that they reach the Bureau without fail, it would be well to deliver them to the respective foreign offices with the request that they be forwarded to the legations in Washington for delivery to this office.

COMPETITION OF ARCHITECTS FOR NEW BUILDING.

In this issue we publish in English and in Spanish the complete " Programme and conditions of competition for the new building of the International Bureau of the American Republics." In Portuguese and French are résumés thereof. The Director hopes that all persons interested in this " American Temple of Peace," as it has been appropriately named by Mr. ANDREW CARNEGIE, will read this programme carefully. It will enable them to comprehend what an appropriate, capacious, and beautiful home the Bureau expects to own within two years. All indications point to a spirited competition among architects for the signal honor of designing this important and historical structure. In addition to ten of the leading firms of architects in the United States who have been specially invited to prepare plans, it is probable that nearly fifty more will enter the open competition. Experts in architecture state that no better opportunity has been afforded in Washington during many years to design a handsome building for a great and noble purpose. The ideas embodied in the correspondence of the Secretary of State of the United States, Mr. ELIHU ROOT, with Mr. ANDREW CARNEGIE and the uses to which the building is to be devoted appeal to all architects who believe that the architectural lines of a structure of this kind should harmonize with the work of the institution of which it is to be the home. Section II, under the head of " Cost and character of construction," in the published programme, outlines in brief general terms the wishes of the Governing Board of the Bureau in this respect.

WHY THE COMPETITION IS LIMITED.

It would have been a pleasure for the Governing Board to have invited the architects of Latin America to participate in the competition, but after mature deliberation it was decided that this would not be feasible.   The opinion is unanimous that no time should be lost in starting construction.   The present quarters of the Bureau are so limited and cramped that it has the greatest difficulty in taking care of its growing work and of housing the additions to the Columbus Memorial Library.   Unless it has its new home in the near future it will be unable to carry into execution the ambitious and broad programme of reorganization and enlargement outlined and authorized by the Third Pan-American Conference held at Rio Janeiro in 1906. Careful calculation shows that the building could not possibly be started until September or October, 1908, if the competition for plans were open to the architects of all the Latin-American countries.   Of course if those of one other country than the United States, where the building is to be erected, were admitted, it would be necessary to permit those of all countries to participate.   This would include the architects of Rio Janeiro, Buenos Ayres, and Santiago, as well as those of Mexico and Havana.   By restricting submission of plans to American architects residing in the United States the competition will close on June 15, 1907, or within forty-five days of the publication of this BULLETIN, and work should start not later than September, 1907.   With due respect to the ability and capacity of Latin-American architects, it is the unanimous opinion of the Governing Board, representing all countries, that it is far better to gain one year in the completion of the much-needed new home of the Bureau than, as a matter of sentiment, to delay its construction for that period simply for a wider competition of architects.

THE BUREAU NOT AN ORNAMENTAL INSTITUTION.

It is a well-known fact that for one reason and another the Bureau has been described and regarded by certain critics in the past as an ornamental institution, or as a fifth wheel to the governmental coach.   While it is doubtful if it ever deserved that description, the most skeptical person can now be convinced of the error of any such judgment by personally visiting its headquarters and seeing with his own eyes what is being done.   The correspondence is growing so rapidly, especially along practical lines of inquiry and answer, that it is almost impossible for the present staff to meet the demands made upon their time.   Powerful business corporations and firms which formerly paid no heed to the Bureau now depend upon it for a great variety of information.   Manufacturing associations, Boards of Trade, Chamber of Commerce, educational institutions, lecturers, students, and travelers are flooding its mail with questions and suggestions that prove beyond doubt the growing interest throughout the United States in Pan-American activities and opportunities.

SOME SPECIAL RESULTS OF WAR.

Much as the troubles in Central America are to be deplored, they have awakened great interest throughout the world in the republics of that section of America. The demand for the printed publications of the Bureau in regard to Nicaragua, Honduras, and Salvador, and, by reflex relationship, concerning Guatemala and Costa Rica, have been almost beyond the capacity of the Bureau to supply. If no other good comes out of the conflict than the spreading of informa-tion about the physical resources and material possibilities of these countries, the contending forces may not have combated each other in vain. The great natural wealth of these five Central American republics has never been fully appreciated and only a few of the opportunities in that field have been thoroughly developed and ex-ploited. There is a wide field there for the use of millions of dol-lars in profitable investment, and the time is not far distant when there will be a progress not unlike that of Mexico.

NAMES AND STANDING OF LATIN-AMERICAN FIRMS.

A large number of inquiries are continually coming to the Bureau in regard to matters which are not directly within its province. For example, many manufacturing firms in the United States ask the Bureau not only to give them the names of representative business houses in different Latin-American cities, but also to pass an opinion on the financial standing of such houses. In view of the responsi-bility involved in answering these questions and of the danger of appearing to indorse particular companies or firms, the Bureau takes pleasure in referring respectively to the Commercial Museums, of Philadelphia, and R. G. Dun & Co., of New York. The former in-stitution publishes an excellent commercial directory of South America, which was prepared by one of its experts, while the latter makes a specialty of rating the standing of business men in South America as it does in the United States. In 1897–98 the Bureau published a commercial directory of Latin-America, which proved a great success, but the demand for the issue was so general that it was soon exhausted, and now, on account of the years that have passed, it hardly seems wise to give the names of firms that were included for fear that they may no longer be doing business.

THE NEW MINISTER OF SALVADOR.

The Bureau welcomes to Washington the latest addition to its Governing Board, Mr. FEDERICO MEJIA, Minister of Salvador to the United States. Mr. MEJIA is one of the most prominent men in his country, and has been for some time Minister of Finance and Public Credit. On Saturday, April 6, he was officially received by President ROOSEVELT.

NOTABLE ADDRESSES ON BOLIVIA AND THE ARGENTINE REPUBLIC.

Particular attention is invited to the addresses delivered by Mr. IGNACIO CALDERÓN and Lieutenant-Commander ATTWELL in regard to Bolivia and the Argentine Republic, respectively. The portions of their addresses quoted give some valuable and recent information concerning the development and resources of these two countries.

FOREIGN TRADE OF THE ARGENTINE REPUBLIC.

The details of Argentine and Brazilian commerce for 1906, compiled from recently issued statistics, give a clear idea of the growth of foreign trade in these two important republics. It is a significant fact indicating the exceptional prosperity of South America that the foreign trade of Argentine Republic last year, including both exports and imports, amounted to over $562,000,000. This is an average of nearly $100 per head of population— a proportion not surpassed by any other country of importance in the world.

GREAT HARBOR IMPROVEMENTS IN BRAZIL.

Engineers will be interested in the vast improvement work planned at Rio Grande do Sul, in Southern Brazil, where a magnificent harbor is to be constructed out of Lago dos Patos, so that the largest ships of the world can reach Rio Grande do Sul. The concession for this enterprise has been granted to Mr. ELMER L. CORTHELL, an American engineer. In this connection it can be said that Mr. LINDON W. BATES, a well-known engineer of New York, is submitting plans to the Chilean Government for the improvement of the harbor at Valparaiso, which, he contends, are far more practicable and cheaper than any projects submitted by European engineers.

GENERAL FEATURES OF INTEREST.

Some further features of interest in this issue of the BULLETIN are the messages of the Presidents of Guatemala, Salvador, Uruguay, and the Dominican Republic; regular monthly trade movements of Mexico and of the United States; the monetary law of Panama; consolidation of railroad companies in the Argentine Republic; real estate transactions in Buenos Ayres; Bolivian tin shipments; Brazilian coffee movements in January, 1907, and the trade of Santos, Brazil, for 1906; cultivation of a new fiber plant, "perini;" increase of German trade with Chile in 1906; the establishment of a bureau of information by the Republic of Colombia in New York; Peruvian mining industry in 1906; the reception of Minister LUIS TOLEDO HERRARTE, of Guatemala, and Minister FEDERICO MEJIA, of Salvador, by the President of the United States, and many important matters that are very interesting.

ARTICLES ABOUT LATIN AMERICA IN JUNE MAGAZINES.

In the June issues of "Munsey's Magazine" and the "Bankers' Magazine," respectively, of New York, will appear articles prepared by the Director of the Bureau which answer a great variety of questions that are being continually asked of this office and give considerable information not generally appreciated regarding the Latin-American Republics.

BARON D'ESTOURNELLES DE CONSTANT AND W. T. STEAD.

It is pleasing to record that two of the most distinguished advocates of peace and good will among the nations of the world, Baron D'ESTOURNELLES DE CONSTANT and W. T. STEAD, who recently visited Washington before attending the Peace Congress held in New York City, April 15–18, have expressed great interest in the work and scope of the International Bureau, and have requested that they be supplied from time to time with all its publications. They both commended its practical object of extending commerce and promoting mutual confidence among the nations of the Western Hemisphere, and remarked that it must become a most potent agency in behalf of cooperative influence and harmonious accord of the governments supporting it.

RECEPTION OF THE MINISTER OF GUATEMALA.

Señor Don Luis Toledo Herrarte, Envoy Extraordinary and Minister Plenipotentiary of Guatemala near the Government of the United States, was received in his capacity as such by President Roosevelt on March 18, 1907. On presenting his credentials Señor Herrarte spoke as follows:

" Mr. President: I have the high honor of placing in your hands the autograph letter accrediting me Envoy Extraordinary and Minister Plenipotentiary of the Government of Guatemala near the Government of the United States of America, which you guide with such foresight and wisdom.

. " Rarely has any mission been so valued and pleasing to me as the one that now brings me to the capital of the great and powerful American Republic, since the principal object of my mission, and to which I shall devote all my energies, is to maintain and to bind even more closely, if that be possible, the frank, amicable, and cordial relations that for a long time have united our respective countries, and to earnestly contribute to the cordial and unchanging sympathy which happily now obtains between both peoples.

" The death—deeply lamented by my Government—of my predecessor, Señor Don Jorge Muñoz, gave occasion to your Government to express the esteem in which it held the deceased diplomat, and furnished thereby a cause of sincere gratitude, which, in representation of my Government, I am pleased to acknowledge.

" This solemn occasion permits me also, Mr. President, to recall with pleasure and gratitude that the Government of the United States, in consonance with the noble and lofty ideals of humanitarianism and with the universal concord inspired by your civilizing policy, interposed, in conjunction with the Republic of Mexico, its powerful influence to the end that the conflict in which my country was unfortunately involved a few months ago be terminated in a satisfactory and honorable manner to the belligerent nations, avoiding by this magnanimous act the useless spilling of blood in our sister republics and establishing thereby in a practical manner the philanthropic and redeeming principle of arbitration, which, at no distant day, must unravel and solve all international controversies.

" Accept, Mr. President, the earnest and sincere wishes which, in the name of the people and Government of Guatemala, I proffer you for the prosperity and greatness of the American people and Government and for your personal felicity and happiness."

The reply of President Roosevelt was as follows:

" Mr. Minister: It is with pleasure that I accept from your hands the letters which accredit you near this Government in the capacity of Envoy Extraordinary and Minister Plenipotentiary of Guatemala.

" It has been the unfaltering endeavor of this country to strengthen and draw closer the friendly relation between our countries, in which lofty aim your Government has cooperated, with what result history tells in the unbroken friendship that has existed between the two nations. I am very happy, Mr. Minister, to learn of your avowed intention to continue the efforts of your predecessors toward strengthening those kindly ties.

" I appreciate your reference to the recent occasion which afforded to the Government of the United States and Mexico a gratifying opportunity to testify the disinterested wish of the two Governments and peoples for uninterrupted peace and harmony among their neighbors.

" It is my hope, Mr. Minister, that in your worthy mission you will have that success which its importance merits, as it is also my desire that in its consummation you shall meet with the kindliest cooperation of this Government. I bespeak for you, in your residence among us, the same cordial welcome which your lamented and respected predecessor received, and I pray you to extend to your esteemed President my friendly greeting and my earnest wish for the happiness and prosperity of the people and Government of Guatemala and for his personal well-being."

SKETCH OF MINISTER TOLEDO HERRARTE.

Luis Toledo Herrarte, Minister of Guatemala, was born in the capital of the Republic of Guatemala on March 28, 1871. His first studies were pursued in a private college under the tutorship of the noted Cuban educator, Don José Mª Izaguirre, and were continued in the National Central Institute, where, at the age of 16, he obtained the degree of Bachelor of Science and Letters and was awarded a gold medal given to the most proficient student of that institution.

In 1888, he matriculated in the School of Medicine and Pharmacy, where he remained two years; at the end of which period he obtained by competitive examination, an appointment from the Government of the Republic entitling him to continue his studies in Europe. He remained in Paris five and one-half years under the instruction of Professors Charcot, Dieulafoy, Jaccoud, Verneuil, and Tillaux, and obtained the degree of Doctor of Medicine in the latter part of 1904 on a thesis which was awarded the highest classification of merit granted by the Faculty of Paris.

During his stay in Europe he visited England, Belgium, and Spain. Returning to his country, he held successively the following important posts: Technical Director and First Surgeon of the Military Hospital; Chief of Clinical Surgery of the General Hospital; Chief of the Medico-Legal Bureau of the Republic; Professor of Internal Pathology and Obstetrics of the Faculty of Medicine; Secretary of the Faculty of Medicine and Member of the Board of Directors; Founder and First Director of the School of Midwives; Editor in Chief of the Scientific Review entitled " The School of Medicine; " Chief of the Military Bureau of Sanitation; Secretary of the Superior Board of Hygiene and Sanitation; Chief of the Scientific Commission appointed to study and combat the epidemic of malarial fevers in the Departments of Alta and Baja Varapaz; Secretary of the Committee on Organization of the Fifth Pan-American Medical Congress; Director of the National Central Institute, and Deputy to the National Assembly at several sessions of the Congress.

His diplomatic career began in Madrid in 1892 in the capacity of Attaché to the Special Commission sent by the Government of Guatemala to Spain to take part in the celebration of the Centennial of the Discovery of America. He afterwards served as the delegate of his country to the Fourth Pan-American Medical Congress held in Panama, and it was due to his efforts that Guatemala was chosen as the place of meeting of the Fifth Pan-American Medical Congress to be held in August, 1908. Early in 1906 he was appointed First Secretary of the Legation of Guatemala in Brazil, and a member of the Guatemalan Delegation to the Third Pan-American Conference at Rio de Janeiro. Lastly, in January of the present year, he received from the President of the Republic credentials accrediting him Envoy Extraordinary and Minister Plenipotentiary of Guatemala near the Government of the United States of America to fill the position made vacant by the lamented death of His Excellency Señor Don JORGE MUÑOZ.

Minister LUIS TOLEDO HERRARTE has published numerous articles on science and education, and has, in addition, compiled his investigations concerning various exotic diseases, particularly yellow fever and malaria, to which subjects he has devoted special work and attention. He is also a member of several scientific and literary societies, and is a Lieutenant-Colonel of the Military Sanitary Corps.

RECEPTION OF THE MINISTER OF SALVADOR.

Señor Don FEDERICO MEJIA was received in his capacity as Envoy Extraordinary and Minister Plenipotentiary from the Republic of Salvador to the United States by President ROOSEVELT on April 6, 1907.

On the occasion of presenting his credentials Minister MEJIA spoke as follows:

" Mr. PRESIDENT: I have the honor to place in your hands the autograph letter by which I am accredited as Envoy Extraordinary and Minister Plenipotentiary of the Government of Salvador near the Government of Your Excellency. I present to you at the same time the letters of recall of my distinguished predecessor, Dr. Don José Rose Pacas.

" Nothing could be more pleasing to me than the honor of conveying to Your Excellency the expression of my Government's fervent wish to maintain and draw closer, if that were possible, the friendly relations which happily exist between our two countries, and in the discharge of the duties of the mission which is intrusted to me I shall spare no efforts to voice faithfully the sentiments of the Salvadorean people, trusting that I shall meet in so doing the same cordiality and interest you have manifested in the cause of the welfare of my country and that of the other States of Central America.

- "Accept, sir, the wishes that I make in the name of the President of Salvador and in my own for the prosperity and further aggrandizement of the great American nation and for the health and personal welfare of Your Excellency."

President Roosevelt replied as follows:

" Mr. Minister: I receive with great pleasure the cordial sentiments of friendship to which you give expression both for your Government and the Salvadorean people. Entertaining the most sincere wishes for the prosperity and happiness of your countrymen and having at heart the continuation and strengthening of the good relations which have always subsisted between our two countries, I assure you of my cooperation in your aim to that end. I have no doubt that while worthily representing the Government by which you are accredited, you will so conduct your mission as to merit and receive the sincere friendship and high regard of that of the United States. I am glad, therefore, to greet you as Envoy Extraordinary and Minister Plenipotentiary of Salvador to the United States. I beg that you will convey to the President of Salvador my cordial appreciation of his message of good will to me personally and for the prosperity of the United States, and assure him of my earnest reciprocation of his wishes. For your own good wishes I thank you, and I trust you will find your residence with us to be most agreeable."

PROGRAMME AND CONDITIONS OF COMPETITION FOR THE SELECTION OF AN ARCHITECT FOR THE NEW BUILDING OF THE INTERNATIONAL BUREAU OF THE AMERICAN REPUBLICS, WASHINGTON, D. C.

GENERAL STATEMENT.

I. A building for the International Bureau of the American Republics is to be erected in the city of Washington, on the property known as Van Ness Park, or block south of 173, bounded by Seventeenth and Eighteenth, B and C streets and Virginia avenue, comprising in all about 5 acres, with the east or Seventeenth street frontage on the White Lot or Executive Grounds, and the B street and Virginia avenue frontage on Potomac Park.[a]

II. Architects, or firms of architects, of repute, not exceeding ten, will be specially invited to submit plans for this new building, and each of those accepting the special invitation will be paid the sum of $1,000, to cover the expense of the plans.

III. A general invitation is hereby extended to all architects of the American Republics residing in the United States[b] to enter the said competition and to submit plans for the said building. The plans thus submitted in response to this general invitation will stand upon the same footing with the plans submitted by those specially invited. The names of those purposing to compete must be registered with the Director of the International Bureau of the American Republics, No. 2 Jackson place, Washington, D. C., on or before the 30th day of April, 1907.

To the designer of the plan which is deemed to be first in merit among those submitted by competitors not specially invited but responding to this general invitation, and excluding any plan which may be accepted for construction of the building, the sum of $3,000 will be paid; to the second in merit thereof, $2,000, and to the third, $1,000.

It will be observed that both classes of competitors, those specially invited and those generally invited, have an equal chance to be selected for the construction of the building, and that only those who are specially invited have the certainty of the payment of $1,000 to cover the expense of plans, while only those who respond to the general invitation without being specially invited have a chance for the three prizes.

IV. All the plans submitted under the foregoing invitations and competition will be passed upon by the Chairman of the Governing

Board and the Director of the Bureau, assisted by a committee of architects, who will be selected after consultation with the competitors, and the architect submitting the accepted plan will be chosen as the architect for the building.

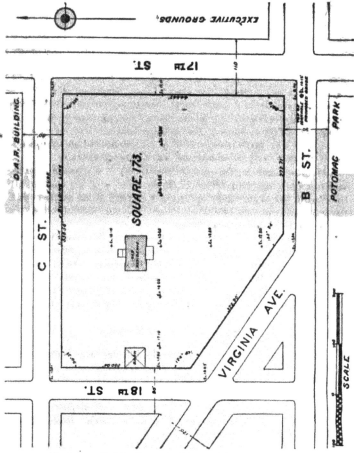

Site of proposed building, International Bureau of the American Republics.

V. The successful architect must be ready to revise his drawings in accordance with any recommendations made by the Committee of Award. If the architect selected should be from those in the open class and should not, in the judgment of the Committee of Award, *be capable of* carrying out the work on account of lack of experience, the committee reserves the right to require him to associate with himself some other architect or firm of wider experience acceptable to the committee.

VI. It is understood that the architect or firm of architects whose design shall be placed first will be awarded the commission for the carrying out of the work to full completion on the basis of the schedule of charges adopted by the American Institute of Architects, said commission to be paid on all work necessary to complete the building ready for occupancy, with the exception of decoration, mural painting, and movable furniture; that no claim shall be made by a competitor for any fee, percentage, or payment whatever, or for any expense incident to or growing out of his participation, other than is expressly provided for in the terms mentioned herein; that a competitor will forfeit all privileges under the regulations who shall violate any of the conditions governing this competition, or who shall seek in any way, directly or indirectly, to gain advantage by influencing in his favor any of those in control of this competition.

VII. The right is expressly reserved to reject any and all designs and to reopen the competition, if, in the opinion of the chairman of the Board, the plans submitted are not suitable in all respects as to design, cost, materials offered, or if any revision recommended shall fail to make the design acceptable.

The Committee of Award shall place out of the competition any set of drawings in which the conditions of these regulations have not been observed, and examine those remaining. No member of the committee above mentioned shall have any interest whatever, directly or indirectly, in the designs submitted in this competition, or any business association with, or employment by, any of the competitors.

CONDITIONS GOVERNING DRAWINGS.

I. All designs must be delivered to the International Bureau of the American Republics, Washington, D. C., on or before 2 p. m., June 15, 1907. Each set thereof, with its accompanying description, must be securely wrapped, sealed, and addressed in typewriting to " The Director, International Bureau of the American Republics, No. 2 Jackson place, Washington, D. C.," with the words " Building competition " on one corner of the cover.

II. Each design submitted must be plainly marked with the name of the building under competition, namely, " New building for the International Bureau of the American Republics," and without any distinguishing mark or device whatever which might disclose or suggest the identity of the competitor.

There must be inclosed with each set of drawings a plain white opaque envelope, within which the competitor will place a card or piece of paper bearing his name and address. The envelope must be securely sealed with a plain wax seal, having no impression, legend, device, or mark upon it which might disclose or suggest the identity of the competitor.

III. Upon opening, as soon as possible and convenient after the conclusion of the competition, the packages containing the drawings, the Committee of Award will number the envelopes containing the names and addresses of the competitors, and will place corresponding numbers, respectively, upon each drawing, plan, specification, etc., submitted by them, and will preserve unopened the envelopes containing such names and addresses until the final selection shall have been made.

Thereupon, all designs of other competitors will be returned to them and no use made of any part thereof, that may be original, without the consent of the author and with compensation therefor. None of the unselected drawings will be exhibited to the public nor to any competitor without the written consent of the maker.

IV. All designs must be on Whatman paper, unmounted, of such size as to permit the presentation of the scheme of the competitor, with a border of clear paper not to exceed six (6) inches all around. Each design submitted shall consist of each of the following drawings only (no alternate designs will be considered), inclosed in a portfolio or between stiff cardboard:

(a) Rendered elevation of east front, scale ¼ inch to 1 foot;
(b) Rendered elevation of south front, scale ¼ inch to 1 foot;
(c) Sketch elevation of north front, scale ⅟₁₆ inch to 1 foot;
(d) Sketch elevation of west front, scale ⅟₁₆ inch to 1 foot;
(e) Plan of each floor, including basement, scale ¼ inch to 1 foot;
(f) Block section through building, showing heights of stories and proportions of principal rooms, scale ¼ inch to 1 foot.

V. A description, not exceeding 1,500 words in length, typewritten on plain legal cap, calling attention to any special points of the design, materials to be used, including heating, lighting, ventilating, plumbing, finish of the building, and other features not clearly set forth in the drawings must accompany the plans.

Perspective sketches must not be included, unless expressly ordered by the Committee of Award in order to reach a final decision.

All drawings except rendered elevations must be in line only, in India ink, the plans and sections blacked in; no objection will be made to putting a slight wash of color over the halls, corridors, stairways, etc., in order to show them more clearly, but there shall be no indication of tiling, mosaic, ceilings, or other embellishments. Furniture, like desks, and their location to lights and doors may be indicated, if desired, but only in outline without tints.

Names and dimensions of rooms shall be lettered on each in black India ink; no script or fancy lettering shall be used. One outstanding figure 6 feet high may be shown on the elvations to give the scale, but no other accessories shall be exhibited.

COST AND CHARACTER OF CONSTRUCTION.

I. The cost of the building when constructed must not exceed, in its entirety, $600,000, including architect's fees, plumbing, gas piping, electric conduits and wiring, lighting fixtures, heating and ventilating apparatus, approved fixtures for library, including steel book stacks, etc., necessary to complete the building for occupancy and use, saving and excepting mural decorations and painting and movable furniture.

II. While the architects are left free to develop their plans as they think best, it is suggested that they bear in mind that the building is to be the home of the International Bureau of the American Republics, an institution supported jointly by the twenty-one republics of America under an organization known as the International Union of American Republics, for the purpose not only of promoting commerce and trade among them, but of developing closer ties of peace, friendship, and association. The peoples of the major portion of these republics are of Spanish, Portuguese, or other Latin extraction, and it therefore may be desirable that the building should have a character and tone in harmony therewith. In this connection attention is called to the ideas embodied in the correspondence between the Chairman of the Governing Board of the Bureau and Mr. Andrew Carnegie, reproduced in the appendix.

If the Spanish or Latin feature of a patio is included, it should have a sliding or rolling glass roof, in part, for protection against inclement weather or cold, but capable of being opened in summer, while the ground surface of the patio should permit of the placing of trees, flowers, and fountains.

The building must be of fireproof construction, the exterior to have such materials as each competitor deems best for the execution of his plans. In short, both the exterior and the interior should be finished with due regard to the specific purpose of the structure as outlined above and not as an average Government office building.

III. The proposed site of the building, already outlined in the " General Statement," is shown by an accompanying diagram, which gives the grades, curb lines, areas, etc., of the ground. The principal frontage will be toward the east, and consideration must be given the fact that the building will stand on a large block of ground, about

5 acres, open to inspection from all sides, especially from the east and southeast, and having space for landscape gardening, driveways, approaches, etc. The land is on one of the principal corners in the scheme for the improvement of the park system of the District of Columbia.

On account of the low elevation of one corner of the ground, 8.70 feet above mean tide, it is probable that some filling in will be required, but the expense of this is not included in the general statement of the cost of the building. The eventual level of the street at this point is indicated by the manhole of a sewer which is nearly 5 feet higher than the present grade.

On the adjoining tract to the north, facing Seventeenth street, is the new building of the Daughters of the American Revolution, and two blocks to the north is the Corcoran Art Gallery.

DIVISIONS OF SPACE, ETC.

Below is a statement covering the wishes of the Governing Board of the International Bureau of the American Republics, as to divisions of space and other arrangements in the building, but no allowance is made for elevators, stairways, hallways, corridors, court-yards, etc. Ample accommodations with abundance of light in these respects must be provided.

The principal necessary divisions of space can be described under the following general heads:

1. Administration section: For the Director of the Bureau, staff, and employees of the Bureau.

2. Library section: For the Columbus Memorial Library, reading rooms, stack room, etc.

3. Assembly section: For a large hall, reception and committee rooms.

4. Service section: For heating apparatus, fuel, mailing rooms, storage, etc.

The following dimensions are by no means absolute, but are intended to give a reasonable idea of the number of square feet required in the different divisions of space and rooms described:

I. Considering "administration section," provision should be made for—

	Square feet.
(a) Office of the Director of the Bureau	600
(b) Cloak and wash and toilet room (60), side room for a private secretary and two clerks (220), and small vault (30), all connecting with office of Director	310
(c) General waiting room between offices of the Director of the Bureau and office of the Secretary of the Bureau	600

Square foet.

(d) Office of the Secretary of the Bureau (300), cloak and wash room (40), with small adjoining room for stenographer (150) _____ 490

(e) Offices of the Chief Clerk (200) and assistants (400)_____ 600

(f) Office of the Translator and assistants_____ 400

(g) Room for Editor of the BULLETIN, statistician expert and assistants _____ 465

(h) Room for Accountant or Bookkeeper and assistant (200), vault for keeping books, records, etc. (25) _____ 225

(i) Room for correspondence archives, etc_____ 300

(j) Two separate rooms, respectively for men and women of office staff, with toilet rooms adjoining_____ 500

(k) Cloak room_____ 150
——— 4,590

Considering the location of this section with reference to the points of the compass, the principal offices should be grouped in the east and south frontages and the southeast corner, with the offices of the Director, Secretary, and immediate staff on the second floor.

II. Considering "library section," provision should be made for—

(a) Stack room _____ 2,000

(b) Public reading room_____ 1,200

(c) Map and photograph room (with plenty of wall space) _____ 800

(d) Periodical room for filing and circulation_____ 800

(e) Receiving and distributing room_____ 480

(f) Three study rooms (180 each)_____ 540

(g) Librarian's office _____ 300

(h) Assistant Librarian _____ 240

(i) Cataloguing room _____ 400

(j) Accessions room _____ 400

(k) Cloak room_____ 150

(l) Lavatories (separate for sexes)_____ 200

(m) Vault for valuable archives_____ 200
——— 7,710

The library section, while having the stack room, reading room, etc., grouped together, should be arranged with reference to easy access and consultation on the part of the administrative, editorial, and statistical staff of the Bureau. For example, the room for the statistical expert and assistants should be convenient to the consultation and reference rooms of the library. The permanent fixtures, which are to be included in the cost of the building, should be modeled after the most modern library arrangements. The stack room should be entirely free of woodwork, with steel stacks in tiers, and adjustable metal shelves, the upper tiers being separated from the

Square feet.

ones beneath by glass or other flooring that will provide plenty of light. The stack space should provide for 200,000 volumes.

III. Considering "assembly section," provision should be made for:

(a) A large, dignified, high-studded assembly hall		6,000
(b) Room for meetings of Governing Board		1,200
(c) Four committee rooms, averaging 20 by 20 feet		1,200
(d) Cloakroom for men		400
(e) Toilet for men		100
(f) Cloakroom for women (300) with toilet (100)		400
(g) A room for caterer's service		400
		9,700

Grand total _____ 22,000

The assembly-hall should be adapted to international conferences or congresses, and to other dignified gatherings, such as receptions to distinguished visitors, addresses of men eminent in various callings at home and abroad, and should permit of decoration, ornamentation, and finish in harmony with the purpose of the International Union of American Republics.

IV. Considering "service section," ample provision should be made for furnaces, fuel, sewerage connections, electric light and gas conduits and meters, janitor's quarters, scrub women's room, lunch room for staff and employees, kitchen facilities (in connection with caterer's room), lesser employees' toilet rooms, mail room, bicycle rack room, binding room, and general distributing, packing, and receiving room. There should be a covered approach to the basement where books and mail matter could be received from and delivered to conveyances without exposure to the rain or weather and with reference to distribution. This should be apart from the point where fuel would be received and ashes or dirt removed.

FURTHER DATA.

This programme sets forth, it is believed, full enough data as to cost and general requirements of the building, its conditions, locations, etc., to permit the competitors to present satisfactory solutions of the problem, but questions may arise or modifications become necessary. Should either of these conditions occur, all inquiries for additional information must be made, in writing only, to the Director of the International Bureau of the American Republics, 2 Jackson place, Washington, D. C., and any answer or additional information, embodying an essential modification, will be simultaneously communicated by mail to eaci competitor, but no information will be given after May 20, 1907.

JOHN BARRETT,
Director International Bureau of the American Republics.
WASHINGTON, D. C., *March 28, 1907.*

APPENDIX.

GOVERNING BOARD OF THE INTERNATIONAL BUREAU OF THE AMERICAN REPUBLICS.

Correspondence and resolutions relating to the gift of Mr. ANDREW CARNEGIE for the building of the International Bureau of the American Republics and the Columbus Memorial Library.

Resolution of the Governing Board and letter of the Secretary of State, Mr. Elihu Root, to Mr. Andrew Carnegie, approved at the meeting of December 19, 1906.

Whereas the Ciairman of the Governing Board of the International Bureau of the American Republics has laid before tiis, the said Board, the following letter sent by him as ciairman to Mr. ANDREW CARNEGIE and has asked for the approval thereof by the Board—tiat is to say:

" DEPARTMENT OF STATE,
"*Washington, December 4, 1906.*

" MY DEAR MR. CARNEGIE: Your active and effective cooperation in promoting better communication between the countries of America as a member of the commission autiorized by the Second Pan-American Conference ield in Mexico, your patriotic citizenship in the greatest of American Republics, your earnest and weighty advocacy of peace and good will among the nations of the earti, and your action in providing a suitable building for the International Tribunal at The Hague embolden me to ask your aid in promoting the beneficent work of the Union American. Republics, wiici was establisied by the Conference of Washington in 1889, continued by the Conference of Mexico in 1902, and has now been made permanent by the Conference of Rio de Janeiro in 1906. Tiere is a general feeling tiat the Rio Conference, the Souti American journey of the Secretary of State, and the expressions of courtesy and kindly feeling wiici accompanied tiem iave given a powerful impulse to the growti of a better acquaintance between the people of all the American countries, a better mutual understanding between them, the establishment of a common public opinion, and the reasonable and kindly treatment of international questions in the place of isolation, suspicion, irritation, strife, and war.

"There is also a general opinion that while the action of the Bureau of American Republics, designed to carry on this work from conference to conference, has been excellent so far as it has gone, the scope of the Bureau's work ought to be enlarged and its activity and efficiency greatly increased.

"To accomplish this, a building adequate to the magnitude and dignity of the great work to be done is indispensable. With this view the nations constituting the Union have expressed their willingness to contribute, and some of them have contributed, and the Congress of the United States has, at its last session, appropriated, to the extent of $200,000, funds available for the purchase of a suitable site in the city of Washington. With this view also the Conference at Rio de Janeiro, on the 13th of August, 1906, adopted resolutions looking to the establishment of a 'permanent center of information and of interchange of ideas among the Republics of this Continent as well as a building suitable for the library in memory of Columbus,' and expressed the hope that 'before the meeting of the next International American Conference the International Bureau of American Republics shall be housed in such a way as to permit it to properly fulfill the important functions assigned to it by this conference.'

"Those functions are, in brief, to give effect to the work of the conference; to carry out its resolutions; to prepare the work of future conferences; to disseminate through each American country a knowledge of the affairs, the sentiments and the progress of every other American country; to promote better communication and more constant intercourse; to increase the interaction among all the Republics of each upon the others in commerce, in education, in the arts and sciences, and in political and social life, and to maintain in the city of Washington a headquarters, a meeting place, a center of influence for the same peaceful and enlightened thought and conscience of all America.

"I feel sure of your hearty sympathy in the furtherance of this undertaking, so full of possibilities for the peace and the prosperity of America and of mankind, and I appeal to you in the same spirit that has actuated your great benefactions to humanity in the past to provide for the erection, upon the site thus to be supplied by governmental action, a suitable building for the work of the Union, the direction and control of which has been imposed by our respective

Governments upon the Governing Board, of which I have the honor
to be Chairman.

" With great respect and esteem, I am, my dear Mr. Carnegie,
    " Very sincerely, yours,
                            " Elihu Root,
    "*Secretary of State and ex officio Chairman of the Governing
    Board of the Bureau of American Republics.*

"Andrew Carnegie, Esq.,
            "*New York City.*"

Now, therefore, be it resolved that the action of the Secretary of
State, as Chairman of this Board, in sending the aforesaid letter be,
and it hereby is, approved.

Mr. Carnegie to Mr. Root.

                        New York, *January 1, 1907.*

Hon. Elihu Root,
    *Secretary of State and ex officio Chairman of the Governing
    Board of the Bureau of South American Republics, Washing-
    ton, D. C.*

Dear Sir: I am greatly pleased that you and your colleagues of
the South American Republics have done me the honor to suggest
that I might furnish a suitable home in Washington for the Bureau
of American Republics.

The approval of your application by the Governing Board of the
International Bureau and President Roosevelt's hearty expressions
of satisfaction are most gratifying.

You very kindly mention my membership of the first Pan-American Conference and advocacy of the Pan-American Railway, the gaps
of which are being slowly filled. The importance of this enterprise
impresses itself more and more upon me, and I hope to see it accomplished.

I am happy, therefore, in stating that it will be one of the pleasures of my life to furnish to the Union of all the Republics of this
hemisphere the necessary funds ($750,000) from time to time as
may be needed for the construction of an international home in
Washington.

The cooperation of our own Republic is seen in the appropriation
of funds by Congress for the purchase of the site, and in the agreement between the Republics for the maintenance of the Bureau we
have additional evidence of cooperation, so that the forthcoming

American Temple of Peace will be the joint work of all of the Republics. Every generation should see them drawing closer together.

It is a cheering thought that all these are for the first time to be represented at the forthcoming Hague Conference. Henceforth they are members of that body, whose aim is the settlement of international disputes by that " High Court of Nations " or other similar tribunal.

I beg to express to each and all of them my heartfelt thanks for being permitted to make such a New Year's gift as this. I have never felt more keenly than I do this New Year's morning how much more blessed it is to give than to receive, and I consider myself highly honored by being considered worthy to provide the forthcoming union home, where the accredited representatives of all the Republics are to meet and, I trust, to bind together their respective nations in the bonds of unbroken peace.

Very truly, yours,   ANDREW CARNEGIE.

The President to Mr. Carnegie.

THE WHITE HOUSE,
Washington, January 2, 1907.

MY DEAR MR. CARNEGIE: I am so much pleased at learning from Secretary ROOT what you are going to do for the Bureau of American Republics. You have already done substantially the same thing for the cause of peace at The Hague. This new gift of yours has an almost, or quite, equal significance as far as the cause of peace in the Western Hemisphere is concerned, for the Bureau of American Republics is striving to accomplish for this hemisphere what The Hague Peace Tribunal is striving to accomplish for both hemispheres. I thank you heartily.

Wishing you many happy New Years, believe me, sincerely, yours,
THEODORE ROOSEVELT.

Resolutions approved by the Governing Board of the International Bureau of the American Republics at the meeting of January 30, 1907.

Resolved, That the letter of Mr. ANDREW CARNEGIE to the Chairman of the Board, dated January 1, 1907, be received and filed and spread upon the minutes of the Board.

Resolved, That the Governing Board of the Bureau of American Republics express to Mr. ANDREW CARNEGIE its acceptance and grateful appreciation of his generous and public-spirited engagement to supply the funds for the proposed new building for the Union of American Republics. The Board shares with Mr. CARNEGIE the hope that the institution whose work will thus be promoted may further the cause of peace and justice among nations and the sincere and helpful friendship of all the American Republics for each other.

Resolved, That the Chairman of the Board communicate a copy of the foregoing resolutions to Mr. CARNEGIE.

The Governing Board of the International Bureau of the American Republics further resolves:

1. That the letter of the Honorable the Secretary of State, Mr. ELIHU ROOT, to Mr. ANDREW CARNEGIE; the answer of this distinguished philanthropist, and the resolution of the Governing Board accepting this splendid gift be kept on file with the important documents of the Bureau; and

2. That the text of these letters and the resolutions thereon be artistically engrossed under the title of "Carnegie's Gift to the International Bureau of the American Republics," and, properly framed, to form a part of the exhibit of the Bureau at the Jamestown Tercentennial Exposition.

ARGENTINE REPUBLIC.

ADDRESS OF LIEUTENANT-COMMANDER ATTWELL.

On March 2, 1907, Lieut. Commander JUAN S. ATTWELL, of the Argentine Navy, delivered an address on the Argentine Republic before the Cosmopolitan Club of Cornell University. In view of the growing interest in the Argentine Republic throughout the United States and the general desire for information concerning its progress and development, the BULLETIN quotes the principal portions of Commander ATTWELL's remarks, as prepared by him:

"The Argentine Republic has made a new record for itself during the year 1906, when its foreign commerce reached the unprecedented total of $563,000,000, in round numbers, of which the imports amounted to $270,000,000 and the exports to $293,000,000. Four years ago the imports and exports only totaled $280,000,000. At this phenomenal rate of increase eight years from now the foreign commerce of the Argentine Republic should pass the $2,000,000,000 mark. The present record, however, is enough to place the Argentine Republic far in the lead of other countries about which we hear much more. The Dominion of Canada, for example, peopled as it is by a sturdy race, equal in numbers to those that toil in the Argentine Republic, has yet to reach the Argentine Republic's total foreign commerce; and

Japan, with its aggressiveness, its industrious and clever population, eight times larger than that of the Argentine Republic, is also behind the Argentine Republic in matters of foreign commerce, and so is China with her 400,000,000 of inhabitants.

"If we turn to other Latin-American countries, we find that Mexico, on the border of the United States, and with a population more than double that of the Argentine Republic, has a foreign commerce nearly three times smaller than the Argentine Republic, while the foreign commerce of that great empire of wealth, Brazil, with a larger population than Mexico, in 1905, was less than two-thirds that of the Argentine Republic.

"We all admire the English people who have made Canada what it is to-day. We all admire the push and energy that characterize the Japanese people, and we are all aware of the great progress made by Mexico and Brazil, so it is far from my mind to speak in any way disparagingly of these countries, nor have I the idea of supposing for an instant that the man reared in the Argentine Republic is any better than the man reared in any other part of the world. It all depends, then, on a condition of soil and climate which permits the raising of diversified crops most needed for the sustenance of man and beast, and, moreover, to the fact that there is in the Argentine Republic a decided willingness of nature to generously respond to the labors of husbandry.

"It is mostly due to this favorable natural condition that while in 1888, there were only 6,000,000 acres under cultivation, in 1905, there were 30,000,000 acres under the plow, an increase that was quite out of proportion with the total increase of population during the same period, which was not much over 1,000,000 inhabitants.

"If we take into consideration the population of different countries and sum up their imports and exports and then calculate the proportion of the total foreign commerce that corresponds to each inhabitant, we find that each person of the Argentine Republic is entitled to over $100, each person of the United States is entitled to $35, each person of Brazil to $20, and each person of Mexico to $15, while the Republic of Uruguay, which is only separated from the Argentine Republic by the River Plata, looms up with $75 per inhabitant.

"When all the arable land of the Argentine Republic shall be cultivated, instead of 30,000,000 we shall have 300,000,000 acres under the plow, leaving a balance of nearly 300,000,000 acres more for the purpose of raising sheep and cattle, so that you can see that the future of the Argentine Republic's agricultural and pastoral industries is practically boundless. It is estimated that 300,000,000 people will be able to live and thrive in the plains of the Argentine Republic, where at present there are only two persons for each square kilometer, while in Germany, for example, the density of population is 104 persons for each square kilometer.

" The Argentine Republic to-day occupies a unique position among the nations that are attracting the attention of mankind as world-producing countries. Its fine system of rivers, which constitute a magnificent means of communication between Buenos Ayres and the very heart of South America, and which come flowing down from the region where the rubber trees grow wild, linking Brazil, Paraguay, and Bolivia with the capital of the Argentine Republic, as well as the railroad lines that cross the country in all directions, and will also join by rail Chile, Bolivia, Brazil, and Paraguay with the mouth of the River Plata, where Buenos Ayres stands, have solved the great problem of transportation and have done more than anything else to hasten the era of great prosperity that the country is now enjoying. The rich soil, the beautiful climate, the means of transportation are there, and these advantages have not been overlooked by the toiling masses of Europe, and more than 2,000,000 foreigners have already gone to the Argentine Republic. The current of immigration has never been larger than at the present time, and last year 260,000 immigrants came into the country, and it is now surmised that this year this figure will be left far behind, since 120,000 immigrants are booked to arrive during the first three months of the present year. Outside of the United States, with its 80,000,000 inhabitants, its immense resources, and situated at a week's distance from Europe, no other country in the world is attracting the number of people that are now flocking to the Argentine Republic, eager to spread themselves over the boundless and fertile plains where land is yet relatively cheap and needs no artificial fertilizer, nor artificial irrigation for that matter, and where the winters are so mild that vegetable life does not perish and shelters are not thought of for our flock of 120,000,000 sheep and our herd of 30,000,000 head of cattle.

" Foreign capital is also pouring into the country at a rapid rate, and it is now known that about $1,300,000,000 of English money alone is invested in the Argentine Republic and enterprises connected with the Argentine Republic and more than $500,000,000 from other European countries. North America alone has so far stood aloof from competing with other countries in the race for high and sure dividends which the Argentine Republic has always yielded to the intelligent investor. I may say that while the Argentine people bought $39,000,000 worth of goods and agricultural machinery from the United States last year, the people of the United States only bought $13,000,000 worth of hides, quebracho, and coarse wool from the Argentine Republic, and yet we are always hearing at this end of the line that the balance of trade between the United States and South America is decidedly against the former. It is precisely the contrary in the case of the Argentine Republic. As a matter of fact, the United States sells nearly as much goods to the Argentine Republic alone (and is increasing its sales at the rate of $10,000,000 per year) as to all the other South American Republics put together, and for this reason, if for no other, we believe that we are entitled to a special hearing when it comes to a question of adjusting commerce. It is also very little known that American imports into the Argentine Republic are now second only to those of England and consequently superior to those of Germany, to which country we send a great quantity of our wool crop, free of duty, while wool is taxed in America at the rate of 11 cents per pound, and hides are also heavily taxed.

"It speaks very well for the excellence of American industry that in spite of serious tariff drawbacks at this end, about $200,000,000 have found their way from the Argentine Republic to the United States during the last decade to pay for American goods, and if we take into consideration the rapid increase of American exports to the Argentine Republic, it is easy to conclude that in the next ten years over $500,000,000 more will also find their way from the Argentine Republic to the American manufacturers, while less than $150,000,000 will leave America to pay for the imports from the Argentine Republic during the same time, therefore leaving a balance in favor of the United States of more than $350,000,000. This is not a theory, but a condition, and these figures show more than anything else the necessity of improving the means of communication between the two countries and of establishing banks to handle the great volume of money that is passing between them, without having to pay unnecessary tolls to London banking houses and to English shipowners, as has been done in the past and is being done at present and will continue to be done until the American people will do something more than merely sell their goods cash down to the persistent Argentine purchaser.

"I shall also leave to clever magazine writers the description of our capital city, Buenos Ayres, with over 1,100,000 inhabitants, larger, therefore, than Baltimore and Boston put together, and which is the second largest sea town in the Western Hemisphere. Buenos Ayres has been called a great city by President Roosevelt in his last annual message to Congress, and it called forth the admiration of the Secretary of State, Mr. Root.

"As an indication of the business activity of the city of Buenos Ayres, it is sufficient to say that the transactions in real estate during the year of 1906 amounted to more than $100,000,000.

"Besides, over $25,000,000 were devoted to the construction of new private dwelling houses.

"The country at large has awakened to a realizing sense of its usefulness, and land values have multiplied during the last five years, the price of living has increased, and labor is scarce from the Atlantic to the Andes and from Tierra del Fuego to the borders of Bolivia. Our port facilities are not sufficient to accommodate all our shipping, our railroads are in want of more rolling stock to carry our crops, booming conditions in this respect being similar to those prevailing at present in the United States.

" We have capital, we have labor, and we have enterprising men, but we need more capital, we need more labor, and we need more enterprising men to help us steer the ship of state through the channels of prosperity. More railroads must be built, canals must be opened, more ships must be constructed for the navigation of our rivers, and new avenues and subways must be cut through our congested cities. These are only a few of our pressing needs, and serve to show the possibilities that the country offers to large investors seeking immediate returns. The cry of progress is always more progress, and we feel that we have just started in the career of producing wealth, possibly because we are only now beginning to realize the full meaning of its attending responsibilities, which we are of course far from wishing to shirk, and are striving to meet in every way.

" The statesman and the husbandman have the country in hand and are doing their best to place it and keep it in the lead of those nations which are fortunately capable of yielding the products needed to feed and clothe a large portion of mankind."

FOREIGN COMMERCE IN 1906.

Details of the foreign trade of the Argentine Republic, received by the Bureau of the American Republics on March 27, 1907, show import valuations of $269,970,521 and export values amounting to $292,253,829 gold, as previously stated in the MONTHLY BULLETIN for March.

The countries of origin and destination for the year were as follows:

Country.	Imports.	Exports.
Africa	$32,269	$3,958,031
Germany	38,416,259	39,417,196
Belgium	12,228,040	25,621,395
Bolivia	134,112	328,598
Brazil	6,641,025	11,891,315
Cuba	679,581	247,391
Chile	828,215	1,358,587
Spain	7,368,269	2,572,576
United States	39,474,894	13,332,112
France	26,744,875	35,768,854
Italy	24,123,636	6,906,124
Holland	1,511,744	2,975,238
Paraguay	1,308,972	206,014
United Kingdom	91,829,988	43,224,038
Uruguay	1,833,241	5,034,440
Various	14,115,451	3,776,722
Orders		95,614,748

The ratio of trade values for the principal participating countries, as compared with 1905, was as follows:

Imports from Germany increased 32 per cent and exports 6.3 per cent; from Belgium, imports show an increase of 40.1 per cent and exports 23.3; from Brazil, imports increased 24.6 per cent and exports declined 9.6 per cent; from Spain, imports increased 28.7 per cent and exports 10.1 per cent; from the United States, imports increased 36.4 per cent and exports declined 15.2 per cent; from France, imports increased 25.8 per cent and exports declined 4.8 per cent; from Italy, imports increased 18.9 per cent and exports 6.7 per cent; from the United Kingdom, imports increased 38.6 per cent and exports declined 3.5 per cent. In the total trade a loss of 9.4 per cent in exports is more than offset by the advance of 31.5 per cent noted for imports.

Import classifications for 1906 show the following values as compared with 1905:

Article.	Value.	Comparisons.
Live stock	$2,526,602	—$1,218,794
Foodstuffs	17,662,548	+ 3,926,632
Tobacco and manufactures	4,911,079	+ 455,671
Wines, spirits, liquors, etc	11,794,039	+ 2,626,197
Textiles:		
Silk goods	3,701,422	+ 1,098,864
Woolens	10,695,037	— 272,225
Cottons	31,670,629	+ 4,603,897
Various	8,062,951	+ 2,480,562
Total textiles	54,130,039	+ 7,911,068
Oils and grease	7,880,973	+ 2,321,181
Chemicals and drugs	7,582,850	+ 1,307,073
Colors and dyes	1,640,435	+ 198,709
Lumber and manufactures	5,612,222	+ 1,071,399
Paper and manufactures	4,914,737	+ 780,895
Leather and manufactures	2,314,551	+ 517,707
Hardware	34,942,308	+11,133,029
Metallic goods	8,592,130	+ 2,588,256
Agricultural implements	17,158,545	+ 626,993
Locomotion	35,055,364	+11,303,015
Glass, earthenware, etc	20,910,800	+ 7,229,860
Building materials	22,001,698	+ 6,615,307
Electrical goods	3,430,031	+ 1,395,357
Various	6,909,561	+ 1,589,947

The classification of exports and the values, as compared with the preceding year, were:

	Value.	Comparisons.
Pastoral products	$124,136,439	—$16,906,547
Agricultural products	157,654,692	— 12,580,543
Forest products	5,921,859	— 1,203,473
Mineral products	273,816	+ 12,300
Products of the chase	1,098,500	+ 307,766
Various	3,168,523	— 219,515

The customs duties on imports (there being no export duties) produced the sum of $59,277,050 gold and $1,821,990 paper, being an increase, as compared with 1905, of $8,687,726 gold and of $596,556 paper.

Included, under the general head of "Various" on the import list are the following countries: Australia, $117,848; Austria-Hungary, $1,723,761; Bulgaria, $125; Canada, $1,220,964; Colombia, $1,315; China, $507,140; Denmark, $25,161; Ecuador, $44,932; Egypt, $18,618; Greece, $71,869; Japan, $229,530; Mexico, $11,204; Norway, $468,042; Panama, $1,787; Persia, $1,313; Peru, $694; Portugal, $327,043; German colonies, $408; French colonies, $11,804; Dutch colonies, $82,242; British colonies, $4,429,988; North American colonies, $26,227; Roumania, $227,766; Russia, $515,711; Salvador, $2,598; Dominican Republic, $2,750; Sweden, $293,018; Switzerland, $3,033,143; Turkey, $58,982, and Venezuela, $15,523.

On the export list "Various" comprises: Austria-Hungary, $46,-328; Norway, $10,687; Peru, $76,154; German colonies, $155,444; British colonies, $4,480; Russia and colonies, $283,395, and Sweden, $307,656.

During the ten years' period 1897–1906 imports have advanced from $98,283,948 to $269,970,521, and exports from $101,169,299 to $202,253,829, showing a threefold increase.

The great advance in import values as compared with 1905 indicates infallibly the increased purchasing power of the country, and the decreased export valuations are to be in a great measure assigned to delayed shipments of wool and maize.

CONSOLIDATION OF RAILROAD COMPANIES.

From March 1, 1907, the administration of the Argentine railways known as the Buenos Ayres and Pacific and the Argentine Great Western will be united. This union will greatly facilitate travel in the sections traversed, and will obviate the necessity for transfer of cargoes at Villa Mercedes, as was formerly the case.

REAL ESTATE REGISTRATION IN BUENOS AYRES, 1906.

The registration of real estate properties in Buenos Ayres during 1906 numbered 21,888, with a valuation of $279,224,593.97 (national currency), as compared with 18,652, valued at $228,010,843.89, in the preceding year.

COMMISSION FOR THE REVISION OF THE TARIFF.

"La Prensa" (Buenos Ayres) for February 17, 1907, states that the President of the Argentine Republic has appointed a commission charged with the investigation and revision of existing tariff rates in the country. The revision is to be undertaken with special reference to articles of prime necessity, with the ultimate purpose of rendering them cheaper for the consumer.

The Board of Revision is composed of Dr. EMILIO FRERS, President; and Señores LUIS E. ZUBERBHULER, FRANCISCO LATZINA, RICARDO PILLADO, EMILIO LAHITTE, ANTONIO LANUSSE, EMILIO HANSEN, FRANCISCO CAYOL, and PEDRO L. MEDINA.

MARITIME MOVEMENT IN 1905 AND 1906.

The maritime service maintained between the Argentine Republic and the various countries engaged in Argentine trade was represented by the following figures in 1905:

Country.	Number of vessels.	Tons.
Great Britain	1,313	3,014,701
Germany	469	1,250,219
Italy	373	860,659
France	259	627,677
United States	250	518,821
Spain	105	208,447
Belgium	237	497,211
The Netherlands	89	207,507

Returns showing the number of vessels entered and cleared at Argentine ports, other than Buenos Ayres, during 1906 place Rosario at the head of the list with 2,351 vessels entered and 2,305 cleared, with an aggregate registered tonnage of 2,876,780. La Plata is second, with 695 entries and 688 clearances and an aggregate tonnage of 1,410,000. Bahia Blanca follows with 377 entries and 363 clearances and a tonnage of 1,050,000. Parana shows a marked decline in tonnage, 418,700 tons being registered, though the number of vessels both ways is relatively large—1.109 entering and 641 clearing.

The total for the four ports was 4,532 entries and 3,997 clearances, with an aggregate register of 5,754,700 tons.

CEREAL CROP SHIPMENTS, 1906.

The shipments of cereal crops from the Argentine Republic during 1906 are reported as follows: Wheat, 2,621,058 tons, as compared with 2,854,178 in 1905; corn, 2,308,772 tons, as against 2,258,871 in 1905, and linseed, 540, 547 tons, the figures for the previous year being 636,327 tons.

PUBLIC WORKS IN 1907.

An extensive system of public works has been outlined by the Argentine Government for 1907, the sum of $1,200,000 having been voted for the purpose by the National Congress. The projected improvements include the construction and repair of highways and bridges.

PATENTS AND TRADE-MARKS IN 1906.

The Bureau of Patents and Trade-Marks of the Argentine Republic reports for the year 1906: Patents solicited, 670; granted, 637; denied, 46, and transfers, 34. The total revenue from this source was $69,056.77.

Trade-marks solicited during the year numbered 2,565;. granted, 2,107; denied, 64; transfers, 148; the total revenue accruing to the Government being $132,640.

APPROVAL OF THE REPORT OF BOUNDARY COMMISSION WITH BRAZIL.

"*El Boletin Oficial*" of February 13, 1907, publishes the following decree approving the final reports of the International Mixed Commission on Boundaries with Brazil:

" BUENOS AYRES, *February 8, 1907.*

" In view of the final report on the demarcation of the dividing line between the Argentine Republic and the Republic of the United States of Brazil, subscribed by the International Mixed Commission constituted conformably with the protocols of August 9, 1895, October 1, 1898, August 2, 1900; and in view, also, of the general plan of the frontiers demarked, traced, and signed by the said commission in compliance with article 6 of the treaty of October 6, 1898—

" The Provisional President of the Senate, in exercise of the Executive power, decrees:

"ARTICLE 1. The final reports, dated June 8, July 15, and August 8, 1904, of the International Mixed Commission, in which is traced and described the dividing line between the two countries: From the mouth of the Cuareim to the mouth of the Pepiriguazú; from the mouth of the Pepiriguazú to the main headwaters of the River San Antonio, and from this point following the bed of the San Antonio to its disembougement into the River Iguazú; and from the mouth of the San Antonio, following the bed of the Iguazú to its disembougement into the Paraná, are approved.

"ART. 2. Likewise the general plan of demarkation signed by the members of the International Mixed Commission, which plan was approved and subscribed by the Commission in consequence of the act of October 6, 1906, is also approved.

"ART. 3. The Minister of Foreign Relations will celebrate the necessary agreements in order to take possession formally of the parts of territory declared by the report and plans to be Argentine, and to turn over the parts of territory that in like manner are declared to belong to the Republic of the United States of Brazil.

"ART. 4. Let this be communicated, published, and delivered to the National Registry.

" VILLANUEVA.

" E. S. ZABALLOS."

CUSTOMS RECEIPTS AT BUENOS AYRES, 1906.

According to official figures the customs receipts collected at the port of Buenos Ayres during the calendar year 1906 amounted to 111,508,871.96 *pesos* national currency and 3,310,991 *pesos* gold. Comparing these figures with those of the previous year an increase is shown in favor of 1906 of 6,643,894.64 *pesos* gold.

BOLIVIA.

RESOURCES AND GENERAL CONDITIONS.

The MONTHLY BULLETIN for March, 1907, contained the concluding paragraphs of the address delivered by the Bolivian Minister, Señor Don IGNACIO CALDERÓN, before the National Geographical Society on January 25, 1907. These selections contained only sentiments in regard to the general progress of South America. There have been since then so many requests for information regarding the material resources of Bolivia that the BULLETIN takes pleasure in producing that portion of Minister CALDERÓN's excellent address which discusses the general conditions, progress, and development of that country.

" The great geological disturbances that in remote ages transformed the continent of South America and produced the wonderful upliftings of the Andes are very marked in Bolivia.

" This mountain chain, traversing the whole length of the continent, divides itself in Bolivia into two principal branches—the one of the west, forming a kind of wall between the sea and the interior, closely follows the coast; the other, extending toward the east and known as the Cordillera Real, presents a series of peaks eternally resplendent in crowns of snow and lifting their heads to heights of more than 21,000 feet, as the Ilimani and the Illampu, with 21,700, and others equally imposing.

" The high plateau of Bolivia occupies an area of more than 66,000 square miles, with a mean altitude of from 10,000 to 13,000 feet above sea level.

SEÑOR DON IGNACIO CALDERON, MINISTER OF BOLIVIA TO THE UNITED STATES.

" It is difficult to say whether the obstacles offered by the vast mountain walls to free traffic and the communication of the people are not more than compensated by the prodigious quantity of minerals they contain and that make Bolivia one of the richest countries of the globe.

" The forests and vast plains extending eastward, with about 7,000 miles of navigable rivers, comprise a fertile agricultural territory embracing more than 304,000 square miles.

" The total area of Bolivia is 709,000 square miles, more or less, and it is therefore the third nation of South America as regards size, but unfortunately the population does not yet correspond to its extension—amounts only to a little more than 2,250,000.

"As the Spaniards settled first in the mining regions, the section of Bolivia situated east of the Cordillera Real, which includes the extensive territories watered by the tributaries of the Amazon and the Plata, is the least populated. There are found the forests filled with fine woods suitable for all industrial purposes, such as railway ties, building, and cabinetmaking. Some of these woods are as hard as iron. Rubber, peruvian bark, and a multitude of useful and medicinal plants abound in this soil, whose wonderful fertility could easily support many millions of inhabitants. The coffee and cocoa are conceded to be of the finest quality. Fruits and all tropical products are abundant. The climate is generally healthful and suitable for settlement by European races.

" The mean temperature of the lowlands of the Amazon to an altitude of 2,000 feet above sea level is 74°, to an altitude of 8,000 it is 66°, and in the central plain, where the altitude varies from 10,000 to 12,000 feet, it is 50°.

" It is calculated that to every 181 meters of ascent in the mountains there is a drop of one grade in the temperature.

" It may be said that in Bolivia there are only two seasons—the rainy season, which corresponds to summer, and extends from December to May, and the dry or winter season, lasting from May to December. In the latter months it seldom rains, and the sky is clear and bright. The rains are more copious in the east, and at times the rivers overflow and rise as high as 10 meters above their ordinary level.

"Almost all of the navigable rivers of Bolivia flow into the Amazon, the most important being the Beni, which receives the Madre de Dios, the Orton, and others before reaching its confluence with the Mamore, where it takes the name of Madeira, one of the most powerful tributaries of the Amazon. Unfortunately the navigation of this great river is obstructed by a series of very dangerous rapids. The Government of Brazil has agreed by treaty to construct a railroad around these rapids and thus expedite the Amazon route.

"The Pilocomayo and the Bernejo are also rivers of importance that flow toward the southeast and empty into the Paraguay. The eastern region of Bolivia is also rich in grazing lands, where the stock industry promises to be highly lucrative. To-day there are found vast herds of wild cattle roaming over the lands.

"Lake Titicaca on the boundary line between Peru and Bolivia is notable for its great altitude, for its romantic traditions, and for the monuments of that distant epoch yet standing on the island of the Sun. The lake's surface extends over an area of more than 5,900 square miles.

"If the natural exuberance and richness of the eastern section of Bolivia is remarkable for its products, the region of the Cordilleras is, I will say, the great storehouse of mineral wealth. The silver mines of Potosi, Oruro, Colquechaca, Huanchaca, and many others have contributed hundreds of millions to the richness of the world. No less abundant are the deposits of copper, bismuth, zinc, cobalt, gold, and tin. On speaking of the commerce of Bolivia I will mention the quantities of these minerals exported to-day.

"The main causes that hinder the development of Bolivia's wealth are the difficulty and cost of transportation, the lack of capital, and the scarcity of population. To what an extent the high rate of freight hinders the growth of industries in Bolivia, it is enough to state that coal at the seacoast is worth from 18 to 25 shillings, or, say, $4 to $6 more or less per ton; taken to the mines in the interior of Bolivia, according to the distance, though this may not exceed 500 miles, the price will be from $40 to $80. We are trying to overcome this difficulty by means of electric and hydraulic power.

"A large number of mining enterprises, as well as the eight banking institutions, are financed with national funds. Recently two German banks have been established in La Paz.

"The constitution of Bolivia is very liberal, and is based on the unitarian system of central government. The President is elected every four years by direct popular vote. The legislative power is exercised by a Senate and House of Deputies, and the judiciary by a supreme court, appointed by the Senate, and by inferior courts and other judges. Foreigners enjoy the same franchises as the natives, and may hold property, work the mines, etc., all in conformity with the laws.

"Bolivia is the only country in South America that has not suffered from earthquakes; and when felt they were almost imperceptible and of no consequence.

"Within the last few years the international commerce of Bolivia has increased considerably. In 1905, it reached 69,065,000 in Bolivian money, an increase of 30 per cent over the figures of the previous year, and according to the statement of President Montes in his last message to Congress, in 1906 it will reach 80,000,000; and when the railroads now in course of construction are completed these figures could be easily doubled in a short time.

"The commerce with the United States has also grown in recent years, and the construction of the railways will greatly augment the present movement. The importations into Bolivia in 1905 amounted to $1,720,000, and yet this small sum is a large increase compared with previous years.

"On the other hand, the importations of Bolivian products into the United States hardly reached $60,000, while Bolivia produced rubber, tin, cocoa, cocoa leaves, Peruvian bark, and many other articles of great consumption in the United States, and which are purchased in Europe to be brought here.

"The exportation of silver averages 13,000,000 ounces a year; of copper, 5,000 tons, more or less; the production of tin grows from year to year, so that from 1897, or ten years ago, when the production was about 3,000 tons, it had reached 17,000 in 1905, and during the past year it is probable that the exportations exceeded 20,000 tons of pure tin.

"It is impossible to foresee the marvelous development that railway facilities will offer to this industry, as well as to the general progress of the country. Bismuth, zinc, and gold represent quantities no less important.

"In spite of all the obstacles that the Bolivian industries have encountered on passing through the Amazon the exportation of rubber in 1905 amounted to 1,700,000 kilograms. This is a product whose output could easily be increased when the railroads now being built are completed. Sir MARTIN CONWAY calculates as not improbable that there may be about 50,000,000 rubber trees in the region of the upper Beni alone. Each tree is supposed to yield annually from 3 to 7 pounds of rubber.

"Bolivia also exports considerable quantities of alpaca wools, the finest chinchilla and vicuña skins, and other national products.

"I shall now proceed to give you an idea of the means of communication of my country and of the railways whose construction is actively progressing.

"The position Bolivia occupies in the heart of South America gives to her commercial and international importance, and although deprived of her coast on the Pacific, she is in immediate contact with five of the most advanced republics; and it is to their interest to encourage a mutual trade for the benefits that will naturally result. And this is not all; the main railway line under construction in Bolivia has a continental bearing, for it will establish the connection between the Argentine system that is now being extended to the interior of Bolivia with the Peruvian railroads coming from the north and the Pacific coast. Then Lima in Peru, La Paz in Bolivia, and Buenos Ayres in the Argentine Republic will be united within a few years by a continuous railway spanning the 2,500 miles, more or less, that separate the capital of Peru on the Pacific from the capital of the Argentine Republic on the Atlantic, and will form an important section of the Pan-American railway.

"For the first time United States capitalists are taking an interest in the construction of railways in that section of South America. The Argentine roads were built with English capital and the same is the case with those of Brazil and Chile, where the majority of the roads are government property. Peru constructed her railways with national funds, but had to cede them for a term of years to her English creditors. Bolivia, then, is the first country where, in cooperation with the Bolivian national resources, American capital is being invested.

" It has been my aim, and I had the good fortune to succeed in interesting representative New York bankers in the great work of giving life to my country by means of roads through rich deposits of minerals and open to the world her virgin forests. My Government has concluded directly with the bankers a contract that is to-day being executed.

" The lines to be constructed by the American syndicate are from La Paz to Tupiza, 530 miles; Oruro to Cochabamba, 133 miles, and La Paz to Puerto Pando, 200 miles, in all, 863 miles.

" Of these railroads the one from La Paz passing by Oruro and Potosi to Tupiza will form the chain uniting the republics of the Pacific with those of the Atlantic, besides traversing the richest metallic zone that exists, perhaps, in the world. The line from Oruro to Cochabamba will open to commerce the fertile valleys of the interior of that section, the most thickly populated of Bolivia, and make that part of the country accessible to the navigable branches of the Mamore.

" The railroad from La Paz to Puerto Pando, a port situated at the headwaters of the Beni, will open the territories of the Beni, where rubber grows in such abundance; also coffee and all the most precious tropical products, as well as the various classes of woods. This railroad will have the peculiarity of passing in a few hours from the frigid zone of the high plains, where there is practically no vegetation, to the tropical region of the orange and the sugar cane. In a distance of less than 30 miles the traveler will be transported, as if by magic, from a temperature of perhaps 40° or less to one of 70° or more, as he descends through wonderful scenery, to the other side of the great eastern chain of the Andes.

" But these railroads are not the only ones called to transform in *some years the* economic life of Bolivia and give her rank and importance to which her size and position entitle her. By a treaty of peace recently celebrated with Chile that Republic agrees to build, and work has already commenced, a railroad from Arica to La Paz, a distance of some 300 miles. That line will unite Bolivia with the Pacific by a road much more direct than that at present afforded by the Antofagasta line, which is 575 miles long, or that from Mollendo to La Paz via Lake Titicaca, a distance of 563 miles. The Arica road will bring the city of La Paz within eight or ten hours of time of the coast.

"The Bolivian Congress authorized more than a year ago the building of a railway from the borders of the River Paraguay, to Santa Cruz, one of the most mediterranean cities, but destined to become one of great importance. The projectors have deposited the sum of 100,000 *pesos* as a guaranty for the execution of the contract, and the construction material has begun to be transported by way of the Plata and Paraguay rivers. The length of this line will be 497 miles. This route will offer free communication to the rich oriental zone by way of the Plata and the Paraguay and open to immigration and progress a territory more than 242,000 square miles, watered by large rivers and of remarkable fertility. There are on foot other projects of railway construction of no less importance.

"Progress is like oil that spreads itself wherever it touches. Some years more of work and effort in preparing transportation facilities, and by the beneficial influence of steam, electricity, and immigration the future greatness of Bolivia is assured."

EXPORTS OF TIN IN 1906.

According to a report presented to the Department of Finance and Industry of Bolivia on February 14, 1907, and furnished to the Bureau of the American Republics by the Bolivian Minister in the United States, the total shipments of tin from the country, during 1906, aggregated 29,370,367.96 kilograms of tin in bars (60 per cent pure) or 17,622,220.776 kilograms of pure metal.

Export duties on this commodity amounted to 1,561,740.53 *bolivianos*, distributed as follows among the various custom-houses:

	Bolivianos.		Bolivianos.
Oruro	817,007.39	La Paz	68,132.97
Uyuni	193,554.66	Potosi	356,276.32
Tupiza	88,547.29	Colquechaca	38,221.90

The provinces producing the metal in reference were: Potosi (covering the shipments from Uyuni, Tupiza, Colquechaca, and part of that from Oruro), with 15,674,807.74 kilograms; Oruro, 11,910,477.32 kilograms; La Paz, 1,748,190.90 kilograms; and Cochabamba, 36,892 kilograms.

The average price of Straits tin, which is the standard in European markets, during the year, was £179 12s. 5d. per ton of pure metal (1,000 kilograms), making the Bolivian 60 per cent bar tin have a market value of £108 the ton. Allowing for the rate of exchange and the cost of placing on the markets, a net profit of 1.20 *bolivianos* per kilogram is made by Bolivian enterprises.

The 1905 production from Bolivian sources was 27,689,621 kilograms, valued at 26,205,140.95 *bolivianos*.

BRAZIL.

FOREIGN COMMERCE, 1906.

Figures published by the "Bureau of Commercial Statistics" for March 5, 1907, report total trade values of Brazil during 1906 to have aggregated £86,296,271, as compared with £74,473,033 in 1905.

Exports, including specie, are valued at £53,092,230, as against £44,642,983 in 1905, while imports reached a valuation of £33,204,041, as compared with £29,880,050 in the preceding year.

Items of export, the valuations thereof in 1905 and 1906, with their respective gains or losses, were as follows:

Article.	1905.	1906.	Comparison.	Value in *milreis*, gold. 1905.	Value in *milreis*, gold. 1906.	Comparison.
Cotton	£1,167,714	£1,656,730	+ 499,016	10,290,700	11,726,492	+ 4,435,702
Monazite sand	100,036	99,143	− 893	889,231	881,289	− 7,942
Sugar	406,954	606,217	+ 200,263	3,608,476	5,388,596	+ 1,780,120
Castor seed	24,017	37,491	+ 13,414	211,016	333,250	+ 119,235
Rubber:						
Mangabeira	144,751	154,802	+ 10,051	1,286,672	1,376,014	+ 89,382
Maniçoba	831,588	825,285	− 9,303	7,418,550	7,335,870	− 82,680
Seringa	13,436,432	13,075,824	− 390,608	119,434,947	116,229,540	− 8,205,398
Cocoa	1,039,535	1,386,441	+ 346,906	9,240,313	12,3.3,9.22	+ 3,083,609
Coffee	21,420,515	27,615,884	+6,195,369	190,404,576	245,174,525	+55,069,919
Cotton seed	108,458	122,034	+ 13,579	964,074	1,084,742	+ 120,608
Para nuts	232,206	183,895	− 98,311	2,061,040	1,190,177	− 873,872
Carnauba wax	207,818	420,016	+ 212,198	1,817,273	3,733,478	+ 1,886,205
Horns	31,069	31,217	+ 148	276,172	277,188	+ 1,316
Hides:						
Wet	788,681	1,090,258	+ 301,577	7,010,498	9,691,180	+ 2,680,682
Dry	599,674	863,518	+ 263,844	5,330,460	7,675,715	+ 2,345,275
Horsehair	34,594	45,395	+ 10,801	307,565	404,511	+ 96,080
				81,007	110,925	+ 29,318
Meat extract	9,181	12,179	+ 3,298	1,490,312	1,128,761	− 361,551
Bran	167,660	126,986	− 40,674	692,079	789,913	+ 97,834
Flour, manioc, or cassava	77,859	88,863	+ 11,006	55,855	69,318	+ 13,463
Medicinal herbs and roots	6,284	7,799	+ 1,515	606,678	714,332	+ 107,654
Fruits	68,250	80,362	+ 12,112	7,355,168	8,284,150	+ 917,987
Tobacco	825,206	931,854	+ 106,648	11,088,108	16,502,881	+ 5,414,783
Herva-matte	1,296,550	1,856,574	+ 620,024	135,679	193,819	+ 58,140
Ipecacuanha	15,264	21,805	+ 6,541	142,414	354,045	+ 211,631
Wool	16,022	39,831	+ 23,809	390,070	318,873	− 71,197
Lumber	43,883	35,874	− 8,009	2,958,152	1,594,185	− 1,363,976
Manganese	332,827	179,380	− 153,447	263,506	382,073	+ 118,567
Scrap metal	29,644	42,983	+ 13,339	3,734,469	4,379,160	+ 644,691
Gold, bar	420,128	492,656	+ 72,528	633,916	1,180,260	+ 846,344
Stones, precious	71,316	166,529	+ 95,213	4,117,590	4,639,512	+ 521,922
Skins	463,229	521,945	+ 58,716	336,668	347,323	+ 10,656
Piassava	37,875	39,074	+ 1,199	2,177,512	2,225,163	+ 47,651
Sundries	241,970	230,332	+ 8,362	....	....	....
Total merchandise	44,632,252	53,059,480	+8,427,228	396,827,679	471,639,822	74,812,143
Specie	10,731	32,750	+ 22,019	95,384	291,107	195,723
Grand total	44,642,983	53,092,230	+8,439,247	396,923,063	471,930,929	75,007,866

Imports are divided into four general classes, the values of which, for the two years under comparison, were:

	1905.	1906.
Live animals	£313,806	$141,585
Raw materials and unfinished manufactures	5,031,863	6,325,800
Manufactures	14,203,319	16,426,019
Foodstuffs and forage	10,281,062	10,250,687
Total	29,830,050	33,204,041

Coffee represents the greatest export increase, and forms over 50 per cent of the total exports of the country. Rubber comes next, with an export ratio of 24.6 per cent, the slight decrease in quantity and value noted in maniçoba and seringa being due to impeded navigation on the rivers, whereby part of the December shipments were of necessity transferred to the following year. Third on the export list comes herve-matte, 3.4 per cent of the total, followed by cotton, 3.1; cacao, 2.6; tobacco, 1.7, while the other 200 articles which form trade items account for 13.5 per cent of the total export values.

Import increases were made in raw materials and semimanufactured articles, while foodstuffs and cattle show a decrease, which is satisfactory evidence that in spite of a larger population the Republic is able to supply itself with said articles.

The nature of the exports noted is indicated as follows:

	Milreis.	
Animals and their products	40,954,005 =	£2,732,270
Minerals and their products	15,372,563 =	1,028,521
Agricultural and forest products	743,345,124 =	49,298,689
Total	799,070,295 =	53,059,480

The 1906 totals are greater by more than £8,000,000 than those of the previous year and exceed those of 1901 by more than £12,000,000, 1905 and 1901 having until the present time outranked all other periods covered by a five years' record.

DETAILS OF FOREIGN TRADE IN 1905.

The Bureau of Commercial Statistics of Rio de Janeiro has just published detailed statistics of the foreign trade of Brazil for 1905, compared with that for 1904. According to these figures the total value of the foreign trade in 1905 was 661,983,684 *milreis* gold, against 580,849,415 *milreis* gold in 1904, showing an increase in 1905 of 81,134,269 *milreis* gold.

Imports in 1905 amounted to 265,156,005 *milreis* gold, against 230,359,319 *milreis* gold in 1904, or an increase of 34,796,686 *milreis*. The increase in imports by classes was as follows: Imports of cattle increased from 939,896 *milreis* gold in 1904 to 2,198,858 *milreis* in 1905; imports of horses, asses, and mules increased from 271,825 *milreis* in 1904 to 350,052 *milreis* in 1905. Under Class II (articles applied· to the arts and ·industries) an increase of 3,397,176 *milreis* gold is noted, being due to increased imports of the following articles: Lead, tin and its alloys, copper and its alloys, hoofs, horns, etc., of animals, iron and steel, jute and hemp, wool, perfumery, dyeing substances, stone, earths, coal and cement, hides and skins. The imports of cotton thread show a considerable decrease.

The imports of manufactured articles show an increase of 17,-933,140 *milreis* gold. There was an increase of 798,279 *milreis* gold in war and hunting ammunition; 688,701 *milreis* in cars and other vehicles; 5,098,265 *milreis* in iron and steel; 366,843 *milreis* in musical·instruments; 653,401 *milreis* in woolen manufactures; 254,868 *milreis* in flax, jute, and hemp; 732,917 *milreis* in stoneware, china ware, and glassware; 3,840,638 *milreis* in machinery, apparatus, tools, and instruments; 1,071,594 *milreis* in paper and paper manufactures; 1,004,000 *milreis* in stone, earths, bricks, earthenware, and marble tiles, the increase in imports of bricks alone amounting to 710,728 *milreis;* 792,486 *milreis* in chemical and pharmaceutical products, and 255,381 *milreis* in manufactures of silk. There was a slight increase noted in imports·of miscellaneous articles.

The imports of provisions show an increase of 11,103,704 *milreis* gold, of which 1,097,602 *milreis* represent the gain in· wheat flour; 566,971 *milreis*, in butter; 1,185,241 *milreis*, in wheat, and 3,960,016 *milreis* in dried beef, notwithstanding the quantity imported in 1905 is only 508,460 kilograms greater than in 1904, being due mainly to the increase in price of this article (293 *reis* per kilo in 1905, against 219 *reis* in 1904. The imports of rice, lard, and potatoes show a considerable decrease over those of 1904.

The imports of specie and foreign bank notes show an increase of 18,707,380 *milreis* over those of 1904.

The imports by classes were as follows:

Class.	Articles.	1904.	1905.
		Per cent.	*Per cent.*
I	Animals, live and dried	0. 02	1. 05
II	Raw materials	17.51	16. 87
III	Manufactured articles	47.02	47. 61
IV	Provisions, etc	34. 85	34. 47

The imports by principal countries of origin were as follows:

Country.	Value in *milreis* gold.	
	1904.	1905.
Germany	29,203,817	35,253,966
Argentine Republic	23,702 252	31,210,143
Belgium	7,465,071	9,660,183
United States	25,642,448	27,400,622
France	20,593,542	23,883,265
Great Britain	63,914,377	70,499,965
Italy	8,375,551	8,835,506
Portugal	16,872,618	19,411,497
Uruguay	11,282,814	13,079,362

The exports of national merchandise and reexports of foreign merchandise in 1905 show an increase of 46,377,609 *milreis* gold over those for 1904.

The following table shows the exports by classes in the two years under comparison:

Class.	Articles.	Value in *milreis* gold.	
		1904.	1905.
I	Animals and animal products................................	23,545,573	18,514,112
II	Mineral products................................	8,337,646	8,753,846
III	Vegetable products................................	318,606,877	369,559,214

The imports of animals and animal products show a decrease of 5,031,461 *milreis* gold compared with those for 1904, the decrease occurring in the following articles: Whale oil, wax, hides of different kinds, hair, meat extracts, wool, preserved tongues, goat and deer skins. There was an increase in the imports of lard, horns, and glycerin.

The exports of minerals and mineral products show an increase of 416,200 *milreis* gold in 1905. The exports of manganese show an increase of 15,117 tons in quantity and 231,360 *milreis* in value; gold in bars, 16,060 *milreis;* old metal, 97,337 *milreis*. There was a loss of 78,106 *milreis* in the value of monazitic sands exported.

The exports of vegetable products show an increase of 50,952,844 *milreis* over those for 1904. The largest increases were noted in the following articles:

Articles.	Quantity.		Value in *milreis* gold.	
	1904.	1905.	1904.	1905.
Cotton, raw................................tons..	13,262	24,081	7,346,728	10,290,790
Sugar (different grades) ....do....	7,861	37,746	831,004	3,608,476
Rubber (different grades)................do....	31,865	35,393	99,780,081	128,140,178
Coffee................................bags..	10,024,536	10,820,661	177,400,617	190,404,576
Cotton seed................................tons..	26,601	37,494	791,498	964,074
Chestnuts................................hectoliters..	92,580	198,226	943,878	2,064,049
Bran................................tons..	21,152	26,432	797,279	1,490,312

There was a considerable decrease in the exports of cacao and tobacco, as may be seen from the following figures:

Articles.	Quantity.		Value in *milreis* gold.	
	1904.	1905.	1904.	1905.
Tobacco................................tons..	23,963	20,390	7,453,477	7,335,103
Cacao................................do.....	23,160	21,090	9,738,002	9,240,313

The exports were distributed as follows:

Country.	Milreis gold.		Percentage of total.	
	1904.	1905.	1904.	1905.
Germany	48,825,562	60,001,034	13.981	15.120
Argentine Republic	9,920,568	12,105,502	2.830	3.050
Austria-Hungary	9,826,809	13,621,325	2.804	3.432
Belgium	5,834,261	8,033,252	1.665	2.025
United States	176,640,681	163,208,995	50.898	41.127
France	17,767,385	29,028,512	5.069	7.315
Great Britain	56,663,964	72,967,401	16.157	18.386
British possessions	1,531,850	2,104,678	.437	.531
Holland	6,793,951	11,773,460	1.938	2.967
Italy	3,318,340	3,662,369	.947	.924
Portugal	3,073,284	2,324,792	.877	.586
Uruguay	5,066,962	6,487,014	1.446	1.632

A comparison of the maritime movement of 1905 with that of 1904 shows an increase in the number of national steamers of 1,289, having a tonnage of 564,524 tons, and a decrease in the number of sailing vessels of 1,079, or a decrease in tonnage of 66,455 tons.

FOREIGN DUTIES ON BRAZILIAN COFFEES.

The "Brazilian Review" for March 5, 1907, publishes the following table showing the various rates imposed upon Brazilian coffees at points of import, per 100 kilograms:

	Francs.		Francs.
France	135	Germany	50
Italy	130	Norway	41
Spain	105	England	34
Austria	92.50	Denmark	33.50
Portugal	100	Sweden	16.70
Russia	95	Switzerland	3.50

The United States, Holland, and Belgium levy no tax on coffee.

IMPROVEMENT WORK AT RIO GRANDE DO SUL.

Press dispatches report the formation of an improvement company, incorporated under the laws of the State of Maine, United States, with a capital stock of $14,500,000, for the purpose of utilizing the concessions originally granted to ELMER L. CORTHELL for harbor and other developments in south Brazil. The work includes the construction and operation of docks, wharves, and warehouses, the building and working of electric railways, and the removal of the sand bar at the entrance of the large lake known as Lagoa dos Patos. This sheet of water is about 200 miles long and 50 miles wide, and upon it are located Rio Grande do Sul, Porto Allegre, and Pelotas. The freight handled at Rio Grande do Sul, is valued at $12,000,000 annually, and under present conditions great expense and possible losses are entailed in lading and unlading.

UNITED STATES AND CANADIAN INVESTMENTS.

Consul-General G. E. ANDERSON, of Rio de Janeiro, reports that an American and Canadian syndicate has purchased the São Paulo and Rio Grande Railroad, which connects the São Paulo country with the Rio Grande do Sul country.

" This railroad represents the future railway interests of southern Brazil, in some respects the richest and most valuable portion of Brazil. It means the extension of American interests, and will lead to a general disposition of industrial and transportation concerns to look to the United States for support and supplies, and offers the beginning of a great trade opportunity, if American manufacturers will take advantage of it. . This railroad purchase is one of the promising movements in behalf of American capital and enterprise in this country. The syndicate, which controls several enterprises in Brazil and in Mexico, has spent upward of $25,000,000 in the purchase of concessions, franchises, and tangible property."

SUBSIDY FOR CULTIVATION OF PERINI FIBER.

The Acting British Consul-General at Rio de Janeiro has reported to his home Government that the Brazilian legislature has voted the grant of an annual subsidy of 30 *contos of reis* (about $9,000) during a period of five years to Doctor PERINI, the discoverer and holder of patent rights for Brazil in connection with the utilization of the perini fiber. The subsidy will be paid as soon as Doctor PERINI shall have inaugurated the manufacture of articles made from the plant in Brazil. It is proposed to form a limited liability company for the exploitation of the plant, and Doctor PERINI has already issued his prospectus. The capital is to be 1,200 *contos of reis* ($375,000) in 6,000 shares, valued at 200 *milreis* each.

RESCINDING OF COASTING TRADE CONCESSION.

The Brazilian "*Diario Official*" for January 29, 1907, contains a copy of a law rescinding the concession for a coasting service between the ports of Brazil, granted on April 19, 1904, to the *Companhia de Navegação Cruzeiro do Sul*, this company having leased its vessels to the " Lloyd Brazileiro."

THE PORT OF SANTOS IN 1906.

The total tonnage entering the port of Santos during the year 1906, aggregated 2,120,781, as compared with 1,694,641 in 1905. The clearances for the two periods were represented by 2,122,950 and

1,687,468 tons, respectively. The nationalities of the vessels and their respective cargoes were as follows:

Nationality.	Entries:		Clearances.	
	No.	Tonnage.	No.	Tonnage.
British	267	695,777	269	698,392
German	130	352,226	129	349,568
Italian	122	317,657	122	317,657
French	129	299,863	129	299,861
Brazilian	468	295,773	471	297,906
Others	75	159,487	93	159,536

It is thus shown that while vessels under the Brazilian flag greatly preponderated, the greater tonnage was carried in British bottoms. The articles shipped abroad are reported as follows:

	Milreis.		Milreis.
Coffee	306,355,949	Bran	415,546
Hides (salted)	428,513	Pineapples	46,731
Rubber (mangabeira)	334,377	Bananas	184,472

Imports figure as follows:

	Milreis.		Milreis.
Cotton, raw; yarn, and manufactures	6,565,511	Wool, raw; yarn, and manufactures	2,990,143
Iron and steel, and manufactures	10,990,084	Coal	3,530,981
Machinery:		Kerosene	1,760,030
Industrial	925,557	Rice	2,400,616
Agricultural	333,803	Codfish	1,728,480
Paper and manufactures	1,646,407	Wheat flour	6,695,830
Drugs and chemicals	1,968,898	Wheat	8,220,852
Leather	2,414,697	Wine	6,886,563
Jute yarn	4,702,314	Sundry foodstuffs	7,758,917
		Specie and bullion	6,269,766

The official value of the milreis is given as $0.546, but locally its value is about $0.35.

The countries of origin and destination of the foregoing were as follows:

Countries.	Imports.	Exports.	Countries.	Imports.	Exports.
	Milreis.	Milreis.		Milreis.	Milreis.
Germany	16,138,691	83,119,401	Holland	626,907	27,294,981
Argentine Republic	15,907,874	2,393,159	India	1,764,757	
Austria-Hungary	905,300	22,583,100	Italy	8,054,595	5,402,477
Belgium	4,541,889	11,003,473	Portugal	4,934,328	
Canada	1,106,664		Sweden	459,985	
United States	8,407,821	92,002,529	Norway	545,269	
France	7,346,783	53,142,947	Switzerland	709,267	
Great Britain	22,338,063	4,694,329	Other countries	840,825	6,468,207
Spain	720,344				

It is estimated that the State of São Paulo, of which Santos is the seaport, receives 20 per cent of the total imports of the Republic of Brazil and ships 40 per cent of the exports. Of the total value of exports from São Paulo in 1906, 99 per cent were supplied by coffee, *10,166,257* bags being reported.

THE TEXTILE MARKET.

A recent German consular report states that the manufacture of cotton goods in Brazil is developing to an amazing extent, thus causing a marked decline in importations from abroad. A high protective tariff on cotton manufactures and free entry for all machinery and apparatus adapted to textile growing and manufacturing further handicaps the imports under this classification.

Figures issued by the British and United States Governments covering their export trade for the year 1906 further establish the fact of the general falling off in Brazilian imports of tissues. For the twelve months ending December 30, 1906, shipments of cotton cloths from the United States to Brazil amounted to but $479,338 in value, as against $743,492 in the corresponding period of the preceding year, while wearing apparel declined from $65,323 to $54,928. British shipments of cotton manufactures remained practically stationary, £1,611,580 and £1,675,596 being the figures for 1905 and 1906, respectively. Worsted tissues show a slight decline from £83,137 in 1905 to £71,625 in 1906, while linen piece goods, woolen tissues, etc., show slight, if any, increase.

Sales from Germany are reported to have increased a trifle but French manufactures have lost ground. Good quality prints of Alsatian origin find ready sales, but imported tapestries whether French or German have no market, as the demand is met by a local product of poor quality. Imitation silk linings come, for the most part, from England, as do also batistes. Muslins are introduced in varying quantities from Germany and France and shirtings from England and Austria. Sheetings and napery come largely from Germany and Austria-Hungary, and cretonnes for upholstery purposes are mainly of German origin, the preference being given to richly colored, up-to-date designs. Sewing thread is introduced from Great Britain and Germany, the former being preferred, and the demand for German and French cotton lace is good. Large consignments of transparent mosquito netting are imported from Germany and the United Kingdom, and printed cotton handkerchiefs are in great demand, being worn on the head by native women and by the Austrian and Italian settlers. This latter trade is in the hands of Great Britain and Germany, the British goods being very cheap and made in imitation of Japanese silk.

White or colored woolen blankets are imported from Germany and as mixed qualities pay exactly the same duty as pure wool, the demand for the former is very restricted. Silk imports have declined and linens for handkerchiefs, table, and bedroom use, as well as for ecclesiastical purposes, are very little called for.

THE SUGAR INDUSTRY AT PERNAMBUCO.

During the first six months of 1906, the quantity of sugar of native production reaching the Pernambuco market was 96,978,880 kilograms, the amount exported being 95,334,887 kilograms. · Of the quantity reported for export, 11,250,662 kilograms were shipped to the north of Brazil, 56,912,864 kilograms to the south of the Republic, and 27,171,371 kilograms were sent abroad.

An estimate of the sugar output of the various producing States, made with a view to facilitating the export of the crop, has fixed the quantities, respectively, as follows:

	Bags.
Pernambuco	100,000
Bahia	30,000
Campos (Rio de Janeiro)	30,000
Alagoas	12,000
Parahyba	9,000
Sergipe	3,000

At a meeting held on August 24, 1906, the "*Société Auxiliaire d'Agriculture de Pernambuco*" suggested to the sugar manufacturers that they should agree to an undertaking whereby they would bind themselves to manufacture Demerara sugar to the amount of 15 per cent of their production, with a view to creating a stock and to obtaining a more advantageous price for their merchandise. The agreement was assented to by twenty-two manufacturers, in consequence of which a sale of 100,000 bags of Demerara sugar was concluded with two important firms at Pernambuco. On September 28, 1906, one-half of this quantity had been shipped to its destination in the United States.

A central committee has been created at the Federal capital charged with the following duties, tending to a development of sugar interests:

1. With collecting precise information as to the price of sugar and the position of the sugar industry in Brazilian markets and on the foreign markets.

2. With transmitting regularly to the committees of the States and to agricultural associations all information relative to the production and consumption of sugar, using for this purpose a special telegraphic code.

3. With facilitating direct sales in foreign markets by making known to each State the number of bags of sugar to be sent away by a given date.

4. To gather all necessary data for fixing statistics as to the production and consumption of sugar at home and abroad.

With publishing every fortnight a bulletin with regard to the commercial fluctuation of sugar, alcohol, and brandy in the home *markets.*

CHILE.

TRADE WITH GERMANY IN 1906.

The Consul-General of Chile in Germany, Señor Don Pio Puelma Besa, has forwarded to his home Government statistical information concerning the trade between Chile and the port of Hamburg in 1906.

Total shipments from Hamburg destined to Chilean ports were valued at 63,471,591.39 *marks* ($15,116,239.75), as compared with 42,-101,961.73 *marks* in 1905. The shipments in December of 1906 were almost double those recorded for the corresponding month of 1905, and, in fact, a comparison by months throughout the two years shows a remarkable scale of increase in the later period.

CUSTOMS DUTIES, JANUARY, 1907.

Total customs duties collected at the various ports of Chile during the month of January, 1907, aggregated $9,900,585.55 (national currency), of which $5,109,331.44 were credited to exports and $4,588,-366.76 to imports. Other branches of the service contributed $202,-887.35 to the general total.

CUSTOMS TARE FOR 1907.

A circular issued by the Superintendent of Customs of the Chilean Republic, on December 20, 1906, announces that the following tare shall be allowed, during 1907, on the gross weight of such articles of merchandise as are hereinafter specified:

IMPORTATION.

	Per cent.
Oils:	
In barrels or iron jars	18
In cans inclosed in wooden boxes (4 cans in a box)	22
Sugar:	
In ordinary bags	1
In double bags	2
In barrels	9
Coffee:	
In ordinary bags	1,500
In double bags	3
Havana cigars: In wooden or tin boxes containing 5,000 cigars or more	60
Cigars from other countries	40
Tobacco:	
Cuban, in bales wrapped in sackcloth, palm leaves, or the like	10
From other countries, in bales wrapped in sackcloth	1
Textiles:	
In bales with iron hoops and wooden boards or strips	6
Without wooden boards or strips	5
With neither iron hoops nor wooden boards or strips	3
Containing wooden boards within the piece goods, besides the iron hoops and wooden boards or strips	8
In bales of any kind	8
Flannel, in bales of any kind	

	Per cent.
Tea: In bulk in boxes of any kind, the gross weight of which does not exceed 60 kilograms	23
Shag: In bales of any kind	4
Yerba-maté or Paraguay tea:	
In barrels containing 50 kilograms	18
In barrels containing more than 50 kilograms	15

EXPORTATION.

Nitrate: In bags	70
Iodine: In barrels	14

When the packing containing such articles of merchandise is other than those specified in this circular, its weight shall be taken and stated in the custom-house permit.

RAILWAY CONSTRUCTION FROM SANTIAGO TO ARICA.

In a bill presented to the Chilean Congress in December, 1906, regarding the construction of the Longitudinal Railway from Santiago to Arica the Executive, Señor Don PEDRO MONTT, urges the importance of the work in reference and states that the Government is firmly resolved to do everything in its power to promote it. The approximate length of the road is 2,353 kilometers—from Santiago to Arica, to which must be added 26 kilometers from Ligua to Papudo, a contemplated branch line to be operated in connection with the main road, so that the grand total is 2,379 kilometers.

Of the Longitudinal line, there are now being worked 390 kilometers of State ownership, with 149 kilometers in course of construction, leaving 1,840 kilometers to be put into operation. To facilitate the completion of the enterprise, it is proposed that the contractors shall rent the State lines running into and forming part of the Longitudinal. The 258 kilometers of roadway, privately owned, to the north of Copiapo, can not be utilized owing to their gauges.

The bill consists of six articles, as follows:

"ARTICLE 1. The President of the Republic is hereby empowered for the term of three years to contract for a fixed sum, wholly or by sections, the study, construction, and equipment of the railways to unite the city of Ligua with the port of Papudo and that of Arica. The locomotive must arrive at Copiapo within five years.

" ART. 2. The total price of the works shall not exceed £7,500,000, and it shall be paid with a cumulative amortisation of not less than one-half per cent per annum.

"Until such time as the said price is paid the contractors shall exploit for their account the railways, subject to tariffs approved by the Government, and the State shall guarantee them interest at the rate of 5 per cent per annum.

"ART. 3. The lease is hereby authorized of the intermediate State *railways between* Ligua and Chanaral, during the construction of the railways referred to in article 1, and during their exploitation by the contractors.

"The tariffs shall be subject to the approval of the Government.

"ART. 4. The President of the Republic is hereby authorized for the term of one year to contract for a fixed price for the construction of the railways from Curico to Llico and from Del Arbol to Pichilemu, for sums not to exceed $7,500,000 (of 18 *pence* each) for the first, and of $2,500,000 (same money) for the second.

"ART. 5. Private or municipal lands required for the construction of the aforesaid railways, their stations, and annexes, in conformity with the plans approved by the President of the Republic, are hereby declared of public utility.

"The expropriation shall be carried out in conformity with the law of June 18, 1857, and the initiatory steps may be taken during the term of five years.

"ART. 6. An expenditure of $3,000,000 is hereby authorized in expropriation of lands, technical inspection and other expenses of the railways authorized by the foregoing articles, and of $300,000 for studies of ports."

COLOMBIA.

EDUCATIONAL STATISTICS.

During the last half of the year 1906, scholastic attendance at the various schools and colleges of the Republic was recorded as follows:

Province of Antioquia, 50,691; Atlántico, 4,916; Bolívar, 14,984; Boyacá, 8,691; Caldas, 18,690; Cundinamarca, 6,368; Cauca, 26,121; Federal District, 12,793; Galán, 8,088; Huila, 5,606; Magdalena, 2,670; Nariño, 13,313; Quesada, 11,723; Santander, 12,605; Tolima, 8,164; Tundama, 7,560; El Meta, 872; Putumayo, 532; Goajira, 4,080; Tierradentro, 1,000; making a total of 218,941.

ESTABLISHMENT OF AN INFORMATION BUREAU IN NEW YORK.

A circular issued from New York under date of February 7, 1907, announces that the Colombian Government has established in that city an agency for the promotion of native enterprises. Dr. ALIRIO DÍAZ GUERRA is in charge of the Bureau and he has requested that all Colombian land, mine, and concession proprietors shall place at his disposition exact information concerning their holdings, geographical position, resources, means of communication, etc., it being designed, by means of this information, to interest capitalists and investors of the United States. The address of the agency is 15-25 Whitehall street, New York.

THE GULF OF URABA OR DARIEN RAILWAY TO THE CITY OF MEDELLIN.

The National Assembly of Colombia decrees:

SOLE ARTICLE. The contract made by the Department of Public Works with Mr. HENRY G. GRANGER for the construction and operation of a railway from the Gulf of Uraba or Darien, the tenor of which is as follows, is hereby approved:

"The undersigned, to wit: MODESTO GARCÉS, Secretary of Public Works, duly authorized by the President of the Republic, in the name of the Government, party of the first part, designated in the text of this contract as 'the Government,' and HENRY G. GRANGER, in his own name, party of the second part, known hereinafter as 'the Contractor,' have made the following contract:

"ARTICLE 1. The Government grants to the contractor, for the term of ninety-nine years, a franchise for the construction, equipment. and operation of a railway from a point on the Gulf of Uraba or Darien to the city of Medellin, in accordance with the provisions of article 45 of this contract.

"ART. 2. The contractor shall have the right to construct branches from the main line to the principal towns in the vicinity whose industries warrant said construction and which towns are not excluded under the provisions of previous franchises.

"ART. 3. The Government grants the right to construct the telegraph and telephone lines that may be needed for the use of the company, in accordance with the rules and regulations of the Government. During the construction of the railway the contractor shall have the free use of the national telegraph and telephone lines in matters relating to the railway.

"ART. 4. The Government guarantees to the contractor that during the term of the franchise it will not permit the construction of any parallel railway within a zone of fifty kilometers on either side of the line, but railways or roads having prior franchises may run through or cross this zone, provided they are not intended to connect between themselves the ends or points of the line referred to in this concession.

"ART. 5. For the legal effects thereof the construction of the railway to which this contract refers is declared a work of public utility, and therefore the contractor shall enjoy all the rights and actions granted under the laws to undertakings of this class.

"ART. 6. The contractor may use the public roads in places where it is indispensable to the construction of the roadbed, but is bound to construct for the public another road having the same conditions. Should the railway traverse any town and be obliged to pass through any of its streets the contractor is not bound to replace the street occupied by the roadbed.

"Art. 7. The contractor is likewise authorized to take from the property of the nation the zones or strips of land that he may need for the roadbed, railway stations, and annexes, as well also to take from such lands the timber, materials, etc., that he may need for the works of the railway.

"Art. 8. On lands belonging to the nation the contactor may make use of such waterfalls and streams of water as he finds in the vicinity of the line for the purpose of using them in the production of electric energy or motive power for the railway.

"Art. 9. During the construction of the railroad, the Government exempts from import duties into Colombia, or from export duties to the country of origin, all materials, tools, utensils, machinery, apparatus, tents, telegraph and fence wires, telegraph and telephone instruments, furniture for stations, and other articles required in the construction and preservation of the work. Under the franchise preservation shall mean only the replacement of rolling stock and fixtures.

"Art. 10. The company is exempt from the payment of all taxes, Federal, departmental, or municipal, now levied or which may hereafter be levied on the property of the company destined for the use of the railway, as well as on the earnings of the latter.

"Art. 11. The employees, workmen, and other personnel of the company are exempt from military service in time of peace and in time of war, except in the case of a foreign war, and from any other onerous civil or police service.

"Art. 12. The Government agrees to furnish free the police or military force that may be necessary to protect persons or property at any point on the line.

"Art. 13. The company shall be called the Colombia Central Railroad.

"Art. 14. The work shall begin within six months after the approval of this contract by the President of the Republic, and shall be completed within six years thereafter, but if the work shall have been completed over half of its length, the right to extend the concession four years longer is thereby acquired.

"Art. 15. The contractor shall erect, at his own expense, in the port from which the railway starts, the necessary buildings, with proper accommodations and of sufficient size, for the custom-house and for the national guards, as soon as the railway reaches the frontier of Antioquia.

"Art. 16. The place at which the line begins on the Gulf of Uraba shall be called Ciudad Reyes, and there shall be reserved therein, free of charge, sufficient space for the encouragement of industry and manufactures, and for schools and public offices.

"ART. 17. On lands belonging to private persons the contractor may obtain, at his own expense, the lands necessary for the roadbed and other uses. Should he not be able to arrange with private persons for the acquisition of said lands, the Government shall secure the necessary expropriation judgments, but the expense of the proceedings shall be for account of the contractor.

"ART. 18. The contractor shall have the exclusive use of the coal mines and petroleum springs found in a zone of ten kilometers on either side of the railway on the condition that he pay to the Government as a national tax 15 per cent of the net profits of the same.

"ART. 19. The Government grants the contractor a subvention of thirty thousand dollars, American gold, for each kilometer constructed and opened to public service. This subvention shall be paid, at the option of the Government, in money or public lands, soil and subsoil, at the rate of three dollars, gold, per hectare on either side of the road on opening to public service each section of three kilometers. For this purpose the Government shall suspend the adjudication of public lands in the region referred to in this contract.

"ART. 20. Public lands shall be delivered in accordance with the plans, drawn up at the expense of the contractor, after the completion of each section of three kilometers. The contractor may occupy, and the Government will temporarily adjudicate to him by virtue of this contract, the lands that correspond to three kilometers of railway. Said adjudication shall be made permanent and in perpetuity in conformity with the legal obligations to cultivate it when the completed section corresponding thereto is delivered. The parcels of land shall be delivered as follows: Ten thousand hectares to the east of the Gulf of Darien, where Ciudad Reyes is situated, between Bobal Creek and Caiman Nuevo; five thousand hectares in lower Atrato, between the Gertrudis and Pelle ravines, at which place the Contractor has established his property called "Jankolomba;" fifteen thousand hectares on the western side of the gulf, between La Miel Creek and the place called "Tolo," where the property called "La Carolina" is situated. All this without injury or damage to the rights of third parties.

"ART. 21. In accordance with the wishes of the Government the contractor shall encourage European and American immigration. Colonists naturalized in Colombia shall enjoy the rights of municipal suffrage, etc., shall be free from military service after the lapse of one year's residence, and their property shall be exempt from military expropriation. Natives of Colombia shall be preferred for colonization purposes and in the development of industries on public lands adjudicated to the contractor.

"ART. 22. The contractor agrees to cultivate within the term of twenty-five years one-half of the public lands adjudicated to him by virtue of this contract. The excess of double the quantity of land cultivated shall then revert to the nation without any remuneration whatever.

"Art. 23. No new manufacturing or agricultural company that makes use of this railway shall pay an export tax greater than two per cent for a period of twenty-five years on the original value. The banana industry shall pay in this place, as in all the Republic, a tax of three cents American gold on each bunch exported, which shall be considered to cover port dues and tonnage of shipments on the high sea levied on the banana trade with the port of Ciudad Reyes, so that said commerce shall not in this place pay any other export tax.

"Art. 24. The Government may liquidate any debt made with the contractor for any cause whatsoever in the form stipulated for the payment of the subvention referred to in article nineteen.

"Art. 25. The railway shall be constructed in accord with the police and railway security regulations now in force or which may be put in force in future.

"Art. 26. The railway may be constructed in all or in part with one or two tracks, according to needs of the traffic of the line and of that of the stations.

"Art. 27. If with respect to any line it should be necessary to deviate from the provisions of the rules and regulations, the technical changes shall be made with the approval of the Department of Public Works.

"Art. 28. The contractor shall complete the definite survey of the line to Medellin within the term of two years from the date of the approval of this contract.

"Art. 29. A copy of the plans and reports of the general survey of the line and the outlines and the plans of construction of stations shall be furnished to the Department of Public Works, which Department shall approve them if they are in conformity with the stipulations of the contract, and shall retain them on file in its office.

"Art. 30. The changes subsequently made to the plans, outlines, drawings, engineering works, etc., are subject to the same conditions.

"Art. 31. The width of the track shall be one meter between rails if a narrow gauge is adopted, or four feet eight and one-half inches if a wide gauge is adopted. The rails shall be steel, of the American type, and shall weigh at least from eighteen to twenty-five kilos per linear meter.

"Art. 32. The sleepers or ties shall be of good foreign or native wood, and shall be laid at the rate of at least one thousand six hundred and fifty per kilometer.

"Art. 33. The clearing shall be of sufficient width to permit the easy construction of embankments and cuts with their ditches. The width of the roadbed at the top shall be at least three meters sixty centimeters at the base of the cuts.

"ART. 34. The ballast shall consist of gravel or other appropriate material, and shall be of a sufficient width to cover the ties.

"ART. 35. The maximum gradient shall not exceed three per cent, and curves shall not be of a shorter radius than one hundred meters, except at stations and points where electricity is used, at which places they may be diminished to such a degree as will insure safety and good service.

"ART. 36. The rolling stock must be first class and sufficient in quantity to meet the needs of the traffic. In no case shall the railway company have a smaller number of locomotives than two for each fifty kilometers, and shall provide a service for first, second, and third class passengers, and after the completion of the railway cars sufficient to handle double the traffic.

"ART. 37. The principal stations shall be constructed of materials of iron, masonry, or fine wood.

"ART. 38. The Government shall appoint an inspector for the purpose of examining the works, to receive the sections of kilometers opened to public service, and to deliver the public lands corresponding thereto.

" Paragraph. It is understood that a section of ten kilometers has been opened to the public when the line constructed in a permanent manner, without works of a temporary character, is traversed by a locomotive whose traction power on a level track is from six hundred to one thousand tons, and which can draw an ordinary train consisting of ten cars of a weight of ninety tons each at a speed of not less than from thirty to forty kilometers per hour on a level track without difficulty.

"ART. 39. The transportation tariffs shall be made by the contractor, with the approval of the Government.

"ART. 40. Public employees traveling by order of the proper authority, and members of the Army traveling under the same conditions, shall pay half the tariff rates.

"ART. 41. First-class mail matter, with mail clerks and guards, shall be transported gratis.

ART. 42. The contractor may fix his residence at such place as he may desire, but he shall maintain permanently a representative in Bogota, having sufficient powers to transact business with the Government on all matters concerning the present concession.

"ART. 43. The present contract may be assigned to the original company that the company may organize, but all subsequent transfers must have the approval of the Government, and in no case shall an assignment be made in favor of a foreign nation or Government.

"ART. 44. The concessionary now accepts in all its parts the provisions of article fifteen of the law of eighteen hundred and eighty-eight, number one hundred and forty-five, ' concerning foreigners and naturalization,' in which it is declared that contracts made in Colombia, between the Government and foreigners, are subject to the laws of Colombia, and hence it is an express condition of this contract that the concessionaire renounce, as in effect he does renounce, the attempt to make any diplomatic claim respecting the duties and rights growing out of this contract, except in the case of a denial of justice.

" Paragraph. Denial of justice is understood only to mean the fact that the Government prevent the concessionaire, or his representative, the right to arbitrate questions of difference arising out of this contract.

"ART. 45. The Government reserves the right to buy the railway, the subject of this contract, with all its branches, annexes, and appurtenances, and the Contractor, or his representatives, agree to sell the same at any time after the expiration of the first forty years following the definite approval of this contract.

" Paragraph. If the Government or the contractor fail to agree concerning the price of the sale, the price shall be fixed by expert appraisers, appointed, one by the Government and the other by the Contractor, these appraisers selecting a third in case of disagreement.

"ART. 46. On the expiration of the franchise the railway, with all its appurtenances and annexes, free from all incumbrance or mortgage, shall become the property of the Government, without any indemnity whatever being paid to the contractor or his representatives.

"ART. 47. This contract shall lapse, and may be so declared by the Government through the medium of the Department of Public Works, in any of the following cases:

" 1. If work is not begun within the term fixed in article fourteen.

" 2. If the plans should not be completed in accordance with the provisions of article twenty-eight.

" 3. If the line to Medellin is not completed and delivered within the term fixed by article fourteen.

" 4. If the construction is not in accordance with the technical conditions prescribed by this contract.

"ART. 48. Should this contract be declared forfeited for any of the causes mentioned, the contractor shall become owner of the works constructed, but on the condition of selling them to the Government at the appraised price made by the experts appointed, one by the Government and the other by the company, which experts, in case of disagreement, shall appoint a third.

"ART. 49. The contractor agrees to construct a wooden wharf at Ciudad Reyes, large and strong enough to accommodate the arrival of vessels navigating the high seas, in order to facilitate the loading and unloading of exports and imports of merchandise and to maintain said wharf in good condition during the life of the franchise. As compensation therefor the Government will credit, after the wharf is constructed, at the price of the subvention referred to in this contract, the equivalent of two and one-half kilometers of railway. A like concession is granted for the construction of a bridge for the Cauca River, which the line must cross in order to arrive at Medellin, and provided said bridge be of iron or steel and embody the conditions of resistance and stability necessary for the needs of the railway traffic.

"ART. 50. The railway must be completed to Medellin within a period of six years. If the contractor fulfills this condition he has the right to continue the line to the south of Antioquia in accordance with the provisions of this contract. Should this new section be completed within a period of six years, he shall likewise have the option of extending the railway to the southern boundary of the department of Cauca.

"Paragraph. In case of forfeiture there shall be deducted from the value of the property of the company the value of the public lands at the price stipulated in this contract.

"ART. 51. The approval of the President of the Republic is necessary for the validation of this contract.

"In witness whereof this contract is signed in duplicate at Bogota on February 20, 1905.

"MODESTO GARCES.

"HENRY G. GRANGER.

"The National Executive Power, Bogota, February 27, 1905. Approved.

"R. REYES.

"The Minister of Public Works.

"MODESTO GARCES."

Submitted to the Honorable National Assembly on March 30, 1905, by the undersigned Minister of Public Works.

MODESTO GARCES.

Office of the Assembly, March 30, 1905. Read and approved on this date. Let it be recorded, circulated, and published.

D. RUBIO PARIS.

CUBA.

FOREIGN COMMERCE IN 1906.

The Bureau of Statistics of the Cuban Treasury Department has published recently the figures relating to the foreign commerce of the Republic during the calendar year 1906, as compared with those of the previous year. The total value of imports in 1906 amounted to $98,530,622, as against $94,971,518 in 1905, an increase of $3,570,-104. The exports in 1906 were valued at $106,258,618, as compared with $110,167,484 in the previous year, a decrease of $3,908,867.

The principal countries of origin were the following:

Country.	1906.	1905.
United States	$47,717,618	$43,118,040
United Kingdom	14,821,054	13,508,273
Spain	9,167,669	10,179,558
Germany	6,414,694	5,915,920
France	5,598,984	5,242,901

The leading countries of destination were:

Country.	1906.	1905.
United States	$88,175,451	$95,330,475
United Kingdom	5,899,734	5,793,850
Germany	3,671,198	3,905,471
Spain	2,234,279	786,844
France	1,198,652	1,513,139

The imports and exports of money during the years under comparison were as follows:

Country.	Imports.		Exports.	
	1906.	1905.	1906.	1905.
United States	$6,800	$552,348	$4,464,112	$1,194,360
Spain	73,589	317,672	685,679	916,854
France	1,264,232	7,372,387	36,654	570
Total	1,344,621	8,241,407	5,286,445	2,111,784

SUGAR CROP OF 1906 AND 1907.

The Bureau of Statistics of the Treasury Department (*Secretaría de Hacienda*) of Cuba has issued figures of the sugar production of the Republic in 1905–6 and the estimate for 1906–7. The total crop in 1905–6 is stated at 8,561,017 sacks, or 1,225,799 tons, as compared with 1,183,347 tons in the preceding year.

the country. With order and economy in the management of the public revenues, the Republic may consider itself saved. Order is the watchword of the present political situation, and order is being observed and will continue to be observed so long as men who are willing to sacrifice all in their desire to duly serve their country, remain at the head of the Government.

FINANCIAL MATTERS.

The revenues to December 31, 1906, amounted to more than $3,800,000. The amount deposited in the National City Bank, of New York, in conformity with the decree of March 31, 1905, together with interest to that date, was $2,317,607.40. The cash on hand in the auditor's office, in the departments of the Treasury, and in other public offices, aggregated more than $280,000.

This is the first time that the annual balance of the public treasury of the nation has shown an amount equal to that mentioned in the memorial of the Secretary of the Treasury—a guarantee of the indisputable advantages of that peace and credit that we shall attain as the basis of our future economic redemption of the Republic, finding therein the means of freeing ourselves from debt and of undertaking all the improvements that will tend to increase the productiveness of the Republic on which the certain development of its material prosperity and political stability depends.

EXPORTS.

The exports for the year represented a value of $6,543,872 and the imports a value of $4,281,337.

FUTURE OF THE REPUBLIC.

The era that opens before the Republic is, therefore, a brilliant one, and the Dominicans intend to utilize it, in so far as possible, endeavoring to maintain and strengthen it by the virtues of industry and the abhorrence of political dissensions, the latter of which encourage peculation, consume the energies of the country, and bring upon it ruin and desolation.

DEPARTMENTS OF JUSTICE AND PUBLIC INSTRUCTION.

The Department of Justice and Public Instruction requires, perhaps, more than any other, your especial attention. Legislation needs to be reformed by purging it of the many errors from which it suffers, and to which the Secretary of State calls attention in his memorial.

My Government desires that the Department of Justice attain its most complete organization, for which purpose it depends upon the support of the Congress which exerts such a direct influence over it. I recommend that you give this subject your particular attention, and that you do all in your power to the end that said Department may fulfill the high mission that it is called upon to occupy in society. The radical reform of the present judicial system is demanded, and the same may be said of the law of public instruction.

Two things are essential to the life of a people. Without justice social order ceases, society totters on its base and falls into corrupt hands and into disorder. Without education ignorance reigns, and in the place of citizens pariahs only are found, and liberty falls smothered without defense into the arms of tyranny. If we want free men and a progressive and prosperous republic, we must look after education, and found it upon a liberal, honorable, and just law that responds to the high ideals and advances of modern progress.

INTERNAL AFFAIRS.

As a natural consequence of the enormous and inevitable expenditures imposed upon the public treasury by the war, which has lasted almost the entire year in some parts of the Republic, the Department of Fomento was neglected, much to the regret of the Government, since the Government not only sees in the work of that Department means that tend to the embellishment of the towns and to the encouragement of useful services, but also means for the relief of poverty, because many families will draw therefrom the sustenance necessary for their support. It is to be regretted that the misconduct of a few should cause so much injury, retard progress, and originate so many public calamities. Notwithstanding this, the Department of Fomento, utilizing the funds in its possession, proceeded to the construction of various public works, some of them in the District of Monte Christi, and others in this capital and at other places in the Republic.

The plan for the construction of various bridges will probably be realized in the course of the present year, and the railroads from Santiago to Moca, and from Sebo to Romana, in the building of which a large part of the internal revenue is being inverted, are now in course of construction.

The current year opens under better auspices, and it is the intention of the Government to effectively further progress in the Republic through all its executive orders and decrees, by endeavoring to stimulate industry in all its forms, proposing not only to elevate the condition of the laborer and the artisan, but also to increase production, which is the source of the maintenance of the State.

* * * * * * * *

POSTS AND TELEGRAPHS.

The definite organization of the Department of Posts and Telegraphs, in which experience never fails to demonstrate the necessity of reforms, since the importance of this Department grows with the industrial and commercial development of the country and becomes a medium of communication, is the work of time, and I can not now affirm, in spite of the efforts exerted in its favor by the Department, that the organization has attained the end desired.

My Government has faith in the future of the Republic, which on a day like this sprang into existence through the decision and patriotism of our fathers, and without hatred and without prejudice relies upon the cooperation of all Dominicans in support of the work of maintaining the liberties of the Republic and of redeeming as soon as possible its economic independence by means of peace, order, and industry.

GUATEMALA.

MESSAGE OF PRESIDENT MANUEL ESTRADA CABRERA TO THE NATIONAL LEGISLATIVE ASSEMBLY, DELIVERED MARCH 1, 1907.

CONDITION OF PEACE.

The profound peace of the Republic since the happy termination of the events of the middle of last year has enabled the Government to continue to devote its entire attention and zealous efforts to the encouragement of that progressive evolution in Guatemala that is becoming more noticeable day by day.

  *   *   *   *

PUBLIC SCHOOLS.

During the previous year, there were in session throughout the Republic 1,276 primary schools, and I earnestly cooperated with the authorities in securing the attendance of pupils in conformity with the requirements of the law. The examinations at the end of the term, generally speaking, were held in an impartial manner and showed that the sacrifices made in favor of the regeneration of the people were not sterile, and the results obtained increase the incentive to perseveringly continue the patriotic work undertaken.

  *   *   *   *   *   *

PUBLIC HEALTH.

The public health has merited due attention, and thanks to the organization formed by means of the Superior Board, with branches throughout the Republic, the sanitary condition of the country has been good, and although some diseases broke out in Chimaltenango, Baja Verapaz, Zacapa, and Izabal, such opportune measures were taken that the diseases were promptly checked without serious injury to said towns.

Decree No. 659 promulgated the Organic Code of the Department of Public Health, which code governs this important branch of the public service and is in conformity with the resolutions of the Sanitary Convention of Washington of October 14, 1906.

*   *   *   *   *   *   *

FOREIGN RELATIONS.

On more than one occasion and in this same place, on informing you of the acts of the Executive in the Department of Foreign Affairs, it has been my pleasure to declare publicly that the sole object of said acts was to enlarge and strengthen the relations of Guatemala with all the countries of America and Europe without allowing any unfortunate circumstances to dissuade me therefrom.

Now, on discussing that point in this message, I regret that I am unable to express myself in like terms, since you well know that about the middle of last year a hostile faction appeared on the frontier of Salvador and soon afterwards reached the frontier of Honduras. The support that its leaders obtained in those Republics and the complications arising therefrom gave rise first to a suspension of diplomatic relations, and soon thereafter to a complete rupture and open hostilities between Guatemala and Salvador, an event that can never be sufficiently lamented by all good Central Americans, but which was unavoidable, since all my efforts to prevent it were unsuccessful in view of the offensive attitude which the then hostile armies maintained.

Fortunately the disagreeable spectacle that Central America presented to the world at that time was relatively of short duration, and terminated in a manner honorable to Guatemala with the Treaty of Peace of July 20, 1906, signed on board the North American cruiser *Marblehead* and ratified by the Honorable Legislative Assembly in August of the same year.

Neither the Government nor the Guatemalan people will ever forget that the celebration of that compact was brought about by the timely mediation of Presidents Roosevelt and Diaz, who, occupied in the development of their respective countries—the United States and Mexico—under the protection of peace which both Presidents endeavor to maintain unalterable in their Republics, view with displeasure the presence of serious difficulties among the peoples of Central America, to whom they are bound by ties of sincere friendship.

The Department of State will report to you concerning the treaty of peace, amity, and commerce that, in accord with the treaty to which I have already alluded and of which it is an extension, was celebrated at San Jose, Costa Rica, September 25 last, by delegates of Guatemala, Costa Rica, Salvador, and Honduras.

I would state that one of the things that caused me the greatest satisfaction was to have been able to communicate to the Pan-American Congress, which met for the third time at Rio de Janeiro on July 23 last, the news that peace had been established in Central America, because—I say it with all frankness—I was greatly preoccupied on seeing my country involved in a fratracidal war at the very time that said Congress opened its sessions, and the more so when I recalled that, in the Conference of 1902, Guatemala figured so prominently as a defender of compulsory arbitration, obtaining, as you will remember, the most flattering results.

How that news was greeted in the Rio Conference, and the many manifestations of sympathy that Guatemala, and the Government of Guatemala, through its delegates at the Conference, received because of it is well known to you. I flatter myself that if you find that my conduct presents a notable contrast, showing me energetic when the defense of the honor of Guatemala was at stake and the first to rejoice over the restoration of peace, you will also find that my conduct does not deviate in the least from that which I should observe as the President of a people whose Government, by their own free will, has been placed in my hands, and that I have endeavored to comply with my duty.

In closing my remarks in connection with Central America, I must, unfortunately, allude to the present conflict between Honduras and Nicaragua, in which, from the beginning, I interposed my friendly mediation, yielding to the sentiments that made me observe a like attitude when Costa Rica and Nicaragua were involved in controversy immediately after I entered upon the performance of my duties as President of the Republic.

Presidents ROOSEVELT and DIAZ, again guided by their policy of peace, also offered to mediate, in conjunction with the Governments of Guatemala, Salvador, and Costa Rica, for the purpose of avoiding a war between the contending Republics; and although up to the present time, the satisfactory results that it was hoped would be secured from such friendly mediation have not been obtained, nevertheless the efforts in favor of peace are at present being multiplied, and I believe and sincerely desire that Honduras and Nicaragua will conclude to amicably settle their difficulties for the sake of the well-being and good name of Central America.

It is easy to understand that the questions I have discussed up to the present time have occupied a large part of the attention of the Executive, but I have not for that reason neglected to attend to all other matters belonging to the important and delicate branch of the Department of Foreign Relations. Said Department will, however, soon submit to the consideration of the Honorable Assembly certain treaties and conventions, such as the treaty of peace, amity, and commerce of San Jose, Costa Rica, already referred to; the convention for the mutual protection of patents with the United States of America, and the Geneva convention of July 6, 1906, concerning the amelioration of the condition of the wounded in arms in the field, as well as the resolutions of the Third International American Conference at Rio.

Our relations with the United States and Mexico, whose Governments never fail to give evidence of their friendship and sympathy toward Guatemala, have been strengthened, and my Government is earnestly striving for the continuance of these relations and at the same time is observing a like policy with respect to the other governments of America and with those of Europe, endeavoring at all times to insure the utmost good will and cordiality.

*.   *   *   *

INTEROCEANIC RAILWAY.

The arrival at the Capital of the locomotive from the Atlantic Coast upon the completion of our interoceanic railway will assume, in the course of the present year, the proportions of an event that will tend to radically transform the face of the Republic. It is necessary, then, that we should give strict attention to the immediate consequence of such an important occurrence and prepare the country at once for the benefits that will be derived therefrom.

Convinced of the importance of that event, I have given the necessary orders to the Department of Fomento, since it is to be expected that from the efforts of that Department will principally come that powerful and inevitable economic evolution that awaits Guatemala because of her location, her elements of natural wealth, and the earnest desire of her Government for industrial development.

AGRICULTURE.

The respective Department will report to you in detail concerning the formation of a Code of Agriculture, of a proposed law governing workmen, of the establishing of a normal school at Aurora, of the proposed mining law framed so as to effectively stimulate this infant industry, of the improvement of rapid means of communication, of the committees for embellishment and public works to be established in all of the principal towns, of the erection of the Palace of the Legislative Department, of the new National Theater of Guatemala, and of many other projects recently undertaken for the purpose of placing the country in a condition to realize in a short

antages that may logically be expected from the
1 in which we find ourselves on coming into closer
lations of America and of Europe.

state to you that agriculture, that important foun-
)f the nation, has merited my especial attention, and
have been taken that were-considered useful to its
ipment. It is a pleasure for me to inform you that
growing out of the past emergency did not prejudice
;hat was to be expected from the proper management of
?partment, owing to Executive orders opportunely issued by
;sident through the respective offices.

addition, earnest efforts have been made to increase and improve
uction by substituting modern and scientific for old and outworn
ctuods and by the settlement of disputes between landowners and
n a strictly equitable manner, for which purpose the labor
.ly mentioned was framed with the object of meeting the
.ts or both parties, in accordance with the principles of liberty
justice espoused by the present administration.

RAILROAD FROM PUERTO BARRIOS.

'e from Puerto Barrios, and which will run in a short
time from the Atlantic to the Pacific Ocean, is knocking at the doors
of Guatemala, consummating in this manner one of the most laudable
and beautiful aspirations of the Guatemalan people and one of my
most ardent and constant desires, inasmuch as the completion of this
iron highway will open new and broader fields for the production
of public wealth and for the growth and progress of our country.

Every assistance and protection tending to the rapid advancement'
of the work has been accorded the constructing company, and it is a
notable and significant fact that on the 21st of last June, in the midst
of the hazards of war, the first rails leading from this capital toward
the north to unite with the road being built from that side to this city
were laid. The expropriation of the necessary lands, in accordance
with the respective contract for said railroad, has been scrupulously
paid by the Government. The other railroad enterprises of the Republic have continued to operate satisfactorily and the Executive has
been careful to see that they were treated in the proper manner.

*　　　*　　　*　　　*　　　*　　　*　　　*

FINANCES IN 1906.

The federal revenues for the year were $30,500,772.98, or an in-
crease of six millions of dollars over the amount of the budget of the
National Legislative Assembly, notwithstanding the marked fall in
exchange.

The expenditures of the different administrative departments amounted to $27,030,761.36, and there was assigned, in addition, to cover the disbursements of the special bureau of public credit, the amount of $18,702,226.15, making the total payment during the year 1906 $45,732,987.51, the deficit having been covered out of the funds of the Government deposit with the American syndicate.

The fact of the payment during the year of loans prior to 1908, some of which were in gold, sufficiently explains the increase in the expenditures, as well as the fact of having made large payments, also in gold, for account of the American syndicate. Other payments were likewise made in national money.

The financial condition of the country, as will be seen, is good, since these results were obtained without increasing the present imposts and in spite of the emergency to which I have several times alluded.

HAITI.

PROPAGANDA FOR HAITIAN PRODUCTS.

A law has been recently promulgated by President NORD ALEXIS, the purpose of which is to give an impulse to Haitian commerce. The provisions of the law are:

"ART. 1. Every Haitian consul or consular agent shall set apart in his office a section to be devoted to the exposition of such samples of native products as shall be forwarded from Haiti, mainly through the chamber of commerce.

"ART. 2. The above-mentioned agents shall transmit to the Haitian Department of Commerce and to the Chamber of Commerce all communications, requests for information, etc., which they may receive regarding said samples."

HONDURAS.

ALIEN LAW.

The law governing aliens in the Republic of Honduras became operative on March 1, 1906, and is to the following effect:

MANUEL BONILLA, President of the Republic of Honduras, by virtue of the authority delegated to the Executive Power by Decree No. 76 of the National Constituent Assembly, issued January 19, 1906, decrees the following:

CHAPTER I.—*Aliens.*

ARTICLE I. Aliens are:

1. Those not born in the Territory of the Republic nor naturalized therein.

other Central American republics residing in the
y of Honduras who do not (do?) declare before the
Governor their intention to preserve their nati-

icans who, having resided one year in Honduras
before the indicated authority their desire to
in the country.
who have become naturalized in another country
the to their residence.
se who may officially serve foreign governments without
er authority. from the Government of Honduras.

ART. 2. The nationality of the children of aliens born in Hondu-
mean territory and of Honduraneans born in foreign territory
ll be determined by the treaties.   en there are no treaties, the
children born in Honduras of alien parents domiciled in the country
are Honduraneans.

ART. 3. For the purpose of determini | the place of birth in cases
under the preceding article, it is declare_ that national vessels are a
part of the territory of Honduras.

ART. 4. The children of ministers and employees of the legations
of the Republic shall not, for the purpose of this law, be considered as
born outside of it.

ART. 5. Honduranean women who contract matrimony with aliens
shall preserve their nationality, if they continue resident in the
country.

ART. 6. The change of nationality of the husband does not import
the change of nationality of the wife and minor children under pater-
nal control, provided the wife and children reside in Honduras.

ART. 7. The nationality of corporations is regulated by the law
authorizing their formation. Consequently, all such as are constituted
according to the laws of the Republic shall be Honduranean, provided that, in addition, they have their legal domicile in Honduras.

ART. 8. Foreign corporations enjoy in Honduras rights conceded
them by the laws of the country of their domicile, provided that these
be not contrary to the laws of Honduras, and that the said corporations have been recognized by the Executive Power.

CHAPTER II.—*Expatriation.*

ART. 9. In like manner as Honduraneans may expatriate themselves, becoming naturalized in another country by virtue of their free
will, so foreigners may acquire Honduranean citizenship in conformity
with the laws of the Republic.

ART. 10. Expatriation, pursuant to naturalization obtained in a
foreign country, does not exempt the criminal from extradition, trial,

and punishment to which he is subject by treaties, international customs, and the laws of the State.

ART. 11. No Honduranean shall be exempt from the duties imposed upon him by the Constitution and the laws, although he may have acquired foreign nationality, so long as he may have his domicile in the Republic.

ART. 12. Persons naturalized in Honduras, notwithstanding they may be in a foreign country, have the right to the same protection as Honduraneans by birth either as to their persons or their property.

ART. 13. The Government of the Republic, in order to protect Honduraneans resident in foreign countries, shall employ the procedures and means set out in the treaties, and in default of treaties, it shall abide by the principles of the law of nations.

CHAPTER III.— *Naturalization.*

ART. 14.. Every foreigner may acquire Honduranean citizenship by obtaining a letter of naturalization from Congress or from the Executive Power if Congress is not in session.

ART. 15. A foreigner who wishes to become naturalized shall solicit the same, personally or by a representative specially empowered in writing, setting out that he renounces all submission, obedience, and fidelity to any other government, and especially to the country of which he may have been a citizen, and also to all foreign protection against the laws and authorities of Honduras and to all rights conceded by treaties or international law to foreigners, making also protestation of allegiance and obedience to the laws and authorities of Honduras.

ART. 16. The following shall be considered as naturalized in Honduras:

1. Spanish Americans who, having resided one year in the country, declare their desire to become naturalized before the Political Governor of the Department in which they may reside.

2. Other foreigners who having resided two years in the country may declare their purpose to become naturalized before the authority set out in the preceding clause, and have fulfilled the requirements set out in the second article of this chapter.

ART. 17. Letters of naturalization shall not be granted to the subjects or citizens of a country with which the Republic may be at war.

ART. 18. Nor shall they be granted to those reputed and judicially declared in other countries to be pirates, slave dealers, incendiaries, makers of false money, or counterfeiters of bank notes or other papers passing as money, nor to murderers, kidnappers, or thieves.

ich may have been obtained by a foreigner from
of law, is entirely void.

s or certificates of naturalization are issued with
, under any construction, may be collected for the
alization of a foreigner in Honduras becomes
ay following that on which is fulfilled the require
for acquiring the same. Vested or acquired right
outher, shall be governed by its laws, but rights in expe
y shall be governed by the laws of Honduras.

CHAPTER IV.—*Registry and its effects.*

ART. 21. Re — of ———————s of the inscription of the
names and nationalities   n   kept for that purpose in the
Ministry of Foreign Relation   ublic.

ART. 22. A foreigner   u   o register, and being in the
capital of the Republic, must   e Ministry of Foreign Rela
tions; but if he be away from   ital, to the governor of the
respective Department, provi   h cases his nationality by
means of one of the documents herein   out:

1. The certificate of the respective   iplomatic or consular agent
accredited in the Republic, provide   t therein is set out that the
party is a native of the country in whose name the agent acts.

2. The passport, legalized in the proper form, with which the applicant may have come into the Republic.

3. The letter of naturalization, legalized in the same manner.
Only when its destruction or loss is sufficiently proven, or this document is not necessary by the law of the country which would have to
issue it, shall other proof of equal value be admitted that the party
interested has legally acquired the naturalization claimed. No
expense shall attach to this proof other than the stamped paper.

ART. 23. Registry establishes only a legal presumption that the
foreigner is of the nationality therein imputed, proof to the contrary
being therefore admissible.

ART. 24. Registry is proved by the certificate thereof issued and
signed by the Minister of Foreign Relations, who alone may issue it.

ART. 25. No authority or public functionary can recognize as of a
particular foreign nationality any person who does not present his
certificate of registry.

ART. 26. The certificate of registry does not serve its holder to
make valid any right or action claimed under it, if the right or action
claimed is prior to the date of the registry.

ART. 27. The rights of foreigners are—

1. To invoke the treaties and conventions existing between Honduras and their own country;

2. To recur to the protection of their country by diplomatic channel, conformably to the precepts established by the Constitution; and

3. The benefit of reciprocity.

ART. 28. The legal status of the registered foreigner is changed by the express or tacit renunciation of the interested party or by a state of war between Honduras and the foreign country.

CHAPTER V.—*Rights and obligations of foreigners.*

ART. 29. The Republic of Honduras is a sacred asylum for all persons who may take refuge in its territory (Constitution).

ART. 30. Foreigners are obliged upon their arrival in the territory of the Republic to respect the authorities and observe the laws (Constitution).

ART. 31. Foreigners enjoy in Honduras all the civil rights of Honduraneans (Constitution).

ART. 32. They may acquire all kinds of property in the country, subject, however, to all the ordinary and extraordinary burdens of general character which may be imposed upon the property of Honduraneans (Constitution).

ART. 33. Foreigners domiciled in Honduras shall be permitted to hold municipal offices, and those simply administrative.

ART. 34. They shall not present claims against the State nor demand any indemnity, except in the cases and in the manner in which Honduraneans may do so (Constitution).

ART. 35. Foreigners shall not resort to diplomatic intervention except in case of manifest denial of justice, unnecessary delay, or evident violation of the principles of international law. The fact that a final decision is not favorable to the claimant shall not be construed as a denial of justice. If in violation of this provision claims are presented and not amicably adjusted, injury to the Government being sustained thereby, the claimant shall lose the right to live in the country.

ART. 36. Extradition of strangers resident in Honduras shall be granted only by virtue of law or treaty for ordinary crimes, but never for political crimes, even though in consequence thereof an ordinary crime may have resulted.

ART. 37. Foreigners resident in Honduras enjoy in like manner as natives the following guaranties:

1. Inviolability of human life;
2. Individual security;
3. Liberty;
4. Equality; and
5. Property rights.

ART. 38. They may consequently utter and publish their ideas, within the limitations imposed by the laws, as well by spoken word as in writing. They may also be responsible agents, owners, or representatives of newspapers or periodical publications, whatever may be the character thereof; but, on the other hand, they must submit themselves to the laws of the country, putting themselves for this purpose upon the footing of natives, without power to recur to diplomatic intervention for the responsibilities incurred.

ART. 39. Foreigners may, without losing their nationality, become domiciled in the country for all legal purposes. Acquisition, change, or loss of domicile is governed by the laws of Honduras. They may likewise acquire residence in any municipality of the Republic, complying with the requisites of law, and consequently they shall have the corresponding rights and obligations.

ART. 40. Transients are exempt from all merely personal taxes, but not from taxes and imposts upon their property, commerce, profession, or industry.

ART. 41. The suspension of individual guaranties being declared in the manner allowed by the laws of war, foreigners, as well as Honduraneans, shall be subject to the dispositions of the law decreeing the suspension, except as provided by the stipulations of preexisting treaties.

ART. 42. Foreigners do not enjoy political rights on a par with Honduraneans. They may not exercise the suffrage, nor seek public office, nor associate themselves in order to treat of political affairs of state, nor take any part therein, nor exercise the right of petition in matters of this kind.

ART. 43. The foreigner who voluntarily exercises the rights set out in the preceding article shall be, by this act, made responsible for his acts and the consequences thereof, as is every Honduranean, without being understood by this to become naturalized.

ART. 44. Foreigners are exempt from military service, but such as are domiciled are liable to such municipal services as have not attached thereto authority, jurisdiction, or deliberative vote, and must lend their services to the armed police when engaged about the security of property and for the preservation of order in the locality in which they reside.

ART. 45. Every foreigner is obliged to respect the neutrality of the Government of the Republic in case of foreign war. Should he violate the same in any manner he will incur the same responsibility as natives.

ART. 46. Strangers shall not take part in the civil dissensions of the country. Those violating this prohibition may be administratively expelled from the territory as pernicious foreigners by the Executive Power being moreover subject to the laws of the Republic for offenses committed against it; without prejudice, that their rights and obligations during a state of war may be governed by international law and treaties.

ART. 47. Continuing offenses, begun first in a foreign country and continuing to be committed in the Republic, shall be punished according to the laws of the Republic, be the delinquents citizens or aliens, provided that they be apprehended within Honduranean territory.

ART. 48. Offenses committed by citizens or foreigners in the territory of the Republic shall be prosecuted and punished according to the laws of the Republic.

ART. 49. Offenses shall be considered as occurring in the territory of the Republic which are committed—

1. On the high seas on board national merchant or war vessels.

2. On board a Honduranean war vessel in port or in foreign waters.

3. On board a Honduranean merchant vessel in port or in foreign waters, when the offense affects the discipline or interior government of the ship, unless help be demanded of the authorities of the port.

" CHAPTER VI.—*Expulsion.*

ART. 50. For reasons of public order or social morality, and when State interests demand it, foreigners may be denied entrance into the territory of Honduras, or their expulsion therefrom ordered.

ART. 51. If aliens, having taken refuge in Honduras, abuse the asylum, conspire against the Republic, or work to destroy or change its institutions, or to disturb in any manner public tranquillity and peace in a friendly country, the Government may order their expulsion.

ART. 52. Transient foreigners or emigrants who may have been prosecuted or sentenced in another country for crimes or grave offenses, and who may be a menace to society, may be expelled from the Republic. In the same manner the foreigner may be expelled, who, not being able to prove his identity, presents himself under an assumed name, or, as of condition, profession or office not possessed by him. The expulsion is without prejudice to prior criminal prosecution by the proper authority.

ART. 53. The Executive Power alone may deny foreigners entrance into the territory of the Republic or may order their expulsion.

ART. 54. In matters of expulsion for any of the reasons set out in the preceding articles, on the initiative of the President of the Republic the political governor of the Department in which the foreigner resides shall institute a verbal process, in order to show the facts or reasons upon which the expulsion must be based, which being concluded he shall forward to the ministry of Government in order that proper action in view thereof and upon its merits may be taken. The procedure for expulsion shall be administrative and discretional, the testimony of foreigners being received in the process.

der of expulsion shall be served upon the person
giving him twenty-four hours at the least for its

"FINAL PROVISIONS.

ovisions of this law shall not change in any man-
as and guaranties that international law and the
;ions which the Government may have entered into
 υ ω   iplomatic representatives and the consular body,
     s that in the said treaties may have been granted espe-
 ɔ ɪoreigners of a particular country.
   law shall take effect on March 1 of the present year, from
h date are repealed prior laws governing this subject in so far as
may be contrary to this law.
'en at Tegucigalpa, February 8, 1906.

MANUEL BONILLA.

IMMIGRATION LAW.

The law governing immigration into the Republic of Honduras
became operative on March 1, 1906, and is as follows:

MANUEL BONILLA, President of the Republic of Honduras, by virtue
of the authority delegated to the Executive Power by Decree No.
76, of the National Constituent Assembly, issued January 19, 1906,
decrees the following:

CHAPTER I.—*Immigration in general and the different kinds of
immigrants.*

ARTICLE 1. Immigration shall be carried on and regulated according to the provisions of this law.

ART. 2. The Executive Power shall promote and aid the immigration of foreigners versed in agriculture, trade, cattle raising, the arts,
business, and all kinds of industry.

ART. 3. Persons of more than sixty years of age shall not be engaged
nor accepted as immigrants, except in the case of a father or mother
arriving with a family or having a family already settled in the
country.

ART. 4. Nor shall persons morally unfit or not in good health be
accepted.

ART. 5. Every foreigner, who before beginning his voyage to the
Republic shall signify before the Immigration Agent or before the
proper consul his intention to accept the benefits granted by this law
and to comply with the obligations imposed thereby, shall be considered as an immigrant.

ART. 6. Immigrants are divided into the following classes:

1. Immigrants, not under contract, in search of employment in the
country.

2. Immigrants under contract with the Government.

3. Immigrants under contract with private persons, associations, or companies for colonization or to be engaged in any enterprise.

CHAPTER II.—*Board of immigration and agriculture.*

ART. 7. A board composed of the following members is established: The Minister of Fomento, the Minister of the Interior, an expert in cattle raising, a scientific agriculturist, and a merchant. The last three will be appointed by the Executive Power.

The board shall elect a president, a vice-president, a secretary, and an under secretary from among the members appointed by the Executive Power.

The board shall hold its ordinary sessions on the 1st and 15th of each month and extraordinary sessions whenever called by the president.

ART. 8. The board shall work conformably to this law and to the regulations issued on immigration and shall have the following functions:

1. To advise the Executive Power, whenever requested, upon projects or matters relative to immigration.

2. To endeavor, in accord with the Executive, to establish in this capital and in other localities model farms on which to test modern agricultural machines and for the crossing of native cattle, bovine and other kinds, with foreign cattle.

3. To formulate projects of immigration and colonization, and to submit the same to the consideration of the Government.

4. To collect seeds of grain and useful plants and shoots or cuttings for cultivation on the model farms, and to distribute the same to persons engaged in agricultural pursuits.

5. To maintain constant relations with the boards of the model farms which may be established in the Departments, in order that there may be mutual help in the work.

6. To obtain reports from the Departments upon the industries which may be suitable to establish or to improve therein, and upon the national lands situated therein, determining their extent and quality in regard to the cultivation suitable therefor, and all particulars in regard to mineral deposits, materials of construction, and especially upon dyewoods and cabinet woods.

7. To look after the course of immigration and colonization and the performance of the consequent duties on the part of the colonists or immigrants as well as on the part of the contractors and authorities, and to give an account of the same to the proper authority.

8. To indicate to the Executive Power the reforms that from time to time should be made for the regulation of the colonies, to stimulate immigration, and to guarantee the enjoyment of franchises and rights granted to colonists and immigrants.

CHAPTER III.— *Franchises, aids, and guaranties granted by the Government to immigrants of the first-class.*

ART. 9. To immigrants of the first-class the Government will grant the following aids, franchises, and guaranties:

A. Exemption from import duties upon clothing in use, household goods, seeds, domestic animals, machinery, tools, and instruments of their trade.

B. Exemption from payment of consular fees, including the fee for issuing, by the respective consul, the passport with which they must come provided and in which is set out their status of immigrants.

C. The Government will grant to immigrants, whether the heads of a family or not, lots of public lands of three or more hectares, according to the conditions as to fertility, healthfulness, and distance from centers of population, on condition that they agree to cultivate, at the least, the third part of the said lands with plantations of industrial or other utility for the period of two years, counting from the day on which they may obtain possession of the lands. Having performed these conditions the Government will grant the property right in the lands, issuing to the immigrants the title thereto without any cost.

D. The immigrant grantees may make use of the waters, of the wood, and other building material needed for their works, buildings, offices, and roads, and which may be found on the public lands or on the commons of the villages or towns in which they may reside, without paying anything therefor.

They shall enjoy the same right after having acquired the final title to the ceded lands.

Immigrants may not transfer by contract *inter vivos* the rights granted to them by the Executive in conformity with this law prior to having acquired full ownership in the ceded lands for the purposes and in the terms indicated. In case of death their successors shall be subject to the same prescriptions.

If the immigrants, prior to having acquired full property in the ceded lands, shall abandon the work for a period of one year without the consent of the Government, they shall lose the lands with the crops and other results of labor, all reverting to the State without any obligation to indemnify.

The Government may authorize the suspension of the said work for such time as it may deem proper, taking into account the reasons and occasions presented by the interested parties.

CHAPTER IV.— *Franchises, aids, and guaranties granted by the Government to immigrants of the second class.*

ART. 10. Consuls accredited to the countries of America and of Europe may, in the name and under instructions of the Government, enter into contracts of immigration and colonization with the subjects or citizens of the said countries.

ART. 11. The Executive may likewise enter into immigration and colonization treaties with the said governments whenever he deems the same opportune.

ART. 12. The rights and obligations of the contracting parties and of the immigrants or colonists shall be such as are determined in the respective agreements.

ART. 13. In such as are entered into by the Government there may be granted the same franchises, aids, and guaranties granted to immigrants of the first-class, and these may be enlarged when suitable without other limitation than that established by the constitution and laws.

CHAPTER V.—*Franchises, aids, and guaranties granted by the Government to immigrants of the third class.*

ART. 14. Persons engaged in agriculture or any other kind of industry may engage foreigners for the carrying on and extension of their works under the authority of the Government, to which shall be given notice of the enterprise, of the number of immigrants needed, of the nationality to which they belong, and of the work for which they are intended, as also of the conditions under which they are contracted. The Government shall also intervene in like manner in the organization of colonies established by private persons.

ART. 15. The Government, by means of its respective subaltern employees, shall be informed upon the strict compliance of the obligations contracted for by the employers and by the immigrants.

ART. 16. The immigrants treated of in this chapter shall enjoy the same guaranties, franchises, and exemptions accorded to immigrants of the first-class.

ART. 17. If immigrants at the expiration of the time of their contracts, or the same having been rescinded, shall resolve to remain in the country as colonists they shall enjoy the same favors and privileges as immigrants of the first-class. They may also, if they so desire, contract with other employers without thereby losing the protection of the Government accorded them on entering the country.

ART. 18. The Government, for the better performance of the present law, may prescribe the regulations, instructions, and ordinances which it may deem proper.

ART. 19. This law shall become operative on March 1 of the current year, from which date all prior laws upon this subject in conflict with this law shall be inoperative.

Given at Tegucigalpa, February 8, 1906.

"MANUEL BONILLA."

MEXICO.

COMMERCE, FIRST HALF OF 1906-7.

ures published by the Statistical Di
'tment of Mexico, the foreign commerce of
t half of the fiscal year 1906-7 (July–December)
the following valuations:

v. . f the trade during the first half of 1906-7 was
J.22, as compared with $219,360,068.81 in 1905-6.

: total value of imports during the period under review was
)8,506.04 Mexican currency, as compared with $87,495,560.85
le corresponding period of the preceding year. The exports were
valued at $117,883,937.18 Mexican currency, against $131,864,507.96
in the first half of 1905-6.

A comparison of these figures show that the general trade, import
and export combined, during the first half of the fiscal year 1906-7
increased $7,122,374.41, as compared with the same period of the previous fiscal year.

Taken separately the imports of the first six months of 1906-7
increased $21,102,945.19, while the exports decreased $13,980,570.78,
as compared, respectively, with the corresponding half of 1905-6.

The details of the imports during the period under review were as
follows:

Animal substances	$10,013,379.29
Vegetable substances	13,471,596.62
Mineral substances	37,028,191.07
Dry goods	13,240,840.87
Chemicals, drugs, etc	4,145,493.60
Beverages	3,372,205.48
Paper and applications	2,992,831.28
Machinery and apparatus	13,661,040.53
Vehicles	4,090,064.94
Arms and explosives	2,058,156.83
Miscellaneous	4,524,705.53
Total	108,598,506.04

The countries of origin of the above imports were the following:

United States	$67,275,176.63
Germany	12,573,055.12
Great Britain	10,303,207.60
France	8,891,869.10
Spain	3,817,785.60
Belgium	1,434,761.94
Other countries	4,302,650.05
Total	108,598,506.04

The exports of mineral products during the period in reference were as follows:

Gold:

In bars	$9, 897, 281. 94
In other forms	2, 822, 062. 47
In Mexican coin	29, 990. 00
In foreign coin	7, 269. 00
Total	12, 756, 603. 41

Silver:

Mexican pesos, old coinage	11, 566, 774. 00
Foreign coin	64, 891. 00
Bars	31, 751, 759. 35
In other forms	5, 362, 215. 30
Total	48, 745, 639. 65

Other mineral products:

Antimony	687, 778. 00
Copper	13; 335, 173. 00
Marble	21, 080. 00
Plombagina	45, 820. 00
Lead	1, 875, 124. 56
Zinc	623, 221. 12
Other mineral products	1, 055, 196. 38
Total	79, 145, 636. 12

Compared with a total of $95,227,111.04 in the corresponding six months of 1905–6, this shows a decrease of $16,081,474.92 in the first half of 1906–7.

The value of vegetable products exported during the first half of 1906–7 was:

Coffee	$1, 711, 055. 00
Barks for tanning	7, 824. 00
Rubber	2, 070, 499. 00
Chicle	633, 070. 00
Frijol beans	374, 943. 00
Fresh fruits	169, 068. 48
Garbanzo beans	2, 603, 581. 00
Guayule	8, 599. 00
Haba beans	2, 550. 00
Henequen in leaf	17, 097, 429. 77
Ixtle in leaf	2, 144, 861. 00
Woods	1, 029, 390. 50
Corn	3, 038. 80
Moral hard wood	39, 210. 00
Dye wood	208, 438. 12
Broom root	854, 117. 00
Tobacco in leaf	867, 125. 35

Vanilla _____ $910, 100. 00
Other vegetable products_____ 980, 324. 20

    Total, first half, 1906–7_____ 31, 715, 224. 17
    Total, first half, 1905–6_____ 29, 363, 577. 40

      Increase in 1906–7_____ 2, 351, 646. 77

The principal article of export under this heading continues to be henequen fiber from Yucatan. In the first half of 1905–6 it amounted to $15,467,436, showing an increase of $1,629,993.77 in 1906–7.

The exports of animal products in the first six months of the fiscal year 1906–7 were as follows:

Cattle _____ $757, 379. 00
Rawhides _____ 4, 232, 428. 03
Other animal products_____ 303, 031. 99

    Total first half of 1906–7_____ 5, 292, 839. 02
    Total first half of 1905–6_____ 5, 607, 898. 26

      Decrease in 1906–7_____ 315, 059. 24

The exports of manufactured articles during the first half of 1906–7 amounted to $1,366,966.22 as compared with $1,315,186.06, an increase of $51,780.16. The exports of miscellaneous articles were valued at $363,271.65, as against $350,735.20 in the corresponding period of the previous fiscal year, an increase of $12,536.45.

SILVER BASIS OF THE STAMP AND CUSTOMS TAXES, APRIL, 1907.

The usual monthly circular issued by the Treasury Department of the Mexican Government announces that the legal price per kilogram of pure silver during the month of April, 1907, is $44.76, according to calculations provided in the decree of March 25, 1905. This price will be the basis for the payment of the stamp tax and customs duties when silver is used throughout the Republic.

POSTAL RECEIPTS, SEVEN MONTHS OF 1906–7.

The movement of the Mexican mail service for January, 1907, and for the seven months of the fiscal year 1906–7, ending January, 1907, is reported as follows:

The total for the seven months' period was $2,343,359.76, as compared with $2,114,684.59 in the same months of the preceding year. For the month of January the receipts were $387,881.61, as compared with $357,543.29 in the preceding month of December and $339,420.69 in the same month of last year.

REGISTRY OF BUSINESS TRANSACTIONS, JANUARY AND FEBRUARY, 1907.

During the month of February the value of business transactions registered in the archives of the public registrar of the City of Mexico was $23,131,195.42, an increase over the preceding month of $5,001,412.87, the figures for the month having been $18,129,782.55. The February operations were distributed as follows:

132 mercantile and railway	$11, 843, 905. 00
257 transfers by deed	6, 546, 309. 26
204 mortgages and attachments	2, 088, 540. 41
9 leases	1, 192, 000. 00
129 judicial orders	1, 356, 210. 02
77 private contracts	18, 437. 82
32 public deeds	85, 792, 91

CUSTOMS REVENUES, FIRST SEVEN MONTHS OF 1906-7.

Official statistics recently published show that the revenues collected by the various custom-houses of the Republic of Mexico during the first seven months of 1906-7 were as follows, the figures for the corresponding period of 1905-6 being also given by way of comparison:

	First seven months.	
	1906-7.	1905-6.
	Pesos.	*Pesos.*
Import duties	29, 203, 819. 31	24, 574, 548. 26
Export duties	630, 713. 38	561, 850. 49
Port dues	608, 396. 88	510, 841. 14
Total	30, 442, 429. 57	25, 677, 239. 89

SUGAR PRODUCTION IN 1906.

The total production of sugar in the Republic of Mexico, as reported by the "*Revista Azucarera*" for 1906-7, was 107,500 tons in 1905-6 and 115,000 tons (estimated) for 1906-7. Morelos is the leading center of production, being credited with 35,661,720 kilos of sugar and 21,256,962 kilos of molasses. The output for the season was 2,500 tons of sugar in excess of the estimate.

Following is a list of the sugar-producing States and their respective quotas for the 1905-6 crops:

State.	Molasses.	Sugar.	State.	Molasses.	Sugar.
	Kilos.	*Kilos.*		*Kilos.*	*Kilos.*
Campeche	658, 913	542, 159	Puebla	6, 037, 000	16, 549, 000
Chiapas	621, 700	371, 700	San Luis Potosí	3, 594, 000	1, 925, 000
Colima	1, 330, 000	1, 740, 000	Sinaloa	3, 860, 000	8, 540, 000
Guerrero	2, 652, 200	2, 096, 450	Tabasco	1, 064, 500	1, 967, 000
Jalisco	6, 448, 060	6, 196, 400	Tamaulipas	1, 529, 500	1, 694, 000
Mexico	747, 480	157, 720	Tepic	2, 000, 000	3, 500, 000
Michoacán	13, 674, 986	6, 658, 723	Veracruz	9, 312, 166	16, 296, 934
Morelos	21, 256, 962	35, 661, 720	Yucatan	2, 130, 304	1, 241, 041
Nuevo Leon	350, 000	913, 918			
Oaxaca	2, 133, 913	1, 477, 820	Total	79, 396, 684	107, 529, 085

COINAGE ISSUE UNDER NEW MONE

A statement issued by the President of th
Commission of Mexico records in detail th
formed currency which has been coined a
during the two years' life of the commissio

The law of March 25, 1905, decreasing
came effective on May 1, 1905, since whicl
and standard currency issued under the a
has reached the sum of $80,454,646.90 in
entirely distinct from the old *pesos fuertes*,
in circulation or hoarded, is variously esti
$30,000,000.

Gold in coins of $10 (hidalgos) and $5
issued to the value of $57,946,500; silver, in
$20,970,000; nickel, in 5-cent pieces, $601,
1 and 2 cents, $936,418.90.

In addition to this metallic or specie circ
rency issued and rigidly secured by the
banks of issue operate, consisted, on Janua
being everywhere accepted at par in all
cash equivalent to the metallic currency.

Of this total, $178,638,041, the chartered
January 31 the sum of $63,574,518, leavin
lic the sum of $115,064,523.

FLOUR MACHINERY SHIPPED TO T

The Torreon "Star" states that a Dura
the manufacture of middlings mills and
that the middlings mill is destined to sup
in flour mills, because, it is claimed, it does
with one-fourth of the power, and with the
it does work no rolls can do and solves th
millers, that of grinding sharp middling
invention will become a big factor in the
world.

The nixtamal mill is having a big sale.
so that each will properly fulfill its own pe
ing business. With the combination of th
unexcelled for grinding food products, su
spices, malt, cotton-seed meal, salt, sugar, c

An Austin (Texas, U. S. A.) company re
some of these mills. The Austin concern
chili con carne and 10,000 cans of *tamales* e

[...] to purchase from first hand chili and beans. While
[...] the mills mentioned above and gave an order for a
[...] to be sent to Austin.

COMMERCIAL TRAVELERS' LICENSES.

[...]ing are the regulations governing commercial travelers in
[...]e States of the Mexican Republic:

[...]scalientes, every agent or commercial traveler who endeav-
[...] goods of any kind to commercial houses is subject to the
[...] of a municipal tax of from $50 to $100 whether successful
[...]g sales or not.

[...] State of Campeche, no taxes are levied on traveling agents.
[...] State of Coahuila, taxes are levied on traveling agents in
[...]e with the local ordinances of the different municipalities.
[...]illo, the following taxes are collected:

[...]o one hundred dollars of agents who carry their wares with
[...] make sales at residences of jewelry, dry goods, or other
[...] articles not specified.

[...] three dollars for the sale of rubber stamps or stationery.
[...] to forty dollars for the sale of sewing machines.
[...]llars for soliciting insurance of all kinds.
[...] five dollars for the sale of lottery tickets.

[...]clova and Parras, (State of Coahuila) traveling agents pay
[...] per month or fraction of a month. In the latter town the
[...] apply for a permit subjects the agent to a fine of from $10

[...]dad Porfirio Diaz, traveling agents pay from $10 to $25 per
[...] fraction thereof, lottery agents from $2 to $5 per month,
[...]s for publications $3 per month.

[...]eon, traveling agents pay from $5 to $10 per month, accord-
[...]e article sold and the importance of the commercial house
[...]esent. The tariff is fixed by the president of the municipal

[...]te of Chiapas levies no taxes on traveling agents.
[...]huahua, agents who sell from samples pay no taxes. Only
[...]nts pay taxes who make actual sales from wares on hand,
[...] class ambulant agents are included. The tariff is 2 per
[...]les, plus the Federal tax.

[...] Federal district and territories, agencies and commission
[...]y from $3 to $75 per month, in accordance with the pro-
[...] the census law. As the laws of the Federal district govern,
[...]t differences, in the territories, it is probable that taxes
[...] those collected in the Federal district are levied on agents
[...]goods in the Territories.

ᵥeling agents pay no taxes.

aveling agents are required to report to the city
municipality visited the name of the house they
ᵤ ᵗ class of merchandise they propose to sell. The
nt ᵤᵢ ᵗ municipal council shall issue a license, good for
  ᵣₗ ing from $5 to $10 for the same.

Hidalgo, according to information obtained from
artment, agents pay from $1 to $100 for the privi-
ᵢ ᵢ.ᵤr a period of one month.

ı Jalisco, no taxes are levied on sales agents.

ı México, traveling agents pay no taxes, but must procure a
ⁿᵍe issued by the General Bureau of Rents. Ambulant salesmen
offer their wares to private persons must register and pay 10 per
ıt on the value of the merchandise.

In Michoacan, the payment of a monthly tax of from $5 to $30,
according to the importance of the house represented, is required.

In Morelos, no tax is levied on traveling agents. The law includes
ambulant merchants only, and these are not specifically mentioned.
This law will probably be changed during the present year.

In the State of Nuevo Leon, traveling agents pay $10, plus a
Federal tax of 25 per cent on the amount of the license, or a total
tax of $12.50 for permission to work in any part of the State for a
period of one month.

In Oaxaca, the municipal law requires traveling agents to list or
manifest the merchandise they propose to sell, and to give bond or
security to the end that, on completing their operations, a payment
of 1½ per cent on the amount of the sales may be collected.

At Puebla, there is a classification board whose duty it is to levy a
tax on traveling agents, according to circumstances and the importance of the business operations represented.

In Queretaro, in conformity with the previous declaration or
manifest of the Department of Rents of the State, a tax of 1 per cent
is levied on the amount of the sales made in the State.

In San Luis Potosi, traveling agents representing houses located
outside the State pay a tax of from $5 to $25, according to the importance of the business transacted.

In Sonora, a municipal tax of from $50 to $100 is levied on traveling
agents, according to the classification made by the president of the
municipal council of each locality visited.

In Sinaloa, traveling agents pay a tax of from $2 to $10, in conformity with the classification of the collector of revenues in each
place, a declaration having been previously made by the agent and
the tax fixed in accordance with the importance of the business
transactions.

In Tabasco, no tax is levied on agents.

In Tamaulipas, the fiscal law of the State imposes a tax of from $5 to $10 a month on agents and commercial travelers who transact business in the different towns. In the city of Tampico the municipal law levies an additional tax on said agents of from $5 to $10 per month.

The State of Veracruz imposes no taxes on agents.

Yucatan levies no tax on traveling agents.

In Zacatecas, traveling agents representing commercial houses are subject to no tax in the State. Ambulant merchants must pay a tax of 1½ per cent, plus the Federal tax, on the amount of the sales made in any part of the State.

FISHING CONCESSION GRANTED TO A NORWEGIAN COMPANY.

A British official report from Christiania states that a Norwegian company in Mexico "*La Compañia Norvega Mexicana*" has been granted a valuable concession by the Mexican Government carrying the sole right to fishing privileges of every description in the Gulf of Mexico for fifteen years.

In addition to supplying fresh fish for local consumption, it is purposed to establish canning factories and to carry on oyster breeding as well as lobster and prawn fisheries. The equipment of the business will be purchased in Norway.

POSTAL CONVENTION WITH ITALY.

In the "*Diario Oficial*" of March 7, 1907, is published the convention for exchange of postal money orders between Mexico and Italy, approved by the Mexican Senate October 24, 1906, ratified by President Diaz January 31, 1907, and which has also been ratified by the Italian Government.

The exchange offices established for Mexico are Mexico City, Nuevo Laredo, and Tamaulipas, and for Italy, Naples.

The maximum limit of postal orders is 200 *pesos* and 500 *lire*, respectively.

NICARAGUA.

INCREASED EXPORT DUTY ON COFFEE.

On February 24, 1907, the President of the Republic of Nicaragua promulgated a decree whereby the export duty on native coffee was advanced from 40 *centavos* gold per quintal to $2 (national currency) per quintal.

This is practically double its former rate of duty, and will continue in effect so long as the coffee market is in its present state.

For the purposes of the decree the gold-bearing bonds of the Republic will be received at the exchange rate of 630 per cent.

PANAMA.

MONETARY LAW.

The law establishing the gold monetary standard for the Republic of Panama and also providing for gold and silver coinage is contained in an act passed by the National Convention on June 26, approved by President AMADOR on June 28, 1904 (known as "Law 84 of 1904"), and in the decree of President AMADOR pursuant to that law, issued December 6, 1904, and known as "Decree 74 of 1904." The two are herewith given:

"*Law 84 of 1904.*

" The National Convention of Panama decrees:

"ARTICLE 1. The monetary unit of the Republic shall be the balboa, that is, a gold coin of one gram six hundred and seventy-two milligrams (1.672 grams) weight, nine hundred thousandths (0.900) fine, divided into one hundred hundredths ($\frac{100}{100}$).

"*Paragraph.* The present gold dollars of the United States of America, and the multiples thereof, shall be legal tender in the Republic for their face value equivalent to the balboa.

"ART. 2. When the Executive Power orders the coinage of national gold coin this coinage shall be made in pieces of one, two and a half, five, ten, and twenty balboas, selecting the denominations of greater circulation in commerce.

"ART. 3. Silver coins shall be of an alloy of nine hundred thousandths pure silver and one hundred thousandths copper.

"ART. 4. The designation, weight, diameter, and equivalence of silver coins shall be the following:

" The peso: A coin that shall weigh twenty-five grams, have a diameter of thirty-seven millimeters, and be equivalent in value to fifty-hundredths of a balboa.

" The half peso: A coin that shall weigh twelve and a half grams, have a diameter of thirty millimeters, and be equivalent in value to twenty-five hundredths of a balboa.

" The fifth of a peso: A coin that shall weigh five grams, have a diameter of twenty-four millimeters, and be equivalent in value to ten-hundredths of a balboa.

" The tenth of a peso: A coin that shall weigh two and a half grams, have a diameter of eighteen millimeters, and be equivalent in value to five-hundredths of a balboa.

" The twentieth of a peso: A coin that shall weigh one and a quarter grams, have a diameter of ten millimeters, and be equivalent in value to two and a half hundredths of a balboa.

"*Paragraph.* Therefore two silver pesos shall be equivalent in value to one balboa, which is the monetary unit. The fractions of the peso shall have the same proportional fractional equivalence with respect to the said unit.

"ART. 5. National silver coins shall be legal tender for their face value in all transactions.

"ART. 6. Colombian silver coins of standard not less than 835 thousandths fine and those of 666 thousandths fine now in circulation in the Republic shall be exchanged for the new national money at the rate of 312.50 pesos for each 100 balboas or the equivalent in Panama silver. But the conversion of Colombian silver coins 666 thousandths fine shall be limited to the pieces of five centavos and to the quantity of twenty thousand pesos agreed on in the first clause of the contract number 36, entered into by the government of the late Department of Panama on behalf of the National Government of the Republic of Colombia with Messrs. Isaac Brandon & Bros., of this city, for coinage of Colombian silver money, which contract was approved by Señor General Victor Manuel Salazar, Civil and Military Chief of the then Department of Panama, on October 10, 1902, and which was published in number 1399 of the *Gaceta de Panamá* of October 9 of the same year.

" *Paragraph.* Obligations, contracted before the going into operation of this law, payable tacitly or expressly in Colombian silver coin not less than eight hundred and thirty-five thousandths (0.835) fine, shall be redeemable in the new national coinage at the rate set out in this article.

"ART. 7. The Colombian silver coin mentioned in this law shall continue to be legal tender until the day on which begins to be put into effect the exchange thereof, and from this day forward it shall have the value herein set out for the exchange thereof.

" *Paragraph.* The Executive Power shall begin the conversion of the coin spoken of in article 6 on the first day of next September. For this purpose the Executive Power shall designate the public offices in the capital and in the provinces in which the exchange shall be made, and shall give notice thereof thirty days prior to the time set. This conversion shall be carried into effect within the sixty days following the time set, after which the Colombian coin shall cease to be legal tender in the Republic.

"ART. 8. For the purpose of effecting the exchange of the silver coin now in circulation in the Republic, the Executive Power is authorized to have coined and to emit up to the sum of three million pesos (3,000,000 pesos) Panama coin, as provided by this law.

"ART. 9. In order to guarantee in legal use the parity of silver coin with gold coin, the Executive Power shall deposit in a reliable banking institution in the United States an amount in gold equivalent to fifteen per cent of the emission.

"ART. 10. The Executive Power shall give an account, by monthly reports published in the 'Gaceta Oficial,' of the amount of Colombian silver coin taken in for the purpose of conversion. The period of conversion having ended, the Executive Power is authorized to sell the coin taken in in any foreign market at the rate most beneficial to the Treasury. The product of this sale shall be covered into the funds of the general Treasury of the Republic.

"ART. 11. The design of the Panama coins to which this law refers shall be the following:

" For the obverse: The bust of VASCO NÚÑEZ DE BALBOA, the discoverer of the Panama coasts on the Pacific Ocean, in profile looking to the right, with a fillet on which appears the words ' Dios,' ' Ley,' ' Libertad.'

" Surrounding the head, close to the edge of the coin, the phrase ' República de Panama;' at the base of the bust the word ' Balboa' in capital letters, but of less size than those of the other inscriptions. At the bottom of the coin, below the bust, the year of coinage in numerals.

" For the reverse: The coat of arms of the Republic of Panama in the center; surrounding this in the upper part the value of the coin in letters, and in the lower part, to the right, the weight of the coin in grams; and to the left the alloy in thousandths of fineness.

"ART. 12. The introduction into the territory of the Republic of all kinds of silver money, except that imported by the Executive Power in order to make effective this law, is prohibited.

"ART. 13. The Executive Power is authorized to celebrate with the Government of the United States of North America a monetary convention, which shall have as a basis this law and the agreement entered into at the conference celebrated in Washington the 18th day of the present month of June between the Commissioners of the Government of the United States and the Commissioner of the Republic of Panama.

"ART. 14. The expenses occasioned by the carrying into effect this law shall be considered as included in the budget of expenses.

" Given at Panama the 27th of June, 1904.

" Let it be published and put into effect.

" M. AMADOR GUERRERO.

" PANAMA, June 28, 1904.

"Decree Number 74 of 1904.

" The President of the Republic, by virtue of the authority conferred upon him by Article 13 of Law 84 of 1904 in regard to coinage, decrees:

ARTICLE 1. The Convention entered into at Washington on June 20 of the present year between the Secretary of War of the United States of America and the Fiscal Commissioners of the Republic of Panama, set out in the following two communications, is approved in all its parts:

" WASHINGTON, *June 20, 1904.*

" Messrs. RICARDO ARIAS and EUSEBIO A. MORALES,
  "Special Fiscal Commissioners of the Republic of Panama,
  "New York.

" GENTLEMEN : I understand that there is now pending in the Convention of the Republic of Panama, exercising legislative power for the Republic, a bill to establish a monetary standard and to provide for the coinage necessary in the Republic. The Isthmian Canal Commission, whose action, by direction of the President of the United States, I am authorized to supervise and direct, is vitally interested in the maintenance in the Canal Zone of a stable currency based upon the gold standard.

" I conceive it to be of common benefit to the Republic and to the Isthmian Canal Commission that the currency used in the Republic and in the Canal Zone should be the same. I am informed that the Convention of the Republic has under consideration a measure which in substance provides:

" I. That the monetary unit of the Republic shall be a gold peso of the weight of 1 gram 672 milligrams and of nine hundred one-thousandths fineness, divisible into 100 cents, to be issued as and when considered by the Republic necessary or convenient for its requirements.

" II. That the present gold dollar of the United States of America and its multiples shall also be legal tender in the Republic of Panama for its nominal value as equivalent to one gold peso of the Republic.

" III. That fractional silver coins shall be issued by the Republic, of various denominations, all to be of an alloy composed of nine hundred one-thousandths of pure silver and one hundred one-thousandths of copper, the declared values of the same bearing a ratio to the same weight of gold of approximately 1 to 32, and that such fractional silver currency shall be legal tender in all transactions.

" IV. That the silver to be coined shall be in fractional denominations of the gold peso or dollar, and, except as hereinafter specifically provided, shall be coined only in exchange or conversion of the Colombian silver peso and fractional currency now legally in circulation in the Republic, and that the amount thus converted shall not exceed $3,000,000 of such Colombian silver pesos.

" V. That after July 1, 1905, there shall be coined and issued by the Republic such additional amount of fractional silver currency to the limit in the aggregate in value of 1,500,000 pesos or gold dollars,

equivalent to 3,000,000 half-dollar pieces, as may be deemed
Secretary of War of the United States necessary or advisabl
construction of the Isthmian Canal and as may be requested
of the Executive Power of the Republic.

" VI. The Republic of Panama, in order to secure the lega
and equivalence with the gold standard of such fractions
coins, shall create a reserve fund by deposit with a responsib
ing institution in the United States of a sum in lawful cur:
the United States equivalent to 15 per cent of the nominal ·
the silver fractional currency issued by the Republic, and as 1
is issued, together with an amount equal to the seigniorage on
ver coins issued at the request of the Secretary of War as a1
less all necessary costs of coinage and transportation.

" VII. That after conference with the Isthmian Canal (
sion, or its representatives or fiscal agents, the Republic of
will take such steps with respect to exchange by drafts 1
reserve fund as will tend to prevent the disturbance of t
parity of the silver fractional currency of the Republic of
with the gold standard.

" VIII. That the Republic of Panama shall cause its co:
be executed at the mints of the United States.

"Assuming that legislation will be enacted substantiall)
foregoing effect, I agree, on behalf of the Isthmian Canal (
sion and by direction of the President of the United States—

" First. That the Isthmian Canal Commission will make 1
and silver coin of the Republic of Panama legal tender wi
Canal Zone by appropriate legislation.

" Second. That it will employ such gold and silver coir
Republic in its disbursements in the Canal Zone and in the]
as the Canal Commission shall find practicable and convenie

" Third. The Isthmian Canal Commission shall cooperate ·
Republic of Panama to maintain the parity of the fraction
coinage of the Republic of Panama with the gold standard
of drafts upon its funds at reasonable rates and on terms wl
tend to prevent the disturbance of such parity.

" Fourth. It is mutually agreed that nothing herein c
shall be construed to restrict the right of the Republic to re
silver currency after the opening of the canal to commerce
an amount as it may deem advisable and thereupon to red
withdraw, pro rata, the reserve fund corresponding to the r
of the amount of silver coinage outstanding.

" Will you please confirm your accord with the foregoing?

" Very respectfully,

" WM. II. TAFT.

"*Secretary o*|

" NEW YORK, *June 20,.1904.*

" Hon. WILLIAM H. TAFT,
   "*Secretary of War, Washington.*

" SIR: Pursuant to the powers that the Republic of Panama has conferred upon us, and subject to the laws of the Republic, we hereby declare our complete assent to the convention contained in your communication of this date and declare that we are in complete accord with that therein stipulated.

   " We are, sir, very truly, yours,
   " RICARDO ARIAS,
   " EUSEBIO A. MORALES,
   "*Fiscal Commissioners of the Republic.*

"ART. 2. Coinage of fractional silver coin of the Republic shall be limited—

   " 1. To the quantity necessary to carry into effect the exchange of the Colombian silver coin, as provided in Law 84 of this year, without this coinage exceeding three million *pesos* (3,000,000 *pesos*).

   " 2. After the first of next June a further coinage and emission up to three million pesos (3,000,000 pesos) Panama coin, equivalent to one million five hundred thousand balboas (1,500,000 balboas), shall be made upon the request of the Secretary of War of the United States at such times and in quantities as he may determine.

"ART. 3. In order to guarantee in legal use the parity between the new gold and silver coin in the Republic, there shall be deposited in a banking institution of the United States fifteen per cent of the face value of each coining, together with an amount equal to the seigniorage produced by the second coining, after deducting the cost and transport of the money to this Republic.

" These deposits shall be made in proportion as the coin is issued.

" Given at Panama December 6, 1904.

   " M. AMADOR GUERRERO."

TARIFF LEGISLATION, 1907.

Two legislative measures affecting the customs tariff of Panama have been enacted by the National Assembly during the present session. The first act imposes a duty of 50 cents gold for each 1,000 or fraction thereof of cocoanuts exported from the Republic. The second act provides that sugar known as " *moscovado*," sugar-cane molasses, or any mixture imported into that country that is available for the distillation of spirits shall pay.duty at the rate of 2 *balboas* and 50 cents for each 50 kilograms.

The *balboa* is equivalent to 1 dollar American gold.

PERU.

THE MINING INDUSTRY IN 1906.

"*El Comercio*" for January 1, 1907, states that during the year 1906 the mining claims taken up in Peru numbered 9,485, as compared with 8,840 in 1905 and 7,763 in the preceding year.

Excluding the output of the Cerro de Pasco mines, which aggregates 40 tons of pure copper daily, the exportation of metals for the year 1906 reached 22,331,802 kilos, valued at £623,082, as against 20,058,606 kilos, with a value of £466,592, in 1905.

Companies formed during the year for the exploitation of the mineral and other resources of the Republic had a capital amounting to £2,884,320, the various organizations being capitalized as follows:

	Capital.
The Inca Rubber Company	£1, 000, 000
The Esquilaya Rubber Company	200, 000
The Inambari Dredging Company	300, 000
The Peruvian Mining, Smelting, and Refining Company	1, 000, 000
The Exploration Syndicate	120, 000
The Humboldt Gold Placers Company	20, 000
The American Vanadium Company	12, 320
Sociedad Explotadora	132, 000
Societé des Mines de Tuco Cheyna	100, 000
	2, 884, 320

CUSTOMS REVENUES AT MOLLENDO, 1906.

Official statistics recently received, show that the custom-house of Mollendo, Republic of Peru, collected during the calendar year 1906 a total revenue of £162,372 6s. 15d., as against £145,364 1s. 82d. in 1905, an increase in favor of 1906 of £15,008 4s. 33d. The revenue in 1903 and 1904 was £132,510 1s. 46d. and £135,453, 0s. 40d., respectively.

IMPROVEMENT OF PERUVIAN LIVE STOCK.

The Peruvian Consul-General at New York, having been authorized by his Government to take steps for the inspection and shipment to Peru of improved breeds of live stock, has announced through "*El Agricultor Peruano*" that he has executed his first order at advantageous prices and values.

Having established satisfactory connection with breeders and stockmen in the United States, he has offered his services for the further development of this line of trade intercourse.

Shipment of orders has been arranged for by the "Kosmos" line, the point of embarkation being San Francisco.

COASTWISE SERVICE TO SAN FRANCISCO.

A Peruvian shipping company, to take over a concession from the Government of Peru, offered a year ago with the grant of a large subsidy, is reported by the Berlin "*Boerson' Courier*" to have been formed with a paid-up capital of $1,500,000, of which $150,000 has been subscribed by the Peruvian Government. It is proposed to purchase the necessary steamers in Europe, but in the meantime the Government has placed at the disposal of the company several steamers of from 2,000 to 3,000 gross registered tonnage. The object of the · company is not only to undertake a regular coasting service off Peru, but also freight and passenger services from Calao to Ecuador, Colombia, Panama, Costa Rica, Nicaragua, Salvador, Guatemala, Mexico, and California to San Francisco. It is intended later on also to establish a steamship line to Europe.

SALVADOR.

INAUGURATION OF PRESIDENT FIGUEROA.

On March 1, 1907, General FERNANDO FIGUEROA was formally inaugurated as President of the Salvadorean Republic, succeeding Señor Don PEDRO JOSÉ ESCALÓN, who had been Chief Executive of the Nation from March 1, 1903.

The ceremonial of transfer of office was marked by enthusiasm of the people and was accompanied by expressions of patriotic feeling on the part of both the retiring and incoming President.

MESSAGE OF PRESIDENT ESCALÓN TO THE NATIONAL ASSEMBLY AT THE OPENING OF ITS REGULAR SESSION ON FEBRUARY 16, 1907.

*

PEACE AND TRANQUILLITY.

Profoundly convinced that peace and transquillity constitute the greatest blessings that can be enjoyed by nations, since these conditions are the indispensable foundations for the development and prosperity of States, I have omitted no effort, however costly it may have been, to secure both these blessings, adjusting my conduct as President to all that has tended to maintain unalterable these conditions, not only in the affairs of our sister Republics, but also in those concerning the interior régime of the nation.

*　　*　　*　　*　　*

RELATIONS WITH GUATEMALA.

There occurred in June of last year events of such gravity with the neighboring Republic of Guatemala that we were placed under the sad alternative of resorting to arms in the protection of our rights and had to engage in an open conflict with that Government, aided by the alliance of our firm and loyal friend, the Government of Honduras.

* * * - * * *

Since the termination of the war our relations with Guatemala have been resumed, and the respective diplomatic representation has now been established.

In conformity with the peace convention celebrated on board the *Marblehead*, a general treaty of peace, amity, commerce, extradition, etc., among the Republics of Salvador, Honduras, Guatemala, and Costa Rica was signed in September last by our delegates, Dr. SALVADOR GALLEGOS and Dr. SALVADOR RODRIGUEZ G., as well as the conventions for the establishing of an International Office and a Central American Pedagogic Institute and a convention ad referendum concerning the boundary treaty between Honduras and Salvador, and it gives me pleasure to inform you that at the present time we are on most amicable terms with all the countries with whom we have relations, and especially with the sister Republics of Central America.

FOREIGN RELATIONS.

In April last Baron VON SEEFRIED AUS BUTTENHEIM was received as Envoy Extraordinary and Minister Plenipotentiary of Germany; in June, LIONEL EDWARD GRESLEY as Resident Minister of His Britannic Majesty; at the end of July, FRANCISCO J. HERBOSO as Envoy Extraordinary and Minister Plenipotentiary of the Government of Chile; at the beginning of the present month (February, 1907), Dr. LUIS ANDERSON as Envoy Extraordinary and Minister Plenipotentiary of Costa Rica, and during the last few days Dr. JOAQUIN SANSON as Minister Plenipotentiary of the Government of Nicaragua.

Through our chargé d'affaires in Guatemala a commercial convention was celebrated with the representative of the Government of Belgium and a treaty of amity, commerce, and navigation with the Minister of Italy. All these documents will soon be submitted by the respective departments to your superior consideration.

Salvador, having accepted the invitation to be represented at the Pan-American Congress at Rio de Janeiro, appointed as her delegates Dr. MANUEL DELGADO and Dr. FRANCISCO A. REYES, also making the former Envoy Extraordinary and Minister Plenipotentiary in *special* mission near the Government of Brazil. But on the termination of the war it was necessary to recall Doctor DELGADO to continue in the performance of his duties as Secretary of Foreign Relations, leaving thereby the delegation in the Congress to the second appointee, Dr. FRANCISCO A. REYES.

In consideration of the friendly and magnanimous action of the Governments of Mexico and the United States as mediators with reference to the past conflict, and as a measure of international expediency, Salvador and Honduras, by common agreement, established legations of the first rank near the governments of Mexico and the United States, appointing as envoys extraordinary and ministers plenipotentiary, respectively, Dr. BALTASAR ESTUPIAN and Dr. JOSÉ ROSA PACAS.

* *

MILITARY AFFAIRS.

The efforts of the Government to continue the policy of the former administration with respect to making out of the army of the republic an institution that shall correspond to its high calling as the protector of national rights, institutions, and public order, have been unceasing.

* * * * . * .

Special attention has been given to the construction of new and the repair of old barracks as a necessary measure for the health and comfort of the troops.

The Polytechnic School is now permanently established in the large and well-ventilated Zapote building, in charge of the Chilean mission, and in August last an annex was established for corporals and sergeants, which, judging from the results already obtained, will largely contribute to the organization of the army.

* * * * * *

INTERNAL AFFAIRS.

Concerning the general health, I am pleased to state that no disease of an epidemic or contagious character has developed, notwithstanding the fact that we have been threatened at times by the existence in neighboring countries of the bubonic plague, yellow fever, and smallpox. Even endemic diseases at certain periods of the year, such as those of a paludic origin, have not, up to the present time, been accentuated, in spite of the torrential rains of October, the time of the year in which these diseases are most prevalent. This is largely due to the sanitary measures taken by the authorities, through the offices in charge of this branch of the public service and through private persons, immediately following the close of the rainy season.

*   *   *   *   *   *   *

My Government has rendered continued aid to the municipalities of the Republic during the last four years, as well as to the inspection and control that the law prescribes for the administration and proper employment of their revenues. This has occasioned a progressive increase in the revenues, and, in general, works of importance have been realized in many places. Well-known economic causes prevented the Executive Power from continuing to issue new laws on municipal arbitration, the drafts of which have been submitted to him. These causes were the loss of the cereal crops and the consequent high price of grains of prime necessity, first when it was not thought equitable to make changes under those circumstances, in the local.imposts, and afterwards the war and the rainy season continued to aggravate those difficulties.

As to national and local highways, the legislature is aware from former messages and memorials of the inadequateness of the special revenues available for this important service. The Government, therefore, has had to divert to this purpose other funds in order to maintain said highways in good condition, and it is fitting to state here that even after the severe rainy season referred to was over, leaving nearly all the roads greatly damaged, traffic suffered but little, due, it is just to say, to the activity of the governors and municipal authorities and the willingness with which the neighbors made the necessary repairs.

*   *

POSTS.

Considerable improvements have been made in the Department of Posts, and the business has increased. Inasmuch as this Department is supported out of its own revenues, the service has been extended and improved, while the credit of the Central Office has been maintained by punctuality in the payments of the foreign postal service. Lately, conventions have been celebrated with Mexico for the exchange of parcels and money orders.

A triweekly postal service has been established with Guatemala via Jerez, and negotiations are in progress for reestablishing the postal service via Zacapa. It should be borne in mind that scarcely any interruptions occurred, not even during the rainiest weather of this winter, due to the activity of the officials and employees of the Department.

In 1902, the expenditures in the postal service amounted to $87,084; in 1903, they rose to $102,787; in 1904, to $121,756; in 1905, to $142,855, and in 1906, to $161,662.

TELEGRAPH AND TELEPHONE.

The telegraph and telephone service has also increased progressively, especially since 1903, at which time, as an economic measure and for the convenience of the public, the amount of the charges and telephonic connections were reduced. Many new offices have been established, and the old ones have been considerably improved, necessitating large outlays for this purpose as well as for works and materials.

The number of telegraph and telephone offices have increased by 36 and 28, respectively, and 535 miles of new telegraph and 856 miles of new telephone lines have been added to the system. The increase in telegraph and telephone apparatus has been 53 and 363, respectively, and there has been an increase of 124 in the personnel of the system.

Two beautiful towers have been constructed in this capital and another tower in Santa Ana for the introduction of wires to the central offices. The expense for materials, which, in 1902, was $14,045.61, has increased year by year up to 1906, when it rose to $161,437.56. The general budget for telegraph and telephones, which in 1902, was $260,221, has likewise increased up to the present time and now amounts to $428,986.

ELECTRIC-LIGHT SERVICE.

In like manner, the electric-light service used by the Government has also increased. The total cost, which, in 1902, was $24,144, has greatly increased up to the present time, and now is $49,144, not including the value of the subventions with which some of the companies have been aided. * * * A similar increase has occurred in the Department of Agriculture.

* * *

PORTS.

A few months ago, and for the special protection of the agriculture of the eastern part of the Republic, the port of Triunfo was again opened to imports and exports, so that that zone now has a quicker route for the shipment of its coffee and other products, overcoming in this manner many difficulties and the enormous cost incurred by the Union route.

WATER SUPPLY.

:n special attention to the introduction of systems
nto the towns as one of the things most urgently
to confine myself to the consideration of towns of
'tance, I shall only review the water supply of this
the largest and most expensive system yet planned
ıd one estimated to be sufficient to meet the needs of
;ithstanding the increase in population; that of
ɔf large size and excellent arrangement, the pipes of
to be laid; that of La Union, the pipes of which are
ıl.   ı: ɩo be used, and those of San Vicente, Cojutepeque,
and San Pedro Nonualco, which have been opened to
...e for some time. The· towns close to the metropolis—
:   ıs of hydraulic installations and others by the force of
'lɩ,ɟ—   properly supplied with water.

BRIDGES.

ges have   ıwise been constructed, such as the ones so needed
ıa, and Sumpul rivers and other streams of less
nrst-mentioned bridge, which was already in use,
ıvas washeu away by the fierce October rains, and the second, which
was in course of construction, was damaged. Plans have been made
and funds provided to repair them in such a manner that they will
withstand these unforeseen but probable disasters.

*   *   *   *   *

NATIONAL EXPOSITION.

A pleasant recollection to me of my administration will always be
the fact of having been able to hold with such success, and relatively at so little expense, the first National Exposition in Salvador.

*   *   *   *   *   *   *

PUBLIC BUILDINGS.

With respect to public edifices, the Government, in addition to the
palace and the building for the School of Agronomy, has constructed two large and well-built houses for the Administration of
Rents—one in Santa Ana and the other in Ahuachapan. As early
as 1903 the Government acquired on very favorable terms the house
that belonged to the London Bank. It was properly repaired and
to-day it is an elegant and durable edifice in which the general treasury office with all its branches is established. Its cost, which in the

'pinion of everyone was very reasonable, was $60,000, payable in three years, with interest at 6 per cent.

* * * *

PUBLIC INSTRUCTION.

Public instruction, and particularly primary instruction, has received my special attention, and I have employed, in so far as possible, all the efforts of my Government, without being discouraged by great financial difficulties, to the promotion of education. Since the beginning of my administration two normal schools have been founded, in addition to that in the capital—one at Santa Ana and the other at San Miguel.

* * * * * * *

The amount expended for text-books and apparatus to be used for higher instruction at the beginning of 1903 was $20,000. This amount was increased during the first, second, and third years of my administration to $30,000 and during the fourth year to $100,000.

In 1903 the budget allowed for the general expense of public instruction $413,592. During the first year of my administration the amount was increased to $543,592, during the second year to $73,048, during the third year to $847,244, and during the fourth year to $1,016,544.

*

Finances in 1906.

The net revenues collected by the Government in 1906 amounted to	$8,484,419.78
Cash on hand, etc	4,038,744.20
Gross receipts	12,523,163.98
Expenditures of public administration in 1906	12,246,825.76
Repayments, deposits, etc	40,855.85
Total expenditures	12,287,681.61
On December 31, 1906, the public debt amounted to	3,397,775.81
The amount of the Burrell claim in American gold on December 31, 1905, was	211,887.33
The balance of bonds of different classes and denominations on December 31, 1906, was	7,035,625.27

CUSTOMS REVENUES, FIRST HALF OF 1906.

During the first six months of 1906, the customs receipts at the various ports of Salvador aggregated $3,234,770.69, a gain over the corresponding period of the preceding year of $267,781.22.

receipts, $2,452,978.29 were for import dues;
xports; receipts from stamps, etc., $38,396.10, the
livided among the regular port services and rents.

'ORT TRADE, FIRST HALF OF 1906.

r.th.   st half of 1906, the foreign merchadise imported
  or   s valued at $2,173,584.05, the weight of the 187,226
    ıg ı 3,563,112 kilograms.
countries furnishing the bulk of the imports were Great
ıın, the United States, Germany, France, and Belgium, and the
ıs supplied included cotton thread, hardware, flour, materials for
. manufacture of soap and candles, shoemaking materials, drugs,
icines, and wines.

PORT MOVEMENTS, MARCH–DECEMBER, 1906.

ɜ entries of vessels at Salvadorean ports, during the last nine
_uutns of 1906, comprised 347 steam and 207 sailing craft, whose
cargoes aggregated 27,271 tons, and carrying 3,582 passengers and
5,413 sacks and 594 packages of correspondence.
The clearances during the same period covered exports of native
products, comprised in 454,920 packages, the number of passengers
being 3,736. Mail matter consisted of 1,597 sacks and 893 packages.

BANK STATEMENT, 1906.

The following table shows the condition of the three leading banks
of the Republic of Salvador on December 31, 1906, the figures of the
previous year being also given for purposes of comparison:

Bank.	December 31, 1905.		December 31, 1906.	
	Cash.	Paper.	Cash.	Paper.
	Pesos.	*Pesos.*	*Pesos.*	*Pesos.*
Banco Salvadoreño	1,575,126	1,010,659	1,679,558	1,111,287
Banco Occidental	955,269	1,047,113	900,646	1,296,351
Banco Agrícola Comercial	548,161	621,172	816,998	936,071
Total	3,078,556	2,678,944	3,397,202	3,343,709

UNITED STATES.

TRADE WITH LATIN AMERICA.

STATEMENT OF IMPORTS AND EXPORTS.

Following is the latest statement, from figures compiled by the
Bureau of Statistics, United States Department of Commerce and
Labor, showing the value of the trade between the United States and

the Latin American countries. The report is for the month of February, 1907, with a comparative statement for the corresponding month of the previous year; also for the eight months ending February, 1907, as compared with the same period of the preceding year. It should be explained that the figures from the various custom-houses, showing imports and exports for any month, are not received by the Treasury Department until about the 20th of the following month, and some time is necessarily consumed in compilation and printing, so that the returns for February, for example, are not published until some time in April.

IMPORTS OF MERCHANDISE.

Articles and countries.	February—		Eight months ending February—	
	1906.	1907.	1906.	1907.
Cocoa (*Cacao; Coco ou cacao; Cacao*):	*Dollars.*	*Dollars.*	*Dollars.*	*Dollars.*
Central America	6,227	3,765	11,773	28,271
Brazil	211,526	876,452	1,018,673	1,958,379
Other South America	212,005	124,840	1,239,174	1,211,462
Coffee (*Café; Café; Café*):				
Central America	1,041,944	1,250,845	8,001,255	2,473,214
Mexico	313,335	186,243	1,357,901	681,677
Brazil	3,298,018	4,027,289	38,677,739	41,109,500
Other South America	1,564,541	793,792	6,629,846	6,031,673
Copper (*Cobre; Cobre; Cuivre*):				
Mexico	1,486,719	1,785,138	11,695,140	12,189,427
Cuba	6,493	6,907	51,970	51,566
South America	90,335	39,543	368,760	482,127
Fibers:				
Cotton, unmanufactured (*Algodón en rama; Algodao em rama; Coton non manufacturé*):				
South America	48,461	77,832	260,229	470,157
Sisal grass (*Henequén; Henequen; Henequen*):				
Mexico	763,631	788,626	9,903,217	10,013,275
Fruits:				
Bananas (*Plátanos; Bananas; Bananes*):				
Central America	379,958	298,343	2,663,579	3,285,008
Cuba	33	14,714	270,109	533,874
South America	26,101	26,884	235,106	74,643
Oranges (*Naranjas; Laranjas; Oranges*):				
Mexico	780	970	46,281	35,587
Cuba	650	1,035	5,899	7,354
Hides and skins (*Cueros y pieles; Couros e pelles; Cuirs et peaux*):				
Mexico	450,250	418,813	2,616,148	3,218,677
Cuba	21,988	9,718	79,262	205,903
Brazil	174,616	169,216	1,240,421	1,273,044
Other South America	1,402,312	1,199,700	7,810,799	8,028,520
India rubber, crude (*Goma elástica; Borracha cruda; Caoutchouc*):				
Central America	82,094	87,063	514,296	529,726
Mexico	40,530	306,969	280,580	1,278,442
Brazil	3,563,700	4,685,756	15,898,637	21,425,134
Other South America	109,317	138,481	878,812	1,001,526
Iron ore (*Mineral de hierro; Mineral de ferro; Mineral de fer*):				
Cuba	164,329	197,148	1,107,318	1,406,831
Lead, ore (*Plomo; Chumbo; Plomb*):				
Mexico	326,447	224,670	2,080,805	1,787,598
Sugar, not above No. 16 Dutch standard (*Azúcar, inferior al No. 16 del modelo holandés; Assucar, não superior ao No. 16 de padrão hollandez; Sucre, pas au-dessus du type hollandais No. 16*):				
Mexico	564	69,904	27,006	164,011
Cuba	6,458,008	9,574,917	29,490,151	31,731,018
Brazil	161,002	86,728	398,140	912,351
Other South America	134,450	87,331	1,671,800	1,815,335

IMPORTS OF MERCHANDISE—Continued.

(countries.	February—		Eight months ending February—	
	1906.	1907.	1906.	1907.
* (*Tabaco y sus manufac-inufacturas; Tabac et ses*	Dollars.	Dollars.	Dollars.	Dollars.
....	2,096,674	1,387,758	11,606,482	13,209,124
2oba; Mogno; Acajou):				
....	55,943	92,842	356,069	340,064
....	26,164	98,892	278,045	445,459
....	11,838	2,859	76,838	112,562
'aine):				
2)C	2,245,086	686,325	4,701,836	1,566,068
Class 3 (C....)	....	51,780	160,562	298,162
....	3,485	47,198	477,640	466,619

EXPORTS OF MERCHANDISE.

Agricultural implements (*Instrumentos agricolas; Instrumentos de agricultura; Machines agricoles*):				
Mexico	43,236	34,913	308,064	282,615
Cuba	10,235	2,084	135,399	40,208
Argentine Republic	255,191	249,308	4,660,386	3,157,045
Brazil	3,154	17,147	62,279	78,381
Chile	5,536	14,543	274,041	322,680
Other South America	25,301	10,700	227,079	157,844
Animals:				
Cattle (*Ganado vacuno; Gado; Bétail*):				
Mexico	31,548	64,100	414,128	615,302
Cuba	30,783	4,796	1,331,794	317,257
South America			77,273	37,289
Hogs (*Cerdos; Porcos; Porcs*):				
Mexico	11,179	5,688	107,116	151,454
South America	....	64	1,320	776
Horses (*Caballos; Cavallos; Chevaux*):				
Mexico	18,960	81,621	169,390	327,044
Sheep (*Ovejas; Orelhas; Brebis*)				
Mexico	3,670	1,650	28,325	58,268
Books, maps, etc. (*Libros, mapas, etc.; Livros, mappas, etc.; Livres, cartes, etc.*):				
Central America	4,557	2,856	38,949	34,459
Mexico	25,893	25,745	257,880	189,033
Cuba	26,155	39,569	235,231	232,574
Argentine Republic	7,932	4,011	44,882	64,572
Brazil	15,951	5,564	82,980	64,398
Chile	4,764	31,281	116,838	224,490
Other South America	5,594	22,208	61,447	80,155
Breadstuffs:				
Corn (*Maíz; Milho; Mais*):				
Central America	8,996	2,615	81,357	19,613
Mexico	78,818	55,394	598,196	762,949
Cuba	86,612	136,698	869,628	940,856
South America	2,893	1,032	15,684	6,920
Oats (*Avena; Aveia; Avoine*):				
Central America	1,641	1,486	20,875	16,146
Mexico	3,354	4,837	19,803	38,340
Cuba	19,339	30,920	151,916	255,599
South America	1,247	905	17,832	9,567
Wheat (*Trigo; Trigo; Blé*):				
Central America	3,116	3,440	35,124	22,903
Mexico	235,338	131,098	1,255,930	559,797
South America	2,892	18,278	386,536	317,207
Wheat flour (*Harina de trigo; Farinha de trigo; Farine de blé*):				
Central America	108,678	190,218	1,203,200	1,141,459
Mexico	7,918	9,284	130,231	81,861
Cuba	298,618	233,329	2,186,622	1,946,757
Brazil	117,066	90,179	851,565	866,675
Colombia	5,919	15,406	476,589	108,984
Other South America	128,217	157,964	1,640,479	1,418,565

EXPORTS OF MERCHANDISE—Continued.

Articles and countries.	February—		Eight months ending February—	
	1906.	1907.	1906.	1907.
Carriages, etc.:	*Dollars.*	*Dollars.*	*Dollars.*	*Dollars.*
Automobiles (*Automóbiles; Automoviles; Automobiles*):	21,331	96,262	166,510	561,385
Mexico	21,331	96,262	166,510	561,385
South America	7,551	6,260	48,041	137,641
Carriages, cars, etc., and parts of (*Carruages, carros y sus accesorios; Carruagens, carros e partes de carros; Voitures, wagons, et leurs parties*):				
Central America	148,228	328,150	669,612	983,547
Mexico	78,018	167,613	680,244	1,520,941
Cuba	122,215	77,577	726,188	545,482
Argentine Republic	5,991	225,645	272,448	1,511,733
Chile	24,000	1,879	389,635	80,828
Other South America	80,786	115,808	284,781	397,174
Cycles and parts of (*Bicicletas y sus accesorios; Bicyclos e partes; Bicyclettes, et leurs parties*):				
Mexico	6,368	5,229	51,394	64,962
Cuba	2,315	3,529	25,592	23,066
Argentine Republic	2,574	556	12,627	12,555
Brazil	376	655	5,365	6,413
Other South America	1,155	1,128	11,889	14,066
Clocks and watches (*Relojes de pared y bolsillo; Relogios de bolso e parede; Horloges et montres*):				
Central America	2,641	918	12,497	10,785
Mexico	3,940	3,308	37,885	82,396
Argentine Republic	4,480	2,742	50,466	39,518
Brazil	3,408	6,023	53,281	62,194
Chile	5,913	5,825	47,817	31,617
Other South America	1,942	4,258	34,376	28,799
Coal (*Carbón; Carvão; Charbon*):				
Mexico	265,616	267,797	1,963,704	4,737
Cuba	144,295	170,398	1,236,347	71,814
Copper (*Cobre; Cobre; Cuivre*):				
Mexico	98,229	60,450	873,281	600,818
Cotton:				
Cotton, unmanufactured (*Algodón en rama; Algodão em rama; Coton non manufacturé*):				
Mexico	184,147	2,730	1,477,212	36,418
Cotton cloths (*Tejidos de algodón; Fazendas de algodão; Coton manufacturé*):				
Central America	117,311	137,496	1,026,829	1,188,292
Mexico	14,077	24,104	192,805	172,750
Cuba	50,336	53,184	795,705	714,117
Argentine Republic	11,956	13,745	226,051	193,125
Brazil	47,281	21,322	409,518	281,719
Chile	39,911	73,118	710,623	761,827
Colombia	52,505	50,143	365,911	565,781
Venezuela	22,472	28,866	229,214	323,358
Other South America	35,167	48,277	318,353	365,473
Wearing apparel (*Ropa de algodón; Fazendas de algodão; Vêlements de coton*):				
Central America	21,251	27,279	170,709	227,197
Mexico	10,537	25,749	192,595	169,115
Cuba	15,916	18,918	165,579	218,666
Other South America	4,382	5,690	59,518	75,576
Fibers:				
Twine (*Bramante; Barbante; Ficelle*):				
Argentine Republic	4,081	4,501	2,145,352	1,100,120
Other South America	7,380	8,455	187,406	190,445
Electric and scientific apparatus (*Aparatos eléctricos y científicos; Aparatos elctricos e scientificos; Appareils électriques et scientifiques*):				
Central America	14,044	27,817	129,201	182,595
Mexico	131,264	95,471	600,650	916,891
Cuba	48,829	45,679	426,141	472,893
Argentine Republic	49,287	17,779	221,943	304,770
Brazil	79,484	83,922	407,676	582,083
Other South America	36,018	117,686	406,611	564,131
Electrical machinery (*Maquinaria eléctrica; Machinas electricas; Machines électriques*):				
Central America	2,125	6,602	18,059	37,738
Mexico	72,528	119,970	603,679	781,526
Cuba	135,218	892	379,751	74,517

EXPORTS OF MERCHANDISE—Continued.

ıcıes and countries.	February—	Eight months ending February—	
		1906.	1907.
Continued.			
....	4, 891		
....	11, 301		
ca..	8, 733		
⁻¹ ⁻ʲanufactures of: *de acero; Trilhos de aço; Rails*			
....			
merica			
hardware, etc. (*Materiales de metal para ruceión; Ferragems; Materiaux de construc- . en fer et acier*):			
⁻al America	360	405	
eo....	885	556	
ʹtine Republic.........................	078	322	
	253	779	
....	655	038	
.ŀḷa	758	709	
ḷⁱ	456	901	
; ̴ ̓	879	2, 665	
	736	49, 829	
i (*Máquinas de coser de coser e accesorios; arties*):			
....	949	195	76, 696	
....	364	103	400, 880	
....	243	481	210, 478	
⁻e R c..............................	828	346	503, 015	
....	757	753	132, 311	
a	359	440	43, 526	
rts of (*Locomotoras y accesorios; ocomotivas e accesorios; Locomotives et leurs parties*):	605	023	239, 131	
Central America...........................		512, 475	367, 638	874, 565
Mexico....................................	13, 716		189, 000	988, 696
Cuba.....................................	17, 331			684, 095
Argentine Republic.......................	142, 165	8, 172		404, 948
Brazil....................................	18, 300	12, 900	120, 508	135, 580
Other South America......................		326, 717	82, 974	549, 647
Typewriting machines and parts of (*Mecanógrafos y accesorios; Machinas de escribir e accesorios; Machines à écrire et leurs parties*):				
Central America...........................		2, 491		28, 668
Mexico....................................	17, 587	25, 407	201, 480	246, 273
Cuba.....................................	7, 218	4, 125		51, 183
Argentine Republic.......................		8, 240		81, 015
Brazil....................................		4, 251		41, 572
Colombia				11, 783
Other South America......................	6, 172	18, 878	89, 510	135, 854
Pipes and fittings (*Cañería; Tubos; Tuyaux*):				
Central America...........................	35, 211	84, 167		429, 120
Mexico....................................	106, 962			846, 041
Cuba.....................................				397, 242
Argentine Republic.......................				80, 499
Other South America......................			182, 609	163, 862
Leather, other than sole (*Cuero distinto del de suelo; Couro, nao para solas; Cuirs, autres que pour semelles*):				
Central America...........................	21, 014	18, 938	117, 575	143, 473
Cuba	22, 028	9, 127	164, 758	86, 041
Argentine Republic.......................	31, 932	20, 620	285, 258	163, 018
Brazil....................................	10, 963	6, 258	90, 317	83, 802
Other South America......................	14, 368	12, 120	144, 777	181, 703
Boots and shoes (*Calzados; Calçados; Chaussures*):				
Central America...........................	34, 595	33, 801	272, 321	374, 306
Mexico....................................	124, 579	110, 474	1, 034, 088	1, 003, 274
Colombia	3, 767	1, 852	81, 679	30, 189
Other South America	17, 743	17, 701	194, 688	263, 086
Meat and dairy products: *Beef, canned (Carne de vaca en latas; Carne de vaca em latas; Bœuf conservé):*				
Central America...........................	4, 819	4, 232	24, 975	46, 014
Mexico	2, 165	1, 610	19, 738	19, 541
Cuba.....................................	2, 092	1, 518	18, 789	12, 756
South America............................	4, 040	3, 136	29, 862	29, 688

EXPORTS OF MERCHANDISE—Continued.

Articles and countries.	February—		Eight months ending February—	
	1906.	1997.	1906.	1907.
Meat and dairy products—Continued.				
Beef, salted and pickled (*Carne de vaca salada ó adobada; Carne de vacca, salgada; Bœuf salé*):	*Dollars.*	*Dollars.*	*Dollars.*	*Dollars.*
Central America	8,469	18,548	65,005	89,916
South America	15,942	20,491	177,716	175,882
Tallow (*Sebo; Sebo; Suif*):				
Central America	10,438	16,424	113,494	93,698
Mexico	1,656	3,466	75,978	17,506
Cuba	2,326	8,163	7,848	12,448
Chile	5,638	2,082	46,704	54,172
Other South America	4,209	4,833	37,296	38,178
Bacon (*Tocino; Toucinho; Lard fumé*):				
Central America	1,893	2,578	12,922	21,707
Mexico	3,969	4,020	31,067	37,889
Cuba	18,878	40,367	275,827	398,006
Brazil	13,340	7,791	116,235	128,962
Other South America	2,638	5,108	9,591	8,552
Hams (*Jamones; Presuntos; Jambons*):				
Central America	8,682	16,729	56,711	99,288
Mexico	9,871	8,437	89,525	75,761
Cuba	39,794	45,495	330,347	398,599
Venezuela	1,945	2,360	35,139	31,546
Other South America	6,253	8,968	50,137	39,822
Pork (*Carne de puerco; Carne de porco; Porc*):				
Cuba	39,594	72,606	385,320	459,026
South America	28,314	34,231	164,784	170,276
Lard (*Manteca; Banha; Saindoux*):				
Central America	17,309	52,874	285,778	448,888
Mexico	73,431	59,658	422,212	441,774
Cuba	243,652	264,006	1,696,385	1,963,261
Brazil	10,294	96,734	80,695	668,132
Chile	5,225	16,687	51,368	128,442
Colombia	7,394	3,688	280,770	32,187
Venezuela	24,603	6,818	268,803	160,180
Other South America	39,119	42,181	374,967	383,404
Butter (*Mantequilla; Manteiga; Beurre*):				
Central America	10,121	9,529	76,348	109,692
Mexico	8,769	15,127	80,524	96,752
Cuba	3,635	6,623	27,605	43,276
Brazil	20,200	6,349	102,259	58,568
Venezuela	6,843	704	78,503	38,660
Other South America	2,887	8,002	23,855	36,882
Cheese (*Queso; Queijo; Fromage*):				
Central America	5,066	7,772	43,128	54,065
Mexico	4,843	8,298	27,862	27,428
Cuba	1,475	2,750	8,132	13,702
Naval stores:				
Rosin, tar, etc. (*Resina, alquitrán, etc.; Resina e alcatrão; Résine et goudron*):				
Cuba	6,071	6,289	48,712	57,911
Argentine Republic	58,216	27,825	341,109	334,348
Brazil	15,767	48,142	368,113	356,319
Other South America	3,932	22,744	190,432	173,088
Turpentine (*Aguarras; Aguaraz; Térébenthine*):				
Central America	4,311	2,047	36,137	26,992
Cuba	5,875	6,811	45,060	56,740
Argentine Republic	33,881	19,043	155,866	134,337
Brazil	11,137	9,425	70,975	104,014
Chile	5,116	14,968	55,357	75,542
Other South America	8,322	6,497	40,771	51,098
Oils:				
Mineral, crude (*Aceites minerales, crudos; Oleos minerais, crús; Huiles minérales, brutes*):				
Mexico	89,229	185,174	468,534	779,368
Cuba	36,759	23,389	235,711	281,321
Refined or manufactured (*Aceites refinados ó manufacturados; Oleos refinados ou manufacturados; Huiles raffinées ou manufacturées*).				
Central America	23,688	19,196	161,451	173,770
Mexico	17,925	20,391	109,224	186,697
Cuba	28,370	93,620	211,715	460,242
Argentine Republic	70,031	180,987	1,334,724	1,540,321
Brazil	258,974	229,216	1,856,234	1,998,289
Chile	46,823	115,178	548,214	519,499
Other South America	54,474	113,169	735,740	788,605

EXPORTS OF MERCHANDISE—Continued.

and countries.	February—		Eight months ending February—	
	1906.		1906.	1907.

ltes vegetales; Oleos vegetaes; Huiles végé-				
....			687	
....			206	
....			374	
....			980	
....			182	
....			565	
o America.................................			196	
Papel; Papel; Papier):				
"o...		909	448	
'ine Republic.................................	11,767	940	667	
....	475	388	147	
....	4,908	278	648	
South America.................................	4,592		184	
			420	
1 {1 Paraffina; Paraffine):				
....		6,974		
ix		66,226		
....		7,456		
abaco en rama; Tobaco c non manufacturé):				
Republic.................................				
....				
abaco elaborado; Tabaco manufacturé):				
Wood and manufactures of:				
Wood, unmanufactured (Madera sin labrar; Madeira ndo manufacturada; Bois brut):				
Central America.................................	20,980	48,048	310,120	435,964
Mexico.................................	75,220	108,965	594,946	878,118
Cuba.................................	5,611	21,175	115,690	96,861
Argentine Republic.................................	26,643	3,836	123,099	112,170
Other South America.................................	806	69,318	106,414	282,894
Lumber (Maderas; Madeiras; Bois de construction):				
Central America.................................	68,853	73,282	394,453	820,815
Mexico.................................	139,910	262,750	1,066,026	1,440,836
Cuba.................................	226,576	252,457	1,506,907	1,458,740
Argentine Republic.................................	426,765	761,144	2,387,944	4,523,675
Brazil.................................	5,797	107,759	248,208	837,514
Chile.................................	61,095	169,504	390,933	700,451
Other South America.................................	59,548	93,104	485,697	868,422
Furniture (Muebles; Mobilia; Meubles):				
Central America.................................	18,978	28,684	201,174	196,260
Mexico.................................	60,740	75,022	495,799	602,614
Cuba.................................	58,510	51,708	515,717	353,495
Argentine Republic.................................	21,381	27,182	224,018	267,150
Brazil.................................	2,461	8,373	31,560	50,707
Chile.................................	2,118	7,102	48,283	55,189
Colombia.................................	1,344	1,194	14,620	10,636
Venezuela.................................	466	1,151	27,333	15,608
Other South America.................................	14,230	13,772	57,436	79,589

IMPORTS AND EXPORTS OF TOBACCO, 1906.

The following figures, compiled by the Bureau of Statistics, United States Department of Commerce and Labor, show the imports and exports of leaf tobacco and its manufactures during the calendar year 1906, the figures for the previous year being also given for comparison:

Imports of foreign leaf and its manufactures.

Articles and countries.	Calendar year—	
	1905.	1906.
Leaf tobacco—		
Suitable for cigar wrappers	$5,514,042	$7,974,338
All other	13,162,097	18,652,809
Total leaf	18,676,139	26,627,147
Imported from—		
Germany	522,564	1,498,092
Netherlands	5,310,691	7,556,097
Other Europe	493,866	1,451,313
British North America	191,638	171,810
Mexico	11,121	54,604
Cuba	11,879,988	15,333,786
Asia and Oceania	262,054	543,804
Other countries	4,267	23,641
Manufactures of—		
Cigars, cigarettes, and cheroots	3,943,613	4,538,779
All other	93,954	120,190
Total manufactures of	4,037,567	4,658,969

Exports of domestic leaf and its manufactures.

Articles and countries.	Calendar year—	
	1905.	1906.
Leaf tobacco	$26,623,136	$31,866,198
Stems and trimmings	178,064	254,302
Exported to—		
United Kingdom	7,563,563	11,492,738
Belgium	1,367,195	843,587
France	2,966,750	3,121,117
Germany	3,849,693	4,117,763
Italy	2,355,779	4,382,439
Netherlands	1,213,341	1,433,253
Spain	1,318,614	577,275
Other Europe	431,914	460,061
British North America	1,488,100	1,563,582
Central America	70,115	68,427
Mexico	108,980	110,086
West Indies and Bermuda	282,694	217,972
Argentine Republic	58,596	81,454
Colombia	10,617	15,128
Other South America	79,981	88,689
Japan	962,180	629,427
British Australasia	1,068,047	1,286,602
Other Asia and Oceania	703,947	443,456
British Africa	606,778	727,527
Other Africa	342,316	518,967
Manufactures of—		
Cigars	51,148	41,853
Cigarettes	2,689,887	2,649,470
Plug	7,243,688	1,904,539
All other	990,277	954,883

COTTON REPORT, 1906.

The final census report on cotton for the year 1906, issued by the Census Bureau of the United States on March 21, shows 13,290,677 bales, as compared with 10,725,602 for 1905 and 13,697,310 for 1904. The average gross weight of the bale for 1906 is 510.70 pounds, and the crop expressed in 500-pound bales is 13,573,226. The items entering into the totals for the 1906 crop are 13,099,927 square bales, 266,793 round bales, 57,352 Sea Island bales, and 321,160 linters.

URUGUAY.

.GE OF PRESIDENT BATLLE Y ORDOÑEZ.

15, 1907, the retiring President of Uruguay, Señor
ez, presented his final message to the Uruguayan
:h he felicitated his country upon the high degree of
liberty enjoyed at present. Public works have re-
c   .ble impulse, higher education is moving in new
:uons,   he principal industries of the country—agriculture
sto   eding—are being conducted on more scientific lines.
national revenues have advanced in an unprecedented manner,
data being given in proof thereof.
                        its for 1905–6 were $6,057,000, and for 1906–7 they
nc   ·   600—an increase of $166,600. From direct taxa-
i f   ivenues, both internal and territorial, were $2,891,232, ad-
ii   u 1906–7 to $3,206,191—an increase of $314,959. Receipts
,   sources are estimated at $11,420,168.40 for 1906–7 and ex-
         pe at $9.116,728.23, leaving a possible surplus of $2,303,440.17.
              benefits derived from the conversion loan, Presi-
         nated that the value of the 6 per cent bonds changed at
par amounted to $6,001,560.67, while the result of the change to 5 per
cent bonds and 3 per cent cash bonus produced $6,322,289.33, the sur-
plus being applied to the construction and organization of a Veterinary and Agricultural College and to the development of secondary
education in the rural districts.

The law of January, 1906, creating the conversion loan, is being
carried out in all its particulars, especially with relation to the port
works of Montevideo, sanitation claims arising out of war operations,
roads and public works, agriculture, veterinary, and educational
establishments.   .

Activity is reported in the movement of the railroads, and for the
year ended June 30, 1906, the transport of animals numbered 829,537,
with a weight of 229,494 tons, as compared with 780,168 in the preceding year—an increase of 49,369, or 6.33 per cent.

Returns from the Immigration Bureau indicate a satisfactory in-
flux of foreigners, as compared with 1905.

Owing to a period of drought which lasted three months, the maize
crop suffered considerably, as did also wheat and other cereals.

In regard to the public debt, it is stated that on January 1, 1906,
this stood at $121,455,747. During the year amortization was ef-
fected for $3,402,519, and by the operations of the conversion loan a
reduction of $12,083,350. Of the conversion loan $32,488,300 were

issued ($11,346,660 remaining to be issued), as also $164,414 of the amortizable debt, second series. This leaves the net total of the public debt on January 1, 1907, at $127,275,933, an increase of $5,820,-126. The internal debts withdrawn under the conversion operations amounted to $12,304,050, and of this $6,001,560 were redeemed in cash, and $6,322,289 converted into bonds of the new loan with a cash bonus of 3 per cent. Owing to the reduced rate of interest the addition to the annual debt service is about one-half million dollars.

NEW CABINET.

The cabinet selected by President WILLIMAN, the recently inaugurated Executive of Uruguay, has the following personnel: Minister of the Interior, Señor Don ALVARO GUILLOT; Minister of Foreign Affairs, Señor Don JACOBO VARELA; Minister of Public Instruction, Señor Don GABRIEL TERRA; Minister of War, General EDUARDO VASQUEZ, and Minister of Public Works, Señor Don LAMOLLE.

IMMIGRATION LAW.

Concerning immigration service.

ARTICLE 1. On and after the promulgation of this law, the immigration service annexed to the Department of Stockraising and Agriculture, in accordance with the law of December 6, 1896, is discontinued.

The corresponding section shall continue in operation as part of the Bureau of Colonization.

ART. 2. The administrative immigration service shall be under the direction of a board composed of five members, with their respective substitutes, who shall hold office for three years, and are eligible for reelection. The office of member of the board is honorary.

ART. 3. The Honorary Immigration Board shall be under the immediate direction of the Department of Fomento.

ART. 4. For the purpose of transacting the business of the Bureau the Executive shall appoint, on the recommendation of the Board, the necessary personnel, having the salaries assigned in the General Budget of Expenses.

The personnel shall be removable at the request of the Board.

ACT. 5. The expenses of the immigration service shall be paid, in the first instance, out of the receipts from the tax on passage tickets created by the present law, and any deficit that may result shall be provided for in the corresponding General Budget of Expenses.

ncerning the duties of the Board.

:ral duties of the Board are those specified in the
80, governing the former Bureau of Immigration
'ontained in chapters 1, 2, 4, 5, and 6.
transact all business and 'exercise all the inherent
) the performance of its general duties, the extent
, modify in each case in conformity with the expediency
ie moment, the circumstances of the case, and the instructions
en by the Department of Fomento with the object of facilitating a
'nt of industrious immigrants, and of properly lodging and
ing them employment.

ART. 7. The Honorary Immigration Board may communicate directly with the administrative and judicial authorities of the country, and with the bureaus of departments as well as with the diplomatic representatives and consuls on matters relating to immigration, and said functionaries shall furnish without delay such data, information, and assistance as may be required.

ART. 8. The Board shall communicate its instructions direct to the consuls and consular agents of the Republic in order that they may comply with their duty in furnishing the information and in making the propaganda required of such officers in accordance with chapter 1 of the law of June 18, 1890, subject to the limitations and restrictions prescribed therein.

The Board shall also send to the consuls blank forms of certificates of fitness that must be issued in conformity with the provisions of article 2 (paragraph 4) and article 9 of said law.

The Board shall report to the Department of Foreign Relations any delay, neglect, or failure committed by consuls in their capacity as information and propaganda agents.

ART. 9. The Board shall prepare instructions for immigrants, giving such data, information, and suggestions as may be of interest to them; shall print said instructions in Spanish, have them translated into other languages and widely distributed in European centers of population.

ART. 10. The Honorary Immigration Committee, composed of the governor, chairman of the administrative board, the district judge, and three citizens appointed by the said functionaries for the purpose of attending to immigration matters in their respective departments, in cooperation with the Honorary Board at Montevideo, is hereby established.

ART. 11. The correspondence of the Honorary Board of Immigration, that of the departmental committees, as well as that received from immigrants or persons in the interior who need their cooperation, and also that directed to or received from persons lodged in the Immigrants Hotel during their stay there, shall be considered official.

Concerning the Immigrants Hotel.

The Honorable Board of Immigration shall, immediately after its formation, proceed to open the Immigrants Hotel, intended for the use of immigrants and their families who come to the Republic.

Free lodging may be had for fifteen days, after the expiration of which time permission to remain will be extended five days, at the rate of 25 cents a day per person over 12 years of age and 15 cents a day per person under 12 years of age.

ART. 13. Immigrants shall be furnished at the hotel with lodging, food, hygienic care, medical attendance, and medicine.

ART. 14. In case of sickness at the Immigrants Hotel, board and medical attendance at the hotel shall be for account of the State, even though the time granted may have expired.

ART. 15. The landing inspector shall personally direct the official and free landing not included in the category of the rejected clause (articles 26 and 27 of the law of 1890, amended by the law of June 23, 1906) and shall see to the comfortable landing of the persons and the proper landing of their baggage.

The unloading inspector shall utilize the river steamers in this service.

ART. 16. The Board shall submit to the Executive Power the rules and regulations for the organization, administration, and government of the hotel.

The prohibitive provisions adopted shall be strictly observed, the infringer or violator being subject to such penalties as may be prescribed in the rules and regulations, and which shall be enforced through administrative channels.

Revenues for immigration service.

ART. 17. To defray the expenses of the service, a tax or stamp, called the immigration tax or stamp, is hereby created. This shall be affixed to the tickets of all passengers going to foreign ports by sea or river, with the exception of Argentine, Paraguayan, and Brazilian ports.

ART. 18. Said tax shall also be applicable to tickets acquired abroad, but which may be used in traveling through the Republic to the taxable foreign ports designated in the preceding article.

ART. 19. The passage tax shall be as follows, and applies to all European ports without distinction of countries:

First-class passage	$5
Second-class passage	3
Third-class passage	1

G of the office of direct taxes shall deliver to the
f Immigration a correct account of the stamps nec-
d shall distribute them to the steamship agencies,
themselves, without preventing either the agencies
from acquiring them at the general office or duly
s.

amship agencies shall keep an account of the pas-
·dance with the form furnished by the board, and
a m·   ily statement thereof to Bureau G of the office of
taxes.

т. 22. The impost stamps on each ticket shall be canceled with a
p perforator showing the date of the passage.

ʀт. 23. The owner or holder of a passage ticket not in accordance
with the conditions specified in the foregoing article shall be subject
to a fine.

Aʀт. 24. Bureau G of the office of direct taxes shall deliver monthly
to the Honorary Board of Immigration the receipts from the sale of
stamps, which shall be applied, in the first instance, to the payment of
the budget (art. 5).

Aʀт. 25. The consuls of the Republic in foreign ports shall remit
monthly to Bureau G of the office of direct taxes statements of passengers landed, which statements shall serve to check the lists of the
agencies.

Aʀт. 26. Each violation of the provisions concerning this tax on
the part of agencies, owners, or possessors of tickets, or by those aiding in their acquisition, shall be subject to a fine of $200, collectible
through administrative channels.

Half the amount of the fine shall go to the informer and the other
half to the reserve fund of the Immigrant's Hotel.

Aʀт. 27. Should it be necessary to obtain and execute a judgment
by the sale of property, the infringer shall be punished to the full
extent of the law.

General and supplementary provisions.

Aʀт. 28. The Honorary Board of Immigration shall grant to
navigation companies the largest privileges and immunities that
ships which transport immigrants should enjoy in Uruguayan ports,
in conformity with the provisions of chapter 4 of said law.

For the location of immigrants and their transportation for
account of the State to the interior of our territory, the Board shall
likewise confer with the fluvial and river transportation companies
in accordance with the provisions of this law. None of these agreements or arrangements shall be put in force without the approval
of the President.

ART. 29. The Honorable Immigration Board shall also submit special rules and regulations concerning the inspection of immigrants and the duties of the landing inspector prescribed in articles 26 and 31 of the law of 1880, already partially regulated by executive decrees of December 10, 1894, and August 10 and November 16, 1900.

Likewise the provisions of the law of June 23, 1906, shall also be borne in mind.

ART. 30. The Board shall also render to National Auditing Office G a monthly account of the funds handled in the same form and by the same methods as that employed in the distribution of other public funds.

ART. 31. After all the expenses of the immigration service have been covered, should any excess exist, the Board shall preferably employ it in useful works and services toward the encouragement of immigration to the country.

ART. 32. The Board shall submit to the President a comprehensive annual report of the administrative and financial work entrusted to it.

ART. 33. Until expense budget G is approved, the following provisional budget for the service of the Board and the maintenance of the Immigrants' Hotel, shall govern:

	Monthly.		Monthly.
Rent of building for hotel	$250	Three servants, at $20 each	$60
Manager	150	Gardener and stable and carriage man, etc	70
Secretary	60		
Auditor-treasurer	100	Laborer	20
Three clerks, at $40 each	120	Coal, light, and other expenses	150
Doctor	50	Meat and other provisions for 250 persons	1,000
Assistant to doctor	40		
Landing inspector and interpreter to go aboard	120	Unforseen expenses	230
Two cooks	70	Total	2,510
Assistant cook	20		

ART. 34. The assigning of the offices abolished in the budget of the section of Immigration and Colonization of the Department of Stock-Raising and Agriculture (Table 14) shall be added to the resources of the new service created by this law.

ART. 35. All laws and provisions contrary to the present law are hereby repealed.

ART. 36. Let it be communicated, etc.

ALFONSO PACHECO.

)m customs reported for the Uruguayan Republic
10ttn of January, 1907, aggregated $1,095,635.25, of
.453.75 are credited to imports; $117,181.50 to exports,
1.J (estimated) to posts' duties.

1 .J of $25,000 over the same month of 1906 is shown,
.J returns for the seven months' period, July–January,
shows an advance of $2,167,390.50 over the same period ten
previous.

VENEZUELA.

CUSTOMS MODIFICATIONS, 1905, 1906.

I.—*Ordinance of May 29, 1905, respecting the classification of cash-registering machines.*

[*"Diario Oficial"* No. 126, of May 31, 1905.]

Cash-registering machines shall be classed in No. 340 of the tariff,
at the duty rate of 30 *centavos* per kilogram.

II.—*Ordinance dated June 13, 1905, relating to lard originating from the Central American Republics.*

[*"Diario Oficial"* No. 138, of June 14, 1905.]

Lard originating from the Central American Republics shall on
importation be admitted duty free. This privileged treatment shall
be applicable during three months from the date of the present
ordinance. In order to receive the benefit of this favor, persons
interested will have to produce certificates of origin legalized by the
competent authorities.

III.—*Ordinance of June 15, 1905, relating to lard proceeding from the United States and Mexico.*

[*"Diario Oficial"* No. 140, of June 16, 1905.]

The exemption granted by ordinance of June 13, 1905, shall also
apply to lard imported from the United States and Mexico; during
three months it shall be admitted free of the duties and taxes applicable thereto. Lard originating from these two countries, and also
from Central American ports, shall previously be submitted to a
chemical analysis and can only be admitted duty free if found to be
sufficiently pure.

IV.—*Ordinance of July 13, 1905, relating to the exemption applicable to hypochlorite of lime.*

[*"Diario Oficial"* No. 163, of July 13, 1905.]

Hypochlorite of lime used as a disinfectant shall be exempted from all import and other duties.

V.—*Decree of August 21, 1905, as to the payment of customs duties and to the exportation of coffee.*

[*"Diario Oficial"* No. 194, of August 21, 1905.]

ARTICLE 1. From and after September 1, 1905, the proportion of import duties for the time being, levied in silver at the rate of 94 per cent of the duties, shall be reduced to 68 per cent, and the difference, namely, 26 per cent, shall be converted into 12 per cent of American gold, to be payable in specie or by sight bank drafts on the United States.

ART. 2. From and after November 1, 1907, the duty of 87½ *centavos* per 100 kilograms on exported coffee shall be substituted by a duty of 45 *centavos* in American gold, also payable in the form stated in article 1 above.

VI.—*Ordinance dated January 18, 1906, relating to the customs treatment of tin plates.*

[*"Diario Oficial"* No. 16, of January 19, 1906.]

Tin plate in varnished, gilt, or enameled sheets, whether plain or with embossed ornaments, shall be classed in No. 105, at the rate of 10 *centavos* per kilogram.

VII.—*Ordinance of January 24, 1906, fixing the duty on paper and cardboard for lithography.*

[*"Diario Oficial"* No. 21, of January 25, 1906.]

Paper and cardboard for lithography shall be erased from tariff No. 150, and classed in No. 154, like other similar articles for printing, at 10 *centavos* per kilogram. This rule applies also to stocks on hand.

VIII.—*Ordinance dated February 20, 1906, granting duty-free importation to sheepskins from the Central American Republics.*

[*"Diario Oficial"* No. 44, of February 21, 1906.]

Raw sheepskins, the origin of Central American Republics, intended to be tanned in the country, shall be admitted free of all import and other duties.

*f March 2, 1906, fixing the duty on tissue labels to be
d to clothing for indicating maker's*

["*Diario Oficial*" No. 53, of March 3, 1906.]

issue used to indicate the name of tailors, to be sewn on
.ning, ul be comprised in No. 15 of the tariff and pay
;am, no account being taken whether they are of cotton, linen,
, silk, or any other material, and whether embroidered or not.

*—Ordinance of April 18, 1906, establishing the customs treatment of
certain cloth.*

["*Diario Oficial*" No. 90, of April 19, 1906.]

By way of assimilation, linen or cotton cloth, whether oiled or covered with paper, for painters and draftsmen, and oilcloth for school
slates, unenumerated in the tariff, shall, as to the former, be charged
with a duty of 20 *centavos*, and as to the latter 5 *centavos*, under tariff
Nos. 155 and 373.

XI.— *Ordinance of April 19, 1906, exempting from duty unbarbed fence
wire.*

["*Diario Oficial*" No. 91, of April 20, 1906.]

By assimilation to barbed fence wire, unbarbed fence wire, Page's
system, manufactured in sections of from 100 to 200 meters in length,
ready for use, is exempt from all import and other duties.

XII.—*Decree dated April 30, 1906, modifying the customs treatment
of certain goods.*

[" *Diario Oficial*," No. 101, of May 2, 1906.]

ARTICLE 1. The following goods shall be dutiable as follows:

	Pesos.
Cotton tissues of all kinds, white or bleached, of which the plain tissue has not been altered, common, containing up to 20 threads in warp or woof, in a space of 7 millimeters (one-fourth foot).	0.40
The same tissues containing over 20 threads in the conditions above stated.	1.00
Lace, insertions, ornaments, galloons, and trimmings embroidered with cotton, of any width not exceeding 25 centimeters.	1.00
The same, having over 25 centimeters in width.	3.00
"Brin" or "bramante" for packing, containing up to 6 threads in warp or woof in a space of 7 millimeters (one-fourth foot).	.05
If such tissues contain more than 6 threads, under the conditions stated above, they will be classed in No. 22 of the tariff in force.	
Nonmilled silk in skeins, and milled silk on wooden or cardboard spools for weaving looms, provided the latter be of the Spanish description of silk of one or two strands.	.25
Coleta of pure or mixed linen.	.60

Pesos.

Tissues: Burat, crape, piqué or other tissues of silk pure or mixed in any proportion, and of whatever quality, for use in the manufacture of shawls, mufflers, tissues and mantles of any kind, size or shape; milled silk of any thickness in skein, for sewing, embroidering, or any other purpose; shawls, mufflers, mantles, fichus, and semifichus, and all similar articles for women, plain, figured or embroidered, of whatever shape and mixture; galloons, ribbons, nettings, ornaments, and fringes, of pure or mixed silk, for shawls, fichus and other similar wearing apparel specified in this number 7. 00

Revolvers, .38 bore or less... 3. 00

ART. 2. With the view of facilitating examination of the cotton goods and "brin" or "bramante" referred to in the present decree, importers must specify in their consular invoices, the number of threads which such tissues contain in warp or woof in the abovementioned space; this rule shall apply as regards the measure of lace, insertions, ornaments, galloons, and edgings.

ART. 3. Nos. 8, 13, 15, 18, 22, 45, 46, 48, 49, 52, and 389, of the tariff in force are modified in accordance with article 1.

ART. 4. The present decree shall be applicable forty days after the date of its publication.

XIII.—*Ordinance of May 8, 1906, relating to the importation of iron bridges.*

["*Diario Oficial*," No. 106, of May 8, 1906.]

Importation of iron bridges by private persons is exempt from all import and other duties.

XIV.—*Ordinance dated May 8, 1906, as to the classification of marble statues, etc.*

["*Diario Oficial*," No. 106, of May 10, 1906.]

The duty of 2 *centavos* on statues, etc., of marble, alabaster, porphyry, jasper, granite, and other similar stones, shall apply to those measuring in height 50 centimeters or upward. Tariff No. 344 is amended accordingly. The present ordinance shall enter into force on the day of its publication.

XV.—*Ordinance of May 31, 1906, extending the limit for the duty-free admission of apparatus for employing denaturated alcohol.*

["*Diario Oficial*," No. 128, of June 2, 1906.]

This ordinance extends for one year the time limit allowed by the law of April 21, 1904, for the duty-free admission of apparatus and implements for employing denaturating alcohol, such as lamps, cooking stoves, heaters for various household and industrial purposes, vessels,

ll kinds of machines, and generally any unenumer-
:h alcohol is used as fuel, or for illuminating pur-
ver.

*ice dated August 10, 1906, relating to the classification
of jute, cocoanut, or hemp carpets.*

["*Diario Oficial,*" No. 187, of August 11, 1906.]

'pets of jute, cocoanut, or hemp are dutiable under No. 286 at 10
'os per kilogram.

II.—*Ordinance of September 27, 1906, modifying the tariff items
affecting aluminium goods.*

["*Diario Oficial,*" No. 227, of September 28, 1906.[

Nos. 116 to 118 are modified as follows:

		Pesos.
nium:		
6. Bars, sheets, wire, powder, and cooking utensils	kilos	0.50
117. Pens, table services, and other objects not specified	do	.80
118. Wares of all kinds, with ornaments or attachments or some other metal of finer quality	kilos	2.00

The present ordinance shall enter into effect on the date of its publication.

XVIII.—*Ordinance dated October 10, 1906, assessing with duty mineral
or aerated water bottle stoppers.*

["*Diario Oficial,*" No. 238, of October 11, 1906.]

Stoppers of gutta-percha or any other material provided with a
notch or screw used in connection with mineral or aerated water bottles are dutiable under tariff No. 413 at the rate of 1 *centavo* per
kilogram.

XIX.—*Ordinance dated October 10, 1906, as to the régime applicable
to machines classed in tariff Nos. 101 and 339.*

["*Diario Oficial,*" No. 238, of October 11, 1906.]

The machines classed in tariff Nos. 101 and 339, including their
duplicate parts and attachments are exempted from the payment of
all import and other duties. This treatment shall not apply to any
kind of pipes and conduits required for the machines referred to.

XX.—*Ordinance of October 16, 1906, exempting from duty unbarbed iron fence wire.*

["*Diario Oficial,*" No. 243, of October 17, 1906.]

Unbarbed galvanized iron fence wire of two twisted ends is assimilated to barbed fence wire mentioned in tariff No. 100 and is free of all import and other duties.

I.—*Resolution of November 5, 1906, assessing duty on "platilla" (cotton tissue).*

["*Gaceta Oficial*" No. 9916, of November 5, 1906.]

Black or colored "platilla" (cotton tissue), generally used as lining for clothing, shall be assessed to duty under Class V of the tariff as white "platilla" of cotton classed in No. 394 of the customs tariff in force.

II.—*Resolution of November 5, 1906, relating to the classification of chrome alum and impure or denatured formic acid.*

["*Gaceta Oficial*" No. 9916, of November 5, 1906.]

The substances known under the name of "chrome alum (sulphate of aluminium and chrome)" and impure or denatured formic acid, for use in tanning hides, shall pay the import duties fixed in Class III of the tariff.

III.—*Resolution of November 5, 1906, respecting the treatment of vaporizer or sprayer receptacles.*

["*Gaceta Oficial*" No. 9916, of November 5, 1906.]

Vaporizer or sprayer receptacles, whether or not provided with parts of rubber, are to be dutiable under Class V, as also the same articles without any part of gold or silver, which are not specially mentioned in the tariff.

IV.—*Resolution dated November 19, 1906, fixing the duty applicable to "cotton serge or prunello."*

["*Gaceta Oficial*" No. 9929, of November 20, 1906.]

Cotton serge or prunello, generally used in the manufacture of footwear, and similar to the tissue known under the name of "alepin" shall, on importation, be dutiable according to Class VI of the tariff.

n of November 19, 1906, relating to naphtha.

iceta Oficial " No. 9929, of November 20, 1906.]

.ll, on importation, pay the duties of Class I of the

!esolution dated November 24, 1906, classifying for duty port-
able " Thermos " bottles.

[" *Gaceta Oficial "* No. 9933, of November 24, 1906.]

:tles known under the name of portable "Thermos" bottles
ised of a nickel receptacle similar in shape to a bottle, wholly
d with leather, shall be comprised in Class V under No. 411
he import tariff in force.

PORTO RICO.

Porto Rico, Governor: ... The report of the governor of Porto Rico ... Washington, Government Printing Office, 1906. 200 p. plates. 8°.

UNITED STATES.

Chicago public library: Thirty-fourth annual report of the Board of Directors of the Chicago public library. June, 1906. Chicago, The Chicago public library, 1906. 62 p. plates.

Field Columbian Museum: ... A catalogue of the collection of the mammals in the Field Columbian Museum by Daniel Girand Elliot ... Chicago, 1907. viii 604 p. plates. 8°.

Jackson, Sheldon: Fifteenth annual report on introduction of domestic reindeer into Alaska, with maps and illustrations, by Sheldon Jackson, general agent of education in Alaska, 1905. Washington, Government Printing Office, 1906. 174 p. maps. plates. illus. 8°. (Publication of the Bureau of Education.)

Memorial service in honor of Volney William Foster. Died August 15th, 1904 ... Held at the First Presbyterian Church, August 28th, 1904, Evanston, Illinois. Printed at the Lakeside Press by R. R. Donnelley & sons co., 1906. 46 p. 8°.

National convention for the extension of the foreign commerce of the United States: Programme, resolutions, and delegates. National convention ... called by the N. Y. Board of Trade and Transportation. New Willard Hotel, Washington, D. C., January 14th, 15th, and 16th, 1907. No imprint. nar. 8°.

Newberry library: Report of the trustees of the Newberry Library for the year 1906. Chicago, [1907]. front. 28 p. 8°.

Smithsonian institution: Report of the acting secretary of the Smithsonian institution for the year ending June 30, 1906. Washington, Government Printing Office, 1906. 91 p. 8°.

Thompson, Slason: Railway statistics of the U. S. of America for the year ending June 30, 1906. Compared with the official reports of 1905 and recent statistics of foreign railways. Prepared for the General Manager's Association of Chicago. By Slason Thompson, Bureau of railway news. Chicago, Gunthorp-Warren Printing company, 1907. 66 p. 8°.

United States Bureau of the Census: Census of manufactures, 1905. Petroleum refining. Washington, Government Printing Office, 1907. 57 p. plates. 4°. (pp. 29–57, "Digest of U. S. Patents relating to petroleum refining.)

——— **Interstate commerce commission:** 18th annual report on the state of railways in the U. S. for the year ending June 30, 1905. Prepared by the division of statistics and accounts. Washington, Government Printing Office, 1906. 728 p. map. 8°.

——— *Treaties, etc.:* ... Convention bet. the U. S. and the Dominican Republic providing for the assistance of the U. S. in the collection and application of the customs revenues of the Dominican Republic, signed at Santo Domingo city on the 8th day of February, 1907. [Washington, Government Printing Office, 1907.] 5 p. 8°.

——— ... Convention signed at Buenos Aires July 10, 1899, bet. the U. S. and the Argentine Republic, under authority of "An act to provide revenue for the government and to encourage the industries of the U. S." Approved July 24. 1897. [Washington, Government Printing Office, 1899.] 5 p. 8°.

ONAL BUREAU OF THE AMERICAN REPUBLICS.

Y OF SCIENCES: Directory of the . . . Academy . . . and
ocieties. Washington, D. C., Press of Judd & Detweiler,
8, 1907. 87 p. 8°.

URUGUAY.

on: Constitución de la república O. del Uruguay com-
i los documentos de la asamblea constituyente y las leyes
posteriores, con un repertorio de la misma constitución por Pablo
V. Goyena. 2ª edición. Montevideo, Imprenta "El Siglo Ilustrado,"
1900. 155, iii p. 24°.

JERAL WORKS, REFERENCE BOOKS, AND BIBLIOGRAPHIES.

DOS UNIDOS DE CENTRO AMÉRICA: Constitución política de los Estados
. Unidos de Centro América. Managua, Tip. Nacional, 1898. 55 p. 8°.
AT BRITAIN. Colonial reports. British Guiana. Report for 1905–6. Lon-
don, Darling & son, 1906. 44 p. ·8°.
———————Emigrants information office: Summary of consular reports,
1905–6. North and South America. Issued by the Emigrants
information office . .·. London, Darling & son, 1907. 138 p. 8°.
IKRNATIONAL AMERICAN CONFERENCE, 1906: Report of the delegates of the
United States to the Third international conference of the American
states held at Rio de Janeiro, Brazil, July .21 to August 26, 1906.
Washington, Government Printing Office, 1907. 180 p. 8°. (59th
Cong., 2d sess., Sen. doc. no. 365.)
INTERNATIONAL BUREAU OF THE AMERICAN REPUBLICS: Monthly Bulletin. Vol.
24, No. 2, February, 1907, Washington, Government Printing Office,
1907. Pp. 261–563, 8°.

CONTENTS.

Reception of Señor Don Enrique C. Creel, as Mexican Ambassador to
the United States.
New building for the Bureau of the American Republics.
The development of intellectual and educational relations between the
countries of America.
Dr. Jose Ignacio Rodriguez.
Tercentenary of English settlement in the United States.
Argentine Republic. Foreign trade, first nine months of 1906; trade
with Brazil; collection of crop statistics; national railway revenues;
customs receipts at Buenos Ayres, November and first eleven months
of 1906; immigration during November and first eleven months of
1906; railway mileage and gauge; railway consolidation; budget of
Buenos Ayres for 1907; census of Rosario; census of Bahia Blanca.
Bolivia. Commercial movement of various custom-houses.
Brazil. Foreign commerce, first nine months of 1906; customs revenues, first nine months of 1906; budget law and customs provisions
for 1907; rubber exports, 1905–6; coffee movement, November, 1906;
creation of conversion office; premiums offered to growers of cacao;
expulsion of foreigners; the Brazilian Lloyd; rubber forests in the
State of Piauhy; new department created; prizes offered for agricultural machinery; estimate of coffee crop for 1907–8; factories of
Bello Horizonte; exports from Pernambuco, November, 1906; immigration; tariff modification, 1906; commercial agreement with Italy;
improvement works at Para; contract for printing new notes; new
State loans; tariff surtax on merchandise; adherence to The Hague
convention.
Chile. Customs revenues, November and first eleven months of 1906;
discovery of deposits of graphite or plumbago; the rebuilding of Valparaiso; approval of immigration contract; uniformity of consular
reports; factory census of Santiago, 1906.
Colombia. Tariff modifications; prohibited exportation of silver and
gold coins; improvement of the Cauca and Nechi rivers.
Costa Rica. Tariff modifications; export trade of Puntarenas, April to
November, 1906.
Cuba. The public treasury on December 31, 1906; sugar crop of
1905–6; exports of tobacco during 1906; fiscal revenues during 1906;
concession for a submarine cable; extradition treaty with the Domin-
ican Republic; American and English capital in the Republic.
Ecuador. Inauguration of President Eloy Alfaro.
Guatamala. Concession for the exploitation of national forests.

and Michoacan; consular trade reports, January, 1907; the henequen market in 1906; customs revenues, January, 1907; postal receipts, November, 1907; copper mining in the Republic; quicksilver in the Republic; railroad concessions; railroad in the municipality of Mexico; railroad in the State of Veracruz.

Nicaragua. Arbitral award of the boundary question between Honduras and Nicaragua; concession of land and water privileges; increased price of public lands; budget for the years 1906 and 1907.

Panama. Trade with the United States; installation of telephones at Panama.

Paraguay. Budget estimates for 1907; postponement of agricultural exhibition; new stamp law.

Peru. Foreign commerce, first four months of 1906; exports to New York, first ten months of 1906; export duty on silver coins.

Salvador. Foreign commerce, first quarter, 1906; subsidy for German steamships; propaganda for Salvador coffee; qualifications for the practice of medicine.

United States. Trade with Latin America; foreign commerce, January, 1907; ratio of trade increase with Latin America; internal revenue, February, 1907; the leather industry in 1906; Army supervision of the Panama Canal construction; Philippine commerce in 1906; exports of manufactures, 1906; convention for the equitable distribution of waters of the Rio Grande.

Uruguay. The new President of the Republic; customs revenues, 1906; promotion of immigration; sealing regulations; additional duty on imports; the cereal and flax crop of 1905–6.

Venezuela. Commercial movement of the Republic during 1905–6.

Cacao production and consumption.

The world's copper output.

The world's wheat crop.

Library accessions and files.

PHILADELPHIA COMMERCIAL MUSEUM: Foreign trade figures. A collection of statistics covering some features of the World's commerce and indicating the share in it of the U. S. Issued by the Bureau of Information of the Philadelphia Commercial Museum. No imprint. 24 p. sq. 8°.

REINSCH, PAUL S.: The Third international conference of American states. [By] Paul S. Reinsch, member of the American Delegation. pp. 187–199. 8°. Caption title. (Reprinted from the American Political Science Review, February, 1907.)

MAPS.

CHILE. Arica. Por el "Almirante Condell." Comandante Sr. Neftalí Molina en 1905. . . . Publicado por la Oficina Hidrográfica, Valparaíso, junio de 1906. Escala 1 : 20,000. 16¼ x 22¼ inches.

———— Canales Mayne i Gray. Por la Marina de Chile hasta 1904. Publicado por la oficina hidrográfica, Valparaíso, marzo de 1906. Escala 1 : 30,000. 17½ x 30 inches.

COLOMBIA. Map of the valley of the river Magdalena, . . . showing line of Cartagena-Magdalena Railway, and its connections with the river service. n. d. 7¾ x 18 inches.

UNITED STATES. Maryland, District of Columbia, Virginia. Washington quadrangle. U. S. Geological survey. Edition of July 1900, reprinted, 1904. Scale 1 : 62,500. 17½ x 27½ in.

URUGUAY. Bahia de Montevideo. n. d. 5¾ x 6¾ inches.

PERMANENT LIBRARY FILES.

Those publications marked with an asterisk have no recent numbers on file.

Persons interested in the commercial and general news of foreign countries will find the following among the official and periodical publications on the permanent files in the Columbus Memorial Library, International Bureau of the American Republics:

ARGENTINE REPUBLIC.

Boletín de la Cámara Mercantil. Barracas al Sud. Weekly.
Boletín Consular. (Ministerio de relaciones exteriores.) Buenos Ayres. Irregular.
Boletín de la Unión Industrial Argentina. Buenos Ayres. Monthly.
*Boletín del Instituto Geográfico Argentino. Buenos Ayres.
*Boletín Demográfico Argentino. Buenos Ayres. Monthly.
Boletín Oficial de la República Argentina. Buenos Ayres. Daily.
Boletín de Precios Corrientes. [Buenos Aires.] Weekly.
Bollettino Mensile della Camera Italiana di Commercio ed Arti in Buenos Aires. Buenos Ayres. Monthly.
Buenos Aires Handels-Zeitung. Buenos Ayres. Weekly.
Buenos Aires Herald. Buenos Ayres. Daily and weekly.
*El Comercio Exterior Argentino. Buenos Ayres.
La Ilustración Sud-Americana. Buenos Ayres. Semimonthly.
Monthly Bulletin of Municipal Statistics of the City of Buenos Ayres. Buenos Ayres. Monthly.
La Nación. Buenos Ayres. Daily.
Patentes y Marcas, Revista Sud-Americana de la Propiedad Intelectual é Industrial. Buenos Ayres. Monthly.
La Prensa. Buenos Ayres. Daily.
Review of the River Plate. Buenos Ayres. Weekly.
Revista Mensual de la Cámara Mercantil. Barracas al Sud. Monthly.
Revista de Derecho, Historia y Letras. Buenos Aires. Monthly.
Revista Nacional. Buenos Ayres. Monthly.
The Standard. Buenos Ayres. Mail supplement.

BELGIUM.

Recueil consulaire. Bruxelles. Quarterly.

BOLIVIA.

*Boletín de la Oficina Nacional de Inmigración, Estadística y Propaganda Geográfica. La Paz. Quarterly.
Boletín de la Sociedad Geográfica de la Paz. La Paz. Irregular.
El Comercio. La Paz. Daily.
El Estado. (Diario Oficial.) La Paz. Daily.
*Revista Comercial é Industrial de la República de Bolivia. La Paz. Monthly.
Revista del Ministerio de Colonización y Agricultura. La Paz. Quarterly.

BRAZIL.

Boletim da Agricultura. Secretario·da Agricultura, Comercio e Obras Publicas do Estado de São Paulo. Sao Paulo. Monthly.
Boletim do Museo Goeldi. Pará. Irregular.
Boletim da Secretaria de Agricultura, Viação, Industria e Obras Publicas do Estado da Bahia. Bahia. Monthly.
*Boletim de Serviço da Estatistica Commercial da Republica dos Estados Unidos do Brazil. Rio de Janeiro. Irregular.
*Brazilian Mining Review. Ouro Preto. Irregular.
Brazilian Review. Rio de Janeiro. Weekly.
Diario da Bahia. Bahia. Daily.
Diario do Congresso Nacional. Rio de Janeiro. Daily.
Diario Oficial. Rio de Janeiro. Daily.
*Gazeta Commercial e Financeira. Rio de Janeiro. Weekly.
*Jornal do Commercio. Rio de Janeiro. Daily.
Jornal do Recife. Pernambuco. Daily.
Jornal dos Agricultores. Rio de Janeiro. Semimonthly.
O Paiz. Rio de Janeiro. Daily.
Provincia (A) do Pará. Belem. Daily.
Revista Agricola. Sao Paulo. Monthly.
Revista Maritima Brazileira. Rio de Janeiro. Monthly.

CHILE.

Anales de La Universidad. Santiago. Monthly.
Boletín del Ministerio de Relaciones Esteriores. Santiago. Monthly.
Boletín de la Sociedad Agrícola del Sur. Concepción. Semimonthly.
Boletín de la Sociedad de Fomento Fabril. Santiago. Monthly.
Boletín de la Sociedad Nacional de Agricultura. Santiago. Weekly.
Boletín de la Sociedad Nacional de Minería. Santiago. Monthly.
Chilian Times. Valparaiso. Semiweekly.
*Diario Oficial de la República de Chile. Santiago. Daily.
El Mercurio. Valparaiso. Daily.
El Noticiero Comercial. Santiago de Chile. Monthly.
El Pensamiento. Santiago. Monthly.
*Revista Comercial ó Industrial de Minas. Santiago. Monthly.

COLOMBIA.

Diario Oficial. Bogotá. Daily.
Revista de la Instrucción Pública de Colombia. Bogotá. Monthly.

COSTA RICA.

Boletín Judicial. San Jose. Daily.
La Gaceta. [Diario Oficial.] San Jose. Daily.

CUBA.

Boletín Oficial de la Cámara de Comercio, Industria y Navegación de la Isla de Cuba. Habana. Monthly.
Boletín Oficial del Departamento del Estado. Habana. Monthly.
Derecho y Sociología. Habana. Monthly.
El Estudio. Boletín de Derecho, Legislación, Jurisprudencia y Administración. Habana. Trimonthly.
La Gaceta Económica. Habana. Semimonthly.
Gaceta Oficial de la República de Cuba. Habana. Daily.

Informe Mensual Sanitario y Demográfico de la República de Cuba. Habana. Monthly.
Informe Mensual Sanitario y Demográfico de Cienfuegos. Cienfuegos. Monthly.
Informe Mensual Sanitario y Demográfico de Matanzas. Matanzas. Monthly.
Revista Municipal y de Intereses Económicos. Habana. Semimonthly.

DOMINICAN REPUBLIC.

Gaceta Oficial. Santo Domingo. Weekly.
Revista de Agricultura. Santo Domingo. Monthly.

ECUADOR.

Anales de la Universidad Central del Ecuador. Quito. Monthly.
Gaceta Municipal. Guayaquil. Weekly.
Registro Oficial de la República del Ecuador. Quito. Daily.

GREAT BRITAIN.

Board of Trade Journal. London. Weekly.
Commercial Intelligence. London. Weekly.
Diplomatic and Consular Reports. London.
Geographical Journal. London. Monthly.
Mining (The) Journal, Railway and Commercial Gazette. London. Weekly.
The Scottish Geographical Magazine. Edinburgh. Monthly.
South American Journal. London. Weekly.
Times (The). London. Daily. (Filed for one year.)
Tropical Life. London. Monthly.

FRANCE.

L'Amérique Latine. Paris. Daily.
Les Annales Diplomatiques et Consulaires. Paris. Monthly.
Le Brésil. Paris. Weekly.
Bulletin American Chamber of Commerce. Paris. Monthly.
Bulletin de la Chambre de Commerce de Paris. Paris. Weekly.
Bulletin de la Société de Géographie Commerciale de Paris. Paris. Irregular.
La Géographie. Bulletin de la Société de Géographie. Paris. Semimonthly.
Journal d'Agriculture Tropicale. Paris. Monthly.
Moniteur Officiel du Commerce. Paris. Weekly.
Le Nouveau Monde. Paris. Weekly.
Rapports commerciaux des agents diplomatiques et consulaires de France. Paris. Irregular. [Sup. to "Moniteur Officiel du Commerce."]
La Revue. Paris. Semimonthly.
*Revue du Commerce Extérieur. Paris. Semimonthly.

GERMANY.

Berichte über Handel und Industrie. Berlin. Irregular.
*Deutsche Kolonialzeitung. Berlin. Weekly.
Petermann's Mitteilungen. Gotha. Monthly.
Südamerikanische Rundschau. Berlin. Monthly.
Der Tropenpflanzer. Berlin. Monthly.
Zeitschrift der Gesellschaft für Erdkunde zu Berlin. Berlin. Monthly.

GUATEMALA.

Boletín de Agricultura. Guatemala. Irregular.
El Guatemalteco. Guatemala. Daily. (Diario Oficial.)
La Locomotora. Guatemala. Monthly.
*La República. Guatemala. Daily.

HAITI.

*Bulletin Officiel de l'Agriculture et de l'Industrie. Port au Prince. Monthly.
*Le Moment. (Journal politique.) Port au Prince, Haiti. Weekly.
Le Moniteur. (Journal officiel de la République d'Haiti.) Port au Prince, Haiti. Biweekly.
Revue de la Société de Législation. Port au Prince, Haiti. Monthly.

HONDURAS.

Boletín Legislativo. Tegucigalpa. Daily.
El Estado. Tegucigalpa. (3 nos. per week.)
La Gaceta. Tegucigalpa. Daily. (Official paper.)
*Gaceta Judicial. Tegucigalpa. Semiweekly.
*El Pabellón de Honduras. Tegucigalpa. Weekly.
*El Republicano. (Semi-official.) Tegucigalpa. Three times a week.
Revista del Archivo y Biblioteca Nacional de Honduras. Tegucigalpa, Honduras. Monthly.

ITALY.

Bollettino del Ministro degli Affari Esteri. Roma. Irregular.

MEXICO.

El Agricultor Mexicano. Ciudad Juarez. Monthly.
Anales del Museo Nacional de México. Mexico. Monthly.
Boletín de Estadística. Merida. Semimonthly.
Boletín del Instituto Científico y Literario. Toluca. Monthly.
Boletín Oficial del Distrito sur de la Baja California. La Paz. Weekly.
Boletín de la Secretaría de Fomento, colonización é industria. Mexico. Monthly.
Boletín Oficial de la Secretaría de Relaciones Exteriores. Mexico. Monthly.
Diario Oficial. Mexico. Daily.
El Economista Mexicano. Mexico. Weekly.
*El Estado de Colima. Colima. Weekly.
El Hacendado Mexicano. Mexico. Monthly.
Mexican Herald. Mexico. Daily. (Filed for one year.)
Mexican Investor. Mexico. Weekly.
Mexican Journal of Commerce. Mexico City. Monthly.
Periódico Oficial del Gobierno del Estado de Guerrero. Chilpancingo. Mexico. Weekly.
Periódico Oficial del Gobierno del Estado de Michoacán de Ocampo. Morelia. Mexico. Semiweekly.
*Periódico Oficial del Gobierno del Estado de Oaxaca. Oaxaca de Juarez, Mexico. Semiweekly.
Periódico Oficial del Gobierno del Estado de Tabasco. San Juan Bautista, Mexico. Semiweekly.
El Republicano. Aguascalientes. Weekly.
Semana Mercantil. Mexico. Weekly.

NICARAGUA.

The American. Bluefields. Weekly.
El Comercio. Managua. Daily.
Diario Oficial. Managua. Daily.

PANAMA.

Gaceta Oficial. Panama. Daily.
Star and Herald. Panama. Weekly.

*La República. Panama. Weekly.
Registro Judicial, Organo del Poder Judicial de la República. Panama. Irregular.

PARAGUAY.

*Boletín Quincenal de la Cámara de Comercio de la Asunción. Asuncion. Semimonthly.
Diario Oficial. Asuncion. Daily.
Paraguay Rundschau. Asuncion. Weekly.
*Revista del Instituto Paraguayo. Asuncion. Monthly.
Revue Commerciale. Assumption. Semimonthly.

PERU.

Auxiliar del Comercio. Callao. Biweekly.
Boletín de Minas, Industrias y Construcciones. Lima. Monthly.
Boletín del Ministerio de Fomento. Dirección de Fomento. Lima. Monthly.
——— Dirección de Obras Públicas. Lima. Monthly.
Boletín de la Sociedad Geográfica de Lima. Lima. Quarterly.
Boletín de la Sociedad Nacional de Agricultura. Lima. Monthly.
Boletín de la Sociedad Nacional de Minería. Lima. Monthly.
* El Economista. Lima. Weekly.
* El Peruano. (Diario Oficial.) Lima. Daily.
Padrón General de Minas. Lima. Semiannual.
Revista de Ciencias. Lima. Monthly.
Revista Pan-Americana. Lima. Monthly.

PHILIPPINE ISLANDS.

Boletín de la Cámara de Comercio Filipina. Manila. Monthly.
El Mercantil. Manila. Daily.
Official Gazette. Manila. Weekly. (Also issued in Spanish.)

PORTO RICO.

La Correspondencia de Puerto Rico. San Juan. Daily.

EL SALVADOR.

Anales del Museo Nacional. San Salvador. Monthly.
Boletín de Agricultura. San Salvador. Semimonthly.
Boletín de la Dirección General de Estadística. San Salvador. Irregular.
Diario del Salvador. San Salvador. Daily.
Diario Oficial. San Salvador. Daily.
* Revista de Derecho y Jurisprudencia. San Salvador. Monthly.

UNITED STATES.

American Druggist. New York. Semimonthly.
American Exporter. New York. Semimonthly. (Alternate Spanish and English editions.)
American Historical Review. New York. Quarterly.
American Made Goods. New York. Quarterly.
American Review of Reviews. New York. Monthly.
Annals of the American Academy of Political and Social Science. Philadelphia. Bimonthly.
El Boletín Comercial. St. Louis. Monthly.
Bookman (The). New York. Monthly.
Bulletin of the American Geographical Society. New York.
Bulletin of Books added to the Public Library of the City of Boston. Boston. Monthly.

graphical Society of Philadelphia. Philadelphia. Monthly.
York Public Library. Monthly.
ew York. Semimonthly. (Alternate Spanish and English

New York. Monthly.
York. Monthly.
New York. Monthly.
N York. Weekly.
ernational edition. New York. Monthly.
ine. New York. Monthly.
ning Journal. New York. Weekly.
-    New York. Weekly.
nent Age. Philadelphia. Monthly.
—..... ..... Importers Journal. New York. Monthly.
bian Museum Publications. Chicago.
.... .e). New York. Quarterly.
Independent (The). New York. Weekly.
ber World. New York. Monthly.
. Geography. New York. Monthly.
. Library I nal. New York. Monthly.
New York. Weekly.
eview. Chicago. Monthly.
Scranton, Pa. Monthly.
York. Monthly.
Weekly.
..... Mexico. St. Louis. Monthly.
Monthly Consular and Trade Reports. (Department of Commerce and Labor.
Washington. Monthly.
National Geographic Magazine. New York. Monthly.
North American Review. New York. Monthly.
Las Novedades. New York. Weekly.
Outlook (The). New York. Weekly.
Pan-American Review. New York. Monthly.
Patent and Trade Mark Review. New York. Monthly.
Records of the Past. Washington, D. C. Monthly.
Scientific American. New York. Weekly.
Scientific American. Export Edition. New York. Monthly.
Sister Republics. Denver, Colo. Monthly.
Tea and Coffee Trade Journal. New York. Monthly.
*Technical World (The). Chicago. Monthly.
United States Tobacco Journal. New York. Weekly.
World To-day (The). Chicago. Monthly.
World's Work. New York. Monthly.

URUGUAY.

Anales del Departamento de Ganadería y Agricultura. Montevideo. Monthly
*Montevideo Times. Montevideo. Daily.
Revista de la Asociación Rural del Uruguay. Montevideo. Monthly.
Revista de la Unión Industrial Uruguaya. Montevideo. Semimonthly.

VENEZUELA.

Boletín de Estadística. Caracas. Monthly.
El Fonógrafo. Maracaibo. Daily.
El Heraldo Industrial. Caracas. Semimonthly.
Gaceta Oficial. Caracas. Daily.
*Venezuelan Herald. Caracas.

HONORARY CORRESPONDING MEMBERS OF THE INTERNATIONAL UNION OF AMERICAN REPUBLICS.

Countries.	Names.	Residence.
Argentine Republic..	Señor Dr. Don Estanislao S. Zeballos.......	Buenos Ayres.
Bolivia..............	Señor Don Manuel V. Balliviána..........	La Paz.
Brazil..............	Dezembargador Antonio Bezerra...........	Pará.
	Firmino da Silva.....................	Florianopolis.
Chile...............	Señor Don Moisés Vargas.................	Santiago.
Colombia...........	Señor Don Rufino Gutiérrez..............	Bogotá.
Costa Rica..........	Señor Don Manuel Aragón................	San José.
Cuba...............	Señor Don Antonio S. de Bustamante......	Havana.
	Señor Don Lincoln de Zayas..............	Havana.
Dominican Republic.	Señor Don José Gabriel Garcíab..........	Santo Domingo.
Ecuador............	Señor Don Francisco Andrade Marín.......	Quito.
	Señor Don Luis Alberto Carbo............	Guayaquil.
Guatemala..........	Señor Don Antonio Batres Jáuregui........	Guatemala City.
	Señor Don Rafael Montúfar...............	Guatemala City.
Haiti...............	Monsieur Georges Sylvain................	Port au Prince.
Honduras..........	Señor Don E. Constantino Fiallos.........	Tegucigalpa.
Mexico.............	Señor Don Francisco L. de la Barra.......	City of Mexico.
	Señor Don Antonio García Cubas..........	City of Mexico.
	Señor Don Fernando Ferrari Pérez........	City of Mexico.
Nicaragua..........	Señor Don José D. Gámez.................	Managua.
Paraguay...........	Señor Don José S. Decoud................	Asunción.
Panama............	Señor Don Samuel Lewis.................	Panama.
	Señor Don Ramón M. Valdés..............	Panama.
Peru...............	Señor Don Alejandro Garland.............	Lima.
Salvador............	Señor Dr. Don Salvador Gallegos.........	San Salvador.
Uruguay............	Señor Don José I. Schiffiano..............	Montevideo.
Venezuela..........	Señor General Don Manuel Landaeta Rosales.	Caracas.
	Señor Don Francisco de Paula Alamo.......	Caracas.

a Honorary corresponding member of the Royal Geographical Society of Great Britain.
b Corresponding member of the Academia Nacional de la Historia de Venezuela

IAN REPRESENTATIVES IN THE UNITED STATES.

AMBASSADORS EXTRAORDINARY AND PLENIPOTENTIARY.

ll..............................Mr. Joaquim Nabuco,
Office of Embassy, 1710 H street, Washington, D. C.

xico..............................Señor Don Enrique C. Creel,
Office of Embassy, 1115 I street, Washington, D. C.

ENVOYS EXTRAORDINARY AND MINISTERS PLENIPOTENTIARY.

Argentine Republic ....Señor Don Epifanio Portela,
Office of Legation, 2108 Sixteenth street, Washington, D. C.

Bolivia ....Señor Don Ignacio Calderón,
Office of Legation, 1633 Sixteenth street, Washington, D. C.

Chile..............................Señor Don Joaquín Walker-Martínez,
Absent.

Colombia..............................Señor Don Enrique Cortes,
Office of Legation, 1312 Twenty-first street NW., Washington D. C.

Costa Rica..............................Señor Don Joaquín Bernardo Calvo,
Office of Legation, 1329 Eighteenth street NW., Washington, D. C.

Cuba..............................Señor Don Gonzalo de Quesada,
Office of Legation, "The Wyoming," Washington, D. C.

Ecuador..............................Señor Don Luis Felipe Carbo,
Absent. Office of Legation, 1222 Connecticut avenue, Washington, D. C.

Guatemala..........................Señor Dr. Don Luis Toledo Herrarte,
Office of Legation, "The Highlands," Washington, D. C.

Haiti..............................Mr. J. N. Léger,
Office of Legation, 1429 Rhode Island avenue, Washington, D. C.

Honduras ....Señor Dr. Don José Rosa Pacas,
Absent.

Nicaragua ....Señor Don Luis F. Corea,
Office of Legation, 2003 O street, Washington, D. C.

Panama ....Señor Don J. Domingo de Obaldía,
Office of Legation, "The Highlands," Washington, D. C.

Peru ....Señor Don Felipe Pardo,
Office of Legation, 2171 Florida avenue, Washington, D. C.

Salvador..............................Señor Federico Mejía,
Office of Legation, " The Arlington."

Uruguay ....Señor Dr. Don Luis Melian Lafinur,
Office of Legation, 1116 Twenty-first street, Washington, D. C.

MINISTER RESIDENT

Dominican Republic ....Señor Don Emilio C. Joubert,
"The Shoreham," Washington, D. C.

CHARGÉS D'AFFAIRES.

Chile..............................Señor Don Alberto Yoacham,
Office of Legation, "The Rochambeau," Washington, D. C.

Honduras..............................Señor Dr. Salvador Córdova,
Office of Legation, care of Consulate-General of Honduras, New York City.

Venezuela ....Señor Dr. Rafael Garbiras Guzman,
"The Rochambeau," Washington, D. C.

UNITED STATES REPRESENTATIVES IN THE LATIN-AMERICAN REPUBLICS.

AMBASSADORS EXTRAORDINARY AND PLENIPOTENTIARY.

Brazil ....IRVING B. DUDLEY, Rio de Janeiro.

Mexico ....DAVID E. THOMPSON, Mexico.

ENVOYS EXTRAORDINARY AND MINISTERS PLENIPOTENTIARY.

Argentine Republic ....A. M. BEAUPRÉ, Buenos Ayres.

Bolivia ....WILLIAM B. SORSBY, La Paz.

Chile ....JOHN HICKS, Santiago.

Colombia ....THOMAS C. DAWSON, Bogotá.

Costa Rica ....WILLIAM L. MERRY, San José.

Cuba ....EDWIN V. MORGAN, Havana.

Ecuador ....WILLIAMS C. FOX, Quito.

Guatemala.............................JOSEPH W. J. LEE, Guatemala City.

Haiti..................................HENRY W. FURNISS, Port au Prince.

Honduras..............................(See Guatemala.)

Nicaragua.............................(See Costa Rica.)

Panama ....HERBERT G. SQUIERS, Panama.

Paraguay ....(See Uruguay.)

Peru ....LESLIE COMBS, Lima.

Salvador...............................(See Costa Rica.)

Uruguay...............................EDWARD C. O'BRIEN, Montevideo.

Venezuela ....W. W. RUSSELL, Caracas.

MINISTER RESIDENT AND CONSUL-GENERAL.

Dominican Republic.....................FENTON R. MCCREERY, Santo Domingo.

.GE FROM THE UNITED STATES TO LATIN-AMERICAN COUNTRIES,

postage from the United States to all foreign countries and colonies (except Canada, . ~uba) are as follows:

	Cents.
***** per 15 grams (1 ounce)	5
~**l cards, each	2
il cards, each	4
and other printed matter, per 2 ounces	1
Commercial papers... { Packets not in excess of 10 ounces	5
Packets in excess of 10 ounces, for each 2 ounces or fraction thereof	1
.mples of merchandise .. { Packets not in excess of 4 ounces	2
Packets in excess of 4 ounces, for each 2 ounces or fraction thereof	1
...gistration fee on letters and other articles	8

·inary letters for any foreign country (except Canada, Mexico, and Cuba) must be forwarded, ** any postage is prepaid on them or not. All other mailable matter must be prepaid, at least ·.

·mailed in the United States addressed to Mexico is subject to the same postage rates and con- ·s it would be if it were addressed for delivery in the United States, except that articles of eous merchandise (fourth-class matter) not sent as *bona fide* trade samples should be sent by Post;" and that the following articles are *absolutely excluded* from the mails without regard w ···· .mount of postage prepaid or the manner in which they are wrapped:

All sealed packages, other than letters in their usual and ordinary form; *all* packages (including packages of second-class matter) which weigh more than 4 pounds 6 ounces, except such as are sent by "Parcels Post;" publications which violate any copyright law of Mexico.

Single volumes of printed books *in unsealed packages* are transmissible to Mexico in the regular mails without limit as to weight.

Unsealed packages of mailable merchandise may be sent by "Parcels Post" to Bolivia, British Guiana, British Honduras, Chile, Colombia, Costa Rica, Guatemala, Honduras, Mexico, Nicaragua, Salvador, and Venezuela, at the rates named on page xv.

PROHIBITED ARTICLES TO ALL FOREIGN COUNTRIES.

Poisons, explosives, and inflammable articles, live or dead animals, insects (especially the Colorado beetle), reptiles, fruits or vegetable matter liable to decomposition, and substances exhaling a bad odor, excluded from transmission in domestic mails as being in themselves, either from their form or nature, liable to destroy, deface, or otherwise injure the contents of the mail bags, or the persons of those engaged in the postal service; also obscene, lewd, or lascivious books, pamphlets, etc., and letters and circulars concerning lotteries, so-called gift concerts, etc. (also excluded from domestic mails); postal cards or letters addressed to go around the world; letters or packages (except those to Mexico) containing gold or silver substances, jewelry or precious articles; any packet whatever containing articles liable to customs duties in the countries addressed (except Cuba and Mexico); articles other than letters which are not prepaid at least partly; articles other than letters or postal cards containing writing in the nature of personal correspondence, unless fully prepaid at the rate of letter postage; articles of a nature likely to soil or injure the correspondence; packets of commercial papers and prints of all kinds, the weight of which exceeds 2 kilograms (4 pounds 6 ounces), or the size 18 inches in any direction, except *rolls* of prints, which may measure 30 inches in length by 4 inches in diameter; postal cards not of United States origin, and United States postal cards of the largest ("C") size (except as letters), and except also the reply halves of double postal cards received from foreign countries.

There is, moreover, reserved to the Government of every country of the Postal Union the right to refuse to convey over its territory, or to deliver, as well, articles liable to the reduced rate in regard to which the laws, ordinances, or decrees which regulate the conditions of their publication or of their circulation in that country have not been complied with.

☞ Full and complete information relative to all regulations can be obtained from the United States Postal Guide.

FOREIGN MAILS.

TABLE SHOWING THE RATES OF POSTAGE CHARGED IN LATIN-AMERICAN COUNTRIES ON ARTICLES SENT BY MAIL TO THE UNITED STATES.

Countries.	Letters, per 15 grams, equal to one-half ounce.		Single postal cards, each.a		Other articles, per 50 grams, equal to 2 ounces.		Charge for registration.	Charge for return receipt.
	Currency of country.	Centimes.	Currency of country.	Centimes.	Currency of country.	Centimes.		
Argentine Republic	15 centavos	35	6 centavos	15	3 centavos	10	24 centavos	12 ctos.
Bolivia via Panama	22 centavos	55	8 centavos	20	6 centavos	15	20 centavos	10 centavos.
Bolivia via other routes	20 centavos	50	6 centavos	15	4 centavos	10		
Brazil	300 rels	35	100 rels	10	50 rels	5	400 rels	200 rs.
Chile	10 centavos	50	3 centavos	15	2 ctos.	10	10 tamos	5 centavos.
Cuba	20 centavos	50	4 centavos	15	2 centavos	10	10 centavos	t ctos.
Costa Rica	10 centimos	25	3 centimos	7½	2 ctos.	5	10 centimos	5 ctos.
Dominican Republic (Santo Domingo)	10 centavos	25	5 centavos	10	2 centavos	5	dies	5 centavos.
Ecuador	10 centavos	50	2 centavos	10				
Falkland Islands	4 pence	40	1 py	15	1 py	10	2 pence	2½ ps.
Guatemala	10 centavos	50	3 centavos	15	1 centavo		10 centavos	5 centavos.
Haiti	10 ohmes de gourde	50	3 ohmes de rde.		2 ohmes de gourde.	10	2 ohmes de gourde.	5 ohmes de gourde.
Honduras	15 centavos	50	3 centvos	15	2 centavos	10	10 centavos	5 ctos.
Honduras, British	5 cents	25	2 cents	10	1 centavo		10 cents.	6 cts.
Mexico	5 centavos	50	5 centavos					
Nicaragua	15 centavos		3 centavos	15	5 centavos	10	5 centavos	5 centavos.
Paraguay	60 centavos		3 centavos	15	8 centavos	10	40 centavos	20
Peru via San Francisco	20 centavos	50	6 centavos	15	1 tamos	10		
Peru via Panama	22 centavos	55	8 centavos	20	6 centavos	15	10 centavos	tamos.
Porto Ricob								
Salvador via Panama	11 centavos	35	3 centavos	15	3 centavos	15	10 tamos	5 centavos.
Salvador via other routes	10 centavos	50	3 centavos	15	2 centavos	10	10 centavos	5 centavos.
Uruguay	50 centavos	50	2 centavos	15	2 centavos	10	50 centimos	25 t cts.
Venezuela	5 cents	25	15 centimos	15	10 centimos			
Dutch Guiana	25 cents Dutch	25	7½ cents Dutch	15	5 cents Dutch	5	10 cents Dutch	10 cents.
French Guiana	25 centimes	50	10 centimes	15	5 centimes	10	25 centimes.	10 centimes.

a The rate for a reply-paid (double) card is double the rate named in this column.
b United States domestic rates and conditions.

'ARCELS-POST REGULATIONS.

SHOWING THE LATIN-AMERICAN COUNTRIES TO WHICH PARCELS MAY BE SENT
M THE UNITED STATES; THE DIMENSIONS, WEIGHT, AND RATES OF POSTAGE APPLI-
E TO PARCELS, AND THE EXCHANGE POST-OFFICES WHICH MAY DISPATCH AND
IVE PARCELS-POST MAILS.

COUNTRIES.	ALLOWABLE DIMENSIONS AND WEIGHTS OF PARCELS.				POSTAGE.		EXCHANGE POST-OFFICES.	
	Greatest length.	Greatest length and girth combined.	Greatest girth.	Greatest weight.	For a parcel not exceeding 1 pound.	For every additional pound or fraction of a pound.	UNITED STATES.	LATIN AMERICA.
	Ft. in.	Ft.	Ft.	Lbs.	Cents.	Cents.		
Bolivia	3 6	6	......	11	20	20	New York and San Francisco.	La Paz.
Chile	3 6	6	......	11	20	20	New York and San Francisco.	Valparaiso.
Colombia	2 0	......	4	11	12	12	All offices authorized to exchange mails between the two countries.	
Costa Rica	2 0	......	4	11	12	12		
Ecuador	3 6	6	......	11	20	20		
Guatemala	3 6	6	......	11	12	12	New York, New Orleans, and San Francisco.	Guatemala City, Retalhuleu, and Puerto Barrios.
Guiana, British	3 6	6	......	11	12	12	All offices authorized to exchange mails.	
Honduras	3 6	6	......	11	12	12	New York, New Orleans, and San Francisco.	Tegucigalpa, Puerto Cortez, Amapala, and Trujillo.
Honduras, British	3 6	6	......	11	12	12	New Orleans	Belize.
Mexico	2 0	......	4	11	12	12	All offices authorized to exchange mails.	
Nicaragua	3 6	6	......	11	12	12	New York, New Orleans, and San Francisco.	Bluefields, San Juan del Norte, and Corinto.
Salvador	3 6	6	......	11	12	12	New York and San Francisco.	San Salvador.
Venezuela	3 6	6	......	11	12	12	All offices authorized to exchange mails.	

UNITED STATES CONSULATES IN LATIN AMERICA.

Frequent application is made to the Bureau for the address of United States Consuls in the South and Central American Republics. Those desiring to correspond with any Consul can do so by addressing "The United States Consulate" at the point named. Letters thus addressed must be delivered to the proper person. It must be understood, however, that it is not the duty of Consuls to devote their time to private business, and that all such letters may properly be treated as personal, and any labor involved may be subject to charge therefor.

The following is a list of United States Consulates in the different Republics (consular agencies are given in italics):

ARGENTINE REPUBLIC—
 Bahia Blanca.
 Buenos Ayres.
 Cordoba.
 Rosario.
BRAZIL—
 Aracaju.
 Bahia.
 Ceara.
 Maceio.
 Manaos.
 Maranhao.
 Natal.
 Para.
 Pernambuco.
 Rio de Janeiro.
 Rio Grande do Sul.
 Santos.
 Victoria.
CHILE—
 Antofagasta.
 Arica.
 Caldera.
 Coquimbo.
 Coronel.
 Iquique.
 Punta Arenas.
 Talcahuano.
 Valdivia.
 Valparaiso.
COLOMBIA—
 Barranquilla.
 Bogotá.
 Bucaramanga.
 Cali.
 Cartagena.
 Cucuta.
 Honda.
 Santa Marta.
 Quibdo.
COSTA RICA—
 Puerto Limon.
 Punta Arenas.
 San José.
CUBA—
 Banes.
 Baracoa.
 Caibarien.
 Cardenas.
 Cienfuegos.
 Habana.
 Manzanillo.
 Matanzas.
 Nuevitas.
 Sagua la Grande.
 Santa Clara.
 Santiago.
DOMINICAN REPUBLIC—
 Azua.
 Macoris.
 Monte Christi.
 Puerto Plata.

DOMINICAN REPUBLIC—Cont'd.
 Samana.
 Sanchez.
 Santo Domingo.
ECUADOR—
 Bahia de Caraquez.
 Esmeraldas.
 Guayaquil.
 Manta.
GUATEMALA—
 Champerico.
 Guatemala.
 Livingston.
 Ocos.
 San José de Guatemala.
HAITI—
 Aux Cayes.
 Cape Haitien,
 Gonaives.
 Jacmel.
 Jeremie.
 Miragoane.
 Petit Goâve.
 Port au Prince.
 Port de Paix.
 St. Marc.
HONDURAS—
 Amapala.
 Bonacca.
 Ceiba.
 Puerto Cortes.
 San Juancito.
 San Pedro Sula.
 Tegucigalpa.
 Trla.
 Trujillo.
 Ruatan.
 Utilla.
MEXICO—
 Acapulco.
 Aguascalientes.
 Alamos.
 Campeche.
 Cananea.
 Chihuahua.
 Ciudad Juarez.
 Ciudad Porfirio Diaz.
 Coatzacoalcos.
 Durango.
 Ensenada.
 Frontera.
 Guadalajara.
 Guanajuato.
 Guaymas.
 Hermosillo.
 Jalapa.
 Laguna de Terminos.
 La Paz.
 Manzanillo.
 Matamoras.
 Mazatlan.
 Mexico.

MEXICO—Continued.
 Monterey.
 Nogales.
 Nuevo Laredo.
 Oaxaca.
 Parral.
 Progreso.
 Puebla.
 Saltillo.
 San Luis Potosí.
 Sierra Mojada.
 Tampico.
 Tlacotalpan.
 Topolobampo.
 Torreon.
 Tuxpan, Vera Cruz.
 Veracruz.
 Victoria.
 Zacatecas.
NICARAGUA—
 Bluefields.
 Cape Gracias á Dios.
 Corinto.
 Managua.
 Matagalpa.
 San Juan del Norte.
 San Juan del Sur.
PANAMA—
 Bocas del Toro.
 Colon.
 David.
 Panama.
 Santiago.
PARAGUAY—
 Asunción.
PERU—
 Callao.
 Chimbote.
 Eten.
 Iquitos.
 Mollendo.
 Paita.
 Salaverry.
SALVADOR—
 Acajutla.
 La Libertad.
 La Unión.
 San Salvador.
URUGUAY—
 Montevideo.
VENEZUELA—
 Barcelona.
 Caracas.
 Carupano.
 Ciudad Bolívar.
 Coro.
 La Guayra.
 Maracaibo.
 Puerto Cabello.
 Tovar.
 Valera.

PAN-AMERICAN CONSULATES.

OF THE LATIN-AMERICAN REPUBLICS IN THE UNITED STATES.

	Mobile.
	San Francisco.
	Washington.
	Fernandina.
	Pensacola.
	Savannah.
	Chicago.
	New Orleans.
	Portland.
	Baltimore.
	Boston.
	Gulf Port and Ship Island.
	Pascagoula.
	St. Louis.
	New York City.
...ania	Philadelphia.
...e Islands	Manila.
...ia	Norfolk.

BOLIVIA.

California	San Diego.
	San Francisco.
Illinoi	Chicago.
Maryland	Baltimore.
Missouri	Kansas City.
New York	New York City.
Pennsylvania	Philadelphia.

BRAZIL.

Alabama	Mobile.
California	San Francisco.
Florida	Fernandina.
	Pensacola.
Georgia	Brunswick.
	Savannah.
Lonisiana	New Orleans.
Maine	Calais.
Maryland	Baltimore.
Massachusetts	Boston.
Mississippi	Gulfport.
	Pascagoula.
Missouri	St. Louis.
New York	New York City.
Pennsylvania	Philadelphia.
Porto Rico	San Juan.
Virginia	Norfolk.
	Richmond.

CHILE.

California	San Francisco.
Canal Zone	Panama.
Georgia	Savannah.
Hawaii	Honolulu.
Illinois	Chicago.
Maryland	Baltimore.
Massachusetts	Boston.
New York	New York City.
Oregon	Portland.
Pennsylvania	Philadelphia.
Philippine Islands	Manila.
Porto Rico	San Juan.
Washington	Port Townsend.
	Tacoma.

COLOMBIA.

Alabama	Mobile.
California	San Francisco.
Connecticut	New Haven.
Florida	Tampa.
Illinois	Chicago.
Louisiana	New Orleans.
Maryland	Baltimore.
Massachusetts	Boston.
Michigan	Detroit.
Missouri	St. Louis.
New York	New York City.
Pennsylvania	Philadelphia.
Porto Rico	San Juan.
Virginia	Norfolk.

COSTA RICA.

Alabama	Mobile.
California	
Canal Zone	
Colorado	
Illinois	
Louisiana	
Maryland	
Massachusetts	
Missouri	
New York	
Oregon	
Pennsylvania	Philadelphia.
Porto Rico	San Juan.
Texas	
Virginia	Norfolk.

CUBA.

Alabama	Mobile.
California	
Florida	
Georgia	Savannah.
Illinois	Chicago.
Kentucky	Louisville.
Louisiana	New Orleans.
Maine	Portland.
Maryland	Baltimore.
Massachusetts	Boston.
Michigan	Detroit.
Mississippi	Gulfport.
Missouri	St. Louis.
New York	New York City.
Ohio	Cincinnati.
Pennsylvania	Philadelphia.
Porto Rico	Arecibo.
	Mayagües.
	Ponce.
	San Juan.
Texas	Galveston.
Virginia	Newport News.
	Norfolk.

DOMINICAN REPUBLIC.

Illinois	Chicago.
Maryland	Baltimore.
Massachusetts	Boston.
New York	New York City.
North Carolina	Wilmington.
Pennsylvania	Philadelphia.
Porto Rico	Aguadilla.
	Arecibo.
	Humacao.
	Mayagüez.
	Ponce.
	San Juan.
	Vieques.

ECUADOR.

California	Los Angeles.
	San Francisco.
Illinois	Chicago.
Louisiana	New Orleans.
Massachusetts	Boston.
New York	New York City.
Ohio	Cincinnati.
Pennsylvania	Philadelphia.
Philippine Islands	Manila.
South Carolina	Charleston.
Virginia	Norfolk.

GUATEMALA.

Alabama	Mobile.
California	San Diego.
	San Francisco.
Florida	Pensacola.
Illinois	Chicago.

CONSULATES OF THE LATIN-AMERICAN REPUBLICS—Continued.

GUATEMALA—Continued.

Kansas	Kansas City.
Kentucky	Louisville.
Louisiana	New Orleans.
Maryland	Baltimore.
Massachusetts	Boston.
Missouri	St. Louis.
New York	New York City.
Pennsylvania	Philadelphia.
Porto Rico	San Juan.
Texas	Galveston.
Washington	Seattle.

HAITI.

Alabama	Mobile.
Georgia	Savannah.
Illinois	Chicago.
Maine	Bangor.
Massachusetts	Boston.
New York	New York City.
North Carolina	Wilmington.
Porto Rico	Mayagüez.
	San Juan.

HONDURAS.

Alabama	Mobile.
California	Los Angeles.
	San Diego.
	San Francisco.
Illinois	Chicago.
Kansas	Kansas City.
Kentucky	Louisville.
Louisiana	New Orleans.
Maryland	Baltimore.
Michigan	Detroit.
Missouri	St. Louis.
New York	New York City.
Ohio	Cincinnati.
Pennsylvania	Philadelphia.
Texas	Galveston.
Washington	Seattle.

MEXICO.

Alabama	Mobile.
Arizona	Bisbee.
	Clifton.
	Douglas.
	Naco.
	Nogales.
	Phoenix.
	Solomonsville.
	Tucson.
	Yuma.
California	Calexico.
	Los Angeles.
	San Diego.
	San Francisco.
Canal Zone	Ancon.
Colorado	Denver.
Florida	Pensacola.
Hawaii	Honolulu.
Illinois	Chicago.
Kentucky	Louisville.
Louisiana	New Orleans.
Maryland	Baltimore.
Massachusetts	Boston.
Mississippi	Pascagoula.
Missouri	Kansas City.
	St. Louis.
New York	New York City.
Ohio	Cincinnati.
Oregon	Portland.
Pennsylvania	Philadelphia.
Philippine Islands	Manila.
Porto Rico	Mayagüez.
	Ponce.
	San Juan.
Texas	Brownsville.
	Eagle Pass.
	El Paso.
	Galveston.
	Laredo.
	Port Arthur.
	Rio Grande City.
	Sabine Pass.
	San Antonio.
	Solomonsville.

MEXICO—Continued.

Virginia	Norfolk.
Washington	Tocoma.

NICARAGUA.

Alabama	Mobile.
California	Los Angeles.
	San Diego.
	San Francisco.
Illinois	Chicago.
Kansas	Kansas City.
Kentucky	Louisville.
Louisiana	New Orleans.
Maryland	Baltimore.
Massachusetts	Boston.
Michigan	Detroit.
Missouri	St. Louis.
New York	New York City.
Pennsylvania	Philadelphia.
Philippine Islands	Manila.
Porto Rico	Ponce.
	San Juan.
Texas	Galveston.
Virginia	Norfolk.
	Newport News.
Washington	Seattle.

PANAMA.

Alabama	Mobile.
California	San Francisco.
Georgia	Atlanta.
Hawaii	Hilo.
Illinois	Chicago.
Louisiana	New Orleans.
Maryland	Baltimore.
Massachusetts	Boston.
Missouri	St. Louis.
New York	New York City.
Pennsylvania	Philadelphia.
Porto Rico	San Juan.
Tennessee	Chattanooga.
Texas	Galveston.
	Port Arthur.
Washington	Puget Sound.

PARAGUAY.

Alabama	Mobile.
Delaware	Wilmington.
District of Columbia	Washington.
Georgia	Savannah.
Illinois	Chicago.
Indiana	Indianapolis.
Maryland	Baltimore.
Michigan	Detroit.
Missouri	Kansas City.
	St. Louis.
New Jersey	Newark.
	Trenton.
New York	Buffalo.
	New York City.
	Rochester.
Ohio	Cincinnati.
Pennsylvania	Philadelphia.
Porto Rico	San Juan.
Virginia	Norfolk.
	Richmond.

PERU.

California	Los Angeles.
	San Diego.
	San Francisco.
Canal Zone	Panama.
Georgia	Savannah.
Hawaii	Honolulu.
Illinois	Chicago.
Louisiana	New Orleans.
Maryland	Baltimore.
Massachusetts	Boston.
New York	New York City.
Oregon	Portland.
Pennsylvania	Philadelphia.
Porto Rico	San Juan.
South Carolina	Charleston.
Washington	Port Townsend.

WEIGHTS AND MEASURES.

The following table gives the chief weights and measures in commercial use in Mexico and the Republics of Central and South America, and their equivalents in the United States:

Denomination.	Where used.	United States equivalents.
Are	Metric	0.02471 acre.
Arobe	Paraguay	25 pounds.
Arroba (dry)	Argentine Republic	25.3171 pounds.
Do	Brazil	32.38 pounds.
Do	Cuba	25.3664 pounds.
Do	Venezuela	25.4024 pounds.
Arroba (liquid)	Cuba and Venezuela	4.263 gallons.
Barril	Argentine Republic and Mexico	20.0787 gallons.
Carga	Mexico and Salvador	300 pounds.
Centaro	Central America	4.2631 gallons.
Cuadra	Argentine Republic	4.2 acres.
Do	Paraguay	78.9 yards.
Do	Paraguay (square)	8.077 square feet.
Do	Uruguay	2 acres (nearly).
Cubic meter	Metric	35.3 cubic feet.
Fanega (dry)	Central America	1.5745 bushels.
Do	Chile	2.575 bushels.
Do	Cuba	1.599 bushels.
Do	Mexico	1.54728 bushels.
Do	Uruguay (double)	7.776 bushels.
Do	Uruguay (single)	3.888 bushels.
Do	Venezuela	1.599 bushels.
Frasco	Argentine Republic	2.5096 quarts.
Do	Mexico	2.5 quarts.
Gram	Metric	15.432 grains.
Hectare	do	2.471 acres.
Hectoliter (dry)	do	2.838 bushels.
Hectoliter (liquid)	do	26.417 gallons.
Kilogram (kilo)	do	2.2046 pounds.
Kilometer	do	0.621376 mile.
League (land)	Paraguay	4.633 acres.
Libra	Argentine Republic	1.0127 pounds.
Do	Central America	1.043 pounds.
Do	Chile	1.014 pounds.
Do	Cuba	1.0161 pounds.
Do	Mexico	1.01465 pounds.
Do	Peru	1.0143 pounds.
Do	Uruguay	1.0143 pounds.
Do	Venezuela	1.0161 pounds.
Liter	Metric	1.0567 quarts.
Livre	Guiana	1.0791 pounds.
Manzana	Costa Rica	1.73 acres.
Marc	Bolivia	0.507 pound.
Meter	Metric	39.37 inches.
Pie	Argentine Republic	0.9478 foot.
Quintal	do	101.42 pounds.
Do	Brazil	130.06 pounds.
Do	Chile, Mexico, and Peru	101.61 pounds.
Do	Paraguay	100 pounds.
Quintal (metric)	Metric	220.46 pounds.
Suerte	Uruguay	2,700 cuadras. (See Cuadra.)
Vara	Argentine Republic	34.1208 inches.
Do	Central America	33.874 inches.
Do	Chile and Peru	33.367 inches.
Do	Cuba	33.384 inches.
Do	Mexico	33 inches.
Do	Paraguay	34 inches.
Do	Venezuela	33.384 inches.

RIO WEIGHTS AND MEASURES.

METRIC WEIGHTS.

m) equals 0.0154 grain.
n) equals 0.1543 grain.
equals 1.5432 grains.
rains.
agram (10 grams) equals 0.3527 ounce.
ctogram (100 grams) equals 3.5274 ounces.
ogram (1,000 grams) equals 2.2046 pounds.
myriagram (10,000 grams) equals 22.046 pounds.
Quintal (100,000 grams) equals 220.46 pounds.
Millier or tonneau—ton (1,000,000 grams) equals 2,204.6 pounds.

METRIC DRY MEASURE.

Milliliter (1/1000 liter) equals 0.061 cubic inch.
Centiliter (1/100 liter) equals 0.6102 cubic inch.
Deciliter (1/10 liter) equals 6.1022 cubic inches.
Liter equals 0.908 quart.
Decaliter (10 liters) equals 9.08 quarts.
Hectoliter (100 liters) equals 2.838 bushels.
Kiloliter (1,000 liters) equals 1.308 cubic yards.

METRIC LIQUID MEASURE.

Milliliter (1/1000 liter) equals 0.27 fluid dram.
Centiliter (1/100 liter) equals 0.338 fluid ounce
Deciliter (1/10 liter) equals 0.845 gill.
Liter equals 1.0567 quarts.
Decaliter (10 liters) equals 2.6417 gallons.
Hectoliter (100 liters) equals 26.417 gallons.
Kiloliter (1,000 liters) equals 264.17 gallons.

METRIC MEASURES OF LENGTH.

Millimeter (1/1000 meter) equals 0.0394 inch.
Centimeter (1/100 meter) equals 0.3937 inch.
Decimeter (1/10 meter) equals 3.937 inches.
Meter equals 39.37 inches.
Decameter (10 meters) equals 393.7 inches.
Hectometer (100 meters) equals 328 feet 1 inch.
Kilometer (1,000 meters) equals 0.62137 mile (3,280 feet 10 inches).
Myriameter (10,000 meters) equals 6.2137 miles.

METRIC SURFACE MEASURE.

Centare (1 square meter) equals 1,550 square inches.
Are (100 square meters) equals 119.6 square yards.
Hectare (10,000 square meters) equals 2.471 acres.

PRICE LIST OF PUBLICATIONS.

Prices.

Bulletin of the Bureau, published monthly since October, 1893, in English, Spanish, Portuguese, and French. Average 225 pages, 2 volumes a year.

Yearly subscription (in countries of the International Union of American Republics and in Canada)... $2.00

Yearly subscription (other countries)................................... 2.50

Single copies.. .25

Orders for the Bulletin should be addressed to the Chief Clerk of the Bureau.

American Constitutions. A compilation of the political constitutions of the independent States of America, in the original text, with English and Spanish translations. Washington, 1906. 3 vols., 8°.

Paper ....each.. 1.00

Bound in cloth..do.... 1.50

Bound in sheep ....do.... 2.00

> Vol. I, now ready, contains the constitutions of the Federal Republics of the United States of America, of Mexico, of the Argentine Republic, of Brazil, and of Venezuela, and of the Republics of Central America, Guatemala, Honduras, El Salvador, Nicaragua, Costa Rica, and Panama. Vols. II and III will be ready shortly.
>
> Vol. II will contain the constitutions of the Dominican Republic, Haiti, Cuba, Uruguay, Chile, Peru, Ecuador, Colombia, Paraguay, and Bolivia.
>
> Vol. III will contain Articles of Confederation of the United States, First Constitution of Venezuela 1811, Fundamental Law of Republic of Colombia 1819, Ditto of 1821, Constitution of Colombia of 1821, Constitution of Central American Confederation of 1824, Constitution of the Grenadian Confederation of 1858, Constitution of the United States of Colombia of 1863, Pro Constitution of Guatemala of 1876, Convention between United States and Republic of Panama for construction of ship canal to connect the waters of the Atlantic and the Pacific Oceans.

Code of Commercial Nomenclature, 1897. (Spanish, English, and Portuguese.) 645 pages, 4°, cloth... 2.50

Code of Commercial Nomenclature, 1897. (Portuguese, Spanish, and English.) 640 pages, 4°, cloth... 2.50

> Note.—Designates in alphabetical order, in equivalent terms in the three languages, the commodities of American nations on which import duties are levied. The English, Spanish, and Portuguese edition is entirely exhausted.

Leyes y reglamentos sobre privilegios de invención y marcas de fábrica en los países hispano-americanos, el Brasil y la República de Haití., Revisado hasta agosto de 1904. Washington, 1904. 415 pages, 8°..................... 1.00

Patent and trade-mark laws of the Spanish American Republics, Brazil, and the Republic of Haiti. Revised to Aug., 1904, Washington, 1904.......... 1.00

The above two works bound together in sheep 3.00

SPECIAL BULLETINS.

Money, Weights, and Measures of the American Republics, 1891. 12 pages, 8°. .05

Report on Coffee, with special reference to the Costa Rican product, etc. Washington, 1901. 15 pages, 8°..................................... .10

El café. Su historia, cultivo, beneficio, variedades, producción, exportación, importación, consumo, etc. Datos extensos presentados al Congreso relativo al café que se reunirá en Nueva York el 1° de octubre de 1902. 167 páginas, 8°... .50

Coffee. Extensive information and statistics. (English edition of the above.) 108 pages, 8°.. .50

Intercontinental Railway Reports. Report of the Intercontinental Railway Commission. Washington, 1898. 7 vols. 4°, three of maps............... 25.00

PUBLICATIONS.

BOOKS (GENERAL DESCRIPTION AND STATISTICS).

A geographical sketch, with special reference to economic
evelopment, and prospects of future growth. Washing-
rations, 3 maps, 366 pages, 8° $1.00
l sketch, natural resources, laws, economic conditions,
1 ...   . , prospects of future growth. Washington, 1904. Illus-
—ges, ' 1.00
graphical sketch, with special reference to economic conditions
—pects of future development. 1901. 233 pages, 8° 75
hort sketch of physical and economic conditions, government, laws,
lu......s, finances, customs tariff, etc., prepared by Señor Gonzalo de
esada, minister from Cuba, with bibliography and cartography of 198
tes. Washington, November, 1905.' Map and 42 illustrations, 541 pages, 8°. 1.00
nala. 1897. (2d edition revised.) Illustrated, 119 pages, 8° 25
iras. Geographical sketch, natural resources, laws, economic condi-
..s, actual development, prospects of future growth. Washington, 1904.
astrated, economic and telegraphic maps, 252 pages, 8° ....
ico. Geographical sketch, natural resources, laws, economic conditions,
actual development, prospects of future growth. Washington, 1904. Illus-
rated, 454 pages, 8° 1.00
raguay. Second edition, revised and enlarged, with a chapter on the native
tces. 1902. Illustrated, map, 187 pages, 8°. Bibliography, page 141 .... .75
ezuela. Geographical sketch, natural resources, laws, economic condi-
.ons, actual development, prospects of future growth. Washington, 1904.
Illustrated, railway map, 608 pages, 8° 1.00

BIBLIOGRAPHICAL BULLETINS.

Chile. A list of books, magazine articles, and maps relating to Chile. Washington, 1903. 110 pages, 8° 1.00
Paraguay. A list of books, magazine articles and maps relating to Paraguay.
53 pages, 8°. Washington, 1904 .... 1.00

MAPS.

Guatemala. From official and other sources. 1902. Scale of 12.5 miles to
1 inch (1:792,000). In 2 sheets, each sheet 71 x 76 cm. No. 1. General
features. No. 2. Agricultural 1.00
Mexico. From official Mexican and other sources. 1900. Scale of 50 miles
to 1 inch. In 2 sheets, each sheet 108 x 80 cm. No. 1. General map.
No. 2. Agricultural areas 1.00
Nicaragua. From official and other sources. 1904. Scale of 12.5 miles to
1 inch (1:192,000). In 2 sheets, each sheet 80 x 80 cm. No. 1. General
map. No. 2. Agricultural 1.00
Bolivia. Mapa de la república de Bolivia, mandado organizar y publicar por
el Presidente Constitucional General José Manuel Pando. Scale 1:2,000,000.
La Paz, 1901. (Reprint International Bureau of the American Republics,
1904) 1.00
Costa Rica. From official and other sources. 1903. Scale of 12.5 miles to 1
inch (792,000) .... .50
Brazil. From official and other sources. 1905. Scale of 75 miles to 1 inch
(1:4,752,000). In one sheet 96 x 93 cm 1.00

LAW MANUALS.

Leyes Comerciales de América Latina: Código de Comercio de España comparado
con los Códigos y Leyes Comerciales de Pan América.
Land and Immigration Laws of American Republics. (To replace edition of 1898.)

HANDBOOKS.

Chile.
Dominican Republic.

MAPS.

Maps are in course of preparation of the Republics of Honduras and Salvador.
Payment is required to be made in cash, money orders, or by bank drafts on banks
in New York City or Washington, D. C., payable to the order of the INTERNATIONAL
BUREAU OF THE AMERICAN REPUBLICS. Individual checks on banks outside of New
York or Washington, or postage stamps, can not be accepted.

FOR FREE DISTRIBUTION.

The Bureau has for distribution a limited supply of the following, which will be
sent, free, upon written application:

The case of the United States of Venezuela before the Tribunal of Arbitration to
convene at Paris under the provisions of the Treaty between the United States of
Venezuela and Her Britannic Majesty, signed at Washington, February 2, 1897, in
10 vols., of which 2 are maps.

Message from the President of the United States, transmitting a communication from
the Secretary of State submitting the report, with accompanying papers, of the
delegates of the United States to the Second International Conference of American
States, held at the City of Mexico from October 22, 1901, to January 22, 1902.
Washington, 1902. 243 pages. 8°. (57th Congress, 1st session, Senate Doc. No.
330.)

Message from the President of the United States, transmitting a report from the Secretary of State, with accompanying papers, relative to the proceedings of the International Congress for the study of the production and consumption of coffee, etc.
Washington, 1903. 312 pages. 8° (paper). (57th Congress, 2d session, Senate
Doc. No. 35.)

Message from the President of the United States, transmitting a report by the Secre-
tary of State, with accompanying papers, relative to the proceedings of the First
Customs Congress of the American Republics, held at New York in January, 1903.
Washington, 1903. 195 pages. 8° (paper). (57th Congress, 2d session, Senate
Doc. No. 180.)

Brazil at St. Louis Exposition. St. Louis, 1904. 160 pages. 8° (paper).

Chile—A short description of the Republic according to official data. Leipzig, 1901.
106 pages. Map and 37 illustrations. 8° (cloth).

Chile—Breve descripción de la República escrita según datos oficiales. Leipzig,
1901. 106 páginas. Mapa y 36 grabados. 8° (en tela).

Chile at Pan-American Exposition. Buffalo, 1901. 252 pages (paper).

Guatemala—The Country of the future. By Charles M. Pepper. Washington,
1906. 80 pages. 8° (paper).

NOTE.—Senate documents, listed above, containing reports of the various International American
Congresses, may also be obtained through members of the United States Senate and House of Representatives.

shows the value, in United Stat...
the Central and South Ameri...
a Director of the United States...

ESTIMATE APRIL 1, 1907.

	Standard.	Unit.	Value in U.S. gold or silver.	
...BLIC.	Gold	Peso	5...	Gold—... ...Ar... Silver—...
VIA	Silver ...	Boliviano	.510	Silver—... sions.
....	Gold	Milreis ..	.545	Gold—... Silver—...
1 ...AMERICAN				Gold—d...
... Rica	Gold	Colon ...	.455	(\$9.3..) Silver—5, ... sions.
...temala ....duras	Silver ...	Peso	.500	Silver—Peso and ...
...Nicaragua ...... Salvador				
CHILE	Gold	Peso	.365	Gold—Escudo (\$1.825), double loon (\$3.650), and condor (\$7.300). Silver—Peso and divisions.
COLOMBIA...........	Gold	Dollar...	1.000	Gold—Condor (\$9.647) and double condor. Silver—Peso.
ECUADOR	Gold	Sucre....	.487	Gold—10 sucres (\$4.8665); Silver—Sucre and divisions.
HAITI	Gold	Gourde..	.965	Gold—1, 2, 5, and 10 gourdes. Silver—Gourde and divisions.
MEXICO.............	Gold	Peso a ...	.498	Gold—5 and 10 pesos. Silver—Dollar b (or peso) and divisions.
PANAMA	Gold	Balboa ..	1.000	Gold—1, 2½, 5, 10, and 20 balboas. Silver—Peso and divisions.
PERU	Gold	Libra ...	4.866½	Gold—½ and 1 libra. Silver—Sol and divisions.
URUGUAY	Gold	Peso	1.034	Gold—Peso. Silver—Peso and divisions.
VENEZUELA	Gold	Bolivar..	.193	Gold—5, 10, 20, 50, and 100 bolivars. Silver—5 bolivars.

a 75 centigrams fine gold. b Value in Mexico, 0.498.

O

International Union of American Republics

Monthly Bulletin

OF THE

International Bureau

OF THE

American Republics

VOL. 24, NO. 5

MAY, 1907

WHOLE NO. 164

WASHINGTON, D. C., U. S. A.

GOVERNMENT PRINTING OFFICE

1907

JOHN BARRETT

ctor of the International Bureau of the American Republics.

FRANCISCO J. YÁNES,   WILLIAM C. WELLS,
        Secretary.   Chief Clerk.

II

GENERAL TABLE OF CONTENTS.

TABLE OF CONTENTS.

ÍNDICE.

INDICE.

INDICE.

TABLE DES MATIÈRES.

SEÑOR DON ENRIQUE CORTES, MINISTER OF COLOMBIA TO THE UNITED STATES.

MONTHLY BULLETIN

OF THE

INTERNATIONAL BUREAU OF THE AMERICAN REPUBLICS,

International Union of American Republics.

| VOL. XXIV. | MAY, 1907. | No. 5. |

On Wednesday, May 1, the Director of the International Bureau of the American Republics, in a statement to the Governing Board covering the estimates and budget for the year 1907-8, called attention to the broadening work of the Bureau in the following terms:

"While this statement is not in any sense a report on the work of the Bureau, the Director takes advantage of the opportunity to point out the gratifying growth in the correspondence and work of the Bureau along practical lines. Careful calculation shows that the number of inquiries received and answered during the first three months of the present administration, or from January 11 to April 11, was nearly three times greater than it was in the corresponding period of last year, while the demand for the printed matter of the Bureau in the same period was quadrupled. Approximately 3,000 letters have been received and answered during the last three months, coming from and going to all parts of the Western Hemisphere and certain sections of Europe and Asia.

"Although naturally the increase has been largely in the United States, where exists the chief need, the growth of interest in the Bureau throughout Latin America has been quite noticeable.

"It is worthy of note that at least twenty-five of the great exporting and business firms of the United States have decided, as a result of interest in Latin America awakened by the Bureau, to send representatives to that part of the world for the purpose not only of selling the products of the United States, but of purchasing those of Latin America. There has been a marked increase in the number of persons seeking information about Latin America with reference to traveling there instead of going to Europe or Asia. The requests of

libraries, both college and public, in all parts of the United States
for lists of books relating to Latin America have grown to such an
extent that the Director has been obliged to order the printing of a
circular bibliograph that can be sent out in answer to these inquiries.

"The BULLETIN has been changed in a number of respects and
made more attractive and practical, with the result that there has
developed a large increase in the demand for it, not only in the United
States but in Latin America. The Director has additional plans
for its improvement, which will soon be put into practice. In the
course of a few months he hopes to have the mailing list confined to
those persons who really make use of it and appreciate it, and to do
this he has cut off the names of a large number of persons who have
been receiving the BULLETIN for the last ten years without making
any new request for its continuance.

"One of the best evidences of practical interest in the commercial
relations of the United States with Latin America is the number of
invitations that are continually pouring into the Bureau for the
Director or some other qualified person to address chambers of commerce, boards of trade, and similar organizations on this subject.
The Director accepts these invitations when, it·is possible to do so
without neglecting the general management of the Bureau."

PRESIDENT ALCORTA'S OPINION OF SECRETARY ROOT'S VISIT.

The newspapers of the United States published, on Thursday, May
9, 1907, an interesting dispatch from Buenos Aires. It was a quotation from the address of President ALCORTA, of the Argentine Republic, at the opening of the National Congress. He took this opportunity
to make a complimentary reference to Mr. ROOT, Secretary of State
of the United States and Chairman of the Governing Board of the
International Bureau of the American Republics, as follows:

"The most notable diplomatic event of the past year was the visit
of the American Secretary of State, Mr. ROOT, to this and other Latin-
American Republics. That eminent statesman brought messages of
cordiality and friendship from the American people and their illustrious President, Mr. ROOSEVELT, and made statements on every possible
occasion which could only have the effect of assisting in the progress
of the Republics and bringing about closer relations between them and
the United States. The visit of Mr. ROOT has already begun to bear
fruit in the genuine friendship established, in a better understanding,
and in the frank relations existing between the Argentine Republic
and the United States, and the firm desire of both Republics to promote their mutual commerce."

THE HISPANIC SOCIETY OF AMERICA.

It gives the Director much pleasure to publish in this issue some data about the Hispanic Society of America, together with photographs of the President, Mr. ARCHER M. HUNTINGTON, and two views of the new building of the society. Although the world in general may not be familiar with the work that Mr. HUNTINGTON has been doing, it will surely, in time, give him credit for accomplishing more than any other North American for the awakening of interest in Hispanic languages, literature, art, and history. He has practically devoted his life and energies and a large portion of his income to developing interest in these subjects, and he has earned the gratitude of all people who wish to promote the study of them in the United States by organizing this Society and providing it with a beautiful and practical home. No visitor to New York has seen all the attractions of that metropolis unless he has visited the building of the Hispanic Society in Audubon Park, where it occupies a commanding position overlooking the Hudson River. On the original advisory board were such distinguished names as Porfirio Díaz, John Hay, Arthur Twining Hadley, Bartolomé Mitre, Morris K. Jesup, Marcelino Menendez y Ielayo, James Fitzmaurice-Kelly, R. Foulche-Delbosc, and Hugo A. Rennert. The board of trustees includes Charles Harrison Tweed, Isaac Edwin Gates, Francis Lathrop, John Ten Broeck Hillhouse, and Mansfield Lovell Hillhouse. Elsewhere in this issue are given further details of the Hispanic Society. The Director of the International Bureau of the American Republics takes advantage of this opportunity to thank President HUNTINGTON for his assurance of the cooperation of the Hispanic Society with the Bureau for the development throughout the United States of interest in the Latin-American Republics, and for important publications of that society, which he has forwarded to the Columbus Memorial Library.

THE NEW LABOR BUREAU OF THE ARGENTINE REPUBLIC.

The International Bureau of the American Republics is glad to have had the opportunity of cooperating with the Government of the Argentine Republic in the organization of its new Bureau of Labor. In response to a request received from His Excellency, the Argentine Minister of the Interior, Señor Don M. A. MONTES DE OCA, the Bureau has communicated not only with the Department of Commerce and Labor of the United States Government, but with the Bureaus of the States of New York, Massachusetts, and Illinois, and has secured from them all their important publications, which have been forwarded to Buenos Ayres. This South American capital is growing so rapidly and the conditions of labor there are demanding

that this new bureau of the Argentine Govern-
rge and interesting field of activity.   The Director
rnor CHARLES E. HUGHES, of New York; Governor
of Massachusetts; Governor CHARLES S. DENEEN,
Hon. CHARLES P. NEILL, Commissioner of Labor
the quick response made to his letters asking that
ireaus of Labor be instructed to provide the Argen-
ith all material at hand.   Inquiries have also been
by the international Bureau from representative men and
ls in the Argentine Republic with reference to the establish-
of an agricultural college in that country, and, in response to
ector's request, the Secretary of Agriculture of the United
and the presidents of a number of North American agricultural
ges have provided the Bureau with data on this subject, to be
forwarded to those concerned.

this connection the Director begs to state that the International
au will be glad to cooperate at all times with any department
different Latin-American governments in securing information
iata in the United States which may be needed, or in giving
assistance in its power for the execution of their respective
programmes.

THE SOUTH AMERICAN TOUR OF PROFESSOR SHEPHERD.

Prof. WILLIAM R. SHEPHERD, of Columbia University, New York,
sailed from New York on May 11 for his tour of South America.   His
itinerary includes Panama, Ecuador, Peru, Bolivia, Chile, the Argentine Republic, Uruguay, and Brazil, in the order named.   He will
be gone four or five months and will endeavor in this period to
visit the principal cities of each one of the Republics named.   It is his
purpose to study carefully not only the educational, intellectual, and
literary status and progress of these Republics, but to familiarize himself with their material, commercial, and economic development.
Upon his return he will use the information he has gained for a
series of lectures before Columbia University and other institutions
in the United States which are desirous of becoming more familiar
with South American countries and affairs.   Although Professor
SHEPHERD goes under the auspices of Columbia University, he will
incidentally represent the International Bureau of the American
Republics in securing special data which is necessary for carrying on
the work of the Bureau.   The statement given out by the New York
papers that he would represent the International Conciliation Committee in spreading its peace propaganda is not true.   At one time
negotiations were under way for him to execute a mission for this

Committee, but later it was decided that he would not have time to attend to that as well as to carry out the programme of Columbia University and the Bureau.

PROFESSOR ROWE'S TRAVELS IN SOUTH AMERICA.

Prof. L. S. Rowe, of the University of Pennsylvania, and one of the delegates of the United States to the Third Pan-American Conference at Rio Janeiro, is now in Chile, and will soon proceed to La Paz, where he will advise the Bolivian Government, in response to a special invitation, in regard to the reorganization of its educational system. Professor Rowe has been the recipient of great attentions from the leading educators of the Argentine Republic during his extended stay in that country. He was a member of the committee of the Pan-American Conference which considered the enlargement of the work of the International Bureau of the American Republics, and he has done much on his trip to awaken interest throughout different South American countries in the practical usefulness of that institution.

POSSIBLE VISITS OF SOUTH AMERICAN STATESMEN TO THE UNITED STATES.

It is a pleasure to announce that progress is being made toward securing a visit to the United States of two such distinguished South American statesmen and scholars as RUY BARBOSA, of Brazil, and Luis M. Drago, of the Argentine Republic. The International Bureau of the American Republics is in correspondence with different universities and representative institutions in the United States for the purpose of arranging that invitations be extended to these representative South American leaders of public opinion to deliver addresses on subjects of interest alike to the United States and Latin America.

THE NEW SPANISH CLUB OF YALE UNIVERSITY.

Special credit is due Yale University for the development of interest in the study of the Spanish language and of Latin-American countries, their history and development. A Spanish society whose membership is made up of students taking a course of study along these lines has been organized by Prof. RUDOLPH SCHEVILL, and its membership has grown so rapidly that it already numbers nearly 100. Prof. SCHEVILL reports a remarkable increase of interest in everything pertaining to the Latin-American Republics, and he believes

r will show still more progress in this direction.
uspices of this club that the Director of the Inter-
! the American Republics recently made an address
before the students of Yale University.

LATIN AMERICA VERSUS ASIA.

. CHARLES M. PEPPER, who was one of the delegates of the
ed States to the Second Pan-American Conference in Mexico, and
; book, "From Panama to Patagonia," has attracted so much
ition, has recently returned from a tour of commercial investi-
-on, on behalf of the Department of Commerce and Labor, in
, and has just submitted a report or his observations. Mr. PEP-
ι found his journey very interesti   but he has informed the
зau of the American Republics thaι he is more convinced than
ω before that the great opportunity for the trade expansion of
United States is in Latin America rather than in Asia.

THE COMPETITION FOR THE NEW BUILDING.

On April 30, the registration of architects for the new building of
the International Bureau of the American Republics was closed. In
addition to the 8 men and firms specially designated, 128 have entered
the open competition. If all these 136 submit drawings it will be
the largest competition which Washington has known and will result
in providing the Bureau with a building both beautiful and practical.
The list of architects is made up of men living in all parts of the country, and therefore the Committee of Award will have a wide variety of
designs upon which to base its conclusions. The competition closes
on June 15 and the decision as to the best plan ought to be reached
not later than June 30. The contract for the actual construction
should be let by the middle of summer, while the first breaking of
ground should take place late in the summer or early in the fall.

THE REPRESENTATIVES OF COLOMBIA AND SALVADOR IN THE UNITED STATES.

The members of the Governing Board of the International Bureau
of the American Republics, whose photographs are published in this
issue, include the Colombian Minister, Señor Don ENRIQUE CORTES,
and Señor FEDERICO MEJÍA, the Minister of Salvador. Mr. CORTES
represents both the highest culture and the best business quality of
his country and has distinguished himself not only in Bogota but in
London as a successful financier. He has served as Minister of For-

eign Affairs in his own country, and was selected by President REYES as Minister to the United States for the special purpose of conducting the negotiations for a new treaty.   Señor MEJÍA has occupied the position of Minister of Finance and Public Credit in Salvador and has been intimately associated with the development of that country to its present prosperous condition.

THE DEATH OF A LEADING EXPORT AUTHORITY.

It is with great sorrow that all those who are interested in the extension of the foreign commerce of the United States have learned of the recent death of Mr. W. J. JOHNSTON, proprietor of the "American Exporter," of New York City.   Few men in the United States have shown more sincere concern for the development of foreign markets for American products, or have worked harder to make American manufacturers and exporters appreciate their opportunities abroad. In frequent conferences between the Director of the International Bureau of American Republics and Mr. JOHNSTON, the former learned to appreciate his deep study of the problems of export trade and his familiarity with its important details.   The present influence, prosperity, and quality of the "American Exporter" are largely due to his personal efforts.   He was a man of untiring energy, good business insight, and devotion to the field of activity in which he was engaged.

APPRECIATION EXPRESSED FOR COURTESIES TO THE DIRECTOR.

The Director of the International Bureau of the American Republics takes advantage of this opportunity to express his sincere appreciation of the courtesies shown him at different places where he has been invited to deliver addresses during the past month upon the relations of the United States and Latin America.   He refers with particular pleasure to President ARTHUR T. HADLEY, Prof. HERBERT E. GREGORY, and Prof. RUDOLPH SCHEVILL, of Yale University; Hon. CHARLES SPRAGUE SMITH, of the *People's Institute*, New York City; Mr. ANDREW CARNEGIE, Mr. ROBERT ERSKINE ELY, and Mr. HAYNE DAVIS, of the New York Peace Congress; President WM. A. LYTLE, Mr. IRVING E. COMINS, and Mr. GEORGE F. BOOTH, of the Worcester Board of Trade; Dr. D. W. ABERCROMBIE, principal of Worcester Academy, Worcester, Massachusetts; President CHARLES W. NEEDHAM, Dean W. R. VANCE, and Prof. E. G. LORENZEN, of George Washington University, Washington, District of Columbia; Mr. B. IRVING, Secretary of the Society of the Oregon Country, Washington, District of Columbia, and Miss HELEN NORRIS CUMMINGS, of the *Cameron Club*, Alexandria, Virginia.

BOLIVIA'S INDUCEMENTS TO IMMIGRANTS.

be congratulated on the practical steps it is taking for
int of immigration.   Few countries in the world have
eral offers for the assistance of new settlers.   The Min-
oi   .   zation and Agriculture gives them free transportation
noth   railroads and highways of the country, and free passage
ir   ects from the port where they land to the point of their
it   All heads of families will receive, at a minimum price,
nectares, or about 125 acres of land, while each son over 18 years
a like amount, and each son over 14 years will receive 14
vares, or about 25 acres.   The report of the Ministry further states
t the popi ju in   was reported as 2,226,935.

PRESIDENT DÍAZ'S MESSA   TO HE MEXICAN CONGRESS.

The message which President Díaz submitted to the Twenty-third
Congress of the Mexican Government, April 1, 1907, is most interesting
and shows the remarkable progress and prosperity of that Republic.
The résumé of the message given in the BULLETIN should be read
carefully by all those who are watching Mexico's growth.   In referring to the currency situation, he calls attention to the fact that the
present coinage of gold amounts to $60,000,000 against $43,000,000
in September, 1906, while the silver subsidiary coins aggregated
$22,000,000.

THE FORWARD MOVEMENT IN CHILE.

Reports from Europe and Chile give evidence of the confidence of
foreign capital in the resources and possibilities of that Republic.
New companies are being organized both in Santiago and in European
cities to develop its mines, its industries, its agricultural lands, and to
build railroads in different directions.   For example, there was
authorized by the Chilean Government on February 14, 1907, the
establishment of an Anglo-Chilean mining corporation, with a capitalization of $1,000,000, whose main offices will be in Santiago.   Not-
withstanding the fact that Chile suffered terribly from the earthquake,
neither the Government nor the people appear the least daunted by
the difficulties of reconstruction.   Everybody is showing a spirit of
courage and activity that compares well with the attitude of the
people of San Francisco and all California in the United States.

THE NEW BUDGET OF URUGUAY.

The prosperous condition of Uruguay is shown by the Budget for 1907–8, which has recently been sanctioned by the Senate and published In this the expenditures and receipts are fixed at nearly $20,000,000, and show a slight surplus in favor of revenues. As evidence of Uruguay's determination to keep up her high financial standing, it can be noted that, among the principal items of expenditure, is the sum of $10,746,189 for national obligations, covering public debt, railway guarantees, etc.

NEW RAILROAD PROJECTS IN PERU.

Peru is showing much activity in railroad work. Some eight important extensions or new lines have recently been authorized by the Congress of that Republic, while the project of building a railroad from Payta to the Upper Amazon is being discussed. In this undertaking the Government will make large territorial grants, which will be an inducement for the investment of capital.

OPPORTUNITIES FOR CAPITAL IN BRAZIL.

Brazil at the present time is offering exceptional opportunities for the investment of foreign capital. New plans for railroad construction, the development of rubber plantations, mining operations, river and harbor improvements, and the utilization of water power, are being constantly reported and should attract the attention of North American capital. All indications now point to a remarkable industrial and commercial advancement throughout Brazil during the next few years.

GROWING INTEREST IN COLOMBIA.

The requests which the International Bureau of the American Republics is receiving for information concerning the mining, agricultural, and timber resources, and the opportunities for railroad construction in the Republic of Colombia, prove the growth of interest in that country which President REYES is striving earnestly to place on a lasting basis of peace and prosperity. Its great material wealth, combined with its unsurpassed location on both the Atlantic and the Pacific, and its proximity to the markets of the United States and of Europe alike, justify a close study of its opportunities and possibilities.

W BRAZILIAN IMMIGRATION LAWS.

published a new law governing immigration and
important State of São Paulo, Brazil. In view of
rity of South America and the greater tendency of
:ope to take advantage of opportunities offered in
blics, it is interesting to note what is being done to
ise of their population. The provisions of the law
od will probably tend to bring people in greater
ulo. That the Brazilian authorities intend to get
best class of people is indicated by the provision that "age,
and morality of the immigrant must be proved by certificates
uthorities at his last place of re nce, or by other trustworthy
ients." Those persons classed as migrants must be foreigners
than 60 years of age who, in amilies or singly, come to
a State territory as agricultural la orers, day laborers, artisans,
we ." Provision is made for free transportation and
rt where they to the district where they
southe ere are also l. l regulations for providing
employment, and financial or other aid until they can fully
themselves.

DEVELOPMENT OF HAITIAN IRON ORE RESOURCES.

Haiti has long been known as a country which has important
resources capable of extensive development, even though its area is
somewhat limited. Among its riches are the extensive iron ore
deposits, which are now attracting considerable attention. The
Government of Haiti has just granted a valuable concession for the
exclusive right and privilege of exploiting these deposits in the district
of Limonade, and it seems probable that further concessions will be
presently granted that will develop other valuable fields of ore.

BRIGHT MINING OUTLOOK IN NICARAGUA.

Reports from Nicaragua show that its mining future is very bright. ·
The new Nicaraguan Mining Code is considered favorable to mining
interests, for by its provisions those intending to develop mines are
allowed to import everything required practically free of duty.
Various companies organized in the United States are installing
plants or making preparations to work the ore bearing districts on an
extensive scale.

about fourteen years Mr. ARCHER MILTON HUNTINGTON
i⁓ nd means to collecting rare Spanish books, maps,
anuscripts, and objects of archæological interest.
)out 40,000 books had been brought thus together

ay of May, 1904, Mr. HUNTINGTON and his wife
of foundation to which reference has been made,
dowing a free public library, museum, and educa-
ithin the city of New York. Eight lots of land in
u⌐r   rk w re conveyed and $350,000 granted as an endow-
leed.
⌐ to⌐⌐o⌐ ⌐   named as trustees: Charles Harrison Tweed,
win   , rancis Lathrop, John Ten Broeck Hillhouse,
n   ⌐ ..ell Hillhouse.
tne tollowing day these gentlemen met Mr. HUNTINGTON at
venth Street, New York City, and proceeded to
f Trustees of the Hispanic Society, electing a
iry. Other officers also—a Treasurer, an Art
1   nervisor of Buildings and Grounds—were elected.
es formally received the grant and accepted for
⌐ves a⌐   ⌐ successors the trusts imposed.
"The Hispanic Society, though its home and headquarters are in
America, and its origin is American, is an international organization
in membership and in the scope and character of its work."

RÉSUMÉ OF CONSTITUTION AND BY-LAWS ADOPTED NOVEMBER 17, 1904.

The object of the society is the advancement of the study of the
Spanish and Portuguese languages, literature, and history, and advancement of the study of the countries wherein Spanish and Portuguese are, or have been, spoken languages.

Its purposes are to promote the public welfare by actively advancing learning, and providing means for encouraging and carrying on the
before-mentioned work within the State of New York; also by issuing
publications from time to time, and by otherwise doing such things as
may be necessary to fully accomplish its work.

A free public library, museum, and educational institution, containing objects of artistic, historic, and literary interest is to be
established.

The management and control of the institution is in the hands of a
board of five trustees. The trustees may receive gifts, bequests, or
devises of property in harmony with the purposes of the institution, and
in particular are constituted to receive from the founder, ARCHER
MILTON HUNTINGTON, or from his wife, HELEN HUNTINGTON, such
gifts under conditions to be prescribed in a foundation deed from
Mr. HUNTINGTON.

The trustees are appointed by Mr. HUNTINGTON and named in the foundation deed, and vacancies in the board occurring during the life of the founder are to be filled by him, and after his death by election by the remaining trustees. Citizens of the United States only are eligible as trustees, who serve without compensation.

The board of trustees elects the President and Vice-Presidents of the Hispanic Society, a Secretary, a Foreign Corresponding Secretary, an Art Director, a Treasurer, a Supervisor of Buildings and Grounds, a Librarian, Curators, assistants, and such other officers or employees as may be necessary.

The powers and duties of the officers are such as the Board of Trustees shall determine.

The members of the Hispanic Society of America constitute an international body, limited in number to 100, in which number the members of the Board of Trustees are included *ex officio*. The members are elected by the Board of Trustees. An unlimited number of corresponding members may be elected by the Board of Trustees. An Advisory Board of 10 from the body of 100 members is to be elected. The Board of Trustees may also elect at their discretion honorary fellows of the Society. The constitution may be amended by the Board of Trustees or by the founder.

The Board of Trustees shall elect from among their number a chairman and an Executive Committee and such other committees as may be necessary.

The Executive Committee shall take charge of and invest the funds of the society in its name, and take all proper measures to provide means for its support; and they shall have the custody of the securities belonging to the invested funds of the society, subject to the order of the Board of Trustees.

The name of any person proposed as a candidate for election to membership of the Board of Trustees shall be submitted first to the Executive Committee.

THE STUDY OF SPANISH-AMERICAN LAW IN THE UNITED STATES.

Hon. JOHN BARRETT, Director of the International Bureau of the American Republics, entered a strong plea for the awakening of greater interest throughout the United States in the Latin-American Republics at a meeting on April 30 at George Washington University, the first of a series planned to advance the study of Spanish-American law in the university. Mr. BARRETT declared that the people of this country greatly underestimated the intellectual advancement of the Latin-Americans.

ARGENTINE REPUBLIC.

AND AGRICULTURAL STATISTICS, 1906.

2,253,829 reported as the valuation of Argentine
r 1906, pastoral and agricultural products repre-
the former figuring for $124,136,439 and the latter
n92. Data issued by the Department of Agriculture
show the following export values of the leading items,
pared with 1905:

Articles.	1906.	
	Tons.	
....	2,357,718	
....	522,323	
....	2,500,275	2,555,213
....	172,036	179,068
....	128,161	147,446
....	70,784	60,037
....	14	236
in lots	285,775	303,034
....	42,319	33,162
(wool)	2,771,403	2,236,038
....	161,087	165,761
....	186,283	182,328
....	25,788	26,837
hides	20,745	21,800
....	325	855
Dried horsehides	1,448	1,164
Jerked beef	7,678	24,670
Butter	4,172	5,424
Tallow	25,978	42,172
Horsehair	2,300	2,338

The destinations of the wheat, linseed, and maize shipments were
as follows during 1906:

Country.	Wheat.	Linseed.	Maize.
	Tons.	*Tons.*	*Tons.*
United Kingdom	266,988	36,344	265,786
France	29,246	31,043	124,354
Belgium	350,643	64,604	214,360
Germany	96,507	104,475	183,901
Italy	47,964	3,865	57,503
Spain	54,598	1,044	31,444
Holland	59,811	38,542	46,851
Russia			
Portugal	15,640	1,817	9,807
Denmark			
Orders	1,175,741	235,855	1,497,402
United States		5	330
Africa	16,713		7,463
Australia			
Mexico			
Cuba			4,334
Brazil	224,525	485	28,101
Chile	837	368	
Bolivia			2
Paraguay	10,530	2,536	1,507
Uruguay	682	1	15,558
Various	7,293	2,717	11,204
Total	2,357,718	523,333	2,500,275

Of the exports of cereals shipped "for orders" the greater share go to the United Kingdom. The same destination is covered for frozen meat, as out of a total numbering 2,771,402 mutton carcasses the United Kingdom received 2,716,672 and of 161,087 quarters of beef, 140,632 were shipped to British ports. Brazil and Cuba took most of the jerked beef.

Uncleansed wool destinations were as follows:

	Tons.		Tons.
United Kingdom	14,508	United States	9,071
France	62,917	Brazil	119
Belgium	22,737	Chile	7
Germany	43,940	Uruguay	366
Italy	1,024		
Spain	46	Total	155,283
Holland	548		

The closure of the ports to exports of live cattle worked havoc in this branch of trade, the figures for the year being 2,945 head of cattle, 37,465 sheep, 4,345 horses, 1,665 donkeys, 14,854 mules, and 27 pigs. Most of the cattle and sheep went to Uruguay. On the other hand, among the animals imported for breeding purposes were: Cattle, 2,448; sheep, 7,802; horses, 975; donkeys, 273, and pigs, 313.

Large quantities of cattle were slaughtered, the various *frigoríficos* totaling 564,171 carcasses for their frozen-meat trade.

An estimate published in the *Boletín del Centro Nacional de Ingenieros Agrónomos* gives the following as the number of animals on the various ranges of the Republic:

Cattle	21,000,000	Goats	3,000,000
Sheep	80,000,000	Mules and donkeys	500,000
Horses	5,600,000	Pigs	800,000

The total value of these animals is estimated at $1,500,000,000, and the same authority considers that the increase in national wealth produced by live stock can not be less than $500,000,000 annually.

Total areas under cultivation in 1906 are given as 13,897,693 hectares, of which 5,692,268 were in wheat, 2,851,300 in maize, and 1,244,182 in linseed. In 1895 the total cultivated area was 4,862,005 hectares, wheat figuring for 2,049,668, maize for 1,246,182, and linseed, 1,020,715.

Railway lines have an extent of 19,794 kilometers and population statistics number the inhabitants as 5,960,595.

IMPORTS OF RAW SUGAR.

To offset the deficit caused by frost in the Argentine sugar crop the *Refinería Argentina* has imported 15,000 tons of raw sugar. Of the quantity imported, 4,500 tons are from Peru, 4,800 tons from Brazil, 3,500 tons from Mauritius, and 2,000 tons of beet sugar from Germany. The Brazilian sugar is reported very superior both as to quality and condition, less loss in weight being also reported.

EPORT ON THE MAIZE CROP.

al report on the maize crop of the year 1906–7 in
ublic states that the protracted drought and the
have had so disastrous effect on the yield that the
r is reduced from 5,500,000 tons—the preliminary
1,̄ ̄,000 tons. Of this quantity, Buenos Ayres will
ˌ ',000 ̄ons; Santa Fé, 555,000 tons; Cordoba, 18,000 tons,
ᴜᴇʀ districts the remaining 200,000 tons.

official estimate of the crop of the preceding year was 4,950,000
, though the final results totaled about 1,000,000 tons below that
ᴜre. The quantity available for export is estimated at 300,000
of which 100,000 tons have alrea been dispatched.

the valuation of the year's maize crop has been $247,000,000,
ᴖad of the $82,035,000 reported at present, a great loss is indi-
l in this branch of agriculture.

RENEWED SHIPMENT OF CATTLE.

n March 14, 1907, the embargo on ipments of live stock from
nos Ayres in accordance with the dᴖree of April 20, 1906, was
oved by governmental action, the disease which had necessitated
ᴜᴜᴏ restriction of exports having been officially declared no longer
existent.

This measure reopens the British market to Argentine cattle, and
efforts are to be made to meet British requirements in the matter of
animal products in general.

PROJECTED RAILROADS.

Various railroad companies of the Argentine Republic, such as the
Southern, Western, Buenos Aires and Rosario, and Argentine Central
have in project the construction of several railroad lines, authorization
for part of which has already been requested from Congress, and that
for the rest will be at the beginning of next session. The amounts
which each company intends to invest in said lines are the following,
in national currency: Southern Railroad, 80,971,400 *pesos;* Buenos
Aires and Rosario, and Argentine Central railroads, 53,499,400
pesos; Buenos Aires and Pacific Railroad, 53,919,800 *pesos;* Buenos
Aires Western Railroad, 46,963,100 *pesos;* Rural Steam Tramway,
20,617,900 *pesos;* total, 255,971,600 *pesos.*

The total number of kilometers of these projected lines is 4,334.

NEW LAND-LAW REGULATIONS.

The Argentine land law gives the lessee of public lands who has complied with the conditions of his lease the right to purchase up to one-half
of the land so leased. The new regulations recently enacted state that
the price to be paid for the land shall be fixed in the lease, as it would

not be fair to expect the tenant to pay a greater price at the end of his term as a result of improvements and increased value given to the land from his own work. The right of purchase was, however, only intended for the original lessee, and article 42 of the regulations now provides that half the land belonging to the State is to be free from such obligation if it should be decided to renew the lease of the land at the expiration of the former contract. All lots up to 2,500 hectares (1 hectare=2.47 acres) which are offered for direct sale for pastoral purposes must be duly measured and surveyed, and the sale must take place within ninety days of the publication of these details. The purchaser of a lot must within two years place thereon 500 sheep or goats and 80 cows, put up the necessary buildings, and plant 100 trees, also pay cost of measurement of the lot. , No person or syndicate can lease more than 20,000 hectares; the term is for five years, and leases are nontransferable.

WOOL EXPORTS, 1900–1906.

The Argentine Department of Agriculture has published recently statistics relating to the wool exports of the country, and a report on the conditions of the wool industry since 1885 and up to 1906. From 1900 to 1906 these exports were as follows:

Year.	Exported.	Official value in gold.	Year.	Exported.	Official value in gold.
	Tons.			*Tons.*	
1900	101,113	$27,991,561	1903	192,989	$50,424,168
1901	228,358	44,666,483	1904	168,599	48,355,002
1902	197,936	45,810,749	1905	191,007	64,312,927

In 1906 there were exported 394,253 bales of wool (1 bale = 400 kilograms), no value being given therefor.

THE BANK OF THE ARGENTINE NATION IN 1906.

In February, 1907, the president of the "Bank of the Argentine Nation" submitted his report for the year 1906 to the Minister of Finance of the Republic. The figures contained therein show that the year was closed with a net profit of 4,413,996 *pesos*, national currency, the largest ever obtained up to the present date, and which represents an $8\frac{1}{2}$ per cent on the capital. In accordance with the respective law, this sum has been added to the capital and reserve fund, which amount to 53,773,388 *pesos*, national currency, and 3,695,796 *pesos*, gold. Private deposits have increased nearly 20,000,000 *pesos*, national currency. The amount of internal drafts bought and sold was 578,000,000 *pesos*, national currency, an increase over the previous year of 176,000,000 *pesos*. The general movement of capital amounted to 7,664,000,000 *pesos*, national currency, an increase of 2,100,000,000 *pesos*.

ROHIBITION OF BRITISH HAMS.

special to the "London Times" says that, in con-
erior quality of some of the hams which come from
intine Ministry of Agriculture has decided not to
Juction after April 15, unless accompanied by a
quality issued by the British sanitary authorities
he Argentine consulates in England.

BOLIVIA.

FOREIGN TRAD1   1905.

United States Minister SORSBY has reported from La Paz concerning the foreign trade of Bolivia during the year 1905, the latest year
for which complete statistics are available. The figures given differ
somewhat from those supplied the International Bureau of the
American Republics by the Minister from Bolivia to the United States,
Señor Don IGNACIO CALDERÓN, and published in the MONTHLY BUL-
LETIN for December, 1906. As stated in the latter report, the values
were the official values according to customs appraisements and not
the real or commercial values, which are naturally somewhat greater.
This may explain the discrepancy observable by a comparison of the
two sets of statistics, as Minister SORSBY's figures are much in excess
of those previously published.

The international commerce of Bolivia is valued at $33,439,429 in
American currency, as against $25,249,396 for the year 1904, an
improvement in the position of the country's commerce of $8,190,033
for the period stated. The imports for the year 1905 are stated at
$13,377,380 in value, as against $10,145,751 for the year 1904, and
the exports for the year 1905 at $20,062,049, as against $15,103,645
for 1904, thus demonstrating an increase of $3,231,629 and $4,958,404,
respectively, in the imports and exports of the country for the
one year, 1904–5. The origin of the imports are classed in the
following order: Germany first, Great Britain second, Chile third,
Peru fourth, the United States fifth, Argentine Republics sixth,
France seventh, Italy eighth, Belgium ninth, Spain tenth, Ecuador
eleventh, and all other countries combined not reaching $48. There
is no classification of the imports, but the exports are classed as
follows for 1905: Tin, $12,582,467; india rubber, $3,516,515; silver,
$1,847,205; copper, $1,187,842; bismuth, $722,978; gold, $18,776; and
lead, antimony, wolfram, cobalt, coca, quina, coffee, etc., $186,266.

IMMIGRATION LAW PROMULGATED MARCH 18, 1907.

SECTION I.—*Concerning the immigrant and his privileges.*

ARTICLE 1. An immigrant is any alien agricultural or industrial worker, under 60 years of age, who, upon proof of good moral character and efficiency, desires to locate in the Republic.

ART. 2. The immigrant who comes to locate in the country shall enjoy, at the present time, the following privileges:

(a) The right to travel to his place of destination over the railways and highways of the Republic.

This right extends to his wife and male children over 18 years of age.

(b) The right to transport his baggage free of duty.

By baggage is understood: His bed and domestic kitchen and household utensils; the tools of his trade or profession, and a firearm for hunting purposes.

(c) The right to occupy public lands for agricultural purposes, stock raising, or useful industries.

Each immigrant may occupy 50 hectares, the valuation of which is fixed at 10 cents per hectare.

(d) Children over 14 years of age shall have the right to 25 hectares.

(e) The right to enjoy easy terms in the payment of the land that he occupies.

These terms are understood to be the following: The immigrant may pay in cash or in five yearly installments. In the latter case, 5 per cent annually will be added to the value of the lands occupied. The immigrant may commence to pay the yearly installments beginning with the third year of his occupancy, with a 5 per cent reduction on the amounts paid in advance.

(f) The right to request of the Immigration Office such data, suggestions, recommendations, and accommodations as may be granted him in conformity with these rules and regulations.

SECTION II.—*Concerning the distribution and ownership of lands.*

ART. 3. The immigrant who observes the requisites prescribed by these rules and regulations has the right to acquire public lands under the conditions hereinafter mentioned.

ART. 4. The lots shall be surveyed and marked by the engineers commissioned by the Department of Colonization and Agriculture, and the adjudication shall be made by means of a deed.

ART. 5. The immigrants may freely select the land they desire in the designated immigration zones, paying the price fixed, and in accordance with the conditions specified in article 2.

ART. 6. Children over 18 years of age shall have the right to acquire lots to locate upon separately whenever they so request.

ART. 7. The immigrant who possesses a certain lot may acquire,

regular means, not exceeding two more lots, but
ars of residence or actual cultivation of his lot.
ligrant shall possess more than three lots by pur-
no   r any other means.
            of a division of an inheritance the division of a lot
            tares shall not be permitted.
            ts shall be delivered with their respective measure-
            'cation.

ART. 11. On measuring the lots an intervening lot shall be left ween each adjudication.

ART. 12. Deeds or titles for immigrants are divided into two classes— provisional and definite.

(a) The first class of titles shall be signed by the agent of the Government and delivered to the immigrants who acquire lands on time payments. The second class of titles shall be signed by the Government, and in the presence of the Notary of the Treasury, and shall be delivered to such immigrants as shall have paid their indebtedness.

(b) The provisional or definite titles shall be delivered without charge to the immigrants at their request.

(c) In case of a purchase on time, the immigrant shall not alienate, hypothecate nor subject the lands or improvements made thereon to any incumbrance, it being understood that both the lands and the improvements are pledged to the Public Treasury until complete payment of the lot is made.

This provision does not include the case of a legitimate inheritance, in which the property will pass to the heir with its mortgages and incumbrances.

(d) The provisional and definite titles shall be recorded in a special book in the Bureau of Labor, and shall also be registered in the Notarial Office of the Treasury.

(e) In the premise or body of the definite titles there shall be set forth: First, the exact description of the boundaries of the lot; second, the length and directions of the dividing lines; third, the square surface and the names of the adjoining lots, and fourth, the conditions and obligations to which the purchasing colonists are subject. Each deed must contain a small plan of the property.

ART. 13. Every immigrant who, within two years from acquiring his title calculated from the date of entry into possession, has not established his permanent residence nor begun the cultivation of the land, shall lose the right to the lot, which shall be sold at public auction, after having been duly advertised.

From the product of the sale there shall be deducted, in the first place, the amount of the indebtedness to the State, then the indebtedness to which the property is subject, and the remainder shall be *delivered* to the immigrant, and in his absence deposited in the *National Treasury.*

SECTION III.—*Concerning the bureau of information and the reception of immigrants.*

ART. 14. The consulates of the Republic in general, and especially the consular offices at Hamburg, Vienna, Antwerp, Barcelona, Paris, Bordeaux, Havre, Marseilles, Lyon, London, Liverpool, Genoa, Naples, Rome, Turin, Milan, Lisbon, Stockholm, Berne, and Geneva, hereby become emigration offices for emigrants, and direct agents of the Government.

ART. 15. It is the duty of these offices to procure for immigrants and industrial workers who so request detailed information concerning the country and its natural, commercial, and industrial conditions; to use their influence in negotiating for accommodations for moving the immigrant and advantageous conditions of transportation, especially with the steamship companies, with whom they may treat for a reduction, which is generally granted to groups of immigrants.

To this end the Department of Colonization will forward propaganda publications in the principal languages, and all the suggestions and instructions that may be necessary.

ART. 16. The bureaus of information shall have a special subvention to pay the expenses of propaganda.

ART. 17. The emigration agents shall send with each group of immigrants a list of the persons who compose the group, giving the following information: Name of the steamer carrying the group, date of sailing, Christian and surname of the immigrant, his age, sex, condition (single, married, or widowed), nationality, occupation, whether he can read or write, point of embarkation, and place of destination. It shall also be indicated whether the immigrants come in a private capacity or whether they are contracted for by immigration or colonization companies.

ART. 18. The emigration agents shall require of the free immigrants a certificate of the municipal district from which they come, setting forth their character, trade, or profession, and their known personal conditions.

ART. 19. If the emigration should be made collectively under the direction of companies or at the request of a private person, the official agent of the Government shall intervene in the contract and shall attend to the embarking of the immigrants and other matters related thereto. In addition he shall see that the emigration companies state the truth to the immigrants and explain the conditions of the contract, so that they may not be deceived by promises and exaggerated statements which would result in injury to the country.

ART. 20. There shall be established in the Department of Colonization and Agriculture a special office called the "Bureau of Labor," which shall have exclusive charge of immigration matters.

ART. 21. The Bureau of Labor shall arrange to receive the immigrants, arrange for the transportation of their persons and baggage, designate the lots of land they are to occupy, and find occupation for them if they are artisans or professional men. The Bureau of Labor shall register them in the proper book and obtain for them all kinds of accommodations until they are settled.

ART. 22. Said Bureau shall keep a registration book of immigrants, giving all particulars in each case; also a register book of the lots of land adjudicated, and a book or books of receipts and disbursements.

ART. 23. The funds appropriated for the promotion of immigration shall be disbursed by this Bureau.

ART. 24. Persons desiring to contract immigrants among individuals who privately set out for this country as well as in the immigration centers of Europe must negotiate with the Bureau of Labor if they wish to enjoy the privileges of these rules and regulations, in which case they shall request permission in writing of the Department of Colonization before landing the immigrants, stating the number of individuals they desire to bring in, the work at which they are to be employed, and their submission to the provisions of these rules and regulations.

ART. 25. Private contracts with immigrants made without fulfilling the foregoing conditions shall not enjoy any of the privileges granted by these rules and regulations.

ART. 26. In the capitals of the Department immigration committees shall be formed, composed of the prefect of the Department, a member of the municipal council, and a secretary of election, the latter officer being salaried, and these committees shall ·cooperate with the main office of the Bureau of Labor in all of their works, especially in the location and settlement of the immigrants in the zones and regions to which they are destined.

SECTION IV.— *Funds for propaganda.*

ART. 27. The following shall be considered special funds for the promotion of immigration: Those set aside in the budget of the respective Department for this purpose.

ART. 28. The inversion of these funds and of others that may be appropriated for the purpose shall be for publications of propaganda, the payment of passage to private transportation companies, and expenses of the Bureau of Labor and of the immigration offices in Europe.

SECTION V.—*Rights and obligations of immigrants.*

ART. 29. In addition to the special privileges granted in these rules and regulations immigrants shall enjoy the guarantees conceded to foreigners by the political constitution of the State.

ART. 30. Immigrants must obey the laws of the country and observe the special immigration and colonization rules and regulations that the authorities may enact.

ART. 31. Centers of immigration having one hundred families shall have schools for both sexes supported by the State.

ART. 32. The Department of Colonization and Agriculture is charged with the execution of the present decree.

IMPORTS FROM THE UNITED STATES IN MARCH AND APRIL, 1907.

The merchandise imported into Bolivia from New York and San Francisco during the months of March and April, 1907, according to reports from the Bolivian consuls at the mentioned ports, was as follows:

	March.		April.	
	Packages.	Value.	Packages.	Value.
New York via—	*Number.*	*Dollars.*	*Number.*	*Dollars.*
Mollendo	19,396	156,191.68	13,022	128,873.40
Antofagasta	1,827	30,683.90	1,502	28,097.42
Arica	32	1,658.13	92	2,107.31
Rosario	354	10,982.00	177	5,166.70
Para	5	111.00	230	1,350.87
Montevideo	22	410.06	133	2,385.93
Total	21,626	199,986.77	15,256	167,981.63
San Francisco via—				
Mollendo		94,129.40		28,689.02
Antofagasta		310.90		2,877.40
Arica		75.00		
Total		94,515.30		31,066.42

The total value of merchandise imported into Bolivia from New York and San Francisco during the first four months of 1907 was $1,151,442.35.

BANK STATEMENT, 1906.

According to the reports for the year 1906, the net profits of Bolivian banks were as follows:

Bolivianos.
National Bank.. 508,274.13
Argandoña Bank... 369,923.06
Industrial Bank.. 265,454.31
Agricultural Bank.. 115,408.85
Hypothecary Bank of Bolivia...................................... 68,082.76

TELEGRAPH SERVICE IN 1905-6.

The annual report of the Director-General of the Bolivian telegraph service covering the year 1905-6 states that from July 1, 1905, to July 1, 1906, eight new lines were established within the Republic.

Bull. No. 5—07——3

',159,753 words were transmitted, and during the of 1906 a total of 2,495,808.

)05 were 82,359 *bolivianos*, and for the first four 9,640 *bolivianos*.

---

*.—At the request of the Bolivian Minister the following cor-
..on is made: In the April BULLETIN, page 837, under the heading
)orts of Tin in 1906;" in line 5, for "kilograms of tin in bars,"
·ad "kilograms of *barrilla* of tin."

BRAZIL.

COMMERCIAL TREATIES.

According to information published in the *Revue Diplomatique*
of April 21, 1907, the Brazilian Government, on April 13, 1907,
denounced all the perpetual clauses—still in effect—of the treaty of
commerce and navigation of January 8, 1826, between Brazil and
France, and the additional articles of June 7 of the same year. These
clauses and articles will become ineffective on July 13, 1907.

As proof that the trade and maritime relations between the two
countries will in no wise suffer from this denunciation, it is cited
that the treaties of the same nature which Brazil then concluded with
other powers lapsed a long time ago without prejudice to the countries signing them nor will this denunciation be prejudicial to a new
commercial agreement.

TARIFF REGULATIONS.

The Brazilian Budget Law for 1907 contains the following provisions:

ARTICLE 1. The import consumption duties established under the
tariff sanctioned by decree No. 3617 of March 19, 1900, as modified
by the laws—No. 1144, dated December 30, 1903, No. 1313 of December 30, 1904, and No. 1452 of December 30, 1905, except as regards
the unamended tariff Nos. 704, 705, 707, and 740 (solely in respect of
barbed fence wire and hooks for the same)—are to remain in force,
with the following alterations:

The duty fixed by the above-named law—No. 1452—on grape juice
is to be levied per kilogram, gross weight. The duties leviable on
the undermentioned articles are fixed at the following rates:

		Reis.
Asses, mules, and horses, except sucking animals and animals for breeding purposes, which are admitted free of duty	head..	60
Mutton preserved by a refrigerating process	kilogram..	200

Reis.

Straw of rye, wheat, oats, and other straw for bottle or demijohn envelopes,
and various other packing purposes..........................kilogram.. 200
Dried and salted meat (xarque)....................:......................do.... 200
Paper for unrolling (de descarga) on reels, to protect the printing of newspapers
on rotary machines...kilogram.. 10
Sisal for reapers and binders..do.... 40
Automobiles (carts or vessels) destined for industrial services, the conveyance
of materials and transport of goods..........................ad valorem.. 5 p. ct.
Kinosol (placed in class 11, in the lysol, etc., group), when recognized by offi-
cial analysis to be solely a disinfectant..........25 per cent, viz kilogram.. 600
Trunks of the black poplar, asp, white poplar, and other white woods suitable
for the manufacture of match wood (under tariff No. 330)....cubic meter.. 20,000
Metallic frit or glazing, white or colored, for ceramic or iron wares (under tar-
iff No. 659)..................................20 per cent, viz kilogram.. 60
Rubberoid, assimilated to galvanized sheets for roofs (tariff No. 728).kilogram.. 100
Typewriters, linotypes, and cash registers are to be dutiable under tariff No. 1009.

ART. 2. Goods enumerated in Nos. 93 and 95 (barley in the grain),
96, 97, 98, 100, and 101 of Class VII of the tariff (cereals), according
to article 1 of the law No. 1452 of December 30, 1905, continue to
be liable to the tax of 2 per cent in gold.

PATENT AND TRADE-MARK LAWS.

The Brazilian law governing patents of invention and the regulations covering the application therefor are contained in decree No.
8820 of December 30, 1882. This decree provides that applicants
for patents in Brazil shall deposit in the first section of the head office
of the Ministry of Industry in Rio de Janeiro a report or description,
in duplicate, in which the invention, its use and purpose, shall be
accurately described; and therewith there shall be deposited, in duplicate, all plans, drawings, and models necessary for the perfect comprehension of the invention, so that, with the explanation in the
report, any competent person can understand the claims of the
inventor and employ his discovery, apply it to further discoveries, or
make use of the improvements it introduces. The concluding paragraph should sum up the claims of the inventor and the limits of the
rights sought. At the beginning of the first page of the report there
must be a description of the invention, in the shape of a title paragraph, written in Portuguese, without correction, underlining, or
erasures, initialed on each sheet and dated and signed by the inventor
or his representative. The report itself may be in any language,
subject to the requirement that certified translations of it must be
furnished, but this title paragraph must be in Portuguese, authenti-
cated as indicated. The report describing the invention, together
with all the plans and papers connected with it, must be deposited
as indicated. The inventor or his representative shall then petition
the minister of industry for the patent, referring to the report
deposited.

on must be filed for each invention. The petition
1ame, nationality, profession, domicile or present
)ner, the nature of his invention, with its purpose
.ccordance with the documents accompanying the
.he department, without any restriction or reserve.
i patent in Brazil involves an expense of from $65
:luding the attorneys' fees, the difference depend-
ue nature of the invention and the ease or difficulty of prov-
ie claims, publication expenses, and fees for experts, as well as
:ng.

; or temporary patent rights will be granted in
in cases. It is provided that if an inventor, before obtaining
patent rights, proposes to make experiments with his invention
make exhibition of the same in an official or semiofficial way,
iall deposit a report upon his invention as in the case of regular
s, except that it need not be in duplicate, and shall then peti-
or a provisional title or patent for whatever period he may wish,
t to exceed three years. The provisional title will thereupon
en without further formality by the Minister of Industry; but
vided that if the inventor shall use his invention for industrial
.ses without obtaining a regular patent, he shall lose his right to
priority guaranteed from the date of the deposit of his original papers.

If within the term of his provisional title the inventor shall petition for full patent rights, he shall be allowed to add to, subtract
from, or substitute in the deposits he has already made, or may withdraw them altogether at the close of the term, with the permission
of the Government. In the case of an official or semiofficial exhibition the Government may grant, upon its own initiative, provisional
titles for inventions exhibited, when the necessary papers have been
filed with the department.

TRADE-MARKS.

The rights secured by trade-marks are regulated by law No. 1336
of September 24, 1904, which modified decree No. 8343 of October 14,
1887, and by decree No. 5424 of January 10, 1905, which approved
the regulations for the execution of said law.

As defined by the law in reference, a registered trade-mark shall
consist of anything that the law does not prohibit and which distin-
guishes the article from others which are identical or similar, but of
different origin, including any name, essential or common denomination, firm, or company, letter or number, provided it is of distinc-
tive nature.

The trade-mark may consist of any sign or illustration which shall
distinguish the article from others which are identical or similar, but

of different origin, provided that the regulations governing the case be observed (article 21).

Size and colors alone can not constitute a trade-mark.

Trade-marks may be employed both on articles themselves and on wrappers or receptacles which are to contain them.

The wrappers or receptacles which are to be stamped with the trade-mark should be of typical or characteristic type to distinguish them from those in common use for the wrapping or packing of products and merchandise and can not be registered for exclusive use as they are already public property.

If the trade-mark asked for contains any facsimile, design, representation, etc., of medals, prizes, or diplomas obtained at exhibitions, the interested parties must show proof that they have really obtained such awards and shall present the original titles or authentic certificates which will be restored to them after the registration of the mark.

No marks will be registered which consist of (1) public, official, national, or foreign arms, blazons, or orders whose use has not been distinctly authorized; (2) names of firms or companies which the petitioner has no right to employ; (3) the name of a locality or establishment which is not the origin of the article, whether this name is fictitious, remote, or not; (4) words, pictures, or designs which offend private or public decency; (5) reproductions of another mark which is already registered for similar articles; (6) exact or partial imitation of a mark already registered for a similar article which might mislead or confuse the purchaser, such imitation to be declared to exist if the two marks can not be distinguished without careful examination.

In the authorization referred to above, in No. 1, the national arms are not included, since they may not be used for any trade-mark, their use being confined to the Departments and establishments of the Republic. No marks may bear fancy medals which might be confused with those granted by exhibitions.

Trade-marks will not be granted (1) for chemical preparations without the name of the manufacturer of the article and the place of origin; (2) for national manufactures in a foreign language without the name of the manufacturer, of the factory, and the locality of the same or the declaration *Industria Nacional* written in clear characters, which declaration, however, is insufficient when the marks are intended to distinguish alimentary articles or substances.

The registration will hold good for fifteen years, after which period it may be renewed. The registration will, however, lose its effect if the owner does not make use of the mark within a period of three years after registration.

gistration of a trade-mark the party interested or
tive must send in a petition, accompanied by three
, containing (1) a description of what the mark is,
         ons as to its characteristics; (2) a reproduction in
    or a drawing, design, impression, or similar process of the
  with all accessories, including the ink which it is proposed to
    a d   ration as to the character of the trade or industry for
   it   to be employed, together with the profession of the peti-
  and his domicile; (4) the petitioner or his legal representative
  in describing the mark may declare that the same mark may vary
    size or colors and arrangement of the colors.
   th the petition and the copies of   mark should be on strong
   r 33 centimeters in height and 22 centimeters in breadth, with a
   gin, for binding purposes, without folds or joints, all to be stamped
   ed, and signed. These dispositions are applicable to foreign trade-
marks.

The secretary of the *Junta Comercial* (Board of Trade) or the
official appointed by the chief inspector shall, so soon as any petition
is presented to him for registration, certify the day and hour of presentation on each of the models, and shall also give a receipt for the
same, if requested to do so, and after the annotation of the petition
shall submit it for dispatch.

So soon as the registration is granted, the secretary of the junta or
the official of the Commercial Inspection Department shall certify
the same on each copy of the mark and shall cause the petition to be
filed, together with one of the said copies, marking it with a number,
which shall be noted on the remaining copies and handed back to the
petitioner.

Within thirty days from the date of registration of the mark the
interested party shall publish in the Federal or State official organ
the certificate of said registration, together with the explanation of the
characteristics of the mark, both to be transcribed textually from the
description treated of, and shall, within the period of sixty days from
said date, deposit in the *Junta Comercial* of Rio de Janeiro one of the
models and one copy of the official organ in which the publication
referred to in the first part of this article has been made.

If desired, the publication may include the design or reproduction
of the mark.

So soon as the registration of the mark has been made in any State
in accordance with the clauses of this article and the subsequent
deposit made a certificate of the same shall be published in the *Diario
Oficial* of the Union.

If the periods in this article are exceeded the deposit of the mark
can not be made, but the owner of the mark has a right to deposit it
afresh.

Further, the deposit of the mark which is to be registered can not be made unless the above rules are complied with.

TRADE CLASSIFICATION OF COFFEES.

Associations of coffee men in Brazil have formally adopted the New York Coffee Exchange classifications of the berry for all their purposes, the *Associação Commercial* of Santos recently adding its final indorsement. The New York method is actually in vogue in the largest consuming market in the world. The committee of the Santos association took occasion in its report to formally outline the rules of classification thus adopted and prepared a table showing the equivalents of the several grades and their more common defects. There are nine grades of coffee recognized by these coffee authorities, as follows:

Type.	Quantity of imperfect beans per half-pound tins.	Extra margin allowed.
1	0	No imperfect beans (green, broken, etc.).
2	6	About 6 imperfect beans (green, broken, etc.).
3	13	About 25 imperfect beans (green, broken, etc.).
4	29–30	About 40 imperfect beans (green, broken, etc.).
5	57–58	About 50 imperfect beans (green, broken, etc.).
6	115–118	About 70 imperfect beans (green, broken, etc.).
7	200	⎫
8	450	⎬ In these low qualities the classification of the coffee is influenced by its appearance.
9	850	⎭

NEAREST EQUIVALENTS OF IMPERFECT BEANS.

3 shells (conchas) equal to 1 black bean.
5 green beans equal to 1 black bean.
5 broken beans equal to 1 black bean.
2 scorched beans equal to 1 black bean.
5 soft or badly threshed beans equal to 1 black bean.
1 large stone equal to 2 to 3 black beans.
1 medium-sized stone equal to 1 black bean.
2 to 3 small stones equal to 1 black bean.
1 large twig equal to 2 to 3 black beans.
1 medium-sized twig equal to 1 black bean.
2 to 3 small twigs equal to 1 black bean.
1 large husk equal to 1 black bean.
2 to 3 small husks equal to 1 black bean.
1 pod (coco) equal to 1 black bean.
2 sailors (Marinheiros) equal to 2 black beans.

CUSTOMS REVENUES, JANUARY, 1907.

The customs revenues of the principal Brazilian ports for the month of January, 1907, were as follows, the figures for the corresponding period of the preceding year being given for purposes of comparison:

Custom-house.	1907.	1906.
Rio de Janeiro	9,366:400$971	6,358:166$368
Santos	3,947:367$574	2,475:183$865
Ceara	501:895$657	317:827$036
Pernambuco	1,970:171$915	1,454:011$120
Espirito Santo	80:417$035	14:196$124
Recebedoria de Rio de Janeiro	2,275:638$103	1,861:273$206
Collectoria Federal São Paulo	501:254$213	420:278$708
Paranagua	297:617$764	138:943$724

s for other Brazilian ports have not yet been

N AND COLONIZATION IN SÃO PAULO.

ing immigration and colonization in the State of
regulated by law No. 1045 of December 27, 1906,

SECTION I.

rICLE I. There shall be considered as immigrants, as regard this
ich foreigners of less than 60 years of age who, in families or
come to settle on State territory as agricultural laborers, day
tisans or skilled workmen and who have produced proof
ir morality and fitness for work; the said foreigners having been
l as third-class passengers either at their own expense or with
ussages paid in full or in part by the State, by municipalities
r ite agricultural or colonizing societies.

morality, and fitness of the immigrant must be proved
s from the authorities at his last place of residence or
trustworthy documents.

. 2. The shipping companies or shippers who convey immigrants to the State may not book any persons for conveyance on
their vessels who are suffering from any contagious disease or having
any organic or physical defect which would incapacitate them for
work; lunatics, beggars, vagabonds, criminals nor persons over 60
years of age except when they come with their families.

For the infraction of this article the agent of the shipping company
or shippers to whom the ships belong and consignees in the State will
be held responsible and will pay a fine of from 100$000 to 1:000$000
which will be doubled on the repetition of the offense.

ART. 3. To every immigrant arriving under the conditions of
Article I shall be granted the following advantages:

I. Disembarkation of himself and his belongings free of duty as
laid down in the fiscal law of the Union.

II. Transport from the quay to the *hospedería* or quarters at
his destination in the interior of the State.

III. Board and lodging at State expense for a period of six days
counting from the day of disembarkation.

IV. Granting of employment, through the official agency of colonization and work in such branch of business or industry as is most
fitted to the ability and capacity of the immigrant.

V. Transport from the hotel to the railway station nearest to the
district of the State where employment is to be given.

ART. 4. In case the immigrant is prevented by illness from leaving
for his destination within the period referred to in No. III of the pre-

ceding article, he will be given board and lodging and medical attention at the expense of the State so long as the illness lasts.

Except in case of illness, the immigrant shall not remain in the
hotel for more than six days unless granted special leave by Government when board and lodging will be paid for according to the rate
laid down by decree.

ART. 5. Such immigrants as are on their way to State and municipal colonies, or colonies belonging to private individuals having
contracts with the Government, shall have the right to board and
lodging in the hotels until sent to their destinations.

ART. 6. Such immigrants as do not desire to participate in the
advantages granted by this law shall expressly declare the fact to
the Inspector of Immigration or one of his officers at the time when
inspection is made, either on board the vessel or in such place as is
appointed for the reception and examination of third-class passengers
at Santos.

ART. 7. The agents and consignees of the ships which are bringing
immigrants to this State must advise the Inspector of Immigration
in the port of Santos at least three days before the arrival of the
vessel or vessels as to their number, in order that he may have sufficient time to arrange for their disembarkation and dispatch to the
interior.

If no such advice is given, the immigrants have the right to remain
on board for thirty-six hours after the arrival of the vessel on which
have traveled.

ART. 8. No company or private person may, without the authorization of the Inspector of Immigration undertake the disembarkation
of the immigrants, their clothes or their baggage. Any person
infringing this rule will be fined 50$000 for each immigrant and
100$000 if the offense is repeated.

ART. 9. The following persons have a right to repatriation at the
expense of the State:

I. Widows and orphans of immigrants who as agricultural laborers
employed on estates or as themselves possessors of lots in the colonies,
when the death of the head of the family takes place within two
years after his arrival in the State and provided that they are without means of sustenance.

II. Such immigrants as, within the same period, fall ill or are the
victims of accidents which incapacitate them from work when they
are employed as mentioned in the foregoing section.

ART. 10. The Government will allow for repatriation, besides a
third-class passage to the port nearest to their destination, a sum of
100$000 to 200$000 according to the size of the immigrants' family.

ART. 11. During the two years after their arrival in the State, free
support shall be given to immigrants employed as agricultural

ate persons or in the colonies by the general defend-
f orphans and absent persons, in actions and other
by law for the collection of wages for agricultural
ribunal of Justice this aid shall be given by the
al of the State.

:h actions as are referred to above, the cost will be
₂ half.

)ayment of these costs can only be exacted after the
process by sentence, agreement, renunciation of the action
other legal measure which fixes the responsibility in the actions
ted of in article 11.

if the action goes to a higher court, he preparation of the briefs
when payable by the laborer, be at half price.

ART. 14. Agricultural immigrants who come at their own expense
and are employed on estates or are themselves possessors of lots in
the colonies, shall have refunded to them by the Government the
amount which they spent on their passages from the port of embarkation to Santos, so long as it is a question of families composed of at
least three persons fit for work and over the age of 12 years.

The same concession will be granted to a bachelor of less than 21
years of age who comes out to join his parents already employed in
agriculture in the State.

ART. 15. Immigrants who have resided in the country previously
but who have remained less than five years in the employ of private
planters or in the colonies, will have no right to the enjoyment of the
above privilege on their return to the State.

ART. 16. Immigrants can not claim the refunding of their passage
money unless they apply for the same within two years from the date
of their arrival.

SECTION II.

ART. 17. The Government shall, for the fostering of immigration,
either for paid labor or for concessions in the colonies, take the following measures:

ART. 18. They shall grant a subsidy of so much per head for each
immigrant to the shipping companies or shippers, who possess vessels
with the necessary qualifications, in accordance with the special dispositions laid down by decree.

ART. 19. This subvention shall be granted free to any company or
shippers who conform to the regulations in force, provided the number of immigrants marked for any one year is not exceeded.

The Government shall, if it considers advisable, suspend the shipping of immigrants and reduce the subvention before the number
referred to above is reached, provided that 60 days' notice be
given before such suspension or reduction to all the companies or
shippers interested.

Art. 20. When it is judged convenient to foster immigration from new sources the Government shall make contracts for conditions as shall best guarantee the interests of the State.

Art. 21. The Government shall issue orders, in agreement with the shipping companies, for tickets for calling immigrants for employment by private planters or in the colonies in accordance with the regulations in force for the execution of this service.

Art. 22. When agricultural or colonizing societies or private individuals introduce into the State, at their own expense, immigrants fit for agricultural labor, whether as paid laborers or as possessors of lots in the colonies, the Government shall refund to such societies or private individuals the whole or part of the sum expended by them for the immigrant, together with his third-class passage from his port of embarkation to Santos, after the immigrants have been settled and all regulations complied with which are established for the best interests of the State.

*   *   *   *   *   *   *

Art. 41. So soon as the definite titles have been granted to the concessionaries the colonies shall be declared emancipated.

The Government will then give up the administration of the colony but will, if deemed convenient, maintain the instruction camp.

Animals for breeding purposes, the mill, implements, plows, and cattle in the colony will be transferred gratis to a syndicate to be formed by all the concessionaries of the lots and to be worked and maintained on the cooperative system.

Art. 42. So long as the colony is not emancipated the Government will maintain on it besides the personnel and laborers:

1. A director to look after the good order and proper carrying out of regulations in the colony, with a salary of 5:000$ per annum.

A physician who will periodically visit the colony, come when summoned and attend sick persons, charging for the same a stipulated fee.

3. An assistant to look after the clerical work of the administration with a salary of 2:400$ per annum.

Art. 43. The Government shall nominate from the numbers of the agricultural class or other fit residents in the State, Brazilians or foreigners, a special delegate for each nationality represented among the immigrants settled in the colonies. This delegate, who shall serve without salary, shall be called Director of Colonization of the respective nationality and shall act as intermediary between the administration of the colony or Government and the concessionaries for any claims that they may wish to make, and shall also act as their adviser and guide and help them when newly arrived to get accustomed to the country.

Art. 44. The extension of dates for the payment of installments

led for in this law will only be granted to conces- tivate their own lots and live on the same.

...id payment of installments will be extended over ...of ...years to colonies which the Government shall create ...Sorocabana railway line or in the districts which are fallow or stant from means of transport while the lots may be of 50 res.

Government may, however, grant a definite title to all con- ...aries who shall have completed three years of continuous dence and cultivation and have improved the land to the extent :000$ in value.

r. 46. The Government is empowered to found colonies in con- n with the owners of the land; the Government to mark out ...nts and pay the owner the price for the half acquired by it, the livided alternately and evenly between the two parties.

...proprietor of the land shall have to submit to certain con- ...as ror the sale of the lots which shall fall to him, as also to the ...erted in the contract that shall be drawn up, which will ...ne best guaranty for the carrying out of the said contract.

...n the creation of such colonies, the rules for their administra- ...the concession of the lots to the Government, and the advan- tages and aid to be granted to the colonists to be settled there shall be fixed by decree in every case.

Art. 47. When companies or private individuals propose to found and maintain colonies on their own estates, under the same condi- tions and with the same advantages as the Government offers to official colonies, they shall be granted, besides the refunding of the passage money of the immigrants and other favors allowed by this law, a premium of 10:000$ for every fifty families settled on such colonies.

These favors will only be granted as laid down in the contracts in which the Government will insert clauses to guarantee the best interests of the State.

Art. 48. When companies propose to colonize uncultivated lands on such of their lines as are open to traffic, the Government will grant them the right to disappropriate the said lands if they belong to pri- vate individuals and also will grant them a free concession for fallow lands within a radius of 20 kilometers on each side of the said line, provided that they measure it out and divide it into lots and settle thereon families of agricultural colonists on conditions to be laid down by contract.

Fallow lands, after having been measured and divided into lots by the companies, shall be divided equally between the Government and the concessionaries into alternate lots, each party to pay half expenses.

ART. 49. The Government will pay part of the expenses of measuring and dividing up lands to such municipalities as propose to found and maintain colonies at their own expense, on conditions which will assure the founding of such colony.

ART. 50. For the division and populating of private estates, the Government may make contracts on the following conditions:

1. The owner must show a clear title to the land which is to be colonized and shall undertake to perform the following at his own expense—

(a) To divide the land into lots of 25 or 50 hectares according as the lots are at a maximum distance of 12 kilometers from the railway or nearest touching point for steamers or from lands far distant from means of transport.

(b) To build roads connecting the lots and the colonies with the main highways.

(c) To build a house on each lot in accordance with the type approved by the Government.

(d) To clear the ground, cultivate it, and make pastures on an area to be determined by the contract.

2. When the lots are prepared in this manner and the proper number of families of colonists or immigrants, as arranged in the contract, are settled, the Government will pay for each lot with its improvements and cultivation a price which shall not exceed 2:500$000.

3. The Government shall grant the period of from five to ten years, according to the position of the lot, to the recently arrived immigrants for the payment of installments to the State for the said lot and a provisional title shall be granted on the payment of the first installment and the definite title on the payment of the last.

4. In contracts made in accordance with this article, the Government shall insert such clauses as shall make for the best interests of the State.

ART. 51. The Government shall give preference for the sale of fallow lands to such persons as are Brazilians or naturalized Brazilians who have lived on and cultivated such lands for more than five years, the price to be 10$000 per hectare of cultivated or forest lands; 2$000 for land for grazing, and 20$000 per hectare for lands in the suburb and lots, together with the expense of measuring and marking out the same.

No occupier may purchase more than 500 hectares of land for cultivation, 4,000 of grazing land, and 50 in the suburban lots.

Suburban lots are those situated within a radius of 18 kilometers from the governor's palace in the capital and 12 kilometers from the municipal chambers in the cities and towns of the State.

lides from the port of Rio Grande do Sul for the
a very gratifying increase over the exports of the
ng exceeded only by those of 1904, an exceptional
's to the United States during the year were almost
)05, but are still much below the amount taken by
during the beginning of the current decade. The
hides exported to Europe in 1896 was 230,719 and
y nides 11˙ 59, while in 1906 the salted hides numbered 447,719
the dry 385,378. In 1896 no hides were exported to the
d State 'y in 1901 the dry hides numbered 79,657, and in
the numr v 79,420, which 1 nber fell to 14,513 in 1905
28,000 in The total exports of all hides in 1896 was
)78 ai in 1906, while in 904, the banner year, they
reached 920,738.

The increased exports to the United ates seem to be due largely
to shipments made in December. During the same month there was
a marked increase in the shipments of animal hair to all points, and
especially to the United States. The United States now is the
heaviest importer of animal hair from Brazil, the United States and
Germany together taking three-fourths of the country's exports
thereof. Germany continues to take the greater portion of Brazil's
exports of horns, France of its glycerine, Great Britain of its bone
ash and fish glue. Brazil's lard and tallow products are practically
all consumed at home.

MISCELLANEOUS NOTES.

Mr. RUSSION and Mr. TOMSON, representing an English syndicate,
recently made a visit to the interior of the State of Bahia to study
and report on the rubber plantations of that district. As a result
of the investigations, Mr. RUSSION purchased for the company seven
large plantations in the region of Rio do Contas and took an option
on nine other plantations in this region. He calculates that 500
tons of rubber can be produced on these plantations during the first
year, and that this production can be greatly increased in time by
the use of modern methods of extraction.

A recent number of the *Minas Geraes* calls attention to the
excellent fiber obtained from the plant known in Brazil as *Páo de
Jangada*, of which the botanical name is *Apeiba tibourbou* Aubl.
This plant is found not only in the State of Minas Gereas, but in nearly
all parts of South America. The fiber of this plant is white and very
resistant, qualities which make it of great value for industrial purposes.

The President of Brazil has authorized a credit of 200 contos to be
opened for the construction of a railway from Cruz Alta to the mouth

of the Ijuhy River. By the decree of February 14, 1907, a credit of 600 contos was authorized in order to broaden the gauge of the São Paulo branch of the Brazilian Central.

Mr. WM. A. F. NEUMANN, representing the Buffalo Forge Company, the Buffalo Steam Pump Company, and the Geo. L. Aquier Manufacturing Company, is now in Brazil making a special study of the machinery in use in that country in the manufacture of sugar and in the preparation of coffee, cacao, rice, cotton, and fibers. Mr. NEUMANN is also representing *La Hacienda*, the agricultural and industrial review published at Buffalo, New York.

It is reported that the Agricultural and Live Stock Exposition, which is to be held at Pelotas, State of Rio Grande do Sul, next May, will be one of the finest ever held in Brazil. The number of persons who have already signified their intention of taking part in the exhibition exceeds 300.

It is reported that work is far advanced on the five steamers which the Lloyd Brazileiro is having built in English shipyards. The *Pará* is expected to be finished ready for launching the current month. The other four vessels will be named *Acre*, *Ceará*, *Bahia*, and *Rio de Janeiro*.

Señor HENRIQUE SÁNCHEZ, a distinguished chemist of Bucaramanga, Republic of Colombia, has recently made the discovery that a very good quality of alcohol could be obtained from the pulp surrounding the coffee bean, which has hitherto been considered useless. This discovery is considered of great significance to coffee-producing countries, inasmuch as it will take the place of petroleum for lighting and power purposes.

The Société Financière et Comerciale Franco-Brésilienne, having its headquarters at Paris, has recently obtained permission from the Brazilian Government to operate in that country. This company has a capital of 5,000,000 francs. The main object of the company is to continue the business of the firm of Nathan & Co. established at São Paulo, but it will also engage in other commercial and industrial operations in connection with the same.

The *Ceará*, one of the new vessels which the Brazilian Lloyd is having built for its coasting service, was launched from the shipyards of Messrs. WORKMAN, CLARK & Co., of Belfast, Ireland, on March 16 last. This is the largest vessel of the Brazilian merchant marine, registering 5,300 tons. In addition to having large freight capacity, it has excellent accommodations for about 170 first-class passengers.

The President of Brazil has issued a decree creating a commission of public works for the Acre Territory, with headquarters at Cruzeiro do Suloon, the Upper Juruá. The Commission will have charge of the building of roads, the work of removing obstructions in rivers, the construction of public buildings, the establishment of industrial and agricultural schools, and any other works which the Federal Government may order.

A new mining company, known as The Minas Geraes Gold Fields Company, was recently organized in London for the purpose of acquiring and working mines in Brazil—among others, the S. Luiz and Juca Vieira mines. The company has a capital of £150,000.

The National Agricultural Association of Brazil has called a Third Sugar Conference to be held at Campos, State of Rio de Janeiro, on June 30 of the current year.

The Government of Brazil has appointed Dr. JOAQUIM NABUCO, the Brazilian ambassador to the United States, and Dr. RUY BARBOSA to serve as Delegates of Brazil at the coming Hague Conference.

The President of Brazil has authorized a credit of 785,365 *milreis* gold for the purchase of silver for the new Brazilian coins.

CHILE.

IMPORT TAX ON MATCHES.

Under date of January 13, 1907, the following law establishing a sliding scale of duties on match imports into Chile was promulgated:

SOLE ARTICLE. Wooden matches, during the space of three years from date, shall pay an import duty at the rate of 20 *centavos* per kilogram of gross weight.

At the expiration of the specified time the duty shall be diminished at the rate of 2 *centavos* annually, per kilogram, until it shall have reached 14 *centavos* per kilogram, gross weight.

CUSTOMS DUTIES, FEBRUARY, 1907.

Total customs duties collected at the various ports of Chile during the month of February, 1907, aggregated $8,092,231.18 (national currency), as compared with $9,900,585.55 in the preceding month. Of the February receipts, import dues are credited with $3,673,179.16 and exports, $4,211,341.98; other branches of the service contributing $207,707.04 to the general total.

For the corresponding month of 1906, total receipts for customs were $6,269,394.28, a marked increase being thus shown for the later period.

THE ANGLO-CHILEAN MINING COMPANY (LIMITED).

The establishment of the Anglo-Chilean Mining Corporation *(Limited)* was authorized by the Chilean Government on February 14,

1907, the object of said corporation being to promote native industrial enterprises in foreign markets. The capitalization is $1,000,000 issued in bonds of $200 each. The main office is to be in Santiago.

LATEST LIVE-STOCK STATISTICS.

Supplementary to the figures published in the MONTHLY BULLETIN for January, 1907, covering live-stock statistics of Chile, the following data, including certain provinces for which returns had not been received at that time, are published.

Cattle of all kinds within the Republic number 8,768,533, distributed as follows:

Horses, asses, and mules, 746,150; kine, 2,674,666; sheep, 4,528,109; goats, 436,739; hogs, 338,993; unclassified, 3,876.

SAVINGS BANKS IN THE REPUBLIC.

Consul ALFRED A. WINSLOW, of Valparaiso, reports that in order to encourage thrift on the part of the laboring classes in the Republic of Chile, the Government has entered into an agreement with the *Caja de Crédito Hipotecaria*, a strong financial institution of Chile, to take charge of the Government savings bank branches at Serena, Curico, Temuco, and Punta Arenas, the Government having found it too expensive to conduct them itself.

An appropriation of 100,000 *pesos*, or $25,000 United States gold, has been made by the Government to open up new branches in other parts of the Republic. The move is being well received and promises much. It is proposed to make use of the post-offices, fiscal treasuries, etc., to advance and encourage the saving habit.

FLAX CULTIVATION IN CHILE.

The British legation at Santiago reports that a German flax-growing expert, acting on behalf of two of the largest flax-spinning firms in Reichenbach, has, during the past four years, been conducting exhaustive experiments in the districts in south Chile round Lake Llanquihue and the island of Chiloe, and has now succeeded in determining the species of plant most suitable to the climatic conditions of the country. The flax grown is said to be of exceedingly good quality and of greater length than the flax ordinarily grown in Europe. Unusually heavy crops have been obtained from the land on which the experiments have been made. The German expert hopes to obtain a bounty from the Chilean Government on the export of flax in order to stimulate its cultivation. It is expected that Puerto Montt will be the center from which the raw material will be exported.

SALT MINES.

ne in its issue of March 13, publishes an interest-
alt mines of the Chilean Republic.
s authority, the salt deposits, as well as the greater
il deposits, are inexhaustible. The Salar Grande
of Huanillos, is the most important one in Chile, and
re is pure in the proportion of 99 per cent of chlorure
deposit is 32,000 hectares in area and 20 meters
without, however, the bottom of the layer having been
ed. The quantity of salt contained in this deposit is estimated
,000,000,000 tons, and in spite of this unheard-of abundance salt
is only exploited on a small s . are several other deposits
in Chile similar to the preceding which could fulfill the ex-
igencies of the world's consumption several centuries.

The following statistics on the wo nportations of this product
show the great possibilities of this co nerce in the hands of big
capitalists:

The yearly imports of common salt by France amount to from
500,000 to 600,000 *francs;* Bulgaria, 1,000,000 *francs;* Norway, from
2,500,000 to 3,000,000 *francs;* Sweden, 2,000,500 *francs;* Brazil, Argentine Republic, Uruguay, and other South American countries, more
than 7,000,000 *francs;* while England exports from 12,000,000 to
15,000,000 *francs* yearly, and Spain from 3,000,000 to 4,000,000
francs.

The Chilean deposits alone can furnish all the salt consumed in the
entire world and at half the price of the European product.

COLOMBIA.

RAILWAY CONTRACT.

The *Diario Oficial* for February 13, 1907, publishes the contract entered into December 19, 1906, between the Minister of Public Works
and Fomento, Señor Don FRANCISCO DE P. MANOTAS, and ALFRED B.
MASON and EDWARD H. MASON, and approved by President REYES
on December 24, 1906, for the construction of a railway between the
cities of Palmira and Cartago, in the Department of Cauca.

The line will be single track, 3 English feet gauge.

Plans must be submitted within six months after approval of contract and work begun immediately on approval of plans, to be terminated within five years.

One-fifth at least of the line must be constructed each year.

The Government guarantees 5 per cent interest upon $40,000
gold per kilometer of road constructed and also 2 per cent in addition
for sinking fund.

Free importation of material for construction is granted.

PAPER MILLS IN THE REPUBLIC.

The *Diario Oficial* of February 26, 1907, publishes the text of an agreement entered into on December 6, 1906, between the Government of Colombia and José A. Pagés and José Pons for the establishment of paper mills in the Republic.

ESTABLISHMENT OF A SUGAR FACTORY.

The *Diario Oficial* of February 25, 1907, publishes the text of an agreement made on July 27, 1906, and approved by President Reyes July 31, 1906, between the Government of Colombia and Vélez, Danies & Co., for the establishment of a central and sugar refinery in the Department of Bolivar.

The cost of the central and the refinery is to be $750,000 gold, of which amount the Government contributes $150,000.

NEW RAILWAY.

United States Consul Luther T. Ellsworth, of Cartagena, reports that a contract has been entered into between the Minister of Public Works and Thomas J. Ribon for the construction of a railway from Nemocon to Santa Rosa de Viterbo, with a branch line to Sogamoso. The territory through which this line will pass is considered very rich in agricultural possibilities, and great industrial development is expected to follow the completion of the line. Mr. Ribon has just finished a line of railway from Honda to Ambaloma, which will be turned over to the Government during the present year.

TARIFF MODIFICATIONS.

A decree issued on January 20, 1907, by the President of Colombia exempts certain merchandise from the payment of import duties and reduces the import duties on other articles desirable to use in the industrial development of the country.

The President of the Republic of Colombia, in exercise of the powers vested in him, decrees:

Article 1. The payment of import duties is hereby removed on chemical fertilizers and bases for chemical fertilizers consisting of phosphates and superphosphates of lime; that is to say, phosphates treated with sulphuric acid; on the salts of potash, namely, chlorate of potash, known in commerce as muriate of potash, sulphate of potash, and kainit; on azo-fertilizers, consisting of nitrate of soda and sulphate of ammonia, calcium cyanide or cyanide of calcium, also called nitrogenous lime; on sulphate and bisulphate of carbon, and pitch or varnish for the manufacture of waterproof cardboard or tropæolin.

ax on fence wire is hereby reduced from 100 p
, but said reduction shall be made by tenth;
e provisions of article 205 of the Constitution.
lecree amends paragraph 3 of sole article of dec
28, 1906.

DECREE CREATING THE PROVINCE OF CAMILO TORRES

President of the Republic of Colombia, in exercise of the
ers vested in him, and considering—

, st, that it is expedient to the better administration of the public
vice to divide into two provinces the present province of Santander,
the Department of Cauca, and

Second, that it is likewise highly d[ ]ble to settle sundry differences concerning the boundary betwe[ ]he districts of the various
provinces of that Department, and ta[ ] advantage of the meeting
of the Administrative Board to which is fitting to delegate said
powers during the recess of the Congress decrees:

ARTICLE 1. That the province of Camilo Torres, consisting of the
districts of Caloto, Espejuelo, Corinto, and Toribio, the former of
which shall be its capital, and all of which are segregated from the
province of Santander, is hereby created.

ART. 2. The Governor of the Department of Cauca is hereby
appointed to fix, with the approval of the Administrative Board, the
boundary at points that have not hitherto been clearly defined by
official acts between the provinces of Popayam, Santander, and
Camilo Torres, particularly between the districts of Santander and
Buenos Ayres and Santander and Caloto.

The decisions made by the board are subject to review by the
Government.

ART. 3. This decree became effective on February 1, 1907.

COSTA RICA.

CUSTOMS RECEIPTS, FISCAL YEAR 1906-7.

La Gaceta for April 11, 1907, publishes the schedule of customs
receipts of the ports of Costa Rica during the fiscal year 1906-7
(April, 1906, to March, 1907, inclusive), the total revenue from this
source being given as 4,346,977.49 colones, as compared with
3,970,285.74 colones for the preceding twelve months.

An increase of 376,791.75 colones is thus indicated for 1906-7, and
as the estimate for the year was only 4,200,000 colones, an advance
over the budget estimate of 146,977.49 colones is reported.

The latest valuation fixes the colón of Costa Rica as equivalent to
$0.465 United States currency.

ABOLITION OF CONSULAR FEES.

According to article 8 of the new consular law approved by the House of Representatives and published in the *Gaceta Official* of Costa Rica of January 30, 1907, consular invoices for Costa Rican ports are to be viséed gratuitously from the 1st of March. For the value of the visé has been substituted a tax which the receivers of the goods must pay to the customs of the Republic.

COSTA RICA AND THE BANANA TRADE.

From a letter written by Hon. ERNEST F. ACHESON, Member of the Congress of the United States representing Pennsylvania, the following data, as published in the "Observer," of Washington, Pennsylvania, for April 8, 1907, is reproduced:

"The population of Costa Rica is estimated at 350,000. The area is 18,400 square miles, or equal to that of New Hampshire and Vermont combined. The foreign population is about 7,000, and this is increasing slightly by immigration. The Government has begun to encourage immigration by the sale of land on easy terms.

"Costa Rica is the most advanced country in Central America, with a desirable population and stable Government. No revolution has occurred here for thirty-five years. The gold standard has been adopted, and business is on a solid basis. The people are peaceful and do not want to go to war. They have the reputation of being more industrious and honest than their neighbors in other States. Most of them take little interest in politics, do not vote, and care little who governs them, so that peace is maintained. While they probably work more than the inhabitants of other countries in the Tropics, they are not hustlers. The country has immense resources—agricultural, mineral, and timber—but the greater part of its territory is unoccupied. Here, as in all Spanish countries, there is no land tax. That is the reason the country has not made progress. Immense tracts of land are held under ancient grants, and as there is no tax to pay it is held in rich families who do not use it and will not subdivide and sell it. Import duties are levied on tobacco, liquors, and various kinds of goods.

"Port Limon was named by Columbus, who sailed along this coast on his last voyage vainly searching for a passage to the western sea. The old navigator explored the shore lines of each gulf and bay and sailed into each river between Yucatan and Trinidad. This portion of the land was well named Costa Rica, or rich coast, and the harbor in which our good ship anchored was called 'Puerto de Limon,' because the islands near by were covered with lime trees. Limon has a population of 8,000, a large proportion being negroes from Jamaica, who are employed in loading and unloading ships and upon the immense banana plantations near by. English is the exclusive

in all the coast country of Costa Rica. Indeed,
ow in all the schools throughout the country, and
ilsory. It must also be used in all the stores.
tself on being the only country of Central America
iool teachers than soldiers.
. inecting Port Limon with San Jose, the capital,
eet. The distance is 102 miles. For 6 miles after
Limon the road skirts the coast, most of the way within
of the breaking billows, and then turns up the valley of the
ntizan River. For many miles it passes through the wonderful
a farms which have made Costa Rica famous. Here the
grows all the year around. A banana shoot, or branch, as it
d, starts to produce at the age of 9 months. The branches
it down each season. Then the laborer cuts the shoots with
hete, or corn cutter, sticks the machete into the ground, twists
s in a shoot, stamps it, and that is all the cultivation the
a inch gets. The underbrush, however, which grows in trop-
iance, is cut three times each year. The banana bunches
ired by hands. Each perfect hand has 22 bananas. The
inds on a bunch ranges from 7 to 22. The average num-
ir bananas on a bunch is 144, though a few bunches have been
found with upward of 500.

"The land along this coast is peculiarly adapted to banana raising.
While the banana trees thrived for awhile in other countries of Central America, no soil seemed rich enough to stand the continuous cultivation of bananas save Costa Rica and upper Panama. Land can
be bought here at $12 per acre. It costs $40 per acre to clear it and
put it into condition to raise bananas. It will yield 15 bunches of
bananas per acre every month. Taking the average of 144 bananas
to the bunch it will be seen that each acre will produce 25,920 bananas
annually. The vegetation is so rank and its growth so rapid that it
takes one man to every 3 acres to clear the brush and grass every four
months, pick the fruit, dig the ditches, build the bridges, and do all
the necessary work. Farm laborers are paid from 85 cents to $1.50
per day American money. As $1 of our money is equivalent to 215
centavos or $2.15 Costa Rica money, the laborers can live luxuriously
on these wages if they choose. Here, as in Panama, the Jamaicans
are indolent and will not work regularly. If engaged to go to work
at 7 a. m. they may not appear until 8 or 9 o'clock, and after three or
four days' work will lay off for two or three days. Frequently they
go off into the bush or jungle, as it is called, build a shack, and clear a
piece of ground. Under the law these squatters must be paid for
their improvements if the owner of the land wishes to take possession.
The land is divided into hectares or 2.47 acres, and all calculations
as to production are based on this measurement.

"The United Fruit Company owns 150,000 acres of land susceptible of banana culture. The greater portion of this, remote from the railroad, is not yet used for the production of bananas. Last year the company purchased about half the bananas it shipped. Many banana growers own their own farms. During 1906 no less than 8,500,000 bunches were shipped from Port Limon, of which 5,000,000 went to the United States. There is no export duty on bananas. About 400 ships, or an average of more than one ship per day, loaded with bananas, left Port Limon last year. This year it is confidently believed 10,000,000 bunches will be exported. A ship of 3,000 tons sometimes takes from 40,000 to 50,000 bunches. While the Jamaica bananas are pronounced better by epicures, the Costa Rica or Limon bananas sell better in the market because they look better. They have a fine appearance, and four customers out of five will choose them. A good many settlers have come here from the United States and have been very successful in banana raising.

"It is said, broadly, that everything will grow in Costa Rica. By far the larger part of the population and production is on the Pacific side of the mountains, yet nine-tenths of all its exports are from Port Limon. Sixty-five per cent of these exports go to the United States. While bananas are the principal export, still last year the value of coffee exported was $3,350,000. Thirty-two thousand bunches or over 4,600,000 bananas are about an average load. Then if one considers that the United Fruit Company has 102 ships carrying fruit to the United States and Europe he gets a faint idea of the tremendous growth of the business. Of course many of the ships ply between Cuba, Jamaica, and other fruit-producing countries to ports of the United States and England. This company gives work to 7,000 persons, including railroad employees.

"What has been accomplished by the United Fruit Company shows what American energy and enterprise can do in a tropical country. It is over four hundred years since Europeans first set foot in Costa Rica. It was the first country on the mainland of the continent to be discovered, but as yet its marvelous resources are scarcely touched. Extensive prairies affording fine pasturage are found in the northern part of the country and vast forests of valuable timber in the north-eastern section. Sugar, corn, cocoa, and tropical fruits flourish. The coffee is of superior quality. The land held by the Government is sold at a nominal figure with a long time allowed for payment. Costa Rica only needs more enterprising Americans with capital, such men as manage the United Fruit Company, to bring it into the first rank of prosperous communities of this continent.

" Passing through vast banana farms, one of which, belonging to one company, is 9 miles in length, the train reaches the foothills of the Cordilleras and begins its winding climb to the summit, a mile above in the clouds.   The road follows the valley of the Reventizan, which soon becomes a dashing torrent.   For 40 or 50 miles there is a succession of horseshoe bends.   The route is tortuous and the grade at many points heavy.

"This line is a great revenue producer.   Last year it earned over $1,700,000.   It was built by an English syndicate, but has been taken over by the United Fruit Company.   The Reventizan is a considerable stream, and as it falls again and again over the rocks for mile after mile, the thought comes that some day this power, now wasted, will be utilized.   It would undoubtedly be sufficient to generate electricity which would operate the railroad, light many towns, and run thousands of machines.

"The train winds through picturesque mountain passes and deep gorges, where mighty walls of solid rock rise for hundreds of feet.   The mountains are fertile to their very tips.   Gardens are planted on slopes as steep as the roof of a house.

"As the summit is approached a good view of Irazu, a volcano on a peak said to be 14,000 feet above the sea, is obtained.   It is one of a group in this neighborhood which are now quiescent, but sometimes emit sulphur, lava, and ashes.   Two miles from the summit is Cartago, a town of 10,000 people, which was destroyed by an eruption nearly sixty years ago.   It is 90 miles from the coast and about 5,000 feet above sea level.   The air is cool and bracing, and one can scarcely believe that it is only a few hours from tropical heat at Port Limon.   Many persons from the Canal Zone go to Cartago to recuperate when worn out by continuous hot weather.   It takes only a day from Colon to reach this mountain top.   Accommodations for boarders are at a premium, and it has been suggested that the Canal Commission build a sanitarium at Cartago.   A few weeks here would do as much to revitalize a man as his six weeks' annual vacation spent in the States, and the trip would be much less expensive.   A peculiarity of this region is that it will rain for weeks on the Atlantic side of the mountains and never a drop fall on the Pacific side.   Going down to San Jose the descent is about 150 feet to the mile.   Switches and sidings for runaway trains are provided, the tracks of the sidings running at a stiff upward grade for some distance to allow a runaway train which is switched to it to expend its force and enable the crew to get control of it.

"After a delightful seven hours' ride San Jose, the capital of Costa Rica, is reached.   San Jose has a population of 25,000 and is a solidly built town of clean and attractive appearance.   The streets are narrow as in all Spanish towns, but are well paved.   The bulk of the population of Costa Rica is in the country around San Jose.   It was settled by immigrants from provinces in Spain where the people were Caucasians and had never mingled with the Moors.   When they settle to Costa Rica they kept their blood pure and refused to intermarry with the Indians, as most of the Spanish settlers did.

"San Jose boasts of one of the most magnificent theaters in the world. Only Paris and Milan have structures which exceed it in grandeur. It was built by the Government and cost over $1,500,000. The money was raised by a coffee tax. The best mechanics and decorators in Italy were brought here to do the work. Although only 10° from the Equator, the mercury never rises above 84°, while in Canada it reaches 104°. Perpetual spring reigns and the flowers are perennial. The days are warm and the nights cool enough to sleep under a blanket. No one has an overcoat, and the houses have no chimneys. Shoes are not worn by the women of the lower classes. Education is free and compulsory between the ages of 8 and 14. On account of earthquakes the houses are one and two story structures with thick adobe walls.

"The sanitary and quarantine regulations are better enforced in Costa Rica than in any State in Central America. The buzzards help to protect the public health, and great flocks of these scavengers of the air can be seen from the car windows. San Jose is over 4,000 feet above the sea, on the Pacific slope of the mountains, and its surroundings are picturesque and beautiful. The valleys between the mountain ranges near by are exceedingly rich and fertile."

CUBA.

RECEIPTS OF CUBAN LUMBER AT NEW YORK, 1906.

Mahogany and cedar logs from Cuba were received at the port of New York during 1905 and 1906 in the following quantities, according to figures furnished the "Cuba Review and Bulletin" for April, 1907:

Year.	Mahogany.	Cedar.
1905	14,628	88,350
1906	31,063	136,449

Prices for Cuban mahogany ranged from 8 to 12 cents, the highest price being for the Santiago wood. Cedar prices ranged between 11 and 14 cents, the wood from Santa Cruz, Santiago, and Manzanillo bringing the highest price.

NATIONAL STATUS OF THE ISLE OF PINES.

The decision of the Supreme Court of the United States rendered on April 8, 1907, declares:

"The Isle of Pines is a part of Cuba, and therefore a foreign country within the meaning of the enacting clause of the tariff act of 1897, and importations therefrom are subject to the tariff laws of the United States."

ECUADOR.

REGULATIONS FOR THE PURCHASE AND SALE OF SALT.

The regulations adopted by the National Assembly of the Republic of Ecuador for the purchase and sale of salt, which is a Government monopoly, were issued on January 17, 1907.

The salt consumed in the Republic is produced by evaporation in pits at Salinas and other districts. The price for purchase at the pits has been fixed at 40 *centavos* (about 18 cents) per 100 kilograms. At the salt deposits throughout the provinces of Guayas, Manabi, Esmeraldas, Los Rios, the coast cantons of El Oro, and the station of Huigra, on the Guayaquil and Quito Railway, the price has been fixed at 2 *sucres* (about 98 cents) per 46 kilograms. Prices at other places in the interior are to be arranged on this basis, plus expense of transport, etc.

EXPORT TAX ON IVORY NUTS.

President ALFARO, on February 14, 1907, approved the following law:

The National Assembly of the Republic of Ecuador decrees:

ARTICLE 1. The exportation of ivory nuts from the ports of the Republic shall be taxed 6 *centavos* per kilogram if the nuts are hulled and 4 *centavos* if in the shell.

This shall be the only impost upon the exportation of this product.

In case the tax should prove excessive, the Executive Power is authorized to restrict the same to the amount now collected.

ART. 2. The collection of the impost on the exportation of ivory nuts shall be made directly. Credit is prohibited.

Done at Quito, capital of the Republic, February 6, 1907.

CONTRACT FOR THE CONSTRUCTION OF THE AMBATO TO CURARAY RAILROAD.

The Department of the Interior and Public Works of Ecuador has contracted with A. MONCAYO for the formation of a company to construct a railway from Ambato to a point on the Curaray River accessible to steamers and to establish a regular steamship service between said railway terminus and Para, Brazil. The plan includes the establishing of steam navigation on all of the navigable rivers of the Oriental Region; the acquisition temporarily or in fee simple of public lands, and the exploitation of mines, waterfalls, etc.; the bringing of foreign immigrants, especially of Europeans, to the Oriental *Region* of Ecuador, and the settling of Ecuadorian agriculturists in *other* provinces and territories. The company is to be incorporated

in London under the name of the Eastern Ecuador Explorati
Company.

The Oriental Region of Ecuador comprises all of the territory of t
eastern slopes of the Ecuadorian Andes lying between the northea
east, and southwest frontiers of the Republic. The Government
Ecuador may at any time fix the precise western limits of the Orien
Region.

The Exploration Company agrees to make, within five years fr
the date on which it begins work, correct hydrographic and topograpl
maps of the Eastern Region, said maps to be the property of t
Government. In compensation for this service the Government
Ecuador grants to the Exploration Company the exclusive right
explore the Oriental Region for five years and the further right
exploit for a period of fifty years all the vegetable wealth that it m
discover, definitely locate, and denounce during the five yei
referred to.

With respect to wild vegetable products the denouncements sl
be made by zones, and shall only include the forests within si
zones and not the land, the land being subject to denouncement
cultivation without prejudicing the rights of the company. 'I
Government also gives the company the preference in the acquisiti
of Government lands for agricultural or industrial purposes in acco
ance with the laws of the Republic. The land granted to the coj
pany shall always be in alternate sections.

The Exploration Company also has the preference in the denounc
ment of mining zones and may, in conformity with the law, acqui
mining property. Employees of the Exploration Company are pi
hibited from making denouncements, unless they obtain a speci
license, until ten years after the expiration of their term of servi
The company also has the preference in the denouncement of wate
falls, but the waterfalls denounced must be exploited within ti
years from the date of the denouncement.

The company must maintain immigration offices in Europe ai
the United States and in other places where it may deem advisab;
and agrees to advance the necessary capital to immigrants to enal
them to become established in the Oriental Region.

For a period of fifty years from the date the company begins opei
tions in the Oriental Region the exportation of the natural produc
of that region, via the eastern rivers, together with the exportati
of articles produced, manufactured, or imported through the wi
coast, is free.

A bid for the construction of the railroad from Ambato to Curar
must be submitted to the Government within one year from the da
of this contract.

FUNDS FOR THE CONSTRUCTION OF THE AMBATO AND CURARAY RAILWAY.

The National Assembly of Ecuador decrees the following amendments to the legislative decree of October 19, 1904:

ARTICLE 1. The following revenues are to be converted in the construction of a railroad from Ambato to Curaray:

1. Ten per cent of the imposts on *aguardiente*.

2. Thirty cents per kilogram of the import duties on matches.

3. Fifty per cent of the import duties on cigarette paper.

4. A tax on imitations made in the country of foreign wines and liquors sold as such, whether in bottles or other vessels of larger size.

5. A license of 100 *sucres* ($48.70) on traveling agents who propose to sell goods in the country.

Whoever infringes the foregoing provision shall pay double the amount of the license. The Executive is empowered to issue rules and regulations governing the collection of this tax.

6. The receipts from the railway.

ART. 2. The receipts of the railroad shall be collected by the treasury collectors and deposited fortnightly in the Bank of Ecuador, which shall be the depository for said funds.

ART. 3. The bank is hereby authorized to invest—authority of the board having been previously obtained—said funds in mortgage bonds at par or at a discount, for the purpose of converting them into productive capital, and when necessary shall make advances on these mortgage bonds in order to facilitate the payments of the board.

ART. 4. All orders of payment concerning the funds of the railway shall be signed by the Secretary of State, who is a member of the board, and by the chairman of the board.

ART. 5. The offices of member of the board, treasurer of the board, and other employments that the board may create in its organization, are honorary.

The paid employees shall be the secretary, engineers, inspectors of works, lawyers, etc., who shall be appointed by the Secretary of Public Works on the recommendation of the board, and their respective salaries fixed by mutual agreement.

ART. 6. The Administrative Board referred to in article 7 of legislative decree of October 19, 1904, is hereby authorized to contract loans for the carrying on of the said work, securing said loans with the revenue derived by virtue of this decree.

ART. 7. The board shall undertake, for its own account, the construction of the railway, or shall definitively contract the construction of the same by means of bids approved by the State Board, and shall invert only the funds provided for this purpose and the receipts from the sale of public lands in the Oriental Region.

ART. 8. The Nation guarantees the fulfillment of the obligations contracted by the board, in conformity with the powers or authority granted it in the present decree.

ART. 9. If the railroad should be constructed by contractors who should employ their own capital in the work, upon payment of the annual interest and amortization, any surplus revenue remaining by virtue of this decree, shall be applied as an additional payment of said capital at the end of the year.

ART. 10. The loans negotiated by the Patriotic Board, in order to be valid, shall be approved by the Executive.

ART. 11. The Secretary of Public Works shall be *ex officio* member of the board.

ART. 12. The Patriotic Board charged with the construction of the railway to Curaray shall order the line to pass through the town of Pelileo, at which point a station shall be established.

ART. 13. The 10 per cent impost on *aguardiente* referred to in paragraph 1 of article 1 of this decree shall be deducted, in the first instance in each one of the provinces, from the total receipts of said impost.

ART. 14. The treasury collectors shall be subject to the provisions contained in article 22, subdivision 5, and article 28 of the fundamental treasury law, concerning any delay in the forwarding of the funds for the construction of the railway to the depositary bank.

The foregoing decree was passed by Congress on January 28, 1907, and was promulgated by the President on January 30 of the same month.

RAILWAY PROJECT.

The *Registro Oficial* of February 23, 1907, publishes the text of the concession to Baron BAUDOUIN VAN DEDEM for the construction of a railway from a port on the Pacific, to be determined by a commission, to Quito, the capital.

POTABLE WATER SUPPLY IN QUITO.

The National Legislative Assembly of the Republic of Ecuador decrees:

ARTICLE 1. The potable water and canalization board of Quito is hereby empowered to negotiate a loan not to exceed 1,700,000 *sucres* ($827,900), in the manner most suitable to its interests, securing said loan with that portion of the maritime customs duties corresponding to said board.

ART. 2. The board is hereby authorized, if necessary, to pledge as a guaranty the work or works undertaken.

ART. 3. The payment of the interest and the amortization of the loan shall be made from the fund specified in article 1, and out of the receipts from potable water until the entire loan is paid.

ART. 4. The supreme decrees of May 19 and October 4, 1906, are hereby amended in conformity with the foregoing, and are approved in all other respects not in conflict with this decree.

The foregoing decree was passed by Congress on February 7, 1907, and approved by the President on February 14 of the same year.

THE AMBATO AND EASTERN RAILWAY CONCESSION.

El Telégrafo, of Guayaquil, in its issue of March 28, 1907, publishes the full text of the contract made by the Government of Ecuador with Count CHARNACÉ for the construction of the Ambato and Eastern Railway from the city of Ambato to the navigable tributary waters of the Marañon or Amazon rivers, the entire construction to be within the boundaries of the Republic of Ecuador. The construction company must be organized in Europe or the United States within a year from the date of this concession. The Government of Ecuador grants to the company 35,000 hectares of public lands for each kilometer of railway constructed from Ambato to the Amazon River or the navigable tributaries thereof.

The railway company has the privilege of exporting domestic products, such as caoutchouc, ivory palm, coffee, toquilla straw, etc., free of export duties. The Government will also aid the company in establishing all kinds of industrial factories, such as plants for the manufacture of sugar, factories for the making of toquilla straw hats, etc., and the products of these industries shall also be exempt from export duties.

If, after the lapse of a period of one year from the organization of the company, it should not construct at least 40 kilometers of railway yearly, the Government of Ecuador may declare the concession forfeited and enter into possession of that part of the railway already constructed, but even in this event the company shall retain its ownership in the lands acquired under the terms of the concession.

FUNDS FOR THE HUIGRA AND CUENCA RAILWAY.

The National Assembly of the Republic of Ecuador, considering that it is necessary to provide the proper funds for the interest and payment of the 6,000,000 *sucres* ($2,922,000) to be invested in a railway from Huigra to Cuenca, decrees:

ARTICLE 1. The following revenues shall be used for that purpose:

(a) Ten per cent additional on import duties formerly applied to the service of Worship;

(b) Ten cents a liter on the fiscal revenues on *aguardientes* (brandies) produced in the provinces of Cañar and Azuay.

(c) An impost of two per thousand on rural property in the aforesaid provinces, to be collected for a period of five years from the promulgation of this decree.

ART. 2. These revenues shall be collected by the respective collectors, and shall be deposited fortnightly in such bank in Guayaquil as may be designated by the Executive.

ART. 3. The Secretary of the Treasury shall be pecuniarily responsible for the investment of these funds in any other manner than that prescribed in article 1 of this decree.

ART. 5. When interest and amortization payments are to be made out of the proceeds of the railway, any surplus of the revenues referred to in article 1 shall be paid into the common treasury funds.

FINAL ARTICLE. From the funds mentioned in paragraph (a) of article 1 there shall be applied, once only, and during the first year in which this decree is in force, the sum of 100,000 *sucres* ($48,700) to the construction of a road from Loja to Santa Rosa.

The collector of customs at Guayaquil shall deposit these funds in a bank, subject to the order of the board of directors of that road.

The foregoing decree was passed by Congress on January 9 and promulgated by the President on January 12, 1907.

GOVERNMENT TRAFFIC IN TOQUILLA STRAW.

The Ecuador Government has decided to buy toquilla straw in Marabi for the purpose of selling it at a low price in the provinces of Azua in order to save the hat-manufacturing industry from annihilation, inasmuch as that industry was threatened with destruction because of the high price and monopoly of this raw material by speculators. The first shipment under this arrangement has already been received at Narajal, and is being sold at 80 cents a pound. Not only have the speculators secured a monopoly of this article, but they have also sold the straw in a wet condition, of short weight, and adulterated with Gualaquiza straw. The Government has therefore ordered that straw for the manufacture of hats be sold under the immediate inspection of the police.

SALE OF LOCOMOTIVES.

The board of directors of The Inca Company has sold 10 locomotives, Nos. 17 to 26, inclusive, now in the Republic of Ecuador, to the Guayaquil and Quito Railway Company, for $176,175.55. The terms of the sale are $1,175.55 cash and the balance in promissory notes of $5,000 each, dated New York, December 3, 1906, payable at the Oriental Bank of New York City, and bearing interest at the rate of 6 per cent per annum.

GUATEMALA.

THE AMERICAN BANK OF GUATEMALA IN THE SECOND HALF OF 1906.

According to the report of the board of directors of the American Bank of Guatemala for the second half of the calendar year 1906, the account of profit and loss, after deducting therefrom unearned interests, administration expenses, fees of members of board of directors, salaries, and other authorized payments, shows a net profit of $546,578.63. The board of directors passed a resolution providing for the payment of $125 per share—1,200 shares—a total of $150,000; for the distribution of a dividend of $100 per share, a total of $120,000; for the deposit of $240,000 with the reserve fund, and for the creation of a new contingent fund amounting to $36,578.63. Grand total, $546,578.63.

RAILWAY TRAFFIC BETWEEN EL RANCHO AND SANARATE.

El Guatemaltico of March 9, 1907, publishes the announcement of the general agent of the Guatemala Railway to the Minister of Fomento of the opening to traffic of the new line between El Rancho and Sanarate.

HAITI.

EXPLOITATION OF IRON-ORE DEPOSITS.

Le Moniteur, official journal of the Haitian Republic, publishes in its issue of March 6, 1907, the terms of the contract recently granted by the Government to Gen. F. EUGÈNE MAGLOIRE for the exclusive right and privilege of exploiting, according to conditions established by law, the iron-ore deposits in the district of Limonade formerly granted to Mr. TURENNE LACONTE, whose concession lapsed through failure to fulfill the conditions of the contract. For the other metals which may be found in the same radius the concessionnaire will be granted the preference in the awarding of the concession.

Before beginning work, and within six months following the publication of the contract in the official journal, the concessionnaire or his representatives must deposit in the National Treasury a guaranty of $1,000 American gold in cash, and this guaranty will be refunded without interest at the end of the year if the terms of the contract have been fulfilled; otherwise it will revert to the State.

The concessionnaire or his representatives, as well as the personnel employed, are exempt from all tax for licenses. All material and all

indispensable implements which the concessionnaire or his representatives may introduce into the country for the exploitation of the
mine are exempt from duties. The concessionnaire can form a stock
company under the form and rules established by the Code of Commerce on the subject.

The concessionnaire or his representatives will pay the State a fixed
amount and a bonus, as prescribed by law. The fixed amount is
established at $2 American gold yearly per square kilometer. The
payments will be made from the commencement of the exploitation.
The bonus is 5 per cent of the net product, and will be paid to the
Government either in kind or in specie (American gold), as preferred,
but after the receipt of the bills of sale, which will be sent to it. These
bills of sale must bear the visé of the Haitian representative in the
industrial centers where the sales are made and the minerals treated.

COMMERCIAL CONVENTION WITH FRANCE.

Le Moniteur for February 20, 1907, contains the text of the new
commercial convention between France and Haiti which was signed
at Port au Prince on January 30.

Under the provisions of this convention, the principal Haitian
products, including rum and tafia, are entitled on importation into
France to pay duty under the French minimum tariff. In return,
certain natural and manufactured products of French or Algerian
origin will enjoy, on importation into Haiti, a reduction of 33⅓ per
cent from the duties of the Haitian minimum tariff. Haitian customs duties on certain specified articles and on French wines are not
to be increased while the convention remains in force. French vessels
are not exempted (as they were under the previous convention of
1900) from paying the supplementary tonnage dues on import duties,
and consequently vessels of all nationalities will now receive the same
treatment. These tonnage dues are not to be increased during the
continuance of the convention.

Pending ratification, the convention went into operation provision-
ally on February 1, 1907. It is to remain in force for a period of three
years, and, unless denounced six months before the expiration of that
period, until six months after denunciation by either contracting
party.

The text of the convention is reproduced in the French section of
the BULLETIN for May, page 1280.

COMMERCIAL MOVEMENT FOR THE FISCAL YEAR 1904-5.

According to a general report on the situation of the Haitian
Republic published in *Le Moniteur* of March 16, the commercial

Bull. No. 5—07——5

movement of this country for the fiscal year (from October, 1904, to September, 1905) shows the following results:

Merchandise of all nationalities entering the eleven open ports is valued at $3,871,061.39 gold, distributed as follows:

United States	$2,746,851.00
France	406,076.96
England	509,793.01
Germany	88,116.58
Other countries	120,223.84
Total	3,871,061.39

In comparing this result with that of the preceding fiscal year 1903–4, or $3,753,934.35, an increase of $117,126.84 is noted for 1904–5.

Statistics show that during the fiscal year 1904–5 the commercial movement increased as follows:

United States	$282,351.98
France	12,827.65
England	151,167.06
Total	446,346.69

A decrease is noted with the following countries:

Germany	$215,420.36
Other countries	113,799.49
Total	329,219.85

The shipments of specie from New York to the eleven open ports during the six months of the fiscal year 1904–5 amount to the sum of $223,123.65.

The provisions and products shipped abroad by the eleven open ports are valued at $8,967,862 national money, while those exported during the fiscal year 1903–4 were estimated at $17,871,925.97, or a a difference of $8,904,063.97, nearly 50 per cent in favor of the fiscal year 1903–4.

The following products show a decrease in the quantity exported: Coffee, campeachy, campeachy roots, yellowwood, cedar, cacao, mahogany, hides, goatskins, wax, old copper, honey, cattle, and guaiac gum.

On the other hand, the following provisions and products exported show a decided increase: Guaiac wood, pitch, horns, orange peel, and cotton.

The exports of cotton seed increase constantly. Of this product 48,876 bags were exported in 1904–5, while 31,312 bags were shipped in 1903–4, or a difference of 17,564 bags. The greatest precautions having been taken to prevent fraud, it must be believed that this advance has its principal source in the increased cotton production.

EXPLOITATION OF MANGANESE MINES.

Le Moniteur of March 2, 1907, publishes the terms of the contract awarded Mr. ALEXANDRE POUJOL for the exploitation of the deposit of manganese ore in the county of the Coteaux. The terms of this contract are similar to those for the iron-ore concession, of which mention is above made.

MEXICO.

MESSAGE OF PRESIDENT DÍAZ.

At the opening of the second session of the Twenty-third Congress of the Mexican Government, President Díaz presented in his message delivered on April 1, 1907, his usual review of national affairs, covering conditions during the preceding half year.

In regard to foreign intercourse it was stated that relations between Mexico and other Governments continue to be characterized by the greatest harmony and cordiality. The convention with the United States for the equitable distribution of the waters of Bravo River and the construction of a great international dam at Engle, United States, 100 kilometers north of Ciudad Juarez, having been duly approved, was promulgated on January 26, 1907.

The difficulties arising from the long-standing questions between the dwellers on the opposite banks of that river, due to the frequent changes in its course, rendered almost impracticable the application of articles 1 and 2 of the convention of November, 1884, between Mexico and the United States. The International Boundary Commission suggested to the two Governments that the dividing line should be determined by the river, regardless of certain changes that take place in its course, and that certain fragments of territory known as *bancos* and separated from both shores should be left out of consideration. After careful consideration and prolonged studies, two articles were agreed on to take the place of the first and second articles of the convention of 1884; the arrangement was signed at Washington on March 20, 1905, and, having been approved by the Senate of both nations, it will, as soon as ratifications have been exchanged, be duly promulgated.

The Federal authority was successfully employed in the settlement of the labor questions which agitated the Republic at the close of the year, and effective sanitary measures were applied for the combating of yellow and typhus fever and for the treatment of tuberculosis. Improvements at the capital during the half year cover the laying of about 40 kilometers of new mains for the supply of drinking water,

In compliance with the law on the subject, verification of instruments and apparatus for weighing and measuring throughout the Republic was effected by the Department of Fomento, and correct models were distributed to the various States.

Water concessions for different industrial purposes were granted, conveying the right to the use of 123.780 liters of water per second for motive power and 32.267 liters per second for irrigation, also 30 new title deeds for the use of more than 40.000.000 liters. Concessions for fishing privileges in both the waters of the Pacific and the Gulf were granted, and agricultural stations maintained in several sections of the Republic.

Patents of invention to the number of 585 were granted, also 10 patents for industrial designs, while 475 trade-marks and 44 commercial names and announcements were registered.

Apart from the opening of the Tehuantepec Railroad, which was elevated into a function of national importance, the Department of Communications reports work accomplished on the water route between Tuxpam and Tampico, port and sanitation work at Coatzacoalcos and Salina Cruz, while the general plans for similar development at Mazatlan have been made and the work begun.

Railways subject to Federal jurisdiction were extended more than

200 kilometers in the half year under review, the present length of the system now aggregating 17,647 kilometers, which, added to the lines constructed under State concessions, gives a total extent of 21,906 kilometers in the Republic. Rolling stock and repairs on the lines received attention.

From July to December, 1906, 14 new local post-offices, 57 agencies, and 6 itinerant offices were established, the total number of offices now aggregating 2,715. The number of pieces of correspondence handled was 86,000,000, as compared with 84,000,000 in the corresponding period of the preceding year, while internal money orders had a valuation of $22,209,000, an increase of $609,000 for the later period. The interchange of postal drafts with foreign countries also shows an increase, that with the United States being 65 per cent; with England, 106½ per cent, and with Germany, 119 per cent. Money-order services have recently been established with the French Republic and with Salvador. Conventions have also been entered into with the postal and telegraph administration of France for the direct interchange of correspondence between the offices of New Laredo, Mexico, and the French offices at Beyrouth and Tripoli, Syria, with the postal administration of the German Empire and with England whereby the maximum amount of a money order shall be 200 *pesos* (Mexican) or its equivalent in German and English money, instead of 100 *pesos* as formerly.

Telegraph lines have been strung aggregating 2,893 kilometers for repair and new systems, and six new telegraph and three new telephone offices opened. A convention with regard to wireless telegraphy is shortly to be submitted to the Senate as a consequence of participation in the International Wireless Telegraph Conference held in Berlin in October, 1906. Earnings of the telegraph system were 8 per cent in excess of those reported for the corresponding six months of the preceding year.

The customs collections during the first half of the current fiscal year (July–December) exceeded those of the first half of 1905–6 by more than $3,000,000, and during January and February, 1907, collections show another $1,000,000 increase.

The new stamp law reducing the rate of the former schedule came into force on November 1, 1906, and notwithstanding the diminution, collections under the new régime exceeded those of the corresponding period of the previous fiscal year by $400,000. Further amendments in this branch of the service of the Government are now contemplated.

The currency situation is reported as satisfactory. As against $43,000,000 gold that had been coined by September, 1906, the present coinage amounts to $60,000,000 gold. The mintage of silver subsidiary coins aggregates $22,000,000.

Among the new measures to be presented to the action of Congress are: Reduction of taxation, the increase of salaries, and the proposed consolidation of railway systems under Federal authority.

FOREIGN COMMERCE IN JANUARY, 1907.

According to figures issued by the Statistical Division of the Treasury Department of the Republic of Mexico, the foreign commerce of the Republic for January, 1907, and for the first seven months of the current fiscal year, 1906–7, was represented by the following valuations, the figures for the corresponding periods of the preceding year being also given for purposes of comparison:

The total value of importations during the seven months under review was $129,341,643.95 in Mexican currency, as declared in the custom-houses, an increase of $16,788,035.84 as compared with the preceding year.

The exports for the seven months were valued at $140,184,883.20, showing a decrease of $16,788,035.84 as compared with the same period of 1905–6.   Imports and their valuation were as follows:

IMPORTS.

[Silver valuation.]

Articles.	January—		First seven months—	
	1906.	1905.	1906–7.	1905–6.
Animal substances	$1,626,137.15	$1,372,440.72	$11,486,616.44	39,383,849.98
Vegetable substances	2,939,082.82	3,581,482.16	16,440,678.44	17,765,676.05
Mineral substances	8,647,362.93	14,245,542.80	46,676,664.90	42,071,671.46
Dry goods	2,100,137.13	1,574,851.47	15,340,978.00	13,862,652.71
Chemical and pharmaceutical substances	756,227.15	756,964.76	4,801,730.75	4,367,576.14
Beverages	564,599.05	696,135.46	3,926,304.59	4,356,368.34
Paper and its applications	458,805.76	453,951.90	3,441,697.04	5,155,552.06
Machinery and apparatus	1,857,257.99	1,808,817.46	15,516,392.69	10,648,656.82
Vehicles	697,022.87	633,880.96	4,767,067.51	2,265,577.36
Arms and explosives	280,184.14	326,687.82	2,338,342.97	2,331,994.50
Miscellaneous	826,320.92	623,608.71	5,352,026.46	4,445,971.73
Total	20,743,137.91	25,761,364.26	129,341,643.95	112,386,625.11

EXPORTS.

[Silver valuation.]

Articles.	January—		First seven months—	
	1907.	1906.	1906–7.	1905–6.
Precious metals	$11,129,196.88	$17,382,029.12	$72,631,439.84	92,922,928.76
Other articles	11,171,749.14	7,725,781.96	67,563,442.55	64,062,630.28
Total	22,300,946.02	25,108,411.08	140,194,883.39	156,972,919.04

The details of the export trade for the periods in reference sl the following classification and figures:

Articles.	January—		First seven months of fi year—	
	1907.	1906.	1906-7.	1905-(
Mexican gold coin....................			$29,990.00	
Foreign gold coin....................	$262.00	$247.00	7,531.00	$4,:
Gold in bars.........................	1,506,094.89	1,428,736.58	11,405,376.83	17,975,:
Gold in other forms.................	432,854.90	495,380.38	3,254,917.37	1,400,(
Total gold......................	1,941,211.79	1,924,363.96	14,697,815.20	19,380,
Mexican silver coin.................	2,824,896.00	10,712,875.00	14,391,660.00	29,697,:
Foreign silver coin.................	17,918.00	25,336.00	82,809.00	76,
Silver in bars......................	4,868,243.37	3,705,806.66	36,620,002.72	38,443,:
Silver in other forms..............	1,476,937.72	1,014,247.50	6,839,153.02	5,289,:
Total silver....................	9,187,965.09	15,458,265.16	57,933,624.74	73,506,
Total gold and silver...........	11,129,196.88	17,382,629.12	72,631,439.94	92,886,
Antimony..........................	120,089.00	2,071.00	807,867.00	595,
Copper............................	1,894,540.00	1,118,096.44	15,229,713.00	16,974,
Marble............................			21,080.00	73,
Plumbago.........................	10,800.00	18,430.31	56,620.00	51,
Lead..............................	272,697.00	206,317.17	2,147,821.56	3,075,
Zinc........................,.....	267,772.00	31,695.00	890,993.12	142,
Other metals......................	18,584.30	35,481.25	1,073,780.68	223,
Total......................	13,713,679.18	18,796,720.29	92,859,315.30	114,023,
Vegetable products:				
Coffee...........................	791,567.34	652,194.30	2,502,622.34	3,388,:
Cascalote and tanning barks......			7,824.00	20,
Rubber..........................	691,374.00	196,474.00	2,761,873.00	694,
Chicle..........................	287,925.00	223,766.10	920,995.00	668,
Beans...........................	84,001.00	57,697.00	458,944.00	-463,
Fruits..........................	21,254.00	14,650.00	190,322.43	210,
Chick peas......................	90,303.00	74,136.75	2,693,884.00	1,784,
Guayule.........................	15,200.00	5,787.00	23,799.00	31,
Horse beans.....................		250.00	2,550.00	110,
Heniquen........................	3,892,582.00	2,735,012.00	20,990,011.77	18,202,
Ixtle...........................	233,644.00	230,254.00	2,378,505.00	2,176,
Woods........................,...	125,269.00	260,956.00	1,154,659.50	1,238,:
Maize...........................	65.00	7,766.00	3,103.80	33,:
Mahogany........................	7,622.00	7,620.00	46,832.00	36,:
Dyewoods........................	38,972.00	40,582.25	246,510.12	220,:
Xacaton.........................	129,371.00	121,686.00	983,488.00	1,134,:
Leaf tobacco....................	105,061.00	36,334.00	972,186.35	543,:
Vanilla.........................	37,300.00	188,365.00	947,400.00	2,505,:
Other vegetables................	239,223.00	100,876.30	1,219,547.20	845,:
Total......................	6,789,833.34	4,956,406.70	38,505,057.51	34,319,(
Animal products:				
Cattle..........................	81,275.00	134,683.00	838,654.00	1,987,:
Skins and hides.................	1,153,499.00	891,939.08	5,385,927.03	4,398,:
Other animal products...........	55,560.00	44,395.34	358,591.99	292,:
Total......................	1,290,334.00	1,071,017.42	6,583,173.02	6,679,(
Manufactured articles:				
Sugar...........................	212,119.00	240.00	367,168.00	260,(
Flour and pastes................			697.00	
Rope............................	48,589.00	36,385.00	407,118.00	276,:
Dressed skins...................	203.00	16,703.00	31,604.00	126,:
Straw hats......................	81,179.00	34,732.00	395,663.80	298,(
Manufactured tobacco............	41,891.00	26,232.00	294,299.60	198,:
Other manufactures..............	54,591.50	79,948.17	308,988.32	348,:
Total......................	438,572.50	194,240.17	1,805,538.72	1,509,·
Miscellaneous articles..............	68,527.00	90,026.50	431,798.65	440,:

Following is a résumé of the valuations of Mexican imports during the periods under comparison, with reference to their countries of origin:

Country.	January—		First seven months—	
	1907.	1906.	1906–7.	1905–6.
Europe	$6,775,396.78	$6,172,042.90	$46,844,036.99	$41,043,290.25
Asia	645,489.89	136,456.99	1,406,754.80	838,780.99
Africa	19,108.11	2,131.00	147,782.59	15,723.38
North America	13,250,807.05	19,417,445.72	80,642,037.22	70,987,992.29
Central America	5,759.58	922.30	17,774.14	18,914.22
South America	19,083.66	10,746.00	117,117.50	164,625.69
West Indies	16,915.54	21,619.35	167,540.91	140,232.67
Oceania	10,577.36		58,599.80	47,305.62
Total	20,743,137.91	25,761,364.26	129,341,643.95	113,256,925.11

Following is a résumé of the valuations of Mexican exports during the periods under comparison, with reference to their countries of destination:

Country.	January—		First seven months—	
	1907.	1906.	1906–7.	1905–6.
Europe	$5,652,684.54	$8,332,540.03	$38,540,572.28	$46,478,576.85
North America	16,398,829.68	16,490,850.80	99,575,066.61	107,212,526.94
Central America	43,210.80	75,032.25	543,448.31	724,107.25
South America	16,230.00	5,254.00	78,779.00	42,717.00
West Indies	189,991.00	204,734.00	1,446,231.00	2,514,391.00
Total	22,300,946.02	25,108,411.08	140,184,883.20	156,972,919.04

AMENDMENTS TO CONTRACT FOR GULF NAVIGATION.

The *Diario Oficial* of April 27, 1907, publishes the text of the agreement of April 6, approved by President Díaz on April 18, between the Government of Mexico and the New York and Cuba Mail Steamship Company, which agreement supplements the agreement of March 31, 1900, for the establishment of navigation service to the ports of the Gulf of Mexico.

The contract is as follows:

"ARTICLE 1. There is added to article 10 of the said contract of March 31, 1900, the following clause:

"If one or more packages intended for a Mexican port or ports shall be shipped in error in a foriegn port or unloaded in error in another port of the Republic than the one intended, the custom-house will permit the company to reembark the package or packages for the port for which intended, provided that the company justifies by custom-house certificate of the last-mentioned port the mistake therein discovered."

ART. 2. All other stipulations not modified by this shall remain in full force and effect.

SILVER BASIS OF THE STAMP AND CUSTOMS TAXES, MAY, 1907.

The usual monthly circular issued by the Treasury Department of the Mexican Government announces that the legal price per kilogram of pure silver during-the month of May, 1907, is $42.84, according to calculations provided in the decree of March 25, 1905. This price will be the basis for the payment of the stamp tax and customs duties when silver is used throughout the Republic.

CONSULAR REPORTS.

The Consul-General of Mexico at New York reports that during the month of February, 1907, 13 vessels proceeding from Mexican ports entered the harbor of New York City, bringing 150,424 packages of merchandise. During the same month the vessels clearing from the port of New York numbered 14, carrying 178,113 packages of merchandise consigned to Mexican ports. The imports in detail from Mexico to New York in February, 1907, were as follows:

Articles.	Quantity.	Articles.	Quantity.
Henequen..................bales..	13,407	Hair..................bales..	61
Coffee....................sacks..	3,949	Lead bullion..............bars..	35,871
Hides.....................bales..	7,028	Metals...................boxes..	453
Hides.....................loose..	1,625	Sarsaparilla.............packages..	143
Ixtle.....................bales..	4,812	Vanilla..................boxes..	44
Goatskins....................do....	2,158	Alligator skins.............do....	15
Deerskins....................do....	114	Honey...................barrels..	426
Rubber.......................do....	8,662	Cedar....................logs..	929
Leaf tobacco.................do....	140	Mahogany.................do....	2,050
Cigars.....................boxes..	30	Copper...................bars..	3,080
Sugar......................sacks..	60,536	Asfalto..................barriles..	2,413
Broom root................bales..	170	Pesos mexicanos.............cajas..	233
Chicle......................do....	2,065		

The Consul of Mexico in Philadelphia reports that the shipments of merchandise from that port to the ports of Tampico, Veracruz, and Progreso in February, 1907, aggregated a value of $121,129.75, and consisted of the following products: Petroleum, $73,248.33; coal, $47,826.80; lumber, $54.62. Total, $121,129.75.

The Mexican Consul at Nogales, Ariz., reports that the exports of merchandise from the State of Sonora, Mexico, to the United States in February, 1907, was as follows:

	Gold.		Gold.
Cane sugar......................	$7	Natural feathers of birds........	$79
Mescal brandy..................	14	Fresh fish......................	25
Leather belting................	56	Lead ore.......................	553
Portland cement...............	13	Potatoes.......................	16
Fresh meats....................	863	Common salt...................	4
Rawhides	17,324	Unmanufactured tobacco.......	511
Spices, not specified.............	5	Gold bullion and dust..........	133,136
Beans..........................	38	Silver bullion..................	157,566
Preserved fruits.................	195	Total..................	310,647
Corn..........................	27		
Oranges.......................	200		

reign merchandise through the custom-house of the State of Sonora in February, 1907, were as

	Silver.		
.....	$52, 209. 97	Paper and paper products....	$8, 032. 02
....	55, 771. 79	Machinery and apparatus....	35, 888. 01
.....	445, 995. 35	Vehicles...................	13, 571. 52
ures		Arms and explosives.......	11, 877. 09
....	58, 778. 25	Miscellaneous..............	21, 592. 93
acts...........	33, 872. 04		
everages.........	5, 657. 15	Total.................	743, 245. 92

untries of origin of the foregoing merchandise are as follows:

	Silver.		
....	$683, 105. 42	Car	$3, 015. 00
....	23, 366. 25	Ger.	9, 359. 87
....	23, 919. 00		
....	78. 38	Total...............	743, 245. 92
....	402. 00		

ms duties collected during the month amounted to n silver.

consul at Nogales, Arizona, reports that the exports of dise from the State of Sonora, Mexico, to the United States in March, 1907, amounted to $136,932 and consisted of the following articles:

Sugar..........................	$46	Oranges......................	$622
Mescal.........................	27	Lead ores....................	1, 842
Rawhides.....................	10, 225	Fresh fish....................	22
Portland cement..............	297	Potatoes......................	13
Fresh meat...................	33	Cheese.......................	8
Spices, not specified...........	7	Ready-made cotton clothing...	17
Preserved fruits...............	1, 193	Common salt..................	5
Horned cattle.................	1, 960	Leaf tobacco..................	494
Chinaware....................	17	Gold bullion and dust..........	78, 239
Lemons......................	5	Silver bullion.................	41, 582
Preserved vegetables..........	138		
Corn.........................	140	Total....................	136, 932

The imports of foreign merchandise into the State of Sonora, Mexico, through the custom-house at Nogales in March, 1907, aggregated $275,195.52, and were from the following countries:

United States..............	$227, 536. 43	Spain......................	$353. 76
England...................	16, 514. 16	China.....................	80. 40
France.....................	16, 303. 10		
Germany...................	12, 721. 28	Total................	275, 195. 52
Japan.....................	1, 686. 39		

These imports consisted of the following merchandise:

Animal products	$37,276.97	Paper and paper products	$5,506.39
Vegetable products	38,748.23	Machinery and apparatus	31,788.15
Mineral products	52,557.67	Vehicles	10,222.86
Textiles, and manufactures thereof	42,686.86	Arms and explosives	22,268.79
		Miscellaneous	22,901.95
Chemical products	6,244.00		
Spirituous beverages	4,993.65	Total	275,195.52

POSTAL RECEIPTS, FIRST HALF OF 1906-7.

The revenues produced by the Mexican mail service during the first half of the fiscal year 1906–7 are thus reported by the Postmaster-General of the Republic to the Secretary of Public Communications and Works, the figures for the corresponding period of 1905–6 being also furnished for purposes of comparison:

	First half fiscal year.	
	1906-7.	1905-6.
	Pesos.	*Pesos.*
Sales of postage stamps	1,712,236.26	1,540,160.08
Rent of post-office boxes	52,410.00	49,473.00
Fines, etc	17,802.43	20,467.18
Premiums on money orders:		
Interior	147,461.36	141,649.19
International	5,797.99	4,382.60
Editors	19,770.11	18,822.85
Total	1,955,478.15	1,775,263.90

Increase in 1906-7, 180,879.25 *pesos*, or 10.15 per cent.

COMMERCE WITH FRANCE.

The exports from France to Mexico in 1906, according to the declared values of the consular invoices viséed by the Mexican consuls in the French Republic, aggregated 55,762,339 *francs*, as compared with 51,015,604 *francs* in 1905, or an increase in 1906 of 4,746,735 *francs*. The imports into France from Mexico have greatly increased, as will be seen from the following table:

	Francs.		*Francs.*
1902	8,266,000	1904	15,622,000
1903	11,272,000	1905	21,631,000

Mexico exported to France in 1905 the following products:

	Francs.		*Francs.*
Copper of first fusion	14,230,000	Volatile oils and vegetable essences	153,000
Cocoa fiber	2,180,000	Tortoise shells	116,000
Woods	1,813,000	Horns, bones, and hoofs	90,000
Coffee	1,116,000	Zinc ores	59,000
Rawhides	942,000	Sponges	51,000
Medicinal roots	209,000	Miscellaneous	283,000
Caoutchouc and crude rubber	198,000		
Vanilla	191,000	Total	21,631,000

France annually consumes enormous quantities of products similar to those produced in Mexico. The number of such products imported and consumed, which exceeds or approximates 100,000 *francs*, is nine, as follows:

Products.	Imports.	Consumed.
	Francs.	*Francs.*
Wool	473,570,000	445,100,000
Cotton	322,400,000	311,400,000
Cereals	221,670,000	151,700,000
Silk and floss silk	320,970,000	257,200,000
Furs and skins	208,500,000	179,700,000
Oleaginous seeds and fruits	199,300,000	192,600,000
Common woods	160,800,000	166,900,000
Copper	112,970,000	108,100,000
Coffee	96,800,000	94,600,000

According to French statistics of 1905, and not including the exports of arms and munitions, the merchandise exported from France to Mexico consisted of 39 classes of articles, the value of 14 of which was from 1,000,000 to 4,000,000 *francs*. These articles were:

Francs.

Jewelry, and manufactures of gold and silver	4,379,000
Cotton goods	4,069,000
Toys, brushes, and buttons	3,407,000
Woolen fabrics	2,335,000
Wines	2,272,000
Clothing and underwear	2,131,000
Silk fabrics and floss silk	1,818,000
Medicines	1,663,000
Paper and paper products	993,000
Wools	933,000
Dressed skins, and manufactures of leather and skins	913,000

Out of the fourteen principal articles which Mexico imported from France in 1905 four exceeded in value 1,000,000 *francs*, one amounted to nearly 1,000,000, and the largest item, consisting of copper of first fusion, was valued at 14,000,000 *francs*, or 66 per cent of the total Mexican imports from France in the year referred to.

ELECTRIC STREET RAILWAY IN MEXICO CITY.

The *Diario Oficial* of April 10, 1907, publishes the text of a contract, dated March 27, 1907, between the Government and the Tramway Electric Company for the construction of a new electric street railway line in the City of Mexico.

RESCINDING OF STEAMSHIP CONTRACT WITH AUSTRIA-HUNGARY.

The *Diario Oficial* of April 8, 1907, publishes the text of an agreement entered into on March 23, and approved by President Díaz, April 3, 1907, whereby the contract of September 5, 1904, between the Government and La Unione Austriaca di Navegazione for the establishment of a line of steamships between the Mexican ports on the Gulf of Mexico, Austria-Hungary, and Central and South America, is rescinded, and the agent of the company is allowed to withdraw the deposit of $10,000.

COMMERCE WITH THE UNITED STATES IN 1906.

From reports published in the "Official Bulletin," March, 1907, of the Department of Foreign Affairs it is shown that the imports of the United States from Mexico in 1905 amounted to $50,218,018, as compared with $51,999,267 in 1906, or an increase in the latter year of $1,781,249. The exports from the United States to Mexico in 1905 aggregated $51,181,674, as compared with $62,273,845 in 1906, or an increase in 1906 of $11,092,171.

The exports from the port of New York to Mexico in 1906 were $11,881,721, as compared with $10,189,816 in 1905. The imports to the United States of Mexican products through the port of New York in 1905 and 1906 are shown in the following table:

	1905.	1906.		1905.	1906.
Heniquen..............bales..	168,471	128,996	Sarsaparilla..........bales..	1,948	1,918
Coffee.................sacks..	109,615	70,177	Alligator skins....number..	332	687
Hides.................bales..	39,683	69,407	Heron plumes.......boxes..	19	19
Do.................loose..	53,456	47,848	Bones............packages..	1,893	3,015
Ixtle.................bales..	30,738	54,945	Honey..............boxes..	5,086	2,963
Goatskins.............do....	11,591	17,582	Cedar..............logs..	1,110	5,976
Deerskins..............do....	33,798	3,453	Mahogany..........pieces..	4,213	5,775
Rubber................do....	3,780	16,993	Jalap..............sacks..	611	521
Leaf tobacco..........do....	99,869	7,682	Copper.............bars..	22,589	46,516
Cigars................boxes..	641	459	Rosewood...........logs..	97	97
Sugar................sacks..	65,035	13,364	Garlic..............sacks..	2,749	1,783
Broom root...........bales..	14,774	3,288	Hats...............boxes..	168	168
Chicle gum...........do....	22,026	27,095	Oranges............do....	5,113	12,584
Fustic...............pieces..	72,278	42,841	Red pepper.........do....	1,729	2,934
Tecali marble.........do....	204	33	Cocoanuts..........bales..	59	....
Hair..................bales..	318	400	Wine...............boxes..	149	....
Lead bullion..........bars..	421,218	360,537	Mexican dollars.......do....	735	3,436
Metals................boxes..	6,064	9,900	Lemons.............do....	....	904
Ores.................sacks..	82,968	100,204	Beans..............sacks..	....	54
Vanilla...............boxes..	1,731	1,501	Asphalt.............bbls..	....	1,355

CONSOLIDATION OF RAILROAD COMPANIES.

In one of the recent sessions of the Mexican Chamber of Deputies the Secretary of Finance of the Republic, Señor LIMANTOUR, delivered a very important and interesting speech explaining the policy pursued by the Government in regard to the railway system of the Republic. The salient features of this speech were as follows:

For the purpose of preventing the absorption of the railroad lines of the Republic by foreign trusts and companies, and in order to reorganize and improve the system, the Government has in view the consolidation in a single company of the National Railway of Mexico and the Central Mexican Railway, and to this end, after long and arduous negotiations, an agreement has been made with the principal banking institutions and persons interested in said companies.

In 1903, in order to exercise control over the National Railway, the Government purchased the majority of the stock thereof.

To carry out this consolidation the Executive has submitted to the approval of Congress a general scheme which consists of the organization of a Mexican stock company which shall issue certificates of indebtedness and shares. The certificates of indebtedness shall be of two kinds: First-mortgage bonds and second-mortgage bonds. The stock representing the capital and property of the enterprise shall be of three kinds: First-preference stock, second-preference stock, and common stock.

In the National Railway the Government holds 47½ per cent of the stock, which is sufficient to control any enterprise. In the new company to be organized, the Government would hold more than 50 per cent of the stock, an actual and effective majority, which would consist of stock of the three kinds. It is not necessary for the realization of this scheme that the Government should make any disbursement of funds, neither will it be necessary therefor to issue public-debt bonds, as all that the Nation would have to do would be to extend its credit, which is superior to that of the two companies, the difference between one and the other serving as basis of the entire transaction.

The first-mortgage bonds, with 4½ per cent interest, do not require any other security; the second-mortgage bonds would be guaranteed by the Government. As the net profits of the two railroads in question (those for the year 1906 amounted to 15,000,000 *pesos*) are sufficient to cover the interest, not only of the first-mortgage bonds but also of those to be guaranteed by the Government, the latter's liability would be merely nominal.

In the new company the Government would hold stock to the nominal value of $113,000,000 American gold, of which the part consisting of first-preference shares would have a real value of very nearly one-half of the nominal value.

AMERICAN INVESTMENTS IN THE REPUBLIC.

A general estimate of American investments in Mexico, made by United States Consul GOTTSCHALK at the City of Mexico, fixes the sum at over $750,000,000 gold value.

A conservative estimate of the American capital brought into Mexico since 1902 and invested in mining and smelting ventures amounts to about $125,000,000 gold.

The following is an approximate investment of American capital in mining and smelting in the States mentioned since 1902:

Aguascalientes..............	$3,000,000	Puebla........................	$5,000,000
Chiapas.....................	1,000,000	Queretaro....................	1,000,000
Guerrero....................	5,000,000	Tabasco......................	1,000,000
Guanajuato.................	12,000,000	Tamaulipas...................	1,000,000
Hidalgo.....................	5,000,000	Veracruz.....................	1,000,000
Jalisco......................	10,000,000	Zacatecas....................	5,000,000
Michoacan..................	2,000,000		
Mexico.....................	2,000,000	Total.................	64,000,000
Oaxaca.....................	10,000,000		

It is also stated that in the States of Sinaloa, Sonora, Coahuila, Durango, and Nuevo Leon at least $60,000,000 of American capital has entered within the last five years.

MANUFACTORY OF ALKALINE CYANIDES.

El Periódico Oficial of the State of Tabasco for March 2, 1907, publishes the text of the contract entered into by the Mexican Government with the Roessler & Hasslacher Chemical Company on November 24, 1906, for the establishment within the Republic of a manufactory of alkaline cyanides of sodium, potassium, or other bases used in the industries, and especially in mining.

The investment by the company shall be at least 200,000 *pesos*, and the construction of the works shall begin within twelve months and be finished within three years.

With the approval of the Secretary of Fomento the company may establish additional works of like kind at other places under the same conditions, except that the capital invested in each of these shall be not less than 100,000 *pesos*.

The company may import free of duty machinery, apparatus, tools, and materials of construction necessary in the establishment of the industry and the construction of the buildings, and, for once only, material necessary for electric lighting of the plant and dependent buildings, and apparatus for the extinction of fires.

CONCESSION FOR ESTABLISHING A STEEL FILE FACTORY.

On December 22, 1906, the Mexican Government granted a concession to ALEXANDER RUEFF, or the company he may organize, to establish a steel file factory in the Federal District. The capital to be invested must not be less than $100,000. The plans must be submitted to the approval of the Department of Fomento within six months from the date of the promulgation of this contract, and the buildings must be constructed within six months from the date of the approval of the plans by the Government. With the consent of the Department of Fomento similar factories may be established at other places in the Republic.

NICARAGUA.

MINING IN THE REPUBLIC.

United States Consul E. W. TRIMMER, of Cape Gracias á Dios, furnishes the following information in regard to the mining industry of Nicaragua:

The mining industry in this district continues to show a steady improvement. Plants for the treatment of tailings by the cyanide process have been installed at a number of mines, and results have proven so satisfactory as to warrant a large increase in capacity. The output of gold bullion from this district now amounts to about 5,000 ounces monthly. The electric power plant installed by one company has been in successful operation since February, 1906, and a new generator is now on the way and will be used to supply power to a group of mines. Transportation has been so much improved since the river steamer of the United States and Nicaragua Company was put in commission that it is now possible to get machinery and supplies into the mines at a fair cost.

The ore-bearing limits of the district have not yet been ascertained, but the location within the past two years of many ore deposits at distances of 20 to 30 miles from the main properties warrants the belief in a fairly continuous ore-bearing zone along 50 miles or more of the foothill region, with a width of from 12 to 20 miles. Owing to the thick tropical growth, prospecting as it is known in the United States is impossible. Natives as guides and machete men are necessary. Several rich placer deposits have been discovered and worked out by crude methods, but in the opinion of mining men the present and future prosperity rests on the large bodies of medium-grade milling ore. The deposits thus far opened occur as replacements along fault lines and fissures, occurring largely in highly altered andesites and other eruptives. The surface soil and grass roots resting on and near the outcrop of ore bodies have been found to contain payable quantities of gold at widely scattered points, and most of the mines have confined their operations to treating this surface soil in Huntington mills.

Very rich shoots of oxidized ore have been found at all the mines near the surface, and below that point very little work has been done; in fact, there is not a "hoist" in the district. Unaltered sulphide ores occur in large quantities, carrying from $8 to $40 per ton in gold, in addition to sulphides of iron, zinc, silver, copper, and lead. The mines are at an altitude of 1,500 feet above sea level and distant some 250 miles by river, or 100 miles air line, from the coast. For many reasons this is not considered a desirable country for a penniless miner, labor being performed very cheaply by natives, but for a mining man who can command a few thousand dollars the district is considered by engineers on the ground to be a most promising field. They also say that many known ore deposits exist which in the United States would be considered worth immediate development, the present operators selecting only those which are the most easily reached and favorably situated.

The new Nicaraguan mining code seems to meet the approval of all interested; by its terms miners are allowed to import everything required for the mines free of duty. Almost the entire mountain country is virgin land open to location, and while one large Pittsburg company has a mineral grant covering almost the entire district, they now grant prospectors terms which are almost as favorable as could be obtained from the Government.

No known coal or oil exists in the district, but the multitude of small streams, with falls and rapids, make possible the use of hydro-electric plants for power purposes.

INCREASE OF DUTIES ON SALTED MEATS, BUTTER, AND SOAPS.

United States Consul RYDER, of Bluefields, Nicaragua, reports, under date of February 26, 1907, that by recent Presidential decree import duties upon the following articles have been increased and made operative:

		Centavos.
Butter	per kilogram	40 to 80
Pork shoulders	do	15 to 30
Salted meats	do	15 to 30
Soap (laundry)	do	5 to 10

Duties on the Atlantic coast of Nicaragua are payable in *soles* at 48 cents; on the Pacific coast in Nicaraguan currency at 5.50 *pesos* ($2.70 American). The above, however, does not apply to San Juan del Norte, where there is a special import duty of 20 per cent ad valorem, United States currency.

The retail price of butter in Bluefields is 77 cents; ham and salted meats, 36 cents; laundry soap, 15 cents per pound, in United States currency.

TRADE OF CAPE GRACIAS Á DIOS, 1906.

United States Consul E. W. TRIMMER, reporting on the commerce and industries of Cape Gracias á Dios, Nicaragua, for the calendar year 1906, says:

Building operations at this port during the past year have been quite extensive. New wharves have been built and old ones rebuilt and extended, and many buildings, both for commercial and residential purposes, have been erected. To carry out the provisions of a

ranted by the Government, the bar at the river
edged to a sufficient depth to allow fruit ships to

1 exports to the United States amounted to $318,-
nsis   f the following articles: Rubber, worth $44,827;
         o; an   gold, $270,161. The imports for the same period
       a   at   80,570, and with the exception of a few cases of
were the products and manufacture of the United States.
cles of import were: Liquors, valued at $34,251; lumber,
merchandise, $83,725; machinery, $95,143; and provisions,

PANAMA.

BUDGET FOR 191 7-8.

January 22, 1907, the National Assembly of Panama adopted
corresponding to the period from January 1, 1907, to
1. 1908. According to this budget, the total estimated
vernment for the period referred to aggregate
,   an   .ne estimated expenditures $4,977,792.27. The
 .udget in detail is as follows:

REVENUES.

Merchandise, taxed 10 per cent	$935,355.00	
Duties on importation of—		
Liquors	409,000.00	
Tobacco	100,000.00	
Cigarettes	100,000.00	
Salt	10,000.00	
Matches	20,000.00	
Coffee	10,000.00	
Opium	12,000.00	
Port dues from steamship companies	16,000.00	
		$1,612,355.00

RECEIPTS.

Distillation of liquors	45,000.00
Sale of liquors at retail	89,906.00
Slaughter of cattle, horses, and mules	154,080.00
Slaughter of sheep	57,550.00
Tax on mines	1,000.00
Patents and trade-marks	1,140.00
Sealed paper and stamps	56,150.00
Registration tax	9,000.00
Export taxes	20,000.00
Real and personal property	40,000.00
Lotteries	100,000.00
Mother-of-pearl fisheries	1,500.00
Property belonging to the nation	35,000.00
Consular fees	126,700.00
Light-houses	4,000.00

Posts and telegraphs	$100,000.00
Miscellaneous receipts	25,000.00
Interest on $6,000,000, at 4½ per cent	540,000.00
Interest on $300,000 parity deposit, at 3 per cent	18,000.00
Interest on $1,400,000, remainder of Canal agreement	35,000.00
Balance of the $3,000,000 former budget of the Canal	1,400,000.00
	4,461,381.00

EXPENDITURES.

Department of the Interior	1,808,170.00
Department of the Treasury	542,537.27
Department of Public Instruction and Justice	1,039,430.00
Department of Fomento	1,587,655.00
Total	4,977,792.27

TARIFF MODIFICATIONS.

Modifications of the customs tariff of Panama as promulgated through the *Gaceta Oficial* of January 27, 1907, provide as follows:

ARTICLE I. *Opium—Tobacco.*—The undermentioned goods, which are ranged under the heading "special classes" in the customs tariff, shall pay the following duties on importation into the Republic:

		Balboas.
Opium (the right to collect this duty may be sold at auction for periods not exceeding four years)	per kilogram	8.00
Tobacco:		
In the leaf, or pressed for manufacture, smoking or chewing	do	0.50
Cigars and cut tobacco	do	1.50
Cigarettes	do	1.00

The duty on tobacco, cigars, and cigarettes is levied on the merchandise alone and not on the exterior packing.

ART. II. Jewelry of all kinds; pearls and precious stones; wares of gold, silver, platinum, and crystal; ornaments of bronze; plated articles, such as table plate; silks of all kinds; fine porcelain, such as that of Sèvres, Dresden, China, and Japan; perfumery and scented soaps shall pay a duty of 15 per cent on the invoice value.[a] This article is not to take effect until it has been secured that the fiscal interests of the Republic shall not be prejudiced. On the goods specified the present duty is 10 per cent ad valorem.

ART. III. A duty of 0.02 *balboa* per kilogram may be levied on imported sugar, white, refined, and centrifugal, as soon as sugar factories in the country produce not less 2,500,000 kilograms annually.

ART. IV. The duty on registries of patents shall be 5 *balboas* for each year of the life of the patent, payable either upon application or in annual installments.

ART. V. The duty on cattle imported for consumption, viz, $20 (silver) for each male and $15 (silver) for each female, is applicable

---

[a] The *balboa* is equivalent to $1 American.

both to live and dead cattle. Four quarters compose a carcass, and the proportional fraction of the duty shall be charged on each quarter. When carcasses are imported cut into smaller sections than quarters, it shall be deemed that a carcass weighs 400 pounds and the duty shall be assessed on that basis.

ART. VI. The duty fixed by the tariff law on coffee ($8 silver per 100 kilograms) shall be applicable to coffee imported ground.

ART. VII. Printed books of all kinds are to be free of import duty.

ART. IX. Methylated alcohol may not be employed in the manufacture of alcoholic beverages, and such alcohol shall be rendered unfit for that purpose on its introduction into the country.

PERU.

IMMIGRATION.

With a view of encouraging foreign immigration into Peru, President JOSÉ PARDO has signed a decree by which free passage is offered to anyone of North American or European origin desiring to go to Peru to establish any industrial enterprise.

A special fund will be devoted to this object.

RAILROAD CONSTRUCTION.

According to information furnished the Bureau of the American Republics through the Peruvian Legation at Washington, the following railroad improvements have been authorized by the Congress of Peru:

Conclusion of the line from Pascamayo to La Viña; extension of the line-to Huancayo; extension to Cuzco; extension to Moquegua; union of the Mollendo and Arequipa lines at Ilo, and the continuation of the Huancayo line as far as Cuzco. The Peruvian Corporation will probably have charge of the work in contemplation. The Government has also been authorized to raise funds for the construction of a road from Oroya to Ucayali. · These funds are to be guaranteed by the tobacco tax, which is worth £200,000 annually.

Another project covers a railroad from Payta to the Upper Amazon, for which the Government will make territorial grants.

PUBLIC WORKS IN THE REPUBLIC.

El Peruano of December 7, 1906, contains copies of laws authorizing the Peruvian Ministry of Fomento to expend $1,035 on the completion of a steel bridge over the River Santa and £1,542 on the construction of a bridge over the River Chalhuanca. The issue of the same journal for December 11 states that the Ministry of Foménto has been authorized to expend £15,000 on canalization works in the town of Iquitos. For the construction of a military hospital £40,000 has also been authorized.

PATENTS AND TRADE-MARKS IN 1906.

Patents issued in Peru during 1906 number 65, as compared with 24 in the preceding year, while the trade-marks registered were 102, of which 75 were foreign and 27 native in their origin. During 1905, of a total aggregating 92, foreign marks numbered 65 and native 27.

GOLD COINAGE IN PERU.

The figures of the coinage of Peruvian pounds (gold) recorded for 1906 make a total of £221,284, and detailed statistics show that since April 16, 1898, the date of the first issue of Peruvian pounds sterling, until December 31, 1906, a total of £917,111.1 have been issued.

The annual quotas from 1900 to 1906 were as follows:

1900	£63,533	1903	£111,639
1901	81,255	1904	86,272
1902	92,356	1905	182,000

RUBBER PRODUCTION, FIRST HALF OF 1906.

The figures published for the rubber production of Peru during the first six months of 1906 indicate an output of 1,062,497 kilograms, valued at £390,554, on which customs duties of £4,386 were paid. In the corresponding period of 1905 the output was 1,033,924 kilograms, whose value was £350,400, and on which customs dues amounting to £13,600 were paid.

RECEIPTS OF PERUVIAN MERCHANDISE AT NEW YORK.

During the eleven months, January–November, inclusive, 1906, receipts of merchandise from Peru at the port of New York were valued at $1,977,710, the leading items being cotton, $476,667; copper in bars, $323,658; alpaca wool, $255,913, and goatskins, $255,386.

THE PORT OF IQUITOS IN 1906.

The United States Consul at Iquitos has reported at length to the Department of Commerce and Labor concerning Peruvian commercial conditions in 1906. He states that all the imports and exports for the vast territory of trans-Andean Peru pass through the custom-house at Iquitos.

nount of imports and exports for the period of five
) 1906, inclusive, together with the duties levied,
as showing the advance made in that time. It is
ve the totals for each year. These are converted
currency:

Year.	Value of imports.	Value of exports.
....	$1,222,019	$1,846,854
....	1,452,646	2,137,488
....	2,780,293	2,610,325
....	2,757,808	4,440,091
....	3,148,713	4,989,899
Total..........................	11,370,479	17,026,658

ie amount of duties collected each year is given in the following
the figures representing United States currency:

....	$301,963
....	266,186
....	661,383
....	636,657
....	812,273
Total	2,678,462

From these figures it will be seen that with the exception of a slight
falling off in imports in 1905 as compared with 1904 there has been a
steady increase in both imports and exports, showing in the five years
an increase of more than 250 per cent, as is also the case in the duties
collected during a similar period.

The annexed table shows imports at Iquitos for the year 1905, value
stated in United States currency:

Countries of origin.	Value.	Percentage.	Countries of origin.	Value.	Percentage.
United States..............	$310,976	0.112	Spain.....................	$12,783	0.0046
England...................	1,077,916	.391	Peru (Government to municipality of Iquitos).....	4,981	.0019
Germany...................	636,846	.231			
France....................	431,679	.1565	China.....................	2,015	.0007
Brazil....................	145,561	.053			
Portugal..................	120,546	.044	Total.................	2,757,932	1.0000
Italy.....................	14,629	.0053			

From the foregoing it will be seen that England is far in the lead,
having furnished in the year referred to 39 per cent of the imports
through Iquitos; Germany is second, with 23 per cent; France third,
with 16 per cent, and the United States fourth, with 11 per cent. It
would be interesting to compare the foregoing with similar data for
the year 1906, but the manner in which the records are kept renders
this almost impossible. While the year shows a substantial increase
over 1905, and the imports from the United States have advanced in

proportion with other countries, it is not thought that the relative positions of the countries importing have been changed.

Imports from the United States have doubled within the past year. These have consisted chiefly of provisions, machinery, preserves, canned goods, patent medicines, firearms, ammunition, beer, shooks, and lumber, which have found a ready market. With systematic and energetic canvassing by intelligent Spanish-speaking representatives of our export houses at home the amount of sales of the above lines of goods could be very largely increased and other lines introduced as well.

A detailed account of the exports of rubber for the years 1905 and 1906, showing ports of destination, is given herewith in metric tons:

Shipments to—	1905.	1906.
Liverpool	1,112,396	912,022
Havre	771,775	1,035,648
Hamburg	128,692	176,875
New York	62,863	45,876
Total	2,075,626	2,171,421

The shipments of ivory nuts in 1905 were, to Liverpool, 12 tons 837 kilograms, and to Havre 44 tons 990 kilograms; in 1906, to Liverpool none, Havre 11 tons 926 kilograms.

In 1905 the exports of dry hides to Liverpool aggregated 10 tons 530 kilograms; in 1906, 7 tons 678 kilograms, and to Havre 7 tons 878 kilograms.

The gain on entire shipments for the year 1906 over that of 1905 was 54 tons 920 kilograms, while in the rubber shipments, 1906 leads by 95 tons 795 kilograms.

THE TELEGRAPH SYSTEM OF THE REPUBLIC.

According to a recent statement of the Director-General of Posts and Telegraphs of the Republic of Peru, the total extension of the telegraph lines of the country is 5,012 kilometers and that of the wires 5,672 kilometers. The Government telephone lines have an extension of 179 kilometers and 49 meters of wire.

The greater part of the telegraph system of the Republic is under Government control and the rest is exploited by the Peruvian Corporation.

All apparatus and other materials for the system are imported from the United States.

SALVADOR.

LIGHTING IN NEW SAN SALVADOR.

al of March 20, 1907, publishes the text of an
. into by La Compañia de Alumbrado Eléctrico, of
he installation in the city of New San Salvador for
7 arc lamps of 1,200 candlepower and 93 incan-
aps (3 candlepower. The agreement is for ten years.

FRENCH EXPORTS TO THE REPUBLIC, 1906.

,rding to the report of the Salvadorean Consul-General at Paris,
year 1906, the value of merchandise exported from France to
norts of the Republic during the same year amounted to
francs, or about $387,446. The total gross weight of
was 796,920 kilograms.

UNITED STATES.

TRADE WITH LATIN AMERICA.

STATEMENT OF IMPORTS AND EXPORTS.

Following is the latest statement, from figures compiled by the
Bureau of Statistics, United States Department of Commerce and
Labor, showing the value of the trade between the United States and
the Latin American countries. The report is for the month of March,
1907, with a comparative statement for the corresponding month of
the previous year; also for the nine months ending March, 1907, as
compared with the same period of the preceding year. It should be
explained that the figures from the various custom-houses, showing
imports and exports for any month, are not received by the Treasury
Department until about the 20th of the following month, and some
time is necessarily consumed in compilation and printing, so that the
returns for March, for example, are not published until some time
in May.

IMPORTS OF MERCHANDISE.

	March—		Nine months ending March—	
	1906.	1907.	1906.	1907.
	Dollars.	*Dollars.*	*Dollars.*	*Dollars.*
Cocoa (*Cacao; Coco ou cacao; Cacao*):				
Central America........................	460	11,354	12,233	39,625
Brazil................................	40,557	211,018	1,054,230	2,109,397
Other South America..................	125,403	99,890	1,364,577	1,311,352
Coffee (*Café; Café; Café*):				
Central America........................	1,545,081	1,081,928	4,546,936	3,555,142
Mexico...............................	345,134	217,031	1,703,035	898,708
Brazil................................	4,928,121	4,554,557	43,605,860	45,664,057
Other South America..................	878,905	1,046,221	7,508,751	7,077,894

IMPORTS OF MERCHANDISE—Continued.

	March—		Nine months ending March—	
	1906.	1907.	1906.	1907.
	Dollars.	*Dollars.*	*Dollars.*	*Dollars.*
Copper (*Cobre; Cobre; Cuivre*):				
Mexico	1,860,771	1,769,706	13,555,811	13,960,135
Cuba	5,068	19,015	57,038	70,581
South America	41,279	314,530	410,039	796,657
Fibers:				
Cotton, unmanufactured (*Algodón en rama; Algodão em rama; coton non manufacturé*):				
South America	....	6,145	36	30,711
Sisal grass (*Henequén; Henequen; Henequen*):				
Mexico	763,746	1,468,055	10,666,963	11,481,330
Fruits:				
Bananas (*Plátanos; Bananas; Bananes*):				
Central America	463,412	432,137	3,126,901	3,717,145
Cuba	93,810	66,041	363,919	509,915
South America	53,317	49,347	288,423	123,900
Oranges (*Naranjas; Laranjas; Oranges*):				
Mexico	990	1,454	47,271	37,041
Cuba	1,879	492	7,778	7,846
Hides and skins (*Cueros y pieles; Couros e pelles; Cuir et peaux*):				
Mexico	412,571	477,973	3,028,714	3,691,650
Cuba	27,224	21,722	106,486	227,625
Brazil	224,436	184,978	1,464,857	1,485,022
Other South America	876,569	701,927	8,687,358	8,730,448
India rubber, crude (*Goma elástica; Borracha cruda; Caoutchouc*):				
Central America	70,067	73,954	584,383	603,680
Mexico	115,766	377,257	396,346	1,655,609
Brazil	2,846,885	4,339,240	18,745,522	25,764,383
Other South America	90,709	79,990	969,611	1,081,516
Iron ore (*Mineral de hierro; Mineral de ferro; Minéral de fer*):				
Cuba	226,239	145,385	1,333,557	1,552,216
Lead, ore (*Plomo; Chumbo; Plomb*):				
Mexico	202,016	213,068	2,282,821	1,950,666
Sugar, not above No. 16 Dutch standard (*Azúcar, inferior al No. 16 del modelo holandés; Assucar, não superior ao No. 16 de padrão hollandes; Sucre, pas au-dessus du type hollandais No. 16*):				
Mexico	1,601	1,306	28,607	165,319
Cuba	7,274,331	8,793,949	36,764,462	40,624,967
Brazil	....	....	398,140	912,361
Other South America	263,818	64,365	1,955,618	1,879,732
Tobacco and manufactures (*Tabaco y sus manufacturas; Tabaco e sus manufacturas; Tabac et ses manufactures*):				
Cuba	1,733,348	1,240,085	13,489,800	14,449,109
Wood, mahogany (*Caoba; Mogno; Acajou*):				
Central America	53,782	38,318	409,851	378,372
Mexico	516	57,858	278,561	503,317
Cuba	2,546	18,151	79,383	130,713
Wool (*Lana; Lã; Laine*):				
South America—				
Class 1 (clothing)	757,528	1,171,333	5,459,384	2,737,416
Class 2 (combing)	29,975	21,799	190,537	319,901
Class 3 (carpet)	61,463	71,180	539,103	537,799

EXPORTS OF MERCHANDISE.

	March—		Nine months ending March—	
Agricultural implements (*Instrumentos agrícolas; Instrumentos de agricultura; Machines agricoles*):				
Mexico	62,882	47,447	370,946	329,462
Cuba	8,145	8,807	143,544	49,110
Argentine Republic	161,368	157,362	4,821,754	3,314,407
Brazil	6,073	15,262	68,352	93,593
Chile	8,652	6,258	282,693	328,888
Other South America	22,038	16,475	249,117	174,319

	March—		Nine months ending March—	
	1906.	1907.	1906.	1907.
	Dollars.	Dollars.	Dollars.	Dollars.

(Partial, mostly illegible upper rows)

Wheat (Trigo; Trigo; Blé):				
Central America	155	2,550	35,279	25,453
Mexico	316,738	144,802	1,572,668	704,689
South America	46	19,986	386,582	337,193

Wheat flour (Harina de trigo; Farinha de trigo; Farine de blé):

Central America	160,251	111,019	1,363,451	1,252,478
Mexico	7,649	17,508	137,880	90,369
Cuba	285,061	323,120	2,471,683	2,269,875
Brazil	88,815	134,122	943,381	1,000,797
Colombia	6,472	13,597	483,061	127,581
Other South America	129,353	117,993	1,769,832	1,536,558

Carriages, etc.:
Automobiles (Automóbiles; Automoriles; Automobiles):

Mexico	34,611	66,908	201,121	628,243
South America	3,991	21,415	52,032	159,086

Carriages, cars, etc., and parts of (Carruages, carros y sus accesorios; Carruagens, carros e partes de carros; Voitures, wagons et leurs parties):

Central America	335,353	252,222	1,004,965	1,235,769
Mexico	83,500	204,435	703,744	1,725,376
Cuba	117,923	91,322	844,111	636,754
Argentine Republic	53,934	140,040	326,382	1,660,773
Chile	1,482	40,334	301,117	121,187
Other South America	10,681	122,204	295,462	519,378

Cycles and parts of (Bicicletas y sus accesorios; Bicyclos e partes; Bicyclettes et leurs parties):

Mexico	12,431	7,922	63,825	72,884
Cuba	2,807	4,376	28,309	27,442
Argentine Republic		1,879	12,627	14,434
Brazil	1,108	2,318	6,473	8,731
Other South America	966	1,881	12,855	15,967

Clocks and watches (Relojes de pared y bolsillo; Relogios de bolso e parede; Horloges et montres):

Central America	909	2,232	13,406	12,967
Mexico	5,315	4,762	43,200	37,760
Argentine Republic	1,496	7,681	51,962	47,199
Brazil	2,388	8,251	55,669	70,445
Chile	8,580	3,762	50,397	35,379
Other South America	3,618	1,465	37,994	30,364

EXPORTS OF MERCHANDISE—Continued.

	March—		Nine months ending March—	
	1906.	1907.	1906.	1907.
Coal (*Carbón; Carvão; Charbon*):	*Dollars.*	*Dollars.*	*Dollars.*	*Dollars.*
Mexico.................................	304,906	336,031	2,258,610	2,381,161
Cuba..................................	271,783	227,316	1,508,130	1,542,115
Copper (*Cobre; Cobre; Cuivre*):				
Mexico.................................	97,799	....	971,080	306,471
Cotton:				
Cotton, unmanufactured (*Algodón en rama; Algodão em rama; Coton non manufacturé*):				
Mexico.................................	76,418	....	1,553,630	36,413
Cotton cloths (*Tejidos de algodón; Fazendas de algodão; coton manufacturé*):				
Central America........................	149,604	129,470	1,176,433	1,267,762
Mexico.................................	16,291	21,101	209,096	193,851
Cuba..................................	70,896	84,080	866,601	798,197
Argentine Republic.....................	6,376	10,660	232,427	203,785
Brazil.................................	61,450	43,028	470,968	324,934
Chile..................................	15,612	51,437	726,240	812,764
Colombia..............................	75,402	66,787	441,313	634,518
Venezuela.............................	44,971	25,491	274,185	348,849
Other South America...................	31,927	32,244	350,280	397,717
Wearing apparel (*Ropa de algodón; Fazendas de algodão; Vêtements de coton*):				
Central America........................	24,464	47,198	195,173	274,395
Mexico.................................	23,830	44,457	216,425	213,572
Cuba..................................	23,944	41,859	189,523	260,525
Other South America...................	3,793	5,380	63,311	80,956
Fibers:				
Twine (*Bramante; Barbante; Ficelle*):				
Argentine Republic.....................	9,902	9,055	2,155,154	1,109,175
Other South America...................	9,141	14,587	196,547	205,032
Electric and scientific apparatus (*Aparatos eléctricos y científicos; Apparatos electricos e scientificos; Appareils électriques et scientifiques*):				
Central America........................	23,120	22,313	152,331	204,908
Mexico.................................	113,752	90,471	714,402	1,007,362
Cuba..................................	99,254	38,272	524,385	511,205
Argentine Republic.....................	28,169	27,296	250,112	332,066
Brazil.................................	79,110	95,020	485,196	628,113
Other South America...................	24,557	60,566	430,268	624,697
Electrical machinery (*Maquinaria eléctrica; Machinas electricas; Machines électriques*):				
Central America........................	3,779	7,776	16,838	45,376
Mexico.................................	111,627	163,656	715,306	945,320
Cuba..................................	22,791	4,882	402,542	79,399
Argentine Republic.....................	5,200	3,590	84,655	113,369
Brazil.................................	31,914	126,590	149,227	409,188
Other South America...................	7,619	24,273	121,730	138,081
Iron and steel, manufactures of:				
Steel rails (*Carriles de acero; Trilhos de aço; Rails d'acier*):				
Central America........................	260,070	702	508,593	169,719
Mexico.................................	16,309	126,983	1,136,922	866,838
South America.........................	342,450	317,482	2,852,757	2,289,205
Builder's hardware, etc. (*Materiales de metal para construcción; Ferragens; Matériaux de construction en fer et acier*):				
Central America........................	30,152	26,976	264,589	264,353
Mexico.................................	149,222	201,647	222,583	1,417,653
Cuba..................................	97,719	66,773	905,360	337,023
Argentine Republic.....................	63,515	51,791	524,978	611,852
Brazil.................................	41,911	51,132	305,913	377,072
Chile..................................	19,315	29,078	171,267	245,797
Colombia..............................	6,236	5,346	46,593	53,706
Venezuela.............................	2,142	4,418	30,209	46,776
Other South America...................	61,023	116,657	483,132	633,814
Sewing machines, and parts of (*Máquinas de coser y sus accesorios; Machinas de coser e accesorios; Machines à coudre et leurs parties*):				
Central America........................	12,124	7,591	88,820	96,774
Mexico.................................	72,509	63,746	473,380	594,038
Cuba..................................	17,961	33,205	228,439	247,481
Argentine Republic.....................	75,279	20,969	578,294	359,161
Brazil.................................	19,256	35,337	151,567	331,713
Colombia..............................	5,580	4,467	49,106	54,047
Other South America...................	42,546	31,613	281,679	300,613

Brazil	9,428	13,871	60,740	67,573
Other South America	23,352	9,310	166,129	191,013
Boots and shoes (*Calzados; Calçados; Chaussures*):				
Central America	32,460	50,950	304,781	625,256
Mexico	111,363	131,359	1,145,451	1,134,633
Colombia	3,855	1,224	35,534	31,413
Other South America	32,915	32,987	227,603	296,073
Meat and dairy products:				
Beef, canned (*Carne de vaca en latas; Carne de vacca em latas; Bœuf conservé*):				
Central America	7,036	3,967	22,011	49,981
Mexico	1,344	1,618	21,082	21,189
Cuba	2,004	1,717	20,793	14,802
Other South America	3,435	2,709	33,300	32,397
Beef, salted and pickled (*Carne de vaca salada ó adobada; Carne de vacca, salgada; Bœuf salé*):				
Central America	12,671	15,944	77,676	105,880
South America	16,109	13,413	193,915	189,294
Tallow (*Sebo; Sebo; Suif*):				
Central America	11,090	6,659	124,584	100,352
Mexico	2,027	2,294	78,005	19,802
Cuba	36	9,305	7,884	21,753
Chile			46,704	54,172
Other South America	4,779	3,509	42,077	41,687
Bacon (*Tocino; Toucinho; Lard fumé*):				
Central America	4,510	3,508	17,432	25,215
Mexico	3,141	7,813	34,208	45,702
Cuba	40,922	55,209	316,740	448,215
Brazil	12,355	19,368	128,500	143,320
Other South America	1,377	3,063	10,968	11,615
Hams (*Jamones; Presuntos; Jambons*):				
Central America	11,007	9,961	68,318	109,240
Mexico	8,356	13,153	97,881	88,914
Cuba	40,943	40,527	371,390	440,086
Venezuela	2,395	3,948	37,404	35,494
Other South America	5,562	6,335	55,690	46,157
Pork (*Carne de puerco; Carne de porco; Porc*):				
Cuba	65,842	80,083	451,162	539,109
South America	22,908	27,254	164,104	234,153
Lard (*Manteca; Banha; Saindoux*):				
Central America	50,545	50,907	345,323	499,745
Mexico	42,572	63,558	464,784	505,332
Cuba	255,821	226,239	1,949,156	2,189,500
Brazil	48,439	192,015	129,134	855,147
Chile	6,105	3,940	57,533	132,382
Colombia	7,182	4,750	287,922	38,937
Venezuela	19,446	15,282	268,252	175,459
Other South America	47,794	31,859	422,171	416,286

EXPORTS OF MERCHANDISE—Continued.

	March—		Nine months ending March—	
	1906.	1907.	1906.	1907.
Meat and dairy products—Continued.				
Butter (*Mantequilla; Manteiga; Beurre*):	*Dollars.*	*Dollars.*	*Dollars.*	*Dollars.*
Central America...	14,181	16,173	90,529	125,865
Mexico...	13,588	16,507	94,112	113,259
Cuba...	5,886	7,306	33,491	55,584
Brazil...	4,733	1,332	106,992	60,000
Venezuela...	9,701	4,149	83,204	42,909
Other South America...	4,349	3,668	28,204	40,550
Cheese (*Queso; Queijo; Fromage*):				
Central America...	7,770	7,243	50,898	61,308
Mexico...	5,758	5,813	33,620	33,236
Cuba...	1,525	2,932	9,657	16,634
Naval stores:				
Rosin. tar, etc. (*Resina, alquitrán, etc.; Resina e alcatrão; Résine et goudron*):				
Cuba...	3,855	6,259	52,567	64,170
Argentine Republic...		4,240	341,190	338,583
Brazil...	88,128	129,809	456,241	496,126
Other South America...	59,372	16,324	249,804	189,412
Turpentine (*Aguarras; Aguaraz; Térébenthine*):				
Central America...	2,103	968	38,240	27,960
Cuba...	7,522	7,664	52,582	66,404
Argentine Republic...	10,116	12,561	155,982	146,998
Brazil...	13,735	15,075	84,710	119,089
Chile...	5,307	2,971	60,664	78,513
Other South America...	2,140	5,353	42,911	56,446
Oils:				
Mineral, crude (*Aceites minérales, crudos; Oleos mineraes, crús; Huiles minérales, brutes*):				
Mexico...	16,931	88,506	485,465	867,876
Cuba...	80,623	63,131	316,334	344,452
Refined or manufactured (*Aceites refinados à manufacturados; Oleos refinados ou manufacturados; Huiles raffinées ou manufacturées*):				
Central America...	33,045	25,503	194,496	199,273
Mexico...	32,937	19,206	142,161	206,903
Cuba...	46,361	42,193	258,163	402,335
Argentine Republic...	255,701	125,647	1,590,425	1,665,968
Brazil...	207,682	302,368	2,064,916	2,296,557
Chile...	53,844	106,814	602,058	626,313
Other South America...	91,227	130,439	826,967	919,044
Vegetable (*Aceites vegetales; Oleos vegetaes; Huiles végétales*):				
Central America...	2,518	5,717	22,555	37,468
Mexico...	19,504	78,223	625,800	757,422
Cuba...	28,693	55,180	128,067	185,383
Argentine Republic...	4,310	5,862	18,270	53,680
Brazil...			129,182	260,993
Chile...	2,732	17,266	15,297	61,462
Other South America...	18,358	19,324	118,554	119,172
Paper (*Papel; Papel; Papier*):				
Mexico...	1,537	2,236	28,963	39,537
Cuba...	10,050	14,594	97,707	146,565
Argentine Republic...	60,141	6,557	182,308	213,584
Brazil...	5,216	4,033	26,184	13,888
Chile...	14,486	7,433	112,670	120,304
Other South America...				
Paraffin (*Parafina; Paraffina; Paraffine*):				
Central America...	4,052	5,904	46,421	50,239
Mexico...	65,076	42,322	367,656	471,529
South America...	2,953	5,814	21,606	45,711
Tobacco, unmanufactured (*Tabaco en rama; Tabacco não manufacturado; Tabac non manufacturé*):				
Central America...	14,252	6,904	104,273	1,781,748
Mexico...	7,803	7,659	71,221	97,531
Argentine Republic...		1,572	43,508	37,285
Colombia...		866	7,485	11,291
Other South America...	4,320	6,163	57,914	72,342
Tobacco, manufactures of (*Tabaco elaborado; Tabaco manufacturado; Tabac manufacturé*):				
Central America...	7,450	4,348	45,135	58,993

EXPORTS OF MERCHANDISE—Continued.

	March—		Nine months ending March—	
	1906.	1907.	1906.	1907.
Wood and manufactures of—	Dollars.	Dollars.	Dollars.	Dollars.
Wood, unmanufactured (*Madera sin labrar: Madeira não manufacturado; Bois brut*):				
Central America	48,623	31,559	366,745	437,328
Mexico	130,368	115,557	714,308	662,570
Cuba	10,618	5,548	126,308	104,304
Argentine Republic	5,302	17,423	135,431	120,693
Other South America	17,423	10,533	123,846	273,647
Lumber (*Maderas; Madeiras; Bois de construction*):				
Central America	76,482	168,522	470,928	569,627
Mexico	228,320	204,963	1,269,340	1,045,719
Cuba	327,474	307,362	1,634,361	1,766,142
Argentine Republic	312,080	407,898	2,655,094	4,921,643
Brazil	22,014	97,517	278,222	388,681
Chile	67,239	122,568	458,172	322,659
Other South America	69,371	158,086	585,068	1,002,480
Furniture (*Muebles; Mobilia; Meubles*):				
Central America	37,364	28,553	228,538	229,312
Mexico	99,631	68,555	805,470	694,169
Cuba	55,470	53,902	874,137	877,327
Argentine Republic	20,693	46,370	344,711	513,559
Brazil	4,285	3,449	35,946	44,176
Chile	3,579	5,438	82,192	69,627
Colombia	970	796	15,399	11,434
Venezuela	1,180	266	28,512	15,813
Other South America	4,366	13,978	61,804	92,987

FOREIGN COMMERCE, MARCH, 1907.

The figures of the Bureau of Statistics for the month of March and nine months of the fiscal year show an unusual increase in foreign trade of the United States, especially in the value of imports. Imports for the month amounted to $133,323,085, the largest on record with the exception of those of December, 1906, which reached $134,349,760. It was an increase of nearly $20,000,000 over March of last year, when the figures were $113,597,577. For the nine months the value was $1,066,059,911, compared with $913,555,097 for the same period ending with March last year, an increase of $152,504,814, which is quite beyond any recent parallel. The increase last year over the corresponding period ending with the same month in 1905 was less than half as much, the gain being from $839,430,114 to $913,555,097.

There was no such gain in exports either for the month or for nine months. For the month of March the value of exports was $162,689,-950, compared with $145,510,707 last year and $136,978,429 the year before. The gain here was a little more than $17,000,000. For the nine months the disparity was still greater. The total was $1,451,904,-971, compared with $1,343,902,090 for the same period a year before, an increase of $108,002,881, or $44,501,933 less than the gain in imports. The excess of exports over imports fell from $430,346,993 for the nine months ending March, 1906, to $385,845,060.

Details of the trade for the periods in reference were as follows:

	March—		Nine months ending March—	
	1906.	1907.	1906.	1907.
IMPORTS.				
Foodstuffs in crude condition and food animals............................	$11,948,511	$13,542,075	$105,828,519	$112,418,200
Foodstuffs partly or wholly prepared.....	12,103,252	14,143,680	101,884,965	110,629,289
Crude materials for use in manufacturing..	41,279,187	47,849,509	303,855,988	355,239,436
Manufactures for further use in manufacturing...............................	18,729,748	24,722,729	159,242,143	203,945,163
Manufactures ready for consumption......	28,382,160	31,602,835	234,913,458	274,712,372
Miscellaneous............................	1,154,719	1,250,224	7,830,024	8,902,151
Total imports...................	113,597,577	133,111,752	913,555,097	1,065,846,611
EXPORTS.				
Foodstuffs in crude condition and food animals............................	16,176,199	14,258,780	144,803,892	126,834,832
Foodstuffs partly or wholly manufactured.	27,836,205	28,653,327	266,349,138	259,562,766
Crude materials for use in manufacturing..	35,265,378	50,851,359	407,320,279	497,905,743
Manufactures for further use in manufacturing...............................	21,226,730	23,227,788	165,038,129	191,627,881
Manufactures ready for consumption......	41,905,295	42,046,238	337,383,104	382,019,365
Miscellaneous............................	951,160	605,003	3,964,185	4,738,752
Total domestic exports.............	143,360,967	159,642,495	1,324,878,727	1,432,689,341
Foreign merchandise exported............	2,149,740	2,108,439	19,023,363	18,276,464
Total exports......................	145,510,707	161,750,934	1,343,902,090	1,450,965,805

The distribution of trade during the periods in reference was as follows:

Countries.	March.			
	Imports.		Exports.	
	1906.	1907.	1906.	1907.
Europe..	$57,491,538	$66,118,437	$98,605,100	$110,305,220
North America................................	22,773,487	25,300,701	27,556,227	30,594,530
South America................................	13,331,132	15,029,563	5,814,021	6,820,204
Asia..	15,139,800	19,591,809	8,534,245	8,797,991
Oceania.......................................	3,529,422	4,017,793	3,523,828	3,950,145
Africa..	1,331,893	3,053,449	1,477,286	1,282,844
Central American States:				
Costa Rica................................	1,008,937	1,136,819	216,185	165,645
Guatemala................................	485,634	142,435	370,112	300,768
Honduras.................................	151,270	154,941	184,919	157,001
Nicaragua.................................	179,225	109,474	202,061	129,997
Panama...................................	141,321	145,076	1,689,718	1,482,133
Salvador..................................	312,072	35,166	135,708	93,798
Mexico.......................................	4,436,008	5,623,444	5,519,646	5,797,902
West Indies:				
Cuba......................................	9,822,954	10,923,694	4,119,505	4,377,470
Haiti......................................	79,555	111,813	237,860	197,554
Santo Domingo...........................	513,138	190,804	168,981	256,553
Argentine Republic...........................	1,516,849	1,877,076	2,366,088	2,178,478
Bolivia.......................................			5,207	122,404
Brazil..	8,253,009	9,521,614	1,309,957	2,142,870
Chile...	1,221,926	1,231,373	487,605	607,723
Colombia.....................................	617,407	801,431	258,906	265,135
Ecuador......................................	238,190	80,409	115,996	132,234
Paraguay.....................................			18,734	7,780
Peru...	240,670	331,395	470,333	487,726
Uruguay......................................	336,681	336,236	275,006	335,859
Venezuela....................................	705,449	772,051	266,265	243,047

Countries.	Nine months ending March.			
	Imports.		Exports.	
	1906.	1907.	1906.	1907.
Europe	$472,918,722	$565,601,075	$930,329,774	$1,025,012,278
North America	164,103,588	178,556,761	234,254,085	261,622,341
South America	111,001,064	121,626,134	55,968,307	62,879,121
Asia	136,764,732	164,090,689	53,680,773	46,298,087
Oceania	18,789,870	20,229,845	25,763,200	31,343,448
Africa	9,977,151	15,742,147	14,965,381	13,946,385
Central American States:				
Costa Rica	3,354,235	3,223,149	1,641,044	1,795,817
Guatemala	2,222,492	1,670,529	2,118,286	2,192,083
Honduras	1,194,060	1,577,868	1,166,841	1,595,293
Nicaragua	1,024,786	793,955	1,405,312	1,529,913
Panama	766,411	1,259,137	8,532,745	11,010,145
Salvador	663,532	555,466	1,009,317	1,048,080
Mexico	37,387,025	41,529,320	42,063,022	47,997,443
West Indies:				
Cuba	54,535,763	60,887,456	36,564,345	36,574,608
Haiti	910,924	829,572	2,853,494	3,275,184
Santo Domingo	1,909,265	1,767,338	1,471,121	1,943,849
Argentine Republic	13,026,566	11,467,869	25,227,447	26,692,782
Bolivia			97,874	865,609
Brazil	66,746,790	77,066,276	10,228,003	13,348,668
Chile	12,473,614	13,238,865	6,070,369	7,637,654
Colombia	5,121,633	4,965,080	2,734,089	2,306,564
Ecuador	1,821,490	2,274,841	1,621,875	1,249,213
Paraguay	760	1,174	34,896	122,810
Peru	1,937,316	3,053,301	3,771,073	4,694,559
Uruguay	2,155,934	2,164,316	2,172,276	2,885,194
Venezuela	6,180,046	5,751,162	3,396,704	2,332,891

RUBBER FROM GUAYULE.

The first factory for the manufacture of rubber from the guayule shrub to be established in Texas is being erected at Marathon, according to information published in the New York "Sun" of April 28, 1907. The shrub grows extensively in the rough region bordering the upper course of the Rio Grande, and it is estimated that it is found in commercial quantities upon more than 20,000,000 acres of land in this State.

A large part of this land is owned by the State, and it is expected that a great revenue will be derived from the sale of the shrub. The money derived from this source will go to the permanent school fund, which already amounts to about $40,000,000.

The guayule rubber industry has passed the experimental stage. There are more than twenty large factories in northern Mexico, some of them representing an investment of more than $500,000 each.

It was only three years ago that the first guayule rubber factory was established in Mexico. Since that time more than $15,000,000 has been invested in the industry in that country, it is estimated. The Continental Rubber Company, of New York, a subsidiary branch of the United States Rubber Company, practically has control of the industry in Mexico, and it is arranging to establish a large factory in Texas.

The present output of rubber from the factories in Mexico is nearly 1,000,000 pounds a month, and this amount will be increased before the close of the current year by the establishment of additional factories. The product is exported to the United States and Europe.

In Mexico the guayule shrub is selling for $100 a ton Mexican money, equivalent to $50 United States gold. The average yield to the acre in Mexico is said to be about 2 tons of the shrub. It will reproduce itself every two years if cut off at the roots.

As a result of the discovery that this shrub is of value the price of land has increased enormously. Before the value of the shrub was known, land upon which it grows could have been purchased for from 20 cents to 30 cents an acre and some of it for 10 cents an acre. This same land is now yielding its owners $100 an acre.

The guayule shrub grows less profusely in Texas than in Mexico. It is estimated that the average yield of the shrub in this State upon the 20,000,000 acres of land upon which it is said to grow will not exceed one-half ton to the acre. Even at this rate there is great wealth for the State in the new industry. The land upon which it grows is worthless for anything else except cattle and sheep grazing.

The factory which is being erected at Marathon will cost about $250,000. Many ranchmen have entered into contracts to sell the guayule shrub upon their lands to this factory.

The rubber which is manufactured from guayule is softer than some other kinds of rubber and does not vulcanize so easily, but these difficulties are overcome by mixing it with other rubber.

COFFEE MOVEMENT, FIRST NINE MONTHS, 1906-7.

The world's visible supply of coffee on April 1, 1907, was 15,397,742 bags, total receipts at Rio de Janeiro and Santos for the nine months being 16,289,061 bags during the first nine months of the crop year 1906-7.

According to the Coffee Exchange report, the total deliveries in the United States from July 1, 1906, to March 31, 1907, were 5,395,412 bags, while Europe received 7,731,897 bags.

Total deliveries in the United States and Europe for the period in reference were 13,127,309 bags, a gain over the corresponding period of the preceding year of 345,629 bags.

For the nine months about 81 per cent of the deliveries were Brazil coffee, and 19 per cent covered all other growths.

Comparative figures issued by the "Brazilian Review" for the two nine months' period of 1906 and 1907 show the following:

World's visible supply of coffee.

	1906-7.	1905-6.		1906-7.	1905-6.
	Bags.	*Bags.*		*Bags.*	*Bags.*
July	9,630,563	11,265,510	December	13,808,836	13,090,349
August	9,948,053	11,465,641	January	14,377,932	12,647,595
September	10,756,653	12,102,496	February	15,133,293	11,931,631
October	12,154,000	1" 624,693	March	15,201,000	11,324,581
November	13,165,786	13,006,841			

B-MARK, AND COPYRIGHT LAWS IN THE CANAL ZONE.

 ." 1907, the following order of the Secretary of War
ııeu ates, extending to the Panama Canal Zone the laws
uts, trade-marks, and copyrights in the United States,
 uu ve:

 .. .uthority of the President, it is ordered that the patent,
.. "rk, and copyright laws of the United States of America are
xtended to and made effective within the Canal Zone, to the
ıat any patent or copyright issued under the laws of the United
 . or any trade-mark duly registered in the Patent Office of the
States, shall vest in the person to whom issued or in whose
 ed, his assigns and licensees, subject to the protection of
 . ...d supreme courts of the Canal Zone, the same exclusive
roperty therein that such person would possess in the United

.OPRIATION FOR DISTRIBUTION OF RIO GRANDE WATERS.

 .t ROOSEVELT, on March 4, 1907, approved the act of Con-
ng an appropriation of $1,000,000 to carry into effect the
s of the treaty between Mexico and the United States pub-
ın the MONTHLY BULLETIN of March, 1907, pages 63–69, for the
equitable distribution of the waters of the Rio Grande.

   The appropriation will be expended under the direction of the
Secretary of the Interior in the construction of a dam for storing and
delivering to Mexico for irrigation purposes 60,000 acre-feet of water
annually in the bed of the Rio Grande at the point where the head
works of the Acequia Madre now exists above the city of Juarez.

FINANCIAL STATEMENT, FIRST QUARTER, 1907.

The monthly statement of the public debt of the United States
shows that at the close of business March 30, 1907, the total debt, less
cash in the Treasury, amounted to $909,106,566, which was a decrease
as compared with March 1 of $11,538,288.

The debt is recapitulated as follows: Interest-bearing debt, $908,-
233,660; debt on which interest has ceased since maturity, $1,095,365;
debt bearing no interest, $402,645,542; total, $1,311,974,568.

This amount, however, does not include $1,130,146,869 in certifi-
cates and Treasury notes outstanding, which are offset by an equal
amount of cash held for their redemption.

The cash in the Treasury is given as follows: Gold reserve,
$150,000,000; trust funds, $1,130,146,869; general fund, $199,520,548;
in national bank depositaries, $165,235,679; in treasury of the Philip-
pines, $3,887,713; total, $1,648,790,810; against which there are
demand liabilities outstanding amounting to $1,245,922,807, which
leaves a cash balance on hand of $402,868,002.

The monthly circulation statement issued by the Comptroller of the Currency shows that at the close of business March 30, 1907, the total circulation of national bank notes was $597,212,063, an increase for the year of $42,545,096, and an increase for the month of $869,041.

The circulation based on United States bonds amounted to $547,-633,063, an increase for the year of $35,411,512 and a decrease for the month of $2,104,310. The circulation secured by lawful money aggregated $49,579,000, an increase for the year of $7,133,584 and an increase for the month of $2,973,351.

The amount of United States registered bonds on deposit to secure circulation was $550,137,900. Bonds on deposit to secure public deposits amounted to $176,324,860, as follows:

Panama Canal, $12,838,000; 2 per cent consols of 1930, $56,523,100; 4 percents of 1907, $9,644,200; 3 percents of 1908–1918, $6,577,500; 4 percents of 1895, $5,403,750; District of Columbia 1924, $1,003,000; State, city, and railroad bonds, $72,883,310; Hawaiian bonds, $1,711,000; Philippine loan, $9,741,000.

The comparative statement of the Government receipts and expenditures for March, 1907, shows the total receipts to have been $54,221,953, and the expenditures $43,602,007, bearing a surplus for the month of $10,619,946. The surplus for the nine months of the present fiscal year is over $51,200,000. One year ago the surplus was a little less than $6,000,000.

As compared with March, 1906, the customs receipts show an increase of $1,300,000; internal revenue an increase of over $2,000,000, and miscellaneous a surplus of $192,000. The expenditures for last month are over $2,000,000 less than for March, 1906.

The coinage executed at the mints of the United States during March, 1907, amounted to $6,630,894, of which $5,874,525 was gold; $326,212 silver, and $430,156 minor coins. This is exclusive of 4,906,057 pieces coined for the Philippine Islands, and 1,955,000, 20-*centavo* pieces executed for the Government of Mexico.

URUGUAY.

NEW CABINET.

Señor Álvaro Guillot, Minister of the Interior.
Señor Blás Vidal, Minister of Finance.
Señor Juan P. Lamolle, Minister of Public Works.
Señor Jacobo Varela Acevedo, Minister of Foreign Affairs.
Gen. Eduardo Vázquez, Minister of War and Marine.
Señor Gabriel Terra, Minister of Industry, Labor, and Public Instruction.

BUDGET FOR 1907-8.

budget for 1907-8 has been sanctioned by the
hed, expenditures for the year being fixed at
, an estimated revenue of $19,185,827. A small
thus indicated.

s are estimated at $10,900,000, though it is more
these figures will be exceeded; city and country
:es, at $2,781,000; business licenses, $1,065,000; profits
:s of the Republic, $370,000; industrial taxes (mainly from
ibacco), $1,266,000; posts and telegraphs, $460,000.

principal items of expenditure are the following:
itrative service, $8,433,747; national obligations, $10,746,189,
1 are included $7,669,664 for public debt service and railway
ntees.

'RODUCTION OF THE CUÑAPIRÚ GOLD MINES IN 1906.

~cording to the report presented by the Chief of the National
'tment of Engineering to the Minister of Improvements of
the production, during 1906, of the French gold mines of
was as follows: Amount of ore treated, 13,962 tons; gold
~ed, at $0.44 per gram, 81,510 grams. The amount paid the
Government for fees, at the rate of 1½ per cent, was $179.32.

VENEZUELA.

LEASE OF ASPHALT MINES.

The *Gaceta Oficial* of the State of Zulia for March 9, 1907, publishes
the text of the lease of February 28, 1907, from the Government of
Venezuela to Señor ANTONIO ARANGUREN, of the city of Caracas, of
the asphalt mines in the Maracaibo and Bolivar districts of the State
of Zulia. The following is a synopsis of the principal points of the
concession:

Grant of all asphalt mines existing in the said districts for a term
of fifty years from the date of the lease; exception being made of
such mines as have heretofore been granted to other persons and
which have not been declared by the Government to be forfeited.
In the last case these mines are also included in the lease. Within
the period of the lease the Government agrees not to grant to any
other person or company asphalt mining rights within the said
districts.

The lessee is to pay to the Venezuelan Government a tax of 2
bolivars annually per hectare of surface area exploited by him in the
asphalt mines, and in addition 2 *bolivars* for each ton of the product
:ploited.

The Government promises to lend to the lessee such assistance as may be compatible with the fiscal laws of the Republic in the dispatch of vessels engaged in export of the products of the enterprise, and to allow entry free of duty, for one time only, of machinery, tools, apparatus, and implements intended for the enterprise, and for all times, of conveyers in shooks necessary for the export of the product.

The lessee is not allowed to assign his contract except with the prior consent of the Federal Executive to any other person or company, foreign or domestic.

IMPORT DUTIES ON FANS USED FOR ADVERTISING PURPOSES.

A decree of February 16, 1907, stipulates that ordinary palm leaf and paper fans upon which advertisements are printed or pasted will be subject, upon their importation into the Republic, to the duties of the fourth class of the tariff (75 *centavos* per kilogram); fans made from cardboard or wood and destined to the same use are subject to duties of the third class (25 *centavos* per kilogram.)

ESTABLISHMENT OF COMMERCIAL AGENCIES BY SPAIN.

The vice-consul of the United States at Madrid reports to the Department of State of the United States that for some time past Spain has been making earnest efforts to find a foreign market for her products and manufactures, and naturally regards her former colonies in South America as the most opportune field. The Minister of Agriculture and Commerce has submitted to His Majesty the King, who has approved same, a decree organizing a "Committee on International Commerce," to be composed of the Minister of Agriculture and Commerce, the Assistant Director of Customs, the Chief of the Commercial Bureau of the Ministry of State, four representatives of the Chamber of Commerce, two of the Chamber of Agriculture, two of the industrial companies legally constituted, two of the Association of Stock Breeders, and the Director of the School of Commerce, who shall be the secretary of said committee.

This committee will make a study of the commercial situations, of the reports of commercial agents of foreign trade in Morocco and America, North and South, and of the organization of commercial propaganda in foreign countries where commercial agents are to be sent.

In order to facilitate the work of this commission four commercial agents will be appointed with residence in Mexico, Buenos Ayres, Valparaiso, and Tangiers, and whose sphere of operations will extend

latemala, San Salvador, Honduras, Nicaragua, Costa
ama Venezuela, Cuba, Porto Rico, Argentine Republic,
y, Br il, Paraguay, Chile, Peru, Bolivia, Ecuador, and
o.

se com rcial agents will be paid by the State and will coop-
onsuls in the furtherance of trade relations.

E OF AMERICA AND GREAT BRITAIN, FIRST QUARTER OF 1907.

e "Accounts relating to Trade and Navigation of the United
dom," published in March, 1907, contain a detailed statement of
commercial intercourse between Great Britain and the various
ries of America during the first quarter of 1907, as compared
the corresponding periods of the two preceding years.
e classification of imports is as follows:

Articles and countries.	1905.	1906.	1907.
Animals, living (for food).			
United States...............................	£2.024.735	£1,955,505	£1,716,326
Sheep and lambs:			
United States...............................	114,730	32,186	63,461
Articles of food and drink.			
Wheat:			
Argentine Republic.........................	1,487.774	1,124,173	1,237,918
Chile......................................	45.006	285	96
United States..............................	561,800	1,885,472	2,052,272
Wheat flour:			
United States..............................	540,790	1,522,456	1,010,260
Barley:			
United States..............................	280,252	466,157	427,028
Oats:			
United States..............................	3,096	468,865	8,984
Maize:			
Argentine Republic.........................	504,968	295,110	882,982
United States..............................	1,960,255	3,034,648	1,633,442
Beef, fresh:			
Argentine Republic.........................	709,286	1,073,795	1,048,961
United States..............................	1,223,974	1,319,438	1,271,616
Uruguay...................................	....	6,785	7,800
Mutton, fresh:			
Argentine Republic.........................	571,208	536,177	491,418
Uruguay...................................	....	24,203	12,337
Pork, fresh:			
United States..............................	100,538	132,279	79,766
Bacon:			
United States..............................	1,773,918	2,079,817	2,066,005
Lard:			
United States..............................	810,835	1,049,865	1,270,282
Beef, salted:			
United States..............................	42,470	54,220	38,303
Hams:			
United States..............................	582,081	671,892	637,916
Cheese:			
United States..............................	154,589	143,355	170,947
Coffee:			
Brazil.....................................	42,368	33,393	287,496
Central America............................	218,273	164,131	172,634
Sugar, unrefined:			
Brazil.....................................	15,407	214,066	74,439
Peru......................................	333,171	90,520	42,726
Tobacco, unmanufactured:			
United States..............................	423,654	504,306	505,840
Tobacco, manufactured:			
United States..............................	331,915	304,692	261,419

Articles and countries.	1905.	1906.	1907.
Metals and articles manufactured therefrom.			
Copper:			
Chile........	£115,847	£75,568	£85,169
United States........	1,202	....	7
Regulus and precipitate:			
Chile........	60,409	27,475	50,430
Peru........	48,588	44,475	55,150
United States........	31,795	41,513	2,655
Wrought and unwrought:			
Chile........	286,148	239,500	377,485
United States........	633,422	401,063	700,771
Iron, pig:			
United States........	3,466	9,543	2,940
Lead, pig and sheet:			
United States........	62,640	67,719	63,840
Tin ore:			
South America........	242,186	202,516	307,352
Scientific apparatus:			
United States........	98,753	106,009	80,553
Clocks:			
United States........	16,573	14,416	19,093
Raw materials for textile manufactures.			
Cotton, raw:			
Brazil........	55,089	618,950	689,109
United States'........	9,485,198	12,539,210	20,071,172
Wool, sheep or lambs':			
Argentine Republic........	500,635	558,489	1,013,069
South America........	239,928	270,693	213,639
Uruguay........	55,319	67,641	86,113
Alpaca, vicuña, and llama:			
Chile........	24,209	23,479	3,304
Peru........	20,080	86,339	65,111
Raw materials for sundry industries.			
Hides, wet:			
Argentine Republic and Uruguay........	23,384	52,031	88,709
Brazil........	....	....	21
Sheepskins:			
Argentine Republic........	59,950	35,196	44,825
Tallow and stearin:			
Argentine Republic........	68,781	70,914	44,883
United States........	108,481	81,001	197,907
Manufactured articles.			
Paper:			
United States........	71,939	104,252	100,278
Leather:			
United States........	708,244	817,930	786,772
Miscellaneous articles.			
Horses:			
United States........	19,466	7,696	8,988
Flax or linseed:			
Argentine Republic........	300,176	212,606	577,295
United States........	....	9,825	13,646
Bullion and specie.			
Gold and silver:			
Brazil........	101,371	72,223	93,503
Mexico, Central and South America........	310,539	212,472	212,053
United States........	2,453,653	5,244,196	3,240.258

The classification of exports is as follows:

Articles and countries.	1905.	1906.	1907.
Articles of food and drink.			
Beer and ale:			
United States........	£69,979	£74,004	£73,554
Salt, rock and white:			
United States........	12,585	18,429	12,947
Spirits:			
United States........	94,471	101,847	119,838
Raw materials.			
Coal, coke, etc.:			
Argentine Republic........	270,575	397,067	437,602
Brazil........	159,840	219,189	245,896
Chile........	86,962	49,071	130,266
United States........	14,907	8,986	7,750
Uruguay........	57,519	90,233	174,155

	1906.	1906.	1907.
...*raw materials*—Continued.			
nbs':			
ressed:	....	....	....
manufactured wholly or in part.			
packing:			
bale	20,619		20,45
bale	2,634		2,364
a, all classes:			
bale	797,316		846,533
America	383,853		406,343
110,705		117,49
...la and Panama	100,788		201,45
86,537		107,71
...nd Santo Domingo	43,920		80,52
72,899		148,38
108,180		66,57
...States.	474,698		975,79
...y	110,091		83,39
...ela	52,637		204,775
...d States.			221,133
...ufactures:			22,647
...ntine Republic	21,562		42,998
1,940		3,577
...d States.	239,445		390,684
a:			
...t States.	14,475		27,382
...goods:			
...ne Republic	20,055	32,912	21,729
17,308	19,915	29,676
...la and Panama	7,482	7,278	6,728
6,745	7,692	10,584
United States	091,830	792,651	858,936
Woolen tissues:			
Argentine Republic	115,967	150,185	152,213
Brazil	41,131	40,095	53,854
Chile	59,964	75,697	108,653
Mexico	16,525	24,195	35,178
Peru	20,537	21,941	24,245
United States	117,415	131,908	133,154
Uruguay	19,467	37,927	28,483
Worsted tissues:			
Argentine Republic	93,899	68,607	76,151
Brazil	27,936	16,444	23,874
Chile	22,923	26,499	55,357
Mexico	14,331	17,796	18,958
Peru	5,520	6,859	4,876
United States	413,424	340,215	350,258
Uruguay	13,393	16,380	12,088
Carpets:			
Argentine Republic	44,252	53,253	51,919
Chile	10,931	23,536	24,034
United States	9,404	38,568	14,295
Saddlery and harness:			
Central and South America	14,367	22,019	21,214
United States	12,628	16,044	15,934
Metals and articles manufactured therefrom.			
Cutlery:			
Argentine Republic	7,317	8,528	6,536
Brazil	8,937	8,613	13,314
Chile	2,528	3,567	4,715
Cuba	858	1,752	2,149
United States	19,814	19,482	22,512
Hardware, unenumerated:			
Argentine Republic	29,670	41,201	28,043
Brazil	39,063	27,002	33,225
Chile	7,936	10,254	14,123
Cuba	5,811	6,271	5,511
United States	6,160	8,453	8,638
Iron, pig:			
United States	142,613	284,307	824,038
Iron, bar, angle, bolt, and rod:			
Argentine Republic	12,180	17,028	16,858
Brazil	8,161	9,741	8,874
Chile	5,934	7,104	13,666
United States	14,712	22,681	15,414

Articles and countries.	1905.	1906.	1907.
Metals and articles manufactured therefrom—Continued.			
Railroad iron:			
Argentine Republic..............................	£104,600	£306,633	£147,321
Chile.....:..	28,079	31,429	47,009
Wrought and cast iron:			
Argentine Republic..............................	24,933	29,026	52,229
Brazil........	9,515	8,996	12,063
Wire of iron or steel:			
Argentine Republic..............................	24,425	51,903	31,941
Brazil..............	4,312	3,981	11,402
United States..............	19,709	21,063	54,201
Galvanized sheets:			
Argentine Republic..............................	192,824	302,903	176,108
Central America............	9,078	9,855	9,958
Chile...........	8,169	7,808	10,482
Cuba..........	28,287	48,744	66,092
Mexico........	24,845	16,961	16,843
Uruguay........	22,728	26,916	24,341
Pipes and fittings:			
Argentine Republic..............................	7,373	37,508	70,141
Tin plates and sheets:			
United States........	238,086	137,916	219,955
Manufactures of steel, unenumerated:			
United States........	22,682	23,442	26,538
Machinery and millwork.			
Locomotives:			
South America............	53,965	260,603	C38,453
United States.....:	205	401	768
Agricultural machinery (engines):			
South America............	10,130	38,506	25,765
United States........	....	2,788	15
Machinery, various:			
South America............	77,406	97,879	116,202
United States........	4,319	1,309	2,253
Agricultural implements:			
South America............	27,548	48,543	43,468
United States........	18	632	561
Sewing machines:			
South America............	13,510	18,818	16,432
Mining machinery:			
South America............	6,325	8,988	21,945
United States........	672	77	770
Textile machinery:			
South America............	39,127	52,442	88,908
United States........	93,234	136,346	178,716
Apparatus, miscellaneous:			
South America............	162,445	262,451	342,366
United States........	149,109	30,998	30,000
Miscellaneous.			
Cement:			
Argentine Republic..............................	6,625	12,517	36,040
Brazil..............	3,958	8,730	19,773
United States........	669	3,611	35,522
Earthen and china ware:			
Argentine Republic..............................	35,703	49,077	50,169
Brazil..............	23,798	27,288	35,995
United States........	145,436	139,367	144,627
Rice:			
Cuba..........	113,369	121,699	88,794
Seed oil:			
Brazil..............	10,344	14,998	17,621
Bullion and specie.			
Gold and silver:			
Brazil..............	602,650	468,200	3,227,673
Central and South America..............	1,399,444	2,104,864	3,293,525
United States........	69,000	296,500	155,407

BOOK NOTES.

lets sent to the Bureau of the American Republics, and
__.ject-matter bearing upon the countries of the Inter-
¹ᵒⁿ of American Republics, will be treated under this caption
y Bulletin.

⎪　⁾ title " What I Saw in the Tropics," Mr. Henry Pearson,
⎪　　" India Rubber World," has published a record of im-
⎪ ⁱᵗ　ceived during journeys to many little-known rubber-pro-
⎪ - s　ıons of the globe. While a study of production methods
main object of the book in reference, the writer has included
any personal and typical adventures that the fund of really
vɪ　ᵈle information contained in it is imparted through a charming
ɪrary medium. With Ceylon as a first objective point, Mr. Pear-
ɪ narrates the incidents of his voyage thither, and, as a result of
siɪ　ᵉ *Hevea* plantations, reports that the first year's tapping
ɪ　, cases, paid the cost of the original investment, while the
ᵈs production shows a profit of 120 per cent. The whole
ɪ ᵗ　ᶜal world in the East is profoundly interested in these
Ceylon experiments and is fully alive to the opportunities that rubber
offers. Proceeding to the Malay States, the Singapore Botanic Gardens were the object of a special report, it being found that while
Hevea responds to cultivation with a phenomenal growth, less promising results are obtained from *Castilloa* and *Ceará*. The Chinese
method of preparing gutta-percha for European markets is described
and several plantations owned by Chinamen were visited at Selangor.
French Indo-China, British North Borneo, Sumatra, and Formosa
are all deeply interested in rubber culture, and experimental plantations are underway. A careful study of Tehuantepec plantations
showed that rubber growing in this section would be more profitable
than coffee production, and in Nicaragua one locality alone is credited
with 400,000 *Castilloa* plants. In Costa Rica one plantation has a
growth of more than 100,000 *Castilloas*, although bananas are the
chief growth of the country. The healthy condition of the Panama
trees, in spite of defective tapping, is remarked on and the response
to care on the part of the Colombian Choco plantations is note-
worthy, the product of the latter being in the main the output of
standing cultivated trees. Jamaican and Hawaiian cultivation of
rubber is still largely experimental in spite of numerous efforts to
advance profitable interest in the work.

La Revue (Paris) for March 15, 1907, publishes as its initial article
a critique of *Le Panaméricanisme*, following the development of an

all-American policy from the time of its origin in the proposition for
a Pan-American Congress inaugurated by SIMON BOLIVAR, down to
the meeting at Rio de Janeiro in 1906. In the opinion of the writer,
S. L. ROCCA, it is from the propaganda of the ardent BOLIVAR that the
Monroe Doctrine drew its fundamental inspiration of a continental
policy. Following upon the invitation of BOLIVAR, addressed to Mexico, Chile, Peru, and the Argentine Republic to unite in friendly conclave, came the Monroe message in 1823 for the ratification of which
the States of America were again urged to assemble. Mexico
Guatemala, Colombia, and Peru sent representatives to this Congress,
but the delegates of the United States did not arrive until after the
date of adjournment. Importance is attached to the reciprocal establishment of embassies in Mexico, Brazil, and the United States, and
the development of a pan-American civilization along lines parallel
to that of the Old World, is noted, the special purpose of which is the
segregation and defense of American interests rather than the forwarding and adoption of European methods. Evidence of the world
power of the United States and of the value attached to the national
policies of the other countries of the New World are indicated in
the postponement of the Hague Peace Conference in deference to the
desire of America to take part, as a whole, in the deliberations of that
Congress. The Conference at Rio de Janeiro, while stated as not
having accomplished as great results as had been anticipated, is found
to have gained in value through the active participation of the Secretary of State of the United States and the cordial greeting extended
to him throughout the various countries of South America.

The second edition of "The Problems of the Panama Canal"
(March, 1907), by Brig. Gen. HENRY L. ABBOT, has been received by
the Columbus Memorial Library, the prefatory note to the first edition stating that the volume is an unbiased and truthful statement of
" how the work appears to a retired officer of the Corps of Engineers,
United States Army, who has spent his life in the prosecution of
public works confided to that corps." The present issue covers the
progress of events since the transfer of the work to the United States,
extending the history of the enterprise from its French beginnings
through the date of purchase by the United States. It also explains
the new studies and resulting plans for the canal and the final action
of the Government thereon; adds two years and a half to the
climatological and hydraulic records, including a new and formidable
flood of the Chagres, and describes the method adopted for the construction of the canal by contract, with the reasons therefor. The
history and technology of the work is thus brought up to the beginning of 1907. The physical conditions of the Isthmus are reported
on and recognition is made of the energetic and valuable services

rendered by Colonel GORGAS in bringing the health record to its present fine status.

Hon. PAUL S. RIENSCH, one of the United States delegates to the Third Pan-American Conference at Rio de Janeiro, contributes to the " World To-Day ".for May, 1907, an appreciation of the beauties of that city. The beautiful entrance into the Rio Harbor was but a forecast of the romantic charm which Mr. REINSCH found everywhere, the quaint mixture of tropical restfulness and modern enterprise being a predominating feature of the street life. Reference is made to the splendor of public and private entertainments and to the intellectual seriousness which characterizes Brazilian literary life. In view of the vast extent of Brazil and the widely divergent economic interests of such regions as the Amazon basin and the agricultural States of the south, the writer finds it not surprising that the national life of the country can not, as yet, be said to embrace all its varied characteristics, many elements of the colonial régime being mingled with the achievements of the " New Brazil."

The " Board of Trade Journal " (British) for March 28, 1907, reproduces an extract from the report of Mr. MAX MULLER, of the British Legation in Mexico City, concerning the guayule rubber industry and its development. This industry has now passed from the experimental to the practical stage, and while it is not anticipated that the gum extracted from the guayule shrub will ever take the place of rubber. it may, however, be used as a substitute for it in many forms of manufacture. Extraction processes have been and still are being registered in the Mexican Patent Office, none of which are regarded as entirely perfected. The quantity of gum contained in the plant is rated as high as 18 per cent, whereas the patented processes obtain from 10 to 12 per cent only. Numerous companies have been formed and factories have sprung up all over the north of Mexico for the utilization of this plant which was formerly regarded not only as worthless, but a veritable scourge.

An interesting bit of Haitian history is touched upon in the " Century Magazine " for April, in which ERNEST E. JOHNSON narrates the incidents connected with his visit to the ruins of the citadel and palace constructed by the one-time king of Haiti, Christophe. These ruins, situated in the vicinity of Melot, consist of a stronghold " La Ferrière," occupying the leveled summit of a steep mountain, and the palace " Sans Souci," on a grassy plateau below. The fortifications, hewn from solid rock, were regarded as impregnable, and the various chambers and galleries which honeycombed the mountain were used as storehouses and treasure caves during the short reign of the slave king. Even in decay these ruins are a remarkable monument to the skill of the French engineer who planned the original construction, while the columns, terraces, and galleries of the palace below are of unusual architectural and historic interest.

The Buenos Ayres " Standard " for March 7, 1907, publishes a paper on Argentine fisheries in which the development of pisciculture in the Republic is outlined by E. A. TULLIAN. The first cultures were inaugurated early in the year 1904 at Lake Nahuel Huapi, the eggs being brought from the United States. The original plants consisted of whitefish, brook trout, lake trout, and salmon, and all were hatched with small losses. Subsequent experiments were successfully carried out in establishing oyster beds within a short distance of Buenos Ayres. it being demonstrated that the North American oyster can live and propagate in Argentine waters. The artificial culture of the pejerry has been attended with most satisfactory results, the eggs having been planted in various waters of the Provinces of Buenos Ayres, Cordoba, San Luis, Salta, Tucuman, and Jujuy.

The third edition of *Progrès et Développement de la Bolivie*, prepared by J. DE LEMOINE, Consul-General for Bolivia in Belgium, has been received by the Columbus Memorial Library. The writer states that for the greater part of his data he is in debt to Presidential messages and Reports of the Ministry of Public Works, certain additions having made in accordance with the need for specified information. A list of the highways and railroads under construction and in operation is furnished to show the interest taken by the Government in opening up the country, while other public enterprises receiving national aid include navigation of the lakes, water supply for various cities, the utilization of the waterways of the Republic as motive power, electric lighting, and geologic and geographic explorations. Interesting information is furnished concerning the mineral wealth of the Republic based upon scientific and disinterested reports, while it is stated that no other country contains within a similar area so great an abundance of agricultural and tropical products.

A consideration of the economic value of explorations in such sections of South America as are practically unknown forms the bulk of a pamphlet recently issued by the Royal Geographical Society (London), the paper on the subject being contributed by Col. GEORGE EARL CHURCH. Apart from the great Chaco region, at least 2,000,-000 square miles of South America have been only partly explored and mapped, all of which offer a splendid field for study. The work of the various boundary commissions has added much to the world's knowledge, and Chile, the Argentine Republic, and Uruguay have been well mapped; but Colonel CHURCH laments the fact that vast reaches of river valleys and mountain heights are cut off from our comprehensive geographical knowledge.

[Philade]lphia Commercial Museum has issued its 1906 foreign [gu]ide of South America, in which a careful résumé is [giv]en .. [of the condi]tions prevailing throughout the various countries of part [of] the Western Hemisphere. Courts, customs duties, com[mer]cial travelers' licenses, shipping and internal communication, re[sources, ind]ustries, and commerce are all covered, with the purpose of [aiding t]rade development between the United States and South

PANAMA.

GILBERT, JAMES STANLEY: Panama patchwork. Poems by James Stanley Gilbert. With an introduction by Tracy Robinson. 2d ed., revised & enlarged. Panama, The Star and Herald Company, 1905. xv, 162 p. front. 12°.

TOMES, ROBERT: Panama in 1855. An account of the Panama railroad, of the cities of Panama, and Aspinwall, with sketches of life and character on the isthmus. By Robert Tomes. New York; Harper & Bro., 1855. 246 p. front., illus. 16°.

PARAGUAY.

CÁMARA DE COMERCIO DE ASUNCIÓN: . . . Memoria correspondiente al ejercicio de 1906. Asunción, Tall. tip. "La Patria," 1907. 40 p. 12°.
Cover title.

PERU.

MAURTUA, VICTOR M. (Comp.): . . . Anales del Perú publicados por Victor M. Maurtua, del Instituto histórico del Perú. Madrid, Imp. de Gabriel L. y del Horno, 1906. 2 v. 4°.
At head of title: "Fernando Montesinos."

PERU. EXPOSICIÓN DE LA REPÚBLICA del Perú presentada al Excmo. Gobierno Argentino en el juicio de límites con la República de Bolivia conforme al tratado de arbitraje de 30 de diciembre de 1902. Barcelona, Imprenta de Henrich y Comp., 1906. 2 v. 4°.

—— JUICIO DE LÍMITES entre el Perú y Bolivia. Prueba Peruana presentada al Gobierno de la República Argentina por Victor M. Maurtua, abogado y plenipotenciario especial del Perú. Barcelona, Imprenta de Henrich y Comp., 1906. 12 v. 8°.
Vol. 8, 9, and 10 have imprint, "Madrid, Imprenta de los hijos de G. M. Hernández."

CONTENTS.

Vol. 1, Virreinato Peruano; v. 2, Organización audiencial Sud-Americana; v. 3, Audiencia de Charcas; v. 4, Virreinato de Buenos Aires y documento de Caravantes; v. 5, Gobernaciones diversas y Rupa-Rupa; v. 6, Gobernaciones de Alvarez Maldonado y Laegui Urquiza; v. 7, Vilcabamba; v. 8, Chunchos; v. 9, Mojos, pt. 1; v. 10, Mojos, pt. 2; v. 11, Obispados y audiencia del Cuzco; v. 12, Misiones.

—— —— Same. Cartas geográficas. Primera serie. [Contains 34 maps published between 1598 and 1904, showing Peru and Bolivia.]

—— —— Same. Cartas geográficas. Segunda serie. Barcelona, Tip. de Henrich y Comp., 1906. atlas, 48 maps. f°.

— —— —— Same. Conclusiones de la exposición del Perú. Barcelona, Imprenta de Henrich y Comp., 1906. 43 p. 8°.

RENAULT, LOUIS (and others): Consultation pour le gouvernement du Pérou par MM. Louis Renault, A. de Lapradelle et N. Politis . . . Paris, A. Pedone, 1906. 27, (1) p. 4°.
Opinions of the French press on "Juicio de límites entre Bolivia y Perú."

PHILIPPINE ISLANDS.

BLAIR, E. H. and ROBERTSON, J. A.: The Philippine Islands. Vol. 48 and 49. 1751 to 1765. Cleveland, The Arthur H. Clark Company, 1907. 2 v. 8°.

SALVADOR.

SALVADOR. PRESIDENT: Á la Asamblea nacional del Salvador, el General don Fernando Figueroa al encargarse de la Presidencia constitucional de la República. 1° de marzo de 1907. [San Salvador, Imprenta Nacional.] iii p. 4°.

—— —— —— P. José Escalón á sus conciudadanos. Marzo 1° de 1907. [San S vador, Imprenta nacional.] iii p. 4°.

UNITED STATES.

K WEBB: ... Handbook of American Indians north of
by Frederick Webb Hodge. In two parts, pt. 1. Washington,
nent Printing Office, 1907. ix, 972 p. illus., maps. 8°.
] of the Bureau of American Ethnology.

AND HARBORS CONGRESS: Report of the proceedings of the Nati
and Harbors Congress. Washington, D. C., January 15–16, 1906.
No imprint. 167 p. 8°.
Cover-title.

YORK PRODUCE EXCHANGE: Annual statistical report of the New York Produce
Exchange for the year 1906, with comparisons with preceding years. Prepared by the statistical department of the exchange. New York, John Pol-
hemus Printing Company, [1907]. 147 p. 8°.

IVIDENCE PUBLIC LIBRARY: Twenty-ninth annual report. ... comprising reports
of the treasurer and librarian for the year ending December 31, 1906.
. [Providence], Snow and Farnham Co., printers, 1907. front., 74 p. 8°.

PUBLIC SCHOOL LIBRARY, COLUMBUS, OHIO: Thirtieth annual report. Sept. 1, 1905 to
Aug. 31, 1906. No imprint. 30 p. 8°.

BUREAU OF THE CENSUS: Estimates of population 1904, 1905, 1906, including
the census returns of states making an intercensal enumeration. Washington, Government Printing Office, 1907. 28 p. 4°. (Bull. 71.)

BUREAU OF STATISTICS: Foreign commerce and navigation of the U. S. for the
year ending June 30, 1906. Washington, Government Printing Office, 1907.
1291 p. 4°.

——— ——— Statistical abstract of the United States, 1906 ... Washington, Government Printing Office, 1907. 716 p. 8°.

——— Laws, statutes, etc.: Copyright enactments of the United States. 1783–1906.
Compiled by Thorvald Solberg. Washington, Government Printing Office,
1906. 174 p. 8°.
Copyright office bulletin no. 3.
At head of title: "Library of Congress."

——— ——— The copyright law of the U. S. of America in force November 15, 1906
... Prepared by Thorvald Solberg, register of copyrights ... Wash-
ington, Government Printing Office, 1906. 30 p. 8°.
Bull. no. 1 of the Copyright office, Library of Congress.

UNIVERSITY OF CALIFORNIA: Shoshonean dialects of California. By A. L. Kroeber.
Berkeley, The University Press, February, 1907. 66–165 p. 8°.
Amer. archæology and ethnology. v. 4, no. 3.

——— ——— The Yokuts language of South Central California. By A. L. Kroeber.
Berkeley, The University Press, January, 1907. 166–377 p. 8°.
Amer. archæology and ethnology. v. 2, no. 5.

VAN TYNE, C. H. and LELAND, W. G.: Guide to the archives of the Government of the
U. S. in Washington. By Claude Halstead Van Tyne and Waldo Gifford
Leland. Published by the Carnegie Institution of Washington, 1904. xiii,
215 p. 8°.

URUGUAY.

URUGUAY. UNIVERSIDAD DE MONTEVIDEO: Programa de la Sección de Agronomía de
la Universidad de Montevideo. Montevideo, Imp. "El Siglo Ilustrado,"
de Mariño y Caballero, 1906. 17, (5) p. 8°.

VENEZUELA.

Landaeta Rosales, Manuel: Una calle histórica de Caracas. [Caracas]. Lit. y tip. del Comercio, 1907. 14 p. 8°.
Cover title.

N. Bolet-Peraza. Memoratissimus. No imprint. [1907.] vii. 77 p. front., port. 8°.

[Venezuela. Ministerio de instrucción pública]: La instrucción en el Estado Tachira. Diciembre de 1906. San Crístóbal, Imprenta del Estado. 48 p. 8°.

—— Ministerio de obras públicas: Memoria . . . 1895, 1896. Caracas, 1895–96. 4 v. 4°.

GENERAL WORKS, REFERENCE BOOKS, AND BIBLIOGRAPHIES.

Annual American catalog, 1906. . . . New York. Office of the Publishers' weekly, 1907. xxxvi, 354, (1). 352 p. 8°.

Annual Library index, 1906. . . . New York, Office of the Publishers' weekly, 1907. vii, (1), 380 p. 8°.

Butler, Nicholas Murray: True and false democracy. An address delivered before the University of California, Berkeley, California, on Charter Day, March 23, 1907. By Nicholas Murray Butler, president of Columbia University. No imprint. 19 p. 8°.
Cover-title.

Calvo, Carlos: Colección completa de los tratados, convenciones, capitulaciones, armisticios y otros actos diplomáticos de todos los Estados de la América Latina. Comprendidos entre el golfo de Méjico y el cabo de Horno, desde el año de 1493 hasta nuestros días . . . por Carlos Calvo . . . 1° período, tomos 1–9. Paris, A. Durand, etc., 1862–1866. 9 v. 8°.

—— Same. 2° período, tomos 1–4. Paris, A. Durand, etc., 1864–1865. 4 v. 8°.

Cattell, James Edward: . . . South America. Edited by James Edward Cattell, assisted by H. S. Morrison and A. C. Kauffman. Published by the Philadelphia Commercial Museum. Philadelphia, [1906]. 284, 21 p. maps. 4°.

CONTENTS.

Argentine Republic, Chile, Peru, Bolivia, Paraguay, Uruguay, Brazil, Ecuador, Venezuela, Colombia, and the Guianas.

Church, George Earl: Desiderata in exploration. 1907. . . . [pt.] 2, South America by Col. George Earl Church. London, The Royal Geographical Society, 1907. 15 p. 8°.
Cover-title.

Colnett, James: A voyage to the South Atlantic and around Cape Horn into the Pacific Ocean, for the purpose of extending the spermaceti whale fisheries, and other objects of commerce, by ascertaining the ports, bays, harbours, and anchoring births, in certain islands and coasts in those seas at which the ships of the British merchants might be refitted. Undertaken and performed by Captain James Colnett, of the Royal Navy, in the ship Rattler. London, Printed for the author by W. Bennett, 1798. xviii, 179 p. front. 4°.

Herrera, Manuel Antonio: América; su pasado, presente y porvenir políticos . . . por Manuel Antonio Herrera . . . Guatemala, Tip. de Amos y Anderson, 1906. 20 p. nar. 12°.

ARLOS: Technological dictionary in the English, Spanish, German, ich languages; containing technical terms and locutions employed trades, and industry in general, military, and naval terms. By s Huelin y Arssu . . . Madrid, Adrian Romo, 1906. xv, 609 p.

RCHAEOLOGIC COMMISSION: Meeting of the diplomatic represent-
l the American Republics at the Department of State, Monday,
er 21, 1903, at 3 p. m., in the interest of the organization of an
ional Archaeologic Commission, and in pursuance of the motion
carrie t the meeting of April 15, 1903. 12 p. 4°.
Caption title.

RNATIONAL BUREAU OF THE AMERICAN REPUBLICS: Monthly Bulletin. April, 1907. Washington. Government Printing Office, 1907. pp. 801—1080. 5 plates.

CONTENTS.

Editorial Section. Photographs of progress and development—Competition of architects for new building—Why the competition is limited—The Bureau not an ornamental institution—Some special results of war—Names and standing of Latin-American firms—The new Minister of Salvador—Notable addresses on Bolivia and the Argentine Republic—Foreign trade of the Argentine Republic—Great harbor improvements in Brazil—General features of interest—Articles about Latin America in June magazines—Baron D'Estournelles de Constant and W. T. Stead.
Reception of the Minister of Guatemala. Sketch of Minister Toledo Herrarte.
Reception of the Minister of Salvador.
Architectural Competition for New Bureau Building. Correspondence and resolutions regarding the Carnegie gift.
Argentine Republic. Address of Lieutenant-Commander Atwell—Foreign commerce in 1906—Consolidation of railroad companies—Real estate registration in Buenos Ayres, 1906—Commission for tariff revision—Maritime movement, 1905 and 1906—Cereal crop shipments, 1906—Public works in 1907—Patents and trade-marks in 1906—Approval of the report of the boundary commission with Brazil—Customs receipts at Buenos Ayres, 1906.
Bolivia. Resources and general conditions—Exports of tin, 1906.
Brazil. Foreign commerce, 1906—Details of foreign trade in 1905—Foreign duties on Brazilian coffees—Improvement work at Rio Grande do Sul—United States and Canadian investments—Subsidy for cultivation of perini fiber—Rescinding of coasting trade concession—The port of Santos in 1906—The textile market—The sugar industry at Pernambuco.
Chile. Trade with Germany in 1906—Customs duties, January, 1907—Customs tare for 1907—Railway construction from Santiago to Arica.
Colombia. Educational statistics—Information bureau in New York—Railway from Darien to Medellin.
Cuba. Foreign commerce in 1906—Sugar crop of 1906 and 1907.
Dominican Republic. Message of President Cáceres.
Guatemala. Message of President Estrada Cabrera.
Haiti. Propaganda for Haitian products.
Honduras. Alien law—Immigration law.
Mexico. Foreign commerce, first half, 1906-7—Silver basis of stamp and customs taxes, April, 1907—Postal receipts, seven months of 1906-7—Registry of business transactions—Customs revenues, seven months of 1906-7—Sugar production in 1906—Coinage issue under the new monetary system—Flour machinery shipped to the United States—Commercial travelers' licenses—Fishing concession to Norwegian Company—Postal convention with Italy.
Nicaragua. Increased export duty on coffee.
Panama. Monetary law—Tariff legislation, 1907.
Peru. Mining industry in 1906—Customs revenues at Mollendo, 1906—Improvement of Peruvian live stock—Coastwise service to San Francisco.
Salvador. Inauguration of President Figueroa—Message of President Escalón—Customs revenues, first half of 1906—Import trade, first half of 1906—Port movements, 1906—Bank statement, 1906.
United States. Trade with Latin America—Imports and exports of tobacco, 1906—Cotton report, 1906.
Uruguay. Message of President Batlle y Ordoñez—New cabinet—Immigration law—Customs receipts, January, 1907.
Venezuela. Customs modifications, 1905-6
Library Accessions and Files.

—— Program and conditions for the new building of the International Bureau of the American Republics. Washington, [Byron S. Adams]. March, 1907. 21 p. front. 8°.

MAURTUA, VICTOR M.: Antecedentes de la recopilación de Yndias. Publicados por Victor M. Maurtua. Madrid, Imprenta de Bernardo Rodríguez, 1906. 245 p. 4°.

PEARSON, HENRY C.: What I saw in the Tropics. A record of visits to Ceylon, the Federated Malay states, Mexico, Nicaragua, Costa Rica, Republic of Panama, Colombia, Jamaica, Hawaii. By Henry C. Pearson, editor of "The India Rubber World." New York, The India Rubber Publishing Company, 1906. [6], 288, [14] p. illus. 8°.

U. S. LIBRARY OF CONGRESS . . . Preliminary check-list of American almanacs. 1639–1800. By Hugh Alexander Morrison, of the Library of Congress. Washington, Government Printing Office, 1907. 159 p. 4°.

MAPS.

BARTHOLOMEW, F. G. (ed.): Atlas of the World's commerce. A new series of maps with descriptive text and diagrams showing products, imports, exports, commercial conditions and economic statistics of the countries of the world. Compiled from the latest official returns at the Edinburgh Geographical Institute and edited by J. G. Bartholomew . . . London, George Newnes, [1907]. lvi p., 42 p. 176 maps. f°.

CRAM'S STANDARD AMERICAN railway system atlas of the World. Showing all the railway systems in colors and numbers . . . A concise and original ready reference index of the United States, Canada, Mexico, and Cuba, accurately locating all counties, county seats, cities, post-offices, railroad stations, villages, etc. . . . New York & Chicago, George F. Cram, 1907. 625, [32] p. f°.

SOUTH AMERICA. [A collection of reprints of old maps of South America accompanies "Juicio de límites entre el Perú y Bolivia," listed in this "Bulletin."]

PERIODICAL FILES.

se publications marked with an asterisk have no recent num
ᴊ on file.

---

ns interested in the commercial and general news of foreign
⸱⸱ ᴎs will find the following among the official and
ations on the permanent files in the Columbus
', International Bureau of the American Republics:

ARGENTINE REPUBLIC.

cantil, ᴮ⸱ ᴜs al Sud. Weekly.
de ᴉones exteriores.) Buenos Ayres. Irregular.
ana. Buenos Ayres. Monthly.
⸱⸱⸱ᴜᴄᴄ ⸱⸱⸱ᵧᴇntino. Buenos Ayres.
ᴊ Aᴉ ao. Buenos Ayres. Irregular.
ᴉ Argentina. Buenos Ayres. Daily.
ᴜ ⸱⸱⸱⸱ [Buenos Aires.] Weekly.
ꜱtuno Mensue dena Camera Italiana di Commercio ed Arti in Buenos Aires.
ᴅuenos Ayres. Monthly.
Buenos Aires Handels-Zeitung. Buenos Ayres. Weekly.
Buenos Aires Herald. Buenos Ayres. Daily and weekly.
*El Comercio Exterior Argentino. Buenos Ayres. Irregular.
La Ilustración Sud-Americana. Buenos Ayres. Semimonthly.
Monthly Bulletin of Municipal Statistics of the City of Buenos Ayres. Buenos Ayres.
Monthly.
La Nación. Buenos Ayres. Daily.
Patentes y Marcas, Revista Sud-Americana de la Propiedad Intelectual é Industrial.
Buenos Ayres. Monthly.
La Prensa. Buenos Ayres. Daily.
Review of the River Plate. Buenos Ayres. Weekly.
Revista Mensual de la Cámara Mercantil. Avellaneda. Monthly.
Revista de Derecho, Historia y Letras. Buenos Aires. Monthly.
Revista Nacional. Buenos Ayres. Monthly.
The Standard. Buenos Ayres. Mail supplement.

BELGIUM.

Recueil consulaire. Bruxelles. Quarterly.

BOLIVIA.

*Boletín de la Oficina Nacional de Inmigración, Estadística y Propaganda Geográfica.
La Paz. Quarterly.
Boletín de la Sociedad Geográfica de la Paz. La Paz. Irregular.
El Comercio. La Paz. Daily.
El Estado. (Diario Oficial.) La Paz. Daily.
*Revista Comercial é Industrial de la República de Bolivia. La Paz. Monthly.
Revista del Ministerio de Colonización y Agricultura. La Paz. Quarterly.

Boletim da Agricultura. Secretario da Agricultura, Comercio e Obras Publicas do Estado de São Paulo. São Paulo. Monthly.
Boletim do Museo Goeldi. Pará. Irregular.
Boletim da Secretaria de Agricultura, Viação, Industria e Obras Publicas do Estado da Bahia. Bahia. Monthly.
*Boletim de Serviço da Estatistica Commercial da Republica dos Estados Unidos do Brazil. Rio.de Janeiro. Irregular.
*Brazilian Mining Review. Ouro Preto. Monthly.
Brazilian Review. Rio de Janeiro. Weekly.
Diario da Bahia. Bahia. Daily.
Diario do Congresso Nacional. Rio de Janeiro. Daily.
Diario Oficial. Rio de Janeiro. Daily.
*Gazeta Commercial e Financeira. Rio de Janeiro. Weekly.
Jornal do Recife. Pernambuco. Daily.
Jornal dos Agricultores. Rio de Janeiro. Semimonthly.
O Paiz. Rio de Janeiro. Daily.
Provincia (A) do Pará. Belem. Daily.
Revista Agricola. São Paulo. Monthly.
Revista Maritima Brazileira. Rio de Janeiro. Monthly.

Anales de La Universidad. Santiago. Monthly.
Boletín del Ministerio de Relaciones Esteriores. Santiago. Monthly.
Boletín de la Sociedad Agrícola del Sur. Concepción. Semimonthly.
Boletín de la Sociedad de Fomento Fabril. Santiago. Monthly.
Boletín de la Sociedad Nacional de Agricultura. Santiago. Weekly.
Boletín de la Sociedad Nacional de Minería. Santiago. Monthly.
Chilian Times. Valparaiso. Semiweekly.
*Diario Oficial de la República de Chile. Santiago. Daily.
El Mercurio. Valparaiso. Daily.
El Noticiero Comercial. Santiago de Chile. Monthly.
El Pensamiento. Santiago. Monthly.
*Revista Comercial é Industrial de Minas. Santiago. Monthly.

Diario Oficial. Bogota. Daily.
Revista de la Instrucción Pública de Colombia. Bogota. Monthly.

Boletín Judicial. San Jose. Daily.
La Gaceta. [Diario Oficial.] San Jose. Daily.

Boletín Oficial de la Cámara de Comercio, Industria y Navegación de la Isla de Cuba. Habana. Monthly.
Boletín Oficial del Departamento del Estado. Habana. Monthly.
Derecho y Sociología. Habana. Monthly.
El Estudio. Boletín de Derecho, Legislación, Jurisprudencia y Administración. Habana. Trimonthly.
La Gaceta Económica. Habana. Semimonthly.

ECUADOR.

Anales de la Universidad Central del Ecuador. Quito. Monthly.
Gaceta Municipal. Guayaquil. Weekly.
Registro Oficial de la República del Ecuador. Quito. Daily.

GREAT BRITAIN.

Board of Trade Journal. London. Weekly.
Commercial Intelligence. London. Weekly.
Diplomatic and Consular Reports. London.
Geographical Journal. London. Monthly.
Mining (The) Journal, Railway and Commercial Gazette. London. Weekly
The Scottish Geographical Magazine. Edinburgh. Monthly.
South American Journal. London. Weekly.
Times (The). London. Daily. (Filed for one year.)
Tropical Life. London. Monthly.

FRANCE.

L'Amérique Latine. Paris. Daily.
Les Annales Diplomatiques et Consulaires. Paris. Monthly.
Le Brésil. Paris. Weekly.
Bulletin American Chamber of Commerce. Paris. Monthly.
Bulletin de la Chambre de Commerce de Paris. Paris. Weekly.
Bulletin de la Société de Géographie Commerciale de Paris. Paris. Irregul
La Géographie. Bulletin de la Société de Géographie. Paris. Semimonthl;
Journal d'Agriculture Tropicale. Paris. Monthly.
Moniteur Officiel du Commerce. Paris. Weekly.
Le Nouveau Monde. Paris. Weekly.
Rapports commerciaux des agents diplomatiques et consulaires de France

GUATEMALA.

Boletín de Agricultura. Guatemala. Irregular.
El Guatemalteco. Guatemala. Daily. (Diario Oficial.)
La Locomotora. Guatemala. Monthly.
*La República. Guatemala. Daily.

HAITI.

*Bulletin Officiel de l'Agriculture et de l'Industrie. Port au Prince. Monthly.
*Le Moment. (Journal politique.) Port au Prince, Haiti. Weekly.
Le Moniteur. (Journal officiel de la République d'Haïti.) Port au Prince, Haiti.
    Biweekly.
Revue de la Société de Législation. Port au Prince, Haiti. Monthly.

HONDURAS.

Boletín Legislativo. Tegucigalpa. Daily.
El Estado. Tegucigalpa. (3 nos. per week.)
La Gaceta. Tegucigalpa. Daily. (Official paper.)
*Gaceta Judicial. Tegucigalpa. Semiweekly.
Revista del Archivo y Biblioteca Nacional de Honduras. Tegucigalpa, Honduras.
    Monthly.

ITALY.

Bollettino del Ministro degli Affari Esteri. Roma. Irregular.

MEXICO.

El Agricultor Mexicano. Ciudad Juarez. Monthly.
Anales del Museo Nacional de México. Mexico. Monthly.
Boletín de Estadística. Merida. Semimonthly.
Boletín del Instituto Científico y Literario. Toluca. Monthly.
Boletín Oficial del Distrito sur de la Baja California. La Paz. Weekly.
Boletín de la Secretaría de Fomento, colonización é industria. Mexico. Monthly.
Boletín Oficial de la Secretaría de Relaciones Exteriores. Mexico. Monthly.
Diario Oficial. Mexico. Daily.
El Economista Mexicano. Mexico. Weekly.
*El Estado de Colima. Colima. Weekly.
El Hacendado Mexicano. Mexico. Monthly.
Mexican Herald. Mexico. Daily. (Filed for one year.)
Mexican Investor. Mexico. Weekly.
Mexican Journal of Commerce. Mexico City. Monthly.
Periódico Oficial del Gobierno del Estado de Guerrero. Chilpancingo, Mexico.
    Weekly.
Periódico Oficial del Gobierno del Estado de Michoacán de Ocampo. Morelia, Mexico.
    Semiweekly.
*Periódico Oficial del Gobierno del Estado de Oaxaca. Oaxaca de Juarez, Mexico.
    Semiweekly.
Periódico Oficial del Gobierno del Estado de Tabasco. San Juan Bautista, Mexico.
    Semiweekly.
El Republicano. Aguascalientes. Weekly.
Semana Mercantil. Mexico. Weekly.

NICARAGUA.

The American. Bluefields. Weekly.
El Comercio. Managua. Daily.
Diario Oficial. Managua. Daily.

PANAMA.

il. Panama. Daily.
rald. Panama. Weekly.
ntica. Panama. Weekly.
licial, Organo del Poder Judicial de la República. Panama. Irregular

PARAGUAY.

..ncenal de la Cámara de Comercio de la Asunción. Asuncion.

.. .al. Asuncion. Daily.
iguay Rundschau. Asuncion. Weekly.
vista del Instituto Paraguayo. Asuncion. Monthly.
i Commerciale. Assumption. Semimonthly.

PERU.

.uxiliar del Comercio. Callao. Biweekly.
boletín de Minas, Industrias y Construcciones. Lima. Monthly.
oletín del Ministerio de Fomento. Dirección de Fomento. Lima. Monthly.
—— Dirección de Obras Públicas. Lima. Monthly.
itín de la Sociedad Geográfica de Lima. Lima. Quarterly.
i de la Sociedad Nacional de Agricultura. Lima. Monthly.
de la Sociedad Nacional de Minería. Lima. Monthly.
ia Economista. Lima. Weekly.
El Peruano. (Diario Oficial.) Lima. Daily.
Revista de Ciencias. Lima. Monthly.
*Revista Pan-Americana. Lima. Monthly.

PHILIPPINE ISLANDS.

Boletín de la Cámara de Comercio Filipina. Manila Monthly.
El Mercantil. Manila. Daily.
Official Gazette. Manila. Weekly. (Also issued in Spanish.)

PORTO RICO.

La Correspondencia de Puerto Rico. San Juan. Daily.

EL SALVADOR.

Anales del Museo Nacional. San Salvador. Monthly.
Boletín de Agricultura. San Salvador. Semimonthly.
Boletín de la Dirección General de Estadística. San Salvador. Irregular.
Diario del Salvador. San Salvador. Daily.
Diario Oficial. San Salvador. Daily.
*Revista de Derecho y Jurisprudencia. San Salvador. Monthly.

UNITED STATES.

American Druggist. New York. Semimonthly.
American Exporter. New York. Semimonthly. (Alternate Spanish and English editions.)
*American Historical Review. New York. Quarterly.
American Made Goods. New York. Quarterly.
American Review of Reviews. New York. Monthly.

Annals of the American Academy of Political and Social Science. Philadelphia. Bimonthly.
El Boletín Comercial. St. Louis. Monthly.
Bookman (The). New York. Monthly.
Bulletin of the American Geographical Society. New York.
Bulletin of Books added to the Public Library of the City of Boston. Boston. Monthly.
Bulletin of the Geographical Society of Philadelphia. Philadelphia. Monthly.
Bulletin of the New York Public Library. Monthly.
Buyer's Index. New York. Semimonthly. (Alternate Spanish and English editions.)
Century Magazine. New York. Monthly.
El Comercio. New York. Monthly.
Current Literature. New York. Monthly.
Dun's Review. New York. Weekly.
Dun's Review. International edition. New York. Monthly.
Engineering Magazine. New York. Monthly.
Engineering and Mining Journal. New York. Weekly.
Engineering News. New York. Weekly.
Export Implement Age. Philadelphia. Monthly.
Exporters and Importers Journal. New York. Monthly.
Forum (The). New York. Quarterly.
Independent (The). New York. Weekly.
India Rubber World. New York. Monthly.
Journal of Geography. New York. Monthly.
Library Journal. New York. Monthly.
Literary Digest. New York. Weekly.
Mines and Minerals. Scranton, Pa. Monthly.
Mining World. Chicago. Weekly.
Modern Mexico. St. Louis. Monthly.
Monthly Consular and Trade Reports. (Department of Commerce and Labor.) Washington. Monthly.
National Geographic Magazine. New York. Monthly.
North American Review. New York. Monthly.
Las Novedades. New York. Weekly.
Outlook (The). New York. Weekly.
Pan-American Review. New York. Monthly.
Patent and Trade Mark Review. New York. Monthly.
Records of the Past. Washington, D. C. Monthly.
Scientific American. New York. Weekly.
Scientific American. Export Edition. New York. Monthly.
Sister Republics. Denver, Colo. Monthly.
Tea and Coffee Trade Journal. New York. Monthly.
United States Tobacco Journal. New York. Weekly.
World To-day (The). Chicago. Monthly.
World's Work. New York. Monthly.

URUGUAY.

Anales del Departamento de Ganadería y Agricultura. Montevideo. Monthly.
*Montevideo Times. Montevideo. Daily.
Revista de la Asociación Rural del Uruguay. Montevideo. Monthly.
Revista de la Unión Industrial Uruguaya. Montevideo. Semimonthly.

VENEZUELA.

adística. Caracas. Monthly.
Maracaibo. Daily.
lustrial. Caracas. Semimonthly

zuelan Herald. Caracas.

ADDITIONS TO THE PERIODICAL FILES DURING APRIL, 1907.

rs' Magazine. New York. Monthly.
...an de las cámaras de comercio, industria y navegación y de las cámaras agrícolas.
drid. Monthly.
al of American History. New Haven, Conn. Quarterly.
)greso Latino. Mexico. Weekly.
...azón. Buenos Aires. Daily.
vista de la Liga de Defensa Comercial. Buenos Aires. Semimonthly.
ento. Buenos Aires. Daily.
na. Buenos Aires. Daily.

HONORARY CORRESPONDING MEMBERS OF THE INTERNATIONAL UNION OF AMERICAN REPUBLICS.

Countries.	Names.	Residence.
Argentine Republic..	Señor Dr. Don Estanislao S. Zeballos	Buenos Ayres.
Bolivia	Señor Don Manuel V. Balliviána	La Paz.
Brazil	Dezembargador Antonio Bezerra...........	Pará.
	Firmino da Silva	Florianopolis.
Chile..............	Señor Don Moisés Vargas	Santiago.
Colombia..........	Señor Don Rufino Gutiérrez...............	Bogotá.
Costa Rica	Señor Don Manuel Aragón	San José.
Cuba	Señor Don Antonio S. de Bustamante	Havana.
	Señor Don Lincoln de Zayas...............	Havana.
Dominican Republic.	Señor Don José Gabriel Garcíab...........	Santo Domingo.
Ecuador...........	Señor Don Francisco Andrade Marín.......	Quito.
	Señor Don Luis Alberto Carbo	Guayaquil.
Guatemala.........	Señor Don Antonio Batres Jáuregui........	Guatemala City.
	Señor Don Rafael Montúfar	Guatemala City.
Haiti..............	Monsieur Georges Sylvain	Port au Prince.
Honduras	Señor Don E. Constantino Fiallos	Tegucigalpa.
Mexico............	Señor Don Francisco L. de la Barra........	City of Mexico.
	Señor Don Antonio García Cubas..........	City of Mexico.
	Señor Don Fernando Ferrari Pérez	City of Mexico.
Nicaragua	Señor Don José D. Gámez.................	Managua.
Paraguay..........	Señor Don José S. Decoud	Asunción.
Panama	Señor Don Samuel Lewis..................	Panama.
	Señor Don Ramón M. Valdés..............	Panama.
Peru	Señor Don Alejandro Garland.............	Lima.
Salvador..........	Señor Dr. Don Salvador Gallegos	San Salvador.
Uruguay..........	Señor Don José I. Schiffiano	Montevideo.
Venezuela	Señor General Don Manuel Landaeta Rosales.	Caracas.
	Señor Don Francisco de Paula Alamo.......	Caracas.

a Honorary corresponding member of the Royal Geographical Society of Great Britain.
b Corresponding member of the Academia Nacional de la Historia de Venezuela

AN REPRESENTATIVES IN THE STATES.

AMBASSADORS EXTRAORDINARY AND PLENIPOTENTIARY.

zil ....Mr. Joaquim Nabuco,
        Office of Embassy, 1710 H street, Washington, D. C.

ico.................................Señor Don Enrique C. Creel,
        Office of Embassy, 1415 I street, Washington, D. C.

ENVOYS EXTRAORDINARY AND MINISTERS PLENIPOTENTIARY.

e Republic ....Señor Don Epifanio Portela,
        Office of Legation, 2108 Sixteenth street, Washington, D. C.

via............................Señor Don Ignacio Calderón,
        Office of Legation, 1638 Sixteenth street, Washington, D. C.

ile.............................Señor Don Joaquín Walker-Martínez,
        Absent.

lombia.......................Señor Don Enrique Cortes,
        Office of Legation, 1312 Twenty-first street NW., Washington, D. C.

ica...........................Señor Don Joaquín Bernardo Calvo,
        Office of Legation, 1329 Eighteenth street NW., Washington, D. C.

ba............................Señor Don Gonzalo de Quesada,
        Office of Legation, "The Wyoming," Washington, D. C.

Ecuador.......................Señor Don Luis Felipe Carbo,
        Absent. Office of Legation, 1222 Connecticut avenue, Washington, D. C.

Guatemala....................Señor Dr. Don Luis Toledo Herrarte,
        Office of Legation, "The Highlands," Washington, D. C.

Haiti.........................Mr. J. N. Léger,
        Office of Legation, 1122 Rhode Island avenue, Washington, D. C.

Honduras ....Señor Dr. Don José Rosa Pacas,
        Absent.

Nicaragua ....Señor Don Luis F. Corea,
        Office of Legation, 2003 O street, Washington, D. C.

Panama ....Señor Don J. Domingo de Obaldía,
        Absent.

                        Señor Don José Agustín Arango,
        Office of Legation, "The Highlands," Washington, D. C.

Peru ....Señor Don Felipe Pardo,
        Office of Legation, 2171 Florida avenue, Washington, D. C.

Salvador.......................Señor Don Federico Mejía,
        Office of Legation, "The Arlington."

Uruguay ....Señor Dr. Don Luis Melian Lafinur,
        Office of Legation, 1116 Twenty-first street, Washington, D. C.

MINISTER RESIDENT

Dominican Republic ....Señor Don Emilio C. Joubert,
        "The Shoreham," Washington, D. C.

CHARGÉS D'AFFAIRES.

Chile...........................Señor Don Alberto Yoacham,
        Office of Legation, "The Rochambeau," Washington, D. C.

Honduras........................Señor Dr. Salvador Córdova,
        Office of Legation, care of Consulate-General of Honduras, New York City.

Venezuela ....Señor Don Augusto F. Pulido,
        "The Rochambeau," Washington, D. C.

UNITED STATES REPRESENTATIVES IN THE LATIN-AMÉRICAN REPUBLICS.

AMBASSADORS EXTRAORDINARY AND PLENIPOTENTIARY.

Brazil ....IRVING B. DUDLEY, Rio de Janeiro

Mexico ....DAVID E. THOMPSON, Mexico.

ENVOYS EXTRAORDINARY AND MINISTERS PLENIPOTENTIARY.

Argentine Republic ....A. M. BEAUPRÉ, Buenos Ayres.

Bolivia ....WILLIAM B. SORSBY, La Paz.

Chile ....JOHN HICKS, Santiago.

Colombia ....THOMAS C. DAWSON, Bogotá.

Costa Rica ....WILLIAM L. MERRY, San José.

Cuba ....EDWIN V. MORGAN, Havana.

Ecuador ....WILLIAMS C. FOX, Quito.

Guatemala ....JOSEPH W. J. LEE, Guatemala City.

Haiti ....HENRY W. FURNISS, Port au Prince.

Honduras.....................................(See Guatemala.)

Nicaragua.....................................(See Costa Rica.)

Panama ....HERBERT G. SQUIERS, Panama.

Paraguay ....(See Uruguay.)

Peru ....LESLIE COMBS, Lima.

Salvador.....................................(See Costa Rica.)

Uruguay.....................................EDWARD C. O'BRIEN, Montevideo.

Venezuela ....W. W. RUSSELL, Caracas.

MINISTER RESIDENT AND CONSUL-GENERAL.

Dominican Republic.....................................FENTON R. McCREERY, Santo Domingo.

! OF POSTAGE FROM THE UNITED STATES TO LATIN-AMERICAN COUNTRIES.

rates of postage from the United States to all foreign countries and colonies (except Canada, !, and Cuba) are as follows:

		Cents.
ams (⅓ ounce)		5
ds, each		2
, each		4
ner printed matter, per 2 ounces		1
	Packets not in excess of 10 ounces	5
Commercial papers	Packets in excess of 10 ounces, for each 2 ounces or fraction thereof	1
	Packets not in excess of 4 ounces	2
Samples of merchandise	Packets in excess of 4 ounces, for each 2 ounces or fraction thereof	1
Registration fee o	ers and other articles	8

country (except Canada, Mexico, and Cuba) must be forwarded, on them or not. All other mailable matter must be prepaid, at least

d in the United States addressed to Mexico is subject to the same postage rates and com- if it were addressed for delivery in the United States, except that articles of indise (fourth-class matter) not sent as *bona fide* trade samples should be sent by that the following articles are *absolutely excluded* from the mails without regard to the amount of postage prepaid or the manner in which they are wrapped:

All sealed packages, other than letters in their usual and ordinary form; *all* packages (including packages of second-class matter) which weigh more than 4 pounds 6 ounces, except such as are sent by "Parcels Post;" publications which violate any copyright law of Mexico.

Single volumes of printed books *in unsealed packages* are transmissible to Mexico in the regular mails without limit as to weight.

Unsealed packages of mailable merchandise may be sent by "Parcels Post" to Bolivia, British Guiana, British Honduras, Chile, Colombia, Costa Rica, Guatemala, Honduras, Mexico, Nicaragua, Salvador, and Venezuela, at the rates named on page xv.

PROHIBITED ARTICLES TO ALL FOREIGN COUNTRIES.

Poisons, explosives, and inflammable articles, live or dead animals, insects (especially the Colorado beetle), reptiles, fruit or vegetable matter liable to decomposition, and substances exhaling a bad odor, excluded from transmission in domestic mails as being in themselves, either from their form or nature, liable to destroy, deface, or otherwise injure the contents of the mail bags, or the persons of those engaged in the postal service; also obscene, lewd, or lascivious books, pamphlets, etc., and letters and circulars concerning lotteries, so-called gift concerts, etc. (also excluded from domestic mails); postal cards or letters addressed to go around the world; letters or packages (except those to Mexico) containing gold or silver substances, jewelry or precious articles, any packet whatever containing articles liable to customs duties in the countries addressed (except Cuba and Mexico); articles other than letters which are not prepaid at least partly; articles other than letters or postal cards containing writing in the nature of personal correspondence, unless fully prepaid at the rate of letter postage; articles of a nature likely to soil or injure the correspondence, packets of commercial papers and prints of all kinds, the weight of which exceeds 2 kilograms (4 pounds 6 ounces), or the size 18 inches in any direction, except *rolls* of prints, which may measure 30 inches in length by 4 inches in diameter; postal cards not of United States origin, and United States postal cards of the largest ("C") size (except as letters), and except also the reply halves of double postal cards received from foreign countries.

There is, moreover, reserved to the Government of every country of the Postal Union the right to refuse to convey over its territory, or to deliver, as well, articles liable to the reduced rate in regard to which the laws, ordinances, or decrees which regulate the conditions of their publication or of their circulation in that country have not been complied with.

☞ Full and complete information relative to all regulations can be obtained from the United States Postal Guide.

FOREIGN MAILS.

TABLE SHOWING THE RATES OF POSTAGE CHARGED IN LATIN-AMERICAN COUNTRIES ON ARTICLES SENT BY MAIL TO THE UNITED STATES.

Countries.	Letters, per 15 grams, equal to one-half ounce.		Single postal cards, each.[a]		Other articles, per 50 grams, equal to 2 ounces.		Charge for registration.	Charge for return receipt.
	Currency of country.	Centimes.	Currency of country.	Centimes.	Currency of country.	Centimes.		
Argentine Republic	15 centavos	35	6 centavos	15	3 centavos	10	24 centavos	12 centavos.
Bolivia via Panama	22 centavos	50	8 centavos	20	6 centavos	10	}20 centavos	}10 centavos.
Bolivia via other routes	20 centavos	50	6 centavos	15	4 centavos	10		
Brazil	300 reis	35	100 reis	10	50 reis	5	400 reis	200 reis.
Chile	10 centavos	50	3 centavos	15	2 centavos	10	10 centavos	5 centavos.
Colombia	20 centavos	50	4 centavos	10	2 centavos	10	10 centavos	5 centavos.
Costa Rica	10 centimos	25	3 centimos	7½	2 centimos	5	10 centimos	5 centimos.
Cuba[b]								
Dominican Republic (Santo Domingo)	10 centavos	25	3 centavos	10	2 centavos	5	10 centavos	5 centavos.
Ecuador	10 centavos	50	3 centavos	10	2 centavos		10 centavos	5 centavos.
Falkland Islands	4 pence	40	1 penny	10	1 penny		2 pence	2½ pence.
Guatemala	5 centavos	50	8 centavos	15	2 centavos	10	10 centavos	5 centavos.
Haiti	10 centièmes de gourde		3 centièmes de gourde		3 centièmes de gourde		2 centièmes de gourde	5 centièmes de gourde.
Honduras	15 centavos	50	3 centavos	15	2 centavos	10	10 centavos	5 centavos.
Honduras, British	5 cents	25	2 cents	10	2 cents	10	10 cts.	6 centavos.
Mexico	5 centavos		2 centavos		1 centavo		10 centavos	5 centavos.
Nicaragua	15 centavos	50	5 centavos	15	2 centavos	10	10 centavos	10 centavos.
Paraguay	60 centavos		6 centavos	15	8 centavos	10	40 centavos	20 centavos.
Peru via San Francisco	20 centavos	50	6 centavos	15	4 centavos	10	10 centavos	10 centavos.
Peru via Panama	22 centavos	55	8 centavos	20	6 centavos	15	40 centavos	20 centavos.
Porto Rico[b]								
Salvador via Panama	11 centavos	55	3 centavos	15	3 centavos	15	10 centavos	5 centavos.
Salvador via other routes	10 centavos	50	8 centavos	15	2 centavos	10	10 centavos	5 centavos.
Uruguay	10 centavos	50	8 centavos	15	2 centavos	10	10 centavos	5 centavos.
Venezuela	50 centimos	50	15 centimos	15	10 centimos	10	50 centimos	25 centimes.
British Guiana	5 cents		2 cents		1 cent	10	10 centavos	5 centavos.
Dutch Guiana	25 cents Dutch	50	7½ cents Dutch		5 cents Dutch		10 cents Dutch	10 cents Dutch.
French Guiana	25 centimes		10 centimes		5 centimes		25 centimes	10 centimes.

a The rate for a reply-paid (double) card is double the rate named in this column.
b United States domestic rates and conditions.

	Ft in	Ft		Cents.	Cents.			
Bolivia	3 6	6			20	20	New York and San Francisco.	La Paz.
Chile	3 6	0	1.	20	20		New York and San Francisco.	Valparaiso.
Colombia	2 0		4	11	12	12	All offices authorized to exchange mails between the two countries.	
Costa Rica	2 0		4	11	12	12		
Ecuador	3 6	6		11	20	20		
Guatemala	3 6	6		11	12	12	New York, New Orleans, and San Francisco.	Guatemala City, Retalhuleu, and Puerto Barrios.
Guiana, British	3 6	6		11	12	12	All offices authorized to exchange mails.	
Honduras	3 6	6		11	12	12	New York, New Orleans, and San Francisco.	Tegucigalpa, Puerto Cortez, Amapala, and Trujillo.
Honduras, British	3 6			11	12	12	New Orleans	Belize.
Mexico	2 0		4	11	12	12	All offices authorized to exchange mails.	
Nicaragua	3 6	6		11	12	12	New York, New Orleans, and San Francisco.	Bluefields, San Juan del Norte, and Corinto.
Salvador	3 6	6		11	12	12	New York and San Francisco.	San Salvador.
Venezuela	3 6	6		11	12	12	All offices authorized to exchange mails.	

UNITED STATES CONSULATES IN LATIN AMERICA.

Frequent application is made to the Bureau for the address of United States Consuls in the South and Central American Republics. Those desiring to correspond with any Consul can do so by addressing "The United States Consulate" at the point named. Letters thus addressed must be delivered to the proper person. It must be understood, however, that it is not the duty of Consuls to devote their time to private business, and that all such letters may properly be treated as personal, and any labor involved may be subject to charge therefor.

The following is a list of United States Consulates in the different Republics (consular agencies are given in *italics*):

ARGENTINE REPUBLIC—
Bahia Blanca.
Buenos Ayres.
Cordoba.
Rosario.

BRAZIL—
Aracaju.
Bahia.
Ceara.
Maceio.
Manaos.
Maranhão.
Natal.
Para.
Pernambuco.
Rio de Janeiro.
Rio Grande do Sul.
Santos.
Victoria.

CHILE—
Antofagasta.
Arica.
Caldera.
Coquimbo.
Coronel.
Iquique.
Punta Arenas.
Talcahuano.
Valdivia.
Valparaiso.

COLOMBIA—
Barranquilla.
Bogotá.
Bucaramanga.
Cali.
Cartagena.
Cucuta.
Honda.
Santa Marta.
Quibdo.

COSTA RICA—
Puerto Limon.
Punta Arenas.
San José.

CUBA—
Banes.
Baracoa.
Caibarien.
Cardenas.
Cienfuegos.
Habana.
Manzanillo.
Matanzas.
Nuevitas.
Sagua la Grande.
Santa Clara.
Santiago.

DOMINICAN REPUBLIC—
Azua.
Macoris.
Monte Christi.
Puerto Plata.

DOMINICAN REPUBLIC—Cont'd.
Samana.
Sanchez.
Santo Domingo.

ECUADOR—
Bahia de Caraquez.
Esmeraldas.
Guayaquil.
Manta.

GUATEMALA—
Champerico.
Guatemala.
Livingston.
Ocos.
San José de Guatemala.

HAITI—
Aux Cayes.
Cape Haitien,
Gonaives.
Jacmel.
Jeremie.
Miragoane.
Petit Goave.
Port au Prince.
Port de Paix.
St. Marc.

HONDURAS—
Amapala.
Bonacca.
Ceiba,
Puerto Cortes.
San Juancito.
San Pedro Sula.
Tegucigalpa.
Tela.
Trujillo.
Ruatan.
Utilla.

MEXICO—
Acapulco.
Aguascalientes.
Alamos.
Campeche.
Cananea.
Chihuahua.
Ciudad Juarez.
Ciudad Porfirio Diaz.
Coatzacoalcos.
Durango.
Ensenada.
Frontera.
Guadalajara.
Guanajuato.
Guaymas.
Hermosillo.
Jalapa.
Laguna de Terminos.
La Paz.
Manzanillo.
Matamoras.
Mazatlan.
Mexico.

MEXICO—Continued.
Monterey.
Nogales.
Nuevo Laredo.
Oaxaca.
Parral.
Progreso.
Puebla.
Saltillo.
San Luis Potosi.
Sierra Mojada.
Tampico.
Tlacotalpan.
Topolobampo.
Torreon.
Tuxpan, Vera Cruz.
Veracruz.
Victoria.
Zacatecas.

NICARAGUA—
Bluefields.
Cape Gracias á Dios.
Corinto.
Managua.
Matagalpa.
San Juan del Norte.
San Juan del Sur.

PANAMA—
Bocas del Toro.
Colon.
David.
Panama.
Santiago.

PARAGUAY—
Asunción.

PERU—
Callao.
Chimbote.
Eten.
Iquitos.
Mollendo.
Paita.
Salaverry.

SALVADOR—
Acajutla.
La Libertad.
La Unión.
San Salvador.

URUGUAY—
Montevideo.

VENEZUELA—
Barcelona.
Caracas.
Carupano.
Ciudad Bolivar.
Coro.
La Guayra.
Maracaibo.
Puerto Cabello.
Tovar.
Valera.

CONSULATES OF THE LATIN-AMERICAN REPUBLICS IN THE UNITED STATES.

ARGENTINE REPUBLIC.

Alabama	Mobile.
California	San Francisco.
District of Columbia	Washington.
Florida	Fernandina.
	Pensacola.
Georgia	Savannah.
Illinois	Chicago.
Louisiana	New Orleans.
Maine	Portland.
Maryland	Baltimore.
Massachusetts	Boston.
Mississippi	Gulf Port and Ship Island.
	Pascagoula.
Missouri	St. Louis.
New York	New York City.
Pennsylvania	Philadelphia.
Philippine Islands	Manila.
Virginia	Norfolk.

BOLIVIA.

California	San Diego.
	San Francisco.
Illinois	Chicago.
Maryland	Baltimore.
Missouri	Kansas City.
New York	New York City.
Pennsylvania	Philadelphia.

BRAZIL.

Alabama	Mobile.
California	San Francisco.
Florida	Fernandina.
	Pensacola.
Georgia	Brunswick.
	Savannah.
Louisiana	New Orleans.
Maine	Calais.
Maryland	Baltimore.
Massachusetts	Boston.
Mississippi	Gulfport.
	Pascagoula.
Missouri	St. Louis.
New York	New York City.
Pennsylvania	Philadelphia.
Porto Rico	San Juan.
Virginia	Norfolk.
	Richmond.

CHILE.

California	San Francisco.
Canal Zone	Panama.
Georgia	Savannah.
Hawaii	Honolulu.
Illinois	Chicago.
Maryland	Baltimore.
Massachusetts	Boston.
New York	New York City.
Oregon	Portland.
Pennsylvania	Philadelphia.
Philippine Islands	Manila.
Porto Rico	San Juan.
Washington	Port Townsend.
	Tacoma.

COLOMBIA.

Alabama	Mobile.
California	San Francisco.
Connecticut	New Haven.
Florida	Tampa.
Illinois	Chicago.
Louisiana	New Orleans.
Maryland	Baltimore.
Massachusetts	Boston.
Michigan	Detroit.
Missouri	St. Louis.
New York	New York City.
Pennsylvania	Philadelphia.
Porto Rico	San Juan.
Virginia	Norfolk.

COSTA RICA.

Alabama	Mobile.
California	San Francisco.
Canal Zone	Colon.
	Panama.
Colorado	Denver.
Illinois	Chicago.
Louisiana	New Orleans.
Maryland	Baltimore.
Massachusetts	Boston.
Missouri	St. Louis.
New York	New York City.
Oregon	Portland.
Pennsylvania	Philadelphia.
Porto Rico	San Juan.
Texas	Galveston.
Virginia	Norfolk.

CUBA.

Alabama	Mobile.
California	Los Angeles.
Florida	Fernandina.
	Jacksonville.
	Key West.
	Pensacola.
	Tampa.
Georgia	Brunswick.
	Savannah.
Illinois	Chicago.
Kentucky	Louisville.
Louisiana	New Orleans.
Maine	Portland.
Maryland	Baltimore.
Massachusetts	Boston.
Michigan	Detroit.
Mississippi	Gulfport.
Missouri	St. Louis.
New York	New York City.
Ohio	Cincinnati.
Pennsylvania	Philadelphia.
Porto Rico	Arecibo.
	Mayagüez.
	Ponce.
	San Juan.
Texas	Galveston.
Virginia	Newport News.
	Norfolk.

DOMINICAN REPUBLIC.

Illinois	Chicago.
Maryland	Baltimore.
Massachusetts	Boston.
New York	New York City.
North Carolina	Wilmington.
Pennsylvania	Philadelphia.
Porto Rico	Aguadilla.
	Arecibo.
	Humacao.
	Mayagüez.
	Ponce.
	San Juan.
	Vieques.

ECUADOR.

California	Los Angeles.
	San Francisco.
Illinois	Chicago.
Louisiana	New Orleans.
Massachusetts	Boston.
New York	New York City.
Ohio	Cincinnati.
Pennsylvania	Philadelphia.
Philippine Islands	Manila.
South Carolina	Charleston.
Virginia	Norfolk.

GUATEMALA.

Alabama	Mobile.
California	San Diego.
	San Francisco.
Florida	Pensacola.
Illinois	Chicago.

CONSULATES OF THE LATIN-AMERICAN REPUBLICS—Continued.

GUATEMALA—Continued.

Kansas	Kansas City.
Kentucky	Louisville.
Louisiana	New Orleans.
Maryland	Baltimore.
Massachusetts	Boston.
Missouri	St. Louis.
New York	New York City.
Pennsylvania	Philadelphia.
Porto Rico	San Juan.
Texas	Galveston.
Washington	Seattle.

HAITI.

Alabama	Mobile.
Georgia	Savannah.
Illinois	Chicago.
Maine	Bangor.
Massachusetts	Boston.
New York	New York City.
North Carolina	Wilmington.
Porto Rico	Mayagüez.
	San Juan.

HONDURAS.

Alabama	Mobile.
California	Los Angeles.
	San Diego.
	San Francisco.
Illinois	Chicago.
Kansas	Kansas City.
Kentucky	Louisville.
Louisiana	New Orleans.
Maryland	Baltimore.
Michigan	Detroit.
Missouri	St. Louis.
New York	New York City.
Ohio	Cincinnati.
Pennsylvania	Philadelphia.
Texas	Galveston.
Washington	Seattle.

MEXICO.

Alabama	Mobile.
Arizona	Bisbee.
	Clifton.
	Douglas.
	Naco.
	Nogales.
	Phoenix.
	Solomonsville.
	Tucson.
	Yuma.
California	Calexico.
	Los Angeles.
	San Diego.
	San Francisco.
Canal Zone	Ancon.
Colorado	Denver.
Florida	Pensacola.
Hawaii	Honolulu.
Illinois	Chicago.
Kentucky	Louisville.
Louisiana	New Orleans.
Maryland	Baltimore.
Massachusetts	Boston.
Mississippi	Pascagoula.
Missouri	Kansas City.
	St. Louis.
New York	New York City.
Ohio	Cincinnati.
Oregon	Portland.
Pennsylvania	Philadelphia.
Philippine Islands	Manila.
Porto Rico	Mayagüez.
	Ponce.
	San Juan.
Texas	Brownsville.
	Eagle Pass.
	El Paso.
	Galveston.
	Laredo.
	Port Arthur.
	Rio Grande City.
	Sabine Pass.
	San Antonio.
	Solomonsville.

MEXICO—Continued.

Virginia	Norfolk.
Washington	Tocoma.

NICARAGUA.

Alabama	Mobile.
California	Los Angeles.
	San Diego.
	San Francisco.
Illinois	Chicago.
Kansas	Kansas City.
Kentucky	Louisville.
Louisiana	New Orleans.
Maryland	Baltimore.
Massachusetts	Boston.
Michigan	Detroit.
Missouri	St. Louis.
New York	New York City.
Pennsylvania	Philadelphia.
Philippine Islands	Manila.
Porto Rico	Ponce.
	San Juan.
Texas	Galveston.
Virginia	Norfolk.
	Newport News.
Washington	Seattle.

PANAMA.

Alabama	Mobile.
California	San Francisco.
Georgia	Atlanta.
Hawaii	Hilo.
Illinois	Chicago.
Louisiana	New Orleans.
Maryland	Baltimore.
Massachusetts	Boston.
Missouri	St. Louis.
New York	New York City.
Pennsylvania	Philadelphia.
Porto Rico	San Juan.
Tennessee	Chattanooga.
Texas	Galveston.
	Port Arthur.
Washington	Puget Sound.

PARAGUAY.

Alabama	Mobile.
Delaware	Wilmington.
District of Columbia	Washington.
Georgia	Savannah.
Illinois	Chicago.
Indiana	Indianapolis.
Maryland	Baltimore.
Michigan	Detroit.
Missouri	Kansas City.
	St. Louis.
New Jersey	Newark.
	Trenton.
New York	Buffalo.
	New York City.
	Rochester.
Ohio	Cincinnati.
Pennsylvania	Philadelphia.
Porto Rico	San Juan.
Virginia	Norfolk.
	Richmond.

PERU.

California	Los Angeles.
	San Diego.
	San Francisco.
Canal Zone	Panama.
Georgia	Savannah.
Hawaii	Honolulu.
Illinois	Chicago.
Louisiana	New Orleans.
Maryland	Baltimore.
Massachusetts	Boston.
New York	New York City.
Oregon	Portland.
Pennsylvania	Philadelphia.
Porto Rico	San Juan.
South Carolina	Charleston.
Washington	Port Townsend.

OF THE LATIN-AMERICAN REPUBLICS—Continued.

SALVADOR.		URUGUAY—Continued.	
ia	San Diego.	Mississippi	Pascagoula.
	San Francisco.	Missouri	St. Louis.
.....	New Orleans.	New York	New York City.
setts	Boston.	Ohio...................	Cincinnati.
....	St. Louis.	Pennsylvania	Philadelphia.
....	New York City.	Philippine Islands	Manila.
		South Carolina	Charleston.
!.		Texas	Galveston.
			Port Arthur and
....	Mobile.		Sabine Pass.
....	San Francisco.	Virginia	Norfolk.
....	Apalachicola.		Richmond.
	Fernandina.	VENEZUELA.	
	Jacksonville.		
	Pensacola.	California	San Francisco.
	St. Augustine.	Illinois	Chicago.
....	Brunswick.	Louisiana	New Orleans.
	Savannah.	New York	New York City.
....	Chicago.	Pennsylvania	Philadelphia.
.a	New Orleans.	Philippine Islands...........	Cebu.
....	Bangor.	Porto Rico...................	Arecibo.
	Calais.		Mayaguez.
	Portland.		Ponce.
....	Baltimore.		San Juan.
....	Boston.		

WEIGHTS AND MEASURES.

The following table gives the chief weights and measures in commercial use in Mexico and the Republics of Central and South America, and their equivalents in the United States:

Denomination.	Where used.	United States equivalents.
Are	Metric	0.02471 acre.
Arobe	Paraguay	25 pounds.
Arroba (dry)	Argentine Republic	25.3171 pounds.
Do	Brazil	32.38 pounds.
Do	Cuba	25.3664 pounds.
Do	Venezuela	25.4024 pounds.
Arroba (liquid)	Cuba and Venezuela	4.263 gallons.
Barril	Argentine Republic and Mexico	20.0787 gallons.
Carga	Mexico and Salvador	300 pounds.
Centaro	Central America	4.2631 gallons.
Cuadra	Argentine Republic	4.2 acres.
Do	Paraguay	78.9 yards.
Do	Paraguay (square)	8.077 square feet.
Do	Uruguay	2 acres (nearly).
Cubic meter	Metric	35.3 cubic feet.
Fanega (dry)	Central America	1.5745 bushels.
Do	Chile	2.575 bushels.
Do	Cuba	1.599 bushels.
Do	Mexico	1.54728 bushels.
Do	Uruguay (double)	7.776 bushels.
Do	Uruguay (single)	3.888 bushels.
Do	Venezuela	1.599 bushels.
Frasco	Argentine Republic	2.5096 quarts.
Do	Mexico	2.5 quarts.
Gram	Metric	15.432 grains.
Hectare	do	2.471 acres.
Hectoliter (dry)	do	2.838 bushels.
Hectoliter (liquid)	do	26.417 gallons.
Kilogram (kilo)	do	2.2046 pounds.
Kilometer	do	0.621376 mile.
League (land)	Paraguay	4.633 acres.
Libra	Argentine Republic	1.0127 pounds.
Do	Central America	1.043 pounds.
Do	Chile	1.014 pounds.
Do	Cuba	1.0161 pounds.
Do	Mexico	1.01465 pounds.
Do	Peru	1.0143 pounds.
Do	Uruguay	1.0143 pounds.
Do	Venezuela	1.0161 pounds.
Liter	Metric	1.0567 quarts.
Livre	Guiana	1.0791 pounds.
Manzana	Costa Rica	1.73 acres.
Marc	Bolivia	0.507 pound.
Meter	Metric	39.37 inches.
Pie	Argentine Republic	0.9478 foot.
Quintal	do	101.42 pounds.
Do	Brazil	130.06 pounds.
Do	Chile, Mexico, and Peru	101.61 pounds.
Do	Paraguay	100 pounds.
Quintal (metric)	Metric	220.46 pounds.
Suerte	Uruguay	2,700 cuadras. (*See* Cuadra.)
Vara	Argentine Republic	34.1208 inches.
Do	Central America	33.874 inches.
Do	Chile and Peru	33.367 inches.
Do	Cuba	33.384 inches.
Do	Mexico	33 inches.
Do	Paraguay	34 inches.
Do	Venezuela	33.384 inches.

METRIC WEIGHTS AND MEASURES.

METRIC WEIGHTS.

Milligram (1/1000 gram) equals 0.0154 grain.
Centigram (1/100 gram) equals 0.1543 grain.
Decigram (1/10 gram) equals 1.5432 grains.
Gram equals 15.432 grains.
Decagram (10 grams) equals 0.3527 ounce.
Hectogram (100 grams) equals 3.5274 ounces.
Kilogram (1,000 grams) equals 2.2046 pounds.
Myriagram (10,000 grams) equals 22.046 pounds.
Quintal (100,000 grams) equals 220.46 pounds.
Millier or tonneau—ton (1,000,000 grams) equals 2,204.6 pounds.

METRIC DRY MEASURE.

Milliliter (1/1000 liter) equals 0.061 cubic inch.
Centiliter (1/100 liter) equals 0.6102 cubic inch.
Deciliter (1/10 liter) equals 6.1022 cubic inches.
Liter equals 0.908 quart.
Decaliter (10 liters) equals 9.08 quarts.
Hectoliter (100 liters) equals 2.838 bushels.
Kiloliter (1,000 liters) equals 1.308 cubic yards.

METRIC LIQUID MEASURE.

Milliliter (1/1000 liter) equals 0.27 fluid dram.
Centiliter (1/100 liter) equals 0.338 fluid ounce.
Deciliter (1/10 liter) equals 0.845 gill.
Liter equals 1.0567 quarts.
Decaliter (10 liters) equals 2.6417 gallons.
Hectoliter (100 liters) equals 26.417 gallons.
Kiloliter (1,000 liters) equals 264.17 gallons.

METRIC MEASURES OF LENGTH.

Millimeter (1/1000 meter) equals 0.0394 inch.
Centimeter (1/100 meter) equals 0.3937 inch.
Decimeter (1/10 meter) equals 3.937 inches.
Meter equals 39.37 inches.
Decameter (10 meters) equals 393.7 inches.
Hectometer (100 meters) equals 328 feet 1 inch.
Kilometer (1,000 meters) equals 0.62137 mile (3,280 feet 10 inches).
Myriameter (10,000 meters) equals 6.2137 miles.

METRIC SURFACE MEASURE.

Centare (1 square meter) equals 1,550 square inches.
Are (100 square meters) equals 119.6 square yards.
Hectare (10,000 square meters) equals 2.471 acres.

PRICE LIST OF PUBLICATIONS.

Prices.

Bulletin of the Bureau, published monthly since October, 1893, in English,
Spanish, Portuguese, and French. Average 225 pages, 2 volumes a year.
  Yearly subscription (in countries of the International Union of American
    Republics and in Canada)... $2.00
  Yearly subscription (other countries).................................... 2.50
  Single copies.. .25
  Orders for the Bulletin should be addressed to the Chief Clerk of the
  Bureau.
American Constitutions. A compilation of the political constitutions of the
  independent States of America, in the original text, with English and Span-
  ish translations. Washington, 1906. 3 vols., 8°.
    Paper...each.. 1.00
    Bound in cloth...do.... 1.50
    Bound in sheep..do.... 2.00

> Vol. I, now ready, contains the constitutions of the Federal Republics of the United
> States of America, of Mexico, of the Argentine Republic, of Brazil, and of Venezuela, and
> of the Republics of Central America, Guatemala, Honduras, El Salvador, Nicaragua, Costa
> Rica, and Panama. Vols. II and III will be ready shortly.
> Vol. II will contain the constitutions of the Dominican Republic, Haiti, Cuba, Uruguay,
> Chile, Peru, Ecuador, Colombia, Paraguay, and Bolivia.
> Vol. III will contain Articles of Confederation of the United States, First Constitution
> of Venezuela 1811, Fundamental Law of Republic of Colombia 1819, Ditto of 1821, Consti-
> tution of Colombia of 1821, Constitution of Central American Confederation of 1824, Con-
> stitution of the Grenadian Confederation of 1858, Constitution of the United States of
> Colombia of 1863, Pro Constitution of Guatemala of 1876, Convention between United
> States and Republic of Panama for construction of ship canal to connect the waters of the
> Atlantic and the Pacific Oceans.

Code of Commercial Nomenclature, 1897. (Spanish, English, and Portuguese.)
  645 pages, 4°, cloth.. 2.50
Code of Commercial Nomenclature, 1897. (Portuguese, Spanish, and English.)
  640 pages, 4°, cloth.. 2.50

> NOTE.—Designates in alphabetical order, in equivalent terms in the three languages,
> the commodities of American nations on which import duties are levied. The English,
> Spanish, and Portuguese edition is entirely exhausted.

Leyes y reglamentos sobre privilegios de invención y marcas de fábrica en los
  países hispano-americanos, el Brasil y la República de Haití. Revisado hasta
  agosto de 1904. Washington, 1904. 415 pages, 8°............................ 1.00
Patent and trade-mark laws of the Spanish American Republics, Brazil, and
  the Republic of Haiti. Revised to Aug., 1904, Washington, 1904.......... 1.00
    The above two works bound together in sheep.......................... 3.00

SPECIAL BULLETINS.

Money, Weights, and Measures of the American Republics, 1891. 12 pages, 8°. .05
Report on Coffee, with special reference to the Costa Rican product, etc.
  Washington, 1901. 15 pages, 8°.. .10
El café. Su historia, cultivo, beneficio, variedades, producción, exportación,
  importación, consumo, etc. Datos extensos presentados al Congreso relativo
  al café que se reunirá en Nueva York el 1° de octubre de 1902. 167 páginas,
  8°.. .50
Coffee. Extensive information and statistics. (English edition of the above.)
  108 pages, 8°.. .50
Intercontinental Railway Reports. Report of the Intercontinental Railway
  Commission. Washington, 1898. 7 vols. 4°, three of maps................ 25.00

PUBLICATIONS.

HANDBOOKS (GENERAL DESCRIPTION AND STATISTICS).

PRICE.

Argentine Republic. A geographical sketch, with special reference to economic conditions, actual development, and prospects of future growth. Washington, 1903. 28 illustrations, 3 maps, 366 pages, 8° $1.00

Bolivia. Geographical sketch, natural resources, laws, economic conditions, actual development, prospects of future growth. Washington, 1904. Illustrated, 214 pages, 8° 1.00

Brazil. Geographical sketch, with special reference to economic conditions and prospects of future development. 1901. 233 pages, 8° .... .75

Cuba. A short sketch of physical and economic conditions, government, laws, industries, finances, customs tariff, etc., prepared by Señor Gonzalo de Quesada, minister from Cuba, with bibliography and cartography of 198 pages. Washington, November, 1905. Map and 42 illustrations, 541 pages, 8°. 1.00

Guatemala. 1897. (2d edition revised.) Illustrated, 119 pages, 8° .... .25

Honduras. Geographical sketch, natural resources, laws, economic conditions, actual development, prospects of future growth. Washington, 1904. Illustrated, economic and telegraphic maps, 252 pages, 8° ....: 1.00

Mexico. Geographical sketch, natural resources, laws, economic conditions, actual development, prospects of future growth. Washington, 1904. Illustrated, 454 pages, 8° 1.00

Paraguay. Second edition, revised and enlarged, with a chapter on the native races. 1902. ' Illustrated, map, 187 pages, 8°. Bibliography, page 141 .... .75

Venezuela. Geographical sketch, natural resources, laws, economic conditions, actual development, prospects of future growth. Washington, 1904. Illustrated, railway map, 808 pages, 8° 1.00

BIBLIOGRAPHICAL BULLETINS.

Chile. A list of books, magazine articles, and maps relating to Chile. Washington, 1903. 110 pages, 8° 1.00

Paraguay. A list of books, magazine articles and maps relating to Paraguay. 53 pages, 8°. Washington, 1904 .... 1.00

MAPS.

Guatemala. From official and other sources. 1902. Scale of 12.5 miles to 1 inch (1:792,000). In 2 sheets, each sheet 71 x 76 cm. No. 1. General features. No. 2. Agricultural 1.00

Mexico. From official Mexican and other sources. 1900. Scale of 50 miles to 1 inch. In 2 sheets, each sheet 108 x 80 cm. No. 1. General map. No. 2. Agricultural areas 1.00

Nicaragua. From official and other sources. 1904. Scale of 12.5 miles to 1 inch (1:792,000). In 2 sheets, each sheet 80 x 80 cm. No. 1. General map. No. 2. Agricultural 1.00

Bolivia. Mapa de la república de Bolivia, mandado organizar y publicar por el Presidente Constitucional General José Manuel Pando. Scale 1:2,000,000. La Paz, 1901. (Reprint International Bureau of the American Republics, 1904) 1.00

Costa Rica. From official and other sources. 1903. Scale of 12.5 miles to 1 inch (1:792,000) .... .50

Brazil. From official and other sources. 1905. Scale of 75 miles to 1 inch (1:4,752,000). In one sheet 96 x 93 cm 1.00

LAW MANUALS.

Leyes Comerciales de América Latina: Código de Comercio de España comparado con los Códigos y Leyes Comerciales de Pan América. Land and Immigration Laws of American Republics. (To replace edition of 1898.)

HANDBOOKS.

Chile.
Dominican Republic.

MAPS.

Maps are in course of preparation of the Republics of Honduras and Salvador. Payment is required to be made in cash, money orders, or by bank drafts on banks in New York City or Washington, D. C., payable to the order of the INTERNATIONAL BUREAU OF THE AMERICAN REPUBLICS. Individual checks on banks outside of New York or Washington, or postage stamps, can not be accepted.

FOR FREE DISTRIBUTION.

The Bureau has for distribution a limited supply of the following, which will be sent, free, upon written application:

The case of the United States of Venezuela before the Tribunal of Arbitration to convene at Paris under the provisions of the Treaty between the United States of Venezuela and Her Britannic Majesty, signed at Washington, February 2, 1897, in 10 vols., of which 2 are maps. Sent only to libraries and educational institutions.

Message from the President of the United States, transmitting a communication from the Secretary of State submitting the report, with accompanying papers, of the delegates of the United States to the Second International Conference of American States, held at the City of Mexico from October 22, 1901, to January 22, 1902. Washington, 1902. 243 pages. 8°. (57th Congress, 1st session, Senate Doc. No. 330.)

Message from the President of the United States, transmitting a report from the Secretary of State, with accompanying papers, relative to the proceedings of the International Congress for the study of the production and consumption of coffee, etc. Washington, 1903. 312 pages. 8° (paper). (57th Congress, 2d session, Senate Doc. No. 35.)

Message from the President of the United States, transmitting a report by the Secretary of State, with accompanying papers, relative to the proceedings of the First Customs Congress of the American Republics, held at New York in January, 1903. Washington, 1903. 195 pages. 8° (paper). (57th Congress, 2d session, Senate Doc. No. 180.)

Brazil at St. Louis Exposition. St. Louis, 1904. 160 pages. 8° (paper).

Chile—A short description of the Republic according to official data. Leipzig, 1901. 106 pages. Map and 37 illustrations. 8° (cloth).

Chile—Breve descripción de la República escrita según datos oficiales. Leipzig, 1901. 106 páginas. Mapa y 36 grabados. 8° (en tela).

Chile at Pan-American Exposition. Buffalo, 1901. 252 pages (paper).

Costa Rica—Some Facts and Figures. Compiled and arranged by J. B. Calvo. 1894. 56 pages. 8° (paper).

Guatemala—The Country of the future. By Charles M. Pepper. Washington, 1906. 80 pages. 8° (paper).

PUBLICATIONS.

Revised to September 1, 1893.
Revised to March 1, 1894.
Revised to September 1, 1893.

e Bureau of the American Republics, in 6 vols., of which there are
and IV remaining. Vol. II contains Haiti and Santo Domingo above,
public, 1892, revised to February 1, 1894, and Paraguay, 1892, revised
1894. Vol. IV contains Ecuador above, Peru, 1892, revised to
and Bolivia, 1892, revised to July 1, 1893.

of the Second International Sanitary Convention of the American
Washington, 1906.

Senate documents, listed above, containing reports of the various International American
meas. may also be obtained through members of the United States Senate and House of Repre-

VALUE OF LATIN-AMERICAN COINS. -

The following table shows the value, in United States gold, of coins representing the monetary units of the Central and South American Republics and Mexico, estimated quarterly by the Director of the United States Mint, in pursuance of act of Congress:

ESTIMATE APRIL 1, 1907.

Countries.	Standard.	Unit.	Value in U. 3. gold or silver.	Coins.
ARGENTINE REPUBLIC.	Gold	Peso	$0. 965	Gold—Argentine ($4.824) and ½ Argentine. Silver—Peso and divisions.
BOLIVIA	Silver ...	Boliviano	.510	Silver—Boliviano and divisions.
BRAZIL	Gold	Milreis ..	.546	Gold—5, 10, and 20 milreis. Silver—½, 1, and 2 milreis.
CENTRAL AMERICAN STATES— Costa Rica......	Gold	Colon ...	.465	Gold—2, 5, 10, and 20 colons ($9.307). Silver—5, 10, 25, and 50 centimos.
Guatemala...... Honduras ...... Nicaragua ...... Salvador	Silver ...	Peso	.500	Silver—Peso and divisions.
CHILE	Gold	Peso	.365	Gold—Escudo ($1.825), doubloon ($3.650), and condor ($7.300). Silver—Peso and divisions.
COLOMBIA..........	Gold	Dollar...	1. 000	Gold—Condor ($9.647) and double condor. Silver—Peso.
ECUADOR	Gold	Sucre....	.487	Gold—10 sucres ($4.8665). Silver—Sucre and divisions.
HAITI	Gold	Gourde..	.965	Gold—1, 2, 5, and 10 gourdes. Silver—Gourde and divisions.
MEXICO............	Gold	Peso ᵃ ...	.498	Gold—5 and 10 pesos. Silver—Dollar ᵇ (or peso) and divisions.
PANAMA	Gold	Balboa ..	1. 000	Gold—1, 2½, 5, 10, and 20 balboas. Silver—Peso and divisions.
PERU	Gold	Libra ...	4. 866½	Gold—½ and 1 libra. Silver—Sol and divisions.
URUGUAY	Gold	Peso	1. 034	Gold—Peso. Silver—Peso and divisions.
VENEZUELA	Gold	Bolivar..	.193	Gold—5, 10, 20, 50, and 100 bolivars. Silver—5 bolivars.

ᵃ 75 centigrams fine gold. ᵇ Value in Mexico, 0.498.

O

International Union of American Republics

Monthly Bulletin

OF THE

International Bureau

OF THE

American Republics

VOL. 24, NO. 6

JUNE, 1907

WHOLE NO. 165

WASHINGTON, D. C., U. S. A.

GOVERNMENT PRINTING OFFICE

1907

Secretary.   Chief Clerk.

II

GENERAL TABLE OF CONTENTS.

INDEX.

TABLE OF CONTENTS.

ÍNDICE.

INDICE

TABLE DES MATIÈRES.

SEÑOR DON LUÍS F. COREA, MINISTER OF NICARAGUA TO THE UNITED
STATES.

MONTHLY BULLETIN

OF THE

INTERNATIONAL BUREAU OF THE AMERICAN REPUBLICS,

International Union of American Republics.

VOL. XXIV.	JUNE, 1907.	No. 6.

There is such a growing demand from all parts of the world for information regarding the work, scope, and character of the International Bureau of American Republics that it has been thought best to include in this issue of the BULLETIN a general sketch of the Bureau that gives sufficient data to answer the majority of inquiries. Even those who are more or less familiar not only with what the International Bureau has accomplished, but with what it has before it, may find in this résumé some facts in regard to the Bureau's importance, opportunity, and responsibility which they have not before appreciated.

LATIN AMERICA AT THE LAKE MOHONK CONFERENCE.

Perhaps the most striking feature of the Lake Mohonk Conference on International Arbitration, which met May 22–24, 1907, was the prominence given to Latin America. In none of the twelve annual preceding meetings has there been manifested such an interest in what Central and South American countries have done for the promotion of international arbitration. The addresses of Ambassador CREEL, of Mexico, and of Minister CALDERÓN, of Bolivia, were among the most notable, important, and significant that were delivered at the conference. They attracted wide attention throughout the United States, and were generally commented upon by the leading newspapers. Brief addresses by Hon. FRANCIS B. LOOMIS, former United States Minister to Venezuela and former Assistant Secretary of State of the United States, and by the Director of the International Bureau of the American Republics, took up various phases of Latin-American efforts at peace and progress. The BULLETIN prints in this issue extracts from some of the speeches delivered at Lake Mohonk.

1301

THE NEW MEMBER OF THE GOVERNING BOARD.

The International Bureau of the American Republics welcomes to membership on its Governing Board Señor Don José Augustin Arango, the new Minister of Panama to the United States, who was received by President Roosevelt on May 13. Mr. Arango is well known to the Director of the Bureau, who enjoyed his friendship and profited by is advice during the Director's experience as United States M r to Panama. The new Minister is one of the foremost men c he young Republic, and will prove a worthy representative of its itions at Washington. The Director takes advantage of this op mity, moreover, to express his regret at the departure of Ministe , as alw taken a deep interest in the work a Bureau. e retiring Minister, however, returns n greater responsibilities than he had in Washi l act as C ief Executive of Panama during th ce of Presia nt Amador.

EXC HONORS FOR MBASSADOR CREEL.

It is to be l the exceptional honor which has been conferred upon the Ambassador of Mexico, Señor Don Enrique C. Creel, by the people of the Province of Chihuahua, who have just elected him governor, will not take him away from Washington. Not only has Ambassador Creel manifested practical interest in the enlarged scope and work of the Bureau and cooperated to make its efforts of advantage alike to Mexico and the United States, but he has done much in a very short time to make Mexico better known and more respected than ever before throughout the United States. It is indeed a rare honor for a man to hold the dual position of Ambassador from his country and of governor of one of its principal provinces. There could be no better evidence of the esteem in which he is held in his own country, not only by his Government at large, but also by the people of a special section remote from the capital.

BUENOS AIRES' CENTENNIAL EXPOSITION IN 1910.

In this era of expositions, which have become such a feature of the national life of the United States, it is most interesting to note that the Government of the Argentine Republic is preparing to hold, at Buenos Aires in 1910, the centennial year of Argentine independence, a great exhibition of arts, industries, agriculture, and cattle. The Argentine Congress has just passed a law providing for the appointment of a national commission which shall formulate plans for the exposition and the awakening of general interest not only in the Argentine Republic but throughout the world in the exposition. As the announcement has just been made there has not been time for much attention to be given this project in the United States or in Europe, but it is to be hoped that if foreign nations are invited to participate, the United States will not fail to make a liberal appropriation for a comprehensive exhibit. The Argentine Republic is growing so rapidly and is becoming so important a factor in the world's trade that the manufacturers and exporters of the United States should not fail to improve this opportunity to exploit their products. If the average American, who might otherwise not be interested in the exhibition at Buenos Aires, will remember that that city has now a population of over 1,000,000 and that the foreign commerce of the Republic amounted last year to $563,000,000, or an average of nearly $100 per head of population, he will be convinced that the opportunity for the United States to strengthen its material position there should not be neglected. It is needless to prophesy that the exhibition will be a success. The Argentine Republic is so progressive and the people of Buenos Aires are so energetic that they are sure to make it one of the most ambitious undertakings of its kind that the world has known. Incidentally, it may be added that 1910 would be a good year for Americans, who wish to see South America, to plan a visit to that part of the world. In this connection it will be interesting to read the published extracts from the message of the President of the Argentine Republic, delivered May 8, 1907, on the occasion of the convening of the Forty-sixth National Assembly. He points out many things which are worthy of consideration by all those who are interested in Latin-American affairs as demonstrated by Argentine development.

MINING REGULATIONS IN BOLIVIA.

The International Bureau of the American Republics is constantly receiving inquiries in regard to mining legislation and regulations in the different Latin-American countries. The BULLETIN in this issue gives a new decree, issued by the Bolivian Government on April 20, 1907, relating to mining concessions and applications, the survey and settling of land, oppositions, approvals, registered titles, and jurisdiction in full. It is the purpose of the BULLETIN to publish, from time to time, all new mining regulations or changes in old laws which are enacted in the different American Republics, so that the growing mining interests of the world may be familiar with the conditions in each country.

PROGRESS AND PROSPERITY OF BRAZIL.

The message of President AFFONSO PENNA, of Brazil, which was delivered at the opening session of the National Congress May 3, 1907, should be carefully read by all persons who are watching the onward movement of the largest Latin-American country. The extracts from it which appear in this BULLETIN show that the country is moving rapidly forward along all lines of development and has before it a remarkable future. The President of Brazil declares that a careful examination of public affairs confirms the belief which he expressed in a former message that the country is marching steadfastly toward a great destiny, and that this opinion is shared by prominent foreigners who'have visited the country and examined its resources and have watched its progress for many years. He says that the wonderful progress that has been made in Rio Janeiro astonished all who have visited it. Trade statistics prove that production has increased, while the statistics of the Treasury—which reflect the economic conditions—are satisfactory. He makes special reference to the International Bureau of the American Republics; to the visit of Secretary Root to South America; to the participation of Brazil at The Hague Conference; to the negotiation of a boundary treaty with Colombia, and to the progress being made in the settlement of questions with Ecuador, Peru, Uruguay, and Bolivia. Great emphasis is laid upon the importance of developing the railways of the country, and he advises Government aid and cooperation to carry out different enterprises. Statistics of foreign trade of Brazil for 1906 show that the exports were worth approximately $265,000,000 and the imports $165,000,000, or a total foreign trade of $430,000,000, an increase of between $60,000,000 and $70,000,000 over 1905.

FINANCIAL STATUS OF CHILE.

The BULLETIN publishes in this issue extracts from a financial publication of Santiago containing a statement sent to the Department of the Interior of Chile by its Bureau of Statistics, which shows a very favorable condition of affairs in that progressive Republic. For instance, the total valuation of property subject to taxation in 1904 was $1,512,591,127, an increase of $112,507,766 over the valuation of 1897. The bank deposits, according to latest reports, were $314,240,433, or an increase of $193,078,147, or 159 per cent, over the deposits of December 31, 1901. Stock companies were incorporated in 1905, to the amount of $25,000,000, or an increase of 800 per cent over 1901. The number of industrial establishments in 1905 was 10,152, against 7,315 in 1901, while there were 35,018 commercial establishments in 1905 against 32,944 in 1901.

MESSAGE OF PRESIDENT REYES, OF COLOMBIA.

Colombia is now forging so rapidly to the front that the reprint of portions of the message of President REYES, delivered April 1, 1907, before the National Assembly of that country, will be read with interest. The nearness of Colombia to the United States, its location on both the waters of the Atlantic and the Pacific, its remarkable variety of resources, and its good fortune in having at its head a man of such statesmanlike qualities as President REYES, are proving to the world that it is a field for great material progress.

OTHER FEATURES OF PARTICULAR INTEREST.

There is not space in the introductory portion of the BULLETIN to comment on all the subjects covered of particular interest in each of the countries, but attention is invited to the message of the President of Costa Rica, delivered on May 1, 1907, to the Costa Rican Congress; the mining report from the Province of Santiago in Cuba; provisions regarding colonization and irrigation in the Dominican Republic; the reception of United States Minister Fox by President ALFARO, of Ecuador; the trade of Guatemala with New York in 1906; commercial, mining, and general conditions in Mexico; organization of a Panama Bureau of Statistics; improved port facilities of Paraguay; new land and irrigation laws in Peru; general commerce of the United States with Latin America; foreign trade of Venezuela, and a paper on the ratio of trade values between Latin America and the United States.

SKETCH OF THE INTERNATIONAL BUREAU OF THE AMERICAN REPUBLICS.

The International Bureau of the American Republics has its headquarters in Washington, D. C. It is maintained by the joint action and contributions of all the Republics of the Western Hemisphere, for the purpose not only of promoting commerce and trade, but of developing among them better acquaintance, closer relations, and more intimate intercourse along material, educational, intellectual, and social lines.

It is an organization which has no counterpart in the world. It is not a bureau subordinate to any one Department of the United States Government, as many people suppose, but it is the independent office of the Governments of Latin America as much as of the United States. Its control is in the hands of a Governing Board, made up of all the diplomatic representatives in Washington of the American

Republics and presided over by the Secretary of State of the United States. This Board, in turn, chooses the Director, who is the chief administrative officer and responsible to the Board for the management of the Bureau. The Director is an officer of twenty-one Republics, but, as the headquarters of the Bureau are in Washington, he is nominated, as a matter of courtesy and precedent, by the Secretary of State of the United States and then voted upon by the Ambassadors and Ministers of the other countries.

The funds for its maintenance are provided by appropriations of the American Republics made in proportion to their population, so that the smallest of the nations in area have as much interest in its support as the larger countries, like the United States. The twenty-one Republics represented on the Governing Board are, in order of population, United States, Brazil, Mexico, Argentin Republic, Chile, Peru, Colombia, Venezuela, Bolivia, Cuba, Haiti, Guatemala, Ecuador, Salvador, Uruguay, Paraguay, Dominican Republic, Honduras, Nicaragua, Costa Rica, and Panama.

THE BUREAU FIRST ESTABLISHED IN 1890.

The Bureau was first established in 1890 by the action of the First International Conference of American Republics, which assembled at that time in Washington and was presided over by JAMES G. BLAINE. The motive which prompted its establishment was the desire of the delegates to dispel the ignorance which they discovered existed in the United States about her sister Republics and, in turn, among the latter concerning the United States. It was first described as a "Bureau of Information," and it was the intention of its founders that it should acquaint manufacturers, exporters, importers, merchants, and all classes of people seeking reliable data for the upbuilding of trade, with the kind of information that would bring about a new era in the material relations of the American Republics.

Its first Director was the distinguished newspaper correspondent, WILLIAM E. CURTIS. In a short time he gave the Bureau a prominence that caused it to be recognized among all the countries as a useful and practical institution. Succeeding him until the Second Pan-American Conference, held in Mexico in 1901, were, in the order of their terms, CLINTON FURBISH, JOSEPH P. SMITH, FREDERIC EMORY, and W. W. ROCKHILL, now United States Minister to China. At the Mexican Conference the plan and scope of the Bureau was enlarged so that it should become the agency for the carrying out of the resolutions of this international gathering.

When Mr. ROCKHILL went to China, in 1905, he was succeeded by WILLIAMS C. FOX, now United States Minister to Ecuador. Under the various administrations of these different Directors the Bureau gradually grew in influence and utility, but there was lacking the

direct interest and hearty support of all the Governments concerned
to make it as powerful and useful an institution as desired for the
good of the nations supporting it. Some new force was required to
give it added influence, popularity, and practical value.

SECRETARY ROOT'S VISIT TO SOUTH AMERICA.

When ELIHU ROOT became Secretary of State he immediately
recognized that something should be done on new and broader lines
to bring about closer diplomatic, commercial, and social relations
between the United States and her sister American Republics. It
was, therefore, decided by the Administration that Mr. ROOT should
make a tour of South America and that at the Third Pan-American
Conference, held in Rio de Janeiro in the summer of 1906, steps
should be taken to reorganize the International Bureau and enlarge
its scope and usefulness. In the discussions that took place in
Washington at the sessions of the Governing Board, prior to the
Rio Conference, the Latin-American representatives cordially recipro-
cated the interest of the Secretary of State in Latin America and in
the plans for the Bureau, with the result that, when the Conference
assembled, it unanimously passed resolutions that will make the
Bureau a powerful and practical institution for the building up of
international American trade, for providing avenues of approach to
each other on political, educational, and intellectual lines, and for
developing more general acquaintanceship and closer intercourse.

THE ELECTION OF DIRECTOR BARRETT.

In December, 1906, JOHN BARRETT, then United States Minister
to Colombia, and prior to that United States Minister, respectively, to
Siam, the Argentine Republic, and Panama, was unanimously chosen
by the Governing Board as Director to succeed WILLIAMS C. FOX, who
was appointed United States Minister to Ecuador. To Mr. BAR-
RETT's hands was intrusted the carrying out of the new programme
of the Rio Conference for the reorganization and enlargement of the
Bureau. Mr. BARRETT was also Delegate of the United States to
the Second Pan-American Conference in Mexico, 1901, where he was
a member of the subcommittee having in charge the resolutions pertaining to the Bureau and passed at that Conference.

SPECIAL RESOLUTIONS REGARDING THE BUREAU.

The following quotation from the resolutions of the Third Conference gives some idea of the scope of its work:
"The Third International American Conference resolves:
"ARTICLE 1. The Third International Pan-American Conference
resolves to continue the International Union of the American ¯
lics created by the First Conference and confirmed by the Se

"The purposes of the International Bureau of the American Republics, which will represent said Union, are the following:

"1. To compile and distribute commercial information and prepare commercial reports.'

"2. To compile and classify information respecting the treaties and conventions between the American Republics and between the latter and non-American States.

"3. To supply information on educational matters.

"4. To prepare reports on questions assigned to it by resolutions of the International American Conferences.

"5. To assist in obtaining the ratification of the resolutions and conventions adopted by the Conferences.

"6. To carry into effect all resolutions the execution of which may have been assigned or may hereafter be assigned to it by the International American Conferences.

"7. To act as a permanent committee of the International American Conferences, recommending topics to be included in the programme of the next Conference; these plans must be communicated to the various Governments forming the Union at least six months before the date of the meeting of the next Conference.

"8. To submit within the same period a report to the various Governments on the work of the Bureau during the term covered since the meeting of the last Conference, and also special reports on any matter which may have been referred to it for report."

ADDITIONAL RESOLUTIONS COVERING NEW WORK.

Further resolutions, which · placed new responsibilities on the Bureau, provided that steps should be taken for housing the institution "in such a way as shall permit it to properly fulfill the important functions assigned to it by this Conference;" that a committee should be appointed in each Republic to assist the Bureau in carrying out its work; that there should be established, as subordinate to it, a special section of commercial statistics; that the Bureau should elaborate the project for providing better steamship facilities between the principal ports of the American Republics for the purpose of facilitating trade, travel, commerce, and general communication; that it should investigate the question of the Inter-Continental Railway and confer with the different Governments with a view to determining as soon as possible what concessions of land, subventions, interest guaranties, exemptions of duty on material for the construction and rolling stock, and any other concessions they may deem it advisable to grant in connection therewith; that it should make a study of the monetary systems of the American Governments for the purpose of submitting to the next Conference a report on the systems in force in each of the Governments, its history, fluctuations and type of exchange which have taken place within the last twenty years, including the preparation of tables showing the influence of said fluctuations on commerce and industrial development; that it should study the laws that regulate public concessions in the various Republics of America, with a view to obtaining information that might be useful to it; and that, finally, it should prepare a programme for the Fourth International Conference, which is to be held within the next five years.

THE COLUMBUS MEMORIAL LIBRARY.

One of the important features of the International Bureau, which is not yet fully appreciated, is the Columbus Memorial Library. It now contains about 13,000 volumes, covering a great variety of commercial, historical, and general information concerning the different American Republics. It is intended to enlarge this Library so that it will be the most complete collection of Americana in the world. The resolution of the Second Pan-American Conference, approved by the Third, recommends that each Government shall provide this Library with copies of all its official publications. Such a collection alone would make it invaluable for consultation and reference. To-day, it is being used by statesmen, writers, students, travelers, business men, and others who wish to obtain reliable information about any American country.

THE GIFT OF MR. CARNEGIE FOR A NEW BUILDING.

On New Year's Day, 1907, Hon. ELIHU ROOT, Secretary of State of·the United States, and Chairman *ex-officio* of the Governing Board of the Bureau, announced a generous gift by Mr. ANDREW CARNEGIE, of $750,000, to be used in the construction of a new building or home for the International Bureau.

The different Governments supporting the Bureau, including the United States, had already appropriated about $250,000 for the purchase of a beautiful site on the corner of Seventeenth and B streets, in the city of Washington. This location comprises 5 acres, facing the Executive Grounds on the east and Potomac Park on the south. The competition for the selection of an architect is now going on, and it is probable that the ground for this "American Temple of Peace," as Mr. CARNEGIE describes it, will be broken early in the fall of 1907.

THE PRACTICAL WORK NOW BEING DONE.

As evidence of the practical work of the Bureau under the present administration, the following facts can be cited:

1. During the first five months of 1907, the Bureau received nearly 6,000 letters from all parts of the world, asking for specific and

ition on various subjects pertaining to Latin Amer-
period there were sent out nearly 6,000 letters
special data which required careful preparation.
m 1 hese, there were received over 2,000 letters request-
a matter, and there were distributed over 60,000 BULLE-
ih, 1, pamphlets, and circulars.

nonth, the Bureau sends out 10,000 BULLETINS, of not
nai 300 pages each, which contain all the latest descriptive and
tic information concerning the commerce and trade and the
t development of the twenty-one American Republics,
lanabooks, averaging 200 to 400 pages each, on the principal
un countries have already been published or are in process
eparation. which are distributed free or at a charge covering
ie (printing and paper.

t d circulars containing accurate information in
-r inini immigration, tariff, and land laws, reports of con-
rs, ai s and addresses by diplomats or specialists about
unuus com s and their characteristics are published and dis-
here v will do the most good.

h exporters, and merchants wishing to exploit the
ts in c ies other than their own are being informed of the
conditions prevailing in the field to be entered and the best ways to
become acquainted with it, while persons wishing to travel for business or pleasure are told the best routes to follow.

7. In the intellectual and educational field of intercourse the systems of the universities and colleges of North and South America are
being studied and an effort is being made to bring about an exchange
of representative scholars and publicists.

8. The study of Spanish and Portuguese is being strongly urged in
the different schools of North America and of English in similar
schools and institutions of South America, while both colleges and
public libraries are being provided with lists of books which will give
information regarding the historical, political, intellectual, and material development of each country.

9. Practical steps have been taken to carry out in detail the programme outlined at the Rio de Janeiro Conference, as described in this
sketch under the head of "Special resolutions regarding the Bureau"
and "Additional resolutions covering new work." While it is somewhat difficult to advance this broad programme as rapidly as desirable, on account of the fact that neither the income nor the staff of the
Bureau have yet been increased, enough has been accomplished to give
an indication of the great good that will result to all the American
Republics from the enlarged scope of the Bureau, which will reach its
fulfillment as the different Republics increase their appropriations,

or quotas, as the staff shall be strengthened by the addition of more experts, and as the new building shall be completed and ready for occupancy.

THE LAKE MOHONK CONFERENCE ON INTERNATIONAL ARBITRATION.

The Lake Mohonk Conference on International Arbitration held its thirteenth annual meeting on May 22–24, 1907.

On the latter date the conference was addressed by Señor Don ENRIQUE CREEL, Mexican Ambassador in the United States; Señor Don IGNACIO CALDERÓN, Minister from Bolivia to the United States; Hon. JOHN BARRETT, Director of the International Bureau of the American Republics, and Hon. FRANCIS B. LOOMIS, former United States Minister to Venezuela and Assistant Secretary of State of the United States.

Under the caption "Latin America and the World," the "Tribune," of New York, comments as follows, on the distinguished speakers and the effect of arbitration verdicts and awards as evidenced by the American nations:

"Yesterday's proceedings at the Lake Mohonk Conference of International Arbitration were agreeably suggestive of the place lately filled in the world by those countries which, for lack of an entirely correct and convenient term, are commonly but not quite accurately called Latin America. A few years ago it was not as it is now. 'Mexicanized' was a term of extreme reproach, used to describe one of the worst states into which the government of a country could fall, and most of the Central and South American Republics were spoken of with either pity or contempt. A marked change has come over those countries in the last generation, and to-day they are entitled to stand as peers in the councils of the nations.

"The Mexican Ambassador, Mr. CREEL, was amply entitled to speak as he did of Mexico's record of abstention from aggressive wars, of her readiness to resort to arbitration, and of her active work for the success of the congress at The Hague. His observations on the possibilities and limitations of international arbitration at the present time were also instinct with temperance and judgment and compare favorably with the utterances which any other responsible statesmen have made in advance of and in preparation for the congress at The Hague. Nor did Mr. CALDERÓN, the Bolivian Minister, overstate the case in dwelling upon the widespread practice of arbitration among the South American Republics. We have frequently taken opportunity to remark upon that very point. If that continent was once the home of wars and revolutions, it has of late been the chief scene of international arbitrations, the verdicts and awards of which have in nearly every case been loyally accepted without demur.

"These circumstances and considerations will invest the appearance of practically all of the Latin American countries at The Hague with special interest and with no small degree of authority. They deserve, most of them, well of the world. They have more than once set examples which other older and more pretentious nations might profitably follow. They are committed to a course at the congress which commends itself to reason and justice, and we may confidently expect that their voices, strange in a European conclave, will be welcomed and will be heard with the respect and courtesy which self-respecting powers accord to their peers."

Ambassador CREEL spoke, in part, as follows:

"Mr. CHAIRMAN, LADIES, and GENTLEMEN: You need not wonder that a Mexican should address you in this hall where so many eminent men have spoken. Mexico, during her entire political life, has always shown her willingness to submit all of her international differences to a friendly arbitration. Never in her wars did Mexico play the part of the aggressor. You will doubtlessly recall that it was Mexico, conjointly with the United States, who first suggested and then obtained the awakening of The Hague Tribunal from its lethargy, thereby becoming a practical institution worthy of entire faith and confidence and to which could be intrusted the adjudication of matters of vital importance.

"No one can fail to recognize the fact that the world rushes steadily onward in our times, whether it be in the solution of material problems, or political, intellectual, moral, or social questions.

*   *   *   *   *   *   *

"For a long time there has been in medicine, law, and diplomacy a school which may be called a prophylactic school, whose doctrine it is to prevent and forestall rather than to repress and punish. In olden times, at the end of a bloody and costly war, the diplomats determined which were the territories to be ceded to the conqueror and what the indemnity to be paid by the conquered one. In our day diplomacy, which, according to Mr. ROOSEVELT, is 'a school of right and truth,' mediates only to prevent war, to allay its hardships, to hasten its termination, thus preventing abuse on the part of the proud, haughty conqueror.

"The greatest thinkers, the most distinguished statesmen, the men who are the pride of mankind, all join now in anathematizing war as a destroyer of activities, a mower of lives, the antagonist of industry, and the enemy of the home. Count MOURAVIEFF, Secretary of Foreign Affairs of Russia, not long ago, when transmitting the views of his Sovereign, stated that the maintenance of general peace and a possible reduction of armaments were the ideals toward which the endeavors of all governments should be directed. 'The financial charges,' continues the distinguished statesman, 'following an upward march strike at the public prosperity at its very source. The intellectual and physical strength of the nations—labor and capital—are for the major part diverted from their natural application and unproductively consumed. Hundreds of millions are devoted to acquiring terrible engines of destruction, which, though to-day regarded as the last word of science, are destined tomorrow to lose all value in consequence of some fresh discovery in the same field.

"'National culture, economic progress, and the production of wealth are either paralyzed or checked in their development. Moreover, in proportion as the armaments of each power increase so do they less and less fulfill the object which the governments have set before themselves.

"To put an end to these incessant armaments and to seek the means of warding off the calamities which are threatening the whole world—such is the supreme duty which is to-day imposed on all states.'

"I do not think it amiss to stop for a moment to consider how far the noble initiative of His Majesty Alexander II has developed and how much has been accomplished by The Hague Conference.

"At a first glance, one may feel inclined to doubt its results, since the armies and navies have considerably increased, on the one hand, and, on the other, the Russo-Japanese war took place soon after the Conference.

"With regard to the first proposition we must agree that the creation of the means of defense is the *effect* of a *cause*—the danger of war—which still exists, and as long as the cause does not disappear the results are bound to continue. For this same reason, the benefits of disarmament will not be effective until the principle of international arbitration has become deeply rooted, and until the several governments have grown confident of the results of such pacific means of determining a controversy.

"The Russo-Japanese war was the result of preexisting causes, and of a state of things which was fatally destined to produce such strife.

"After this explanation, and coming back to the main point of my address, we must feel satisfied with the beneficent influence of The Hague Tribunal, as from the time when Gladstone advocated arbitration of the Alabama claims to this day great strides have been made, both in public opinion and in the mind of the statesman. This is shown by the propaganda made by the different peace congresses, the work of the Interparliamentary League, the four cases submitted to The Hague Tribunal by eight dignified, civilized states, and by the forty-four treaties made among nations to submit certain differences to arbitration. The meetings of the Pan-American Congresses are a further proof of this fact, which is also shown in the call issued for a Second Hague Conference.

* * * * * * *

"As for Mexico, I have to reiterate the statement that she has always upheld the principle of international arbitration. We do not believe, in Mexico, that the time is ripe for unrestricted arbitration as a means for the settlement of disputes, but we believe that certain limitations should be established in such cases as involve territorial integrity and national honor. Of course it must be understood that our aim is to arrive at the specification, in unmistakable terms, of those cases affecting national honor, by avoiding ambiguous, general, and metaphorical phrases such as *matters of vital importance,, subjects involving questions of a special nature*, and other similar expressions which, in the majority of cases, as is well known, are nothing but a mask behind which bad faith and a quarrelsome spirit lurk.

"Later on, when by the number of adjudged cases, the methods established, and the results accomplished a perfect knowledge of the system is obtained, it may then seem prudent to continue the work until the high and noble ideal of justice has been attained.

"In my country also—and in saying this I am confident that I am rightly interpreting the general opinion—the desire exists to see the doctrine of the distinguished Secretary of State, the Hon. ELIHU ROOT, prevail—that is, that the armies and navies of the world must not be used to exact, by force, the payment of debts contracted by the claimant powers, leaving such extreme methods for cases of denial of justice and evident and notorious bad faith. Mexican statesmen have struggled for over fifty years against such methods fraught with arbitrariness. The protests entered by different secretaries of foreign relations of my country against Napoleon's intervention and the French claims of the time of Louis Philippe are still fresh in the memory of all.

"To compel, by force, the payment of a debt, when the person or the State who loaned the amount in question was fully cognizant of the economic and political conditions of the borrower, and his facilities for discharging the obligation, is a complete misapplication of the general conception and principles of credit. In such cases, one of the principal points which is always borne in mind, is the possibility that payment may not be made in due time, because of the insolvency of the debtor, hence the more or less high rates of interest and securities exacted.

"In a matter of such importance I give my cordial support to the sense of justice and right expounded by CALVO in his work on International Law, and also agree with the Drago Doctrine as expressed

in the communication which he authorized as Secretary of Foreign
Relations of the Argentine Republic, on December 29, 1902.

"Any method by which countries may be led to the peaceful settlement of their international difficulties, is of the greatest and highest
importance, not only for the preservation of peace but also to make
international arbitration more solid and stable. It is, therefore, an
all-important matter that treaties made between friendly nations
should always, in provision of any disagreement, stipulate the obligation to refer to The Hague Tribunal all cases after diplomatic exer-
tions are exhausted. The views and the influence of modern statesmen in this connection are most gratifying, as in less than four years
forty-four treaties of arbitration have been signed, many of which
provide for the submission to The Hague Tribunal of any differences
that may arise. May such example be followed by others, and its
application become more universal.

"This current of public opinion, this great love of justice which
grows daily in both hemispheres, lend support to the action of the
President of the United States and his Secretary of State, in asking
that a group of civilized nations, decided to settle by peaceable means
their differences, come together to ask justice before a permanent
court formed by men who by their independence, honorability, learning, and disinterestedness, offer ample security that their judgment
shall be just, right, and impartial.

"By this means the world will attain a superior organization,
where day by day the necessities for armies and navies shall decrease,
thus lessening the public charges; confidence shall be reestablished
among governments and nations; industry shall demand the aid of
idle hands and of the energies which she now lacks, and lastly peace
and good will shall exert their noble influence in the development and
happiness of the human family.

"The best proof that Mr. ROOT's views on the subject are irresisti-
bly gaining ground lies in the fact that not a day passes without a new
problem demanding solution.

"Which are the obligations and which the rights of neutrals,
minutely described so as to leave no room for doubt or discussion?
What rules should control the transmission of wireless messages, both
in time of peace and in time of war, between private individuals,
between a belligerent power and its citizens, and between the inhabitants of a neutral country? Can the right of free use of space in the
air be curtailed by intercepting the hertzian waves, the wireless messages, and what are the requisite conditions for so doing?

"The attention of the new Peace Conference must also be called to
the determination of such delicate points as that of declaration of war,
because while some believe it to be a relic of mediæval chivalry, others
hold that it is an indispensable requisite, the violation of which

imports treachery and deceit. The same applies to the use of submarine mines on the high seas, which, in my judgment, ought to be unanimously condemned, because of the damages inflicted thereby to commerce and navigation, and because of the constant menace to the merchant marine of the world from such mines as also from those that may become detached from their places. It should also be definitely determined whether neutrals having no navy to protect their coasts, may place mines in their waters to insure their neutrality.

"The Hague Conference has established very important rules in the matter of the protection to which the property of neutrals is entitled on the high seas, the necessity to defend honest commerce and to employ all possible means to the end that those engaged in the interchange of the products of the world may not suffer the contingencies and dangers of war, while performing their mission of peace and harmony.

"This, Ladies and Gentlemen, is a great deal, but certainly it is not all. There remains still, that private property on land be fully protected in time of war, specially stipulating the inviolability of railroads, which are to the social body like the arterial system; and stoppage means death.

"I am fully aware of the fact that this is not an easy matter to deal with, since railroads may transport men and other elements intended to prolong and increase war, thus reducing the probabilities of peace, or again, they may be the property of one of the belligerents. However, means could be found to arrange matters by exercising necessary vigilance so that commerce be not interrupted and both the rolling stock and other property be amply protected. The stipulations contained in article 54 of The Hague Regulations regarding war on land sadly contrasts with those on war on the seas, because of the brevity and deficiency of the former and the minute and wise provisions of the latter. I hope, however, that the learned members of the coming conferences may consider such an important subject.

"In the matter of treatment of prisoners of war, we have as precedents the code approved by President LINCOLN in 1863, the Convention of Geneva in 1864, the Brussels Convention in 1874, the resolutions of the First Hague Conference, the instructions issued by Count KATSURA, Japanese Secretary of the Interior, in the Russo-Japanese war, and other dispositions on special and particular cases. But we still need the preparation by The Hague Conference of an international code complete in all details, inspired by new advances in humanitary sentiments, developed by the progress of civilization, which tends to minimize the suffering of the victim and to preserve human life.

"It may sound strange, but one other factor which will contribute toward the termination of war is the number of scientific institutions capable of destroying the greatest armies, the most powerful navies, by the mere agency of a few engineers, the application of chemical formulas, and some simple mechanical contrivance. 1.

"Nothing, however, will so effectively work toward the complete success of international arbitration as these gatherings devoted to free from all other questions, on a scientific basis, the very foundations of international law, to create public opinion, to cast the figure of Peace in the molds of altruism, to spread the gospel of Right in both hemispheres, and to write in glowing characters the glorious words: 'Justice—International Arbitration!'"

Señor CALDERÓN addressed the Conference in the following terms:

"I do not propose to speak of the powerful and noble influence in favor of the cause of international peace and justice which this great nation exercises. This is too well known, and for it mankind renders a tribute of admiration, and recognizes its influence in favor of the oppressed of all nations, and respect for their rights.

"But I am going to ask that you give me your kind attention for a few moments longer, in order to tell of the progress made by the South American Republics in the humanitarian and moral principle of international arbitration.

"Much has been said of the revolutions and the lack of order supposed to reign in these countries, by people little aware of their true conditions; and by writers, who, assuming a contemptuous air, speak of the Latin-American countries as little less than the home of savages.

"One of the wisest and most fortunate moves which has confirmed the sagacity of the illustrious Secretary of State, Hon. ELIHU ROOT, is without doubt the historic visit he made last year to the various Republics, on the occasion of the Pan-American Congress at Rio.

"Mr. ROOT knew that south of the Isthmus of Panama there were young nationalities established under the same democratic principles that have served as the fundamental base of progress of the United States, and perceived that false reports and perhaps intentional misrepresentations had fostered a spirit of mistrust against this country, and he decided to correct it. His frank statements soon changed this feeling and succeeded in inspiring the confidence of the sister Republics and in assuring them of this Government's respect for their sovereignty and of its good intentions. On the other hand, he has acquainted his fellow countrymen with, and revealed to them, the progress and the true condition of these Republics.

"I can confidently affirm that the principle of international arbitration is a doctrine more generally practiced and accepted in South American countries than anywhere else. Brazil has established arbitration among her constitutional precepts and has submitted to this method of settlement territorial questions with England, France, the Argentine Republic, and other countries.

Republic also furnishes very conspicuous examples
...ce and peace. After a sanguinary conflict, in which
...the male population of Paraguay perished, and when
... country lay at the mercy of the victors—Brazil, the
... public, and Uruguay—the Argentine Republic declared
...he victory did not create rights and submitted the dispute
possession of the territory of Villa Occidental to the President
States for arbitration. When President HAYES decided
... Argentine Republic, it accepted the decision in good faith.
...epublic did even more, and condoned to Paraguay the war
...

...uestion with Brazil over the territory of Misiones both
... mitted the matter to the arbitration of President CLEVE-
... the Argentine Republic bowed to the award, which was in
... Brazil.

...er, wh ... lar passions reached a point in which a war
... d all of the neighboring Republics seemed
... nies and fleets of Chile and the Argentine
...u the signal to begin the combat, both countries
... great example of good sense in submitting the
...d v ... disputes over their boundaries to the arbitration of
the King of England. The decision of that Sovereign has been
accepted and carried out, and there on one of the highest accessible
peaks of the Cordilleras, dividing the two nations, the noble impulses
animating them have caused to be raised one of the most beautiful
monuments that has ever been erected.

"This monument is not built over the bloody spoils of martyrs
sacrificed before the altar of their country; neither is it a reminder
of the submission of one people to the other. It is the emblem
of peace abiding within the souls of the sons of the American
Republics, who have lifted up the image of Christ, the Redeemer, as a
mark of tribute to His doctrines. It inspires neither revenge nor a
sense of humiliation to the beholder. A symbol of love, and the pedestal of the Prince of Peace it is the eternal guide under whose
inspiration must grow the human brotherhood. The inscription on
the pedestal reads:

> "Sooner shall the mountains crumble
> to dust than Argentines and Chi-
> lians break the peace which at
> the feet of Christ, the Redeemer,
> they have sworn to maintain.

"Bolivia, my country, has submitted to arbitration important
boundary questions with Peru, Paraguay, and Brazil. Peru also has
arbitration agreements with Bolivia, Brazil, Ecuador, and Italy.

"The boundary disputes have been the main cause of the disagreements among the Latin American Republics.   Such is at present the popular sentiment in favor of arbitration that all of those questions have been submitted to that honorable way of settlement.

"The Pan-American Congresses, especially that of Mexico, have recorded this noble aspiration of the American Republics in explicit declarations.

"Uruguay and the Argentine Republic celebrated, in 1902, a general treaty of arbitration, stipulating the submission to arbitration all controversies of whatever kind and for any cause arising among them which would not affect the precepts of their constitutions.

"Besides this treaty, Uruguay has similar ones with Spain, and has approved a treaty of obligatory arbitration entered into in the Pan-American Conference in Mexico by the Argentine Republic, Bolivia, Guatemala, Salvador, Santo Domingo, Peru, and Paraguay.

"And this is the work of countries commonly considered as always playing at revolutions and without the least idea of order or justice.

"The principal efforts to popularize the adoption of arbitration must be directed toward educating public opinion, and in substituting the sentiments of justice for the false pride of brute force.   We must teach the masses to respect the rights of others as the best agency for protecting our own.

"It is useless to speak of disarmament when first of all the rival nations have more confidence in their fighting strength than in the justice of their cause or the love of peace of their neighbors.

"To a certain extent the democratic doctrine of government by the people and for the people affords greater security against wars, provided the public sentiment is properly guided and the nation as a whole has a true love for fair play and honest dealing.

"When the Venezuelan ports were bombarded by the combined fleets of some of the great powers of Europe, the Argentine Republic, through her minister of foreign affairs, called attention to the great injustice and the menace to the sovereignty of the victim Republic that such action implied.

"Señor DRAGO in his famous note, among others, made the following statements: 'The acknowledgment of a debt and the liquidation of its amount must be made by the country without curtailment of its fundamental rights as a sovereign entity; but the compulsory demand at a given time, by means of force, would only be the destruction of the weak nations and the absorption of their Governments with all of their faculties by the strong nations of the world.   The principles acknowledged in the American Continent are different.'   The illustrious HAMILTON said: 'The contracts entered into as between nations and individuals are obligations subject to the conscience of the sovereign and can not be an object of compulsory claim.   They do not confer any right of action outside of the will of their sovereign.'

ifully for their own welfare, conquering and dominating
ficent gifts, free from military thraldom and in the full
the rights with which God has endowed our immortal

ITT spoke as follows:
its not generally known in the United States should
itention of the American people in forming a true and
ion of the Latin American Republics. Secretary Roor's
e visit to South America and the recent political conditions
tral America have awakened a new interest throughout the
id States in her sister Republics which is in danger of being
ced by wrong impressions.
st. Latin America, judged as a whole, is not a land of civil
and revolutions, despite the popular idea in the United States
pe to the contrary. It is unfair, unjust, and untrue to con-
scribing Latin America in these days as characteristically
usionary, or as being a part of the world which is in a state of
ti more than in a condition of peace. Nearly five-sixths of
ipulation and area of Latin America has known no serious
i or civil war for over ten years, while the major portion of
not been afflicted with a serious revolution, involving great
bloodshed or destruction of property, in twenty years. The trouble
is that so much prominence and attention has been given to revolutions in the small countries of Central and South America that both
press and people of the United States and Europe have overlooked
the fact that the larger and richer nations have been enjoying almost
undisturbed peace for a long period of years. It is as unjust to call
Latin America the home of revolutions because now and then a civil
struggle breaks out in some country as it is to say that riots and bloodshed predominate all over the United States because there have been
serious troubles at times in Idaho, Colorado, and Louisiana.

"Brazil, which is as large as the United States proper, the Argentine Republic, which has half the area of the United States; Chile,
which is larger than the combined area of our Pacific Coast States,
plus the first tier of States; Peru, which is as large as all our Atlantic
Coast States from Maine to Georgia; Bolivia, which is three times as
large as Texas, and Mexico, which would include our whole Central
West, all enjoy such stable conditions of government, prosperity, and
peace that to-day European financial papers are discussing them as
providing fields for the investment of capital equally as safe as those
of the United States. South America and Mexico resent keenly the
constant repetition of the charge that Latin America is given over to
revolutions. It is high time that the American people and press
familiarized themselves with the actual facts and gave the greater
portion of Latin America credit for evolving good government and

order out of disturbed conditions of the past and thereby merit the confidence of the United States in its future progress.

"Second. No group of nations in the world has done more than Latin America to promote the cause of international arbitration. In other words, the United States and the nations of Europe, Asia, and Africa combined have not by practical tests and the referring of disputes to arbitration equaled the record of Latin America in this respect. The long list of boundary disputes between the different countries of Latin America which have been adjudicated by arbitration is evidence of this contention. There have been many cases where the decision to arbitrate their cause of dispute has prevented prominent South American countries from going into an expensive war. There is no better evidence of the forward movement of Latin America in this line than the avoidance of war between the Argentine Republic and Chile just as they were on the point of engaging in a struggle that would probably have been one of the bloodiest in the history of the world and which would have reduced both countries to a state of desolation and poverty and burdened them with a public debt that would have retarded their progress a quarter of a century. Now, instead of suffering with such a fearful handicap, they are making astounding progress, not only in trade and commerce, but in general educational, intellectual, and social lines.

"Last year the Argentine Republic enjoyed a commerce with the outer world amounting to $563,000,000, which is nearly $100 per head of population—more than that of any other prominent nation—and which would have been impossible if she had carried on her shoulders a mighty foreign debt. In this connection it is interesting to note that the progressive Argentine Republic, with a population of only 6,000,000, enjoyed a greater commerce with the outer world in 1906 than did progressive but warlike Japan with 40,000,000 people. Chile, likewise, has gone ahead with such strides in material and political development that her trade has grown over 100 per cent in the last ten years and her people are able to recover financially from a disastrous earthquake with the same ease as the residents of San Francisco and California. What would have been her status if she had been almost ruined by a war with the Argentine Republic it is difficult to imagine.

"Third. The only great and impressive monument on the Western Hemisphere erected as a result of arbitration stands on the boundary line of the Argentine Republic and Chile amid the summits of the Andean Cordillera. At an altitude of nearly 15,000 feet, or 3 miles, above the placid level of the Atlantic and Pacific, commanding a mighty prospect of the Argentine Republic on one side and Chile on the other, and seeming to breathe forth the spirit of peace, is a dignified, gigantic, bronze statue of the Christ, which was erected by the

joint order and expense of the two Governments and was dedicated
in the presence of the leading statesmen of both countries who journeyed from their homes to the cold altitudes of the Andes to witness
its unveiling and to testify to their support of its everlasting significance. The very fact that the bronze out of which the statue is cast
is from the molten cannon, gives additional meaning to its presence
on the mountain tops. It is located on the principal pass between
the two countries which is used by all travelers going back and forth,
while directly under it—when the railroad is completed—will pass a
tunnel—the longest in the world—that is to bring Chile and the Argentine Republic as close together in communication as they have been
united by the arbitration that made this monument possible."

TREATY OF PEACE, AMITY, AND COMMERCE BETWEEN SALVADOR AND NICARAGUA.

The undersigned, RAMÓN GARCÍA GONZÁLEZ, Secretary of Foreign
Relations of the Republic of Salvador, and JOSÉ DOLORES GAMEZ,
Secretary of Foreign Relations of the Republic of Nicaragua, each in
representation of their respective Governments, duly authorized, as
shown by the full powers they have produced, and which were found
to be in proper form, after long interviews with and through the
friendly mediation of Mr. PHILIP BROWN, Chargé d'Affaires of the
United States near the Government of the Republic of Honduras,
have agreed to conclude the Treaty of Peace, Amity, and Commerce
contained in the following stipulations:

"I. The perfect harmony and relations between the signatory Governments having been altered in consequence of the late war between
Honduras and Nicaragua, in which the Government of Salvador was
compelled to intervene because of the alliance entered into with the
Government of Honduras under the administration of General MAN-
UEL BONILLA, and taking into consideration the powerful reasons of
necessity and convenience to reestablish peace between both countries, and after thoroughly discussing the matter, have agreed and
hereby mutually agree to reestablish their temporarily interrupted
relations on the basis of the good faith that should exist in the friendly
relations of the two sister Republics.

"II. Peace being reestablished by the present treaty, the signatory Governments agree that Nicaragua shall invite the other Central
American Governments to a Central American Congress to be held
in Corinto, in accordance with the proposal of the representatives
of the Governments of these Republics, together with the Secretary
of State of the United States, said Congress to be composed of the

representatives of the five sister Republics, and with full powers to conclude a General Treaty of Peace and Amity having compulsory arbitration for its fundamental basis, substituting the previous pacts of the same character, made in Corinto, and in San José, Costa Rica, to the end that armed conflicts between sister Republics may in future be avoided. In addition, the representatives of the five Republics shall be able to agree upon stipulations relating to commerce, navigation, and other matters they deem beneficial to Central American interests.

"III. Until the provisions of the foregoing article are complied with, it is hereby agreed that any controversy that may hereafter arise between Salvador and Nicaragua, and which might alter their friendly relations, shall be settled by means of compulsory arbitration applied by the joint action of the Presidents of the United States and Mexico, who shall have power full to appoint an umpire whose award shall be final. The President of Mexico may delegate his powers as arbitrator to the Mexican Ambassador in Washington or to such other person as he may designate.

"IV. As evidence of the sincerity with which the signatory Governments have acted and also of the confidence which they have in the compliance of what has been agreed upon, they cheerfully promise to issue, in their respective countries, a decree granting full and unconditional amnesty to such citizens as have been hostile in the late war in Honduras.

"V. Salvador and Nicaragua solemnly agree to conclude a Treaty of Commerce based on an interchange of ratifications.

"VI. The present contract shall be ratified and its ratifications shall be exchanged in the city of Managua, or in that of San Salvador, a month after the last ratification, or at an earlier 'date, if that be possible.

"In testimony whereof the contracting parties sign the present treaty in triplicate, jointly with Mr. PHILIP BROWN, Chargé d'Affaires of the United States near the Governments of Honduras and Guatemala, who has interposed his good offices and the moral support of the country he represents, at Amapala, April 23, 1907.

[L. S.]   RAMÓN GARCÍA GONZÁLEZ.
[L. S.]   JOSÉ DOLORES GÁMEZ.
                                   PHILIP BROWN.

EXECUTIVE PALACE,
San Salvador, April 26, 1907.

In view of the foregoing Treaty of Peace, Amity, and Commerce, concluded at Amapala, April 23 of the current year, between the Secretaries of Foreign Relations of Salvador and Nicaragua, in representation of their respective Governments, and with the friendly

mediation of Mr. PHILIP BROWN, Chargé d'Affaires of the United
States of America near the Government of the Republic of Honduras, said treaty consisting of a preamble and six articles, the
Executive Power finding the same to be in accordance with the
instructions given to that effect to the Secretary, Dr. RAMÓN GON-
ZÁLEZ GARCÍA, resolves to approve said treaty in all its parts and
submit it to the ratification of the National Assembly during its
present sessions.

(Rubricated by the President.)

The Assistant Secretary of Foreign Relations,

CAÑAS.

RECEPTION OF THE MINISTER OF PANAMA IN THE UNITED STATES.

Señor Don JOSÉ AGUSTÍN ARANGO, Envoy Extraordinary and
Minister Plenipotentiary of Panama near the Government of the
United States, was received in his capacity as such by President
ROOSEVELT on May 13, 1907. On presenting his credentials Señor
ARANGO spoke as follows:

"Mr. PRESIDENT: High will be the gratification I shall find in the
discharge of the mission with which I have been intrusted by the
Government of my country, to represent it, jointly with the honorable Minister, Señor OBALDÍA, near the Government of Your
Excellency, as accredited by the autograph letter which I have the
honor to place in Your Excellency's hands.

"The benevolence Your Excellency's Government has shown us

"Since the advent of your country into the family of independent States, the Government of the United States has given frequent evidence of its friendly disposition; and it shall be our aim, within those bounds of equity and justice of which you speak, to still further strengthen the good relations now subsisting.

"I thank you for the personal good wishes which you express on behalf of the President, Government, and people of Panama, as well as on your own account, and beg you in turn to assure your worthy President of the high regard which the Government and people of the United States and myself entertain for him and the Panaman people."

RATIO OF TRADE VALUES BETWEEN LATIN AMERICA AND THE UNITED STATES.

According to the latest available statistics, the ratios of trade values between the various countries of Latin America and the United States are as follows:

Total imports by the Argentine Republic in 1906, are given as $269,970,521, of which $39,474,894, or 14.62 per cent, were of United States origin; whereas of total exports valued at $292,253,829 only $13,332,112, or 4.56 per cent, were sent to that country. In 1905, out of a total import valuation of $197,974,000, $27,902,000, or 14.62 per cent, were from the United States, that country taking $15,167,000, or 4.87 per cent, out of a total export valuation of $311,544,000.

Of Bolivian imports, valued in 1905 at $13,377,000, the United States furnished $756,000, or 5.6 per cent, and took $27,000, or 0.13 per cent, out of a total export value of $20,062,049. United States statistics report exports to Bolivia, in 1906 (calendar year), valued at $242,616, but Bolivian statements quote a much larger sum.

In 1906, Brazil received $19,000,000, or 11.46 per cent, from the United States, out of a total import value of $165,000,000, and sent thither $93,000,000, or 36 per cent, out of a total export value of over $265,000,000. The 1905 figures indicate imports from the United States of $14,961,000, or 10.33 per cent of the total ($144,775,000), while exports thither were $89,108,000, or 41.13 per cent, out of a total of $216,000,000.

Total Costa Rican imports, in 1905, are reported as $5,239,000, of which $2,706,000, or 51.65 per cent, were from the United States, and that country received $3,836,000, or 47.14 per cent, out of a total export value of $8,138,000. Export figures from the United States to Costa Rica during the calendar year 1906 are placed at $2,473,281 and imports are valued at $4,715,510.

Guatemala's total imports are valued, in 1905, at $6,844,000, of which $2,707,000, or 39.55 per cent, were of United States origin, and her exports were worth $8,238,000, of which $2,875,000, or 34.90 per cent, went to the United States. For 1906, (calendar year), United States export values to Guatemala are placed at $2,980,072, while imports from that country were $2,822,020.

Total imports by Honduras in 1905 were $2,293,000, of which $1,690,000, or 73.70 per cent, were from the United States, while of the total exports, worth $5,564,000, the share taken by the United States was $4,623,000, or 83.09 per cent. For 1906, United States export values to Honduras are placed at $1,896,204, while imports from that country were $2,204,692.

Nicaragua's total imports were valued at $3,202,000 in 1904, the latest year for which full statistics are available, and of that sum, the United States furnished $1,668,000, or 52.09 per cent, while of total exports worth $3,926,000, the United States received $2,089,000, or 53.21 per cent. For 1905 and 1906, United States export values to Nicaragua were $1,833,595 and $2,041,231, respectively, and imports for the two years were $1,433,815 and $1,331,172.

In 1906, the United States export values to Panama were $14,239,471 as compared with $7,831,564 in 1905, while imports from that country were $1,448,686 in 1906 as against $879,145 in the preceding year.

Salvador, in 1905, took imports from abroad worth $4,346,000, of which $1,355,000, or 31.18 per cent, were of United States origin, and exported to the value of $5,640,000, sending $1,225,000, or 23.49 per cent, to that country. In 1906, United States export values to Salvador were $1,321,765, imports being placed at $1,216,262.

Cuba's imports in 1906 were worth $98,530,622, of which $47,717,618, or over 48 per cent, were from the United States, while of a total export value of $106,258,618 that country took $88,175,451, or over 82 per cent.

The total import of Haiti from October, 1904, to September, 1905, inclusive, were valued at $3,871,069, of which the United States contributed $2,746,851, or over 71 per cent. For 1906, United States export values to Haiti are placed at $3,266,425, and imports from that country at $1,036,330, as compared with $2,916,379 and $1,171,303 in 1905.

The Dominican Republic imported, in 1906, merchandise valued at $4,065,437, the United States furnishing $2,271,292, or over 48 per cent, the exports being reported for $6,536,379, of which the United States took $3,464,425, or 53 per cent. In 1905, imports by the Republic figured for $2,737,000, the United States furnishing $1,961,000, or 71.65 per cent, while of total exports of $6,881,000 the United States took $4,484,000, or 65.16 per cent.

Chile's total imports in 1905 were valued at $71,868,000, of which the United States furnished $7,129,000, or 9.92 per cent, and exports were valued at $103,223,000, the United States taking $15,693,000, or 15.20 per cent. In 1906, United States export values to Chile were $9,392,453, imports from that country being reported for $18,146,232.

Export figures from the United States to Colombia in 1906 were $2,961,671, as compared with $3,635,417; in 1905, imports were reported as $6,669,461 and $6,268,939 in the two years, respectively. Colombian imports in 1904 were valued at $14,453,000, the United States supplying $4,936,000, or 34.15 per cent, while of exports valued at $12,658,000, that country took $6,837,000, or 54.01 per cent.

Ecuador's import values, in 1905, were $7,657,000, the United States supplying $2,210,000, or 28.86 per cent, and of exports valued at $9,468,000 the total shipments to that country were $2,468,000, or 27.32 per cent. In 1906, United States export values to Ecuador were $1,834,756 while imports were valued at $3,281,684.

Total Mexican imports in 1906 (fiscal year) were valued at $109,884,000, of which $72,509,000, or 65.99 per cent, were of United States origin, and exports were worth $135,027,000, of which the United States took $92,633,000, or 68.6 per cent.

Paraguay imported merchandise from abroad to the value of $3,566,000 in 1904, the latest for which complete figures are available, the United States furnishing $125,000, or 3.51 per cent, while total exports are reported at $3,179,000 for the year in question—the percentage received by the United States not being noted. The United States reports exports to Paraguay in the calendar year 1906 valued at $110,496, as compared with $6,719 in 1905, the imports for the same periods being $1,200 and $2,205, respectively.

In 1904, Peruvian imports were valued at $20,916,000, of which the United States supplied $3,761,000, or 17.98 per cent, and exports were rated at $19,790,000, of which the United States took $1,849,000, or 9.34 per cent. United States statistics report exports to Peru, in 1906, valued at $5,193,455, as compared with $4,287,228 in 1905, the figures for imports from Peru in the two periods being given as $2,933,508 and $2,608,665, respectively.

Uruguay's import trade in 1904 was reported for $21,938,000, the United States furnishing $2,121,000, or 9.67 per cent, while exports were valued at $39,793,000, the United States receiving $2,137,000, or 5.37 per cent. United States exports to Uruguay in 1906 are stated as $3,160,606, as compared with $2,703,761 in 1905, the figures for imports in the same periods being $2,453,013 and $3,529,495, respectively.

For the fiscal year 1906, the total value of imports received by Venezuela was $8,676,000, the United States furnishing $2,622,000, or 30.22 per cent, while exports were valued at $15,630,000, of which the United States took $4,862,000, or 31.11 per cent. In the calendar year 1906 United States exports to Venezuela are quoted at $3,310,518, as compared with $3,208,864 in 1905, the figures of imports for the two periods being $7,789,893 and $7,010,357, respectively.

ARGENTINE REPUBLIC.

MESSAGE OF PRESIDENT FIGUEROA ALCORTA.

In his annual message delivered to the Argentine Congress, on May 8, 1907, President FIGUEROA ALCORTA stated that prosperity and advancement in all departments of the public service were evident to the entire world, and that as regards 1906, the year was marked by complete political harmony between the Nation and the provinces. In general, public order remained intact.

The hundredth anniversary of the independence of the Republic occurs in 1910, and it is purposed to celebrate it with the completeness its historical significance demands.

The postal and telegraph services of the Republic throughout the year were in harmony with general progress, the statistics relating thereto being beyond all expectations. The total number of postal communications was 552,014,897, representing an increase of 51,627,034 over the preceding year. The telegrams numbered 9,977,887, against 8,934,652 in 1905. Revenues derived from both services amounted to $9,086,593, an increase of $1,086,593 over the sum estimated in the budget. The present telegraph system is insufficient to meet the extensions made, in spite of the extensions made, which represent a total of 398 kilometers of line and 1,668 kilometers of conductors, the total present system being 24,757 kilometers of line and 55,283 kilometers of conductors. Eighty-eight new offices were opened during the year, bringing the total thereof to 2,012. During 1907 there will be constructed a line between Saavedra and Bahia Blanca, a conductor will be added between Tucuman and Recreo, and two between San Agustin and Cordoba, besides new underground cables. The obstacles to the continuation of the construction of the new building for the General Post-Office and Telegraph Department have been removed.

The condition of public health throughout the year was satisfactory; the cases of sparodic diseases which were registered at Buenos Ayres, Rosario, and Salta were of slight sanitary importance, owing to the readiness with which they yielded to treatment. The new pharmacy act has resolved a most important medico-social problem and has begun to bear its fruits in the efficacy of the guaranties it affords to the pharmaceutical retail trade. As a beginning in the programme of fluvial sanitary service, the works for the erection of the Corrientes Station have been initiated.

Relations of the most cordial character have been maintained with other nations. The most notable diplomatic event of the year was the visit of the Secretary of State of the United States, Mr. ROOT, to various South American Republics, including the Argentine Republic. The eminent statesman brought a message of peace and amity from his great Nation and its President, Mr. ROOSEVELT; Mr. ROOT himself at every opportunity expressed sincere hopes for the future peace and prosperity of these Republics. President FIGUEROA stated that he retained the most pleasant recollections of Mr. ROOT's visit and of the cordial reception accorded to him, and that the visit has given signs of bearing fruit in positive abundance.

Commercial relations with the United States are constantly increasing. The European powers in turn offer the most unequivocal proofs of friendship and goodwill. The Kings of England and Spain have raised their legations to the first grade. Sweden and Norway, since their separation, have hastened to improve the friendly relations which have always existed between the Republic and those nations. Various foreign countries with which the Argentine Republic had not previously cultivated direct relations have now accredited representatives at the capital. The relations with Paraguay and Bolivia have improved, due to the arbitration treaty signed at Buenos Aires on January 12, 1907. On the occasion of the inauguration of the new President of Uruguay, which took place on March 4, 1907, the Argentine Government deemed it just to give that nation a proof of friendship by sending a naval division to participate in the ceremony at Montevideo. The Argentine Government took part in the Pan-American Conference at Rio Janeiro, giving in this manner a further proof of friendship to Brazil. Representatives will also be sent to The Hague Peace Conference, in accordance with an invitation received in 1905, from the Russian Emperor, and more recently from the Queen of Holland. The Government has initiated a movement for the assembling of an international conference at Buenos Aires in 1910 for the purpose of rendering uniform the Code of International Law in so far as it relates to the principle of domicile. The nations that have incorporated this principle in their private legislation will be invited. Invited by the Government of the United States to take part in the Jamestown Exposition, the Executive decided to send the frigate *Presidente Sarmiento* and a delegation of officers. The mutual relations of the South American Republics continue to be most cordial. Notwithstanding the immense number of foreign residents in the country, not a single case has arisen to warrant diplomatic intervention. Relations with the Holy See have

acquired a greater degree of cordiality and the Argentine representative to the Vatican has been accredited as a First Class Minister
Plenipotentiary.

The economic prosperity of the country continues unabated, and
the balance sheet of the year's working shows a saving of $5,100,000.
The internal and foreign credits of the nation has been maintained
and the Argentine Legation in London has more than sufficient
funds to meet the service of the external debt and other expenditures abroad up to July, 1907. The internal debt has been reduced
by $12,698,460 gold, and now amounts to $88,243,800 (national
currency) and $3,701,540 gold. The consolidated external debt was
lowered by $4,834,825, gold.

The foreign commerce of the country amounted to $562,224,350 gold,
as against $527,998,261 in 1905. Import figures were $269,970,521
and export $292,253,829, the former showing an increase of $64,816,101
and the latter a decrease of $30,590,012 over 1905. The increase in
imports was due to the exceptional crops of the three last years
and the consequent increased purchasing power of the agriculturists,
while the decrease in export values was due to the prevalence of
disease in cattle and to atmospheric conditions coupled with the invasion of locusts.

While increased imports are usually an indication of prosperity on
the part of the consuming nation, it is not, however, desirable that
the greater proportion of increase should be in articles of consumption
rather than of reproduction. The advance of the Argentine Republic
in this regard is shown by the fact that ten years ago articles of actual
consumption represented 67.2 per cent of total imports and those
capable of reproduction or development 32.8 per cent. In 1906,
however, the former class of imports figured for 45.5 per cent and the
latter 54.5 per cent. Special attention is called to the importation
of horticultural items, which President FIGUEROA ALCORTA points
out might easily be raised in the Republic.

In spite of the drought and locusts, agriculture, which is the principal source of Argentine prosperity, responded to the national hopes,
and, though the value of exports fell below those of the preceding
year by over $30,000,000, the general trend of commercial move-
ments during the past five years has been decidedly upward. The
five years' annual average for exports was exceeded by $36,000,000,
and shipments of wheat, linseed, and maize were far in excess of the
local consumption, the proportions of export to home consumption
being 3¾ to 1 for wheat, 5 to 1 for linseed, and 5½ to 1 for maize.

The year 1906 was one of great development in all branches of
public instruction, the number of primary schools having advanced
from 5,199 in 1905 to 5,941, while teachers numbered 16,192 in 1906,
as compared with 13,971 in the preceding year. The total number

of pupils registered was 557,658, against 538,732 in 1905. Higher branches of education have been encouraged, and during the year there were established in the Province of Buenos Aires four national and two normal schools; in the Province of Santa Fe a national college and a normal school, while in the city of Buenos Aires a professional school for women and an academy of fine arts were inaugurated. The industrial schools at Rosario and national college for young women at the capital are prospering. A national Department of Labor, created by the budget law of 1906–7, was organized by decree of March 14, 1907, and has entered upon its duties.

The execution of public works was retarded by the labor crisis, but the communication services by land and water have been improved and other necessary developments executed.

The railways in operation at the close of 1906 aggregated 20,814 kilometers, an increase for the year of 555 kilometers, while the few months of 1907 have added 404 kilometers to this extent. Under construction, 5,547 kilometers are reported, of which a large portion will be completed during 1907. Railway traffic indicates increased prosperity, passenger service advancing 25 per cent and merchandise transit 15 per cent. Net profits from railroad operations show, however, a gain of only 4 per cent by reason of the increased cost of labor and material, especially coal.

Rolling stock includes 2,116 locomotives, an increase of 452, and freight cars now have a capacity of 872,000 tons, an increase of 186,000 tons, while shed areas cover 748,000 cubic meters.

Work on the State lines has been pushed, especial effort being directed toward reaching the Bolivian frontier, this line being part of a vast programme of international connections. It is, however, necessary that the Argentine Congress should pass the Quiaca and Tupiza railway bill, whose completion will supplement the vast system of the Central Northern, whose outlet to a port on the San Cristobal and Santa Fe will be opened this year. This line will carry the trade of central and southern Bolivia and will facilitate exchange with the north and center of the Argentine Republic.

The completion of this line will make the Argentine nation the first in South America to fulfill one of the principal proposals of the United States at the American International Congress at Washington, namely, the construction of the great Pan-American Railway.

The channels leading to the ports of Buenos Aires, Rosario, and Uruguay have been dredged, and at Rosario $2,083,597 have been spent on port works during the year. Other works connected with education, sanitation, irrigation, etc., are progressing; bridges have been constructed; roads repaired; drainage and waterworks completed or new systems inaugurated in Cordoba, Mendoza, Santiago, Santa Fe, and many other cities. Since 1903 $16,694,500 have been spent in sanitary improvements, the expenditures for last year covering $1,392,688 in the capital and $4,349,680 in the provinces.

President FIGUEROA ALCORTA states that all that has been accomplished in the past year is but a part of the vast programme that has been laid out for future operations for the welfare and development of the country and he urges upon Congress the necessity of providing amply for the furtherance of the measures proposed.

DESTINATION OF EXPORTS, FIRST QUARTER OF 1907.

The "Review of the River Plate," in its issue for April 12, 1907, publishes the figures showing the details of exportation from the Argentine Republic during the first quarter of 1907, as compared with the same period of the preceding year, the principal articles and the points of destination being furnished. In the statement in reference the average weights are as follows: 1 bale of sheepskins, 400 kilograms; 1 bale of wool, 400 kilograms; 1 bale of hair, 400 kilograms; 1 bale of goatskins, 370 kilograms; 1 bale of hay, 50 kilograms; 1 pipe of tallow, 400 kilograms; 1 hogshead of tallow, 200 kilograms; 1 cask of tallow, 160 kilograms; 1 case of butter, 25 kilograms.

The number of dry oxhides for the first quarter of 1907 reported as shipped abroad was 515,094, as compared with 587,610 in the corresponding period of 1906, with the following destinations: United Kingdom, 2,500; United States, 308,506; France, 4,044; Germany, 69,912; Belgium, 15,283; Italy, 62,207; orders, 2,755; and other countries, 49,887.

Salt oxhides numbered 414,163 on the export lists for the first quarter of 1907, as compared with 364,553 in the corresponding period of the previous year. The following were the destinations thereof: United Kingdom, 54,378; United States, 21,686; France, 26,764; Germany, 219,580; Belgium, 77,548; Italy, 1,914; orders, 9,380; other countries, 2,913.

Dry horsehides exported numbered 23,274, as compared with 31,396 in 1906, destined as follows: France, 32; Germany, 23,242. Salt horsehides were exported to the number of 2,179, against 1,050 in the first quarter of 1906, the whole amount being destined to Germany.

The bales of sheepskins sent abroad amounted to 13,781 and 12,662 in the first quarters of 1907 and 1906, respectively, destined as follows in 1907: United Kingdom, 339; United States, 818; France, 11,358; Germany, 347; Belgium, 155; Italy, 722; Brazil, 42.

Hair to the amount of 1,147 and 830 bales was sent abroad in the first quarters of 1907 and 1906, respectively, with the following destinations in 1907: United Kingdom, 56; United States, 234; France, 31; Germany, 167; Belgium, 384; Italy, 251; Brazil, 24.

Shipments of tallow in the first quarter of 1907 aggregated 5,148 pipes, 18,619 casks, and 3,937 hogsheads, as compared with 4,390 pipes, 22,039 casks, and 768 hogsheads in the corresponding period of 1906. The countries of destination for the first-mentioned period were: United Kingdom, 1,878 pipes, 12,171 casks, and 3,837 hogsheads; France, 108 pipes; Germany, 577 pipes and 1,402 casks; Belgium, 404 pipes and 1,992 casks; Italy, 2,077 pipes and 315 casks; Brazil, 104 pipes, 785 casks, and 100 hogsheads; and other countries, 1,954 casks.

Goatskins to the amount of 699 bales were shipped abroad in the first quarter of 1907, as compared with 3,993 in the corresponding period of 1906, distributed as follows: United Kingdom, 29; United States, 507; France, 156; Belgium, 7.

Shipments of wool aggregated 195,013 bales and 185,958 bales in the first quarters of 1907 and 1906, respectively, with the following destinations in 1907: United Kingdom, 19,426; United States, 11,088; France, 82,280; Germany, 49,592; Belgium, 24,809; Italy, 2,607; other countries, 4,211.

Frozen wethers numbering 625,939 and 648,935 were shipped abroad in the first quarters of 1907 and 1906, respectively, of which in 1907, the United Kingdom took 596,775; Italy, 300; South Africa, 28,854.

The exports of oats in the first quarter of 1907 amounted to 81,779 tons, as compared with 32,384 in the corresponding period of 1906, with the following destinations: United Kingdom, 29,317; United States, 60; France, 10,068; Germany, 2,081; Belgium, 15,868; Italy, 2,646; Brazil, 3; orders, 7,974.

The shipments of wheat in 1907 and 1906 aggregated 1,118,429 tons and 963,159 tons for the first quarters, respectively, the 1907 shipments being distributed as follows: United Kingdom, 203,328; France, 20,037; Germany, 79,626; Belgium, 123,411; Italy, 6,598; South Africa, 6,118; Brazil, 73,185; orders, 450,158; other countries, 155,328.

Maize shipments aggregated 108,280 tons and 90,527 tons in the first quarters of 1907 and 1906, respectively, the destinations for 1907 being as follows: United Kingdom, 31,510; France, 15,759; Germany, 6,575; Belgium, 20,344; Italy, 891; South Africa, 204; Brazil, 1,032; orders, 22,047; other countries, 9,918.

In the first quarter of 1907 there were shipped abroad 401,120 tons of linseed, as compared with 214,407 tons in the same period of the previous year, the destinations being as follows: United Kingdom, 46,354; France, 28,721; Germany, 117,621; Belgium, 27,848; Italy, 10,721; South Africa, 57; Brazil, 4; orders, 127,780; other countries, 43,014.

Flour shipments in the first quarters of 1907 and 1906, respectively, amounted to 29,209 tons and 27,383 tons, the 1907 shipments being destined as follows: United Kingdom, 301; Brazil, 28,758; orders, 150.

Bran shipments amounted to 38,745 tons and 37,603 tons for the first quarters of 1907 and 1906, respectively, with the following destinations in 1907: United Kingdom, 950; France, 1,803; Germany, 31,221; Belgium, 1,192; Brazil, 1,000; orders, 1,698; other countries, 881.

Pollard shipments amounted to 19,640 bags in the first quarter of 1907, as compared with 16,648 bags in the corresponding period of the previous year, the destinations being as follows: United Kingdom, 13; France, 18,347; Belgium, 1,100.

Oilseed shipments for the first quarter of 1907 amounted to 24,231 bags, as compared with 43,102 bags for the same period of 1906, being destined as follows: United Kingdom, 5,000; France, 2,128; Germany, 15,600; Italy, 1,504.

In the first quarter of 1907, beef shipments amounted to 439,191 quarters, as compared with 543,931 quarters in the same period of the previous year, the destinations being as follows: United Kingdom, 425,110; Italy, 612; Brazil, 13,069.

During the first quarter of 1907, hay was sent abroad to the amount of 94,441 bales, as compared with 358,343 bales in the corresponding period of 1906, Brazil taking all the exports of this product for said quarter of 1907.

Quebracho shipments, in the first quarter of 1907, amounted to 81,556 tons, as compared with 89,278 tons in the same period of 1906, and were distributed as follows: United Kingdom, 3,338; United States, 22,998; France, 4,614; Germany, 20,672; Italy, 2,645 orders, 22,422; other countries, 4,867.

Quebracho extract was shipped abroad in the first quarter of 1907 to the amount of 10,310 tons, as compared with 17,053 tons in the same period of the preceding year, distributed as follows: United Kingdom, 1,371; United States, 5,525; France, 39; Germany, 1,574; Belgium, 488; Italy, 813; Brazil, 130; other countries, 190.

Butter shipments in the first quarter of 1907 amounted to 37,741 cases, as compared with 71,209 cases in the corresponding period of 1906, with the following destinations: United Kingdom, 30,149; France, 20; South Africa, 7,440; Brazil, 132.

CENTENNIAL EXPOSITION AT BUENOS AIRES IN 1910.

The necessary measures have been taken by the Argentine Government for the holding of a general exhibition of arts, industries, agriculture, and cattle in Buenos Aires during 1910, the centennial year of that city.

The *Comisión Nacional del Centenario* has been authorized by law to proceed with formulation of plans and the development of general interest in the matter.

RECEIPTS FROM LAND, LICENSE, AND STAMP TAXES, 1906.

According to the report issued by the chief of the Argentine Department of Land, License, and Stamp Taxation, the total receipts from this branch of the public service, during 1906, were $21,238,512.59 paper, as compared with $19,971,243.19 in 1905, an increase of $1,267,069.40.

Of the total amount, $7,211,046.25 was for the land tax, against $6,946,085.21 in 1905; $4,442,512.04 was for licenses, as compared with $3;858,421.17 in 1905 and $9,584,954.30 was for stamp taxes, against $9,166,936.81 in 1905.

A new assessment which has been made for the collection of the land tax will doubtless result in a further increase of this source of revenue—30 per cent being the estimated increase—while the classification recently drawn up of professions, enterprises, and industries subject to the license tax indicates a material increase in that section also.

MARITIME MOVEMENT, 1906.

Entrances and clearances of vessels at Argentine ports in 1906 were: Rosario, entrances and clearances, 4,656 vessels, of 2,876,780 tons; La Plata, entrances and clearances, 1,383 vessels, of 1,410,000 tons; Bahia, Blanca, and Parana, entrances and clearances, 2,490 vessels, of 1,468,700 tons; total entrances and clearances for the four ports, 8,529 vessels, of 5,755,480 tons. The entrances for Buenos Aires were: 258 sailing vessels, of 262,931 tons, and 1,936 steam vessels, of 4,227,367 tons; total sail and steam, 2,194 vessels, of 4,490,298 tons. In the entrances into Buenos Aires the British flag covered 2,580,592 tons, the German flag 506,358 tons, the Italian flag 514,393 tons, and the French flag 309,712 tons. The American flag is not mentioned in the returns.

SUGAR PRODUCTION IN 1906.

According to figures published by the *Boletin de la Union Industrial Argentina* of April 15, 1907, the 39 sugar factories of the Argentine Republic manufactured during the year 1906 1,919,593 bags of sugar, with a total weight of 118,817,528 kilograms, as compared with 1,919,593 bags, weighing 137,090,770 kilograms in 1905; a decrease in 1906 of 224,270 bags, weighing 18,273,242 kilograms.

REDUCTION OF IMPORT DUTIES ON SUGAR.

On April 20, 1907, the Argentine Minister of Finance promulgated a decree of the President of the Republic, whereby item No. 126 of the tariff of values is altered in the following manner:

"Sugar not refined or of less than 96° of polarization, −0.06."

The effect of this is to reduce the specific duty on the sugars mentioned by 1 cent gold per kilogram.

The report of the Minister of Finance states that the action is taken in view of a note from the Ministry of Agriculture recommending the reduction of the duties on raw sugar for refining and of the previous report of the Administration of Internal Taxes in reply to a note of the Ministry of Finance of March 12. It is stated that the stock of sugar in the Republic is insufficient for the necessities of consumption, even without a rise in price above that which is fixed by law. The maximum wholesale price fixed by Law 4288 is $3 per 10 kilograms, put in wagons at the mills, including the tax paid, thus reducing the manufacturer's price to $2.62½ per 10 kilograms, though the market price is now much higher. The year's stock is said to be short by about 20,000 tons, the consumption for 1906 having been 140,000 tons.

PROPRIETARY MEDICINES IN THE REPUBLIC.

Under date of April 16, 1906, a very stringent law was promulgated in the Argentine Republic regarding the sale and introduction of proprietary articles. This provides that all proprietary remedies, domestic and foreign, for external or internal use, must have the authorization of the National Department of Hygiene before they may be placed on sale in the country, in default of which they shall be treated as secret remedies and their sale prohibited.

For the purpose of obtaining such authorization it is provided that application be made to the National Department of Hygiene, the samples necessary for analysis and specimens of labels, bottles or other receptacles, and the prospectuses, advertisements, and circulars of instruction which are to accompany the preparations when sold to the public being submitted with the application. The preparation is then analyzed, its correspondence with the formula and its benefit or utility determined. The advertising matter is also scrutinized with a view to determining whether it is free from deceptive or grossly exaggerated statements regarding the composition or curative properties of the remedy. If the commission shall deem the remedy open to no objection on this score, the proper authorization will be granted.

Thereafter, the remedy may be offered to the public, but only in connection with the prospectuses and other advertisements that have been submitted to the commission. Any modification of any sort introduced into the advertising matter that accompanies or exploits the preparation shall be deemed by the commission a proper ground for withdrawing the authorization and imposing a fine provided by the law. In the case of remedies already authorized to be sold in the Argentine Republic, the space of one year is provided for compliance with the new statute.

REPORT OF THE SOUTHERN RAILWAY.

According to an official statement the receipts of the Southern Railway of the Argentine Republic during the year 1904–5 amounted to £3,350,102, and the expenditures to £1,670,625, the proportion being 49.87 per cent. In 1905–6, the receipts reached the amount of £3,896,888 and the expenditures that of £2,239,387, the proportion being 57.47 per cent. During the first half of the fiscal year 1906–7, the receipts were £1,929,679 and the expenditures £1,125,136, the proportion being 58.31; it is estimated that the proportion of expenditures during the entire fiscal year will be about 60 per cent.

Merchandise was transported on this line in the following quantities: Year ended June 30, 1904, 2,362,197 tons; year ended June 30, 1905, 3,090,703 tons; year ended June 30, 1906, 3,702,477 tons; second half of 1906, 2,110,682 tons.

The passenger traffic was as follows:. Year ended June 30, 1904, 6,924,096 passengers;. year ended June 30, 1905, 7,695,123 passengers;. year ended June 30, 1906, 9,551,772 passengers; second half of 1906, 6,002,186 passengers.

BOLIVIA.

MINING REGULATIONS.

On April 20, 1907, the Bolivian Government issued the following important decree:

"CONCESSIONS.

"ARTICLE 1. Unoccupied ground between mining concessions which can not form a unit—that is to say, a square of one hundred meters, even though the total may exceed the ten thousand square meters contained in said unit—shall also be considered free ground between mining claims.

"ART. 2. The grantee of said deposits, placers, blanket veins, or other surface beds who finds veins in the subsoil of the mining property which he is working must make the proper application for said veins.

"DUTIES OF ADJOINING MINE OWNERS.

"ART. 3. Whenever a more or less numerous group of mining concessions is threatened or is suffering the consequences of an inundation common to all of them, and which endangers their existence and prevents the extraction of their ores, the proper authority shall compel the grantees to jointly execute, at their own expense, the works necessary to drain the flooded mines, in whole or in part, or check the progress of the inundation.

"APPLICATIONS.

"Art. 4. The party in interest must accompany his application with a sketch clearly showing the position in which his mining claims shall be surveyed, as well as their location with regard to the adjoining mining claims.

"Art. 5. Should mining claims which are the subject-matter of an application for adjudication be located within the boundary of two or more departments and extend into the latter, the application may be filed with any of the prefects having jurisdiction, and the respective publications shall be made in the two or more departments comprised in the adjudication.

"Art. 6. The grantee of surface ores who desires to work the veins of the subsoil belonging to him shall file his application in the respective prefecture, stating that he is the grantee of the soil, setting forth the titles he may have, giving the boundaries of the property, etc., and the necessary details.

"The prefect shall issue the decree of concession, and the Administrator of the Treasury shall be advised thereof for the purpose of the payment of the titles. Said decree shall be attached to the original docket, and the certified copy that the party in interest requests shall be granted.

"Art. 7. Any third party may solicit said veins, and should the grantee of the mining claim, after being notified, fail to file his application in due form within ten days, plus the term allowed because of the distance, it shall be understood that he has waived said right.

"Art. 8. Every application should be filed on two sheets of stamped paper of the value of ten Bolivianos, in order that they may be used with the decree of adjudication and cancelled thereon.

"If the petition is made on other than the proper stamped paper the prefect shall order the payment of said stamped paper, plus four times its value, in a term which shall not exceed twenty-four hours. Should the party in interest fail to make such payment his application shall be disregarded.

"Art. 9. Inasmuch as forfeiture is not produced *ipso facto*, a previous decision being necessary to declare the forfeiture, no application shall be taken into consideration for lands previously applied for, even though the first applicant may have perfected his rights, and it is presumed that said rights have been abandoned. Should there be two or more applicants for the same mining claim the one first making application for forfeiture shall be preferred, without taking into consideration that the parties who made application for lands they considered free have the right of priority.

"ART. 10. The survey, fixing of landmarks, and entry, shall be effected within seventy days from date of the first publication.

"ART. 11. In case of an opposition which shall be decided administratively or judicially, the proceedings referred to in the foregoing article shall be effected within the term of forty days from the date on which the decree ordering the execution shall have been notified to the applicant.

"ART. 12. The prefect may likewise grant a reasonable extension of time should the grantee encounter difficulties that he can not possibly overcome.

"ART. 13. The proceedings of survey and entry relating to a single mineral shall be made according to the order of priority of the applications of concession.

"The noncompliance of this strict order will only be dispensed with when the distance and isolation of the mining claims applied for do away with any fear of causing damages.

"OPPOSITIONS.

"ART. 14. When the opposition is made at the time of carrying out the survey and setting of the landmarks, the engineers or experts shall only make a provisional survey showing the location of the new application and of that alleged to have been invaded, and shall make a detailed plan of the section in litigation, which shall be attached to the proceedings.

"ART. 15. If the concession sought to be located contains a greater number of mining claims than that which is the cause of the opposition, final possession shall be given to the part in litigation, and action shall be taken in accordance with the provisions of the foregoing article with regard to that portion which is affected by the litigation.

"ART. 16. In addition to the oppositions based on priority and lack of free land, the oppositions referring to the application for ores in placers, veins, winnowing, and overflow places, the purpose of which is to locate mining claims in arable land, shall be taken into consideration.

"The oppositions to the concessions of clearings, and washings or sweepings of abandoned works and mines shall be admissible if it is alleged that the latter are now being worked or are fenced and walled.

"ART. 17. For the purposes of the oppositions the Departmental Bulletin shall be considered as a genuine document only when the concession that is sought to be protected is acted upon. If the same is consolidated and has titles, a certified copy of the same as well as the authorized plan should be attached to the docket.

"ART. 18. The opposer whose opposition is admitted shall request in writing that the proceedings be forwarded to the regular courts within the term of twenty-five days from the date of the last notification, under penalty of the opposition being declared rejected.

"ART. 19. If after the expiration of the term prescribed in the foregoing article the grantee does not allege the default of the opposer and allows the forty days fixed by article 82 to elapse, his right may be declared forfeited by any person interested in the land.

"ART. 20. The term of six months allowed him to appear before the common courts, when it has not been possible to defend the property by means of the opposition, shall not affect the adjoining mine owner, who having been mentioned in the petition was not notified for the purpose of taking possession.

"ART. 21. In the cases referred to in articles 43, 46, and 58 of the rules and regulations of October 28, 1882, the peremptory term of twenty days shall be granted should there be any evidence to produce.

"APPROVAL AND REGISTRATION.

"ART. 22. Should the prefect fail to attend the operations of survey, placing of landmarks and entry, the docket shall be forwarded to him so that he may approve the same after satisfying himself that the operations were carried out in accordance with the provisions in force and that the titles have been brought down to date.

"If the docket is in proper form, the prefect shall direct that the title to the property be issued.

"ART. 23. Said approval shall be applied for within thirty days from the date on which the proceedings took place.

"ART. 24. The prefect may officially declare the nullity of possession if from an examination of the docket it should appear that such express provisions as the failure to notify adjoining mine owners, irregularity in the survey which does not correspond to the unity and grouping of the hectares, the giving of possession without previous survey, and the like, should not have been complied with.

"ART. 25. The adjoining mine owner who is prejudiced by the survey of the new mine may also request the prefecture to annul the proceedings giving possession whenever it appears that legal requisites have been infringed and as long as the decree of approval of such proceedings has not been issued. If such decree has been issued, the adjoining mine owner shall have no other recourse than an appeal to the common courts.

"TITLES.

"ART. 26. Whenever he who exploits surface ores obtains the concession of the subsoil, he shall only pay the sum prescribed for properties located on veins.

"ART. 27. For the payment of taxes the unoccupied space up to 10,000 square meters or fraction thereof shall be considered as a complete hectare; from 10,000 to 20,000 square meters or fraction thereof, two hectares, and so on.

"FORFEITURE.

"ART. 28. An application shall be considered abandoned if the survey and setting of landmarks are not made within the seventy days prescribed by law.

"ART. 29. The foregoing article shall not apply if an extension of time has been obtained, or if an opposition to the application was made.

"ART. 30. Forfeiture will also be incurred in the proceedings whenever the mine owner does not demand the survey, setting of landmarks and entry, and allows the seventy days granted by article 10 and the forty days granted by article 11 to elapse, even though he may not have been notified of the decree of adjudication.

"ART. 31. Forfeiture is incurred only by a decree for cause issued by the prefecture that made the concession.

"ART. 32. Any person in interest may denounce the abandonment of an application and cause the forfeiture of an application to be declared.

"JURISDICTION.

"ART. 33. In accordance with the fundamental law, the Department of Industry has cognizance of the appeals of the decrees issued concerning mining matters by the departmental prefectures.

"ART. 34. The supreme decrees of July 18 and November 20, 1906 are hereby repealed."

BRAZIL.

MESSAGE OF PRESIDENT AFFONSO PENNA.

The following is a résumé of the message presented by President AFFONSO PENNA to the Brazilian Congress at its opening session, May 3, 1907:

The President began the message by reaffirming the programme which he had announced in his inaugural message of last November, and declared that a more careful examination of public affairs has but confirmed the belief which he then expressed that the country is marching steadfastly toward its great destiny. This opinion is shared by eminent foreigners who have visited the country and by others of unquestioned authority who have been watching its development for many years. The wonderful progress which has recently been made in the capital of the Republic astonishes all who visit it.

Trade statistics show that production has increased, while the situation of the Treasury, which reflects the economic condition, is satisfactory. A breath of new life is felt stirring and impelling the national organism.

The country continues to maintain friendly relations with all nations and efforts will be made to strengthen them and make them more cordial. Referring to the Third International American Conference at Rio, whose sessions extended from July 23 to August 27 of last year, it is stated that the discussions were characterized by the greatest cordiality, and thanks to the wisdom and forethought of the Delegates in excluding from the deliberations subjects which might give rise to disagreements, the conference succeeded in realizing a work rich in results and which it is hoped will be lasting. Among its important deliberations were those bearing upon the reorganization of the International Bureau of the American Republics, which is to become more and more the material expression of this sentiment of solidarity among the peoples of our continent; a convention establishing the status of naturalized citizens who again take up their residence in the country of their origin; a convention extending the Treaty on Pecuniary Claims celebrated in Mexico in 1902; a resolution creating a special section dependent upon the Bureau of American Republics, having for its object the study of the customs legislation of the Continent; a convention for the protection of intellectual and industrial property by means of international registration; the establishment at Montevidéo of a center of sanitary information that shall carry out in South America the recommendations of the International Sanitary Bureau of Washington; resolutions reaffirming the interest of the Republics in the success of the Pan-American Railway project, and recommending the study of the monetary systems in force in each of the American Republics and the fluctuations of the type of exchange which have taken place in the last twenty years. Satisfaction is expressed that the committee of jurists appointed to prepare a code of public international law and private international law will hold its first sittings at Sao Paulo. A resolution was also passed recommending the celebration of an International American Conference of the coffee-producing countries in Rio de Janeiro.

In this connection, touching on the visit of Secretary ROOT, President AFFONSO PENNA said: "It was on the occasion of the meeting of this Conference that Brazil had the pleasure of receiving a visit from the Secretary of State of the United States of America, Mr. ELIHU ROOT, the worthy colleague of the great President, THEODORE ROOSEVELT, who thus had an opportunity of seeing in the different leading cities the esteem in which he is held and the sincere friendship which the Brazilian Republic feels for her great sister of the north. This visit, which began with Brazil on such a distinguished occasion, was extended to almost all the countries of South America, and contributed greatly to the strengthening of the ties of confraternity among the nations of this part of the world."

The Government of Brazil was represented at the International Conference which was held at Geneva in June of last year, for the purpose of revising the Red Cross Convention of August 22, 1864. At this conference a convention was signed July 6, 1906, for improving the lot of the sick and wounded in the armies in campaign; both this and the 1864 convention were ratified by the Brazilian Government on December 20 last. On the same date Congress authorized the adhesion of Brazil to two of the conventions signed at the First Peace Conference of The Hague, one regulating the laws and usages of terrestrial war, the other extending to maritime war the principles of the Geneva Convention of August 22, 1864. In this connection the President stated that it is his intention to shortly send a special message to Congress asking for authority to adhere to the convention signed at The Hague July 29, 1899, for the peaceful sulotion of international conflicts. Brazil will be represented at the Second Peace Conference by Senator RUY BARBOSA and EDUARDO LISBOA.

A treaty establishing the boundary between Brazil, Colombia, and Dutch Guiana was concluded at Rio de Janeiro on May 5, 1906, and has been submitted to the Senate for its approval. A treaty of limits and navigation between Brazil and Colombia was signed at Bogota on April 24 last, which fixes the common frontier line from Cucuhy on the Negro River to the confluence of the Apaporis with the Japury, over the territory south of the Japury to the north bank of the Amazon. Questions regarding the dominion of territory are pending between Colombia, Ecuador, and Peru, and it was therefore decided to delay the negotiations relative to this part of the line until they should be decided. The Brazilian frontier in this region, from the confluence of the Apaporis to the brook Santo Antonio, near Tabatinga, has already been recognized by Peru in the treaty of Lima of October 23, 1851, and by Ecuador in the treaty of Rio de Janeiro of May 6, 1904. On the 24th of last April there was also signed at Bogota a *modus vivendi* with Peru regarding trade and navigation of the Ica River. A treaty of navigation and commerce will shortly be concluded with Ecuador. The instructions to the Brazilian and Bolivian commissions appointed under the treaty of Petropolis to establish the boundary between the two countries were signed at Rio de Janeiro in February last, and the commissions will meet before July 6, 1907. The commissions have been instructed to determine the exact location of the so-called " *Marco da cabeceira do rio Verde*," established under the treaty of March 27, 1867, to see whether it is really near this river, or whether, as some affirm, it is near an affluent of the Paragahu.

The time set for the holding of the sessions of the Brazilian-Peruvian Arbitration Tribunal, created under the agreement of July 12, 1904, has been postponed until January 25, 1908. An agreement has been made with Peru to begin on September 30, 1907, the negotiations relative to the establishment of the frontier between the source of the Javary and parallel 2° as provided for by the treaty of Petropolis. The governments of Brazil and the Argentine Republic have approved the maps presented by the Mixed Commission charged with the demarcation of the common frontier along the Uruguay, Pepiry, Guacu, Santo Antonio, and Iguau rivers, in accordance with the award of Washington of February 5, 1895. On April 13, 1907, the Brazilian Government denounced the treaty of friendship, navigation, and commerce of January 8, 1826, between Brazil and France, to take effect July 13, 1907; also the agreements existing between Brazil and Germany, Belgium, France, Spain, Italy, Portugal, and Switzerland, relating to the collection and administration of inheritances.

On December 12, 1906, a protocol was signed at Rio de Janeiro modifying the agreement of February 15, 1879, between Brazil and the Republic of Uruguay, for the purpose of facilitating the execution by the courts of one country, of the letters rogatory sent to it by the courts of the other country, both in civil and criminal matters. This protocol will become effective as soon as it has been approved by the congresses of the two countries.

Brazil was represented at the International Wireless Telegraph Conference held at Berlin in October, 1906. A convention relating to wireless telegraphy was signed at this conference, which is to be submitted to Congress for its approval.

The President called attention to the urgent need of reorganizing the Department of Foreign Relations, increasing its personnel, which is about the same as it was fifty years ago, notwithstanding the remarkable progress which has been made in political and commercial relations with other countries.

On the subject of education, the President called attention to the great need of professional and technical education and urgently recommended the reorganization of this branch of the public service.

He is of the opinion that some changes should be made in the provisional government provided for the Acre Territory, as experience has shown it to be defective. The powers of the prefects should be more clearly defined and the judicial administration reorganized. A decree of March 8, 1907, created a commission of public works for this territory, which will have charge of the work of opening up roads, removing obstructions from rivers, erecting public buildings, and establishing agricultural and professional schools.

A revision of the Commercial Code of Brazil is recommended so as to meet the needs of the commercial and industrial development.

Statistics of the foreign trade of Brazil for 1906 show that the exports were worth 799,670,295 *milreis*, or $265,000,000, while imports amounted to 499,286,976 *milreis*, or $165,000,000, showing an excess of exports over imports of 300,383,319 *milreis*, or $100,000,000. Statistics of the export trade for the first three months of the current year show a noteworthy gain over the same period of 1906.

There was a notable increase in production last year. Brazil holds the first place among the world's producers of coffee, rubber, herva-maté and cacao. There was a considerable increase in the exports of sugar, cotton, and hides. Trade statistics for 1906 show an increase of £3,374,000 in imports of raw material and manufactured articles, and a decrease of £202,640 in food products. There was an increase in exports of £8,437,000, due mainly to the greater export of coffee, herva-maté, cacao, cotton, hides, and tobacco.

Congress is urged to enact a homestead law in order to attract immigrants and establish them permanently in the country.

A geological and mineralogical service has been created for the purpose of making a study of the geological structure and mineral resources of the country. It will collect and disseminate information in regard to the mineral wealth for the purpose of promoting its development.

Regulations governing forests and waters are being prepared and will shortly be submitted to Congress for its approval.

During the year 1906, 126,683,198 pieces of mail were sent out and 245,982,419 pieces distributed, as compared with 109,109,871 pieces and 196,126,499 pieces, respectively, in 1905. There were issued 141,789 national postal drafts and 27,827 foreign drafts, amounting to over 20,000,000 *milreis*. The number of new post-offices established during the year was 127, making the total number now 2,974.

The length of the telegraph lines of the country now reaches 27,349 kilometers. A commission has been appointed to construct a telegraph line between Guyaba and Santo Antonio on the Madeira River, which is the starting point for the Madeira-Mamore Railway; branch lines will be extended from this latter point to the Acre territory.

Satisfactory progress is being made on the port improvement works at Rio de Janeiro, and it is expected that the first section of the wharf will be ready during the current year and that the entire works will be concluded by December, 1910. The plans and estimates for the port works at Bahia and Belem have been approved and work on the same will shortly be begun.

Great emphasis is laid upon the importance of developing the railways of the country. Congress is urged to make appropriations for the construction of lines connecting State railways. The branch line between Mathilde and Muniz Freire, which will connect the Leopoldina and Victoria-Minas railways, is already under way and should be finished within two years. The survey work on the branc line from Derrubadinha, on the Victoria-Minas Railway, to Sant Ignez, in Bahia, and on the line from Timbo to Propria, has bee concluded; other connecting lines between the States are bein surveyed. Progress is being made on the branch line of the Soroca bana Railway which extends to Itarare and on the section connect ing the Sao Paulo Railway with Rio Grande. The line connectin Rio Grande with Uruguayana will soon be completed. During th year under review the railways were extended 77,420 meters, th present length of the system now aggregating 1,703,714 meter against 1,626,294 meters in 1905. The receipts from freight traffi increased from 15,642,955 milreis in 1905 to 17,441,447 milreis i 1906. The number of passengers transported in 1906 was 21,077,932 as compared with 19,501,622 in 1905. Railway receipts in 190(aggregated 31,156,705 milreis, as compared with 28,641,492 milrei in 1905; expenditures amounted to 30,077,284 milreis in 1906 against 27,823,789 milreis in 1905.

The Conversion Office, created by the law of December 6, 1906 for the purpose of preventing the great fluctuations in the exchang has now been in operation several months, and the experiment thu far has been favorable to the institution. The deposits made up t the present time amount to 88,642,427 milreis.

The law of December 30, 1905, estimated the receipts for 1906 a 69,074,930 milreis gold and 223,825,000 milreis paper. The revenue actually collected during the year amounted to 88,651,568 milrei gold and 261,465,212 milreis paper, which is 19,576,637 milreis gol and 37,640,212 milreis paper in excess of the estimated receipts.

The expenditures for the fiscal year were fixed at 48,311,512 mil reis gold and 286,348,218 milreis paper. Extraordinary credits wer authorized during the year to the amount of 17,181,829 milreis gol and 110,863,720 milreis paper, making the total expenditures 66,064, 333 milreis gold and 332,405,793 milreis paper.

The revenues collected during the first three months of the cur. rent year show an increase over those for the same period of 1906 231,742,021 milreis, of which 18,139,386 milreis represent the increas in customs receipts.

In addition to the payment of bonds of the internal loan of 189 to the amount of 6,000,000 milreis, there have been redeemed sinc November, 1906, recision bonds to the amount of £238,660 o 3,818,560 milreis.

The fund for the redemption of the internal loans, paper, create by act of Congress of April 8, 1902, had on March 31 last 21,45 bonds, worth 21,441,700 milreis.

The amount of paper money in circulation on March 31 last wa 664,667,411 milreis. During the month of April paper money to th amount of 1,000,000 *milreis* was redeemed from the fund established for this purpose and burned.

The foreign debt of Brazil at the present time amounts to £69,-608,351 9s. On December 31, 1906, the paper money guaranty fund amounted to £5,015,181 1s 11d.

INTERNATIONAL COMMERCE IN 1906.

The various countries participating in Brazilian commerce during 1906 are reported as follows with respect to destination and origin of exports and imports by the " Brazilian Review " of April 30, 1907.

Total imports, exclusive of specie, were valued at £33,204,041 ($165,000,000), the percentage supplied by the United States being 11.46, while exports totaled £53,059,480 ($265,000,000), of which the United States took nearly 36 per cent.

The countries of origin for the imports were as follows, the 1905 figures being furnished for purposes of comparison:

IMPORTS.

Country.	1905.	1906.	Ratio in 1906.
Germany	£3,977,321	£4,873,140	14.676
Argentine Republic	3,511,141	3,508,922	10.567
Austria-Hungary	519,209	512,583	1.544
Belgium	1,086,772	1,286,116	3.874
Chile	41,709	44,181	.133
China	31,999	29,124	.088
Cuba	4,703	8,610	.025
Denmark	67,455	65,277	.196
United States	3,082,570	3,805,128	11.460
France	2,686,868	3,057,305	9.208
Great Britain	7,931,245	9,294,707	27.993
Greece	653	790	.002
Spain	214,518	267,596	.805
Holland	130,367	160,770	.484
Italy	993,994	1,094,826	3.297
Japan	10,016	14,281	.043
Paraguay	23,546	21,067	.063
Peru	12,061	2,681	.008
Portugal	2,183,794	2,174,690	6.552
Canada	156,205	170,530	.514
India	539,236	426,943	1.286
New Zealand	1,869	802	.002
Newfoundland	435,357	421,397	1.269
Other British colonies	20,344	23,363	.070
Russia	27,884	39,801	.120
Sweden	} 380,114 {	143,414	.432
Norway		287,950	.867
Switzerland	231,892	299,287	.902
Turkey in Asia	4,325	5,682	.017
Turkey in Europe	5,369	7,245	.022
Uruguay	1,471,428	1,114,374	3.356
Other countries	46,097	41,459	.125
Total	29,830,051	33,204,041	....

Destinations reported for exports during 1905 and 1906 were as follows:

EXPORTS.

Country.	1905.	1906.	Per cent. 1906.
Germany			
Argentine Republic			
Austria-Hungary			
Belgium			
Bolivia			
Bulgaria			
Channel (for orders)			
Chile			
China			
Cuba			
Denmark			
Egypt			
United States			
France			
Great Britain			
Greece			
Spain			
Canary Islands			
Scotland			
Italy			
Morocco			
Paraguay			
Peru			
Portugal			
Madeira Islands	14		
Barbados	12		
Canada			
Cape of Good Hope			
Gibraltar	6,763		
Hongkong	1,713		
India	1		
Malta	2,601	12,066	.023
Newfoundland		518	.001
Algiers	90,509	95,307	.180
Dahomey	386	303	
Delagoa Bay	2,208	4,796	.010
Cape de Verde	158	33	
Tunis	1,281	4,841	.010
Roumania	17,603	17,190	.032
Russia	114,545	139,024	.262
Sweden		68,902	
Norway	33,609	31,876	.060
Tripoli	250	956	.002
Asia Minor	91,867	130,686	.246
Turkey	152,763	164,286	.310
Uruguay	729,799	835,949	1.576
Total	44,643,113	53,050,490	100.000

The total tonnage for steam and sailing vessels entering Brazilian ports, in 1906, was 14,464,937 tons carried in 17,764 ships against 12,927,295 tons in 1905 and 17,072 vessels. Clearances numbered 17,770 vessels and 14,451,157 tons as compared with 17,064 vessels and 12,926,298 tons in the preceding year. Brazilian and British ships are far in excess of all others reported.

The six leading articles of export were: Coffee, £27,615,884; rubber, £14,055,911; hides, £1,953,776; herva maté, £1,856,574; cotton, £1,656,730, and cacao £1,386,441.

The United States, Germany, and France were the leading purchasers of the coffee exported, taking 317,441 tons, 176,863 tons, and 128,362 tons, respectively.

Of mangabeira rubber Germany took 256,208 kilograms, the United States 154,135 kilograms, and Great Britain 132,210 kilograms; of maniçoba rubber 1,530 tons were sent to Great Britain, 433 tons to the United States, and 375 tons to Germany, while seringa shipments were as follows: To the United States, 16,162 tons; Great Britain, 10,760 tons; France, 2,770 tons, and Germany 1,651 tons.

Tanned hides were sent to Great Britain, France, and Germany, the three leading countries, in the following quantities: 11,335 tons, 4,625 tons, and 4,221 tons, respectively, France and Germany being the leading purchasers of dry hides, taking 5,129 tons and 1,010 tons, respectively.

Cacao was exported to the United States to the amount of 8,891 tons; to Germany, 7,190 tons; to France, 5,284 tons; Great Britain, 2,020 tons, and to Holland 423 tons, other countries taking the remaining 1,324 tons out of a total of 25,135 tons shipped.

Cut tobacco was exported to the amount of 679,727 kilograms, Germany purchasing 520,243 kilograms and Great Britain 85,084 kilograms, while 22,947 tons of leaf tobacco were sent abroad. Germany taking practically the entire quantity.

Sugar exports totaled 849,963 kilograms of white sugar and 84,099 tons of other sorts, the Argentine Republic taking the bulk of the white, or 633,308 kilograms, and dividing with the United States and Great Britain the brown and other varieties.

Manufactures form the leading item on the import list, being reported for £16,426,019, or 49.5 per cent of the whole, machinery of all classes and cotton goods ranking all other articles. Great Britain and the United States are the leading competitors in imports of machinery, the first-named country occupying first place, though in one item—locomotives—there was a marked advance on the part of the United States and an equally decided decline on that of Great Britain. In cotton goods Great Britain is easily first in the market, followed by Germany, France, and the United States.

Foodstuffs and forage are quoted as worth £10,250,687, or 34.85 per cent of the whole on the import list, ranking next to machinery in value. Under this heading the leading item is covered by 122,282 tons of wheat flour from the Argentine Republic, followed by wines from Italy, codfish from Newfoundland, rice from India, and wheat flour from the United States.

Materials raw or partly prepared for use in the arts and industries form 19.23 per cent of the total imports, figuring for £6,325,800. Cotton occupies first place on this list, followed by wood and lumber in various forms and iron and steel.

PORTUGUESE ENTERPRISE IN RIO DE JANEIRO.

The permanent exposition of Portuguese products established at Rio de Janeiro under the combined commercial and Government authority of Lisbon, was opened on March 29, 1907, with considerable display, being inaugurated in Brazilian-Portuguese style with a collation, speech making, and entertainment, attended by the Minister of Fazenda and other Brazilian authorities and by a large number of representatives of Rio de Janeiro business circles.

While the exposition, even if it is a great success, is not likely to be of particular importance to American interests, since the goods presented come into competition with no articles from the United States, it is of importance as indicating what might be presented by the United States at the present time with profit, and the idea in its relation to possible trade campaigns elsewhere is worth consideration.

At present the exposition includes divisions as follows: Works of art; wines, liqueurs, champagnes, vinegars and wine products, olive oils, spirits, mineral waters, cork and cork products, dried and prepared fruits, dried vegetables, cheeses, salt, preserved meats and fish; preserved fruits, vegetables, etc.; photography, lithographing, ceramics, shoes, and miscellaneous.

In connection with the exposition of Portuguese products, attention is called to the museum established by the Academy of Commerce, an institution founded for education along business and commercial lines. The principal object of the museum is to collect samples of all native raw materials of industrial utility, which are classed methodically with information as to their place of origin, means of using them, how and where they can be obtained, and cost. It is planned to form duplicate collections of such materials and forward them for display in similar museums in foreign cities for the purpose of disseminating abroad a knowledge of Brazilian products. In connection with the museum there has been organized an information bureau for the collection and spread of commercial information, and a bulletin is to be published later in this connection.

IMMIGRATION AT RIO DE JANEIRO, 1906.

The number of immigrants entered at Rio de Janeiro in 1906 was 27,147, as follows: Portuguese, 16,795; Italians, 4,318; Spaniards, 4,074; Turks, 1,110; Germans, 225; Austrians, 101; Russians, 199; French, 105; English, 72; Americans, 29; Belgians, 15; Argentinas, 14; Swiss, 10; various, 80. This is a considerable increase over the previous year and marks a beginnning of better things in the labor line, in the estimation of Brazilian statesmen.

PROPRIETARY MEDICINES IN THE REPUBLIC.

The "Trade-mark Bulletin" reports that a statute has gone into effect in Brazil requiring that all proprietary remedies for introduction into that country be certified by a licensed druggist in the country of manufacture.

TRADE OF SANTOS, FIRST QUARTER OF 1907.

For the first three months of 1907, total imports at the port of Santos are stated as 33,358:389$ or £2,113,071, as compared with 17,646:786$ or £1,216,813 in the corresponding period of the preceding year. Exports for the quarter were 76,011:952$ or £4,821,956 as against 42,180:150$ or £2,852,444 in the first three months of 1906. The trade of the port is thus seen to have practically doubled in the year.

Great Britain, Germany, the Argentine Republic, and the United States furnished the bulk of the imports, in the order named, though Great Britain is far in advance of her competitors. On the other hand, the United States leads as a receiver of exports, followed by Germany, France, Great Britain, and Holland.

Coffee, hides, rubber, and bran were the four leading items of export, the quantity of coffee exported amounting to 2,415,374 bags, as compared with 1,405,027 bags in the first three months of 1906.

RUBBER EXPORTS, FIRST QUARTER OF 1907.

Shipments of rubber from Amazonas and Para, during the first three months of 1907, are valued at £5,148,282 as compared with £5,290,489 in the corresponding period of 1906.

COFFEE MOVEMENT, MARCH, 1907.

[*Boletim da Associação Commercial* of April 9, 1907.]

The coffee movement at the ports of Rio de Janeiro and Santos, for the month of March, 1907, compared with that of the same month of the previous year, was as follows:

	Rio de Janeiro.		Santos.	
	1907.	1906.	1907.	1906.
	Bags.	*Bags.*	*Bags.*	*Bags.*
Entries................................	382,421	128,784	894,151	222,000
Shipments.............................	165,547	201,672	925,943	306,230
Sales.................................	271,000	103,000	1,026,027	287,548
Daily average of entries.............	11,368	4,153	28,843	7,483
Daily average of shipments...........	5,893	....	29,809	16,330
Entries from July 1..................	3,420,013	2,498,556	12,685,392	6,300,799
Stock on hand Mar. 30	740,749	72,351	2,694,780	665,902

SHIPMENTS OF CARBONS.

Carbon exporters in Brazil pay a tax for doing business as follows: Firms exporting up to $150,000 annually, $1,500; exporting above $150,000, $3,000. In addition to this tax there is an export duty of 7 per cent *ad valorem.*

There are no companies engaged in mining or searching for carbons, that work being done by the natives, individually, or in small parties working together. Prices are not controlled by any trust, but are governed by supply and demand and are subject to frequent changes. The carbon region begins about 267 miles from Bahia, and can be reached in four days, viz: Bahia to Cachoera, 45 miles by water, one day; Cachoera to Bandeira de Mello, 158 miles by rail, one day; thence to Andarahy, 64 miles, on mule back, two days.

EXPORTS FROM PERNAMBUCO, MARCH, 1907.

The *Boletim Mensal* of the Commercial Association of Pernambuco publishes the following statistics of the export movement at that port for the month of March, 1907:

Carnauba wax .... bags..	1,422	Oil.................... boxes..	1,338
Mandioca flour.......... do....	8,160	Do.............. barrels..	865
Rubber..............barrels..	19	Sugar.................. kilos..	7,104,218
Do.................bales..	13	Cotton................do....	8,221,175
Textiles................. do....	899	Rum.................. pipes..	1,260
Corn.....................bags..	13,269	Alcohol................ do....	348
Skins...................bales..	138	Honey................. do....	9
Castor-oil seed...........bags..	359	Hides................bales..	681
Coffee................. do....	970	Cotton seed.......... kilos..	12,681
Soap.................boxes..	5,280		

FIBER CONCESSIONS AND INDUSTRIES.

The "Brazilian Review" states that a contract has been signed by the government of the State of Minas Geraes with the Empire Fiber Company of North America, whose capital is $350,000, for the planting and exploitation of pita and rice by American methods. The government grants the land, while the company establishes a school where ten pupils are to be taught each year the technicalities of the business. If within four years 1,000,000 plants of pita are not growing or if within one year machinery has not been installed for the preparation of the products, the land will revert to the State, with all improvements made, without the government having to pay any indemnity.

It is reported that the two Perini fiber plantations in the State of Rio de Janeiro produced in March 200 tons of fiber and 750 tons of cellulose. English firms have offered Doctor PERINI £40 per ton for all the fiber he is able to furnish and £12 per ton for the cellulose. The Perini plant is capable of yielding three crops per year.

CHILE.

CUSTOMS RECEIPTS, FIRST QUARTER, 1907.

Customs receipts at the ports of the Chilean Republic during the first quarter of 1907 show import duties worth 12,679,442 *pesos* 9 *centavos*, and export duties for 13,607,742 *pesos* 82 *centavos*, while from other branches of the service the receipts were 608,597 *pesos* 28 *centavos*, as compared with the corresponding period of the preceding year, when 9,883,850 *pesos* 44 *centavos* were recorded for imports duties; 13,874,104 *pesos* 26 *centavos* for exports and 507,316 *pesos* 76 *centavos* for other services of the customs, an increase as regards imports of 2,795,591 *pesos* 65 *centavos* is noted; export values declined in the sum of 266,361 *pesos* 44 *centavos*, and other branches of the service show an advance of 101,280 *pesos* 52 *centavos*.

In the aggregate, the receipts for the months of January, February, and March, 1907, show a net increase of 2,630,310 *pesos* 73 *centavos* over the same months of 1906.

FINANCIAL STATUS OF THE COUNTRY.

El Boletín de la Sociedad de Fomento Fabril, of Santiago, Chile, publishes in its issue for April, 1907, the text of a statement sent to the Department of the Interior by the Chilean Bureau of Statistics concerning the financial status of the Republic.

According to the statement referred to, the tax rate paid by each inhabitant during the five years from 1901 to 1905 was as follows: 1901, $11.59; 1902, $11.56; 1903, $11.85; 1904, $11.93; 1905, $11.82; annual average during the period of five years, $11.75. In this calculation, the revenues from Government railroads and posts and telegraphs have not been taken into consideration, as the same are public utilities and not taxes. The duties on nitrate and iodine have also been omitted, as they affect only a very limited number of individuals.

Referring to the tax-paying capacity of the country, the Bureau of Statistics says that the annual tax of $11.75 could easily be increased to a double amount, $23.50, a tax which, compared with those paid in other countries, is not very high. In France each inhabitant pays $36; in Great Britain, $29.66; in Holland, $23.17; in Italy, $23; in Austria, $21.78; in Denmark, $19.78, etc.

In 1897, the total value of property subject to taxation was $1,400,084,362; and in 1904, $1,512,591,127, an increase of $112,507,766.

The bank deposits in 1901, amounted to $121,162,288 and in 1903 to $314,240,435, an increase of $193,078,147, or 159 per cent.

In 1901, stock companies were incorporated to the amount of £475,000; and in 1905, to that of £5,741,240, an increase of 859 per cent.

The number of industrial establishments in 1901, was 7,315; and in 1905, 10,152, an increase of 2,837, equal to 38 per cent. In 1901, there were 32,944 commercial establishments; and in 1905, 35,018, an increase of 2,074, or 6 per cent.

SURVEY OF THE LONGITUDINAL RAILWAY.

By virtue of a presidential decree, dated April 16, 1907, the Chilean Government has accepted the bid presented by the *Société d' Études de Construction et d' Exploitation de Chemins de Fer au Chili* to carry out, for the amount of 400,000 gold *pesos* of 18 shillings, the survey of the Longitudinal Railway between Ligua and Copiapo, for the alteration of the sections of said railway operated at present and situated between the same points, for the connection of the railroad from San Marcos to Paloma with the line from Ovalle to Serena, and for the survey of the branch line from Ligua to Papudo. The payment of the cost of these surveys shall be made only in case the Government should reject the bid which the company may afterwards submit for the construction and exploitation of the line in question.

THE NITRATE INDUSTRY.

The figures given below, taken from the last report presented by the manager of the Association for Nitrate Propaganda, show that the condition of the nitrate industry in Chile is not only very satisfactory but that it also enjoys a rapidly increasing prosperity due mainly to the steady growth of the world's consumption of this valuable fertilizer.

The principal source of revenue of the Republic is the export duty on nitrate, which is about $1.22 gold per *quintal*. From 1880 (the year in which this tax was established) to December 31, 1905, the collections amounted to $273,000,000 gold, approximately. It is reported that a large corporation of capitalists contemplates purchasing a portion of the Government nitrate lands for the price of $73,050,000 gold.

The commercial year for nitrate transactions commences on March 1 of each year and ends on April 30 of the following. During the nitrate years 1904-5 and 1905-6, the production, exportation, and consumption of nitrate were as follows:

	1904-5.	1905-6.
	Quintales.	*Quintales.*
Production	36,661,125	37,810,552
Exportation	34,200,521	36,223,721
Consumption	33,798,013	36,393,078

A comparison of the above figures shows an increase in favor of 1905-6 as follows: Production, 1,149,427 *quintales;* exportation, 2,033,200 *quintales;* consumption, 2,595,065 *quintales.*

During the first half of 1906, the production amounted to 18,252,411 *quintales,* the exportation to 15,656,259 *quintales,* and the consumption to 25,510,285 *quintales.* In the same period of 1905 these items were represented by 18,324,399, 15,242,870, and 24,048,106 *quintales*, respectively. The increase in the first six months of 1906 is, therefore, of 71,988 *quintales* in production, of 413,389 *quintales* in exportation, and of 1,462,179 *quintales* in consumption.

On August 25, 1906, there were 113 plants, with an estimated output of 58,019,000 *quintales*. In 1900 there were 74, with an estimated output of 30,393,000 *quintales*.

TREATY OF FRIENDSHIP, COMMERCE AND NAVIGATION WITH JAPAN.

Under date of May 24, 1907, the International Bureau of the American Republics was informed through the Department of State of the United States of the official promulgation by the Government of Chile, on March 31, 1907, of a treaty of friendship, commerce and navigation between that Government and Japan. The signing of the treaty in reference was carried out in Washington on September 25, 1897, by Señor DOMINGO GANA, at that time Minister from Chile to the United States, and JUSHU TORUHOSHI, Japanese Minister to the United States, the protocol explaining the most-favored-nation clause being executed on the same date, with indorsement at Tokyo October 16, 1899.

PRODUCTION AND CONSUMPTION OF SUGAR IN 1906.

From data furnished by the managers of the sugar factories at Viña del Mar, Penco, and Membrillo, the Bureau of Statistics of Chile has issued tables showing the production and consumption of sugar in the Republic in 1906.

The factory at Viña del Mar produced, during 1906, 19,922,268 kilograms of sugar, as against 22,607,055 kilograms in 1905. With the exception of 800,000 kilograms, more or less, that were kept at the factory, the whole product was consumed in the Republic.

The production of the factory at Penco during 1906 was 18,652,208 kilograms, as compared with 12,404,812 kilograms in 1905. The sales of this factory were 17,368,515 kilograms in 1906 and 13,575,307 in 1905.

The market product, in 1906, of these two factories amounted to 36,890,783 kilograms; adding to this sum the 934,470 kilograms of refined sugar imported in 1905, the total consumption in the Republic during 1906 reached the amount of 37,825,253 kilograms, which, in a population estimated at 4,000,000, shows a consumption of 9½ kilograms, or 20½ pounds, *per capita*. "Mulhall's Statistical Dictionary" gives the following *per capita* sugar consumption of various countries: Great Britain, 69 pounds; France, 23 pounds; Germany, 15 pounds; Austria, 13 pounds; Russia, 8 pounds; Sweden, 18 pounds; Norway, 11 pounds; Holland, 29 pounds; Belgium, 16 pounds; Denmark, 30 pounds; Switzerland, 23 pounds; Italy, 7 pounds; Spain, 6 pounds.

In regard to the factory at Membrillo, its manager has made the following estimates as to its probable production in the years specified: 1908, 45,050 tons; 1909, 39,300 tons; 1910, 71,950 tons.

COLOMBIA.

MESSAGE OF PRESIDENT REYES.

The President of the Republic, Gen. RAFAEL REYES, on April 1, 1907, submitted to the National Assembly his annual message, accompanied by brief reports from the several Cabinet ministers. After congratulating the country on the state of peace and prosperity enjoyed for several years, General Reyes says:

"Our international relations have been cultivated and maintained on a footing of cordiality and correctness, toward which effective help has been given by the honorable diplomatic body at this capital and by our representatives abroad, where it is considered that Colombia has definitively come out from the era of civil wars, through which every country in the world has passed, and that she has now entered upon peace and progress.   *   *   *

"The acute economic crisis which has weighed down the nation since the termination of the late civil war, as a result of the excessive emission of paper money, is still sharp.   The Government, in order to relieve the situation, has applied the greater part of the public revenue so as to recover firmly the credit of the country abroad and by this means to attract foreign capital for the construction of railways and for other industries.   In the interior of the country the Government has given its attention to the improvement of lines of communication, converting mule tracks into cart roads, repairing these and opening new ones.   In this manner the public taxes have been given a reproductive and fruitful employment, which has controlled, in part, the bad economic situation, and will finally control it entirely.

"We have kept to the level of our estimates, and every day the organization of our finances and the regular administration of our public taxes is improving, to the point where we can say that these are properly managed.

"The harvests were abundant last year and promise to be so this year, which will keep the mass of the population from suffering for a lack of provisions.

"Since your last sessions the Assembly has increased the number of its members by twenty-one deputies, corresponding to the six new departments which have been formed, and to the federal district. In this assembly all the different political groups of the country are worthily represented by the most distinguished men of Colombia.

"I have spoken incidentally of the political composition of the National Assembly, but only to give evidence of its representative elements; however, your labors will not be of a political character, as the nation has no problems of that kind pending, and as the actual institutions are accepted by all the political parties, the political labors of these parties will remain for the future, as they already are, in the fruitful field of the Administration, in which all can work for the good of the country; and this will be the principal object of the political groups: they will either change into coincident forces for doing good or they will have to disappear, for the nation can no longer tolerate within its strong organism any disrupting and opposing forces to its progress and well-being under the name of political entities. It is pleasing to me to recognize in you all the patriotic and open spirit required to accept with loyalty and frankness the postulate concerning the mission of political parties which is to-day dominant in all Colombians of good will."

REPORT OF THE MINISTER OF THE INTERIOR.

Señor Don EUCLIDES DE ANGULO, the Minister of the Interior, in his report to the National Assembly, accompanying the message of President REYES, says:

"The failure constantly observed by the authorities of the representatives of some foreign companies domiciled abroad, and who transact business in the Republic, to appear before the magistrates or civil officers of the Government as plaintiffs or defendants, in accordance with our laws, is notorious. In fact, said companies generally have attorneys who represent them, and whenever it is necessary for them to demand the compliance of some obligation from private or juridical persons of the country, they have availed themselves of their powers of attorney and have carried on the proper proceedings to a final result, but whenever the companies themselves have been required to fulfill their own obligations the attorneys have refused to exercise the powers conferred on them, thus excluding from international jurisdiction the legal entity they represent, in order to compel their opponents either to waive their rights or to appear before foreign courts in case it was necessary to exercise them before the latter. Therefore the result has been that, on the one hand, the right of the natives was left in an undecided and inefficient state, while, on the other hand, foreigners have enjoyed all advantages in order to make effective their rights. This difficulty has been overcome by following the modern practice of nations by the issuance of legislative decrees Nos. 2 and 37 of 1906.

"The Government has kept these provisions in force, which are found in the laws of all civilized countries, because it is believed that by so doing it was rendering a tutelary service to the natives and was establishing clear rules for the exercise of the same rights of foreigners doing business in Colombia.

"Many petitions for the repeal of decrees Nos. 2 and 37 had to be rejected, and it should be added that many of said petitions, which were supported by native lawyers, aimed at the elimination of wise provisions, the object of which was to establish, with absolute clearness, the judicial status of foreign companies, and to avoid the disregard, always to be deplored, of the rights of native citizens.

"To further develop legislative decrees Nos. 2 and 37, of 1906, the Government, at the request of the parties in interest, has made several explanatory decisions, the last of which is dated February 22, and was rendered in connection with the petition made by the German subject, CARLOS ARNTZ, and published in No. 12901 of the *Diario Oficial.* There is maintained therein a sound doctrine juridically adapted to our positive law, and the Government should continue along this line, because it is the legal way, and because it is necessary to stop the old tendency to speculate with the condition of internal disorders in matters so delicate as those I have just referred to.

*　　*　　*　　*　　*　　*　　*

"The limited companies established in accordance with the provisions of the Commercial and Civil Codes, are juridical persons by virtue of the law, and do not for their existence need authorization by the Executive, as formerly provided in article 553 of the first-mentioned Code, inasmuch as said article was repealed by law 27 of 1888, this construction having served to reject, in several instances, the petitions made to the Department for the aforesaid purpose.

*　　*　　*　　*　　*　　*　　*

"The Post and Telegraph report covers the period from April, 1904, when the former report was made, to the present time. The Department of Posts has operated regularly after the reorganization made in 1905, in accordance with Executive decrees 317 and 562 of said year. In conformity with that reorganization the Department of Posts has fifteen divisions in the capital of the Republic.

*　　*　　*　　*　　*　　*　　*

"The routes existing when the previous report was made have been increased by four new ones, namely: One from Manizales to Carmen de Atrato; one from Anserma to Istmina; one from Bogota to Agua de Dios, and, lastly, one for the Atlantic, from Bogota via Girardot to Barranquilla.

"The establishment of a confidential agency in Panama for the purpose of receiving and dispatching the mails for the Departments of Cauca and Nariño in the southern part of the Republic, and those sent abroad from the latter places, has also given satisfactory results.

*	*	*	*	*	*	*

"In 1905, there were handled 659,416 prepaid letters, representing a value in stamps of $182,772.21, and 369,879 official communications; in 1906, the pieces of paid mail matter numbered 386,280, representing a postage value of $101,460.57, while the official communications handled numbered 207,677 pieces."

REPORT OF THE MINISTER OF FOREIGN AFFAIRS.

Señor Don A. Vasquez Cobo, the Minister for Foreign Affairs, in his report to the National Assembly accompanying the message of President Reyes, says:

" When our Plenipotentiary at Rio de Janeiro communicated to us the desire of Mr. Root, Secretary of State, to go to the port of Cartagena to make a visit to Colombia as the termination of his trip through South America, the Government prepared to receive that eminent statesman in a manner worthy of him and of the traditions of hospitality and courtesy for which the Republic is noted. The undersigned received from his Excellency the President the pleasing order to go to Cartagena, which he did, to await the arrival of the distinguished guest. Mr. Root arrived at that city on September 24 of last year, and was the object of the usual courtesies. On welcoming Mr. Root in the name of the Republic and of His Excellency the President, I said to him, among other things: 'We receive you as the herald of peace, of justice, and of concord.' Mr. Root, in answer to my remarks, expressed the 'sincere desire that all questions which exist between the United States of Colombia and the United States of America may be settled peacefully, in the spirit of friendship, of mutual esteem, and with honor for both countries.'

"This frank and amicable declaration, as well as the other remarks made by the distinguished Secretary of State in honor of Colombia and its illustrious Chief, inclined the Government to a further continuation of the negotiations begun in Washington by Minister Mendoza Pérez. In order to carry these negotiations to a happy termination, Dr. Enrique Cortés, a citizen who, because of his learning, tact, and long residence in European countries, seemed best fitted to continue this mission, was appointed to take the place of Dr. Mendoza Pérez.

"Mr. Cortés proceeded to Washington and began his duties in accordance with the instructions given him by this Chancellery. In order to obtain the best results in this delicate matter, the Government decided to appoint as the advisers of the legation, Messrs. José María Pasos, Gabriel O'Byrne, and Antonio R. Blanco.

"The negotiations have been conducted in a satisfactory manner, and the Government entertains the hope that it may soon be able to announce the celebration of an agreement suitable to the honor and interests of the nation. It would be a cause of special satisfaction to me if such agreement could be concluded before the termination of your labors, in order that you may take it into consideration.

"I should mention that the distinguished diplomat, Hon. John Barrett, a loyal friend of Colombia and who took upon himself a journey through our Department with fruitful results to the country, has contributed in a large measure, with intelligence and tact, toward the good feeling existing between Colombia and the United States."

PATENTS AND TRADE-MARKS IN 1906.

According to the official publication of the Colombian Department of Public Works and Improvements, 39 patents of invention were issued, and 61 trade-marks registered, during the calendar year 1906.

TRADE OF BARRANQUILLA, 1906.

Of the foreign commerce of Colombia, amounting to some $23,000,000 per annum, 65 per cent is conducted through the port of Barranquilla.

The total foreign trade of the port amounted to $16,030,100 during the year 1906, an increase of $882,955 over the year 1905. There was a decrease in the imports of $493,826 and an increase in exports of $1,376,779, showing a balance of trade in favor of the port of $2,456,000, an increase of $1,870,604 over the balance of the preceding year.

The following statement shows the value of imports through Barranquilla during the year 1906, as per countries of origin: United Kingdom, $2,706,252; United States, $1,217,777; Germany, $1,127,520; France, $1,109,686; Spain, $208,047; all other countries, $367,773; total, $6,787,055; total in 1905, $7,280,879; decrease, $493,824. The duties levied on the foregoing imports for the year 1906 amounted to $4,333,028, an average of 64 per cent ad valorem, and an increase of $228,849 over the year 1905. There was an unusual amount of railroad material imported from the United Kingdom during the year, which contributed largely in obtaining for that Kingdom the first rank among the purveyors to Colombia. On the other hand, as previously reported, the imports of flour have practically ceased on account of the prohibitive duties imposed at the beginning of the year, which fact has solely affected American exporters, and caused our percentage to fall much below our usual share. Of the total exports, the United States took 51 per cent; the United Kingdom, 20 per cent; Germany, 17 per cent; France, 5 per cent; Spain, 1 per cent, and other countries 6 per cent. .

The port proper is Savanilla, also known as Puerto Colombia, but Barranquilla is the official port, wherein the custom-house, warehouses, ships' agencies, and commercial institutions are located. Barranquilla, which has a population of 50,000, is situated on the western bank of the Magdalena River, 17 miles from the Atlantic coast, to which it is connected by a railway owned by English interests. It is the capital of the new department called El Departamento del Atlantico, and is a thriving city, having more than quadrupled its population during the last three decades. While Barranquilla can boast of many flourishing industries, such as the brick (sand-lime and clay), tile, mosaic, cotton ginning, shoe, candle, soap, soda water, beer, ice, lumber, flour milling, cotton manufacture, etc., it is essentially a commercial city, being by far the greatest port in the country, and the main distributing point for the large cities of the interior, such as Bogota, Medellin, Bucaramanga, etc. Three banks—The Banco Central, Banco del Atlantico, and Banco de Barranquilla—are established here, and about 40 large business houses, making a general import, export, and wholesale trade, besides some 200 retailers in the various lines, and varying in importance from the little corner shop to the good sized general merchandise store.

During the calendar year 1906, 326 steamers visited Savanilla, with a total registered tonnage of 691,004 tons, an increase of 150,677 tons as compared with 1905. Of the ship tonnage, 274,141 was German, 245,170 was English, 99,274 was Spanish, and 25,985 was Italian. One fact to be deplored is that not even an American sailing vessel has visited the port during the year. The consular records here show that the last American vessel that called at Savanilla was on April 22, 1903—the American bark *John Stanhope*. Not one ton of American freight to Colombia is carried in American bottoms at present.

The service between the United States and Barranquilla (Savanilla) is as follows: Atlas service of the Hamburg-American Line (German), weekly—New York sailings every Saturday for Savanilla, via Jamaica, trip eight and one-half days, fare $60, about 2,000 miles; Savanilla sailings every Tuesday for New York, via Cartagena, Port Limon, and Jamaica, trip fourteen days; Royal Mail Steam Packet Company (English), semimonthly to New York, via Colon and Jamaica, and vice versa, trip nine days, fare $60; The Leyland and Harrison Line (Liverpool), thrice a month to New Orleans, via Colon and Kingston, trip ten days.

In the European service the Hamburg-American Line (German) has three sailings a month; Royal Mail Steam Packet Company

(English), two sailings a month; Compagnie Générale Transatlantique, (French), two sailings a month; Compañia Transatlantica de Barcelona (Spanish), one sailing a month; Compagnia Italiana de Navigacione (Italian), one sailing a month. The trip to European ports via Venezuela and the West Indies occupies about twenty days. The average freight rate to New York per ton is $9; to European ports, $15.

RIGHTS AND OBLIGATIONS OF FOREIGNERS.

The American Consulate-General at Bogota, Colombia, furnishes the following information for foreigners who intend to enter the Republic of Colombia:

Although each foreigner entering Colombia is requested to present a viséed passport, if one arrives without a pass he may gain entrance to the country by addressing himself to his resident Consul, the collector of customs, and captain of the port.

No invoice is required for or duty collected upon personal baggage, if it does not exceed 330.69 pounds in weight, and is accompanied by the owner, and is consistent with his station in life.

Foreigners coming to Colombia, however will avoid much annoyance, expense, and delay if they provide themselves with properly viséed passports, also with a consular invoice to cover their baggage if it exceeds limitation. Baggage that is in excess and not covered by a consular invoice or that is not accompanied by the owner is assessed duty at the highest rate in the tariff ($1.50 per kilo of 2.20 pounds) and 70 per cent per kilo additional. The penalty for the absence of the invoice is 10 per cent and 5 per cent for making the inventory.

Excess baggage accompanied by the owner and by a consular invoice is assessed duty at the tariff rate of the merchandise of which it may consist.

Invoice fees.—The minimum charge for a Colombian consular invoice is $18 on goods not exceeding $200 in value, and the maximum fee is $30 for each $1,000 or additional fraction of $1,000.

Transportation, etc.—At present and until transportation facilities are much changed and improved all perishable goods destined for the interior of the country should be so packed as to exclude moisture and in packages not exceeding 125 pounds in weight for transportation on mule back, peons, or in canoes.

All merchandise that is transported via the Magdalena River is subject to 100° F. for a period of about ten days. Merchandise, such as photographic films, pharmaceutical preparations, etc., are often ruined through insufficient care in packing. Goods destined for the interior are exposed to the downpour of the tropical rains and may accidentally be submerged in crossing mountain streams or in careless handling in canoes. Goods may now be sent from the Magdalena River to Bogotá by the Cambao cart road, but even by this route there is no assurance of their exemption from damage by water.

IMPROVEMENTS AT CARTAGENA.

The Cartagena Water Works Company (Limited), of London, has completed its pipe lines from the springs of Turbaco to Cartagena and will soon be ready to furnish residences, etc., with a good supply of spring water. The Government palace, which covers an entire block, has been beautified and enlarged by the adding of one story and by remodeling and adorning its many rooms. The municipal electric-light plant has in use new machinery, dynamos, etc., recently received from the United States, England, and Germany, and is producing very satisfactory light for the residences and streets of the city. The light given by a small bulb costs the purchaser $1.50 gold per month.

It is estimated that the new sugar refinery and cane plantation to be put in operation near Cartagena will cost $800,000 gold. A building and loan association, the first one in Cartagena, has been organized by a citizen of the United States.

DEVELOPMENT OF COMMUNICATION FACILITIES.

The Colombian Minister of Public Works and Promotion, in his annual report to the National Assembly, presented on April 1, 1907, gives a detailed account of the plan adopted by the Government for the improvement of the railroad system of the Republic. Besides utilizing many of the lines under construction, or for which contracts have been entered into, this design when carried out will establish close communication among the Departments of Cauca, Caldas, Antioquia, Cundinamarca, the Capital District, Quesada, Boyaca, Tundama, Galán, and Santander; and the extension of the system throughout the Magdalena and toward the Atlantic coast will include the Departments of Atlantico, Bolivar, and Magdalena. It is purposed to consolidate into a single line several of the railroads now under process of construction, thus: From Buenaventura, on the Pacific, to Cali; thence to Medellin, taking a northerly direction, passing through the principal cities on the Cauca River, and proceeding along the course of this river through Caldas and Antioquia; at Medellin it will connect with the railroad that is being built from Puerto Berrio, on the Magdalena River; from this port, in a southerly direction and proceeding along the left bank of the Magdalena River, to La Maria on La Dorada Railroad, which is being extended to Ambalema; a branch line will connect the latter point with the Tocaima station on the Girardot Railroad, which will ascend to Sabana to join at Facatativa with the line connecting the latter with Bogotá;

thence, by means of the Northern Railroad and its extension to Chiquinquira, now under construction, and the line terminating through Bucaramanga at a point near Puerto Wilches, the lower section of the Magdalena River will be reached, whence this stream is navigable at all times. Besides, a line passing through Quindio will establish direct communication between Cartago and Girardot, and another one will be laid out from Medellin to the Gulf of Uraba.

From January, 1906, to April, 1907, extensions have been made in the railroad system of the Republic as follows: Southern Railroad, 2 kilometers, 510 meters, and 40 centimeters; Antioquia Railroad, 19 kilometers, 339 meters, and 15 centimeters; Santa Marta Railroad, 8 kilometers; Tolima Railroad, 5 kilometers; Girardot Railroad, 4 kilometers, and about 40 more that will soon be opened to traffic; Northern Railroad (Zipaquira to Nemecon), 15 kilometers, and La Dorada Railroad (extension), 23 kilometers.

United States Consul-General JAY WHITE, of Bogota, transmits the following report on the construction of railways in Colombia:

"The Girardot Railway has 80 miles under operation and 205 miles contemplated or under construction. The road runs from Girardot on the Magdalena River through Hospicio, and is to connect with the Sabana Railway at Facativa, a distance of 80 miles, and is to be completed January 1, 1908. The Antioquia Railway when finished will consist of the extension of the road from Puerto Berrio to Medellin, 78 miles. The construction of a line is contemplated to join the Dorada Railway with the "Puerto Berrio and Medellin Railway" at Providencia, 75 miles, and the extension of the line from Puerto Berrio to Barranca Bermeja, 50 miles.

"Other engineering works contemplated or in course of construction in Colombia are: The extension of the Dorada Railway from Honda to Ambalema, 66 miles; the Buenaventura Railway, to Buga, and the Cambao wagon road, from Facativa to Cambao, on the upper Magdalena River, 75 miles. Some material is on the ground for the construction of the railway from the Ciudad Reyes, on the Gulf of Darien, to Medellin. A concession has also been granted for the extension of the Northern Railway, from Bogota-Zipaquira to Chiquinquira, 40 miles.

"It is proposed to install a new sewer and water system in the city of Bogota, relay pavements, build new hospitals, public schools, abattoirs, markets, and 2,000 workingmen's model houses. The municipal improvements also contemplate the conversion of the present horse-car service into an electrical line. All the foregoing work is reported to be under the control of English concessionaires, with the exception of the Buenaventura and Colombian Central railways and the Bogota Street Railway, which are controlled by American capital."

The *Diario Oficial* of March 15, 1907, publishes the text of the contract of February 1, 1907, approved by President REYES on February 4, between the Government and Mr. THOMAS GERMAN RIBON for the construction of the Tundama Railroad.

The Government grants to Mr. RIBON the exclusive right of construction and exploitation of a railroad from Nemocon in the Department of Quesada to Santa Rosa de Viterbo in the Department of Tundama, with a branch line from between these two points to Sogamoso.

A subsidy of $9,990 gold per kilometer constructed and put into service is granted by the Government to be paid in Government 6 per cent bonds. In addition, a grant of 300 hectares of public lands per kilometer of road constructed is made.

The *Diario Oficial* of March 9, 1907, publishes the text of the contract of February 20, approved by President REYES February 25, 1907, between the Government and Señor CAMILO CARRIZOSA, and Señor JORGE VÉLEZ for the establishment of a line of steam navigation on the upper Magdalena between the river ports of Girardot and Arraucaplumas. The contract calls for forty-eight round trips a year and for stops at Upito, Guataque, Iguanime, Ambalema, and Cambos.

COMMERCIAL STATUS OF SANTA MARTA.

The value of the articles declared at Santa Marta for export to the United States during the calendar year 1906 amounted to $534,942, consisting of the following items: Alligator skins, $10,674; bananas, $498,142; cacao, $491; coffee, $4,541; copper (old), $2,927; goatskins, $4,148; hides, $13,999; and logwood, $20.

Santa Marta is at present the only Colombian port exporting bananas, sending its entire output to the United States. The industry has developed wonderfully, and although yet in its infancy it is by far the greatest industry in the district, the output having increased from 171,891 bunches in 1892, the first year of any recorded export, to 1,397,388 bunches in 1906.

The present acreage devoted to bananas is about 7,000 acres, of which an American corporation owns 25 per cent, the balance belonging to individuals. All the fruit is purchased and exported by the American company, and the following prices per first-class bunch (nine hands or up) are paid the growers: From the months of August to January, inclusive, 15 cents; in February, 20 cents; in March, 25 cents; April, May, and June, 35 cents; July, 25 cents; or an average price the year around of 22.5 cents. It is believed that the general output will be increased 25 per cent during the year 1907.

The Santa Marta Railway, with an actual mileage of 93 miles, has its lines now to Fundacion and is gradually extending across the banana belt toward the Magdalena River as fast as the lands are taken up and cultivated and expects to reach the river at a point called Tenerife in a couple of years. Santa Marta may then prove to be a serious competitor with the ports of Barranquilla and Cartagena for the foreign traffic of the country, having the advantage of a deep and well-protected harbor, more accessible than either of the other two, and of a quicker ocean service, made necessary on account of the transportation of fruit.

Santa Marta can also boast of being the only district in the country where at present coffee can be grown and exported at a profit, since it has no river transportation to pay. The total amount of banana land conveniently situated for irrigation in the whole district of Santa Marta, including Rio Frio and Fundacion, might possibly reach 50,000 acres, now awaiting transportation facilities before development.

COSTA RICA.

MESSAGE OF PRESIDENT CLETO GONZÁLEZ VÍQUEZ.

President CLETO GONZÁLEZ VÍQUEZ addressed, on May 1, 1907, an important message to the Costa Rican Congress, covering the following information:

"In March, 1905, a statement relating to the award on boundaries, a treaty modifying the frontier between both countries, and a convention on landmarks were signed in Panama by the Plenipotentiary of Costa Rica, Mr. LEONIDAS PACHECO, and General SANTIAGO DE LA GUARDIA, who was then Minister of Foreign Relations of the aforesaid Republic. The Panama Assembly has already approved these three conventions, except the one relating to boundaries, in which some substantial changes were made. These agreements now only lack the consideration of the Costa Rican Congress and its decision as to whether they are acceptable to us with the changes made therein.

*   *   *   *   *   *   *

"The means of communication have been and shall continue to be the object of special attention by my Administration. Without that most essential factor agriculture would be handicapped, inasmuch as the high price of transportation takes from the agriculturist what would constitute his legitimate profit, and, anticipating a loss, his enthusiasm and energy will necessarily be weakened. The lack of roads also necessarily results in the high price of provisions and affects considerably the welfare of the poorer classes, whose cost of living does not bear any proportion to the rate of wages.

*   *   *   *   *   *   *

"On the other hand, the lands of the Central Plateau are commencing to show signs of exhaustion, and therefore it is indispensable to open and establish roads that shall give easy access to the fertile and almost virgin regions of the northern and southern parts of the Republic. The inhabitants of the old lands would settle and cultivate the new ones if the opportunity of transporting their products to central markets at a rate which would leave a profit were given them. In accordance with these veiws, the construction of a road to General is under consideration, and the Government expects within a short time to begin work to that end. These improvements, to which it is proposed to add a telegraph line, will attract to that privileged zone the people south of San José and some from the Cartago district, who at present justly complain of the meager yield of their lands.

"There is no doubt that incalculable advantages would be derived by putting the high plateau where we live in communication with the plains of San Carlos, Sarapaqui, and Santa Clara. The construction of a railroad at least as far as Sarapaqui becomes easier every day because of the progress which the Costa Rica Railroad is making in that direction. In order to carry out the negotiations pending between the Government and the Northern Railway and the United Fruit Company, the Government has stipulated as a condition of settlement that the aforesaid section of the railroad shall be constructed.

* * * * *

"The construction of the railroad to Puntarenas has continued without interruption, notwithstanding the fact that the amount of the loan negotiated had been exhausted. The amount required to complete this work—which amount will continue to be an incumbrance to the State until said work is finished—is more than three million *colones*. The plan of negotiating an internal loan for the purpose of securing funds, should, in my opinion, be abandoned, because it is impossible to raise such funds here on easy installments without positive injury to commerce and agriculture.

* * * * * * *

"The customs receipts, estimated at 4,200,000 *colones*, for the fiscal year 1906 rose to 4,346,977.49 *colones*, an amount larger than that of the preceding year by 332,543.71 *colones*.

"The receipts from liquors, the amount of which was estimated at 1,450,000 *colones*, increased to 1,747,793.54 *colones*, or 421,571.92 *colones* more than the amount collected during the fiscal year 1905–6.

"The receipts from tobacco, calculated at 190,000 *colones*, decreased to 158,115.51 *colones*.

"The receipts from posts and telegraphs aggregated 237,635.64 *colones*, or 12,635.64 more than the amount estimated in the budget, and 25,677.56 *colones* more than the receipts of the previous year.

"The total receipts, which were estimated at 6,623,500 *colones*, rose to 6,951,209.92 *colones*.

"Not including the expenses for the continuation of the railroad, the expenditures of the Treasury, which were estimated on making up the budget at 6,627,731.20, rose to 7,323,775.34 *colones*. The Pacific Railway, which was assigned 703,664.28 *colones* in the budget, required, together with the rolling stock and the plant, the sum of 1,188,900.97 *colones*, or 485,236.29 *colones* more than were estimated in the budget.

* * * * * * *

"The Interior Debt on March 31, 1906, which, together with the amount borrowed from the banks for the railway, aggregated 8,308,178.73, *colones* rose on March 31, 1907, to 8,592,086.77 *colones*, or an increase of 283,908.04 *colones*."

CUSTOMS CLASSIFICATION OF FAT COMPOUNDS.

On April 25, 1907, the Treasury Department issued the following circular to the custom-house officers of the Republic:

"CIRCULAR No. 1.

"Decree No. 15, of June 6, 1902, provides that the classification of lard or tallow shall include not only the genuine article, but also all those substances which are sold in the market under these names, made of substances wholly or partially different from the substances imitated, or of lard or tallow which have lost their original good quality.

"Manterine, vegetole, 'bombera,' etc., should be classified among such substances, these being fats, some of which have the appearance of tallow and some of lard, so that they may be sold under those names, reducing thereby the necessity of employing the national product, which the aforesaid decree was intended to protect. Therefore, in order that the law be properly applied, the necessary order should be given the classifiers to the end that manterine and other fats having the appearance of lard or tallow be classified like the genuine article they most resemble, both as to color or any other detail."

By act of the Constitutional Congress of May 21, approved by President VIQUEZ, May 22, 1907, crude cottonseed oil intended exclusively for industrial uses will pay an import tax of 2 *centimos* per kilogram.

POSTAL CONVENTION WITH GREAT BRITAIN.

La Gaceta, of May 4, 1907, publishes the text of the convention for exchange of postal money orders between Great Britain and Costa Rica, signed by plenipotentiaries of the two countries at San José on April 26 and approved by President VIQUEZ on April 29, 1907. The exchange office for Great Britain will be London and for Costa Rica, San Jose.

CUBA.

RATIFICATION OF THE SANITARY CONVENTION OF 1905.

The *Gaceta Oficial* of May 10, 1907, announces the ratification by Provisional Governor CHARLES E. MAGOON, of the International Sanitary Convention, signed *ad referendum* at Washington October 14, 1905.

MINES OF SANTIAGO PROVINCE.

The following table shows the number of tons of iron, copper, and manganese ores shipped from the Santiago mines and the value of same for the four years 1903–1906:

Year.	Iron ore.		Manganese.		Copper.	
	Tons.	Value.	Tons.	Value.	Tons.	Value.
1903	557,960	$1,389,335	23,610	$97,670	783	$8,888
1904	376,470	849,408	20,214	82,170	10,599	235,764
1905	554,200	1,474,632	6,771	33,856	19,533	599,138
1906	636,960	2,210,331	8,300	83,000	24,558	330,236
Total	2,125,590	5,923,706	58,895	296,696	55,473	1,174,026

Mining is one of the principal sources of wealth of the Province of Santiago de Cuba, owing to the abundance and accessibility of the minerals. Iron is the most abundant, but copper and manganese are found in sufficient quantities for profitable exploitation. Gold, lead, zinc, and asphalt are also said to exist, but so far there has been no development of any of the mines said to contain these minerals.

Four principal companies are engaged in mining and exploiting minerals. From the mines at Daiquiri 3,536,121 tons of ore were produced to December 31, 1906. The production for the year 1906 was 510,500 tons. The ore has all been shipped to the United States except about 75,000 tons, which went to England, Germany, Belgium, and Cape Breton, Nova Scotia.

A company owning several iron mines on the north coast, in the Mayari Mountains back of Nipe Bay, is about to commence the construction of a broad-gauge railroad from the mines to the bay at Cagimaya, at which place will be built two wharves and other necessary equipment for economically handling the ore and exporting it to the United States. It is estimated that it will be possible to ship 1,000,000 tons annually.

Another American company operating near the Daiquiri mines shipped its first ore in 1884, since which time about 5,000,000 tons have been produced, nearly all going to the United States. The ore is transported from the mines to Santiago Bay by rail, where the company has a fine steel pier.

Copper deposits exist throughout almost the whole of the southern portion of Santiago Province, but so far the only attempt that has been made to mine it for exportation is in the vicinity of El Cobre, about 15 miles west of Santiago. A deposit of extraordinary richness exists in this territory.

TAKING OF A CENSUS IN 1907.

The *Gaceta Oficial*, of May 8, 1907, publishes the text of the decree of the same date establishing a census bureau charged with the collection, tabulation, and publication of a census of the population, by name, age, sex, conjugal condition, race, nativity, citizenship, occupation, literacy, and school attendance of children under 18 years of age in each Province, municipality, barrio, and other civil division of Cuba, to be made during the year 1907, and as soon as the necessary preparations therefor can be made.

DOMINICAN REPUBLIC.

PROPRIETARY MEDICINES IN THE REPUBLIC.

The law governing the introduction of proprietary medicines into the Dominican Republic went into effect on January 1, 1907, the text of which, as published in the Official Gazette of the Dominican Republic for June 20, 1906, and furnished the International Bureau of the American Republics by the Dominican Consul-General in the United States, is as follows:

"ART. 65. Pharmaceutical specialties (specifics) coming from foreign countries, patented or not, in order to be sold in this Republic are subject to the conditions established in this circular.

"ART. 66. To obtain permission for the sale of specifics not patented, the manufacturer will furnish, either personally or through power of attorney, to the superior council, through the Minister of the Interior:

"(a) Two bottles, boxes, or cases of the specific.

"(b) The application, which shall consist of (1) the name of the medicine, (2) the base of its composition, (3) the dose and method of administration, (4) the use to be made of it.

"For specifics patented and approved by institutions or foreign faculties it will be sufficient if the persons interested send with the application a copy of the official organ in which is published the decision granting the patent, and deposit with the secretary of the superior council the name of the medicine and the registered trademark by which it is distinguished.

"ART. 67. Simple natural products will be excepted from the conditions of this law if there is received here the method of procedure for the preparation, but in no case must there be mixed with them other substances, nor must they be sent incased in the form of a specific.

"ART. 68. The superior council will send a copy of the certificate issued to the chancellor of the exchequer, who on the receipt of it will authorize or prohibit the introduction of the specific, notifying the custom-house officers to this effect, so that in case articles that have not been authorized are imported they may be subjected to the penalties established in the law of customs and ports regarding all articles whose introduction is prohibited. ·

"ART. 69. In order that manufacturers whose specifics are now on sale in the Republic may comply with the precepts designated in this law, three months' time will be allowed for those of American make and six months for those of other countries. During this time, which will commence from the day of the execution of the present law (January 1, 1907), the officers of the customs will continue to estimate and verify these medicines as they have been doing. After that time they will proceed in conformity with the above articles.

"ART. 70. The applications, which should be addressed to the superior council (*consejo superior*), shall be written on sealed paper with type, and this council will collect for certification and registration the sum of $20 gold for the approbation granted in favor of each specialty not patented and $10 gold for those which have been patented. These · charges will be ·divided between· the superior council and the fiscal council, and must be paid by the manufacturer or the person holding his power of attorney on receipt of notification of the approbation.

"ART. 71. The superior council will open a register in which will be placed in numerical order the name of each specific whose sale has been authorized, the date of the approbation, and the name of the solicitor."

FRONTIER DEVELOPMENT.

President CACERES on April 20, 1907, approved the following law enacted by the National Congress on March 15 for the colonization and development of the frontiers bordering on the Republic of Haiti:

"LAW REGARDING COLONIZATION AND DEVELOPMENT OF THE
FRONTIERS.

"ARTICLE 1. The development of the frontiers bordering on the neighboring Republic of Haiti from the commune of Dajabón, inclusive, to the mouth of the river Pedernales is declared a public service.

"ART. 2. The sum of $40,000 American gold is set apart each year in order to bring into the country, on account of the State, forty families of agriculturalists of the white race.

"ART. 3. For the installation of each family is set apart: (*a*) The sum of $110; (*b*) 200 tareas (tarea, about 1 acre) of uncleared land for cultivation; (c) a monthly stipend of $30 for one year; (d) 3 shovels, 2 picks, 3 hoes, 5 machetes, and 4 axes.

"Art. 4. Immigrants taking advantage of the provisions of this law shall within two years thereafter make exhibit to the commissioner appointed by the Government for that purpose of the half at least of the land which has been granted to them in complete state of cultivation.

"In case of failure to comply with this provision the immigrant shall lose the right and privileges accruing under this law.

"Art. 5. Every agriculturalist, or his heirs, shall enjoy for fifteen years the entire production of the said land; after this time, which can not be extended, the Government shall enter into possession of the farm in order to lease it, giving the first preference to the agriculturalist who improved it, or to his heirs.

"Art. 6. Petitions to migrate to the country addressed by virtue of this law should be sent to the Minister of Foreign Relations through the respective Dominican Consuls and should be accompanied by a certificate of good character issued by competent authority; by a copy, properly legalized, of the register of birth of the father or head of the family; by enumeration of the persons in the family, specifying males and females, and a medical certificate of good health for all the family.

"Paragraph. Males of more than 45 and females of more than 35 years of age are not entitled to the benefits of this law.

"Art. 7. The consuls of the Republic, together with each petition, shall send such information as they can gather separately in respect to the petitioners.

"Art. 8. The Minister of Fomento shall prescribe such rules as may be necessary and those to which the immigrants should be subjected, and shall sign with them the proper contracts.

"Paragraph. The form of these contracts shall be formulated by the Minister of Fomento and approved by the National Congress.

"Art. 9. This law shall become effective so soon as the new Law of Public Expenditures shall be voted.

"Art. 10. This law repeals all others which may be contrary thereto, and will be sent to the Executive power as required by the Constitution."

IRRIGATION WORKS IN THE MONTE CRISTI DISTRICT.

President CACERES on March 23 approved the following resolution passed by the National Congress on March 18, 1907, for carrying into effect the plans for irrigating Monte Cristi district:

"Resolved:

"ARTICLE 1. To appropriate as a charge on the Public Treasury and for the period of two years the sum of $75,000 annually, which shall be set apart to meet the expenses occasioned by the irrigation of Monte Cristi district by the submersion system according to the plans prepared for that purpose and deposited in the Ministry of Fomento and Public Works.

"Paragraph. The amount above set out shall be assigned in the Law of Public Expenditures, annually voted by the National Congress, under the heading of "Fomento and public works."

"ART. 2. The above-mentioned work is under the charge of the Executive power, which shall employ all the means which may be within its power and exercise all necessary diligence tending to bring to a happy issue and in the shortest time the realization of this so important work."

MUNICIPAL IMPROVEMENTS AT SANTO DOMINGO.

The *Gaceta Oficial* of April 20, 1907, publishes the text of the resolution of the National Congress of April 15, approved by President CACERES April 19, 1907, authorizing the municipal government of the city of Santo Domingo to contract a loan of $600,000 gold at 6 per cent interest with a sinking fund of 1 per cent, the proceeds of which are to be employed in building an aqueduct for public and private use of the city, in modernizing the electric plant, in improvement of city streets, in building a public market and a theater. In a circular letter issued by the municipal government of Santo Domingo on April 26 correspondence in regard to the proposed improvements is invited.

ECUADOR.

RECEPTION OF UNITED STATES MINISTER.

Hon. WILLIAMS C. Fox, formerly Director of the International Bureau of the American Republics, was, on April 18, 1907, received in Quito by President ALFARO as Envoy Extraordinary and Minister Plenipotentiary from the United States to Ecuador.

On presenting his credentials, Minister Fox said:

"YOUR EXCELLENCY: In the name of the Government of the United States of America I have the honor to present to Your Excellency the letter of recall of my predecessor, Mr. JOSEPH W. J. LEE, and also that which accredits me as Envoy Extraordinary and Minister Plenipotentiary of my country to the Government of the Republic of Ecuador.

"The distinguished preference of my Government in conferring upon me this duty I consider not only pleasing, but also I esteem it a personal good fortune in that it gives me the opportunity to discharge the friendly duties relating to the official position I come to

occupy. Conformably to the instructions of the :
United States, I shall do all within my power to
extend the cordial relations which happily have
between Ecuador and my country.

"We march together, sir, on the road of progress
recognize likewise that, although civilization cannot
that the aspirations of humanity are the same, we
in the Western Hemisphere there are special interest
national complications, to assure the happiness.
Together, also, we wish for no victories but those of
ritory except our own; for no sovereignty except the
ourselves. It is our desire in the affairs of the wo
mutual respect and just consideration for the rights
for peace, prosperity, and progress.

"You will please, sir, to accept the cordial greet
ROOSEVELT and the sincere good wishes of the peop
States, to which allow me to join the high appreciatic
tain of the honor done me in being chosen as the ol
tive of my Government, near that of your Excellenc

The President of the Republic, Señor General Do
answered.

"Mr. MINISTER: Together with the letter of recal
guished predecessor, Mr. JOSEPH W. J. LEE, you ha
hands the credentials which invest you with the high
Extraordinary and Minister Plenipotentiary of the
America to the Government of Ecuador.

"The relations between our respective countries, n
and each day more cordial and solid, will make you
Minister, that the mission confided to your pers
encounter the most favorable reception from the
people of Ecuador.

"As director of the International Bureau of the
Hemisphere you have come to appreciate our great
confident that the greater part of your diplomatic lal
in strengthening the chains that unite the American
they may work together for the final triumph of jut

"It has pleased me much, Mr. Minister, to hear yo
so much ability the ideas of your eminent statesme
the common interests of America. In accord with th
principles of the Law of Nations, you encounter he
aspire to no other victories than those of peace, for
waged war; you encounter a people who wish for n
but their own, for never have they claimed any oth
you encounter a people who covet no sovereignty
themselves, for they wish to be in the right that they

and upheld in their independence and in their constant desire for their national prosperity and that of their sister nations of the continent. I beg that you will present to President ROOSEVELT my sincere wishes for his personal happiness and the prosperity of the nation he directs. In regard to yourself, be welcome, Mr. Minister, and may your pleasant stay among us make you to remember that we have learned to appreciate your merits."

TARIFF MODIFICATIONS.

According to *El Registro Oficial* No. 280, of January 17, 1907, customs duties in the Republic of Ecuador are modified as follows:

The following articles of primary necessity are exempted from all fiscal and municipal taxes: Maize, barley, potatoes, beans, vetches, lentils, wheat, and sugar.

The import duty on vermicelli shall be at the rate of 1 *centavo* per kilogram.

Rice and flour imported from Peru into the Province of Loja through the land custom-house at Macara are also declared to be free of all fiscal and municipal tax.

Beer manufactured in the sea districts shall be liable to a tax of 2 *centavos* per bottle, and foreign beer shall pay a sole import duty of 3 *centavos* per kilogram, gross weight, in addition to the surtax of 100 per cent, the consumption duty thereon being abolished.

The present law shall become effective throughout the Republic six days after its promulgation in the capital.

REGULATION OF THE CUSTOMS SERVICE.

The *Registro Oficial* of March 21, 1907, publishes the text of the decree of President Alfaro, dated March 20, 1907, reorganizing the custom-house service at Guayaquil and prescribing the duties of the several officers connected therewith.

THE EASTERN ECUADOR EXPLORATION COMPANY.

Information furnished by the United States Consul at Guayaquil states that on March 26, 1907, a contract was signed *ad referendum* by the Minister of the Interior of Ecuador authorizing the formation of the Eastern Ecuador Exploration Company, to be incorporated in London or in such place as shall be approved by the Government. The purposes of the company are:

First, to construct a railroad from Ambato to some point on the Curaray River at or below the head of navigation for this river. Second, to establish a port on the Curaray River at the terminus of the railroad. Third, to establish a regular line of steamers between the terminus of the road and the city of Para, in Brazil; also to establish lines of steamers on any or all of the navigable rivers of the oriental region of Ecuador. Fourth, to explore the oriental region and exploit its riches, both mineral and vegetable. Fifth, to acquire temporary or permanent titles to mines, waterfalls, etc. Sixth, to procure foreign immigration and provide for the settlement in this (oriental) region of Ecuadorian farmers from other Provinces.

The term "oriental region" is defined to be all that territory lying between the eastern watershed of the eastern chain of the Ecuadorian Andes and the northeastern, eastern, and southeastern boundaries of the Republic, but the Government of Ecuador may fix the western limit of this region with greater accuracy if necessary or desirable. Plans for the railroad must be presented within one year from date of contract, and the capital which is used in the construction of the road will be repaid by the Government of Ecuador in bonds secured by special funds. When the plans for the road are accepted, permanent title will be given to the company to alternate tracts of land 4 miles wide along its entire length.

The company through, its own operations or through a subsidiary company, promises to operate a line of steamers between the terminus of its railroad and the city of Para. It will establish hotels and hospitals and an office to facilitate the immigrant in preempting a homestead; this office will furnish the services of a surveyor and an expert agriculturist to the immigrant without charge, except for actual

etc., and to exploit such properties as may be thus located for fifty years; in the case of vegetable products title to the land which such products occupy is not conferred. Titles to mines may be acquired by fulfilling the usual conditions required by the Government of Ecuador and exploiting such property within ten years from date of discovery. Employees of the company are prohibited by the Government from filing upon mining properties until they may have left the service of the company ten years, unless permitted to do so by the company. Provision is made for fair dealing with Indians.

At the end of fifty years the concessions granted by the contract will be canceled by the Government, but this will not affect permanent rights and titles that may have been acquired. The company is authorized to issue preferred stock at 10 per cent not to exceed $2,433,250 in value, provided an equal amount of common stock is issued at the same time. Common stock may be increased at the discretion of the company.

CONTRACT FOR A RAILWAY FROM HUIGRA TO CUENCA.

The *Registro Oficial* of Ecuador for February 21 publishes the text of the contract executed on February 7, 1907, between the Government, as authorized by decree of the National Assembly, and Mr. EDWARD MORLEY, of England, but domiciled in Ecuador, representing also Mr. GEORGE P. ALTENBERG, of New York, for the building of a railroad from Huigra to Cuenca.

The railroad is to be constructed by a company to be known as the "Huigra and Cuenca Railway Company," to be organized in Great Britain or in the United States, and is to be a 3 feet 6 inches gauge.

Importation of machinery, tools, and construction material is to be free of all taxes.

In a letter written to the International Bureau of the American Republics, on the subject, Mr. MORLEY says:

"This railway commences at Huigra, on the Guayaquil and Quito Railway, 72 miles from Guayaquil, and extends to Cuenca, in the southern plateau of Ecuador, crossing near the town of Azogues the immense coal field in that vicinity. This coal is of good quality and easily mined. It stands on edge, and there are ten principal seams, the largest being 10 feet wide, with 6 feet of good coal, the others varying from 1 to 4 feet each. The railway will cross this coal field in three places at a distance of 70 miles from Huigra. The entire length of the line to Cuenca is 90 miles, and the construction will be easy, there being plenty of Indian labor obtainable at 40 cents gold per day. Very few bridges will be necessary, and those small ones. There is also good timber for ties and mining on the line. The climate is temperate, Huigra, where the line starts, being 4,100 feet above sea level, and Cuenca, the end of the route, 8,500 feet. The

latter city is the third largest in Ecuador, with a population
at 50,000, but in the immediate vicinity there is a total po
100,000.   The two provinces traversed by the railway—
Azuay—have a total population of 320,000, all adjacent (
These two provinces are extremely rich in minerals, and sev
mines are close-to the railway.   Coal and iron are very pl

"The Huigra and Cuenca Railway will be built first,
proposed to connect Cuenca with the deep-sea port, Puert
90 miles distant, and then extend the railway by way of
Paute to deep water on the River Morona, thus connecting
zon with the Pacific by a short railway.   The distance (
extension will be about 150 miles, probably less when the
completed.   The grade down to the Morona River via
Paute is less than 2 per cent, and the country is suitable f
work.

"When these lines are completed, the whole traffic of
Amazon will pass by this railway to the Pacific, thence by
Isthmus of Panama to New York and elsewhere, making 1
distance over the route down the Amazon to Para of (
miles."

GUATEMALA.

RATIFICATION OF INTERNATIONAL CONVENTIO1

President ESTRADA CABRERA, on April 18, 1907, approved
the National Legislative Assembly of April 16, 1907, ratifyin
vention signed at San Jose, Costa Rica, on September 24
representatives of the governments of Guatemala, El Salva
duras, and Costa Rica, for the establishment of a Central
Pedagogic Institute, and of an international bureau in C
City.

President ESTRADA CABRERA, on April 19, 1907, approved
the National Legislative Assembly of April 16, 1907, rat
convention adopted at the Third Pan-American Congress
Janeiro in August, 1906, in regard to patents, industrial m
erary and artistic property, etc., and the convention adop
same time and place in regard to international law; and on
1907, approved the act of the National Legislative Assembly
18, 1906, ratifying the convention in regard to pecuniary cl
the act of same date ratifying the convention relating to n
citizens, both signed at the same Congress on August 13, 1

President ESTRADA CABRERA, on April 18, 1907, approve
lowing acts of the National Legislative Assembly, passed
16, 1907:

Act ratifying the general treaty of peace, friendship, and commerce signed at San José, Costa Rica, on September 25, 1906, between representatives of Guatemala, El Salvador,. Honduras, and Costa Rica;

Act ratifying the convention signed on November 10, 1906, between representatives of Guatemala and the United States for the reciprocal protection of patents.

President ESTRADA CABRERA on April 22 approved the act of the National Legislative Assembly of April 19, 1907, ratifying the Geneva Convention signed on July 6, 1906, for bettering the condition of wounded and sick soldiers in the field.

DISCOVERY OF AN OLEAGINOUS PLANT.

According to press dispatches, Doctor SARDÁ has discovered recently in Guatemala a plant possessing valuable properties. Its name is *Myristica sebifera*, and its seed yields a vegetable oil that, it is claimed, has the same odor and taste of the cocoa butter, melts at 37° C., is soluble in alcohol, ether, and turpentine, may be used in the manufacture of soaps, candles, perfumes, sweetmeats, and pharmaceutical products, is a food substance, and never grows rancid.

With such properties this new oil, which its discoverer has named "*myristina*," must be worth at least $150 gold per ton, or perhaps much more, as it is further claimed that the substance in question is made transparent without difficulty, that the soap made therefrom foams in salt water, that it saponifies alkali, and that it illuminates with greater power than other similar oils.

IMPORTS FROM NEW YORK IN 1906.

According to the annual report of the Guatemalan Consul-General in New York for 1906, the total value of merchandise shipped thence to the ports of Guatemala during the year in reference amounted to $1,241,436.96. The export traffic of New York with Guatemala has increased considerably within the period of four years, as may be seen in the following table:

1903	$345,472.06	1905	$1,013,272.18
1904	816,745.16	1906	1,241,436.96

The principal articles exported during the last year were machinery, cotton goods, wool and silk, galvanized wire, hardware, agricultural implements, electric instruments and apparatus, medicines, drugs, railroad materials, furniture, leather, petroleum, paints, oils, iron pipes, paper, books, pianos, phonographs, automobiles, liquors, provisions, etc.

MEXICO.

FOREIGN COMMERCE IN FEBRU

According to figures issued by the Statistical
ury Department of the Republic of Mexico, the
the Republic for February, 1907, and for the fir
current fiscal year 1906-7, was represented by
tions, the figures for the corresponding periods
being also given for purposes of comparison:

The total value of importations during the
review was $149,464,925.18 in Mexican currenc
custom-houses, an increase of $16,144,803.39 a
same period of the preceding year.

The exports for the eight months were value
showing a decrease of $18,314,977.78 as comp
period of 1905-6.   Imports and their valuation

IMPORTS.

[Silver valuation.]

Articles.	February—	
	1907.	1906.
Animal substances.....................	$1,526,694.93	$1,287,193.88
Vegetable substances.................	2,847,861.65	3,290,666.25
Mineral substances....................	8,463,122.64	8,503,117.29
Dry goods.............................	1,943,883.67	1,763,172.33
Chemical and pharmaceutical substances.	737,680.90	322,225.65
Beverages.............................	500,351.20	466,294.78
Paper and its applications............	604,968.80	388,833.97
Machinery and apparatus..............	1,577,709.71	1,600,395.45
Vehicles..............................	827,593.97	276,132.00
Arms and explosives..................	191,341.98	367,794.81
Miscellaneous.........................	675,327.06	846,368.50
Total............................	20,123,251.23	20,003,190.63

EXPORTS.

[Silver valuation.]

Articles.	1907.	1906.
Precious metals.......................	$12,380,969.70	$14,359,100.70
Other articles........................	9,571,783.74	9,120,504.63
Total............................	21,962,753.44	23,479,665.33

The details for the export trade during the period in reference show the following classification and figures:

Articles.	February—		First eight months—	
	1906-7.	1905-6.	1906-7	1905-6
Mexican gold coin......................			$29,990.00	
Foreign gold coin......................			7,531.00	$4,835.98
Gold in bars...........................	$1,600,980.00	$2,417,656.51	13,006,356.83	20,392,971.11
Gold in other forms...................	390,196.35	410,614.28	3,645,113.72	1,810,633.38
Total gold....................	1,991,176.35	2,828,270.79	16,688,991.55	22,208,440.47
Mexican silver coin...................	3,947,217.00	4,193,296.00	18,338,877.60	33,891,126.90
Foreign silver coin...................	13,591.00	3,761.00	96,400.00	79,870.62
Silver in bars.........................	5,321,634.15	6,692,837.04	41,941,636.87	45,136,350.25
Silver in other forms.................	1,107,351.20	641,053.87	7,946,504.22	5,930,262.12
Total silver..................	10,389,793.35	11,530,889.91	68,323,418.09	85,037,608.99
Total gold and silver..........	12,380,969.70	14,359,160.70	85,012,409.64	107,246,049.46
Antimony..............................	134,178.00	98,103.00	942,845.00	668,652.96
Copper................................	1,495,334.00	3,284,069.50	16,725,047.60	20,258,902.22
Marble................................	22,918.00		48,998.00	73,696.00
Plumbago.............................	9,600.00	14,200.00	66,220.00	65,621.51
Lead..................................	304,717.00	570,643.23	2,452,538.56	3,649,398.77
Zinc..................................	9,073.00	5,384.00	900,066.12	148,211.99
Other metals.........................	12,975.74	45,194.50	1,086,756.42	258,754.34
Total......................	14,369,765.44	18,371,754.93	107,229,080.74	132,395,586.26
Vegetable products:				
Coffee............................	874,155.00	1,352,653.60	3,376,778.34	4,741,626.10
Cascalote and tanning barks.....	304.60	600.00	8,218.00	20,747.90
Rubber...........................	665,809.00	176,051.72	3,427,772.00	870,868.74
Chicle...........................	314,965.00	182,090.03	1,235,980.00	851,387.49
Beans............................	57,449.00	57,372.90	515,393.00	520,653.72
Fruits...........................	16,133.00	13,182.00	206,455.43	223,570.90
Chick peas.......................	61,701.00	82,684.00	2,735,585.00	1,856,584.75
Guayule..........................	8,600.00	9,798.00	32,399.00	41,139.00
Horse beans......................			2,550.00	119,540.00
Heniquen.........................	1,612,669.00	835,008.00	22,602,680.77	19,037,456.90
Ixtle............................	327,212.00	279,366.00	2,715,718.00	2,455,519.88
Woods............................	403,972.00	78,614.88	1,558,631.50	1,317,608.74
Maize............................	934.00	24,310.20	4,037.80	58,296.20
Mahogany.........................	4,718.00	18,097.87	51,550.00	54,987.87
Dyewoods.........................	56,606.00	56,801.80	303,116.12	296,885.20
Xacaton..........................	142,418.00	106,921.00	1,125,906.60	1,241,364.00
Leaf tobacco.....................	57,687.00	106,820.32	1,039,822.85	650,411.06
Vanilla..........................	144,476.00	123,501.00	1,091,876.00	2,639,321.99
Other vegetables.................	1,476,278.00	146,448.65	2,695,825.20	992,238.53
Total......................	6,236,238.60	3,651,208.07	44,741,295.51	37,971,187.17
Animal products:				
Cattle...........................	35,208.00	185,064.00	873,922.90	2,173,012.50
Skins and hides..................	849,186.00	805,570.69	6,235,052.63	5,203,676.85
Other animal products...........	57,591.00	47,455.80	416,182.99	340,316.43
Total......................	941,985.00	1,038,090.10	7,525,158.02	7,717,005.78
Manufactured products:				
Sugar............................	116,037.00	99,246.00	483,205.00	389,878.00
Flour and pastes.................			697.00	
Rope.............................	66,319.00	75,958.60	472,437.00	352,821.00
Dressed skins....................	651.00	30,782.00	32,255.00	157,487.00
Straw hats.......................	55,998.00	76,077.00	451,601.80	374,196.29
Manufactured tobacco............	27,758.00	28,063.64	322,087.60	228,803.19
Other manufactures..............	64,948.00	47,751.30	373,986.32	396,589.59
Total......................	330,651.00	357,878.34	2,136,189.72	1,867,806.07
Miscellaneous articles................	74,064.00	60,738.44	505,582.65	501,500.14

Following is a résumé of the valuations of Mexican imports during the periods under comparison, with reference to their countries of origin:

Country.	February—		First eight months—	
	1907.	1906.	1906-7.	1905-6.
Europe	$4,487,871.76	$4,412,491.18	$53,421,482.75	$49,484,782.6
Asia	182,628.70	93,411.90	1,896,304.50	963,193.95
Africa	24,070.00	246.15	171,662.50	15,943.25
North America	13,293,074.79	14,513,196.60	98,983,112.01	85,851,192.29
Central America	1,326.42	2,384.40	19,193.44	22,246.71
South America	15,943.74	16,702.26	123,691.34	141,327.05
West Indies	13,944.73	17,517.42	139,495.64	165,066.9
Oceania		4,944.00	30,562.50	67,348.6
Total	20,123,281.35	30,063,196.08	149,494,526.18	123,235,121.3

Following is a résumé of the valuations of Mexican exports during the periods under comparison, with reference to their countries of destination:

Country.	February—		First eight months—	
	1907.	1906.	1906-7.	1905-6.
Europe	$6,433,719.84	$6,087,674.82	$44,964,392.13	$44,896,482.37
Asia			796.00	
North America	15,365,330.80	15,049,300.60	114,943,564.31	132,441,461.68
Central America	36,534.00	82,551.46	579,962.31	990,945.71
South America		8,310.32	78,779.00	51,027.32
West Indies	123,930.00	260,629.00	1,570,161.00	2,775,020.00
Total	21,952,723.44	23,479,665.38	162,137,606.64	180,452,564.42

MODIFICATION OF EXPORT DUTIES.

In accordance with the provisions of the Mexican Budget for the fiscal year 1907–8, promulgated May 22, 1907, export duties on certain specified articles are modified as follows:

Campeche or dyewood, $0.50 per ton of 1,000 kilograms; mulberry wood, $0.25 per ton of 1,000 kilograms; zacatón root, at the rate of 70 centavos per 100 kilograms gross; chicle, at the rate of 2 centavos per kilogram net; guayule, leaf, in natural state or crushed, 15 pesos per ton of 1,000 kilograms gross; henequen, leaf, 50 centavos per 100 kilograms net; ixtle, leaf, 50 centavos per 100 kilograms net; deer and goat skins, $2.25 per 100 kilograms gross; hides of cattle and others, 75 centavos per 100 kilograms gross.

POSTAL RECEIPTS, NINE MONTHS, 1906–7.

The movement of the Mexican mail service for the nine months ending March, 1907, as reported by the chief of the postal bureau in the Department of Communication and Public Works, shows total receipts from this source of fiscal revenue amounting to $2,984,014.85, as compared with $2,714,637.74 in the same period of the preceding year. An advance of $269,377.11 is thus shown, or 9.92 per cent.

TRADE WITH GALVESTON IN 1906.

cording to the annual report of the Mexican Consul at Galveston, s, for the year 1906, the commercial movement between that port various Mexican Gulf ports during the period covered shows a ierable increase over the previous years. The value of merchan- xported from Galveston to Mexico during the year in reference 2,413,934, the principal articles being maize, lumber, oils, lard, inery and hardware, cotton, hogs, wheat, and cattle. The tation of Mexican products into Galveston, in 1906, was valued)56,487, the greater part of which being for henequen, ',771; other imports consisted of coffee, palm-leaf hats, fine -- ..,..., etc.

During the year under review, 123 steamers were cleared from Galveston to the following Mexican Gulf ports: Tampico, Vera Cruz, Progreso, Coatzacoalcos, Campeche, Frontera, and Laguna del Carmen.

SILVER BASIS OF THE STAMP AND CUSTOMS TAXES, JUNE, 1907.

The usual monthly circular issued, by the Treasury Department of the Mexican Government announces that the legal price per kilogram of pure silver during the month of June, 1907, is $42.73, according to calculations provided in the decree of March 25, 1905. This price will be the basis for the payment of the stamp tax and customs duties when silver is used throughout the Republic.

CUSTOMS RECEIPTS FIRST NINE MONTHS, 1906-7.

The Mexican customs receipts for the first nine months of the fiscal year 1906-7 (July to March, inclusive) aggregated $39,587,950.58 as compared with $34,922,201.65 .in the corresponding period of the preceding fiscal year. Import duties are recorded as $37.986,921.80; export dues, $813,514.89, and port dues, $787,513.89.

SISAL AND MANILA HEMP IN AUSTRIA-HUNGARY.

The Mexican Ministry of Foreign Affairs has been informed by the Mexican Consul-General in Budapest that the Hungarian Govern- ment, with the purpose of facilitating the introduction into the coun- try of manila and sisal cordings, has ordered that the customs duties thereon shall be modified.

Ropes and twines which formerly paid entry dues ranging from 12 to 83 crowns per 100 kilograms, according to their thickness, will henceforth be dutiable only at the rate of 12 crowns per 100 kilograms, without regard to thickness.

This order became effective on April 1, 1907, and it is anticipated that similar measures will be taken by Austria.

CUSTOMS DUTIES DURING FIRST TEN MONTHS OF 1906-7.

Mexican customs receipts for the month of April show a total of $4,690,884.92 (national currency), of which $83,129.81 were for exports and $4,607,755.11 for imports. The port of Vera Cruz led all others as a port of entry, with $1,616,384.85, while Progreso, with $41,578.07, held first rank as a point of shipment abroad.

Total customs duties received at the various ports of the Mexican Republic during the first ten months of 1906-7 (July, 1906–April, 1907) aggregated $44,399,698.33 as compared with $38,088,862.52 in the corresponding period of the preceding year.

Receipts from imports are credited with $42,594,676.91 as compared with $36,554,590.06 in 1905-6, and export duties were $896,644.70 and $751,770.24 in the two periods in reference, respectively.

FISHING CONCESSION ON THE PACIFIC COAST.

The Mexican official journal publishes the text of a contract between the Ministry of Fomento and Señor ENRIQUE OROZCO, by which certain fishing rights on the Pacific coast of the Republic are conceded to the concessionaire. The district included is situated on the west coast of the peninsula of Lower California, between 23° 30′ and 29° N.

The concessionaire undertakes to establish, within two years from the date of the signing of the contract, at least one factory for the canning and preserving of the fish products. An important clause in the contract directs that within a period of two years an establishment for the sale of the canned products shall be opened in the capital. It is further stipulated that not less than 25 per cent of the preserved products of the factory shall be placed on sale, and that they shall be sold at prices not exceeding half those at which similar imported foreign products are sold in the City of Mexico.

The contract also provides that all the machinery necessary for preserving the fish and for the manufacture of the various packages in which it may be offered for sale shall be allowed to enter free of duty.

IMPROVED STEAMSHIP SERVICE WITH THE UNITED STATES.

The "Mexican Herald" for May 2, 1907, states that from May 4 the Mexican-American Steamship Company inaugurated a fast express service between New Orleans and Tampico and Veracruz, which is an advance over any previously existing service between the southern cities of the United States and Mexico.

According to the new schedule, twenty-one days will be required for the round trip between New Orleans, Tampico, and Veracruz, instead of twenty-seven days as previously.

A ship will leave New Orleans every Saturday, and this regular schedule will enable connecting rail lines to depend on the service. Business men of New Orleans will thus be able to compete successfully for Mexican trade, a weekly service making quick deliveries a possibility.

URANIUM ORE IN GUERRERO.

A large deposit of uranium ore has been recently discovered in the State of Guerrero and crystallized specimens have been identified by Prof. José AGUILAR, Director of the Geological Institute of Mexico, as torbernite, a hydrosulphite of copper and uranium. It is the first time that this rare mineral has been observed in the Republic.

The world's total production of uranium in 1906 was but 11 tons, and ores from 5 to 8 per cent are quoted at 50 cents gold per pound, or $1,000 per ton.

RAILROAD FROM QUERETARO TO GUANAJUATO.

By virtue of a contract entered into on the 12th of January, 1907, and published in the *Periodico Oficial* of the State of Tabasco, of April 13, 1907, Mr. MANUEL RUBIO ARRIAGA has been authorized by the Mexican Government to construct and exploit a railroad line between the States of Queretaro and Guanajuato, starting from the capital of the former and terminating at the town of Acambaro in the latter. The whole line must be completed within seven years from the date of the contract. The concessionaire has made a deposit of 10,800 *pesos* in bonds of the Consolidated Public Debt in order to guarantee the fulfillment of the terms of the contract.

MARKET FOR HENEQUEN IN THE ARGENTINE REPUBLIC.

The Consul-General of Mexico in the Argentine Republic is endeavoring to establish direct shipments of henequen from his country to the latter Republic. Large quantities of this fiber are annually received from the United States markets and it is now purposed to establish an importing company in South America which shall work in harmony with an exporting association in Mexico, and which shall be the distributing depot for Mexican henequen throughout Brazil, Uruguay, and Chile. Factories have already been established in the Argentine Republic for the elaboration of henequen into twine, rope, etc.

PREMIUMS AT THE ST. LOUIS EXPOSITION.

In the *Boletín de la Secretaría de Fomento* received by the International Bureau of the American Republics on May 19, 1907, from the Mexican Government is published an account of the ceremonies attending the distribution of the various awards received by Mexican

exhibitors at the St. Louis Exposition. In a total of 2,2
exhibits, 1,677 received premiums, of which 474 were
516 silver, 618 bronze, and 69 first prizes.

The industrial advance of the Republic as evidenced
ing at various Expositions is shown by the fact that at I
31 per cent of her exhibits received awards; in Chicago,
cent; in Paris, 1900, 51 per cent; in Buffalo, 1901, 71 per
St. Louis, 73 per cent.

Agricultural exhibits received the bulk of premiums,
exhibitors 754 were awarded prizes; liberal arts follows
awards out of 327 exhibitors; and manufactures thir
premiums and 391 exhibits.

TRADE OF CIUDAD JUAREZ, 1906.

When the free zone was abolished in June, 1905, it was
the abolition would have a tendency materially to lessen
of trade conducted through this port. On the contrary,
a report made by United States Consul LEWIS A. MARTI
has very materially increased—both imports and exports
ness prospects in the district were never more encoura
various industries more active, and there never was a tii
customs officials were handling more revenues from i
exports.

The imports in 1906 amounted to $8,130,794, an incre
pared with those of 1905, of $1,484,558; while the expor
to $8,815,378, an increase of $4,046,662 over those of
imports by articles, as far as they can be designated from
returns, were as follows:

Articles.	Value.	Articles.
Arms and explosives....................	$156,226	Machinery—Continued.
Boards and deals......................	800,226	All other....................
Cattle...............................	106,604	Shoes........................
Chemicals............................	147,706	Stationery...................
Coal and coke........................	127,534	Vehicles:
Cotton-seed oil.......................	396,634	Railway cars..............
Horses...............................	48,982	Carriages.................
Iron.................................	127,205	All other.................
Ironware.............................	242,537	Other merchand'se...........
Machinery:		
Agricultural......................	68,634	Total merchandise.......
Electrical........................	111,927	Mexican gold coin...........
Sewing machines..................	91,044	
Locomotives......................	272,000	Total imports...........
Mining...........................	98,115	

Of the foregoing, $7,334,810 worth was drawn from
States, $443,839 from Germany, $194,455 from the Unite
and $138,490 from France. The exports for 1906 were
follows: Minerals, $7,110,088; vegetables, $930,861; ar
ucts, $738,434; all other products, $35,995; total exports
of which $8,295,970 went to the United States.

A number of new manufacturing enterprises are being established. One recently started turns out brooms and mattresses from corn shucks, and from the refuse shucks they make daily 600 packages of cigarettes. A large building-brick factory is starting up at Sabinas with machinery from St. Louis, and will make 30,000 bricks daily. A sash and door factory has just been completed.

CONSULAR TRADE REPORTS.

The Consul-General of Mexico at New York reports that during the month of April, 1907, twelve vessels proceeding from Mexican ports entered the harbor of New York City, bringing 86,828 packages of merchandise. During the same month the vessels clearing from the port of New York numbered 16, carrying 206,507 packages of merchandise, consigned to Mexican ports. The imports in detail from Mexico at New York in April, 1907, were as follows:

Articles.	Quantity.	Articles.	Quantity.
Henequen...............bales..	6,385	Lead bullion.............bars..	20,853
Coffee................sacks..	14,918	Sarsaparilla..........packages..	739
Hides................bales..	7,373	Vanilla..............boxes..	99
Hides................loose..	4,496	Alligator skins...........do....	60
Ixtle................bales..	4,996	Bones..............packages..	31
Goatskins..............do....	2,477	Honey................barrels..	229
Deerskins..............do....	244	Cedar................logs..	184
Rubber................do....	5,348	Mahogany..............do....	34
Leaf tobacco............do....	1,321	Jalap................sacks..	100
Cigars................boxes..	50	Copper................bars..	4,061
Broom root............bales..	617	Coin................boxes..	207
Chicle................do....	3,197	Silver ingots............bars..	483
Fustete................logs..	3,374	Garlic................sacks..	1,397
Tecali marble...........slabs..	49	Oranges................box..	1
Hair................bales..	50	Mexican dollars.........boxes..	84

The Mexican Consul at Nogales, Arizona, reports that during the month of April, 1907, the following merchandise was imported through the custom-house of Nogales from the State of Sonora, Mexico:

	Gold.		Gold.
Cane sugar......................	$229	Natural feathers.................	$277
Refined sugar...................	69	Fresh fish......................	25
Leather belts...................	64	Lead ore........................	835
Portland cement...............	24	Potatoes........................	2
Rawhides.......................	12,477	Cheese.........................	9
Fresh meat.....................	22	Ready-made cotton clothing....	8
Articles not specified..........	167	Common salt....................	22
Beans..........................	11	Leaf tobacco....................	683
Canned fruits..................	6,026	Wheat.........................	2
Cattle.........................	14,740	Silver bars.....................	129,528
Preserved vegetables...........	215	Gold bars and dust.............	144,959
Corn...........................	13		
Oranges........................	3,763	Total...................	314,170

The value of the merchandise shipped through the custom-house of Nogales, Mexico, to the State of Sonora in April, 1907, was $396,647.91, and consisted of the following merchandise:

	Gold.		Gold.
Animal products	$65,480.17	Paper and paper products	$6,127.49
Vegetable products	40,104.63	Machinery and apparatus	69,939.96
Mineral products	82,149.42	Vehicles	10,204.77
Textiles, and manufactures		Arms and explosives	14,465.47
thereof	58,169.61	Miscellaneous	20,029.65
Chemical products	24,043.62		
Spirituous beverages	5,953.12	Total	396,647.91

The aforesaid merchandise came from the following countries:

United States	$353,054.12	Austria	$537.88
France	3,039.22	Canada	253.26
Germany	12,538.48	Japan	2,681.34
England	11,742.42		
Spain	12,801.19	Total	396,647.91

The Mexican Consul at Philadelphia advises that the shipments of merchandise from that port to the Mexican ports of Tampico and Veracruz during the month of April, 1907, amounted to $102,460, and consisted of coal and powder invoiced at $74,285 and $28,175, respectively.

The Mexican Consul at Philadelphia advises that the shipments of merchandise from Philadelphia to the Mexican ports of Tampico and Veracruz during the month of May, 1907, amounted to $95,555.74, and consisted of petroleum and coal invoiced at $66,836.49 and $28,719.25, respectively.

Receipts of merchandise at San Diego, California, from Mexican ports are reported by the special deputy collector as furnished by the Mexican Consul for the months of January, February, March, and April, as follows:

Merchandise.	Value.	Merchandise.	Value.
JANUARY.		**MARCH.**	
Cattle	$20,462	Products of the United States re-	
Horses	290	turned	$2,260
Swine	75	Copper ore	560
Products of the United States re-		Beeswax	740
turned	2,839	Tea	380
Pine nuts	101	Horses and mules (18)	1,025
Miscellaneous	567	Cattle (547)	7,863
		Sheep	1,767
Total	24,334	Mexican onyx	2,000
		Bran	828
FEBRUARY.		Panocha	195
Cattle (700)	10,303	Miscellaneous	419
Horses	600		
Mexican onyx	13,302	Total	17,937
Products of the United States re-		**APRIL.**	
turned	6,921	Cattle (173)	1,899
Bran	1,205	Horses (17)	783
Gold bullion	391	Sheep (500)	1,500
Beeswax	351	Mules, swine, and goats	364
Wool blankets	108	Gold bullion	1,595
Fresh beef	93	Bran	1,168
Hides of cattle	92	Beeswax	551
Guano	65	Hides of cattle (4,282 pounds)	621
Miscellaneous	325	Products of the United States re-	
		turned	69,764
Total	33,746	Panocha	200
		Miscellaneous	244
		Total	78,372

Shipments from San Diego to Mexican ports for the first quarter of 1907 were as follows:

	Pieces.	Value.
January	5,005	29,686
February	2,357	7,804
March	5,153	14,600

EXPLOITATION OF IRON PROPERTIES.

President DIAZ, on May 21, 1907, promulgated the act of Congress approving the contract made on February 1, 1907, by the Minister of Fomento granting a concession to the company "A. B. Adams, incorporated," to explore for iron ores in the districts of Jamiltepec, Tlaxiaco, Teposcolula, Nochixtlán, Huajuapam, Justlahuaca, and Juquila, in the State of Oaxaca. The text of the contract is published in the *Diario Oficial* of May 30, 1907.

NICARAGUA.

REDUCTION OF EXPORT DUTY ON COFFEE.

According to information furnished by the United States consul at Managua, the decree published in the MONTHLY BULLETIN for April, page 885, concerning the rate fixed by the Nicaraguan Government for the duty to be paid on coffee exports from the Republic, reduces the duty on that commodity 20 per cent.

Previously the duty was 40 cents gold per quintal, while the decree in reference, issued February 24, 1907, fixes it at $2 national currency. At the rate of exchange indicated in article 3 of the decree (630 per cent), this would be equal to a fraction less than 32 cents gold per quintal (100 pounds).

The text of the decree follows:

The President of the Republic, taking into consideration the unexpected fall in the price of coffee in foreign markets, and being duly empowered, decrees:

ARTICLE 1. From the publication of the present decree, the export duty on each quintal of coffee shall be 2 *pesos* in national currency, instead of 40 cents gold now being paid.

ART. 2. This decree shall remain in force during the existence of the cause that necessitated its issue.

ART. 3. For the purpose of carrying out this law the gold bonds issued for payment of above duty shall be received at their equivalent in national currency, the exchange being effected at the rate of 630 per cent.

ART. 4. All the regulations established in the decrees of January 27, 1894, and October 22, 1904, will remain in full force.

PANAMA.

ORGANIZATION OF A BUREAU OF STATISTICS.

A general statistical office for Panama was organized on May 10, 1907, under the direction of Señor Don LEON FERNÁNDEZ GUARDIA, which will have in charge the collection and publication of the vital, commercial, and agricultural statistics of the Republic.

APICULTURE IN THE REPUBLIC.

The *Gaceta Oficial* of Panama for March 6, 1907, publishes the contract made by the Secretary of Fomento on March 5, and approved by President AMADOR on March 6, 1907, with Señor VICTOR VARGAS GAMALLO, for the introduction of bee culture in the Republic.

APPOINTMENT OF A DELEGATE TO THE CONVENTION OF JURIS-CONSULTS.

The *Gaceta Oficial* of April 5, 1907, publishes the text of the decree of President AMADOR GUERRERO, dated April 1, appointing Dr. BELISARIO PORRAS, delegate from Panama to the Convention of Jurisconsults to meet during the year in Rio de Janeiro, according to the resolution of the Third International American Conference, to prepare codes of public and of private international law for submission to the convention.

PARAGUAY.

INCREASED PORT FACILITIES.

A movement to secure an improvement in the handling of imported merchandise at the Paraguayan custom-house is reported as due to increasing shipments.

Representatives of the commerce of Paraguay have placed in the hands of the Minister of Finance a memorial soliciting that measures be taken for the construction of various provisional sheds for the deposit of merchandise in order that the cargoes which are on their way to the port of Asuncion, representing more than 7,000 tons, may be placed in them after their arrival. The lighting of the custom-house deposits by electricity; establishment of an official gold exchange for the collection of custom-house duties for a reasonable and prudent time, and a dislodgment of the occupants of fiscal lands needed for the improvements are other measures to be carried into execution.

Paraguayan commerce is continually on the increase, and for some time there has been a great need for better accommodations at the custom-house.

PERU.

LAND AND IRRIGATION LAWS.

The forest lands of Peru are in what is known as the "*Montaña*," which is the most extensive territory of the country. It offers a wide field for emigrants by reason of the fertility of its different districts, the variety of its products, and the special franchises conferred by the laws. The emigrant enjoys the same civil rights as the native-born inhabitants, and can readily become a proprietor of Montaña lands under the provisions of the law of December 21, 1898, which establishes as methods of acquisitions: (1) By purchase, at the rate of 5 soles, $2.50 American gold, per hectare (2.47 acres); (2) by contract for colonization; (3) by rental of 1 sol, or 50 cents American gold, per year per hectare; (4) by free grants—only, however, in respect of lots of not over 2 hectares. But it should be noted that, as the law seeks to promote the cultivation of the Montaña lands, there is nothing whatever to prevent any person who may have received and cultivated one lot from acquiring others successively, subject to the same obligation with regard to cultivation. The spirit of the law is such that, in carrying it into effect, the Government endeavors to give the colonists every possible facility and advantage.

On the western slope of the Andes and in the coast region, where irrigation is more or less necessary, the granting of public lands is governed by the irrigation law of October 9, 1893, which provides as follows:

"ARTICLE 1. The Executive power is authorized to make irrigation concessions or contracts with strict subjection to the prescriptions of this law.

"ART. 2. Concession shall only be granted for the utilization of waters when these belong to the public. They may be applied to the irrigation of cultivable lands, and must in no way directly or indirectly affect the right of third parties.

"For the purposes of the law the following are regarded as belonging to the public domain:

"(1) Rivers.

"(2) Torrents, springs, and permanent and periodical streams, presuming always that they have not been subject to previous appropriation.

"ART. 3. The waters referred to in the preceding article may be conceded to the occupiers of uncultivated lands pertaining to the State. In either case, the right to the waters will be perpetual. When the property in the waters is conceded to associations or individuals in order to irrigate lands belonging to private owners, the proprietors of the waters and of the lands will enter into such agreements between themselves as they may deem necessary for the purpose of irrigation.

"If, in the contract, the payment of an annual sum be stipulated for against the use of the waters, such charge can not extend beyond a period of ninety years. On the expiration of this period, the lands shall be exempt from the obligation of paying such annual sum, and the control of the water reservoirs and other works exclusively connected with the irrigation shall pass free of all charge to the irrigation service.

"ART. 4. Petitions presented to the Government for the acquisition of the rights hereby accorded shall set forth—

"(a) The designation of the waters and the method of utilization to be employed.

"(b) The precise jurisdiction of the lands to be irrigated.

"(c) The period within which the work is to be executed.

"(d) The security to be given in order to guarantee its execution.

"(e) The documents showing any right the petitioner may have over the land in case the concession solicited is for irrigation.

"(f) The tariffs upon which owners of land will be required to pay the respective fee (or annual sum) in cases where the concession solicited is for the irrigation of lands belonging to third parties.

"(g) The plan, descriptive report, and estimated cost and income of the enterprise.

"ART. 5. Immigration enterprises will enjoy the following advantages:

"(1) Exemption from import duties on machinery, ironwork, and other material which the enterprise may introduce for the construction of hydraulic works, and exemption from the payment of the alcabala tax on the lands of private individuals purchased for the same.

"(2) The property in the uncultivated lands of the State, or of municipalities which may be adequately irrigated.

"(3) Exoneration from every direct impost during the first three years in favor of all settlers cultivating the irrigated lands.

"(4) Power to alter the course of waters not privately owned, to improve their utilization by means of dams, and to execute the works necessary to connect the public with the irrigation system.

"ART. 6. The contractors shall have the right to use gratuitously public lands when necessary for the construction of dams, aqueducts, and other works indispensable for the irrigation. If the lands required for these works are private property, the Government in virtue of the present law shall declare the work to be of public utility and effect their expropriation in conformity with the laws.

"ART. 7. In case of the work not being carried into execution, the security which may have been deposited with the State shall be forfeited in favor of the latter.

"ART. 8. No concession can be transferred without the consent of the Government.

"ART. 9. The contractor remains subject to the laws of the Republic and shall be incompetent to put forward any claim whatsoever otherwise than before the tribunals therein constituted.

"ART. 10. All concessions with respect to irrigation, granted anterior to the last twenty years, which have not been utilized up to date, are null and void."

PETROLEUM SHIPMENT TO THE ARGENTINE REPUBLIC.

In March, 1907, the British merchant steamer *Circassian Prince* sailed from Callao for Lobitos (oil wells in the north of Peru) to take on 3,000 tons of crude petroleum for a firm which has already placed the order in Buenos Ayres, and it is expected that in view of the price obtained regular shipments of the article will be made.

PROPRIETARY MEDICINES IN THE REPUBLIC.

The medical faculty, which is vested with power to legislate in the matter, has recently issued a decree whereby it is provided that all proprietary medicines introduced into the Republic of Peru shall be subjected to an examination by a pharmacy commission.

Specifics, together with the formula for their compounding, must be submitted to this commission, whose findings, given in the form of a certificate, authorize or prohibit the sale and use of the medicines throughout the Republic.

This decree, it is understood, applies at present only to those proprietary preparations that have not already been introduced to the public or already invoiced to some purchaser in the Republic.

SALVADOR.

IMPORT TRADE DURING THE THIRD QUARTER OF 1906.

During the third quarter of the year 1906, imports of merchandise at the various ports of the Republic of Salvador were reported as follows:

Through Acajutla, 160,158 parcels were received, valued at $1,930,-723.98; through La Libertad, 31,570 parcels, valued at $494,940.19; and through La Union, 65,498 parcels, valued at $700,501.56, the sum total being 257,226 parcels, worth $3,126,165.73.

The origin of the imports reported was: From Great Britain, $1,063,679.92; United States, $979,746.08; France, $267,387.57; Germany, $334,177.35; and Belgium, $120,634.94.

The leading item of import was cotton textiles, valued at $1,941,-661.47.

INTERNAL DEBT OF THE REPUBLIC.

In his report made to the National Assembly on April 26, 1907, by the Salvadorean Minister of the Treasury, the total internal debt of the country is stated as follows:

Payable in gold, $3,550,232.18; payable in silver, $1,590,533.84; Salvadorean bonds, $3,397,775.81 silver.

PAN-AMERICAN RAILWAY CONSTRUCTION.

Press advices state that President FIGUÉROA recently approved the concession secured by J. M. NEELAND for the construction of the Pan-American Railway of Central America, work to begin not later than September 1, 1907. The total length of the road will be 450 kilometers, and it will run through the richest agricultural region of the State of Salvador. The capital for the construction of the road will be furnished by capitalists from the United States and Holland. The company is capitalized at $7,000,000 gold. The road will be known as the Pan-American of Central America, and its completion is expected in four years. The construction of the road will be slow, as the greater part of the route is mountainous. ·

The principal traffic of the line will be coffee, and as the State of Salvador alone produces 2,000,000 bags yearly it will be exceedingly heavy. Another large factor in the traffic will be sugar. From La Union ships will convey this traffic to the United States. La Union is on the Bay of Fonseca, which has been pronounced by Humboldt and other competent authorities the finest natural harbor in the entire Western Hemisphere.

PAYMENT OF IMPORT DUTIES IN GOLD.

The *Diario Oficial* of Salvador for March 26, 1907, publishes the following decree signed by President FIGUEROA on March 22, 1907:

"The Executive Power of the Republic of El Salvador, considering:

"That by virtue of agreements made with various state creditors it has been agreed to reduce to American gold the debts in their favor, and it being indispensable therefore to dictate the means necessary in order to make payment in this kind of money, it is decreed:

"SOLE ARTICLE. From the 1st of next April the imposts with which imported merchandise is taxed, that is, the 8 *pesos* silver per 100 kilograms referred to in article 573 of the present tariff, shall be reduced to $3.70 American gold and shall be collected in cash or in bank drafts at sight on the United States.

"Given in the Executive Palace at San Salvador, March 22, 1907."

INCREASED DUTY ON AGUARDIENTE.

On and after April 1, 1907, the tax on each bottle of aguardiente sold from Government deposits, both with regard to the regular quotas and to additional purchases, was increased 25 cents silver.

UNITED STATES.

TRADE WITH LATIN AMERICA.

STATEMENT OF IMPORTS AND EXPORTS.

Following is the latest statement, from figures compiled by the Bureau of Statistics, United States Department of Commerce and Labor, showing the value of the trade between the United States and the Latin-American countries. The report is for the month of April, 1907, with a comparative statement for the corresponding month òf the previous year; also for the ten months ending April, 1907, as compared with the same period of the preceding year. It should be explained that the figures from the various custom-houses, showing imports and exports for any month, are not received by the Treasury Department until about the 20th of the following month, and some time is necessarily consumed in compilation and printing, so that the returns for April, for example, are not published until some time in June.

IMPORTS OF MERCHANDISE.

	April—		Ten months ending April—	
	1906.	1907.	1906.	1907.
Cocoa (*Cacao; Coco ou cacao; Cacao*):	*Dollars.*	*Dollars.*	*Dollars.*	*Dollars.*
Central America	1,184	3,453	13,417	43,078
Brazil	79,006	207,645	1,133,236	2,377,042
Other South America	182,509	173,152	1,547,066	1,484,504
Coffee (*Café; Café; Café*):				
Central America	708,192	2,195,355	5,255,128	5,750,497
Mexico	318,047	349,206	2,021,082	1,247,914
Brazil	1,968,701	5,086,062	45,574,561	50,750,119
Other South America	776,449	697,566	8,285,200	7,775,460
Copper (*Cobre; Cobre; Cuivre*):				
Mexico	1,588,979	1,899,436	15,144,790	15,859,252
Cuba	8,706	26,425	65,746	97,006
South America	75,334	35,066	485,373	831,723
Fibers: Cotton, unmanufactured (*Algodón en rama; Algodao em rama; Coton non manufacturé*):				
South America	38,157	23,598	339,023	562,497
Sisal grass (*Henequén; Henequen; Henequen*):				
Mexico	1,277,296	982,347	11,944,259	12,463,677
Fruits: Bananas (*Plátanos; Bananas; Bananes*):				
Central America	461,409	422,330	3,588,400	4,139,475
Cuba	133,837	203,343	497,756	803,256
South America	52,429	15,871	340,852	13,861
Oranges (*Naranjas; Laranjas; Oranges*):				
Mexico	1,844	4,768	49,115	41,809
Cuba	2,371	137	10,149	7,963

Wood, mahogany (Caoba; Mogno; Acajou):			
Central America	37,495	19,281	467,398
Mexico	51,682	22,762	330,243
Cuba	23,766	19,916	103,149

Wool (Lana; LA; Laine):				
South America—				
Class 1 (clothing)	879,672	1,326,413	6,339,056	4,
Class 2 (combing)	8,477	92,996	199,014	
Class 3 (carpet)	50,512	37,624	589,615	

EXPORTS OF MERCHANDISE.

Agricultural implements (Instrumentos agricolas; Instrumentos de agricultura; Machines agricoles):				
Mexico	61,956	64,127	422,902	
Cuba	21,412	16,049	144,966	1
Argentine Republic	134,495	106,673	4,956,249	
Brazil	13,992	12,607	62,344	
Chile	8,888	16,031	291,584	
Other South America	14,623	17,722	263,740	
Animals:				
Cattle (Ganado vacuno; Gado; Bétail):				
Mexico	51,189	47,932	504,850	
Cuba	187,104	27,187	1,578,908	
South America	12,179		99,324	
Hogs (Cerdos; Porcos; Porcs):				
Mexico	15,033	11,035	122,543	
South America		205	1,320	
Horses (Caballos; Cavallos; Chevaux):				
Mexico	21,304	31,893	246,882	
Sheep (Ovejas; Ovelhas; Brébis):				
Mexico	19,046	17,066	52,026	
Books, maps, etc. (Libros, mapas, etc.; Livros, mappas, etc.; Livres, mappes, etc.):				
Central America	4,421	6,982	48,700	
Mexico	26,692	25,504	207,732	
Cuba	24,204	26,737	262,963	
Argentine Republic	9,068	7,272	63,469	
Brazil	2,562	13,547	105,764	
Chile	15,154	1,608	187,914	
Other South America	10,122	7,054	76,612	

EXPORTS OF MERCHANDISE—Continued.

	April—		Ten months ending April—	
	1906.	1907.	1906.	1907.
	Dollars.	Dollars.	Dollars.	Dollars.
Breadstuffs:				
Corn (Maiz; Milho; Mais):				
Central America	8,398	9,015	100,646	31,530
Mexico	74,007	73,861	772,530	942,600
Cuba	71,604	124,107	1,025,435	1,184,840
South America	1,048	774	17,806	8,320
Oats (Avena; Avcia; Avoine):				
Central America	6,837	1,650	30,003	23,827
Mexico	6,455	1,745	31,908	44,680
Cuba	25,312	19,438	202,797	288,374
South America	1,740	424	21,705	10,400
Wheat (Trigo; Trigo; Blé):				
Central America	315	2,550	35,504	28,003
Mexico	126,108	333,410	1,668,776	1,038,099
South America	75,300	21,906	461,942	359,099
Wheat flour (Harina de trigo; Farinha de trigo; Farine de blé):				
Central America	151,900	167,634	1,515,351	1,420,112
Mexico	9,234	18,372	147,114	117,741
Cuba	239,176	251,005	2,710,859	2,820,882
Brazil	105,804	127,645	1,049,185	1,128,442
Colombia	6,618	11,530	489,679	134,111
Other South America	417,955	86,767	2,187,787	1,623,335
Carriages, etc.:				
Automobiles (Automóbiles; Automoviles; Automobiles):				
Mexico	91,881	64,409	293,002	692,652
South America	9,748	11,214	61,780	170,270
Carriages, cars, etc., and parts of (Carruages, carros y sus accesorios; Carruagens, carros e partes de carros; Voitures wagons et leurs parties):				
Central America	24,950	309,114	1,029,915	1,544,883
Mexico	71,905	244,073	835,739	1,909,449
Cuba	80,557	42,885	924,668	679,639
Argentine Republic	29,481	181,240	355,863	1,842,013
Chile	13,814	25,110	404,931	146,267
Other South America	3,377	79,256	208,830	508,634
Cycles and parts of (Bicicletas y sus accesorios; Bicyclos e partes; Bicyclettes et leurs parties):				
Mexico	7,361	6,318	71,186	79,202
Cuba	2,461	3,153	30,800	30,595
Argentine Republic	688	1,760	13,315	16,203
Brazil	1,387	1,453	7,860	10,184
Other South America	1,238	1,262	14,093	17,229
Clocks and watches (Relojes de pared y bolsillo; Relogios de bolso e parede; Horlogés et montres):				
Central America	1,671	1,740	15,077	14,707
Mexico	23,309	5,185	66,409	42,345
Argentine Republic	9,838	18,800	61,800	65,999
Brazil	3,763	8,735	59,432	70,160
Chile	2,200	5,918	58,657	41,297
Other South America	2,048	4,238	40,042	34,522
Coal (Carbón; Carrão; Charbon):				
Mexico	225,486	332,206	2,484,096	2,713,367
Cuba	88,076	246,054	1,590,206	1,788,109
Copper (Cobre; Cobre; Cuivre):				
Mexico	87,635	124,647	1,058,715	831,118
Cotton:				
Cotton, unmanufactured (Algodón en rama; Algodao em rama; Coton non manufacturé:				
Mexico	37,365	....	1,590,995	26,413
Cotton cloths (Tejidos de algodón; Fazendas de algodão; Coton manufacturé):				
Central America	143,711	142,561	1,320,144	1,430,323
Mexico	21,912	19,332	231,008	213,183
Cuba	63,243	97,009	929,847	895,206
Argentine Republic	23,942	10,214	256,369	213,990
Brazil	53,336	44,103	524,301	369,037
Chile	63,582	48,402	749,622	861,116
Colombia	80,896	74,565	528,269	709,063
Venezuela	47,037	19,041	321,222	397,890
Other South America	31,938	59,772	382,218	457,489
Wearing apparel (Ropa de algodón; Fazendas de algodão; Vêtements de coton):				
Central America	39,912	64,823	226,085	339,218
Mexico	27,984	34,349	244,409	247,921
Cuba	21,614	40,516	211,137	389,041
Other South America	13,001	6,443	76,332	61,389

EXPORTS OF MERCHANDISE—Continued.

	April—		Two months ending April—	
	1906.	1907.	1906.	1907.

	Dollars.	Dollars.	Dollars.	Dollars.
Argentine Republic	80,162	63,971	575,140	678,0
Brazil	39,620	46,333	345,533	433,0
Chile	18,399	24,634	189,666	270,0
Colombia	7,300	9,270	53,893	62,1
Venezuela	3,008	2,434	33,217	49,2
Other South America	126,733	89,820	609,865	734,0
Sewing machines and parts of (*Máquinas de coser y sus accesorios; Machinas de coser e accesorios; Machines à coudre et leurs parties*):				
Central America	14,098	12,567	102,918	109,1
Mexico	73,260	79,721	546,649	673,2
Cuba	28,151	35,426	256,590	282,9
Argentine Republic	20,196	37,772	607,690	396,9
Brazil	17,267	40,235	166,834	371,6
Colombia	4,273	6,130	53,379	60,1
Other South America	37,072	26,093	318,751	338,7
Steam engines and parts of (*Locomotoras y accesorios; Locomotiras e accesorios; Locomotifs et leurs parties*):				
Central America	456,117	11,307	823,755	1,115,6
Mexico		92,640	298,600	1,112,5
Cuba		31,225	650,421	733,6
Argentine Republic		2,505	189,651	407,4
Brazil	4,250	344,731	255,958	578,1
Other South America	46,751	64,572	307,117	639,3
Typewriting machines and parts of (*Mecanógrafos y accesorios; Machinas de escribir e accesorios; Machines à écrire et leurs parties*):				
Central America	1,905	2,868	43,165	36,5
Mexico	38,114	32,358	274,234	316,5
Cuba	3,538	9,724	59,792	86,1
Argentine Republic	4,839	9,200	81,413	90,6
Brazil	6,764	5,993	32,925	52,5
Colombia	772	1,912	9,649	14,9
Other South America	7,502	18,954	114,075	186,9
Pipes and fittings (*Cañería; Tubos; Tuyaux*):				
Central America	44,266	30,416	323,116	455,1
Mexico	159,565	75,822	1,256,263	1,006,2
Cuba	22,736	69,233	520,192	482,0
Argentine Republic	15,174	9,666	107,226	92,8
Other South America	14,969	7,675	163,149	192,9
Leather, other than sole (*Cuero distinto del de suelas; Couro, não para solas; Cuirs, autres que pour semelles*):				
Central America	14,943	23,657	152,357	183,9
Cuba	13,170	11,511	191,894	104,6
Argentine Republic	22,581	13,784	280,273	198,7
Brazil	71,527	14,263	121,277	111,6
Other South America	71,708	9,533	189,657	300,0

EXPORTS OF MERCHANDISE—Continued.

	April—		Ten months ending April—	
	1906.	1907.	1906.	1907.
	Dollars.	Dollars.	Dollars.	Dollars.
Boots and shoes (*Calzados; Calçados; Chaussures*):				
Central America	39,448	54,282	344,229	479,538
Mexico	135,459	120,808	1,280,910	1,255,441
Colombia	5,251	2,339	40,785	33,752
Other South America	26,672	29,004	254,275	325,077
Meat and dairy products:				
Beef, canned (*Carne de vaca en latas; Carne de vacca em latas; Boeuf conservé*):				
Central America	5,509	6,841	37,520	56,822
Mexico	1,725	1,791	22,807	22,950
Cuba	589	1,553	21,382	16,086
Other South America	2,798	1,635	36,098	34,032
Beef, salted and pickled (*Carne de vaca salada ó adobada; Carne de vacca, salgada; Boeuf salé*):				
Central America	12,536	10,495	90,212	116,355
South America	25,825	8,122	219,740	197,416
Tallow (*Sebo; Sebo; Suif*):				
Central America	10,098	8,285	134,682	108,637
Mexico	2,059	437	80,064	20,239
Cuba	86	15,429	7,970	37,182
Chile	4,500		51,204	54,172
Other South America	2,773	2,432	44,850	44,119
Bacon (*Tocino; Toucinho; Lard fumé*):				
Central America	4,768	6,325	22,200	31,540
Mexico	3,557	6,869	37,765	82,571
Cuba	56,200	64,300	372,949	512,575
Brazil	15,549	15,552	144,139	158,882
Other South America	2,496	709	13,464	12,324
Hams (*Jamones; Presuntos; Jambons*):				
Central America	10,721	10,905	79,039	120,154
Mexico	5,591	10,797	103,472	99,711
Cuba	43,323	62,754	414,613	502,820
Venezuela	4,654	1,829	42,058	37,323
Other South America	4,546	3,013	60,245	49,170
Pork (*Carne de puerco; Carne de porco; Porc*):				
Cuba	41,567	75,233	492,729	614,342
South America	17,358	14,981	196,298	212,681
Lard (*Manteca; Banha; Saindoux*):				
Central America	33,605	76,456	378,928	576,201
Mexico	21,662	70,834	486,445	576,166
Cuba	299,778	243,010	2,248,934	2,432,510
Brazil	98,324	150,577	227,458	1,005,724
Chile	10,030	13,318	67,563	145,700
Colombia	6,554	9,123	294,476	46,000
Venezuela	25,062	6,888	313,334	182,350
Other South America	86,286	30,500	508,457	446,756
Butter (*Mantequilla; Manteiga; Beurre*):				
Central America	15,419	15,707	105,948	141,572
Mexico	14,976	11,878	109,068	125,137
Cuba	7,644	5,245	41,135	60,829
Brazil	10,203	2,366	117,195	62,366
Venezuela	13,084	2,373	96,288	45,182
Other South America	5,480	4,238	33,684	44,788
Cheese (*Queso; Queijo; Fromage*):				
Central America	6,407	7,220	57,305	68,528
Mexico	3,661	2,659	37,281	35,895
Cuba	1,241	3,250	10,898	19,884
Naval stores:				
Rosin, tar, etc. (*Resina, alquitrán, etc.; Resina e alcatrão; Résine et goudron*):				
Cuba	4,412	4,963	56,979	69,133
Argentine Republic	45,898		387,007	338,563
Brazil	64,031	43,324	520,272	539,452
Other South America	14,768	19,162	264,572	208,574
Turpentine (*Aguarras; Aguaraz; Térébenthine*):				
Central America	1,032	2,068	39,272	30,028
Cuba	5,911	5,210	58,493	71,614
Argentine Republic	15,111	15,156	181,093	162,154
Brazil	14,541	6,809	99,251	125,898
Chile	2,457	7,800	63,121	86,313
Other South America	4,033	6,206	46,944	62,692
Oils:				
Mineral, crude (*Aceites minerales, crudos; Oleos mineraes, crús; Huiles minerales, brutes*):				
Mexico	72,308	23,333	557,833	891,209
Cuba	64,557	86,923	380,891	431,375

EXPORTS OF MERCHANDISE—Continued.

	April—		Ten months ending April—	
	1906.	1907.	1906.	1907.
Refined or manufactured (*Aceites refinados ó manufacturados; Oleos refinados ou manufacturados; Huiles raffinées ou manufacturées*):	Dollars.	Dollars.	Dollars.	Dollars.
Central America	33,014	21,577	227,510	
Mexico	33,538	7,751	173,600	
Cuba	28,511	62,233	286,074	
Argentine Republic	27,495	135,841	1,617,600	
Brazil	226,349	207,564	2,301,266	
Chile	30,806	90,425	582,954	
Other South America	73,975	119,250	900,942	
Vegetable (*Aceites vegetales; Oleos vegetaes; Huiles vegetales*):				
Central America	3,014	5,620	25,509	
Mexico	52,320	60,009	678,150	
Cuba	28,869	27,553	196,692	
Argentine Republic	2,093	4,348	31,363	
Brazil	51,302	80,708	180,091	
Chile	3,432	17,390	18,629	
Other South America	14,005	30,578	132,340	
Paper (*Papel; Papel; Papier*):				
Mexico	909	4,574	29,802	
Cuba	9,645	18,714	161,345	
Argentine Republic	6,415	10,990	185,053	
Brazil	461	270	32,500	
Chile	12,294	22,791	134,964	
Other South America	5,053	5,190	78,883	
Paraffin (*Parafina; Parafina; Paraffine*):				
Central America	3,210	3,859	49,651	
Mexico	38,619	56,771	496,275	
South America	2,891	5,302	24,497	
Tobacco, manufactured (*Tabaco en rama; Tabacco nao monufacturado; Tabac non manufacturé*):				
Central America	8,845	2,956	65,085	
Mexico	5,478	8,054	76,009	
Argentine Republic	686	4,860	44,094	
Colombia	987	1,577	5,472	
Other South America	9,006	4,914	66,620	
Tobacco, manufactures of (*Tabaco elaborado; Tabac manufacturé*):				
Central America	4,251	5,920	49,396	
Wood, and manufactures of:				
Wood, unmanufactured (*Madera sin labrar; Madeira não manufacturada; Bois brut*):				
Central America	53,046	54,286	413,780	
Mexico	100,800	145,208	816,104	
Cuba	15,953	10,921	142,161	
Argentine Republic	35,000	4,967	163,401	
Other South America	2,736	4,617	126,382	
Lumber (*Maderas; Madeiras; Bois de construction*):				
Central America	112,350	90,334	983,274	
Mexico	186,784	134,171	1,470,193	
Cuba	187,254	236,001	2,021,835	
Argentine Republic	208,386	251,082	2,856,326	
Brazil	81,783	181,620	552,034	
Chile	60,309	191,970	518,481	
Other South America	76,742	146,544	631,819	
Furniture (*Muebles; Mobilia; Meubles*):				
Central America	41,266	23,837	262,804	
Mexico	85,360	89,811	690,790	
Cuba	50,458	70,351	627,745	
Argentine Republic	10,564	44,408	255,275	
Brazil	7,052	6,168	38,882	
Chile	3,650	1,662	61,812	
Colombia	3,031	1,312	18,639	
Venezuela	4,204	1,767	18,630	

FOREIGN COMMERCE FOR APRIL, 1907.

The foreign commerce of the United States for April 1907, as shown by the statement issued by the Department of Commerce and Labor, made large gains over the corresponding month of 1906, the imports amounting to $129,554,075 and the exports to $157,444,281, as against $107,318,081 for imports and $141,946,383 for exports in April, 1906.

For the ten months' period ending with April, 1907, imports show a recorded value of $1,195,399,276, as compared with $1,020,873,178 in the same period of the preceding year, while exports are valued at $1,608,344,680, against $1,488,282,130 in the first ten months of the preceding year.

Taking the exports by classes, an actual decrease both for the month and the ten months' period is noted in "foodstuffs in crude condition" and in "foodstuffs partly or wholly manufactured" compared with a year ago. The reduction in the former for April was slight, being from $13,770,221 to $13,659,742, but for the ten months the value declined from $158,574,113 to $140,493,914. These include cereal grains and live food animals, meat and flour and meal coming under the head of partly or wholly manufactured foodstuffs. In this class also the decline was slight for the month and relatively greater for the ten months. The figures for April are $28,199,706 in 1906 and $28,031,915 in 1907, and for the ten months the decrease is from $294,546,844 to $287,610,553. The percentage that these foodstuffs constitute of the total exports fell from 30.89 to 26.96 for the longer period.

There was a considerable increase in the export of crude materials for manufacture over 1906 from $38,691,927 to $44,615,629 for the month, and from $446,012,207 to $542,520,911 for the ten months. The part that raw cotton played in this advance may be seen in the separate figures for that material. They were $31,797,617 for April last year and $36,032,382 for April this year, and $366,265,727 last year and $450,626,586 this year for the ten months ending with April. In manufactures for further use in manufacturing the increase for the month was from $19,443,958 to $22,681,453, and for the ten months from $184,482,087 to $214,322,749. Herein copper and mineral oil and some of the important items of iron and steel exports figure prominently. Copper alone shows a gain from $6,059,076 to $7,284,931 for the month, and from $62,520,350 to $73,395,587 for the ten months. Total exports of iron and steel, not including ore, increased from $14,933,495 to $17,684,863 for April, and from $131,214,260 to $149,710,569 for ten months of the fiscal year. This includes both manufactures "ready for consumption," like machinery and builder's hardware, and those for further use in manufacturing, like pig iron, bars, steel billets, etc. The table for leather and leather goods is similarly mixed, the total for ten months showing a gain from $32,995,147 to $37,971,149.

The interesting feature in imports is the increase in materials of manufacture. For those in crude condition the increase for the month was from $41,157,156 to $46,208,637, and for the ten months from $345,013,144 to $401,310,942. Manufactures for further use in manufacturing increased from $18,810,834 to $23,476,930 for April, and from $178,052,977 to $227,945,850 for ten months. The two together for the ten months constitute 52.64 per cent of all imports, against 51.24 a year ago. The most important imports of raw materials are hides and skins, raw silk, india rubber, and wool. For ten months ending with April imports of hides and skins increased only from $66,681,774 to $66,711,687. Raw silk increased from $47,064,022 to $63,565,043, india rubber from $40,846,762 to $53,577,526, and wool from $33,425,262 to $35,010,575. A considerable amount of copper and of iron and steel in various forms was imported. Of the latter the imports amounted to $32,795,503 for ten months, against $23,296,873 for the corresponding period a year before.

Of manufactures "ready for consumption" imports were worth $24,205,423 in April last year and $28,966,427 this year, but in the same month exports of this class were valued at $40,589,137 last year and $45,201,876 this. For the ten months imports of these articles amounted to $259,118,881 last year and $303,678,867 this, and exports show an increase in the same period from $377,974,240 to $397,127,671. These constitute 25.40 per cent of the total imports and 25.01 per cent of the exports. Exports of cotton manufactures for ten months fell from $45,172,807 to $28,166,449, while imports increased from $53,730,480 to $62,532,292. The largest gain in exports of manufactures is in products of iron and steel.

Total trade values for the periods in reference, with the various grand divisions of the earth and with the countries of Latin America, were as follows:

Countries.	April.			
	Imports.		Exports.	
	1906.	1907.	1906.	1907.
North America............................	$23,749,170	$26,857,136	$37,739,449	$62,877,49
Central American States:				
Costa Rica............................	545,366	709,261	323,779	227,599
Guatemala............................	326,420	1,195,584		
Honduras............................	186,495	169,394		111,49
Nicaragua............................	157,397	44,395		
Panama..............................	77,915	128,562	1,692,549	1,...
Salvador.......	63,834	605,013	705,842	
Total Central American States.........	1,327,396	2,783,394	2,358,707	2,...
Mexico.................................	4,564,437	5,345,945	6,284,743	6,...
Cuba.................................	11,469,846	13,372,299	3,549,649	4,...
Haiti.................................	100,342	72,645	127,951	
Santo Domingo.........................	247,649	853,494	104,276	
Total West Indies.....................	12,709,137	14,304,481	4,468,590	4,...
South America:				
Argentina.............................	1,713,104	1,965,965	1,299,492	3,...
Bolivia.............................			1,...	
Brazil.............................	4,685,967	5,994,946		

Countries.	April.			
	Imports.		Exports.	
	1906	1907.	1906.	1907.
South America—Continued.				
Chile	$583,347	$1,639,680	$851,204	$928,219
Colombia	618,547	390,443	241,251	259,860
Ecuador	178,102	160,679	175,829	144,651
Falkland Islands				
Guiana:				
British	844	18,226	163,273	92,079
Dutch	67,278	63,438	66,951	19,051
French	4,875	3,540	18,962	40,980
Paraguay		1,163	4,279	22,235
Peru	110,036	751,626	448,327	478,318
Uruguay	43,907	444,784	173,474	373,218
Venezuela	663,528	686,938	337,877	183,902
Total South America	8,640,275	14,937,516	5,464,119	7,047,176
Europe	53,663,089	61,353,259	98,965,089	103,132,801
North America	23,740,170	28,537,136	27,739,448	32,877,450
South America	8,640,275	14,937,516	5,464,119	7,047,176
Asia	17,010,873	18,831,026	7,530,418	9,983,366
Oceania	3,161,224	3,499,733	2,964,740	3,380,207
Africa	1,082,450	2,395,405	1,696,256	1,023,281

Countries.	Ten months ending April.			
	Imports.		Exports.	
	1906.	1907.	1906.	1907.
North America	$187,843,756	$207,093,897	$251,994,103	$283,819,230
Central American States:				
Costa Rica	3,919,591	4,022,510	1,854,313	2,023,053
Guatemala	2,548,912	2,865,893	2,407,439	2,451,558
Honduras	1,280,546	1,747,192	1,325,877	1,501,707
Nicaragua	1,182,183	838,251	1,552,258	1,681,171
Panama	846,326	1,398,086	9,866,660	12,933,407
Salvador	737,356	962,484	1,208,286	1,184,829
Total Central American States	10,514,914	11,834,418	18,214,833	21,775,725
Mexico	41,952,052	46,773,302	47,926,765	54,085,668
Cuba	66,024,615	73,259,855	40,432,395	40,826,489
Haiti	1,011,266	908,117	2,901,045	2,458,043
Santo Domingo	2,156,914	2,270,762	1,666,399	2,172,814
Total West Indies	77,771,079	87,061,666	55,361,979	56,584,086
South America:				
Argentina	14,740,490	13,421,819	26,617,860	28,040,713
Bolivia			119,545	724,300
Brazil	71,402,677	85,902,325	11,808,311	15,361,665
Chile	13,056,961	14,878,545	6,921,564	8,565,873
Colombia	5,740,180	5,356,523	2,975,340	2,566,444
Ecuador	1,999,562	2,444,520	1,507,404	1,393,864
Falkland Islands			1,166	
Guiana:				
British	1,000,109	1,197,104	1,424,445	1,521,762
Dutch	571,451	481,478	451,212	431,447
French	38,383	26,772	266,943	287,082
Paraguay	750	2,337	38,805	145,045
Peru	2,047,352	3,805,017	4,219,400	5,172,877
Uruguay	2,199,842	2,609,100	2,345,750	2,898,402
Venezuela	6,843,573	6,438,100	2,634,581	2,516,863
Total South America	119,641,330	136,563,640	61,422,326	69,626,317
Europe	526,601,810	626,952,924	1,038,294,833	1,129,161,441
North America	187,843,756	207,093,897	251,994,103	283,819,230
South America	119,641,330	136,563,640	61,422,326	69,626,317
Asia	153,775,605	182,921,685	91,191,191	76,982,333
Oceania	21,951,094	23,729,578	28,748,040	34,765,690
Africa	11,059,581	18,137,552	16,631,637	13,969,689

WOOL IMPORTS FROM LATIN AMERICA DURING 1906.

Figures covering imports of wool, hair of the alpaca, goat, and other like animals, by the United States, during 1906, show the following as regards receipts from Mexico and South America:

For clothing: From Mexico 1,364 pounds were received, valued at $183; from the Argentine Republic, 30,145,400 pounds, valued at $6,645,684; from Brazil, 38,523 pounds, worth $6,694; from Chile, 383,534 pounds, worth $60,536; from Peru, 23,198 pounds, worth $5,711, and from Uruguay, 3,829,868 pounds, worth $847,985.

Carpet wools: From Mexico, 3,403 pounds, valued at $234; the Argentine Republic, 5,747,772 pounds, valued at $781,396; Brazil, 76,075 pounds, valued at $4,528; Chile, 247,012 pounds, valued at $25,300; Uruguay, 3,995 pounds, worth $458, and from Venezuela, 6,569 pounds, valued at $367, while other South American countries supplied 1,884 pounds, valued at $124, making total receipts from South America 6,083,307 pounds, with a valuation of $812,173.

URUGUAY.

FOREIGN COMMERCE FOR THE FIRST HALF OF 1906.

Figures issued by the Statistical Bureau of the Republic of Uruguay state that the imports for the half year January–June, 1906, amounted to $17,052,581, an increase over the same period of the preceding year of $2,356,098 gold.   Exports are given as $20,178,400, an increase of $1,874,786 over 1905.

Great Britain supplied the bulk of the imports, though her percentage of 30 per cent of a few years ago has declined to 27 per cent.   Germany has advanced to second place, with 16 per cent; France, third, with 12.3 per cent; United States fourth, the Argentine Republic fifth, and Italy sixth.

Of the exports France is the principal purchaser, taking about $5,000,000 out of the total $20,000,000.   Belgium and Germany each take about $3,000,000; the Argentine Republic and Brazil, $2,800,000 and $1,800,000, respectively, while the United States is only reported for $750,000 for the half year.

INDORSEMENT OF THE PROJECTED BOARD OF JURISCONSULTS.

Through the Department of State of the United States, the International Bureau of the American Republics was informed under date of May 10, 1907, that on March 27, 1907, the President of the Republic of Uruguay had formally approved the Convention signed on August 23, 1906, in the city of Rio de Janeiro in regard to the assembling of an international board of jurisconsults, subject to final action of the General Assembly.

This board is to be composed of one representative from each of the signatory States, nominated by the respective government, and is to meet for the purpose of preparing a project of a code of international private law and another of international public law.

One of the provisions of the convention was that the nominations of the members of the board be communicated to the Government of Brazil before April 1, 1907, and the President of Uruguay, pending the favorable action of the National Congress in the matter has designated Dr. GONZALO RAMIREZ as the Government's representative.

Doctor RAMIREZ was the organizer of the Montevideo Legal Congress and is a publicist of note, being professor of international private law in the University of Uruguay.

VENEZUELA.

TRADE OF CARUPANO FOR THE FIRST QUARTER OF 1907.

According to the bulletin for the first quarter of 1907, published by the Chamber of Commerce of Carupano, the foreign trade of that port during said period amounted to 1,920,912 *bolivares*, as compared with 1,467,438 *bolivares* in the same period of 1906. The 361,953 kilograms of merchandise imported during the first quarter of 1907 were valued at 258,123 *bolivares*, as against 295,354 *bolivares*, value of 408,995 kilograms of merchandise imported in the corresponding quarter of 1906. One million one hundred and seventy-two thousand and eighty-four kilograms of merchandise, valued at 1,662,789 *bolivares*, were shipped abroad during the quarter in reference, as compared with 1,129,354 kilograms, valued at 1,165,055 *bolivares*, exported in the same period of 1906. The fiscal revenues collected at the custom-house during the first three months of 1907 made a total of 368,695.74 *bolivares*, the principal item being "import duties," which are credited with the amount of 189,662.26 *bolivares*.

TRADE OF CIUDAD BOLIVAR FOR THE FIRST QUARTER OF 1907.

The port of Ciudad Bolivar, for the first three months of 1907, reports a total valuation of imports of 1,767,572.90 *bolivares*, and of exports 1,149,350 *bolivares*. On the foregoing, customs duties amounting to 1,159,887.15 *bolivares* were collected.

Balata rubber was the leading item of export, 150,987 kilograms valued at 643,412 *bolivares* being shipped. Other items were: gold, 174,904 *bolivares;* hides, 146,744 *bolivares*, and 700 heifers worth 70,000 *bolivares*.

FOREIGN TRADE IN 1906.

In a report on Venezuela for the year 1906, the British Minister at Caracas states that the imports amounted to $8,750,500 and exports to $15,763;950. Taking the returns of the past four years, imports may be said on the whole to be decreasing, while exports are almost stationary.

Of the foreign goods imported into Venezuela, about equal values were received from the United States and from Great Britain and her colonies, who sent about 27 per cent and 26 per cent, respectively, Great Britain thus gaining considerable ground as compared with 1905, when the proportions were 28.2 per cent and 23.3 per cent. The third country in importance to supply Venezuela with goods is Germany, whose trade seems somewhat on the decline, having sunk from a position about equal to that of Great Britain to some 17 per cent in 1906.

The principal articles of importation are: From the United States, cereals and kerosene oil; from Great Britain and her colonies, coal, textiles, and hardware; from Germany, rice and cement.

The chief article of export from Venezuela is coffee, which at present amounts to about 40,000 tons per annum, or 45 per cent of the total value of the export trade, followed in value by cocoa, cattle and hides, balata and gold.

TRADE OF PUERTO CABELLO IN 1906.

Foreign trade through the port of Puerto Cabello in 1906 showed some improvement, but was below the figures of two previous years. The following table, prepared from the most reliable figures obtainable, forwarded by the United States Consul, gives the value of imports by countries:

Countries.	1904.	1905.	1906.	Countries.	1904.	1905.	1906.
England..........	$818,987	$444,308	$535,346	Spain............	$141,321	$169,337	$94,493
United States....	474,722	428,146	522,648	Italy............	81,155	45,030	49,347
Germany..........	459,404	271,608	300,907				
France...........	191,037	116,838	16,549	Total......	2,305,919	1,474,838	1,036,558
Holland..........	140,293	67,308	140,133				

The foregoing table shows that the United States is the only country which made a gain over the figures of 1904; the sales of England decreased almost a third, those of Germany show a considerable falling off, while France all but lost the market.

The following table shows the exports, by articles, from Puerto Cabello in 1906:

Articles.	Pounds.	Value.	Articles.	Pounds.	Value.
Cocoa	2,005,733	$237,915	Woods	202,275	$770
Coffee	28,079,407	2,176,265	All other articles	884,896	41,463
Copra	147,545	3,650			
Deerskins	78,542	11,172	Total	33,255,006	2,749,264
Divi-divi	150,827	1,096	Cattle........number	71,806	1,201,008
Goatskins	663,359	102,597			
Hides	1,019,838	173,327	Total		3,950,272
Old copper	21,584	1,009			

The following shows the exports to the United States in 1906:

Articles.	Pounds.	Value.	Articles.	Pounds.	Value.
Bones	250,152	$1,080	Hides	822,138	$152,919
Calfskins	1,225	211	Orchids	728	128
Cocoa	135,578	23,343	Tonka beans	2,504	599
Cocoanuts	437,104	2,196	All other articles	3,525	433
Coffee	3,871,899	347,669			
Deerskins	64,061	11,072	Total	6,653,242	687,775
Goatskins	1,065,056	148,222			

By comparing the foregoing table with the table of imports it may be seen that Venezuela sent to the United States through Puerto Cabello $687,775 worth of goods and bought in return $522,648 worth, leaving a balance of trade in its favor of $165,127. The United States has no rival in the imports of wheat flour, lard, and kerosene, and leads all other countries in hams, barbed wire, and patent medicine. .

The only public work of any importance undertaken during the year in this district was the construction by the Government of a dry dock and machine shops. The dock is one of 3,000 tons; it is being built by an American firm and by American workmen. The principal machinery of the shops and the entire electric-light plant of the works are of American manufacture.

FREE IMPORTATION OF CERTAIN ARTICLES.

On April 18, 1907, President CASTRO, for the purpose of protecting the alcohol distilling industry, deemed advisable to order the free entrance through the custom-houses of the Republic, for two years from the aforesaid date, of the following articles:

Alcohol heating apparatus and their motors.

Lamps especially constructed for alcohol and which do not operate with any other agent, as well as their attachments not adaptable to other lamps.

Alcohol burners for lighting purposes and their attachments, such as manchons or incandescent covers.

Talc and glass chimneys for said lamps and devices used for lighting the same.

IMPORTATION OF POSTAL PACKAGES.

On April 23, 1907, President CASTRO issued the following decree:

"ARTICLE 1. In order to regulate the internal service of postal packages, the number shall not exceed four packages of 5 kilograms each of the same article, brought in the same vessel, for each importer, without prejudice to the tariff duties and other imposts now in force.

"ART. 2. Whenever the importer introduces a greater number of kilograms in postal packages containing the same merchandise on the same vessel he shall pay, in addition to the duties and imposts now in force, 20 per cent of the tariff duties on the total weight of the same merchandise.

"ART. 3. Importers of postal packages are granted the foreign term provided by the Treasury regulations, counting from the date of this decree."

BOOK NOTES.

Books and pamphlets sent to the Bureau of the American Republics, and containing subject-matter bearing upon the countries of the International Union of American Republics, will be treated under this caption in the Monthly Bulletin.

In the opening paragraph of his article on South America—the land of to-morrow—published in "The Munsey Magazine" for June, 1907, Mr. JOHN BARRETT states that the ignorance prevailing generally throughout the United States in regard to this great southern continent is almost appalling. Further, that more attention is given by the press of Europe to South America in a week than by all the papers of the United States in a year. It is with the purpose of dispelling some of this ignorance that the article in reference was prepared. The writer treats his subject *con amore*, and details facts to support his statement that South America has many extraordinary features of natural and artificial development that surprise the uninformed. The vast areas and resources of the southern half of the Western Hemisphere are more or less matters of current knowledge, but that the city of Rio de Janeiro spent, in 1906, more money for public improvements than any city in the United States except New York; that Buenos Aires is the largest city in the world south of the equator, ranking second only to Paris as a Latin city; that it contains as the home of a newspaper the finest and costliest office building in the world; that its opera house is the most magnificent in the Western Hemisphere; its leading clubhouse, the handsomest and largest in the world, and its dock system the most extensive in all America, while at Lima, in Peru, and at Córdoba, in the Argentine

Republic, are universities far antedating Harvard and Yale. These features of national life are neither generally known nor appreciated. It is from its commercial aspects that South America is called the land of to-morrow, and figures are furnished showing the immense strides made during the past few years by Argentine, Brazilian, Chilean, and other national governments in bringing the native products into the markets of the world. That the United States does not take its logical position in this commerce is largely due to differences of language and lineage, which disadvantages have, however, been overcome in other instances and have never yet formed an insuperable barrier to trade intercourse. Illustrations of public buildings, industrial works, and municipal monuments amply indicate the esthetic side of life in South America.

As secretary and subsequent member of the Board of Commissioners appointed in 1884 to study intercontinental trade conditions in America, Mr. WILLIAM ELEROY CURTIS speaks authoritatively in his "Brief History of the Reciprocity Policy," published in the May (1907) number of the "Annals of the American Academy of Political and Social Science." Following the abortive effort to secure reciprocal trade relations with Canada, the United States Government made its first active endeavor to extend its commercial relations in Latin America through a treaty with Mexico in 1882, which, however, expired by limitation on May 20, 1887, without the necessary measures being taken for its enactment. Equally unsuccessful were efforts directed toward Cuba, Porto Rico, and Santo Domingo, and it was not until the Board of Commissioners above mentioned made their tour of Central and South America in 1884 that any tangible results were obtained. As an outgrowth of the international conference recommended by the Commission, the International Bureau of the American Republics was established, and interest in Latin America and its trade possibilities was greatly augmented. Reciprocally advantageous commercial measures were inaugurated with nearly all the Republics of Central and South America and with the British and Spanish colonies in the West Indies, and negotiations with Mexico were renewed. Under these conditions the exports of the United States to Latin America increased from $63,000,000 to $103,000,000. Subsequent legislation altered tariff conditions, and though concessions have been made covering certain specified items of commerce, reciprocity has not taken a prominent place in the policy of the United States Government.

With special reference to the needs of the Spanish-American traveler, a directory and guide of the city of New York has been prepared and issued by JULIO ACEVADO as the organ of the general Spanish-American agency in that city. In addition to a map and general description of New York, the volume contains information as to means of communication, piers, places of amusement and general interest, while the vocabulary of phrases in Spanish and English is a valuable aid to the traveler. The prices charged for telegrams, messenger service, etc., are recorded, and monetary equivalents expressed in the currency of the United States and in that of the various countries of Latin America. The bulk of the volume is devoted, however, to a business directory in which may be found the names and addresses of persons and of commercial and manufacturing houses where Spanish is spoken and where there is more or less interest or connection with the Spanish or Spanish-American people. The information is carefully classified and indexed, so that it is readily available.

From the *Imprenta Nacional* of Bogota, Colombia, comes Volume V of the Library of National History (*Biblioteca de Historia Nacional*), embracing the papers written by Padre Fray PEDRO DE AGUADO on early Colombian settlement and history. Though now published for the first time, they were prepared in the sixteenth century, and have formed the source of authoritative information to students and historians.

A report presented by the President of the Chamber of Commerce, Agriculture, and Industries of Quito, dated March 2, 1907, has been forwarded to the Columbus Memorial Library by Mr. WILLIAMS C. Fox, United States Minister to Ecuador, as the initial publication of that body. The governmental and other reports contained therein indicate a forward movement in the economic conditions of the Republic.

"Dun's Review" for June, 1907, is issued as a special Cuban number and is devoted very largely to setting forth the conditions that exist at present in the Island Republic. Apart from a consideration of the commercial, industrial, and political status of the country, the climatic and artistic values of the "Pearl of the Antilles" are described.

"Costa Rica" as described in the personal journal of SEGARRA Y JULIA, 1907, forms an interesting and instructive volume of travels recently received by the Columbus Memorial Library. Written in a light, almost colloquial style, it narrates with charm and veracity the impressions and experiences of the writers in a trip from sea to sea in Central America.

MEXICO.

GREAT BRITAIN. FOREIGN OFFICE: Report on the Mexican Budget for the fiscal year 1907–8. . . . London, Harrison and Sons, 1907. 15 p. 8°.
(Diplomatic and consular reports, annual series no. 3751.)

MEXICO. MINISTERIO DE HACIENDA Y CRÉDITO PÚBLICO: Memoria . . . correspondiente al año económico de 1° de julio de 1902 á 30 de junio de 1903 . . . México, Tip. de la Oficina Impresora de Estampillas, 1907. xviii, 371, clxi p. 4°.

PANAMA.

PANAMA. MINISTERIO DE GOBIERNO Y RELACIONES EXTERIORES: Memoria presentada á la asamblea nacional de 1906 por el Secretario de gobierno y relaciones exteriores. Panama, Tip. de Torre é hijos, 1907. xcv, 449 p. 4°.

PERU.

[RODRÍGUEZ, P. M. comp.]: César Canevaro. Veinticinco año de general 12 de abril de 1882–12 de abril de 1907. Lima, Imp. Carlos F. Southwell, [1907.] iv p. front. (port.) 8°.

PHILIPPINE ISLANDS.

U. S. PHILIPPINE COMMISSION: Seventh annual report of the Philippine commission. 1906. In three parts. . . . Washington, Government Printing Office, 1907. 3 v. 8°.

UNITED STATES.

AMERICAN POLITICAL SCIENCE ASSOCIATION: Proceedings of the . . . Association, held at Chicago, Ill., December 28 to 30, 1904. Lancaster, Pa., Wickersham Press, 1905. 249 p. 8°.

—— Same. Second annual meeting held at Baltimore, Md., December 26 to 29, 1905. Lancaster, Pa., Wickersham Press, 1906. 232 p. 8°.

FIELD COLUMBIAN MUSEUM: Annual report of the Director to the Board of Trustees for the year 1906. Chicago, January, 1907. 108 p. 8°.
(Publication of the Museum, 119. Report series, vol. 3, no. 1.)

—— Analysis of iron meteorites compiled and classified. By Oliver Cummings Farrington, Curator, Department of Geology. Chicago, March 1, 1907. 59–110 p. 8°.
(Geological series, v. 3, no. 5.)

JOHN CRERAR LIBRARY: . . . Twelfth annual report. For the year 1906. Chicago, 1907. 64 p. 8°.

LEWIS AND CLARK CENTENNIAL EXPOSITION: Report of the . . . exposition commission for the state of Oregon. Held at Portland, Oregon, June first to October fifteenth, 1905. (Salem, J. R. Whitney, 1906.) [64] p. front. 41 pls. 8°.

MARYLAND GEOLOGICAL SURVEY: Calvert county. Baltimore, The Johns Hopkins Press, 1907. 227 p. plates. 8°.
(With case of maps.)

—— St. Mary's county. Baltimore, The Johns Hopkins Press, 1907. 209 p. plates. 8°.
(With case of maps.)

NATIONAL ARBITRATION AND PEACE CONGRESS: American prophets of peace. Souvenir of the National Arbitration and Peace Congress. New York, April, 1907. [42] p. illus. 8°.

TRANS-MISSISSIPPI COMMERCIAL CONGRESS: Official proceedings of the seventeenth session of the Trans-Mississippi Commercial Congress held at Kansas City, Missouri, November 20, 21, 22 & 23, 1906. . . . Kansas City, Union Bank Note Company, 1906. 319 p. illus. 8°.

U. S. BUREAU OF THE CENSUS: Mortality statistics. 1905. Sixth annual report . . . Washington, Government Printing Office, 1907. iv, 354 p. 4°.

—— BUREAU OF STATISTICS: Exports of manufactures and their distribution by articles and countries. 1800 to 1906. Washington, Government Printing Office, 1907. 63 p. 4°.

—— CONGRESS. PRINTING INVESTIGATION COMMISSION: Report of the . . . commission created . . . March 3, 1905 . . . In two volumes. Vol. I. Hearings. Washington, Government Printing Office, 1906. 493, lxxiv p. 8°.

—— LIBRARY OF CONGRESS: The copyright bill . . . . 59th Cong., 1st sess., compared with copyright statutes now in force and earlier U. S. copyright enactments. Washington, Government Printing Office, 1906. 86 p. 4°.
(Copyright office bulletin no. 12.)

—— —— Report on copyright legislation by the register of copyrights . . . Washington, Government Printing Office, 1904. 110 p. 8°.
(Reprinted from rept. of the Librarian of Congress, June 30, 1903.)

—— TREASURY DEPARTMENT: Digest of decisions of the Treasury Department (customs) and of the Board of U. S. general appraisers, rendered during the calendar years 1904, 1905 and 1906 . . . Washington, Government Printing Office, 1907. 461 p. 8°.

URUGUAY.

URUGUAY. Oficina de Crédito Público: Deuda pública de la República O. del Uruguay. 1906. [Montevideo], Imp. "El Telégrafo Marítimo,". [1907]. [20] p. obl. 8°.

—— MINISTERIO DE HACIENDA: . . . Presupuesto general de gastos y cálculo de recursos para 1906-1907. Montevideo, Tall. A. Barreiro y Ramos, 1906. 37 p. 8°.

VENEZUELA.

GREAT BRITAIN. FOREIGN OFFICE: Report for the year 1906 on the trade and commerce of Ciudad Bolívar. . . . London, Harrison & sons, 1907. 6 p. 8°.
(Diplomatic and Consular reports, annual series, no. 3757.)

WEST INDIES.

SIMON, PEDRO. Noticias historiales de las conquistas de tierra firme en las Indias occidentales por Fr. Pedro Simon, del orden de San Francisco del Nuevo Reino de Granada. Bogotá, Medardo Rivas, 1891-1892. 4 v. 8°.

GENERAL WORKS, REFERENCE BOOKS AND BIBLIOGRAPHIES.

AVILES, MAXIMILIANO: Fuerza de acción. Males transitorios de los países Latino-americanos y modo de subsanarlos. Por Maximiliano Avilés. Prólogo de Mariano José Madueño. Nueva York, 1907. 170 p. 8°.

INTERNATIONAL AMERICAN CONFERENCE, 1906: Actas authenticas. Rio de Janeiro, 1906. Various paging. 4°.
(Minutes of each day's proceedings, with signatures of the President and the Secretary of the Conference at the end.)

—— Resolutions. 18 resolutions bd. in 1 v. f°.
(Text in Portuguese, Spanish, and English.)

INTERNATIONAL BUREAU OF THE AMERICAN REPUBLICS: Monthly Bulletin. **May,** 1907.* Washington, Government Printing Office, 1907. pp. 1081-1300. 5 plates. ˊ8°.

CONTENTS.

Editorial Section: Work of the Bureau—President Alcorta's opinion of Secretary Root's visit—The Hispanic Society of America—New Labor Bureau of the Argentine Republic—The South American tour of Professor Shepherd—Professor Rowe's travels in South America—Possible visits of South American statesmen to the United States—The new Spanish Club of Yale University—Latin America versus Asia—Competition for the new building—The representatives of Colombia and Salvador in the United States—Death of a leading export authority—Appreciation expressed for courtesies to the Director—Bolivia's inducements to immigrants—Message of President Diaz to the Mexican Congress—The forward movement in Chile—The new budget of Uruguay—New railroad projects in Peru—Opportunities for capital in Brazil—Growing interest in Colombia—New Brazilian immigration laws—Development of Haitian iron-ore resources—Bright mining outlook in Nicaragua—Chile's efforts to promote popular thrift—A Congressman's view of Costa Rica.
The Hispanic Society of America.
The study of Spanish-American law in the United States.
Argentine Republic: Live-stock and agricultural statistics, 1906—Imports of raw sugar—Report on the maize crop—Renewed shipment of cattle—Projected railroads—New land law regulations—Wool exports, 1900-1906—The Bank of the Argentine Nation in 1906—Prohibition of British hams.
Bolivia: Foreign trade in 1905—Immigration law—Imports from the United States, March and April, 1907—Bank statement, 1906—Telegraph service, 1905-6.
Brazil: Commercial treaties—Tariff regulations—Patent and trade-mark laws—Trade classification of coffees—Customs revenues, January, 1907—Immigration and colonization in São Paulo—Export of hides from Rio Grande do Sul—Miscellaneous notes.
Chile: Import tax on matches—Customs duties, February, 1907—The Anglo-Chilean Mining Company (Limited)—Latest live-stock statistics—Savings banks in the Republic—Flax cultivation in Chile—Salt mines.
Colombia: Railway contract—Paper mills in the Republic—Sugar factory in the Department of Bolivar—Tariff modifications—Creation of the Province of Camilo Torres.
Costa Rica: Customs receipts, fiscal year 1906-7—Abolition of consular fees—Costa Rica and the banana trade.
Cuba: Receipts of Cuban lumber at New York—National status of the Isle of Pines.
Ecuador: Regulations for the purchase and sale of salt—Export tax on ivory nuts—Contract for railway construction from Ambato to Curaray—Funds for the Ambato-Curaray Railway—Railway project—Potable water supply in Quito—The Ambato and Eastern Railway concession—Funds for the Huigra and Cuenca Railway—Government traffic in toquilla straw—Sale of locomotives.
Guatemala: The American Bank of Guatemala—Railway traffic between El Rancho and Sañarate.
Haiti: Exploitation of iron-ore deposits—Commercial convention with France—Commercial movement, fiscal year 1904-5—Exploitation of manganese mines.
Mexico: Message of President Díaz—Foreign commerce, January, 1907—Amendments to contract for Gulf navigation—Silver basis for stamp and customs taxes, May, 1907—Consular reports—Postal receipts, first half of 1906-7—Commerce with France—Electric street railway in Mexico City—Rescinding of steamship contract with Austria-Hungary—Commerce with the United States in 1906—Consolidation of railroad companies—American investments in the Republic—Manufactory of alkaline cyanides—Concessions for establishing a steel file factory.
Nicaragua: Mining in the Republic—Increased duties on salted meats, butter, and soaps—Trade of Cape Gracias a Dios, 1906.
Panama: Budget for 1907-8—Tariff modifications.
Peru: Immigration—Railroad construction—Public works in the Republic—Patents and trade-marks in 1906—Gold coinage in 1906—Rubber production, first half of 1906—Receipts of Peruvian merchandise at New York—The port of Iquitos in 1906—The telegraph system of the Republic.
Salvador: Street lighting in New San Salvador—French exports to the Republic.
United States: Trade with Latin America—Foreign commerce, March, 1907—Rubber from guayule—Coffee movement, first nine months of 1906-7—Patent, trade-mark, and copyright laws in the Canal Zone—Appropriation for the distribution of Rio Grande waters—Financial statement, first quarter, 1907.
Uruguay: New cabinet—Budget for 1907-8—Production of the Cuñapiru mines in 1906.
Venezuela: Lease of asphalt mines—Import duties on fans for advertising.
Establishment of commercial agencies by Spain.
Trade of America and Great Britain, first quarter of 1907.
Book notes.
Library and accessions and files.

PERIODICAL FILES.

Those publications marked with an asterisk have no recent numbers on file.

Persons interested in the commercial and general news of foreign countries will find the following among the official and periodical publications on the permanent files in the Columbus Memorial Library, International Bureau of the American Republics:

ARGENTINE REPUBLIC.

Boletín de la Cámara Mercantil. Barracas al Sud. Weekly.
Boletín Consular. (Ministerio de relaciones exteriores.) Buenos Aires. Irregular.
Boletín de la Unión Industrial Argentina. Buenos Aires. Monthly.
*Boletín del Instituto Georgráfico Argentino. Buenos Aires.
*Boletín Demográfico Argentino. Buenos Aires. Irregular.
Boletín Oficial de la República Argentina. Buenos Aires. Daily.
Boletín de Precios Corrientes. [Buenos Aires.] Weekly.
Bollettino Mensile della Camera Italiana di Commercio ed Arti in Buenos Aires. Buenos Aires. Monthly.
Buenos Aires Handels-Zeitung. Buenos Aires. Weekly.
Buenos Aires Herald. Buenos Aires. Daily and weekly.
*El Comercio Exterior Argentino. Buenos Aires. Irregular.
La Ilustración Sud-Americana. Buenos Aires. Semimonthly.
Monthly Bulletin of Municipal Statistics of the City of Buenos Aires. Buenos Aires. Monthly.
La Nación. Buenos Aires. Daily.
Patentes y Marcas, Revista Sud-Americana de la Propiedad Intelectual é Industrial. Buenos Aires. Monthly.
La Prensa. Buenos Aires. Daily.
La Razón. Buenos Aires. Daily.
Review of the River Plate. Buenos Aires. Weekly.
Revista de la Liga de Defensa Comercial. Buenos Aires. Semimonthly.
Revista Mensual de la Cámara Mercantil. Avelleneda. Monthly.
Revista de Derecho, Historia y Letras. Buenos Aires. Monthly.
Revista Nacional. Buenos Aires. Monthly.
Sarmiento. Buenos Aires. Daily.
The Standard. Buenos Aires. Mail supplement.
Tribuna. Buenos Aires. Daily.

BELGIUM.

Recueil consulaire. Bruxelles. Quarterly.

BOLIVIA.

*Boletín de la Oficina Nacional de Inmigración, Estadística y Propaganda Geográfica. La Paz. Quarterly.

* Boletim de Serviço da Estatística Commercial da Republica dos Esta
   Brazil. Rio de Janeiro. Irregular.
* Brazilian Mining Review. Ouro Preto. Monthly.
Brazilian Review. Rio de Janeiro. Weekly.
Diario da Bahia. Bahia. Daily.
Diario do Congresso Nacional. Rio de Janeiro. Daily.
Diario Oficial. Rio de Janeiro. Daily.
* Gazeta Commercial a Financeira. Rio de Janeiro. Weekly.
Jornal do Recife. Pernambuco. Daily.
Jornal dos Agricultores. Rio de Janeiro. Semimonthly.
O Paiz. Rio de Janeiro. Daily.
Provincia (A) do Pará. Belem. Daily.
Revista Agricola. São Paulo. Monthly.
Revista Maritima Brazileira. Rio de Janeiro. Monthly.

CHILE.

Anales de La Universidad. Santiago. Monthly.
Boletín del Ministerio de Relaciones Esteriores. Santiago. Monthly.
Boletín de la Sociedad Agrícola del Sur. Concepción. Semimonthly.
Boletín de la Sociedad de Fomento Fabril. Santiago. Monthly.
Boletín de la Sociedad Nacional de Agricultura. Santiago. Weekly.
Boletín de la Sociedad Nacional de Minería. Santiago. Monthly.
* Diario Oficial de la República de Chile. Santiago. Daily.
El Mercurio. Valparaiso. Daily.
El Noticiero Comercial. Santiago de Chile. Monthly.
El Pensamiento. Santiago. Monthly.
* Revista Comercial é Industrial de Minas. Santiago. Monthly.

COLOMBIA.

Diario Oficial. Bogotá. Daily.

La Gaceta Económica. Habana. Semimonthly.
Gaceta Oficial de la República de Cuba. Habana. Daily.
Informe Mensual Sanitario y Demográfico de la República de Cuba. Habaná. Monthly.
Informe Mensual Sanitario y Demográfico de Cienfuegos. Cienfuegos. Monthly.
Informe Mensual Sanitario y Demográfico de Matanzas. Matanzas. Monthly.
Revista Municipal y de Intereses Económicos. Habana. Semimonthly.

DOMINICAN REPUBLIC.

Gaceta Oficial. Santo Domingo. Weekly.
Revista de Agricultura. Santo Domingo. Monthly.

ECUADOR.

Anales de la Universidad Central del Ecuador. Quito. Monthly.
Gaceta Municipal. Guayaquil. Weekly.
Registro Oficial de la República del Ecuador. Quito. Daily.

GREAT BRITAIN.

Board of Trade Journal. London. Weekly.
Commercial Intelligence. London. Weekly.
Diplomatic and Consular Reports. London.
Geographical Journal. London. Monthly.
Mining (The) Journal, Railway and Commercial Gazette. London. Weekly.
The Scottish Geographical Magazine. Edinburgh. Monthly.
South American Journal. London. Weekly.
Times (The). London. Daily. (Filed for one year.)
Tropical Life. London. Monthly.

FRANCE.

L'Amerique Latine. Paris. Daily.
Les Annales Diplomatiques et Consulaires. Paris. Monthly.
Le Brésil. Paris. Weekly.
Bulletin American Chamber of Commerce. Paris. Monthly.
Bulletin de la Chambre de Commerce de Paris. Paris. Weekly.
Bulletin de la Société de Géographie Commerciale de Paris. Paris. Irregular.
La Géographie. Bulletin de la Société de Géographie. Paris. Semimonthly.
Journal d'Agriculture Tropicale. Paris. Monthly.
Moniteur Officiel du Commerce. Paris. Weekly.
Le Nouveau Monde. Paris. Weekly.
Rapports commerciaux des agents diplomatiques et consulaires de France. Paris. Irregular. [Sup. to "Moniteur Officiel du Commerce."]
La Revue. Paris. Semimonthly.
*Revue du Commerce Extérieur. Paris. Semimonthly.

GERMANY.

Berichte über Handel und Industrie. Berlin. Weekly.
Petermann's Mitteilungen. Gotha. Monthly.
Südamerikanische Rundschau. Berlin. Monthly.
Der Tropenpflanzer. Berlin. Monthly.
Zeitschrift der Gesellschaft für Erdkunde zu Berlin. Berlin. Monthly.

GUATEMALA.

Boletín de Agricultura. Guatemala. Irregular.
El Guatemalteco. Guatemala. Daily. (Diario Oficial.)
La Locomotora. Guatemala. Monthly.
*La República. Guatemala. Daily.

PARAGUAY.

*Boletín Quincenal de la Cámara de Comercio de la Asunción. Asuncion. Semi-
monthly.
Diario Oficial. Asuncion. Daily.
Paraguay Rundschau. Asuncion. Weekly.
* Revista del Instituto Paraguayo. Asuncion. Monthly.
Revue Commerciale. Assumption. Semimonthly.

PERU.

Auxiliar del Comercio. Callao. Biweekly.
Boletín de Minas, Industrias y Construcciones. Lima. Monthly.
Boletín del Ministerio de Fomento. Dirección de Fomento. Lima. Monthly.
——— Dirección de Obras Públicas. Lima. Monthly.
Boletín de la Sociedad Geográfica de Lima. Lima. Quarterly.
*Boletín de la Sociedad Nacional de Agricultura. Lima. Monthly.
Boletín de la Sociedad Nacional de Minería. Lima. Monthly.
* El Economista. Lima. Weekly.
* El Peruano. (Diario Oficial.) Lima. Daily.
Revista de Ciencias. Lima. Monthly.
* Revista Pan-Americana. Lima. Monthly.

PHILIPPINE ISLANDS.

Boletín de la Cámara de Comercio Filipina. Manila. Monthly.
El Mercantil. Manila. Daily.
Official Gazette. Manila. Weekly. (Also issued in Spanish.)

PORTO RICO.

La Correspondencia de Puerto Rico. San Juan. Daily.

EL SALVADOR.

Anales del Museo Nacional. San Salvador. Monthly.
Boletín de Agricultura. San Salvador. Semimonthly.
Boletín de la Dirección General de Estadística. San Salvador. Irregular.
Diario del Salvador. San Salvador. Daily.
Diario Oficial. San Salvador. Daily.
* Revista de Derecho y Jurisprudencia. San Salvador. Monthly.

SPAIN.

Boletín de las cámaras de comercio, industria y navegación y de las cámaras agrícolas.
Madrid. Monthly.

UNITED STATES.

American Druggist. New York. Semimonthly.
American Exporter. New York. Semimonthly. (Alternate Spanish and English
editions.)
American Historical Review. New York. Quarterly.
American Made Goods. New York. Quarterly.
American Review of Reviews. New York. Monthly.
Annals of the American Academy of Political and Social Science, Philadelphia.
Bimonthly.
Bankers' Magazine. New York. Monthly.
El Boletín Comercial. St. Louis. Monthly.
Bookman (The). New York. Monthly.
Bulletin of the American Geographical Society. New York.
Bulletin of the Geographical Society of Philadelphia. Philadelphia. Monthly.

* Forum (The). New York. Quarterly.
Independent (The). New York. Weekly.
India Rubber World. New York. Monthly.
Journal of American History. New Haven, Conn. Quarterly.
Journal of Geography. New York. Monthly.
Library Journal. New York. Monthly.
Literary Digest. New York. Weekly.
Mines and Minerals. Scranton, Pa. Monthly.
Mining World. Chicago. Weekly.
Modern Mexico. St. Louis. Monthly.
Monthly Consular and Trade Reports. (Department of Commerce ar
    Washington. Monthly.
National Geographic Magazine. New York. Monthly.
North American Review. New York. Monthly.
Novedades (Las). New York. Weekly.
Outlook (The). New York. Weekly.
Pan-American Review. New York. Monthly.
Patent and Trade Mark Review. New York. Monthly.
Scientific American. New York. Weekly.
Scientific American. Export Edition. New York. Monthly.
Sister Republics. Denver, Colo. Monthly.
Tea and Coffee Trade Journal. New York. Monthly.
United States Tobacco Journal. New York. Weekly.
World To-day (The). Chicago. Monthly.
World's Work. New York. Monthly.

URUGUAY.

Anales del Departamento de Gandería y Agricultura. Montevideo. Mont
*Montevideo Times. Montevideo. Daily.
Revista de la Asociación Rural del Uruguay. Montevideo. Monthly.

HONORARY CORRESPONDING MEMBERS OF THE INTERNATIONAL UNION OF AMERICAN REPUBLICS.

Countries.	Names.	Residence.
Argentine Republic..	Señor Dr. Don Estanislao S. Zeballos.......	Buenos Ayres.
Bolivia.............	Señor Don Manuel V. Ballivián[a]..........	La Paz.
Brazil.............	Dezembargador Antonio Bezerra...........	Pará.
	Firmino da Silva	Florianopolis.
Chile...............	Señor Don Moisés Vargas	Santiago.
Colombia...........	Señor Don Rufino Gutiérrez...............	Bogotá.
Costa Rica..........	Señor Don Manuel Aragón	San José.
Cuba...............	Señor Don Antonio S. de Bustamante	Havana.
	Señor Don Lincoln de Zayas...............	Havana.
Dominican Republic..	Señor Don José Gabriel García[b]..........	Santo Domingo.
Ecuador............	Señor Don Francisco Andrade Marín.......	Quito.
	Señor Don Luis Alberto Carbo	Guayaquil.
Guatemala..........	Señor Don Antonio Batres Jáuregui........	Guatemala City.
	Señor Don Rafael Montúfar	Guatemala City.
Haiti...............	Monsieur Georges Sylvain	Port au Prince.
Honduras	Señor Don E. Constantino Fiallos	Tegucigalpa.
Mexico.............	Señor Don Francisco L. de la Barra........	City of Mexico.
	Señor Don Antonio García Cubas..........	City of Mexico.
	Señor Don Fernando Ferrari Pérez	City of Mexico.
Nicaragua	Señor Don José D. Gámez.................	Managua.
Paraguay..........	Señor Don José S. Decoud	Asunción.
Panama	Señor Don Samuel Lewis..................	Panama.
	Señor Don Ramón M. Valdés..............	Panama.
Peru	Señor Don Alejandro Garland.............	Lima.
Salvador...........	Señor Dr. Don Salvador Gallegos	San Salvador.
Uruguay...........	Señor Don José I. Schiffiano	Montevideo.
Venezuela	Señor General Don Manuel Landaeta Rosales.	Caracas.
	Señor Don Francisco de Paula Alamo.......	Caracas.

[a] Honorary corresponding member of the Royal Geographical Society of Great Britain.
[b] Corresponding member of the Academia Nacional de la Historia de Venezuela

Mexico...............................Señor Don ENRIQUE C. CREEL,
        Office of Embassy, 1415 I street, Washington, D. C.

ENVOYS EXTRAORDINARY AND MINISTERS PLENIPOTENTIARY.

Argentine Republic ....Señor Don EPIFANIO PORTELA,
        Office of Legation, 2108 Sixteenth street, Washington, D. C.

Bolivia..............................Señor Don IGNACIO CALDERÓN,
        Office of Legation, 1683 Sixteenth street, Washington, D. C.

Chile...............................Señor Don JOAQUÍN WALKER-MAR
        Absent.

Colombia............................Señor Don ENRIQUE CORTES,
        Office of Legation, 1312 Twenty-first street NW., Washington D. C.

Costa Rica..........................Señor Don JOAQUÍN BERNARDO CAI
        Office of Legation, 1329 Eighteenth street NW., Washington, D. C.

Cuba................................Señor Don GONZALO DE QUESADA,
        Absent.

Ecuador.............................Señor Don LUIS FELIPE CARBO,
        Absent. Office of Legation, 1222 Connecticut avenue, Washington,

Guatemala...........................Señor Dr. Don LUIS TOLEDO HERR
        Office of Legation, "The Highlands," Washington, D. C.

Haiti...............................Mr. J. N. LÉGER,
        Office of Legation, 1429 Rhode Island avenue, Washington, D. C.

Honduras............................Señor Dr. Don JOSÉ ROSA PACAS,
        Absent.

Nicaragua ....Señor Don LUIS F. COREA,
        Office of Legation, 2003 O street, Washington, D. C.

Panama ....Señor Don J. DOMINGO DE OBALDI
        Absent.

                    Señor Don JOSÉ AGUSTÍN ARANGO,
        Office of Legation, "The Highlands," Washington, D. C.

Peru ....Señor Don FELIPE PARDO,
        Summer address, "Overledge," Manchester-by-the-Sea, Mass.

Salvador............................Señor Don FEDERICO MEJÍA,
        Office of Legation, "The Arlington."

Uruguay ....Señor Dr. Don LUÍS MELIAN LAFI
        Office of Legation, 1416 Twenty-first street, Washington, D. C.

MINISTER RESIDENT.

UNITED STATES REPRESENTATIVES IN THE LATIN-AMERICAN REPUBLICS.

AMBASSADORS EXTRAORDINARY AND PLENIPOTENTIARY.

Brazil .... Irving B. Dudley, Rio de Janeiro.
Mexico .... David E. Thompson, Mexico.

ENVOYS EXTRAORDINARY AND MINISTERS PLENIPOTENTIARY.

Argentine Republic .... A. M. Beaupré, Buenos Ayres.
Bolivia .... William B. Sorsby, La Paz.
Chile .... John Hicks, Santiago.
Colombia .... Thomas C. Dawson, Bogotá.
Costa Rica .... William L. Merry, San José.
Cuba .... Edwin V. Morgan, Havana.
Ecuador .... Williams C. Fox, Quito..
Guatemala .... Joseph W. J. Lee, Guatemala City.
Haiti .... Henry W. Furniss, Port au Prince.
Honduras .... (See Guatemala.)
Nicaragua .... (See Costa Rica.)
Panama .... Herbert G. Squiers, Panama.
Paraguay .... (See Uruguay.)
Peru .... Leslie Combs, Lima.
Salvador .... (See Costa Rica.)
Uruguay .... Edward C. O'Brien, Montevideo.
Venezuela .... W. W. Russell, Caracas.

MINISTER RESIDENT AND CONSUL-GENERAL.

Dominican Republic .... Fenton R. McCreery, Santo Domingo.

	Ft. in.	Ft.		Cents	Cents		
Bolivia	3			11	20	20	New York and San Francisco.	La Paz.
Chile	3 6	6		11	20	20	New York and San Francisco.	Valparaiso.
Colombia	2 0	......	4	11	12	12	All offices authorized to exchange mails between the two countries.	
Costa Rica	2 0	......	4	11	12	12		
Ecuador	3 6	6	......	11	20	20		
Guatemala	3 0	6	......	11	12	12	New York, New Orleans, and San Francisco.	Guatemala City, Retalhuleu, and Puerto Barrios.
Guiana, British	3 6	6	......	11	12	12	All offices authorized to exchange mails.	
Honduras	3 6	6	......	11	12	12	New York, New Orleans, and San Francisco.	Tegucigalpa, Puerto Cortez, Amapala, and Trujillo.
Honduras, British	3 6	6	......	11	12	12	New Orleans	Belize.
Mexico	2 0		4	11	12	12	All offices authorized to exchange mails.	
Nicaragua	3 6	6	......	11	12	12	New York, New Orleans, and San Francisco.	Bluefields, San Juan del Norte, and Corinto.
Salvador	3 6	6	......	11	12	12	New York and San Francisco.	San Salvador.
Venezuela	3 6	6	......	11	12	12	All offices authorized to exchange mails.	

FOREIGN MAILS.

Table showing the Rates of Postage Charged in Latin-American Countries on Articles sent by Mail to the United States.

Countries.[‡]	Letters, per 15 grams, equal to one-half ounce.		Single postal cards, each.[a]		Other articles, per 50 grams, equal to 2 ounces.		Charge for registration.	Charge for return receipt.
	Currency of country.	Centimes.	Currency of country.	Centimes.	Currency of country.	Centimes.		
Argentine Republic	15 centavos.	33	6 centavos.	16	3 centavos.	10	24 centavos.	12 centavos.
Bolivia via Panama	22 centavos.	55	8 centavos.	20	6 centavos.	15	20 centavos.	10 centavos.
Bolivia via other routes	20 centavos.	50	6 centavos.	16	4 centavos.	10		
Brazil	300 reis.	35	100 reis.	10	50 reis.	5	400 reis.	200 reis.
Chile	10 centavos.	50	3 centavos.	15	2 centavos.	10	10 centavos.	5 centavos.
Colombia	20 centavos.	50	4 centavos.	10	2 centavos.	5	10 centavos.	5 centavos.
Costa Rica	10 centimos.	25	3 centimos.	7½	2 centimos.	5	10 centimos.	5 centimos.
Cuba[b]								
Dominican Republic (Santo Domingo)	10 centavos.	25	3 centavos.	10	2 centavos.	5	10 centavos.	5 centavos.
Ecuador	10 centavos.	50	2 centavos.	10	1 penny.	10		
Falkland Islands	4 pence.	40	1 penny.	15	1 penny.	15	2 pence.	2½ pence.
Guatemala	10 centavos.	50	3 centavos.	15	2 centavos.	10	10 centavos.	5 centavos.
Haiti	10 centièmes de gourde.	50	3 centièmes de gourde.	15	2 centièmes de gourde.	15	2 centièmes de gourde.	5 centièmes de gourde.
Honduras	15 centavos.	50	3 centavos.	15	2 centavos.	10	10 centavos.	5 centavos.
Honduras, British	6 cents.	25	2 cents.	10	1 cent.	10	10 cents.	5 cents.
Mexico	5 centavos.	25	2 centavos.	10	1 cent.	10	10 centavos.	5 centavos.
Nicaragua	15 centavos.	50	5 centavos.	15	2 centavos.	10	40 centavos.	20 centavos.
Paraguay	60 centavos.	55	8 centavos.	15	8 centavos.	15		
Peru via San Francisco	20 centavos.	50	6 centavos.	15	4 centavos.	10	} 10 centavos.	} 5 centavos.
Peru via Panama	22 centavos.	55	8 centavos.	20	6 centavos.	15		
Porto Rico[b]								
Salvador via Panama	11 centavos.	55	3 centavos.	15	3 centavos.	8	10 centavos.	5 centavos.
Salvador via other routes	10 centavos.	50	3 centavos.	15	2 centavos.	10	10 centavos.	5 centavos.
Uruguay	10 centavos.	50	3 centavos.	15	2 centavos.	10	50 centimos.	25 centimos.
Venezuela	50 centimos.	50	15 centimos.	15	10 centimos.	10		
British Guiana	5 cents.	25	2 cents.	15	1 cent.	6		
Dutch Guiana	25 cents Dutch.	60	7½ cents Dutch.	16	6 cents Dutch.	10	10 cents Dutch.	10 cents Dutch.
French Guiana	25 centimes.	60	10 centimes.	16	5 centimes.	10	25 centimes.	10 centimes.

[a] The rate for a reply-paid (double) card is double the rate named in this column.
[b] United States domestic rates and conditions.

UNITED STATES CONSULATES IN LATIN AMERICA.

Frequent application is made to the Bureau for the address of United States Consuls in the South and Central American Republics. Those desiring to correspond with any Consul can do so by addressing "The United States Consulate" at the point named. Letters thus addressed must be delivered to the proper person. It must be understood, however, that it is not the duty of Consuls to devote their time to private business, and that all such letters may properly be treated as personal, and any labor involved may be subject to charge therefor.

The following is a list of United States Consulates in the different Republics (consular agencies are given in italics):

ARGENTINE REPUBLIC—
Bahia Blanca.
Buenos Ayres.
Cordoba.
Rosario.
BRAZIL—
Aracaju.
Bahia.
Ceara.
Maceio.
Manaos.
Maranhdo.
Natal.
Para.
Pernambuco.
Rio de Janeiro.
Rio Grande do Sul.
Santos.
Victoria.
CHILE—
Antofagasta.
Arica.
Caldera.
Coquimbo.
Coronel.
Iquique.
Punta Arenas.
Talcahuano.
Valdivia.
Valparaiso.
COLOMBIA—
Barranquilla.
Bogotá.
Bucaramanga.
Cali.
Cartagena.
Cucuta.
Honda.
Santa Marta.
Quibdo.
COSTA RICA—
Puerto Limon.
Punta Arenas.
San José.
CUBA—
Banes.
Baracoa.
Caibarien.
Cardenas.
Cienfuegos.
Habana.
Manzanillo.
Matanzas.
Nuevitas.
Sagua la Grande.
Santa Clara.
Santiago.
DOMINICAN REPUBLIC—
Azua.
Macoris.
Monte Christi.
Puerto Plata.

DOMINICAN REPUBLIC—Cont'd.
Samana.
Sanchez.
Santo Domingo.
ECUADOR—
Bahia de Caraquez.
Esmeraldas.
Guayaquil.
Manta.
GUATEMALA—
Champerico.
Guatemala.
Livingston.
Ocos.
San José de Guatemala.
HAITI—
Aux Cayes.
Cape Haitien,
Gonaives.
Jacmel.
Jeremie.
Miragoane.
Petit Godve.
Port au Prince.
Port de Paix.
St. Marc.
HONDURAS—
Amapala.
Bonacca.
Ceiba,
Puerto Cortes.
San Juancito.
San Pedro Sula.
Tegucigalpa.
Tela.
Trujillo.
Ruatan.
Utilla.
MEXICO—
Acapulco.
Aguascalientes.
Alamos.
Campeche.
Cananea.
Chihuahua.
Ciudad Juarez.
Ciudad Porfirio Diaz.
Coatzacoalcos.
Durango.
Ensenada.
Frontera.
Guadalajara.
Guanajuato.
Guaymas.
Hermosillo.
Jalapa.
Laguna de Terminos.
La Paz.
Manzanillo.
Matamoras.
Mazatlan.
Mexico.

MEXICO—Continued.
Monterey.
Nogales.
Nuevo Laredo.
Oaxaca.
Parral.
Progreso.
Puebla.
Saltillo.
San Luis Potosi.
Sierra Mojada.
Tampico.
Tlacotalpan.
Topolobampo.
Torreon.
Tuxpan, Vera Cruz.
Veracruz.
Victoria.
Zacatecas.
NICARAGUA—
Bluefields.
Cape Gracias á Dios.
Corinto.
Managua.
Matagalpa.
San Juan del Norte.
San Juan del Sur.
PANAMA—
Bocas del Toro.
Colon.
David.
Panama.
Santiago.
PARAGUAY—
Asunción.
PERU—
Callao.
Chimbote.
Eten.
Iquitos.
Mollendo.
Paita.
Salaverry.
SALVADOR—
Acajutla.
La Libertad.
La Unión.
San Salvador.
URUGUAY—
Montevideo.
VENEZUELA—
Barcelona.
Caracas.
Carupano.
Ciudad Bolivar.
Coro.
La Guayra.
Maracaibo.
Puerto Cabello.
Tovar.
Valera.

	Jacksonville.	California	San Fran
	Pensacola.	Illinois	Chicago.
	St. Augustine.	Louisiana	New Orle
Georgia	Brunswick.	New York	New Yor
	Savannah.	Pennsylvania	Philadelp
Illinois......................	Chicago.	Philippine Islands............	Cebu.
Louisiana	New Orleans.	Porto Rico....................	Arecibo.
Maine........................	Bangor.		Mayague
	Calais.		Ponce.
	Portland.		San Juan
Maryland	Baltimore.		
Massachusetts.................	Boston.		

WEIGHTS AND MEASURES.

The following table gives the chief weights and measures in commercial use in Mexico and the Republics of Central and South America, and their equivalents in the United States:

Denomination.	Where used.	United States equivalents.
Are	Metric	0.02471 acre.
Arobe	Paraguay	25 pounds.
Arroba (dry)	Argentine Republic	25.3171 pounds.
Do	Brazil	32.38 pounds.
Do	Cuba	25.3664 pounds.
Do	Venezuela	25.4024 pounds.
Arroba (liquid)	Cuba and Venezuela	4.263 gallons.
Barril	Argentine Republic and Mexico	20.0787 gallons.
Carga	Mexico and Salvador	300 pounds.
Centaro	Central America	4.2631 gallons.
Cuadra	Argentine Republic	4.2 acres.
Do	Paraguay	78.9 yards.
Do	Paraguay (square)	8.077 square feet.
Do	Uruguay	2 acres (nearly).
Cubic meter	Metric	35.3 cubic feet.
Fanega (dry)	Central America	1.5745 bushels.
Do	Chile	2.575 bushels.
Do	Cuba	1.599 bushels.
Do	Mexico	1.54728 bushels.
Do	Uruguay (double)	7.776 bushels.
Do	Uruguay (single)	3.888 bushels.
Do	Venezuela	1.599 bushels.
Frasco	Argentine Republic	2.5096 quarts.
Do	Mexico	2.5 quarts.
Gram	Metric	15.432 grains.
Hectare	do	2.471 acres.
Hectoliter (dry)	do	2.838 bushels.
Hectoliter (liquid)	do	26.417 gallons.
Kilogram (kilo)	do	2.2046 pounds.
Kilometer	do	0.621376 mile.
League (land)	Paraguay	4.633 acres.
Libra	Argentine Republic	1.0127 pounds.
Do	Central America	1.043 pounds.
Do	Chile	1.014 pounds.
Do	Cuba	1.0161 pounds.
Do	Mexico	1.01465 pounds.
Do	Peru	1.0143 pounds.
Do	Uruguay	1.0143 pounds.
Do	Venezuela	1.0161 pounds.
Liter	Metric	1.0567 quarts.
Livre	Guiana	1.0791 pounds.
Manzana	Costa Rica	1.73 acres.
Marc	Bolivia	0.507 pound.
Meter	Metric	39.37 inches.
Pie	Argentine Republic	0.9478 foot.
Quintal	do	101.42 pounds.
Do	Brazil	130.06 pounds.
Do	Chile, Mexico, and Peru	101.61 pounds.
Do	Paraguay	100 pounds.
Quintal (metric)	Metric	220.46 pounds.
Suerte	Uruguay	2,700 cuadras. (See Cuadra.)
Vara	Argentine Republic	34.1208 inches.
Do	Central America	33.874 inches.
Do	Chile and Peru	33.367 inches.
Do	Cuba	33.384 inches.
Do	Mexico	33 inches.
Do	Paraguay	34 inches.
Do	Venezuela	33.384 inches.

Decagram (10 grams) equals 0.3527 ounce.
Hectogram (100 grams) equals 3.5274 ounces.
Kilogram (1,000 grams) equals 2.2046 pounds.
Myriagram (10,000 grams) equals 22.046 pounds.
Quintal (100,000 grams) equals 220.46 pounds.
Millier or tonneau—ton (1,000,000 grams) equals 2,204.6 pounds.

METRIC DRY MEASURE.

Milliliter (1/1000 liter) equals 0.061 cubic inch.
Centiliter (1/100 liter) equals 0.6102 cubic inch.
Deciliter (1/10 liter) equals 6.1022 cubic inches.
Liter equals 0.908 quart.
Decaliter (10 liters) equals 9.08 quarts.
Hectoliter (100 liters) equals 2.838 bushels.
Kiloliter (1,000 liters) equals 1.308 cubic yards.

METRIC LIQUID MEASURE.

Milliliter (1/1000 liter) equals 0.27 fluid dram.
Centiliter (1/100 liter) equals 0.338 fluid ounce.
Deciliter (1/10 liter) equals 0.845 gill.
Liter equals 1.0567 quarts.
Decaliter (10 liters) equals 2.6417 gallons.
Hectoliter (100 liters) equals 26.417 gallons.
Kiloliter (1,000 liters) equals 264.17 gallons.

METRIC MEASURES OF LENGTH.

Millimeter (1/1000 meter) equals 0.0394 inch.
Centimeter (1/100 meter) equals 0.3937 inch.
Decimeter (1/10 meter) equals 3.937 inches.
Meter equals 39.37 inches.

PRICE LIST OF PUBLICATIONS.

PRICE.

Bulletin of the Bureau, published monthly since October, 1893, in English, Spanish, Portuguese, and French. Average 225 pages, 2 volumes a year.

Yearly subscription (in countries of the International Union of American Republics and in Canada)... $2.00

Yearly subscription (other countries)................................... 2.50

Single copies.. .25

Orders for the Bulletin should be addressed to the Chief Clerk of the Bureau.

American Constitutions. A compilation of the political constitutions of the independent States of America, in the original text, with English and Spanish translations. Washington, 1906. 3 vols., 8°.

Paper ....each.. 1.00

Bound in cloth...do.... 1.50

Bound in sheep ....do.... 2.00

> Vol. I, now ready, contains the constitutions of the Federal Republics of the United States of America, of Mexico, of the Argentine Republic, of Brazil, and of Venezuela, and of the Republics of Central America, Guatemala, Honduras, El Salvador, Nicaragua, Costa Rica, and Panama.
>
> Vol. II, now ready, contains the constitutions of the Dominican Republic, Haiti, Cuba, Uruguay, Chile, Peru, Ecuador, Colombia, Paraguay, and Bolivia.
>
> Vol. III will contain Articles of Confederation of the United States, First Constitution of Venezuela 1811, Fundamental Law of Republic of Colombia 1819, Ditto of 1821, Constitution of Colombia of 1821, Constitution of Central American Confederation of 1824, Constitution of the Grenadian Confederation of 1858, Constitution of the United States of Colombia of 1863, Pro Constitution of Guatemala of 1876, Convention between United States and Republic of Panama for construction of ship canal to connect the waters of the Atlantic and the Pacific Oceans.

Code of Commercial Nomenclature, 1897. (Spanish, English, and Portuguese.)

645 pages, 4°, cloth... 2.50

Code of Commercial Nomenclature, 1897. (Portuguese, Spanish, and English.)

640 pages, 4°, cloth... 2.50

> NOTE.—Designates in alphabetical order, in equivalent terms in the three languages, the commodities of American nations on which import duties are levied. The English, Spanish, and Portuguese edition is entirely exhausted.

Leyes y reglamentos sobre privilegios de invención y marcas de fábrica en los países hispano-americanos, el Brasil y la República de Haití. Revisado hasta agosto de 1904. Washington, 1904. 415 pages, 8°............................ 1.00

Patent and trade-mark laws of the Spanish American Republics, Brazil, and the Republic of Haiti. Revised to Aug., 1904, Washington, 1904........... 1.00

The above two works bound together in sheep 3.00

SPECIAL BULLETINS.

Money, Weights, and Measures of the American Republics, 1891. 12 pages, 8°. .05

Report on Coffee, with special reference to the Costa Rican product, etc. Washington, 1901. 15 pages, 8°... .10

El café. Su historia, cultivo, beneficio, variedades, producción, exportación, importación, consumo, etc. Datos extensos presentados al Congreso relativo al café que se reunirá en Nueva York el 1° de octubre de 1902. 167 páginas, 8°.. .50

Coffee. Extensive information and statistics. (English edition of the above.) 108 pages, 8°.. .50

Intercontinental Railway Reports. Report of the Intercontinental Railway Commission. Washington, 1898. 7 vols. 4°, three of maps............... 25.00

LAW MANUALS.

Leyes Comerciales de América Latina: Código de Comercio de España comparado con los Códigos y Leyes Comerciales de Pan América.
Land and Immigration Laws of American Republics. (To replace edition of 1893.)

HANDBOOKS.

Chile.
Dominican Republic.

MAPS.

Maps are in course of preparation of the Republics of Honduras and Salvador.
Payment is required to be made in cash, money orders, or by bank drafts on banks in New York City or Washington, D. C., payable to the order of the INTERNATIONAL BUREAU OF THE AMERICAN REPUBLICS. Individual checks on banks outside of New York or Washington, or postage stamps, can not be accepted.

FOR FREE DISTRIBUTION.

The Bureau has for distribution a limited supply of the following, which will be sent, free, upon written application:

The case of the United States of Venezuela before the Tribunal of Arbitration to convene at Paris under the provisions of the Treaty between the United States of Venezuela and Her Britannic Majesty, signed at Washington, February 2, 1897, in 10 vols., of which 2 are maps. Sent only to libraries and educational institutions.

Message from the President of the United States, transmitting a communication from the Secretary of State submitting the report, with accompanying papers, of the delegates of the United States to the Second International Conference of American States, held at the City of Mexico from October 22, 1901, to January 22, 1902. Washington, 1902. 243 pages. 8°. (57th Congress, 1st session, Senate Doc. No. 330.)

Message from the President of the United States, transmitting a report from the Secretary of State, with accompanying papers, relative to the proceedings of the International Congress for the study of the production and consumption of coffee, etc. Washington, 1903. 312 pages. 8° (paper). (57th Congress, 2d session, Senate Doc. No. 35.)

Message from the President of the United States, transmitting a report by the Secretary of State, with accompanying papers, relative to the proceedings of the First Customs Congress of the American Republics, held at New York in January, 1903. Washington, 1903. 195 pages. 8° (paper). (57th Congress, 2d session, Senate Doc. No. 180.)

Brazil at St. Louis Exposition. St. Louis, 1904. 160 pages. 8° (paper).

Chile—A short description of the Republic according to official data. Leipzig, 1901. 106 pages. Map and 37 illustrations. 8° (cloth).

Chile—Breve descripción de la República escrita según datos oficiales. Leipzig, 1901. 106 páginas. Mapa y 36 grabados. 8° (en tela).

Chile at Pan-American Exposition. Buffalo, 1901. 252 pages (paper).

Costa Rica—Some Facts and Figures. Compiled and arranged by J. B. Calvo. 1894. 56 pages. 8° (paper).

Guatemala—The Country of the future. By Charles M. Pepper. Washington, 1906. 80 pages. 8° (paper).

VALUE OF LATIN-AMERICAN COINS.

The following table shows the value, in United States gold, of coins representing the monetary units of the Central and South American Republics and Mexico, estimated quarterly by the Director of the United States Mint, in pursuance of act of Congress:

ESTIMATE APRIL 1, 1907.

Countries.	Standard.	Unit.	Value in U. S. gold or silver.	Coins.
ARGENTINE REPUBLIC.	Gold	Peso	$0.965	Gold—Argentine ($4.824) and ½ Argentine. Silver—Peso and divisions.
BOLIVIA	Silver ...	Boliviano	.510	Silver—Boliviano and divisions.
BRAZIL	Gold	Milreis ..	.546	Gold—5, 10, and 20 milreis. Silver—½, 1, and 2 milreis.
CENTRAL AMERICAN STATES— Costa Rica......	Gold	Colon ...	.465	Gold—2, 5, 10, and 20 colons ($9.307). Silver—5, 10, 25, and 50 centimos.
Guatemala...... Honduras ...... Nicaragua ...... Salvador	Silver ...	Peso	.500	Silver—Peso and divisions.
CHILE	Gold	Peso	.365	Gold—Escudo ($1.825), doubloon ($3.650), and condor ($7.300). Silver—Peso and divisions.
COLOMBIA...........	Gold	Dollar...	1.000	Gold—Condor ($9.647) and double condor. Silver—Peso.
ECUADOR	Gold	Sucre....	.487	Gold—10 sucres ($4.8665). Silver—Sucre and divisions.
HAITI	Gold	Gourde..	.965	Gold—1, 2, 5, and 10 gourdes. Silver—Gourde and divisions.
MEXICO.............	Gold	Peso a ...	.498	Gold—5 and 10 pesos. Silver—Dollar b (or peso) and divisions.
PANAMA	Gold	Balboa ..	1.000	Gold—1, 2½, 5, 10, and 20 balboas. Silver—Peso and divisions.
PERU	Gold	Libra ...	4.866½	Gold—½ and 1 libra. Silver—Sol and divisions.
URUGUAY	Gold	Peso	1.034	Gold—Peso. Silver—Peso and divisions.
VENEZUELA	Gold	Bolivar..	.193	Gold—5, 10, 20, 50, and 100 bolivars. Silver—5 bolivars.

a 75 centigrams fine gold.   b Value in Mexico, 0.498.

Lightning Source UK Ltd.
Milton Keynes UK
UKHW010336120219
337137UK00004B/242/P

9 780331 337518